PRINCIPLES OF FAMILY LAW

AUSTRALIA
Law Book Co.
Sydney

CANADA AND USA
Carswell
Toronto

HONG KONG
Sweet & Maxwell Asia

NEW ZEALAND
Brookers
Wellington

SINGAPORE AND MALAYSIA
Sweet & Maxwell Asia
Singapore and Kuala Lumpur

PRINCIPLES
OF
FAMILY LAW

SEVENTH EDITION

BY

S.M. CRETNEY, DCL, FBA

One of Her Majesty's Counsel honoris causa,
Solicitor, Fellow Emeritus of All Souls College, Oxford

J.M. MASSON, MA, PhD

Professor of Law
University of Warwick

AND

R. BAILEY-HARRIS, MA, BCL

Professor of Law
University of Bristol
Barrister

LONDON
SWEET & MAXWELL
2003

First Edition 1974
Second Edition 1976
Third Edition 1979
Fourth Edition 1984
Fifth Edition 1990
Sixth Edition 1997
Reprinted 1998 (twice), 2000
Seventh Edition 2002
Revised edition 2003

Published by
Sweet & Maxwell Ltd of
100 Avenue Road,
London NW3 3PF
(http://www.sweetandmaxwell.co.uk)
Computerset by Wyvern 21 Ltd, Bristol
Printed in Great Britain
by TJ International Ltd, Padstow, Cornwall

No natural forests were destroyed to make this product;
only farmed timber was used and replanted.

British Library Cataloguing in Publication Data
A CIP catalogue record for this book is available
from the British Library.

ISBN 0421 843 101

PREFACE

The aim of this book continues to be not only to explain the law as it is, but to give an account of its historical background, to analyse the factors underlying its development and to stimulate discussion of its effectiveness as an instrument of social policy in the context of the social realities confronting the legal system at the beginning of the twenty-first century.

The Government's decision not to implement those parts of the Family Law Act 1996 dealing with the ground for divorce leaves the law and those who try to explain it in some difficulty. The task is not made any easier by the apparent reluctance of the Government to give any comprehensive (or even coherent) explanation of the direction of future policy, a reluctance all the more puzzling given the frequent assertions of a commitment to so-called open government. The present text seeks to give a comprehensible explanation of the law as it now is, and to sketch in the main issues for future decision.

There have been major changes in the statutory provisions governing the financial consequences of relationship breakdown: the Welfare Reform and Pensions Act 1999 has made pension sharing a reality. The Child Support, Pensions and Social Security Act 2000 will make significant changes to the law governing the determination and enforcement of the parental obligation to support the child; and the text dealing with the Act was written on the basis that the Government would be able to meet the target of bringing the revised scheme into effect in 2002. Although this proved not to be the case, it is now envisaged that the Act will be phased in with effect from March 2003. So far as case law is concerned, the opinions of the Law Lords in *White v. White* [2001] 1 A.C. 596 are undoubtedly significant for the development of the law governing the financial consequences of divorce, although opinions differ as to whether or not the law has been clarified.

Nor has child law stood still; and regrettably it seems clear from research and practice that the original intentions behind the Children Act of reducing State intervention, increasing family support and reducing delay have not been achieved. In particular, the Human Rights Act 1998 has started to have an impact. The issues of respecting the family life of adults and children, of striking a fair balance between them and ensuring a fair hearing when the exercise of rights is in question are challenging the established decisions and processes.

Law reform in a field such as Family Law which affects people's private lives is almost necessarily a controversial and therefore protracted process. Detailed consideration of adoption law reform began in 1990 and draft legislation was published in 1996. In February 2000 the Prime Minister announced that he would personally lead a thorough review of adoption law and in October 2001 a Bill of 145 clauses was introduced into the House of Commons. Amendments to extend adoption to unmarried and same sex couples were moved and unsurprisingly proved controversial. The Adoption and Children Act 1989 eventually received Royal Assent on November 7, 2002. It is the largest and arguably the most complex piece of Family Law legislation enacted in the last half-century. The Act should bring Adoption in from the cold, and reflects the concept of adoption as being primarily one aspect of the provision for child care made by the community (rather than primarily a matter of transferring a child from one family group to another). The book has therefore been reprinted to include (in Chapter 23) full coverage of adoption law as it will be when the 2002 Act is fully implemented. (This Chapter was issued as a Supplement for those who had purchased the original version of the Book). The text of Chapters 1 to 22 of this book continues to include references to the Bill as it stood on August 1, 2002.

The first edition of this book was published in 1974 and was 369 pages long. By the time of the fourth edition in 1984 it had grown to 1,018 pages. Happily, I was able to persuade Professor Judith Masson to contribute the Chapters dealing with children, and she continued to so so in the fifth and sixth editions. In the present edition she has been responsible for the whole of Part Five (including the new Chapter 23). Professor Rebecca Bailey-Harris also joined the team; and contributed her expertise on financial and property matters. She has been responsible for Chapters 4 to 7, 9, 10 and 14 as well as the whole of Part IV (which deals with Child Support obligations. I have continued to have responsibility for the rest of the book. Future editions will be under the charge of Professors Bailey-Harris and Masson.

I have always taken a particular interest in the choice of the picture appearing on the cover of the book; and the choice for the last edition, published in 1997, of Degas' fine study of the Bellelli family proved particularly apt: in 1998 scholars concluded that the reason why the picture had not been exhibited in the artist's lifetime was that it revealed too clearly the tensions in the subjects' marriage.

The authors hope that they have stated the law in Chapters 1 to 22 on the basis of the materials available to them on August 1, 2002; Chapter 23 is based on sources available at February 3, 2003.

Stephen Cretney
St. Valentine's Day, February 14, 2003.

CONTENTS

INTRODUCTION: THE FAMILY AND THE LAW

PART I: THE FAMILY AND MARRIAGE

PART II: FAMILY PROPERTY

PART IV: CHILD SUPPORT OBLIGATIONS

PART V: CHILDREN AND FAMILY LAW

TABLE OF CASES

TABLE OF STATUTES

TABLE OF STATUTORY INTRUMENTS

TABLE OF ABBREVIATIONS

A. Legislation

A.E.A. 1925	Administration of Estates Act 1925
C.A.	Children Act
CPR	Civil Procedure Rules 1998
C.S.A.	Child Support Act 1991
C.S.P.S.S.A. 2000	Child Support, Pensions and Social Security Act 2000
C.Y.P.A. 1933	Children and Young Persons Act 1933
D. P. M.C.A.	Domestic Proceedings and Magistrates' Courts Act 1978
D.R.A.	Divorce Reform Act
D. V. & M.P.A.	Domestic Violence and Matrimonial Proceedings Act 1976
ECHR	European Convention of Human Rights and Fundamental Freedoms
F.C.(G) Regs	Family Credit (General) Regulations 1987
F.L.A. 1996	Family Law Act 1996
F.L.R.A. 1987	Family Law Reform Act 1987
F.P.C.	Family Proceedings Court (Children Act 1989) Rules 1991
F.P.R.	Family Proceedings Rules 1991
H.F.& E.A.	Human Fertilisation and Embryology Act 1990
H.R.A.	Human Rights Act 1998
I. (P.F.&D.) A	Inheritance (Provision for Family and Dependants) Act 1975
I.S.(G) Regs	Income Support (General) Regulations 1987
L.P.A.	Law of Property Act 1925
M.C.A.	Matrimonial Causes Act
M.C.R.	Matrimonial Causes Rules
M.H.A.	Matrimonial Homes Act 1983
M. & F.P.A.	Matrimonial and Family Proceedings Act 1984
M.P.P.A.	Matrimonial Proceedings and Property Act 1970
S.S.A. 1998	Social Security Act 1998
S.S.A.A. 1992	Social Security Administration Act 1992
S.S.C.B.A.	Social Security Contributions and Benefits Act 1992
T.L.A.T.A.	Trusts of Land and Appointment of Trustees Act
W.R.P.A. 1999	Welfare Reform and Pensions Act 1999

B. Other Abbreviations

CAAC	Children Act Advisory Committee
CAEW	Central Authority for England and Wales
CAFCASS	Children and Family Court Advisory and Support Service
CETV	Cash Equivalent Transfer Value
GALRO	Guardians as litem and Reporting Officers
NAYPIC	National Association for Young People in Care
SFLA	Solicitors Family Law Association
SSI	Social Services Inspectorate

INTRODUCTION

THE FAMILY AND THE LAW

I. MARRIAGE AND THE FAMILY: STATUS

A–001 Books about family law have traditionally focused almost exclusively on marriage and divorce; and this preference could easily be justified. In particular, it could be said that it was by marriage (and generally speaking only by marriage) that men and women automatically acquired legal rights—for example, to be provided with maintenance and to succeed to property—against their partners and other relatives. Marriage—although originating in agreement between the parties—created a status, that is to say "the condition of belonging to a class in society to which the law ascribes peculiar rights and duties, capacities and incapacities."[1] It could even be said that marriage effectively served to define the family, since it was the fact that a child's parents were married which conferred on the child the status of legitimacy—in effect, recognition of the child's family relationship.

These rights and duties which flowed from the status of marriage were of a special nature, in so far as the law refused to allow the parties to the marriage to vary them. It was, for example, impossible at common law for a couple to contract out of the husband's common law obligation to support his wife or to contract that the wife should have the right to decide about the children's upbringing. The position was well explained by a nineteenth century American judge:

> "When the contracting parties have entered into the married state, they have not so much entered into a contract as into a new relation, the rights, duties and obligations of which rest, not upon their agreement, but upon the general law of the State, statutory or common, which defines and prescribes those rights, duties and obligations. They are of law, not of contract. It was of contract that the relation should be established, but, being established, the power of the parties, as to its extent or duration, is at an end, their rights under it are determined by the will of the sovereign as evidenced by law. They can neither be modified nor changed by any agreement of parties ... The reciprocal rights arising from this relation, as long as it continues, are such as the law determines from time to time, and none other."[2]

---

[1] *The Ampthill Peerage* [1977] A.C. 547 at 577, *per* Lord Simon of Glaisdale: and see *Salvesen v Administrator of Austrian Property* [1927] A.C. 641 at 653, *per* Lord Haldane.

[2] *per* Appleton C.J., *Adams v. Palmer* 51 Maine 480, (1863) at 483; see also *Maynard v. Hill* 125 U.S. 190 (1888).

II. CHANGING SOCIAL AND DEMOGRAPHIC REALITIES

A–002 This concentration on marriage as fundamental to family law for long reflected social realities. Of course, it is true that families were created outside marriage[3] and the legal system made special (and discriminatory) provision to secure a measure of support for illegitimate children; but such families were statistically not numerous, and a law which appeared to regard them as deviant may well have reflected popular attitudes. Overwhelmingly marriage was the institution within which family relationships were formed and nurtured[4]; by the mid-1970s 95 per cent of all women and 91 per cent of all men had married by the age of 40; marriage had thus become an almost universal experience—increasingly to be contracted at a young age.[5] Only six or so births in every hundred were illegitimate; and a significant number of those illegitimate children were adopted[6] and thereby[7] legally integrated into a family founded on marriage. Not until 1979 did the official General Household Survey take the step of gathering information about the extent of extra-marital cohabitation.

These social realities have had a strong influence on the development of family law: if marriage was the basis of the family, it followed that for lawyers divorce—the process whereby marriage is legally ended—came to be seen as of equal importance. But the increase in cohabitation outside marriage requires a change of emphasis.

A. The dominance of divorce

A–003 Marriage had traditionally been defined in English law as "the voluntary union for life of one man to one woman to the exclusion of all others"[8]; but the increasing availability of divorce—particularly after the Second World War—made that definition inaccurate: marriage was indeed still a voluntary union, but it could no longer be regarded as lifelong. In the 1980s it was estimated that if the current rate of divorce were to continue in the future no less than one in three marriages would end in divorce.[9] The law might have little direct part to

---

[3] For an eminently readable account of the complex family life of a man who managed not only to run a successful banana importing business but also to perform the role of devoted husband and father to two families (each remaining unaware of the other's existence) at the same time, see *My Father and Myself* (1968) by the celebrated man of letters and dog lover J.R. Ackerley; and for a comparatively recent example of the same phenomenon see *Jessop v. Jessop* [1992] 1 F.L.R. 591.

[4] But extra-marital cohabitation had long been perceived as a problem: see K.E. Kiernan and V. Estaugh, *Cohabitation, Extra-marital childbearing and social policy* (1993), Chap. 1 and the materials there cited.

[5] In 1971 30per cent of spinsters marrying were under 20. For an accessible account of demographic trends, see C. Gibson, "Changing Family Patterns in England and Wales" in *Cross Currents* (S.N. Katz, J. Eekelaar and M. Maclean ed., 2000).

[6] The number of adoptions peaked at 26,986 in 1968: see generally R. Leete, "Adoption Trends, and Illegitimate Births 1951.1977" (1978) 14 *Population Trends*.

[7] Almost invariably: a tiny proportion of adoptions were in favour of an unrelated single person.

[8] *Hyde v. Hyde* (1866) L.R. 1 P. & D. 130 at 133; and generally S. Poulter (1979) 42 *M.L.R.* 409, and C. Hamilton, *Family, Law and Religion* (1995), particularly at pp. 66–73.

[9] See J. C. Haskey. "The proportion of marriages ending in divorce" (1980) 27 *Population Trends*.

play in the ongoing and functioning family unit, but divorce involved legal proceedings and (usually) the involvement of lawyers. For this reason, English Law School syllabuses—at least until the publication of P.M. Bromley's *Family Law*[10] in 1957[11]—tended to deal with the family (if at all) in courses entitled the "law of matrimonial causes", whilst the leading practitioners' text[12] only broadened its title to *Divorce and Family Matters*[13] as recently as 1991.[14] Moreover, the fact that many divorced people remarried—in 1991 over a third of all marriages were remarriages of people one or both of whom had been divorced whereas 30 years ago this proportion was less than one in 10[15]—tended to reinforce the view that family law could be viewed primarily in terms of marriage and divorce.

B. Cohabitation outside marriage

A–004 By the year 2000, it had become clear that this approach could no longer be justified. As Waite L.J. put it in delivering judgment in *Fitzpatrick v. Sterling Housing Association Ltd*[16]:

> Today "25per cent of all women aged between 18 and 49 are unmarried cohabitants, and in the age group most likely to cohabit (women in their late 20s and men in their late 30s) over one third of the population now cohabits. As it became more open, so attitudes towards it became less judgmental. That included the attitude of the courts, where notwithstanding that the encouragement of marriage as an institution remains a well-established head of public policy, the respect due to the sincerity of commitment involved in many such relationships is reflected in judicial terminology—terms like 'partner' now being more generally used than the once-preferred references to 'common-law spouse', 'mistress' or even . . . 'living in sin'."

For some time it seemed possible to argue[17] that much of this cohabita-

---

[10] "Family Law" was the classification favoured by the German pandectists of the 19th century (departing in this respect from the Roman law derived "law of persons" adopted in the *Code Napoleon*).

[11] Publication of this work powerfully influenced acceptance of family law as a proper subject for academic study and research; whilst the Law Commission's commitment (*2nd Programme of Law Reform*, 1968, Item XIX) to the codification of family law perhaps reflected official acceptance of the term.

[12] Rayden on *Divorce*, which went through 15 editions between 1910 and 1988.

[13] Reflecting the wide ranging changes effected by the Children Act 1989.

[14] Rayden and Jackson, *Law and Practice in Divorce and Family Matters* (16th ed. by M. Booth, N. Wall, G.J. Maple and A.K. Biggs, 1991).

[15] See generally C. Gibson, "Changing Family Patterns in England and Wales" in *Cross Currents* (S.N. Katz, J. Eekelaar, and M. Maclean ed., 2000), pp. 32–34.

[16] [1998] Ch. 304, CA. See generally C. Gibson, "Changing Family Patterns in England and Wales" in *Cross Currents* (S.N. Katz, J. Eekelaar and M. Maclean ed., 2000), Chap. 2; and for a full analysis of the demographic material, J. Haskey, "Demographic Aspects of Cohabitation in Great Britain" (2001) I.J.L.&F. 51.

[17] As was done, *e.g.* in the 4th edition of this work (1984), p. 4.

tion was in effect by way of trial marriage[18] but it is now apparent that long-term cohabitation has become more frequent.[19] Moreover, the marriage rate has fallen dramatically over the years[20] and it seems that far more people than in the past are likely to remain unmarried.[21]

The increase in births outside marriage is even more striking. Over a third of all births now take place outside marriage—more than four times the proportion a quarter of a century ago. Most of the parents seem to be in an established relationship: around 80 per cent of births outside marriage are jointly registered by the two parents, and three-quarters of those births are to parents living at the same address.[22] It seems that the trend, first observed many years ago in Sweden and Denmark, towards accepting long-term cohabitation as a socially acceptable alternative to marriage has been replicated in this country.[23]

III. DEFINING THE STATE'S INTEREST

A–005 The traditional understanding is that the state has a vital interest in the legal relationship between couples, so that it is for the state acting through the legal system—rather than for the parties acting through private agreement—to determine such matters as the rules on which they will enter into the relationship and the consequences which should flow from any breakdown. But this doctrine has become increasingly difficult to reconcile with the changing nature of marriage (which, as has been said[24] is now seen as being primarily a concern of the individuals involved, governed by their individual sense of ethics or utility). The traditional doctrine is also inconsistent with the wish of government to curb the massive expenditure (often of public, rather than private, funds) on court hearings and other legal procedures. For these reasons, there has been a significant movement away from universal state regulation and towards a recognition—and even encouragement—of the right of couples to determine for themselves the consequences of the breakdown of their relationship. But the law remains somewhat ambivalent on these matters as will be seen clearly in the chapter dealing with child support and with the limitations on the scope for private ordering in

---

18 It is clear that there is also much cohabitation at later ages amongst the divorced.

19 See Gibson and Haskey, *op. cit.*, n. 16, above.

20 See Gibson, *op.cit.*, Table 2.1. Detailed statistics are published annually: *Marriage and Divorce Statistics 1999* shows that in 1999 263,515 marriages were solemnised in England and Wales — 24per cent fewer than a decade earlier. This downward trend has been consistent since the number of marriages peaked in 1972 at 426,241.

21 *ibid.*

22 (1999) 29 *Social Trends* Table 2.18.

23 There is a substantial and growing literature. Reference may usefully be made to the papers presented at a 1999 conference on "Trends in Cohabitation: Demography, Law and Policy" organised by Professor Jane Lewis. These are collected in Vol. 15, No. 1, of the *International Journal of Law, Policy and the Family*. C. Gibson, "Changing Family Patterns in England and Wales" in *Cross Currents* (S.N. Katz, J. Eekelaar, and M. Maclean ed., 2000) Chap. 2 provides a succinct account of the key demographic factors.

24 See See M. Glendon, *State, Law and Family* (1977), p. 323; and see *Bellinger v. Bellinger* [2001] 2 F.L.R. 1048 and 1082, *per* Thorpe L.J.

relation to the financial consequences of divorce; and the task of exposition becomes correspondingly more difficult.

IV. PARENTAGE AS THE KEY FACTOR IN FAMILY LAW?

A–006 Against this background, the fact that legislation[25] has come to highlight the significance of parentage (rather than the legal relationship between the child's parents) as the most relevant factor in determining a child's legal position is of particular significance; and the Family Law Reform Act 1987 removed most of the legal disadvantages of having been born outside marriage.[26] This change of emphasis—although not intended to affect respect for the institution of marriage[27]—makes continued emphasis on the central role of marriage in family law even less appropriate. However, it remains true that there are far more married than unmarried couples; and that the majority of children live in households formed by their two married parents. It is also true that both statute and reported case law are still (in relation to adults) largely dominated by the problems of the married and formerly married rather than by those of the never married. Any survey of family law will necessarily continue to reflect those facts.

V. ARRANGEMENT OF TEXT

A–007 **Part I** deals with the **Family and Marriage.** Who can (and who cannot) marry; and what are the legal formalities for marriage? What are the legal consequences of marriage? How far is the law coming to equate the legal position of unmarried and married couples? What legal obligations flow from marriage?

Part II deals with **Family Property,** where (at least in theory) case law has come to adopt an attitude of neutrality between the claims of the married and the claims of the unmarried to share in family assets.

Part III deals with **Family Breakdown** (focusing at this stage on the relationship between the adults concerned). This Part of the book includes a consideration of the legal remedies available against violence and molestation, an area in which there are now comparatively few relevant distinctions between marital

[25] Family Law Reform Act 1987; and see now Children Act 1989, Chap. 19, below.
[26] The Family Law Reform Act 1987 also sought to avoid attaching labels (such as "illegitimate") to children born outside marriage, but may not have been wholly successful in that regard. The Act did not remove all legal distinctions between children born in and outside marriage, and the concept of legitimacy remains legally significant, albeit less likely to be relevant. It may be noted that the words "legitimate" and "illegitimate" are used no less than 13 times in the explanatory note to the first commencement order: S.I. 1988 No. 425.
[27] See the Law Commission's Report, *Illegitimacy* (Law Com. No. 118, (1982)), paras 4.6.4.8.

and non-marital relationships. The dissolution of marriage remains of central importance; and an account of the divorce process is given.

Part IV deals with **Child Support Obligations** and the enforcement of financial orders.

Part V deals with **Children and Family Law**; and covers such questions as what is meant by parentage, what rights attach to it, and what rights do the children have? The comprehensive legal structure established by the Children Act 1989 for enabling issues relating to children's upbringing (including the definition of the circumstances in which the state, through the agency of local authorities, is to be entitled to remove children from their parents) is of central importance; but the text also deals with issues of practical and jurisprudential interest, such as the legal remedies for child abduction and the regulation of adoption and surrogacy.

Part I

THE FAMILY AND MARRIAGE

CHAPTER ONE

THE MARRIAGE CEREMONY

I. INTRODUCTION

1–001 This Chapter deals with the rules governing the marriage ceremony, that is to say with the formalities required to establish the legal relationship of husband and wife. To create such a relationship, however, it is not sufficient that the parties should have observed these rules; it is also necessary that each of them should have had legal capacity to marry. The rules governing capacity to marry are discussed in Chapter 2.

The modern law can only be understood in its historical context. An explanation will make it easier to consider the modern law, and to assess how far it achieves the objectives of a good marriage law.

II. HISTORICAL DEVELOPMENT[1]

A. The informal common law marriage

1–002 The common law for many years left the regulation of marriage largely to the church: marriage law was canon law, and under canon law the status of marriage could be created with almost complete absence of formality.

B. Marriage created by consent

1–003 Although the doctrine of the early Church was that consummation was the essential factor in the creation of a marriage,[2] this doctrine gave rise to problems with regard to the marriage of Joseph and the Virgin Mary[3] who, according to one view, had exchanged vows of lifelong chastity. In the twelfth century, therefore, it became accepted that a valid marriage could be formed by the mere exchange of consents. Provided words of consent to marriage in the present tense (*sponsalia per verba de praesenti*) were used there was no need for any other ceremony, since the consent created the marriage.[4]

---

[1] For an accessible introduction, see W.R. Cornish and G. de N. Clark, *Law and Society in England 1750–1950* (1989), pp. 360–365.

[2] The text relied on was Genesis, 2, 24: "Therefore shall a man leave his father and his mother, and shall cleave unto his wife: and they shall be one flesh."

[3] See J.A. Brundage, *Law, Sex and Christian Society in Medieval Europe* (1987), p. 274.

[4] For the modern doctrine of the Catholic Church, see Canons 1055–60 (1983) and for the Anglican position, Canons B30-6.

If the consent was expressed in the future tense (not "I do marry you," but "I promise that I will marry you") and sexual intercourse subsequently took place, the parties then immediately became man and wife. The reason was that the *sponsalia per verba de futuro* "implied such a present consent at the time of the sexual intercourse as to complete the marriage in substance, and give it equal validity with the contract *de praesenti*."[5] Thus the Church reconciled two views: first, its own primitive doctrine that consummation was necessary to form a marriage; and, secondly, the doctrine derived from Roman law, that consent was the vital factor: *consensus non concubitus facit matrimonium*. The result was that the "one contract which . . . should certainly be formal had become the most formless of contracts."[6]

Informal common law marriages continued to be valid in England and Wales until 1753[7]; the old law remained in force in Scotland until 1940,[8] and common law marriages can still be contracted in some parts of the United States.[9]

C. Disadvantages of informality

1–004 The informality permitted by the common law had a number of disadvantages. First, it allowed clandestine marriages—marriages contracted in secret, without witnesses; and there would often be uncertainty about the validity of such a marriage. It was not so much that there might be doubts about the validity of the informal union itself; but rather that indiscreet and quickly forgotten words breathed under the influence of passion would be relied on many years later by one of the parties to a, possibly transient, relationship. The intention underlying such an assertion of an informal marriage might well be to invalidate the other party's subsequent solemn marriage with a third party.[10]

Secondly, hasty and ill-considered marriages were facilitated. The agreement

---

[5] T. Poynter. *A Concise View of the Doctrine and Practice of the Ecclesiastical Courts* . . . (2nd ed., 1824), p. 14.

[6] F. Pollock and F.W. Maitland. *The History of English Law* (2nd ed., 1898 reissued 1968), Vol. 2, p. 369. L. Stone, *Uncertain Unions* (1992), contains fascinating case studies derived from Process Books of the Court of Arches and other sources, and notes (at p. 3) that "very large numbers of perfectly respectable people in the seventeenth and early eighteenth centuries could never be quite sure whether they were married or not".

[7] The decrees of the Council of Trent (1563) required the presence of a priest and independent witnesses, but those rules never became part of English law. It is true that, according to *R. v. Millis* (1844) 10 Cl. & F. 534, H L, the presence of an episcopally ordained clergyman was necessary to the validity in this country of a common law marriage; but that decision is generally thought to be wrong: see J. Jackson, *The Formation and Annulment of Marriage* (2nd ed., 1989), pp. 18–19.

[8] Marriage (Scotland) Act 1939. In *Shaw v. Henderson* 1982 S.L.T. 211 such a marriage was held to have been established in 1978; and is still possible in Scotland to establish retrospectively a marriage "by cohabitation with habit and repute"; see generally E.M. Clive, *The Law of Husband and Wife in Scotland* (3rd ed., 1993), pp. 48–67. Such a marriage may be held to have been created where couples set up a home together as a married couple and are generally accepted as such; but no such marriage can exist where the parties have rejected the institution of marriage: see R(G) 4/84; and see also R(G) 2/82; R(G) 5/83.

[9] See H.D. Krause, *Family Law* (1995), pp. 58–59; and the references in C. Hamilton, *Family. Law and Religion* (1995), p. 44. The expression "common law marriage" is often incorrectly used to refer to a relationship between cohabitants.

[10] See, *e.g. Dalrymple v. Dalrymple* (1811) 2 Hag. Con. 54.

which is all that is necessary to form a valid common law marriage might—as an American writer has put it—have been entered into "in the privacy of one's own bedroom, in an automobile after a picnic in the country, or after a night's debauch."[11] In such cases, it seems unlikely that there would be much point in inquiring whether the promises were in the present or future tense.

Thirdly, the creation of such a marriage might have important and undesirable legal consequences. The American case of *State v. Ward*[12] provides a striking illustration of the potential evil of such "quickie" marriages: the defendant to a charge of unlawful intercourse with a minor successfully asserted that the complainant was his wife at common law.

Marriage had important financial consequences,[13] not least that the rich heiress's property immediately vested in her husband. The fact that the heiress had married in secret made no difference to the validity of the marriage and its possibly devastating effect in terms of the wife's family's property. It was this fact which led to pressure for legislation effectively outlawing the clandestine marriage.

D. Lord Hardwicke's Act and after

1–005 The Clandestine Marriages Act (almost always called Lord Hardwicke's Act), carried in 1753 against strong opposition, did away with the formless common law marriage in England.[14] The Act stipulated a public church ceremony after the calling of banns on three successive Sundays.[15] The consent of a minor's parents or guardians had to be obtained, and entries made in an official register. The Act applied to all except members of the Royal Family,[16] Quakers and Jews. Thus Protestant dissenters and Roman Catholics were compelled to marry according to the Anglican rite, or not at all.[17]

In 1836 the law was changed.[18] Quakers and Jews retained their distinctive

---

[11] H.D. Krause, *Family Law* (1995), p. 57, suggests that marriages between couples who exchanged their vows during a roller coaster ride and a couple who "exchanged their wedding kiss in the heavens, after parachuting out of a plane, along with their wedding party" were validly contracted under U.S. laws requiring compliance with specific formalities.

[12] 28 S.E. 2d 785 (1944).

[13] Below, Chap. 3, and for the move for reform, L. Stone, *Road to Divorce* (1990). Chap. 4; L. Stone, *Uncertain Unions* (1992), Chap. 1.

[14] See generally J.R. Gillis, *For Better, For Worse* (1985); S. Parker, "The Marriage Act 1753. A Case Study on Family Law-Making" (1987) 1 I.J.L. & F 133; S. Parker, *Informal Marriage, Cohabitation and the law, 1750–1989* (1990). Until 1856 it was possible for English residents to go to Scotland and there celebrate a marriage with traditional lack of official form. After that date by the law of Scotland (Marriage (Scotland) Act 1856, s.1) the parties had to reside in Scotland for three weeks.

[15] The Church of England retained the power to grant licences allowing marriage without the prior calling of banns: see below.

[16] Hence, they could continue to contract common law marriages, and it appears that some did so. This exemption from the formal requirements of the law appears to have been preserved, see the Marriage Act 1949, s.74(2); but in practice the freedom of members of the Royal Family to contract marriages has been restricted by the Royal Marriages Act 1772.

[17] See O. Chadwick, *The Victorian Church* (1966), Vol. I, p. 143; and generally R.B. Outhwaite, *Clandestine Marriage in England, 1500–1850* (1995).

[18] An important change had already been made by the Marriage Act 1823. Under Lord Hardwicke's Act, failure to obtain a necessary parental consent or to comply with any other stipulated formality

rights; but anyone else who wished to do so could marry outside the Church of England. Two main systems, operating in parallel, thus became available: (i) marriage in the Church of England, with requirements for banns or licence similar to those laid down by Lord Hardwicke's Act; and (ii) marriages under the provisions of the 1836 Act.[19] Marriages under the 1836 Act could be purely secular (the register office ceremony) or could (subject to certain conditions) be celebrated in non-Anglican places of worship. The law was consolidated by the Marriage Act 1949,[20] but it is still largely based on the pattern established in 1836.

III. FORMALITIES FOR MARRIAGE—THE MODERN LAW

1–006 The law prescribes certain preliminaries which must take place before the celebration of a marriage; it also lays down some rules about the ceremony itself, and about the registration of marriages.

A. Preliminaries to marriage

1. Parental consent[21]

1–007 "Parental" consent is, in principle, required to the marriage of a person who is under 18[22] (and not a widow or widower[23]); but a marriage solemnised without such consent will be valid.

Whose consent is required?

1–008 The legislation for long contained complex, outdated, and unsatisfactory rules defining the persons whose consent was required to the marriage of a minor;

---

invalidated the marriage. Under the 1823 Act formal defects only invalidated a marriage if the parties had "knowingly and wilfully" contravened the Act.

19 Marriage Act 1836. The law was subsequently amended by the Marriage Act 1898 so that a registrar did not need to be present at non-Anglican religious ceremonies.

20 Substantial amendments have been made to the 1949 Act, notably by the Marriage Act 1994.

21 Under the Royal Marriages Act 1772 the consent of the Sovereign in Council is required to the marriage of descendants of George II. A marriage contracted in defiance of the Act is void: note the illuminating article by T.B. Pugh and A. Samuels, "The Royal Marriages Act 1772; Its Defects and the Case for Repeal" (1994) 15 *Statute Law Review* 46 (and note also S.M. Cretney, "The Royal Marriage Act 1772: A Footnote" (1995) 16 *Statute Law Review* 195).

22 See the Marriage Act 1949, s.3, as amended by the Children Act 1989, Sched. 12, para. 5. Consent is only a statutory prerequisite to a marriage after civil preliminaries or by common licence; parental consent is not formally required to a marriage after the calling of banns, but the parent or other third party may object: s.3(3). Moreover the Canons of the Church of England (B32) prohibit a minister from solemnising a marriage "otherwise than in accordance with the requirements of the law relating to the consent of parents or guardians in the case of a person under eighteen years of age".

23 Consent is thus required in the unlikely event of a minor's previous marriage having been terminated by divorce or annulment.

but the law has been modernised by the Children Act 1989, and now substantially gives effect to the principle that the consent required should be that of the person or persons who have had actual day-to-day care of a child.

The rules are now that consent is required from the following:

(a) Each parent of the child who has "parental responsibility", and each guardian of a child. (The term "parental responsibility" is defined in the Children Act[24] so that, effectively, the father and mother of a legitimate child each have parental responsibility, but the father of an illegitimate child does not unless he acquires it in accordance with the provisions of the Act.)

(b) If a court has made a residence order which is in force with respect to the child, the consent of the person or persons with whom the child is to live under the terms of that order is required in substitution for that of the parents or guardians.[25]

(c) If the child is the subject of a care order, then the consent of the local authority designated in the order is required in addition to the consents of the parents and guardians.

(d) If there is no residence or care order in force, but a residence order was in force immediately before the child reached the age of 16, the consent of a person or persons with whom he or she was to live under that residence order is required.[26]

(e) If the child is a ward of court, the consent of the court is required in addition to that of any person specified above.[27]

Dispensing with parental consent

Consent may be dispensed with in two groups of case: **1–009**

(a) Where consent of a prescribed person "cannot be obtained by reason of absence or inaccessibility or by reason of his being under any disability." In such circumstances either the consent may be dispensed with by the superintendent registrar, or the court may consent.[28]

(b) If a person whose consent is required refuses to give it, application can be made to the court.[29]

---

[24] ss.2, 3.
[25] Marriage Act 1949, s.3(1A)(b).
[26] s.3(1A)(c),(d).
[27] s.3(6).
[28] Marriage Act 1949, s.3(1), proviso (a).
[29] s.3(1), proviso (b).

Should the requirement of parental consent be retained?

1–010 The age for "free marriage" was reduced from 21 to 18 by the Family Law Reform Act 1969.[30] There was subsequently a certain amount of discussion[31] about the need to retain any requirement of parental consent to the marriage of teenagers; but such discussions now have a somewhat dated flavour. Far from rushing into marriage in late adolescence, the trend has been towards marriage much later in life. The average age for first marriage[32] by women was 22.6 in 1971 but had risen to 30.1 in 1999; and, whereas in 1971 nearly a third of all brides married as teenagers, by 1999 the proportion had fallen to less than five per cent. The problem of teenage marriages seems thus to have solved itself. In some quarters it has been supplanted by the problem of teenage child bearing: in 1996 there were some 94,000 conceptions to women under 20 (about one third of which led to abortion)[33]; and it seems clear that the law governing the age for marriage has little to offer in respect of that phenomenon.

2. Other preliminaries—civil and anglican

1–011 In 1836, Parliament (as we have seen) allowed marriages to take place outside the Church of England; and it was originally intended that all marriages, wherever they took place, should be preceded by a single form of preliminary—the giving of notice, in a prescribed form, to a superintendent registrar. However, the House of Lords rejected this proposal; and two systems—the traditional Anglican procedures—administered by the Church itself—on the one hand and the state administered registrars' procedure introduced in 1836—continue to exist side by side. (It is important to note the procedure used for the *preliminaries* to marriage does not necessarily determine the way in which the marriage itself is celebrated; in particular, religious marriage ceremonies may well be preceded by civil preliminaries.)

The existence of two systems is a complication which many consider unnecessary and undesirable. In 1973, the Law Commission proposed a single code of preliminaries for all marriages[34] and this was supported by an *Efficiency Scrutiny of the Registration Service* conducted for the Thatcher government by the Marks and Spencer executive Sir Derek Rayner. But the Government adopted a, per-

---

[30] s.2(1)(c), giving effect to the recommendations of the *Committee on the Age of Majority* (Chairman: The Hon Mr Justice Latey) Cmnd. 3342 (1965) (subsequently cited as the *Latey Report*).

[31] By the Kilbrandon Committee. Cmnd. 4011 (1969), and by the Law Commission in P.W.P. No. 35.

[32] See C. Gibson, "Changing Family Patterns in England and Wales" in *Cross Currents* (S.N. Katz, J. Eekelaar and M. Maclean ed., 2000), Table 2.1. The average age for first marriage amongst men in 1999 was 30.1: see *Marriage and Divorce Statistics 1999*.

[33] (1999) 29 *Social Trends* 51. Although the teenage conception rate has fallen somewhat since 1990 (in 1996 there were 63 conceptions per thousand women under 20, as compared with 69 per thousand in 1990). The Government established a target of reducing the pregnancy rate of girls under 16 to 4.8 per thousand by the year 2000, but the rate appears to have remained almost double that figure: *cf.* (1996) 26 *Social Trends* 63.

[34] Law Com. No. 53, (1973).

haps surprisingly, cautious attitude to the proposals; and in the event comprehensive reform was deferred.[35]

In 1998 the Blair Government issued a wide-ranging Consultation Document *Supporting Families*, which indicated support for "measures to strengthen the institution of marriage". These included giving registrars "an enhanced role"[36]; and in 2002 a White Paper, *Civil Registration: Vital Change*[37] indicated that legislation was to be introduced with firm proposals for reform which have not, at the date of going to press, been met.[38] Some important changes were made, without any Parliamentary or other public debate,[39] by the Immigration and Asylum Act 1999.

In the circumstances, all that can be done is to set out, first the so-called "civil" preliminaries; and then the preliminaries laid down by law to govern marriage in the Church of England.

(a) Civil preliminaries

1–012 All marriages other than those to be solemnised in the Church of England have to be[40] preceded by preliminary formalities for which the superintendent registrar[41] of the relevant district[42] is responsible. It should be emphasised that these civil preliminaries have to be used, not only for civil marriages but for all non-anglican religious weddings.

These preliminaries are primarily designed to ensure that notice of the inten-

---

[35] For example, the White Paper *Registration: Proposals for Change*, Cm. 939 (1990), para. 3.2–3 accepted that "many factors other than administrative advantage had to be taken into account, and that "a wider consensus" was needed before "fundamental change" could be made in so sensitive an area. (However, it seems that the Archbishop's Council's Working Group—see below—is enjoying "extremely helpful" relations with the Government's officials: see *Just Cause or Impediment? A Report from the Review of Aspects of Marriage Law Working Group* (General Synod of the Church of England, 2001), p. 3.

[36] *Supporting Families* (1988), para. 4.4. It may be that these words were in part responsible for engendering fears in some quarters that the Government had plans for transferring the control of preliminaries to Anglican marriages to civil registrars; but the *Marriage Law Working Group* (see above) regarded these fears as groundless: para 9.

[37] Cm. 5355.

[38] See below, p. 000. For the Church of England's position see *Just Cause or Impediment? A Report from the Review of Aspects of Marriage Law Working Group* (General Synod of the Church of England, 2001) a discussion by a group set up by the Archbishops' Council to undertake a review of aspects of the law relating to marriage according to the rites of the Church of England. It points out that there is within the Church "a wide variety of influencing factors and different views" (para. 15).

[39] But see *Supporting Families—Summary of Responses to the Consultation Document* (1999), para. 4.7.

[40] Marriages in the Church of England may be preceded by one variant of the civil preliminaries—*i.e.* the issue of a superintendent registrar's certificate—rather than by ecclesiastical preliminaries: Marriage Act 1949, s.5(d).

[41] The office of superintendent registrar of births, death and marriages (which is constitutionally one of some interest: see *Miles v. Wakefield Metropolitan District Council.* [1987] A.C. 539, HL) was created by the 1836 legislation: see the Births and Deaths Registration Act 1836, and the Marriage Act 1836. The legislation is now consolidated in the Registration Service Act 1953.

[42] Superintendent registrars are appointed on a district basis, and are paid by local authorities, Registration Service Act 1953, s.6. The registrar-general (who is appointed by the Crown: *ibid.* s.1) is ultimately responsible for registration services.

ded marriage is given, thus providing publicity and an opportunity for objections to be made (*e.g.* by a parent who believes his or her consent should be obtained, or by a person who claims to be married to one of the intending spouse). There are now two[43] different procedures:

(i) superintendent registrar's certificate;
(ii) registrar-general's licence.

(i) Superintendent registrar's certificate

1–013 The main requirements are:

(i) *Notice*

Each party must give notice in a prescribed form to the superintendent registrar of the district or districts where he or she has resided for at least seven days.[44] All notices are recorded in a marriage notice book which is open to public inspection. The notice must be "suspended or affixed" for 21 days on a noticeboard in "some conspicuous place" in the superintendent registrar's office. The superintendent registrar is under an obligation to report to the Home Office Immigration Department any cases which give rise to suspicion.[45]

(ii) *Objections and inquiries*

1–014 The superintendent registrar will seek to satisfy himself that, on the basis of the evidence before him, the parties are free to marry. For example, if one party

---

[43] The Immigration and Asylum Act 1999, s.160, abolished (with effect from January 1, 2001) the procedure whereby a superintendent registrar could issue a certificate with licence (often, erroneously, called a "special licence". Such a certificate could be issued to permit a marriage at the expiration of one whole day from the giving of notice: if notice were given on Monday, for example, the marriage could take place on Friday. Furthermore, the notice of intended marriage was not required to be displayed in the registrar's office. An enhanced fee was payable for the grant of a certificate with licence; but it had long seemed anomalous that the waiting time could be reduced to 48 hours and publicity virtually eliminated simply by paying a fee which (apart from anything else) bore no relation to the cost of the service provided). However, the licence procedure was widely used and it is not yet clear whether the change in the law will give rise to grievances.

[44] Marriage Act 1949, s.27(1), as amended by Immigration and Asylum Act 1999, s.161(1). The notice must be in the prescribed form (see the Reporting of Suspicious Marriages and Registration of Births Deaths and Marriages (Miscellaneous Amendments) Regulations 2000, S.I. 2000 No. 3164) and will give details of the parties' age, marital status, place of residence, nationality, etc. The person giving notice is warned that to make a false declaration will expose him to prosecution. The 1999 Act introduced a requirement that a person giving notice should provide evidence of the prescribed matters if required to do so: Marriage Act 1949, s.28A inserted by Immigration and Asylum Act 1999, s.162.

[45] Immigration and Asylum Act 1999, s.24; Reporting of Suspicious Marriages and Registration of Births Deaths and Marriages (Miscellaneous Amendments) Regulations 2000, S.I. 2000. No. 3164.

states that she is a widow or has been divorced, proof of the relevant death or divorce will have to be produced.

Members of the public may object to an intended marriage: any person may enter a caveat with the superintendent registrar,[46] and any person whose consent is required to the marriage of a minor may forbid the issue of a certificate by writing "forbidden" by the entry and signing it with a statement of the capacity in which he purports to act.[47] The validity of the objection will then be investigated.

(iii) *Waiting time*

1–015 At the end of 15 days[48] from the giving of notice, the superintendent registrar will issue a certificate which authorises the solemnisation of the marriage within three months from the day when notice was entered in the marriage notice book.[49] This means that a couple must normally have been resident in this country for 22 days before they can marry here, and that they must wait for 15 days after taking the decision to marry before they can do so.[50] If there are "compelling reasons" for reducing the 15 day waiting period because of the "exceptional circumstances of the case"—it was suggested that a call to military service abroad might be such a reason—the Registrar General may, on application, reduce the period.[51]

These provisions may be effective in reducing the number of marriages of convenience contracted in this country. By requiring couples to reside here for three weeks they will certainly make it impossible for this country to exploit the—evidently substantial—market for combined marriage and honeymoon packages which appeal to many.[52]

(iv) *Special provisions for marriage of the house-bound and detained*

1–016 The Marriage Act 1983 introduced a procedure whereby persons who are house-bound by reason of illness or disability or detained in prison or under certain legislation relating to mental health may be married at their place of residence or detention on a superintendent registrar's certificate.

In order to take advantage of these provisions, the notice must be accompanied either by an official certificate giving details of the detention or by a doctor's certificate stating that by reason of illness or disability the person concerned ought not to move or be moved from the place where he or she is at the time, and that the position is unlikely to change for at least three months. Once the certificate has been issued, the marriage may be solemnised in an Anglican or

---

[46] Marriage Act 1949, s.29.

[47] s.30.

[48] Marriage Act 1949, s.31(2) as amended by the Immigration and Asylum Act 1999, s.160(4).

[49] s.33

[50] But a special licence granted by the Archbishop of Canterbury may authorise an Anglican marriage: see below.

[51] Marriage Act 1949, s.31(5A) as inserted by Immigration and Asylum Act 1999, s.160(6). Note also the provisions of the Marriage (Registrar-General's Licence) Act 1970: see below.

[52] Perhaps a tropical climate was thought to be a prerequisite to success in this field.

other religious ceremony, or in a civil ceremony at the place specified in the documents.

By providing facilities for marriages to be solemnised in a prison or hospital the United Kingdom gave effect to its obligations under the European Convention on Human Rights, and made unnecessary the practice of escorting prisoners to a marriage ceremony outside prison. But the Marriage Act 1983 contains some surprising omissions: for example, a person who is likely to die within a few days or weeks will not remain house-bound for the stipulated minimum period of three months. A separate procedure—the registrar-general's licence—may be invoked in such a case.[53]

(ii) Registrar-general's licence

1–017 Until 1971 there was no civil procedure which could be used to authorise marriage[54] outside a register office, or Anglican church, or a registered place of worship. This caused hardship where the parties wanted to contract a so-called "death-bed marriage". The only way of doing this was to obtain a special licence from the Archbishop of Canterbury[55]; but a licence would only be given for an Anglican marriage, and then, it would appear in practice, only to those who were free to marry by Anglican canon law. Thus a special licence would not normally be available where one of the parties had been divorced so long as the former spouse was still alive nor will a special licence be granted if neither party has been baptised.[56]

The Marriage (Registrar-General's Licence) Act 1970 accordingly provides a civil procedure analogous to the Archbishop's special licence. The registrar-general's licence may be issued if there is evidence that one of the persons to be married is seriously ill and not expected to recover, and that he or she cannot be moved to a place at which marriages can be solemnised under the 1949 Act.[57] It is specifically provided—presumably in order to avoid any interference with the traditional use of the Archbishop's licence—that the procedure shall not be used as a preliminary to an Anglican wedding.

In practice, the restrictively drawn provisions of this Act might be thought to have been rendered largely superfluous by the enactment of the Marriage Act 1983 (which establishes a simpler and more far-reaching procedure whereby the disabled may marry).[58] But in 1999, 214 registrar-general's licences were issued[59]; and as we have seen[60] there may be a few cases in which the 1970 Act can be used in circumstances in which the 1983 Act would not be available.

---

[53] See below.

[54] Other than Quaker and Jewish marriages: see below.

[55] See below.

[56] *Just Cause or Impediment? A Report from the Review of Aspects of Marriage Law Working Group* (General Synod of the Church of England, 2001), para. 37.

[57] Marriage (Registrar-General's Licence) Act 1970, s.l.

[58] See above. In particular, marriage under the 1983 Act may be civil or religious (including Anglican) as the parties wish.

[59] *Marriage and Divorce Statistics* 1999, Table 3.34.

[60] See above.

Nevertheless, it seems regrettable that the opportunity was not taken to draw the 1983 Act in terms wide enough to permit the repeal of the 1970 Act.

(b) Anglican preliminaries

1–018 Three procedures (administered exclusively by the church authorities) are available only as a preliminary to marriage according to the rites of the Church of England:

(i) banns;
(ii) common licence; and
(iii) special licence.

(i) Banns

1–019 This procedure is used in 90 per cent of Anglican weddings.[61] The main features of the law are as follows:

Residence

1–020 If the parties reside in the same parish the banns must be published there[62]; if in different parishes, in each of them.[63] They may also be published in any parish church or authorised chapel which is the usual place of worship[64] of one or both of the parties[65] but this will only be necessary if the parties are to be married there.[66]

There is no specific requirement as to length of prior residence, or as to what constitutes residence.[67]

---

[61] *i.e.* in 60,739 out of 67,219 Anglican marriages: *Marriage and Divorce Statistics 1999*, Table 3.34. Banns may, of course, be called in Roman Catholic or Non-conformist churches; but they have no legal significance in such cases.

[62] There is a great deal of case law on the proper publication of banns; see Jackson, *The Formation and Annulment of Marriage* (1969), pp. 169–182.

[63] Marriage Act 1949, s.6.

[64] In order to qualify for this purpose, the applicant must be enrolled on the church electoral roll: s.72.

[65] s.6(4).

[66] s.12(1).

[67] According to the Law Commission's *Working Paper No. 35* (1971) "the residential qualification is often regarded as fulfilled by booking a room in a local hotel and depositing a suitcase in it" (p. 11, n. 52), but *quaere* whether this is legally sufficient: *Fox v. Stirk* [1970] 2 Q.B. 463; *Hipperson v. Newbury District Electoral Registration Officer* [1985] Q.B. 1060. In the circumstances it is perhaps not surprising that one respondent to *Just Cause or Impediment? A Report from the Review of Aspects of Marriage Law Working Group* (General Synod of the Church of England, 2001) said that he spent more time dealing with matters of residence than any other issue so far as preliminaries are concerned, whilst another commented that the present law was "honoured much in the breach", and the Working Group noted "widespread concern at the lack of consistency exercised in the application of the legal rules: *op. cit.*, para. 111.

Publicity

1–021 The banns are entered in a register, and must be published therefrom[68] "in an audible manner and in accordance with the form of words prescribed by the rubric prefixed to the office of matrimony in the Book of Common Prayer" on three Sundays preceding the solemnisation.[69]

Discovery of impediments

1–022 The theory is that banns are primarily "addressed to Parents and Guardians, to excite their vigilance, and afford them fit opportunities of protecting those lawful rights which may be avoided by clandestinity".[70] But whereas in the case of civil preliminaries, the registrar may now require the production of evidence that any necessary consents have been obtained,[71] there is no analogous provision in relation to marriage after banns.[72]

Waiting time

1–023 The parties may marry immediately after the third publication of the banns. The wedding must be solemnised in one of the churches where the banns have been published.[73] The waiting time will depend on whether or not the clergyman requires seven days' notice before the first publication: the absolute minimum would be 15 days if publication were sought and made without prior notice on Sunday, in which event the marriage could take place on Monday fortnight. But in practice the waiting time will almost invariably be in excess of 21 days.

(ii) Common licence

1–024 This is the ecclesiastical counterpart of the superintendent registrar's certificate and licence. Basic rules are laid down in the Marriage Act,[74] but the details are matters of ecclesiastical law and practice.[75] Common Licences are granted

---

[68] "and not from loose papers": Marriage Act 1949, s.7(3).

[69] s.7(1)(2).

[70] T. Poynter, *A Concise View of the Doctrine and Practice of the Ecclesiastical Courts* . . . (2nd ed., 1824), p. 27.

[71] This power was only introduced by the Family Law Reform Act 1969, s.2(3), although it had prior to this been the practice of registrars to ask for such written consent; see *Latey Report,* para. 185. The Immigration and Asylum Act 1999 created an anomaly by giving civil registrars (but not the clergy) power to require the production of documentary evidence: Marriage Act 1949, s. 28A inserted by Immigration and Asylum Act 1999, s. 162.

[72] Canon B32 prohibits a clergyman from celebrating marriages in defiance of the parental consent requirement.

[73] Certificates must be provided of the publication of banns in the other relevant churches: s.11. The marriage must take place within three months of completion of publication: s.12.

[74] ss. 15–16.

[75] Since the grant of a licence is a matter for discretion, it is open to the church to impose conditions, *e.g.* that no licence will be issued unless one party is a baptised Christian: *An Honourable Estate* (1988), para. 178. It is not the practice to issue a licence where a party to the intended marriage is divorced and the former spouse is still living: *Just Cause or Impediment? A Report from the Review of Aspects of Marriage Law Working Group* (General Synod of the Church of England, 2001), p. 12.

by Diocesan Registrars (or by a surrogate appointed by the Chancellor of the Diocese). The main requirements are:

Residence

1–025 The licence can only permit a marriage in either the parish where one of the parties has had his usual place of residence for 15 days immediately before the grant of the licence or in the church which is "the usual place of worship"[76] of either or both parties.[77]

Declaration

1–026 In contrast to the procedure by banns, a common licence can only be granted if one of the parties swears an affidavit[78] that he or she believes there to be no lawful impediment, that the residential qualification is satisfied, and (where one of the parties is a minor and not a widow or a widower) that the requisite consents have been obtained or dispensed with.[79]

Publicity, discovery of impediments, and waiting time

1–027 A caveat may be entered against the grant of a licence; and if it is, no licence can be issued until the caveat has been withdrawn or the ecclesiastical judge certifies that the caveat should not obstruct the grant of a licence.[80]

There is no waiting time: once the licence is issued the marriage can take place immediately. In practice the formalities for obtaining a licence usually take some little time; but there is virtually no publicity or opportunity for objection. The cost is more than for the normal procedure by banns.

Only five per cent or so of Anglican marriages take place on the authority of a common licence.[81]

(iii) Special licence

1–028 By an Act of Parliament of 1533[82] power is reserved[83] to the Archbishop of Canterbury to license marriages at any hour of the day or night in any church or chapel or other meet and convenient place whether consecrated or not. Originally, we are told, licences "were intended exclusively for the use of persons of

---

[76] To qualify, the party's name must be on that church's electoral roll: s.72.

[77] s.15(1).

[78] Thus exposing himself to punishment for perjury if he or she knows that its contents are untrue.

[79] s.16.

[80] s.16(2).

[81] *Marriage and Divorce Statistics 1999*, Table 3.34; *Just Cause or Impediment? A Report from the Review of Aspects of Marriage Law Working Group* (General Synod of the Church of England, 2001), p. 13.

[82] The Ecclesiastical Licences Act. The Act provides a right of appeal to the Lord Chancellor against a refusal without reasonable cause to grant a licence: ss.11, 12.

[83] And see also the express savings in the Marriage Act 1949, s.79(6): Marriage (Registrar-General's Licence) Act 1970, s.19.

noble and illustrious quality". As recently as 1973 it was said that only some 250 were granted each year. But, for a variety of reasons, the use of the special licence procedure increased in the last quarter of the twentieth century. In 1999, 1867 Anglican marriages (2.7 per cent of the total) were by Archbishop's licence.[84] In practice they are today usually granted to permit marriages in places such as college chapels at Oxford and Cambridge and in churches with which neither party has the connections stipulated for marriage after banns or by licence.[85] It has been said[86] that the authorities exercise the jurisdiction to grant special licences "sparingly" and will only normally be used to permit a marriage outside the parish in which one or other of the parties resides if a "clear justification" is shown, and that normally there must be a clear connection between the parties and the place in question.

B. Solemnisation of the marriage

1–029 There are four main[87] categories of marriage ceremony in English law:

(1) civil marriage;
(2) marriage according to a non-Anglican religious ceremony;
(3) marriage according to the rites of the Church of England; and
(4) Quaker and Jewish marriages.

1. Civil marriage

1–030 Traditionally, civil marriages have taken place in a register office; but the Marriage Act 1994[88] provides for such marriages also to take place in "approved premises" (such as stately homes and hotels).

(a) Register office marriages

The ceremony

1–031 A register office ceremony can take place after completion of the civil preliminaries described above. The ceremony, which will take place "with open

[84] 1,051 out of a total of 67,219 Anglican marriages: *Marriage and Divorce Statistics 1999*, Table 3.34.

[85] It is possible to avoid the expense (Currently £120) of obtaining a special licence by taking advantage of the procedure authorised by s.46 of the Act. A marriage takes place after civil preliminaries: the couple then, on production of the Marriage Certificate, have a religious service celebrated: Marriage Act 1949, s.46(1), as amended by the Marriage Act 1983, Sched. 1, para. 12. But the couple are in law married by the civil ceremony: Marriage Act 1949, s.46(2).

[86] *Just Cause or Impediment? A Report from the Review of Aspects of Marriage Law Working Group* (General Synod of the Church of England, 2001), para. 37. The Faculty Office publishes the criteria which are applied in deciding on the grant of Archbishop's licences on its website: www.facultyoffice.org.uk

[87] There are special provisions relating to marriages in naval, military or air force chapels: Marriage Act 1949, Pt V.

[88] Marriage Act 1949, s.26(1)(bb) inserted by the Marriage Act 1994, s.1(2).

doors,"[89] must[90] be purely secular in form, and is in effect the exchange of the *sponsalia per verba de praesenti* in a prescribed modern form: "I call upon these persons here present to witness that I, A.B., do take thee, C.D., to be my lawful wedded wife (or husband)."[91] The parties are also required to declare that they know of no lawful impediment to the marriage.

Registrars sometimes declare[92] that it is their duty to remind the parties "of the solemn and binding character" of the marriage vows and that marriage "according to the law of this country is the union of one man with one woman, voluntarily entered into, for life, to the exclusion of all others." Since a divorced person is involved in more than half of all civil ceremonies[93] this allocution may often be inappropriate.

Which register office?

1–032 The Marriage Act 1949[94] provided that the marriage should take place in the register office serving the district in which one or both of the parties resided; but, in response to complaints that some register offices were mundane places without character,[95] the Marriage Act 1994 sought to give greater choice. It is now provided[96] that a superintendent registrar may issue a certificate for the solemnisation of the marriage in the office of another superintendent registrar, notwithstanding that the office is not within a registration district in which either of the parties resides. No doubt it is anticipated that local authorities (who are responsible for the provision of register offices[97]) will compete to provide attractive facilities.

(b) Marriages on approved premises

The premises

1–033 Until the coming into force of the Marriage Act 1994[98] civil marriages could be celebrated in only a single place in each registration district, namely the

---

[89] Marriage Act 1949, s.45. According to the form of instructions for the solemnisation of marriages in a registered building, the "doors need not actually be open provided they are not so closed as to prevent persons from entering that part of the building": S.I. 1952 No. 1869 Form 12, para. 3.

[90] s.45(2).

[91] ss.45(3), 46(1); but see n. 26 p. 30, below.

[92] The practice was intended to meet criticisms made by the Committee on Procedure in Matrimonial Causes (under the chairmanship of Denning J.) Cmd. 7024 (1947).

[93] In 1999, it appears that 85,686 of the 162,670 civil marriages involved one or two divorced persons: *Marriage and Divorce Statistics 1999*, Table 3.31.

[94] Marriage Act 1949, s.34.

[95] *Hansard* H.C., Vol. 250, col. 1334.

[96] Marriage Act 1949, s.35(2A) inserted by the Marriage Act 1994, s.2(1) (brought into force on January 1, 1995: The Marriage Act 1994 (Commencement No. 1) Order 1994, S.I. 1994 No. 3116).

[97] Registration Services Act 1953, s.10.

[98] The relevant provisions came into force on April 1, 1995: see the Marriage Act 1994 (Commencement No 2) Order 1995, S.I. 1995 No. 424.

register office. In accordance with the Thatcher government's general philosophy, the principle was adopted that people should have a choice of building in which their marriage may be celebrated and that a local authority should be empowered to have several marriage rooms of its own and also to license other suitable buildings (such as stately homes and hotels) as venues for civil marriages.[99] The Marriage Act 1994 accordingly permits civil marriages to be solemnised on "approved premises",[1] *i.e.* premises[2] approved by the local authority in accordance with regulations made by the Secretary of State.[3] The Regulations[4] require the local authority to satisfy itself that the premises provide a "seemly and dignified venue for the solemnisation of marriages; that the premises have no recent or continuing connection with any religion, religious practice or religious persuasion, and that the room or rooms in which ceremonies of marriage will be solemnised are identifiable by description as a distinct part of the building; whilst it is also provided that the marriage room be separate "from any other activity on the premises at the time of the ceremony". Precautions are also taken against some of the fears expressed about the availability of alcoholic drink at marriages by the requirement that no food or drink be sold or consumed in the room in which a marriage ceremony takes place for one hour prior to the cermony or during the ceremony.

It is understood that (in addition to hotels such as the Ritz, the Dorchester and Claridges) premises ranging from Caerphilly Castle, through HMS Warrior and Newnham College, Cambridge to the Newcastle United Football Club have been authorised under the Act.[5] According to *The Times* newspaper,[6] the owners of the London Eye hope that the "£1,700 service will attract thousands of couples" and that, for their money, the "wedding party gets a personal waiter and a pod filled with flowers that contains up to 20 guests. For an extra £299, another 25 guests can watch the ceremony from an adjacent capsule".

---

[99] *Registration: Proposals for Change*, Cm. 939 (1990) (criticised by A. Bradney [1989] *Fam. Law* 408).

[1] Marriage Act 1949, s.26(1)(bb), as inserted by Marriage Act 1994, s.1(1).

[2] Mr Gyles Brandeth, the sponsor of the Marriage Act 1994, stated that it was a basic tenet of English law that marriages should take place in a building; and that, while the idea of a wedding in a garden might seem attractive, it might be difficult to give a sufficiently specific description of the place in which an outdoor wedding was to be celebrated. "We do not want to encourage people to get married behind the bushes" (he said): *Hansard* (HC), Vol 250, col. 1330. However, according to a news story *The Times* on May 11, 2001 a couple were married in a pod on the London Eye; and it recorded that "two members of staff (one on the ground and one in the wedding pod) carried two way radios so that anyone rushing to object at the appropriate time could make their views heard".

[3] Marriage Act 1949, s.78(1) as amended by Marriage Act 1994, Sched. 1, para. 8.

[4] The Marriages (Approved Premises) Regulations 1995, S.I. 1995 No. 510.

[5] According to S. Byrne, *The Sunday Times*, August 27, 1995. It has also been reported that Eurostar has obtained a licence to hold weddings in the First Class Departure Lounge at Ashford International Railway station; and *The Times*, (March 21, 1996), states that guests will have to go through Customs to get to the marriage room. If accurate, it is questionable whether the requirement that marriages be celebrated "with open doors" will be honoured.

[6] May 11, 2001.

The ceremony

1–034 The Marriage Act 1994 is restricted to civil marriages[7]; and it is specifically provided[8] that no religious service[9] is to be used at a marriage on approved premises. It is also provided[10] that each of the parties to the marriage should make the declaration and use the form of words prescribed for register office ceremonies.[11] The marriage must be celebrated in the presence of two witnesses and the superintendent registrar and a registrar of the registration district in which the premises are situated.[12] Members of the public must be permitted to attend.[13]

(c) Use made of civil marriage

1–035 Civil marriages constituted more than 60 per cent of all marriages in England and Wales in 1999, continuing a long established trend towards the secular. Although this trend has been influenced by the refusal of many religious bodies to celebrate marriages if either party had been divorced and had a former spouse living, by 1999 almost half of the marriages between those who had never previously been married were civil marriages.[14] It is possible that the statistics will continue to be influenced by the increased readiness of some religious bodies[15] to provide facilities for remarriage after

---

[7] The rules which confine weddings to the district in which one of the parties resides (or usually worships) thus continues to apply to Anglican and other religious weddings, notwithstanding the fact that this requirement was found "especially irksome" by the public.

[8] Marriage Act 1949, s.46B(4), as inserted by Marriage Act 1994, s.1(2).

[9] The Marriages (Approved Premises) Regulations 1995, S.I. 1995 No. 510. Sched. 2, para. 10, further stipulates that any reading, music, words or performance which forms part of a ceremony of marriage celebrated on the premises must be secular in nature; and that for this purpose any such material used by way of introduction to, in any interval between parts of, or by way of conclusion to the ceremony shall be treated as forming part of the ceremony. In the course of debate on the Marriage Act 1994 it was suggested that popular tunes such as "Sheep may safely graze" might be inappropriate, and that it would even be found necessary to pick the parts of Ravel's *Danses Sacrées et Profanes*" which were profane rather than sacred: *Hansard* H.C. Vol. 250, col. 1339 (Mr Michael Stern). Although the intention to maintain the principle—regarded as of great importance when the facility of civil marriage was introduced in 1836—of purely secular marriage is apparent in practice it may be difficult to uphold it. The writer has been reliably informed that a Bishop of the Church of England, invited as a guest to an authorised premises wedding, responded positively to an invitation from the bride's father at the conclusion of the proceedings to give an episcopal benediction to the marriage.

[10] Marriage Act 1949, s.46B(1), as inserted by Marriage Act 1994, s.1(2).

[11] *ibid.*, ss.44(3), 46B(3).

[12] *ibid.*, s.46D(1), as inserted by Marriage Act 1994, s.1(2). It may be for this reason that Mr Robin Cook (at the time occupant of the Foreign Secretary's country residence at Chevening) apparently resiled from his reported intention to marry there, in the event preferring what the Press described as a "very private and very personal" ceremony at a London Register Office: see *The Times*, April 10, 1998.

[13] Marriage Act 1949, s.46B(2), as inserted by Marriage Act 1994, s.1(2).

[14] 74,244 out of a total of 155,027: see *Marriage and Divorce Statistics 1999*, Table 3.31.

[15] For a case in which a man whose wife had obtained a decree absolute of divorce against him subsequently sought a decree of nullity, in part so that he would thereafter be able to marry in a church, see *W v. W (Nullity: Gender)* [2001] 1 F.L.R. 324. Non-conformist churches are less reluctant than the Established and Roman Catholic churches to solemnise the marriages of the divorced: slightly more than half of the marriages by Methodist ceremonies in 1999 involved a

divorce and the impact of hotel, stately home and wedding-palace marriages but it seems clear that marriage has now, for the majority of the population, become a secular event.

2. Marriage according to a non-Anglican religious ceremony[16]

1–036 Since 1836, places of worship may be registered for the solemnisation of matrimony; and since 1898[17] it has been possible for an authorised person (usually a minister of the religious group concerned) to be nominated to celebrate marriages without the presence of the registrar. The state is thus responsible for the preliminaries to marriage, and licenses both the places where the marriages can take place and those who can solemnise them; but the form of the ceremony is left almost entirely to the parties and the authorities of the registered building.

(a) Preliminaries

1–037 The parties must comply with the civil preliminaries, as set out above. The certificate will state where the ceremony is to be held.[18] This must normally be a registered building in the district where one of the parties resides.[19]

(b) Registration of buildings

1–038 If a building is to qualify for registration, it must be a "separate building"[20] which is "a place of meeting for religious worship." It has been judicially[21] stated that religious worship usually means reverence or veneration of God or of a supreme being, and that the expression used in the legislation connotes a place where people come together as a congregation or assembly to do reverence to a deity. Applying this test, the Court upheld the registrar-general's refusal to register a chapel of the Church of Scientology. Sikh and Hindu temples and Muslim mosques are entitled to be registered, although in fact only a comparatively small number are registered.[22]

---

divorced person. In contrast, some 11per cent of Anglican weddings involved a divorced person (a percentage which has increased in recent years and seems still to be increasing) whereas the Roman Catholic church seems still to uphold its traditional discipline in this matter, with fewer than seven per cent of such marriages: *Marriage and Divorce Statistics 1999*, Table 3.31.

[16] For Jewish and Quaker marriages, see below.

[17] Marriage Act 1898.

[18] Marriage Act 1949, ss.27(3), 31, 32, 35(5).

[19] But there is power to designate a building elsewhere if this is the nearest place in which a particular form of religious ceremony can be conducted, or if it is the usual place of worship of one or both parties: *ibid.*, s.35.

[20] *ibid.*, s.41(1), unless it is a Roman Catholic chapel: Marriage Acts Amendment Act 1958, s.1(1).

[21] *per* Lord Denning M. R., *R. v. Registrar-General. ex p. Segerdal* [1970] 2 Q. B. 697 at 707; and see further *Re South Place Ethical Society* [1980] 1 W.L.R. 1565: [1981] Conv. 150 (St. J. Robilliard).

[22] See A. Bradney [1989] *Fam. Law* 408; Although the sponsor of the Marriage Act 1994, Mr Gyles Brandeth. stated that there were 281 "eastern religious buildings" registered (see *Hansard* H.C. Vol. 250, col. 1330) the *Marriage and Divorce Statistics* 1999. Table 3.42 indicate that 594 mosques, 180 Sikh Temples and 385 "other" buildings were registered in that year.

(c) The celebrant

1–039 Marriages in registered buildings must be attended either by a registrar or an "authorised person"—*i.e.* a person whose authorisation by the trustees or governing body of the building has been duly notified to the authorities.[23] In practice, the authorised person will be a minister of the religion concerned and allowing an "authorised person" to act instead of a registrar is intended to minimise the discrimination against religious groups outside the established church.

(d) The ceremony

1–040 The Act provides that the marriage shall be celebrated with open doors in the presence of two or more witnesses, and a registrar or authorised person. The authorised person will often be the celebrant.[24]

Subject to one important qualification, the marriage may be solemnised "according to such form and ceremony as [the parties] may see fit to adopt",[25]—for example, according to Hindu or Islamic form. The qualification is that it is essential that at some stage in the proceedings the parties make the following[26] statements:

> "I do solemnly declare that I know not of any lawful impediment why I, A.B., may not be joined in matrimony to C.D.";

and:

> "I call upon these persons here present to witness that I, A.B., do take thee, C.D., to be my lawful wedded wife [or husband]."[27]

---

[23] Marriage Act 1949, s.43.

[24] See the Law Commission's *Working Paper No. 35* (1971), para, 87.

[25] Marriage Act 1949, s.44(1).

[26] The Marriage Ceremony (Prescribed Words) Act 1996 provides a modernised alternative forms of words: "I declare that I know of no legal reason why I [name] may not be joined in marriage to [name]" (or the parties may simply answer "I am" to the question "Are you [name] free lawfully to marry [name]?"). The alternative "words of contract" are that the parties may say to each other "I [name] take you [*or* thee] [name] to be my wedded wife [*or* husband]": s.1(1).

[27] *ibid.*, s.44(3). When the marriage is in the presence of an authorised person (instead of a registrar) the formula "I, A. B., do take thee, C. D., to be my wedded wife (or husband)" may be substituted.

3. Marriage according to the rites of the Church of England

(a) Preliminaries

1–041 A marriage can take place either (i) after completion of any of the ecclesiastical preliminaries, or (ii) on the authority of a superintendent registrar's certificate.[28]

It is commonly believed that a clergyman of the Church of England is bound to solemnise the marriage of a parishioner irrespective of the religion (or lack of it) of the parties.[29] But by statute a clergyman is entitled to refuse to marry any person whose former marriage has been dissolved (on whatever ground) if the former spouse is still living, and he may refuse to celebrate marriages permitted by the civil law between persons who are related by affinity. He may also refuse to allow such marriages to be solemnised in his church.[30]

(b) The ceremony

1–042 The marriage must be celebrated by a clergyman in the presence of two or more witnesses[31] according to the rite prescribed in the Book of Common Prayer or other authorised form of service.

4. Quaker and Jewish marriages

1–043 Quaker and Jewish marriages were exempted from the provisions of Lord Hardwicke's Act, but it is now necessary for one of the forms of civil preliminaries to be completed. In the case of Quaker marriages ("marriages according to usages of Society of Friends")[32] a special declaration has to be made when giving notice.[33] There is no statutory requirement in the case of Jewish marriages save that the marriage be between "two persons professing the Jewish religion".[34]

The celebration of Jewish and Quaker marriages is entirely a matter for the rules of those religions. They need not be celebrated in a registered building, by

---

[28] Marriage Act 1949, s.5(d). It seems that very few marriages are celebrated in reliance on a registrar's certificate, and for many years such marriages were extremely rare. However in 1999 there were 1,051 (albeit only 1.6 per cent of the total of Anglican marriages). It appears that some clergy encourage this procedure as an alternative to the calling of banns in cases in which they have agreed to solemnise a wedding involving a divorced person: *Just Cause or Impediment? A Report from the Review of Aspects of Marriage Law Working Group* (General Synod of the Church of England, 2001), p. 13.

[29] *Argar v. Holdsworth* (1758) 2 Lee 515; *Davis v. Black* (1841) 1 Q.B. 900; *An Honourable Estate* (1988), App. I.

[30] Matrimonial Causes Act 1965, s.8(2); Marriage (Prohibited Degrees of Relationship) Act 1986, s.3.

[31] Marriage Act 1949, s.22.

[32] s.47.

[33] *ibid.*, s.47.

[34] *ibid.*, s.26(1)(d). There is no comparable requirement in the case of Quaker marriages provided that the Society of Friends' general rules permit the marriage: s.47(1).

an authorised person, or in public. There are, however, special rules for the registration of such marriages.[35]

Hours for marriage

1–044 Except in the case of Quaker and Jewish marriages, and marriages by special[36] or registrar-general's[37] licence, it is an offence knowingly and wilfully to celebrate a marriage save between 8 a.m. and 6 p.m.[38] However, a marriage contracted outside those hours will be valid.[39]

C. Registration and proof of marriages

1–045 The objects of a system of registration are to ensure that[40]:

> " . . . there is a public record of an event which has important legal consequences both for the parties themselves and for third parties and for the State. The parties need such a record as evidence of their marriage and so that they can present proof of it to others. Third parties need it so that they can determine the status of the parties and the status (*e.g.* legitimacy) of themselves and others in so far as that is dependent on the marriage of the parties. The State needs it because upon it may depend rights and obligations owed by or to the State in relation, for example, to tax, social security, and allegiance. An effective system of registration affords means of proof or disproof and avoids uncertainty where certainty is essential. In addition registration provides statistics regarding marriage which are vital for any serious research into legal, social or demographical problems."

There are statutory provisions facilitating proof of marriage by production of a certified copy of the relevant entry in the register of marriages[41]; but where no such evidence is available the court may, on evidence that the couple had cohabited for such a length of time and in such circumstances as to acquire the reputation of being husband and wife, presume that a marriage ceremony has taken place and that the ceremony complied with the necessary formalities.[42]

---

35 See Marriage Act 1949, Pt IV.

36 *ibid.*, ss.75(1). 79(6).

37 Marriage (Registrar-General's Licence) Act 1970, s.8(1).

38 s.75(1)(a); s.4.

39 See below.

40 Law Com. No. 53 (1973), Annex, para. 104.

41 See Marriage Act 1949, s. 65. Marriages abroad need to be proved, but the need to obtain expert evidence of the local law has been reduced by a provision in the Rules allowing proof of a marriage outside England and Wales the validity of which is not disputed by production of a document purporting to be a marriage certificate issued under the relevant law or a certified copy: Family Proceedings Rules, 10.4 10.4.

42 See *Mahadervan v. Mahadervan* [1964] P. 233; *Pazpena de Vire v. Pazpena de Vire* [2001] 1 F.L.R. 460; *A-M v. A-M (Divorce: Jurisdiction: Validity of Marriage)* [2001] 2 F.L.R. 6. In *Chief Adjudication Officer v. Bath* [2000] 1 F.L.R. 8 the Court of Appeal applied the presumption in a case where the parties had gone through a Sikh marriage ceremony in a Gurdwara in West London in 1956 and thereafter lived together as husband and wife for 37 years until the man's death.

In 2002 the Government announced plans[43] to modernise registration facilities, for example by the provision of computer support for the registration service.[44]

D. Consequences of irregularities

1–046 There are three categories of irregularity: (1) those which invalidate the marriage; (2) those which have no effect on the validity of the marriage; (3) those as to the consequence of which the legislation is silent.

1. Defects invalidating the marriage

1–047 In sharp contrast to the system originally introduced by Lord Hardwicke's Act,[45] the general principle of modern English law is that only contumacious disregard of the marriage formalities will invalidate a marriage. The Act provides that if the parties "knowingly and wilfully" disregard certain requirements the marriage shall be void.[46] It has never been determined whether it is sufficient that the parties know that in fact the formality has not been observed, or whether they must also know that the defect will in law invalidate the marriage.[47]

Examples of irregularities falling within this class (in the case of Anglican marriages) are: (a) marriages celebrated other than in a church or chapel where banns may be published; (b) failure properly to carry out the necessary preliminaries; (c) marriages after parental objection has been duly made or after expiry of the banns; and (d) marriages performed by persons not in Holy Orders.

Examples in respect of other marriage procedures are (a) marriages without due notice or without a certificate; (b) marriages after the certificate has expired; (c) marriages in a place other than that specified in the certificate; and (d) marriages in the absence of a registrar, where such presence is required.[48]

2. Defects not affecting the validity of the marriage

1–048 The legislation specifies certain defects, evidence of which is not to be given in proceedings touching the validity of the marriage; and it would seem to follow

---

However, the building had not been registered nor had any attempt been made to comply with the statutory provisions as to notice and the attendance of a Registrar at the ceremony. It was established that the couple had not intended to break the law, and accordingly the provisions of Marriage Act 1949, s.49 (invalidating marriages "knowingly and wilfully" contracted in breach of these formal requirements) did not apply.

[43] *Civil Registration: Vital Change* Cm. 5355 (2002).

[44] Publication of the Government's proposals was long delayed: see *Just Cause or Impediment? A Report from the Review of Aspects of Marriage Law Working Group.* (General Synod of the Church of England, 2001), p. 4.

[45] Under which failure to comply with the stipulated procedures made the purported marriage void. (Thus the marriage would have no effect on the parties property rights.)

[46] Marriage Act 1949, ss.25 (Anglican marriages), 49 (marriage under certificate).

[47] *Greaves v. Greaves* (1872) L.R. 2 P. & D. 423 at 424–425, *per* Lord Penzance.

[48] Marriage Act 1949, ss.25 (Anglican marriages), 49 (marriage under certificate); and see *Chief Adjudication Officer v. Bath* [2000] 1 F.L.R. 8, and n. 42, above.

that such defects cannot invalidate the marriage. This class includes: (a) failure to obtain parental consent; and (b) failure to comply with the requirements as to the parties' residence.[49]

3. Other defects

1–049 The Marriages Act 1949 is silent as to the consequences of certain irregularities: these include the requirements that the ceremony take place between 8 a.m. and 6 p.m., that it be celebrated with open doors, and that certain prescribed words be used. It seems probable that such irregularities do not affect the validity of the marriage.[50]

Overriding all these rules, there is probably a general principle that a marriage can in English law only be created by something which can be described as "a ceremony in a form known to and recognised by our law as capable of producing . . . a valid marriage[51]; and if this is correct, a purported "marriage" by African customary law in a private house, or an Islamic ceremony outside a registered building, for example, would be wholly ineffective.

E. The case for reform

1–050 One obvious difficulty of the marriage laws is their complexity and obscurity. As long ago as 1988 a Government Green Paper, "Registration: A Modern Service"[52] said that "many of the procedures [relating to marriage] are unnecessarily complex and restrictive and reflect the needs and social conditions of the early nineteenth century rather than those of the late twentieth century", whilst the Law Commission had stated that the "proliferation of procedures" outlined above meant that "the law is not understood by members of the public or even by all those who have to adminster it."[53] Some evidence of this lack of understanding is provided by the Efficiency Scrutiny of the Registration Service: many errors were found in the documentation completed by the Anglican clergy who deal with the preliminaries for some 110,000 marriages each year. This is obviously unsatisfactory; but what other objects should a good marriage code seek to attain? It is suggested that they include the following:

1. Certainty

1–051 There should be no doubt whether or not a marriage has been created. Moreover, the precise moment of time at which the parties become man and wife should

---

[49] *ibid.* s.48.

[50] See the Law Commissions Report on *Solemnization of Marriage in England and Wales* (Law Com. No. 53 (1973), Annex. para. 120).

[51] *R. v. Bham* [1966] 1 Q.B. 159, a criminal prosecution against a celebrant for "knowingly and wilfully" celebrating a Muslim marriage contrary to the provisions of s.75, and see *Gandhi v. Patel* [2002] 1 F.L.R. 603.

[52] Cm. 531, para. 3.2.

[53] Law Com. No. 53, Annex, para. 6.

be ascertainable, since otherwise there may be problems about legitimacy and succession rights.

It is clearly a major defect of English law that it fails to make the consequences of a number of procedural defects clear.[54] The minimal requirements (relating to both preliminaries and celebration) for a valid marriage should be clearly specified.[55]

It is also unsatisfactory that validity or invalidity may depend on a subjective test of the parties' knowledge and intent[56]; while English law even fails to make it clear at what moment of time the marriage is complete.[57] It may be well be that the crucial moment is the formal exchange of consent, as in the Australian case of *Quick v. Quick*[58]:

> The parties had exchanged the marriage promises but as the man was putting the ring on the woman's finger (and before the priest had joined their hands or pronounced them man and wife) she pulled it off, hurled it to the ground and, with the words "I will not marry you," ran out of the church. It was held that the parties had been validly married.

2. Proof and public records

1–052 The system of registration introduced into English law in 1836 provides a reasonably effective means whereby the parties can prove that they have contracted a valid marriage: production of an official sealed copy of the entry in the register is to be received as evidence of the marriage to which it relates.[59]

3. Consents and avoidance of fraud

1–053 The law should seek to ensure that both parties to a marriage are free to marry and do in fact truly consent to the marriage; and it should also ensure that any requisite parental consent has been given. The procedures should ensure that all those with legitimate interests in opposing the marriage—a class which might, for example, extend to the relatives of an elderly and demented person[60]—are discovered. In these respects, the present law is seriously defective.

English law at present seeks to attain the objectives set out above by publicising the intended marriage: banns are called, or a notice is displayed on a public notice board so that the local populace can check that nobody who is ineligible

---

[54] The existing law provides a procedure for retrospective validation of marriages where there is doubt: Provisional Order (Marriages) Act 1905 as amended.

[55] See Law Com. No. 53 (1973). Annex, paras 121–133 for a valuable analysis.

[56] *ibid.* para. 121.

[57] It seems that this question occupied the mind of the celebrated jurist A.V. Dicey during his own wedding: see R.A. Cosgrove, *The Rule of Law: Albert Venn Dicey, Victorian Jurist* (1980).

[58] [1953] V.R. 224.

[59] Marriage Act 1949, s.65(3).

[60] See, *e.g. Re Davey* [1981] 1 W.L.R. 164 (marriage of 92-year-old spinster to employee of care home in which she resided).

is trying to get married.[61] But in fact, in these days of "larger, more mobile and more anonymous populations"[62] the statutory provisions wholly fail to achieve publicity for the intended marriage. The conditions which made the calling of banns in rural English parishes a hundred or more years ago an important and talked about event have vanished, never to reappear; whilst the Efficiency Scrutiny's investigations confirmed that the main use made of the register office's marriage notice boards is by photographers, florists, "salesmen of insurance, babyware and marital aids" in order to identify potential customers.[63] Only one superintendent registrar had ever heard of the display of a notice leading to a valid objection "and that by pure chance."[64] The only remedy likely to have much impact on this problem would seem to be the creation of a national register of civil status on the continental pattern. Although such an idea may be an "anathema to many,"[65] anything less may be thought to be an unsatisfactory compromise.[66]

4. Solemnisation of the marriage

1–054 The parties should obviously be made to understand that they are contracting a marriage according to English law; but the present law does little to achieve this objective—particularly if either party does not understand English. He or she might for example (reasonably but wrongly) think that Islamic law governs a marriage contracted in a mosque in England. Even if the ceremony takes place in a register office there are few effective precautions to ensure that both parties understand that it is a marriage ceremony (as distinct from a betrothal[67]) and that the marriage so created is monogamous.[68] It would require only minor changes in the law to remedy these defects. But the multiplicity of marriage systems is bound to cause confusion, and the question arises whether (as in many foreign countries) a civil ceremony should become the only legally effective way of contracting a marriage—the parties would of course remain free subsequently to go through any religious ceremony they pleased. There is a long history of proposals for reform along these lines, but an equally long history of their being rejected (often, it would seem, on no better ground than that the foreign overtones of such a procedure would, as a Royal Commission put it in 1868, be

---

[61] Efficiency Scrutiny, para. 41.1.
[62] *ibid.*
[63] *ibid.*
[64] *ibid.*
[65] P.W.P. 35, para. 115.
[66] See Kilbrandon Report, para. 128, and the cogent criticism in Law Com. No. 53 (1973), Annex, paras. 116–117.
[67] As in *Parojcic v. Parojcic* [1958] 1 W.L.R. 1280 (marriage of Yugoslavs in Oxford register office).
[68] The Government anticipated that the amendments to the Marriage Act 1949 made by the Immigration and Asylum Act 1999 (and in particular the requirement that both parties to the intended marriage attend to give the requisite notice of their intention) should help ensure that both parties understood the nature of marriage in English law.

"opposed to the habits and feelings of the great majority of the people of Great Britain").[69]

5. An impressive ceremonial

1–055 A marriage ceremony (in the Law Commission's words[70]) "is an important family and social occasion." It should therefore adequately express the significance of the occasion and not be surrounded by "unnecessary and irksome restrictions." A limited move towards this objective was taken by the provisions introduced by the Marriage Act 1994 giving choice about the place in which a civil wedding may be solemnised; but the law about religious weddings remains complex and unsatisfactory; and the Government has failed to find time to give effect to proposals whereby many more buildings (for example, university, college, and school chapels) could be used for weddings without special formality.

In 2002 the Government issued a White Paper, *Civil Registration: Vital Change,*[71] announcing an intention to update the legislation governing the registration of births, deaths and marriages by 2004 with implementation of the changes starting in 2005. It is clear that the Government propose to retain the distinction between civil and religious marriage[72]; but that the system will move towards the registration of *celebrants* rather than the *places* where weddings can take place. It will be left to the celebrant to agree the time at which the wedding is to take place, and (within certain limits) where the wedding takes place. It is also clear that the Government plan to make extensive use of information technology, and that those who provide registration services are to be encouraged. But much else remains obscure, concealed behind the excited rhetoric currently fashionable in Government publications. Will the Church of England be allowed to retain the system of calling banns as an alternative to giving prior notice of the intended marriage, for example? Although it appears that Ministers have given the Church so to understand,[73] the scope of what is intended is far from clear.[74]

---

[69] *Report of the Royal Commission on the Laws of Marriage* (1868, BPP 1867–1868, vol. 32), p. 35. It appears that the Blair Government is well aware of the need to ensure the approval of the Church of England (and no doubt other groups) to proposals for reform: see *Just Cause or Impediment? A Report from the Review of Aspects of Marriage Law Working Group* (General Synod of the Church of England, 2001), pp. 2–6.

[70] Law Com. No. 53 (1973), Annex, para. 4.

[71] *Civil Registration: Vital Change* Cm. 5355 (2002), para. 3.12.

[72] Cm. 5355 (2002).

[73] See *Just Cause or Impediment?* (2001), p. 3; *Civil Registration: Vital Change* Cm. 5355 (2002), para. 3.7. The Church of England is expected to debate its own approach in the course of 2002.

[74] Many other controversial aspects of the registration process are not discussed in detail—for example, will it be possible to amend the registration of a transsexual's birth; are the present rules which restrict the right of a father to have his paternity recorded to be retained?—whilst some proposals seem inconsistent with current government policy (for example the Immigration and Asylum Act 1999 insists on personal attendance to give notice of intended marriage, whilst *Civil Registration: Vital Change* enthusiastically advocates the use of the telephone and internet for registration of births (and deaths)–

CHAPTER TWO

CAPACITY TO MARRY AND NULLITY

I. HISTORICAL INTRODUCTION: THE DISTINCTION BETWEEN VOID AND VOIDABLE MARRIAGES[1]

2–001 For reasons which can only be understood by reference to history, English law draws a distinction between void and voidable marriages.

Until the Reformation, a marriage was either valid or void. The existence of any of the impediments recognised by the canon law—for example, that either party was already married, or that either party was incapable of consummating the marriage—would invalidate a purported marriage. It made no difference that the couple had been through a solemn marriage ceremony and had thereafter lived together as man and wife for many years. There never had been a marriage between them; and their relationship could create none of the legal consequences of marriage. Hence, for example, their children would be illegitimate and disqualified from succeeding to the parents' property.

The right to seek a decree from the ecclesiastical court decree declaring the union "to have been and to be absolutely null and void to all intents and purposes whatsoever"[2] was not confined to the parties; and anyone who had an interest in the matter (such as a relative entitled to property in default of legitimate issue) could dispute the validity of the marriage. This could be done perhaps many years after the death of the parties.[3]

It must also be remembered that there was, until 1857, in general no divorce in English law.[4] A decree of nullity thus provided the only lawful escape from a union which had become intolerable. Not surprisingly, the grounds on which

---

[1] See generally on the early development of the law F. Pollock and F. W. Maitland, *The History of English Law* (2nd ed., 1898 reissued 1968), Vol. 2, pp. 7–30; and for comprehensive accounts R. Phillips, *Putting Asunder, A History of Divorce in Western Society* (1988), Chaps. 1 and 2; J. Jackson, *The Formation and Annulment of Marriage* (2nd ed., 1969), pp. 7–58; and (for the canon law and its impact) J. A. Brundage, *Law, Sex and Christian Society in Medieval Europe* (1987), p. 274. L. Stone, *Uncertain Unions, Marriage in England 1660–1753* (1992) contains interesting case studies; and reference may be made to the same author's *Road to Divorce* (1990) for useful contextual material. For the concept of the voidable marriage, see F. H. Newark (1945) 8 *M.L.R.* 203; E. J. Cohn (1948) 64 *L.Q.R.* 324; D. Tolstoy (1964) 27 *M.L.R.* 385. The development of English law was greatly influenced by the matrimonial problems of Henry VIII: for illuminating accounts see J. Scarisbrick, *Henry VIII* (2nd ed., 1997), Chap. 7.

[2] *De Reneville v. De Reneville* [1948] P. 100.

[3] There were certain limited exceptions: see J. Jackson, *The Formation and Annulment of Marriage* (2nd ed., 1989), pp. 44–53. S.M. Waddams, *Law, Politics and the Church of England, The Career of Stephen Lushington 1782–1873* (1992) is a source of much useful information about the working of the ecclesiastical law in practice.

[4] The so called divorce *a mensa et thoro* was the equivalent of the modern judicial separation.

decrees of nullity could be obtained were considerably extended[5] and it is said that an ingenious lawyer could usually discover some flaw in a marriage. The result was to create great uncertainty about the validity of marriages, and this uncertainty could affect property rights.

This was unsatisfactory; and after the Reformation the common law courts began to prohibit the ecclesiastical courts from impeaching the validity of marriages on certain grounds[6] after the death of either party. This practice effectively created the main conceptual distinction between void and voidable marriages[7]: a decree could be pronounced in relation to a void marriage at any time, even after the death of the parties, but voidable marriages could only be attacked during the lifetime of both parties.

The other distinctions between the two categories can conveniently be tabulated as follows:

Void	*Voidable*
No valid marriage ever existed.	The marriage is valid unless annulled.
Any interested person[8] may take proceedings.	Only the parties to the marriage can take proceedings.
A decree is not necessary since the marriage does not exist.	Unless a decree is obtained the marriage remains in force.

II. SIGNIFICANCE OF DECREE

2–002 The modern legislation defines the grounds on which a marriage is void, and those on which it is voidable[9]; and the distinction between the void and merely voidable still remains of practical importance, not least because it is never *necessary* to obtain a decree annulling a void marriage. But it will now often be in a petitioner's interest to obtain a decree in respect of a purported marriage which was void in law. This is because, in order to avoid hardship, many of the incid-

[5] See, *e.g.* the concept of prohibited degrees of affinity, below. Similar developments have occurred in those modern states where divorce is not available: see, *e.g.* the use of nullity in Ireland (whose constitution prohibited divorce): W.R. Duncan and P.E. Scully, *Marriage Breakdown in Ireland: Law and Practice* (1990); P. O'Connor, "Ireland: Nullity and the Judiciary" (1993–94) 32 Louisville J. Fam. L. 345.

[6] Those subsequently termed "canonical disabilities" (*i.e.* impotence, marriage within the prohibited degrees, lack of age or pre-contract).

[7] See also (i) the distinction suggested by Lord Guest in *Ross Smith v. Ross Smith* [1963] A.C. 280 at 348. "In a void marriage the decision depends upon the ascertainment of a state of facts instantly verifiable at the date of the marriage. ... Where a marriage is voidable the decision depends on supervening circumstances, such as ... impotence which may be *quoad hanc* and therefore not ascertainable till after the parties have cohabited"; and (ii) the justification advanced by Walton J. in *Re Roberts dec'd* [1978] 1 W.L.R. 653 at 656, that void marriages are those which cannot be permitted on social and public policy grounds taking priority over anything that the parties themselves wish, whereas voidable marriages are those where it is appropriate to leave it entirely to the parties whether or not to take advantage of their right to obtain a decree.

[8] As to what constitutes a sufficient interest, see J. Jackson, *The Formation and Annulment of Marriage* (2nd ed., 1969), pp. 100–102.

[9] See below.

ents of a valid marriage have by statute been attached to void marriages provided that a decree of nullity is obtained. Consider, for example, the case of a marriage which is void because the husband was already married to a third party.[10] Unless and until a decree is granted, the wife has none of the legal rights normally attaching to that status, for the simple reason that she is not married. But if a decree is granted[11] she becomes entitled to apply for financial relief orders in the same way as a wife whose marriage has been dissolved.[12]

In effect, therefore, a decree declaring a marriage void gives the parties some at least of the rights and duties flowing from a legal status which they never had.[13]

Void or non-existent?

2–003 The fact that a decree relating to a void marriage has these consequences prompts the question whether the traditional classification into void and voidable marriages is now exhaustive. May there not be certain purported unions which do not even qualify as "void" marriages? It has been said[14] that the word "marriage" used in the legislation is "no more than convenient shorthand for a purported ceremony of marriage"; but it appears that if the ceremony is a manifest sham,[15] or did not purport to be a marriage of the kind contemplated by the Marriage Acts it will not be regarded as a "marriage" such as is capable of being annulled by a decree of nullity[16]:

> In *A-M v. A-M (Divorce: Jurisdiction: Validity of Marriage)*[17] a ceremony was conducted in the couple's London flat by an Islamic Mufti from a London mosque. The ceremony involved the exchange of rings and the taking of vows. Friends attended and the woman wore a wedding dress, hat and veil. A printed document entitled "Certificate of Marriage" was signed by both parties, expressly as "bridegroom" and "bride". The court held that it had no jurisdiction to grant a decree of nullity in respect of this

---

[10] See, *e.g.* the remarkable facts of *R. v. Yacoob* [1981] Crim.L.R. 248, set out at n. 65 below. In practice, if the existence of the "void" marriage is disclosed, it will be necessary to satisfy the authorities of its invalidity.

[11] As to the position if the "husband" dies before a decree is obtained, see below.

[12] See *W v. W (Physical Inter sex)* [2001] Fam. 111, *ST v. J (Transsexual: Void Marriage)* [1998] Fam. 103.

[13] The statement by Nourse L.J. in *Re Spence dec'd* [1990] Ch. 652, CA, that a void marriage is "only an idle ceremony [which] achieves no change in the status of the participants [and] achieves nothing of substance" is an impeccable statement of the position at common law, but cannot be accepted as literally correct in the light of the developments referred to in the text. The same is true of the assertion of the traditional view that if a ceremony is void the court is doing no more than "pronouncing a blinding glimpse of the obvious": *Re Roberts dec'd* [1978] 1 W.L.R. 653 at 655, *per* Walton J.

[14] *per* Potter L.J., *S-T (formerly J) v. J* [1998] Fam. 103.

[15] In *Gereis v. Yagoub* [1997] 1 F.L.R. 854 counsel suggested as other examples a marriage ceremony on stage in the course of a play and a ceremony of betrothal.

[16] *A-M v. A-M (Divorce: Jurisdiction: Validity of Marriage)* [2001] 2 F.L.R. 6 at 24 (Hughes J.).

[17] [2001] 2 F.L.R. 6.

"marriage", since it did not purport to be a marriage under the Marriage Acts.[18] There was "nothing like a marriage".[19]

It is not clear how this test would be applied to cases in which the reason for the manifest invalidity is that the parties were of the same sex.

The real issue in these cases will often be, not whether the court has power to declare that the parties are not married,[20] but whether the court by pronouncing a decree of nullity will create the foundation upon which an application for financial relief may be founded.[21] Even if a decree of nullity is granted the court will not necessarily exercise its discretion to make financial orders.[22]

Is nullity still important?

2–004 The law of nullity is now comparatively unimportant as a method of dealing with the breakdown of a matrimonial relationship: in 1998 there were only 474 nullity decrees, compared with 143,879 decrees of divorce.[23] But the law of nullity remains of fundamental conceptual importance since it effectively answers the question of legal capacity: who may marry whom?

III. THE MODERN LAW OF NULLITY

2–005 The Nullity of Marriage Act 1971 (now consolidated in the Matrimonial Causes Act 1973) implemented most of the recommendations made by the Law Com-

---

18 See also *Gandhi v. Patel* [2002] 1 F.L.R. 603. These cases should be compared with *Gereis v. Yagoub* [1997] 1 F.L.R. 854 (H.H.J. Aglionby): a couple went through a marriage ceremony conducted by a Coptic Orthodox priest in a Coptic Orthodox church in Kensington which was not licensed for marriages under the provisions of the Marriage Act 1949. The judge gave weight to the fact that the ceremony "gave all the appearance of and had the hallmarks of a marriage that would be recognised as a marriage but for the" formal requirements of the Marriage Act 1949 and granted the wife petitioner a decree of nullity. The "decision may have been a merciful one": *per* Hughes J., *A-M v. A-M (Divorce: Jurisdiction: Validity of Marriage)* [2001] 2 F.L.R. 6.

19 See *R v. Bham* [1966] 1 Q.B. 159 (where a prosecution under Marriage Act 1949, s.75(2)(a) failed because the potentially polygamous marriage in accordance with Islamic law which the defendant had solemnised in a private house was not in a form known to and recognised by English law as capable of creating the status of marriage between the parties).

20 The court has no power to make a declaration (otherwise than by a decree of nullity) that "a marriage" was at its inception void: see Family Law Act 1986, s.58; but it would have power to declare that a marriage was at its inception valid: Family Law Act 1986, s.55(1)(a). These provisions were evidently intended to make it impossible to evade the ancillary relief jurisdiction by invoking the power to make declarations of status.

21 It seems clear from the Parliamentary Debates on the relevant provision of the Nullity of Marriage Act 1971 that the Promoters did not intend to give even the recognition implicit in granting a decree of nullity to relationships between persons who were, and knew themselves to be, unequivocally of the same sex: see *Official Report* H.C. April 2, 1971, vol. 814, col. 1838 (Mr Leo Abse); and *Official Report* H.L. April 22, 1971, vol. 317, col. 816-7 (Lord Chancellor Hailsham). But *cf. Bellinger v. Bellinger* [2001] 2 F.L.R. 1048 at 1086–1087, *per* Thorpe L.J.

22 In *Whiston v. Whiston* [1995] Fam. 198 the Court of Appeal held that the rule of public policy debarring a wrongdoer from profiting from his wrong applied so as to deny ancillary relief to a person who had knowingly contracted a bigamous marriage. However, in *S-T v. J (Transsexual: Void Marriage)* [1998] Fam. 103 the majority of the Court of Appeal favoured a flexible approach to the exercise of the discretion. But in neither case was any financial order made.

23 See *Marriage and Divorce Statistics 1998*, Table 4.23.

mission in a comprehensive review of the law[24], and exhaustively[25] codifies English internal law on the subject.

The text analyses the law under four headings:

(a) grounds on which a petition may be presented,
(b) bars to the making of a decree.
(c) the effects of a decree; and
(d) proposals for further reform.

A. Grounds

2–006 The Nullity of Marriage Act 1971 provided[26] that a marriage taking place after July 31, 1971, should be void on the following grounds only[27]:

"(a) that it is not a valid marriage under the provisions of the Marriage Acts 1949 to 1986 (that is to say where—

(i) the parties are within the prohibited degrees of relationship;
(ii) either party is under the age of sixteen; or
(iii) the parties have intermarried in disregard of certain requirements as to the formation of marriage);

(b) that at the time of the marriage either party was already lawfully married;
(c) that the parties are not respectively male or female."

A marriage which has taken place after July 31, 1971, is voidable on the following grounds only[28]:

"(a) that the marriage has not been consummated owing to the incapacity of either party to consummate it;

---

[24] Law Com. No. 33, *Report on Nullity of Marriage*.

[25] Re *Roberts, dec'd* [1978] 1 W.L.R. 653 at 658. However, the Nullity of Marriage Act 1971, s.7(4) (now embodied in the Matrimonial Causes Act 1973, Sched. 1, para. 6) provided that nothing in the Act affected any law or custom relating to the marriage of members of the Royal Family, and thereby preserved the rule that purported marriages contrary to the provisions of the Royal Marriages Act 1772 remain void notwithstanding the fact that the 1772 Act is not mentioned: see for another case where the provisions of the 1772 Act were preserved without that fact being expressly adverted to in parliamentary discussion, S.M. Cretney, "The Royal Marriages Act 1772: A Footnote" (1995) 16 *Statute Law Review* 195.

[26] s.1. The legislation is now consolidated as M.C.A. 1973, s.11(a)–(c) and is reproduced as amended by the Marriage (Prohibited Degrees of Relationship) Act 1986, s.6(4). The Matrimonial Proceedings (Polygamous Marriages) Act 1972 added an additional ground (now M.C.A. 1973, s.11(d)) "in the case of a polygamous marriage entered into outside England and Wales, that either party was at the time of the marriage domiciled in England and Wales." However, as a result of amendment made by the Private International Law (Miscellaneous Provisions) Act 1995, Sched., para. 2(2), "polygamous marriage" no longer includes a marriage which is potentially (as against actually) polygamous.

[27] It is thus impossible for the English courts to follow the example of Ireland, in which nullity has been made available on the ground that a party suffered from an inherent characteristic preventing him from sustaining a proper marital relationship; *UF v. JC [1991]* 2 I.R. 330.

[28] Nullity of Marriage Act 1971, s.2 (now consolidated as M.C.A. 1973, s.12).

(b) that the marriage has not been consummated owing to the wilful refusal of the respondent to consummate it;
(c) that either party to the marriage did not validly consent to it, whether in consequence of duress, mistake, unsoundness of mind or otherwise;
(d) that at the time of the marriage either party, though capable of giving a valid consent, was suffering (whether continuously or intermittently) from mental disorder within the meaning of the Mental Health Act 1983,[29] of such a kind or to such an extent as to be unfitted for marriage;
(e) that at the time of the marriage the respondent was suffering from venereal disease in a communicable form;
(f) that at the time of the marriage the respondent was pregnant by some person other than the petitioner."

The grounds set out in the legislation are exhaustive: there is no other ground on which a decree of nullity can be obtained.[30] The text examines them in turn.

1. Void marriages

(a) Prohibited degrees

2–007 The Marriage Acts 1949–1986[31] declare that marriages between certain relatives are void. Before seeking to summarise the complicated statutory provisions it may be helpful to consider the policy apparently underlying the various prohibitions.

The policy of the law

(i) *Consanguinity and affinity*

2–08 The law effectively distinguishes between relationships of consanguinity (that is to say, those which would be created by a marriage between blood relations, such as a parent and child and a brother and sister) and those of affinity.

Relationship by affinity is a relationship created by a marriage. For the church, marriage[32] made a man and woman one flesh; and accordingly, since it is wrong

---

[29] Mental Health Act 1983, Sched. 4, para. 34.

[30] See *Re Roberts dec'd* [1978] 1 W.L.R. 653, 658 (but see note 16 above). See also Family Law Act 1986, s.55 (as substituted by Family Law Reform Act 1987, s.22) which now governs the court's power to grant declarations.

[31] The legislation may now be so described: Marriage (Prohibited Degrees of Relationship) Act 1986, s.6(2). The prohibited degrees include half-blood and illegitimate relationships: *R. v. Brighton Inhabitants* (1861) 1 B. & S. 447; Marriage Act 1949, s.78(1A) as inserted by F.L.R.A. 1987, Sched. 2, para. 10.

[32] Or even sexual intercourse outside marriage: *Roger Donington's Case,* 2 Co. Inst. 684 (marriage invalid because H had previously had intercourse with third cousin of his future wife). These refinements were abolished at the Reformation: Marriage Act 1540; *Wing v. Taylor* (1861) 2 Sw. & Tr. 278.

to marry a brother or sister it must be equally wrong to marry a spouse's brother or sister—to marry one's brother-*in law* or one's sister-*in law*. Since the brother or sister would be within the prohibited degrees of consanguinity, the spouse's sibling would be within the (correspondingly prohibited) degrees of affinity. Much of the debate about the prohibited degrees in the past 150 years has focused on the rules prohibiting marriage between persons related by affinity.

(ii) *No universally accepted policy*

2–09 Rules prohibiting marriage[33] between certain categories of relatives are probably universal[34] but there is considerable diversity in their content. For example, should first cousins be allowed to marry? English law allows such marriages; but they are prohibited in parts of the United States.[35] Should a man be allowed to marry his niece? English law will not allow him to do so; whereas Jewish law permits uncle/niece marriages without restriction[36] and some systems based on canon law allow such marriages provided a dispensation is obtained.[37]

When we come to affinal relationships the diversity is even more remarkable. Should a man be allowed to marry his deceased wife's sister or deceased brother's widow? Such marriages are encouraged in some cultures, but only since 1907 and 1921 respectively have they been permitted in England.[38] Should a man be allowed to marry his step-daughter or his mother-in-law? For long such marriages would have seemed repugnant to many; yet the Marriage (Prohibited Degrees of Relationship) Act 1986 now permits them, albeit subject to certain conditions.[39] Australia has gone even further, removing all restrictions founded solely on the existence of affinity.[40]

(iii) *Justification for restrictions*[41]

2–010 Religious considerations were for many years seen as overwhelmingly important[42]; but today policy is influenced in part by assumptions about the genetic risks of inbreeding and in part by broader considerations of social policy about the family unit.

---

33 And sometimes also sexual relations outside marriage: see above.

34 See generally, S. Wolfram, *In-laws and Outlaws: Kinship and Marriage in England* (1987).

35 See generally H.D. Krause, *Family Law* (1995), pp. 49–51; C. Hamilton, *Family, Law and Religion* (1995), p.4.

36 See *Cheni v. Cheni* [1965] P. 85.

37 See, *e.g. Catalano v. Catalano* 170 A 2d 726 (1961) (uncle/niece marriage valid under Italian law, but not recognised in Connecticut); and see further *per* Sir J. Simon P., in *Cheni v. Cheni* [1965] P. 85.

38 Deceased Wife's Sister's Marriage Act 1907; Deceased Brother's Widow's Marriage Act, 1921.

39 See para 2–011, below.

40 See H. A. Finlay. "Farewell to Affinity and the Calculus of Kinship" (1976) 5 Univ. of Tas. L. Rev. 16.

41 A fuller discussion can be found in the 5th edition of this work at pp. 36 *et seq*.

42 Canon law (and thus English law) was based on the rather obscure prohibitions contained in Chapter 18 of the book of Leviticus and elsewhere in the Pentateuch.

The genetic risks of inbreeding[43] arises from the possibility that the parties will be carriers of a recessive disease such as cystic fibrosis or sickle cell disease; but it should be remembered that characteristics which may appear in the offspring of a union between blood relatives may also be favourable. (As one scholar[44] has pointed out, "the success of modern agriculture, plant and animals, is based on incest.") Genetic counselling is practised in some countries to minimise the risks in a marriage between, for example, first cousins. But genetic considerations cannot justify a bar on marriage between affines (for example, marriage by a man with his step-daughter or by a woman with her former husband's son); and the main justification for imposing restrictions in such cases is that the prohibition on marriage serves to discourage sexual relationships within the home circle: there can thus be closeness between those who share the same household without the risk that the stability of the family will be disrupted by incestuous courtship. This argument was used to justify the prohibition on marriage between a man and his deceased wife's sister.[45] If a man could look on his wife's sister as a potential spouse, the trusting, intimate, but asexual relationship of brother and sister might well (it was argued) be destroyed. Further, such marriages would cause a confusion of roles when the children of the marriage had to be told that their aunt had become their mother.[46]

Such arguments may appear to be even stronger in the case of marriage between a man and his step-daughter. It might be thought that the law should protect girls from the danger—increasingly recognised as a very real danger—of sexual abuse by those in authority over them.[47]

However, these general arguments have not prevailed against the pressures of changing social circumstances. In 1907, Parliament was persuaded to accept that a man might be allowed to marry his deceased wife's sister[48]; and finally in

---

[43] The scientific background was summarised by the Kilbrandon Committee in its report *The Marriage Laws of Scotland,* Cmnd. 4011 (1969); and see the Scottish Law Commission's Memorandum No. 44 (1980), paras. 3.2–11 and its Report on the Law of Incest in Scotland (Scot, Law Com. No. 69, paras. 3.19–23). The issue is also discussed in V. Bailey and S. McCabe [1979] Crim.L.R. 749 at 757–758.

[44] H.D. Krause, *Family Law* (1995), p. 51.

[45] See the evidence of the Church of England to the Morton Commission (cited at para. 1162): the Kilbrandon Report, para. 33. *Re Woodcock and Woodcock* [1957] N.Z.L.R. 960, *per* Finlay A.C.J.; and the speech of then Bishop of Durham on the Marriage (Enabling) Bill, February 25, 1981 (*Hansard,* H.L., Vol. 417, col. 1121).

[46] Even more so since (as a result of the Marriage (Enabling) Act 1960) their divorced biological mother might still be alive.

[47] See *e.g.* the speeches of Lord Denning, *Official Report H.L.* December 9, 1985, vol 469, col. 47; Lord Mishcon, at col. 54, the Bishop of Birmingham (*Official Report H.L.* February 3, 1986, vol 470, col. 950) and Lord Simon of Glaisdale, *Official Report H.L.* February 3, 1986, vol 470, col. 953. See also *No Just Cause,* pp. 20–23 and pp. 96–99. Under the present law a step-father commits no criminal offence if he has consensual sexual intercourse with his step-daughter; but, for consideration of the case for extending the scope of the criminal law in this context, see the Home Office Consultation Paper, *Setting the Boundaries* (2000).

[48] The argument which ultimately seemed to carry weight was that, if a wife died leaving her husband with young children to bring up, help would be needed urgently from someone prepared to take over the mother's position; and in the days before the State provided comprehensive care for children in need the only available help was often the father's sister-in-law. Physical propinquity could lead to emotional involvement. What could be more natural than marriage? The law was further relaxed over the years—notably by the Marriage (Enabling) Act 1960, which allowed marriage with the former spouse of a divorced brother or sister.

1986 Parliament accepted that marriage with a step-son or step-daughter or with a former spouse's parent[49] could, in certain circumstances, be permitted. The underlying reason for this relaxation[50] of the law was that the increase in divorce and remarriage had greatly increased the likelihood that a couple who have not *in fact* been members of the same family unit would nevertheless be debarred from marriage by reason of a relationship through marriage; and attention was focused on the problem because a number of persons obtained private Acts of Parliament permitting a marriage within the prohibited degrees of affinity.

The prohibited degrees of relationship under the Marriage Acts 1949 to 1986: an unsatisfactory compromise?

The Marriage Acts 1949 to 1986 now contain the following prohibitions: **2–011**

(i) *The prohibited degrees of consanguinity.*

A person may not marry his or her parent, grandparent,[51] child or grandchild, uncle or aunt, nephew or niece.[52]

(ii) *The prohibited degrees of affinity—the first class: step-relations.*

2–012 A person may only marry the child of a former spouse if two conditions are satisfied. First, both parties to the marriage must be 21 or over; and secondly, the younger party must not at any time before attaining the age of 18 have been a child of the family[53] in relation to the other party.

(iii) *The prohibited degrees of affinity—the second class: parents- and children- in law.*

Marriage with a former spouse's parent is only permitted[54] if— **2–013**

(i) Both parties to the intended marriage have attained the age of 21; *and*
(ii) The marriage is solemnised—

---

[49] Or grandparent.

[50] Brought about by the Marriage (Prohibited Degrees of Relationship) Act 1986—an Act significantly influenced by the Report (*No Just Cause,* 1984) of a Review Body established by the Archbishop of Canterbury. For a fuller account of the background to the legislation, see the 4th edition of this work, pp. 53–54 and footnotes.

[51] The draftsman of the English legislation evidently did not think it necessary to prohibit marriages with a great grandparent (or indeed with a great grandchild). Compare the more cautious approach of the Marriage (Scotland) Act 1977, s.2 and Sched. 1.

[52] Marriage Acts 1949–1986, Sched. 1, Pt I. For adoptive relationships, see below.

[53] *i.e.* a person who has "lived in the same household as that person and been treated by that person as a child of his family": Marriage Acts 1949 to 1986, s.78. This definition is similar to that contained in the divorce legislation: M.C.A. 1973, s.52(1): see below. The main difference is that, under the Marriage Acts, there is an additional requirement that the two persons have "lived in the same household."

[54] Marriage Act 1949, Sched. 1, Pt III (as amended).

"(a) in the case of a man marrying the mother of a former wife of his, after the death of both the former wife and the former wife's father;

(b) in the case of a man marrying a former wife of his son, after the death of both his son and his son's mother;

(c) in the case of a woman marrying the father of a former husband of hers, after the death of both the former husband and the former husband's mother;

(d) in the case of a woman marrying a former husband of her daughter, after the death of both her daughter and her daughter's father."

The general policy underlying these complex statutory provisions is reasonably clear: for example, a man is not to be allowed to marry his step-daughter if there has been a parental relationship between them; and he is not to be allowed to marry his daughter-in-law in circumstances[55] where it may be thought his sexual overtures have caused the breakdown of her marriage to his son. But it is not clear that they are likely to be wholly effective in these respects.

First, it is unlikely that there can be any realistic investigation into the parties' declaration that the intended bride[56] has not been a child of the family in relation to the other. Secondly, the conditions do not (and probably could not) cover all the cases to which the policy would require them to apply.

For example:—

> Henry married Winifred in 1955. They had a son, Simon; but Winifred died whilst he was still a baby. Henry married Teresa, who looked after Simon as if she were his mother throughout his childhood. Simon married Doreen in 1978; and the marriage was happy for several years until Henry started an affair with Doreen. Teresa obtains a divorce based on Henry's admitted adultery with Doreen. Simon is so overwhelmed by what has happened that he commits suicide. Henry may nonetheless marry Doreen although he would seem (in so far as such judgments can ever sensibly be

---

[55] See the facts of *Bailey v. Tolliday* [1982] 4 F.L.R. 542; and note the "typical example" suggested by Lord Meston in the course of the debates on the Marriage (Prohibited Degrees of Relationship Act) 1986, *Hansard,* H.L., Vol. 471, col. 891: "A young couple marry. They may go to live with the parents of, say, the young husband. There may be a weak immature perhaps teenage daughter-in-law, who may be very vulnerable to the influence of her father-in-law. There is a situation of proximity and dependence. If a relationship did develop between the young husband's wife and his father, there are two subsisting marriages which potentially would be ended by divorce."

[56] The prohibition relates solely to marriage; and the fact that a person has intercourse with a child of the family does not constitute the crime of incest (but see now the Home Office Consultation Paper, *Setting the Boundaries* (2000)). For example, in *Smith v. Clerical Medical and General Life Assurance Society and others* [1993] 1 F.L.R. 47, CA. a man married the mother of a 13-year-old girl. Six years after the marriage he left the matrimonial home with the girl, and they set up house together, holding themselves out as a married couple. It was apparently intended that they should marry; but in fact it seems clear that such a marriage would have been void before the enactment of the Marriage (Prohibited Degrees of Relationship) Act 1986, and that the provisions of that Act could not validate such a marriage (since the girl had, before attaining the age of 18, lived in the same household with the intended husband, and he had treated her as a child of his family).

made) to have been entirely responsible for the destruction of his son's marriage.

Thirdly, the rule does operate to prevent marriages to which there could be no reasonable objection. As the Scottish Law Commission say[57]:—

> "Suppose that a man aged 40 married a woman aged 25 who has never known her father. The wife is killed in a road accident and, some time later, the man and his former wife's mother, who is closer to his own age, want to get married. Why should it matter whether the former wife's father, who might not even know that she ever existed, is alive or dead? What is the point of this restriction on a marriage between two people who are both unmarried and unrelated by blood?"

Adoption and the prohibited degrees

2–014 A child who is adopted remains within the same prohibited degrees in respect of the natural parents and other relatives as if the adoption order had never been made.[58] An adopter and the adopted person are deemed to be within the prohibited degrees, and they continue to be so notwithstanding that someone else subsequently adopts the adopted child[59]; but there is no other prohibition arising by reason of adoption. Hence, a man may marry his adoptive sister (provided she does not fall into any other of the proscribed relationships), and (subject to the same proviso) a woman may marry her adopted brother.

Consequences of purported marriage within prohibited degrees

2–015 We have seen that marriages within the prohibited degrees are void—whether or not the parties are aware of the relationship which makes them so. Before 1835 such marriages were only voidable; but Lord Lyndhurst's Act (passed in that year for reasons which are obscure and may have been discreditable)[60] declared any future marriage within the prohibited degrees to be void, rather than merely voidable.

The prohibited degrees and the criminal law

2–016 Marriages within the prohibited degrees are often said to be void on the ground of incest, but it does not follow that a criminal offence will have been committed by either party. Thus, although it is a criminal offence for a man

---

[57] *Report on Family Law* (Scot. Law Com. No. 135, (1992)), para. 8.9.

[58] Adoption Act 1976, s.47(1).

[59] Marriage Acts 1949 to 1986, Sched. 1, Pt I. For the background to this apparently unsatisfactory rule see S.M. Cretney, "From Status to Contract?" in *Consensus ad Idem* (F.D. Rose, ed., 1996).

[60] The Act retrospectively validated existing marriages and it was introduced in order to protect the legitimacy of children born to the 7th Duke of Beaufort (who had married his deceased wife's sister in 1822): see *per* Lord Lyndhurst, *Hansard's Parliamentary Debates* (3rd series), July 23, 1858, Vol. 151, cols. 1975–1977; S. Wolfram, *In-laws and Outlaws* . . . (1987), p. 30.

knowingly to have intercourse with his daughter,[61] granddaughter, mother or sister, he may, without infringing the criminal law, have intercourse with his aunt or niece notwithstanding the fact that he could not marry them.

(b) Minimum age

2–017 A marriage is void if either party is under 16.[62] This rule should be distinguished from that[63] requiring parental consent if either party is under 18, failure to comply with which has no effect on the validity of the marriage.[64] It should also be distinguished from the rule under which it is a criminal offence for a man to have unlawful sexual intercourse with a girl who is aged under 16. If he is validly married to her (as he may be if the marriage was contracted abroad) it seems unlikely that intercourse between the man and his wife could be held "unlawful."[65]

The policy of the law

2–018 There are three issues which need consideration. First, what is the purpose of imposing a minimum age for marriage? Secondly, what should that age be? Thirdly, what should be the legal consequences of a purported marriage which infringes the rule?

English law was changed in 1929: until that year, a boy could marry at 14 and a girl at 12; and marriages where one or both parties were under the relevant age were not void but voidable. Either party could avoid the marriage on attaining majority, but unless and until this was done the marriage remained valid.[66]

The issues have subsequently been considered on three occasions[67]; and attitudes concerning the age below which marriage should not be permitted have been affected by changed perceptions of the relevant social and economic issues.[68] At one time, parentally-approved marriage between a couple who had attained the age of puberty may well have seemed unobjectionable: age as such was not important. Then informed opinion became concerned with problems of child sexual abuse and prostitution which were thought to be related to the age at which marriage was permitted.[69] More recently, the focus of concern has

---

[61] But not with his step-daughter, see above.

[62] Marriage Act 1949, s.2. But foreign marriages between parties one or more of whom is under this age may be valid: *Alhaji Mohamed v. Knott* [1969] 1 Q.B. 1.

[63] Marriage Act 1949, s.3, as amended.

[64] s.48 This requirement is regarded as part of the formalities of the marriage ceremony.

[65] *H.M Advocate v. Watson* (1885) 13 S.C. (J.) 6 at 9; *R. v. Chapman* [1959] 1 Q.B. 100; *Alhaji Mohamed v. Knott* (above).

[66] See J. Jackson, *The Formation and Annulment of Marriage* (2nd ed., 1969), p. 26, Blackstone *Commentaries* (1770), Book 1, Chap. 15, p. 436.

[67] *i.e* in 1967, by the Committee on the Age of Majority (the Latey Committee); in 1969, by the Committee on the Marriage Law of Scotland (the Kilbrandon Committee); and in 1970 by the Law Commission (as part of its Report on the Law of Nullity of Marriage, Law Com. No. 33).

[68] The policy arguments are considered in the fourth edition of this work, pp. 56–61.

[69] See the sources cited in the 4th edition of this work at pp. 56–57.

moved towards promoting the stability of marriage; and in the 1960s it was often suggested that the age at which marriage is permitted should be raised.[70] However, since the early 1970s there has been a general upward trend in the age of first marriage in this country[71] and (as already noted[72]) the problem seems to have solved itself.

The question of whether an under-age marriage should be void or voidable is rather more difficult.[73] The present law may well cause some hardship, particularly if the parties—perhaps immigrants from a country with an unreliable birth registration system—believed that they were of age. However, there seems no realistic likelihood of change being made in the law; and the issue is not usually of great importance. If the parties discover the defect, and still wish to be married, they can go through a marriage ceremony and thereby for most purposes remedy the situation; and in any event the law now attaches many of the legal incidents of marriage to a void marriage provided that a decree of nullity is obtained or other appropriate legal action taken.

(c) Defective formalities

2–019 The circumstances in which failure to comply with the formalities laid down by the Marriage Acts 1949 to 1986 will invalidate a marriage have been explained in Chapter 1.

(d) Bigamy

2–020 For English law, marriage is traditionally regarded as "the voluntary union for life of one man and one woman to the exclusion of all others."[74] Hence a purported marriage is void if it is proved that at the time of the ceremony either party was already lawfully married to a third party.[75]

It should be stressed that the marriage will still be void even if the parties had believed on reasonable grounds that the third party was dead.[76] It should also be noted that the crucial date is that of the ceremony.[77] If the former spouse

---

[70] Latey Report, paras. 102–3; and paras 166–177; Kilbrandon Report, paras. 14–21.

[71] See generally K.E. Kiernan, "The structure of families today: continuity or change?" (O.P.C.S.), p. 19; and *Occasional Papers No. 31*, 1983 above.

[72] See para. 1–010 above.

[73] The arguments in favour of preserving the existing rule that under-age marriages are void are cogently summarised in Law Com. No. 33, paras 17–19; but for the view that these arguments are unconvincing, see the 4th edition of this work pp. 60–61.

[74] *Hyde v. Hyde* (1866) L. R. 1 P. & D. 130 *per* Lord Penzance at 133; see the stimulating analysis by S. Poulter, "The Definition of Marriage in English Law" (1979) 42 *M.L.R.* 4.

[75] M. C. A. 1973, s.11(b); as to proof of the existence of a prior marriage, see below and, for a recent example where it only became apparent in the course of divorce proceedings brought after the breakdown of a 15-year relationship that the purported marriage was in fact bigamous, see *Whiston v. Whiston* [1995] 2 F.L.R. 268, CA.

[76] So that there may be a defence to the criminal offence of bigamy.

[77] See, *e.g.* the complicated facts of *R. v. Yacoob* [1981] Crim. L. R. 248, a case decided by the Court of Appeal (Criminal Division), in which the question was whether an intended witness ("W") was the defendant's wife. The facts were that W's marriage to H, was ended by divorce in 1964; in 1965 she "married" H2, who (unknown to her) was already married to X; in 1968,

subsequently dies, the later "marriage" remains void (although the parties could regularise their position by going through a second marriage ceremony, which they would then be free to do).

(e) Parties of same sex

2–021 Statute provides that a marriage is void if the parties are not respectively male and female[78]; and it can be said with certainty that English law will not recognise a relationship between a couple of the same sex as constituting a valid marriage.[79] The question whether a person is male or female is a question of fact, and rarely gives rise to problems.[80]

In recent years, however, the courts have had to consider the position of persons affected by gender identity dysphoria, that is to say "discontent with being a person of the sex to which one was born and discontent with living in the gender role consistent with that birth sex".[81] This may when profound be called transsexualism,[82] a recognised medical condition for which gender reassignment therapy is in principle available under the National Health Service. Such therapy is intended to correct the dissonance between felt sex and physiological structure.[83] The medical procedures will often begin with hormone treatment; but ultimately a so-called "sex-change" operation may take place.[84] Such

---

she married H3, but did not see him after the ceremony: in 1969 she "married" H4 who disappeared. In 1970 she obtained a decree of nullity in respect of the marriage to H2, and (in 1971) "married" the defendant. It was held that this marriage was void, since that to H3 was valid.

[78] Matrimonial Causes Act 1973, s.11(c).

[79] It has been said (see *per* Ward L.J. *S-T (formerly J) v. J* [1998] Fam. 103 at 141) that "single sex unions remain proscribed as fundamentally abhorrent to" the classical understanding of marriage as the voluntary union for life of one man and one woman, to the exclusion of all others whilst in the same case Potter L.J. described a "marriage" between parties of the same sex as "not merely a void but a meretricious marriage". For a discussion of the relevant policies, see R. Wintermute and M. Andenas, *Legal Recognition of Same Sex Relationships* (2001). Note that it does not follow that a sexual relationship between persons of the same sex will be devoid of legal consequences: see *Fitzpatrick v. Sterling Housing Association Ltd* [2001] 1 A.C. 27.

[80] See, however, *W v. W (Physical Inter-sex)* [2001] Fam. 111, where a husband's nullity petition against a wife registered at birth as male was dismissed. The court held that where a person was affected by partial androgen insensitivity (resulting in what is sometimes called "physical inter-sex") the entry in the Birth Register was not conclusive; and, accepting expert evidence that the patient was at the time of the marriage "towards the female end of a midpoint between male and female" and that accordingly the marriage had been valid, and that the court had had jurisdiction to terminate it by granting a decree of divorce.

[81] See the evidence of Professor Green, Consultant Psychiatrist and Research Director of the Gender Identity Clinic Charing Cross Hospital, as cited in *Bellinger v. Bellinger* [2001] 2 F.L.R. 1048 at 1055.

[82] *ibid.* It has been officially estimated that there are between 1,300 and 2,000 male to female and 250 female to male transsexual people in the United Kingdom: *Report of the Interdepartmental Working Group on Transsexual People* (Home Office, April 2000), para. 1.3.

[83] A. Bradney [1987] *Fam. Law.* 350.

[84] But note that the *Report of the Interdepartmental Working Group on Transsexual People* (Home Office, April 2000), para. 1.5.) states that although gender "reassignment is commonly termed a sex change, . . . in reality it is an alteration only in a person's physical characteristics. The biological sex of an individual is determined by their chromosomes, which cannot be changed. What can be achieved through the transsexual person's own efforts, and with counselling, drugs and surgery is social, hormonal and surgical reassignment".

operations give the patient some of the physical attributes of the sex to which he feels he psychically belongs—for example, plastic surgery may be used to remove male genitalia and construct an artificial vagina. There will also be medication with sex hormones to assist in the creation of a female appearance.

What is the legal position if a person who has been treated in this way seeks to "marry" as a woman? The traditional view of English law for the past 30 years[85] has been that a person's sex is fixed for all time at birth; and the only relevant tests of sexual identity are biological. Thus:—

> In *Corbett v. Corbett*,[86] April Ashley—formerly known as George Jamieson—had undergone a sex-change operation. Thereafter, she lived as a woman, and indeed worked successfully as a female model; and she had been recognised as a woman for national insurance and passport purposes.[87] It was nevertheless held that she remained a man for the purpose of the marriage laws; and that her purported marriage to Arthur Corbett was a nullity. She had been born with male genitalia and a male chromosomal structure; and her sexual attribution could not be changed. The facts that she had become philosophically, psychologically and socially a woman,[88] considered herself to be a woman, had lived as a woman and had, as a result of surgical and other treatment, most of the external attributes of a woman were thus irrelevant: secondary sexual characteristics or psychological sexual nature were not material to the issue which the court had to decide.

This approach has serious implications for transsexuals who may reasonably feel that the law denies them the right to establish any securely founded legal relationship.[89] However, in 2001 a majority of the Court of Appeal in *Bellinger v. Bellinger*[90]—whilst recognising the "profoundly unsatisfactory nature of the

---

[85] *i.e.* since the decision in *Corbett v. Corbett* [1971] P. 83.

[86] [1971] P. 83.

[87] However, it is the practice of the registrar-general (which the Divisional Court has refused to review: see *Re P. and G. (Transsexuals)* [1996] 2 F.L.R. 90) not to permit any amendment of the birth register relating to a transsexual's birth; and in the result a person whose sex was recorded at birth as "male" will not be able to obtain a corrected birth certificate. In *Rees v. United Kingdom* [1987] 2 F.L.R. 111, the European Court on Human Rights held (by 12 votes to three, and in this respect not following the unanimous opinion of the European Commission on Human Rights) that such a refusal did not constitute a breach of the applicant's right, guaranteed by Article 8 of the European Convention, to respect for his private life; and and a similar approach was taken by the majority in the later *Cossey* case [1991] 2 F.L.R. 492. But the powerful dissenting opinions should be noted, as should the view of the court that states should keep the law under review in the light of continuing developments. In *B v. France* [1992] 2 F.L.R. 249, the European Court of Human Rights held that France was in breach of the obligations imposed by Article 8—the distinction lying in the consequences attached by French law to an entry in the Register of Civil Status.

[88] *R. v. Tan* [1983] Q.B. 1053 at 1064, *per* Parker J.

[89] For example a male to female transsexual will not only be treated as remaining a male for the purpose of invalidating a "marriage" to a male, whilst the treatment which such a person has undergone would make it impossible for a "marriage" with a female to be consummated, and any such marriage would accordingly be voidable under the provisions of Matrimonial Causes Act 1973, s.12(a), below.

[90] [2001] 2 F.L.R. 1048.

present position", that "the plight of transsexuals requires careful consideration" and that recommendations of an official Working Group "merit action" by the relevant government departments[91]—upheld the *Corbett* interpretation of the law and rejected arguments that it was inconsistent with the provisions of the European Convention on Human Rights. Although Thorpe L.J., in a powerful dissenting judgment, would have held that medical and social developments since the *Corbett* case had destroyed the view of the law to which it gave effect, it appears that it must for the time being[92] be accepted as correct. But there will perhaps be many who find contrary to "reason and common humanity alike" the paradox that society is prepared to provide the drastic surgical and medical treatment of gender reassignment therapy for those who suffer from what is recognised as a serious and distressing medical problem whilst denying those concerned access to the legal status which would enable them to function fully in their new gender.[93]

2. Voidable marriages

(a) Incapacity to consummate

2–022 A marriage is voidable if, owing to the incapacity of either party, it has not been consummated. Statute[94] thus codifies a basic principle of the canon law. Although marriage was formed simply by consent, the contract of marriage implied that the parties had the capacity to consummate it.[95] If this capacity were lacking, the rule prior to the Reformation[96] was that the marriage was void, and thereafter that it was voidable.

It is necessary to emphasise that the theory was that incapacity prevented a marriage from coming into existence at all and that physical capacity was as much a basic requirement of marriage as the intellectual capacity to consent. In practice, there may seem to be little difference between the case of a couple who never succeed in consummating the marriage, and that of a husband who "was not interested in women at all" and had intercourse on some eight occasions in 18 years of marriage.[97] It could well be argued that in each case an unsatisfactory union is to be terminated because the parties are incompatible.

---

[91] *per* Dame Elizabeth Butler-Sloss P., at 1075.

[92] Leave has been given to appeal to the house of Lords. It is also possible following publication of the *Report of the Interdepartmental Working Group on Transsexual People* in April 2000 and the criticisms of government inaction voiced by all three members of the Court of Appeal in *Bellinger v. Bellinger* [2001] 2 F.L.R. 1048 that legislation might attract the necessary government support. Moreover, although challenges in the European courts to English law had been unsuccessful it is apparent that "there is a momentum for change increasingly recognised in the Court at Strasbourg and articulated in judgments critical of the . . . approach of English law" (as Dame Elizabeth Butler-Sloss P. put it in *Bellinger* at 1072).

[93] See *per* Thorpe L.I., (drawing on a paper delivered by Lord Reed to the Anglo-German Family Law Judicial Conference, Edinburgh, September 2000).

[94] M.C.A. 1973, s.12(a).

[95] *per* Sir Samuel Evans, *Dickinson v. Dickinson* [1913] P. 198 at 205.

[96] Above.

[97] *P. v. P.* [1964] 3 All E.R. 919.

But for the canon law there was a vast theoretical difference between (on the one hand) recognising that the marriage was a nullity in cases where incapacity existing at the time of the marriage could be proved and (on the other) dissolving a valid marriage because of some supervening cause.

Some problems of interpretation

Supervening incapacity sufficient?

2–023 It was a basic requirement of the canon law that the incapacity exist at the date of the marriage; and it is clear that the codification of the law in 1971 was not intended to effect any change.[98] However, the legislation does not in terms require that the incapacity should have existed "at the time of the celebration of the marriage." Could a wife whose husband is made impotent as a result of a car accident on the way from the church to the honeymoon therefore petition successfully for nullity on this ground? Perhaps the courts would interpret the provision in the light of the classical concept of the distinction between nullity and divorce,[99] and refuse a decree. But this is by no means certain: in particular it cannot now be argued that nullity is restricted to those cases in which the condition existed at the time of the marriage, since the ground of wilful refusal to consummate[1] is an exception to that principle.

Petitioner's knowledge of own incapacity not a bar?

2–024 Either party to the marriage can petition: there is nothing in the words of the Act to prevent a spouse who is incapable basing a petition on his or her own incapacity. It is true that before the enactment of the Nullity of Marriage Act 1971 such a spouse could not obtain a decree if, at the time of the marriage, he or she knew of the incapacity, or if it would, in all the circumstances, be unjust to allow the petition to succeed.[2] But this rule was (it is submitted) an application of the old bar of approbation, which was abolished by the 1971 Act.[3] If this is correct, a petitioner who knew of the incapacity is entitled to a decree on that ground unless the respondent can establish the modern statutory bar of approba-

---

[98] See the explanatory notes to the Law Commission's draft bill: Law Com. No. 33, p. 47, para. 2. The Report was referred to by Dunn J. in *D. v. D. (Nullity: Statutory Bar)* [1979] Fam. 70 at 77.

[99] *Briggs v. Morgan* (1820) 2 Hag. Con. 324 at 331; *Brown v. Brown* (1828) 1 Hag. Ecc. 523; *B. v. M.* (1852) 2 Rob.Ecc. 580; *Napier v. Napier* [1915] P. 184 at 189–190; *S. v. S.* [1963] P. 162.

[1] See below.

[2] H.K. Bevan, "Limitations on the Right of an Impotent Spouse to Petition for Nullity" (1960) 76 *L.Q.R.* 267; *Harthan v. Harthan* [1949] P. 115; *Pettit v. Pettit* [1963] P. 177; *Morgan v. Morgan* [1959] P. 92. In this last case a man of 72 married a woman of 59 on the basis that their relationship was to be one of companionship only. The husband's subsequent petition on the ground of his own impotence was rejected because, having regard to the agreement, it would have been contrary to justice and public policy to allow him to succeed.

[3] s.3(4) of the Nullity of Marriage Act 1971 provided that the statutory bar of approbation (now to be found in s.13(1) of the Matrimonial Causes Act 1973) "replaces . . . any rule of law whereby a decree may be refused by reason of approbation, ratification or lack of sincerity on the part of the petitioner or on similar grounds." It would be difficult to find words more clearly apt to cover the bar applied in *Morgan v. Morgan* [1959] P. 92. See generally *D. v. D. (Nullity: Statutory Bar)* [1979] Fam. 70 at 76–78.

tion laid down in the Matrimonial Causes Act 1973.[4] Apart from these two matters, the present law is unchanged from the canon law administered in the ecclesiastical court.

Its main features are:

2–025 *(i) The issue is ability to have sexual relations, not the ability to procreate.* The fact that a party is sterile or barren is irrelevant.[5]

What sexual relationship suffices for this purpose? The case law[6] establishes that what is required is capacity for *vera copula,* intercourse which is "ordinary and complete," and not "incipient, imperfect and unnatural."[7] More precisely, this means that there must be erection and penetration for a reasonable length of time[8] but it is not necessary for either party to be capable of orgasm.[9]

2–026 *(ii) Many cases of incapacity are not based on physical abnormality, but on psychological impotence;* and it is no objection that the impotence may only be *quoad hunc* or *hanc—i.e.* that the respondent is capable of having intercourse with other partners.[10] A spouse who suffers from invincible repugnance to the act of intercourse with the other may thus be regarded as incapable of consummating the marriage.[11] But it would seem that a rational decision not to permit

---

[4] M.C.A. 1973, s.13(1). In order successfully to raise this defence, the respondent will have to satisfy the court not only that the petitioner knew of the incapacity, and that it would be unjust to the respondent to grant the decree, but also that the petitioner, with knowledge that it was open to him to have the marriage avoided, so conducted himself in relation to the respondent as to lead the respondent reasonably to believe that he would not seek to do so: see further the 4th edition of this work, p. 65.

[5] This is true even if the inability to procreate results from the voluntary act of the respondent (*e.g.* in undergoing a vasectomy or sterilisation) which has not been disclosed to the other: *Baxter v. Baxter* [1948] A.C. 274.

[6] *D. v. A.* (1845) 1 Rob.Eccl. 279; *Snowman v. Snowman* [1934] P. 186; *Clarke v. Clarke* [1943] 2 All E.R. 540; *White v. White* [1948] P. 330; *R. v. R.* [1952] 1 All E.R. 1194; *G. v. G.* [1952] V.L.R. 402; *B. v. B.* [1955] P. 42; *S. Y. v. S. Y.* [1963] P. 37; *W. v. W.* [1967] 1 W.L.R. 1554; *Corbett v. Corbett* [1971] P. 83.

[7] *per* Dr Lushington, *D. v. A.* (above), at 298, 299. It follows from the accepted definition of consummation that a decree of nullity may be obtained on the ground of incapacity even although a child has been conceived by *fecundatio ab extra: Clarke v. Clarke* [1943] 2 All E.R. 540.

[8] *R. v. R.* [1952] 1 All E.R. 1194; *W. v. W.* [1967] 1 W.L.R. 1554; *cf.* the definition of sexual intercourse for adultery and rape in wluch penetration for however short a period suffices.

[9] *S. Y. v. S. Y.* [1963] P. 37. The cases can be said to have been based on a primitive version of the theory, now underlying the ground on which divorce is permitted, that marriages should be decently buried if they have irretrievably broken down: if the parties do not find sexual satisfaction in marriage, they will be tempted to find solace elsewhere. In the words of Dr Lushington (in *D. v. A.* (1845) 1 Rob.Eccl. 279 at 299) " . . . when the *coitus* itself is absolutely imperfect, and I must call it unnatural, there is not a natural indulgence of natural desire; almost of necessity disgust is generated, and the probable consequences of other connections with men of ordinary self control become almost certain . . . no man ought to be reduced to this state of quasi unnatural connection and consequent temptation. . . . " But the law failed to develop a general doctrine which would have permitted a marriage to be terminated if the parties were incapable of forming a normal sexual relationship.

[10] See, *e.g. G. v. M.* (1885) 10 App.Cas. 171 at 176, where medical evidence was given that if the husband were "encouraged and had plenty of time and was not nervous, and if a little champagne were given him beforehand, he might succeed with any other woman."

[11] *G. v. G.* [1924] A.C. 349.

intercourse is insufficient[12]: there must be some element of psychiatric or sexual aversion.[13] Thus, in *Singh v. Singh*[14]—

> The petitioner, a 17-year-old Sikh girl reluctantly went through a marriage ceremony arranged by her parents with a man she had never previously met. She "never submitted to the physical embraces of the husband, because . . . it does not appear that she saw him again. Having taken the view . . . that she did not want to be married to him, it is [continued Karminski L.J.] understandable that she did not want to have sexual intercourse with him; but that . . . seems to be a very long way from an invincible repugnance."

2–027 *(iii) The fact the parties have had normal intercourse prior to the marriage ceremony is irrelevant.* What is in issue is whether the marriage has been consummated, and intercourse after the marriage is required.[15]

2–028 *(iv) The inability must be permanent and incurable.* It will be deemed to be incurable if any remedial operation is dangerous, or if the respondent refuses to undergo an operation.[16]

2–029 *(v) It is for the petitioner to prove that the incapacity exists.* The court has power to order a medical examination, and may draw adverse inferences against a party who refuses to be examined.[17] It used to be the practice to require the parties to cohabit for three years, but this is no longer true.[18]

(b) Wilful refusal to consummate

2–030 A marriage is voidable if it has not been consummated owing to the wilful refusal of the respondent to consummate it.[19]

Background

2–031 Wilful refusal is something which happens after the marriage; and to have accepted it as a ground for annulment would have offended against the basic principle of the canon law that nullity is "granted for some defect or incapacity existing at the date of the marriage."[20] Hence, wilful refusal was not a ground

---

[12] *Singh v. Singh* [1971] P. 226.
[13] *ibid., per* Karminski L.J. at 232.
[14] [1971] P. 226.
[15] *Dredge v. Dredge* [1947] 1 All E.R. 29.
[16] *S. v. S.* [1956] P. 1; *L. v. L.* (*falsely called W.*) (1882) 7 P.D. 16. If the respondent refuses to undergo an operation, a petition may also be founded on wilful refusal: see *D. v. D.* (*Nullity: Statutory Bar*) [1979] Fam. 70 at 72.
[17] *B. v. B.* [1901] P. 39; *W. v. W.* [1905] P. 231; M.C.R. 1973, r. 30.
[18] *B. v. B.* [1958] 1 W.L.R. 619 (cohabitation for one week).
[19] M.C.A. 1973, s.12(b).
[20] Morton Commission, para. 89. See also *Napier v. Napier* [1915] P. 184 at 189, *per* Pickford L.J.

for annulment under the practice of the ecclesiastical courts inherited by the Divorce Court in 1857 (although refusal or failure to consummate might have been used as *evidence* of incapacity). However, in 1937 Parliament intervened[21] and wilful refusal became by statute a ground on which a marriage might be annulled.

The main features of the law are:

2–032 *(i) Settled and Definite Decision.* A decree can only be granted if the respondent has made "a settled and definite decision . . . without just excuse"[22] not to consummate marriage. This is a question of fact which may involve an examination of the whole history of the marriage. On the one hand:—

> In *Ford v. Ford*[23] the marriage had taken place whilst H was serving a sentence of five years' imprisonment. H and W were left alone on visits for periods of up to two hours. W had heard from other visitors that it was not unusual in such circumstances for intercourse to take place; but H refused. Moreover, he showed no interest in living with W; and when he was granted a home visit he insisted that W take him to a former girlfriend's home. A circuit judge granted a decree on the grounds of wilful refusal. H's behaviour indicated that he had no intention of pursuing a married life with W, even though the refusal to have intercourse (in breach of the Prison Rules) in prison would not by itself have justified the finding that he had wilfully refused to consummate the marriage.

On the other hand, a husband's claim that his wife has wilfully refused to consummate the marriage has failed because the court considered that he had not used appropriate tact, persuasion and encouragement.[24] And:—

> In *Potter v. Potter*,[25] the failure to consummate the marriage originally resulted from a physical defect in the wife. This was cured by surgery; and the husband then made one further attempt to consummate the marriage. The wife's emotional state following the operation was such that this was unsuccessful and thereafter the husband refused to make any further attempts. The wife failed in a petition alleging his wilful refusal. The court held that his failure to consummate resulted from natural and not deliberate loss of ardour. The wife would also, presumably, have failed had she pursued a petition based on the husband's incapacity since at the date of the marriage he apparently did have capacity and it is immaterial that he subsequently became impotent *quoad hanc*.[26]

2–033 *(ii) Absence of "Just Excuse".* A wilful refusal petition must be dismissed if

---

[21] Matrimonial Causes Act 1937, s.7(1)(a)
[22] *Horton v. Horton* [1947] 2 All E.R. 871.
[23] (1987) 17 *Fam. Law* 232 (Goodman J.)
[24] *Baxter v. Baxter* [1947] 1 All E.R. 387 at 388, CA, *per* Lord Greene M.R.
[25] (1975) 5 *Fam. Law* 161, CA.
[26] See *S. v. S.* [1956] P. 1.

the respondent can show a "just excuse" for the refusal to consummate.[27] For example, if the parties have agreed that a civil marriage shall be followed by a religious ceremony, it is a "just excuse" for refusing to consummate the marriage that the religious ceremony has not taken place.

The courts have gone further, and held that one party's refusal to go through the religious ceremony is a failure to implement the agreement and thus itself amounts to wilful refusal to consummate the marriage.[28]

> In *Kaur v. Singh*,[29] a marriage was arranged between two Sikhs. A civil ceremony took place, but by Sikh religion and practice (as the parties well knew) a religious ceremony was necessary in order to perfect the marriage. It was the husband's duty to arrange the religious ceremony, but he refused to make the necessary arrangements. The court held that the wife was entitled to a decree on the grounds of his wilful refusal to consummate. The result would apparently be the same if the husband had tried to have intercourse but the wife refused.[30]

2–034 *(iii) Agreements and "companionship" marriages.* Would it be a defence to a wilful refusal petition that the parties had agreed not to have intercourse? Such an agreements are sometimes said to be invalid as being contrary to public policy,[31] but this has been held not to be a valid objection if the parties are elderly[32] or there is some other good reason for their having made the agreement.

2–035 *(iv) Conditions capable of treatment?* If the respondent is physically unable to consummate the marriage he or she will nevertheless be held wilfully to have refused to do so if the respondent has refused to undergo straightforward curative treatment.

2–036 *(v) What is intercourse?* Consummation involves sexual intercourse; and the word intercourse must be interpreted as generally understood in the light of social circumstances known to exist when the legislation was passed. Hence, the House of Lords held[33] that a refusal to have intercourse unless a condom were used was not a refusal to consummate.

---

[27] For the view that the requirement of "just excuse" is based on dubious authority, has not received sufficient judicial analysis, has been expressed in alternative and confusing terms and that its application has been rare, see A. Borkowski [1994] *Fam. Law* 685.

[28] *Jodla v. Jodla* [1960] 1 W.L.R. 236; *Kaur v. Singh* [1972] 1 W.L.R. 105. In *A v. J (Nullity Proceedings)* [1989] 1 F.L.R. 110, it was held that a wife's uncompromising insistence on the postponement of a religious ceremony because she was disappointed by the husband's cool and inconsiderate behaviour to her constituted a wilful refusal on her part to consummate the marriage.

[29] [1972] 1 W.L.R. 105.

[30] *Jodla v. Jodla* [1960] 1 W.L.R. 236.

[31] *Brodie v. Brodie* [1917] P. 271.

[32] *Morgan v. Morgan* [1959] P. 92; *Scott v. Scott* [1959] P. 103.

[33] *Baxter v. Baxter* [1948] A.C. 274. It should be noted that the decision was based on the fact that this ground for annulment is statutory; the question was not, therefore, to be solved exclusively by reference to the construction given by the courts to the word "consummation" in the (then non-statutory) ground of incapacity. For a criticism of the decision, see (1948) 11 *M.L.R.* 176 (Gower) and *G. v. G.* [1952] V.L.R. 402.

There are conflicting decisions[34] as to whether a marriage is consummated by *coitus interruptus*.

Should wilful refusal be a ground for annulment?

2–037 Since wilful refusal occurs after the marriage, it is not conceptually an appropriate ground for annulment which (as indicated above) is in principle concerned solely with defects existing at the time of the marriage. But attempts (by the Church of England amongst others) to have wilful refusal removed from the grounds for annulment have been unsuccessful.[35]

(c) Lack of consent: duress, mistake, insanity, etc.

Introduction—historical evolution

2–038 For the canon law, marriage was created by the consent of the parties[36]; and if there were no true consent there could be no marriage.[37] Hence, until the Nullity of Marriage Act 1971, lack of consent (whether arising from duress, mistake or insanity) made a marriage void. As a result of the 1971 Act, a marriage celebrated after July 31, 1971 is voidable (rather than void) if either party did not validly consent to it, whether in consequence of duress, mistake, unsoundness of mind or otherwise.[38]

We first of all examine the substance of the law; we then consider the reasons why the law was changed in 1971.

No apparent consent

2–039 If the parties have not apparently given their consent to the marriage, the formalities prescribed by English law[39] cannot have been completed.

Apparent consent but no real consent

2–040 In practice, the difficulties arise because the outward expression of consent may not be accompanied by the necessary intention. For example, a man may

---

[34] *Cackett v. Cackett* [1950] P. 253; *White v. White* [1948] P. 330; *cf. Grimes v. Grimes* [1948] P. 323. The law on this subject is now, in practical terms, of little importance by reason of the readier availability of divorce as a means of dissolving unhappy unions: see below.

[35] This would enable the Church to accept the law applied in the secular courts as being consistent with Christian doctrine: *The Church and the Law of Nullity of Marriage* (1955), pp. 38, 48; and also Morton Commission, paras. 88, 89, 283; *Putting Asunder*, pp. 67. 124–125; *Marriage and the Church's Task* (1978). But the Law Commission in its comprehensive review of the law (see Law Com. No. 33, para. 27) supported the retention of wilful refusal as a ground for annulment, and in the Parliamentary Debates on the Nullity of Marriage Act 1971 the Lord Chancellor refused (notwithstanding powerful support for the abolitionist view) to accept an amendment to the Nullity of Marriage Act which would have abolished wilful refusal as a ground for nullity: see *Hansard* H.L., Vol. 318, col. 940.

[36] p. 11, above.

[37] But the doctrine of ratification might in some cases prevent the validity of the marriage being challenged.

[38] M.C.A. 1973, s.12(c).

[39] *per* Sir Jocelyn Simon P. in *Szechter v. Szechter* [1971] P. 286 at 294–295.

be insane, and not aware of what he is doing. He may believe his bride to be A, whereas in fact she is B: although he intends to marry, he does not intend to marry the person who claims to be his wife. In recent years it has become apparent that problems arise where the traditional norms of a religious, cultural or ethnic group come into conflict with the wish of a young woman to have a free choice of marriage partner.[40] The fact that marriage automatically revokes any will made by either party and that each spouse will have substantial entitlements on the other's intestacy makes marriage to an elderly and mentally failing woman attractive to fortune hunters. Use of the expression "shot-gun marriage" should not conceal the fact that forced marriages are still a significant problem in the twenty-first[41] century.

The policy dilemma

2–041 Cases where a formal consent is said not to have been a real expression of the will present an acute juristic dilemma.[42] If the apparent consent is not real, there should in principle be no marriage: marriage depends on a true consent. But to allow an apparently valid marriage to be avoided by one of the parties alleging the existence of a state of mind or belief which was not evident at the time of the ceremony was traditionally thought to jeopardise the security of marriage.

English law[43] seeks to resolve this dilemma. On the one hand, the law does not allow private reservations or motives to vitiate an ostensibly valid marriage; on the other hand it accepts that there may be cases in which there has been no consent at all.

The application of this subtle distinction can give rise to difficulties in practice; and the cases can best be considered under the three headings specifically referred to in the legislation: (i) insanity; (ii) duress and fear; (iii) mistake.

(i) *Insanity*

2–042 Marriage (it has been judicially asserted)[44] is a very simple contract, which it does not require a high degree of intelligence to understand. Mental illness or lack of mental capacity will only affect the validity of consent if either spouse was, at the time of the ceremony, by reason of the illness or deficiency, incapable of understanding the nature of marriage and the duties and responsibilities it

---

[40] These problems were highlighted by Singer J. in *Re K.R. (Abduction: Forcible Removal by Parents)* [1999] 2 F.L.R. 542. Many such cases involve the young person concerned being taken abroad, and the Foreign and Commonwealth Office has established a dedicated forced marriage desk and help line to provide advice and assistance. But strong pressure may be exercised even in cases where the family intends the marriage to be solemnised in this country, perhaps in a Register Office or perhaps in a Registered Place of Religious Worship.

[41] See *Re Davey* [1981] 1 W.L.R. 164 (92-year-old spinster and employee of care home).

[42] The issues are fully explored, with the aid of much comparative material, by J.H. Wade, "Limited Purpose Marriages" (1982) 45 *M.L.R.* 159.

[43] Other systems adopt a conceptual approach which places greater emphasis on the need for a genuine consent: see *Vervaeke (formerly Messina) v. Smith and Others* [1983] 1 A.C. 145; *Akram v. Akram* 1979 S.L.T. 87.

[44] *per* Sir J. Hannen P. in *Durham v. Durham* (1885) 10 P.D. 80 at 82: see also *per* Hodson L.J., in *Re Park* [1954] P. 112 at 136.

creates.[45] The fact that the illness is such as to make the person concerned totally unfit for marriage is irrelevant.

In 1937 Parliament provided an alternative and more easily established ground for annulment in cases in which one party was unfit to marry because of mental illness[46]; but between 1937 and 1971 proceedings were still occasionally brought on the old ground inherited from the canon law, particularly by relatives who would have been entitled on the deceased's intestacy had the deceased died unmarried.[47]

However, as a result of the Nullity of Marriage Act 1971, marriages celebrated after July 31, 1971 in which there is a lack of consent are no longer void but are merely voidable and accordingly it seems unlikely that any petitions will be brought on the basis of "common law" insanity. This is because if either of the parties wants to terminate the marriage, it will usually be easier (and just as effective) to establish the alternative "unfitness for marriage" mental disorder ground and no third party seeking to establish a succession claim can attack the validity of the marriage on the ground of a spouse's mental incapacity.

(ii) *Duress and fear*

2–043 The underlying principle of the law is that if a formal consent has been "brought about by force, menace or duress—a yielding of the lips, not of the mind—it is of no legal effect."[48]

The traditional view is that public policy requires that marriages should not be lightly set aside[49] and for this reason the principle should be strictly applied and not rashly extended.[50] However, the readier availability of divorce may have affected these assumptions; whilst the tensions between, on the one hand; the emphasis placed by modern West European societies on freedom of personal choice and, on the other hand, the preference of some ethnic groups for a considerable element of parental involvement in the selection of a marriage partner has confronted the courts with cases in which application of the traditional

---

[45] *Re Park* [1954] P. 112; *Hill v. Hill* [1959] 1 W.L.R. 127; and see *Fischer v. Adams* 38 N.W. 2d 337 (1949). In *Re B (A Minor) (Wardship: Sterilisation)* [1988] A.C. 199, the courts were concerned with a 17-year-old epileptic of low intelligence who, amongst other handicaps, could not understand the link between sexual intercourse and pregnancy. The question for decision was whether leave should be given for her to be sterilised: but Lord Hailsham asserted, *obiter,* that she could not have given a valid consent to marriage.

[46] Insanity was also (subject to restrictive conditions) made a specific ground for divorce: Matrimonial Causes Act 1965, s.1(1)(a)(iv). (For a striking illustration of the difficulties of establishing that mental illness had disabled a person from consenting to marriage, see the facts of *Re Park* [1954] P. 112.)

[47] Proof of inability to consent to the marriage rendered it void. The only recent English cases involved disputes about whether or not a will made by the deceased had been revoked by the marriage alleged to be void: *Re Park* [1954] P. 112; *Re Roberts (dec'd)* [1978] 1 W.L.R. 653; *Hill v. Hill* [1959] 1 W.L.R. 127 (a Privy Council appeal from Barbados) was also a succession dispute turning on the validity of the deceased's marriage.

[48] Bishop, *Marriage and Divorce* (6th ed., 1881), p. 177, cited in *Szechter v. Szechter* (above). Since the Nullity of Marriage Act 1971 this statement is no longer technically correct since a valid (but voidable) marriage will have been created.

[49] *per* Butt J., *Scott v. Sebright* (1886) 12 P.D. 21 at 24.

[50] *per* Karminski J., *H. v. H.* [1954] P. 258 at 267.

approach might lead to a denial of justice.[51] In the result, it is difficult to state the law with any confidence, but the main conditions seem to be as follows:

(i) Fear or pressure. There must be fear (or at least pressure) sufficiently grave to override the party's true intent. Thus, in an American "shotgun" marriage case, the marriage was void because "if there had not been a wedding, there would have been a funeral."[52] **2–044**

(ii) Subjective test. The test to be applied is a subjective one: the question is not whether a person of ordinary courage and resolution would yield to the fear, but whether the petitioner did so yield.[53] The will of a weak-minded person may be overcome by threats or pressure which would not have affected the more resolute. Thus:— **2–045**

> In *Hirani v. Hirani*[54] a 19-year-old Hindu girl, who was found to be wholly dependent on her parents, was told by them to break off a friendship she had formed with a young Muslim, and to marry a Hindu selected by them: "You had better marry somebody we want you to—otherwise pick up your belongings and go." The daughter did as she was told, and went through a marriage ceremony with the respondent (whom neither she nor her parents had seen before the wedding). After living with him for six weeks she left and went to her former boy-friend's house. It was held that this was "as clear a case as one could want of the overbearing of the will of the petitioner and thus invalidating or vitiating her consent."[55] The petitioner had been forced into the marriage; and a decree was granted.

On the other hand, the courts have refused to annul marriages deliberately entered into in order to escape from a disagreeable situation such as penury or social degradation[56] or out of a sense of obligation to family or religious tradition. The distinction may be a fine one; as is evident from a comparison of the facts of *Hirani* with those of *Singh v. Singh*.[57] In this latter case:—

---

[51] There were a number of post-war cases in which the parties were held never to have consented to marriages contracted in order to facilitate escape from totalitarian regimes: see *H. v. H.* [1954] P. 258; *Szechter v. Szechter* [1971] P. 286. On the issues raised by ethnic minority marriage customs, see generally S. Poulter, *English Law and Ethnic Minority Customs* (1986).

[52] *Lee v. Lee* 3 S.W. 2d 672 (1928). For other examples, see *Scott v. Sebright* (above) (threats to make petitioner bankrupt, and to shoot her); *Griffith v. Griffith* [1944] I.R. 35 and *Buckland v. Buckland* [1968] P. 296 (prosecution for defilement); *Parojcic v. Parojcic* [1958] 1 W.L.R. 1280 (to return to totalitarian country); *Szechter v. Szechter* [1971] P. 286; and *H. v. H.* [1954] P. 258 (danger of remaining in totalitarian country).

[53] It is true that in *Szechter v. Szechter* [1971] P. 286 at 297–298, Simon P., said that the will of one of the parties must be shown to have been overborne by "genuine and reasonably held" fear. However, Lord Simon has apparently had second thoughts about the validity of this way of formulating the matter: see (1983) 99 *L.Q.R.* 353.

[54] (1982) 4 F.L.R. 232, CA.

[55] *per* Ormrod L.J. at 234.

[56] *Szechter v. Szechter* [1971] P. 286.

[57] [1971] P. 226 (cogently criticised by S. Poulter (1979) 42 *M.L.R.* 408 at 410–418).

A marriage was arranged by the parents of two Sikhs, a girl aged 17 and a boy aged 21. The bride had never seen her husband before the marriage, and only went through the register office ceremony out of a "proper respect" for her parents and the traditions of her people. She then refused to go through the usual religious ceremony, or to live with the husband. The court declined to annul the marriage: there was no evidence at all of fear.[58]

At one time, the cases—perhaps influenced by a desire to ensure that decrees were only granted on this ground in exceptional circumstances—seemed to suggest that nothing less than a threat of immediate danger to life, limb or liberty[59] could be sufficient to justify a finding of lack of consent; but the imposition of any such rigid requirement seems inconsistent with principle. What is in issue is simply whether or not there was a true consent. Since divorce will now sooner or later terminate almost any marriage, there would seem to be no adequate justification for an illogically restrictive policy.

2–046 **(iii) Other party not necessarily responsible.** The fear need not necessarily result from the behaviour of the other party. Pressure from the bride's father has often been involved; whilst threats to life and liberty by totalitarian regimes have been held to suffice.[60]

2–047 **(iv) Relevance of the fear arising in consequence of party's misconduct.** It is sometimes said that the fear must not be justly imposed. A petition will on this view fail if, for example, the petitioner who had had unlawful sexual intercourse with the bride went through a marriage cermony with her because he was frightened that otherwise he might be imprisoned.[61]

However, it is submitted that this view is wrong. It is illogical (because the justice of the threat has nothing to do with the subjective question of whether the threatened person did in fact consent); and it is contrary to principle (because canon law held a marriage void even if the petitioner had been subjected to a just fear arising as a consequence of his own fault).

(iii) *Mistake and fraud*

2–048 Generally neither mistake nor fraud avoids a marriage. The cynic may say that the maxim *caveat emptor* applies just as much to marriage as it does to

---

[58] It may be possible to reconcile the two cases as turning on this crucial finding of fact; the approach in *Hirani* and is not only more humane but more securely founded on principle. In Scotland the decisions in *Mahmood v. Mahmood* 1993 S.L.T. 589 and *Mahmud v. Mahmud* 1994 S.L.T. 599, have approved *Hirani.*

[59] *Szechter v. Szechter; Singh v. Singh; Singh v. Kaur* (above).

[60] *H. v. H.* [1954] P. 258; *Szechter v. Szechter* [1971] P. 286. Strictly, these decisions seem questionable: although the parties were no doubt frightened, their decision to marry was in each case a conscious and indeed a rational one. The parties wanted to be married so that they could enjoy the legal consequences of matrimony.

[61] The man is free to elect between scandal and possible punishment on the one hand, and marriage to the girl he was wronged on the other; *per* Haugh J., *Griffith v. Griffith* [1944] I.R. 35 at 43; *Buckland v. Buckland* [1968] P. 296. On this view, a decree may only be granted if the accusation is shown to be false.

other contracts. Fraud is only a vitiating factor if it procures the appearance without the reality of consent; and it is not sufficient that fraud has induced a genuine consent.[62] Hence, a marriage into which a woman tricked a man by concealing the fact that she was pregnant by a third party was valid.[63]

There are in fact only two groups of case in which mistake has been held sufficient to vitiate consent to marriage:

(i) Mistake as to the person (as distinct from mistake as to that person's attributes). If I marry A under the belief that she is B this is sufficient to found a petition. In contrast, if I marry A erroneously believing her to be a chaste virgin of good family and possessed of ample wealth the marriage will be unimpeachable.[64]

(ii) Mistake as to the nature of the ceremony. It is sufficient to avoid the marriage if one party believes that he or she is appearing in a police court, or that the ceremony is a betrothal[65] or religious conversion ceremony,[66] or if one of the parties is so drunk (or under the influence of drugs) as not to know what is happening.[67]

These principles have been applied to cases where a "sham" marriage has been contracted in order to acquire a nationality or immigration status. If the parties intend to contract a marriage—even though the marriage is only to be for that limited purpose—it will in the absence of fear or duress[68] be unimpeachable[69] in English law.

In Messina v. Smith[70] W went through a marriage ceremony, knowing that it was such a ceremony, and that the purpose of it was to enable her to obtain British nationality and a British passport and thereby protect herself

---

[62] *Moss v. Moss* [1897] P. 263 at 269, *per* Sir F. H. Jeune P.

[63] It would now, by statute, be voidable provided certain conditions are satisfied: see p. 00, below.

[64] There are fine distinctions. In a New Zealand case (*C. v. C.* [1942] N.Z.L.R. 356) H represented to W that he was a well-known featherweight pugilist. Her mistake was as to his attributes and not as to his identity; she intended to marry the man physically present, and his name was not an essential condition of the marriage. Hence the petition failed. In an Australian case, on the other hand, where W believed that H was a member of a particular family with which she was acquainted there was held to be a mistake of identity as against a mere mistake of name: *Allardyce v. Mitchell* (1869) 6 W.W. & A'B. 45.

[65] *Hall v. Hall* (1908) 24 T.L.R. 756 (where an English woman, who thought that marriages could only be celebrated in church, went through a marriage ceremony in Kensington Register Office believing that she was merely registering her name); *Kelly v. Kelly* (1932) 49 T.L.R. 99; *Parojcic v. Parojcic* [1958] W.L.R. 1280; *Ford v. Stier* [1896] P. 1.

[66] *Mehta v. Mehta* [1945] 2 All E.R. 690.

[67] *Sullivan v. Sullivan* (1812) 2 Hag.Con. 238 at 246 (*per* Sir W. Scott). A mistake as to the effects of the relationship produced by the marriage is insufficient: a petition failed where H thought the marriage was polygamous, entitling him to take further wives (*Kassim v. Kassim* [1962] P. 224) and also where H erroneously assumed that his Russian wife would be allowed to leave the Soviet Union and live with him: *Way v. Way* [1950] P. 71.

[68] *H. v. H.* [1954] P. 258; see also *Kurma v. Kurma, The Times*, April 30, 1958.

[69] *Silver v. Silver* [1958] 1 W.L.R. 259; *Vervaeke (formerly Messina) v. Smith and Others* [1983] 1 A.C. 145.

[70] [1971] P. 322. For subsequent proceedings see *Vervaeke (formerly Messina) v. Smith and Others* [1983] 1 A.C. 145.

against the risk of deportation for offences incidental to her engaging in prostitution. A petition to annul the marriage on the ground that the parties had had no intention to cohabit as husband and wife, and that there had thus been no true consent to the marriage, failed.[71]

Should lack of consent make a marriage void or voidable?

2–049 The canon law rule that a marriage was void[72] if one party had not truly consented survived until the Nullity of Marriage Act 1971 rendered such marriages merely voidable. The result is no doubt convenient, but it is conceptually astonishing.[73] The result of holding such a marriage to be merely voidable is that a person who does not understand what he or she is doing may become legally bound to a relationship whose whole juridical basis is the consent of both parties. Moreover, that relationship has important legal consequences, including, for example the right of intestate succession. A man—such as an attendant in a nursing home—may go through a marriage ceremony with a rich elderly woman who is so severely demented that she has no idea what is happening; and such a "marriage" will since 1971 effectively revoke the will she had made some years previously in favour of her family whilst her "husband" will have extensive succession rights on her death intestate.[74] This seems unsatisfactory.

(d) Venereal disease, pregnancy by another and mental illness

2–050 The remaining three grounds on which a marriage may be voidable originate in the Matrimonial Causes Act 1937 and were introduced because of the lack of matrimonial relief for fraudulent or wilful concealment of material facts[75]: a husband who discovered that his wife was carrying another man's child had no ground of matrimonial relief since deceit was not a ground for annulment,[76] and the pregnancy did not establish that she had, since the marriage, committed adultery.

The grounds now are:

(i) that at the time of the marriage the respondent was suffering from venereal disease in a communicable form;

---

[71] *per* Ormrod J., *Messina v. Smith* (1971) as cited and approved by Lord Hailsham of St. Marylebone. *Vervaeke (formerly Messina) v. Smith and Others* [1983] 1 A.C. 145 and 152.

[72] There is some judicial support for the view that marriages affected by force, fear, fraud or drunkenness were voidable only, but this view is convincingly refuted by Tolstoy (1963) 27 *M.L.R.* 385: see J. Jackson, *Formation and Annulment of Marriage* (2nd ed., 1969), p. 285).

[73] A full account of the policy considerations is given in the 4th edition of this work at pp. 79–81; and reference should be made to the Law Commission's Report on *Nullity of Marriage*, Law Com. No. 33.

[74] See Chap. 8, below.

[75] Morton Commission, para. 267.

[76] *Moss v. Moss* [1897] P. 263.

(ii) that at the time of the marriage the respondent was pregnant by some person other than the petitioner[77]; and

(iii) that at the time of the marriage either party, though capable of giving a valid consent, was suffering (whether continously or intermittently) from mental disorder within the meaning of the Mental Health Act 1983[78] of such a kind or to such an extent as to be unfitted for marriage. This was intended to cover the case where the afflicted party is capable of giving a valid consent to the marriage but has a mental disorder[79] which makes a normal married life impossible.[80]

B. Bars

2–051 It is a feature of matrimonial law that it is insufficient for a petitioner merely to establish a ground upon which a decree is granted. This is because in some circumstances there may be a bar to the granting of the relief sought. The text therefore explains the bars which are relevant in the case of nullity petitions.

1. Void marriages

2–052 There are no longer[81] any bars to the granting of a decree on the ground that a marriage is void.

2. Voidable marriages

2–053 The Nullity of Marriage Act 1971 codified the bars which may prevent a decree being granted notwithstanding proof of one of the grounds upon which a marriage is voidable. There are now three such bars:

(a) Time

2–054 It is an absolute bar to the granting of a decree on the ground of lack of consent, venereal disease, or pregnancy by a third party, that proceedings were not instituted within three years of the marriage.[82] Exceptionally, the court may

---

[77] M.C.A. 1973, s.12(e) and (f).

[78] s.12(d) as amended by Mental Health Act 1983, Sched. 4, para. 34.

[79] As defined: Mental Health Act 1983, s.1(2).

[80] *Bennett v. Bennett* [1969] 1 W.L.R. 430 at 434.

[81] Prior to the Nullity of Marriage Act 1971 (see s.6(1)), collusion was a bar to the grant of a decree even where the marriage was void; see Law Com. No. 33, paras. 37, 38. There may also be cases where a party is estopped from putting the validity of a marriage in issue: *Woodland v. Woodland* [1928] P. 169; see generally Tolstoy, "Marriage by Estoppel or an Excursion into Res Judicata" (1968) 84 *L.Q.R.* 245, but note that the divorce courts' jurisdiction is inquisitorial in nature and that the scope for such doctrines is accordingly restricted: see *W. v. W. (Physical Inter-sex)* [2001] Fam. 111 at 324 (concession correctly made that neither estoppel nor laches applicable in case in which court had previously granted respondent to nullity petition decree absolute of divorce in respect of the marriage).

[82] M.C.A. 1973, s.13(2), as substituted by M.&F.P.A. 1984, s.2(2).

give leave for proceedings to be instituted after the expiration of three years if the petitioner has at some time during the three-year period suffered from mental disorder if it would in all the circumstances be just to give leave.[83]

(b) Knowledge of defect

2–055 A petition founded on (a) venereal disease or (b) pregnancy by a third party will fail unless the petitioner can satisfy the court that, at the time of the marriage, the petitioner was ignorant of the facts alleged.[84] A husband's knowledge that the wife is pregnant is not in itself a bar; he must also know that she was pregnant by someone other than himself.[85]

Knowledge is no longer a specific[86] bar to a petition based on the existence of a mental disorder.[87]

(c) Approbation[88]

2–056 For the ecclesiastical courts, approbation could be defined as conduct on the part of the petitioner[89] which so plainly implied a recognition of the existence and validity of the marriage as to render it inequitable and contrary to public policy that the validity of the marriage should subsequently be questioned by the petitioner.[90]

The Nullity of Marriage Act 1971 replaced these uncertain and obscure rules with a statutory code.[91] The court is not to[92] grant a decree of nullity on the ground that a marriage is voidable if the respondent satisfies the court:

> "(a) that the petitioner, with knowledge that it was open to him to have the marriage avoided, so conducted himself in relation to the respondent as to lead the respondent reasonably to believe that he would not seek to do so; and

---

[83] M.C.A. 1973, s.13(4) as inserted by M.&F.P.A. 1984, s.2(3). For the reasons, see the Law Commission's Report on *Time Restrictions on Presentation of Divorce and Nullity Petitions*. Law Com. No. 116.

[84] M.C.A. 1973, s.13(3).

[85] *Stocker v. Stocker* [1966] 1 W.L.R. 190.

[86] But knowledge of the defect may be a bar if, knowing that the marriage could be avoided, the petitioner so conducted himself in relation to the respondent as to lead the respondent reasonably to believe that he or she would not seek annulment: M.C.A. 1973, s.13(1), below.

[87] The bars so far discussed apply only to marriages celebrated after July 31, 1971.

[88] For full discussions of the pre-1971 law see Lasok, "Approbation of Marriage in English Law and the Doctrine of Validation" (1963) 26 *M.L.R.* 249; J. Jackson, *Formation and Annulment of Marriage* (2nd ed., 1969), Chap. 8. The old law can be of no more than historical interest, because the new rules now embodied in M.C.A. 1973 apply to all proceedings instituted after July 31, 1971 (whenever the marriage was celebrated): Nullity of Marriage Act 1971, s.3(4); *cf.* the original draft: Law Com. No. 33, p. 49, para. 6.

[89] *G. v. M.* (1885) 10 App. Cas. 171 at 199, *per* Lord Watson.

[90] *ibid.*, at p. 186, *per* Lord Selborne L.C.

[91] *D. v. D. (Nullity: Statutory Bar)* [1979] Fam. 70 at 72.

[92] The bar is absolute and not discretionary: *D. v. D. (Nullity: Statutory Bar)* [1979] Fam. 70 at 76. For the reasons, see Law Com. No. 33, para. 43.

(b) that it would be unjust to the respondent to grant the decree."[93]

Hence, three separate matters must be proved[94]:

(i) conduct by the petitioner in relation to the respondent which resulted in the respondent reasonably believing that he would not seek to have the marriage annulled;
(ii) knowledge by the petitioner, at the time of the conduct relied on, that he could have the marriage annulled; and
(iii) injustice to the respondent if a decree were to be granted.

There has been no case reported in which this statutory bar has been successfully pleaded; and a spouse wishing to resist the granting of a decree has formidable hurdles to overcome. Even if the petitioner did lead the respondent to believe he would not seek annulment, and the respondent did at the time know that he or she would have been able to have the marriage annulled, it will often be impossible for a respondent to show that he would suffer injustice if a decree were granted. This is because any spouse will usually be able in time to have the marriage terminated by divorce[95] and the respondent in that case will have the same rights to apply for financial provision and property adjustment orders as in nullity proceedings.[96] Finally, it should be noted that public policy is no longer a consideration directly relevant to the operation of the bar.[97] Thus:—

In *D. v. D. (Nullity: Statutory Bar)*[98] a couple had adopted two young children, thereby representing to the court that they were validly married. A decree of nullity was granted: the fact that the couple had held themselves out as married was no longer relevant; nor was it relevant that it might be contrary to public policy to allow a couple who had acted in this way to have their marriage annulled.[99]

---

[93] M.C.A. 1973, s.13(1).
[94] The requirements of the section are cumulative: *D. v. D. (Nullity: Statutory Bar)* [1979] Fam 70, 78.
[95] See Chap. 11, below.
[96] *D. v. D. (Nullity: Statutory Bar)* [1979] Fam. 70 at 78.
[97] *D. v. D. (Nullity: Statutory Bar)* [1979] Fam. 70. Under the old law there was authority for the view that the court might hold that a marriage had been approbated in spite of the absence of injustice to the parties if public policy so required (see *Tindall v. Tindall* [1953] P. 63 at 72; *Slater v. Slater* [1953] P. 235 at 244); for the policy underlying the change see Law Com. No. 33, para. 44—a passage cited by Dunn J. in *D. v. D. (Nullity: Statutory Bar)* [1979] Fam. 70 at 77, who added (at 78) "parties are to be encouraged to resolve their differences, and to do that, certainty in the law is a requisite, untrammelled by considerations of public policy which may vary from judge to judge."
[98] [1979] Fam. 70.
[99] *cf. W. v. W.* [1952] P. 152 (a decision under the old law). It is submitted that the change in the law was clearly desirable: the policy of protecting the child in such cases is better secured by the statutory requirement that the court consider whether to exercise its powers to make residence or other orders, in respect of the children (M.C.A. 1973, s.41) rather than by asserting the continuance of the marriage.

C. Effects of a decree[1]

2–057 At common law (a) any children of a void marriage would be illegitimate, because their parents had never been married; and (b) none of the legal consequences associated with marriage could flow from the relationship which by definition had no legal existence. For example, a person whose marriage was void would not have the right of a spouse in relation to the other's British citizenship,[2] nor would he or she have any right to succeed to the other's property on intestacy; whilst no duty to provide maintenance could arise from the purported marriage. In the eyes of the law, the couple were merely cohabitants.

The same consequences followed if the marriage were voidable. This was because, although the marriage would be valid until avoided, the decree when made, operated retrospectively and declared the marriage "to have been and to be absolutely null and void to all intents and purposes whatsoever,"[3] and once the decree had been pronounced the marriage became void *ab initio*.

Over the years the law has been reformed, and the position is now radically different in relation to both voidable and void marriages:

1. Voidable marriages

2–058 The fact that a decree operated retroactively was anomalous and inconvenient, and created hardship; and the Nullity of Marriage Act 1971 now[4] provides that a decree operates to annul the marriage only as respects any time after it has been made absolute, and that "the marriage shall, notwithstanding the decree, be treated as if it had existed up to that time." This new rule undoubtedly removes anomalies; but its application will not always produce a result which seems conspicuously just. For example:—

> In *Ward v. Secretary of State for Social Services*[5] the widow of an army officer went through a ceremony of marriage; but the marriage was a disaster and lasted for less than a week. It was never consummated and in due course a decree of nullity was granted on that basis. But it was held that the marriage which had been annulled brought to an end the petitioner's status as a widow and that she had therefore lost her entitlement to an army widow's pension.

---

[1] Every decree is in the first instance a decree nisi which is not generally to be made absolute before the end of six weeks from its grant: M.C.A. 1973 s.15. It follows that a voidable marriage will not be legally terminated until the decree *nisi* has been made absolute; quite what effect a decree *nisi* has on the status of the parties to a marriage held to be void is not clear.

[2] See, *e.g. R. v. Hillingdon Borough Council, ex p. Streeting* [1980] 1 W.L.R. 1425.

[3] *De Reneville v. De Reneville* [1948] P. 100 at 111.

[4] The legitimacy of the children of a voidable marriage was preserved notwithstanding the fact that the parents' marriage had been declared never to have existed: see M.C.A. 1937, s.7(1) (2) and Law Reform (Miscellaneous Provisions) Act 1949, s.4.

[5] [1990] 1 F.L.R. 119. (The Pensions Act 1995, s.168, preserves the rights of women whose remarriage is terminated by death, divorce or annulment to certain war pensions; but it does not affect the general principle stated in the text.)

2. Void Marriages

Even more striking is the fact that a void marriage may now have some of the legal consequences of a valid marriage. **2–059**

(a) Legitimacy of children

Since 1959 English law has accepted that the offspring of a void marriage may be "treated as" the parent's legitimate child if at the time of conception (or the time of the marriage ceremony if later) both or either of the parties reasonably believed that the marriage was valid.[6] **2–060**

(b) Financial provision after decree[7] of nullity

If a "marriage" does not exist, it logically follows that none of the rights and duties of marriage subsist between the parties. If a man fails to maintain his "wife", it was at common law an answer to her claim for maintenance that the "marriage" was void (and it is still an answer if a spouse seeks maintenance in proceedings under the Domestic Proceedings and Magistrates' Courts Act 1978 or in the High Court on the ground of failure to provide reasonable maintenance).[8] This is because those remedies depend upon the existence of the relationship of husband and wife. However, provided that a decree of nullity is obtained, the court now[9] has exactly the same powers[10] to order one party to make financial provision for the other as it would have when dissolving a valid marriage.[11] Similarly, a "wife" or "husband" who has obtained such a decree can apply to the court for reasonable provision out of the estate after the other's death.[12] **2–061**

---

[6] The rule is now contained in Legitimacy Act 1976, s.1 (as amended by F.L.R.A. 1987, s. 28). But this provision only applies to a child born *after* the void marriage has taken place: *Re Spence (dec'd)* [1990] Ch. 652, CA. For the history of the law's refusal to recognise the canon law doctrine of the putative marriage, see: F.H. Newark (1944) 8 *M.L.R.* 203; E.J. Cohn (1948) 64 *L.Q.R.* 324.

[7] An applicant cannot effectively oust the court's jurisdiction to make such ancillary orders by seeking a bare declaration that the marriage was void *ab initio:* see F.L.A. 1986, s.55(1), and, for a full discussion of the background, the Law Commission's Report on *Declarations in Family Matters,* Law Com. No. 132.

[8] Relief is only available to a "party to a marriage," and a party to a void union is not such: see *Ivett v. Ivett* (1930) 94 J.P. 237; 143 L.T. 680.

[9] M.C.A. 1973, ss.23, 24, as substituted by the F.L.A. 1996, Sched. 2.

[10] *D. v. D. (Nullity: Statutory Bar)* [1979] Fam. 70.

[11] It does not however follow that the court will exercise its discretion: see *Whiston v. Whiston* [1995] Fam. 198 (criticised by S.M. Cretney (1996) 112 *L.Q.R.* 33) but note that in *S.T. v. J. (Transsexual: Void Marriage)* [1998] Fam. 103 a majority of the Court of Appeal (whilst denying in that case the applicant's claim for relief) none the less favoured a flexible approach to applications even when the applicant had been guilty of some wrongdoing (for example, making a false declaration when giving notice for the marriage) in contracting it.

[12] Inheritance (Provision for Family and Dependants) Act 1975, ss.1(1)b, 25(1). This presupposes that a person whose void marriage has been annulled is within the definition of former spouse—*i.e.* "a person whose marriage with the deceased was . . . annulled". In the light of decisions such as *S.T. v. J. (Transsexual: Void Marriage)* [1998] Fam. 103 it seems improbable that an argument that there has never been a marriage capable of being annulled could succeed.

(c) Financial provision from estate if no decree

2–062 If a spouse only discovered that the "marriage" was void for bigamy after the other spouse's death, the survivor would have no right to succeed on intestacy; and it would be too late to obtain a decree which would enable an application to be made to the court under the legislation referred to above.[13] The Law Reform (Miscellaneous Provisions) Act 1970[14] dealt with this problem: a person who in good faith entered into a void marriage with a person since deceased may apply to the court for reasonable provision out of the deceased's estate, in exactly the same way as if the applicant were the deceased's surviving spouse (or a person who had obtained a decree of nullity carrying with it the right to be considered for financial provision).

D. Proposals for further reform

2–063 The law of nullity has lost much of its practical importance for two main reasons. First, as we have seen, many of the legal consequences of marriages have now been attached to even a void[15] marriage. Secondly almost all marriages can now be dissolved by divorce if either party wishes it. Before the Divorce Reform Act 1969 a divorce could only be obtained if one party could prove that the other had committed a matrimonial offence[16]; and if he or she could not do so, the only way of escape[17] was by obtaining a decree of nullity. Now a spouse separated for many years[18] will usually be able to divorce and remarry, whatever the views of the other spouse. The reality is that nullity has ceased to provide a statistically significant form of relief for couples who wish to be free from the legal consequences of marriage; and it is sometimes suggested that, there would be much to be said for abolishing the concept of the voidable marriage (with the attendant full hearings and sometimes unpleasant medical examination) and allowing the parties to seek a divorce based on the breakdown of their marriage.[19] However, the Law Commission rejected this proposal; and it seems unlikely that further reform of the law governing the annulment of marriage will be on the agenda in the foreseeable future.

---

[13] In some cases she might have been able to recover damages for breach of contract from the estate: *Shaw v. Shaw* [1954] 2 Q.B. 429; see Law Com. No. 26.

[14] See now Inheritance (Provision for Family and Dependants) Act 1975, ss.1(1)(a),25(4).

[15] See above.

[16] See Chap. 11, below.

[17] In practice (but not in theory) if the other party were prepared to accept divorce it could usually be obtained, the husband providing "evidence" of the commission of an offence (*e.g.* adultery) on the basis of which his wife would petition.

[18] See, *e.g. Clifford v. Clifford* [1948] P. 187 (marriage in 1919; never consummated; H left in 1937; petition presented in 1946); see also *Notley v. Notley, The Times,* November 4, 1960 (marriage in 1927; never consummated; H left in 1954).

[19] This has been done in Australia.

CHAPTER THREE

THE LEGAL CONSEQUENCES OF MARRIAGE

INTRODUCTION

3-001 In the opening pages of this book the emphasis traditionally given to marriage in expositions of family law was explained by the fact that marriage created a status from which certain legal rights and duties automatically stemmed. The reader having learned in Chapters 1 and 2 how marriage comes into existence in English law, might therefore reasonably expect now to be told what those rights and duties are. After all, if one looks at the codified systems of law in force in many of the other countries of the European Union[1] one finds statements (albeit often cast in rather general terms[2]) about the rights and duties of spouses, and dealing with such matters as the choice of the family home,[3] as well as the effects of marriage in relation to the parties' property.[4] This Chapter should surely contain the English counterpart.

It has to be admitted at once that (notwithstanding the commitment made by the Law Commission[5] to the systematic reform and eventual codification of family law, and the cascade[6] of legislation[7] affecting the family) no such comprehensive statement is to be found; and that it is virtually impossible to give an account of the legal consequences of marriage which is coherent, much less comprehensive. Indeed, those coming to the English legal system from a different cultural background might well describe English family law as "little more than a jumble of procedures, couched almost entirely in terms of remedies rather than rights, moving directly from the formation of marriage to divorce or death, pausing only to give the parties the right to apply to the court for protection from violence".[8] It would be difficult to deny the charge that the statute book fails to deal in any systematic or comprehensive manner with such matters as

---

[1] See, for example, the French *Code Civil,* Chap. VI.

[2] See, *e.g.* the French *Code Civil,* Art. 212: "Les epoux se doivent mutuellement fidélité secours, assistance".

[3] *Code Civil,* Art. 215.

[4] *Code Civil,* Title V.

[5] *Second Programme of Law Reform* (Law Com. No. 14 (1967)) Item XIX; and see now the Commission's *Sixth Programme of Law Reform* (Law Com. No. 234 (1995)), Item 8.

[6] *Hewer v. Bryant* [1970] Q.B. 357 at 371, *per* Sachs L.J.

[7] The achievements of the Law Commission are summarised in the Commission's *Twenty-Eighth Annual Report 1993* (Law Com. No. 233 (1994)). Pt III and see also Dame B. Hale, "Family Law Reform: Whither or Wither?" (1995) C.L.P. 217.

[8] The words put into the mouth of a foreign enquirer by S.M. Cretney, "The Codification of Family Law" (1981) 44 *M.L.R.* 1,9; *cf.* B. Hale (above).

the legal consequences of marriage, the mutual rights and duties of the spouses, and of parent and child.[9]

In order to understand the background to the law—and by way of a prelude to an attempt to highlight the more important legal consequences of marriage—it may be helpful to say a little about its development, and specifically about three features of the common law which have a particular significance: (a) the doctrine of the legal unity of husband and wife; (b) the notion of consortium; and (c) the common law duty to maintain a wife. The text examines these in turn.

A. The doctrine of the legal unity of husband and wife

3–002 A common law, husband and wife were said[10] to be one person; and (as Blackstone put it):

> [the] "very being or legal existence of the woman is suspended during the marriage, or at least is incorporated and consolidated into that of the husband: under whose wing, protection, and *cover* she performs everything . . . Upon this principle, of an union of person in husband and wife, depend almost all the legal rights, duties, and disabilities, that either of them acquire by marriage."[11]

In reality, the doctrine was not consistently applied; but it did provide an attractively simple explanation for many of the distinctive rules relating to the legal relations between spouses ranging from the common law rule[12] that one spouse

---

[9] The Children Act 1989—in many ways a model of a well-drafted statute—exemplifies the reluctance of English statutory texts to specify the rights and obligations stemming from family membership: the key concept of "parental responsibility" is defined as "all the rights, duties, powers, responsibilities and authority which by law a parent of a child has in relation to the child and his property" and thus leaves the user to find out the content and true meaning of "parental responsibility" from other sources (and in particular from case law).

[10] The doctrine in reality imperfectly represented the common law: see G. Williams, *The Legal Unity of Husband and Wife* (1947) 10 *M.L.R.* 16, 18; *Midland Bank Trust Co. Ltd v. Green (No 3)* [1979] Ch. 496 (Oliver J).

[11] Blackstone, *Commentaries on the Laws of England* (8th ed. 1824), Vol. 1, p. 449. This explains the use until well into the twentieth century of the Norman French expression "feme covert" to refer to a married woman. "Feme sole" means an unmarried woman, whether spinster, widow or divorced.

[12] Abolished by the Law Reform (Husband and Wife) Act 1962 giving effect to recommendations of the Law Reform Committee (9th Report, Cmnd. 1268). However, the court has a discretionary power to stay an action in certain circumstances (for example, if it appears that no substantial benefit would accrue to either party from the continuance of the proceedings, or if the action relates to property and could more conveniently be disposed of by an application under the Married Women's Property Act 1882); and the legislation thus reflects a cautious approach to the desirability of litigation within the family. It may be noted that it has apparently become common in some United States jurisdictions for tort actions to be used in an attempt to secure the financial benefits denied by a refusal to take matrimonial conduct into account in settling the financial outcome of marital breakdown: see Bagshaw (2001) 117 *L.Q.R.* 571 at 574; but in England it seems that most actions between spouses are in substance actions by the two of them to recover compensation from an insurance company—see for example the case (reported as news item in *The Times*, April 26, 1994), of *Ginder v. Ginder* in which a husband who admitted that he had undertaken responsibility for "man's work" in the house was held liable in damages (perhaps as

could not sue the other in tort[13] to the rule that a married woman automatically had the same legal domicile as her husband.[14] For years the unity doctrine continued to rear its head "hydra-like" and to be applied with surprising results.[15] For example, in 1945 a magistrates' court was reported[16] to have acquitted a man of an offence in using his wife's non-transferable railway ticket because they were in law one person, whilst as recently as 1978 the courts had to decide whether it was a good defence to a tort action in conspiracy that those involved were husband and wife and thus one person.[17] It is certainly true that the unity doctrine was a legal fiction; and it has been said[18] that it had been so eroded by the judges (who created exception after exception to it) and cut down by statute after statute that "little of it remains". But this statement encapsulates one of the difficulties of providing a coherent account of the law: although it is true that usually answers will be found to questions about the legal consequences of marriage in one or more of a range of ill-related statutes, the difficulty is to know how much the "little that remains" of the doctrine of unity is still significant.[19]

B. The notion of consortium

3–003 The difficulty of giving a coherent account of the common law rules relating to the legal consequences of marriage is well exemplified by an attempt to state the contemporary relevance of the common law doctrine that husband and wife became entitled to one another's *consortium*—in effect the right to the other's society, assistance, comfort and protection.[20] The main practical significance of

much as £500,000) for personal injuries suffered by his wife in trying to rescue her son from the roof of a carport onto which he had been able to climb because of the husband's negligent failure to carry out repairs.

[13] *Manby v. Scott* (1660) Smith's Leading Cases (13th ed.), p. 417. Disputes between spouses were exclusively within the province of the ecclesiastical court, and any historical treatment of the subject would contain an extended coverage of this topic. The Matrimonial Causes Act 1857, s.22, provided that (subject to statutory provision to the contrary) the court should give relief on principles as nearly as may be conformable to the principles applied by the ecclesiastical courts; and this principle—preserved by the Supreme Court of Judicature (Consolidation) Act 1925, s.32—remained, in theory at least, part of English law until the relevant provision was repealed by the Supreme Court Act 1981, s.152(4), Sched. 7

[14] Described "the last barbarous relic of a wife's servitude": *Gray v. Formosa* [1963] P. 259 at 267, *per* Lord Denning M.R. The rule was abolished by the Domicile and Matrimonial Proceedings Act 1973, s.1.

[15] *Lush on the law of Husband and Wife* (4th ed. by S.N. Grant-Bailey, 1933), p. 58.

[16] The reports were in fact inaccurate: see G. Williams (1947) 10 *M.L.R.* 16

[17] *Midland Bank Trust Co. Ltd and Another v. Green and Another (No. 3)* [1982] Ch. 529, CA.

[18] *ibid.* at 538, *per* Lord Denning M.R.

[19] Note *e.g.* the principle that one spouse has an unlimited insurable interest in the life of the other (so that a spouse may insure the other's life and recover the sum insured without needing to prove that the death has caused any financial loss): see Life Assurance Act 1774; *Griffiths v. Fleming* [1909] 1 K.B. 805, CA.

[20] *Best v. Samuel Fox & Co. Ltd* [1952] A.C. 716 at 729, *per* Lord Goddard, and at 735, *per* Lord Reid. It appears that a father was also entitled to the physical possession of his legitimate children, to their services and certain other rights but that whilst he could claim damages for interference with the right to services and assert his right to physical possession by the writ of *habeas corpus* there was no right to damages for mere interference with the right to the child's company: see *F. v. Wirral Metropolitan Borough Council and Another* [1991] Fam. 69, C.A.; and note *Lough v. Ward* [1945] 2 All E.R. 338 at 346–347, *per* Cassels J.

this rather nebulous concept[21] was that it came to provide the basis on which compensation might be claimed by a husband whose rights had been injured by the defendant's act—so that if a defendant negligently injured a wife she would have her own right of action in tort for the damage she had suffered and her husband would have a corresponding (but independent) right to damages for the loss of her society brought about by her hospitalisation or even by the change in her personality consequent on the accident.[22] The Administration of Justice Act 1982[23] abolished the right to bring such actions providing that no person should be liable in tort[24] on the ground only of the defendant "having deprived him of the services or society of his wife."[25] But no statute has ever abolished the principle that spouses are entitled to consortium and this principle may still be relevant in some circumstances. For example, in interpreting statutes in which the expression "living together" has been used (in the criminal law[26] and in relation to taxation[27] as well as in divorce matters[28]) it has been said[29] that

> "[the] law has regard to what is called the consortium of husband and wife, which is a kind of association only possible between husband and wife. A husband and wife are living together, not only when they are residing together in the same house, but also when they living in different places, even if they are separated by the high seas, provided the consortium has not been determined."

The difficulty is, therefore, that under the case law system judges may still reach decisions on the basis that the relationship of husband and wife is in some sense "special"; but it is not always easy to predict when they will do so. It seems improbable that the technical rules developed by the common law will ever be relevant today; but the notion that the relationship of husband and wife has a distinctive character remains pervasive and may influence developments in the

---

[21] At one time it had significance in the context of the husband's supposed right to beat his wife and to control her movements: *Lush on the law of Husband and Wife* (4th ed., by S.N. Grant-Bailey, 1933), pp. 24 *et seq.* By the end of the nineteenth century such rights were obsolescent and only relevant to the extent that a husband might be held to have some right to control the ambit and nature of his wife's social life (see *R. v. Jackson* [1891] 1 Q.B. 671, C.A; *Place v. Searle* [1932] 2 K.B. 497) and they are now obsolete: *R v. Reid* [1973] Q.B. 299.

[22] See *e.g. Oakley v. Walker* (1977) 121 S.J. 619.

[23] The Law Reform (Miscellaneous Provisions) Act 1970 had abolished the right to claim damages for enticement, harbouring, and adultery.

[24] There may apparently still be liability for loss of a wife's services if the loss is attributable to breach of contract: *Jackson v. Watson & Sons* [1909] 2 K.B. 193.

[25] The question of whether damages should be available for the loss of a relative's society was a controversial one; and the Administration of Justice Act 1982 followed the recommendation of the Law Commission (Law Com. No. 56) that a spouse or parent should be entitled to a fixed sum of damages for "bereavement" against a person who had wrongfully caused death: Administration of Justice Act 1982, s.3 inserting s.1A into the Fatal Accidents Act 1976.

[26] *R v. Creamer* [1919] 1 K.B. 564, C.A.

[27] *Eadie v. I.R.C.* [1924] 2 K.B. 198; *Nugent-Head v. Jacob* [1948] A.C. 321, H.L.; *Holmes v. Mitchell* [1991] 2 F.L.R. 301.

[28] See, *e.g. Santos v. Santos* [1972] Fam. 247, C.A.

[29] *R v. Creamer* [1919] 1 K.B. 564 at 569, C.A., *per* Darling J.

law.[30] In this limited but important sense the concept of consortium (and indeed some equitable doctrines giving special protection to married women) may thus be found not only to remain alive, but not to have passed the age of child-bearing.[31]

C. The common law right to maintenance

3–004 One aspect of the common law which remained of real significance until well into the twentieth century was the principle (perhaps flowing from the doctrines of property law under which a husband became entitled to substantial interests in his wife's property[32]) that a husband had an obligation, "whether he wished that result or no" to support his wife "according to his estate and condition".[33]

The duty to maintain was conceptually important; but the extent of the wife's right was limited, and the methods of enforcing it were inadequate. First, so long as husband and wife lived together, it was entirely for the husband[34] to fix the standard of living. The common law did not give a wife a right to an allowance but only a right to be supported by being given "bed and board"[35] (although it is true that if the husband deserted the wife, or if his misconduct[36] drove her away from the matrimonial home, the rule was modified to the extent that the husband was no longer sole judge of what was appropriate but came under an obligation to provide reasonable expenses for necessaries for the wife "according to her husband's degree"[37]).

Secondly, a wife was not entitled to be maintained if she and her husband were living apart by agreement, or indeed for any reason other than his misconduct. Moreover, if the wife committed even a single act of adultery,[38]

---

[30] See notably the decision in *Barclays Bank Plc v. O'Brien* [1994] 1 A.C. 180, CA, and HL

[31] But it has been said that such progeny must be "legitimate—by precedent out of principle": *Cowcher v. Cowcher* [1972] 1 W.L.R. 425 at 430, Bagnall J.

[32] See below, para. 4–004.

[33] *Lush on the law of Husband and Wife* (4th ed., by S.N. Grant-Bailey, 1933), p. 381. Chapter 12 of that work contains an exhaustive account of the subject; and see *Manby v. Scott* (1660) Smith's Leading Cases (13th ed.), p. 417; and (for a modern echo of the rule) *Povey v. Povey* [1972] Fam. 40. For a lucid account of developments in the century following the introduction of judicial divorce see J.L. Barton, "The Enforcement of Financial Provisions" in *A Century of Family Law* (R.H. Graveson and F.R. Crane ed., 1957), Chap. 14.

[34] At least in the absence of totally unreasonable behaviour on his part: consider *Gollins v. Gollins* [1964] A.C. 644; and *Carter-Fea v. Carter-Fea* (1987) 17 *Fam. Law* 131. For a striking application of this principle, see *McGuire v. McGuire* 59 N.W. 2d 336 (1953) (Nebraska Supreme Court) at 342; see also *Commonwealth v. George* 56 A. 2d 228 (1948).

[35] *per* Hodson L.J., *Lilley v. Lilley* [1960] P. 169 at 178.

[36] As distinct from a reasonable exercise of his marital right: see *Jackson v. Jackson* [1932] All E.R. 553 where the husband's insistence on occupying a house next door to his mother's and taking the housekeeping out of the wife's hands did not justify her leaving him.

[37] *per* Blackburn J., *Bazeley v. Forder* (1868) L.R. 3 Q.B. 559 at 562.

[38] Unless the husband had condoned it or connived at it: *Wilson v. Glossop* (1888) 20 Q.B.D. 354; *Harris v. Morris* (1801) 4 Esp. 41.

she forfeited all rights to maintenance at common law, whatever the extenuating circumstances.[39]

Thirdly, even if the wife could establish that she was entitled to be maintained under these rules, the methods available for enforcing her right were limited in the extreme.[40] It is true that her right to have a roof over her head could be enforced by an injunction restraining the husband from carrying out any transaction which would deprive her of her entitlement, but in relation to other financial support the common law only provided indirect assistance. In particular, the court would not order the husband to maintain his wife, much less to pay her a specific allowance.[41] All that the law did do was to permit the wife in some circumstances to pledge her husband's credit for the supply of "necessaries" under the doctrine of agency of necessity.[42] But since the agency of necessity was only available so long as the wife was entitled to be maintained under the common law rules, a shopkeeper could only rely on the doctrine if he were confident that the wife had not committed adultery[43] and was not in desertion. Shopkeepers were reluctant to take this risk.

Common law right to maintenance now of no practical relevance?

3–005 When the Law Commission came to investigate this area of the law, they concluded[44] that the agency of necessity had become an anachronism: the court (it was thought) had extensive powers to enforce maintenance obligations directly in legal proceedings, whilst state benefits were available to a wife faced with destitution. The Matrimonial Proceedings and Property Act 1970 accordingly abolished[45] the agency of necessity. Although the common law duty to maintain lingered on as a subject of practical significance to the family lawyer it would seem that the abolition of the domestic rating system (under which the common law duty might on occasion be relevant in determining whether a husband was still in rateable occupation of the house in

---

[39] For instance, the fact that the husband had treated her with great cruelty, driving her from the matrimonial home, and had himself frequently committed adultery: *Govier v. Hancock* (1796) 6 Term. 603: see also *Stimpson v. Wood & Sons* (1888) 57 L.J.Q.B. 484.

[40] *Northrop v. Northrop* [1968] P. 74 at 116; *Gray v. Gray* [1976] Fam. 324 at 328.

[41] In certain circumstances, financial remedies might be available in the ecclesiastical court. The wife's primary remedy was a decree for Restitution of Conjugal Rights founded on her husband's desertion: see generally *Manby v. Scott* (1660) Smith's Leading Cases (13th ed.), p. 417. If the husband disobeyed, he could be excommunicated (or, after the Ecclesiastical Courts Act 1813, imprisoned). If he were guilty of other matrimonial offences the wife could seek a divorce *a mensa et thoro* (*i.e.* judicial separation) on making which the ecclesiastical court could order payment of alimony: see *National Provincial Bank v. Ainsworth* [1965] A.C. 1175; *Weldon v. Weldon* (1883) 9 P.D. 52.

[42] Although referred to as an "agency" this is part of matrimonial law, rather than agency. Distinguish agency arising by the application of normal contractual principles as explained in the 4th edition of this book, n. 18, p. 738.

[43] An isolated act of adultery was sufficient, even if unknown to the creditor and husband: *Wright (H.S.) and Webb v. Annandale* [1930] 2 K.B. 8.

[44] Law Com. No. 25, paras 108–9.

[45] s.40.

which his wife was living[46]) effectively if unceremoniously ended any practical significance the subject may have possessed. In this as in the other areas so far discussed, statute has rendered the common law doctrines largely irrelevant. As Ward J. has put it[47]:

> "The strange state of our law is that there may be a so-called common law duty to maintain, but when one analyses what that duty is it seems effectively to come to nothing. Like so many rights, the right extends only so far as the remedy to enforce it extends . . . the common law has no remedy. The remedies to enforce a duty to maintain are the statutory remedies which are variously laid down in numerous statutes."

Once again, however it should be noted that no statute has ever abolished the common law duty, or replaced it by any comprehensive up-to-date statement of the mutual rights and duties of members of the family; and that accordingly it is not inconceivable that the common law duty may turn out still to have some residual relevance.

The obligation not to allow a spouse to be a charge on public funds

3–006 It is convenient to mention at this stage one particular development of the common law principle which reinforces the view that today the common law has been effectively supplanted by statute. The common law rule requiring a man to maintain his wife was in part founded on a concern that individuals should not be allowed to abandon their families to be cared for at the public expense; and there are echoes of the common law duty to maintain in provisions of modern social security legislation requiring a man to maintain his wife, and a woman to maintain her husband.[48] But the legislation limits the application of this principle to the recovery from one spouse of income support and related benefits paid to the other[49]; and in other important respects the echo of the common law duty is a faint one. In particular, the existence of factors which would have relieved a husband from the common law obligation do not conclude the question of whether he is under an obligation to reimburse the authorities (although those factors are relevant to the exercise of the discretion as to whether that obligation should be enforced).[50]

---

[46] See *Cardiff Corporation v. Robinson* [1957] 1 Q.B. 39; *Mourton v. Hounslow L.B.C.* [1970] 2 Q.B. 362; and *cf. Brown v. Oxford City Council* [1979] Q.B. 607; *Harrow L.B.C. v. Brady* [1980] R.A. 168; and *Routhan v. Arun District Council* [1982] Q.B. 502, C.A., particularly at 517 (*per* Eveleigh L.J.) and 521 (*per* Brandon L.J.); and *R. v. Harrow Justices, ex p. Harrow L.B.C.* (1983) 81 L.G.R. 514. The provisions of the Matrimonial Homes Act 1967 would seem to have made the common law duty on a husband to provide his wife with a roof over her head largely irrelevant.

[47] *Re C (A Minor) (Contribution Notice)* [1994] 1 F.L.R. 111 at 116.

[48] Social Security Administration Act 1992, s.78(6) and Pt V reproducing the effect of provisions dating back to the National Assistance Act 1948.

[49] There is a similar obligation in respect of children.

[50] See *National Assistance Board v. Parkes* [1955] 2 Q.B. 506.

HUSBAND AND WIFE: THE STATUTORY FRAMEWORK

3–007 Notwithstanding this Chapter's insistence that statute has overridden other sources of family law the reader would be ill advised to assume that the common law will never be relevant, even in those areas (such as maintenance obligations) in which the legislature has been active. There are surprisingly large areas in which statute remains silent; and whilst English statutes seek to provide answers to all possible questions on issues within the scope of a particular Act of Parliament, they do not seek to lay down general principles which might be used as the basis for solving problems not part of the draftsman's remit at the time. The fact that there is no comprehensive codification of English family law[51] means that important matters are not covered by statute; and in many areas it is difficult to state the law save by reference to the underlying principle—implicit in the doctrine of the rule of law as conventionally expounded—that the law permits anything which is not expressly prohibited. This characteristic results in English law appearing somewhat undeveloped compared with many other systems; and this is nowhere better exemplified than in the treatment of the law of names. In most European states, the question of the name by which a spouse or child is to be known is governed by elaborate statutory provision[52]; whereas in contrast English statute law is silent on the subject of an adult's choice of name,[53] and merely prohibits the taking of any formal step to change the name of a child subject to a residence order without leave of the court.[54]

---

[51] Note the Law Commission's gradual retreat from the commitment to provide a comprehensive and logical formulation of the law governing family support obligations (see Working Paper No. 9, 1967): S.M. Cretney, "The Codification of Family Law" (1981) 44 *M.L.R.* 1 at 11, n. 56. The Law Commission remains committed to the notion of codification in the sense of the systematic examination of various topics; and in evidence to the Special Public Bill Committee on the Family Homes and Domestic Violence Bill Hale J. (a Law Commissioner from 1984 to 1993) explained the Commission's approach to codification as exemplified by the Children Act 1989 and subsequent legislation: see H.L. 55 (1994/5) *Minutes of Evidence* March 9, 1995, question 7; B. Hale (1995) C.L.P. 217; the Law Commission's *Sixth Programme of Law Reform* (Law Com. No. 234 (1995)) Item 8.

[52] See, *e.g.* the provision of the German Civil Code BGB 1355 providing that if the spouses did not choose a name on marriage the husband's name became the family name. The Federal Constitutional Court declared that this provision infringed the principle of equality of men and women asserted by Article 3(2) of the Basic Law (Grundgesetz): see generally R. Frank, "Germany: Revolution from the Federal Constitutional Court" (1993) 31 J. Fam. L. 347. Note also the decision of the European Court of Human Rights in *Burghartz v. Switzerland* (1994) 18 E.H.R.R. 101 that a provision of Swiss Law regulating the choice of family name infringed the provisions of the European Convention on Human Rights, Arts. 14 and 8.

[53] See *Halsbury's Laws of England* (4th ed., reissue), Vol. 35, para. 1273 and generally the discussion in the Law Commission's Report on *Illegitimacy* (Law Com. No. 118, (1982), para. 9.21; and note the general principle stated by Lord Chelmsford in *du Boulay v. du Boulay* (1869) L.R.2 P.C. 430 at 431–433 that the assumption of a particular name by a stranger is not a grievance for which the law affords redress whatever cause of annoyance it may be to the family whose name has been taken. See also *Cowley v. Cowley* [1900] P. 305 (CA upheld by HL [1901] A.C. 450) in which the Earl Cowley unsuccessfully sought to restrain his divorced wife from using the name "Countess Cowley".

[54] Children Act 1989, s.13(1). It has been said that a change of name is an important matter: see *W v. A (Child: Surname)* [1981] Fam. 14; *Re F (Child: Surname)* [1993] 2 F.L.R. 837. The fact that a surname has been changed may be evidenced by Deed (and the law prescribes a procedure whereby such deeds may be enrolled) but the Deed is merely formal evidence of what has taken place.

For these reasons, the reader cannot conscientiously be advised that the law governing the position of husband and wife is entirely founded on statute; but the statutory framework remains the main source of law. It may be helpful to give an outline of the legal consequences of marriage; and then outline moves to harmonise the legal position of husband and wife by way of contrast. In tabular form, the text is arranged as follows:

A. Statutory Rights and Duties; finance and property **3–008–9**

(a) Court orders for maintenance

(i) Financial orders in magistrates' courts
(ii) Orders in the High Court and County Court on the ground of failure to provide reasonable maintenance
(iii) Orders ancillary to judicial separation.

(b) Separation and maintenance agreements
(c) Occupation of the matrimonial home
(d) Entitlement to property
(e) Miscellaneous economic consequences flowing from the status of marriage

(i) Taxation
(ii) Pensions

B. Other legal consequences of the marriage relationship

(a) The criminal law
(b) Contract and tort
(c) Evidence
(d) Citizenship and immigration

C. Moves to harmonise the legal position of husband and wife

A. Statutory rights and duties: finance and property of husband and wife

Rights to economic support

3–010 As already stated, no statute has ever abolished the common law duty imposed on a husband to support his wife; but in fact that duty has for practical purposes been supplanted by statutes which give spouses a right to apply to the court for financial orders. Statute also limits the extent to which husband and wife are free to regulate their financial affairs by private agreement; and the Matrimonial Homes Act 1967 conferred on spouses certain rights in relation to the occupation of the matrimonial home effectively supplanting the common law. The text outlines in turn the right to seek court orders for financial support; the law governing separation and maintenance agreements; and finally the statutory occupation rights conferred by the matrimonial homes legislation.

(a) Court orders for maintenance

3–011 There are three main statutory procedures available to a spouse who seeks financial support from the other. These procedures are in practice only available when a marriage has broken down[55]; and in those circumstances couples often prefer to petition for a divorce decree and seek the exercise of the wide range of powers available to the court to make financial orders ancillary to the grant of that decree.[56] But, although of much less importance than when divorce was in practice not easily available to the less affluent, a brief account of the court's powers to make maintenance orders outside the divorce context must be given.

The three procedures are as follows:

(i) Application may be made under the Domestic Proceedings and Magistrates' Courts Act 1978 to magistrates sitting as a family proceedings court.[57]

(ii) Application may be made to a County Court or High Court under section 27 of the Matrimonial Causes Act 1973 on the ground that the respondent has failed to provide reasonable maintenance for the applicant or for a child of the family.

(iii) A spouse may seek a decree of judicial separation and the court may exercise wide powers to make orders for financial provision and property adjustment in such cases.

These procedures are dealt with in turn.

(i) Financial orders in magistrates' courts[58]

3–012 The court has power to make financial[59] orders if the applicant[60] can establish one of the grounds set out in section 1 of the Domestic Proceedings and Magistrates' Courts Act 1978. The court is also given power to make certain financial

---

[55] By reason of the restrictions on the availability and enforceability or orders when the spouses are still living together: see, *e.g.* Domestic Proceedings and Magistrates' Courts Act 1978, s.28.

[56] See Chap. 14, below.

[57] Magistrates' Courts Act 1980, ss.65(1)(j), 67, as amended.

[58] For the history see the *Report of the Committee on One-Parent Families* (Cmnd. 5629 (1974)); and for a brief account, the 5th edition of this book work, p. 353. The Domestic Proceedings and Magistrates' Courts Act 1978 gave effect to recommendations made by the Law Commission in its *Report on Matrimonial Proceedings in Magistrates' Courts* (Law Com. No. 77, (1976)).

[59] For the court's powers to make residence and other orders relating to children, see Part V, below.

[60] Notwithstanding "some misgivings" expressed in consultation on the provisional proposals (Law Com. No. 77 (1976), para 2.8) the Act accepts the principle of equality between husband and wife; and either party to a marriage may apply for an order. The procedure for applications is now laid down by the Family Proceedings Courts (Matrimonial Proceedings, etc.) Rules 1991, S.I. 1991 No. 1991.

orders in cases where the parties are living apart by agreement, and to make orders for payments which have been agreed by the parties.

Grounds of application under section 1 of the 1978 Act

An applicant may seek a financial order on either of the following grounds[61]: **3–013**

(i) *The other party has failed to provide reasonable maintenance for the applicant*[62]

The Act gives no guidance as to what has to be established to make out this ground; but it seems clear that the court may find that there has been a failure even though the applicant has been guilty of some matrimonial misconduct (such as adultery or desertion) and even though the parties have separated without having made any agreement about continued financial support. **3–014**

(ii) *The other party has failed to provide, or to make proper contribution towards, reasonable maintenance for any child of the family*[63]

The expression "child of the family" is very widely defined in the Act,[64] and extends to any child of the parties[65] and to other children—most obviously, step-children—"treated" as a child of the spouses' family.[66 68] **3–015**

(iii) *The other party has behaved in such a way that the applicant cannot reasonably be expected to live with the other party*[69]

(iv) *The other party has deserted the applicant*[70]

Desertion has the same meaning as in the law of divorce,[71] but it is not necessary under the 1978 Act to show that the desertion has continued for two **3–016**

[61] The 1978 Act also introduced a complex provision empowering the court to make an order in favour of a spouse living apart from the other by agreement for periodical payments of a similar amount to those made voluntarily in the previous three months: D.P. & M.C.A. 1978, s.7. But it appears that this well intentioned provision is rarely invoked in practice; and for that reason it is not discussed in the text of this edition. For the background and a brief discussion see the 5th edition of this book, pp. 361–362.

[62] D.P. & M.C.A. 1978, s.1 (a).

[63] *ibid.* s.3(1).

[64] s.88.

[65] The provisions of the Child Support Act 1991 will often prevent the court from exercising its powers to make any periodical payments order against a parent in respect of his or her own child.

[66–8] In practice, orders will now rarely be made in favour of a child because of the provisions of Child Support Act 1991, s.8(1). But it seems that the court could make an order in favour of the mother on proof that there had been neglect of the child (see *Northrop v. Northrop* [1968] P. 74) and that its power to do so is not affected by the fact that a child support officer has jurisdiction to make a maintenance assessment: see Child Support Act 1991, s.8(11) defining "maintenance order" in terms of orders "to or for the benefit of the child".

[69] D.P. & M.C.A. 1978, s.1(c). This provision is prospectively repealed by the Family Law Act 1996 but it seems that the 1996 Act is not to be brought into force: see Chap. 11, below.

[70] D.P. & M.C.A. 1978, s.1(d).

[71] M.C.A. 1973, s.1(2)(c).

years or indeed any other period. In most cases, an applicant who could show desertion would also be able to show failure to provide maintenance and it seems improbable that the repeal of this provision will materially affect an applicant's prospects of obtaining an order.

Orders that can be made

3–017 If the applicant satisfies the court of a ground of complaint the court may make any of the following orders[72]:

(i) *An order that the other party shall make to the applicant such periodical payments, and for such term, as may be specified in the order*

3–018 This provision gives the court a flexible power to make weekly, monthly or other periodical orders[73]; and in particular the court may (like the divorce court) make a limited term order (*e.g.* to pay a weekly sum for six months).[74] However, a magistrates' court (unlike the divorce court) has no power to order that the periodical payment be secured.

(ii) *An order that the other party shall pay to the applicant such lump sum (not exceeding £1000) as may be so specified*

3–019 The Act specifically provides that a lump sum order may be made for the purpose[75] of enabling any liability or expenses reasonably incurred in maintaining the applicant, or any child of the family, before the making of the order to be met[76] but the lump sum awarded must not exceed £1,000.[77]

(iii) *Orders to make periodical payments in respect of a child of the family and/or an order for a lump sum payment (not exceeding £1,000) to or for the benefit of each child of the family.*[78]

---

[72] D.P. & M.C.A. 1978, s.2.

[73] If a magistrates' court exercises this power over someone resident in this country it must consider the method of payment, and may make (*e.g.*) an order attaching the debtor's wages: Magistrates' Courts Act 1980, s.59(1), (2), as substituted by Maintenance Enforcement Act 1991, s.2; see generally Chap. 16 below.

[74] See, *e.g. Khan v. Khan* [1980] 1 W.L.R. 355.

[75] D.P. & M.C.A. 1978, s.2(2).

[76] D.P. & M.C.A. 1978, s.2(3); Magistrates' Courts (Increase of Lump Sums) Order 1988, S.I. No. 1069.

[77] It has been held that the power to award a lump sum is not to be limited to cases where the other party has capital available since in an appropriate case the payment could be made out of earnings: *Burridge v. Burridge* [1983] Fam. 9.

[78] Although the provisions of the Child Support Act prevent the court from exercising its power to make periodical payments orders if a child support officer has jurisdiction to make an assessment under that Act there is no impediment to the making of a lump sum order in favour of a child, whilst the power to make periodical payments orders may in some circumstances be exercised in favour of step-children and other "children of the family".

Exercise of the court's discretion

3–020 The Act provides[79] that where an application is made for a financial order on one of the grounds set out above the court must have regard to all the circumstances of the case, first consideration being given to the welfare while a minor of any child of the family who has not attained the age of 18.

The Act also sets out a number of factors—similar to those governing the exercise of the court's powers in divorce proceedings[80]—to which the court is required to have particular regard.[81] The emphasis is in practice likely to be on determining how the reasonable needs of the family can best be met[82] in the light of the resources which are available. Thus:—

In *Titheradge v. Titheradge*[83] magistrates increased[84] an order against a husband from a total of £14 weekly to a total of £80 weekly. On appeal it was held that such an order could not be justified since its net effect would be disastrous to the family unit in which the husband was living. The Court substituted periodical payment orders totalling £35 weekly, which could be met by the husband without reducing his living standard below a "reasonable level". It appears that the financial position of the wife and children would remain unaltered, since any payments would simply reduce their welfare benefit entitlement.

In *E v. C (Child Maintenance)*[85] magistrates made an order that an unemployed man, living with a cohabitant and her two children, should make payments of £5 weekly in respect of his children. It was held that they had been wrong to do so. The father's income from welfare benefits only provided a bare subsistence, he had a new family and new responsibilities, and should not have been subjected to a "crippling" order. Moreover, it was relevant to take account of the fact that if his liability were assessed under the Child Support Act, there would have been a *nil* assessment.

In *B v. B (Periodical Payments: Transitional Provisions)*[86] magistrates had made an order against a man with a significant overdraft who had been out of work for more than two months. It was held that, although the magistrates were entitled to take account of the fact that he was being supported by his partner, it had been quite wrong to make an order which would in

---

[79] The court may order payment by instalments: Magistrates' Courts Act 1980, s.75(1); and the instalments may be varied: D.P. & M.C.A. 1978, s.22; D.P. & M.C.A. 1978, s.3(1), as amended.

[80] M.C.A. 1973, s.25(2).

[81] D.P. & M.C.A. 1978, s.3(2) and (in relation to orders in favour of children of the family) ss.3(3), (4). The court should make findings in respect of each of the matters referred to in the statute: *Vasey v. Vasey* [1985] F.L.R. 596 at 603.

[82] *Stockford v. Stockford* [1981] 3 F.L.R. 58 at 63, *per* Ormrod L.J.

[83] (1983) 4 F.L.R. 552.

[84] The case concerned a variation of an existing order.

[85] [1996] 1 F.L.R. 472 (Douglas Brown J.)

[86] [1995] 1 F.L.R. 459, Douglas Brown J.

effect have required her to make payments for the children of the first marriage.

Consent orders

3–021 The 1978 Act gives magistrates the power to make consent orders. Either party may apply to the court on the ground that the applicant or his spouse has agreed to make financial provision for a spouse or a child of the family.[87] The court may order that the agreed financial provision be made,[88] provided, first, that there is proof of the agreement,[89] and secondly that the court has no reason to think that it would be contrary to the interests of justice to do so.[90]

At one time, the making of a consent order could result in significant tax saving but changes in tax law have now virtually extinguished this advantage. A consent order does still give the payee the advantage of having a comparatively easily enforceable right; and it gives the payer some limited security against allegations that he has failed to provide for the family. But these advantages will rarely justify incurring the expense involved in obtaining a court order.

Effect of cohabitation, divorce and remarriage

3–022 Orders do not automatically determine on divorce,[91] and in practice were often allowed to continue in force.

An order can be obtained notwithstanding that the parties to the marriage are living with each other[92] at the date of the making of the order.[93] But if they continue to live with each other or subsequently resume living with each other for a continuous period of six months or more any periodical payment order for a spouse[94] ceases to be enforceable.[95]

Periodical payment orders in favour of a spouse[96] automatically determine if that spouse remarries.[97] This is so even if the "remarriage" is void or voidable.[98]

---

[87] D.P. & M.C.A. 1978 s.6, as amended by M. & F.P.A. 1984, s.10, to enable an order to be made on the application of either the payer or the payee.

[88] s.6(1)(**a**).

[89] s.6(1)(a); s.6(8).

[90] D.P. & M.C.A. 1978, s.6(1)(b).

[91] *Wood v. Wood* [1957] P. 254.

[92] *i.e.* "living with each other in the same household": D.P. & M.C.A. 1978, s.88(2). This is the same formula as that used in M.C.A. 1973, s.2(6).

[93] D.P. & M.C.A. 1978, s.25(1).

[94] But not orders for children: *ibid.* s.25(2).

[95] *ibid.* s.25(1). Certain orders in respect of children are unaffected unless the court otherwise directs. The question whether the court should have the power to make an order whilst the parties were living under the same roof was for long controversial: see S.M. Cretney, *Law, Law Reform and the Family* (1998), p. 172; and see the discussion in Law Com. No. 77 (1976), paras 2.58—2.65.

[96] But not orders for a child.

[97] D.P. & M.C.A. 1978, s.4(2).

[98] *ibid.* s.88(3).

Variation of orders

3–023 The court has power to vary or revoke periodical payment orders[99] (including interim orders)[1] but it has no power to vary a lump sum order. It may increase or decrease periodical payments, and add a lump sum order[2] (not exceeding the maximum of £1,000).[3] There is power to suspend any periodical payments order[4] (*e.g.* while the other party is unemployed[5]) and subsequently to revive it.

(ii) Orders in the High Court and county court on the ground of failure to provide reasonable maintenance

Grounds of application

3–024 Section 27 of the Matrimonial Causes Act 1973 provides that either party to a marriage may apply to the court for an order on the ground that the other party has failed to provide reasonable maintenance for the applicant, or to provide (or to make a proper contribution towards) reasonable maintenance for any child of the family. In exercising this discretion the court is directed to have regard to all the circumstances of the case (including those specified when a court is considering applications in divorce proceedings). Where an application is also made in respect of a child of the family under 18 "first consideration" must be given to the child's welfare.[6]

Orders that can be made

3–025 The court may make orders for periodical payments, unrestricted in amount, secured or unsecured. If secured, payments may continue during the applicant's life.[7] The court may also order payment of a lump sum.[8]

The powers of the High Court and county court are thus wider than those of the Magistrates, since in the superior courts there is no restriction on the size of lump sum awards. But the courts' powers are narrower than those available in divorce or judicial separation in that there is no power to make any other capital provision order (*e.g.* to transfer a house or shares).

Duration of orders

3–026 The fact that the spouses cohabit after the making of an order is not a bar to its being enforced. Orders do not automatically determine on divorce, but a

---

[99] D.P. & M.C.A. 1978, s.20(1).
[1] *ibid.* s.20(3).
[2] *ibid.* s.20(1).
[3] Or such larger amounts as may be specified at the time: D.P. & M.C.A. 1978, s.20(7).
[4] *ibid.* s.20(6).
[5] Law Com. No. 77 (1976) para. 4.53.
[6] M.C.A. 1973, s.27(3).
[7] M.C.A. 1973, s.27(6)(b), s.28(1)(b).
[8] M.C.A. 1973, s.27(6)(c).

subsequent marriage automatically brings any order for periodical payments to an end.[9]

Use made of neglect proceedings in the superior courts

3–027 This jurisdiction is very little used.[10]

(iii) Orders in judicial separation

The court has power to make financial provision and property adjustment orders in judicial separation proceedings in the same way as in divorce proceedings.[11] However, there is no power to make pension sharing orders in judicial separation proceedings.[12]

(b) Separation and maintenance agreements

3–028 A couple whose relationship is in difficulties might prefer to separate and to regulate their financial affairs by private agreement rather than taking legal proceedings; and this was particularly true before divorce became readily available and acceptable. But as we have seen, marriage created a status and no agreement between the parties about financial support could be conclusive. The general principle which has emerged is that husband and wife may make legally enforceable agreements regulating their financial affairs; but that any such agreement may be varied by the court. It is not possible by private agreement to oust the court's jurisdiction; but the outcome of the conflicting pressures which have led to this result is that the law governing the enforceability of separation and maintenance agreements between husband and wife is by no means straightforward.

Binding contract?

3–029 The first question to be asked is whether the agreement made between husband and wife is entitled to be regarded as an enforceable contract. The initial assumption is that spouses do not, in their ordinary day-to-day lives, usually intend to enter into enforceable contracts with one another[13] (even on such matters as the making of a regular housekeeping allowance[14]); and accordingly when it is alleged that an agreement between husband and wife is legally enforceable the court will first ask whether what took place between

---

[9] M.C.A. 1973, s.28.
[10] The Judicial Statistics no longer provide any relevant data.
[11] M.C.A. 1973, s.23.
[12] Welfare Reform and Pensions Act 1999, s.19, Sched. 3, para. 2.
[13] *Pettitt v. Pettitt* [1970] A.C. 777 at 816, *per* Lord Upjohn.
[14] *Balfour v. Balfour* [1919] 2 K.B. 571 at 578, *per* Atkin L.J. Note that in *Pettitt v. Pettitt* [1970] A.C. 777 at 816, Lord Upjohn said that the facts of that case stretched the doctrine that spouses living together do not intend to create legal relations "to its limits."

the parties was merely a domestic arrangement or whether it was intended that it should give rise to legally enforceable obligations.[15] When husband and wife decide to separate and make an agreement to govern their future financial relationship, the court will usually be prepared to impute to them an intention to create legal relations.[16]

There may be other aspects of contract law which are relevant to the validity of an agreement to provide financial support—in particular, such an agreement (if not by deed) must be supported by consideration. In the case of agreements between spouses,[17] consideration will normally be found in each party giving up claims which might otherwise have been pursued (or, traditionally, by one spouse releasing the other from the duty to cohabit); and in practice disputes about consideration now rarely arise, no doubt because most separation and maintenance agreements are made by deed.

Public policy

3–030 Maintenance agreements between spouses are also susceptible to attack on the ground that a particular provision is contrary to public policy[18]; and the authorities seem to support the following propositions. First, agreements or dispositions which tend to encourage the violation of the marriage tie[19] are void. Secondly, it is said to follow from this that an agreement between husband and wife whereby they make arrangements in the event of a future separation is void. But, thirdly, if the husband and wife, while living apart, agree to resume cohabitation, enforceable financial arrangements may be made in the same agreement to take effect in the event of a future separation. This exception to the general principle is justified on the basis that such an agreement will promote rather than hinder reconciliation.

---

[15] *Balfour v. Balfour* [1919] 2 K.B. 571, particularly at 577, *per* Duke L.J.; *Jones v. Padavatton* [1969] 1 W.L.R. 328 at 332, *per* Salmon L.J. See also *Burns v. Burns* [1984] F.L.R. 216 at 232, *per* May L.J. However the distinction may sometimes be a fine one: *Connell v. Motor Insurers' Bureau* [1969] 2 Q.B. 494 at 505; *Gould v. Gould* [1970] 1 Q.B. 275.

[16] *Merritt v. Merritt* [1970] 1 W.L.R. 1211 (but *cf. per* Lord Denning M.R. at 1213, presumption in such circumstances of intention to create legal relations, and *per* Widgery L.J. at 1214, no presumption against creating such a relationship). See also *Peters (Executors) v. I.R.C.* [1941] 2 All E.R. 620; *Gould v. Gould* [1970] 1 Q.B. 275.

[17] In the case of agreements between parents to support a child, it seems that consideration will often be found in one parent's undertaking to maintain the child if the agreed payments are made or to refrain from taking proceedings: *Ward v. Byham* [1956] 1 W.L.R. 496; *cf. Williams v. Roffey Bros & Nicholls (Contractors) Ltd* [1991] 1 Q.B. 1.

[18] See generally *Fender v. St John-Mildmay* [1938] A.C. 1; and see *per* Lord Atkin, *Hyman v. Hyman* [1929] A.C. 601 at 625; such agreements sometimes "looked at askance and enforced grudgingly" but the true position is that separation agreements "are formed, construed and dissolved and to be enforced on precisely the same principles as any respectable commercial agreement, of whose nature indeed they sometimes partake."

[19] See, *e.g. Re Johnson's Will Trusts* [1967] Ch. 387: annuity to testator's daughter to be increased if she were divorced or separated, evidence that testator concerned to protect his daughter against her husband. Held void, because the condition might well influence the daughter's mind if she were contemplating separation or divorce.

Fraud, duress, undue influence

3–031 Finally, an agreement may be attacked by one of the parties on the ground that it had been obtained by fraud,[20] duress, undue influence, or by misrepresentation[21] (and in some circumstances that the agreement was vitiated by mistake[22]). However, in practice, the existence of the statutory power to vary maintenance agreements, coupled with the statutory rule that an agreement ousting the jurisdiction of the court is void—both of which matters are dealt with below[23]—mean that it is rarely necessary to invoke these contractual doctrines in order to obtain a review of a private agreement.

Final and conclusive?

3–032 Although the object of making a maintenance agreement was traditionally to settle the extent of a husband's obligations to his wife once and for all whilst giving her the assurance that come what may she would be entitled to the stipulated provision, the law now makes it impossible to achieve such finality by private agreement. This was originally because of the common law's reluctance to enforce an agreement ousting the financial jurisdiction of the court,[24] and since 1957 various statutory provisions have allowed the court to vary maintenance agreements.

Variation of maintenance agreements

3–033 The statutory power[25] to vary maintenance agreements reflects the belief that in principle maintenance agreements should be binding and enforceable; but that either party should be able to seek a variation if fresh circumstances making the agreement inequitable had arisen. The salient features of the law are:—

(i) *To what agreements do the provisions of Matrimonial Causes Act ss 34 to 36 apply?*

3–034 It is provided[26] that for the purposes of these provisions a maintenance agreement means:—

---

[20] *Allsop v. Allsop* (1980) 124 S.J. 710.

[21] See *Barclays Bank plc v. O'Brien* [1994] 1 A.C. 180, H.L.; *Simpson v. Simpson* [1992] 1 F.L.R. 602; *Bank of Commerce and Credit International SA v. Aboody* [1990] 1 Q.B. 923, C.A.; and see *Wales v. Wadham* [1977] 1 W.L.R. 199.

[22] *Galloway v. Galloway* (1914) 30 T.L.R. 531.

[23] See below, paras 3–033—3–036.

[24] *Hyman v. Hyman* [1929] A.C. 601; and see for a more recent illustration *Sutton v. Sutton* [1984] Ch. 184. The impact of this rule is much reduced by the practice of embodying agreements related to divorce and other matrimonial proceedings in consent orders: see Chap 15, below. For the power of the magistrates' court to make consent orders under Domestic Proceedings, and Magistrates' Courts Act 1978, s.6.

[25] Now contained in M.C.A. 1973, ss.34–36. Provision for the variation of agreements was first made by the Maintenance Agreements Act 1957, enacted to give effect to the recommendations of the Royal Commission on Marriage and Divorce (Cmd. 9678 (1956)), Pt X.

[26] M.C.A. 1973, s.34(2).

"... any agreement in writing made, whether before or after the commencement of this Act, between the parties to a marriage, being—

(a) an agreement containing financial arrangements, whether made during the continuance or after the dissolution or annulment of the marriage; or
(b) a separation agreement which contains no financial arrangements in a case where no other agreement in writing between the same parties contains such arrangements."

The expression "financial arrangements" means,[27] for this purpose:—

"... provisions governing the rights and liabilities towards one another when living separately of the parties to a marriage (including a marriage which has been dissolved or annulled) in respect of the making or securing of payments or the disposition or use of any property, including such rights and liabilities with respect to the maintenance or education of any child, whether or not a child of the family."

The scope of the Act is therefore broad. In particular (provided the agreement is in writing)[28] no other formality is required; and a letter (for example) may fall within the definition.[29] Moreover the definition of "financial arrangements" (particularly in its reference to the "disposition or use of property") goes far beyond terms for the payment of periodical maintenance, so that apparently an agreement about furnishings[30] would, for example, fall within it.

(ii) *Void provisions*

3–035 Any provisions purporting to restrict the right to apply to the court for financial provision are void,[31] but any other financial arrangements contained in the agreement are valid (unless they are void or unenforceable for some other reason).[32] The agreement need not be made for the purpose of the parties living separately.[33]

---

27 *ibid.*

28 An oral maintenance agreement is enforceable (see *Peters v. I.R.C.* [1941] 2 All E.R. 620), but falls outside the provisions of the Act. Of much greater practical importance is the doctrine that the legal effect of an agreement which has been embodied in an order of the court derives from the *order*; and the terms of such an order cannot be varied under the provisions of M.C.A. 1973, ss.34–36: see *De Lasala v. De Lasala* [1980] A.C. 546 at 560; *Livesey (formerly Jenkins) v. Jenkins* [1985] A.C. 424; *Thwaite v. Thwaite* [1982] Fam. 1. It is on this basis that clean break settlements are routinely made in divorce: see generally Chap 14 below.

29 *M.H. v. M.H.* [1981] F.L.R. 429.

30 See *D. v. D.* (1974) 118 S.J. 715 (agreement to pay instalments for half-share of matrimonial home); *Sutton v. Sutton* [1984] Ch. 184.

31 See, *e.g. Jessel v. Jessel* [1979] 1 W.L.R. 1148 at 1152.

32 M.C.A. 1973, s.34(1).

33 s.34(2). But the definition of "financial arrangements" still stipulates that they be provisions "governing the rights ... towards one another when living separately of the parties to a marriage": M.C.A. 1973, s.34(2).

(iii) *Power to vary agreements*

3–036 The Act provides[34] that if a maintenance agreement[35] is for the time being subsisting[36] either party[37] may apply to the court[38] for a variation order. The court's powers on such an application are sweeping. It may vary or revoke "financial arrangements" contained in the agreement or insert such arrangements for the benefit of a spouse or a child of the family.[39] But as a condition precedent to the exercise of these powers, the court must be satisfied either that there has been a change in the circumstances in the light of which the agreement was made or that the agreement does not contain proper financial arrangements with respect to any child of the family.[40] However, the court may act even if the parties had directed their minds to the possibility of a particular change of circumstances.[41] A spouse who has chosen to accept a lower but consistent income in preference to a higher, but perhaps speculative and problematical income will be entitled to apply for a variation if the choice turns out to have been the wrong one. But the fact that there is jurisdiction to entertain the application does not mean that it will be granted: the court will not act unless the change of circumstances has made the agreement unjust[42]; and generally the courts are reluctant to interfere with freely negotiated agreements entered into on the basis of a full knowledge of the relevant circumstances and on proper advice.[43]

(c) Occupation of the matrimonial home

3–037 At common law, a wife had a right to be provided by her husband with a suitable home; but in 1965 the House of Lords held[44] that this right was a purely personal right, not attaching to any particular house and of its nature incapable of binding third parties. The Matrimonial Homes Act 1967 was enacted to remedy this situation, which it did by conferring on a spouse who lacked any proprietary interest in the matrimonial home a right not to be evicted or excluded from the home without leave of the court, and by providing machinery whereby

---

34 s.35

35 *i.e.* a written agreement which either (a) contains "financial arrangements" (as defined, see above) or (b) is a separation agreement which does not itself contain financial arrangements, where no other written agreement does so: s.34(2).

36 See *Pace (formerly Doe) v. Doe* [1977] Fam. 18 at 22. Whether a maintenance agreement is "subsisting" is to be determined at the time of the application. An agreement is no longer "subsisting" for the purposes of this definition if its terms have been embodied in a court order: see *Thwaite v. Thwaite* [1982] Fam. 1.

37 If one party has died, provision is made for application by personal representatives: M.C.A. 1973, s.36.

38 A magistrates' court can only vary a periodical maintenance payments: s.35(3).

39 M.C.A. 1973, s.35(2). For the extent of the court's powers, see *Pace (formerly Doe) v. Doe* [1977] Fam. 18 at 23.

40 s.35(2).

41 *cf. K. v. K.* [1961] 1 W.L.R. 802; *Ratcliffe v. Ratcliffe* [1962] 1 W.L.R. 1455.

42 Hence voluntary reduction in earning capacity would not justify a variation: *K. v. K* [1961] 1 W.L.R. 802; *Gorman v. Gorman* [1964] 1 W.L.R. 1440.

43 See generally *Edgar v. Edgar* [1980] 1 W.L.R. 1410.

44 *National Provincial Bank Ltd v. Ainsworth* [1965] A.C. 1175.

that right could, by registration, be made to bind purchasers (such as mortgagees) or other third parties. Those rights (now called "matrimonial homes rights") are preserved in the codification of the law governing occupation of the family home and domestic violence; and it is relevant to note that, although the legislation now seeks to give cohabitants, former cohabitants and others the right to apply to the court for a so-called "occupation order" in respect of a home, it does not provide any machinery whereby such persons may protect occupation rights against third parties dealing with the property.[45]

(d) Entitlement to property

3–038 Since 1882[46] it has been a cardinal feature of English property law that marriage, as such, has no effect on the parties' entitlement to property during their joint lifetimes. There are a few unimportant statutory exceptions to the principle,[47] but the legislature has resisted pressures to create a statutory regime of community of property. This subject is dealt with elsewhere in this book.[48]

In contrast, when a married person dies without leaving a will disposing of all his or her property[49] the status of marriage assumes great importance. A surviving spouse is entitled to the first £125,000[50] of the deceased's estate; a surviving cohabitant is in contrast not entitled to anything on the deceased partner's intestacy. These rules are dealt with elsewhere in this book; but at this stage it suffices to notice that the law still confers important rights on the married and denies similar rights to those whose relationship may have been factually indistinguishable from that of a person happily married to the deceased.

(e) Miscellaneous economic consequences flowing from the status of marriage

(i) Taxation

3–039 The influence of the common law doctrine that husband and wife became one person was for many years exemplified by the statutory provision that the

---

[45] See the discussion in the evidence of Hale J. to the Special Public Bill Committee on the Family Homes and Domestic Violence Bill (H.L. Paper 55, March 15, 1995, p. 73).

[46] Married Women's Property Act 1882

[47] Matrimonial Proceedings and Property Act 1970, s.37; see Chap. 6, below. The right given to a wife to share in savings made from a housekeeping allowance is also relevant; Married Women's Property Act 1964.

[48] See Chap. 9, below. There are, however, a number of statutory provisions which facilitate the creation of property rights in a spouse—notably Married Women's Property Act 1882, s.11, which provides that a life policy expressed to be for the benefit of the assured's spouse creates a trust for the spouse. This provision is important in that the policy proceeds are, in the absence of fraud, not subject to claims by the life assured's trustee in bankruptcy or creditors.

[49] It is relevant to note that marriage revokes a will (other than one expressed to be made in contemplation of marriage): Wills Act 1837, s.18 as substituted by Administration of Justice Act 1982, s.18. For the effect of *divorce* on wills, see the Law Reform (Succession) Act 1995, Chap. 8, below.

[50] Or £200,000 if the deceased died without issue. For the survivor's additional rights where the estate exceeds these amounts, see Chap. 8 below.

income of a married woman living with her husband was "deemed for income tax purposes to be his income and not to be her income".[51] It was widely (but erroneously[52]) thought that this rule imposed a tax on marriage; and in any event the fact that a married woman's existence was often ignored by the Revenue—who would[53] communicate with her husband about a woman's financial affairs—seemed offensive to many. After protracted campaigning, the rule was eventually abolished from 1990.[54] However, the tax system has not adopted a consistent policy of neutrality as between married couples[55] and those living together outside marriage.

Transfers (whether on death or by way of lifetime gift) between spouses are exempt from inheritance tax[56]; whereas transfers between a cohabiting couple are not. A transfer between spouses does not give rise to a chargeable gain for the purposes of capital gains tax[57]; but there is no comparable provision for transfers between the unmarried. Conversely, there are certain situations in which a married couple are treated less favourably than an unmarried couple: for example, there is an exemption from capital gains tax on the disposal of a dwelling house which has been the only or main residence[58]; but, whereas husband and wife are only allowed one residence for this purpose,[59] both partners in a relationship outside marriage are entitled to relief on a residence. Many of these rules have their origins in specific responses to particular needs (or abuses) rather than in any coherent policy towards the taxation of the family unit.

(ii) Pensions

3–040 Legislation makes provision for the payment by the state of pensions to a widow, that is to say to a woman who was married to the deceased at the date of his death. No comparable provision is made for a woman who was not validly married to her partner.

---

[51] Income and Corporation Taxes Act 1970, s.31(1).

[52] A married couple would pay less tax than an unmarried couple in the same financial position unless either their income took them into the higher rates of tax or a substantial part of their income was derived from investments: see the explanation in the 4th edition of this book at p. 956.

[53] At least until administrative changes were introduced in 1979: see [1979] B.T.R. 481.

[54] Finance Act 1988, s.32. Thereafter each spouse became responsible for making a return of income and paying the relevant tax.

[55] The position of a married couple is stated on the basis that they are living together: see Income and Corporation Taxes Act 1988, s.282; *Gubay v. Kington* [1984] 1 W.L.R. 163, HL; *Holmes v. Mitchell* [1991] F.L.R. 301.

[56] Inheritance Taxes Act 1984, s.18. There are also limited exemptions from Inheritance Tax in respect of gifts in consideration of marriage: Inheritance Taxes Act 1984, s.22.

[57] Taxation of Chargeable Gains Act 1992, s.58.

[58] *ibid.* s.222.

[59] *ibid.* s.222(6).

B. Other legal consequences of the marriage relationship

3–041 Marriage has many other legal consequences; but only a few examples can be given from those of most importance to the lawyer.

(a) The criminal law

3–042 At common law a husband could not be convicted of rape on his wife; but in 1991 the House of Lords held that the supposed marital exemption in rape today forms no part of the law of England.[60] Again, at one time neither husband nor wife could be convicted of stealing the other's property; but under the modern law[61] husband and wife are to be regarded as separate persons (although prosecutions for "marital theft" usually require the consent of the Director of Public Prosecutions). But it remains the law that husband and wife cannot be convicted of the criminal offence of conspiring with one another[62] (although as we have seen they can be held liable for the tort of conspiracy[63]) and there are circumstances in which a wife will be able to escape criminal liability on the ground that she committed the offence in the presence of and under the coercion of her husband.[64]

(b) Contract and tort

3–043 Statute[65] now provides that a married woman is capable of rendering herself and being rendered liable in respect of any contract, debt or obligation, and of suing and being sued in contract as if she were a femme sole.[66] The same statute also provided that a married woman should be equally liable to enforcement and bankruptcy proceedings.[67] No statute has interfered with the common law rule under which it was presumed that a wife had her husband's authority to pledge his credit for necessary goods and services.[68]

We have seen that in principle spouses are liable to one another and to third parties in tort without regard to their marital status; but it is possible that some relics of the unity theory which can be justified by broader policy considerations—for example, the rule that a spouse who communicates a defamatory statement about a third party to the other spouse is not liable to be sued by the third party[69]—will linger on.

---

[60] *R v. R* [1992] 1 A.C. 599, HL.
[61] Theft Act 1968, s.30(1).
[62] Criminal Law Act 1977, s.2(2)(a); *Mawji v. R* [1957] A.C. 126, P.C.
[63] See para. 3–002, above.
[64] Criminal Justice Act 1925, s.47.
[65] Law Reform (Married Women and Tortfeasors) Act 1935, s.1.
[66] See above para. 3–002.
[67] There are certain provisions which evidently seek to prevent husband and wife from obtaining unfair advantages against creditors: Insolvency Act 1986, ss. 339, 423.
[68] As distinct from her agency of necessity: see para. 3–004, above.
[69] *Wennhak v. Morgan* (1888) 20 Q.B.D. 635.

Since 1846[70] certain specified categories of dependant have had the right to sue a person whose wrongful act, neglect or default brought about a death which has caused the claimant financial loss. The category of dependant has always included a surviving spouse; but in 1982 the class was extended to enable an unmarried partner who satisfied certain conditions to sue in respect of the loss flowing from the death.[71]

(c) Evidence

3–044 The common law rule which denied the competence of spouses to give evidence has been whittled away over the years[72]; and spouses are now *compellable* witnesses for the accused in all cases. But a spouse is only compellable to give evidence for the prosecution if the offence charged involves an assault on, or injury or a threat of injury on the person concerned (typically wife battering) or on a person under the age of 16; or if the offence charged is a sexual offence against a person under the age of 16; or the offence charged consists of an attempt to commit such an offence or conspiring, aiding and abetting, etc., the commission of such an offence.[73]

(d) Citizenship and immigration

3–045 Entitlement to British citizenship is now governed by the provisions of the British Nationality Act 1981; and, broadly speaking marriage no longer confers any entitlement to British citizenship nor does the marriage of a British citizen to a foreign national automatically deprive him or her of British citizenship. But a person married to a British citizen may apply for naturalisation under conditions which are less onerous than those governing applications by others.[74]

British citizens have the right of abode, that is "the right to live in, and to come and go into and from, the United Kingdom without let or hindrance".[75] But it does not follow that a citizen's spouse or partner has the same right[76]; and a spouse who is not a British citizen may only enter and remain in the United Kingdom in accordance with rules made by the Home Secretary.[77] Although leave to enter and remain is in practice often given to a spouse[78] there

---

70 Fatal Accidents Act ("Lord Campbell's Act").

71 Administration of Justice Act 1982, s. 3(1).

72 The only surviving restriction on *competence* seems to be the rule that where husband and wife are jointly charged with a criminal offence neither is competent to give evidence for the prosecution so long as he or she is liable to be convicted: Police and Criminal Evidence Act 1984, s.80.

73 Police and Criminal Evidence Act 1984, s.80(2)(3)(4).

74 British Nationality Act 1981, s.6(2) and Sched. 1, para. 3.

75 Immigration Act 1971, s.1(1).

76 *ibid.* s.2 as substituted by British Nationality Act 1981, s.39(1); *R v. Secretary of State for the Home Department, ex p. Rofathullah* [1989] Q.B. 219. Under s.2(2) of the 1971 Act as originally enacted the wife or former wife of a person with the right of abode herself had the right of abode.

77 Immigration Act 1971, s.3(1), (2). The Rules as laid before Parliament in accordance with the Immigration Act are at present to be found in the *Statement of Changes in Immigration Rules* (H.C. 251. 1990).

78 *Statement of Changes in Immigration Rules,* paras. 46, 122–124, 127–129.

are certain rules restricting the entry of spouses—for example, a person under the age of 16 cannot, for these purposes,[79] be regarded as a spouse; whilst entry will be refused unless the authorities are satisfied that the marriage was not entered into primarily to obtain permission to enter the United Kingdom.[80] These attempts to distinguish between genuine marriages and marriages of convenience have given rise to difficulty, particularly in cases in which the parties come from a culture in which arranged marriages are the norm.[81]

C. Moves to harmonise the legal position of married and unmarried couples

(i) Statutory provisions

3–046 Since the First World War[82] statutes have, under the pressure of social realities, increasingly contained provisions equating the position of a couple "who are living together as husband and wife" with that of a married couple. The statutory provisions governing entitlement to income support where the resources and needs of couples are aggregated[83] are well known; but other examples abound. Thus, an "unmarried couple"[84] are treated similarly to a married couple in respect of succession to public sector tenancies, and remedies in respect of the occupation of the family home (not to mention liability to pay council tax[85]). In some cases—notably the right to claim reasonable financial provision out of a deceased partner's estate and the right to make a claim under the Fatal Accidents Act 1976—an unmarried partner will only qualify if he or she has lived with the deceased as an unmarried couple in the same household for a specified period—for example, two years.

These attempts to equate the position of an unmarried couple with that of a married couple seem to involve a major conceptual difficulty. This is because marriage is a legally recognised status, and the question whether a couple are "married" does not involve any investigation of their personal relationship or any resolution of the question which of the normal incidents of such a relationship (such as the use of a common name or the existence of sexual relations)

---

[79] Contrast the general law under which the marriage of a person under 16 will be valid if it was valid under the parties' personal law: *Mohammed v. Knott* [1969] 1 Q.B. 1.

[80] See generally *Halsbury's Laws of England* (4th ed. reissue, 1992), Vol 4(2), paras. 95–97.

[81] See, *e.g. R. v. Immigration Appeal Tribunal, ex p. Iqbal,* [1993] Imm. A.R. 270 (absence of passionate relationship or indeed of being "in love" not of itself indicative of it being primary purpose of marriage to obtain admission to the United Kingdom: "Marie Antoinette married Louis XVI for dynastic reasons rather than as a love match but no one would regard that fact was indicating that the primary purpose of the marriage was for her to secure admission to France", *per* Schiemann J.).

[82] The problem first became of acute concern in the context of service pensions payable under the Naval and Military War Pensions Acts.

[83] See Chap. 7, below.

[84] This convenient expression is used in the Social Security Contributions and Benefits Act 1992, s.137(1).

[85] Local Government Finance Act 1992, s.9.

are essential and which are superfluous.[86] In contrast the question whether or not a couple are "living together as husband and wife" does involve a value judgment on that question. In cases—such as claims under the inheritance legislation—in which the exercise of a discretion is involved, the court may be given additional guidelines in an attempt to structure the exercise of the discretion. But whatever the conceptual difficulties, the courts have found little difficulty[87] in applying "unmarried couples" legislation and in many cases—notably the Fatal Accidents Act, for example—the need to provide for a major social problem must outweigh the claims of juristic precision.

(ii) Case law developments

3–047 Common law and equity have over the years been able to develop some protection for married couples on the basis of a judicial understanding of the obligations or marriage. A good example is to be found in the development of the law governing the disclosure of confidence:—

> In *Argyll (Duchess) v. Argyll (Duke)*[88] the Duchess successfully sought an injunction restraining the husband from making available for publication secrets of her life communicated to him during their marriage. The court held that the confidential nature of the relationship of husband and wife was of its very essence; and that accordingly the Duchess was entitled to have her confidences protected.

That decision was squarely based on a clear perception about the attributes of the relationship between spouses; but the court have increasingly had to ask how far factually similar relationships outside marriage will give rise to similar consequences. Thus:—

> In *Stephens v. Avery*[89] the court granted the plaintiff an injunction restraining a former close friend from disclosing to a newspaper details of the plaintiff's lesbian relationship with a woman subsequently killed by her husband. On the facts, the information had been disclosed on the expressed basis that the information was secret, confidential and private; but part of the defence was that information about relationships outside marriage was not protected by the law (to some extent because the behaviour was immoral) and it is possible that the case will be seen to support the view

[86] See the reference to *R v. Immigration Appeal Tribunal, ex p. Iqbal,* [1993] Imm. A.R. 270 at above for an illustration of the difficulties which can arise in defining the essence of a relationship such as marriage; and similar difficulties arise in the application of the so-called cohabitation rule in social security legislation: see *Re J. (Income Support: Cohabitation)* [1995] 1 F.L.R. 660.

[87] See *e.g. Re Watson (dec'd)* [1999] 1 F.L.R. 878, where Neuberger J. said the proper approach was to ask how a reasonable person with normal perceptions would have regarded the couple, and that consideration of that question should not ignore the multifarious nature of marital relationships.

[88] [1967] Ch. 302.

[89] [1988] Ch. 449.

that a sexual relationship is itself capable of creating an obligation of confidence between the parties.

It is true that the law's approach to claims to privacy is now (in part because of the influence of the Human Rights Act 1998) much more broadly based[90]; but it appears that marriage still enjoys a special status in this respect.[91]

The view that the law should look at the factual reality of a couple's relationship rather than confining themselves to issues of legal status has been remarkably demonstrated in the development of the law relating to the circumstances in which a person who has guaranteed repayment of a loan made to a spouse or cohabitant may be allowed a defence based on the emotional pressures arising from the couple's relationship. The leading case is *Barclays Bank Plc v. O'Brien*[92] (dealt with more fully in Chapter 5 below): in which the House of Lords accepted that a transaction could be vulnerable if the lender was aware that the relationship between the parties involved what Lord Browne-Wilkinson called "the underlying risk of one cohabitee exploiting the emotional involvement and trust of the other." In his view:—

> "Now that unmarried cohabitation, whether heterosexual or homosexual, is widespread in our society, the law should recognise this. Legal wives are not the only group which are now exposed to the emotional pressure of cohabitation. Therefore if, but only if, the creditor is aware that the surety is cohabiting with the principal debtor, . . . the same principles should apply to them as apply to husband and wife."[93]

The case raises difficult issues in the law of contract, but this clear recognition of the desirability of looking to the substance of a family relationship rather than to its legal form is of great significance for the future development of family law, since it raises (if it does not answer) the question of whether marriage is becoming a redundant legal concept.[94] Indeed one eminent jurist[95] wrote as long ago as 1980—

> "Family law no longer makes any attempt to buttress the stability of marriage or any other union. It has adopted principles for the protection of children and dependent spouses which could be made equally applicable to

---

[90] See *e.g.* the discussion in *Douglas, Zeta-Jones, Northern & Shell plc v. Hello! Ltd* [2001] 1 F.L.R. 982.

[91] See the discussion in *A v. B plc and Another* [2002] 1 F.L.R. 1021, 1039.

[92] [1994] 1 A.C. 180; noted by B. Fehlberg (1994) 47 *M.L.R.* 467 and by J.R.F. Lehane (1994) 110 *L.Q.R.* 167.

[93] [1994] 1 A.C. 180, 198. The Court of Appeal has held that a person who has not cohabited but has had a stable sexual and emotional relationship with the principal debtor is equally protected: *see Midland Bank plc. v. Massey* [1994] 2 F.L.R. 342. The question is apparently whether the emotional ties between the parties impaired the defendant's judgmental capacity: see *per* Steyn L.J. at 345.

[94] See "Marriage: An Unnecessary Legal Concept" by E.M. Clive, in J.M. Eekelaar and S. Katz (eds) *Marriage and Cohabitation in Contemporary Societies* (1980).

[95] B. Hoggett, "Ends and Means: The Utility of Marriage as a Legal Institution" in J.M. Eekelaar and S. Katz (eds), *Marriage and Cohabitation in Contemporary Societies* (1980), pp. 94, 101.

> the unmarried. In such circumstances, the piecemeal erosion of the distinction between marriage and non-marital cohabitation may be expected to continue. Logically, we have already reached a point at which, rather than discussing which remedies should now be extended to the unmarried, we should be considering whether the legal institution of marriage continues to serve any useful purpose."

But at the same time (in the view of many) English law fails to provide an adequate legal regime for the large and apparently increasing number of couples who live together in a relationship which is factually similar to that of a married couple but do not have the legal status of husband and wife.[96] Contrary to a widely held belief, merely living together does not create a "common law marriage"; and unmarried cohabiting couples "face immense and distressing difficulties in securing legal recognition of their caring and enduring family lives:

> they do not enjoy full rights to communal property, or the right to be treated as next of kin by state agencies such as hospitals in the event of serious illness . . . [The survivor of a cohabiting couple] cannot even register her partner's death or sign for his funeral".[97]

If the law has been cautious in its attitude to the consequences of heterosexual unmarried partnerships it has been even more so where the couple are gay or lesbian. But in *Fitzpatrick v. Sterling Housing Association Ltd*[98] the question was whether the applicant, who had had for nearly 20 years a close loving and faithful homosexual relationship with the tenant of a West London flat, was entitled to succeed to the tenancy on his partner's death. To do so he had to show either that he and the tenant had been living together "as husband and wife" or that he had been a "member of the deceased tenant's family". The House of Lords unanimously rejected the first claim, but a 3–2 majority held that the applicant was entitled to be treated as a "member of the family" for this purpose.[99]

All these issues are controversial[1] and it is desirable to keep a sense of proportion. It will have become clear from reading this Chapter that marriage does in

---

[96] See C. Gibson, "Changing Family Patterns in England and Wales" in *Cross Currents* (S.N. Katz, J. Eekelaar, and M. Maclean, ed., 2000), pp. 32–34.

[97] Lord Lester of Herne Hill Q.C. moving the Second Reading of the Civil Partnerships Bill, *Official Report* H.L. January 25, 2002, vol. col.

[98] [2001] 1 A.C. 27.

[99] See also *Barclays Bank plc v. O'Brien* [1994] 1 AC 180 at 198, *per* Lord Browne-Wilkinson.

[1] Bills introduced by Members of the two Houses of Parliament in 2001 with the objective of improving the status of cohabiting couples were received sympathetically. In October 2001 the House of Commons, by 179 votes to 59, gave Jane Griffiths leave to introduce a Bill (*Official Report* HC October 24, 2001 vol. col.); and on January 25, 2002 the House of Lords gave a Second Reading to a professionally drafted Civil Partnerships Bill: *Official Report*, HL January 25, 2002, vol. col. Although neither Bill is likely to reach the statute book, it appears that the Government is investigating the implications of setting up a scheme of civil partnership registration and in January 2001 no fewer than 60 civil servants from different government departments attended a meeting to begin the task of working through the "large number of questions, many of which have not [previously] been exhaustively explored": see Lord Williams of Mostyn: *Official Report* HL January 25, 2002, and see para 9–005, below.

fact still have important legal consequences in English law; and it is hoped that the reader will be in a better position to make an informed judgment on the social and political issue of how far it should remain the policy of the law to preserve these distinctions after reading the pages which follow.

Part II

FAMILY PROPERTY

CHAPTER FOUR

INTRODUCTION—ENTITLEMENT TO FAMILY ASSETS[1]

I. PROPERTY OWNERSHIP IN CONTEMPORARY SOCIETY

4–001 The effect of marriage or other family relationships on legal entitlement to property must be seen in the context of patterns of property-ownership in society. A striking feature of the last half-century has been the great extension of home-ownership financed by building society and bank credit. Between 1961 and 1998 the number of owner-occupied dwellings more than doubled; in 2001 there were twice as many owner-occupied as rented dwellings.[2] Almost seven in 10 households in the United Kingdom are now owner-occupied,[3] just above the European Union average.[4] A factor contributing to this trend has been the sale of social sector housing to tenants under the right to buy legislation of the 1980s.[5]

Housing represents a significant proportion of many people's assets, although—as we shall see—no longer the largest. House prices have increased since the end of the Second World War by far more than the rate of inflation. Despite a housing recession between 1990 and 1993, prices began to stabilise again in 1993.[6] Between 1999 and 2000 the average price of a dwelling in the United Kingdom rose by 12 per cent, although there were marked regional variations, with buyers in London paying on average more than double the price paid in North-East England.[7] Credit to finance house purchase has been readily available in recent years: people have borrowed most of the capital required to buy a house, and watched the value of the house increase while their debt remained the same[8] in money terms (and less and less if allowance is made for the effect of inflation). The average mortgage payment as a per centage of average income has ranged between 12 and 20 per cent for most of the period

---

[1] The most useful up-to-date text on family property law is K. Gray and S. Gray, *Elements of Land Law* (3rd ed., 2001).

[2] (2002) 32 *Social Trends* 166.

[3] *ibid.*

[4] Belgium, Finland, Portugal, Sweden, Denmark, France, the Netherlands, Austria and Germany all have lower proportions of owner-occupied dwellings than the U.K.— (2002) 32 *Social Trends* Table 10.6.

[5] Discussed in Chap. 7. By the end of 1998, 2.3 million council, housing association and new town development corporation housing in Great Britain had been sold into owner-occupation: (2000) 30 *Social Trends* 168.

[6] (2000) 30 *Social Trends* 177.

[7] (2002) 32 *Social Trends* Table 10.24.

[8] Most mortgages in fact required regular repayment of capital over the years (either directly or by the payment of premiums under an endowment life policy which would produce sufficient on maturity to repay the loan); but these repayments are comparatively small. Some mortgages are interest-only.

between 1971 and 2000.[9] The extension of building society financed home-ownership, and inflation of house values over the years, has enabled many families to acquire a substantial capital asset. The wealth of the household sector has grown strongly in recent years, averaging 4.6 per cent between 1987 and 2000, adjusted for inflation.[10]

In the last few years the significance of pension entitlements as a family resource has increased, due both to political and fiscal/economic considerations. From 1996 pensions and life assurance funds represented the most important component of the household sector's wealth—38 per cent in 1998, compared with 25 per cent residential buildings net of loans and 15 per cent securities and shares. It remains to be seen whether threats to the long-term viability of occupational pension provisions apparent at the time of writing will reverse this trend. In fact non-financial assets, such as the value of homes, were in 2000 the most important components once again.

II. A VARIETY OF LEGAL REGIMES APPLICABLE

4–002 A number of chapters in this book deal with entitlement to family assets in the broad sense.[11] But the reader must be forewarned that the pattern of English law in this field is complex and that a variety of different regimes apply in a variety of situations. Thus the regime applicable may vary according to the status of the parties concerned, to the point in time at which entitlement is considered, and the parties between whom the question of entitlement arises. A particular regime is not necessarily exclusive to one situation. In order to provide the reader with a map of a somewhat complex legal landscape, this Chapter will briefly outline of the position in relation to the unmarried, to marriage, to divorce and to termination of a family relationship by death, indicating which of the ensuing chapters of this book provide detailed discussion of each topic.

The expression "family assets" itself has no single or agreed meaning in English law. It is sometimes used to describe "those things which are acquired by one or other or both of the parties, with the intention that there should be continuing provision for them and their children during their joint lives, and used for the benefit of the family as a whole."[12] As will be seen later in this Chapter, a matrimonial property regime is an institution unknown to English law, and the phrase "family assets" has been said to have "no legal meaning" as a method of solving questions of title.[13]

---

[9] (2002) 32 *Social Trends* 176.
[10] (2002) 32 *Social Trends* 103.
[11] Chaps 5, 6, 7, 8, 9, 14.
[12] *Wachtel v. Wachtel* [1973] Fam. 72 at 90, *per* Lord Denning M.R. For another definition of "family assets", see *Gissing v. Gissing* [1971] A.C. 886, *per* Lord Diplock at 904.
[13] *Pettitt v. Pettitt* [1970] A.C. 777 at 809, 810, 817; *Gissing v. Gissing* [1971] A.C. 886 at 899.

The unmarried

4–003 A large number of people now live together outside marriage,[14] but cohabitation does not without more affect the parties' legal position in relation to ownership of property, nor is there (as yet) a regime permitting an adjustment of property and pension rights[15] on the breakdown of an unmarried relationship comparable to that which operates on divorce, nullity and judicial separation.[16] The property entitlements of unmarried persons (including those of current and former cohabitants) are governed by the general law determining beneficial ownership, namely ordinary principles of property and contract law. The relevant principles of law and equity identify the parties' existing beneficial entitlements; their objective is not to effect a transfer of entitlement from one party to another in the interests of achieving a fair outcome.[17] Yet these principles of law and equity are (in the absence of a statutory adjustive regime) used as the means of dispute resolution on relationship breakdown, and thus a jurisdiction which is in nature declaratory is in practice invoked as a vehicle for asset distribution. Whether the law should be reformed, and what direction future reform might take, is discussed in Chapter 7.

Entitlement during marriage

4–004 Under many legal systems the coming into existence of marriage has an important effect on the parties' property rights: in particular, in many systems, some or all of the parties' property becomes, as a result of their marriage, subjected to legal joint ownership.

English law never accepted a community regime in this sense, nor to date has it permitted spouses to enter into pre-nuptial agreements which are effective conclusively to determine their property rights and financial obligations.[18] However, until the late nineteenth century, marriage had a most profound effect on property entitlement at common law: husband and wife became legally one—although as Lord Denning has put it in *Williams & Glyn's Bank Ltd v. Boland,*[19] the husband was that one. In the absence of specific provision by settlement, much of the wife's property vested in him; but in compensation she acquired a right to be supported by the husband and she also had certain rights to property after his death. In the nineteenth century there was a powerful movement of opinion[20] against the injustice caused by the common law rules; and in a series of

---

14 For some trends and statistics, see Chap. 9.

15 But see the transfer of certain tenancies under F.L.A. 1996, s. 53 and Sched. 7, discussed in Chap. 14.

16 Matrimonial Causes Act 1973, ss.24, 24B.

17 As is the objective of an order for ancillary relief under the Matrimonial Causes Act 1973; *Piglowska v. Piglowski* [1999] 2 F.L.R. 763; [1999] 1 W.L.R. 1360; [1999] 3 All E.R. 632; *White v. White* [2000] 2 F.L.R. 981, [2000] 3 W.L.R. 1571; [2001] 1 A.C. 596, HL; *Cowan v. Cowan* [2001] EWCA Civ. 679; [2001] 2 F.L.R. 192; [2001] 3 W.L.R. 684, CA; *Cordle v. Cordle* [2002] E.W.C.A. Civ.1791; 1 F.L.R. 207, CA.

18 The effect of such agreements in law is discussed in Chap. 5.

19 [1979] Ch. 312 at 432, CA.

20 The 4th edition of this work, pp. 625–634, contains a fuller account with more extensive references. For a recent account of the movement for reform in the 19th century, see L. Holcombe,

enactments culminating in the Married Women's Property Act 1882 Parliament adopted the regime of "separate property"—which had long been familiar to the upper and middle classes whose marriage settlements provided that the wife's capital should remain her separate property and not become subject to the common law rules. One result of the 1882 reform was that marriage no longer had any immediate effect on entitlement to property.

The 1882 reform was intended to be beneficial to married women, and the introduction of separate property certainly did have advantages—for example, a married woman's earnings were thenceforth her own to do with as she wished, whereas at common law her earnings belonged to her husband. Nevertheless, the Act introduced only a system of formal equality between husband and wife, in respect of legal capacity to acquire and retain property, leaving untouched the socio-economic background whereby the respective roles conventionally taken by spouses determined their respective capacities to benefit from the legal system. The Act's shortcomings in achieving fairness in economic terms at the time of divorce eventually necessitated the creation of a statutory adjustive jurisdiction, discussed in the next section and in Chapter 14.

The effect of the adoption of separation of property as the principle governing proprietary entitlement was put very clearly by Lord Upjohn in 1970. In the absence of any relevant statutory provision (he said):

> "... the rights of the parties [to a marriage] must be judged on the general principles applicable in any court of law when considering questions of title to property, and though the parties are husband and wife these questions of title must be decided by the principles of law applicable to the settlement of claims between those not so related, while making full allowances in view of the relationship."[21]

4–005 However, as we shall demonstrate in Chapter 5, as a result of the operation of doctrines such as the constructive trust, legal title is not necessarily co-terminous with equitable ownership. Furthermore, the purity of the regime of separation of property during marriage in English law has been eroded by a number of piecemeal statutory reforms of the latter part of the twentieth century, which are discussed in Chapter 6. The Married Women's Property Act 1964 gave a wife a proprietary interest in savings from housekeeping, and section 37 of the Matrimonial Proceedings and Property Act 1970 made it clear that contributions in money or money's worth by a spouse to the improvement (as opposed to the acquisition) of property will (under certain conditions) give rise to a proprietary right. Neither of these provisions retains any real significance in practice, given

---

Wives and Property (1983); and, for an excellent brief account, W.R. Cornish and G. de N. Clark, *Law and Society in England 1750–1950* (1989), pp. 398–402.

[21] *Pettitt v. Pettitt* [1970] A.C. 777 at 813, *per* Lord Upjohn; see also *per* Lord Morris at 803, and *per* Lord Diplock at 821. This case unequivocally decided that—contrary to the views of Lord Denning and some other judges—the provisions of the Married Women's Property Act 1882, s.17 empowering the judge to "make such order ... as he thinks fit" in disputes about title to or possession of property did not give the court a free hand to do what was just in all the circumstances.

the existence of the "ancillary relief"[22] jurisdiction conferred on courts by Part II of the Matrimonial Causes Act 1973 to make a fair distribution of assets on divorce. Of greater significance during marriage has been the creation of "matrimonial home rights", originating in the Matrimonial Homes Act 1967 and finding contemporary expression in Part IV of the Family Law Act 1996. This too is discussed in Chapter 6.

On making a decree of divorce, nullity or judicial separation, the court has extensive powers under sections 22 to 25C of the Matrimonial Causes Act 1973 to redistribute the parties' assets according to the criteria therein specified, the implicit over-arching objective being the achievement of a fair outcome.[23] These provisions override the general law in the sense that once the Matrimonial Causes Act 1973 has been invoked it is dominant in determining the spouses' respective rights and interests. Where there are no substantive third party interests to be determined in proceedings between husband and wife on divorce, the general law (either common law, equity or statute) should not be invoked.[24] However, as Thorpe L.J. observed in *Tee v. Tee and Hillman,*[25] the general principles of property law continue to be of primary importance to married couples when the dispute involves a third party[26]—for example, a creditor of the husband. The creditor may be able to enforce his legal rights of recovery against the property of the husband[27]; but he will not usually be entitled to attack property which is beneficially owned by the wife unless she has joined in the transaction or done something else to render herself liable. For example, in both *McHardy and Sons (A Firm) v. Warren*[28] and *Midland Bank plc v. Cooke,*[29] the plaintiffs were owed money by the husband who had charged the matrimonial home (legal title to which was in his sole name) to secure his indebtedness. The court in each case held that the wife was entitled in equity to a 50 per cent beneficial interest in the property,[30] and the plaintiffs could not have recourse to that share in satisfaction of their claim.[31]

It is for this reason that questions of beneficial entitlement to property are particularly important when a spouse[32] is adjudicated bankrupt. In that case all

---

[22] Defined by the Family Proceedings Rules 1991, r.1.2.

[23] See the cases cited in n. 17, above.

[24] See *Laird v. Laird* [1998] 1 F.L.R. 791; *Tee v. Tee and Hillman* [1999] 2 F.L.R. 613, where there was a "diversionary excursion" into the Trusts of Land Act 1996, described by Thorpe L.J. as "about as appalling a litigation history as it would be possible to dicover" (at 618).

[25] [1999] 2 F.L.R. 613 at 619.

[26] In certain circumstances a disposition may subsequently be set aside under the bankruptcy legislation: see Insolvency Act 1986, ss. 339–342, 423.

[27] Or other claimant: see *e.g. Re Sharpe (Bankrupt)* [1980] 1 W.L.R. 219 in which the bankrupt's aunt who had contributed money to the purchase of a house in the belief that she would be able to live there was held to have acquired an interest under a constructive trust such as would bind the legal owner's trustee in bankruptcy.

[28] [1994] 2 F.L.R. 338, CA.

[29] [1995] 2 F.L.R. 915; [1995] 4 All E.R. 562, CA.

[30] The interest bound the creditors because they were treated as having notice of her equitable interest: see the discussion in Chap. 5.

[31] The fact that property owned by a debtor's wife or partner cannot be taken in enforcement proceedings by the creditor does not necessarily mean that the proceedings will have no effect on the property. In particular, a creditor may obtain a charging order on a debtor's interest in the family home. See the discussion in Chap. 5, below.

[32] Or cohabitant.

the property to which the bankrupt spouse is beneficially entitled vests by operation of law in the trustee in bankruptcy; and it is the trustee's duty to realise the property for the benefit of the bankrupt's creditors. The other spouse's property, in contrast, does not vest in the trustee; and he or she is in principle entitled to keep it.[33]

As will be explained in Chapter 5, in current English law couples are not permitted on public policy grounds conclusively to resolve the financial consequences of marriage breakdown by private contract, whether embodied in a pre-nuptial or a separation agreement.

Divorce

4–006 For many years, the question of beneficial ownership remained of crucial importance to divorce practitioners. This was because the divorce court had virtually no powers to adjust the entitlement of family members to capital assets when a marriage broke down; and questions of entitlement therefore had to be solved by reference to the ordinary law of property in which the fact of marital breakdown would be irrelevant. The injustice of the separate property doctrine was made apparent in a series of cases dealing with the matrimonial home where the conveyance was taken in the name of one spouse and the nature of the contributions made by the other to the family were insufficient to give rise to an equitable interest. In the 1950s and 1960s the Court of Appeal under the leadership of Lord Denning M.R. developed a jurisprudence permitting discretionary allocation of "family assets" under section 17 of the Married Women's Property Act 1882.[34] However, in *Pettitt v. Pettitt*[35] and *Gissing v. Gissing*[36] orthodoxy was conclusively reasserted by the House of Lords, as is discussed in Chapter 5. Statutory intervention was therefore necessary to recognise a wider range of contributions made to the welfare of the family by spouses. The Matrimonial Proceedings and Property Act 1970 was later consolidated as Part II of the Matrimonial Causes Act 1973. This statutory jurisdiction to make "ancillary relief" orders is discussed in Chapter 14.

However, there are still people who, for religious or other reasons, do not want to divorce; and if a couple choose not to bring matrimonial proceedings the court will have to resolve any questions about the beneficial entitlement to their property without using the divorce court's adjustive powers.[37] Moreover, in a very rare case, a spouse may find herself or himself denied access on divorce to the ancillary relief jurisdiction under Part II of the Matrimonial Causes Act

---

[33] See *H v. M (Property: Beneficial Interest)* [1992] 1 F.L.R. 229 at 231, *per* Waite J.: ascertaining the parties' strict entitlements is (in contrast to the forward looking approach of the divorce court's adjustive jurisdiction) "a process which is anything but forward looking and involves, on the contrary, a painfully detailed retrospect".

[34] *Jones v. Maynard* [1951 Ch. 572; *Bendall v. McWhirter* [1952] 2 Q.B. 466; *Rimmer v. Rimmer* [1953] 1 Q.B. 63; *Cobb v. Cobb* [1955] 2 All E.R. 696; *Hine v. Hine* [1962] 3 All E.R. 345.

[35] [1970] A.C. 777.

[36] [1971] A.C. 886.

[37] MCA 1973, s.28(3), although a married couple may use separation proceedings as a way of invoking the court's powers.

1973.[38] In such a case the remedies under the general law will be the only available option.

Death

4–007 The majority of marriages are terminated by death, and not by divorce. Devolution of family property on death is discussed in Chapter 8, which deals will the effects of marriage and divorce on wills, with intestacy, and with claims under the Inheritance (Provision for Family and Dependants) Act 1975.

III. PROPERTY RIGHTS AND PERSONAL RIGHTS

4–008 For the lawyer, a property right must be:

> "definable, identifiable by third parties, capable in its nature of assumption by third parties, and have some degree of permanence or stability."[39]

Apparently similar rights may be either proprietary or purely personal; but the difference is crucial. If my right is proprietary I can, in principle, assert it against third parties—even in many cases against an innocent purchaser. If it is personal, then in principle I cannot enforce it against a third party at all, and the fact that the third party knew of my claim will not necessarily affect the position. It is, of course, true that I may be able to sue the grantor of the right (for example, for damages for breach of contract) but that right of action may not be an adequate remedy, particularly if the grantor turns out to be insolvent.

The leading case illustrating this fundamental notion is *National Provincial Bank Ltd v. Ainsworth*[40]:

> H had deserted W. It was conceded that she had a right to be provided with housing by her husband, and that she could have obtained an injunction from the courts to stop him interfering with her right. Unfortunately, W only found out that H had mortgaged the house after the transaction had been completed. H become insolvent. The House of Lords held that W's right to be provided with housing by her husband—the so-called "deserted wife's equity"—was intrinsically incapable of binding the bank: "the rights

---

[38] *Whiston v. Whiston* [1995] 2 F.L.R. 268; [1995] Ch. 198; [1995] 3 W.L.R. 405; *J. v. ST* (formerly *J. (Transsexual: Ancillary Relief)* [1997] 1 F.L.R. 402; discussed in Chap. 14.

[39] *per* Lord Wilberforce, *National Provincial Bank v. Ainsworth* [1965] A.C. 1175 at 1248; and see *Ashburn Anstalt v. Arnold* [1989] Ch. 1, CA. (in which, it is submitted, the analysis of this conceptual framework remains good law, notwithstanding the fact that the decision was overruled in *Prudential Assurance Co. Ltd v. London Residuary Body* [1992] 2 A.C. 386, HL).

[40] See above. The decision of the House of Lords in *Lloyds Bank plc v. Rosset* [1991] 1 A.C. 107 also illustrates this principle; the fact that there is a common intention that a home be shared throws no light on the parties' intentions in relation to beneficial ownership: see at 130, *per* Lord Bridge of Harwich.

of husband and wife must be regarded as purely personal ... these rights as a matter of law do not affect third parties."[41]

The policy of the general law has been to restrict the number of property interests capable of being recognised by the law. The more interests there are which are capable of binding purchasers unaware of their existence the less confidence will be placed in the system of property rights. Moreover, the greater the number of proprietary rights the greater the time spent in, and thus the cost of, investigating titles. Cheaper and more efficient conveyancing necessitates a reduction in the number of rights to be examined. This policy of the general law is strongly reflected in the recent Land Registration Act 2002, discussed briefly in Chapter 5. On the other hand, family law seeks to achieve fairness, in the occupation and ownership of assets, between parties who have shared a variety of different roles during their relationship. It has pursued this objective not by extending or altering the orthodox concept of property rights but by other forms of statutory intervention. As we shall see in Chapter 6, the effect of *National Provincial Bank plc v. Ainsworth*[42] has been reversed by the creation of statutory[43] "matrimonial home rights" which are personal[44] in character but through the device of registration can be made to bind third parties.

[41] *per* Lord Upjohn at 1233. This case should be distinguished from *Williams & Glyn's Bank v. Boland* [1981] A.C. 487 where it was conceded that the wife had a proprietary interest, of its nature capable of binding purchasers. In *National Provincial Bank v. Ainsworth* (above) the question was whether the wife's interest (which was merely the right to be housed by her husband, rather than a beneficial interest in the property) was capable of binding a purchaser. The House of Lords held that it was not.

[42] [1965] A.C. 1175.

[43] Matrimonial Homes Act 1967; Matrimonial Homes Act 1983; Family Law Act 1996, ss. 30–31.

[44] See *Hunter v. Canary Wharf* [1997] 2 F.L.R. 342; see the reservations expressed on this point by S. Cretney in [1997] *Fam. Law*. 601–602.

CHAPTER FIVE

BENEFICIAL ENTITLEMENT AT LAW AND IN EQUITY

I. INTRODUCTION

5–001 Property law is concerned with the answer to the general question "to whom does this belong?" However, most family property law has developed in connection with land; and the following analysis therefore focusses primarily on the rules relating to land, with some reference where appropriate to distinctive rules relating to other property.

The relevant general principles of property law are of two kinds, formal and substantive. The rules governing formalities have had an important impact on the way in which the law has developed.

II. FORMAL REQUIREMENTS—INTERESTS IN LAND

5–002 The imposition of formal requirements on legal transactions has a number of objectives: the achievement of certainty, the provision of evidence of intention, and an indication to the parties of the serious nature of the transaction and its consequences.[1]

A. Deed needed for transfer of legal estate

5–003 Section 52 of the Law of Property Act 1925 stipulates that a deed is necessary to convey or create any legal estate in land. If the conveyance of the family home is taken in the name of one partner it follows that the other cannot successfully claim to be entitled to the legal estate.[2]

B. Writing necessary for creation of other interests in land

5–004 Section 53 (1) of the Law of Property Act 1925 stipulates that no interest in land can be created or disposed of except by a signed written document.[3]

[1] Hill and Howard, "The Informal Creation of Interests in Land" (1995) *Legal Studies* 356 at 357.

[2] Any assignment of any legal leasehold interest must—irrespective of its duration—be effected formally by deed: see *Crago v. Julian* [1992] 1 W.L.R. 372; [1992] 1 All E.R. 744; [1992] 1 F.L.R. 478; (where failure to attend to the conveyancing formalities meant that a woman, entitled under a divorce court consent order to the tenancy of her former husband's flat, could be evicted by the landlord).

[3] The beneficial title to property may of course pass on intestacy or under a duly executed will: see Chap. 8, below.

Hence:—

In *Gissing v. Gissing*[4] the matrimonial home had been conveyed into the husband's sole name. When the marriage broke up he told her: "Don't worry about the house—it's yours. I will pay the mortgage payments and all other outgoings." The wife had no claim on the basis of that statement: there was no deed which could displace the legal estate and no written document which could give her any other interest. Similarly, in *H v. M (Property: Beneficial Interest)*[5] the legal title to a bungalow was taken in the name of the man (who explained that his tax and divorce problems dictated this course); but he said to his partner "Don't worry about the future, because when we are married it will be half yours anyway, and I'll always look after you and our child." This statement had no effect on the legal title to the property.

C. Contracts for the Disposition of Land

5–005 Writing is also required for contracts for the sale or other disposition of interests in land: Law of Property (Miscellaneous Provisions) Act 1989, s.2 discussed later in this Chapter.

III. BENEFICIAL INTEREST MAY BE CLAIMED BY WAY OF RESULTING, IMPLIED OR CONSTRUCTIVE TRUST

5–006 The legal system nevertheless recognises that absolute compliance on formal requirements would produce injustice, particularly if the parties have in fact agreed to create proprietary rights. Section 53(2) of the Law of Property Act 1925 provides that the requirement of a signed written document for the creation or disposal of any interest in land does not affect the "creation or operation of resulting, implied or constructive trusts," so that a spouse who cannot show any entitlement to the legal estate may nonetheless be able to establish a claim to a beneficial interest under these equitable doctrines; and if there is nothing in writing to satisfy the requirements of section 53(1) a person claiming an interest under an asserted trust has to rely on this exemption.[6] Furthermore, section 2 (5) of the Law of Property (Miscellaneous Provisions) Act 1989 declares that "nothing in this section affects the creation or operation of resulting, implied or constructive trusts".

Hence the document of title or the formal contract is the starting point in relation to real property, but if the document does not expressly declare the shares in the equitable as well as the legal interests, there is scope for argument

---

[4] [1971] A.C. 886.
[5] [1992] 1 F.L.R. 229, Waite J.
[6] *Springette v. Defoe* [1992] 2 F.L.R. 388 at 397, *per* Sir Christopher Slade.

about their existence and extent.[7] Despite the increasingly common conveyancing practice of expressly declaring the proportions of both legal and beneficial interests when a family home is acquired,[8] there nevertheless remain situations, particularly in the context of informal family relationships, where there is no express declaration of equitable interests on the title document of the house in which the parties live.

The terms "implied, resulting and constructive trust" are not used consistently There has been considerable controversy[9] as to the correct usage of these terms and, furthermore, as to the interrelationship of the institutions involved, notwithstanding the bold statement of Lord Diplock in *Gissing v. Gissing*[10] that it may for certain purposes be unnecessary to distinguish between them. In *Drake v. Whipp*[11] Peter Gibson L.J. observed that:

> " . . . it is not easy to reconcile every judicial utterance in this well-travelled area of law. A potent source of confusion, to my mind, has been suggestions that it matters not whether the terminology used is that of constructive trust . . . or that of resulting trust . . . "[12]

A further contentious issue (discussed later in this Chapter) has been the relationship between the doctrines of constructive trust and proprietary estoppel and the extent of their assimilation.[13]

Is the debate purely terminological, or is it substantive, with both doctrinal and practical significance? The following issues have arisen:

(a) Is intention (actual, implied or presumed) the basis of all informal trusts,[14] or does the resulting trust stand apart?
(b) Should the term "constructive trust" properly be confined in usage to the remedial constructive trust imposed on the parties by the court irrespective of their intentions (actual or implied), such as was advocated by Lord Denning in the 1970s[15] and is currently utilised in some

---

7 *Pettit v. Pettit* [1970] A.C. 777 at 813 *per* Lord Upjohn; *Goodman v. Gallant* [1986] Fam 106.
8 *The Family Lawyer's Handbook* (Bailey-Harris ed., The Law Society 1997), pp. 145–152; Land Registration Rules 1925 (as amended), rr. 19(1), 98, Sched. 1.
9 N. Glover and P. Todd, "The Myth of Common Intention" (1996) 16 *Legal Studies* 324, especially at 335–338, 339–341.
10 [1971] A.C. 886 at 905.
11 [1996] 1 F.L.R. 826; [1996] F.C.R. 298.
12 At 827.
13 *Lloyds Bank plc v. Rosset* [1991] A.C. 107 at 132 *per* Lord Bridge; *Grant v. Edwards* [1986] Ch. 638 at 656 *per* Browne-Wilkinson V.-C.; *Stokes v. Anderson* [1991] 1 F.L.R. 391 at 399 *per* Nourse L.J.; D. Hayton, "Equitable Rights of Cohabitees" (1990) 54 *Conveyancer* 370; S. Gardner, "Rethinking Family Property" (1993) 109 *L.Q.R.* 263; P. Ferguson, "Constructive Trusts—A Note of Caution" (1993) 109 *L.Q.R.* 114; D. Hayton, "Constructive Trusts of Homes—A Bold Approach" (1993) 109 *L.Q.R.* 485; T. Lawson-Cruttenden and A. Odutola [1995] *Fam. Law* 560 at 561-2; Palowski [1996] *Fam. Law* 484 at 486; Lawson, "The Things We Do For Love: Detrimental Reliance in the Family Home" (1996) 16 *Legal Studies* 218 at 220, 224–231; C. Davis, "Informal acquisition and loss of rights in land: what justifies the doctrines?" (2000) 2 *Legal Studies* 198.
14 *per* Peter Gibson L.J. in *Drake v. Whipp* [1996] 1 F.L.R. 826 at 827.
15 *Williams & Glyn's Bank Ltd v. Boland* [1979] Ch. 312 at 329; and *Hussey v. Palmer* [1972] 1 W.L.R. 1286.

overseas jurisdictions? This was the position advocated in earlier editions of this book . Or has it now become acceptable to use the term "constructive trust" in cases where the courts infer an intention from the parties' words and conduct? The latter (despite a certain linguistic infelicity) appears consistent with current judicial practice and will be adopted in this edition. In *Lloyds Bank plc v. Rosset*[16] Lord Bridge stated that the making of direct contributions to the purchase price would "readily justify the inference necessary to a constructive trust".[17] In *Drake v. Whipp* Peter Gibson L.J. asserted that in a constructive trust "the intention, actual or imputed, of the parties is crucial".[18]

(c) What is the proper characterisation of the trust imposed in cases such as *Midland Bank v. Cooke*[19] and *Drake v. Whipp*: a resulting or a constructive trust?

It is impossible to argue in the light of the opinions of the Law Lords in *Pettitt v. Pettitt, Gissing v. Gissing* and *Lloyds Bank plc v. Rosset*[20] that the doctrine of remedial constructive trust (imposed irrespective of the parties' intentions, actual or inferred) forms any part of the law of England and Wales. Although the doctrines of implied, resulting and constructive trusts are all based on the underlying principle that it would in the circumstances be unconscionable to allow the legal owner to assert the absolute ownership which appears on the title documents, the element of unconscionability is a necessary but not a sufficient condition for the establishment of an equitable interest. In particular, it remains a cardinal principle of the law that the mere fact that a person expends money or labour on another's property does not by itself entitle the person making the contribution to any beneficial interest in that property.[21]

In English law, common intention and agreement are vital elements in the creation of many legal and equitable interests in property, whether the creation be formal or informal. The doctrines of resulting and constructive trust which permit interests in land to be created without compliance with formalities continue to be based—in principle at least—on the existence of agreement between the parties, actual, presumed, express, implied or inferred.[22] English law has not accepted the concept of the remedial constructive trust imposed, irrespective of the parties' actual or presumed intentions, to achieve a just result in relation to beneficial ownership which has found favour in some other jurisdictions.[23]

---

16 [1991] 1 A.C. 107 at 132–133, per Lord Bridge of Harwich.

17 See also the use of the term "institutional constructive trust" *per* Lord Browne-Wilkinson in *Westdeutsche Landesbank Girozentrale v. Islington LBC* [1996] A.C. 669 at 714–715.

18 [1996] 1 F.L.R. 826 at 827.

19 [1995] 2 F.L.R. 915; (1995) 4 All E.R. 562, CA.

20 [1991] 1 A.C. 107.

21 *Thomas v. Fuller-Brown* [1988] 1 F.L.R. 237, CA; and see *Grant v. Edwards* [1986] Ch. 638, CA.

22 *Pettit v. Pettit* [1970] A.C. 770; *Gissing v. Gissing* [1971] A.C. 886. For criticism of the common indention requirement in constructive trusts, see Law. Com. Discussion Paper *Sharing Homes* (July 2002) (www.law.com.gov.uk), para. 2.106.

23 Courts in other commonwealth countries have adopted a more flexible approach: see D.J. Hayton, "Remedial Constructive Trusts of Homes" [1988] *Conv.* 259; S. Gardner, "Rethinking Family Property" (1993) 109 *L.Q.R.* 263; and note, *e.g. Pettkus v. Becker* (1981) 117 D.L.R. (3d) 257;

Hence the preponderance of the principles which we are about to describe in this section are (in theory at least) limited to defining what the parties intended their proprietary rights to be. As mentioned in the last Chapter, the general principles of law and equity do not in the main operate as a means of resource redistribution, *i.e.* they do not transfer entitlement from one party to another in order to achieve a just result. Thus their very nature and origins render these doctrines imperfect vehicles for achieving social justice in the context in which they are now commonly invoked, namely the resolution of property disputes on the breakdown of unmarried relationships, an issue which will be discussed further in Chapter 9.

What, then, are the circumstances in which a person will be able successfully to assert an equitable interest by way of informal trust? As will be seen, the case-law from which the answer must be provided is complex.

A. Payment of purchase price—resulting trust

5–007 The presumption of resulting trust operates where one person makes a direct financial contribution to the purchase of property[24] conveyed into the name of the other. He or she will, in the absence of admissible evidence that some other result was intended, be entitled in equity to a share in the property proportionate to the amount of the contribution.[25] There is some debate as to the doctrinal basis of the resulting trust: is presumed intention, as stated by Peter Gibson L.J. in *Drake v. Whipp*,[26] or the supposition that a person who receives money gratuitously is obliged[27] to account for it?

Sorochan v. Sorochan (1986) 29 D.L.R. (4th) 1; *Peter v. Beblow* (1993) 101 D.L.R. (4th) 621 (Canada—unjust enrichment basis of doctrine; beneficial interest awarded to women who had lived with men for substantial periods and made indirect contributions to the family wealth); and a similar approach has been adopted in New Zealand (see, *e.g. Hayward v. Giordani* [1983] N.Z.L.R. 75—*Pettkus v. Becker* doctrine accepted—and more recently *Gillies v. Keogh* [1989] 2 N.Z.L.R. 327, discussed in (1990) 106 *L.Q.R.* 213. In Australia, the High Court has adopted the principle that one party to a relationship is not to be allowed to retain the benefit of property when it would be unconscionable to do so: see *Baumgartner v. Baumgartner* (1987) 164 C.L.R. 137, and this has allowed the Australian courts to find that property is jointly owned when a couple have pooled their earnings (or perhaps simply spent money for the purposes of their joint relationship) if one of those purposes was the purchase of the house in which they lived: see *Hibberson v. George* [1989] D.F.C. 95–064. Finlay, Bailey-Harris and Otlowski, *Family Law in Australia* (5th ed., Butterworths, ed, 1997), pp. 320–324.

[24] The presumption applies to transfers of money or other personal property: *Tinsley v. Milligan* [1994] 1 A.C. 340 at 371, *per* Lord Browne-Wilkinson referring (*inter alia*) to *Dewar v. Dewar* [1975] 1 W.L.R. 1532 at 1537; and *Snell's Equity* (29th ed., 1990), p. 182. In the case where land is transferred by a donor to a donee it is sometimes suggested that the provisions of Law of Property Act 1925, s.60(3)(4)—resulting trust not to be implied in voluntary conveyance "by reason that the property is not expressed to be conveyed for the use or benefit of the grantee"—will prevent a presumption of resulting trust from arising, but this seems questionable: see Megarry and Wade, *The Law of Real Property* (6th ed., 2000), p. 541. In any event, the court will be satisfied on very little evidence that the transferor did not intend to lose the beneficial interest: *Hodgson v. Marks* [1971] Ch. 892.

[25] See generally *Cowcher v. Cowcher* [1972] 1 W.L.R. 425; [1972] 1 All E.R. 943; *Re Vandervell's Trusts (No. 2)* [1974] Ch. 269.

[26] [1996] 1 F.L.R. 826 at 827; and if so, whose intention, and as to what? *Carlton v. Goodman* [2002] E.W.C.A. Civ. 545, [2002] 2 F.L.R. 259 at [23]–[26], *per* Mummery L.J.

[27] Equitable institutions seek to give the force of law to moral obligations: *Sekhon v. Alissa* [1989] 2 F.L.R. 94 at 99 *per* Hoffmann J.

Whatever its doctrinal basis, the practical application of the resulting trust can be seen in the Court of Appeal's decision in *Springette v. Defoe*[28]:—

> Two mature people met in 1979, and lived together as man and wife—at first in the woman's local authority flat, but subsequently in a local authority house. They were given the opportunity to buy the house under a statutory "right to buy" policy; and the price was discounted by 41 per cent because the woman had been the local authority's tenant for 11 years. They financed the purchase by borrowing, 12,000 from a building society, and were jointly liable under the loan.[29] It was not disputed that the woman should be treated as having contributed 75 per cent of the purchase price (by way of the discount which she had earned and her half share of the mortgage) and the man 25 per cent; and the Court of Appeal held that, since there was no evidence that they had agreed between themselves on some other division, their beneficial interests were accordingly 75 per cent for the woman and 25 per cent for the man.

In such a case, exactly how the discount should be taken into account when considering financial contributions has been controversial; arguably it is not part of the purchase price but merely affects the amount to be paid. In *Evans v. Hayward*[30] the Court of Appeal advanced two alternatives: either the discount can be regarded as part of the purchase price or[31] as a matter capable of giving rise to an inference as to the parties' intentions.

A party may have an improper motive[32] in placing property in the name of another; does this affect the presumption of resulting trust? In *Tinsley v. Milligan*[33] Kathleen Milligan had run a bed-and-breakfast business with her lover Stella Tinsley. They each put money into the acquisition of the house, but title to their house was in Stella's sole name, as were the bank and building society accounts. This was done so that Kathleen could claim various means-tested welfare benefits on the basis that she had no stake in the property but was simply a lodger. The couple's relationship broke down, and Stella gave Kathleen notice to quit. It was held that Kathleen had an interest in the property by way of resulting trust; and the majority of the House of Lords held that the fact that the property had been put into Stella's sole name to facilitate the making of fraudulent claims for welfare benefits made no difference to her right to enforce her proprietary claim.[34] Kathleen was entitled by way of resulting trust to an interest in equity by virtue of her contributions to the purchase, and did not have to rely on the illegal purpose in order to establish her claim: in effect all that she needed to do was to show

---

[28] [1992] 2 F.L.R. 388, CA; see also *Evans v. Hayward* [1995] 2 F.L.R. 511.

[29] In the present case, it was conceded that each party was to be treated as having made a contribution of half the amount borrowed; but see below.

[30] [1995] 2 F.L.R. 511, CA.

[31] *per* Staughton L.J. at 517B.

[32] R. Buckley, "Illegal transactions: chaos or discretion?" (2000) 2 *Legal Studies* 155.

[33] [1995] 1 A.C. 340; followed in *Lowson v. Coombes* [1999] 1 F.L.R. 799; [1999] Ch. 373; [1999] 2 W.L.R. 720, CA.

[34] See below on the relevance of illegality in relation to the presumption of advancement.

that she had paid money to acquire an interest in the property. Accordingly, it would not be contrary to public policy to give effect to her entitlement. *Tinsley v. Milligan* was followed in *Lowson v. Coombes,*[35] where properties were purchased jointly but conveyed into the woman's sole name to defeat any potential claims by the man's wife for financial relief under the Matrimonial Causes Act 1973. It was held that the man was entitled to a beneficial interest notwithstanding the illegality of purpose; he did not need to rely on the illegality but only on the resulting trust that arose in his favour on the transfer.[36] These "no reliance" cases have been the subject of criticism by the Law Commission.[37]

According to the traditional concept of resulting trust, both the existence and the quantum of the equitable interest is determined by direct financial contributions to the purchase price. Equating assumption of liability under a mortgage with a cash contribution has given rise to some difficulties[38] in the authorities. It has been traditional to distinguish the resulting trust from a constructive trust, where evidence of common intention that a trust be created is inferred from the parties' conduct. The pitfalls of incorrect characterisation, on the traditional analysis, were highlighted by Peter Gibson L.J. in *Drake v. Whipp,*[39] who also drew attention to the controversy over the distinction between the various categories of "informal" trust and the terminology appropriate to them.[40] In reality, cases such as *Drake v. Whipp, Midland Bank v. Cooke* and *The Mortgage Company v. Shaire* challenge the orthodoxy of the traditional concept of the two types of informally created trust. If these cases are to be categorised as examples of resulting trust, then it is difficult to see how the entire course of the parties' conduct both at the time of purchase of property and thereafter can be taken into account in determining the *quantum* of the beneficial interests. It may be that they are better characterised as examples of constructive trusts of the second type described by Lord Bridge in *Lloyds Bank plc v. Rosset,*[41] namely those where the parties' common intention as to the beneficial interests is inferred from conduct. We return to these difficulties later in this Chapter.

---

[35] [1999] 1 F.L.R. 799; [1999] Ch. 373; (1999) 2 W.L.R. 720, CA.

[36] One may ask in these case what has become of the principle that he who seeks an equitable remedy must come with clean hands: see *Winkworth v. Edward Baron Development Co. Ltd* [1987] 1 F.L.R. 825, HL (not referred to in *Tinsley v. Milligan*). The Court of Appeal in *Tribe v. Tribe* [1995] 2 F.L.R. 966; [1995] 3 W.L.R. 713; [1995] 3 All E.R. 236 [1996] Ch. 103 was critical of *Tinsley v. Milligan.*

[37] Consultation Paper No. 154 *Illegal Transactions: The Effect of Illegality on Contracts and Trusts* (1999), para. 3.23; Consultation Paper No. 160 *The Illegality Defence in Tort* (2001), para. 5.35.

[38] The principal issue being whether the *quantum* of the contribution is the entire mortgage debt or the payments made; the authorities are not easy to reconcile. See *e.g. Walker v. Hall* [1984] F.L.R. 126; *Young v. Young* [1984] F.L.R. 375; *Marsh v. Sternberg* [1986] 1 F.L.R. 526; *Stokes v. Anderson* [1991] 1 F.L.R. 391, *Huntingford v. Hobbs* [1993] 1 F.L.R. 736; *Irvin v. Blake* [1995] 1 F.L.R. 70; *The Mortgage Company v. Shaire* [2000] 1 F.L.R. 973, Ch. D. See also *Carlton v. Goodman* [2002] E.W.C.A. Civ. 545, [2002] 2 F.L.R. 259, CA, where a joint mortgagor was in the circumstances not entitled to a beneficial interest.

[39] [1996] 1 F.L.R. 826.

[40] See in particular *per* Peter Gibson L.J. at 827.

[41] [1991] A.C. 107.

B. Presumption of resulting trust sometimes rebutted by presumption of advancement

5–008 The presumption of resulting trust will yield to the (itself rebuttable) presumption of advancement. Equity presumes that the transferor intends to make a gift of the property. The presumption of advancement applies when a husband purchases property in his wife's name[42] or a parent in the name of a child (legitimate or illegitimate) or to a person to whom the donor stands *in loco parentis,* but to no other categories of family relationship. Obviously outmoded in a contemporary social context, the presumption now rarely holds sway[43] and will yield to slight evidence suggesting a contrary intention.[44] Nevertheless there is one context in which the presumption of advancement retains significance and produces results which appear anomalous: where property is transferred for an illegal purpose. Thus in *Tinsley v. Milligan,*[45] discussed above, the illegal purpose was held by the House of Lords not to defeat Kathleen's claim to an interest by way of resulting trust, since she did not need to rely on the illegal purpose.[46] However, if the property has been transferred by a husband/father to a wife or child, the presumption of advancement applies and he cannot avoid disclosing the illegal purpose in order to rebut the presumption of advancement, and so the claim will fail,[47] unless the illegal purpose has not yet been carried out.[48] This result may seem curious and little more than an accident of history.[49]

C. Constructive trust: common intention acted on to claimant's detriment

5–009 If there is admissible evidence that, at the date of the acquisition or exceptionally at some later date, the parties intended the home to be jointly owned, the court will imply/impute a trust of the proceeds of sale to that effect, provided that the claimant has acted to his or her detriment. It is arguable how closely the conduct evidencing detriment must be referable to the acquisition of the property in question.[49a]

There are two stages in this analysis:

---

[42] *Mercier v. Mercier* [1903] 2 Ch. 98; *Silver v. Silver* [1958] 1 W.L.R. 259.

[43] Reliance on it came under attack as long ago as *Pettitt v. Pettitt* [1970] A.C. 777 *per* Lord Reid at 793, *per* Lord Hodson at 811, *per* Lord Diplock at 824; see also *Harwood v. Harwood* [1991] 2 F.L.R. 274 *per* Sir Christopher Slade at 294.

[44] *Loades-Carter v. Loades-Carter* (1966) 110 S.J. 51; *McGrath v. Wallis* [1995] 2 F.L.R. 114.

[45] [1995] 1 A.C. 28.

[46] Applied in *Lowson v. Coombes* [1999] 1 F.L.R. 799; [1999] 2 W.L.R. 720, CA.

[47] *Gascoigne v. Gascoigne* [1918] 1 K.B. 223; *Chettiar v. Chettiar* [1962] A.C. 294; *Tinker v. Tinker* [1970] P. 136.

[48] See *Tribe v. Tribe* [1995] 2 F.L.R. 966 *per* Nourse L.J. at 977 and *per* Millett L.J. at 984.

[49] *ibid.* at 974. See also the criticism of the Law Commission, n. 37, *supra.*

[49a] There may be some difference in legal consequence between a right to share in property founded on a resulting trust stemming from contributions to the purchase price and a right to share based on an agreement or arrangement: see *Re Densham (A Bankrupt)* [1975] 1 W.L.R. 1519 (evidence clearly established parties intended joint-ownership of matrimonial home; but their agreement was void under the Bankruptcy Act 1914, s.42 in so far as it was not for valuable consideration. But the wife had made contributions from their earnings to the mortgage and other acquisition costs; and the court computed the wife's contributions at £585 towards a purchase price of £5,783, and accordingly she was entitled—by way of resulting trust, in the present analysis—to

1. Is there evidence of intention?

5–010 The speech of Lord Bridge of Harwich in *Lloyds Bank plc v. Rosset*[50] articulated two methods of establishing the intention that a property be jointly owned: discussions, and inferences drawn from conduct.

(a) Discussions[51] evidencing agreement or understanding

5–011 The first and fundamental question which must always be resolved[52] is whether there have:

> "at any time prior to the acquisition of the disputed property, or exceptionally at some later date, been discussions between the parties leading to any agreement, arrangement or understanding reached between them that the property is to be shared beneficially. The finding of an arrangement or arrangement to share . . . can only . . . be based on evidence of express discussion, however imperfectly remembered and however imprecise their terms may have been."[53]

Rarely, there may be clear evidence that the parties had made an agreement about beneficial entitlement. Thus in *Barclays Bank v. Khaira*[54] a husband and wife, in the presence of a witness, signed a Land Registry form which purported to transfer their house to the wife. Although the document was stamped, it was never presented to the Land Registry for registration and was thus ineffective to transfer the legal estate to the wife. However, the trial judge held that the transfer was "the best evidence a court could reasonably expect of an express domestic arrangement as to the sharing of a beneficial interest", and that accordingly it was capable of being effective to give the wife an equitable interest in the property.

However, in most of the cases which have come before the courts the matter has been much less clear cut; the evidentiary problems in relation to discussions alleged to have occured years earlier are self-evident. In recent years this means of evidencing intention that a property be jointly owned has been less commonly invoked in the reported case-law than the alternative of drawing inferences from conduct. Occasionally the problem is merely one of reconciling conflicting accounts of the discussions between the parties and thereby ascertaining their intentions. In *Ungurian v. Lesnoff*[55] a Polish woman came to England to live

---

a one-ninth share as against the trustee in bankruptcy, since her entitlement to that share was not dependent on the agreement with her husband but was an acquisition for value).

[50] [1991] A.C. 107 at 132.

[51] The "actual" intention referred to by Peter Gibson L.J. in *Drake v. Whipp* [1996] 1 F.L.R. 826 at 827.

[52] *Lloyds Bank plc v. Rosset* [1991] 1 A.C. 107 at 132, *per* Lord Bridge of Harwich.

[53] *per* Waite J., *H. v. M. (Property: Beneficial Interest)* [1992] 1 F.L.R. 229 at 231 (following the substance of Lord Bridge of Harwich's speech in *Lloyds Bank plc v. Rosset* (above)).

[54] [1993] 1 F.L.R. 343. For a case where the evidence of common agreement was less clear, see *Re Share (Lorraine)* [2002] 2 F.L.R. 89, Ch.D.

[55] [1990] Ch. 206, Vinelott J.

with the plaintiff; and he bought a house in which they lived. The judge rejected her claim that the plaintiff had promised that if she burnt her boats (by giving up her career and housing in Poland) and threw in her lot with him he would buy a house which would be her absolute property; but the judge was satisfied on the evidence that it had been understood that the plaintiff would provide her with a home in which she would be entitled to live for her life.[56]

However, the more common question is whether any sufficient understanding can be found on which the parties have relied. Illustrative are two examples of intention evidenced by representations cited by Lord Bridge in *Lloyds Bank plc v. Rosset*[57] in the context of unmarried cohabitation where:

> "the female partner had been clearly led by the male partner to believe, when they set up home together, that the property would belong to them jointly".[58]

In *Eves v. Eves*[59] a man told the woman with whom he was living that the house was to be their joint home, but that the conveyance would be taken in his sole name because she was under 21 (then the legal age of majority). The court held that it could properly find that there had been an understanding between them or a common intention that she was to have a proprietary interest,[60] because if this had not been so it would have been unnecessary to make the excuse.[61] In *Grant v. Edwards*[62] the woman was told by the man that the only reason for not acquiring the property in joint names was her involvement in divorce proceedings, and the potential of joint-ownership to operate to her detriment in those proceedings. *H. v. M. (Property: Beneficial Interest)*[63] was decided after *Rosset,* the significance of which we have already emphasised. There, legal title to a bungalow was taken in the man's sole name; but the judge was satisfied that the express discussions which had taken place established the existence of mutual expectations of a shared beneficial interest. It is not wholly clear on which

---

[56] The result was that the house was held on trust for her during her lifetime; and was thus settled land within the Settled Land Act 1925. Accordingly Mrs Lesnoff had the right to sell the house and have a replacement purchased with the proceeds. The Trusts of Land and Appointment of Trustees Act 1996 put an end to the problems of informal rights of life occupancy resulting in accidental strict settlements under the Settled Land Act 1925: no new settlements can be created, expressly or impliedly.

[57] [1991] A.C. 107.

[58] *ibid.* at 133.

[59] [1975] 1 W.L.R. 1338, CA.

[60] In this case, the woman did "a great deal of work to the house and garden. She did much more than many wives would do." See [1975] 1 W.L.R. 1338, *per* Lord Denning M.R. at 1340. Not surprisingly the case was often seen as one in which the claim to a beneficial interest was founded on the making of contributions to the value of the property; but in *Lloyds Bank plc v. Rosset* [1991] 1 A.C. 107, HL, Lord Bridge of Harwich regarded it as an "outstanding example" of a case founded on a common understanding that the woman was to have a proprietary interest and said that her conduct "fell far short of such conduct as would by itself have supported the claim in the absence of an express representation that she was to have such an interest."

[61] But note P. Clarke, "The Family Home: Intention and Agreement" [1992] *Fam. Law* 72 for the view that this was not an agreement but a disagreement, and that the court converted what was in fact the intention of one party into an agreement.

[62] [1987] 1 F.L.R. 87.

[63] [1992] 1 F.L.R. 229 at 231, *per* Waite J. (and see the further facts stated at p. 110, above).

"limb" of Lord Bridge's speech in *LLoyd's Bank plc v. Rosset*[64] the Court of Appeal in *Drake v. Whipp*[65] founded the constructive trust by which the woman held a one-third interest in the property, but there is reference in the judgment to discussions "at the time of the purchase".[66]

The question of whether there has been an agreement or understanding is essentially one of fact for the trial judge; and it has been said[67] that the primary emphasis accorded by the law to actual discussions[68] between the parties (however imperfectly remembered and however imprecise their terms):—

> " . . . means that the tenderest exchanges of a common law[69] courtship may assume an unforseen significance many years later when they are brought under equity's microscope and subjected to an analysis under which many thousands of pounds of value may be liable to turn on fine questions as to whether the relevant words were spoken in earnest or in dalliance and with or without representational intent. This requires that the express discussions to which the court's initial inquiries will be discussed should be pleaded in the greatest detail, both as to language and to circumstance."

(b) Drawing inferences from conduct

5–012 In the absence of express discussions to support a finding of an agreement or arrangement to share, the court will consider:

> "the conduct of the parties both[70] as the basis from which to infer a common intention to share the property beneficially and as the conduct relied on to give rise to a constructive trust."[71]

---

64 [1991] 1 A.C. 107 at 132–133.

65 [1996] 1 F.L.R. 826.

66 *ibid.* at 829. " . . . she said that when he was going to get the barn that he promised to put her name on the title, that Mr Whipp's evidence was that he told her at the time of the purchase that he would put the matter right and by that he meant that since he was using her money, she would get a percentage of the value of the property in proportion to her contribution". *Sed quaere* why her interest was declared to be one third, when she had contributed over 40% of the purchase price.

67 *H. v. M. (Property: Beneficial Interest)* [1992] 1 F.L.R. 229 at 242–243, *per* Waite J.

68 *Lloyds Bank plc v. Rosset* [1991] 1 A.C. 107 at 132–133, HL *per* Lord Bridge. The common intention means a shared intention, not an intention which each party happened to have in his or her own mind but never communicated to the other: *Springette v. Defoe* [1992] 2 F.L.R. 388 at 393, 395, *per* Dillon and Steyn L.JJ.

69 The citation has to be read in the context of a case dealing with the relationship between a couple who never married, and the allusion is therefore presumably to a so-called common law marriage: see p. 9, above. But precisely the same attention needs to be given to the evidence in cases in which entitlement to property is in issue between spouses; see *e.g., Midland Bank v. Cooke* [1995] 2 F.L.R. 915, CA.

70 The language may appear to suggest that a constructive trust may arise from conduct irrespective of intention.

71 *Lloyds Bank plc v. Rosset* [1991] A.C. 107 at 133 *per* Lord Bridge. It seems that the inference sought to be drawn is that the parties had at the time of acquisition communicated to one another a common intention to acquire the property in specified shares, and that it is not sufficient to show that each thought they were acquiring equal shares without communicating their intention:

The crucial question is the nature of the conduct which will be held sufficient. Here the case-law has adopted a restrictive approach in relation to the existence (as opposed to the *quantum*) of an equitable interest. Where one partner has made a direct contribution to the acquisition costs the court will readily[72] infer an intention that both parties should have a proprietary interest in the family home. A cash contribution to outright purchase,[73] or to the initial deposit[74] will give rise to the necessary inference of intention. Most family homes are now acquired with the assistance of a mortgage. Both the assumption of liability under the mortgage[75] and regular and substantial direct contributions to the mortgage instalments will also suffice.[76] The making of occasional payments seems less likely to lead the court to draw the necessary inference about the parties' intentions.[77]

But what of the wide range of other contributions to family life, some at least of which can be said to be indirectly related to the acquisition of property? Even before the decision in *Rosset,* there had been a number of cases in which such contributions were held to be insufficient to give rise to the inference that a constructive trust had been created. For example, in *Burns v. Burns*[78] the woman took her partner's name, lived with him for 19 years, looked after their children for 17 years, put her earnings into the housekeeping, and bought fixtures and fittings for the house, a washing machine and tumble drier. In *Layton v. Martin*[79] the parties were lovers for 13 years and lived together for five years. The woman provided house-management, love, companionship, and secretarial assistance in his business; as the judge put it, the "services she was expected to supply were, to all intents and purposes, those of a wife". In *Thomas v. Fuller-Brown*[80] the plaintiff designed and built a two-storey extension to the defendant's house, constructed a through lounge, did some electrical and plumbing work, replastered and redecorated the property throughout, landscaped and reorganised the garden, laid a driveway, carried out repairs to the chimney and roof and repointed the gable end, constructed an internal entry hall, and created a newly rebuilt kitchen. He was held to have acquired no beneficial interest in the property.

In *Lloyds Bank plc v. Rosset*[81] Lord Bridge of Harwich (with whom all the

---

see *Springette v. Defoe* [1992] 2 F.L.R. 388, CA, particularly *per* Steyn L.J., at 392–393: "our trust law does not allow property rights to be affected by telepathy." See also *Evans v. Hayward* [1995] 2 F.L.R. 511; *Sed quaere* the common intention as to the *quantum* of shares and the point in time at which this is established: *Midland Bank v. Cooke* [1995] 2 F.L.R. 915, CA.

[72] *Lloyds Bank plc v. Rosset* [1991] 1 A.C. 107 at 133 *per* Lord Bridge of Harwich. See also *Re Densham* [1975] 1 W.L.R. 1519.

[73] As in *Drake v. Whipp* [1996] 1 F.L.R. 826; *quaere* whether this is a resulting or a constructive trust.

[74] In some cases this initial contribution is received by way of gift from a third party: *Halifax Building Society v. Brown* [1996] 1 F.L.R. 103; *Midland Bank plc v. Cooke* [1995] 2 FLR 915.

[75] *The Mortgage Co. v. Shaire* [2000] 1 F.L.R. 973; but see *Carlton v. Goodman* [2002] E.W.C.A. Civ. 545, [2002] 2 F.L.R. 259, CA, where it was held that in the circumstances one of the joint mortgagors was not entitled to a beneficial interest.

[76] *per* Lord Diplock *Gissing v. Gissing* [1971] A.C. 886 at 908, and note *Re Gorman (A Bankrupt)* [1990] 2 F.L.R. 284; see also the cases referred to in nn. 68 and 69, above.

[77] *per* Buckley L.J., *Kowalczuk v. Kowalczuk* [1973] 1 W.L.R. 930 at 935.

[78] [1984] Ch. 317.

[79] [1986] 2 F.L.R. 227 and see *Windeler v. Whitehall* [1990] 2 F.L.R. 505.

[80] [1988] 1 F.L.R. 237.

[81] [1991] A.C. 107.

other Law Lords expressed agreement) went so far as to say that he thought it to be "extremely doubtful" whether contributions other than direct contributions to the purchase price initially or by way of mortgage liability or instalments would justify the inference necessary to the creation of a constructive trust. There would thus appear to be little distinction between the evidence required for the creation of a resulting trust and that for a constructive trust of this second limb of Lord Bridge's speech.[82] In *Rosset* the wife (who was a skilled decorator and painter) spent all her time over a period of seven weeks trying to make a newly-acquired but semi-derelict farmhouse ready for occupation as the family home by Christmas. The House of Lords rejected as "quite untenable" the trial judge's view that her contributions were sufficient evidence of a common intention that she should have a beneficial interest in the property. However, certain reported decisions subsequent to *Rosset* require close consideration if they are to be reconciled with the speech of Lord Bridge.

In *Midland Bank v. Cooke*[83] the couple married in 1971 and moved into a house purchased in the husband's name. The purchase price of £8,500 was raised by a mortgage of £6,450 with the balance made up by the husband's own savings and £1000 in the form of a wedding gift from the husband's parents. The wife, a teacher, made considerable financial contributions to the upkeep of the home and to household expenses. In 1978 the mortgage was replaced with a bank loan granted to the husband to secure a business guarantee. A year later the wife agreed to the mortgage having priority over any interest she might have in the home. In 1981 the couple executed a further charge in joint names. The property was subsequently transferred into their joint names as tenants in common. In 1987 the couple defaulted on payments and the bank sought possession. The county court judge found that the wife's equitable interest took priority over the bank's claim; but he held that her interest was 6.7 per cent of the house's value, being the proportion of the purchase price represented by her half-share of the beneficial interest. But the Court of Appeal held that she was entitled to half the beneficial interest. Waite L.J. stated the law thus:

> "When the court is proceeding, in cases like the present where the partner without legal title has successfully asserted an equitable title through direct contribution, to determine (in the absence of express evidence of intention) what proportions the parties might be assumed to have intended for their beneficial ownership, the duty of the judge is to undertake a survey of the whole course of dealing between the parties relevant to their ownership and occupation of the property and their sharing of its burdens and advantages. That scrutiny will not confine itself to the limited range of direct contributions that are needed to found a beneficial interest in the first place. It will take into consideration all conduct which throws light on the question what shares were intended."[84]

---

[82] *Sed contra: Le Foe v. Le Foe and Woolwich plc; Woolwich plc v. Le Foe and Le Foe* [2001] 2 F.L.R. 970, FD, Nicholas Mostyn Q.C. For criticisms of the case-law adopting a restrictive approach to contributions, see Law Com. Discussion Paper, *Sharing Homes* (July 2002), paras. 2.107–2.108.

[83] [1995] 2 F.L.R. 915; (1995) 4 All E.R. 562, CA.

[84] [1995] 2 F.L.R. 515 at 926.

Drake v. Whipp[85] (in which the couple were unmarried) illustrates the converse in outcome, namely where the *quantum* of the woman's beneficial interest was determined to be a lower proportion of the property's value than that of her initial contribution to the purchase price. A barn was purchased for conversion in the man's name; the woman provided 40 per cent of the purchase price. After conversion, the woman had contributed 19.4 per cent of the total financial costs, as well as 30 per cent of labour, and contributions to household expenses out of her modest income. The judge held that she was entitled to a 19.4 per cent share in the barn. The Court of Appeal held on the basis of a constructive trust that her "fair" share was 33 per cent; the matter was to be approached "broadly, looking at the parties' entire course of conduct".[86] In *The Mortgage Co. v. Shaire,*[87] as part of the settlement of ancillary relief proceedings, the woman's husband transferred his interest in the family home to her and her cohabitant. The woman and her cohabitant jointly assumed liability under a mortgage secured on the home; repayment was primarily made by him. In determining the *quantum* of the equitable interests at 75 per cent for the woman and 25 per cent for the man, Neuberger J. held that in the absence of express agreement at the time of purchase the court had to rely on the contemporary and subsequent conduct of the parties. The primary focus in these cases is the *quantum* rather than the existence of an equitable interest; there was a clear cash contribution to the purchase price (whether by way of deposit, mortgage liability or repayment) satisfying the criterion expounded by Lord Bridge in the second limb of *Rosset*. The emerging principle appears to be that once a claimant has established some beneficial interest by making a contribution to the purchase price,[88] the quantification of that interest is determined by reference to broader considerations of the whole course of dealings between the parties over the course of their relationship, including a range of different contributions to family life. The problems created by this "broad-brush" approach to quantification are discussed below.

2. Has there been detrimental reliance by the claimant?

5–013 Common intention that a property be jointly-owned is necessary to the establishment of a beneficial interest by way of constructive trust, but it is not sufficient *per se;* equity will not assist a volunteer. It must also be shown that the claimant acted to his or her detriment or in some other way significantly altered his or her position in reliance thereon.[89] The question of what conduct will suffice is one of fact.

---

[85] [1996] 1 F.L.R. 826.
[86] *ibid.* at 831.
[87] [2000] 1 F.L.R. 973.
[88] *Sed contra Le Foe v. Le Foe* [2001] 2 F.L.R. 970, Nicholas Mostyn Q.C., which appears to hold this initial contribution unnecessary.
[89] *Gissing v. Gissing* [1991] A.C. 886; *Lloyds Bank v. Rosset* [1991] A.C. 107.

In *Midland Bank plc v. Dobson and Dobson*[90] the court accepted that husband and wife had a common intention to share the beneficial interest in the matrimonial home; but the wife nonetheless failed in her claim to a beneficial interest because there was no evidence that she had acted to her detriment on the basis of that intention. She had made no direct contribution to the acquisition costs or mortgage instalments, and her contributions in buying domestic equipment and in decorating the house were unrelated to the intention that the ownership of the house be shared. In *Lloyds Bank plc v. Rosset* (where the wife's contributions were held to be insufficient to give rise to an inference of intention that the property be jointly owned) Lord Bridge expressed "considerable doubt" as to whether the wife's "trifling" contributions (described above) were capable of constituting the necessary detriment. It was (said Lord Bridge of Harwich[91]) "the most natural thing in the world for any wife . . . to spend all the time she could spare and to employ any skills she might have . . . in doing all she could to accelerate progress of the work". The explanation in both these cases may well be that the court regarded (rightly or wrongly) the contributions to be insignificant (whatever their precise nature).

Some commentators[92] see the authorities as drawing a distinction between cases based on express common intention[93] (discussions) and those based on inferred common intention. In relation to the former, a wide range of contributions may suffice to establish detrimental reliance, including acts not inherently referable to the acquisition of property,[94] provided they are not so trifling as to be negligible. In relation to the latter (common intention inferred from conduct) the test is arguably a stricter one, and it appears that the contribution must be referable to the acquisition of the property. But in reality, detriment has rarely been a real issue in the recent reported case-law. A more significant development has been the willingness of courts to construe the whole course of the parties' dealings with each other at the stage of determining the *quantum* of beneficial interests, which is discussed below.

D. Quantification of the beneficial interest

The existence of a beneficial interest is one issue; its *quantum* is another. **5–014**

---

[90] [1986] 1 F.L.R. 171.

[91] [1991] 1 A.C. 107 at 131.

[92] Howard and Hill, *loc. cit.* n. 1 *supra*, at 363–364, 372.

[93] See also, in the context of an express trust of personalty, *Rowe v. Prance* [1999] 2 F.L.R. 797.

[94] *per* Lord Bridge in *Lloyds Bank v. Rosset* [1991] A.C. 107 at 132; *per* Nourse L.J. in *Grant v. Edwards* [1987] 1 F.L.R. 87 at 100; *Hammond v. Mitchell* [1991] 1 W.L.R. 1127; *Ungurian v. Lesnoff* [1990] 1 Ch. 206; *Stokes v. Anderson* [1991] 1 F.L.R. 391; T. Lawson-Cruttenden and A. Odutola "Constructive Trusts: A Practical Guide" [1995] *Fam. Law* 560 at 561-2.

Express declaration of beneficial interest in the conveyance

The straightforward case is that in which property is conveyed to two or more parties, and contains an express and explicit[95] declaration[96] of the beneficial interests. In the absence of fraud or common mistake such a declaration will normally be conclusive[97] of the parties' beneficial interests. It is thus highly desirable conveyancing practice that such an express declaration be routinely made.[98]

In *Goodman v. Gallant*[99] Mr Gallant and Mrs Goodman negotiated with Mrs Goodman's husband to buy out his interest in the former matrimonial home; and Mr Goodman's conveyance of the fee simple (which had been vested in him alone) was expressed to be to "the purchasers as beneficial joint tenants." The conveyance also incorporated a declaration by Mr Gallant and Mrs Goodman that they were to hold the net proceeds of sale "upon trust for themselves as beneficial joint tenants". Five years later Mrs Goodman claimed that she and her husband had each had a 50 per cent beneficial interest in the property; and that the effect of the conveyance of Mr Goodman's interest to Mr Gallant and herself was simply to deal with Mr Goodman's half share, with the result that she had become beneficially entitled to a three-quarter interest in the house, whilst Mr Gallant had one-quarter. The Court of Appeal rejected this argument: the declaration of trust concluded the question of the respective beneficial interests of the two parties.

Where there is no express declaration of trusts of the beneficial interests in

---

[95] See *Goodman v. Gallant* [1986] 1 F.L.R. 513 at 524. If the conveyance contains a provision dealing with the parties' beneficial interests it is simply a question of construction as to what those words mean: see *Huntingford v. Hobbs* [1993] 1 F.L.R. 736 at 742, *per* Sir Christopher Slade. It is certainly undesirable to rely on the common form declaration in a Land Registry transfer that the survivor of two or more registered proprietors can give a valid receipt for capital monies because such a declaration is not explicit, and does not preclude the possibility that a proprietor may be a nominee for third parties: see *Harwood v. Harwood* [1991] 2 F.L.R. 274, CA; and *Huntingford v. Hobbs* [1993] 1 F.L.R. 736, CA (but compare *Re Gorman (A Bankrupt)* [1990] 2 F.L.R. 284, CA, where the declaration incorporated an assertion that the transferees were entitled for their own benefit thus—so it was held—negativing any third party involvement).

[96] It appears unnecessary that the declaration should have been signed by the parties: *Roy v. Roy* [1996] 1 F.L.R. 541, CA.

[97] But note that there may—apart from cases of fraud and common mistake—be circumstances in which a court will be prepared to rectify a conveyance which does not give effect to the parties' true intentions: see, *e.g. Wilson v. Wilson* [1969] 1 W.L.R. 1470, Buckley J., and *Pink v. Lawrence* (1978) 38 P. & C.R. 98 (both referred to without adverse comment in *Goodman v. Gallant* [1986] 1 F.L.R. 513 at 524, *per* Slade L.J.); *Roy v. Roy* [1996] 1 F.L.R. 541, CA; and see also the other cases referred to in n. 5 on p. 656 of the 4th edition of this work.

[98] See D. Hodson in *The Family Lawyers' Handbook,* n. 8, *supra*. See now Land Registration Rules 1925, rr. 19(1), 98, Sched. 1, as inserted by the Land Registration Rules 1997, r. 2(2). Solicitors have been judicially reminded that it is highly desirable that the conveyance should set out expressly the parties' beneficial interests, whether as beneficial joint tenants or as tenants in common: *Cowcher v. Cowcher* [1972] 1 W.L.R. 425, Bagnall J.; *Bernard v. Josephs* [1982] Ch. 391, *per* Griffiths L.J. at 403; *Walker v. Hall* [1984] F.L.R. 126, CA; *Goodman v. Gallant* [1986] 1 F.L.R. 513 at 524; *Huntingford v. Hobbs* [1993] 1 F.L.R. 736, CA; *Carlton v. Goodman* [2002] E.C.W.A. Civ. 545, [2002] 2 F.L.R. 259, CA. Solicitors who fail to take steps to find out and declare the beneficial interests are failing in their professional duty: *Walker v. Hall* (above); *Springette v. Defoe* [1992] 2 F.L.R. 388, CA.

[99] [1986] 1 F.L.R. 513, CA. This decision resolved a long-standing conflict of opinion between Lord Denning on the one hand (see *Bedson v. Bedson* [1965] 2 Q.B. 666; *Bernard v. Josephs* [1982] Ch. 391) and others (see, *e.g. Leake v. Bruzzi* [1974] 1 W.L.R. 1528; *Wilson v. Wilson* [1963] 1 W.L.R. 601).

the conveyance, the mere fact that the property is in joint names does not does not necessarily[1] indicate that the parties are to be equally entitled.[2] The principles for determining the *quanta* of the beneficial interests in the absence of express declaration are discussed in the next section.

No express declaration of the beneficial interests in the conveyance

5–015 In cases where there is no express declaration in the conveyance of the trusts of the beneficial interests, the court asks first whether there is an express agreement or understanding as to the extent of the beneficial interests. If there is no such express agreement, the court will look to the parties' conduct to see what intention may be inferred as to the proportions in which the equitable interests are to be held. Whether the legal estate is held in joint names or one name is of significance,[3] but not conclusive. Recent case-law has cast considerable doubt on the traditional distinction drawn in earlier editions of this book between resulting trusts[4] and implied trusts in the quantification process. It is at least arguable that a single approach now applies to all cases where it is necessary to determine the respective beneficial interests of two persons living in a house together, whether as man and wife or in a close relationship, succinctly summed up by Neuberger J. in *The Mortgage Co. v. Shaire*.[5]

5–016 *(i) Is there evidence (written or oral) of express agreement as to the shares in which the equitable interests are held?* If so, that is normally conclusive[6]; a court will depart from such agreement only for very good reason, such as a subsequent renegotiation or evidence of a variation or cancellation.

The court may find that the agreement was for equal ownership. Thus in *Savill v. Goodall*[7] the Court of Appeal held that the trial judge had been wrong to assume that the shares of the parties could only be ascertained by reference to their contributions in all the circumstances. The court must first ask itself whether there has been an agreement, arrangement or understanding between the parties[8]; and if so the beneficial interests would be governed by what they had decided. No further inquiry was appropriate. On the facts, the parties had acquired the property with the intention that it be their joint property; and if "an ordinary, sensible couple, without more, declare an intention to own their home jointly, they can only be taken to intend that they should own it equally." Other examples where the court found an agreement for joint-ownership are *Grant v.*

---

[1] Although it may be one of the factors to be taken into account; see *e.g. Huntingford v. Hobbs* [1993] 1 F.L.R. 736 at 743, *per* Sir Christopher Slade.

[2] See *e.g. Crisp v. Mullings* (1976) 239 E.G. 119; *Bernard v. Josephs* [1982] Ch. 391; *Harwood v. Harwood* [1991] 2 F.L.R. 274 at 291–292, CA; *The Mortgage Co. v. Shaire* [2000] 1 F.L.R. 973.

[3] *Lloyds Bank plc v. Rosset* [1991] 1 A.C. 107 at 128D and 159F; *Stokes v. Anderson* [1991] 1 F.L.R. 391 at 394 D - E; *The Mortgage Co. v. Shaire* [2000] 1 F.L.R. 973 at 980.

[4] R. O'Hagen, "Quantifying Interests Under Resulting Trusts" (1997) 60 *L.Q.R.* 420.

[5] [2000] 1 F.L.R. 973 at 979–980.

[6] *Lloyds Bank plc v. Rosset* [1991] 1 A.C. 107 at 132F and 163F.

[7] [1993] 1 F.L.R. 755, CA.

[8] *i.e.* in accordance with the principles laid down in *Lloyds Bank plc v. Rosset* [1991] 1 A.C. 107 at 132, above.

Edwards[9] and (in the context of an express trust of personal property) *Rowe v. Prance*.[10] However, the court's reasoning process is not always very clear, and cases with apparently similar facts may produce different outcomes. In *Eves v. Eves*[11] the court held that a woman who had lived with a man for some years was only entitled to one-quarter of the sale proceeds of the property. As Sir Nicolas Browne-Wilkinson subsequently said in *Grant v. Edwards*,[12] the court in *Eves v. Eves* "felt able to find a lesser beneficial interest" than the one-half which might have been thought to be what the parties had intended "without explaining the legal basis on which it did so." In *The Mortgage Co. v. Shaire*[13] Neuberger J. was unable to find sufficient evidence of express agreement from conversations or in the terms of a transfer agreement.

5–017 *(ii) Where there is no express agreement the court must rely on the whole course of conduct between the parties, contemporaneous with the purchase and subsequent to it, to determine the parties' intentions as to the shares in which the beneficial interests are held.* This broad-brush approach is the product of recent case-law[14] which has posed considerable challenges to more orthodox methods of determining the *quanta* of beneficial interests.

The respective financial contributions are of relevance in "illuminating the common intention as to the extent of the beneficial interest."[15] It is arguable that the extent of financial contributions is now less decisive than it appeared to be in earlier case-law. The more traditional authorities adopted a well-established approach to cases classified as examples of resulting trust, applying the principle that a person who advances the purchase money is entitled to the property[16]; and the person who advances part of the purchase money is entitled to a proportionate part of the property.[17] Thus in *Springette v. Defoe*[18] it was agreed that a woman should be treated as having contributed 75 per cent and the man 25 per cent of the purchase price of the house in which they lived together; and the Court of Appeal held that (since there was no evidence that they had agreed between themselves on some other division) their beneficial interests were 75 per cent for the woman and 25 per cent for the man.[19] Yet even the application of this apparently simple principle was made difficult by the contemporary realities of home-buying; the situation in which a couple simply put up cash to meet the purchase price of the prop-

---

9 [1986] Ch. 683.

10 [1999] 2 F.L.R. 787, ChD (discussed in section XII, below).

11 [1975] 1 W.L.R. 1338, CA; a case which was expressly classified in *Lloyds Bank plc v. Rosset* as being one in which there had been an arrangement between the parties, rather than as one in which the court inferred the existence of an agreement from the surrounding circumstances.

12 [1986] Ch. 638 at 657.

13 [2000] 1 F.L.R. 973.

14 *Midland Bank v. Cooke* [1995] 2 F.L.R. 515; *Drake v. Whipp* [1996] 1 F.L.R. 826; *The Mortgage Co. v. Shaire* [2001] 1 F.L.R. 973.

15 *per* Nourse L.J. in *Stokes v. Anderson* [1991] 1 F.L.R. 391 at 400B; cited by Neuberger J. in *The Mortgage Co. v. Shaire* [2000] 1 F.L.R. 973 at 980.

16 *Dyer v. Dyer* (1788) 2 Cox 92 at 93.

17 *Pettitt v. Pettitt* [1970] A.C. 777 at 814; *Walker v. Hall* [1984] F.L.R. 126 at 133, *per* Dillon L.J.; *Huntingford v. Hobbs* [1993] 1 F.L.R. 736 at 744, *per* Sir Christopher Slade.

18 [1992] 2 F.L.R. 388, CA; *cf. Evans v. Hayward* [1995] 2 F.L.R. 511.

19 The same approach was adopted in cases involving other family relationships: *Sekhon v. Alissa* 1989] 2 F.L.R. 94 (mother and daughter); *Dewar v. Dewar* [1975] 1 W.L.R. 1532 (brother).

erty are relatively uncommon and in many cases a substantial part of the purchase money will be provided by a bank or building society by way of a mortgage.[20] Such contributions might be regarded as a contribution to the purchase price, such as will found a claim by way of resulting trust; but they might equally be regarded as a direct financial contribution such as will—in the absence of agreement or understanding—justify the drawing of an inference about the parties' intentions.[21] If the view is taken that the mortgage should be regarded as a contribution to the purchase price it is—assuming the traditional resulting trust doctrine is to be applied—crucially important to know whether the value of that contribution to the purchase price is to be taken as the whole amount of the mortgage debt or whether the value of the contribution is to be restricted to the amounts of the payments actually made. The authorities are difficult to reconcile.[22]

However, a number of recent decisions challenge both the classic categorisation of informal trusts and the orthodox approach to quantification of the beneficial interests.[23] It is unclear whether these cases are correctly characterised as examples of resulting or of constructive trust of the second limb in *Rosset*. If they are the former, then it would appear that there will be few cases in which the purely arithmetical approach adopted in the conventional resulting trust cases will now be applied. If they are the latter, then a distinction[24] is now to be drawn between the initial establishment of a beneficial interest and its subsequent quantification. What emerges—provided a claimant can surmount the stringent test laid down in the *Rosset* case[25] and is able to establish an entitlement to some beneficial interest—is a subsequent broad-brush approach to quantification which draws inferences as to the parties' probable common understanding about the ownership of the property from the whole course of dealings between them. As a result, the quantification of the respective beneficial interests will not necessarily correspond to the proportion of the initial cash contributions to the purchase. Contributions of the "indirect" kind held in the *Rosset* case to be insufficient to give rise to an inference of common intention at the initial stage of

---

[20] It has been suggested that the discount allowed to a local authority tenant under the "right to buy" legislation constitutes a cash contribution equivalent to the amount of the discount (see *Springette v. Defoe* [1992] 2 F.L.R. 388, CA, particularly *per* Steyn L.J. at 395), but this is open to question: see *Evans v. Hayward* [1995] 2 F.L.R. 511, *per* Staughton L.J.

[21] See above; and note *Evans v. Hayward* [1995] 2 F.L.R. 511. In *Costello v. Costello* [1996] 1 F.L.R. 805, CA, a son contributed the money necessary to enable his parents to exercise their right to buy; but the outcome of the case (that his mother was tenant for life under the Settled Land Act (1925) depended on the construction of a deed of trust they had executed. No further settlements under the Settled Land Act can be created, either formally or informally, after the coming into force of the Trusts of Land and Appointment of Trustees Act 1996. For circumstances in which it was held not to be intended that a joint mortgagor acquire a beneficial interest, see *Carlton v. Goodman* [2002] 2 F.L.R. 259, CA.

[22] Compare the differing views expressed in the judgments in *Huntingford v. Hobbs* (above); and see *Harwood v. Harwood* (above); *Passee v. Passee* (above); *Marsh v. von Sternberg* (above); *Young v. Young* [1984] F.L.R. 375, CA; *Walker v. Hall* (above); *Bernard v. Josephs* (above); and *Crisp v. Mullings* (1976) 239 E.G. 119. In *Springette v. Defoe* [1992] 2 F.L.R. 388 the parties were treated as having agreed that they should be treated as each contributing half the principal secured by a joint mortgage. But see *The Mortage Co. v. Shaire* [2000] 1 F.L.R. 973.

[23] The new broad-brush approach to quantification described in this section has greatly reduced the need for equitable accounting, discussion of which has therefore been omitted from this edition.

[24] *Sed contra Le Foe v. Le Foe* [2001] 2 F.L.R. 970.

[25] *Lloyds Bank plc v. Rosset* [1991] A.C. 107, HL.

founding common intention that property be jointly owned are nevertheless relevant at the subsequent stage of quantification of the beneficial interests. It has been said[26] that the court can properly take any relevant evidence into account at the quantification stage,[27] including the making of indirect contributions, for example by way of contributions to household expenses, which would be insufficient at the initial stage. Moreover, it appears[28] that the court can take into account contributions made over the whole period of ownership; and the Court of Appeal has accepted that the agreement which is inferred could (and perhaps often will) be to divide the shares in such proportions as seem equitable at the date of sale.[29] The distinction between entitlement and quantification has received a mixed reception, on the one hand being criticised for its doctrinal confusion[30] and its capacity to produce illogical results,[31] on the other being welcomed as a liberalisation.[32] Conceptually, the new broad-brush approach remains founded on inferred intention and is thus wholly different from saying that the court (under the so-called remedial constructive trust doctrine) imposes a trust to give effect to what would be fair and reasonable, but in practice the result may be not altogether dissimilar.[33] The new approach may be illustrated by a number of decisions.

5–018 In some cases where the broad brush approach to quantification has been applied the legal title has been in the sole name of one of the parties. The facts of *Midland Bank v. Cooke*,[34] have been described earlier in this Chapter[35]; for present purposes it will be recalled that the wife contributed only 6.7 per cent of the purchase price but the Court of Appeal held her entitlement to the beneficial interest was equal to that of her husband. Once it had been established that some beneficial interest had been acquired by both parties the court was entitled to draw inferences as to the parties' probable common understanding about the ownership of the property.[36] This involved a survey of the whole course of

---

26 *Grant v. Edwards* [1986] Ch. 638, and see *Gissing v. Gissing* [1971] A.C. 886 at 908–909, HL; *Bernard v. Josephs* (1983) 4 F.L.R. 178 at 188, *per* Griffiths L.J.; *Passee v. Passee* [1988] 1 F.L.R. 263, CA; *Springette v. Defoe* [1992] 2 F.L.R. 388 at 396, *per* Sir Christopher Slade.

27 Many cases decided before the decision in *Lloyds Bank plc v. Rosset* attached great significance to contributions made after the acquisition, *e.g.* by carrying out heavy manual improvement work: see *e.g. Eves v. Eves* (p. 118, above) and *Cooke v. Head* [1972] 1 W.L.R. 518, CA. (where a woman "worked very hard with her hands, did heavy work, including the use of a sledgehammer and a wheelbarrow loaded with heavy material", *per* Karminski L.J.), *Midland Bank v. Cooke* [1995] 2 F.L.R. 915, CA suggests that such contributions would be highly material in quantifying a beneficial interest: see below.

28 *Passee v. Passee* [1988] 1 F.L.R. 263 at 270–272.

29 See *Bernard v. Josephs* [1983] 4 F.L.R. 178 at 188, *per* Griffiths L.J.; *Passee v. Passee* [1988] 1 F.L.R. 263, CA: *Springette v. Defoe* [1992] 2 F.L.R. 388 at 396, *per* Sir Christopher Slade; *Huntingford v. Hobbs* [1993] 1 F.L.R. 736, CA. (where the intention of the parties was held to have been in proportion to the woman's cash contribution to the purchase of the family home and the man's liability under a mortgage, *i.e.* 61% and 39%).

30 N. Glover and P. Todd (1996) 16 *Legal Studies* at 340–341; Battersby [1996] 8 *Child & Family Law Quarterly* 261. See also Law Com. Discussion Paper *Sharing Homes* (July 2002), para. 2.109.

31 Wragg "Constructive Trusts and The Unmarried Couple" [1996] *Fam. Law* 298 at 300.

32 Lawson-Cruttenden and Odutola [1995] *Fam. Law* 560 at 563.

33 In *Drake v. Whipp* [1996] 1 F.L.R. 826 the assessment of the woman's entitlement was said to be "fair".

34 [1995] 2 F.L.R. 915.

35 See page 121.

36 *Gissing v. Gissing* [1971] A.C. 886, *per* Lord Diplock.

dealing between the parties relevant to their ownership and occupation of the property and their sharing of its burdens and advantages; and that scrutiny would not be confined to the limited range of acts of direct contribution of the sort needed to found a beneficial interest in the first place. Moreover, the fact that the parties had stated that they had not made any agreement about the ownership of the property was not conclusive: it would be wrong to put someone beyond the pale of equity's assistance in formulating a fair presumed basis for the sharing of the beneficial interests simply because they had been honest enough to admit that they had never given ownership a thought.[37] The decision received a mixed reception from commentators,[38] some criticising it as doctrinally heterodox and productive of anomalies, others welcoming it as liberalisation of the law. The view[39] that different criteria apply to the threshold condition ("is there a beneficial interest at all?") and to the question of quantifying that interest may seem somewhat artificial. It is certainly difficult to understand how a women who has given 18 years of her life to caring for her partner, his home and their children should be entitled to nothing,[40] whereas another (in all respects in identical circumstances, save that her partner's parents had paid £100 towards the deposit on a house) should be entitled to half the proceeds of sale. In *Drake v. Whipp*[41] (the facts of which have been described earlier in this Chapter[42]) the woman's contribution to the pre-conversion purchase price of property in the man's name was 40 per cent and her financial contributions overall were 19.4 per cent; looking at the parties' entire course of conduct, the Court of Appeal held that her entitlement was 33 per cent. It is not easy to determine how this *quantum* was arrived at on facts which appear similar to those in *Midland Bank plc v. Cooke*; the broad-brush approach is inevitably conducive to unpredictability of outcome.

The new approach to quantification of the beneficial interests may also be applied where the legal estate is in joint names. In *The Mortgage Co. v. Shaire*[43] (again, see earlier in this Chapter for the facts[44]) joint legal title and joint assumption of mortgage liability by the woman and her cohabitant were by no means conclusive of the *quanta* of the parties' respective beneficial entitlements. Looking to the whole course of conduct in the absence of express agreement, including the particular circumstances of the ancillary relief settlement between the woman and her former husband from which the property in question was

---

[37] The Court of Appeal distinguished *Springette v. Defoe* [1992] 2 F.L.R. 388, CA on the basis that it was an example of part pooling of resources by a middle-aged couple already established in life whose house-purchasing arrangements were clearly regarded as having the same formality as if they had been the subject of a joint venture or commercial partnership.

[38] Battersby, "How not to judge the quantum (and priority) of a share in the family home" (1996) 8 *Child & Family Law Quarterly* 261; D. Wragg, "Constructive Trusts and the Unmarried Couple" [1996] *Fam. Law* 298; Pawlowski, "*Midland Bank v. Cooke*—A New Heresy?" [1996] *Fam. Law* 484; N. Glover and P Todd, "The Myth of Common Intention" (1996) 16 *Legal Studies* 325 at 340.

[39] Not adhered to in *Le Foe v. Le Foe* [2000] 2 F.L.R. 970.

[40] See *Burns v. Burns* [1984] Ch. 317, CA.

[41] [1996] 1 F.L.R. 826.

[42] See para. 5–012.

[43] [2000] 1 F.L.R. 973.

[44] See para. 5–012.

derived, Neuberger J. held that the woman's beneficial entitlement was 75 per cent and her cohabitant's 25 per cent.

While the court may on particular facts find that the beneficial interests are held equally, this will usually be as a result either of a finding of actual agreement or an inference of intention from conduct, rather than by application of the maxim "equality is equity",[45] which remains a last resort.[46]

IV. CLAIMS FOUNDED ON CONTRACT

5–019 A couple may decide to regulate their affairs in relation to family property by contract; and in appropriate cases the court may be able to infer the existence of a legally enforceable agreement between them. In order to establish a contract the following elements must be established:

(i) A genuine meeting of minds between the parties—*i.e.* an offer and an acceptance.
(ii) The parties' intention to create a legally enforceable relationship.[47]
(iii) Terms of the agreement which are sufficiently precise. There is a relationship here with the last rule: lack of precision may indicate that a legally binding agreement is not envisaged.[48]
(iv) Unless the agreement is contained in a deed or document under seal, there must be consideration.[49]
(v) The contract must not be affected by fraud, duress or undue influence.
(iv) Any additional formal requirement prescribed by law in respect of the subject-matter of the contract must be satisfied.
(vii) The terms which it is sought to enforce must not be illegal or contrary to public policy.

Of these general rules, (ii), (vi) and (vii) are of particular significance in the context of agreements relating to family property and require further explanation.

1. *Intention to create legal relations*

5–020 Older authorities (which now appear to come from a different world) suggested that a distinction could be drawn between intentions during the existence of a domestic relationship and those on its breakdown. If the parties were not

[45] *H. v. M. (Property: Beneficial Interest)* [1992] 1 F.L.R. 229 at 239, *per* Waite J.; and see the cases cited in p. 653, n. 90 of the 4th edition of this work.
[46] It was applied in the alternative in *Rowe v. Prance* [1999] 2 F.L.R 787, Nicholas Warren Q.C. having found an express agreement of equal ownership.
[47] *Jones v. Padavatton* [1969] 1 W.L.R. 328.
[48] *Gould v. Gould* [1970] 1 Q.B. 275.
[49] See *Hemmens v. Wilson Browne (A Firm)* [1994] 2 F.L.R. 101 (the facts have been given in Chap. 4, above) for a case in which an agreement intended to be legally binding failed to have any legal effect for this and other reasons.

living in amity or are separated, or about to separate, it was readily presumed that they intended to create legal relations[50] or at least there was no presumption against their having intended to create such relationship.[51] But what of the situation where the relationship was current? Was it to be presumed that parties did not intend to create legal relations while emotionally involved? Two decisions may be contrasted.

> In *Tanner v. Tanner*[52] the male partner purchased a house for occupation by the defendant and the twin daughters of their relationship. The defendant moved into the house; but subsequently the parties' relationship broke down, and the plaintiff claimed possession on the basis that the defendant was only a bare licensee under a licence which he had revoked. The Court of Appeal held that there was an implied contractual licence under the terms of which the defendant was to be entitled to occupy the house so long as the children were of school age, or until some other circumstance arose which would make it unreasonable for her to retain possession.

On the other hand, in *Layton v. Martin* and Others[53]:—

> A woman accepted a man's offer that if she would live with him he would give her what emotional security he could, plus financial security on his death. She failed in an action against his estate after his death because the court refused to find that there had been any intention to create a legally enforceable contract—a decision which seems harsh on the facts.[54]

An assumption against intention to create legal relations by parties in an ongoing relationship must now be called in question by the policy adopted by successive governments in recent years of promoting resolution of family responsibilities by private agreement. It is possible that in the future contracts will assume centre stage in the regulation of financial responsibilities in relationships both married and unmarried. Public policy in this area is discussed below.

2. *Formal requirements for contracts relating to land*

5–021 If the contract relates to an interest in land, there are two statutory provisions which may affect its enforceability. First, a document which is a "contract by an estate owner . . . to convey or create a legal estate" must be protected as a Class C (iv) Land Charge,[55] otherwise it will be void against a purchaser of a legal estate for money or money's worth.[56] However, this provision will rarely be in point because the agreement will usually only relate to a transfer of an

---

[50] *Merritt v. Merritt* [1970] 1 W.L.R. 1211 at 1213, *per* Lord Denning M.R.
[51] *per* Widgery L.J., *ibid.* at 1214.
[52] [1975] 1 W.L.R. 1346.
[53] [1986] 2 F.L.R. 227.
[54] See also *Horrocks v. Foray* [1976] 1 W.L.R. 230 where again a woman claimant failed.
[55] Land Charges Act 1972, s.2(4).
[56] *ibid.* s.4(5).

equitable interest in the land; and even if the agreement is to transfer a legal estate, this provision would not affect its enforceability as between the parties.

Secondly, the Law of Property (Miscellaneous Provisions) Act 1989[57] imposes a general requirement that a contract for the disposition of land or any interest in land should be in writing.[58] This rule replaces the much more flexible rule formerly contained in the Law of Property Act 1925, which merely required such a contract to be evidenced in writing, and permitted contracts not so evidenced to be enforced if the plaintiff could show an act of part performance on his part such as would render it inequitable for the defendant to rely on the lack of formality. The objective of section 2 of the 1989 Act was to introduce certainty where uncertainty existed before.[59] At first glance it might appear that the 1989 Act had done much to restrict reliance on informal contracts as a source of entitlement to property. Would a claim of the type brought in *Tanner v. Tanner, supra,* now be invalidated?[60] However, section 2(5) declares that "nothing in this section affects the creation or operation of resulting, implied or constructive trusts". The implications of this provision are now beginning to manifest themselves in the case-law—in particular, a claimant who could before the introduction of the legislation have relied on an informal contract[61] may now on appropriate facts assert an interest by estoppel. Hence the result may in many cases be no different.

In *Yaxley v. Gotts and Gotts*[62] a builder made an oral agreement with the defendants that, in return for his conversion and management work in relation to a house to be divided into six flats, he would own two of the flats. The parties eventually had disagreements and the plaintiff was excluded from the property. He claimed a long lease and rents of the two flats, relying on the oral agreement or representations in reliance on which he had expended money and carried out work. The judge held that he had a good claim by virtue of the doctrine of proprietary estoppel. The defendants appealed on the ground that the judge should have held the oral agreement void under section 2 (1) of the Law of Property (Miscellaneous Provisions) Act 1989, and that the doctrine of proprietary estoppel could not operate to save it. The Court of Appeal[63] dismissed the appeal, holding that the facts justified a finding that a constructive trust had arisen whereby the plaintiff was entitled to a long leasehold interest. On the authority of *Lloyds Bank plc v. Rosset*[64] there had been an agreement in reliance on which the plaintiff had acted to his detriment. Beldam L.J. held that the plaintiff's interest could equally well be claimed under proprietary estoppel. The

[57] See the preceding Law Com. No. 164 *Formalities and Contracts for the Sale Of Land* and earlier Working Paper 92.

[58] s.2. For an analysis of the effect of this provision see *United Bank of Kuwait plc v. Sahib* [1995] 2 All E.R. 973, Chadwick J.; and as to what constitutes an "interest in land" see *Pitt v. P.H.H. Asset Management Ltd* [1993] 4 All E.R. 961, CA.

[59] *per* Phillips L.J. in *Bank of Kuwait v. Sahib* [1997] Ch. 107 at 143–144; [1996] 3 W.L.R. 372; [1996] 2 F.L.R. 666, CA.

[60] [1975] 1 W.L.R. 1346 (assuming, without deciding, that *Tanner* involved a contract relating to an "interest" in land in terms of s. 2(1) of the 1989 Act).

[61] *Tanner v. Tanner* [1975] 1 W.L.R. 1346.

[62] [1999] 2 F.L.R. 941; [2000] Ch. 162; [1999] 3 W.L.R. 1217; [2000] 1 All E.R. 711, CA.

[63] Beldam, Robert Walker and Clarke L.JJ.

[64] [1991] A.C. 107.

implications of this decision remain to be further explored in future case-law. Would a court hold that an express contract over land comes within the exception? If not, would a plaintiff with a specifically enforceable contract be—somewhat paradoxically—in a worse position, in that the court would feel that the express provision of the 1989 Act would prevent it from holding that a constructive trust arose?[65]

3. *Rules of public policy*

5–022 Contractual resolution of the financial consequences of relationship breakdown (whether of marriage or unmarried cohabitation) appeals in principle to the interests of party autonomy, individual responsibility and diversity. The circumstances of family relationships are so diverse that a particular rather than a generalised solution has obvious attraction; moreover, such contracts may, if carefully drawn, achieve clarity in the definition of legal rights. But inherent problems are also readily apparent. Private contracts permit parties to contract out of a general regime which (particularly if statutory) is expressive of State paternalism and community norms; a system of unqualified contractual freedom will not necessarily meet the objectives of achieving economic justice between parties on relationship breakdown, nor of protecting the public purse. Thus the essential conflict lies between State paternalism and party autonomy.

Current English law is ambivalent in its attitude towards regulation of financial consequences of relationship breakdown by private contract. In recent years there has been a heavy promotion both by courts and governments of a "settlement culture"[66] in the resolution of financial disputes on divorce, and parties are discouraged from proceeding to full litigation and trial. New procedural rules governing financial proceedings on divorce encourage pre-trial settlement by agreement. However, a number of policy rules are to the opposite effect. It is, for example, still the law that a married couple cannot by contract preclude the court from exercising its jurisdiction or make financial provision and property adjustment orders.[67] The public interest in preserving the public purse has long held primacy of position; the court's jurisdiction to intervene and enforce personal financial obligation where resources permit has been jealously guarded. It is true that in exercising its statutory powers to reallocate property on or after divorce the court will give appropriate consideration—either under the rubric of "all the circumstances" in section 25(1) of the Matrimonial Causes Act 1973, or as conduct which it would be inequitable to disregard for the purposes of section 25(2)(g)—of any agreement about financial matters which has not subsequently been embodied in a court order.[68] Nevertheless, the *ex post facto* deter-

---

[65] See the discussion of *Lloyds Bank plc v. Carrick and Carrick* [1996] 2 F.L.R. 600; [1996] 4 All E.R. 630 by Robert Walker L.J. in *Yaxley v. Gotts and Gotts* [1999] 2 F.L.R. 941 at 954. See I. Moore, "Proprietary Estoppel, Constructive Trusts and s 2 of the Law of Property (Misc Provisions) Act 1989" (2000) 63 *M.L.R.* 912.

[66] Discussed further in Chap. 14.

[67] See *Hyman v. Hyman* [1929] A.C. 601; *Sutton v. Sutton* [1984] Ch. 184.

[68] For an illustration of the (substantial) weight accorded to a separation agreement, see *G. v. G. (Financial Provision: Separation Agreement)* [2000] 2 F.L.R. 18, F.D.

mination of an agreement's significance in subsequent court proceedings has been described by judicial authority[69] as the worst of all worlds. In short, the only secure method under current English law of ensuring the conclusive effect of an agreement about the financial consequences of divorce is to have the agreement embodied in a consent order.[70] Here the courts have consistently articulated the paternalistic role for the State by declaring that it is the order of the court and not the agreement *per se* which is operative and binding upon the parties, and in claiming—in principle and theory if more questionably in practice—the obligation of judicial scrutiny of the terms of an agreement embodied in a consent order. The Court of Appeal in *Xydhias v. Xydhias*[71] emphasised that ordinary contractual principles do not determine financial proceedings following divorce. Yet the real extent of scrutiny of consent orders is open to doubt, given the very real pressures of crowded lists and timetables, particularly at county court level.[72]

Under the current law, pre-nuptial contracts[73] are not binding as contracts between spouses, but are a consideration to be taken into account by a court in the exercise of its discretion in ancillary relief on divorce, whether as part of "all the circumstances" in section 25 of the Matrimonial Causes Act 1973 or as conduct under section 25(2)(g).[74] The weight to be given to the existence and to the terms of the contract will depend entirely on the circumstances of the case, even where it was entered into by nationals of an overseas country in which such contracts are binding.[75] Pre-nuptial contracts were addressed in the Government's Green Paper *Supporting Families* released in 1998. The proposal to give pre-nuptial contracts greater validity in English law was located in a Chapter entitled "Strengthening Marriage", but there was no attempt to set the issue in the context of competing values of State paternalism and party autonomy. The paper made the questionable assumption that providing greater security on property matters in this way could make it more likely that some people would marry rather than live together.[76] It proposed six safeguards designed to protect the interests of a party to the agreement who is economically weaker and the interests of children,[77] although these were not divided into those pertaining to initial validity and those permitting subsequent variation of terms by a court. The

---

[69] *per* Hoffmann L.J. in *Pounds v. Pounds* [1994] 1 F.L.R. 775 at 791.

[70] Matrimonial Causes Act 1973, s. 33A.

[71] [1999] 1 F.L.R. 683; [1999] All E.R. 386, CA.

[72] See the discussion in Chap. 14 at pp. 323–324.

[73] See Harcus "Prenuptial Agreements" [1997] *Fam. Law* 669; Barton, "Premarital Contracts and Equal Shares on Divorce" [1998] *Fam. Law* 423; Milligan, "Prenuptials Beware" [1999] *Fam. Law* 483; Creamer, "Prenuptial Agreements: An Idea Whose Time has Come?" [2000] *Fam. Law* 359; Hooker, "Prenuptial Contracts and Safeguards" [2001] *Fam. Law* 57; Leadcrammer, "Pre-Nuptial Contracts—New Safeguards, New Problems?" [2001] *Fam. Law* 295; Bruce, "Premarital Agreements following White v. White" [2001] *Fam. Law* 305.

[74] *M. v. M. (Financial Provision: Pre-Nuptial Agreement)* [2002] 1 F.L.R. 654, F.D.

[75] *F. v. F. (Ancillary Relief:Substantial Assets)* [1995] 2 F.L.R. 45 at 66 *per* Thorpe L.J.; *M. v. M. (Financial Provision: Pre-Nuptial Agreement)* [2002] 1 F.L.R. 654, Connell J.; but contrast with the approach of Wilson J. in *S. v. S. (Divorce: Staying Proceedings)* [1997] 2 F.L.R. 100 at 102; [1997] 1 W.L.R. 1200 at 1202.

[76] para. 4.22.

[77] para. 4.23.

suggested vitiating factors were lack of independent legal advice, non-disclosure, significant injustice, and the existence of a child of the family, whether or not that child was alive or a child of the family at the time the agreement was made. Arguably the last two of these grounds of invalidity were too wide[78] and had the potential to reduce the attraction of contractual resolution. At the time of writing there appear to be no government plans to implement these proposals. In *M. v. M. (Financial Provision: Pre-Nuptial Agreement)*[79] Connell J. questioned whether such pre-nuptial agreements can be seen as diminishing the importance of the marriage contract, now that divorce is so commonplace.[80] However, his Lordship regarded the case as a vivid illustration of the problems with which pre-nuptial contracts are beset. The wife had signed notwithstanding legal advice that the terms were unfair to her, since she was pregnant at the time and wanted marriage. On the other hand the husband would not have entered his second marriage without such an agreement. The wife was awarded a lump sum of £875,000 (excluding child maintenance) whereas the terms of the pre-nuptial agreement had purported to limit her entitlement to £275,000. Notwithstanding the limited effect of pre-nuptial agreements in the law of England and Wales, the Solicitors' Family Law Association has published a book of precedents to assist practitioners who are requested to draw them up.[81]

Contracts between the unmarried ("cohabitation contracts") attract no general principle of invalidity, although this may simply reflect English law's laissez-faire attitude to the regulation of unmarried relationships rather than to any considered promotion of party autonomy. There is a general rule that a contract "founded on an immoral consideration" or likely to prejudice the status of marriage will not be enforced. Although at one time a contract between a man and a woman to live together[82] might have been regarded as contrary to public policy,[83] it is inconceivable that the English courts would today strike down an agreement regulating the financial rights and duties of a cohabiting couple.[84] Case law gives no support to any broad rule that such contracts are outside the

---

[78] For critiques of the proposals, see *e.g.* Hooker, "Pre-Nuptial Contracts and Safeguards" [2001] *Fam. Law* 57.

[79] [2002] 1 F.L.R. 654, F.D.

[80] *ibid.* at para. [21].

[81] *Separation and Premarital Agreements Precedents* (SFLA, 2000); for snapshot research on their use, see [2001] *Fam. Law* 725.

[82] See the assertion by Lord Wright in *Fender v. St John Mildmay* [1938] A.C. 1 at 42; and for examples of such contracts as promoted in the U.S. see L.J. Weitzman, *The Marriage Contract: Spouses, Lovers and the Law* (1981), Chap. 12, *e.g.* "We recognise the central importance of sex in human relationships and commit ourselves to putting time and creative energy into realising our sexual potential" [but] "we do not intend that our love and commitment to each other should exclude other relationships in work, friendship or sex"; and many further examples are given in the empirical study of intimate contracts contained in the Appendix. H.D. Krause, *Family Law* (1995), Chaps. 6 and 7 contains a useful account of the relevance in the U.S. of contract to both marital and extra-marital relationships.

[83] See generally J.L. Dwyer, "Immoral Contracts" (1977) 93 *L.Q.R.* 386; and see also S. Poulter, "Cohabitation Contracts and Public Policy" (1974) 124 *New Law Journal* 999 at 1034.

[84] For discussion see C. Barton, *Cohabitation Contracts* (1985); M. Parry, *The Law Relating to Cohabitation* (3rd ed., 1993).

law,[85] and books of legal precedents are available[86] to guide those who wish to enter into them and their legal representatives (although the extent to which such agreements are made in practice is unclear). Similarly, in the United States and elsewhere in the common law world the old rules have been restrictively interpreted.[87] The Committee of Ministers of the Council of Europe recommended that "contracts relating to property between persons living together as an unmarried couple, or which regulated matters concerning their property either during their relationship or when their relationship has ceased, should not be considered invalid solely because they have been concluded under these conditions".[88] The Civil Partnerships Bill introduced in the House of Lords by Lord Lester on January 10, 2002 (discussed in Chapter 9) would make provision for a property agreement setting out the partners respective entitlements to specified property.[89]

V. ESTOPPEL

5–023 The doctrine of estoppel prevents a person from asserting strict legal rights when it would be unconscionable or unjust to do so.[90] For many years,[91] the doctrine has recognised[92] that if a party to a relationship incurs expenditure or does some other act to his or her detriment in the belief, encouraged by the other, that he or she already owns or would be given some proprietary interest, an equity will arise to have the expectations which have been encouraged made good so far as may fairly be done between the parties. Estoppel thus enables the court to go some way in giving effect to a party's reasonable assumptions (even if they are not shared by the other partner) if to do otherwise would be unfair or unjust, without going as far as to introduce a general doctrine of remedial constructive trust whereby the courts would have discretion to do whatever they might consider to be just or reasonable in the circumstances of every individual case. The doctrine is of particular utility when one party moves into property owned by

---

[85] Note that in *Heghbiston Establishment v. Heyman* (1978) 36 P. & C.R. 351 the court refused to follow earlier authority (*Upfill v. Wright* [1911] 1 K.B. 506) rendering a lease subject to forfeiture on the basis that allowing cohabitants to reside constituted immoral user.

[86] D. Lush, H. Wood and D. Bishop, *Cohabitation: Law, Practice and Precedents* (2nd ed, Family Law, 2001).

[87] See notably *Marvin v. Marvin* 557 P. 2d 106 (1976) (USA); and *Seidler v. Schallhofeer* [1982] 2 N.S.W.L.R. 80, (N.S.W. Court of Appeal). H.D. Krause, *Family Law* (1995), pp. 73–87 contains a valuable and critical account of the influence of the Marvin decision in the U.S.

[88] R(88)3. Mrs T. Gorman introduced the Cohabitation (Contract Enforcement) Bill under the 10-minute rule on June 11, 1991. The bill was intended to remove doubts about the validity of such contracts: see *Hansard,* H.C., Vol. 192, col 791.

[89] Civil Partnership Bill, Clause 10.

[90] *Crabb v. Arun R.D.C.* [1976] Ch. 179, *per* Scarman L.J.; *Gillett v. Holt* [2001] Ch. 210; [2000] 2 F.L.R. 266; [2000] 3 W.L.R. 815; [2000] 2 All E.R. 289 *per* Robert Walker L.J. See P. Milne, "Proprietary Estoppel and the Element of Unconscionabilty" (1997) 56 *M.L.R.* 34.

[91] See the (dissenting) speech of Lord Kingsdown in *Ramsden v. Dyson* (1866) L.R. 1, 129 at 170, HL, and generally on the evolution of the doctrine *Taylors Fashions Ltd v. Liverpool Victoria Trustee Co. Ltd* [1982] Q.B. 133, Oliver J.

[92] Adapted from the formulation by E. Nugee Q.C. in *Re Basham dec'd* [1987] 2 F.L.R. 264 at 269; and see *Wayling v. Jones* (1996) 2 F.L.R. 455.

another—a situation not uncommon in the context of family relationships,[93] although it is by no means confined to that factual situation.

The doctrine of estoppel and those of implied, resulting and constructive trust have developed separately, but it is well recognised that there is a substantial degree of overlap. In *Grant v. Edward,*[94] Sir Nicholas Browne-Wilkinson V.-C. said that in both cases:—

> "the claimant must to the knowledge of the legal owner have acted in the belief that the claimant has or will obtain an interest in the property. In both, the claimant must have acted to his or her detriment in reliance on such belief. In both, equity acts on the conscience of the legal owner to prevent him from acting in an unconscionable manner by defeating the common intention. The two principles . . . rest on the same foundations and have on all other matters reached the same conclusion."

Robert Walker L.J. observed in *Yaxley v. Gotts and Gotts*[95] that:

> "at a high level of generality, there is much common ground between the doctrines of proprietary estoppel and the constructive trust . . . [Both] are concerned with equity's intervention to provide relief against unconscionable conduct . . . In the area of a joint enterprize for the acquisition of land (which may be, but is not necessarily, the matrimonial home) the two concepts coincide."

Nevertheless, the two doctrines have not been assimilated. It can be powerfully argued that there are fundamental distinctions[96] between the two: in this view (shared by the authors of this book) estoppel is a remedial concept centred on the intervention of the court whereas the constructive trust is a means of creating a proprietary right which operates entirely independently of the court. The basis of informal trusts is agreement or understanding (actual, inferred or presumed) that property is to be shared beneficially, whereas estoppel gives effect to the disappointed expectations of one party whether or not shared by the other.[97] That a mutual understanding or bargain as to what particular interest

---

[93] G. Batterbury, "*Matharu v. Matharu*—a hard case, but does it make bad law?" (1995) 7 *Child and Family Law Quarterly* 59.

[94] [1986] Ch. 638 at 656, CA. See also *Lloyds Bank plc v. Rosset* [1989] Ch. 350 at 387, *per* Nicholls L.J.; *Lloyds Bank plc v. Rosset* [1991] 1 A.C. 107 at 132 *per* Lord Bridge; *Austin v. Keele* [1987] A.L.J.R. 605 at 609, PC, *per* Lord Oliver of Aylmerton; *Re Polly Peck International plc* [1998] 3 All E.R. 812 at 832 *per* Nourse L.J.

[95] [1999] 2 F.L.R. 941 at 951; for academic perspectives on the underpinning principle of unconscionability, see D.J. Hayton, "Equitable Rights of Cohabitees" [1990] *Conv.* 370; and Browne Wilkinson, "Constructive Trusts and Unjust Enrichment" (Birmingham, Holdsworth Club, 1991).

[96] See for a persuasive analysis, P. Ferguson, "Constructive Trusts—A Note of Caution" (1993) 109 *L.Q.R.* 114; and compare the reply by D.J. Hayton, "Constructive Trusts of Homes—A Bold Approach" (1993) 109 *L.Q.R.* 485; I. Moore "Proprietary Estoppel, Constructive Trusts and s 2 of the Law of Property (Miscellaneous Provisions) Act 1989" (2000) 63 *M.L.R.* 912. The Law Commission's Discussion Paper *Sharing Homes* (July 2002) (www.lawcom.gov.uk), discusses both the similarities and differences between the two doctrines: see paras 2.101–2.104 and 2.2110.

[97] On the distinction, see Beldam L.J. in *Yaxley v. Gotts and Gotts* [1999] 2 F.L.R. 941 at 966.

is to be granted, or when or how, is not essential[98] to the operation of the doctrine of estoppel was emphasised by the Court of Appeal in *Gillett v. Holt*[99]: one consequence of these distinctions is that the basis for quantifying a successful claimant's interest may differ in a case founded on estoppel from that which applies in a case founded on implied, resulting or constructive trust.[1]

This is not to say that the present doctrinal basis of the law is wholly satisfactory—indeed, it would be difficult to deny that it remains full of anomalies, fictions, and unfairness.[2] It remains to be seen whether, at some time in the future, the House of Lords will seek to resolve the conceptual difficulties in the present law, whether by assimilating the principles of *Gissing/Rosset* type constructive trusts and those of proprietary estoppel, or even "by following the recent trend in other commonwealth jurisdictions towards more generalised principles of unconscionability and unjust enrichment".[3]

The trend of recent authority is to emphasise a broad approach to the doctrine of proprietary estoppel, its fundamental grounding in unconscionability, and the interrelation of its constituent elements.[4] The court (having analysed the conduct and relationship of the parties) asks, first, whether an equity has been established; secondly, if so, what is the extent of that equity; and thirdly, what is the relief appropriate to satisfy the equity?

In establishing the equity, the formulation of Mr Edward Nugee Q.C. in *Re Basham (Dec'd).*[5] has been widely adopted in the modern case-law[6]:

> "Where one person (A) has acted to his detriment on the faith of a belief, which was known to and encouraged by another person (B) that he either has or is going to be given in or over B's property, B cannot insist

---

[98] However, as Robert Walker L.J. observed in *Gillett v. Holt* [2000] 2 F.L.R. 266 at 285, where the detriment involves the claimant moving house or otherwise taking some course of action at the other party's request, the link between the promise relied on and the detriment will resemble the process of offer and acceptance leading to a mutual understanding.

[99] [2000] 2 F.L.R. 266 at 285 *per* Rober Walker L.J. (with whom Waller and Beldam L.JJ. agreed).

[1] See *Baker v. Baker* [1993] 2 F.L.R. 247, CA; and the discussion at p. 141, below. But note that the flexible approach to quantification of the beneficial interest adopted in cases such as *Midland Bank v. Cooke* [1995] 2 F.L.R. 915 (discussed earlier in this Chap.) may in practice have somewhat eroded the distinction in practical outcome.

[2] R. Bailey-Harris "Dividing the Assets of Relationships Outside Marriage" in *Dividing the Assets on Family Breakdown* (Family Law, 1998) at pp. 76–80. The Law Commission's Sixth Programme of Law Reform (Law Com. No. 234, 1995), p. 34 stated that the "present legal rules are uncertain and difficult to apply and can lead to serious injustice"; and in *Midland Bank v. Cooke* [1995] 2 F.L.R. 915, CA, Waite L.J. said that the Law Commission's proposal to examine the property rights of home-sharers was "well-timed and has the potential to save a lot of human heartache as well as public expense". The Law Commission's Discussion Paper *Sharing Homes* (July 2002) (www.lawcom.gov.uk) has voiced criticisms of the current law: see paras 2.105-2.114. It nevertheless refrained from recommending statutory reforms: see Chap. 9, below.

[3] *Stokes v. Anderson* [1991] 1 F.L.R. 391 at 399, *per* Nourse L.J.

[4] See *e.g. Greasley v. Cooke* [1980] 2 W.L.R. 1306; *Taylor Fashions v. Liverpool Victoria Trustees Ltd; Old & Campbell v.Liverpool Friendly Society* [1982] Q.B. 133; *Re Basham (dec'd)* [1986] 1 W.L.R. 1498; *Wayling v. Jones* [1995] 2 F.L.R. 1029; *Gillett v. Holt* [2000] 2 F.L.R. 266; *cf. Coombes v. Smith* [1987] 1 F.L.R. 352; *Taylor v. Dickens* [1998] 1 F.L.R. 806, disaproved in *Gillett v. Holt, supra.*

[5] [1987] 2 F.L.R. 264 at 269.

[6] See *e.g. Wayling v. Jones* [1995] 2 F.L.R. 1029 at 1031 (Balcombe L.J.); *Gillett v. Holt* [2000] 2 F.L.R. 266 at 280 (Robert Walker L.J.).

on his strict legal right if to do so would be inconsistent with A's belief."

In *Gillett v. Holt*[7] Robert Walker L.J. observed that:

> " . . . it is important to note . . . that the doctrine of proprietary estoppel cannot be treated as subdivided into three or four watertight compartments . . . the quality of the relevant assurances may influence the issue of reliance . . . reliance and detriment are often intertwined, and . . . whether there is a distinct need for a 'mutual understanding' may depend on how the other elements are formulated and understood. Moreover, the fundamental principle that equity is concerned to prevent unconscionable conduct permeates all elements of the doctrine. In the end the court must look at the matter in the round."

The owner must know that the claimant is acting on the basis of an misapprehension[8] about his or her legal rights, created encouraged or acquiesced in by the owner. In *Pascoe v. Turner*[9]:

5–024

> The defendant and his former housekeeper had lived as man and wife for many years. He then formed another relationship, and told the plaintiff that the house and its contents were hers. In reliance on that statement the plaintiff made substantial improvements to the house and bought furnishings for it, using for these purposes a large proportion of her small capital. The statement that the property was to be the plaintiff's was held to be ineffective as a transfer because the appropriate formalities had not been observed[10]; but the court held that an equitable estoppel arose in the plaintiff's favour by reason of the defendant's encouragement and acquiescence in the actions which she had taken in reliance on it, and that this estoppel could only be satisfied by transferring the legal estate in the property to her. It is not necessary that the assurances made be irrevocable in nature, a matter of considerable importance in the context of testamentary promises[11]; indeed, estoppel claims by their nature concern promises which are initially revocable.[12] There must be a sufficient link between the promises relied upon and the conduct which constitutes the detriment,[13] but the nature of the link will depend upon the factual context: a mutual understanding is not essential.[14]

---

[7] [2000] 2 F.L.R. 266 at 279.

[8] There was no misapprehension in *Coombes v. Smith* [1986] 1 W.L.R. 808; [1987] 1 F.L.R. 352, Ch D.

[9] [1979] 1 W.L.R. 431.

[10] See also *Greasley v. Cooke* [1980] 1 W.L.R. 1306.

[11] *Gillett v. Holt* [2000] 2 F.L.R. 266, disapproving *Taylor v. Dickens* [1998] 2 F.L.R. 806, ChD, criticised by M. Thompson in [1998] *Conveyancer and Property Lawyer* 210 and G. Douglas in [1998] *Fam. Law* 191.

[12] W. Swadling [1998] *Restitution Law Review* 220.

[13] *Eves v. Eves* [1975] 1 W.L.R. 1338, in particular *per* Brightman J. at 1345C-F; *Grant v. Edwards and Edwards* [1986] Ch. 638, [1987] 1 F.L.R. 87 *per* Nourse L.J. at 648–649 and 94–95 respectively, and *per* Browne-Wilkinson V.-C. at 655–657 and 98–100 respectively, *Wayling v. Jones* [1995] 2 F.L.R. 1029 at 1031 *per* Balcolme L.J.

[14] *Gillett v. Holt* [2000] 2 F.L.R. 266 at 284–285 *per* Robert Walker L.J.

To what extent must detriment or change of position by the claimant have been induced or caused by the promises made by the owner? One ground for dismissal of the claim in *Coombes v. Smith*[15] was that the woman changed her position because she chose to live with the defendant, not in reliance on any representation made by him; however, that decision arguably represents a stricter approach to the doctrine of proprietary estoppel which is now out of line with the preponderance of current authority. In *Wayling v. Jones*[16] the plaintiff lived with the deceased for some 16 years. During their relationship they changed residence several times and the deceased ran several businesses. The plaintiff acted as the deceased's companion and chauffeur and helped run the deceased's business, in return receiving only pocket money and expenses. The deceased repeatedly promised to leave the plaintiff his business and to update his will, but failed to do so. After the deceased's death the plaintiff received no more than a car and some furniture. At first instance the plaintiff's claim based on proprietary estoppel was dismissed on the ground that he had failed to prove that the detriment he had suffered (not receiving adequate wages) had in fact been suffered in reliance on the belief that he would inherit the deceased's property. One problem the plaintiff faced was that in cross-examination he had stated that had the deceased made no promises he would still have remained with him. The Court of Appeal allowed his appeal. The decision[17] confirms that the promise relied upon does have to be the sole inducement for the conduct,[18] and that if there is conduct from which inducement can be inferred, the burden of disproving reliance shifts to the defendant.[19]

Current authority takes a broad approach to the detriment[20] which must be established by the claimant under proprietary estoppel. According to the Court of Appeal in *Gillett v. Holt,*[21] the authorities:

> " . . . show that it is not a narrow or technical concept. The detriment need not consist of the expenditure of money or other quantifiable financial detriment, so long as it is something substantial. The requirement must be approached as part of a broad enquiry as to whether repudiation of an assurance is or is not unconscionable in all the circumstances."

In that case the appellant became from the age of 12 the protegé of the respondent, a rich farmer with a large farming business. The appellant worked for the respondent, eventually as his business partner, for 40 years. The respondent made assurances that he would leave his estate to the appellant, but eventually made a will in favour of another person. The judge at first instance[22] dismissed

---

[15] [1986] 1 W.L.R. 808.

[16] [1995] 2 F.L.R. 1029.

[17] Criticised by E. Cooke in (1995) 112 *L.Q.R.* 389.

[18] *Amalgamated Investment & Property Co. (In Liquidation) v. Texas Comerce International Bank* [1982] Q.B. 84 at 104–105.

[19] *Greasley v. Cooke* [1980] 1 W.L.R. 1036; *Grant v. Edwards and Edwards* [1986] Ch. 638 at 657.

[20] R. Wells "The Element of Detriment in Proprietary Estoppel" [2001] 65 *Conveyancer* 13.

[21] [2000] 2 F.L.R. 266.

[22] Carnwath J. [1998] 2 F.L.R. 470.

the claim, holding in the alternative that the appellant had failed to establish sufficient detriment. The Court of Appeal held *inter alia* that the judge had taken too narrowly a financial view of the requirement of detriment. The appellant and his wife had in reliance on repeated assurances of testamentary assurances and because they trusted the respondent devoted the best years of their life to working for him, and had been loyal both to his business interests and to his social life. The cumulative effect of the evidence was that appellant had an exceptionally strong claim on the respondent's conscience.

At the third stage of determining the relief appropriate to satisfy the equity,[23] the restrictions on the doctrine of estoppel as currently applied, as well as its flexibility, become apparent. A wide range of possible relief is available. Nevertheless, recent[24] authority predicates a cautious approach: the task of the court is to seek the minimum required to do justice between the parties.[25] The court may decide that this is satisfied by transfer of the entire legal estate,[26] or proceeds of sale,[27] by a proportion of the beneficial interest,[28] or an occupation right,[29] or compensation. In *Gillett v. Holt*[30] the minimum required to satisfy the equity was the transfer to the appellant of the freehold of the farmhouse and surrounding acreage plus a sum to compensate for his exclusion from the rest of the farming business. Nevertheless, the result may be very different in other situations.[31] For example:—

> In *Baker v. Baker*[32] a man of 75 who was in frail health gave up his secure council flat in London to move into a house purchased by his son and daughter-in-law. The father, who was to have a bed-sitting room in the house rent free for the rest of his life, contributed £33,950 in all to the purchase, the balance being provided by way of a building society mortgage contracted by the son and daughter-in-law (to whom the house was conveyed). The parties lived together for a year, but the son then made a serious (and unjustified) allegation against the father, who left. The trial judge held that the father was entitled by way of equitable estoppel to recover the £33,950 he had contributed to the purchase of the property with interest from the date when the plaintiff had left; but the Court of Appeal held that the judge should have quantified what it was that the plaintiff had

---

[23] M. Pawlowski, "Proprietary Estoppel—Satisfying the Equity" (1997) 113 *L.Q.R.* 232; S. Gardener, "The Remedial Discretion in Proprietary Estoppel" (1999) 115 *L.Q.R.* 438.

[24] Compare the broader formulation of Sir Arthur Hobhouse in *Plimmer v. Wellington Corporation* (1884) 9 App. Cas. 699 at 714: to look at the circumstances of each case to decide in what way the equity can be satisfied.

[25] *Crabb v. Arun District Council* [1976] Ch. 179 at 198 *per* Scarman L.J.; *Pascoe v. Turner* [1979] 1 W.L.R. 431 at 438, CA, *per* Cumming-Bruce L.J.; *Gillett v. Holt* [2000] 2 F.L.R. 266 at 290 *per* Robert Walker L.J.

[26] *e.g. Pascoe v. Turner* [1979] 1 W.L.R. 431; *Matharu v. Matharu* [1994] 2 F.L.R. 597.

[27] *Wayling v. Jones* [1995] 2 F.L.R. 1029, CA.

[28] *Baker v. Baker* [1993] 2 F.L.R. 247.

[29] *Greasley v. Cooke* [1980].

[30] [2000] 2 F.L.R. 266.

[31] See also *Matharu v. Matharu* [1994] 2 F.L.R. 597, forcefully criticised by G. Battersby [1995] *C.F.L.Q.* 59.

[32] [1993] 2 F.L.R. 247, CA.

lost, based only on his loss of the right to rent-free accommodation. This would be less than the amount he had paid towards the purchase, which included (and was intended to include) an element of gift to the appellants.

VI. SIGNIFICANCE OF RELATIONSHIPS IN ESTABLISHING ENTITLEMENT TO PROPERTY UNDER EQUITABLE DOCTRINES

5–025 The issue of the parties' relationship arises in three contexts: first, the nature of the evidence giving rise to an inference of intention that ownership be shared in the doctrine of constructive trust; secondly, conduct constituting detrimental reliance in both constructive trust and proprietary estoppel; and thirdly, conduct relevant to the quantification of beneficial interests under the trust doctrines. It is not surprising that interpretation of the equitable doctrines differs somewhat in the family context from the purely commercial.[33] However, a number of more specific questions arise.

(a) The general law purports to be indifferent to marital status, and in English law there is no distinct matrimonial property regime, but do the authorities in reality draw a distinction between married and unmarried relationships? The starting point (as stated by Lord Upjohn, in *Pettitt v. Pettitt*[34]) is that property disputes between husband and wife have to be decided by ordinary principles "while making full allowance" in view of the relationship between the parties; and it follows from this that the question becomes "what allowances have to be made?" Ideally, the answer should depend on the content of the parties' relationship rather than their legal status, and the role-divisions which they have assumed during that relationship. However, in the absence of express agreement,[35] certain authorities may seem to suggest a greater willingness to draw the inference of intention to share beneficial ownership in the case of a married than an unmarried couple.[36] Secondly, again in the absence of actual agreement,[37] when it comes to the issue of *quantum,* the courts may be more willing to draw the inference of intention that beneficial ownership should be equal in the case of a married than an unmarried couple.[38] Nevertheless, these interpretations must be regarded as no more than tentative, and in any event susceptible to changes of judicial direction in the context of contemporary mores.

(b) It has been suggested that notwithstanding the apparent formal neutrality of the equitable doctrines, the case-law in reality reflects an element of gender bias. This may consist of a stereotyping of women's traditional role: allegedly,

---

[33] On the different interpretations of reliance in estoppel, see E Cooke, "Reliance and Estoppel" (1995) 111 *L.Q.R.* 389, at 393–394.

[34] [1970] A.C. 777 at 813.

[35] Examples: *Grant v. Edwards* [1987] 1 F.L.R. 87; *Eves v. Eves; Rowe v. Prance* [1999] 2 F.L.R. 787.

[36] Contrast *Midland Bank v. Cooke* [1995] 2 F.L.R. 915 with *Bernard v. Josephs* [1982] Ch. 39i; *Burns v. Burns* [1984] Ch. 317; *Layton v. Martin* [1986] 2 F.L.R. 227; *Windler v. Whitehall* [1990] 2 F.L.R. 505 and *Thomas v. Fuller-Brown* [1988] 1 F.L.R. 237.

[37] See *e.g. Rowe v. Prance* [1999] 2 F.L.R. 787.

[38] Contrast, in particular, *Midland Bank v. Cooke* [1995] 2 F.L.R. 915 with *Drake v. Whipp* [1996] 1 F.L.R. 826.

in order to succeed, female claimants must show that they did much more than the judges would expect most women to do.[39] It has been further suggested that in a male homosexual relationship, quasi-domestic contributions are treated differently than if they had been performed by a woman.[40] These views remain somewhat controversial.

VII. SEVERANCE: CONVERTING A JOINT TENANCY INTO A TENANCY IN COMMON

5–026 If the parties are beneficial joint tenants, the interest of the one will on death accrue automatically, by operation of law, to the survivor.[41] But either may sever the joint tenancy, thus converting it into a beneficial tenancy in common,[42] *i.e.* co-ownership in distinct although undivided shares.[43] The interest of a tenant in common passes, on death, under his or her will or intestacy. The conversion of a joint tenancy into a tenancy in common by severance will thus be important if either party wishes to control the devolution of the property after death. In particular, a joint tenant who knows that a relationship is breaking down may well want to prevent his or her share in the property from passing automatically on death to the other; and a joint tenant who has children by a previous relationship will often want to be sure that the asset goes to those children (whether under a will or on intestacy) rather than to the other joint tenant. There are four ways of severing a beneficial joint interest in land.

A. By giving written notice to the other spouse under section 36(2) of the Law of Property Act 1925

5–027 Such a notice need not be in any particular form, but it must be intended to take effect forthwith, and must show an intention that the property be thenceforth held under a tenancy in common. Hence in *Harris v. Goddard*[44] it was held that a wife's application that the court make a property adjustment order over the former matrimonial home did not suffice to sever the joint tenancy, since it merely invited the court to consider exercising its powers in one of a number of

---

39 See *e.g.* A. Lawson, "The Things We Do For Love: Detrimental Reliance in the Family Home" (1996) 16 *Legal Studies* 218, 224–226; L. Flynn and A. Lawson, [1995] 3 *Feminist Legal Studies* 105.

40 L. Flynn and A. Lawson [1995] 3 *Feminist Legal Studies* 105 at 119 and 121, interpreting *Wayling v. Jones* [1995] 2 F.L.R. 1029, CA.

41 Where two or more persons die in circumstances rendering it uncertain which of them survived the other, the younger is deemed to have survived the elder: Law of Property Act 1925, s.184; and accordingly the younger of two beneficial joint tenants killed in a common accident will (in the absence of evidence to the contrary) succeed to the severable share. For an example of the difficulties to which this presumption may give rise, see *Re McBroom (dec'd)* [1992] 2 F.L.R 49.

42 See *Re Draper's Conveyance* [1969] 1 Ch. 486; *Harris v. Goddard* [1983] 1 W.L.R. 203.

43 Law of Property Act 1925, ss. 1(6) ans 36(2).

44 [1983] 1 W.L.R. 1203.

different ways at some time in the future.[45] Severance is effective on proof that the notice has been posted, even though it is never read or received by the other tenant.[46]

This method of effecting a severance is extremely simple, and it should be standard practice for solicitors to discuss the desirability of severance with any joint tenant who is contemplating divorce.[47] Severance cannot prejudice the client's interests in ancillary relief proceedings[48]; and will effectively prevent what is often the whole of the family capital passing to the other if death occurs before the final ancillary order.[49]

B. By mutual agreement

5–028 The law "has been willing to mitigate the hazards of survivorship by allowing severance to occur relatively easily",[50] and mutual agreement exemplifies the law's readiness to allow severance to occur.[51] For example, an agreement will be effective notwithstanding the fact that it is not in writing[52]; and the fact that the agreement would not be specifically enforceable is irrelevant. Even an unimplemented and unenforceable agreement in the course of divorce negotiations may constitute a sufficient "agreement" for this purpose. Thus:—

> In *Hunter v. Babbage*[53] the parties had been divorced, and the wife gave the appropriate notice of intention to proceed with her application for ancillary relief. Calderbank negotiations[54] took place in the course of which the wife's solicitors agreed to the sale of the former matrimonial home on terms that she would have a lump sum from the proceeds; but the husband died before all the financial negotiations had been completed. It was held that the joint tenancy had been severed by agreement. The fact that the negotiations were originally on a "without prejudice" basis was not material since both husband and wife had subsequently accepted the proposals; and the court rejected an argument that the fact the agreement was to be

---

[45] An application to the court may constitute a sufficient notice in writing provided that the relevant documents clearly indicate a desire to sever: see *e.g. Re Draper's Conveyance* [1969] 1 Ch. 486, Plowman J. (application under Married Women's Property Act 1882 for sale and division of proceeds effective to sever; approved in *Burgess v. Rawnsley* [1975] Ch. 429, CA).

[46] *Kinch v. Bullard* [1999] 1 W.L.R. 423; [1999] 1 F.L.R. 66; [1998] 4 All E.R. 650.

[47] And *a fortiori* if the parties are not married to one another, since in that case the divorce court will have no power to vary their beneficial interests.

[48] The court can make whatever order is appropriate, whether the spouses' interests be as beneficial joint tenants or beneficial tenants in common.

[49] *Re Palmer (dec'd) (Insolvent Estate)* [1994] 2 F.L.R. 609; [1994] Ch. 316; [1994] 3 W.L.R. 420; [1994] 3 All E.R. 835, CA.

[50] K. Gray and S. Gray, *Elements of Land Law* (3rd ed., 2001), p. 851.

[51] *Williams v. Hensman* (1861) 1 John and H. 546; *Burgess v. Rawnsley* [1975] Ch. 429.

[52] *cf.* the usual requirement of writing for any dealing in interests in land.

[53] [1994] 2 F.L.R. 806, Ch D, J. McDonnell Q.C.

[54] *i.e.* negotiations "without prejudice save as to costs": see Chap. 14.

(but had not yet been) incorporated in a consent order prevented the agreement from severing from the tenancy.[55]

C. By alienation[56] or other "act of any one of the persons interested operating upon his own share"

5–029 Such acts destroy a joint tenancy because they are inconsistent with the unities of title and interest which are an essential part of joint tenancy,[57] or they evidence an intention on the part of the person concerned to treat the severable share as his or her separate share. Even a concealed or dishonest act suffices. For example:—

> In *Ahmed v. Kendrick*[58] H and W were (so it was held) joint tenants of the matrimonial home in law and equity. H agreed to sell the house to A, but did not tell W. H subsequently forged her signature on the land registry transfer. It was held that the effect of H's actions was to sever the beneficial joint tenancy and to transfer to A the beneficial tenancy in common to which he thereby became entitled. Accordingly the property was held on trust for W and A.[59]

The separate dealing may be involuntary; and in a number of cases it has been accepted that a joint tenant's bankruptcy severs the joint tenancy, the bankrupt's severable share vesting in his or her trustee in bankruptcy.[60]

D. By "any course of dealing sufficient to intimate that the interests of all were mutually treated as constituting a tenancy in common"

5–030 Severance by mutual conduct is difficult to distinguish from severance by mutual agreement[61]; but it seems that there is a distinction between the two: it is not necessary to show a concluded agreement provided a sufficient common intention is shown to treat the tenancy as severed—for example, severance will occur in the absence of agreement if the parties have over a long period of time acted

---

[55] An agreement does not have to be enforceable between the parties to effect a severance provided that it indicated a common intention to sever: *Burgess v. Rawnsley* [1975] Ch. 429 at 446, *per* Sir J. Pennycuick.

[56] B Crown, "Severing of Joint Tenancy by Partial Alienation" [2001] 117 *L.Q.R.* 477.

[57] See generally K.J. Gray and S. Gray, *Elements of Land Law* (3rd ed., 2001), p. 856 ff.

[58] [1988] 2 F.L.R. 22; distinguished on the facts in *Penn v. Bristol and West Building Society* [1995] 2 F.L.R. 938, Ch D.

[59] See also of *First National Securities Ltd v. Hegerty* [1985] F.L.R. 850.

[60] See, *e.g. Re Gorman (A Bankrupt)* [1990] 2 F.L.R. 284, DC. A bankrupt is only divested of his estate when a trustee is appointed (s.306) and this will normally be some time after the making of the bankruptcy order. As to when severance takes place see *Re Dennis (A Bankrupt)* [1995] 2 F.L.R. 387; [1996] Ch. 80, [1995] 3 W.L.R. 367; [1995] 3 All E.R. 171, CA; and *Re Palmer (Insolvent estate)* [1994] Ch. 316; [1994] 2 F.L.R. 609; [1994] 3 W.L.R. 420; [1994] 3 All E.R. 835, CA.

[61] *Burgess v. Rawnsley* [1975] Ch. 429.

on the assumption that each owns a severed share rather than an interest liable to accrue to the other tenant on death.[62]

It is impossible to sever a joint tenancy by will; by the time the will has taken effect the deceased's share will have accrued to the other. This rule creates an important practical problem. A spouse whose marriage is on the verge of break-up may want to sever in order to protect the interest of his or her children; but giving notice to the other may be seen as a hostile step and precipitate a crisis.

VIII. RESOLVING DISPUTES ABOUT THE EXERCISE OF PROPRIETARY RIGHTS

A. The statutory framework

5–031 By virtue of the Trusts of Land and Appointment of Trustees Act 1996,[63] all co-ownership (whether concurrent or successive) of real property is regulated by the trust of land, a structure which replaced the trust for sale[64] under section 30 of the Law of Property Act 1925. The 1996 Act introduced some long-awaited substantive changes into the law as well as providing a uniform model regulating all forms of co-ownership. Detailed exposition of the Act's provisions may be found in the standard works on land law[65]; the present discussion highlights the main features of interest for family law purposes.[66]

Under the 1996 Act, the trustees have, for the purposes of exercising their functions as trustees, all the powers of an absolute owner.[67] Their wide powers include sale, mortgage, lease, purchase of further land for investment or occupation purposes,[68] partition between beneficiaries,[69] and exclusion and restriction of beneficiaries' occupation rights.[70] Their powers extend to proceeds of sale.[71] In addition, trustees can apply to court under section 14 for an order resolving a dispute between co-owners; this is discussed below.

One aim of the 1996 Act was to do away with obsolete concepts and doctrines. To this end the Act abolished[72] the doctrine of conversion and the trust

---

[62] See *Gore and Snell v. Carpenter* (1990) 60 P. & C.R. 456 at 462.

[63] In force January 1, 1997.

[64] Harwood, "Gathering Moss: Trusts for Sale" [1996] *Fam. Law* 290.

[65] See D. Barnsley, "Co-Owners' Rights to Occupy Land" [1998] *C.L.J.* 123; L. Clements, "The Changing Face of Trusts: The Trusts of Land and Appointment of Trustees Act 1996" (1998) 61 *M.L.R.* 56; N. Hopkins, "The Trusts of Land and Appointment of Trustees Act 1996" [1996] *Conveyancer* 411.

[66] See S. Baughen, "Trusts of Land and Family Practice" [1997] *Fam. Law* 736; M. Harwood, "A Home for Life—The New Trusts of Land Act" [1997] *Fam. Law* 182.

[67] Trusts of Land and Appointment of Trustees Act 1996, s.6(1). These may be excluded by express provision in a disposition: s.8(1). The Trustee Act 2000 brings the powers of other trustees into conformity.

[68] Trusts of Land and Appointment of Trustees Act 1996, s.6(3),(4).

[69] *ibid.* s.7(1).

[70] *ibid.* s.13(1).

[71] Reversing *Re Wakeman; Wakeman v. Wakeman* [1947] Ch. 607.

[72] Trusts of Land and Appointment of Trustees Act 1996, s.3.

for sale, whereby property owned jointly or in common was subject to a trust (*i.e.* an imperative obligation) to sell, although the trustees also had power to postpone sale. The power to sell and to postpone sale are now comprised in the new trust for land. Section 12 declares[73] that any beneficiary who is beneficially entitled to an interest in possession[74] has the right to occupy the land.[75] Section 13 permits the trustees to exclude and regulate occupation rights as between one or more (but not all) beneficiaries. One beneficiary may be excluded from occupation[76] and conditions[77] (such as payment of outgoings, mortgage instalments or compensation) imposed on another beneficiary who occupies the property. However, where a beneficiary is already in occupation, the section 13 powers cannot be exercised, in the absence of that beneficiary's consent, without a court order.[78] Thus section 13 will have little application where a couple share the family home. Beneficiaries have the right to be consulted on the exercise of trustees' functions.[79]

The courts have wide powers to resolve disputes between co-owners. Any trustee or any person with an interest in property subject to a trust of land[80] may apply to court for an order, and the court can make such order as it thinks fit relating to the exercise of trustees' functions or declaring the nature or extent of beneficiaries' interests in the land or its proceeds.[81] Section 14 contains the powers; section 15, discussed below, lists the factors relevant to the exercise of the court's discretion, except in cases where the application for an order is made by a trustee in bankruptcy and section 335A of the Insolvency Act 1986 applies.[82]

B. Exercise of the court's discretion

5–032 The Trusts of Land and Appointment of Trustees Act 1996 preserves the distinction, established in earlier case-law and subsequently reinforced by changes made by the Insolvency Act 1986, between those cases in which the dispute involves only family members and those cases in which the order is sought by a trustee in bankruptcy.[83] A more controversial question is whether the new

---

[73] *ibid.* s.12(1). Rights of occupation had been recognised as an incident of equitable entitlement in the case-law prior to the Act: see *e.g. Bull v. Bull* [1955] 1 Q.B. 234; *Williams and Glyn's Bank v. Boland* [1981] A.C. 487. See also s.33 of the Family Law Act 1996.

[74] On the nature of such an interest, see *IRC v. Lloyds Private Banking* [1999] 1 F.L.R. 147, ChD.

[75] Unless the land is used purely for investment purposes, or is unsuitable for occupation: Trusts of Land and Appointment of Trustees Act 1996, s.12(1) and (2).

[76] Where a single building lends itself to physical partition, the s.13 power permits the trustees to exclude or restrict beneficiaries' rights in different parts of the building: *Rodway v. Landy* [2001] E.W.C.A. Civ. 471, [2001] Ch. 703, [2001] 2 W.L.R. 1775, CA. This case concerned the partition of a doctors' surgery.

[77] Trusts of Land and Appointment of Trustees Act 1996, s.13(5),(6). These may include contribution to costs of adaptation in cases of partition: *Rodway v. Landy, supra.*

[78] *ibid.* s.13(7).

[79] *ibid.* s.11(1).

[80] *ibid.* s.14(1). Secured creditors and personal representatives are included.

[81] *ibid.* ss.14(2) and 17(2).

[82] *ibid.* s.15(4).

[83] See *Re Citro (A Bankrupt)* [1991] Ch. 142, CA.

law distinguishes between bankruptcy cases and those involving, for example, a chargee.

1. Family disputes

5–033 Under section 15, the matters to which the court is to have regard in determining an application for a section 14 order include:

(a) the intentions of the person or persons (if any) who created the trust,
(b) the purposes for which the property subject to the trust is held,
(c) the welfare of any minor who occupies or may reasonably be expected to occupy the land subject to the trust as his home, and
(d) the interests of any secured creditor of any beneficiary.

The interpretation of this provision is of course a matter for the courts, in particular the extent to which the legislation is evolutionary or revolutionary. The express reference to the purpose for which the property is held may be seen as an express endorsement of the collateral purpose doctrine developed in earlier case-law on section 30 of the Law of Property Act 1925: was there a "secondary or collateral" purpose (beyond sale) concerning the interests of adults or children which subsisted?[84] The express reference to the welfare of minors may be interpreted as an elevation of children's interests in purely intra-family disputes; on their status in other disputes, see the discussion below.

2. Other disputes

5–034 Distinct statutory provisions apply when a dispute over property involves a trustee in bankruptcy of a family member. On bankruptcy, the whole of the bankrupt's property[85] vests by operation of law in a trustee in bankruptcy[86]; and the trustee comes under an obligation to realise the debtor's assets (including the bankrupt's interest in the matrimonial home) for the benefit of the creditors. Where the family home is jointly-owned, bankruptcy severs the joint tenancy[87];

---

[84] *Jones v. Challenger* [1961] 1 Q.B. 176; *Rawlings v. Rawlings* [1964] P. 398 at 419, *per* Salmon L.J.; *Burke v. Burke* [1974] 1 W.L.R. 1063, *per* Lawton L.J.; *Jones (A.E.) v. Jones (E.W.)* [1977] 1 W.L.R. 438; *Williams (J.W.) v. Williams (M.A.)* [1976] Ch. 278; *Chhokar v. Chhokar* [1984] F.L.R. 313, CA. *Re Evers Trust* [1980] 1 W.L.R. 1327 at 1330, *per* Ormrod L.J.; *Dennis v. McDonald* [1981] 1 W.L.R. 810; *Bernard v. Josephs* [1982] Ch. 391.

[85] *i.e.* the bankrupt's "estate" as defined by Insolvency Act 1986, s.283. But note that the definition excludes things which are necessary to the bankrupt for use personally by him in his employment, business or vocation (s.283(2)(a))—a definition wide enough in appropriate circumstances to extend to motor cars, computer equipment, etc.—and also clothes, bedding, furniture, household equipment and provisions "necessary for satisfying the basic domestic needs of the bankrupt and his family" (s.283(2)(b)).

[86] Insolvency Act 1986. In addition to the rules relating to the vesting of the bankrupt's property in the trustee, it should be noted that any disposition of property by the bankrupt is void, except to the extent that it was made with the consent of the court or was subsequently ratified by the court: Insolvency Act 1986, s.284.

[87] See *e.g. Re Gorman (A Bankrupt)* [1990] 2 F.L.R. 284, DC.

and the bankrupt's severed share vests in the trustee. The result will therefore be that the family home is owned by the trustee and the bankrupt's spouse or partner as tenants in common.

Obviously, the trustee will not usually wish to take up residence in the property, and the question of how the trustees will realise the bankrupt's interest for the benefit of the creditors arises. In practice, it appears[88] that in many cases the trustee will often first negotiate with the bankrupt's spouse or partner; and that in some cases the wife or relatives are able to buy out the bankrupt's interest thereby preserving the family home intact. But in many cases such a buy-out is not practicable; and the trustee will apply to the court under the Trusts of Land and Appointment of Trustees Act 1996 for an order for sale.

The exercise of the court's discretion on such an application is governed not by section 15 of the 1996 Act but instead by the provisions of the Insolvency Act 1986, s.335A.[89] The court is to make such order as it thinks just and reasonable having regard to (a) the interests of the bankrupt's creditors; (b) the conduct of the spouse or former spouse "so far as contributing to the bankruptcy"; (c) the needs and financial resources of the spouse or former spouse; (d) the needs of children; and (e) all the circumstances of the case other than the needs of the bankrupt. After one year from the bankruptcy the court is obliged to "assume, unless the circumstances of the case are exceptional, that the interests of the bankrupt's creditors outweigh all other circumstances."[90]

Very few applications for sale are in practice made within a year from the bankruptcy.[91] Although the Insolvency Act 1986 was intended[92] to give greater weight to the desirability of giving a measure of preference to personal as against property interests,[93] the courts have rarely be able to find that "exceptional circumstances" exist.[94] The *locus classicus* is *Re Citro,*[95] where Hoffmann J. took into account the fact that the half share which the bankrupt's wife would receive on sale would not enable her to find proper accommodation for herself and the children, and noted the evidence that the children's education would suffer if their home were sold. He thought that a fair solution would be to make an order for sale and possession, but not allow it to be enforced until the youngest child was 16. The Court of Appeal allowed the trustee in bankruptcy's appeal against this order and held that an immediate sale should have been ordered. Eviction of a wife and young children with all the consequent educational problems to which that would give rise was not in any way exceptional, but rather one of the

---

[88] From research funded by the E.S.R.C. and carried out at Bristol by Cretney, Clark, Davis, Furey, Wadsley and others.
[89] See the Trusts of Land and Appointment of Trustees Act 1996, s.15(4).
[90] Insolvency Act 1986, s.335A(3).
[91] From the Bristol Research referred to at n. 88 above.
[92] See (1991) 107 *L.Q.R.* 177 (S.M. Cretney) where the legislative history is summarised.
[93] *Re Citro (A Bankrupt)* [1991] Ch. 142 at 161, *per* Sir T. Bingham M.R.
[94] See, *e.g. Re Holliday (A Bankrupt) ex p. the Trustee of the Property of the Bankrupt v. Holliday* [1981] Ch. 405, CA. For a full analysis of the case law, see A. Clark, "Children of Bankrupts" (1991) *Child Law* 116.
[95] [1991] Ch. 142, CA. The decision was taken under the law as it was before the coming into force of the 1986 legislation, but the Court of Appeal specifically held that the result would be the same under that code.

"melancholy consequences of debt and improvidence with which every civilised society has been familiar."[96]

Weighing the competing interests of families and creditors necessarily involves a value judgment[97]; and the effect of the case-law continues to give weight to the view that the policy of the law is that "a man has an obligation to pay his debts and to pay them promptly, even if discharging this duty affects his liability to maintain his wife and family."[98] The effect of the legislation is that the bankrupt's family will in practice be given one year's grace but in the absence of truly exceptional circumstances, no more. Examples of judicial findings of exceptional circumstances are comparatively rare,[99] but serious illness of the bankrupt's spouse maybe held to constitute such.[1]

At the time of writing an appeal is pending[2] on the question whether the construction and application of section 335A of the Insolvency Act 1986 in the authorities discussed above are compliant with Article 8 of the European Convention for the Protection of Human Rights and Fundamental Freedoms incorporated into domestic law by the Human Rights Act 1998, or whether a different balance should be struck between the competing interests of the family and the creditors.

What of other disputes, for instance those between a family member and a chargee[3]? The case-law on section 30 of the Law of Property Act 1925 in this context generally[4] applied the same principles as in the bankruptcy cases, namely that a sale would be ordered on the chargee's application unless exceptional circumstances existed.[5] In *TSB Bank plc v. Marshall, Marshall and Rogers*[6] (a county court decision) it was held that the principles established in this context under section 30 continued to be applicable under the Trusts of Land and Appointment of Trustees Act 1996, and that in cases of conflict between the interests of the chargee and an innocent spouse, those of the chargee would prevail save in exceptional circumstances. However, in *The Mortgage Corpora-*

---

96 *per* Nourse L.J. at 157. In *Re Gorman (A Bankrupt), ex p. the trustee of the bankrupt v. The bankrupt* [1990] 2 F.L.R. 284, DC, the court postponed enforcement of an order for sale until the conclusion of an action by the bankrupt's ex-wife for negligence against her former solicitor, thereby enabling her to put forward proposals to the trustee to purchase the bankrupt's interest from the damages awarded to her. It should be noted that some protection is given to a bankrupt with whom a child is residing: Insolvency Act 1986, s.337.

97 by Hoffmann J. in *Re Citro* (above) at first instance: see [1991] 1 Ch. 142 at 150.

98 *Re Bailey* [1977] 1 W.L.R. 278 at 284 *per* Walton J.

99 *Re Holliday (A Bankrupt) ex p. the Trustee of the Property of the Bankrupt v. Holiday* [1981] Ch. 405 is an example; the court postponed the sale for five years. In *Re Bailey (A Bankrupt)* [1977] 1 W.L.R. 278, Walton J. seemed prepared to accept that the fact that a house which had been specially converted to meet the needs of a disabled child might justify a finding of exceptional circumstances.

1 *Re Raval (A Bankrupt)* [1998] 2 F.L.R. 719, CA; *Claughton v. Charalambous* [1999] 1 F.L.R. 740, Ch D; *Re Judd v. Brown, Bankrupts (Nos 9587 and 9588 of 1994)* [1998] 2 F.L.R. 360.

2 *Jackson v. Bell* [2001] EWCA Civ. 387 [2001] *Fam. Law* 879.

3 Charging Orders Act 1979.

4 But contrast *Abbey National v. Moss* [1994] 1 F.L.R. 307, where Peter Gibson L.J. sought to distinguish the bankruptcy cases and attached weight to the continuing collateral purpose of the trust.

5 *Lloyds Bank plc v. Byrne and Byrne* [1993] 1 F.L.R. 369, CA; *Barclays Bank v. Hendricks* [1996] 1 F.L.R. 258; *Bank of Baroda v. Dillon* [1998] 525, CA.

6 [1998] 2 F.L.R. 769. It is unclear the extent to which this point was argued.

tion v. Shaire[7] Neuberger J. considered that the law had been changed by section 15 of the 1996 Act, subsection (4) of which provides:

> "This section does not apply to an application if section 335A of the Insolvency Act 1986 . . . applies to it."

According to Neuberger J. this indicated that a different approach applied to disputes between family members and the trustee in bankruptcy than to disputes between family members and others. In relation to the latter, Parliament had intended to tip the balance somewhat more in favour of families and against banks and other chargees,[8] and the old authorities should be treated with caution. This distinction has received some endorsement from the Court of Appeal in *Bank of Ireland Home Mortgages Ltd v. Bell and Bell,*[9] where Peter Gibson L.J. observed that the 1996 Act, by requiring the court to have regard to the particular matters specified in section 15, appeared to have given scope for some change in the court's practice. The extent of that change is not however clear; the facts of that case were extreme (large arrears owing on the mortgage, the marriage long since broken down and the child nearly adult); the Court of Appeal allowed the bank's appeal against refusal of sale. Even if the balance has been tipped somewhat in favour of families, it seems likely that case where sale is refused as opposed to postponed will continue to be rare.

IX. PROTECTION AGAINST UNDUE INFLUENCE AND MISREPRESENTATION

5–035 The fact that their home is often the family's only substantial asset and that it has almost invariably come to be owned jointly has meant that couples have increasingly been asked to join in a mortgage or other transaction necessary to secure credit for the family's business. Against this social and economic background, a series of cases have addressed the question whether one partner could escape from liability.[10] The argument on one side is that a vulnerable party has been unfairly taken advantage of by a person with whom she has a close relationship, either through misrepresentations to the nature and extent of liability, or through the application of pressure. On the other hand, it would not be in the interests of either family or commercial life if banks and other lenders were over-reluctant to advance money on the family home. There is thus a need to strike a balance between the competing interests. The risk of misrepresentation

---

[7] [2000] 1 F.L.R. 973; [2001] 3 W.L.R. 639.

[8] The court was prepared to refuse a sale on condition of agreement between the chargee and the wife as to conversion of the chargee's equity into a loan on which she would pay interest

[9] [2001] 2 F.L.R. 809.

[10] It is impossible in a family law textbook to give a full account of these matters; and reference should be made to J. Wadsley and G. Penn *The Law Relating to Domestic Banking* (2nd ed., Sweet & Maxwell, 2000), Chap. 18 and Treitel *The Law of Contract* (10th ed., Sweet & Maxwell, 1999), Chap. 10.

and undue influence in personal relationships cannot be wholly eliminated without making lenders' business practices unworkable.[11]

The origin of the current law is *Barclays Bank plc v. O'Brien*,[12] in which the wife of an accountant executed a charge over the jointly-owned matrimonial home securing her husband's liabilities as guarantor of a company's overdraft to the Bank. She claimed that she had succumbed to undue pressure on her husband's part, that he had misrepresented to her the effects of the charge, and that accordingly it was not enforceable against her. These defences were unsuccessful at first instance; but the Court of Appeal held that wives (and other "especially vulnerable" persons) were entitled to rely on a special equity protecting them from liability provided that (i) the relationship between debtor and surety and the consequent likelihood of influence and reliance was known to the creditor; (ii) the surety's consent to the transaction was procured by undue influence or material misrepresentation on the part of the debtor, or the surety lacked an adequate understanding of the nature and effect of the transaction; and (iii) the creditor had failed to take reasonable steps to ensure that the surety's consent was a true and informed one. The House of Lords denied the existence of any such special equity. However, it dismissed the Bank's appeal because the husband had misrepresented the extent of the liabilities assumed by the wife; and the Bank should, on the facts, have been put on inquiry as to the circumstances. Accordingly, it was fixed with constructive notice of the husband's misrepresentation; and the charge in its favour securing the husband's liability to the Bank was set aside.

Lord Browne-Wilkinson said that the House of Lords should seek to restate the law in a form which was principled, reflected the current requirements of society and provided as much certainty as possible; and the decision seeks to go back to first principles.[13] There are now two questions to be asked in this type of case.[14] First, does the party seeking to escape from liability have an equity as against the other owner to set the transaction aside; and secondly, if so, does the lender or other person seeking to enforce the transaction have actual or constructive notice of that equity?

---

[11] *Royal Bank of Scotland plc v. Etridge (No 2); Barclays Bank plc v. Harris; Midland Bank plc v. Wallace; National Westminster Bank plc v. Gill; Barclays Bank plc v. Coleman; UCB Home Loans Corporation Ltd v. Moore; Bank of Scotland v. Bennett; Kenyon-Brown v. Desmond Banks and Co.* [2001] UKHL 444; [2001] 2 F.L.R. 1364; [2001] 3 W.L.R. 1021; [2001] 4 All E.R. 449 at para. [2] *per* Lord Bingham and para. [98] *per* Lord Hobhouse.

[12] [1994] 1 A.C. 180.

[13] The extension of the law was not initially accepted in Scotland: *Mumford v. Bank of Scotland; Smith v. Bank of Scotland* [1996] 1 F.L.R. 344. However, in *Smith v. Governor and Company of Bank of Scotland* [1997] 2 F.L.R. 862 the House of Lords held that there were no social or economic considerations which would justify a difference in treatment in the two jurisdictions.

[14] For general discussion of the development of the case-law, see M. Oldham, "Neither a Borrower nor a lender be: the life of O'Brien" (1995) 7 *C.F.L.Q.* 104; Haley, "Sureties, Banks and the Family Home" (1997) 9 *C.F.L.Q.* 173; Richardson, "Protecting Wives Who Provide Security for a Husband's, Partner's or Child's Debt" [1996] 16 *Legal Studies* 368; Fehlberg, "Money and Money: Sexually Transmitted debt in England" (1997) 11 *International Journal of Law, Policy and the Family* 320.

A. The equity to set aside

5–036 In most cases, the basis on which the defendant will seek to escape liability is that the transaction had been induced by a misrepresentation or by the exercise of undue influence.

1. Misrepresentation

5–037 There is little conceptual difficulty in understanding the concept of misrepresentation which renders the transaction voidable. In *Barclays Bank plc v. O'Brien, supra,* the husband had deliberately misrepresented to the wife both the extent of the security and the duration of the borrowing period. The case-law provides numerous examples of knowing misrepresentation,[15] but a charge may equally be set aside where the misrepresentation was innocent. In *TSB Bank plc v. Camfield*[16] a wife joined with her husband in a charge over the matrimonial home, the effect of which was to impose on her beneficial interest an unlimited liability to meet the debts of a business in which the husband was a partner. The husband had innocently misrepresented to her that her liability would be limited to £15,000; and if a higher figure had been contemplated she would not have executed the charge. It was held that she was entitled as against her husband to set aside the charge.[17]

2. Undue influence

5–038 There is more difficulty in defining what is meant by "undue" influence, but it is now well established[18] that the cases fall into two categories. In Class 1 there is proof of actual undue influence.[19] In cases where actual undue influence is exerted, there is no need to show that the transaction was not readily explicable

---

[15] *Midland Bank plc v. Massey* [1994] 2 F.L.R. 342; [1995] 1 All E.R. 929, CA; *Allied Irish Bank plc v. Byrne* [1995] 2 F.L.R. 238, ChD; *Bank Melli Ian v. Samadi-Rad* [1995] 2 F.L.R. 367; *Bank of Cyprus (London) v. Markon* [1999] 2 F.L.R. 17; [1999] All E.R. 707, ChD.

[16] [1995] 1 F.L.R. 751; [1995] 1 W.L.R. 430; [1995] 1 All E.R. 951, CA.

[17] And that, on the second stage of the O'Brien test, that her equity to do so bound the Bank.

[18] *BCCI SA v. Aboody* [1990] 1 Q.B. 923, CA; *Barclays Bank plc v. O'Brien* [1993] 1 F.L.R. 124; *Credit Lyonnais Bank Nederland NV v. Burch* [1997] 1 F.L.R. 11; [1997] 1 All E.R. 144.

[19] According to *BCCI SA v. Aboody* at 967, a person relying on a plea of actual undue influence must show: (a) that the other party to the transaction . . . had the capacity to influence the complainant; (b) that the influence was exercised; (c) that its exercise was undue; (d) that its exercise brought about the transaction. The court rejected suggestions that the complainant had to show that the influence exercised was accompanied by some "malign intent" or that it was necessary to show some positive action whether by way of coercion or otherwise; and would (on the facts of that case) have been prepared to find that the elements set out above were present. For examples of findings of actual undue influence, see *CIBC Mortgages plc v. Pitt* [1994] 1 A.C. 200; *Langton v. Langton* [1995] 2 F.L.R. 890; *Bank of Scotland v. Bennett* [1999] 1 F.L.R. 115 (although no constructive notice).

by the relationship of the parties.[20] In Class 2 cases there is a rebuttable[21] presumption of undue influence arising from the relationship between two persons. In Class 2A, certain relationships are as a matter of law deemed to give rise to the presumption; principally, these are solicitor and client, and medical practitioner and patient. Class 2B is very broad: the presumption arises from the existence of a relationship where one party has acquired over the other a measure of influence or ascendancy of which unfair advantage is taken.[22] The *O'Brien* principle is not confined to cases of abuse of trust and confidence but extends to reliance, dependency and vulnerability; there is no single touchstone for determining its applicability.[23] This makes it difficult to encapsulate its essence,[24] but it appears to apply in all cases in which the lender has reason to know that there is an underlying risk of one person exploiting another's emotional involvement and trust.[25] It is not possible to list exhaustively the relationships in which it applies, since, as Lord Nicholls observed in *Royal Bank of Scotland plc v. Etridge (No. 2)*[26] " . . . the reality of life is that relationships are infinitely various" and "Human relationships do not lend themselves to categorisations of this sort". The principle's application is not confined to sexual relationships, although that is in reality its main sphere.[27] It is applied to spouses[28] and cohabitants (whether heterosexual or homosexual),[29] but neither cohabitation nor a sexual relationship is essential.[30] The principle applies in other family relationships[31] and even to employer/employee.[32] In short, a lender is put on notice "in every case where the relationship between the surety and the debtor is non-commercial."[33]

In cases of presumed undue influence, the complainant has traditionally been required to show that the transaction was to his or her "manifest disadvantage"; the burden then shifts to the alleged wrongdoer to rebut the presumption by

---

20 The expression "manifest disadvantage" was regarded as unhelpful and was discarded by the House of Lords in *Royal Bank of Scotland v. Etridge* [2001] 2 F.L.R. 1364; [2001] 3 W.L.R. 1021; [2001] 4 All E.R. 449: see *per* Lord Nicholls at paras [21]–[30].

21 In *Allied Irish Bank v. Byrne* [1995] 2 F.L.R. 325, ChD the judge held that Mrs Byrne had shown such independence of judgment and behaviour as to make it impossible to presume that she was acting under her former husband's influence.

22 *per* Lord Nicholls in *Royal Bank of Scotland v. Etridge (No. 2)* [2001] 2 F.L.R. 1364; [2001] 3 W.L.R. 1021; [2001] 4 All E.R. 449 at para. [8].

23 *ibid.* para. [11].

24 *Royal Bank of Scotland plc v. Etridge* [2001] 2 F.L.R. 1358; [2001] 3 W.L.R. 1021; [2001] 3 All E.R. 449 *per* Lord Nicholls at para. [11].

25 *Midland Bank plc v. Massey* [1994] 2 F.L.R. 342.

26 [2001] U.K.H.L. 44; [2001] 2 F.L.R. 1364; [2001] 3 W.L.R. 1021; [2001] 4 All E.R. 449 at para. [86].

27 *ibid.* para. [82].

28 In most of the cases it is a wife who asserts the equity, but this is not invariably so: see *Barclays Bank plc v. Rivvett* [1999] 2 F.L.R. 731.

29 See *Barclays Bank plc v. O'Brien per* Lord Browne-Wilkinson.

30 *Midland Bank plc v. Massey* [1994] 2 F.L.R. 342; see Stryn L.J. at 345 F -G.

31 *Bainbridge v. Browne* (1881) 18 Ch. D. 188 (father and children); *Mahoney v. Purnell* [1996] 3 All E.R. 61; [1997] 1 F.L.R. 612 (elderly man and son-in-law); father and daughter *per* Lord Nicholls in *Etridge, supra* at para. [84].

32 Such as employer and employee: *Re Craig (Dec'd)* [1971] Ch. 95; *Credit Lyonnais Bank Nederland plc v. Burch* [1997] 1 F.L.R. 11; [1997] 1 All E.R. 144, CA; *Staples v. Lee* [1998] 1 F.L.R. 138.

33 *Royal Bank of Scotland v. Etridge (No. 2), supra, per* Lord Nicholls at para. [87].

showing that the transaction was freely entered into.[34] The existence of that requirement was questioned in *Barclays Bank plc v. Coleman*,[35] in which the Court of Appeal held that in any event manifest meant clear and obvious and not substantial. In *Royal Bank of Scotland v. Etridge (No. 2)*[36] the House of Lords stopped short of holding that the requirement was not necessary, but urged that the label "manifest disadvantage" be discarded and that the doctrine return to the substantive approach articulated in *Allcard v. Skinner*[37] and *National Westminster Bank v. Morgan*,[38] namely whether the transaction was readily explicable by the relationship of the parties.

B. Will the equity bind the lender or other third party?

5–039 If a lender has notice,[39] actual or constructive, of the right to impugn a transaction, then the equity binds[40] the lender as well as the wrongdoer.[41] Cases of actual notice are rare, but there has been a considerable amount of case law on the circumstances in which a lender will be held to have constructive notice. First the lender must be put on inquiry; this will occur when the transaction is not on its face explicable by the relationship of the parties,[42] and where (through the existence of a personal relationship of which the lender is aware) there is a substantial risk that the other party has committed a legal or equitable wrong entitling the transaction to be set aside.[43] The second question is whether the creditor had taken reasonable steps to satisfy himself that the surety had entered into the obligation freely and in knowledge of the true facts. What constitutes reasonable steps was initially set out in *O'Brien* but more comprehensively articulated by the House of Lords in *Royal Bank of Scotland plc v. Etridge*.[44] As the House of Lords emphasised in the latter case, the procedures henceforth to be followed are intended to be the minimum necessary to reduce the risk of pressure in a personal relationship to an acceptable level, not to eliminate it completely (which would be commercially unrealistic). Since the circumstances in which banks are put on inquiry are very wide:

---

[34] *Langton v. Langton* [1995] 2 F.L.R. 890, ChD.

[35] [2000] 1 F.L.R. 343; [2001] Q.B. 20; [2000] 3 W.L.R. 405; [2000] 1 All E.R. 385.

[36] [2001] 2 F.L.R. 1364; [2001] 3 W.L.R. 1021; [2001] 3 All E.R. 449.

[37] (1887) 36 Ch.D. 145 at 185 *per* Lindley L.J.

[38] [1985] A.C. 686 at 704 *per* Lord Scarman.

[39] The burden of proof is on the debtor: *Barclays Bank v. Boulter and Boulter* [1999] 2 F.L.R. 986; [1999] 1 W.L.R. 1919; [1999] 4 All E.R. 513, HL.

[40] Partial enforcement is not appropriate, although terms may be imposed when a charge is set aside: *TSB Bank v. Camfield* [1995] 1 F.L.R. 751; *Bank Melli Iran v. Samadi - Rad* [1995] 2 F.L.R. 367; *Dunbar Bank plc v. Nedeem* [1997] 1 F.L.R. 318; [1997] 2 All E.R. 513.

[41] The claim against the lender is secondary to and parasitic upon the existence of the claim by one debtor against the other: *First National Bank plc v. Walker* [2001] 1 F.L.R. 505.

[42] This will not be the case where a loan is jointly granted for joint purposes and joint benefit: *CIBC Mortgages v. Pitt* [1984] 1 A.C. 200; *Brittania Building Society v. Pugh* [1997] 2 F.L.R. 7; *Dunbar Bank v. Nadeem* [1998] 2 F.L.R. 457, this may be so notwithstanding that some risk is involved: *Society of Lloyds v. Khan* [1999] 1 F.L.R. 246.

[43] *Barclay's Bank plc v. O'Brien* [1994] 1 A.C. 180 at 196; *Royal Bank of Scotland v. Etridge (No. 2)* [2001] 2 F.L.R. 1364; [2001] 3 W.L.R. 1021; [2001] 3 All E.R. 449.

[44] [2001] 2 F.L.R. 1364; [2001] 3 W.L.R. 1021; [2001] 3 All E.R. 449.

> "The furthest a bank can be expected to go is to take reasonable steps to satisfy itself that the wife has had brought home to her, in a meaningful way, the practical implications of the proposed transaction."[45]

The lender who follows the procedures outlined by the House of Lords in *Etridge* will be entitled (save in exceptional cases) to assume that the security is enforceable.[46] The lender must insist that the surety attends a private meeting with its representative to warn her of the extent of liability and risks and to advise her to take independent legal advice and receive written certification[47] that she has done so. It is not unreasonable for a lender to prefer that the advice and information be given by an independent adviser. A solicitor is obliged to give advice covering at least the nature and consequences of documents to be signed, extent of liability and risks, and the essential choice whether to sign or to to refuse to sign. A solicitor may also act for the bank, absent any conflict of duty, but in advising the surety he is acting for her alone and in no way as the bank's agent. The bank itself has various obligations as to the provision of information.

The leading cases have undoubtedly had an influence on banking practice; the Banking Code[48] contains similar requirements (minus the independent interview). The latest version of the Code stipulates that unlimited guarantees are no longer to be taken.[49] Ultimately however, it is not self-evident how far any system of regulation should seek to protect a person who signs documents "blindly and without a care" because she considers that if her husband "tells me to sign it, it is for the good of the business and indirectly for the good of me . . . I never interfered with his work and he never interfered with running the house."[50]

---

45 *per* Lord Nichols at para. [54].

46 Cases where a bank has been fixed with constructive notice have prior to *Etridge* been comparatively rare. Examples are *Allied Irish Bank plc v. Byrne* [1995] 2 F.L.R. 238; *Bank Melli Iran v. Samadi-Rad* [1995] 2 F.L.R. 367; *Credit Lyonnais Bank Nederland NV v. Burch* [1997] 1 F.L.R. 11; *Dunbar Bank plc v. Nadeen* [1997] 1 F.L.R. 318; *Bank of Scotland v. Bennett* [1997] 1 F.L.R. 801; *Bank of Cyprus (London) v. Markon* [1999] 2 F.L.R. 17. Note that in *Etridge* itself the House of Lords on the old guidelines allowed the appeals of four wives and dismissed those of three. An action may lie against the solicitor, the success of which will of course be dependent on satisfying the usual elements of liability in negligence, including breach of duty and causation: *Mahoney v. Purnell* [1997] 1 F.L.R. 612; *Royal Bank of Scotland v. Etridge (No. 2)* [1998] 2 F.L.R. 843; *Mercantile Credit Co. Ltd v. Fenwick* [1999] 2 F.L.R. 110. It is difficult to envisage how a solicitor who complies with the obligations set out by the House of Lords in *Royal Bank of Scotland plc v. Etridge (No. 2), supra* could be held to be in breach of duty.

47 This may be signed by a legal executive acting within the authority of his principal: *Barclays Bank plc v. Coleman* [2000] 1 F.L.R. 343.

48 *The Code of Banking Practice,* first adopted in 1992; the current version dates from 1999.

49 See J. Wadsley and G. Penn, *The Law Relating to Domestic Banking* (2nd ed., Sweet and Maxwell, 2000), at paras 18–029, 18–030 and 18–033.

50 The quotation is from the evidence of Mrs Aboody, as cited in *BCCI SA v. Aboody* [1990] 1 Q.B. 923, CA. S.M. Cretney, "Mere Puppets, Folly and Imprudence: Undue Influence for the Twenty-First Century" [1994] *R.L.R.* 3 is an attempt to analyse some of the different policies articulated in the case law.

X. WILL A BENEFICIAL INTEREST BIND PURCHASERS?

5–040 We have already seen that an important consequence of the classification of an interest as a property right (as distinct from a merely personal right) is that the interest is of its nature considered to be capable of binding third parties. Anyone considering a transaction involving land will therefore be concerned to ascertain whether there are any such interests which could affect the purchaser's property. This is not the place for a full discussion of overriding interests, for which the reader is referred to the comprehensive land law texts.[51] Furthermore, the Land Registration Act 2002[52] will repeal the Land Registration Act 1925. In time the new legislation will eliminate unregistered title completely and make electronic conveyancing compulsory. The Act also aims to reduce the number of overriding interests. Within the confines of a family law text, the following briefest of accounts is offered.

The Land Registration Act 2002 will put an end to unregistered title, although this will take some years. Where title is unregistered, the purchaser's position has depended on the doctrine of notice: a person who purchases[53] a legal estate in land in good faith and for value takes the land free of any equitable right (such as a spouse's or partner's equitable beneficial interest) unless he has actual or constructive notice of that right. Broadly speaking, a person has actual notice of such a right if he or she knows about it; there is constructive notice if he or she ought to have known about it—if, for example, a purchaser would have known about it had he made such inquiries[54] and inspections as ought reasonably to have been made.[55] In *Kingsnorth*

---

[51] See *e.g.* E Burn, *Cheshire and Burn's Modern Law of Real Property* (16th ed., Butterworths, 2000), pp. 862–878; C. Harpum, *Megarry and Wade: The Law of Real Property* (6th ed., Sweet and Maxwell, 2000); K. Gray and S. Gray, *Elements of Land Law* (3rd ed., 2001) pp. 989–1032.

[52] Preceded by the Law Commission's extensive discussion in *Land Registration for the Twenty-First Century* (Law Com. No. 254) and *Land Registration for the Twenty-first Century: A Conveyancing Revolution* (Law Com. No. 271). For a succinct account, see E. Cooke, "The Land Registration Bill 2001" [2002] 66 *Conveyancer* 11.

[53] This expression includes a person who lends money on mortgage.

[54] On the extent of inquiries necessary to avoid constructive notice, see *Williams & Glyn's Bank Ltd v. Boland* [1981] A.C. 487 (this case was exclusively concerned with registered land; references to the position in unregistered conveyancing are *obiter*). The doctrine followed in *Caunce v. Caunce* [1969] 1 W.L.R. 286 and *Bird v. Syme-Thompson* [1979] 1 W.L.R. 440 that a wife's occupation of the matrimonial home is insufficient to put a purchaser on notice of her rights (*e.g.* on the ground that her occupation is "consistent" with her husband's title) was treated with scepticism by Russell L.J. in *Hodgson v. Marks* [1971] Ch. 892 at 934 and was rejected in *Boland* both by Lord Denning in the Court of Appeal [1979] Ch. 312 at 332 and by Lord Wilberforce.

[55] "Constructive" notice is now in effect defined by s.199(1) of the Law of Property Act 1925 which (under the rubric "Restrictions on constructive notice") provides that a purchaser is not prejudiced by notice of anything which under the Land Charges Act 1972 is unenforceable for non-registration or of "any other instrument or matter of fact or thing unless—(a) it is within his own knowledge, or would have come to his knowledge if such inquiries and inspections had been made as ought reasonably to have been made by him; or (b) in the same transaction with respect to which a question of notice to the purchaser arises, it has come to the knowledge of his counsel, as such, or of his solicitor or other agent, as such, or would have come to the knowledge of his solicitor or other agent, as such, if such inquiries and inspections had been made as ought reasonably to have been made by the solicitor or other agent." Restrictive construction has been given to the doctrine of constructive notice by the Court of Appeal in *B. v. B. (P. Ltd Intervening) (No.*

Trust Ltd v. Tizard[56] a husband told the lender that he was single. The lender's surveyor had seen no evidence that the house was occupied by the wife or any other female. But the judge held that the lender was bound by the wife's interest since an inspection by the lender's surveyor by prior appointment on a Sunday afternoon did not satisfy the test of reasonable inquiry set out above.

Under the Land Registration Act 2002 registration of title will be compulsory. For registered land, the general principle is that a registered proprietor takes free of any interest not disclosed on the register[57] and title to land is in principle to be regulated by and ascertainable from the register.[58] However, there is an important qualification of this principle, in so far as the registered title is made subject to a number of "overriding interests" set out in Schedules 1 and 2 of the Land Registration Act 2002. Schedule 1 contains those unregistered interests which override first registration, Schedule 3 those which override registered dispositions. Amongst these are (subject to certain qualifications) the interests of those in actual occupation, which may include an equitable interest of a family member not appearing on the register.[59]

Schedule 1 includes "an interest belonging to a person in actual occupation of the land." Under the repealed legislation the courts were troubled by what degree of physical presence sufficed to constitute "actual occupation".[60] The increasing trend of case-law was to emphasise that occupation must be apparent as well as actual.[61] According to Schedule 2 of the Act of 2002, the interest of a person in actual occupation will not override if inquiry was made of such a person before the disposition and he unreasonably failed to disclose the right; this reproduces the old law. Schedule 3 also exempts an interest if the occupation would not have been obvious on a reasonably careful inspection of the land at the time of the disposition and the person to whom the disposition is made did not have actual knowledge of the interest. In the words of one commentator[62] "this rules out the old conundrum about undiscovered occupation, whereby a purchaser's protection could be weaker in registered land." In other words, something akin to the doctrine of notice now applies on registered dispositions. No doubt the new provisions will generate case-law.

---

2) [1995] 1 F.L.R. 374 and *Halifax Mortgage Services Ltd v. Stepsky* [1996] 1 F.L.R. 620; [1996] Ch. 207; [1996] 2 W.L.R. 230; [1996] 2 All E.R. 277.

56 [1986] 1 W.L.R. 783.

57 See Land Registration Act 2002, ss. 11,12.

58 *Abbey National Building Society v. Cann* [1991] 1 A.C. 56 at 78 *per* Lord Oliver of Aylmerton.

59 *Williams & Glyn's Bank Ltd v. Boland* [1981] A.C. 487; *Le Foe v. Le Foe and Woolwich plc; Woolwich plc v. Le Foe and Le Foe* [2001] 2 F.L.R. 970 (wife). In *Hypo-Mortgage Services Ltd v. Robinson* [1997] 2 F.L.R. 71 the Court of Appeal held that young children could not be in actual occupation. Since they could not give an informed reply to an inquiry, a lender or purchaser could never be protected.

60 *Abbey National Building Society v. Cann* [1991] A.C. 56; *Stockholm Finance Ltd v. Garden Holdings Inc* [1995] N.P.C. 162.

61 By analogy with the doctrine of notice: see *per* Robert Walker L.J. in *Ferrishurst Ltd v. Wallcite Ltd* [1999] 2 W.L.R. 667.

62 E Cooke, "The Land Registration Bill 2001" [2002] 66 *Conveyancer* 11 at 28.

XI. PERSONAL PROPERTY

5–041 The family home will often be the only substantial asset at issue between the parties to a relationship; but there may also for example be disputes about the ownership of chattels[63] and entitlement to funds in a bank account. The law on these matters is far from clear."[64]

Sections 52 and 53 of the Law of Property Act 1925 have no application to personal property, and therefore entitlement to a chattel may in appropriate circumstances[65] be determined on the basis of an express trust evidenced by oral statements. In *Rowe v. Prance*[66] a couple made plans to buy a boat and sail the world. The boat was registered in the man's sole name on the excuse that the woman did not have an Ocean Master's Certificate, but he frequently referred to it as 'ours' and indicated that it was her security. The woman gave up her flat and stored her furniture. The world trip never transpired and the relationship eventually foundered. It was held that the man had constituted himself an express trustee of the boat. Furthermore, the shares were held to be equal; the regular use of the word "our" indicated that no distinction was to be drawn between the parties' ownership, or alternatively the maxim "equality is equity" applied.[67]

In the case of land or chattels, the claim which the courts often have to decide is whether the beneficial interest belongs to both husband and wife, even though the legal title is only in one. In the case of bank accounts, the claim is often the converse—*i.e.* that although husband and wife have had a joint account, the balance in it and any investments made out of it belong only to one of them.

The courts have established a number of guidelines applicable to such cases. First, it seems that if the parties pool their resources in a common fund, then each will have an interest as beneficial joint tenant in the whole of the fund.[68] Thus if both husband and wife pay their incomes into a joint bank account, each party is to be treated as equally entitled. On the death of one, the survivor will normally be entitled to the whole balance by operation of the right of survivorship generally applicable to joint ownership. However, if funds are withdrawn from a common pool account, property which is purchased with the proceeds will prima facie belong to the person who acquires the title: thus if a wife buys shares in her own name paying for them by drawing on a joint bank account they will prima facie belong to her absolutely.[69] This will not be so if

---

[63] Where title normally depends on the question of who has provided the purchase price and whether there has subsequently been an effective delivery of the property by way of gift to the other: *Re Cole* [1964] Ch. 175.

[64] The Law Commission concluded that the rules for determining the ownership of property during marriage are "arbitrary, uncertain and unfair" Law Com. No. 175 (1985), *Matrimonial Property*, para. 1.4.

[65] An express trust was found in *Paul v. Constance* [1991] A.C. 103 (repeated statements that "the money is as much yours as mine").

[66] [1999] 2 F.L.R. 787.

[67] For a critical evaluation, see S. Baughen [2000] 64 *Conveyancer* 58.

[68] *Jones v. Maynard* [1951] Ch. 572; *cf. Gage v. King* [1961] 1 Q.B. 188.

[69] *Re Bishop (dec'd)* [1965] Ch. 450.

there is evidence that the assets acquired were intended to be held in the same way as the fund,[70] but this would be unusual.

These principles of the common fund will only apply in cases where there has been a pooling of resources. If, in contrast, virtually all the funds are provided by one party the presumptions of advancement and resulting trust will (in the absence of other evidence) be applied to determine the ownership. It is for this reason that if a husband has his salary paid into a joint bank account, prima facie the account will belong to the spouses as joint tenants,[71] whereas if such an account were fed solely by a wife's earnings the result might well be different.

It is sufficient to rebut any presumption if it can be shown that the account was in joint names for reasons of convenience or for some limited purpose only.[72] One common reason for having a joint bank account is to enable the wife to continue to draw cash after the husband's death before probate has been granted. It has been held[73] that such an account (on which the husband continued to draw) has for the purposes of this rule been opened for convenience only; and that accordingly the wife acquired no interest before the husband's death.

Although an account may originally have been put into joint names for convenience only, the intention may change so that a beneficial joint interest arises.[74]

---

[70] *Jones v. Maynard* (above).

[71] *Re Figgis (dec'd)* [1969] 1 Ch. 123; *cf. Heseltine v. Heseltine* [1971] 1 W.L.R. 342, where a joint account was fed largely with the wife's capital; assets bought out of it were held to belong exclusively to her.

[72] *Re Figgis (dec'd)* [1969] 1 Ch. 123; *Marshall v. Crutwell* (1875) L.R. 20 Eq. 328; *Hoddinott v. Hoddinott* [1949] 2 K.B. 406; *Harrods Ltd v. Tester* [1937] 2 All E.R. 236; *Heseltine v. Heseltine* (above) (account only in joint names "for convenience of administration for the family purposes": *per* Lord Denning M.R. at 347).

[73] *Thompson v. Thompson* (1970) 114 S.J. 455.

[74] *Re Figgis* (above). Semble such a new intention will only affect monies subsequently paid into the account: *cf.* L.P.A. 1925, s.53(1)(c). Where there has been an agreement to marry—and this means a clear agreement, not merely a vague recognition of the possibility of a marriage at some unspecifed time in the future: *Bernard v. Josephs* [1982] Ch. 391 at 406—and this agreement has been terminated, the Law Reform (Miscellaneous Provisions) Act 1970, governs the situation. The Act (s.2(1)) applies "any rule of law relating to the rights of husbands and wives" to the resolution of disputes relating to property in which either party had an interest during the engagement.

CHAPTER SIX

STATUTORY REFORMS RELATING TO FAMILY PROPERTY

INTRODUCTION

6.001 This Chapter outlines six statutory reforms—of widely differing scope and varying degrees of practical significance—which directly affect ownership and occupation rights over family property. Each has been enacted piecemeal in response to a particular problem. These reforms fall far short of a co-ordinated fundamental reform of family property law as a whole,[1] which remains in an unsatisfactory and unco-ordinated state.[2] As will be seen, most of the reform enacted to date affords protection to spouses, and thus evidences a policy of privileging the institution of marriage over other relationships.

Chapter 9 addresses the question of future legislative reform of family property law.[3]

I. THE MARRIED WOMEN'S PROPERTY ACT 1964

6.002 At common law, if a husband provided his wife with an allowance out of his income for housekeeping, any sums not spent on this purpose remained his, and he was entitled to any property bought with such savings.[4]

This rule seemed symptomatic of the injustices done to married women (particularly those who devoted their lives to looking after the home). The Morton Commission[5] therefore recommended that savings made out of a housekeeping allowance should belong half to the husband and half to the wife; and the Married Women's Property Act 1964[6] now provides:

---

[1] Notwithstanding the investment by the Law Commission of considerable skill and effort in the subject over 30 years or more: see the publications cited in this chapter and Chap. 9.

[2] Commented on by the Court of Appeal in *Midland Bank v. Cooke* [1995] 2 F.L.R. 915; [1995] 4 All E.R. 562, CA and *Drake v. Whipp* [1996] 1 F.L.R. 826.

[3] In practice, for many families, the private law (with which this Part of the book has been almost exclusively concerned) has been of less importance than the public law; see R. Probert, "Cohabitants and the Family Home" [2000] *Fam.Law* 925. In recent years the legislation requiring local authorities in certain circumstances to provide housing for homeless persons has become of major significance when relationships break down. The homelessness legislation is discussed, briefly, in the following Chapter.

[4] *Blackwell v. Blackwell* [1943] 2 All E.R. 579; *Hoddinott v. Hoddinott* [1949] 2 K.B. 406. The law was reviewed by the Law Commission, *Matrimonial Property*, Law Com. No. 175 (1989).

[5] *Royal Commission on Marriage and Divorce Report 1951–1955* (Cmd. 9678 (1956)), para. 701.

[6] See O.M. Stone (1964) 27 *M.L.R.* 576.

> "If any question arises as to the right of a husband or wife to money derived from any allowance made by the husband for the expenses of the matrimonial home or for similar purposes, or to any property acquired out of such money, the money or property shall, in the absence of any agreement between them to the contrary, be treated as belonging to the husband and wife in equal shares."

This provision therefore confers a genuine proprietary interest in such savings: it applies not only if a marriage breaks down, but generally, and may assume some importance on death and insolvency. But it will be noted that the legislation perpetuates the stereotype under which a husband provides an allowance for his wife; and that it has no effect on provision made by a wife for her husband (much less on provision made between people who live together outside marriage).

The interpretation of the section gives rise to difficulty, for example[7]:—

(i) What is an "allowance" for this purpose? Does the expression cover the case where the wife has a power to draw on the husband's bank account?

(ii) What does "for the expenses of the matrimonial home or for similar purposes" mean? It is not, for example, clear whether payment of mortgage instalments is to be regarded as "an expense of the matrimonial home" or an expense of acquiring it.[8]

(iii) It is not clear whether the Act operates retrospectively[9]—*i.e.* whether it applies to savings made out of an allowance before the Act came into force or not. (It is, however, fair to say that this problem seems unlikely to be of great practical importance after the passage of 30 years.)

(iv) The Act applies to property acquired out of the allowance. However, the meaning of that expression is not clear: if, for example, part of the allowance is "invested" in a ticket in the National Lottery or in an entry on the football pools, are any winnings "derived from" the allowance?[10] Might it even be said that if money is given to pay mortgage instalments, the Act would not apply to give the wife a beneficial interest because the house was not bought with money derived from the allowance but rather from the allowance itself?[11]

Even when the legal effect of the Act is clear, the consequences sometimes seem bizarre. First, the Act creates a tenancy in common, so that the fund will

---

[7] The defects of the law were fully analysed by the Law Commission in PWP No. 90, *Transfer of Money between Spouses* (1985); and note that the Family Law (Scotland) Act 1985, s.26, reformulated this provision in its application to Scotland in an attempt to remove some of the defects referred to below.

[8] *Tymosczuk v. Tymosczuk* (1964) 108 S.J. 656.

[9] So held in *Tymosczuk v. Tymosczuk* (above), but doubted in *Re John's Assignment Trusts* [1970] 1 W.L.R. 955.

[10] *cf. Hoddinott v. Hoddinott* (above).

[11] Law Commission PWP No. 90, *Transfer of Money between Spouses* (1985), para. 4.7.

be held jointly by the spouses during their lives, but on death the share passes under the deceased's will or intestacy. Secondly, if a wife buys something obviously intended for her own personal use (perhaps, for example, jewellery) the Act apparently entitles the husband to a half share in it (unless the courts find there is an implied agreement to the contrary).

In all the circumstances, it may be doubted whether this Act (which was intended to redress a particular grievance of married women[12]) has had any great significance: in the almost four decades for which it has been on the statute book it has rarely been referred to, and seems to have had little effect on decisions. The Law Commission recommended repeal of the Act, and its replacement by a statutory presumption that property bought for the joint use or benefit of spouses should (subject to some exceptions) be jointly-owned by them, but those somewhat controversial proposals have never been implemented. It may be that the more limited approach adopted by the Family Law (Scotland) Act 1985—which creates a presumption that household goods (as narrowly defined) are to be jointly owned—would command more general support. In any event, the 1964 Act is of very little practical importance given the ancillary relief jurisdiction which operates on divorce[13] and is the principal forum in which disputes over property between husband and wife are detemined.

II. THE MATRIMONIAL PROCEEDINGS AND PROPERTY ACT 1970, s.37

6.003 One of the ways in which the courts tried to give effect to the partnership idea of marriage was to hold that a spouse who contributed in money or in labour to the improvement of the matrimonial home should be given credit on any realisation of the house for a proportion of the value, in so far as it was attributable to the work done in improving the property.[14] But it was never clear on precisely what juristic basis such a claim could be founded[15] and the Matrimonial Proceedings and Property Act 1970 was an attempt to remove uncertainty.[16] Section 37 provides:

[12] The Act originated in a Private Member's Bill introduced by Baroness Summerskill to give effect to a recommendation of the Morton Commission (para. 701).

[13] Discussed in Chap. 14.

[14] See *Appleton v. Appleton* [1965] 1 W.L.R. 25 at 28 and 29; *Jansen v. Jansen* [1965] P. 478.

[15] But see the explanation given by Lord Denning M.R. in *Davis v. Vale* [1971] 1 W.L.R. 1022 at 1025–1026.

[16] See Law Com. No. 25 (1969), para. 56. The Act is declaratory; and in *Re Pavlou (A Bankrupt)* [1993] 2 F.L.R. 751 a decision about giving a co-owner credit for improvements was resolved without any specific reference to the legislation; and again in *Midland Bank v. Cooke* [1995] 2 F.L.R. 915; [1995] 4 All E.R. 562, CA, no references were made to the provision notwithstanding the fact that the wife's claim to a beneficial interest in that case appears to have been largely founded on the improvements she had carried out. Nor was reference made to it in *Le Foe v. Le Foe and Woolwich plc*; *Woolwich plc v. Le Foe and Le Foe* [2001] 2 F.L.R. 970, where the wife appears to have made paid for some improvements to the home for the purposes of running a bed and breakfast business.

"It is hereby declared that where a husband or wife contributes in money or money's worth to the improvement of real or personal property in which or in the proceeds of sale of which either or both of them has or have a beneficial interest, the husband or wife so contributing shall, if the contribution is of a substantial nature and subject to any agreement between them to the contrary express or implied, be treated as having then acquired by virtue of his or her contribution a share or an enlarged share, as the case may be, in that beneficial interest of such an extent as may have been then agreed or, in default of such agreement, as may seem in all the circumstances just to any court before which the question of the existence or extent of the beneficial interest of the husband or wife arises (whether in proceedings between them or in any other proceedings)."

The following points should be noted:

(i) The Act only deals with contributions to the improvement (as distinct from the acquisition[17]) of property.
(ii) The Act only applies to contributions by husband or wife. The cohabitee (or child) has no claim under this provision.
(iii) The contribution must be in money or money's worth. A spouse who pays a contractor[18] for an extension to the house will be entitled, as will a spouse who carries out such an improvement himself. The test seems to be: is it the sort of work for which one would normally expect to have to pay?
(iv) The contribution must be "of a substantial nature." This is intended to prevent a claim arising in the case of the "do-it-yourself job which husbands often do."[19] The Act has been held to apply to payments made to have a house connected to the electricity supply, and for installing a water heater, sink unit, three fireplaces, a wall and iron gates,[20] and to the installation of a central heating system.[21]
(v) The contribution must effect an "improvement"; and this word seems to be used in contra-distinction to "maintenance."[22] The distinction may result in some curious anomalies: if a husband who is a jobbing builder takes time off from work to carry out extensive repairs to the roof or structure of the house or is an electrician who rewires the house, neither of these expensive services seems to give him any claim under the Act. But he does have a claim if he installs a prefabricated garage, although the value of this work is much less.

[17] For the rules applicable in such cases, see Chap. 5, above.
[18] *Griffiths v. Griffiths* [1974] 1 W.L.R. 1350 and *Re Nicholson (dec'd)* [1974] 1 W.L.R. 476.
[19] *per* Lord Denning M.R., *Button v. Button* [1968] 1 W.L.R. 457 at 461.
[20] *Davis v. Vale* (above).
[21] *Re Nicholson (dec'd)* (above).
[22] In *Re Nicholson (dec'd)* (above), Pennycuick V.-C. suggests that a replacement may not constitute an improvement. This must, however, be a question of degree.

(vi) The contribution must be identifiable with the relevant improvement; mere general contributions to looking after the home will not suffice.[23]

(vii) The Act applies to all types of property, real or personal; and it is not limited to a house bought as a matrimonial home. There seems to be no reason why it should not be invoked in relation to business assets, for example—although no doubt in the nature of things it is most likely to be invoked in respect of home improvement.[24]

(viii) The provisions of the Act yield to agreement between the spouses, whether express or implied from their conduct. The agreement may be negative—*i.e.* that, notwithstanding the work, no interest shall be acquired,[25] or positive—*e.g.* that the shares shall be a certain percentage of the proceeds of sale. On the strict wording of the Act, the agreement must be contemporaneous with the improvement.

(ix) The Act confers a genuine proprietary right which will be recognised in bankruptcy or for succession[26] purposes.

(x) The court is given a limited discretion in assessing the extent of the interest to which the contribution gives rise. However, this discretion is limited[27] and it seems that the court will in principle assess the outcome by reference to the increase in the value of the property which can be attributed to the improvements.[28]

(xi) If the spouses are joint tenants the acquisition of an enlarged share under the Act would apparently operate to sever the joint tenancy by destroying the unity of interest.[29]

In conclusion, section 37 now appears to be of little practical significance, particularly in view of (a) the broad-brush approach to quantification of benefi-

---

[23] *Harnett v. Harnett* [1973] Fam. 156 (appeal dismissed [1974] 1 W.L.R. 219); *Kowalczuk v. Kowalczuk* [1974] 1 W.L.R. 933.

[24] *Kowalczuk v. Kowalczuk* [1973] 1 W.L.R. 930. It was not referred to in relation to the enhancement of the home for the purposes of running a bed-and-breakfast business in *Le Foe v. Le Foe and Woolwich plc; Woolwich plc v. Le Foe and Le Foe* [2001] 2 F.L.R. 970.

[25] As, perhaps, in *Re Holliday (A Bankrupt)* [1981] Ch. 405 where the bankrupt claimed no interest in the matrimonial home of his second marriage, notwithstanding the fact that he had spent "considerable sums in or towards extensive alterations and redecoration of those premises."

[26] *Re Nicholson, (dec'd)* (above). *cf. Samuel's Trustee v. Samuel* (1975) 233 E.G. 149.

[27] Law Com. No. 25 (1969), para. 58, and explanatory note to draft clause 27.

[28] *Re Nicholson (dec'd)* (above); *Griffiths v. Griffiths* [1973] 1 W.L.R. 1454 (Arnold J.). Strictly, it may be that the court should assess the value of the property prior to each improvement, calculate the increase in value then brought about by the improvement, and enlarge the share of the improving spouse accordingly. But a calculation of this kind would be difficult to carry out in cases where there has been a series of improvements, and particularly if there is no satisfactory evidence of value. In such cases the court will probably "look at the situation in the round, to see what has been achieved by means of the improvements" in relation to the value of the house: *Griffiths v. Griffiths* (above) at 1457, *per* Arnold J.; and see *Re Nicholson, (dec'd)* (above) at 482–483. Of course, improvements "may add not one penny to the value of the house. Indeed, the alteration may well lower its value, for the alteration, though convenient to the owner, may be highly inconvenient in the eyes of a purchaser," *per* Lord Greene M.R., *Re Diplock* [1948] Ch. 465 at 546.

[29] See Chap. 5, section VI, above.

cial interests adopted in *Midland Bank v. Cooke,*[30] and (b) the existence of the ancillary relief jurisdiction which divides assets on divorce[31] and requires the court to consider *inter alia* the contributions made by each spouse to the welfare of the family.[32]

III. THE LAW REFORM (MISCELLANEOUS PROVISIONS) ACT 1970[33]

6.004 This Act was primarily concerned to abolish the action for breach of promise of marriage. As a consequence, it introduced a special code to deal with some of the proprietary problems which may arise when an agreement to marry[34] is terminated; and these rules may be of significance in cases where a couple who have lived together have also, at some stage, agreed to marry.[35]

The Act is complex. First, it introduces rules dealing with gifts between the betrothed. It provides that a gift of an engagement ring is rebuttably presumed to be absolute[36] but the Act retains the old rules of law under which most other gifts would be construed as conditional on the marriage taking place.[37] Secondly, the Act applies section 17 of the Married Women's Property Act 1882[38] "to any dispute between, or claim by, one [sic] of them in relation to property in which either or both had a beneficial interest while the agreement was in force"[39] provided that proceedings are instituted within three years of the termination of the agreement. However, this provision is of somewhat limited effect,[40] and does no more than to make the advantages of a summary procedure[41] available.

The Act also applies the rules of law governing the rights of husbands and wives in relation to property to the determination of beneficial interests in property acquired during an engagement.[42] These rules include not only the presumption of advancement[43] and the other principles, outlined above, whereby a beneficial interest in property may be obtained by financial contribution to its

---

[30] [1995] 2 F.L.R. 915; [1995] 4 All E.R. 562, discussed in full in Chap. 5.

[31] Discussed in Chap. 14.

[32] Matrimonial Causes Act 1973, s. 25(2)(f).

[33] The Act gives rise to a large number of problems of interpretation; but since the Act is in practice rarely invoked those difficulties are not dealt with in this or the previous edition: see for a detailed consideration the 4th edition of this work at pp. 689–692; and Cretney (1970) 33 *M.L.R.* 534.

[34] It has been held to be immaterial that the agreement might have been unenforceable before 1970 (*e.g.* on the ground that one or both parties were married to others at the relevant time): see *Shaw v. Fitzgerald* [1992] 1 F.L.R. 357, Scott Baker J.

[35] See *Bernard v. Josephs* [1982] Ch. 391 at 399, 402. The mere possibility of ultimate marriage being in a party's mind is insufficient to bring the provisions of the Act into play; what is required is a clear agreement or common fixed intention: *ibid.* at 406, *per* Kerr L.J.

[36] s.3(2). The term "engagement ring" is not defined; *cf. Elkington and Co. Ltd v. Amery* [1936] 2 All E.R. 86.

[37] *Cohen v. Sellar* [1926] 1 K.B. 536; *Jacobs v. Davis* [1917] 2 K.B. 532.

[38] As extended by s.7 of the Matrimonial Proceedings (Property and Maintenance) Act 1958.

[39] s.2(2); *Marsh v. von Sternberg* [1986] 1 F.L.R. 526.

[40] *Mossop v. Mossop* [1988] 2 F.L.R. 173.

[41] *Marsh v. von Sternberg* [1986] 1 F.L.R. 526; *Mossop v. Mossop* [1988] 2 F.L.R. 173 at 178, *per* Sir Frederick Lawton.

[42] s.2(**1**).

[43] *Mossop v. Mossop* [1988] 2 F.L.R. 173 at 176, *per* Balcombe L.J.

acquisition or improvement,[44] but also the statutory principle embodied in the Matrimonial Proceedings and Property Act 1970[45] whereby a substantial contribution in money or money's worth to the improvement of property may entitle the contributor to a beneficial interest in the property.

What the Act does not do is to give the parties any right to apply to the court for financial relief or property adjustment orders under the Matrimonial Causes Act 1973 or otherwise, since those powers are only exercisable in marital proceedings, *i.e.* as ancillary relief.[46]

IV. "MATRIMONIAL HOME RIGHTS" UNDER THE FAMILY LAW ACT 1996

A. Historical background

6.005 In 1965, the House of Lords held[47] that a married woman's common law right to be provided by her husband with a roof over her head[48] was a personal right and that it was accordingly incapable of binding a third party, even if the third party had notice of the wife's rights. A man might therefore, without consulting his wife, mortgage the family home and the wife would—unless she could establish that she was entitled to a beneficial interest which bound the purchasers[49]—have no defence to an action for possession brought by the lender to enforce the security. The Matrimonial Homes Act 1967 was primarily intended to remedy this defect in the law. It did so by giving spouses in occupation of the matrimonial home rights of occupation (including the right not to be evicted during the marriage unless the court otherwise orders) and by providing machinery—registration of a Class F Land Charge—whereby a spouse could make those rights bind third parties.

The Matrimonial Homes Act[50] was subsequently transformed by judicial

---

[44] Above, Chap. 5.

[45] s.37 of the Matrimonial Proceedings and Property Act 1970, above. *See Mossop v. Mossop* [1988] 2 F.L.R. 173 at 176, *per* Balcombe L.J.

[46] *Mossop v. Mossop* [1988] 2 F.L.R. 173 at 176–177 *per* Balcombe L.J.; *cf. Bernard v. Josephs* [1982] Ch. 391 at 403, 406.

[47] *National Provincial Bank Ltd v. Ainsworth* [1965] A.C. 1175.

[48] At common law the wife acquired, by virtue of the marriage, the right to cohabit with her husband and the right to support according to his estate and condition: see *National Provincial Bank v. Ainsworth* [1965] A.C. 1175, *per* Lord Wilberforce at 1244. The right to support included a right to be provided with housing, but this right was restricted in two main respects. First, the wife had no right to live in a particular house (see now *Syed v. Syed* (1980) 1 F.L.R. 129). Secondly, the right was only enforceable by the wife obtaining a decree of restitution of conjugal rights and seeking her husband's committal to prison for non-compliance: *Weldon v. Weldon* (1883) 9 P.D. 52.

[49] Usually under the doctrines of implied, resulting or constructive trust: see *Williams & Glyn's Bank Ltd v. Boland* [1981] A.C. 487.

[50] The Act was substantially amended (notably by the Matrimonial Homes and Property Act 1981, giving effect to recommendations about property law in the Law Commission's *Third Report on Family Property* (Law Com. No. 86); the legislation was eventually codified in the Matrimonial Homes Act 1983.

decision[51] into a codification of the law governing the jurisdiction of the court to make orders excluding one spouse from the home; and in that respect it has been replaced by the provisions contained in Part IV of the Family Law Act 1996.[52] Nevertheless, the provisions originally contained in the 1967 Act which created what have now come to be called "matrimonial home rights" remain important as part of property law; and the relevant provisions—amended in some respects by the 1996 Act and other legislation—are accordingly appropriately considered here in that context. Moreover, as will be seen, the existence of matrimonial home rights is relevant to the nature of the application to be made for an occupation order under Part IV of the Family Law Act 1996.[53]

B. When matrimonial home rights arise

6.006 A spouse's matrimonial home rights are defined by the Family Law Act[54] as:

(a) if in occupation, a right[55] not to be evicted or excluded from the dwelling house[56] or any part of it by the other spouse except with the leave of the court;
(b) if not in occupation, a right with the leave of the court so given to enter into and occupy the dwelling house.

C. Who is entitled to matrimonial homes rights?

6.007 As explained above, the concern of the Matrimonial Homes Act 1967 was to protect a spouse (usually a wife) who was vulnerable because she had no recognised property right in the home; and this concern is reflected in the definition

---

[51] *Richards v. Richards* [1984] 1 A.C. 174, HL, holding that the Matrimonial Homes Act 1983 codified and spelt out the jurisdiction of the court in relation to ouster proceedings between spouses and that applications during the marriage for orders relating to the occupation of the matrimonial home should accordingly be made under that Act. The real significance of what may appear to be an arid decision on procedure is that the 1983 Act laid down a principle to be applied by the court in exercising the discretion to make ouster and other orders, and this principle attached more weight to the conduct of the parties and the justice of the case (and correspondingly less weight to the interests of the children) than had sometimes been thought appropriate.

[52] F.L.A. 1996, Pt IV, "Family Homes and Domestic Violence". These provisions were originally intended to be enacted in the Family Homes and Domestic Violence Bill, but that Bill was withdrawn at a late stage in its passage through Parliament: see Chap. 10, below.

[53] Discussed in Chap. 10.

[54] s. 30(2). The definition is in substance identical to the definition of "rights of occupation" contained in the Matrimonial Homes Act 1983, s.1(1)(a). For a penetrating analysis of the concept, see *Wroth v. Tyler* [1974] Ch. 30, *per* Megarry J.

[55] The nature of which was discussed by Thorpe L.J. in *Foulkes v. Chief Constable of Merseyside Police* [1998] 2 F.L.R. 789 at 796.

[56] "Dwelling house" is defined as including "(a) any building or part of a building which is occupied as a dwelling, (b) any caravan, house-boat or structure which is occupied as a dwelling, and any yard, garden, garage or outhouse belonging to it and occupied with it": F.L.A. 1996, s.63(1). Matrimonial home rights do not arise in respect of a house which has at no time been, and which was at no time intended by the spouses to be, a matrimonial home of the spouses in question: s.30(7). A spouse may be entitled to matrimonial home rights in respect of more than one house—for example, a town house and a country cottage—but registration may only be effected in respect of one of them: F.L.A. 1996, Sched. 4, para. 2.

now embodied in the Family Law Act 1996.[57] A spouse has matrimonial home rights if the other spouse "is entitled to occupy a dwelling house by virtue of a beneficial estate or interest or contract" or "by virtue of any enactment giving that spouse the right to remain in occupation" and the other spouse is not so entitled. In effect, therefore, it is only a "non-owning spouse" who is entitled to matrimonial homes rights since the spouse who has a beneficial interest in the property is, by virtue of that fact, thought to be adequately protected against dispositions in favour of third parties.[58]

D. Making the matrimonial home rights bind third parties

6.008 Although, on a strict analysis, matrimonial home rights are personal in nature[59] (so that they cannot be assigned[60] and will come to an end on termination of the marriage by death or legal process[61] unless the court has otherwise ordered[62]) the legislation provides machinery whereby they may be protected, almost as if they were property rights, against third parties. The Family Law Act 1996[63] provides that where at any time during the subsistence of a marriage, one spouse is entitled to occupy a dwelling house by virtue of a beneficial estate or interest, then the other spouse's matrimonial home rights[64] are a charge on that estate or interest which has the same priority:—

> "as if it were an equitable interest created at whichever is the latest of the following dates—
>
> (a) the date on which the [entitled spouse] acquires the estate or interest,
> (b) the date of the marriage, and
> (c) January 1, 1968 . . ."[65]

---

[57] s. 30(1).

[58] In principle a beneficial interest will bind third parties. But F.L.A. 1996, s.30(9) provides that a spouse who has only an equitable interest shall be treated "for the purpose only of determining whether he has matrimonial home rights as not being entitled to occupy the dwelling-house by virtue of that interest", thus ensuring that such a person will be entitled to matrimonial home rights capable of protection by registration. For the evolution of the law, see the 4th edition of this work at pp. 247–248.

[59] Considered in the context of entitlement to bring an action in private nuisance by the House of Lords in *Hunter v. Canary Wharf Ltd* [1997] A.C. 666; for a critical comment on the decision, see S.Cretney [1997] *Fam. Law* 601.

[60] *Wroth v. Tyler* [1974] Ch. 30 at 45, *per* Megarry J.

[61] *O'Malley v. O'Malley* [1982] 1 W.L.R. 244.

[62] F.L.A. 1996, s.33(5).

[63] s.31(1), (2), (3) reproducing the effect of provisions in the Matrimonial Homes Act 1983.

[64] F.L.A. 1996 reproduces a number of complex provisions dealing with the (unusual) case where the dwelling house is a trust property and a married couple are living there because one of them is a beneficiary. These refinements are ignored in the explanation given in the text.

[65] The date of the commencement of the Matrimonial Homes Act 1967. For example, if H buys a house in July 1994, and gets married on November 1, 1995, the wife's charge will attach as from the latter date.

The charge must, if it is to bind third parties, be protected by registering[66] a notice under the Land Registration Act 2002[67] or (if the title is not registered under the 1925 Act) by registering it as a Class F Land Charge under the provisions of the Land Charges Act 1972.[68] Unless and until so registered the charge will be void against a purchaser[69] of the land or of any interest therein.[70]

The legislation thus reconciles the conflicting policies of giving protection to a wife and yet enabling transactions in land to take place without the purchaser having to make difficult and embarrassing inquiries about the vendor's matrimonial status. An intending purchaser searches for land charges as a matter of routine. If the search[71] reveals no charge the purchaser can be confident that no matrimonial home right can be asserted against the title.

It may be helpful to give an illustration of the working of these provisions:—

> Suppose that H (who is married to W) buys[72] Blackacre as a matrimonial home. At that moment a charge attaches to it in W's favour. But if, as is commonly done, H immediately on the same day (and indeed in fact, as distinct from traditional legal theory,[73] as part of the same transaction) mortgages the property to a building society, the wife's charge will not bind the building society.[74] This is because the charge was not protected by registration at the time that the mortgage was created. Hence, if H defaults on the mortgage payments, the building society will be entitled to enforce the mortgage by possession, sale, or other means.[75]
>
> If W does register a Class F charge after completion of the purchase and

---

[66] In order to comply with the Human Rights Act 1998, from May 28, 2001 the Land registry will automatically serve a notice informing the registered proprietor that an entry relating to a matrimonial home right has been made: see [2001] *Fam. Law* 414; Land Registration Rules 2001.

[67] F.L.A. 1996, s.31(10).

[68] Land Charges Act 1972, s.2(7) as amended by F.L.A. 1996, Sched. 8, para. 47.

[69] *i.e.* including a mortgagee.

[70] Land Charges Act 1972, s.4(8). It is expressly provided that the wife's rights do not constitute an overriding interest under the Land Registration Act 2002: F.L.A. 1996, s.31(10)(b). It is possible that an unregistered charge may affect priorities between competing equitable interests: *McCarthy & Stone v. Julian S. Hodges & Co.* [1971] 1 W.L.R. 1547; but *cf. Lloyd's Bank Ltd v. Rosset and Rosset* [1989] 1 F.L.R. 51, CA, particularly *per* Nicholls L.J.

[71] A purchaser will only be protected by an official certificate of search: *cf. Kaur v. Gill* [1988] *Fam. Law* 110, CA, where a purchaser who (apparently now a frequent practice) relied on a telephone inquiry was not protected. For a discussion of the advantages and disadvantages of the registration requirement, see the 4th edition of this work at pp. 259–60.

[72] Note that the protection afforded to a tenant is also limited in the absence of registration: *Sanctuary Housing v. Campbell* [1999] 2 F.L.R. 383.

[73] Legal theory seems now to have been brought (albeit with some difficulty) into line with reality: see *Abbey National Building Society v. Cann* [1991] 1 A.C. 56, not following *Church of England Building Society v. Piskor* [1954] Ch. 553.

[74] Although the wife will be entitled to meet the mortgage payments (F.L.A. 1996, s.30(5)), and has certain procedural protection in possession proceedings: see F.L.A. 1996, ss.54–56.

[75] However, the legislation contains important provisions whereby a spouse may make payments of mortgage instalments, rent and other outgoings which (in effect) have to be accepted as if made by the mortgagor or tenant; a spouse may thus be able to avoid a default situation arising: see now F.L.A. 1996, s.30(3). The court has power to order a party to make payments: s.40, although this provision is apparently unenforceable: *Nwogbe v. Nwogbe* [2000] 2 F.L.R. 744, CA. The Act also confers certain procedural protection in respect of mortgage enforcement: see ss.54–56.

mortgage, her right will bind subsequent purchasers—so that if, for example, H were to contract a second mortgage, the second mortgagee would take subject to W's rights.

In practice it is of course most improbable that a mortgagee would knowingly grant a mortgage subject to the wife's rights of occupation.[76] Accordingly, in practice—but not in theory—registration of a wife's rights under the Act may well prevent the husband from dealing with the property at all without the wife's consent.[77] One spouse may, therefore, be tempted to register a charge as a tactical device to exert pressure on the other to come to some financial arrangement. To act in this way is to misuse the legislation[78]; but it is not easy to ensure that such misuse does not occur.

E. Matrimonial home rights and bankruptcy

6.009 As originally enacted, the Matrimonial Homes Act gave effect to the policy of the law that a debtor's obligations to creditors took priority over the debtor's family obligations, and the matrimonial home rights were—even if registered—void against a debtor's trustee in bankruptcy. However, the Insolvency Act 1986 now provides some limited protection for the bankrupt and his or her family. It is provided that the spouse's charge on the bankrupt's estate or interest in the home continues to subsist, and binds the trustee in bankruptcy.[79] But the trustee in bankruptcy is empowered to apply to the bankruptcy court for an occupation order under section 33 of the 1996 Act, and it is provided that the court may then make such order as it thinks just and reasonable having regard to all the circumstances (some of which are specified[80]) "other than the needs of the bankrupt". Where the application is made more than one year from the bankruptcy, the court is required to assume, unless the circumstances of the case are exceptional,[81] that the interests of the bankrupt's creditors outweigh all other considerations.[82] The effect of this provision, as interpreted by the courts, is that the bankrupt's family have been given a year's grace in the absence of truly exceptional circumstances.[83] As noted in Chapter 5, whether this is compliant with

---

[76] But for an unusual case in which a purchaser was bound by the wife's matrimonial home right, see *Kaur v. Gill* [1988] Fam. 110, CA (in which under the legislation then in force the Court of Appeal refused to make an order in favour of the wife giving her an exclusive right to occupy).

[77] The legislation provides that a person entitled to a charge may postpone or release it: F.L.A. 1996, Sched. 4, paras 5, 6 (and, for an example of a case in which this was done, see *Banco Exterior Internacional v. Mann* [1995] 1 F.L.R. 602). The Act also contains a provision protecting the position of a contracting purchaser; Sched. 4, para. 3.

[78] *Barnett v. Hassett* [1981] 1 W.L.R. 1385.

[79] Insolvency Act 1986, s.336(2) as amended by F.L.A. 1996, Sched. 8, para. 57.

[80] Insolvency Act 1986, s.336(4), as amended.

[81] For an illustration of exceptional circumstances, see *Re Bremner (A Bankrupt)* [1999] 1 F.L.R. 912 (elderly wife caring for elderly and infirm bankrupt husband; bankrupt's state of health taken into account only as relevant to the distinct needs of the wife)

[82] *ibid.* s.336(5).

[83] See the discussion in Chap. 5.

Article 8 of the European Convention for the Protection of Human Rights and Fundamental Freedoms is currently under challenge.[84]

F. Matrimonial home rights and court orders relating to occupation of the matrimonial home

6.010 The reader should be reminded that this Chapter is concerned with property law (using that term to mean rights capable of binding third parties). The power of the court to make orders as between the parties relating to the occupation of the property is dealt with in Chapter 10 below, whilst the powers of the divorce court to re-adjust beneficial interests in property is dealt with in Chapter 14.

V. COURT'S POWERS TO ORDER TRANSFER OF CERTAIN TENANCIES

6.011 By virtue of section 53 of and Schedule 7 to the Family Law Act 1996,[85] the court has power to transfer[86] a statutory, protected, secure or assured tenancy[87] on divorce or on separation of cohabitants. In relation to the latter, these provisions represent a not insignificant policy development, given the stormy legislative history of the original Family Homes and Domestic Violence Bill 1995 and the suspicions of Conservative MPs towards the extension of rights to the unmarried. Nevertheless, the provisions are limited in their scope. The Act stops short of giving a generalised power to transfer tenancies of the family home, much less giving a power to transfer the fee simple. Moreover, the powers are exercisable only between heterosexual partners.[88]

Where the court exercises the power of transfer it may direct the transferee to make a compensation payment to the other.[89] Guidelines are given for the exercise of the discretion to transfer, and on the question of whether a compensation order should be made.[90] The court must consider all the circumstances, including the parties' (and children's) housing needs and resources, financial resources, the effects of any order, their suitability as tenants, and, in relation to cohabitants, the nature of their relationship and the duration of their cohabitation.

---

[84] *Jackson v. Bell* [2001] EWCA Civ. 387 [2001] *Fam. Law* 879 (permission to appeal given).

[85] S. Bridge, "Transferring Tenancies in the Family Home" [1998] *Fam. Law* 26; A. Woelke, "Transfer of Tenancies" [1999] *Fam. Law* 72.

[86] Transfer by a sole tenant and by a joint tenant may be ordered: Sched. 7, paras 2(1), 3(1), 6; *Gay v. Sheeran* [1999] 2 F.L.R. 519.

[87] The power applies to protected or statutory tenancies under the Rent Act 1977, secure tenancies under the Housing Act 1985, statutory tenancies under the Rent(Agricultural) Act 1976, and assured tenancies under the Housing Act 1998: Sched. 7, para. 1.

[88] See the definition of cohabitant in s. 62(1) of the Family Law Act 1996.

[89] Sched. 7, para. 10.

[90] Sched. 7, para. 5.

VI. RIGHT FOR SPOUSES, ETC., TO INVOKE SUMMARY PROCEDURE

6.012 In 1882, the Married Women's Property Act provided a summary procedure (available, irrespective of the value of the property in issue, in the county court as well as in the High Court) for the determination of disputes about the title to or possession of property. This summary procedure has been made available to former spouses[91] and (as already mentioned[92]) to those who have been engaged.[93] The Married Women's Property Act procedure does not enable the court to vary property rights[94]; but it is said[95] that the summary procedure will be quicker, simpler and cheaper than an ordinary action.

---

[91] Matrimonial Property and Proceedings Act 1970, s.39.

[92] See section III, above.

[93] Law Reform (Miscellaneous Provisions) Act 1970, s.2. In 1995 the Government accepted the Law Commission's recommendation that the summary procedure should be made available to cohabitants and former cohabitants; and provision to that effect was included in the Family Homes and Domestic Violence Bill. However, this provision came to be seen by some as symptomatic of that Bill's failure to uphold the institution of marriage; and it is not reproduced in the 1996 Act. It may be that opposition to the proposed change did not appreciate its extremely limited scope.

[94] *Pettitt v. Pettitt* [1970] A.C. 777, HL.

[95] By the Law Commission in its *Report on Domestic Violence and Occupation of the Family Home* (Law Com. No. 207 (1992)), para. 6.0014.

CHAPTER SEVEN

STATE SUPPORT FOR FAMILIES

7–001 This Chapter contains a short account of two aspects of state support for families in need: public sector housing and welfare benefits. For more detailed discussion beyond the scope of a family law text, the reader is referred to the standard works on these topics.[1]

PART I: HOMELESSNESS AND PUBLIC SECTOR HOUSING[2]

INTRODUCTION

7–002 The pattern of property tenure in this country has changed dramatically, particularly since the end of the Second World War. There has been a dramatic fall in the number of lettings and a correlative steep rise in home-ownership. By 1995 only 10 per cent of the population rented privately.[3] In recent years there has been a virtual cessation of local authority house building, coupled with the disposal of much local authority stock through the right to buy scheme instituted in the 1980s.[4] Voluntary housing associations have played some (albeit limited) role in remedying the shortfall, especially since the mid 1990's. Despite the reduced availability of accommodation,[5] the duties imposed on local authorities in respect of housing the homeless remain significant in the context of relationship breakdown. Many of the cases accepted as having a "priority need"[6] arise from the breakdown of a relationship with a partner.

Although it is impossible in a book of this kind to give an adequate account even of those aspects of housing law which are primarily relevant to family breakdown, the reader may find a short account of the following topics of assistance in putting the law in context:

---

[1] To which reference is made where appropriate in footnotes in this Chap.

[2] See D. Cowan, *Housing Law & Policy* (Macmillan, 1999); J. Morgan, *Housing Law* (Blackstone Press., 1998). Both these works contain excellent analysis of the social and political background which is essential to an understanding of the details of the complex legal regulation.

[3] Cowan, *supra*, n.2, at p. 57.

[4] The right to buy scheme is discussed later in this Chap.

[5] In [2002] *Fam. Law* 179 G Douglas commented that cases such as *R v. Northavon D.C. ex parte Smith* [1994] 2 A.C. 402, *The Queen on the Application of G v. Barnet LBC* [2001] EWCA Civ. 540; [2001] 2 F.L.R. 877 and *The Queen* on the *Application of A. v. Lambeth LBC* [2001] EWCA Civ. 1624; [2002] 1 F.L.R. 353 "illustrate that there continues to be a dearth of suitable accommodation, and very limited resources available to local authorities to meet the diverse needs of the populations living within their boundaries".

[6] For the meaning of "priority need" see below.

(1) Local authorities and homelessness.
(2) The right to security of accommodation in public sector housing.
(3) The right to buy local authority accommodation.

The fall in the number of private lettings means that only the briefest note of the protection afforded to private sector lettings is appropriate in this text. It is provided at the conclusion of Part I of this Chapter.

I. LOCAL AUTHORITIES AND HOMELESSNESS

7–003 The Housing Act 1996 requires a local authority to provide assistance to certain eligible[7] persons who are homeless or threatened with homelessness. Local authorities are required to maintain a register of qualifying persons[8] and an allocation scheme operates.[9] One explanation for homelessness is simply that the resources from the disposal of one owner-occupied home are inadequate to provide housing for two families. Another common situation is where a victim of domestic violence is restricted to short-term relief under the domestic violence legislation[10] and seeks help from the local authority.[11]

A. The local authority's duty

7–004 The Housing Act 1996[12] prescribes in detail the duties[13] which local authorities owe to the homeless, the most significant being the duty to secure that accommodation is available for the applicant's occupation.[14] "Homeless or threatened homelessness" is defined in the statute. The Act provides[15] that a person is homeless if he has no accommodation available for his occupation which he is

---

[7] Housing Act 1996, s.185; applicants are not eligible for assistance if they are subject to immigration control under the Asylum and Immigration Act 1996, unless they come within the exceptions prescribed by the Housing Accommodation and Homelessness (Persons Subject to Immigration Control Order) 1996, S.I. 1996 No. 1982 as amended by the Homelessness (Persons Subject to Immigration Control (Amendment)) Order 1997, S.I. 1997 No. 628. For illustrations of ineligibility, see *R. v. Hammersmith and Fulham LBC ex p. Damoah* (1999) 2 C.C.L.R. 18 and *The Queen on the Application of G v. Barnet LBC* [2001] EWCA Civ. 540; [2001] 2 F.L.R. 877. On the local authority's duty to provide suitable interim accommodation for asylum-seekers under s.188 of the Housing Act 1996, see *R. v. Ealing LBC ex p. Surdonja* [1999] *Fam. Law* 85.

[8] Housing Act 1996, s.162.

[9] Housing Act 1996, ss.159, 167.

[10] See Chap. 10, below.

[11] Research has indicated that 15% of those statutorily homeless are victims of domestic violence: Morley and Pascal, "Women and Homelessness" [1996] *J.S.W.F.L.* 327.

[12] A duty to formulate a homelessness strategy will be added by the Homelessness Act 2002, ss.1–4.

[13] Including the duty to provide advice and information: Housing Act 1996, s.179. There is a duty to provide interim accommodation for an applicant considered to be eligible pending investigation: Housing Act 1996, s.188.

[14] Housing Act 1996, s.193(2). Even if an applicant is in this category, only limited duties have arisen if there is other suitable accommodation available in the area: s.197; but this provision will cease to have effect under the Homelessness Act 2002, s.9.

[15] Housing Act, 1996, s.175(1).

entitled to occupy by virtue of an interest in it or by court order, or by licence or statutory right. A person is not to be treated as having accommodation unless it is accommodation which it would be reasonable for that person to continue to occupy.[16] The Act further provides that is not reasonable for a person to continue to occupy accommodation if it is probable that this will lead to violence[17] against him or a member of his family residing or expected to reside with him. Violence is now defined so as to include threats of violence which are likely to be carried out[18] from a person with whom he is associated. In the case of domestic violence the persons must be associated[19]; this is defined in the Housing Act 1996[20] in the same way as in the Family Law Act 1996.[21]

The duty to secure that accommodation is available for occupation[22] is owed only to those with priority need who are not homeless intentionally.[23] The two-year limit[24] on this duty will be abolished by the Homelessness Act 2002.[25] Priority need is defined; the statutory criteria most likely to be relevant on relationship breakdown are that the applicant is (a) a person with whom dependent children reside or might reasonably be expected to reside[26]; (b) vulnerable as a result of old age, mental illness, handicap etc[27] (c) a pregnant woman or a person with whom she resides.[28] The commonest priority qualification is that the household has dependent children. It has been held that it is wrong for a local authority to require that a parent obtain a residence order as a means of proving that she satisfies the requirement of the Act.[29]

---

[16] *ibid.* s.175(3). A restrictive interpretation was given in *R. v. Hillingdon LBC ex p. Pulhofer* [1986] A.C. 484. In *R. v. Brent LBC ex p. Awua* [1996] A.C. 55 it was held that the accommodation need not be settled or permanent.

[17] Housing Act, s.177 (1); extended from domestic violence to "other violence" by the Homelessness Act 2002, s.10(1). In *R. v. Ealing LBC ex p. Sidhu* (1983) 3 F.L.R. 438 it was held that a woman who has fled to a refuge may be classified as homeless; but see *per* Lord Hoffmann in *R. v. Brent LBC ex p. Awua, supra.* On local authority practice in relation to proof of violence, see Malos and Hague, *Domestic Violence and Housing: Local Authority Responses to Woman and Children Escaping from Violence* (1993).

[18] Housing Act 1996, s.177 (1A), as substituted by s.10(1) of the Homelessness Act 2002.

[19] *ibid.*

[20] *ibid.* s.178.

[21] Family Law Act, s.62(3); see Chap. 10.

[22] Lesser duties are owed to persons becoming homeless intentionally (s.190) and to those not in priority need who are not homeless intentionally (s.192); these mainly concern the provision of advice and assistance in obtaining accommodation.

[23] Housing Act 1996, s.193.

[24] *ibid.* subs. (3).

[25] s.6.

[26] Housing Act 1996, s.189(1)(b). For a case in which a father (unsuccessfully) claimed priority need founded on his having a joint custody order, see *R. v. Port Talbot B.C., ex p. McCarthy* (1990) 23 H.L.R. 207, CA; but in *R. v. Lewisham LBC, ex p. Creppy* (1991) 24 H.L.R. 121 the fact that the child was being informally fostered did not negative entitlement. There is no requirement that the children be exclusively dependent on and resident with the applicant: *ex p. Vaglivi-ello* [1991] *Fam. Law* 143.

[27] *ibid.* s.189 (1)(c); this also encompasses vulnerable persons residing with the applicant. In *Ortiz v. City of Westminster* (1995) 27 H.L.R. it was held that the applicant must show both that he is less able to obtain accommodation than the ordinary person and that if he files to obtain it he will suffer more than most.

[28] *ibid.* s.189(1)(a).

[29] *R. v. Ealing London Borough, ex p. Sidhu* (1982) 80 L.G.R. 534, DC.

An Authority has only limited duties[30] to a person who has become homeless intentionally.[31] The Act provides[32] that a person becomes homeless intentionally if he deliberately does or fails to do anything in consequence of which he ceases to occupy accommodation which is available for his occupation and which it would have been reasonable for him to occupy. There is a vast amount of case-law on the interpretation of the statutory provisions, but in practice non-payment of rent or mortgage interest is often the crucial factor.[33] In the context of relationship breakdown it has been claimed that many authorities require women who have been subjected to harassment by their former partners to use all available matrimonial remedies—notably to apply to exclude the partner from the home—if the woman is to avoid being classified as intentionally homeless.[34]

B. To whom is the duty under the housing legislation owed?

7–005 The duty to secure that accommodation is available[35] is owed only to the person who is homeless and in priority need:—

> In *R v. Oldham Metropolitan Borough Council, ex parte Garlick*[36] the local authority found that an applicant was in priority need, but that he had—by deliberately omitting to make mortgage payments—become homeless intentionally. The applicant did not challenge that decision, but made a fresh application under the Act in the name of his four-year-old son. The House of Lords held that this application had been properly rejected: a healthy four-year-old child living with his or her parents[37] was owed no duty under the Act because dependent children were not amongst those classified as in priority need; and it was the intention of the Act that the child's accommodation be provided by the parents or those looking after

---

[30] Housing Act 1996, s.190. Difficult questions can arise where intentional homelessness could be made out against one partner but not against the other: contrast *Lewis v. North Devon D.C.* [1981] 1 W.L.R. 328 and *R. v. Mole Valley D.C., ex p. Burton* [1989] *Fam. Law* 64.

[31] And to persons who are not homeless intentionally but are not in priority need: Housing Act 1996, s.192.

[32] *ibid.* s.191(1).

[33] See *R. v. Salford City Council, ex p. Devonport* (1983) 8 H.L.R. 54, CA; *R v. Eastleigh Borough Council, ex p. Beattie (No. 2)* (1984) 17 H.L.R. 168, Q.B.D; cf. R. v. Wandsworth LBC, ex p. Hawthorne [1995] 2 All E.R. 331.

[34] The findings from the sample analysed by R. Thornton, "Housing through Relationship Breakdown: The Local Authorities' Response" [1988] *J.S.W.L.* 67 can be supported by reference to reported cases. In *R. v. Wandsworth London Borough, ex p. Nimako-Boateng* [1984] F.L.R. 192 at 196, Woolf J. said: "There is all sorts of protection that a women can get if her husband misbehaves. The local authority could perfectly properly in many cases in this country take the view that it would be reasonable for the wife to continue to occupy the accommodation and to say to a wife, if she thinks it right: 'If you are having trouble with your husband, go to the appropriate authority, be it a magistrates' court or the Family Division, and get protection against your husband."' And see *Thurley v. Smith* [1984] F.L.R. 875, CA, where the local authority made the exercise of its discretion turn on the question of whether an ouster order were made.

[35] Housing Act 1996, s.193.

[36] [1993] 2 F.L.R. 194, HL.

[37] It was accepted that a child under 16 who left home might be vulnerable and able to establish a priority need: see *per* Lord Griffiths at 197.

the child. If the application were successful, the "intentional homelessness" provisions could rarely if ever be applied to a family with dependent children.

C. Relationship with other local authority duties

7–006 If a housing authority makes a finding of intentional homelessness under the homelessness legislation, it has not been obliged[38] to comply with a request[39] from a social services department to help a child in need by providing housing for a child in need, if to do so would not be compatible with the housing authority's duties and obligations. For example:—

> In *R v. Northavon District Council, ex parte Smith*[40] Mr Smith applied to the housing authority (Northavon) for housing for himself and his five dependent children; but Northavon determined that he had become homeless intentionally. Mr Smith then approached Avon as the relevant social services authority with a view to their performing their duty to safeguard the welfare of the children by making cash payments to cover rent and deposits.[41] Avon refused to do so; but instead invoked the power to ask the Housing Authority (Northavon) to help with the provision of housing. Northavon said they had performed their duties under the Housing Act 1985, and that it would be a "contradiction" to offer the Smiths a tenancy in the light of the intentional homelessness decision. Mr Smith's application to quash Northavon's decision failed. There was a duty for the authorities to co-operate the one with the other, but an action for judicial review was not the way to obtain that co-operation. The authorities[42] "must together do the best they can".

The relationship between local authorities' duties under the Housing Act 1996 as currently framed and those under the Children Act 1989 has been explored in recent case-law. In *The Queen on the Application of G v. Barnet London Borough Council*[43] the mother of a young child was ineligible for assistance with accommodation under the Housing Act 1996 as a homeless person because she did not satisfy the habitual residence requirement. After providing her with temporary accommodation the local authority gave her notice that she would not be given further accommodation but offered to accommodate the child (who was assessed as being in need). The Court of Appeal held *inter alia* that the provisions of the Children Act 1989[44] did not impose a duty to provide accommodation for child and mother together. Such a far-reaching duty would leave

---

[38] Under the Housing Act 1996: see *The Queen on the Application of G v. Barnet LBC* [2001] EWCA Civ. 540 [2001] 2 F.L.R. 877.

[39] Made under Children Act 1989, s.27.

[40] [1994] 2 A.C. 402, HL.

[41] See Children Act, s.17(6).

[42] *per* Lord Templeman at 410.

[43] [2001] EWCA Civ. 540; [2001] 2 F.L.R. 877.

[44] ss. 17(3),(6), s. 20, s. 23(6).

the authority with virtually no discretion and would make Part VII of the Housing Act 1996 irrelevant whenever an intentionally homeless person was parent of a young child. In *The Queen on the Application of A v. Lambeth London Borough Council*[45] the Court of Appeal confirmed that the accommodation to be provided to a child in need under section 20 of the Children Act 1989 is confined to situations where there is no intact family unit. The Court held that section 17 of the Children Act was not itself directed to the provision of accommodation and was not a duty enforceable in judicial proceedings at the suit of an individual. The Court held further that there was no power to provide accommodation for a family under section 17. In reaction to this decision, Parliament enacted section 12 of the Homelessness Act 2002, requiring housing authorities to provide social services departments with advice and assistance in respect of families otherwise ineligible for housing assistance. However, in *The Queen on the Application of W v. Lambeth London Borough Council*[46] a differently constituted Court of Appeal held that section 17 did give the local authority the power to provide accommodation for a family.[47]

II. THE RIGHT TO SECURITY OF ACCOMMODATION IN PUBLIC SECTOR HOUSING

7–007 The homelessness legislation thus gives some people a right to have housing provided for them by a local authority; but before the enactment of the Housing Act 1980 (now consolidated in the Housing Act 1985) tenants of local authority housing had virtually no legal security of tenure (although in practice they could reasonably expect that the authority would not terminate their tenancy except for good cause). Because of this, it was often possible for a local authority to bring to an end a couple's joint tenancy, and re-allocate the property to the man or woman alone.[48]

The Housing Act 1985[49] gives security of tenure to most public sector tenants who satisfy the condition that they occupy the property as their only or principal home.[50] However, a tenancy granted under a housing authority's duty to provide accommodation for the homeless is not a secure tenancy unless the tenant has been notified that it is regarded as secure.[51] Where a tenancy is secure, the general principle[52] is that a tenant's right to protection from eviction is only lost in the following cases:

---

45 [2001] EWCA Civ. 1624; [2002] 1 F.L.R. 353, CA.
46 [2002] EWCA Civ 613; [2002] 2 F.L.R. 328.
47 Comment by G. Douglas in [2002] *Fam. Law* 592.
48 See *Davis v. Johnson* [1979] A.C. 264 at 343, HL, *per* Lord Salmon.
49 Pt IV, as amended by the Housing Act 1996.
50 Housing Act 1985, s.81. *Crawley B.C. v. Sawyer* (1988) 20 H.L.R. 98.
51 Housing Act 1985, Sched. 1, para. 4.
52 It is possible that a person ousted from the home by court order for a substantial period will no longer satisfy the condition that the tenant occupy the home as his or her only or principal home: see *Fairweather v. Kolosine* (1984) 11 H.L.R. 61 (where the order was for five years); and note the dicta of Ralph Gibson L.J. in *Wiseman v. Simpson* [1988] 1 F.L.R. 490 at 498.

(i) where the authority obtains a possession order founded on one of the grounds (for example, non-payment of rent,[53] nuisance, domestic violence[54]) specified in the Act.[55]

(ii) where the court makes an order under statute[56] transferring the tenancy while it is subsisting.

(iii) where the tenant agrees, and assigns the tenancy in accordance with the provisions of the Act[57]; and

(iv) if the other joint tenant gives the local authority notice to quit. The local authority may then grant a tenancy in the sole name of the tenant who gave notice to quit, which can be a desirable outcome for the victim of domestic violence. From another perspective, the former joint tenant who loses his home through the other giving notice to quit is in a vulnerable position.[58]

III. THE RIGHT TO BUY LOCAL AUTHORITY HOUSING[59]

7–008 The right to buy, introduced by the Housing Act 1980,[60] was perhaps the most fundamental change of recent years in relation to publicly funded housing policy. Basically, a secure tenant of public sector housing has the right (provided that he or she has held the tenancy for a short period) to acquire the freehold in the rented property at a price which may usually be left on mortgage, and which is discounted (up to 65 per cent in London, 75 per cent elsewhere) of the average value of local authority houses and flats in each government region. The promotion of home-ownership by successive governments, the ready availability of credit facilities and the attractions of the right to buy scheme as a means of

---

[53] In *Burrows v. Brent LBC* [1997] 1 F.L.R. 178 the House of Lords held that in the absence of special circumstances an agreement by a landlord not to enforce strictly an order for possession—based here on non-payment of rent—did not create a new secure tenancy or licence under Pt IV of the Housing Act 1985; followed in *Brent LBC v. Knightley* [1997] 2 F.L.R. 544.

[54] Housing Act 1996, s. 145.

[55] Housing Act 1985, s.84 and Sched.2 (Ground One).

[56] Family Law Act 1996, s. 53, Sched. 7; Matrimonial Causes Act 1973, s.24; Children Act 1989, Sched. 1. Such orders do not infringe the prohibition on assignment contained in the Housing Act 1985: see s.91(3)(b)5.

[57] Housing Act 1985, s.91(3).

[58] In *Hammersmith and Fulham LBC v. Monk* [1992] A.C. 478, HL a man and woman were joint tenants of a local authority flat. The woman had discussions with the authority in the light of which she gave the authority notice to quit. Subsequently the authority granted her a tenancy in her own name. However, the effect of that decision is somewhat restricted by the requirement that the necessary formalities be complied with: see *Hounslow LBC v. Pilling* [1993] 2 F.L.R. 49, CA (notice to quit had to be given at least four weeks before the date on which it was to take effect by reason of the provisions of Protection from Eviction Act 1977). It is difficult to reconcile *Burton v. Camden LBC* [1998] 1 F.L.R. 681 with *Hammersmith, supra*. There is no statutory duty for one joint tenant to consult the other before giving notice to quit: *Crawley B. C. v. Ure* [1995] 1 F.L.R. 806, CA. See also *Harrow LBC v. Johnstone* [1997] 1 F.L.R. 887, where a husband had an injunction prohibiting his exclusion; the House of Lords held that the wife could still give notice to quit to the landlord, and that this was not a contempt of court.

[59] Davis and Hunter "Purchase of the Family Home Under the Right to Buy Provisions" (1996) 8 *C.F.L.Q.* 313.

[60] Now Housing Act 1985, Pt V.

acquisition in the low-cost sector have given rise to social problems, not the least the dramatic reduction of stock available for those in real need of public sector accommodation.[61]

If the right to buy is exercised, it might be thought that the former tenant would be in exactly the same position as any other owner of property, and that the rights of the former tenant and the family would be governed by the private law of property adjustment discussed in Chapter 13, below. However, a complication arises because some or all of the discount allowed on the purchase is repayable if there is a "relevant disposal which is not an exempted disposal" within three years.[62]

What is the position if the owner's marriage breaks down, and the property becomes subject to the divorce court's adjustive jurisdiction within the three year period? Generally speaking, a disposal under the terms of a property adjustment order in divorce proceedings will be an exempt transfer[63] and no question of a liability to repay the discount will arise. However, in *R. v. Rushmoor Borough Council, ex parte Barrett*[64] the Court of Appeal held that a sale pursuant to a court order under the Matrimonial Causes Act 1973, s.24A was not within this exemption (which, it was said, Parliament had intended to confine to cases where there had been a property adjustment within the family rather than an out-and-out sale). This decision was excessively technical and gave scope for avoidance measures. For example, if the court settled the house on trust for H and W until the expiration of six months from the order a subsequent sale would qualify as an exempt transfer, whereas if an immediate sale were ordered the discount would be repayable. The anomaly was removed by section 24A of the Matrimonial Causes Act 1973 being added to the list of exempt disposals by the Housing Act 1996.[65]

IV. REGULATION OF PRIVATE SECTOR TENANCIES

7–009 As noted at the beginning of this Chapter, the number of private sector tenancies has declined sharply from the position in the early years of the twentieth century. Until 1988, the Rent Act 1977 provided rent control plus a high degree of security of tenure (through protected and statutory tenancies), as well as succession rights, in the private sector. The Housing Act 1988 put an end to the creation of new regulated tenancies under the Rent Act 1977. The 1988 Act created assured and assured shorthold tenancies,[66] but the measure of protection offered falls well short of that under the Rent Act 1997.

---

[61] On the extent of uptake of the option of home-ownership by this means, and the policies of successive governments, see D. Cowan *Housing Law and Policy* (Macmillan, 1998), pp. 340–357.

[62] Housing Act 1985, s.155(2).

[63] *ibid.* s.160(1)(c).

[64] [1988] 2 F.L.R. 252, CA.

[65] Housing Act 1996, s. 222, Sched. 18, para. 15(3).

[66] Section 96 of the Housing Act 1996 provides that a tenancy satisfying the criteria is (subject to certain exceptions) presumed to be an assured shorthold tenancy.

The number of protected and statutory tenancies under the Rent Act 1977 has now ben closed for some years, and numbers are naturally greatly diminished and still diminishing. However, in 1998 a case concerning succession to a Rent Act tenancy attracted much professional and popular attention. In *Fitzpatrick v. Sterling Housing Association Ltd*,[67] the applicant lived with his same-sex partner for 18 years in a flat of which the partner was the protected tenant. On his partner's death he sought a declaration that he was entitled to succeed to the tenancy. The First Schedule to the 1977 Act entitles a person who was "living with the original tenant as his or her wife or husband" to become the statutory tenant[68] and "a member of his or her family residing with him or her in the dwelling-house at the time of an for a period of two years before the death" to be entitled to an assured tenancy.[69] In the Court of Appeal[70] Waite and Roch L.JJ. held that the applicant did not qualify under either definition; according to Ward L.J.,[71] dissenting, he qualified under both. The House of Lords was unanimous in rejecting the claim under the first definition, but by a majority[72] held that the applicant was a member of the deceased tenant's "family" at the relevant time. The speeches made it clear[73] that the case concerned only a narrow issue of statutory interpretation under this particular legislation, and not the rights of homosexuals in the law generally.

According to their Lordships, the 1988 amendment extending the category of those entitled to become statutory tenants was intended to cover those who although not legally husband and wife lived together as such without being married. The terminology employed—"his or her or wife or husband"—indicated cohabitation between members of the opposite sex.[74] Parliament in 1988 had not intended[75] that terminology to include "my same-sex partner".[76]

By a majority of three to two, it was held that the applicant was entitled to an assured tenancy as having been a member of the deceased's "family" residing in the home at the relevant time. The interpretation of the statutory terminology was held to be one of mixed law and fact.[77] The majority considered that Parliament had deliberately left the term "family" undefined in the Rent Act 1977,

---

67 [2000] 1 F.L.R. 271; [1999] 3 W.L.R. 1113.

68 Rent Act Sched. 1, para. 2(2); Housing Act 1988, s. 39(2), Sched. 4, Pt 1, paras 2 and 3.

69 ibid. para. 3. This category had existed since 1920.

70 [1998] Ch. 304; [1998] 1 F.L.R. 6.

71 Strongly criticised by Lord Hobhouse for overstepping the legitimate bounds of the judicial function in relation to statutory interpretation: [1999] 3 W.L.R. 1113 at 1152.

72 Lord Slynn of Hadley, Lord Nicholls of Birkenhead and Lord Clyde, Lord Hutton and Lord Hobhouse of Woodborough dissenting.

73 [1999] 3 W.L.R. 1113 at 1118 (Lord Slynn), 1129 (Lord Hobhouse), 1136, 1138 (Lord Clyde).

74 See *e.g.* Lord Slynn at 1118, Lord Nicholls at 1127, Lord Clyde at 1131, Lord Hutton at 1140, Lord Hobhouse at 1153.

75 Lord Hutton and Lord Hobhouse asked why it had not done so: [1999] 3 W.L.R. 1113 at 1141, 1151-3 and 1155-6.

76 Contrast the view of Ward L.J. in the Court of Appeal: [1998] 1 F.L.R. 6 at 38–40; see comments by N. Wikeley (1998) 10 *Child and Family Law Quarterly* 191 and R. Bailey-Harris [1997] *Fam. Law* 784.

77 See the criticism of this distinction by S. Cretney and F. Reynolds in "Limits of the Judicial Function" (2000) 116 *L.Q.R.* 181.

and had intended the term to be interpreted broadly and flexibly.[78] The purpose[79] of the statutory provision was to provide a measure of security for those who shared their lives with the tenant on the premises in a way which characterises a family unit. That unit is characterised by mutual interdependence, sharing, caring, affection, commitment and support between the members, and can be brought into existence by choice as well as by virtue of kinship.[80] It is a question of fact whether a particular relationship satisfies those characteristics. The sexual element of the relationship in the instant case appeared to be of crucial significance to the majority.[81] The minority adopted a narrower construction of "family" in this context, one limited to those in a legal or *de facto* relationship to the tenant of blood or affinity[82] and were concerned about floodgates potential if a wide definition were to be adopted.[83]

PART II: STATE FINANCIAL SUPPORT: THE WELFARE BENEFIT SYSTEM AND FAMILY BREAKDOWN

7–010 It would be impossible to give a comprehensive account[84] of state financial provision[85] in a book of this kind; but this Part of the Chapter attempts to outline the main features likely to be relevant in situations of family breakdown.

I. HISTORICAL INTRODUCTION

7–011 Family breakdown has always involved the risk of destitution; and for many years the Poor Law provided a measure of relief to the casualties—sometimes by the provision of a subsistence level of support in "outdoor" relief to those (for example, widowed mothers and their children[86]) considered "deserving", but otherwise by committal to the workhouse[87] in an attempt to ensure that the

---

78 *ibid.* [1999] W.L.R. 1113 at 1119 (Lord Slynn), 1124–5 and 1129 (Lord Nicholls), 1132 and 1138 (Lord Clyde).

79 *ibid.* at 1125–7 (Lord Nicholls), 1132 (Lord Clyde).

80 *ibid.* at 1122 (Lord Slynn), 1127 (Lord Nicholls), 1135 (Lord Clyde).

81 Criticised by R. Bailey-Harris in "New Families For a New Society?" in *Family Law at the Millennium,* (S. Cretney ed., Family Law, 2000) 67 at 73.

82 [1999] W.L.R. 1113 at 1144, 1153, 1155. See *Carega Properties v. Sharrat* [1979] 1 W.L.R. 928 (elderly tenant and young man who regarded themselves as aunt and nephew did not qualify).

83 *ibid.* at 1147; see also *per* Lord Hutton. See also Lord Hobhouse at 1155.

84 See Ogus, Barendt and Wilkeley, *The Law of Social Security* (4th ed., N.J. Wilkeley *et al.* ed., 1995); *Social Security Legislation* Vols I, II and III (Sweet and Maxwell, 2001); *Supplement, 2001–2*; *Welfare Benefits Handbook 2002–2003* (Child Action Poverty Group); *The Law Relating to Social Security* (Stationery Office, 11 Volumes).

85 The child support scheme is dealt with in Chap. 15 and enforcement procedures in Chap. 16.

86 The single mother and her children were generally treated unfavourably—notably by being denied outdoor relief and being required to enter the workhouse—in comparison with the widow and her children: see App. 5, "The History of the Obligation to Maintain" by M. Finer and O.R. McGregor in *Report of the Committee on One Parent Families* (Cmnd. 5629, (1974)), Vol. 2, pp. 121 *et seq.*

87 Which imposed "severely deterrent conditions upon its inmates, as well as subjecting them to loss of civic rights, separation from their spouses, and a deliberately imposed stigma of pauperism": Finer and McGregor, *op. cit.*, para. 55.

pauper's condition was less eligible than that of the poorest labourer and that the poor law did not provide a "bounty on indolence and vice".[88] In the first half of the twentieth century further provision was made by the creation of state-provided insurance-based pensions for the widows and families of those who had made sufficient contributions in their working lives[89]; but proposals to bring other unsupported mothers and their families into the scheme were rejected.[90]

The Beveridge Report, published in 1942,[91] was the origin of the modern social security system. It comprehensively explored the possibility of extending insurance-based contributory benefits to cover the risk of family breakdown brought about by events other than the death of a husband[92]; but in the event no progress was made. The result was that widows whose husbands had made the necessary contributions over the years became entitled to pensions, but no comparable provision was available for divorced, deserted or separated wives or for unmarried mothers. However, the creation of the Welfare State aimed to ensure that adequate support would be available for all who were truly poor. In 1948, the Poor Law was repealed,[93] and replaced by the National Assistance Act 1948. The legislation provided that every person in Great Britain whose resources (as defined) were insufficient to meet his or her requirements (also as defined) became entitled to receive a supplementary allowance[94]; and it was[95] the policy of the law to eradicate the stigma attached to the Poor Law by insisting that supplementary benefits were the subject of rights and entitlement, and that no shame attached to the receipt of them. However, the supplementary benefit system preserved one important principle derived from the Poor Law: although the state might provide financial support for a claimant, it was also entitled to recover the amounts disbursed from any person legally bound to support the claimant (the so-called "liable relative"[96]). In practice, therefore, supplementary benefit law came to constitute a third system of family law, at

---

[88] *Report of the Poor Law Commissioners* (1834) as cited in Finer and McGregor, *op cit.*, para. 54.

[89] Widows', Orphans' and Old Age Contributory Pensions Act 1925; and provision for widows' pensions was extended by statute in 1929, 1937 and 1940.

[90] M. Finer and O.R. McGregor, "The History of the Obligation to Maintain" (App. 5 to the *Report of the Committee on One Parent Families* (Cmnd. 5629, (1974)), Vol. 2, para. 84.

[91] Social Insurance and Allied Services, (Cmnd. 6404, (1942)).

[92] See generally J. Harris, *William Beveridge: A Biography* (1977); and, for the place of the Beveridge Report in the context of the welfare state, R. Lowe, *The Welfare State in Britain since 1945* (1993). An account of the reactions of officials and others can be found in M. Finer and O.R. McGregor, "The History of the Obligation to Maintain" (App. 5 to the *Report of the Committee on One Parent Families* (Cmnd. 5629 (1974)), Vol. 2, pp. 136–149).

[93] National Assistance Act 1948, s.1.

[94] Supplementary Benefits Act 1976, s.1(1).

[95] *per* Finer J., *Reiterbund v. Reiterbund* [1974] 1 W.L.R. 788 at 797; see also *Reform of the Supplementary Benefits Scheme* (Cmnd. 773, 1979), para 4.

[96] The "liable relative" principle was stated with admirable clarity in Social Security Act 1976, s.17; but although the meaning has remained substantially unaltered the consolidating legislation (Social Security Administration Act 1992) succeeds in obscuring the principle in a series of inter-related provisions: see notably ss.78(6)–(9) and 105. An excellent history of the liable relative procedure is given in the *Report of the Committee on One Parent Families* (Cmnd. (5629, (1974)) (hereinafter referred to as "Finer Report"), paras 4.173 *et seq.* (and see also M. Finer and O.R. McGregor, "The History of the Obligation to Maintain" App. 5 to the Finer Report, particularly para. 112).

least as important as the codes of family law administered in the divorce court and in the magistrates' domestic jurisdiction.

Changing political philosophies—in particular, the commitment of successive governments to the values of economic self-reliance and personal responsibility—coupled with economic conditions have led to many changes in the social security system. For many years, lawyers and the courts developed schemes which maximised the availability of welfare benefits on divorce, particularly in the context of the so-called "clean break" settlement.[97] Dependance on welfare assistance—and government disapproval thereof—appeared to reach its height in the late 1980s and early 1990s. The number of single-parent families apparently grew at an unprecedented rate—from eight per cent of all families in 1971 to 21 per cent in 1992.[98] Three quarters of a million lone parents came to depend on income support,[99] and it was estimated that benefits paid to lone parents had risen from £1.75 billion in 1981–2 to £3.6 billion in 1990.[1] By 1989, less than a quarter of those families who were receiving income support were in receipt of any provision by way of maintenance payments (whereas in 1981–2 about half such families had some support from this source); and the proportion of lone parents in work seemed to be falling, with only 23 per cent of lone parents in full time (and 17 per cent in part time) employment.[2] In the light of these matters, the Conservative Government made significant changes in the social security system, some intended to increase the effectiveness of the liable relative procedure, and some intended to improve the employment prospects of parents. The most far-reaching change was the enactment of the Child Support Act 1991 and the creation of the Child Support Agency intended to create an efficient system whereby absent parents would be required to support their children at a realistic level. We discuss the merits—and failings—of the system of child support in Chapter 14. The Labour Government elected in 1997 has continues to promote a philosophy[3] of economic self-reliance and the strategy of encouraging a shift from "welfare to work" by individuals wherever possible, thus reducing dependence on public assistance. To this end there has been some move from the payment of benefits to the provision of tax credits,[4] such as the Working Families Tax Credit and the childcare tax credit described below. Conditions for entitlement to benefits have been made more rigorous and amounts available to assist with housing costs (both rent and mortgage interest) strictly controlled. The one-parent benefit was abolished in 1998.

The principal statutes are the Social Security Contributions and Benefits Act

---

[97] Chap. 14, below.

[98] See General Household Survey 1992; and for a survey, commissioned by the Government and heavily influential in the policy changes culminating in the enactment of the Child Support Act 1991, see J. Bradshaw and J. Millar, *Lone Parent Families in the U.K.* (1991).

[99] Children Come First (Cm. 1263 (1990)).

[1] See K. Kieman and M. Wicks, *Family Change and Future Policy* (1990).

[2] J. Bradshaw and J. Millar, *Lone Parent Families in the U.K.* (1991).

[3] HM Treasury *Work Incentives* (1998); DSS *New Ambitions for our Country: A New Contract for Welfare*, Cm. 3805 (1998).

[4] *Work Incentives, supra*, Chap 3.

1992[5] and the Social Security Administration Act 1992. The Jobseekers Act 1995 introduced the Jobseekers Allowance to replace unemployment benefit and income support for the unemployed, and imposed demanding eligibility criteria based on availability for work, particularly in the case of young people. The Social Security Act 1998 reformed the system of decisions and appeals. Some further changes of substance were made by the Welfare Reform and Pensions Act 1999 and the Child Support, Pensions and Social Security Act 2000.[6] In Chapter 14, we describe the abolition of the child maintenance bonus and its replacement by a new incentive intended to encourage parents with care to work. The remaining part of this Chapter provides a brief outline of the range of tax credits and benefits most relevant to family breakdown.

II. TAX CREDITS

7–012 Certain tax credits are available to families in full-time but low paid work; they are intended to act as an incentive to take up even low paid work rather than remaining dependent on welfare benefits.[7] In October 1999 Family Credit was replaced by the Working Families Tax Credit.[8] The benefit is administered by the Tax Credit Office of the Inland Revenue. The claimant or partner must be engaged and normally engaged in remunerative work for not less than 16 hours per week. The claimant or partner must be responsible for a child or young member of the household.[9] Income and capital must be below prescribed levels—*i.e.* a means test applies. The capital limit is £8000.[10] If the relevant net income of the family is below an "applicable amount" calculated by reference to the number of children in the family, then "maximum family credits" are payable. If income exceeds the applicable amount, the maximum credit is reduced by 55 per cent of the excess.[11] Maintenance paid regularly is treated as income and is disregarded for the purpose of this benefit.[12] However, no mortgage assistance is available with this tax credit.

A family receiving Working Families Tax Credit is eligible for a childcare tax credit.[13] This provides 70 per cent of actual costs of up to £135 a week for one child and £200 for two or more. It was introduced as an incentive to mothers—and single mothers in particular—to work rather than remain on benefit; the former family credit scheme had made no allowance for child care costs.

---

[5] Consolidating and updating the Social Security Act 1986.

[6] For details of the primary legislation, see the references in n. 3, *supra,* which also contain details on the vast amount of delegated legislation.

[7] *Work Incentives, supra,* para. 3.19.

[8] HM Treasury *The Modernisation of Britain's Tax and Benefit System; Number 3: The Working Families' Tax credit and work incentives* (1998). See S.S.B.A. 1992, s. 128, and the Family Credit (General) Regulations 1987 (S.I. 1987 No. 1973) as amended.

[9] Family Credit (General) Regulations 1987, reg. 7.

[10] S.S.C.B.A. 1992, s. 134.

[11] S.S.C.B.A., s. 128(2)(b); FC (G) Regs, reg. 48.

[12] F.C.(G) Regs, reg. 16(2) and para. 47.

[13] F.C (G) Regs, reg. 46A.

III. SOCIAL SECURITY BENEFITS

7–013 Social security benefits can be classified as means-tested and non-means tested (although the term "income -related" is often preferred to "means-tested" in official circles). Means-tested benefits are paid to those below thresholds of income and capital and require a detailed investigation of the claimant's financial circumstances. Benefits may also be classified as contributory and non-contributory, entitlement to the former depending on contributions to the National Insurance Scheme paid by the individual or a spouse or dependant. The following brief discussion adopts the first classification. The means test is described separately.

Means tested benefits

Income support

7–014 This used to be the main benefit for the unemployed, but was replaced as such by the Jobseekers Allowance created by the Jobseekers Act 1995 (see below). Income support[14] (which is a non-contributory benefit) nevertheless retains significance for lone parent families. Lone parents are not absolutely obliged to be available for employment and therefore do not receive Jobseekers' Allowance.[15] The claimant for income support must be over 16, not be in "remunerative work" (defined as not less than 16 hours per week paid work),[16] and not be entitled to a Jobseekers' Allowance. This means that some part-time work can be undertaken without removing eligibility, but earnings affect the amount payable. The claim is made not simply for an individual but for a family unit, including a spouse, partner and dependent children under 19 living in the home. Income support supplements income by an "applicable amount"[17] set by regulation. It is available to those with childcare responsibilities such as lone parents and those on parental leave from work.[18] Only one member of a family can claim income support.[19] The "cohabitation rule" is discussed below.

A claimant's eligible housing costs are included in the "applicable amount"; and this is of particular significance in the context of marital breakdown since those costs include mortgage interest payments[20] on a loan used to "acquire an interest in the dwelling occupied as the home." It was, as explained elsewhere in this book,[21] possible in this way to arrange divorce settlements under which a wife would remain in the former matrimonial home and the costs—potentially

---

[14] For qualifications, see S.S.C.B.A. 1992, s. 124; Income Support (General) Regulations 1987 (S.I. 1987 No. 1967) as amended, especially reg. 21.

[15] However, entitlement to income support is now conditional upon attending a work-focussed interview: WRPA 1999, s. 57, inserting new s. 2A–2C in the S.S.A.A. 1992.

[16] I.S.(G) Regs, regs 2, 4, 6.

[17] S.S.C.B.A. 1992, s.124(4).

[18] I.S.(G) Regs, Sched. 18, paras 1–6 and 14 and 12A.

[19] S.S.C.B.A. 1992, s.134(2).

[20] A "qualifying home loan" is defined in the Income Support (General) Regs, Sched. 3 para. 15.

[21] See Chap. 13, below.

very large—of the mortgage interest would fall on the taxpayer through the income support scheme. The fact that an income support claimant would be entitled to housing costs of substantial amounts which would be forfeited if the claimant went into full-time employment came to be seen as a substantial disincentive to self-sufficiency attained through employment.[22] Not surprisingly, therefore, the availability of income support in this context has been progressively restricted. The same restrictions apply to the Jobseekers' Allowance. No mortgage interest has been payable on new housing loans contracted from October 1, 1995 during the first 39 weeks on benefit.[23] Since April 10, 1995 the maximum ceiling on loans has been £100,000.[24] There are restrictions on excessive housing costs.[25]

Housing costs other than mortgage interest—for example, rent payable to a private landlord—are now, generally speaking, recoverable if at all through the housing benefit scheme.[26]

Jobseekers' Allowance

7–015 The Jobseekers' Allowance[27] is the main benefit for the unemployed and for those employed for less than 16 hours a week who are seeking full-time employment. It is available to all persons who are unemployed and required to seek employment, and therefore its details are outside the scope of a family law text. If the family unit comprises two adults who are unemployed, Jobseekers' Allowance will be the principal benefit. The qualifications[28] are that a person is not in full-time work but is capable of work, is actively seeking it and otherwise satisfies labour market conditions. The "applicable amount" payable is the same as under income support. The system[29] requires a claimant to attend a new Jobseeker's Interview, to sign a Jobseeker's Agreement and and thereafter to attend fortnightly interviews to ensure continued compliance with the labour market requirements, *e.g.* of availability for work.

Eligible housing costs are available—and restricted—in the same way for the Jobseekers' Allowance as for income support.[30]

The means test

7–016 Both income support and income-based Jobseekers' Allowance are means-tested.[31] If the total of a claimant's capital assets exceeds a specified amount

---

[22] "The generosity of the scheme for those out of work can create huge disincentives to move back into work—but to extend help with mortgages to people in work would be immensely costly": Mr Peter Lilley, Hansard H.C. Vol. 246, col. 1207.
[23] Income Support (General) Regs, Sched. 3 para. 1(2).
[24] Income Support (General) Regs 1987, Sched. 3, para.11(4) and (5).
[25] Income Support (General) Regs, Sched. 3 para 13.
[26] See below.
[27] Jobseekers' Allowance may also be contributory where National Insurance payments have been made.
[28] Jobseekers' Act 1995, s.1.
[29] For details, see the Jobseekers' Allowance Regs 1996, S.I. 1996 No. 207.
[30] See *e.g.* the Jobseekers' Allowance Regs 1996, Sched. 2, paras 1 (2), 10(3) and (4), 12 and 14.
[31] The details are beyond the scope of the present discussion. See Income Support (General) Regs 1987, reg. 35, 36, 45, 47, 53, Scheds 9, 10; Jobseekers' Allowance Regs 1996, reg. 98, 107, 116, Scheds 6, 7.

(currently £8,000) the claimant is not entitled to the benefit. If it exceeds £3,000 the capital is deemed to give rise to a so-called tariff income of £1 per week for each £250. The regulations lay down a general rule that the whole of the claimant's capital shall be taken into account and assessed at its current market value, save in so far as certain specified assets are disregarded. Disregards which are particularly relevant in the context of relationship breakdown include the dwelling occupied as the home, personal chattels, and the surrender value of life policies

As to income, the general principle is that the whole of the earnings and other income of members of the family is calculated on a weekly basis and goes to reduce the amount of benefit entitlement. "Earnings" is widely defined, but certain income is disregarded; the amount of disregard (there are three levels) depends on the circumstances.[32]

The cohabitation rule

7–017 The capital and income of both married and unmarried couples are aggregated for the purpose of Income Support and Jobseekers' Allowance. The legislation provides[33] that "married couple" means a man and woman who are married to each other and are members of the same household. It follows from this that when a couple separate they cease to be within this definition and in practice a wife whose husband leaves will often have recourse to income support. The expression "unmarried couple" is defined[34] to mean a man and a woman who are not married to each other "but are living together as husband and wife otherwise than in prescribed circumstances." The underlying policy is clear: where a couple live together as husband and wife the fact that they are not legally married should not make their position either better or worse than a couple who are in fact married.[35] If there were no such rule an unmarried couple would be significantly better off than a married couple.

The need to make investigations (often in secret) into a couple's private life in an attempt to ascertain the whether they are cohabiting is commonly seen as offensive by those concerned. It is not surprising that the application of the rule has given rise to much controversy; but case-law has accepted a number of criteria.

It is clear that in order to establish that a couple are living together as husband and wife it is not sufficient to show that they are living in the same household. The fact that they are doing so may well be strong evidence, but it has been said to be necessary to go on and ascertain, in so far as this is possible, the manner in which and the reason why the couple are living together in the same household.[36] Thus, for example, a person who lives in a household simply as a

---

[32] Income Support (General) Regs 1987, Sched. 8, paras 5, 6, 9; Jobseekers' Allowance Regs 1996, Sched. 6, paras 6, 11–12.

[33] S.S.C.B.A. 1992, s.134; J.S.A. 1995, s.35.

[34] S.S.C.B.A. 1992, s.137; J.S.A. 1995, s.35.

[35] See *Crake v. Supplementary Benefits Commission* [1982] 1 All E.R. 498 at 501, 502, *per* Woolf J.; see also *Paterson v. Ritchie* 1934 S.C. (J.) 42, *per* Lord Anderson.

[36] *ibid.*

housekeeper, or to look after a sick or incapable person, would not fall within the definition.[37] It is clear that the intention of the parties is a highly relevant factor[38]; but on the other hand it has been doubted whether a person's intention can be ascertained otherwise than by what he or she does and says at the relevant time.[39] On that view, conduct is the decisive factor.

It is for the authority which is seeking to establish that aggregation of the means of the two people concerned is justified to prove that cohabitation is occurring. Guidance is given in the Adjudication Officers' Guide, as amended from time to time. The main criteria to be taken into consideration are as follows, although the list is not exhaustive[40]:

(a) Members of the same household. The parties must be living in the same household, apart from periodical absences due to illness, holidays, or work.[41] **7–018**

(b) Sharing daily life. This means "mutuality in the daily round" of tasks and duties.[42] **7–019**

(c) Stability. Living together as husband and wife clearly implies more than an occasional or very brief association. When a couple first live together, it may be clear from the start that the relationship is similar to that of husband and wife (for example, if the woman has taken the man's name and has borne his child), but in cases where at the outset the nature of the relationship is less clear it may be right not to regard the couple as living together as husband and wife until it is apparent that a stable relationship has been formed. **7–020**

(c) Financial support. In most husband and wife relationships one would expect to find financial support of one party by the other, or sharing of household expenses, but the absence of any such arrangement does not of itself prove that a couple are not living together. **7–021**

(d) Sexual relationship. A sexual relationship is a normal part of a marriage and therefore of living together as husband and wife. But its absence at any particular time does not necessarily prove that a couple are not living as husband and wife, nor does its presence prove that they are. If a couple have never had such a relationship, it may be wrong to regard them as living together as husband and wife.[43] **7–022**

---

[37] *ibid.*

[38] R(G) 3/81; see also *Kaur v. Secretary of State for Social Services* [1981] 3 F.L.R. 237; *Robson v. Secretary of State for Social Services* [1981] 3 F.L.R. 232; *Kimber v. Kimber* [2001] 1 F.L.R. 232

[39] *Crake v. Supplementary Benefits Commission* [1982] 1 All E.R. 498 at 505, *per* Woolf J.

[40] *Kimber v. Kimber* [2001] 1 F.L.R. 383 (a case on cessation of maintenance under the Matrimonial Causes Act 1973, discussed in Chap. 14), but nevertheless arguably useful guidance in the social security context).

[41] *Kimber v. Kimiber* [2000] 1 F.L.R. 383.

[42] *ibid.*

[43] *Re J. (Income Support: Cohabitation)* [1995] 1 F.L.R. 660 at 666 *per* Social Security Commissioner M. Rowland.

(e) Children. When a couple are caring for a child or children of their union, there is a strong presumption that they are living as husband and wife.

7–023 **(f) Public acknowledgment.** Whether the couple have represented themselves to other parties as husband and wife is relevant. However, many couples living together do not wish to pretend that they are actually married. The fact that they retain their identity publicly as unmarried people does not mean that they cannot be regarded as living together as "husband and wife". What is important is the public acknowledgement of their common life.

Finally, it should be noted that once the necessary relationship has been shown to exist, it may be difficult to rebut the presumption that it is continuing.[44]

Maintenance and the liable relative procedure

7–024 In principle, all payments made by a "liable relative" are taken into account as income for the purpose of the means test. Payments made by way of income support or jobseekers' allowance made for separated wives and children is recoverable from "liable relatives". The Social Security Administration Act 1992 provides[45]:

> "(a) a man shall be liable to maintain his wife and any children of whom he is the father, and (b) a woman shall be liable to maintain her husband and any children of whom she is the mother."

Liability to maintain for these purposes is not directly affected by any financial order made in matrimonial proceedings. In *Hulley v. Thompson,*[46] a consent order in divorce proceedings provided that the husband transfer the matrimonial home to the wife, but that he pay no maintenance to the wife or children. It was held that this did not exclude his liability to maintain them under the supplementary benefit provisions. So far as children are concerned, for practical purposes the provisions of the Social Security Administration Act 1992 have been overtaken by the Child Support Act 1991[47]; in other words, the liable relatives procedure is now relevant only in respect of spouses.

The Benefits Agency traces and contacts the person concerned and ask him or her to make voluntary payments. The aim is to ensure that the liable relative pays the amount which would remove the dependant's need for income support altogether, but in practice the Agency exercises wide discretion to negotiate an appropriate sum.[48] If no acceptable offer is forthcoming, recourse may be had to legal action. The Secretary of State may apply to a magistrates' court for an order,[49] and the court must have regard to all the circumstances and, in particu-

---

[44] *Crake v. Supplementary Benefits Commission* [1982] 1 All E.R. 498–502, *per* Woolf J.
[45] ss. 78(6) and 105(3).
[46] [1981] 1 W.L.R. 159; and see *Crozier v. Crozier* [1994] 1 F.L.R. 126.
[47] Described in Chap. 15.
[48] See National Audit Office *Report on Support for Lone Parent Families* (1990, H.C. 328), para. 4.3. Officials used an administrative formula.
[49] Social Security Administration Act 1992, s. 106(1); Jobseekers' Act 1995, s. 23.

lar, to the income of the liable person, and may order the liable person to pay such sum, weekly or otherwise, as it may consider appropriate.[50]

A spouse may take proceedings for financial relief against the other; and the traditional policy was for long to "encourage and assist" a woman to take such proceedings herself: only in cases in which a claimant is unwilling to take proceedings is direct action by the Secretary of State considered.[51] Under a long-standing practice known as "the diversion procedure", arrangements are made for payments due under the order to be made or transferred to the Benefits Agency[52]; and in this way the regularity of a claimant's income is not affected by the fact that the payments due under the order are not made regularly. Where the claimant is a lone parent the Secretary of State may take enforcement action whether the claimant agrees to his doing so or not.[53]

Housing benefit

7–025 Housing benefit is non-contributory and is available to those on low incomes who pay rent. The importance of housing to the welfare of families has long been reflected in government policy. From 1915 central government provided financial assistance with the costs involved, but the main responsibility was transferred to local authorities by the Social Security and Housing Benefit Act 1982. The current housing benefit scheme derives from the Social Security Act 1986[54] (now consolidated in the Social Security Contributions and Benefits Act 1992[55]) the principal objective of which was to achieve a greater harmonisation between housing benefit and other welfare benefits. Under the 1986 Act a person on income support was originally entitled to a maximum of 100 per cent of the eligible rent.

In the changed political climate of the 1990s the housing benefit scheme was seen to be excessively generous. The Secretary of State[56] regarded the cost as being unacceptable, and pointed out that a scheme which gave full indemnity for tenants' rents meant that they had no incentive to choose the more economical of two dwellings or to negotiate over their rent level, while landlords were tempted to increase rents accordingly. It was said that taxpayers meeting their own rents resented subsidising higher rents than they could themselves afford; and that people on housing benefit should have similar incentives to those paying their own rents when deciding what they could afford. Accordingly, with effect from the January 2, 1996,[57] the general principle of a "maximum housing benefit"

---

[50] Social Security Administration Act 1992, s. 106(2); Jobseekers' Act 1995, s. 23. Regulations—the Income Support (Liable Relatives) Regs 1990, S.I. 1990 No. 1777 and the Jobseekers' Allowance Regulations 1996, reg. 169—prescribe the amounts which may be included in an order made in respect of a claimant/parent who is not married to the liable relative.

[51] See *Children Come First*, Cm. 1263, (1990), Vol. 2, para. 1.3.4.

[52] For the history of the so-called diversion procedure see the 4th edition of this book, p. 342.

[53] Social Security Administration Act 1992, s. 108; Jobseekers Act 1995, s. 23

[54] The legislation is now consolidated in S.S.C.B.A. 1992; see in particular s. 130.

[55] See also the Housing Benefit (General) Regs 1987. On both primary and delegated legislation, see *CPAG's Housing Benefit and Counciul Tax Benefit Legislation* (13th ed., 2001).

[56] Mr Peter Lilley, *Hansard*, H.C., Vol. 246, col. 1206.

[57] Housing Benefit (General) Amendment Regs 1995, S.I. 1995 No. 1644, reg. 1(1).

has been fixed which takes account of local circumstances; and broadly speaking that is the top limit of a person's rent eligible for consideration under the scheme. Entitlement to housing benefit is now conditional upon attending a work-focussed interview.[58]

The Social Fund[59]

7–026 At one time, the social security system contained elaborate provisions giving entitlement to single payments to meet exceptional needs. These provisions have now been repealed; and the legislation instead provides that payments may be made out of the Social Fund in certain circumstances.[60] The legislation deals separately on the one hand with payments for maternity expenses, funeral expenses and payments made in cold weather to the elderly, the disabled and to persons caring for young children,[61] and on the other hand payments in respect of other needs (such as to ease a domestic crisis or to visit a child who is with the other parent pending a court decision).[62] Such payments are to be made in accordance with Social Fund Directions issued by the Secretary of State. Social Fund Officers have a wide discretion in respect of decisions whether or not to make payments under the Directions; and it is provided that needs must be prioritised, and payments kept within a stipulated overall local budget.[63]

IV. NON MEANS-TESTED BENEFITS

7–027 Child benefit and guardian's allowance are non-contributory benefits which are not means-tested,[64] but entitlement to most non-means-tested benefits depends on sufficient contributions to the National Insurance scheme.

Child benefit

7–028 The Child Benefit Act 1975 made provision for the payment in cash of non-contributory benefits in respect of all children in a family. The legislation has now been consolidated in the Social Security and Contributions Act 1992[65] which lays down the general principle of entitlement: "a person who is responsible for one or more children in any week . . . shall be entitled to a benefit (to be known as 'child benefit') for that week in respect of the child or each of the

---

[58] W.R.P.A. 1999 s. 52, inserting new s. 2A–2C into S.S.A.A. 1992.

[59] T Buck *The Social Fund: Law and Practice* (Sweet & Maxwell, 2nd ed., 2000).

[60] S.S.C.B.A. 1992, s.138.

[61] Social Fund Maternity and Funeral Expenses (General) Regs 1987, S.I. 1987 No. 481; Social Fund Cold Weather Payments (General) Regs 1988, S.I. 1988 No. 1724; Social Fund Winter Fuel Payment Regs 2000 (S.I. 2000 No. 729).

[62] Social Fund Direction No. 4, para. (b). No payment can be made to help with contact arrangements for children after the court has made its definitive decision.

[63] Social Fund Direction Nos. 40, 41.

[64] This aspect of the scheme is somewhat controversial: see the discussion of policy in Ogus, Barendt and Wilkeley, *The Law of Social Security* (4th ed., N.J. Wilkeley *et al.* ed., 1995).

[65] Pt IX.

children for whom he is responsible."[66] The provisions of the Act are supplemented by detailed regulations.[67]

A person is "responsible for a child"[68] if either (a) he or she has the child living with him[69] or (b) is contributing to the cost of providing for the child at a weekly rate not less than the child benefit rate. It will often be the case, particularly after a relationship breakdown, that several people qualify for benefit under that test. The Act therefore lays down a code of priorities.[70] For example, a person who has the child living with him is entitled as against one who contributes to his maintenance,[71] and where husband and wife reside together, the wife is entitled.[72] As between two unmarried parents, the mother is entitled.[73] A person is a child for any week in which he is under the age of 16, or under 18 if certain prescribed conditions are met, or under 19 and receiving full-time "non-advanced" education (GCSE, AS and A levels, NVQ Level 3 and below). Benefit is not payable for children receiving "advanced" education,[74] or for apprentices and other employed trainees, or for those benefiting from the youth training scheme.[75]

The one parent benefit—an additional amount payable to a lone parent in receipt of child benefit—was abolished in 1998.

Guardian's allowance

7–029 This long-standing[76] non-contributory benefit is available to a person responsible for a child who is either an orphan or whose links with a surviving parent can for practical purposes be treated as non-existent. Eligibility is not limited to legal guardianship.

Contributory benefits[77]

7–030 There is a large number of benefits, entitlement to which depends on contributions made by the "insured person" or his spouse. The legislation is now consol-

---

66 Social Security Contributions and Benefits Act 1992, s. 141.
67 Principally the Child Benefit (General) Regs 1976 S.I. 1976 No. 965.
68 S.S.C.B.A. 1992, s. 143.
69 This expression is a broad one: a child may be "living with" a parent even if he is in care and only returns home at weekends: see *England v. Supplementary Benefits Commission* [1981] 3 F.L.R. 222; a child may also be regarded as "living with" a parent who enjoys staying contact R(F) 2/79.
70 S.S.C.B.A. 1992 s. 144; Sched. 10.
71 *ibid.* Sched. 10, para. 2.
72 *ibid.* Sched. 10, para. 3.
73 *ibid.* Sched, para. 4(2).
74 Child Benefit (General) Regs 1976, S.I. 1976 No. 965, reg. 7A.
75 *ibid.* regs. 7B, 8.
76 The allowance was introduced in 1946 to replace the orphan's pension payable since the enactment of the Widows', Orphans' and Old Age Contributory Pensions Act 1925. Eligibility is now governed by S.S.C.B.A. 1992, s 77, and the Social Security (Guardians' Allowances) Regs 1975, S.I. 1975 No. 515.
77 For a discussion of the historical background, see Ogus, Barendt and Wilkeley, *The Law of Social Security* (4th ed., N.J. Wilkeley *et al.* ed., 1995), Chap. 5. *Report of the Committee on One Parent Families* (Cmnd. 5629 (1974)) App. 5 (particularly pp. 126–147).

idated in the Social Security Contributions and Benefits Act 1992. Contributory benefits include incapacity benefit, maternity allowance, bereavement payment, widowed parent's allowance, and retirement pensions. The legislation is daunting in its complexity; and details may be found in the comprehensive specialist texts.[78]

[78] See D. Bonner, I. Hooker, P. Smith, and R. White *Social Security Legislation Vol I: Non-Means Tested Benefits* (Sweet & Maxwell, 2001/2); and the references in n. 83 *supra*.

CHAPTER EIGHT

DEVOLUTION OF FAMILY PROPERTY ON DEATH[1]

I. WILLS

8–001 Any adult person of sound mind may dispose of all his or her property on death by making a will complying with the formalities prescribed by the Wills Act 1837.[2] Until 1938 this power to disinherit the testator's spouse and children was absolute. The Inheritance (Family Provision)[3] Act 1938 gave the court a limited power to override the deceased's testamentary provisions by ordering provision to be made out of a deceased's estate for the maintenance of a surviving spouse and a limited category of other dependants; the Inheritance (Provision for Family and Dependants) Act 1975 now gives the court more extensive powers, but it remains the case that in principle a man or woman is free to dispose of property by will in whatever way the testator chooses.[4]

Although a comparatively small proportion of the population make wills—only 33 per cent of a sample interviewed on behalf of the Law Commission had done so—will making is often simply deferred until old age; and 60 per cent of those aged 60 or over in the Law Commission's interview sample had made wills. The evidence supports the hypothesis that the greater part of the wealth transmitted on death passes under a will rather than on intestacy.[5]

Effects of marriage and divorce on wills

8–002 A will is revoked by the testator's marriage,[6] but until January 1, 1983[7] the testator's divorce did not have any direct effect on his or her will[8] However,

---

[1] For fuller accounts, see Parry and Clark, *The Law of Succession* (11th ed., 2002 by R. Kerridge); A. Borkowski, *Textbook on Succession* (1997); and see J. Finch *et al*, *Wills, Inheritance, Families* (1996).

[2] As amended by Administration of Justice Act 1982, Pt IV.

[3] For the historical background, see S.M. Cretney, *Law, Law Reform and the Family* (1998), Chap. 10.

[4] *Re Coventry (dec'd)* [1980] Ch. 461 at 474.

[5] See *Distribution on Intestacy* (Law Com. No. 187, (1989)), App. C; and J.M. Masson, "Making Wills, Making Clients" [1994] Conv. 267 at 268–270.

[6] Wills Act 1837, s.18. (A new provision to the same effect has been substituted by Administration of Justice Act 1982, s.18.)

[7] The date on which the relevant provision of the Administration of Justice Act 1982 came into force: ss.18(2), 76(11).

[8] Nor did the fact that the marriage had been annulled.

statute now provides[9] that unless a testator has shown a different intention, any property given to the former spouse will pass as if he or she had died on the date on which the marriage is dissolved[10] (and accordingly legacies and other gifts will lapse[11]). It is however, specifically provided[12] that the former spouse may make a claim for reasonable financial provision under the Inheritance (Provision for Family and Dependants) Act 1975.

II. INTESTACY[13]

8–003 Under the system of intestate succession introduced by the Administration of Estates Act 1925 the whole of the deceased's property (after payment of debts, etc.) is distributed in accordance with the following rules.

A. Where the intestate leaves[14] a spouse[15] and issue[16]

8–004 The surviving spouse takes[17]:

(a) The personal chattels[18] absolutely.

---

[9] See Law Reform (Succession) Act 1995, ss.3 and 4; and for the background see the Law Commission's Report *The Effect of Divorce on Wills* (Law Com. No. 217 (1993)).

[10] Or annulled: Law Reform (Succession) Act 1995, s.4. The operative date is that of decree absolute: see n.15, below.

[11] The appointment of the former spouse as executor trustee or donee of a power of appointment is also to take effect as if the former spouse had died.

[12] *ibid.* s.18A(2). For a critique of the legislation, see R. Kerridge [1995] Conv. 12.

[13] C.H. Sherrin and R.C. Bonehill, *The Law and Practice of Intestate Succession* (2nd ed., 1994) is a comprehensive text; while the main principles of the law are fully analysed in *Distribution on Intestacy,* Law Commission P.W.P. No. 108 (1988). The evolution of the law is considered in S.M. Cretney, *Law, Law Reform and the family* (1998), Chap. 10.

[14] The Law Reform (Succession) Act 1995 (giving effect to the substance of a recommendation in the Law Commission Report on *Distribution on Intestacy* (Law Com. No. 187, (1989), para. 57), amends s. 46, of the Administration of Estates Act 1925 so that a spouse will not inherit (or be treated as having survived) unless he or she survives the deceased for a period of 28 days. The general rule is that where two or more persons die in circumstances rendering it uncertain which of them survived the other, the younger is deemed to have survived the elder: Law of Property Act 1925, s.184. For an example of the difficulties to which this presumption could give rise, see *Re McBroom (dec'd)* [1992] 2 F.L.R. 49.

[15] "Spouse" does not include a former spouse: but spouses remain married until decree *absolute* of divorce: see *Re Seaford* [1968] P. 53 (where the husband was found dead, apparently as a result of a drug overdose, on the day on which the wife applied for the decree to be made absolute, and it was held that his death brought the marriage to an end, the court had no jurisdiction to make the decree absolute, and that the wife was entitled to succeed as his widow); *Re Collins (dec'd)* [1990] Fam. 56 (where the husband was entitled on the wife's intestacy, notwithstanding the fact that she had been granted a decree nisi of divorce founded on his violent behaviour to her during a short marriage). However, if a spouse dies intestate while a judicial separation is in force and the parties remain separated, his property will devolve as if the other spouse were dead: M.C.A. 1973, s.18(2).

[16] However remote. Broadly speaking, illegitimacy is no longer relevant in determining intestate succession rights: Family Law Reform Act 1987, s.18.

[17] Subject to the rule of public policy which debars a wrongdoer from benefiting from his own wrong: *Re Giles (dec'd)* [1972] Ch. 544; *Jones v. Roberts* [1995] 2 F.L.R. 422 (H.H. Judge Kolbert); but the application of this rule may be affected by the Forfeiture Act 1982, which gives the court a discretionary power to relieve against forfeiture: see *Re H (dec'd)* [1990] 1 F.L.R. 441.

[18] Defined (widely) in s.55(1)(*x*), A.E.A. 1925.

(b) A "statutory legacy", currently amounting to £125,000.[19]
(c) A life interest in one-half of the balance of the estate.

Subject to the spouse's rights, the estate is held on the "statutory trusts" for the issue of the intestate. These trusts are defined in the Act.[20] For present purposes it suffices to note that the intestate's children may receive maintenance out of income until they are 18, and will then receive the capital; and that if any child of the intestate predeceases the intestate leaving issue the issue will take the child's presumptive share.

B. Where the intestate leaves a spouse but no issue

8–005

(a) If the deceased also leaves a parent, or a brother or sister[21] the surviving spouse takes:

  (i) the personal chattels absolutely;
  (ii) a "statutory legacy" of £200,000[22];
  (iii) one-half of any balance absolutely. The other half is held for the intestate's surviving parent or parents (in equal shares) absolutely; but if the intestate leaves no parent, the property is held on the statutory trusts for the brothers and sisters (or the issue of any predeceased brother or sister).

(b) If the deceased leaves no relatives within these categories, the whole estate goes to the surviving spouse.

C. Where the intestate leaves no surviving spouse

8–006

(a) If the deceased leaves issue, the whole estate is held on the statutory trusts for their benefit.
(b) If he leaves no issue but is survived by one or both parents, then they take (in equal shares if both survive) absolutely.
(c) If he leaves neither issue nor parent the following relatives take in order:

  (i) brothers and sisters of the whole-blood (the issue of any predeceased brother or sister taking their share);
  (ii) brothers and sisters of the half-blood (and their issue, as above);
  (iii) grandparents, equally;
  (iv) uncles and aunts (*i.e.* brothers and sisters of the whole-blood of a

---

[19] See Family Provision (Intestate Succession) Order 1993, S.I. 1993 No. 2906. Interest is payable on the legacy from the date of death until payment at such rate as the Lord Chancellor fixes from time to time by order: Administration of Justice Act 1997, s.28(1); Intestate Succession (Interest and Capitalisation) Order 1983, S.I. 1983 No. 1374.

[20] A.E.A. 1925, s.47, as amended.

[21] Or issue of such. Only brothers and sisters of the whole-blood are eligible to take under these rules; half brothers and sisters become entitled only if the intestate left no spouse: see below.

[22] Family Provision (Intestate Succession) Order 1993, S.I. 1993 No. 2906.

parent of the intestate). The issue of a predeceased uncle and aunt take his or her share on the statutory trusts.

(d) In default the estate passes as *bona vacantia* to the Crown.[23] In this event, the Crown may as a matter of grace make provision for "dependants" (whether kindred or not) of the intestate and for other persons for whom the intestate might reasonably have been expected to make provision.[24] This power may be used to provide some part of the estate for the deceased's cohabitant who has no entitlement on the deceased partner's intestacy. Although the Inheritance (Provision for Family and Dependants) Act 1975 would sometimes enable a cohabitant to obtain an order for financial provision out of the estate, it appears that *ex gratia* payments are still often made thus avoiding the expense of an application to the court.[25]

English intestacy law generous to surviving spouse

8–007 The salient feature of this code of distribution is the generosity with which it treats the surviving spouse[26]: it is only in the case of comparatively large estates that the survivor will not inherit the whole of the intestate's property.[27] There may be cases where this generosity causes injustice, particularly where a parent with dependent children has married more than once: since the person married to the deceased at the date of death will take the estate perhaps to the prejudice of children of an earlier marriage or other dependants.[28] Moreover, it will be noted that sibling relationships of the whole-blood are given substantial priority over those of the half-blood. The intestate's half-brother will not be entitled to any share of his property if the intestate left a surviving spouse, a surviving brother or sister of the whole-blood or any issue of such a brother or sister.

Rights in respect of the matrimonial home

8–008 The surviving spouse has the right to require the intestate's interest in the matrimonial home in which the surviving spouse was resident at the time of the

---

[23] See for example *Cameron v. Treasury Solicitor* [1996] 2 F.L.R. 716.

[24] A.E.A. 1925, s.46(1)(vi).

[25] See *Distribution on Intestacy,* Law Commission P.W.P. No. 108 (1988), p. 8, n. 15.

[26] The Law Commission recommended that a surviving spouse should be entitled to the whole of the intestate's estate: *Distribution on Intestacy* (Law Com. No. 187, (1989)), but the Government (see *Hansard,* H.L., Vol. 547, col. WA 38) rejected this much criticised proposal: see R. Kerridge, "Distribution on Intestacy, The Law Commission's Report" (1990) 54 Conv. 358; Sherrin and Bonehill, *The Law of Intestate Succession* (2nd ed., 1994), p. 24 (proposals "naive and simplistic") and the debates in *Hansard,* H.L., Vol. 538, cols. 170–178 and in *Hansard* H.L., Vol. 561, col. 502. It appears that the Law Commission continued to believe that the Government should have accepted their proposal or at least raised the amount of the statutory legacies to "a figure which resolves the serious injustices of the present law in modern times": Law Commission 28th Annual Report 1993, (Law Com. No. 223, (1993)), para. 3.8; and, for a discussion of the policy issues, see S.M. Cretney, *Law, Law Reform and the Family* (1998), p. 273, ff.

[27] See, for a particularly striking case *Re Collins (dec'd)* [1990] Fam. 56; *Sivyer v. Sivyer* [1967] 1 W.L.R. 1482.

[28] *Distribution on Intestacy* (Law Com. No. 187, (1990)). The Law Commission's proposal is all the more surprising in the light of a Public Attitude Survey which showed little support for treating a second spouse so generously: see para. 41.

intestate's death to be appropriated in or towards satisfaction of his or her share.[29] The survivor also has the right to have the entitlement to a life interest capitalised in accordance with a statutory formula.[30]

III. THE INHERITANCE (PROVISION FOR FAMILY AND DEPENDANTS) ACT 1975[31]

8–009 The Inheritance (Family Provision) Act 1938, which first gave the court a discretion to award reasonable provision out of a deceased's estate for the maintenance of certain dependants if the will or intestacy failed to make such provision for them, was a controversial measure enacted only after prolonged campaigning. For this reason, it was somewhat limited in scope.[32] Experience of the operation of the law (and perhaps changes in public attitudes) suggested that much of the opposition to the legislation was not well-founded; and proposals made by the Law Commission[33] for substantial changes in, and extensions to the scope of, the law were implemented by the Inheritance (Provision for Family and Dependants) Act 1975.[34]

Not a remedy for unjust enrichment

8–010 The Act does not confer rights to a particular share of the deceased's estate on any of his dependants.[35] The court may, it is true, in a proper case direct that the whole of the deceased's estate be allocated to someone who would not have received anything under the will or intestacy; but the statute is not concerned to remedy unjust enrichment. It is not the function of the court to decide how the available assets should be fairly divided[36]; instead it is concerned with

---

[29] Intestates' Estates Act 1952, Sched. 2. The surviving spouse may require the personal representatives to exercise this power of appropriation partly in satisfaction of his or her interest in the estate and partly in return for a payment of money: *Re Phelps (dec'd)* [1980] Ch. 275.

[30] Administration of Justice Act 1977, s.28; Intestate Estates (Interest and Capitalisation) Order 1977, S.I. 1977 No. 1491.

[31] See R.D. Oughton, *Tyler's Family Provision* (3rd ed., 1997) for an excellent and important account, drawing on departmental records, of the genesis and legislative history of the legislation.

[32] See S.M. Cretney, *Law, Law Reform and the Family* (1998), p. 250–252 and the sources there cited.

[33] See Law Com. No. 61 (1974). *Family Provision on Death.*

[34] The Act largely follows the draft Bill annexed to Law Com. No. 61 (1974). The draft is copiously and helpfully annotated. It has been said that the 1975 Act forms part of a continuum, and that the legislature did not intend to put on one side and ignore the body of case law on the 1938 Act in so far as it gives guidance on the exercise of the discretion to award reasonable provision: *Re Coventry (dec'd)* [1980] Ch. 461 at 487, CA; but the Court of Appeal has subsequently held that the earlier authorities should be approached with caution because of the substantial changes which have been made in the legislation itself and that this is particularly true of claims where a surviving spouse is concerned: *Moody v. Stevenson* [1992] Ch. 486, CA.

[35] The Law Commission considered a system under which a surviving spouse would have fixed rights of inheritance: see P.W.P. No. 42, pp. 215–259 and n. 26, above.

[36] *Re Coventry (dec'd)* [1980] Ch. 461 at 486, *per* Goff L.J.

dependency, and in particular (it has been said[37]) to remedy "wherever reasonably possible, the injustice of one, who has been put by a deceased person in a position of dependency upon him, being deprived of any financial support, either by accident or by design of the deceased, after his death." Accordingly certain specified "dependants" may apply to the court,[38] which has a discretion to order financial provision for the applicant if it is satisfied that the disposition of the deceased's estate[39] effected by his will or the law relating to intestacy, or a combination of his will and the intestacy, is not such as to make reasonable provision for him. It is not sufficient to show that it would have been reasonable for the deceased to have provided for the applicant; the court must be satisfied that, looked at objectively, the disposition of the estate is unreasonable.[40]

1. Who may apply

8–011 The Act does not distinguish between male and female applicants; and there is no especially heavy burden on a male applicant.[41] The fact that a person is of full age in good health and economically self-sufficient is not a bar to the making of an application under the 1975 Act.[42] The Act provides[43] that any of the following persons who survive the deceased may apply.[44]

---

[37] *Jelley v. Iliffe and Others* [1981] Fam. 128–138, Stephenson L.J; *Bishop v. Plumley and another* [1991] 1 F.L.R. 121 at 123, CA.

[38] The Family Division and Chancery Division of the High Court both have jurisdiction. The Law Commission had recommended that the Family Division alone should have jurisdiction, and the decision to preserve the role of the Chancery Division seems to have reflected the need to compensate the Chancery Division for the loss of the wardship jurisdiction: see the Parliamentary Debates on the Administration of Justice Act 1970, *Hansard,* H.C., Vol. 801, cols. 109–117.

[39] It has been said that litigation in respect of small estates should be discouraged as far as justly possible: *Re Coventry* [1980] Ch. 461; *Jelley v. Iliffe and Others* [1981] Fam. 128 (where, however, the court refused to strike out a claim), settlements are to be encouraged (see *e.g. Bouette v. Rose* [2000] 1 F.L.R. 363) and that appeals concerning modest estates should not be dissipated by pursuing an appeal against a sensible judgment at first instance: see *Re Goodchild (dec'd)* [1997] 2 F.L.R. 644. In order to discourage unmeritorious litigation it has been suggested that judges should reconsider the conventional practice of ordering that the costs of all parties be paid out of the estate: *Re Fullard (dec'd)* [1982] Fam. 42, *per* Ormrod L.J.

[40] *Re Coventry (dec'd)* [1980] Ch. 461 at 488–489.

[41] See *Re Dennis (dec'd)* [1981] 2 All E.R. 140 at 145.

[42] See *Re Jennings (dec'd)* [1994] Chap. 286 at 299, *per* Henry L.J.

[43] s.1(1).

[44] No application may be made without leave of the court more than six months after the grant of administration. For a full consideration of the factors to be taken into account in deciding whether or not to grant such leave, see *Re Salmon (dec'd)* [1981] Ch. 167 (which should be read in the light of *Re Dennis (dec'd)* [1981] 2 All E.R. 140); and (on the factors governing applications made under this provision on behalf of a minor) see *Re C (dec'd) (Leave to Apply for Provision)* [1995] 2 F.L.R. 24, Wilson J. For a remarkable case in which leave was given six years after the grant of probate, see *Stock v. Brown and Another* [1994] 1 F.L.R. 840, Thorpe J. It should be noted that the grant of administration may not be made until long after the death: see, *e.g. Re Collins (dec'd)* [1990] Fam. 56. (death in 1980; letters of administration taken out in 1987); and no application under the 1975 Act can be made unless and until a grant has been taken out: see *Re McBroom (dec'd)* [1992] 2 F.L.R. 49, Eastham J.

(a) The wife or husband of the deceased[45]

8–012 This category of applicant does not include persons whose marriage has been terminated by decree absolute[46] of divorce or nullity. However, it does include persons whose "marriage" was void, provided that they entered into the marriage in good faith, did not obtain a divorce or annulment, and did not remarry during the deceased's lifetime.[47]

(b) A former wife or former husband of the deceased who has not remarried[48]

8–013 Increasingly the Divorce Court has sought to make comprehensive orders at the time of the divorce; and has powers which are broad enough to enable it to do so. In the light of this trend, it has been suggested that there will now be only a few cases (perhaps, for example, where periodical payments had continued for some time and on the husband's death it was discovered that he had had capital available, or where capital—for example from an insurance policy—was produced as a result of his death) in which it would be appropriate for an application by a former spouse to succeed.[49]

The divorce court now has power, if it considers it just to do so, to order that a former spouse shall not be entitled to apply, on the other's death, for provision under the Inheritance (Provision for Family and Dependants) Act 1975. This power can be used, in appropriate cases, whether or not the parties agree, to secure a "clean break" between the parties to a marriage on their divorce.[50]

---

45 Spouses who are separated, whether by decree of judicial separation or otherwise, remain married; but the court may in proceedings for judicial separation, if it considers it just to do so, order that neither party to the marriage should be entitled on the death of the other to apply: s.15, as substituted by M. & F.P.A. 1984, s.8(1).

46 *Re Collins (dec'd)* [1990] Fam. 56.

47 I. (P.F.& D.) A., s.25(4). If it were not for this provision a woman who (for example) discovered that her marriage was bigamous after her husband's death would have no right to succeed on his intestacy, and could at most only qualify for "maintenance" level financial provision envisaged by the Act as appropriate for persons who were being maintained by the deceased at his death: s.1(1)(e). As to what constitutes a "void marriage", see *Gandhi v. Patel* [2002] 1 F.L.R. 603, and para. 2–003, above.

48 s.1(b). For these purposes a person has remarried even if the marriage is void or voidable: s.25(5). For a case vividly demonstrating the potential for injustice of such a provision, see *Ward v. Secretary of State for Social Services* [1990] 1 F.L.R. 119.

49 *Re Fullard (dec'd)* [1982] Fam. 42; *Cameron v. Treasury Solicitor* [1996] 2 F.L.R. 716; but *cf. Re Farrow* [1987] 1 F.L.R. 205—lump sum awarded in divorce dissipated; further provision held appropriate.

50 s.15, as amended. For the factors to be taken into account by the court in determining whether or not to exclude the right to apply under I. (P.F.& D) A. see *Whiting v. Whiting* [1988] 2 F.L.R. 189; but note that in *Cameron v. Treasury Solicitor* [1996] 2 F.L.R. 716 at 723, Thorpe L.J. observed that orders dismissing claims for ancillary relief under M.C.A. 1973 which did not also bar claims under I. (P.F.& D) A. would now "be so irregular as to suggest fundamental error in the drafting". The court may make an order debarring a spouse from applying if (but only if) payments are made from the other's pension fund: *H. v. H. (Financial Provision)* [1988] 2 F.L.R. 114.

(c) A child of the deceased

8–014 This class extends to illegitimate,[51] adopted[52] and posthumous children of the deceased.[53] This Act does not impose any restriction of age or marital status: an adult married child may apply, but it has been said[54] that claims for maintenance by able-bodied and comparatively young men in employment and able to maintain themselves should be "relatively rare", and are to be "approached with a degree of circumspection". This does not mean that a claim by a son (or daughter[55]) is viewed with disfavour; it simply means that, faced with a claim by a person who is physically able to earn his or her own living, the court will be inclined to ask "why should anybody else make provision for you if you are capable of maintaining yourself?"[56]

(d) Any person (not being a child of the deceased) who, in the case of any marriage to which the deceased was at any time a party, was treated by the deceased as a child of the family in relation to that marriage

8–015 This provision follows the precedent of the divorce law[57] in enabling children who have in fact formed part of a deceased's family to apply, even though they are not biologically related to him and have not been adopted by him.

The definition is in one important respect restricted: it requires that the child should have been treated as a child of the family *in relation to a marriage* to

---

[51] s.15(1); and note *In the estate of McC.* (1978) 9 *Fam. Law* 26; *C A. v. C.C.* (1979) 123 S.J. 35.

[52] See *Williams v. Johns* [1988] 2 F.L.R. 475.

[53] s.25(1)(b). A child of the deceased who is adopted after the deceased's death is to be treated in law as the child of the adopters, and is not entitled to make a claim as the deceased's child: *Re Collins (dec'd)* [1990] Fam. 56.

[54] *Re Coventry (dec'd)* [1980] Ch. 461 at 495; and see *Re Jennings (dec'd)* [1994] Ch. 286 at 301, *per* Henry L.J. (where this approach is taken to apply to all those of full age in good health and economically self-sufficient); *Re Goodchild (dec'd) and Another* [1996] 1 F.L.R. 591 at 608–613, *per* Carnwath J. (exceptional case where some provision should be made).

[55] The principle of the earlier decisions expressed in relation to a son is "applicable no less to the case of a daughter and, with developments in the structure of society, instances of its application in such cases may become more common": *Re Jennings (dec'd)* [1994] Ch. 286 at 295, *per* Nourse L.J. In *Espinosa v. Bourke* [1999] 1 F.L.R. 747 the Court of Appeal held that, on the facts, the deceased's 55 year old married daughter had shown the existence of factors sufficiently weighty to justify a substantial award in her favour.

[56] *Re Dennis (dec'd)* [1981] 2 All E.R. 140 at 145, *per* Browne-Wilkinson J; and note *Re Jennings (dec'd)* [1994] Ch. 286 at 295, *per* Nourse L.J.: on an application by an adult son there must be some special circumstance, "typically a moral obligation" if a claim is to succeed; but the Court of Appeal has subsequently held that these are not threshold requirements but merely indicate circumstances indicating that the deceased was under a weighty obligation to provide for the person concerned: see *Re Hancock (dec'd)* [1998] 2 F.L.R. 346; *Re Pearce (dec'd)* [1998] 2 F.L.R. 705; and *Espinosa v. Bourke* [1999] 1 F.L.R. 747. See also *Re Goodchild (dec'd)* [1997] 2 F.L.R. 644 (parent's promise to make provision a weighty factor); and note the decision in *Re Abram (dec'd)* [1996] 2 F.L.R. 379 (where the fact that a son had worked without reward in the family business was held to be one of the factors establishing an "overwhelming" obligation to provide for him).

[57] M.C.A. 1973, s.52(1). But the definition is not identical: under the divorce legislation, the child must have been treated as a child of the family by both parties to the marriage; under the inheritance legislation the criterion is treatment by the deceased in relation to his marriage: see *Re Leach* [1986] Ch. 226, CA—successful application for provision from step-mother's estate although most of the "treatment" had occurred after the father's death.

which the deceased was a party; and it follows that a child cannot make a claim as a child of the family for provision out of the estate of the mother's cohabitant, notwithstanding the fact that the cohabitant may have been the only father figure in the child's life.[58]

In considering applications by children and children of the family the court is given additional[59] guidelines[60] which (in the case of children of the family) are similar to those applied in divorce proceedings.

(e) Any person (not being a person included in the foregoing paragraphs of this subsection) who immediately before the death of the deceased was being maintained, either wholly or partly, by the deceased

8–016 This category extends to all those who were in fact dependent on the deceased at the date of death, whether relatives or not. The most obvious example of a person who would be eligible to apply under this head was a cohabitant[61] for whom the deceased provided support.[62] An elderly but impoverished relative or friend taken into the deceased's household and given free board and lodging and treated as a member of the family would however, also qualify,[63] as would a man who had been supported by the woman with whom he had lived.[64] In one case,[65] the Court of Appeal accepted that a woman who had cared for her brain-damaged child, using the damages the daughter had been awarded to provide housing and other facilities for the two of them, was entitled to make an application for provision out of the daughter's estate as someone being maintained by the deceased child.

The qualifying condition is economic dependence: the applicant must be a person who was "being maintained"[66]; and the courts at one time took the view that in those cases in which there had been some mutual provision of support (for example, where the deceased had provided rent-free housing,[67] and the

---

[58] See *J v. J (Property Transfer)* [1993] 2 F.L.R. 56, Eastham J.

[59] *i.e.* to those applied to all applications: see s.3, below.

[60] s.3(3); see below.

[61] *Jelley v. Iliffe* [1981] Fam. 128 at 135.

[62] This provision was concerned with financial dependence, and not with the quality of the relationship between the parties: provided that support was provided it was immaterial that the applicant was never a *de facto* wife or sole mistress, but merely "a woman who it was the deceased's pleasure to visit and relax with and have occasional sexual intercourse with ... ": *Malone v. Harrison* [1979] 1 W.L.R. 1353 at 1360, *per* Hollings J.

[63] *Jelley v. Iliffe* [1981] Fam. 128 at 135.

[64] *Re Beaumont (dec'd)* [1980] Ch. 444; *Jelley v. Iliffe* [1981] Fam. 128.

[65] *Bouette v. Rose* [2000] 1 F.L.R. 363. (The mother was entitled to half the child's estate under the rules of intestate succession: see above. It appears however that she spent the whole of the assets received as her daughter's administrator notwithstanding the fact that she knew the child's father was legally entitled to a half share).

[66] And s.1(3) of the Act contains a definition of that concept—for "the purposes of subsection (1)(e), above, a person shall be treated as being maintained by the deceased either wholly or partly, as the case may be, if the deceased, otherwise than for full valuable consideration, was making a substantial contribution in money or money's worth towards the reasonable needs of that person"—to which the court gave a restrictive interpretation: *Re Wilkinson (dec'd)* [1978] Fam. 22; *Re Beaumont (dec'd)* [1980] Ch. 444; *Jelley v. Iliffe* [1981] Fam. 128; *Re Kirby* [1981] 3 F.L.R. 249.

[67] *Jelley v. Iliffe* [1981] Fam. 128 at 138; see also *Harrington v. Gill* [1981] 4 F.L.R. 265.

applicant had done the cooking and domestic chores) the court had to weigh up the value of the respective contributions, strike a balance, and then say whether the balance of contributions (if any) was substantial. In short, the courts would ask the question, "has the deceased contributed more than the applicant?"[68] In effect, the more deserving the applicant the less chance he or she appeared to have of establishing a claim to share in the deceased's estate. But more recently the Court of Appeal came to urge the value of common sense and to criticize the use of "fine balancing computations involving the normal exchanges of support in the domestic sense".[69] In *Bishop v. Plumley and another*[70] the Court accordingly allowed an appeal against a decision that the services provided by the woman who had lived with the deceased for many years and provided exceptional care for him in his last illness equalled the benefits of secure housing which he had provided for her so as to disqualify her from putting forward a claim under this head.

Finally, it should be noted that the relevant time for ascertaining whether the condition is satisfied is immediately before the death of the deceased; and if this provision had been given a literal interpretation it would have created absurd anomalies—for example, suppose that the deceased had been supporting an aged parent in a nursing home, but that the parent had been admitted to a national health hospital for urgent treatment a week before the deceased's death. In such circumstances, it might seem quite wrong to deny the parent a claim for provision; and the courts have taken the view that what is in question is the settled basis or general arrangement between the parties, rather than the actual, perhaps fluctuating, variation of it which exists immediately before the death. A relationship of dependence which has existed for years will not be treated as no longer subsisting, for example during a few weeks of mortal sickness.[71] On the other hand, if it can be clearly shown that the deceased had divested himself of financial responsibility for the applicant before his death, the application must fail.[72]

(f) A person living with the deceased as a spouse

8–017 The Law Commission, in its review of the law governing distribution on intestacy,[73] rejected suggestions that the intestacy rules should automatically provide for cohabitants[74] because of the complexity, cost and delay which would inevitably be involved. However, the Commission accepted that cohabitants

---

[68] See, *e.g. Re Kirby (dec'd)* [1981] 3 F.L.R. 249 (couple pooled earnings; deceased said to have contributed 50% more than applicant).

[69] *Bishop v. Plumley* [1991] 1 F.L.R. 121 at 126, *per* Butler-Sloss L.J., CA.

[70] [1991] 1 F.L.R. 121, CA.

[71] *Re Beaumont, (dec'd)* [1980] Ch. 444; *Jelley v. Iliffe* [1981] Fam. 128; *Re Kirby, (dec'd)* [1981] 3 F.L.R. 249.

[72] See, *e.g. Kourkgy v. Lusher* [1981] 4 F.L.R. 65 where the applicant had been the deceased's mistress intermittently for more than 10 years; applicant established general arrangement by deceased for her maintenance up to July 14, 1979; deceased held to have abandoned responsibility on return from holiday with wife on July 29; deceased died on August 7; claim failed.

[73] Law Com. No. 187, 1989.

[74] *op. cit.* para. 58.

should be able to apply for discretionary provision without the need to show dependence; and it is now[75] provided that a person who:—

(a) was living with the deceased in the same household immediately before the date of the death; and
(b) had been living with the deceased in the same household for at least two years before that date; and
(c) was living during the whole of that period as the husband or wife of the deceased—

may apply to the court for an order.[76] Although, as we shall see, such an applicant must show that provision is required for maintenance[77] it has been said[78] that the express recognition of cohabitation as a qualification may reduce the problems faced by elderly unmarried couples in demonstrating a qualification based solely on their having been maintained by the deceased. However, there is nothing in the Inheritance (Provision for Family and Dependants) Act 1975 permitting the court to distribute the family assets in order merely to achieve a fair distribution.

2. What has to be established

8–018 The court, if it is to have discretion to make an order, must first be satisfied as a threshold or condition precedent to the exercise of the jurisdiction[79] "that the disposition of the deceased's estate effected by his will or the law relating to intestacy, or the combination of his will and that law is not such as to make reasonable financial provision for the applicant".[80] This is essentially a question of fact (albeit one involving a value judgment); and the Court of Appeal will thus be reluctant to interfere with a decision on this point unless satisfied that it is plainly wrong.[81]

A number of points require further comment.

(a) Disposition effected by will or intestacy

8–019 It is usually assumed that the family provision legislation is most commonly invoked where the deceased has made a will excluding (or making only small provision for) the applicant, in favour of more extensive provision for others.

---

75 Inheritance (Provision for Family and Dependants) Act 1975, s.1(6)(a). 1A as inserted by Law Reform (Succession) Act 1995, s.2. Spouses and former spouses are excluded.
76 Additional guidelines for the exercise of the courts discretion in such applications are provided by Inheritance (Provision for Family and Dependants) Act 1975, s.3(2A) as inserted by Law Reform (Succession) Act 1995, s.2(4).
77 See *Re Jennings (dec'd)* [1994] Ch. 286, CA.
78 *Bouette v. Rose* [2000] 1 F.L.R. 363 at 372.
79 *Re Fullard (dec'd)* [1982] Fam. 42.
80 s.2(1).
81 *Re Coventry (dec'd)* [1980] Ch. 461 at 487 *per* Goff L.J.; *Espinosa v. Bourke* [1999] 1 F.L.R. 747 (where the Court of Appeal was satisfied the decision below was plainly wrong).

However, the legislation is not limited to such cases, and would equally be available where a testator has tried by his will to make provision for the applicant but failed. For example, the testator may (miscalculating the size of his estate) have given large legacies to strangers and a residuary gift to his surviving spouse. Under the general law the legacies are paid in full before the widow (or widower) is entitled to anything. The test is easy to state: what testamentary provision would a reasonable person in the position of the deceased have made for the applicant in all the circumstances, including those specified in section 3 of the Act?[82]

The fact that the deceased died intestate is no bar to an application.[83] It seems, at first sight, strange that a court should ever hold that the rules laid down by law to govern the devolution of estates are capable of operating so as to produce an unjust result. However, the inflexibility of the general rules inevitably means that there will be such. For example, a cohabitant or other dependant without legal links with the deceased can never, as such, benefit on intestacy; and, as we have seen, the law treats an intestate's surviving spouse with generosity so that the whole of all but the largest estates will go to the deceased's surviving spouse to the exclusion of any dependent children (particularly children of a former marriage). Thus:—

> *In Re Sivyer*[84] the intestate left a widow, and a 13-year-old daughter by his previous marriage. Under the intestacy laws the widow was entitled to the whole of his estate. It was held that the daughter should receive provision.[85]

The question of whether reasonable provision has been made is entirely objective.[86] The court is not to ask whether the deceased knew all the material facts: the issue is not whether the deceased has been reasonable or unreasonable, but whether the provision in fact made is reasonable or not.[87] It follows that the question whether the operative dispositions make or fail to make reasonable provision must be approached in exactly the same way whether the court is dealing with a will or an intestacy or with a combination of the two.[88]

(b) What is "reasonable financial provision"?

8–020 The Act draws a crucial distinction between two categories of applicant[89]:

---

[82] *Harrington v. Gill* [1981] 4 F.L.R. 265 at 271, *per* Dunn L.J. For the matters specified in section 3 of the Act, see below.

[83] See, *e.g. Re Cook* (1956) 106 L.J. 466; *Re Sivyer* [1967] 1 W.L.R. 1482; *Re Coventry* [1980] Ch. 461; *Re Kirby (dec'd)* [1981] 3 F.L.R. 249; *Harrington v. Gill* [1981] 4 F.L.R. 265, *Bouette v. Rose* [2000] 1 F.L.R. 36.

[84] [1967] 1 W.L.R. 1482.

[85] For an even more striking example, see *Re Collins (dec'd)* [1990] Fam. 56.

[86] *Moody v. Stevenson* [1992] Ch. 486 at 494, *per* Waite J., CA.

[87] *Re Coventry (dec'd)* [1980] Ch. 461 at 474–5, 488–9.

[88] *Re Coventry (dec'd)* [1980] Ch. 461 at 488, *per* Goff L.J.

[89] See *Malone v. Harrison* [1979] 1 W.L.R. 1353; *Re Coventry (dec'd)* [1980] Ch. 461.

(i) Criterion to be applied in the case of applications by the surviving spouse[90]

8–021 The question is whether such financial provision has been made as it would be reasonable in all the circumstances of the case for a husband or wife to receive, whether or not that provision is required for his or her maintenance.[91]

(ii) Criterion to be applied in the case of all other applicants

8–022 The question is whether the provision is such as it would be reasonable for the applicant to receive for his or her maintenance.[92] Maintenance may for this purpose, be defined as "such financial provision as could be reasonable in all the circumstances of the case to enable the applicant to maintain himself in a manner suitable to those circumstances."[93] Maintenance does not extend to cover all provision for the well-being or benefit of the applicant[94]; but rather what is needed to meet the recurring expenses of living[95] (such as housing, food, clothing and entertainment). Thus:—

> In *Re Jennings (deceased)*[96] the applicant was a 50-year-old who had been brought up from the age of four by his mother and stepfather. There was no contact between father and son after the divorce and the only thing the father did for his son was to send him 10 shillings in a birthday card on his second birthday. The father left the residue of his estate (which amounted to some £300,000 after payment of inheritance tax) to charities. The son had been successful in business; and the Court of Appeal held that because the son was in reasonably comfortable financial circumstances and there was no evidence that he was likely to encounter financial difficulties in the future, it was impossible to show that he required "maintenance".[97]

---

[90] Although a judicially separated spouse qualifies (in the absence of any order to the contrary made under I. (P.F.& D.) A., s.15: see para. 8–012 above) as a "dependant" for the purposes of making an application under the Act he or she is not treated as a surviving spouse for the purpose of the basis of provision if at the date of death the decree is in force and the separation was continuing: s.1(2)(a). Claims by the judicially separated are thus assessed by reference to provision for *maintenance:* see below.

[91] I. (P.F.& D.) A., s.1(2)(a).

[92] s.1(2)(b).

[93] *Re Coventry (dec'd)* [1980] Ch. 461 at 494, *per* Buckley L.J.

[94] For example, payment of the applicant's debts solely to remove the threat of bankruptcy proceedings: *Re Dennis (dec'd)* [1981] 2 All E.R. 140; and see *Re Abram (dec'd)* [1996] 2 F.L.R. 379. Payment of business debts, thereby enabling the applicant to carry on remunerative activity, may be regarded as provision for maintenance: see *Re Goodchild (dec'd)* [1997] 2 F.L.R. 644.

[95] *Re Dennis (dec'd)* [1981] 2 All E.R. 140 at 145, *per* Browne-Wilkinson J.

[96] [1994] Ch. 256, CA. Compare *Re Callaghan (dec'd)* [1985] Fam. 1, Booth J., where the applicant could show that he needed money to exercise the right to buy his council house without the burden of a substantial mortgage which he could not easily support.

[97] In *Re Jennings (dec'd)* [1994] Ch. 286, CA, both Nourse and Henry L.JJ. state that the provision must be "required" for the applicant's maintenance, following in this respect a dictum in *Re Coventry (dec'd)* [1980] Ch. 461 at 472, *per* Olivier J. But the word "required" does not appear in this provision of the Act, and it seems questionable whether Oliver J. was correct in thinking that it should be read into it.

However, the fact that the provision is intended to provide maintenance does not mean that the provision ordered must be restricted to income; the simplest method of providing housing, for example, may be to provide a lump sum with which the applicant can buy himself a house. Moreover, if the estate is very small, the only sensible way of making provision for the applicant may be to award a lump sum,[98] or to direct that the deceased's house be transferred to the applicant.[99]

3. Circumstances to be taken into consideration

8–023 The Act provides[1] that the court shall in considering both whether the disposition of the deceased's estate makes reasonable financial provision for the applicant and in determining whether and in what manner to exercise its powers to make orders to "have regard" to a series of matters, on the basis of the facts as they are known at the date of the hearing.[2]

Some matters are to be considered in all cases and additional considerations have to be taken into account in the case of certain applicants.[3]

(a) Matters to be considered in all cases

8–024 The first group (to be considered whatever the head of dependency upon which the application is based) is as follows[4]:—

> (a) the financial resources and financial needs which the applicant has or is likely to have in the foreseeable future;
> (b) the financial resources and financial needs which any other applicant for an order . . . has or is likely to have in the foreseeable future;

---

[98] *cf. Kusminow v. Barclays Bank Trust Co. Ltd* [1989] *Fam. Law* 66 where expenses of administering a trust pointed to provision by outright payment rather than settlement; and see also *Harrington v. Gill* [1981] 4 F.L.R. 265 where the contents were also transferred to the applicant absolutely; *Millward v. Shenton* [1972] 1 W.L.R. 711.

[99] As in *Rajabally v. Rajabally* [1987] 2 F.L.R. 390, CA (where the matrimonial home was vested in the deceased's widow subject to a charge for a lump sum legacy for a mentally disabled son).

[1] I.(P.F.& D.)A., s.3(1).

[2] s.3(5); and note *Re Hancock (dec'd)* [1998] 2 F.L.R. 346 (six-fold increase in value of land between testator's death and date of hearing; *held*, court to determine application on basis of values as known at date of hearing.

[3] Statements made by the deceased are admissible under the Civil Evidence Act 1968 as evidence of any fact stated therein: Inheritance (Provision for Family and Dependants) Act 1975, s.21; and see *Kourkgy v. Lusher* (1983) 4 F.L.R. 65; *cf. Williams v. Johns* [1988] 2 F.L.R. 475, where the court emphasised the objective nature of the test to be applied, and in consequence seemed to discount the importance to be attached to the deceased's statement of reasons.

[4] s.3(1); and *Espinosa v. Bourke* [1999] 1 F.L.R. 747 (where the deceased's will included a statement that he made no provision for his daughter because she had been adequately provided for and had shown "a degree of irresponsibility"; the Court of Appeal held these matters were appropriate to be considered, but that they did not outweigh the obligation on the deceased to give effect to a promise to let the daughter have shares he had inherited from his wife).

(c) the financial resources and financial needs which any beneficiary of the estate of the deceased has or is likely to have in the foreseeable future[5];
(d) any obligations and responsibilities[6] which the deceased had towards any applicant for an order . . . or towards any beneficiary of the estate of the deceased;
(e) the size and nature of the net estate[7] of the deceased;
(f) any physical or mental disability of any applicant for an order . . . or any beneficiary of the estate of the deceased;
(g) any other matter, including the conduct of the applicant or any other person, which in the circumstances of the case the court may consider relevant.[8]

The "conduct" which the court is required to consider is not limited to misconduct. The court will wish to consider such matters as whether any of those affected had, for example, been generous in providing the deceased with financial support,[9] whether the applicant has given up his own house to live with the deceased, how far two competing parties had helped the deceased in his business, and so on.[10]

Inevitably, however, there will be cases in which the allegation is of morally culpable conduct, either by the applicant (in which case the suggestion will be that the applicant should get less than might otherwise be the case), or by the deceased in relation to the applicant (in which case the applicant might expect to get more), or by other beneficiaries under the deceased's will or intestacy (in which case it may be argued that the applicant should be allotted some or all of the benefits to which the beneficiary would otherwise be entitled). How far are such matters relevant?

---

[5] This will include payments under the deceased's pension scheme, for example, even though such payments are not part of his "net estate" for the purposes of the Act: see *Re Cairnes, (dec'd)* [1982] 4 F.L.R. 225.

[6] In *Re Jennings* [1994] Ch. 286, C.A., the Court of Appeal held that this referred to obligations and responsibilities subsisting at the date of the deceased's death; and accordingly held that the failure of a father to retain contact with, or support, his son during infancy was not relevant to a claim by the son on the father's death many years later. The mere existence of the relationship of father and son is insufficient to constitute such an obligation. The Court of Appeal seems to have treated the statutory list of specified "circumstances" as an exhaustive enumeration of conditions, at least one of which must be satisfied if the court is to be able to find that the deceased's provision was not reasonable, but this approach seems questionable and more recent decisions have taken a flexible approach: see notably *Re Hancock (dec'd)* [1998] 2 F.L.R. 346; *Espinosa v. Bourke* [1999] 1 F.L.R. 747.

[7] See, *e.g. Re Rowlands dec'd* [1984] F.L.R. 813 (estate consisted largely of Welsh hill farm). "Net estate" is defined in s.25 of the Act; and s.8 provides that *donationes mortis causa* and nominated property are to be treated as part of the net estate. (However, the definition of nominated property relates to nominations under statutory powers; and the deceased's right to nominate a beneficiary under a private pension scheme has been held not to fall within the definition: *Re Cairnes, dec'd* [1982] 4 F.L.R. 225.) If the deceased was a joint tenant of property the court may treat his severable share as forming part of the net estate: s.9; and see *Kourkgy v. Lusher* [1981] 4 F.L.R. 65; *Jessop v. Jessop* [1992] 1 F.L.R 591, C.A.; *Powell v. Osbourne* [1993] 1 F.L.R. 1001; *Re McBroom, dec'd* [1992] 2 F.L.R. 49, Eastham J. (this power cannot be exercised unless and until a grant of administration has been taken out to the deceased's estate).

[8] This will extend to divorce and its financial consequences: *Re Fullard dec'd* [1982] Fam. 42

[9] See *Jelley v. Iliffe and Others* [1981] Fam. 128 at 140.

[10] *Re Thornley* [1969] 1 W.L.R. 1037.

The conduct which the court takes into account may extend to a daughter's neglect to care for her father in his last years and indeed her lifestyle.[11] In the context of applications by a surviving spouse, it has been observed,[12] that the reference to conduct is in much wider and more general terms than the terms used in the divorce legislation embodied in the Matrimonial Causes Act 1973[13] and in divorce cases discussion of conduct inevitably engenders bitterness, distress and humiliation. This is not true to the same extent where one of the parties is dead. Conduct will, however, only be one of the factors for consideration.

(b) Matters to be considered in relation to particular categories of applicant

8–025 There are further statutory guidelines applicable to particular categories of applicant:

(i) Spouses and former spouses

The divorce expectation

8–026 In the case of an application by the deceased's wife or husband the court must[14] have regard to the provision which the applicant might reasonably have expected to receive if the marriage had been ended by divorce on the day of the deceased's death[15]; and this "divorce expectation" may well be a very important consideration.[16] It has been said that the minimum posthumous provision for a surviving spouse should correspond as closely as possible to the inchoate rights enjoyed by that spouse in the deceased's lifetime by virtue of his or her prospective entitlement under matrimonial law.[17] But this is not to say that the divorce expectation will determine the outcome—even although it may be the "logical starting point".[18] For example, in divorce cases the parties' respective needs are often of overriding importance; and the fact there is only one person's need to be considered that when the marriage is ended by death may justify a larger

---

[11] *Espinosa v. Bourke* [1999] 1 F.L.R. 747 at 757.

[12] *Malone v. Harrison* [1979] 1 W.L.R. 1353 at 1364, per Hollings J.; *cf. Re Snoeck, dec'd* [1982] 13 *Fam. Law* 18, where Wood J. refused to interpret the reference to conduct in a sense different from that of the divorce legislation. Accordingly, with some hesitation, it was held that the wife's conduct, at a time when the deceased was terminally ill, in throwing water over him on three occasions, driving a car at him, striking him over the head with a rolling-pin milk bottle and umbrella, puncturing the tyres of his car, and writing abusive and offensive letters to his business colleagues, did not justify a failure to make any provision at all for her, since it did not cancel out her contributions in the early part of the 20-year marriage and her contributions in managing the home and bringing up the children.

[13] s.25(2)(g); see below.

[14] Unless judicial separation was in force and the separation was continuing.

[15] s.3(2).

[16] *Re Besterman (dec'd)* [1984] F.L.R. 503, CA; and see *Kusminow v. Barclays Bank Trust Co. Ltd* [1989] *Fam. Law* 66; *Moody v. Stevenson* [1992] 1 F.L.R. 494; *Davis v. Davis* [1993] 1 F.L.R. 54, CA: *Powell v. Osbourne* [1993] I F.L.R. 1001, CA.

[17] *Moody v. Stevenson* [1992] 1 F.L.R. 494 at 505, CA. *per* Waite J.

[18] *ibid.*

award than could have been expected on divorce[19]; whilst the considerations which point to the clean break on divorce are not all present when a marriage is ended by death.Thus, on the one hand:—

> In *Moody v. Stevenson*[20] the deceased's 81-year-old husband continued to live in the former matrimonial home, which had been given to the deceased by her mother. The deceased's will gave her entire estate to her daughter by a previous marraige, and stated that she considered her husband had adequate resources of his own. The daughter sought possession of the house; and the husband applied for reasonable provision out of the estate. The Court of Appeal held that the starting point should have been to look at the provision a divorce court would have made for the husband; and this would undoubtedly have included provision for his housing. Accordingly he should be given the right to occupy the house for so long as he was able and willing to do so.

In contrast:—

> In *Davis v. Davis*[21] the applicant's husband had given his wife of seven years £15,000 shortly before his death; and his will gave her a life interest in the residue of his estate (amounting to something in the region of a quarter of a million pounds). The trustees (who were directed by the will to have regard to his widow's expressed wishes) arranged for the purchase of a house for the widow's occupation; but she applied to the court for the house to be transferred to her absolutely. Although it was clear that if the marriage had been ended by divorce the court would have ordered an outright clean break capital payment, the Court of Appeal considered that a life interest was a perfectly reasonable provision in all the circumstances.

Other factors in relation to spouses and former spouses

The court must also have regard to[22]: **8–027**

"(i) the age of the applicant and the duration of the marriage;
(ii) the contribution made by the applicant to the welfare of the family of the deceased, including any contribution made by looking after the home or caring for the family."[23]

---

[19] *Re Krubert (dec'd)* [1996] 3 W.L.R. 959; *Re Bunning (dec'd)* [1985] F.L.R. 1 (and *cf. Smith v. Smith (Smith and Others Intervening)* [1991] 2 F.L.R. 432, CA).
[20] [1992] Ch. 486, CA.
[21] [1993] 1 F.L.R. 54, CA.
[22] I.(P.F.& D.)A., s.3(2).
[23] *cf.* M.C.A. 1973, s.25(1)(d), (f).

(ii) Children and children of family

8–028 The court must have regard to the manner in which the applicant was being or in which he might expect to be educated or trained.[24] In the case where the applicant is a child of the family[25] the court is also directed[26] to have regard:—

(a) to whether the deceased had assumed any responsibility for the applicant's maintenance and, if so, to the extent to which and the basis upon which the deceased assumed that responsibility and to the length of time for which the deceased discharged that responsibility;
(b) to whether in assuming and discharging that responsibility the deceased did so knowing that the applicant was not his own child;
(c) to the liability of any other person to maintain the applicant.

(iii) Persons being maintained by deceased

8–029 Where the applicant's claim is based on the fact that the applicant was being maintained by the deceased at the time of the death, the court is to "have regard" not only to the factors set out above but also "to the extent to which and the basis upon which the deceased assumed responsibility for the maintenance of the applicant and to the length of time for which the deceased discharged that responsibility."[27]

(iv) Cohabitants

8–030 Where an application is made under this head the court, in addition to the matters specifically mentioned,[28] is directed to have regard to:

(a) the age of the applicant and the duration of the cohabitation;
(b) the contribution made by the applicant to the welfare of the family of the deceased, including any contribution made by looking after the home or caring for the family.[29]

---

[24] s.3(3). *cf.* M.C.A. 1973, s.25(3)(4). There are special provisions for children of the family: s.3(3)(a), (b), (c), as to which see *Re Leach* [1986] Ch. 226, CA.

[25] See *Re Leach* [1986] Ch. 226, CA; *Re Callaghan* [1985] Fam. 1, Booth J.; and *Re Debenham* [1986] 1 F.L.R. 404, Ewbank J.

[26] s.3(3); and see *Re Leach* [1986] Ch. 226, CA. Compare the provisions of M.C.A. 1973, s.25(4).

[27] s.3(4); and note *Harrington v. Gill* [1983] 4 F.L.R. 265, CA: the court will under this head consider the standard of living enjoyed by the applicant during the deceased's lifetime and the extent to which the deceased contributed to that standard of living.

[28] See s.3(1)(a) to (f).

[29] Inheritance (Provision for Family and Dependants) Act 1975, s.3(2A) as inserted by Law Reform (Succession) Act 1995, s.2(4); compare Matrimonial Causes Act 1973, s.25(2)(f), Chap. 14, below.

4. Orders that can be made

8–031 The court has extensive powers. In addition to periodical payments and lump sums,[30] the court may make orders:

(a) for the transfer or settlement of property[31];
(b) that property (*e.g.* a house) be bought and transferred to the applicant or settled for his benefit[32];
(c) varying ante-nuptial or post-nuptial settlements (subject to certain restrictions).[33]

In deciding whether to exercise these powers, and if so in what manner the court is directed to have regard to the "guidelines" referred to above. [34] The objective is to ensure that the applicant will receive the reasonable financial provision which the deceased has failed to make; and the powers are sufficiently flexible to ensure, for example, that the applicant is enabled to live in the deceased's house for the rest of his or her life.[35]

Orders for periodical payments in favour of a former spouse must determine on remarriage, as under the divorce legislation. Orders in favour of a widow or widower need not do so.[36]

Orders for periodical payments (but not for lump sums or transfer of property) can be varied.[37]

There is a wide range of ancillary powers,[38] including a power to order interim payments,[39] powers to vary maintenance agreements made by the deceased, and maintenance orders.[40]

The Act also contains provisions giving the court extensive powers where the deceased has made dispositions[41] or contracts[42] intended to defeat applications under the Act. It is not clear that the Act has been wholly successful in preventing avoidance of its provisions.[43]

---

[30] I.(P.F.& D.)A., s.2(1)(a), (b). A lump sum may be payable by instalments: s.7.
[31] s.2(1)(c), (d).
[32] s.2(1)(e).
[33] s.2(1)(f).
[34] s.3(1).
[35] *Re Abram (dec'd)* [1996] 2 F.L.R. 379 (where the applicant had made an Individual Voluntary Arrangement with his creditors under the provisions of Insolvency Act 1986; and the court directed that provision be made for the applicant by protective trusts which would benefit him and his family rather than the creditors).
[36] s.19(2).
[37] s.6 This provision is narrowly drawn: see *Fricker v. Personal Representatives of Fricker* [1981] 3 F.L.R. 228.
[38] See, *e.g.* ss.2(4), 19, 20.
[39] See Re *Besterman (dec'd)* [1981] 3 F.L.R. 255.
[40] See ss.16–18.
[41] s.10.
[42] s.11.
[43] See generally C.H. Sherrin, "Defeating the Dependants" [1978] Conv. 13.

CHAPTER NINE

REFORM OF FAMILY PROPERTY LAW: THE FUTURE

INTRODUCTION

9–001 It can be forcefully argued that family law—including the rules governing property rights—is an instrument to secure and safeguard the values which society upholds in the family.[1] In modern society, there is an increasing degree of plurality in those values.[2] Furthermore, the socio-economic context in which legal rules operate has become increasingly complex, as the roles assumed by men and women in the family and in society have progressively become less stereotyped. It may seem uncontroversial that the law should endeavour to give fair recognition to the varied contributions which partners make to their common life. Nevertheless, the means by which that goal is best achieved, and the precise content of fairness,[3] continue to generate much debate. For instance, should equality rights in relation to family assets be defined during the currency of a relationship, or only realised at the time of breakdown? Further, the distinction between formal equality and substantive equality is now well recognised in the literature.[4] These complex issues inevitably underpin any discussion of future reform of family property law.

The Married Women's Property Act 1882[5] was a classic example of the formal equality model. It marked the successful conclusion of a long campaign for reform of the law governing married women's property; and the regime of separation of property remedied many of the injustices which had troubled the nineteenth-century reformers. But the problems of a formal equality model became increasingly apparent. By the end of the Second World War it was

---

[1] J.Eekelaar, "Family Law and Social Control", in *Oxford Essays in Jurisprudence* (3rd Series, OUP, 1987), Chap. 6; Houlgate, "Must the Personal be Political?: Family Law and the Concept of Family" (1998) 12 *International Journal of Law, Policy and the Family* 107; J. Dewar, "The Normal Chaos of Family Law" (1998) 61 *M.L.R.* 467; J. Dewar a Family Law and Its Discontents" (2000) 12 *International Journal of Law, Policy and the Family* 59; Lord McGregor of Durris, *Hansard*, H.L., Vol. 437, col. 653.

[2] See the comments of Lord Hoffmann in *Piglowski v. Piglowski* [1999] 2 F.L.R. 763 at 785; R.Bailey-Harris "Lesbian and Gay Family Values and the Law" [1999] *Fam. Law* 560.

[3] R Bailey-Harris, "Dividing the assets on Family Breakdown: The Content of Fairness" in *Current Legal Problems* (Freemen, ed., OUP, 2001), p. 533.

[4] M Fineman, "Implementing Equality: Ideology, Contradiction and Social Change. A Study of Rhetoric and Results in the Regulation of the Consequences of Divorce" [1983] *Wisconsin Law Review* 789; J. Scutt, "Equal Marital Property Rights" (1983) 18 *Australian Journal of Social Issues* 128; E. Cox, "Beyond Community of Property: A Plea for Equity" (1983) 18 *Australian Journal of Social Sciences* 142; A. Diduck and H. Orton "Equality and Support for Spouses" (1994) 57 *M.L.R.* 681; R. Bailey-Harris, "The Role of Maintenance and Property Orders in Redressing Equality" (1998) 12 *Australian Journal of Family Law* 3.

[5] Discussed in Chap. 4.

obvious that separate property was not always effective in achieving justice for married women,[6] and it increasingly came to be urged that the law failed to deal adequately with the economic realities of twentieth-century married life, especially in relation to the matrimonial home, the value of which might have increased dramatically during the marriage. In particular the law seemed to deny any share in the house to the wife unless she was shown by the title documents to be a joint owner, or she could show that she had made a financial contribution to its acquisition. The law of property thus failed to recognise that a housewife's contribution to the marriage partnership was comparable to that of her husband, who (in the social and economic circumstances which were then thought to prevail) was freed to engage in paid work by reason of her assumption of domestic responsibilities. Accordingly, in 1970 a comprehensive statutory adjustive regime[7] was enacted, designed to achieve a fair allocation of assets between spouses on divorce and to remedy the shortcomings of the law of property.

Changes in social and economic conditions in the last three decades have created a more complex pattern of role-division in relationships and in society. In most relationships the parties adopt mixed roles, with each assuming responsibilities both domestic and income-generating. As Lord Nicholls observed in *White v. White*[8]:

> "Typically, a husband and wife share activities of earning money, running the home and caring for the children".

It is now usual for both spouses to make financial contributions to the acquisition of the family home, which is in any event usually[9] now vested in husband and wife jointly. Taking a cohort of woman at age 30, 47 per cent of those born in the 1900s had paid employment during that year; this rose to 56 per cent for those born in the 1940s and to 67 per cent for those born in the early 1960s.[10] Between 1984 and 1999 the number of women in full-time employment in the United Kingdom increased by one fifth, while the number of males remained static.[11] Nevertheless, women have not yet achieved full equality with men in the employment market, and—given the continuing demands of the traditional parenting role—may never do so.[12] The cohort study (cited above) of the working patterns of women aged 30 showed that employment rates for women without children have been consistently

---

[6] See R. Deech, "Matrimonial property and divorce: a century of progress", in *State, Law and the Family* M.D.A. Freeman ed., (1984).

[7] Matrimonial Proceedings and Property Act 1970, now consolidated as Pt II of the Matrimonial Causes Act 1973. See Chap. 4, and the detailed discussion in Chap. 14.

[8] [2000] 2 F.L.R. 981 at 989.

[9] "virtually all" matrimonial homes are now taken in joint names according to Law Com. No. 175, para. 4.3.

[10] (2000) 30 *Social Trends* 71 and Table 4.11.

[11] (2000) 30 *Social Trends* 71.

[12] See generally *Women, Gender and Work* (M.F. Loutfi, ed., International Labour Office, Geneva, 2001).

higher than for those with children.[13] In the early 1990s, 92 per cent of childless women in that cohort were in employment, compared to 54 per cent of those with children. Women remain disproportionately represented in part-time jobs in comparison with men.[14] In 1999 80 per cent of women said they worked part-time because they did not want a full-time job, compared with 40 per cent of men; the principal reason given was family and other domestic commitments.[15] Also marked is the continuing predominance of women in skilled non-manual occupations (such as clerical and secretarial) as compared to men in professional occupations.[16] In 2001 there were more than twice as many men as women managers and officials, although the proportion of managers and administrators who are women increased modestly from 30 per cent in 1991 to 33 per cent in 1999.[17] Women are more likely than men to work in temporary employment.[18] It is thus not surprising that the gender differential in relation to income from employment persists.[19] Furthermore, there is some evidence that women continue to shoulder the greater share of responsibilities within the home.[20]

9–002 The increased plurality of contemporary society is reflected in the growing acceptance of different family forms. Almost a decade ago a survey[21] concluded with the suggestion that attitudes to cohabitation reflected the process whereby the taboo of the day before yesterday becomes the controversial of yesterday, the accepted of today and the wanted norm of tomorrow. More recent research bears out this view[22]:

> "Marriage is still widely valued as an ideal, but is regarded with much more ambivalence in terms of its role in partnering and (especially) parenting. Views have changed markedly over time and, for many, marriage is no longer seen as having any advantage over cohabitation

---

[13] (2000) 30 *Social Trends* 71 and Table 4.11.

[14] (2002) 32 *Social Trends* Table 4.3.

[15] (2000) 30 *Social Trends* 70–71.

[16] (2002) 32 *Social Trends* 26 and Table 4.14.

[17] (2000) 30 *Social Trends* 72 and Table 4.13; (2002) 32 *Social Trends* Table 4.14.

[18] (2002) 32 *Social Trends* 85.

[19] (2002) 32 *Social Trends* Chart 5.7. Figures issued by the Office for National Statistics in January 2002 revealed that women working full-time were paid 81.5per cent as much as their male counterparts *The Times* January 25, 2002, p.26.

[20] S. Witherspoon, "Interim Report: A Woman's Work" in R. Jowell, S. Witherspoon and L. Brook, *British Social Attitudes, the Fifth Report* (1988), pp. 182–183; and see for a detailed analysis, "The Domestic Labour Revolution: a Process of Lagged Adaptation?" by J. Gershuny, M. Godwin and S. Jones in *The Social and Political Economy of the Household* (M. Anderson *et al.* ed., 1994), Chap. 5.

[21] See K.E. Kieman and V. Esthaugh, *Cohabitation, Extra-marital Childbearing and Social Policy* (1993), p. 70.

[22] See the discussion in *Something to Celebrate* (1995) Church of England Board of Social Responsibility; J. Lewis *et al. Individualism and Commitment in Family and Cohabitation*, LCD Research Paper Series 8/1999; J. Lewis "Marriage, Cohabitation and the Nature of Commitment" (1999) 11 CFLQ 355; A. Barlow *et al. Family Restructuring, the Common Law Marriage Myth and the Need for Legal Realism* (Nuffield Foundation, 2002); A. Barlow *et al. Family Affairs: Cohabitation, Marriage and the Law* (Nuffield, 2002); A Barlow *et al.* "Just a Piece of Paper? Marriage and Cohabitation" [2001] *British Social Attitudes: The 18th* Report (Sage, 2001) 129; J. Haskey "Cohabitation in Great Britain: Past, Present and Future Trends—and Attitudes" (2001) *Population Trends 103*. 4–25.

> in everyday life . . . Meanwhile, cohabitation is now widely accepted both as a prelude to married life and as an alternative to it, even where there are children."[23]

In Great Britain[24] 26 per cent of men and 25 per cent of women aged from 16 to 59 now cohabit,[25] compared with one in eight men and one in six women at the time of the last edition of this book, and there is an increasing separation between marriage and childbearing.[26] Furthermore, partners living together in a personal relationship may be of the same sex.

Despite widespread social acceptance of different family forms, the current law generally accords an inferior status to cohabitation than to marriage, and same-sex partners are treated even less favourably than their heterosexual counterparts.[27] The law is confusing, with the result that many unmarried couples are unaware of their rights[28] and popular misconceptions—for instance that cohabitants have the same legal rights as married couples—abound.[29] The current law has been much criticised,[30] but the precise direction law reform should take is controversial and involves some complex issues of social policy. Couples now express varying degrees of commitment through a variety of family forms of varying duration. Should the law continue to distinguish between the consequences it attaches to different relationships, or should it assimilate them? Should the ethos of equality apply generally, whatever the formal status of a relationship? If so, does equal treatment necessarily mean identical treatment? In the remainder of this Chapter we address some of these issues facing potential law reformers. The first part discusses the case for reform of matrimonial

---

[23] A. Barlow *et al.*, "Just a Piece of Paper", n. 22, *supra*, p.23.

[24] J. Ermisch and M. Franconi, *Cohabitation in Great Britain: Not For Long But Here to Stay* (1999, Colchester: Institute of Social and Economic Research); J. Haskey "Demographic Aspects of Cohabitation in Great Britain" (2001) 15 *International Journal of Law, Policy and the Family* 51.

[25] (2000) 30 *Social Trends* 40 and Table 2.10.; J. Haskey and K. Kiernan, "Cohabitation—Some Demographic Statistics" [1990] *Fam. Law* 442. For the pattern Europe-wide, see K Kiernan, "The Rise of Cohabitation and Childbearing Outside Marriage in Western Europe" (2001) 15 *International Journal of Law, Policy and the Family* 1.

[26] K.E. Kiernan and V. Esthaugh, *Cohabitation: Extra-Marital Childbearing and Social Policy* (1993), p. 6; (2002) 32 *Social Trends* Chart 2.14.

[27] R. Bailey-Harris and J. Masson, "Family Laws's Futures", Chap. 20 in *Law's Futures,* (Hayton ed., Hart, 2001); R. Bailey-Harris "New Families for a New Society?' in *Family Law: Essays for the Millennium* ed., (Cretney ed., 67–77; R. Bailey-Harris, "Same-Sex Partnerships in English Family Law", in *Legal Recognition of Same-Sex Partnerships.* (R. Wintemute and M Andenas, ed., Hart, 2001), Chap 34.

[28] S. Arthur, J. Lewis, M. Maclean, S. Finch and R. Fitzgerald *Settling Up: making financial arrangements after divorce or separation* (National Centre for Social Research, 2002).

[29] A Barlow *et al.*, n. 22 *supra*.

[30] See *e.g.* The Rt Hon Lord Justice Thorpe, "The English System of Ancillary Relief" in *Dividing the Assets on Family Breakdown* (Bailey-Harris ed., *Family Law,* 1998) 1 at 8–9; R. Bailey-Harris "Dividing the Assets on Breakdown of Relationships Outside Marriage", *op cit* Chap. 5; District Judge Taylor, "Section 25: Quick, Cheap and Conciliatory" [1995] *Family Law* 403; Mark Harper "Cohabitation Law Reform: The Way Forward" [1999] *Family Law* 435; R. Bailey-Harris, "Lesbian and Gay Family Rights and the Law" [1999] *Family Law* 560; Probert "Cohabitants and the Family Home" [2000] *Fam. Law* 925; Gouriet, "Cohabitation Update" [2000] *Fam. Law* 210; Bessant, "Cohabitation, Reform and the Human Rights Act 1998" [2001] *Fam. Law* 525; Law Com. Discussion Paper *Sharing Homes* (July 2002), paras 2.105–2.112.

property law, and the second the case for reform of property rights in other relationships. Reform of the law on ancillary relief is discussed at the conclusion of Chapter 14.

I. THE CASE FOR REFORM OF MATRIMONIAL PROPERTY LAW

9–003 The Law Commission from 1965 to 1988 published a number of extensive and careful discussions of various reform issues in family property law.[31] The Commission summarised the case for a reform of matrimonial property in its 1988 report on the subject.[32] The three principal reasons identified were the unfairness and lack of clarity in the existing rules, the need for justice between spouses not only on divorce but also during the existence of the marriage, and the effect on negotiation of settlements[33] of a backdrop of defined property rights.[34]

There are three main kinds of matrimonial property regime which have been proposed in an attempt to meet criticisms of the separate property regime.[35] The first is a community of property regime. The essence of a community system is that, by virtue of the marriage, the spouses' property is at some stage subjected to joint-ownership. Such systems—widespread particularly in the civil law world—take different forms.[36] It is now common for the regime to be confined to property acquired or built up after the marriage.[37] Most schemes now give both parties management powers, and the regimes now predominantly adopt the model of deferred rather than immediate community, whereby the parties' proprietary rights are unaffected until something (commonly, divorce) occurs requiring a dissolution of the community. Such a scheme is perhaps better classified as a regime of separa-

---

[31] Law Com. No. 53: *First Report on Matrimonial Property: A New Approach;* Law Com. 1973 (joint ownership); Law Com. No. 86 *Third Report on Family Property* (1978); Law Com. No. 115 *Report on the Implications of Williams and Glyn's Bank v. Boland;* Law Com. PWP No. 42; Law Com. No. 175, *Family Law: Matrimonial Property* (1988). The Discussion Paper *Sharing Homes* (July 2002) was not confined to the property rights of married couples.

[32] *Family Law: Matrimonial Property* (Law Com. No. 175, (1988)), para. 1.4. For another cogent account of the case for reform, see the *Report of the Australian Law Reform Commission Matrimonial Property* (1987) extracted in Finlay, Bradbrook and Bailey-Harris, *Family Law, Cases Materials and Commentary* (2nd ed., 1993), pp. 669–675.

[33] For the operation of the current ancillary relief jurisdiction, further Chap. 14, below; on unpredictability of outcomes, see Davis, Cretney and Collins *Simple Quarrels* (1994).

[34] See the 5th edition of this book at pp. 221–223 for a full account of the Law Commission's reasoning.

[35] Discussed in greater detail in the 6th edition of this book, pp. 223–230.

[36] See *International Encyclopedia of Comparative Law* (1980) P. IV, Chap. 4 by M. Rhenstein and M.A. Glendon, passim. Many of the issues raised in the text are considered in Freedman, Hammond, Masson and Morris, *Property and Marriage—An Integrated Approach* (Institute of Fiscal Studies, 1988) the conclusions of which are briefly summarised by J. Masson, "A New Approach to Matrimonial Property" [1988] *Fam. Law* 327.On the German Civil Code, see H. Lucke *The German Civil Code,* Chap. 3 in R. Bailey-Harris, ed. *Dividing the Assets on Family Breakdown* (Family Law, 1998); on the French Civil Code, see A. Batteur *Droit Des Personnes et de la Famille* (LGDJ, 1998), Chap. 2.

[37] See the discussion of a mixed community of gains in Freedman, Hammond, Masson and Morris, *Property and Marriage—An Integrated Approach* (Institute of Fiscal Studies, 1988).

tion of property coupled with a claim for equalisation of property rights on the termination of marriage. Arguably, its objectives can equally well be achieved in this country through reform of the law on ancillary relief, which is discussed in Chapter 14.

The second main option is one of special rules for the matrimonial home, involving restraints on disposition and a form of statutory-co-ownership.[38] The introduction of a system of community of property limited to what is often in practice a couple's only significant asset was in 1973 advocated by the Law Commission on the ground *inter alia* that it would reflect the realities of family life. There were, nevertheless, powerful objections both of principle and detail to the Law Commission's proposals.[39] In any event, changes in the pattern of home-ownership in subsequent years have greatly reduced the need for such legislative reform, since for some time now virtually all matrimonial homes have been purchased in joint names.[40]

The third option is one whereby beneficial title to property is made to depend on intended use. In 1985 the Law Commission published a Working Paper on the subject of *Transfer of Money between Spouses,* which was primarily concerned with reform of the Married Women's Property Act 1964. But apparently the response to that Paper encouraged the Commission to put forward potentially far-reaching proposals designed to give effect to the policy that the beneficial ownership of property acquired during a marriage should in principle depend on the purpose for which it was acquired (or transferred), and specifically on whether the acquisition or transfer was wholly or mainly for the use or benefit of one or both spouses.[41] Despite the fact that the scheme was only to apply in the absence of a contrary intention, and that some assets and transfers (notably business transfers) were to remain outside the scheme, objections still remained.[42]

It is thus obvious that extensive debates on matrimonial property over several decades failed to produce any consensus in favour of a particular reform.[43] In England and Wales there has been very little recent call for such reform, and attention has instead shifted to the question whether the principles governing asset distribution on divorce are in need of reform in order to achieve a greater degree of justice. This is discussed in Chapter 14.

---

[38] See *First Report on Family Property: A New Approach* (Law Com. No. 52), para. 25; J.E. Todd and L.M. Jones, *Matrimonial Property* (1972), p. 20. These proposals assume that the spouses' rights of occupation of the matrimonial home (Chap. 6, above) would continue to be protected.

[39] See *e.g.* the debate on the Law Commission's *Third Report on Family Property* (1978), Law Com. No. 86: *Hansard,* H.L., Vol. 401, col. 1432; the *Report of the Scottish Law Commission on Matrimonial Property* (Scot. Law Com. No. 86, (1984)), paras 3.9 *et seq.*

[40] Law Commission Report, *Family Law: Matrimonial Property* (Law Com. No. 175 (1988)), para. 4.3.

[41] Law Com. No. 175.

[42] See the note of dissent by Mr Davenport Q.C., Law Com. No. 175, p. 4.

[43] In 1984 the Scottish Law Commission found very little support for major reform: see Scot. Law Com. No. 86, (1984), para. 1.1.

II. REFORM OF PROPERTY RIGHTS IN OTHER RELATIONSHIPS

9–004 In other countries, increasing plurality in family forms has stimulated considerable law reform activity.[44] Details naturally differ, but generally speaking there are two main models[45] of statutory regulation. The first is dominant in mainland Europe,[46] the second in the Antipodes but is not unknown elsewhere.

The first model is that of registered partnership,[47] with defined consequences for the registered relationship in particular areas of law. In some countries the registration option is available only to same-sex partners[48] (who save in the Netherlands[49] do not have the option of marriage) but in others also to heterosexual partners.[50] The legal consequences to which registration gives rise is necessarily a question of social policy for the domestic legislature, in particular the extent to which they mirror or differ from those attached to marriage. Registered partnership is the attractive model to proponents of party autonomy and also serves a symbolic function as a public expression of commitment, but since it is wholly dependent on mutual registration,[51] it may fail to protect a vulnerable party. The Netherlands is the first state in the world to make marriage available to all couples irrespective of sex.[52]

---

44 A detailed description of the many different regimes are beyond the scope of the present work, but the reader is referred to *Marriage and Cohabitation in Contemporary Society* (J. Eekelaar and S. Katz ed., 1980); J. Eeekelaar and T. Nhlapo (eds) *The Changing Family* (Hart, 1998); *Legal Recognition of Same-Sex Partnership: a Study of National, European and International Law,* R. Wintemute and M. Andenas (ed., Hart, 2001).

45 R. Bailey-Harris "New Families For a New Society" in *Family Law: Essays for the New Millennium,* (S. Cretney ed., Family Law, 2000) pp. 67 at 74–77.

46 For an overview of developments in Europe see (2001) 15 *International Journal of Law, Policy and the Family: Special Edition: Unmarried Cohabitation in Europe* 1–184. The registered partnership model has been adopted in Vermont from April 1, 2000: Act Relating to Civil Unions (15 Vermont Statutes Annotated, Chap. 25).

47 Linda Nielson, "Family Rights and the Registered Partnership Act in Denmark" (1990) 4 *International Journal of Law and the Family* 297; Morten Broberg, "The Registered Partnership For Same-Sex Couples in Denmark" (1996) 8 *Child and Family Law Quarterly* 149; Craig Lind, "Pretended Families and the Local State in Britain and the USA" (1996) 10 *International Journal of Law, Policy and the Family* 134; Ingrid Anderson, "Registered Personal Relationships" [1997] *Family Law* 175; Ingrid Lund-Anderson, "Cohabitation and Registered Partnership in Scandinavia" in *The Changing Family* (Eekelaar and Nhapo ed., Hart Publishing, 1998); J. Eekelaar, "Registered Same-Sex Partnerships and Marriages—A Statistical Comparison" [1998] *Family Law* 561); A. Barlow and R. Probert, "Reforming the Rights of Cohabitants: Lessons from Across the Channel" [199] *Fam. Law* 477; Steiner, "The Spirit of the new French registered partnership law—promoting autonomy and pluralism or weakening marriage?" (2000) 12 *C.F.L.Q. 1; R. Probert and A. Barlow, "Displacing marriage—diversification and harmonisation with Europe?" (2000) 12 CFLQ 153, D. Bradley "Regulation of Unmarried Cohabitation in West-European Jurisdictions—Determinants of Legal Policy" (2001) 15 International Journal of Law, Policy and the Family* 22; Gradually More C. Martin and I. Thery, "The Pacs and Marriage and Cohabitation in France" (2001) 15 *International Journal of Law, Policy and the Family* 135; and see generally *Legal Recognition of Same-Sex Partnerships: A Study of National, European and International Law,* (R. Wintemute and M. Andenas ed., Hart, 2001).

48 *e.g.* Denmark, Norway, Iceland, Greenland, Finland , Germany, Luxembourg, Vermont.

49 Act No. 950, November 9, 2000.

50 Netherlands, France, Belgium.

51 Low take-up rates were noted by J. Eekelaar in "Registered Same-Sex Partnership and Marriage" [1998] *Fam. Law* 561.

52 See n. 49, above.

The second model (widely adopted in Australia[53] and in New Zealand[54] but also by some European legislatures[55]) is to attach specific consequences to a defined relationship (usually after a minimum duration, such as two years) by operation of law. This falls short of a truly status approach, since the legal consequences are not comprehensive. The qualifying relationship can be defined either in terms of cohabitation ("living together as"), or in a form of words which does not imply the necessity of a sexual relationship (although one may in fact exist), such as "domestic relationship"[56] or "close personal relationship".[57] Legislative definitions of the qualifying relationship in the States and Territories in Australia were originally exclusively heterosexual, but New South Wales,[58] Queensland,[59] Victoria[59a] and New Zealand[60] have now extended protection to same-sex relationships.[61] The legislative schemes in Australia and New Zealand differ in detail as to the financial consequences of the recognised relationship. The Australian Capital Territory, Queensland and New Zealand have gone furthest in assimilating financial consequences to those of marriage.[62] This model of legal regulation offers a high degree of protection to the vulnerable, but may be criticised on the basis that it seeks to impose legal consequences on those who seek to avoid them by choosing not to marry. A contractual "opt out"

---

[53] De Facto Relationships Act 1984 (N.S.W.), later renamed the Property (Relationships) Act 1984 by the Property (Relationships) Legislation Amendment Act 1999; Property Law Act 1958 (Vic.) as amended by the Property Law (Amendment) Acts 1987 and 1998 and the Statute Law Amendment (Relationships) Act 2001 (Vic.); De Facto Relationships Act 1991 (N.T.); Domestic Relationships Act 1994 (A.C.T.); De Facto Relationships Act 1996 (S.A.) Property Law Act 1974 as amended by the Property Law Amendment Act 1999 (Qld.); De Facto Relationships Act 1999 (Tas.); Property (Relationships) Act 1976, as amended by the Property Relationships Amendment Act 2001(N.Z).; R. Bailey-Harris "Financial Rights in Relationships Outside Marriage: A Decade of Reforms in Australia" [1995] *International Journal of Family Law* 233–255; R. Bailey-Harris, "Dividing the Assets of the Unmarried Family—Recent Lessons From Australia" [2000] *International Family Law* 90; N. Peart, M. Brigs and M. Henegan, *Relationships Property* (Brooker, 2001).

[54] Property (Relationships) Amendment Act 2001.

[55] Sweden, Catalonia, Aragon and Navarra; see also the definition of "concubinage" in the French Civil Code Arts 515–518, as amended by Act No. 99–944, November 15, 1999.

[56] See *e.g.* Domestic Relationships Act 1994 (Australian Capital Territory). The Victorian legislation uses the term "domestic partner".

[57] Property (Relationships) Act 1984 (NSW) as amended, s. 5(1)(b).

[58] Property (Relationships) Legislation Amendment Act 1999 (N.S.W), inserting a new s. 4(1) into the Property Relationships Act 1984.

[59] Property Law Amendment Act 1999 (Qld.) s. 260 which uses the term "de facto spouse".

[59a] Property Law Act 1958 (Vic.) as amended, s.275(1).

[60] Property (Relationships) Act 1976, amended and renamed by the Property (Relationships) Amendment Act 2001, s. 2D; N. Peart, "Property Rights For Married, De Facto and Same-Sex Couples—Proposals for Reform in New Zealand" [2001] *International Family Law* 93; N.Richardson "Recent New Zealand Legislation Affecting De Facto Couples" [2001] *International Family Law* 114; N. Peart, M. Brigs and M. Henegan, *Relationships Property* (Brookers, Wellington, 2001).

[61] For a discussion of the complex social policy issues involved, see J. Millbank "Lesbian and Gay Families" (1998) 12 *Australian Journal of Family Law* 99 at 134–136; J. Millbank and W. Morgan "Let Them Eat Cake and Ice Cream: Wanting Something 'More' From the Relationships Recognition Menu" in *Legal Recognition of Same-Sex Partnerships* (R. Wintemute and M. Andenas, Hart, 2001), Chap. 14.

[62] R. Bailey-Harris "Dividing the Assets of the Unmarried Family: Recent Lessons from Australia" [2000] *International Family Law* 90 at 91–92.

facility available in the Australian and New Zealand models seeks to meet this criticism.

9–005 What of current developments within the United Kingdom?[63] The Scottish Law Commission over a decade ago recommended[64] that a former cohabitant should be able to apply to a court within one year after the end of the cohabitation for financial provision (by way of a capital sum, but not periodical payments) on the basis of one of the principles used in Scotland in resolving the financial consequences of divorce—namely that fair account should be taken of any economic advantage derived by either party from contributions made by the other and of any economic disadvantage suffered by either party in the interests of the other party or of any child of the family. The Scottish executive announced in 2000 that it intended to enact these proposals, but at the time of writing legislation has yet to appear. In England and Wales, proposals for reform have come primarily from non-government sources. Both the Law Society[65] and the Solicitors' Family Law Association[66] in 1999 formulated proposals similar in principle to those of the Scottish Law Commission, and each recommended that the defined relationship should be inclusive of both heterosexual and same-sex partnerships. Each recommended an "opt" out facility through cohabitation contract, subject to certain safeguards. A further paper published by the Law Society in July 2002 recommended similar extensive rights for cohabitants (inclusively defined). It further recommended that same-sex partners be able to opt for registration, with the same rights as married couples.[66a] In 1995, the Law Commission's Sixth Programme of Law Reform[67] committed the Commission to an examination of the property rights of home-sharers. The Discussion Paper *Sharing Homes* (July 2002) was critical of the current law but declined to make specific proposals for legislation, regarding difficult questions of social policy as matters for political debate and decision outside the remit of a law reform body.

There has been support—again from non-government sources—for the enactment of a registered partnership model of regulation. Lord Lester of Herne Hill introduced a Civil Partnership Bill[68] in the House of Lords in January 2002.[69] The Bill proposed that two adults who had lived together for a minimum of six months should be able to register their civil partnership; a sexual relationship

---

[63] See J. Lewis "Debates and Issues Regarding Marriage and Cohabitation in British and American Literature" (2001) 15 *International Journal of Law, Policy and the Family* 169.

[64] See the Scottish Law Commission's Discussion Paper No. 86, *The Effects of Cohabitation in Private Law* (Discussion Paper No. 86, 1990) and the Commission's *Report on Family Law* (Scot. Law Com. No. 135, (1992)), Pt XVI., paras 16.14–16.23.

[65] Family Law Committee of the Law Society *Proposals for Reform of the Law of Cohabitation* (April 1999).

[66] SFLA *Cohabitation Report* (April 1999); M. Gouriet, "Cohabitation Update" [2001] *Fam. Law* 210.

[66a] *Cohabitation: The Case for Clear Law: Proposals for Reform* (July 2002).

[67] Law Com. No. 234, (1995), item 8.

[68] See M. Harper "Cohabitation" *SFLA Review* Issue 93, March 2002, pp. 32–33. The much shorter Partnerships Civil Registration Bill was introduced by Jane Griffiths MP as a Private Member's Bill in the House of Commons on October 24, 2001. There is a return date in April 2002, but in reality the Bill is unlikely to proceed further.

[69] Introduced on January 10, 2002; Second Reading on January 25, 2002.

would not be a necessary prerequisite. The Bill—inclusive of both heterosexual and same-relationships—proposed a wide range of consequences of registering a civil partnership. For the purposes of this Chapter, the most significant included a form of statutory co-ownership in equal shares of communal property (defined as the partners' principal home and certain of the contents), subject to a registered property agreement providing for different entitlements to such property. On cessation of the relationship, a partner would be able to apply to the court for an intervention order distributing communal property otherwise than in accordance with the co-ownership provision or the terms of an agreement, and for a financial provision and/or pension-sharing order. The considerations on which the court was to exercise its discretion were to be similar to those found in section 25 of the Matrimonial Causes Act 1973.[70] There was to be a general principle that each partner should be financially independent of the other on the cessation of the civil partnership, and to this end a financial provision order would have a maximum duration of two years. The Bill received much popular support[71] but has now been withdrawn, apparently in the light of government promises to consider the whole issue of legal regulation of family relationships outside marriage. The Cabinet Office has instigated a cross-Departmental review and has established a Civil Partnership and Sexual Orientation Team within the Women and Equality Unit. Only time will tell whether the Government will in fact promote law reform in this field, and if so, what model will be adopted, or whether the anxiety that to address any "family values" issue is a potential vote-loser will prevail.

---

[70] Discussed in Chap. 14.

[71] See *e.g. The Times,* Leading Article, January 11, 2002.

Part III

FAMILY BREAKDOWN

CHAPTER TEN

PROTECTION FROM VIOLENCE AND HARASSMENT

I. INTRODUCTION

10–001 This Chapter deals with the remedies available to those who suffer violence or other forms of harassment by members of their family or others with whom they have had a relationship. Remedies afford both personal protection and security of accommodation, through non-molestation and occupation orders. This Chapter poses terminological problems which are underpinned by serious policy dilemmas. The conventional term "domestic violence" has in recent years come under increasing criticism, as has the alternative "family violence", particularly from feminist jurisprudence.[1] It is argued that the term "domestic" downgrades the seriousness of the violence in question, an effect reinforced by the so-called ideology of privacy which has permeated much of recent family policy[2]—the notion that the family is sacrosanct and that the home is a private place, to be guarded against outside intervention.[3] The "privatisation" debate moreover raises the issue of the respective roles of the criminal and civil laws in this sensitive field, discussed further below. The term "family violence" may suggest a complicity and its gender-neutrality downplays the unarguable fact that most (although not all) intra-family violence is directed against women and children by men. Moreover, the term "victim" is itself not without controversy on the ground of its negative stereotyping, much feminist literature preferring that of "survivor" with its connotations of empowerment.[4] The public/private debate and the identification of violence with the inequality axiomatic in a power imbalance has led to questions about the appropriateness of some methods of dispute resolution, such as mediation.[5] In recent years an increasingly broad view has

---

1 The critique and substantial literature is well summarised by J. Conaghan in "Tort Litigation in the Context of Intra-familial Abuse" (1998) 60 *M.L.R.* 132 at 132–136 and accompanying footnotes.

2 See K. O'Donovan, *Sexual Divisions in Law* (1985); S.S.M. Edwards, *Sex and Gender in the Legal Process* (1996), Chap. 5; J. Bridgeman and S. Millns, *Feminist Perspectives on Law* (Sweet & Maxwell, 1998), Chap. 1; A. Diduck and F. Kaganas, *Family Law, Gender and the State: Text, Cases and Materials* (Hart Publishing, 1999), Chap. 10.

3 On the relative infrequency with which matters are brought to court, see Report on *Domestic Violence and Occupation of the Family Home* (Law Com. No. 207,(1992)), para. 2.4–2.6.

4 See *e.g.* L. Kelly, *Surviving Sexual Violence* (Cambridge: Polity, 1988).

5 See A. Diduck and F. Kaganas, *op cit. supra* n. 2, Chap. 11; F. Kaganas and C. Piper, "Domestic Violence and Divorce Mediation" [1994] JSWFL 265; F. Raitt, "Domestic Violence and Divorce Mediation" (1966) 18 *J.S.W.F.L.* 11; M. Richards, "Domestic Violence and Mediation" [1997] *Fam. Law* 127; Frickers, "Mediation, Domestic Violence and the USA Approach" [1997] *Fam. Law* 125 at 201. Note however that in *Re L; Re V; Re M; Re H (Contact: Domestic Violence)* [2000] 2 F.L.R. 334 at 366–367, Thorpe L.J. questioned the value of litigation as the conventional mode of enforcing contact disputes.

been taken of the impact of violence across the whole range of family proceedings. Much attention—including empirical research as well as doctrinal analysis—has been directed to the relevance of violence in proceedings under the Children Act 1989.[6] There has been an increasing recognition that (perhaps as an unintended consequence of the aim to eradicate considerations of fault from family proceedings) violence has tended to be downplayed by judges, welfare officers and other agents of the family justice system,[7] and remedial steps have been suggested.[8]

As the Law Commission pointed out,[9] "domestic violence" can take many forms.[10] The term has a wider meaning (in addition to the narrower meaning of the use or threat of physical force)—

> "which extends to abuse beyond the more typical instances of physical assault to include any form of physical, sexual or psychological molestation or harassment which has a serious detrimental effect upon the health and well-being of the victim . . . Examples of such 'non-violent' harassment or molestation cover a very wide range of behaviour. Common instances include persistent pestering and intimidation through shouting, denigration, threats or argument, nuisance telephone calls, damaging property, following the applicant about and repeatedly calling at her home or place of work. Installing a mistress into the matrimonial home with a wife and three children, filling car locks with superglue, writing anonymous letters and pressing one's face against a window whilst brandishing papers"

---

[6] Hester and Radford, *The Impact of the Children Act: Women, Violence and Male Power* (Open University Press, 1995); Hester and Radford, *Domestic Violence and Child Contact in England and Denmark* (Bristol University Press, 1996) Jaye (1996) 8 *C.F.L.Q.* 285; Smart & Neale [1997] *Fam. Law* 332; Conway [1996] *Fam. Law* 499; Hester & Pearson [1997] 11 *C.F.L.Q.* 281; Parkinson & Humphreys [1998] 10 *C.F.L.Q.* 147; Peacock "Domestic Abuse Research" [1998] *Fam. Law* 628; Humphreys, "Judicial Alienation Syndrome" [1999] *Fam. Law* 313; Barnett, "Disclosure of Domestic Violence in Child Contact disputes" [1999] *Fam. Law* 104; R. Bailey-Harris, J. Barron and J. Pearce "From Utility to Rights: The Presumption of contact in Practice" (1999) *I.J.L.P.&F.* 111; Hester, Pearson and Harrison, *Making an Impact: Children and Domestic Violence* (Kingsley Publishes Ltd, 2000) for a male perspective on the relevant research, see Yarwood, "Domestic Abuse Research" [1999] *Fam. Law* 114.

[7] *Re L;Re V;Re M;Re H (Contact: Domestic Violence)* [2000] 2 F.L.R. 334; [2001] 2 W.L.R. 339; [2000] 4 All E.R. 609; [2000] 2 F.C.R. 404, CA; F. Kaganas, "Contact and Domestic Violence" (2000) 12 *C.F.L.Q.* 311; *Re M (Interim Contact: Domestic Violence)* [2000] 2 F.L.R. 377; [20001] 1 F.C.R. 124, F.D; *Re G (Domestic Violence: Direct Contact)* [2000] 2 F.L.R. 865.

[8] Advisory Board on Family Law Children Act Sub-Committee *A Report to the Lord Chancellor on the Question of Parental Contact in Cases Where there is Domestic Violence* (April 12, 2000), summarised in [2000] *Fam. Law* 388. The issue is discussed in more detail in Chap. 20.

[9] *Report on Domestic Violence and Occupation of the Family Home* (Law Com. No. 207, (1992)), para. 2.3. There is a vast literature on the subject of domestic violence, to which an excellent introduction is provided by L.J.F. Smith, *Domestic Violence: an overview of the literature* (Home Office Research Study No. 107, 1989). The Law Commission's Report also contains extensive references whilst S.S.M. Edwards, *Sex and Gender in the Legal Process* (1996) (especially Chap. 5) contains a valuable feminist perspective. See also the references in nn. 1–3 *supra*.

[10] See G. Jones, D. Lockton, R. Ward and E. Kashefi, "Domestic violence applications: an empirical study of one court" (1995) 17 *J.S.W.F.L.* 67 for an analysis of the cases coming before a county court over a four year period.

have all been held in decided cases to constitute molestation.[11] Nevertheless, as we shall see, not all forms of intimidation are encompassed.

This Chapter will describe both criminal and civil remedies for violence and harassment. Their respective roles have not been without controversy, and difficult issues can also arise in defining the proper limits of legal (as against social) sanctions. The primary objectives of the criminal law are the punishment and deterrence of offenders[12] in the interests of the community as a whole; prosecution may be felt to contribute to the final breakdown of the family. Imprisonment of the aggressor may well lead to unemployment and consequent financial hardship for the victim and the children, and may exacerbate the problem by provoking further violence.[13] By contrast, the civil law focuses on protection and compensation. Moreover, "family law" remedies are directed to preserving, or reconstructing, so far as is possible, an ongoing relationship between the individuals concerned. The appropriate balance is difficult to strike. The primacy of family law remedies in this field is not without its critics,[14] since this type of violence is a crime like any other and should be recognised as such. On the other hand there are strong adherents to the view that intra-family disputes involving violent or aggressive behaviour require management by processes distinct from the general legal process.[15]

II. THE ROLE OF THE CRIMINAL LAW

10–002 An incident of domestic violence may involve the commission of a criminal offence. It is now well settled that marriage does not constitute a licence to

---

[11] *Report on Domestic Violence and Occupation of the Family Home* (Law Com. No. 207, (1992)), para. 2.3 (the footnotes are omitted).

[12] However, a claim may be made under the Criminal Injuries Compensation Act 1995 for compensation notwithstanding the fact that the victim and the person responsible for the injuries were living in the same household at the time, provided (in the case of violence between adults in the family) that the person responsible and the applicant stopped living together in the same household before the application was made and seem unlikely to live together again: see generally *R. v. Home Secretary and Criminal Injuries Compensation Board, ex p. P.* [1994] 2 F.L.R. 861; [1995] 1 W.L.R. 845; [1995] 1 All E.R. 870; (1995) 2 F.C.R. 553, CA. On the different objectives of criminal charges and contempt proceedings respectively, see *DPP v. Tweddle* [2001] E.W.C.A. Admin. 185, [2002] 2 F.L.R. 400.

[13] See the Law Commission's *Report on Domestic Violence and Occupation of the Family Home* (Law Com. No. 207, 1992), paras 2.8 *et seq.* for a sensitive and perceptive account of the relationship between the criminal and civil law procedures in the context of domestic violence.

[14] A. Kewley, "Pragmatism Before Principles: The Limitation of Civil Law Remedies For Victims of Domestic Violence" (1996) 18 *J.S.W.F.L.* 1.

[15] *Foulkes v. Chief Constable v. Merseyside Police*, [1998] 2 F.L.R. 798; [1998] 3 All E.R. 705; (1999) 1 F.C.R. 98 *per* Thorpe L.J. (arrest for breach of the peace not appropriate for a dispute between spouses in the matrimonial home; note that this procedure was on the particular facts held to violate Art. 8 of the E.C.H.R.: *McLeod v. U.K.* [1998] 2 F.L.R. 1048; [1998] Crim. L.R. 155; (1999) 1 F.C.R. 193, ECHR. The Law Commission recommended its abolition: Report *Binding Over* (Law Com. No. 222 (1994), especially paras 6.9–6.19. However, the concept of breach of the peace and power to bind over survived the scrutiny of the ECHR in *Steel and Others v. U.K.* (1999) 28 E.H.R.R. 603; see also *Chief Constable of Cleveland Police v. McGrogan* [2002] 1 F.L.R. 707.

assault a spouse against his or her will[16] and the supposed common law doctrine which would allow a husband to beat his wife provided he used a stick no thicker than his thumb[17] has long since been consigned to the museum of legal folklore.[18] The criminal law may accordingly be invoked for offences ranging from murder and manslaughter, through unlawful wounding,[19] grievous bodily harm,[20] assault occasioning actual bodily harm[21] and aggravated assault,[22] to common assault.[23] It was long thought that a man could not be convicted of raping his wife,[24] but in 1991 the House of Lords held[25] that this rule no longer formed part of English law. Statute has subsequently confirmed and clarified this position,[26] whilst the courts have laid down that the fact that a rapist is married to his victim does not justify a lenient sentence.[27] More generally, the Court of Appeal has stated that marital disharmony does not of itself excuse let alone justify the commission of acts of violence.[28]

Nevertheless, in practice the criminal law has been criticised for its apparent failure through traditional offences to afford real protection from intra-family violence. Much depends on police discretion and police practice, and although determined efforts at improvement have been evident,[29] there are continuing anxieties that the culture of non-intervention in so-called "private" disputes has not been wholly dispelled.[30] There are often problems in obtaining convincing

---

16 See *R. v. Jackson* [1981] 1 Q.B. 671 at 679, 682; *R. v. Reid* [1973] Q.B. 299; [1972] 3 W.L.R. 395; [1972] 2 All E.R. 1350. The extent to which consent is capable of being a defence to a charge of sexual assault presents considerable difficulties: see *R. v. Brown* [1994] 1 A.C. 212, HL; and the Law Commission's Consultation Paper, *Consent in the Criminal Law* (Law Com. C.P. No. 139 (1995)).

17 See *per* Lord Denning M.R., *Davis v. Johnson* [1979] A.C. 264 at 270; [1978] 2 W.L.R. 553; [1978] 1 All E.R. 1132, HL.

18 See generally M. Doggett, *Marriage, Wife Beating and the Law in Victorian England* (1992).

19 Offences against the Person Act 1861, s.20.

20 *ibid.* s.18.

21 *ibid.* s.47.

22 *ibid.* s.43.

23 *ibid.* s.42.

24 See J.L. Barton, "The Story of Marital Rape" (1992) 108 *L.Q.R.* 260 for a provocative historical account.

25 *R. v. R.* [1992] 1 A.C. 599; [1991] 3 W.L.R. 767; [1991] 4 All E.R. 481; [1992] 1 F.L.R. 217, CA.

26 Criminal Justice and Public Order Act 1994, s.142 giving effect to proposals made by the Law Commission in its *Report on Rape within Marriage* (Law Com. No. 205 (1992)).

27 *R. v. W.* (1993) 14 Cr. App. R. (S.) 256.

28 *R. v. Rossiter* [1994] 2 All E.R. 752 at 753, *per* Russell L.J.

29 See the Government's evidence to the House of Commons Home Affairs Select Committee (Third Report (1992/3) H.C. 245-i) and note the Statement of Prosecution Policy on Domestic Violence incorporated as Annex A to the Government's Reply to that Report (Cmnd. 2269 (1993)). Note also that Home Office Circular 60/1990 had (amongst other things) reminded police forces of the effectiveness of arrest in defusing a situation of domestic tension.

30 See S.S.M. Edwards and A. Halpern, "Protection for the Victim of Domestic Violence: Time for Radical Revision?" [1991] *J.S.W.F.L.* 94; and see S.S.M. Edwards, *Sex and Gender in the Legal Process* (1996), pp. 192–213; S. Wright, "Policing Domestic Violence: A Nottingham Case Study" (1998) 20 *J.S.W.F.L.* 397.

evidence,[31] and defendants are often charged with comparatively minor offences.[32]

However, recent years have witnessed some innovative legislation offering criminal law protection from molestation. Offences in respect of communications exist under the Telecommunications Act 1984[33] and the Malicious Communications Act 1988. The offence of intentional harassment was created by the Criminal Justice and Public Order Act 1994,[34] but of most significance in this field was the Protection from Harassment Act 1997. The genesis of this legislation was widespread public concern over "stalking", which gave rise first to unsuccessful private members' bills and subsequently to government action.[35] That the Act was passed with the phenomenon of stalking in mind was confirmed by the Court of Appeal in *R. v. Colohan*.[36] Clearly the protection afforded by this legislation was never intended to be relationship-specific and its application is not limited by the concept of "persons associated"[37] found in Part IV of the Family Law Act 1996. Stalking has been described thus:

> "The essential characteristics of this phenomenon are the obsessive harassment of a victim, normally female, by someone who pursues her by following her movements, telephoning and so on. Any relationship between the parties has ended, if, indeed, it ever existed outside the imagination of the perpetrator."[38]

10–003 In *R. v. Colohan*[39] the conduct in question was threatening letters; the sender raised mental illness as a defence. The Court of Appeal, adopting a purposive constructive of legislation which was designed to protect victims from conduct likely to be pursued by those of obsessive or unusual psychological make-up, adopted an objective test of harassment—what a reasonable person would

---

31 Although a spouse is now a competent and compellable witness against the other in proceedings involving an assault on the other or on a person under 16 (Police and Criminal Evidence Act 1984, s.80) research carried out by A. Cretney and G. Davis at Bristol University confirms that many domestic violence prosecutions fail because the complainant withdraws or fails to give evidence: see A. Cretney and G. Davis, "Prosecuting 'Domestic' Assault" [1996] *Crim. L.R.* 162.

32 *ibid.*

33 s.43.

34 s.154, inserting a new s.4A into the Public Order Act 1986.

35 A Bill intended to give protection against stalking by creating a criminal offence failed to make progress in the House of Commons: see *Official Report* H.C. May 10, 1996, Vol. 277, col. 609; and the Government stated that a similar Bill (a Stalking (No. 2) Bill) which received a second reading in the House of Lords on June 12, 1996) was unacceptable because its scope was too wide and would criminalise the lawful activities of persons such as journalists and debt collectors. On the history of the government's own legislation, see [1996] *Fam. Law* 527; Lawson Cruttenden, "The Government's Proposed Stalking Law—A Discussion Paper" [1996] *Fam. Law* 755; [1997] *Fam. Law* 4; royal assent June 21, 1997; Protection From Harassment Act 1997 (Commencement No. 1) Order 1997 (S.I. 1997 No. 1418); Lawson-Cruttenden and Addison, "Harassment and Domestic Violence" [1997] *Fam. Law* 429; H. Conway, "Protection from Harassment Act 1997" [1997] *Fam. Law* 714.

36 [2001] EWCA Crim. 1251; [2001] 2 F.L.R. 757.

37 Family Law Act 1996, s.62(3).

38 R. Bird, *Domestic Violence and Protection from Harassment: The New Law* (Family Law, 2nd ed., 1997), p.109.

39 [2001] EWCA Crim. 1251; [2001] 2 F.L.R., C.A. Crim. Div.

think—and accordingly rejected the defence. Despite its origin, the Act's application would not appear to be confined to stalking. In *Thomas v. News Group Newspapers Ltd*[40] it was held (in the civil context) that the publication of press articles likely to incite racial hatred of another was a course of conduct capable of amounting to harassment under the Act. Whether in accordance with legislative intention or not, the Protection from Harassment Act 1997 has created civil remedies which to an extent overlap with those under Part IV of the Family Law Act 1996; that relationship is discussed in the next section, together with the interpretation of the terms "molestation" and "harassment".

The Protection from Harassment Act 1997 is however distinctive in its creation of criminal remedies against harassment, a term it leaves undefined. Section 1 (1) provides that:

> "A person must not pursue a course of conduct[41]—
>
> (a) which amounts to harassment of another, and
> (b) which he knows or ought to know[42] amounts to harassment of the other"

There are two levels of offence. Section 2(1) provides that a person who breaches section 1 commits an arrestable offence, with a maximum term of imprisonment of six months or a fine not exceeding level 5 on the standard scale, or both.[43] Section 4 is directed to the more serious offence of putting people in fear of violence. Thus a person whose course of conduct causes another to fear, on at least two occasions, that violence will be used against him is guilty of an offence if he knows or ought[44] to know that this will be the effect; the penalty for an offence under this section is liable if convicted on indictment to a maximum term of five years imprisonment or a fine or both, or on summary conviction to a maximum term of six months imprisonment or a fine or both.[45] The availability of the two levels of offence is useful both in terms of the punishment and deterrence of harassment but nevertheless Lord Steyn in *obiter dicta* in *R. v. Ireland; R. v. Burstow*[46] drew attention to certain (clearly unintended) weaknesses in the drafting of the relevant provisions. The maximum penalty under the first level offence might be inadequate to deal with persistent offenders who cause serious psychiatric injury to victims, whilst there may be difficulty in securing convictions under section 4 in respect of a silent telephone caller (a serious social problem): the victim in such cases may have cause to fear that violence *may* be used against her but no more. More generally, the operation of the Act in relation to both offences is limited by the need to establish a "course of conduct."[47] In *Lau v. DPP*[48] (where a conviction for the lower

[40] *The Times*, July 25 2001; [2001] EWCA Civ. 1233 , CA.
[41] Defined to include speech: s.7(4).
[42] According to the objective test of the reasonable person: s.1(2).
[43] s.2(2).
[44] The same objective test of the reasonable person applies: s.4(2): *R. v. Colohan* [2001] (No. 1377).
[45] s.4(4).
[46] [1998] 1 F.L.R. 105 at 107–108; comment by S. Cretney in [1997] *Fam. Law* 137; [1977] 4 All E.R. 225, HL.
[47] Protection from Harassment Act 1997, ss.4(1) and 7(3).
[48] [2000] 1 F.L.R. 799, QB; comment by G. Douglas in [2000] *Fam. Law* 799.

level offence based on two incidents separated by four months was quashed) it was held that the fewer the incidents and the wider they are spread, the less likely it will be that a finding of harassment will be made. A nexus is required to link the acts complained of, which was absent in this case, as it was in *R. v. Hills*[49] (two assaults some six months apart). A comprehensive consideration of the criminal provisions of the 1997 Act is beyond the scope of the present work.[50]

III. THE ROLE OF THE CIVIL LAW

10–004 Violence or other psychological pressures of a collapsing relationship may necessitate remedies directed both to the future behaviour of the parties and to the future use of property. These have been identified as:

> "two distinct but inseparable problems: providing protection for one member of the family against molestation or violence by another and regulating the occupation of the family home when the relationship has broken down either temporarily or permanently".[51]

These matters are generally regarded as the stuff of the civil rather than the criminal law, since what is primarily in issue is the relationship between the individuals involved, rather than the relationship between a particular individual and the community as a whole. Moreover, it is generally agreed that[52] the main aim of the civil law (in contrast with the criminal law) in this context is to regulate and improve matters for the future, rather than making judgments upon or punishing past behaviour. Nevertheless, a number of not uncontroversial policy issues arise, concerned essentially with the degree to which the civil law remedies should privilege marital status and proprietary rights. Should the nature of the remedies available differ according to whether the parties are or were married or in another relationship? To what extent should accommodation orders reflect existing legal and equitable rights in the property concerned? Should a distinction be drawn in this respect between personal protection orders and those which confer—and interfere with—occupation rights? As will be seen, the current law adopts some uneasy compromises on these issues, having been driven in part by political pressures.

By the middle of the 1990s a hotchpotch of remedies had developed piecemeal over the years, and the resulting law was complex,[53] confusing and riddled with anomalies both substantive and jurisdictional. Protection was provided both

---

[49] [2001] 1 F.L.R. 580; [2001] 1 F.C.R. 596, CA.

[50] For full discussion, see Bird, *op cit., supra*, Chap. 10; T. Lawson Cruttenden, *The Protection From Harassment Act* (Blackstone Press, 1997).

[51] Law Commission Report on *Domestic Violence and Occupation of the Family Home* (Law Com. No. 207, (1992)), para. 1.1.

[52] *Report on Domestic Violence and Occupation of the Family Home* (Law Com. No, 207, (1992)), para. 2.11.

[53] On the complexities of the pre-1996 law, see Verduyn "Ouster Orders Now" [1996] *Fam. Law* 36.

by the so-called inherent jurisdiction[54] inherited from the Court of Chancery, and by various statutes[55] of limited scope to meet specific situations or to strengthen the powers of specified courts.[56] The matter was referred to the Law Commission, upon whose Report *Domestic Violence and Occupation of the Family Home* (Law Com. No. 207 (1992) the reforming legislation was based. The Commission identified three objectives[57] in reforming the civil law[58] in this field: first, to remove gaps, anomalies and inconsistencies with a view to synthesising the available remedies so far as possible into a clear, simple and comprehensive code; secondly to provide adequate protection; and thirdly to avoid exacerbating hostilities between the adults involved, so far as this would be compatible with providing proper and effective protection both for adults and for children. The Report's major proposal was for a single consistent set of civil law remedies, to be contained in one statute and to be available to family members in all family courts. It is important to note that as a matter of policy the Commission drew a distinction[59] between orders for personal protection on the one hand and ouster orders on the other; the former in no way prejudice the respondent's legitimate interests whereas the latter will (albeit temporarily) where the respondent has proprietary or other legal rights over the property in question. The Report therefore recommended[60] that the new statute embody two distinct types of remedy—the non-molestation order and the occupation order—which could of course be combined in appropriate circumstances. In 1995 the Government introduced the Family Homes and Domestic Violence Bill which closely followed the Law Commission's recommendations and was initially thought to be non-controversial. However, the Government eventually decided, amidst an angry campaign by some MPs[61] and others[62] who

---

[54] In *Richards v. Richards* [1984] A.C. 175; [1983] 3 W.L.R. 173; [1973] 2 All E.R. 807, HL the House of Lords held that the inherent jurisdiction had been codified in the Supreme Court Act 1981, s.37 which gives the court power to grant an interlocutory or final injunction "in all cases in which it appears to the court to be just and convenient to do so"; but the conventional view is that this provision (which dates from 1873) is merely declaratory of the court's inherent power, and did not extend it in any way: see *Bremer Vulkan Schiffbau und Maschinenfabrik v. South India Shipping Corporation* [1981] A.C. 909, particularly *per* Lord Scarman, at 995 For this reason, the jurisdiction is much more restricted than might at first appear: see further p. 260, below.

[55] The most important statutes empowering the court to grant orders were: (i) The Matrimonial Homes Act 1983 (consolidating the provisions of the Matrimonial Homes Act 1967 and subsequent amendments); (ii) The Domestic Violence and Matrimonial Proceedings Act 1976; and (iii) The Domestic Proceedings and Magistrates' Courts Act 1978.

[56] *Richards v. Richards* [1984] A.C. 174 *supra* at 206–207, *per* Lord Scarman. The Introduction to the Law Commission's Report, *Domestic Violence and Occupation of the Family Home* (Law Com. No. 207, (1992)) provides a useful succinct explanation of the interrelationship between the different statutory provisions.

[57] Report No. 207, para. 1.2.

[58] The Report did not address the criminal law.

[59] Report para. 2.48.

[60] *ibid.*

[61] According to the Labour Party's shadow Lord Chancellor, Lord Irvine of Lairg, the Government had allowed itself to be "blown off course by an irrational reaction on the part of a tiny unrepresentative minority . . . trying to claim a spurious moral high ground for party political reasons": Official Report H.L., January 30, 1996, Vol. 568, col. 1397.

[62] The *Daily Mail* conducted an outspoken and evidently effective campaign against the Bill (and the Law Commission); but as the Law Commission points out the broadsheet press "saw the

believed the Bill would erode the distinction between the legal rights of married and unmarried couples and thereby undermine the institution of marriage, to withdraw the Bill for further consideration—notwithstanding the fact that the Bill had received a most thorough examination by a House of Lords Special Public Bill Committee,[63] had been passed by the House of Lords, and had virtually completed its passage through the House of Commons. Some modifications were made, largely motivated by political expediency (namely the Government's desire to secure the passage of the Bill in the Commons) and as will be seen, their genesis is, in terms of substance, all too evident.

The relevant provisions are now found in Part IV of the Family Law Act,[64] which swept away earlier legislation and created[65] a set of remedies available in the courts[66] having jurisdiction in family matters.[67] This part of the Family Law Act 1996 is the most important source of law in this area and its provisions are considered in detail in the next section. However, the Law Commission's aspiration of this legislation providing a *single* set of remedies available to family members has not been wholly realised. A separate, subsequent legislative initiative produced the Protection from Harassment Act 1997, which provides *inter alia* a civil remedy[68] for harassment in the form of injunctive relief (non-molestation order) and damages. Whilst not originally designed to provide protection from harassment by family members,[69] 1997 Act is nevertheless capable of being invoked in that context as well as being more generally available. The extent of overlap between the two Acts—in particular, the legal content of the terms "molestation" and "harassment" respectively—is not wholly clear and was not fully explored in government literature or Parliamentary debates on the later legislation. The issue is discussed later in this Chapter.[70] It may be that in time the courts will in practice assert the exclusivity of the remedies in Part

benefits that the changes would bring": Law Commission Thirtieth Annual Report 1995, (Law Com. No. 239 (1996)), para. 1.20.

[63] 1995, H.L. 55. For a full account of the history, see the speech by Lord Brightman (who had chaired the committee) Official Report H.L., March 11, 1996, col. 618.

[64] See the debates in the House of Lords (Official Report January 30, 1996 and March 11) and House of Commons (Standing Committee E, Official Report, Third and Ninth Sittings, April 30, and May 16, 1996).

[65] R. Bird, "The Family Law Act Part IV: Ist October Overview" [1997] *Fam. Law* 67; J. Murphy "Domestic Violence: The New Law" (1996) 59 *M.L.R.* 845.

[66] The general principle embodied in the Act is that remedies are available in the High Court, the County Court and a magistrates' courts: s.57(1). However, it is provided (s.59(1)) that a magistrates' court is not competent to entertain any application, or make any order, involving any disputed question as to a party's entitlement to occupy any property by virtue of a beneficial estate or interest or by virtue of an enactment giving him the right to remain in occupation, unless it is unnecessary to determine the question in order to deal with the application or make the order; and it is intended to exercise the rule-making power to provide a flexible system (analogous to that established under the Children Act 1989) for the transfer of cases between different courts and different levels of court: see the Lord Chancellor's statement to the Special Public Bill Committee on the Family Homes and Domestic Violence Bill (1995, H.L. 55), March 9, 1995, p. 6.

[67] Applications constitute "family proceedings" for the purpose of the Children Act 1989. An application for an order under Part IV may also be made in the course of other family proceedings: s.36(2).

[68] The criminal provisions of the Act have already been outlined at pp. 234–235 *supra*.

[69] The social mischief against which the 1997 Act was directed was stalking: see p. 233, *supra*.

[70] See pp. 250–253 below.

IV of the Family Law Act 1996 between family members,[71] but that point has not yet been reached. Finally, there remains jurisdiction to issue injunctions under the general law, albeit of greatly diminished practical significance in a family context due to the existence of specialised legislation.

The following sections discuss occupation orders and non-molestation orders separately, followed by measures available for their enforcement.

A. OCCUPATION ORDERS[72]

1. Introduction

10–005 Part IV of the Family Law Act 1996 empowers the court[73] to make *inter alia* orders regulating the occupation of a home.[74] The statutory provisions are (on their face at least[75]) complex,[76] both as regards who is entitled to seek the orders[77] and the criteria governing the exercise of the court's discretion. These complexities are in part the result of policies espoused by the Law Commission

---

[71] There may be hints to be inferred from the judgment of the Court of Appeal in *Checchi v. Basheer* [1999] 2 F.L.R. 528.

[72] The Act defines occupation orders in s.39(1). There was comparatively little debate on the provisions of this part of the Act; but a great deal of useful material is to be found in the parliamentary proceedings on the Family Homes and Domestic Violence Bill in 1995, especially the House of Lords Special Public Bill Committee, (1995, H.L. 55). Where the provisions of the 1996 Act are identical to those of those of the 1995 Bill these proceedings are referred to without further explanation.

[73] See the definition in s.57(1) and n. 46 above.

[74] The hearing of an application for an order under Part IV of the Act (whether for an occupation or a non-molestation order) will usually take place only after the respondent has been notified of the proceedings so that he will be able to attend and state his case. However, the Act accepts the policy—discussed by the Law Commission in its *Report on Domestic Violence and Occupation of the Family Home* (Law Com. No. 207 (1992)), paras 5.5–5.10—that the court needs power to intervene immediately and without notice in some cases. The Act accordingly provides that the court may in any case where it considers that it is just and convenient to do so make an order *ex parte:* s.45(1). However, in determining whether to exercise the power to make orders *ex parte*—which case law had emphasised should be done "with great caution and only in circumstances in which it is really necessary to act immediately": *Ansah v. Ansah* [1977] Fam. 138 at 142–143, *per* Ormrod L.J.—the court is required to have regard to all the circumstances including (a) any risk of significant harm to the applicant or a relevant child attributable to the conduct of the respondent if the order is not made immediately, (b) whether it is likely that the applicant will be deterred or prevented from pursuing the application if an order is not made immediately, and (c) whether there is reason to believe that the respondent is aware of the proceedings but is deliberately evading service and that the applicant or a relevant child will be seriously prejudiced by the delay in taking the normal steps to serve the respondent: F.L.A. 1996, s.45(2). Where the court does decide to make an *ex parte* order under these provisions it must afford the respondent an opportunity to make representations relating to the order as soon as just and convenient at a hearing of which proper notice has been given to all parties: s.45(3); and t is to be assumed that such orders will continue to be made only for short periods: *Ansah v. Ansah* (above).

[75] It is however questionable whether that apparent complexity is reflected in the everyday practice of courts at first instance.

[76] See J. Murphy, "Domestic Violence: The New Law" (1996) 57 *M.L.R.* 845.

[77] The Act provides that a child under the age of 16 may not apply for a non-molestation order or an occupation order except with the leave of the court; and that the court may grant leave only if it is satisfied that the child has sufficient understanding to make the proposed application: s.43.

and in part of the political controversy which dogged the original Bill's later parliamentary history.[78]

The sophisticated drafting of the legislation makes the precise extent of the court's powers depend in part on the nature of the applicant's interest (if any) in the property.[79] To this end the Act draws an important distinction between an applicant who is "a person entitled" and persons who are not so entitled.[80] The underlying policy is that the court's powers should be more extensive in the case of an applicant who can point to some recognised legal, equitable, or statutory right than in the case of a person who merely has the use of a family home, although the court's powers to make orders in respect of persons entitled are not restricted merely to giving effect to that entitlement. As the ensuing discussion will demonstrate, in essence the complex provisions privilege marriage over unmarried cohabitation, and occupation by virtue of a proprietary, contractual or statutory right over mere use. This privileging is found both in the factors relevant to the exercise of the court's discretion and the duration of the orders that can be made. These policies—not wholly uncontroversial from the point of view of the victim of violence[81] or in the opinion of all commentators[82]—stem both from distinction drawn by the Law Commission between occupation and non-molestation orders as regards prejudice to legitimate interests,[83] and from amendments with a political motivation made following the withdrawal of the original Family Homes and Domestic Violence Bill 1995.[84] The latter added to the complexity of distinctions now embodied in the legislation.

2. Who is a "person entitled"?

10–006 There are two main categories of person who come within the definition of "person entitled"[85]:

(i) *A person with matrimonial home rights*

The Act incorporates provisions originating in the Matrimonial Homes Act 1967 whereby a spouse who had no ownership rights in respect of a matrimonial

---

[78] See pp. 236–237, *supra*.

[79] For a succinct summary of the complex differences, see Horton [1996] *Fam. Law* 49 especially at 51.

[80] It may be difficult for an applicant to decide whether he is "entitled" or not; but as already mentioned the Act provides, first, that a court which considers it has no power to make orders under the provision invoked by the applicant may make an order under the section it believes to be relevant; and secondly that bringing proceedings for an occupation order as a non-entitled person does not stop the applicant from subsequently claiming a legal or equitable interest in the property: s.39(3), (4).

[81] Not all comparable legal systems observe such distinctions as to status and ownership where ouster orders are necessary in the context of intra-family violence: see Part XV of the Family Law Act 1975 (Cth) in Australia.

[82] See J. Eekelaar and M. Maclean, *The Parental Obligation* (Hart Publishing,1997), p. 144.

[83] Law Commission *Report on Domestic Violence and the Family Home* (Law Com. No 207 (1992)), para. 2.48.

[84] See p. 237, *supra*.

[85] s.33(1)(a).

home was given what were originally described as "occupation rights"—essentially the right not to be evicted during the marriage unless the court otherwise ordered. Those rights have been re-named "matrimonial home rights"[86]; and their significance has been explained in Chapter 6.

(ii) *A person entitled to occupy a dwelling house by virtue of a beneficial estate or interest or contract or by virtue of any enactment giving him the right to remain in occupation.*

10–007 The crucial element of this definition is that the applicant should have the right to occupy a dwelling house.[87] Examples include the person who owns the fee simple absolute in possession, the person who has a legal tenancy, the person entitled to be in occupation of a house under the Rent Acts and a tenant for the life under the Settled Land Act 1925. The Trusts of Land and Appointment of Trustees Act 1996 made it clear beyond all doubt that a person entitled to a beneficial interest only in equity (for example by reason of an implied resulting or constructive trust) is thereby "entitled to occupy" the land.[88]

3. The property concerned

10–008 The dwelling house in question must either be or have at some time been or at some time been intended to be[89] the home of the person entitled and of another person with whom he or she is "associated"—an expression which is widely defined[90] to include a spouse or former spouse, a cohabitant[91] or former cohabitant, relative, people who live or have lived in the same household,[92] the

---

[86] As defined in F.L.A. 1996, s.30(2).

[87] As defined, s.63(1).

[88] Trusts of Land and Appointment of Trustees Act 1996, s. 12 . The Family Law Act 1996 (ss. 30(9) , 35(11), and 36(11)) seek to minimise difficulties which might arise from any uncertainty about the status of the equitable owner by a provision which specifically entitles such a person to apply for the more limited relief available to non-entitled persons, whilst also leaving it open for a person who is prepared to assume the burden of convincing the court that he or she has a right to occupy to apply for the more extensive provision available to an entitled person. See the evidence of Hale J. to the Special Public Bill Committee on the Family Homes and Domestic Violence Bill (1995, H.L. 55), March 15, 1995, questions 68–72; see p. 246 below. The distinction between the entitled and the non-entitled is of greater importance under Part IV of the Family Law Act 1996 than under the 1995 Bill since the remedies available to a non-entitled cohabitant have been made less extensive. See further below.

[89] Compare the Matrimonial Homes Act 1983 which only extended to a property which had at some time actually been the matrimonial home.

[90] In F.L.A. 1996, s.62(3); see for a full explanation pp. 253–256, below. In *G v. G (Non-Molestation Order: Jurisdiction)* [2000] 2 F.L.R. 533 Wall J. held that Part I of the Act must be given a wide, purposive construction so as not to exclude borderline cases from the swift and effective protection it provides for victims of domestic violence.

[91] *i.e.* a man and a woman who, although not married to each other, are living together as husband and wife. The expression "former cohabitants" does not include cohabitants who have subsequently married: F.L.A. 1996, s.62(1).

[92] Otherwise than merely by reason of one of them being the other's employee, tenant, lodger or broader: s.62(3) (c).

engaged or formerly engaged[93] a certain children,[94] and parties to the same family proceedings.[95]

4. Orders the court can make on application by an entitled person

10–009 The Act[96] gives courts jurisdiction to make two main types of order, described by the Law Commission[97] as declaratory and regulatory orders.

A declaratory order is an order declaring that the applicant is entitled to occupy a dwelling house[98]; as such it merely declares the nature of the interest claimed. The court may also enforce the applicant's entitlement to remain in occupation against the respondent[99] by making an order for possession.

However, in practice regulatory orders are much more commonly sought, and a wide range of powers is available. The Act provides that such an order may:—

> ... require the respondent to permit the applicant to enter and remain in the dwelling house or part of the dwelling house[1]
>
> regulate the occupation of the dwelling house by either or both parties[2]
>
> "prohibit, suspend or restrict" the exercise by a person who is entitled to occupy the dwelling house by reason of a beneficial interest, etc.[3]
>
> require the respondent to leave the dwelling house or part of the dwelling-house[4]
>
> exclude the respondent from "a defined area in which the dwelling-house

---

[93] s.62(3)(e). In this case, there must be evidence of the kind prescribed by the Act: s.44, and no application can be made for an occupation order more than three years after the termination of the agreement: s.33(2).

[94] For the definition see F.L.A. 1996, s. 62(3) (f), 62(4), 62(5). For an example of a case in which a parent successfully sought to oust a 19-year-old son, see *Egan v. Egan* [1975] Ch. 218 where the parents' case was based on the fact that an adult child is only entitled to occupy the family home by reason of his parents' licence, that once that licence was revoked the son became a trespasser, and that accordingly an injunction could be granted restraining the son from remaining in or entering the house.

[95] F.L.A. 1996, s.62(3) (g); and s.63(1) and (2).

[96] F.L.A. 1996, s.33(4) (declaratory orders); s.33(3) (regulatory orders).

[97] *Domestic Violence and Occupation of the Family Home* (Law Com. No. 207 (1992)), para. 4.2.

[98] The court may also declare that the applicant is entitled to "matrimonial home rights" and may also, where it considers that it is in all the circumstances just and reasonable to do so, make an order that those rights should not be brought to an end by the death of the other spouse or by divorce or other termination of the marriage (s.30(5), 30(8)).

[99] F.L.A., s.33(3).

[1] s.33(3)(b).

[2] s.33(3)(c)—for example, by providing that one party should have the right to be in the home on certain days of the week or between certain times.

[3] *i.e.* under s.30(1)(a)(i). This power can be exercised by ordering one joint tenant to leave the house altogether, or to leave it for 48 hours, or only to exercise the rights to which the respondent is entitled if someone else is present (for example, whilst a child is living in the house).

[4] s.33(3)(f).

is included"[5]—for example, excluding the respondent from the block of flats in which the home is situated or from the surroundings.[6] This provision may also be used to prohibit the respondent from coming into the street (or perhaps even the neighbourhood) in which the home is situated.[7]

The Act contains guidelines which structure the exercise of its discretion in relation to the broad range of its powers, which are discussed below.

5. Exercise of the discretion[8] on applications by entitled person

10–010 Section 33(6) of the Act provides that, in deciding whether to exercise its powers to make regulatory orders[9] and, if so, in what manner, the court shall "have regard to all the circumstances including:—

(a) the housing needs and housing resources of each of the parties and of any relevant child,[10]
(b) the financial resources of each of the parties,
(c) the likely effect of any order, or any decision by the court not to exercise its powers to make regulatory orders, on the health, safety or well-being of the parties and of any relevant child, and
(d) the conduct of the parties in relation to each other and otherwise.[11]

However, section 33(7) (which is drafted in complex terms) requires the court to make an order if it appears that the applicant or any relevant child is likely to suffer "significant harm" should an order not be made, unless the respondent (or a relevant child) would suffer harm as a result of the making of an order and it appears that the harm likely to be suffered by the child or respondent in that event "is as great as or greater than the harm attributable to conduct of the

---

[5] s.33(3)(g).

[6] See the evidence of Hale J. to the Special Public Bill Committee on the Family Homes and Domestic Violence Bill (1995 H.L. 55), March 15, 1995, question 39.

[7] The Law Commission's draft Bill referred to "a defined area in the vicinity of the home" (see Law Com. No. 207 (1992)), para. 4.2; but the draftsman of the 1995 Bill and 1996. Act evidently preferred to follow the precedent of the Domestic Violence and Matrimonial Proceedings Act 1976, s.2(1)(c). In *Burris v. Azadani* [1996] 1 F.L.R. 266; [1995] 1 W.L.R. 1372; [1995] 1 All E.R. 802; [1996] 1 F.C.R. 618, CA, the defendant was restrained (under the so-called inherent jurisdiction) from coming within 250 yards of the home of a woman whom he had harassed and threatened. In *Vaughan v. Vaughan* [1973] 1 W.L.R. 1159 the court ordered a husband not to go within 50 miles of the home; but *quaere* whether this would be a "defined area".

[8] See G. Basse, "Property and Hardship in Divorce Proceedings—the Operation of the Family Law Act 1996, s 33" [1999] *Fam. Law* 757.

[9] *i.e.* orders under s.33(3), which includes an order enforcing the applicant's right to remain in occupation: see above.

[10] Defined by s.62(2) as (a) any child who is living with or might reasonably be expected to live with either party to the proceedings, (b) any child in relation to whom an order under the Adoption Act 1976 or the Children Act 1989 is in question in the proceedings, and (c) any other child whose interests the court considers relevant.

[11] F.L.A. 1996, s.33(6)(d). The reference to conduct did not appear in the 1995 Bill or in the Bill for the 1996 Act when introduced. Its implications are discussed at pp. 244–245 below.

respondent likely to be suffered by the applicant or child if the order is not made".

Thus section 33(6) sets out the general considerations governing the exercise of the court's discretion, whereas section 33(7) imposes the "balance of harm test" once certain preconditions are met. The interrelationship between these two provisions has been explored in case-law and requires some explanation.

The precondition for the operation of subsection (7) is proof of the likelihood of "significant harm". This term, borrowed from the Children Act 1989[12]—is of crucial importance. In relation to children, the Family Law Act embodies precisely the same test as that used in the 1989 Act[13]—*i.e.* harm is defined to mean ill-treatment[14] or the impairment of health[15] or development. If the issue is one of a child's health or development, the test is that which could reasonably be expected of a similar child.[16] However, in relation to adults the definition of "significant harm" contains no statutory reference to "development"[17]; and, secondly, there is no requirement of comparison with a similar person. "Significant" has been interpreted in the context of the Children Act 1989 as "considerable, noteworthy or important"[18] and this has been adopted in relation to the Family Law Act 1996.[19] In *Chalmers v. Johns*[20] the Court of Appeal held that the "slight" nature of the domestic violence involved (minor violence on occasions in the course of a tempestuous relationship) meant that it had not been open to the trial judge to find that it fell within the ambit of subsection (7). In *Banks v. Banks*[21] it was held that the behaviour of an elderly wife who suffered from manic depression and dementia was not unreasonable and would not cause her husband significant harm.

10–011 Where significant harm is an issue on the facts, subsection (6) and (7) are not simultaneously applicable on the facts.[22] The order in which they are to be considered is, according to the authorities, the reverse of that in which they appear on the statute-book The court should first consider whether the criterion of "significant harm" in subsection (7) is satisfied, in which case the "balance of harm" test contained therein applies; if it is not, then the exercise of discretion is governed solely by subsection (6).[23] The latter exercise is a precise one strictly

---

[12] ss. 31(9), 31(10) and 105.

[13] s.63(1), (3).

[14] Including sexual abuse and forms of ill-treatment which are not physical: s.63(3).

[15] Including physical or mental health.

[16] s.63(3).

[17] "... the concept of development is very important when one is considering harm to children because the sort of harm the children suffer is very frequently the impairment of their developments, whereas on the whole one hopes that adults have done their developing and what then they have happened to them is an impairment of their physical or mental health", *per* Hale J., Evidence given to the Special Public Bill Committee on the Family Homes and Domestic Violence Bill (1995, H.L. 55), March 15, 1995, question 47.

[18] *per* Booth J. in *Humberside CC v. B* [1993] F.L.R. 357.

[19] *Chalmers v. Johns* [1999] 1 F.L.R. 392 at 399 *per* Otton L.J.

[20] [1999] 1 F.L.R. 392; comment in [1999] *Fam. Law* 16; F. Kaganas (1999) 11 *C.F.L.Q.* 193.

[21] [1999] 1 F.L.R. 726; comment in [1999] *Fam. Law* 209.

[22] *Chalmers v. Johns* [1999] 1 F.L.R. 392; *cf.* the erroneous approach adopted in *Banks v. Banks* [1999] 1 F.L.R. 726.

[23] *Chalmers v. Johns* [1999] 1 F.L.R. 392, CA; *G v. G (Occupation Order: Conduct)* [2000] 2 F.L.R. 36, CA.

governed by the specific factors listed in the checklist, to which adequate reference must be made in the judgment.[24]

Where the "significant harm" criterion is met, what is the nature of the "balance of harm" test? According to the Law Commission:

> "It is highly likely that respondent threatened with ouster on account of his violence would be able to establish a degree of hardship (perhaps in terms of difficulty in finding or unsuitability of alternative accommodation or problems in getting to work). But he is unlikely to suffer significant harm, whereas his wife and children who are being subjected to his violence or abuse may very easily suffer harm if he remains in the house."[25]

It is important to appreciate that the balance of harm test—which tends prima facie to favour the applicant[26]—applies only where the application is made by an entitled person or (with a very subtle variation[27]) a non-entitled former spouse; it is thus an example of the privileging, simultaneously, of marital status and legal rights in relation to property. The test requires a comparison of the harm which would be suffered by the applicant and any relevant child if the order were not made with that which would be suffered by the respondent and any relevant child if the order were made; it is erroneous to compare the two situations from the applicant's perspective.[28] A graphic illustration of the comparative exercise is *B v. B (Occupation Order)*.[29] After suffering serious violence from the husband, the wife moved out of their council house with their two-year-old-daughter, and they were provided with unsatisfactory bed-and-breakfast accommodation. The husband remained in the home with his six-year-old son from an earlier relationship. The husband appealed an order under section 33 that he vacate the home. The Court of Appeal set aside the order; weighing the respective likelihoods of harm to each of the children, the balance came down clearly in favour of the husband's child, who if an exclusion order were made would have to change schools, and separating him from his father was not an option.[30]

The criteria in section 33 include—contrary to the recommendations of the Law Commission—references to "conduct", both as one of the factors under subsection (6), and also by restricting the court's consideration under the balance of harm test in subsection (7) to harm attributable to conduct of the respondent.

---

[24] *G v. G (Occupation Order: Conduct)* [2000] 2 F.L.R. 36; [2000] 2 F.C.R. 53.

[25] *Domestic Violence and Occupation of the Family Home* (Law Com. No. 207 (1992)), para. 4.34.

[26] It appears that the Family Law Bar Association and the Society of Conservative Lawyers were opposed to the balance of harm test because they considered that it would lean too far in the favour of applicants and could lead to occupation orders almost on demand: see *Domestic Violence and Occupation of the Family Home* (Law Com. No. 207 1992), para. 4.23; and see in particular the Evidence of East London Families Need Fathers to the Special Public Bill Committee on the Family Homes and Domestic Violence Bill (1995, H.L. 55).

[27] See pp. 248–249 below.

[28] *G v. G (Occupation Order: Conduct)* [2000] 2 F.L.R. 36, CA.

[29] [1999] 1 F.L.R. 715; comments in [1999] *Fam. Law* 208 and [1999] *C.F.L.Q.* 193. See also *Banks v. Banks* [1999] 1 F.L.R. 726.

[30] Note however that the Court of Appeal observed *obiter* that Part I of the Family Law Act 1996 is designed to protect family members from domestic violence, and that nothing in its judgment in this case which turned on its particular facts should be read as weakening that objective.

How has this been interpreted in the case-law? As to the attribution issue in subsection (7), it has been made clear that the conduct in question need not necessarily be intentional; it is its effect which the court must assess, although lack of intention to cause harm may be a relevant consideration.[31] More generally, conduct of both parties forms part of the consideration of whether it is just and reasonable to make an ouster order. The case-law on the 1996 Act continues the trend of authorities decided under the repealed legislation[32] by emphasising that an exclusion order is draconian in nature[33] because it affects proprietary rights and should not be lightly made—even going so far as to suggest that it should be restricted to exceptional cases, at least where the final determination of ancillary relief matters is only a matter of weeks away.[34] The absence of actual (or substantial) violence may justify the refusal of an ouster order,[35] although conversely its presence will satisfy the criterion in section 33(7). Overall however, the force of the criticism that the Law Commission's proposals made it likely that men would be more likely to be ousted from their homes under the new law than under the law it replaced has been somewhat weakened by the experience of case-law on the 1996 Act.

6. Duration of orders in favour of entitled persons

10–012 Occupation orders in favour of entitled applicants are potentially longer-term than in the case of non-entitled applicants, namely "for a specified period, until the occurrence of a specified event or until further order".[36] It is thus of particular advantage to cohabitants to bring themselves into the category of the "entitled" by virtue of asserting a proprietary or contractual right, because otherwise the order's duration is limited to 12 months, as explained below. Nevertheless, occupation orders in favour of entitled persons are not intended to be permanent; disputes between the parties will most generally be resolved on a long-term basis by ancillary relief proceedings under Part II of the Matrimonial Causes Act 1973 in the case of divorcing couples,[37] and by proceedings for the realisation of equitable interests[38] or by transfer of tenancy for unmarried couples.[39]

---

[31] *G v. G (Occupation Order: Conduct)* [2000] 2 F.L.R. 36, CA; *Banks v. Banks* [1999] 1 F.L.R. 726 (respondent suffering from dementia).

[32] Which apparently may remain of some relevance: *e.g. Richards v. Richards* [1984] A.C. 174; *Wiseman v. Simpson* [1988] 1 W.L.R.490; see S. M. Cretney, "Family Law—A Bit of a Racket" (1996) 146 *N.L.J.* 191.

[33] For a critical perspective, see Humphries, "Occupation Orders Revisited" [2001] *Fam. Law* 542.

[34] *Chalmers v. Johns* [1999] 1 F.L.R. 392; *G v. G (Occupation Order: Conduct)* [2000] 2 F.L.R. 36, CA.

[35] *Chalmers v. Johns* [1999] 1 F.L.R. 392; *G v. G (Occupation Order: Conduct)* [2000] 2 F.L.R. 36, CA.

[36] s.33(10). Orders may not be made after the death of either of the parties; and (save in the case of matrimonial homes rights, which the court may extend: 33(5), (9)) cease to have effect on the death of the party. In contrast to orders in cases of a "person entitled," orders in favor of an applicant with no existing right to occupy are essentially short term: see below.

[37] Discussed in Chap. 14.

[38] Discussed in Chap. 5.

[39] Family Law Act 1996, s. 53 and Sched. 7.

8. Orders in favour of those with no existing right to occupy: non-entitled persons

10–013 The Act[40] allows certain categories of person to apply for an occupation order notwithstanding that they have no existing right to be in occupation of the property either by virtue of a proprietary or contractual right[41] or by having matrimonial home rights. The rationale is their "overriding need for short term protection in cases of domestic violence or for short term accommodation for themselves and their children when a relationship breaks down."[42] However, as we shall see, the protection afforded to non-entitled applicants is less extensive than that enjoyed by their entitled counterparts, reflecting the legislative policies discussed earlier.

9. Who can apply as a non-entitled person?

10–014 The category of non-entitled persons who may apply for an occupation order is limited[43] to former spouses and cohabitants or former cohabitants; and the property in question must be one which the applicant is not (but the other partner is) entitled to occupy[44] by virtue of a beneficial estate or interest, contract, or enactment and be a home in which they live together (or had intended to live together[45]) as husband and wife.[46] The sub-division into former spouses and unmarried couples was the result amendments following opposition in the House of Commons to the Family Homes and Domestic Violence Bill 1995, the inten-

---

[40] ss.35, 36.

[41] The question of whether a person is entitled to occupy may be one of some difficulty; and the Act provides that the court may, in effect, make an order under the appropriate provision even if the application is incorrectly formulated: s.39(3). Moreover, the fact that an application is made on the basis that the applicant is a non-entitled person does not stop the applicant from subsequently asserting a beneficial interest: s.39(4).

[42] Law Commission Report No. 207 *Domestic Violence and Occupation of the Family Home* (1992), para. 4.10.

[43] A party to a subsisting marriage will normally have matrimonial home rights and this be a "person entitled": see pp. 239–240, above.

[44] The Act also makes provision for applications to be made in respect of homes (such as accommodation provided by an employer, or by a relative, or as a squat) which neither party is entitled to occupy: see ss.37, 38. The Act also provides that a person who has an equitable interest but not a legal estate in a dwelling house "is to be treated only for the purpose of determining whether he is to be eligible to apply" under s.35(11) or 36(11) of the Act "as not being so entitled"; and it is apparent that this clause is modeled on the Matrimonial Homes Act 1983, s.1(11) (inserted into that legislation in order to "make it crystal clear that in respect of the matrimonial home a spouse has a registrable right of occupation under the Matrimonial Homes Act . . . notwithstanding that he or she may also be entitled to an equitable interest therein by virtue of a contribution to its acquisition or improvement") (Law Commission *Report on Financial Provision* (Law Com. No. 25 (1969), para. 5)). In the present context, the effect of the provision is simply to make it clear that an equitable owner will be able to apply for a short term occupation order as a non-entitled person, whilst preserving the applicant's right to apply for a longer term order as an "entitled person" if he or she wishes to take on the burden of convincing the court that the equitable interest confers the right to occupy the home.

[45] Or in the case of former spouses have been their actual or intended matrimonial home: s.35(1)(c).

[46] F.L.A. 1996, s.36(1)(c). Note that these criteria were not fulfilled on the facts of *Clibbery v. Allan* [2002] E.W.C.A. Civ. 45, [2002] 1 F.L.R. 565, CA and the county court judge held that the court had no jurisdiction to make the orders sought.

tion being to sharpen the distinction between marriage and other relationships in order to secure the passage of the legislation. As will be explained below, the factors governing the exercise of discretion differ according to the sub-category on non-entitled applicant, and the legislative scheme is complex. It is thus obviously to the advantage of a cohabitant to be able apply as an entitled person by virtue of enjoying for example a proprietary right in the property in question.

It is significant that "cohabitant" is heterosexually defined in the Family Law Act 1996,[47] and thus a homosexual may apply for an occupation order against a partner only if he or she is entitled within the meaning of section 33(1)(a) which in practice will mean having a legal, equitable or contractual right in the property. Moreover the respondent (with whom the applicant must be "associated"[48]) has to be entitled to occupy the property. The limitation on the protection thus afforded to the homosexual applicant, and its discriminatory implications, has not escaped criticism.[49]

10. The exercise of the discretion to make orders on applications by non-entitled persons and the duration of orders

10–015 The Family Law Act 1996 deals separately with applications by former spouses on the one hand[50] and cohabitants and former cohabitants on the other[51]; and the factors governing the exercise of discretion differ according to the category, as does the potential duration of the orders available.

(i) *Applications by non-entitled former spouses*[52]

10–016 Consistent with the legislation's policy of privileging the institution of marriage, former spouses are given the most favourable treatment amongst non-entitled applicants, but they are nevertheless not treated identically with those who are currently married.[53]

The first question is whether the court should make an order at all. If the applicant is already in occupation, the order must contain provision giving the

---

47 Family Law Act 1996, s. 62(1). The provision is similar to that found in para. 2 of Schedule 1 to the Rent Act 1997, which was interpreted by the House of Lords in *Fitzpatrick v. Sterling Housing Association Ltd* [2001] 1 A.C. 27; [1999] 3 W.L.R. 1113 as employing gender-specific language which evidenced an intention to exclude same-sex relationships. See comment by R. Bailey-Harris in [2000] *Fam. Law* 14 and Roberts, "*Fitzpatrick v. Sterling HA* - A Case with Wider Implications?" [2000] *Fam. Law* 417.

48 By virtue of having lived together in the same household: Family Law Act 1996, s. 62(3)(c).

49 J. Murphy "Domestic Violence: The New Law" (1996) 57 *M.L.R.* 845 at 852; R. Bailey-Harris, "Same-Sex Partnerships in English Family Law" in *Legal Recognition of Same-Sex Relationships* (R. Wintemute and M. Andenaes, Hart Publishing, 2001), pp. 612–613.

50 s.35.

51 s.36.

52 It is evidently considered that parties who are married will either have matrimonial home rights or be entitled to occupy as a matter of property law. Parties to a marriage which is actually or potentially polygamous are within the meaning of the word "spouse" for the purposes of this Act: s.63(5).

53 And are "persons entitled" by virtue of having matrimonial home rights: Family Law Act 1996 s. 33(1)(a).

applicant the right not to be evicted or excluded from the home or any part of it by the respondent for the period specified in the order[54]; and it must prohibit the respondent from evicting or excluding the applicant during that period. If on the other hand the applicant is not in occupation, the order must give the applicant the right to enter into and occupy the home for the period specified in the order and require the respondent to permit the applicant to do so.[55]

The exercise of the court's discretion in relation to non-entitled former spouses is structured by section 35(6). "All the circumstances" are defined to include a number of specific considerations.[56] The first four of these are identical to those found in section 33 (a)- (d) in relation to entitled applicants,[57] but the remainder are additional, namely:

(e) the length of time that has elapsed since they ceased to live together;
(f) the length of time which has elapsed since the marriage was ended;
(g) the existence of certain pending proceedings[58] between the parties.

These additional considerations are unobjectionable and indeed sensible and realistic, since they address the essentially factual questions of when the marriage broke down and the how imminent is a final resolution of disputes through *e.g.* an ancillary relief order.[59]

If, on consideration of the above matters, the court decides to make an occupation rights order, namely not to be evicted or excluded by the respondent,[60] the court will then proceed to consider whether the order should in addition[61]:

(a) regulate the occupation of the dwelling house by either or both of the parties;
(b) prohibit, suspend or restrict the exercise by the respondent of his right to occupy the dwelling house;
(c) require the respondent to leave the dwelling house of part of the dwelling house; or
(d) exclude the respondent from a defined area in which the dwelling house is included.

In reaching its decision, the court must consider all the circumstances including those specified in subsection (6). The "balance of harm" test then applies[62] but with a subtle difference when compared with entitled applicants: in relation

---

[54] s.35(3).
[55] s.35(4).
[56] To which specific consideration must be given and specific mention made in judgment: *G v. G (Occupation Order: Conduct)* [2000] 2 F.L.R. 36.
[57] Discussed at p. 242, above.
[58] *i.e.* applications for property adjustment in divorce, applications for financial relief for a child against a parent, or proceedings relating to the ownership of the house: s.35(6)(g).
[59] Note the importance attached to the imminence of such proceedings in *Chalmers v. Johns* [1999] 1 F.L.R. 392 and *G v. G (Occupation Orders: Conduct)* [2000] 2 F.L.R. 36.
[60] Family Law Act 1996, s. 35(3).
[61] *ibid.* s. 35(5).
[62] *ibid* s. 35(8).

to non-entitled former spouses it comes into play as an overriding requirement only when the court has decided to make an order.[63]

Occupation remedies for non-entitled applicants are intended to be "relatively short term measure of protection, just to give sufficient time to find alternative accommodation or to await the outcome of property proceedings."[64] An order in favour of a former spouse can have effect only for a specified period not exceeding six months but may be extended on one or more occasions for further specified periods, each not exceeding six months.[65]

(ii) *Applications by non-entitled cohabitants and former cohabitants*[66]

10–017 There are a number of substantive distinctions between the provisions governing applications for occupation orders by cohabitants or former cohabitants and those governing former spouses, the policy of which is self-evident and was determined by legislative history and political considerations.[67]

First, section 41 requires the court in considering the nature of the parties' relationship[68] "to have regard to the fact that the parties have not given each other the commitment involved in marriage". This section was inserted by amendment after the withdrawal of the original Bill and was clearly intended to satisfy those MPs perturbed by the spectre of the erosion of the institution of marriage. Its linguistic and logical inelegance[69] is as open to doubt as its impact on the everyday practice of the courts.[70]

Secondly, the exercise of the court's discretion is structured by additional considerations,[71] namely:

(i) the nature of the parties' relationship;
(ii) the length of time during which they have lived together as husband or wife;
(iii) whether there are or have been any children who are children of both parties or for whom both parties have or have had parental responsibility[72];
(iv) the length of time that has elapsed since the parties ceased to live together.

The first of these, when taken in conjunction with section 41, purports, on its

---

[63] Bird, *Domestic Violence and Protection from Harassment - New Law* (Family Law, 2nd ed., 1997) pp 43–44.
[64] *Domestic Violence and Occupation of the Family Home* (Law Com. No. 207 (1992)), para. 4.19.
[65] Family Law Act 1996, s. 35(10).
[66] H. Conway, "Abused Cohabitees, Property Disputes and the Family Law Act 1996" [1996] *Fam. Law* 499.
[67] See the discussion at pp. 236–237.
[68] This is a matter to which the court is required to have regard when deciding to make an occupation order under F.L.A. 1996, s.36: see below.
[69] An assumption masquerading as a fact.
[70] The section may be intended to suggest a less enduring right of occupation, but note that the maximum duration of the order is in any event 12 months: s. 36(10).
[71] *ibid.* s. 36(6)(e) - (i).
[72] "Parental responsibility" has the same meaning as in the Children Act 1989: s.63(1).

face at least, to require the making of a value-judgment rather than a merely factual inquiry by the court. Again, its practical impact is questionable.

Thirdly, the "balance of harm" test as such does not apply to the making of occupation orders in favour of non-entitled cohabitants. The court is instead required by section 36(8) to have regard to the "harm questions",[73] that is to the two components of the test, *viz.* (first) whether the applicant or a relevant child is likely to suffer significant harm attributable to conduct of the respondent if no such provision is included; and (secondly) whether the harm likely to be suffered if such a provision is included is as great or greater than the harm attributable to conduct of the respondent which is likely to be suffered if it is not. This is to be contrasted with the duty imposed on the court in relation to other categories of applicant by sections 33(7) and 35(8).

The final way in which non-entitled cohabitants are relatively underprivileged is in relation to duration of an occupation order, which is for a maximum of six months renewable only once for a maximum of six months.[74]

12. Ancillary provisions

10–018 Once an occupation order has been made in respect of a home, the Act contains additional powers which should in principle be very useful, such as the power to grant either party possession or use of the furniture or other contents.[75]

The court may also impose obligations as to repair, maintenance and the discharge of outgoings in respect of the house (including the mortgage[76]), and to pay what is in effect an occupation rent to someone excluded from property which he or she would otherwise have been entitled to occupy.[77] However, in practice these statutory provisions are ineffective because of the absence of an enforcement mechanism[78] and the issue merits urgent Parliamentary attention.[79]

B. Non-molestation orders

1. Introduction: The Nature of Molestation and Harassment

10–019 The Family Law Act 1996 confers on the courts a wide power to make orders prohibiting "molestation", a term it deliberately—in the interests of flexibility—

[73] P. Pearson, "Domestic Violence", Chap. 4 in *The Family Lawyer's Handbook* (The Law Society, 1997), pp. 120, 123.

[74] F.L.A. 1996, s.36(10). The same distinction is drawn in respect of applications in respect of a home which neither party was entitled to occupy: see s.37(5), 38(6).

[75] 40(1)(c)-(e). The power is exercisable at any time after an occupation order has been made. There was no power under the Domestic Violence and Matrimonial Proceedings Act 1976 to make orders in respect of the household goods; and experience showed that the gap in the law enabled a vindictive person to inflict considerable hardship on his former partner—in *Davis v. Johnson* [1979] A.C. 264 for example, it was reported that when the applicant returned to the home she found it empty save for some plastic ornaments and plates.

[76] A. Grand, "Getting the Mortgage Paid" [1999] *Fam. Law* 833.

[77] s.40(1)(b). The Act contains guidelines for the exercise of these discretionary powers: s.40(2).

[78] *Nwgogbe v. Nwgogbe* [2000] 2 F.L.R. 744; [2000] 3 F.C.R. 345, CA.

[79] Humphries, "Occupation Orders Revisited" [2001] *Fam. Law* 542.

leaves undefined.[80] Similarly, injunctive relief[81] restraining harassment is available[82] under the Protection from Harassment Act 1997, but again the term is undefined. Do the two terms overlap or differ completely in scope?

Molestation is certainly wider than but inclusive of physical violence. According to the Law Commission[83] it:

> "... encompasses any form of serious pestering or harassment and applies to any conduct which could properly be regarded as such a degree of harassment as to call for the intervention of the court."

The element of seriousness referred to above appears to be an essential characteristic of "molestation"[84] in the context of the Family Law Act 1996,[85] and hence the protection offered by the 1997 Act against harassment causing anxiety[86] may be—in this respect—wider in scope. However, the concept of "harassment" in the 1997 Act is in another respect narrower than "molestation" in the 1996 Act, since the former is confined to "a course of conduct" on at least two occasions displaying a sufficient nexus.[87]

Case-law[88] demonstrates that each of the terms is wide, albeit not entirely without limitation. In each of the following five cases the behaviour was held to constitute "molestation." In *Vaughan v. Vaughan*[89] a husband called at the wife's house early in the morning and late at night, called at her place of work, and made "a perfect nuisance of himself to her the whole time."[90] In *Horner v. Horner*[91] the husband repeatedly telephoned the school at which the wife taught, and made disparaging remarks about her. He also hung on the school railings scurrilous posters about the wife addressed to the parents of the children she taught. In *George v. George*[92] the husband was a devoted father upset by an order depriving him of care and control of his children. He wrote an abusive letter to the wife, yelled and screamed at her, and used obscene language to her when she came—allegedly in the company of the woman with whom she was sharing a lesbian relationship—to collect the children after a visit. In *Spencer v.*

---

[80] The Law Commission recommended that there should be no statutory definition, in part because the lack of a statutory definition had not given rise to difficulty in the past and in part because of concern that a definition might become over-restrictive or could lead to border-line disputes: see *Domestic Violence and Occupation of the Family Home* (Law Com. No. 207; (1992)), para. 3.1; and see further the evidence of Hale J. to the Special Public Bill Committee on the Family Homes and Domestic Violence Bill (1995, H.L. 550), March 15, 1995, question 96.

[81] Also damages where loss has been caused: Protection from Harassment Act 1997, s. 3(2).The offences created by the Act have been discussed earlier at p. 234.

[82] Protection from Harassment Act 1997, s. 5.

[83] *Domestic Violence and Occupation of the Family Home* (Law Com. No. 207, (1992)), para. 3.1.

[84] H.H.J. Fricker, "Molestation and Harassment after *Patel v. Patel*" [1988] *Fam. Law* 395 at 399.

[85] *C v. C (Non-Molestation Order: Jurisdiction)* [1998] 1 F.L.R. 554; [1998] 2 W.L.R. 599, FD.

[86] Protection from Harassment Act 1997, s. 3(2)

[87] Protection from Harassment Act 1997, ss. 1(1) and 7(3). See *Lau v. DPP* [2000] 1 F.L.R. 799; *R. v Hills* [2001] 1 F.L.R. 580; [2000] 1 W.L.R. 1432.

[88] Much of which pre-dates the two Acts.

[89] [1973] 1 W.L.R. 1159.

[90] *per* Davies L.J. at 1162.

[91] [1982] Fam. 90; [1982] 2 W.L.R. 914; [1982] 2 All E.R. 495; [1983] F.L.R. 50.

[92] [1986] 2 F.L.R. 342.

Camacho[93] a man searched through his partner's handbag. In *Johnson v. Walton*[94] a man sent photographs of the partially nude plaintiff to a national newspaper with the intention of causing her distress. Frightening silent telephone calls made repeatedly to women,[95] threatening letters[96] and newspaper articles inciting racial hatred of an individual[97] all constitute harassment under the Protection From Harassment Act 1997. If the courts give the 1997 Act an application beyond the context of stalking, it will offer civil remedies which to a degree overlap with those in Part IV of the Family Law Act 1996.

10–020 By contrast, the behaviour in *C v. C (Non-Molestation Order: Jurisdiction)*[98] was held to fall outside the scope of "molestation" in section 42 of the Family Law Act 1996. In the course of an acrimonious divorce the wife provided a tabloid newspaper with information about her husband's treatment of his former wives. Sir Stephen Brown P., discharging a restraining order obtained *ex parte* by the husband, held that "molestation" implies some quite deliberate conduct aimed at a high degree of harassment of the other partner so as to justify the intervention of the court. Here the wife's revelations came nowhere near molestation as envisaged by section 42, which—significantly—was located in Part I of the Act concerned with the topic of domestic violence. The husband's real concern was not about molestation but about damage to his reputation, for which the remedy lay in an action for defamation. This decision has been described as "a robust attempt to keep the concept of molestation within bounds."[99]

The implementation of the Human Rights Act 1998 makes it essential that the courts' powers in respect of molestation and harassment be compliant with relevant Articles of the European Convention on Human Rights: Article 5 (right to liberty and security), Article 6 (fair trial), Article 8 (respect for private and family life) and Article 10 (freedom of expression, including press freedom).[1] Issues include ambit (persons and conduct restrained), notice[2] and service,[3] and self-incrimination. The compliance requirements encompass enforcement procedures including committal proceedings.[4] The ambit issue is perhaps less acute in relation to orders under the Family Law Act 1996, which are—as described

---

[93] (1983) 4 F.L.R. 662.

[94] [1990] 1 F.L.R. 350.

[95] *R v. Ireland; R v. Burstow* [1998] 1 F.L.R. 105, HL; [1997] 4 All E.R. 225; accepted *obiter*, although it was doubted whether such conduct would constitute the more serious s.4 offence of putting people in fear of violence: *per* Lord Steyn at 107H–108 B.

[96] *R. v. Colohan* [2001] EWCA Crim. 1251 [2001] *Fam. Law* 757.

[97] *Thomas v. News Group Newspapers Ltd, The Times,* July 25, 2001, CA.

[98] [1998] 1 F.L.R. 554; [1998] 2 W.L.R. 599, FD.

[99] G. Douglas in [1998] *Fam. Law* 254.

[1] H. Swindells, A. Neaves, M. Kushner and R. Skilbeck, *Family Law and the Human Rights Act 1998* (Family Law, 1999), pp. 20, 23 and 56–58. See, from a civil liberties' perspective, the written evidence given to the Special Public Bill Committee on the Family Homes and Domestic Violence Bill (1995, H.L. 55) by S. M. Cretney, p. 13. See also the comments of the Lord Chancellor in introducing an amendment circumscribing the power to make *ex parte* orders (Committee on the Family Homes and Domestic Violence Bill (1995, H.L. 55), April 24, 1995, cols 16–17). For the scope of the Convention in the context of domestic disputes, see the Law Commission's Report on Binding Over (Law Com. No. 222, (1994)), para. 5.4.

[2] *Re W (Ex Parte Orders)* [2000] 2 F.L.R. 927, FD.

[3] Platt, "Human Rights and Part IV of the Family Law Act 1996" [2000] *Fam. Law* 905.

[4] CPR Practice Direction *Committal Applications,* May 28, 1999 (see [2001] *Fam. Law* 309); President's Direction *Committal Applications,* March 16, 2001 (see [2001] *Fam. Law* 333).

below—restricted in availability to those who have had a "family relationship,"[5] albeit widely defined. Such protection is not confined to the accused/defendant: Articles 5 and 8 of the Convention offer protection to the rights of the victim of molestation and harassment. The courts are increasingly engaged, in a wide variety of contexts, in the sensitive exercise of balancing competing rights under the Convention.

A major difference between the Family Law Act 1996 and the Protection from Harassment Act 1997 is that the scope of the former is restricted to "associated persons" whereas the latter is of general application as to the persons concerned.[6] Part IV of the Family Law Act 1996 is the primary[7] source of injunctive relief in cases involving a family relationship. The Protection from Harassment Act 1997 will be used[8] when the parties are not "associated" within the terms of the 1996 Act, or where the sanctions it offers are more attractive to a victim than those offered by the Family Law Act 1996, or where the harassment is not of the degree of seriousness sufficient to satisfy the concept of "molestation" under the 1996 Act.[9] However, the 1997 Act requires proof of a "course of conduct,"[10] and so may be unavailable for protection from isolated incidents of harassment. The two Acts are discussed separately in the following sections.

(a) Non-Molestation orders under the Family Law Act 1996[11]

(i) Applications by "associated persons"

10–021 The Family Law Act[12] provides that the court may make a non-molestation order if an application[13] has been made for the order by a person who is associated with the respondent. The definition of "associated person" is therefore of crucial importance; the underlying policy is that people who have or have had a family or domestic relationship should, by virtue of that fact, be entitled to

---

[5] See the evidence given to the Special Public Bill Committee on the Family Homes and Domestic Violence Bill (1995, H.L. 55) by H. H. J. Fricker Q.C., March 29, 1995, p. 71.

[6] For an illustration of the distinction as to victim, see *Hale v. Tanner* [2000] 2 F.L.R. 879; [2000] 1 W.L.R. 2377; [2000] F.C.R. 62, CA.

[7] But not necessarily exclusive, it being assumed that an "associated person" has the right to elect between remedies. See R. Bird, *Domestic Violence and Protection from Harassment: The New Law* (Family Law, 2nd ed., 1997) pp. 114–115. The Matrimonial Homes Act 1983 was regarded as a comprehensive codification of the law (*Richards v Richards* [1984] 1 A.C. 175, HL), but there is a difference between excluding the pre-existing "inherent" jurisdiction and acknowledging the operation of subsequent legislation. Duality of remedies available to associated persons was enviseaged *obiter* by the Court of Appeal in *R. v Hills* [2001] 1 F.L.R. 580.

[8] For a comparison between the two, see T. Lawson-Cruttenden and N. Addison, "Domestic Violence and Harassment—A Consideration of Part I of the Family Law Act 1996 and the Protection from Harassment Act 1996" [1998] *Fam. Law.* 543 and R. Bird, *Domestic Violence and Protection from Harassment: The New Law* (Family Law, 2nd ed., 1997), pp. 114–115.

[9] In *R. v. Hills* [2001] 1 F.L.R. 185 the Court of Appeal observed *obiter* that the 1997 Act might, on appropriate facts, be used to prevent stalking of a former partner or estranged spouse.

[10] Protection From Harassment Act 1997, ss. 1(1), 4 (1).

[11] On the origins of the current legislative provisions, see S. Gerlis, "The Family Law Bill: Reconsidering Non-Molestation Orders" [1996] *Fam. Law* 52.

[12] F.L.A. 1996, s.42(2)(a).

[13] The application may be "free-standing"—*i.e.* not associated with any application for other relief—or may be made in other family proceedings—*e.g.* in divorce proceedings: s.39(2)(a).

the special legal protection afforded by this legislation if they are in need of it.[14] In short, the nexus of the relationship is the qualification for access to the swift emergency remedies.[15]

That nexus is very widely defined by the Act, which[16] provides that a person is "associated" with another person if:—

(a) they are or have been married to each other,
(b) they are cohabitants or former cohabitants;

This term is defined[17] as a man and a woman who, although not married to each other, are living together as husband and wife. The gender-specific terminology adopts a strong analogy with lawful marriage[18] and must be taken to evidence an intention to exclude same-sex partnerships,[19] which nevertheless are included (somewhat coyly, but with less potential for political controversy) in the next broad definitional category. Case-law in other fields has established useful (though non-exclusive) criteria indicating the existence of cohabitation.[20]

(c) they live or have lived in the same household, otherwise than merely by reason of one of them being the other's employee, tenant, lodger or boarder;

This is a broad category in which a familial element is not necessary.[21] The Law Commission intended it to include those who have lived in the same household other than on a purely commercial basis.[22] The crucial test is the degree of community of life which goes on; there must be an element of shared lifestyle.[23] Once that is satisfied, this category includes not only same-sex partners but also

---

[14] See the discussion in the Law Commission's *Report on Domestic Violence and Occupation of the Family Home* (Law Com. No. 207 (1992)), paras. 3.1–3.27;

[15] See the Second Reading speech of the Lord Chancellor (Official Report) H.L. February 23, 1995, and the discussion in R. Bird, *Domestic Violence and Protection from Harassment: The New Law* (Family Law, 2nd ed., 1999) pp. 15–21.

[16] s.62(3).

[17] s.62(1)(a).

[18] See R. Bailey-Harris, "Dividing the Assets of the Unmarried Family—Recent Lessons From Australia" [2000] Int. *Fam. Law* 91.

[19] See the interpretation of similar provisions in para. 2 of Sched. 1 to the Rent Acts 1977 by the House of Lords in *Fitzpatrick v. Sterling Housing Association* [1999] 3 W.L.R. 1113. See N. Roberts, "*Fitzpatrick v. Sterling*—A Case with Wider Implications?" [2000] *Fam. Law* 417 at 420. "Former cohabitants" does not include cohabitants who have subsequently married: F.L.A. 1996, s.62(1) (b).

[20] See *e.g. Crake v. Supplementary Benefits Commission; Butterworth v. Supplementary Commission* [1982] 1 All E.R. 498; *Atkinson v. Atkinson* [1988] 2 F.L.R. 353; [1988] 2 W.L.R. 204; *Re J (Income Support: Cohabitation)* [1995] 1 F.L.R. 660; *Re Watson (dec'd)* [1999] 1 F.L.R. 878; *K v. K (Enforcement)* [2000] 1 F.L.R. 383, FD.

[21] The expression is wider than that of "member of the . . . family . . . residing in the same household" in para. 3 of Sched. 1 to the Rent Act 1977 discussed in *Fitzpatrick v. Sterling Housing Association* [1999] 3 W.L.R. 1113.

[22] Report on *Domestic Violence and Occupation of the Family Home* (Law Com. No. 207), para 3.21.

[23] *ibid.*

arrangements such as a group of students sharing the one flat or house.[24] On normal principles of statutory interpretation—*expressio unius exlusit alterius* – it must be taken as excluding familial relationships such as a nephew and aunt sharing the same home, since such would fall under the category of "relatives", below.

(d) they are relatives

This term is very expansive, since it included relationships derived from the connection of cohabitation as well as marriage.[25] The authors know of no more extensive statutory definition of a person's kin. The only familial relationship excluded from the definition is that of cousin.

(e) they have agreed to marry each other[26] (whether or not the agreement has been terminated)[27]
(f) they are a child's parents (or connected with a child in other defined[28] ways[29]);
(g) they are parties to the same family proceedings.[30]

A person falling outside the wide definition of "associated person" is not without legal protection , but must seck it elsewhere—principally, either under the Protection from Harassment Act 1997 or under section 37 of the Supreme Court Act 1991, discussed below. The need for the definition has been questioned by

---

[24] Persons who share a flat would be within this definition if they are all joint tenants of the property, but not if one of them has taken a lease and then agrees to allow others to share the flat: *ibid.* para. 3.22.

[25] By F.L.A. 1996, s. 63(1) as meaning: (a) the father, mother, stepfather, stepmother, son, daughter, stepson, stepdaughter, grandmother, grandfather, grandson or granddaughter of the person concerned or of that person's spouse or former spouse, or (b) the brother, sister, uncle, aunt, niece or nephew (whether of the full blood or of the half blood or by affinity) of that person or of that person's spouse or former spouse, and includes, in relation to a person who is living or has lived with another person as husband and wife, any person who would fall within (a) or (b) if the parties were married to each other.

[26] However, no application may be made under this provision after the end of the period of three years from termination: s.42(4).

[27] There must be either evidence in writing of the existence of the agreement to marry s.44(1)(2) or the agreement must be evidenced by the gift of an engagement ring by one party to the agreement to the other in contemplation of their marriage or by a ceremony entered into by the parties in the presence of one or more other persons assembled for the purpose of witnessing the ceremony: s.44(2). The nature of the necessary "evidence in writing" was raised but not answered by Wall J. in *G v. G (Non-Molestation Order: Jurisdiction)* [2000] 2 F.L.R. 533 at 544; [2000] 3 W.L.R. 1202, FD.

[28] The Act (s.62(2),(4)) provides that a person falls within the necessary relationship if he is a parent of the child or has or has had "parental responsibility" for the child. Thus the father of an illegitimate child who has never had parental responsibility for that child is nevertheless associated with the child's mother (who could thus seek an order against him).Two persons are also associated with each other if the child has been adopted or freed for adoption and (a) one is the child's natural parent or that parent's natural parent and (b) the other is the child or any person who has applied for or been granted an adoption order or a person with whom the child has been placed for adoption: s.62(5)

[29] However, a local authority cannot seek these remedies, a body incorporate being expressly excluded: s.62(6).

[30] As defined: s.63(1),(2).

those who advocate giving the court a general power to intervene in appropriate circumstances irrespective of the parties' relationship,[31] as have its details.[32] Nevertheless its very breadth means that in practice a wide range of applicants will have access to the effective remedies provided by Part IV of the Family Law Act 1996, and moreover judicial interpretation suggests that the definition should be broadly construed under a purposive interpretation of the legislation. *Chechi v. Basheer*[33] concerned a family quarrel originating in a land dispute. The appellant originally obtained non-molestation orders *ex parte* under the Family Law Act 1996 against his brother and six nephews, but these were discharged at the full hearing on the basis that the family relationship was incidental and that the case should therefore be dealt with as civil rather than family proceedings. The Court of Appeal disagreed on this point, holding that the dispute was genuinely within the ambit of Part IV of the 1996 Act; although it was in origin about land, it was "patently overlaid and magnified by the family relationship".[34] In *G v. G (Non-Molestation Order: Jurisdiction)*[35] the principal issue in dispute was the nature of the former living arrangements between a man and the woman who applied for a non-molestation order against him under section 42 of the Family Law Act 1996. The justices found that the parties were not "associated" as they had not lived in the same household, had not cohabited and had not agreed to marry. Wall J. allowed the woman's appeal and remitted the case for adjudication on the merits. The evidence was sufficient to satisfy the requirements of "cohabitation" under section 62(3)(b), given that at least three of the recognised[36] indicators of such relationship were present. His Lordship observed that:

> "where domestic violence is concerned, [courts] should give the statute a purposive construction and not decline jurisdiction, unless the facts of the case before them are plainly incapable of being brought within the statute. Part IV of the 1996 Act is designed to provide swift and accessible protective remedies to persons of both sexes who are the victims of domestic violence, provided they fall within the criteria laid down in s 62. It would . . . be most unfortunate if s 62(3) was narrowly construed so as to exclude borderline cases where swift and effective protection for the victims of domestic violence is required".[37]

(ii) Orders made by court of its own motion

10–022 Under section 42(2)(b) of the Family Law act 1996 the court may make a non-molestation order in any family proceedings against any party to those

---

[31] See the Written Evidence given to the Special Public Bill Committee on the Family Homes and Domestic Violence Bill (1995, H.L. 55) by M. Hayes, p. 37; and by S. Edwards and A. Halpern, p. 18; see M. Hayes, "Only Associated Persons Need Apply" [1996] *Fam. Law* 134.

[32] J. Murphy, "Domestic Violence: The New Law" (1996) 59 *M.L.R.* 845 at 850–854.

[33] [1999] 2 F.L.R. 489; comment in [1999] *Fam. Law* 528.

[34] *ibid.* at 493. However the appeal was dismissed on the basis that the mandatory power of arrest under s.42 would have been inappropriate in the circumstances: see p. 264 below.

[35] [2000] 2 F.L.R. 533; [2000] F.C.R. 53, FD.

[36] See n. 20, p. 254 above.

[37] [2000] 2 F.L.R. 553 at 543.

proceedings, if it considers that the order should be made for the benefit of any other party to the proceedings or any relevant child,[38] whether or not any application has been made for the order. In its *Report to the Lord Chancellor on the Question of Parental Contact in Cases Where There is Domestic Violence* (1999), the Children Act Sub-Committee of the Advisory Board on Family Law recommended more robust use of this power in order to secure the safety of the residential parent and child in cases involving domestic violence where interim or longer contact is ordered under section 8 of the Children Act 1989.[39]

(iii) Terms which may be included in non-molestation order

10–023 The Act empowers the court to make orders prohibiting the respondent from molesting a person who is associated with the respondent or from molesting a relevant child.[40] A non-molestation order may[41] refer to molestation in general, to particular acts of molestation, or to both. In practice, orders are commonly worded in terms of prohibitions on threatening, intimidating, harassing or pestering the applicant or named children.[42] Non-molestation orders may be made for a specified period or until further order.[43] The duration of a non-molestation order is a matter for the court's discretion; an order for an indefinite period may be appropriate in the circumstances and courts are not obliged to regard such cases as exceptional or unusual.[44] The issue of the terms and duration of a non-molestation order is anterior to and distinct from that of a power of arrest; the latter cannot be used as a reason for limiting the former.[45] An order made in other family proceedings will cease to have effect if those proceedings are withdrawn or dismissed.[46]

(iv) Matters relevant to the exercise of the court's discretion

10–024 The Family Law Act provides[47] that in deciding whether to exercise its powers to make a non-molestation order, and if so in what manner, the court is to have regard to all the circumstances including the need to secure the health, safety and well-being of the applicant[48] and of any relevant child.[49] The grant of a non-molestation order is obviously much less draconian than the grant of an order excluding a person from his or her home. The Law Commission drew a

---

[38] Defined in s.62(2).
[39] Report, paras 5.4(d) and 5.7(c). See Chap. 20.
[40] s.42(2) (b).
[41] s.42(6).
[42] See the pro forma suggested by D.J. Ashton at [1998] *Fam. Law* 4, 7.
[43] s.42(7).
[44] *Re B-J (Power of Arrest)* [2000] 2 F.L.R. 443; [2000] 2 W.L.R. 107; [2000] 1 All E.R. 325, CA, overruling *M v. W (Non-Molestation Order: Duration)* [2000] 1 F.L.R. 107; comment in [2000] *Fam. Law* 107.
[45] *ibid.*
[46] s.42(8).
[47] s.42(5).
[48] Or, where the court decides to make an order of its own motion, the person for whose benefit it considers the order should be made: s.42(5)(a).
[49] As defined by s.3; see 62(2) above.

distinction of principle between non-molestation orders which can be obeyed without prejudice to the respondent's interests, and ouster orders which obviously prejudice those interests, however temporarily or justifiably.[50] Under the current law as under the old,[51] courts experience little difficulty in exercising their discretion in cases where they have jurisdiction. There may be circumstances in which it is not appropriate to make an order. Thus in *Banks v. Banks*[52] the husband's application for a non-molestation order was dismissed. The respondent wife suffered from manic depression and dementia, and the abuse to which she subjected the husband was a symptom of her condition and something over which she had no control; no order was made.[53] In *Chechi v. Basheeer*[54] it was held that the county court judge had been within the legitimate bounds of his discretion in refusing to make an order under section 42 because the near-mandatory requirement of attachment of a power of arrest[55] would have been inappropriate given the special circumstances of the family dispute in question.

(b) Orders under the Protection From Harassment Act 1997

10–025 The genesis of the Protection from Harassment Act 1997[56] was concern[57] over "stalking". The legislation is an unusual hybrid[58] of criminal[59] and civil remedies; the present discussion is confined to the latter. Whether intentionally or not, the legislature has created civil remedies which to an extent overlap with non-molestation orders under Part IV of the Family Law Act 1996,[60] with the important proviso that the 1997 Act is not limited by the definition of "associated person"[61] but as to persons is of general application. Like "molestation" in the Family Law Act 1996, the term "harassment" is in the interests of flexibility left undefined; their relationship has been discussed earlier.[62] It will be

---

[50] Report on *Domestic Violence and Occupation of the Matrimonial Home* (Law Com. No. 207 (1992)) para 2.48.
[51] See the 5th edition of this book at p. 217.
[52] [1999] 1 F.L.R. 726; [1999] 2 F.C.R. 110, CA; comment in [1999] *Fam. Law* 209.
[53] Even assuming she had capacity to understand an order; see further *P v. P (Contempt of Court: Mental Capacity)* [1999] 2 F.L.R. 897, and Ashton, "Injunctions and Mental Disorder" [2000] *Fam. Law* 39.
[54] [1999] 2 F.L.R. 489.
[55] See p. 264, below.
[56] H. Conway, "Protection from Harassment Act 1997" [1997] *Fam. Law* 714; Lawson-Cruttenden and Addison, "The Protection from Harassment Act 1997" (1997) 147 N.L.J. 983; Lawson-Cruttenden and Addison, *The Protection from Harassment Act 1997* (Blackstone Press, 1997).
[57] "Stalking: Consultation Paper and Government Proposals" [1996] *Fam. Law* 527; Lawson-Cruttenden, "The Government's Proposed Stalking Law - A Discussion Paper" [1996] *Fam. Law* 755.
[58] R. Bird, *Domestic Violence and Protection from Harassment* (Family Law, 2nd ed., 1999), p. 108.
[59] For a discussion of the offences created by the Act, see pp. 234, above.
[60] Lawson-Cruttenden, "Harassment and Domestic Violence" [1996] *Fam. Law* 429; Lawson-Cruttenden and Addison, "Domestic Violence and Harassment: A consideration of Part I of the Family Law Act 1996 and The Protection From Harassment Act 1997" [1998] *Fam. Law* 543.
[61] Family Law Act 1996 s. 62(3).
[62] See pp. 250–252 above.

recalled however that the 1997 Act requires a "course of conduct"[63] which must involve conduct on at least two occasions[64] and it has been held that a nexus between them must be established.[65] The test is the objective one of the reasonable person, and mental illness is no defence.[66] It is clear that the conduct in *Khorosandjian v. Bush*[67] would now be within the scope of the Protection from Harassment Act 1997. There a young man could not accept that his relationship (which does not appear to have involved a sexual element, and certainly did not involve cohabitation) with an 18-year-old woman he had met at a snooker club was at an end. He continued to harass and pester her. The Court of Appeal held (controversially) that by telephoning the applicant at her parents' home the defendant had been guilty of the tort of nuisance, and an injunction was available accordingly; that decision was overruled by the House of Lords in *Hunter v. Canary Wharf*[68] which re-asserted conventional restrictions on the title to sue in nuisance. An expansive interpretation of harassment under the Protection from Harassment Act 1997 was adopted by the Court of Appeal in *Thomas v. News Group Newspapers Ltd*,[69] where it was held[70] that the publication of press articles calculated to incite racial hatred of another was conduct capable of falling within the statutory definition.

Civil remedies are created by section 3, which provides that an actual or apprehended breach of section 1 may be the subject of a civil claim by the actual or potential victim.[71] Damages may be awarded for *inter alia* anxiety or financial loss caused by the harassment.[72] More importantly, the High Court and county courts have jurisdiction[73] to grant injunctions restraining the defendant from pursuing any conduct which amounts to harassment.[74] Moreover, a court sentencing the defendant for a section 2 or section 4 offence may issue an order restraining future conduct which amounts to harassment or which will cause fear of violence,[75] and breach of such an order is itself a criminal offence.[76] The exercise of the court's discretion under the 1997 Act is unconstrained by any statutory guidelines. A victim who qualifies as an "associated person" for the purposes of section 62(3) of the Family Law Act 1996 may nevertheless in

---

[63] Protection from Harassment Act 1997, ss. 1(1),4(1).

[64] *ibid.* 7(3); see *Tameside Metropolitan L.B.C. v. M. (Injunctive Relief: County Courts: Jurisdiction)* [2002] 1 F.L.R. 318, Manchester County Court.

[65] *Lau v. DPP* [2000] 1 F.L.R. 799; [2000] 1 F.C.R. 53, QB; *R. v. Hills* [2001] 1 F.L.R. 580.

[66] Protection from Harassment Act 1997, ss. 1(2), 4(2); *R. v. Colohan* [2001] EWCA Crim. 1251; [2001] 2 F.L.R. 757.

[67] [1993] Q.B. 727, CA.

[68] [1998] A.C. 65; see P. Cane (1997) 113 *Law Quarterly Review* 515.

[69] [2001] *The Times*, July 25, 2001.

[70] Dismissing an appeal against a refusal to strike out, and transferring the case for trial to the High Court.

[71] *ibid.* s. 3(1).

[72] *ibid.* s. 3(2).

[73] Under their general powers.

[74] *ibid.* s. 3.

[75] *ibid.* s. 5(1) and (2).

[76] *ibid.* s. 5(5) and (6), which has been described as "an interesting linkage of civil and criminal jurisdictions": H. Conway [1997] *Fam. Law* 715.

an appropriate case be attracted to the criminal sanctions which the 1997 Act provides.[77]

(c) Injunctions under the general civil law

10–026 Part IV of the Family Law Act 1996 and the provisions of the Protection from Harassment Act 1997 will provide remedies against molestation and harassment in the vast majority of cases involving any domestic element, but for the sake of completeness brief mention must be made of the availability of injunctive relief under the general civil law.

Section 37 of the Supreme Court Act 1981 provides that the High Court[78] may grant an interlocutory or final injunction "in all cases in which it appears to the court to be just and convenient to do so". Obviously this power extends far beyond the context of violence and harassment which is the subject of the present discussion. In the context of personal relationships, the inherent jurisdiction can be invoked to restrain the defendant from (for example) communicating with the applicant's employers or disclosing confidential material to the press[79] which would be beyond the powers conferred by the Family Law Act 1996.[80] The jurisdiction may be used to oust a person from premises in order to protect a child.[81] Nevertheless, the extent of the courts' jurisdiction is restricted. The right to obtain an injunction is not itself a cause of action; it must support some pre-existing recognised legal or equitable right,[82] or at least an arguable cause of action.[83] The absence from the common law of a tort of harassment which underpinned the refusal of injunctive relief some of the earlier authorities[84] has in practice been remedied by the enactment of the Protection from Harassment Act 1997.

---

[77] Enforcement of orders under the Protection from Harassment Act 1997 is discussed below at p. 264.

[78] County Courts Act 1984, s.38 (as substituted by the Courts and Legal Services Act 1990) provides that the country court may make an order which could be made by the High Court if the proceedings were in the High Court; it is often said that this provision enables the county court to exercise the so-called inherent jurisdiction of the High Court to grant injunctions: see *e.g. Pearson v. Franklin (Parental Home: Ouster)* [1994] 1 F.L.R. 246. But on one view the Act merely gives the county court power to grant remedies and does not empower the county court to exercise the inherent jurisdiction of the High Court: see *e.g. D. v. D. (County Court Jurisdiction: Injunctions)* [1993] 2 F.L.R. 802. But see *Tameside Borough Council v. M (Injunctive Relief: County Courts: Jurisdiction)* [2002] 1 F.L.R. 318.

[79] See *Argyll (Duchess) v. Argyll (Duke)* [1967] Ch. 302; *Stephens v. Avery* [1988] Ch. 449; and generally the *Report of the Committee on Privacy and Related Matters* (Cmnd. 1102 (1990)) and the Lord Chancellor's Department's Consultation Paper on *Infringement of Privacy* (1993).

[80] See *C v. C (Non-Molestation Order: Jurisdiction)* [1998] 1 F.L.R. 554, discussed above at p. 252, above. But arguably such powers may not beyond the Protection from Harassment Act 1997: *Thomas v. News Group Newspaper Ltd, The Times,* July 2001.

[81] *C.v. K (Inherent Powers: Exclusion Order)* [1996] 2 F.L.R. 506; *Re P (Care Orders: Injunctive Relief)* [2000] 2 F.L.R. 385.

[82] See *e.g. Patel v. Patel* [1988] 2 F.L.R. 179; *C v. K (Inherent Power: Exclusion Order)* [1996] 2 F.L.R. 506; Fricker, "Inherent Jurisdiction, Ouster and Exclusion" [1994] *Fam. Law* 629; K. Barnett, "Inherent Jurisdiction, Ouster Orders and Children" [1997] *Fam. Law* 96.

[83] *Burris v. Adzani* [1996] 1 F.L.R. 266; [1995] 1 W.L.R. 1327; [1995] 4 All E.R. 802, CA; Davey (1996) 8 *C.F.L.Q.* 269.

[84] *e.g. Patel v. Patel* [1988] 2 F.L.R. 179.

C. Enforcement of Occupation and Non—Molestation Orders

10–027 Both the Family Law Act 1996 and the Protection from Harassment Act 1997 contain their own enforcement mechanisms. In addition, there is the general power of courts to sentence for contempt, which will be addressed first.

1. Sentences for contempt

10–028 It is a contempt of court to disobey a court order. A sentence of contempt serves a dual purpose: in the interests of the administration of justice, to signal the court's disapproval of disobedience of its orders and to secure future compliance, and to punish for the breach itself in the light of its gravity.[85] That said, the discretion in sentencing is wide, and in the past the reported authorities have provided little guidance. Although the full range of sentencing options is not available for contempt, there are some alternatives to imprisonment: adjournment, fine and mental health orders.[86] The dilemma facing a judge in committal proceedings[87] involving family members is classically that discussed at the outset of this Chapter: how to reconcile the objectives of the justice system in relation to seriously antisocial conduct[88] with sensitivity to the special character of family proceedings and the continuing relational and emotional ties of the parties commonly involved therein.[89]

The Court of Appeal in *Hale v. Tanner*[90] provided valuable guidance on sentencing for contempt in family proceedings.[91] The court has a discretion whether or not to commit to prison for the first breach of an order,[92] although this is not common practice and much will depend on the nature of the conduct in question. The length of committal should be determined without reference to whether or not it is to be suspended. Suspension[93] is a very useful power and possible in

[85] *Neil v. Ryan* [1998] 1 F.L.R. 1068; *Wilson v. Webber* [1998] 1 F.L.R. 1097; *Rafiq v. Muse* [2000] 1 F.L.R. 820, CA; *Hale v. Tanner* [2000] 2 F.L.R. 879 at 884 *per* Hale L.J.; [2000] 1 W.L.R. 2377; [2000] F.C.R. 62; *Harris v. Harris* [2001] 2 F.L.R. 55, FD; *A-A v. B-B* [2001] 2 F.L.R. 1, CA.

[86] Contempt of Court Act 1981, s.14(1), (2)). Magistrates' courts have powers to punish for disobedience to their orders under Magistrates' Courts Act 1980, s.63(1); and magistrates are given powers (comparable to those of the High Court and county courts) to pass suspended sentences, and to make orders under the Mental Health legislation: F.L.A. 1996, ss.50, 51.

[87] On the nature of committal and the distinction from prosecution, see *M v. M (Committal: Contempt)* [1997] 1 F.L.R. 762 and *DPP v. Tweddle* [2001] E.W.C.A. Admin. 188, 2 F.L.R. 400, QBD.

[88] *Wright v. Jess* [1987] 2 F.L.R. 373; *Brewer v. Brewer* [1989] 2 F.L.R. 251; *G. v. G. (Contempt: Committal)* [1993] *Fam. Law* 335; *Jones v. Jones* [1993] 2 F.L.R. 377; *Hudson v. Hudson* [1995] 2 F.L.R. 72; *Delaney v. Delaney* [1996] 1 F.L.R. 458; *Thorpe v. Thorpe* [1998] 2 F.L.R. 127; *Neil v. Ryan* [1998] 1 F.L.R. 1068; *Wilson v. Webber* [1998] 1 F.L.R. 1098; *Rafiq v. Muse* [2000] 1 F.L.R. 820.

[89] *Ansah v. Ansah* [1977] Fam. 138 at 142–143, *per* Ormrod L.J.; *Hale v. Tanner* [2000] 2 F.L.R. 879 at 884 and 885 *per* Hale L.J. [200] 1 W.L.R. 2377; [2000] 3 F.C.R. 62.

[90] [2000] 2 F.L.R. 879.

[91] Although not on the length of sentence appropriate for particular types of breach, on which no evidence was submitted.

[92] *Thorpe v. Thorpe* [1998] 2 F.L.R. 127, CA.

[93] There is no jurisdiction to release a contemnor on his application to purge the contempt by suspending the unserved balance of the sentence: *Harris v. Harris* [2001] E.W.C.A. Civ. 1645 [2002] 1 F.L.R. 248.

this context in a far wider range of circumstances than in criminal cases. Its length is a separate consideration, although it is often appropriate to link it to compliance with the underlying order.[94] Account should be taken of any concurrent proceedings in order to avoid double punishment. The court should endeavour to explain the nature and purpose of its orders to the contemnor.

The serious nature[95] of committal proceedings and their potential to deprive an individual of liberty necessitate procedural fairness to comply with Article 6 of the European Convention for the Protection of Human Rights and Fundamental Freedoms, incorporated into domestic law by the Human Rights Act 1998.[96] A contemnor is not required to understand the nature of the court's jurisdiction nor the concept of contempt, but must have sufficient mental capacity to understand that an order has been made forbidding him from doing certain things and that if he does them he will be punished.[97] Compliance of committal proceedings with Article 6 has been ensured by Practice Directions.[98] On a contemnor's application to purge his contempt, there are only three possible outcomes: immediate release, deferred release, or refusal.[99]

Nevertheless, the existence of powers to inflict punishment for breach *ex post facto* is less important than the prevention of breach in the first place. Here the power of arrest, discussed below, plays a vital role.

(ii) Enforcement under the Family Law Act 1996

10–029 The Domestic Violence and Matrimonial Proceedings Act 1976 was innovative in empowering the court to attach a so-called "power of arrest" to certain orders. The power of arrest authorised the police to arrest without warrant and bring before the court any person reasonably suspected of being in breach of an order. Nevertheless the courts appeared reluctant to exercise their discretion; in fact it was considered relatively exceptional to attach a power of arrest to an injunction.[1] It had been held that such a power should only be included in an order where a person persistently disobeyed injunctions and made a nuisance of himself to the other party and to others concerned.[2] But the Law Commission's consultations revealed a weight of informed opinion favouring a change of policy, and it recommended that there should be a presumption in favour of a

---

[94] On the terms of suspension, see *Griffin v. Grifin* [2000] 2 F.L.R. 44; [2000] 2 F.C. R. 302. The court has power on an application by a contemnor to purge his contempt to suspend the remaining part of a sentence, to put sincerity to the test: *Harris v. Harris* [2001] 2 F.L.R. 955.

[95] The seriousness of an order for suspended imprisonment for contempt requires the order to be drawn on Form N79: *Couzens v. Couzens* [2001] 2 F.L.R. 701, CA.

[96] *Manchester City Council v. Worthington* [2000] 2 F.L.R. 531.

[97] *P v. P (Contempt of Court: Mental Capacity)* [1999] 2 F.L.R. 897; [999] 3 F.C.R. 547; comment in [1999] *Fam. Law* 690.

[98] CPR Practice Direction *Committal Applications*, May 28, 1999 (see [2001] *Fam. Law* 309); President's Direction *Committal Applications* March 16, 2001 (see [2001] *Fam. Law* 333. Note that a suspended committal order must be served in accordance with Form N79: *Couzens v. Couzens* [2001] EWCA Civ. 992; [2001] 2 F.L.R. 701.

[99] *Harris v. Harris* [2001] EWCA Civ. 1645; [2002] 1 F.L.R. 248.

[1] See the Law Commission's *Report on Domestic Violence and Occupation of the Family Home* (Law Com. No. 207 (1992)), para. 5.10.

[2] *Lewis (A.H.) v. Lewis (R.W.F.)* [1978] 1 All E.R. 729 at 731, *per* Ormrod L.J.

power of arrest in cases where there has been actual or threatened violence.[3] In consequence, this enforcement mechanism is rendered considerably more effective by the Family Law Act 1996.

If the court attaches a power of arrest to an occupation order or to a non-molestation order, a constable may arrest without warrant a person whom he has reasonable cause for suspecting to be in breach of the provision to which the power is annexed[4]; and in practice powers of arrest are registered at a police station so that the applicant should normally be able to summon police assistance with the minimum of difficulty. The person arrested must be brought before the court[5] within the period of 24 hours beginning at the time of the arrest.[6] The court may then remand[7] the person concerned[8] and it may punish for the contempt constituted by the breach of the order.[9] A power of arrest may be attached notwithstanding that the respondent is a minor and committal is not an available option.[10] Notwithstanding the lack of express words in the statute, the position regarding the duration of a power of arrest is the same whether it is made on notice or not; the issue of the terms and length of a non-molestation order should be considered before that of the power of arrest.[11]

The power of arrest is now virtually mandatory in certain circumstances. The Act provides[12] that the court must attach a power of arrest to an occupation or non-molestation order if the respondent has "used or threatened violence" against the applicant or a "relevant child", unless it is satisfied that in all the circumstances of the case the applicant will be adequately protected without the power of arrest. Note that there is no power to attach a power of arrest to an

---

[3] *Report on Domestic Violence and Occupation of the Matrimonial Home* (Law Com. No. 207 (1992)), paras 5.12–5.13.

[4] s.47(6). It should be noted that, although the court has power to accept undertakings in cases in which it has power to make an occupation or non-molestation order, and although such undertakings are enforceable as if they were orders of the court, there is no power to attach a power of arrest to an undertaking and indeed the court is prohibited from accepting an undertaking under the relevant statutory provision in any case where a power of arrest would have been attached to the order: s.46(3).

[5] *i.e.* the "relevant judicial authority" as widely defined in F.L.A. 1996, s.63(1) (so as to extend to a district judge in the case of a county court order and a justice of the peace in the case of a magistrates' order).

[6] In reckoning this period, no account is taken of Christmas Day, Good Friday or any Sunday: F.L.A. 1996, s.47(7).

[7] F.L.A. 1996, s.47(7)(b).

[8] The remand may be in custody or on bail; see F.L.A. 1996, s.47(11) and Sched. 5; Magistrates' Courts Act 1980, ss.128, 129. Conditions may be attached to the grant of bail to secure that the person concerned does not interfere with witnesses or otherwise obstruct the course of justice: F.L.A. 1996, s.47(12). The power to remand may be exercised to enable a medical report to be obtained: s.48.

[9] The courts may in appropriate circumstances make a hospital or guardianship order under the Mental Health Act 1983, ss.37, 38: F.L.A. 1996, s.51; Contempt of Court Act 1981, s.4A.

[10] *Re H (Respondent Under 18: Power of Arrest)* [2001] 1 F.L.R. 641; [2001] 1 F.C.R. 370, CA.

[11] *Re B-J (Power of Arrest)* [2000] 2 F.L.R. 443, overruling *M v. W (Non-Molestation Order: Duration)* [2000] 1 F.L.R. 107.

[12] F.L.A. 1996, s.47(2). Different considerations apply where the order is made *ex parte* since the respondent will not have had an opportunity to state his case. It is accordingly provided that the court may attach a power of arrest to an order made *ex parte* if the respondent has used or threatened violence against the applicant or a relevant child and that there is a risk of "significant harm" to the applicant or child if the power of arrest is not attached to those provisions immediately: s.47(3).

undertaking. In *Chechi v. Basheer*[13] the near-mandatory attachment of a power of arrest was held to be a justified reason for declining to make an order under the Family Law Act 1996, since the use of the power would have been inappropriate in the unusual circumstances of the family dispute in question. However, it should not be assumed that the power of arrest must attach to the order in its entirety. Section 47(2) confers a discretion as to which parts of the order the power of arrest should be attached, and it may be appropriate to draw distinctions between different sorts of behaviour.[14]

(iii) Enforcement under the Protection from Harassment Act 1997

10–030 The distinctive hybrid of criminal and civil remedies which this Act creates has already been noted.[15] Breach of a (civil) restraining order made under the Act is itself a criminal offence, punishable by fine or imprisonment or both.[16] This is intended to be an alternative to civil committal; these avenues of enforcement are mutually exclusive.[17] Enforcement is dealt with more generally in section 3(3)–(6). There is no jurisdiction under the Act to attach a power of arrest to an injunction, but where an injunction has been granted to prohibit harassment and the plaintiff considers that prohibited conduct has occurred, he may apply to court for a warrant for the arrest of the defendant.[18] This procedure also exists under the Family Law Act 1996 as an alternative, available later in time if a power of arrest was not initially attached to an order.[19]

---

13 [1999] 2 F.L.R. 489.

14 *Hale v. Tanner* [2000] 2 F.L.R. 879 at 822 *per* Hale L.J.; Platt, "Human Rights and Part IV of the Family Law Act 1996" [2001] *Fam. Law* 905.

15 See pp. 234, 258–260 above.

16 Protection from Harassment Act 1997, s. 3(6) and (9).

17 *ibid.* s. 3(7),(8).

18 *ibid.* s. 3(3).

19 Family Law Act 1996, s. 47(8).

Chapter Eleven

ENDING MARRIAGE: DIVORCE

I. PRELIMINARY

The nature of divorce

11–001 A decree absolute[1] of divorce ends[2] the legal status of marriage previously existing between the parties, and thereafter neither party has the legal rights or owes the legal duties of a spouse. The divorce court does have extensive powers to make financial and other orders on divorce; but the rights of the parties thereafter flow from the order,[3] and not from the parties' agreement or from the fact that they were once husband and wife. It should also be noted that a divorce order operates prospectively: the parties may have acquired rights in the course of the marriage—for example, in respect of property—which will not be lost merely because the couple cease to be husband and wife.[4] Although divorce may often be for the parties in emotional terms, what an American scholar[5] has described as a "high impact experience" divorce as a matter of legal analysis deals with legal status and with legal rights and duties: it brings to an end a legal relationship, but it has no direct bearing on personal relationships. For example, a couple may have cohabited for only a few days after marriage and

---

[1] All decrees of divorce are in the first instance decrees *nisi* ("unless"). A decree nisi does not legally terminate the marriage. A decree nisi may be made absolute on the application of a party in whose favour it has been pronounced six weeks after the decree nisi has been pronounced; and the party against whom the decree has been granted may apply to the court for it to be made absolute three months later. If the decree is not made absolute within 12 months, the court may require the applicant to file an affidavit or give evidence in open court accounting for the delay. The two stage procedure was originally intended to give time for inquiries to be made into the circumstances surrounding the petition and for the Queen's Proctor or anyone else who considered that the divorce should not be granted to intervene and "show cause" against the decree being made absolute. Now the period between decree nisi and absolute if often used to negotiate about the financial and other consequences of the ending of the marriage.

[2] The court must be satisfied that there is a valid marriage to dissolve, and the burden of proof is on the petitioner: see *R. v. Nottingham County Court, ex p. Byers* [1985] 1 W.L.R. 403. For a case in which it became apparent in the course of divorce proceedings that the "marriage" had been bigamous (and was therefore void) see *Whiston v. Whiston* [1995] 2 F.L.R. 268, CA. Compare *W v. W (Physical Inter-sex)* [2001] Fam. 111, where the court had previously granted the respondent to a nullity petition a decree absolute of divorce in respect of the marriage, and it was conceded that the divorce decree did not found any argument based on estoppel or laches

[3] *De Lasala v. De Lasala* [1980] A.C. 546, PC: *Thwaite v. Thwaite* [1981] 2 F.L.R. 280, CA.

[4] For example, a divorced woman is entitled to rely on her former husband's contribution record in establishing entitlement to the state retirement pension: see Chap. 11, above. However, a divorced woman does not become her husband's widow, see *Ward v. Secretary of State for Social Services* [1989] 1 F.L.R. 119.

[5] F.E. Zimring, foreword to S.D. Sugarman and H.H. Kay (eds), *Divorce Reform at the Crossroads* (1990).

thereafter for years lived separate and apart, consumed with mutual hatred and bitterness; but so far as the law is concerned, they remain a married couple entitled to the rights flowing from the legal relationships. The law will seek to enforce the duties—for example, in respect of financial support—which separated spouses owe one another; but the law has[6] no procedure whereby husband and wife can be compelled to live together, much less to provide the mutual society, help and comfort for which the institution of marriage was traditionally ordained.[7]

Conversely, divorce does not necessarily bring the parties' personal relationship to an end. It is not unknown for a couple to resume cohabitation after divorce[8]; but far more commonly it is the fact that the couple have children which requires them to continue to collaborate to a greater or lesser extent. On one view, therefore, the main consequence of divorce in a monogamous society is that it constitutes a licence to remarry: on divorce each party becomes free to marry again.

In recent years, so much attention has been given to the increase in divorce that there is some danger of forgetting that the majority of marriages are still brought to an end only by death.[8a] Death does of course terminate the status of marriage; but a surviving spouse has important legal rights as a widow or widower. These matters are dealt with elsewhere in this book.[9]

II. DIVORCE RATES

11–002 For many years the conventional view was that the state has a vital interest in the control of marriage and divorce, and that there must be some restriction on the availability of divorce in order to uphold respect for the sanctity of marriage. But over the years since judicial divorce first became available in this country in 1858 there has been a substantial upward trend in the divorce rate. In 1858 there were 244 divorce petitions. In 1914 for the first time the number exceeded 1,000; in 1942 it rose above 10,000. In 1971 (the first year of the operation of the Divorce Reform Act 1969 permitting divorce on the basis of irretrievable breakdown) there were 110,017 petitions; and in 1993, 184,471 divorce petitions were filed.[10] The number of divorce petitions presented in any one year is not a

---

[6] The decree of Restitution of Conjugal Rights in form ordered one spouse to return to the other and render conjugal services; but it was not in recent years capable of literal enforcement; and the right to petition for such a decree was abolished by M.P.P.A. 1970, s.20.

[7] See the Form of Solemnization of Marriage contained in the Book of Common Prayer.

[8] For a remarkable example, see *S v. S (Financial Provision) (Post-Divorce Cohabitation)* [1994] 2 F.L.R. 228. Douglas Brown J. (couple resumed living together after divorce and cohabited for 15 years) and note also *Hewitson v. Hewitson* [1995] 1 F.L.R. 241 (relationship continued for four years after divorce). Cases in which one former partner provides a home when the other is incapacitated by illness are also not unknown; see *e.g. Fuller v. Fuller* [1973] 1 W.L.R. 730.

[8a] *cf. Bellinger v. Bellinger* [2001] 2 F.L.R. 1048, *per* Thorpe L.J. It is believed that the statement in the text is correct (although projections suggest the balance may soon change).

[9] Chaps 8 (Devolution of Family Property on Death) and 14 (Termination of Marriage by Death).

[10] *Judicial Statistics, Annual Report 1993,* Table 5.7. The number of decrees absolute is smaller than the number of petitions: in 1993 162,579 decrees absolute were granted: *ibid.* The estimated figures for 1994 show a small decrease: 176,200 petitions and 158,100 decrees absolute: (1996) 83 *Population Trends* 78.

wholly satisfactory indication of the divorce rate; but whatever statistical measure is adopted it is clear that there has been an enormous increase in recourse to divorce. For example, there were 2.1 divorces per thousand married persons in 1961, 6.0 in 1971, 11.9 in 1981, whilst by 1991 the figure had risen to 13.5.[11] It is true that in recent years there has been some reduction in recourse to divorce,[12] but it remains true that the divorce rate has doubled since the Divorce Reform Act 1969 came into force and quadrupled over the last 30 years; and there has also been a rapid growth in the number of persons divorcing for a second or third time. An increasing divorce rate is a world-wide phenomenon, but the rate in England and Wales is now one of the highest in Europe, and it has increased more rapidly than in almost any other country.[13]

The significance of divorce rates: cause for concern?

11–003 The question of whether the increased divorce rate is a matter for concern is one which has given rise to much discussion. In one respect, it seems that there is no room for dispute: increasingly children will find that they have family relationships—whether close or not—with a greatly extended kinship group; and there are undoubtedly tensions in many relationships between a step-parent and his or her spouse's children.[14] But there is evidently room for considerable dispute about such issues as whether a high divorce rate poses a threat to the institution of marriage, whether an increasing divorce rate necessarily indicates an increase in the rate of marital breakdown, and on the relevance of the law to these matters. Is the liberalisation of the divorce laws a factor in increasing the rate of marital breakdown, or is increase attributable more to social (as distinct from legal) change?

It is of course true (as a Government consultation paper on divorce reform[15] put it in 1993) that no statute, however "cleverly and carefully drafted can make two people love each other, like and respect each other, help, understand and be tolerant of each other or force them to live together in peace and harmony"; and the days when the courts made orders requiring one spouse to return to the

---

[11] *Facing the Future. A Discussion Paper on the Ground for Divorce* (Law Com. No. 170 (1988)), App. A; (1994) 24 *Social Trends* Table 2.14. See for an up-to-date analysis, J. Haskey, "The proportion of married couples who divorce . . ." (1996) 83 *Population Trends* 25.

[12] See generally C. Gibson, "Changing Family Patterns in England and Wales" in *Cross Currents* (S.N. Katz, J. Eekelaar, and M. Maclean ed., 2000), pp. 43–46. In 1999 there were 144,556 divorces in England and Wales, compared with an average of 160,000 in the years 1991–1995: Gibson, *op. cit.* Table 2.4; *Marriage and Divorce Statistics 1999*, Table 4.20.

[13] It appears that of all European Community states only Denmark has a higher divorce rate than the United Kingdom: (1993) 23 *Social Trends* Table 2.15.

[14] See E. Ferri, *Step-children: a national study* (1984); A.J. Cherlin, *Marriage, Divorce, Remarriage* (1991). The number of children under 16 involved in a parental divorce fell from more than 175,000 in 1993 to 147,721 in 1999: *Marriage and Divorce Statistics 1999*, Table 4.27.

[15] *Looking to the future: Mediation and the Ground for Divorce* (Cm. 2424, para.3.4).

other and render conjugal services[16] have long since gone. And it is equally true—to quote the 1993 Consultation Paper[17] again that:—

> "It is pointless, and harmful, not to recognise that many marriages break down. The causes for this lie deep in the fabric of society. Even if it were thought desirable, the ability of the Government to influence family relationships at this level is limited. Certainly, changing the divorce law cannot save . . . marriages."

But this may be thought to confuse two issues. Whether or not it is thought that the law can identify particular marriages which can be "saved",[18] it has been argued that the law does exercise a general influence on attitudes, and that the ready availability of divorce contributes to the growth of "a habit of mind in the people"[19] and thus[20] does play a part in weakening the security of marriage. In this view, the ready availability of divorce leads to an increasing disposition to regard divorce, not as the last resort, but as the obvious way out when things begin to go wrong,[21] and so (it is argued) the law does have some influence in establishing standards and modes of behaviour.[22] In particular, it has been claimed that for Parliament to *change* the law by statute inevitably conveys a certain message about what is, and what is not, acceptable.[23]

---

[16] By means of the decree of Restitution of Conjugal Rights (at one time enforceable by imprisonment: Ecclesiastical Courts Act 1813). See n.6, above.

[17] para. 1.3

[18] The desirability of identifying marriages capable of being saved was a consistent theme in the debates on the Family Law Act 1996; and the "general principles" underlying the Family Law Act 1996 emphasise the desirability of taking all practicable steps to save a marriage which may have broken down: F.L.A., s.1; see further below.

[19] See the dissenting report by the Archbishop of York, Sir William Anson, and Sir Lewis Dibdin to the Gorell Commission Report (Cd. 6478 (1912)), p. 185. A not dissimilar view is expressed by Deech (1990) 106 *L.Q.R.* 229 at 242: "Any increase in the divorce rate results in increased familiarity with divorce and its effects as a solution to marital problems and increased willingness to use it and to make legislative provision for its aftermath."

[20] An eloquent summary of arguments derived from Hume and Paley was given by Lord Stowell in a frequently quoted passage:

> "the general happiness of the married life is secured by its indissolubility. When people understand that they must live together, except for a very few reasons known to the law, they learn to soften by mutual accommodation that yoke which they know they cannot shake off, they become good husbands and good wives from the necessity of remaining husbands and wives . . . If it were once understood that upon mutual disgust married persons might be legally separated, many couples who now pass through the world with mutual comfort, with attention to their common offspring, and to the moral order of civil society, might have been at this moment living in a state of mutual unkindness, in a state of estrangement from their common offspring, and in a state of the most licentious and unreserved immorality . . . The happiness of some individuals must be sacrificed to the greater and more general good": *Evans v. Evans* (1790) 1 Hag. Con. 35 at 36–37.

[21] *Royal Commission on Marriage and Divorce* (Chairman: Lord Morton of Henryton) (Cmd. 9678 (1956)), para. 47.

[22] See A. Allott, *The Limits of Law* (1980), particularly at pp. 168–174 for the view that "the availability of a possibility which was previously unthinkable or not thought about transforms the psychology of the subjects as well as the legal possibilities. Their expectations and tolerances alter." (p. 173).

[23] See *Official Report* H.L. February 29, 1996, col. 1638, *per* Baroness Young: "Law influences behaviour and it sends out a very clear message. There would be no point in legislating at all if the law did not influence behaviour . . . We know from recent experience in the fields of gender,

These considerations have all influenced the development of English law over the years; and some knowledge of the evolution of the law is necessary both to understand the modern law, and to be in a position to evaluate arguments of policy about the law's objectives and its success in attaining them.

Part III of this Chapter therefore summarises the evolution of the law from the enactment of the Matrimonial Causes Act 1857 down to the enactment of the Divorce Reform Act 1969 (which purported to make divorce available on the sole ground that the marriage had irretrievably broke down). Part IV deals with the divorce process under the 1969 Act. Part V deals with the decision to legislate for further reform of the law in the Family Law Act; and with the consequences of the Blair Government's decision announced in January 2001[24] to ask Parliament to repeal the relevant provisions of that Act.

III. THE EVOLUTION OF THE DIVORCE LAW 1857–1969[25]

The doctrine of the matrimonial offence

11–004 Until 1857 no English court had the power to grant a degree of divorce terminating a valid marriage. The ecclesiastical courts had jurisdiction to annul marriages; and they also had jurisdiction to grant decrees of divorce *a mensa et thoro* (which relieved the parties of the duty to cohabit, but did not permit either party to remarry). The only way in which a spouse could obtain the freedom to remarry was by obtaining a private Act of Parliament (having first obtained a divorce *a mensa et thoro* from the ecclesiastical court, and a judgment awarding damages for adultery from the common law courts or providing good reason for failing to do so).[26]

---

of race and of disability . . . that [the law] has not only influenced behaviour, it has also profoundly influenced the culture of our time."

[24] See below. An announcement that implementation was to be deferred had been made on June 17, 1999.

[25] R. Phillips, *Putting Asunder, A History of Divorce in Western Society* (1988) is a detailed, scholarly and comprehensive comparative study of marriage breakdown; whilst L. Stone, *Road to Divorce, England 1530–1987* (1990) presents a historian's account of the response to marital breakdown in this country (and the same author's *Broken Lives, Separation and Divorce in England 1660–1857* (1993) makes illuminating use of case studies to give a picture of divorce before the introduction of judicial divorce in 1857). O. R. McGregor's *Divorce in England, a Centenary Study* (1957) is a work containing much statistical, demographic and historical material of great value by a deeply learned social historian who does not conceal his passionate commitment to reform of the law and impatience with those taking a different view. M. A. Glendon, *State Law and Family: Family Law in Transition in the United States and Western Europe* (1987) contains many illuminating insights. S. M. Cretney, *Law, Law Reform and the Family* (1998) Chap. 2 contains an account, drawing on archival material of the background to the enactment of the Divorce Reform Act 1969.

[26] A full historical account of the private bill procedure is given in the First Report of the Commissioners into the Law of Divorce (1853) ("the Campbell Commission"); and see L. Stone, *Road to Divorce, England 1530–1987* (1990), Chap. 10; and the case studies in L. Stone, *Broken Lives, Separation and Divorce in England 1660–1857* (1993). Historical research has cast fresh light on the realities of the divorce process, and undermined confidence in the accuracy of much previously accepted material: see A. Horstmann, *Victorian Divorce* (1985); S. Anderson, "Legislative Divorce—Law for the Aristocracy" in Rubin and Sugarman, *Law, Economy and Society, Essays in the History of English Law 1750–1914* (1984); and S. Wolfram, "Divorce in England" 1700–1857 (1985) 5 Ox. J.L.S. 155.

The Matrimonial Causes Act 1857, passed in part as a consequence of the rationalisation of the structure of the courts dealing with probate and in part as a response to criticism of the cost and delay of the private Act procedure,[27] created[28] the Court for Divorce and Matrimonial Causes, and conferred on that court jurisdiction to grant decrees of dissolution of marriage, nullity, etc. But the 1857 Act did not change the underlying principles on which divorce had been granted under the Parlimentary procedure.[29] These were:

(a) the only ground upon which divorce could be obtained was the respondent's adultery;
(b) the petitioner had to show that he or she was free from guilt;
(c) the court had to be satisfied that there was no connivance or collusion between parties seeking to escape from the solemn obligations of matrimony.

Divorce was thus a legal remedy available to an injured and legally guiltless petitioner who could establish that the respondent had committed the most serious of matrimonial offences, adultery.[30]

Exclusive reliance on adultery[31] as the ground for divorce was never universally accepted[32] and came under increasing attack over the years,[33] but reform was delayed until 1937. The Matrimonial Causes Act of that year (often known as A.P. Herbert's Act[34]) extended the grounds for divorce and provided that either spouse could petition for divorce on the ground of the other's adultery,

---

[27] Compare the discussion in Wolfram (1985) and Anderson (1984) (*op. cit.* above) with L. Stone, *Road to Divorce, England 1530–1987* (1990), pp. 326–7: some persons following "fairly lowly occupations" (*e.g.* commercial traveller, schoolteacher, slate merchant and a cabinet maker) were able to divorce, but it is suggested that they would need to have been in very comfortable circumstances to afford the costs involved.

[28] s.6.

[29] See App. 5, pp. 102–4, of the *Report of Committee on One-Parent Families* (Cmnd. 5629, (1974)).

[30] Judicial separation was seen as the appropriate relief in cases of cruelty. Moreover, a wife petitioner for divorce could not rely solely on adultery, but had to show either incestuous adultery; adultery and bigamy; rape, sodomy or bestiality; or adultery with cruelty, or adultery and desertion for at least two years. After 1884, failure to comply with a decree of Restitution of Conjugal Rights was treated as statutory desertion, so that a wife who was able to establish adultery could obtain a divorce immediately provided the husband failed to comply with a decree of Restitution: M.C.A. 1884, s.5. It was not until the Matrimonial Causes Act 1923 that a wife was given the right to petition on the ground of adultery alone.

[31] The reasons for exclusive reliance on physical infidelity as the ground for divorce can be summarised: (a) It followed the historical precedent of the private divorce Acts, the justification for which was originally to prevent illegitimate children being foisted on "the unhappy husband whose bed had been violated." (*Mr Lewkenor's Case*, 13 *State Trials* 1308); and (b) Scriptural justification for divorce was usually based on adultery. It was also thought by some, until well into the 20th century, that adultery was regarded with particular opprobrium by public opinion.

[32] See Milton, *The Doctrine and Discipline of Divorce* (Everyman ed.), p. 276 who thought that the canon law should regard spiritual and civil companionship rather than carnal coupling as the true basis of marriage: " . . . he who affirms adultery to be the highest breach, affirms the bed to be the highest end of marriage, which is in truth a gross and boorish opinion. how common soever, so far from the countenance of scripture, as from the light of all clean philosophy or civil nature."

[33] Notably by the Gorell Commission (Cd. 6478, 1912)) whose report was ultimately the basis of the Matrimonial Causes Act 1937, and in some ways foreshadowed the modern concept of breakdown.

[34] See A.P. Herbert, *The Ayes have it* (1937).

cruelty, desertion for a continuous period of three years or more, or incurable insanity. But the Act still conceptualised divorce as a remedy for a legal wrong: to allow divorce by consent would (so it was thought) destroy the institution of marriage and the sanctity of family life; and accordingly the posture of a petitioner for divorce still had to be that of an innocent party willing to perform his or her side of the contract, neither conniving at nor condoning the wickedness of the other party, and above all seeking no deal or understanding with him or her to let the divorce through.[35] In one respect the 1937 Act marked the acceptance of an important change of principle: the Act[36] permitted a petitioner to obtain a divorce on the ground that the respondent was incurably of unsound mind and had been continuously under care and treatment for a period of at least five years preceding the presentation of the petition. Divorce was thus to be available because of misfortune, and a serious inroad[37] had thereby been made into the offence principle.

The decline of the matrimonial offence doctrine

11–005 After 1937, the retention of the matrimonial offence as the basis of divorce law came under increasing attack. This was for three main reasons.

First, although it was a fundamental principle that divorce was so much a matter in which the community was vitally concerned that the parties' mutual agreement was not a basis upon which it could be allowed, and divorce procedure was based on the assumption that the litigation was contentious, the facts were that over 90 per cent of petitions were undefended. It seemed quite clear that in many cases the parties had agreed on divorce.[38]

Secondly, as we have seen, the 1937 Act allowed divorce for misfortune; and, in 1964, decisions of the House of Lords[39] established that a respondent who was in no way morally blameworthy might nonetheless be divorced for the matrimonial offence of cruelty. Increasingly the crucial question seemed to be simply whether the petitioner could reasonably be expected to endure the marital situation.

Finally, although it usually remained necessary to prove that the respondent had committed a matrimonial offence, it ceased to be essential to establish that the petitioner was an aggrieved and innocent victim. This was because statute[40] made collusion into a discretionary[41] rather than an absolute bar, and restricted

---

[35] Sir Harold S. Kent, *In On The Act* (1979), pp. 78–84 which contains much interesting background.

[36] s.2.

[37] *Field of Choice*, para. 21.

[38] And might even have agreed to provide false evidence of adultery for this purpose, as in the so-called "Hotel Cases" where the husband would arrange to provide evidence of adultery (possibly never committed) sometimes with the assistance of a professional companion: see A.P. Herbert, *Holy Deadlock* (1934).

[39] *Gollins v. Gollins* [1964] A.C. 644; *Williams v. Williams* [1964] A.C. 698.

[40] Matrimonial Causes Act 1963, s.4.

[41] *i.e.* the court was not obliged to grant a divorce, but might do so if on consideration of all the circumstances it considered it to be right to do so. In effect, the fact that both parties were agreed in wanting a divorce was no longer a sufficient reason for preventing their obtaining one (always provided that there was acceptable evidence of the commission of a matrimonial offence): see *Nash v. Nash* [1965] P. 266; *M. v. M.* [1967] P. 313; *Gosling V Gosling* [1968] P. 1.

the scope of the bar of condonation.[42] Where the court did have a discretion to refuse a divorce because the petitioner had committed a matrimonial offence, it became increasingly accepted that no public interest was served by keeping legally in existence a marriage which had in fact broken down.[43] If full and frank disclosure were made,[44] the court's discretion would normally be exercised and a divorce granted.[45] Increasingly, in these circumstances, a decree was awarded to both parties and in consequence "the guilty/innocent dichotomy" became blurred.[46]

The post Second World War campaign for reform and the enactment of the Divorce Reform Act 1969

11–006 In spite of these developments, the law still caused hardship. A common situation was that of the couple who had lived together as man and wife for many years but were unable to marry because a prior marriage could not be dissolved. It did not matter that this marriage had manifestly broken down beyond any hope of retrieval: if the "innocent" partner refused to petition for divorce, and abstained from committing any matrimonial offence, the marriage would remain legally in existence until death.

The Second World War inevitably imposed a great strain on many family relationships. There were hasty weddings, separations—lasting sometimes for years—and all the tensions of life in an uncertain, dangerous and deprived world. There was a divorce explosion. In 1939 there had been 8,517 divorces, but by 1947 the number had soared to an unprecedented 47,041.[47] Yet there remained a large and increasingly vocal number of people who wanted to escape from a relationship which had become meaningless to them but who were unable to do so because their legal spouse refused to petition for divorce and could not be shown to have committed a matrimonial offence. Particular hardship was caused to people who had formed what came to be called "stable illicit unions" and who wanted to marry, not least to legitimize their children. Not surprisingly, there was mounting pressure to reform the divorce law so that marriages which had ceased to exist in fact could be terminated in law.

In 1951, after a Bill which would have permitted divorce after seven years' separation had been given a Second Reading in the House of Commons, a Royal

---

[42] Matrimonial Causes Act 1963, ss. 1 and 2, containing the so-called "kiss and make-up" provisions designed to facilitate reconciliation.

[43] *Blunt v. Blunt* [1943] A.C. 517; *Masarati v. Masarati* [1969] 1 W.L.R. 393; *cf. Bull v. Bull* [1968] P. 618.

[44] A respondent seeking the exercise of discretion had to file a "discretion statement"; it was the duty of the petitioner's solicitor to make clear to his client the duty of full disclosure; see *Pearson v. Pearson* [1971] P. 16. This rule sometimes led to absurd and embarrassing results: *Barnacle v. Barnacle* [1948] P. 257, where the petitioner had not understood the meaning of adultery, and the trial judge gave examples of misunderstanding on other occasions: "it is not adultery if she is over 50." . . . "I did not think it was adultery during the daytime"; "I thought it meant getting a girl into trouble": "I thought it meant drinking with men in public houses" (at. 261).

[45] *per* Sachs L.J., *Masarati v. Masarati (above)* at 396.

[46] *Field of Choice*, para. 21.

[47] *Royal Commission on Marriage and Divorce, Report 1951–1955* (Cmd. 9678 (1956)), Table 1.

Commission was appointed[48] to inquire into the law. However, the Commissioners were divided and did not accept the case for radical reform—indeed, all except one[49] of the 19 members favoured the retention of the matrimonial offence principle while nine members opposed breakdown of marriage even as an alternative ground for divorce. The proper function of the law (it was said) was to give relief where a wrong had been done, not to provide a dignified and honourable means of release from a broken marriage. The publication of the Royal Commission Report in 1956 was thus a check to hopes for speedy reform; but the campaign nonetheless continued. In 1963 Mr Leo Abse presented a bill which amongst other things would have allowed divorce after seven years' separation. Although this Bill did not become law, the Archbishop of Canterbury announced in the House of Lords debate[50] that he had decided to appoint a Committee to investigate the formulation of a principle of breakdown of marriage. The report of this group, *Putting Asunder*, was published in 1966, and was the catalyst for the divorce reforms effected by the Divorce Reform Act 1969.[51]

Irretrievable breakdown: the compromise

11–007 *Putting Asunder* favoured, as the lesser of two evils,[52] the substitution of the doctrine of breakdown for that of the matrimonial offence; and the Archbishop's Committee accepted that a divorce decree should be seen simply as a judicial recognition of this state of affairs, with a consequent redefinition of status.[53] But breakdown was not to be established on the mere say-so of the parties. Rather, the court would in every case have to carry out a detailed inquest into the alleged fact and causes of the "death" of a marriage relationship. It would have to be made possible for the court to inquire effectively into what attempts at reconciliation had been made, into the feasibility of further attempts, into the acts, events, and circumstances alleged to have destroyed the marriage, into the truth of statements made (especially in uncontested cases), and into all matters bearing upon the determination of the public interest.[54]

The principle that divorce should be based on irretrievable breakdown came to be accepted by other church bodies; and it has been said[55] that the former Christian lobby against divorce was effectively silenced or converted.

The Lord Chancellor, Lord Gardiner, was able[56] to refer *Putting Asunder* to the recently established Law Commission (some of whose members had been active supporters of the move for reform[57]). The Law Commission's report, *The*

[48] The Royal Commission on Marriage and Divorce under the chairmanship of Lord Morton of Henryton (a Lord of Appeal in Ordinary).
[49] Lord Walker.
[50] *Hansard* (H.L.), Vol. 250, col. 1547.
[51] S.M. Cretney, *Law, Law Reform and the Family* (1998), Chap. 2 contains a full account.
[52] *Putting Asunder*, para. 68.
[53] *ibid.* para. 66.
[54] *ibid.* para. 84.
[55] L. Stone, *Road to Divorce, England 1530–1987* (1990), p. 406.
[56] Under Law Commissions Act 1965, s. 3(1)(e).
[57] See S.M. Cretney, *Law, Law Reform and the Family* (1998), p. 57. The Commission had included matrimonial law in its *First Programme of Law Reform* (Law Com. No. 1, 1965), Item X.

Field of Choice, published in 1966, took, as its starting point, the view that[58] a good divorce law should seek "(i) To buttress, rather than to undermine, the stability of marriage; and (ii) When, regrettably, a marriage has irretrievably broken down, to enable the empty legal shell to be destroyed with the maximum fairness, and the minimum bitterness, distress and humiliation." The Commission concluded that the offence-based divorce law failed to satisfy these criteria[59]:—

> "It does not do all it might to aid the stability of marriage, but tends rather to discourage attempts at reconciliation. It does not enable all dead marriages to be buried, and those that it buries are not always interred with the minimum of distress and humiliation. It does not achieve the maximum possible fairness to all concerned, for a spouse may be branded as guilty in law though not the more blameworthy in fact. The insistence on guilt and innocence tends to embitter relationships, with particularly damaging results to the children, rather than to promote future harmony. Its principles are widely regarded as hypocritical."

The Law Commission therefore favoured reform: but it did not accept the proposal made by the Archbishop's group that divorce should be available only after a full inquest into the alleged breakdown. The Law Commission thought that such an inquiry would be humiliating and distressing to the parties; and that it would be impracticable, in the absence of a vast increase in expenditure of money and human resources,[60] to have a full inquiry in every case.

The Law Commission therefore put forward various options which, it considered, provided a practicable basis for reform.[61] Discussions took place between representatives of the Law Commission and the Archbishop's group,[62] and agreement was reached on the principles ultimately embodied in the Divorce Reform Act 1969:—

(i) the basic principle was to be that breakdown should be the sole ground for divorce; but—
(ii) breakdown should not be the subject of a detailed inquest by the court; instead it should be inferred, either from one of several specified facts akin to the traditional matrimonial offences, or from the fact that the parties had lived apart for two years if the respondent consented or five years if there were no consent.

In 1967, Mr William Wilson obtained a favourable place in the ballot for

---

[58] *Reform of the Grounds of Divorce: The Field of Choice* (Law Com. No. 6 (1966) (subsequently cited as *Field of Choice*), para. 15.
[59] *ibid.* paras 23–28.
[60] *ibid.* para. 2.
[61] *ibid.* paras 54–55.
[62] For a detailed account of the negotiations, see S.M. Cretney, *Law, Law Reform and the Family* (1998), pp. 63–69. See also *Third Annual Report of the Law Commission*, Appendix, where the agreement between the two bodies is set out.

private member's bills; and the Government—whilst refusing to commit itself to any view on the policy of the Bill—made drafting facilities available to the Bill's cross-party sponsors. The Wilson Bill failed for lack of parliamentary time; but in 1968 Mr Alec Jones drew a place in the ballot and took over the Bill. On this occasion, the Government—whilst still maintaining its position of neutrality on the merits of the Bill—agreed to make parliamentary time available; and the Bill eventually received Royal Assent on October 22, 1969.[63]

IV. DIVORCE UNDER THE DIVORCE REFORM ACT 1969[64]

11–008 The Divorce Reform Act 1969[65] provided that "the sole ground on which a petition for divorce may be presented to the court . . . shall be that the marriage has broken down irretrievably"; and (as we have seen) the Act was presented to Parliament as if irretrievable breakdown were the basis on which divorce would be granted. But for three reasons the reality was very different.

First the provision asserting that breakdown was to be the ground for divorce was immediately followed by a statement that the court should not hold the marriage to have broken down irretrievably unless the petitioner satisfied it of one or more of five "facts".[66] These facts are:—

(a) that the respondent had committed adultery and the petitioner found it intolerable to live with the respondent;
(b) that the respondent had behaved in such a way that the petitioner could not reasonably be expected to live with the respondent;
(c) that the respondent had deserted the petitioner for a continuous period of at least two years immediately preceding the presentation of the petition;
(d) that the parties to the marriage had lived apart for a continuous period of at least two years immediately preceding the presentation of the petition and the respondent consented to a decree being granted;

---

[63] The Parliamentary debates were protracted, and the organisational skills of Mr Leo Abse (who effectively managed the Bill's passage) made a significant contribution to the evental success. Part of the price which opponents of the Bill exacted was that it should not be brought into force until January 1, 1971, to enable the Government to introduce legislation intended to protect the financial position of divorced spouses: see further Chap. 14, below. For a detailed account of the Parliamentary debates see B.H. Lee, *Divorce Reform in England* (1974), Pt 3.

[64] The act was consolidated in the M.C.A. 1973 and subsequent references are to that Act unless otherwise stated.

[65] s.1 The Act also retained the bar introduced in 1937 on starting divorce proceedings within the early years of marriage.

[66] M.C.A. 1973, s.1(2). The provisions of ss. 1–7 of this Act (and other provisions dealing with the ground for divorce) would have been repealed by F.L.A. 1996, Sched 10; but (as explained above) those provisions of the 1996 Act are not to be brought into force and the provisions of M.C.A. 1973, s.1(2) continue in force. There is a substantial body of case-law on the interpretation of the "facts"; and although this will, for the reasons set out below, usually be largely irrelevant a brief account is given below.

(e) that the parties to the marriage had lived apart for a continuous period of at least five years immediately preceding the presentation of the petition.

Almost inevitably, there was a tendency to see these facts (rather than the breakdown of the marriage) as the true grounds for divorce. The real question therefore seemed to be whether the petitioner could establish[67] that the respondent had committed adultery[68] or been guilty of what was (inaccurately[69]) usually called "unreasonable behaviour", or that the parties had lived apart"[70] for the requisite period. It was insufficient to establish that the marriage had broken down irretrievably. For example:—

In *Buffery v. Buffery*[71] the parties had been married for more than 20 years. They had grown apart, had nothing in common, and could not communicate. The Court of Appeal accepted that the marriage had irretrievably broken down, and also accepted that the husband had been insensitive about money matters. But this was insufficient to establish the "behaviour" fact and, accordingly, a decree could not be granted.

Secondly, the Act provided that if a "fact" were proved the court was to grant a divorce decree "unless it is satisfied on all the evidence that the marriage has not broken down irretrievably".[72] The petitioner does not have to show that the marriage had broken down *by reason* of the "fact" in question; and it was virtually impossible for one spouse to prove that the marriage had not broken down irretrievably if the other persisted in the claim that it had.[73]

---

[67] After the introduction of the so-called "special procedure" (see below) the great majority of divorce petitions would be processed without either party having to answer questions about the allegations made; and the opportunity to present a false case cannot always have been resisted: see, *e.g. Callaghan v. Hanson-Fox* [1991] 2 F.L.R. 519 (where a husband claimed, after his wife's death, that he had been living with his wife at the date of her petition based on living apart and had continued to so to the date of her death) and (for a remarkable example of how fraud may be perpetrated) *Moynihan v. Moynihan (No. 1 and 2)* [1997] 1 F.L.R. 52.

[68] And that the petitioner found it intolerable to live with the respondent.

[69] Because it was not the behaviour but the expectation of cohabitation which had to be intolerable: see below.

[70] Petitions based on desertion—a highly technical concept: see the 5th edition of this work, pp. 116–122—were rare. But the courts gave a technical interpretation even to the apparently simple concept of living apart: see below.

[71] [1988] 2 F.L.R. 365; and see for another example *Richards v. Richards* [1972] 1 W.L.R. 1073

[72] M.C.A. 1973, s.1(4). In *Cotterell v. Cotterell* (1998) 3 F.C.R. 199, CA, the Court of Appeal held that the court should always first consider whether the marriage has irretrievably broken down and only then go on to consider what it regarded as the subsidiary question of whether one of the "facts" had been made out but this decision stands on its own and is difficult to reconcile with the language of the statute.

[73] Burgoyne, Ormrod and Richards, *Divorce Matters* (1987). pp. 57–58. As the then President of the Probate, Divorce and Admiralty Division, Lord Simon of Glaisdale, put it (in the Riddell Lecture, reprinted in the 11th edition of *Rayden on Divorce,* at p. 3233) "If even one of the parties adamantly refuses to consider living with the other again, the court is in no position to gainsay him or her. The court cannot say, 'I have seen your wife in the witnessbox. She wants your marriage to continue. She seems a most charming and blameless person. I cannot believe that the marriage has really broken down.' The husband has only to reply, 'I'm very sorry; it's not what you think about her that matters, it's what I think. I am not prepared to live with her any more.' He may add for good measure, 'What is more, there is another person with whom I

11–009 Thirdly, the creation of the so-called special procedure effectively transformed the decision whether a marriage should be ended from a judicial process (involving, it was said, judicial care as distinct from rubber stamping[74]) into what seemed to be an administrative act, dependent solely on the filing of the appropriate forms correctly completed[75] and, in particular, the filing of a petition alleging one or more of the "facts" prescribed by the legislation. In outward form English law still attempted to emphasise the institutional solemnity of marriage by insisting that it could be ended only by a judicial pronouncement, but the reality is that[76] most of the procedural steps on the path to the grant of a decree had become administrative and automatic, albeit complex.[77]

It is not surprising that lay people involved in divorce found the process very different from the "careful and dignified proceedings" envisaged by the Denning Committee in 1947.[78] Even for members of the Royal Family, the legal procedure obtained in dissolving a supposedly life-long union is routine:—

---

prefer to live.' The court may think that the husband is behaving wrongly and unreasonably; but how is it to hold that the marriage has not nevertheless irretrievably broken down?" However, it has held that a solicitor should not file a petition stating that the marriage has broken down irretrievably unless and until the client gives express instructions to that effect: *R v. R (Divorce: Stay of Proceedings)* [1994] 2 F.L.R. 1036, 1038, *per* Ewbank J.

[74] The "special procedure" only applied to undefended divorces, but there was strong pressure not to defend a petition. First (as has been officially recognised) the "court itself discourages defended divorce not only because of the futility of trying a contention by one party that the marriage has not broken down despite the other party's contention that it has, but also because of the emotional and financial demands that it makes upon the parties themselves and the possible harmful consequences for the children of the family: *Report of the Matrimonial Causes Procedure Commitee* (Chairman, Mrs Justice Booth, D.B.E.) (1985), para 2.16. Secondly, notwithstanding judicial criticism (see the comments of Sir J. Donaldson, M.R., *McCarney v. McCarney* [1986] 1 F.L.R. 312) public funding is not normally available simply to defend a divorce petition in cases in which the marriage appears to have broken down irretrievably. Thirdly, most solicitors would discourage a client from seeking to defend a petition: see Davis and Murch, *Grounds for Divorce* (1988), Chap. 7.

[75] *Santos v. Santos* [1972] Fam. 247 at 262. The petition and other pleadings are considered by a district judge who decides whether the petitioner has made out a case and is entitled to a decree: it is the district judge's duty to be satisfied about the essentials of the petition and proof of its contents. In principle the district judge carries out in his chambers the same function of inquiry once performed by the judge (even although in practice the district judge's ability to perform this function is tempered by the fact that only affidavit evidence is available).

[76] *Pounds v. Pounds* [1994] 1 F.L.R. 775 at 778, *per* Waite L.J.

[77] The procedure was summarised by Waite L.J. in *Pounds v. Pounds* [1994] 1 F.L.R. 775 at 776: "Following presentation of the petition, the petitioner's solicitor lodge an application for directions for trial together with a standard affidavit in the form required to verify the particular ground alleged in the petition. In routine cases . . . the [district judge] gives directions for trial by entering the cause in the special procedure list and thereafter considers the evidence filed by the petitioner. If he is satisfied that the petitioner has sufficiently proved the contents of the petition and is entitled to the decree sought and any costs prayed for, he will make and file a certificate to that effect. The court then sends notification to the parties of the date, time and place fixed for the pronouncement of the decree nisi. The parties are also told that their attendance at the pronouncement of decree is not necessary. The actual process of pronouncement of the decree has become reduced to a very brief ceremony of a purely formal character in which decrees are listed together in batches for a collective mention in open court before a judge who speaks (or nods) his assent. The right to a decree absolute six weeks thereafter is automatic . . . [T]he sole truly judicial function in the entire process is that of the [district judge] when granting his certificate. Everything that follows is automatic and administrative, and the open court pronouncement of the decree is pure formality, to which the pronouncing judge . . . has no option but to consent . . ."

[78] Second Interim Report of the *Committee on Procedure in Matrimonial Causes* (Cmd. 6945, 1946), para. 4.

"The standard procedure as it operated in Court Three of Somerset House on the morning of 23 April 1992 was documented by the national newspapers. Judge Angel took four minutes to pronounce 30 decrees nisi—the first of which formally ended the marriage of Princess Anne and Captain Phillips. The clerk gave proper dignity to the proceedings, reading the Princess's full name, title and honours; meanwhile the petitioner was carrying out royal engagements in Hampshire. All citizens, be they patricians or plebeians, are swept quickly and invisibly through the common process of dissolution. The state's direct and visual regulatory capacity has all but disappeared."[79]

Ground for divorce irrelevant?

11–010 The Divorce Reform Act was passed by Parliament on the basis that the court would consider petitions with care—so that, for example, the court would need to be satisfied[80] not only that the respondent had committed adultery, but that there was evidence to justify a finding that this was "so offensive and deeply wounding . . . that any further married life" with the respondent would be intolerable.[81] It may well have been difficult for a court to carry out any meaningful inquiry into this question; but at least there was the possibility that it would do so. In some cases at least the petitioner might have been questioned, and it is even possible that occasionally a possibility of reconciliation might have emerged.[82] But under the special procedure the petitioner merely has to write the word "yes" on the form which asked whether he or she finds it intolerable to live with the other spouse; and it is difficult to envisage that anyone who had gone so far as to start divorce proceedings would do otherwise. Again, the introduction of the special procedure makes a mockery of the law's traditional insistence that adultery is a serious matrimonial offence which accordingly requires a high standard or proof.[83] The prescribed form merely asks the respondent whether the adultery was admitted, and an affirmative answer constituted sufficient proof.[84] It was no longer necessary to name the third party allegedly involved, even if the petitioner knew his or her identity.[85]

The result seems to be that a person seeking advice on divorce will be advised that the marriage can be quickly dissolved[86] provided that the other party is not

---

[79] C.S. Gibson, *Dissolving Wedlock* (1994), p. 2.

[80] In the case of petitions founded on M.C.A. 1973, s.1(2) (a).

[81] *per* Lord Stow Hill, *Official Report* H.L. Vol. 303, col. 296.

[82] The legislation gave the court power to adjourn the proceedings to enable reconciliation attempts to be made: M.C.A. 1973, s.6(2).

[83] See, *e.g. Bastable v. Bastable* [1968] 1 W.L.R. 1684.

[84] *Report of the Matrimonial Causes Procedure Committee* (Chairman: the Hon. Mrs Justice Booth DBE) (1985), para. 2.15.

[85] F.P.R. 1991 (S.1. 1991 No. 1247), r. 2.7.

[86] "A solicitor will ask a wife seeking divorce whether, over the life of the marriage, she can think of occasions on which her husband has been difficult. It is a pretty unusual marriage which has not had a fair number of difficult moments over 10 years. The solicitor will then crystallise and distil those examples into 10 or so incidents which, when put together, read in a lurid way, as if the marriage was especially wicked and abnormal, whereas in fact it was probably very normal". (Mr Donald Anderson M.P., *Official Report* H.C. April 24, 1996, col. 477.)

obstructive; whilst the other party will be told that—however unjustly, as he or she might think—sooner or later there would be a divorce; and that it was probably best to accept that fact. The real issues came to be seen to be the financial consequences of the divorce and the arrangements to be made about the children; and to these matters the ground for divorce was largely irrelevant. Indeed, it seems that sometimes serious discussion about financial matters does not take place until the decree of divorce has been granted, if only because the court had no power to make binding orders unless and until a decree had been granted.

In this way the special procedure transformed the whole basis of divorce almost without anyone noticing the fact. Whereas an allegation of adultery might once have been bitterly contested—not only to avoid the stigma of being branded the "guilty party" in the divorce courts but also because such a finding would for long have debarred a wife from entitlement to financial provision and might even have resulted in her being denied the right to care for the childen—the law now seems to be unconcerned about such matters.

No divorce proceedings to be started in first year of marriage

11–011 Between 1937[87] and 1984 no petition for divorce could be presented before the expiration of the period of three years from the date of marriage unless it was shown that the case was one of exceptional hardship suffered by the petitioner or one of exceptional depravity on the part of the respondent. In 1984[88] Parliament accepted the Law Commission's view[89] that this provision was unsatisfactory not least because it involved the making of distressing and humiliating allegations in more than a thousand cases each year. But it was thought desirable to retain some restriction on the availability of divorce early in marriage so as to assert (symbolically at least) the state's interest in upholding the stability and dignity of marriage, and to prevent divorce being apparently available within days of the marriage ceremony.[90] The legislation was therefore amended to provide[91] that no petition for divorce shall be presented to the court before the expiration of the period of one year from the date of the marriage.

This rule prevents *divorce* proceedings being *started* within one year of the marriage. The rule does not affect the ground upon which divorce may be obtained. It is specifically provided[92] that the rule does not prevent the presentation of a petition based on matters[93] which occurred before the expiration of the year. Nor does the rule prevent other proceedings (such as a petition for a decree of judicial separation,[94] an application for a financial order based on failure to provide maintenance,[95] an application under the Children Act 1989 for orders

[87] Matrimonial Causes Act 1937, s.1.
[88] Matrimonial and Family Proceedings Act 1984, s.1.
[89] *Time Restrictions on Presentation of Divorce and Nullity Petitions* (1982) Law Com. No. 116.
[90] For the background to the 1984 legislation, see the fifth edition of this work at pp. 95–97.
[91] M.C.A. 1973, s.3(1), as substituted by Matrimonial and Family Proceedings Act 1984, s.1.
[92] M.C.A. 1973, s.3(2), as substituted.
[93] For example, the respondent's adultery or behaviour: see below.
[94] See Chap. 12, below.
[95] Under M.C.A. 1973, s.27; see para. 3–024, above.

relating to the upbringing of children,[96] or an application for a non-molestation or for an occupation order relating to the family home[97]) being started to provide legal remedies during the first year of the marriage.

Judicial interpretation of the five "facts"

11–012 Between 1971 (when the Divorce Reform Act 1969 came into force) and 1977 (when the "special procedure" was made available in all[98] undefended divorces the courts gave a considerable amount of guidance on the interpretation of the statutory language describing the "facts" on the basis of which the inference of irretrievable breakdown would be drawn. As explained above, the use of the "special procedure" has in practical terms greatly reduced the value and relevance of this case-law guidance. In the great majority of cases there will be no dispute between the parties—indeed, the Solicitors' Family Law Association *Code of Practice* suggests that the parties and their advisers will often confer in advance about the "facts" to be alleged and the particulars which are to be given—and (although practice may to some extent differ from court to court) it seems that the courts do not usually seek to investigate statements made in a petition which is undefended. Nevertheless, no decree of divorce can be granted unless the court is satisfied that one of the "facts" has been established to its satisfaction,[99] and the hence the practising lawyer still needs to have an understanding of the statutory provisions if only so as to give appropriate advice to the client and to be able to ensure the relevant forms have been completed correctly. Moreover, the law student may find that judicial interpretation of the "facts" remains important in the examination room. For these reasons, a brief[1] account follows.

(a) The respondent has committed adultery and the petitioner finds it intolerable to live with the respondent

11–013 The petitioner must show (i) that the respondent has in fact committed adultery, and (ii) that the petitioner finds it intolerable to live with the respondent.

11–014 *The fact of the respondent's adultery.* Adultery involves voluntary or consensual sexual intercourse between a married person and a person (whether married or unmarried) of the opposite sex not being the other's spouse. In reality, the court[2]has no way of investigating whether uncontested allegations of adultery

---

[96] Children Act 1989, s.10(4), (5); see Part V, below.

[97] Under Family Law Act 1996, Part IV; see Chap. 10, above.

[98] In the absence of special circumstances.

[99] See *e.g. Buffery v. Buffery* [1988] 2 F.L.R. 365.

[1] For a fuller account, reference may be made to the 5th (1990) edition of this book pp. 101–129; whilst a full citation of authorities will be found in the standard practitioner work, *Rayden & Jackson's Law and Practice in Divorce and Family Matters* (17th ed. N. Wall *et al.*, ed., 1997)

[2] If the court's suspicions are aroused, it may refer the matter to the Queen's Proctor (in effect, the office of the Treasury Solicitor) and detailed inquiries will be made in appropriate circumstances: see M.C.A. 1973, s. 8; *Moynihan v. Moynihan (No. 1 and 2)* [1997] 1 F.L.R. 52 at 68.

are true. Although the courts have emphasised the overriding importance of honesty and the fundamental seriousness of the divorce process a petition based on the adultery "fact" will almost invariably, if undefended, lead to a speedy divorce by consent. Perhaps for this reason adultery is the fact relied on in a large proportion (more than a quarter of the total) of divorce petitions.

11–015 *The petitioner finds it intolerable to live with the respondent.* The policy of the Divorce Reform Act was that adultery should be relevant only in so far as it was a symptom of marital breakdown; and the Act was influenced by the philosophy that adultery should "not in itself . . . be regarded as demonstrating breakdown unless the petitioner can in addition satisfy the court that the act of adultery is so offensive and deeply wounding to him or her that any further married life with the respondent is unthinkable".[3] But the legislation does not require the petitioner to allege "that the respondent has committed adultery by reason of which the petitioner finds it intolerable to live with the respondent", and it accordingly fails to achieve that objective:

> In *Cleary v. Cleary and Hutton*[4] the Court of Appeal held that the adultery fact can be established provided the petitioner genuinely finds it intolerable to live with the respondent, even if the adultery has not played any significant part in the breakdown of the marriage.

The fact that there need be no link of this kind could lead to apparently bizarre results;[5] but the Court of Appeal's interpretation gives effect to the plain words of the statute and is consistent with the aim of the legislation that breakdown of marriage should be the sole ground for divorce. Breakdown is not, but adultery is, a justiciable issue.

11–016 *Six months living together a bar.* If one spouse knows that the other has committed adultery, but has continued thereafter to live with him or her for six months or more, a divorce petition cannot be based on that act of adultery.[6] Conversely, if they have lived together for less than six months that fact is to be disregarded "in determining . . . whether the petitioner finds it intolerable to live with the respondent." This was intended to make it clear that a couple could seek a reconciliation without running the risk that by living together for a short period the innocent party would be held to have forgiven the adultery and could thus no longer be held to find living with the respondent intolerable.

---

[3] Lord Stow Hill, *Hansard H.L.* Vol. 303, col. 296.
[4] [1974] 1 W.L.R. 73.
[5] In *Roper v. Roper* [1972] 1 W.L.R. 1314 at 1317, Faulks J. suggested that a wife might even divorce a husband who had committed a single act of adultery because he blew his nose more than she liked.
[6] M.C.A. 1973, s.2(1).

(b) The respondent has behaved in such a way that the petitioner cannot reasonably be expected to live with the respondent.

11–017 This so-called "behaviour" fact is frequently relied on in divorce petitions. In the debates leading up to the Divorce Reform Act 1969 it was accepted that "cruel and intolerable conduct" could "sound the death knell" of a marriage; and that it would be wrong to require the parties to separate for a lengthy period before allowing them to divorce. On the other hand, the need to make allegations of such behaviour seems inconsistent with the policy of enabling marriages which have irretrievably broken down to be dissolved with the "minimum bitterness, distress and humiliation"[7] The rules require a petitioner to give brief particulars of the individual facts relied on,[8] and although good practice[9] suggests that the parties' advisers will confer about what is to be included in the petition, this does not always occur.

Sometimes, it is true, the allegations may be trivial: for example

> In *Livingstone-Stallard v. Livingstone-Stallard*[10] the court had to consider the parties' methods of washing their underwear.
>
> In *Richards v. Richards*[11] it was alleged that the husband never remembered the wife's birthday or wedding anniversary, did not buy her Christmas presents, failed to give her flowers on the birth of their child and failed to notify her parents of the event, refused to take her to the cinema, and refused to dispose of a dog which had caused considerable damage to the matrimonial home.

But for one party to make such allegations may cause the other great distress—particularly if the respondent believes that it is the petitioner who is truly responsible for the breakdown. Sometimes, of course, serious allegations are made. Physical violence (for example, blacking the wife's eye on two occasions and striking her in the face on another[12]) is a common complaint. Petitions may allege such matters as the practice of perversions, the making of excessive sexual demands, or that the husband has abused a child of the family. Sometimes there seems to be an element of mental unbalance on the part of the respondent:

> In *O'Neill v. O'Neill*[13] the husband, a retired airline pilot, had a withdrawn personality and the marriage had never been entirely satisfactory; but the

---

[7] One of the objectives of a good divorce law as stated by the Law Commission in its Report *Reform of the Grounds of Divorce, The Field of Choice* (1966, Cmnd. 3123) para. 17

[8] Family Proceedings Rules 1991, App. 2, para. 1(m).

[9] As laid down in the Solicitors' Family Law Association *Code of Practice.*

[10] [1974] Fam. 47, CA,

[11] [1984] A.C. 174, HL. The case was reported on the issue whether the wife could obtain an interlocutory order excluding the husband from the matrimonial home, and these allegations—described by one judge as "rubbishy"—would perhaps not have sufficed as the basis for a decree on this ground.

[12] *Bergin v. Bergin* [1983] F.L.R. 344.

[13] [1975] 1 W.L.R. 1118.

"last straw" for the wife was that for two years the husband carried out a prolonged renovation programme in the flat which they had bought, and this involved mixing cement on the living room floor, having no door on the lavatory for eight months, and so on.

What has to be established?

11–018 The court needs to be satisfied first, that the respondent has behaved in a certain way; and secondly, that on the basis of such facts as are proved about the respondent's behaviour, the petitioner cannot reasonably be expected to live with him or her[14]. "Behaviour" petitions are more likely than others to be defended; and for this reason, the case law discussing the interpretation of the "behaviour" fact cannot be regarded as entirely academic. The more important doctrinal points may be summarised as follows:

(a) "Unreasonable behaviour" not the test

11–019 The abbreviation "unreasonable behaviour" (although often used) is incorrect, and gives a misleading impression of what is required. As Eekelaar put it[15], it "is not the behaviour that needs to be unreasonable, but the expectation of cohabitation." Thus—

> In *Bannister v. Bannister*[16] the wife's undefended petition alleged that the husband had not taken her out for two years, did not speak to her except when it was unavoidable, stayed away for nights giving her no idea where he was going, and had been living an entirely independent life ignoring her completely. She failed at first instance because the judge considered that the behaviour alleged did not constitute "unreasonable behaviour," but the Court of Appeal allowed the wife's appeal on the ground that the husband's behaviour did make it unreasonable to expect the wife to live with him.

(b) Must be "behaviour"

11–020 The Act requires that the respondent should have "behaved" in such a way that the petitioner cannot reasonably be expected to live with him; and it has been said that "behaviour is something more than a mere state of affairs or a state of mind . . . [it] is action or conduct by the one which affects the other."[17] Thus if an accident or illness rendered a spouse comatose and totally passive (a "cabbage existence") it could be that a petitioner would be unable to rely on the behaviour "fact."[18]

---

[14] *Andrews v. Andrews* [1974] 3 All E.R. 643 at 644.

[15] [1975] A.S.C.L. 188.

[16] (1980) 10 *Fam. Law* 240.

[17] *Katz v. Katz* (above) at p. 960, *per* Sir George Baker P.

[18] So held in *Smith v. Smith* (1973) 118 S.J. 184 (wife suffering from Alzheimer's disease) not followed in *Thurlow v. Thurlow* (above) in so far as it decided that involuntary behaviour caused by disease of the mind could not constitute behaviour for the present purpose.

Yet negative or passive conduct can still constitute "behaviour". For example:

> In *Carter-Fea v. Carter-Fea*[19] the husband was unable to manage his affairs. The wife suffered much stress and unhappiness, and ultimately decided that she could not go on living in a world of fantasy with "unpaid bills, bailiffs at the door, and second mortgages." She was held to be entitled to a decree.

(c) Test objective; but reasonableness judged through eyes of the parties

11–021 The test is objective in so far as the question to be answered is: can the petitioner "reasonably be expected" to live with the respondent? But the court must consider the particular parties to the suit before it, not "ordinary reasonable spouses". The question is:

> ". . . can this petitioner, with his or her character and personality, with his or her faults and other attributes, good and bad, and having regard to his or her behaviour during the marriage reasonably be expected to live with this respondent?"[20]

It seems to follow that mere incompatibility is not sufficient[21]; and that—

> "a violent petitioner may reasonably be expected to live with a violent respondent; a petitioner who is addicted to drink can reasonably be expected to live with a respondent similarly addicted; a taciturn and morose spouse can reasonably be expected to live with a taciturn and morose partner; a flirtatious husband can reasonably be expected to live with a wife who is equally susceptible to the attractions of the other sex; and if each is equally bad, at any rate in similar respects, each can reasonably be expected to live with the other".[22]

The test is what could reasonably be expected of these parties; but the determination of what is "reasonable" in this context would seem to requires the making of value judgments about the nature of marriage and about the obligations and standards of behaviour implicit in the marriage contract.[23] The Court of Appeal[24] has favoured an approach which puts the issue in terms of a direction to a jury:—

---

[19] [1987] *Fam. Law* 130.

[20] *Ash v. Ash* [1972] Fam. 135, *per* Bagnall J. at 140.

[21] *Pheasant v. Pheasant* [1972] Fam. 202.

[22] *Ash v. Ash* [1972] Fam. 135

[23] The courts (for example in *O'Neill v. O'Neill* [1975] 1 W.L.R. 1118) have deprecated reference to the wording of the marriage service in the Book of Common Prayer ("for better or for worse, in sickness and in health"); but it is not clear that the test of "reasonableness" can be applied without some view as to the nature of the mutual commitment implied in marriage.

[24] *O'Neill v. O'Neill* [1975] 1 W.L.R. 1118.

> "Would any right-thinking person come to the conclusion that this husband has behaved in such a way that his wife cannot reasonably be expected to live with him, taking into account the whole of the circumstances and the characters and personalities of the parties?"

But this is not always easy to answer, especially where the behaviour in question is attributable to mental or physical illness. On the one hand, there are certainly cases in which it is clear that, whatever the excuse, the petitioner cannot reasonably be expected to live with the other. For example:—

> In *White v. White*[25] the husband was, by his own account, intending to kill himself by jumping from a balcony. However, he then heard a message from God telling him not to kill himself but to kill his wife instead. He told the wife that he would obtain a shotgun, use it to blow her head off and then play football with the severed head. On such facts a decree would be granted, and it would be immaterial that the husband was affected by mental illness to such an extent as not to be responsible for his actions.

But other cases may be more difficult. For example:—

> In *Thurlow v. Thurlow*[25a] a husband was granted a decree against his epileptic and bed-ridden wife. The court declared that it would take full account of the obligations of the married life, including "the normal duty to accept and share the burdens imposed upon the family as a result of the mental or physical ill-health of one member"; but the underlying question remains: can the petitioner reasonably be expected to go on living with the respondent?

In practice the fact that the health of the petitioner or that of the family as a whole is likely to suffer is a powerful factor influencing the court in favour of granting a decree. Many of the most obvious difficulties arise in cases of mental illness, but similar considerations would presumably apply if the respondent's behaviour was attributable to physical disease such as disseminated sclerosis, or cerebral thrombosis.

(d) Relevance of continued cohabitation

11–022 Does the fact that the petitioner has in fact gone on living in the same household mean that the petitioner can be expected to continue to live with him? The Act contains a provision[26] (s.2(3)) which is intended to facilitate reconciliation by enabling the parties to live together for a short period without losing the right to seek divorce if the attempt is unsuccessful[27]: in deciding whether the peti-

---

[25] [1983] Fam. 54; and see also *Katz v. Katz* [1972] 1 W.L.R. 955.
[25a] [1976] Fam. 32.
[26] M.C.A. 1973, s.2(3)
[27] See the comparable provision of s.2(1) in relation to the adultery "fact": above, para. 11–016.

tioner can reasonably be expected to live with the respondent the court must disregard cohabitation for up to six months. Longer periods do not constitute an absolute bar; and the longer the period the more likely it is that the court will draw the inference that the petitioner could reasonably be expected to put up with the respondent's behaviour. But the petitioner is entitled to refute any such inference; and in *Bradley v. Bradley*[28] (where the wife was still living in a four-bedroomed council house with the husband and seven children) the Court of Appeal held that she should be allowed to prove that it would be unreasonable to expect her to go on doing so.

(c) The respondent has deserted the petitioner for a continuous period of at least two years immediately preceding the presentation of the petition.

11–023 For many years the courts, in administering the matrimonial offence based divorce law gave adopted a restrictive attitude to the concept of desertion for fear that too wide a definition would lead to divorce by consent after a period of separation. The effect of the courts' struggles with changing policy considerations over the years was to introduce what Lord Diplock[29] called "metaphysical niceties" into the law; and it is virtually impossible to make clear statements of principle without over-simplification.[30]

Although the Divorce Reform Act retained desertion as one of the facts from which the court will infer the irretrievable breakdown of the marriage, it is rarely the basis for a divorce petition.[31] If a couple have lived apart for two years and both consent to a divorce that is sufficient to establish a "fact" evidencing breakdown; if they have lived apart for five years that is of itself a "fact".[32] For these reasons desertion can only be relevant in exceptional cases, for example where the couple have lived apart for at least two (but not five) years and the respondent is unwilling to agree to a divorce, and where they have lived apart for five years, but the petitioner fears that the grant of a decree based on that fact might be opposed on one of the "hardship" grounds available in such cases.[33] Against this background it seems justifiable to give only the briefest explanation of the essence of desertion.

The main elements of desertion are: (i) the fact of separation; (ii) the intention to desert. The intention to desert involves: (a) lack of consent to the separation

---

[28] [1973] 1 W.L.R. 1291.

[29] *Hall v. Hall* [1962] 1 W.L.R. 1246 at 1254.

[30] One complication which can now be ignored is the doctrine of constructive desertion, i.e. where one party drives the other out it is that party who is guilty of "constructively" deserting the other. Where (as is usually the case) it is the behaviour of the party concerned which is said to have made continuance of the common life intolerable the "behaviour" fact discussed above will almost always be available as the foundation for a divorce petition. In cases where one party simply orders the other to leave it has been held that the case must be dealt with as one of desertion (see *Morgan v. Morgan* (1973) 117 S.J. 223,

[31] In no year since 1973 for which a breakdown of the facts relied on is available has the proportion of desertion petitions exceeded five per cent of the total.

[32] M.C.A. 1973, s.1(2)(d) and s.1(2)(e).

[33] M.C.A. 1973, s.10(2): see below.

on the part of the petitioner; (b) lack of any justification for the separation; and (c) the respondent having the mental capacity to form the intent.

The fact of separation

11–024 The requisite factual separation can be established even if the couple remain under the same roof. Is there one household or two? Is there still any sharing (however minimal) of a common life—for example, sharing a common living room, or taking meals together. If so, the parties are not, for this purpose, separated:

> In *Le Brocq v. Le Brocq*[34] the wife excluded her husband from the matrimonial bedroom by putting a bolt on the inside of the door. There was no avoidable communication between them, but the wife continued to cook the husband's meals, and he paid her a weekly sum for housekeeping. The court held that the necessary factual separation had not been established: there was, as Harman L.J. put it, "separation of bedrooms, separation of hearts, separation of speaking: but one household was carried on . . .

The mental element: animus deserendi

11–025 The greatest difficulty in deciding whether a person is in desertion lies in the mental element, the *animus deserendi*. What is required is an intention (usually of course inferred from the words and conduct of the spouse alleged to be in desertion) to bring the matrimonial union permanently to an end. By no means every separation will constitute desertion, since: (i) the separation may be consensual; (ii) there may be good cause for the separation—for example where a mentally ill husband terrified the children, or where the husband has behaved badly to the wife; or (iii) the respondent may lack the mental capacity necessary to form the intention to desert.

11–026 **(i) Separation consensual.** If and so long as[35] both parties consent to a separation, there can be no desertion. Whether or not there is such consent is a question of fact.[36] Consent may also be implied.[37] But the court makes allowance for the emotional realities of the situation: a wife who told her husband "Go if you like, and when you are sick of her, come back to me" was not giving a consent to his living apart from her[38] and the fact that one spouse is glad that the other has gone does not mean that he or she has consented to the separation.

11–027 **(ii) Good cause for separation.** The respondent may be justified in leaving the

---

[34] [1964] 1 W.L.R. 1085.

[35] *Nutley v. Nutley* [1970] 1 W.L.R. 217.

[36] *Bosley v. Bosley* [1958] 1 W.L.R. 645.

[37] As in *Joseph v. Joseph* [1953] 1 W.L.R. 1182, where the wife obtained a *get* (a Jewish divorce). Although this was ineffective in English law to dissolve her marriage the fact that she had done so showed that she had no objection to the husband living apart from her.

[38] *Haviland v. Haviland* (1863) 32 L.J.P.M. & A. 65.

petitioner against the latter's will, either by necessity; or because of the petitioner's behaviour. Such cases could perhaps more sensibly be described as cases of "reasonable excuse"—for example, the reason for the separation may be that one of the spouses is in prison, or separation may be justified in the interests of the children's mental health—for example in *G.v.G.*[39] the court held that where the husband's behaviour, a symptom of mental illness, terrified the children the wife was justified in not allowing him into the matrimonial home notwithstanding the fact that he was no longer morally responsible for his actions. In other cases the other spouse's behaviour is the justification for leaving. The court held that only "grave and weighty" behaviour would suffice for this purpose.[40]

11–028 **(iii) Mental incapacity.** Mental illness may prevent the formation of the intention to desert.[41] If by reason of insanity one spouse has deluded beliefs about the conduct of the other, the rights of the parties in relation to the charge of desertion are to be adjudicated on as if that belief were true. For example:

> In *Perry v. Perry*[42] the wife believed that her husband was trying to murder her. She left him. If the deluded belief had been true she would have been justified in doing so Hence she was not in desertion.

Desertion may be terminated

11–029 Desertion is an inchoate offence: spouses owe a duty to one another to live together and if they do so they cannot be in desertion. But desertion would also be terminated if the necessary mental element is ended, even if the parties remain apart. In the days of the matrimonial offence divorce it was common for lawyers to draft "bona fide" offers to return in an attempt to demonstrate that the client no longer had the necessary intention to desert. If the parties remained factually separated after such an offer had been unreasonably refused the courts might well hold that the person refusing to live with his spouse had become guilty of desertion.

The requirement that desertion be for a continuous period of two years

11–030 Desertion only constitutes the "fact" from which the court may infer that the marriage has irretrievably broken down if it has lasted for a continuous period

---

[39] [1964] P. 133.

[40] A husband's conduct in taking a second wife has been held to justify his first wife in leaving him notwithstanding the fact that he was legally entitled to contract such a marriage: *Quoraishi v. Quoraishi* [1985] F.L.R. 780.

[41] At common law the onset of mental illness would terminate desertion if the person concerned had ceased to be capable of forming the necessary intention. Statute now provides that the court may treat desertion as having continued if the evidence would have lead it to infer that the desertion would in fact have continued: M.C.A. 1973, ss.2(4), 17(1). But this provision does not affect the need to show that there was an intention to desert at the start of the period.

[42] [1964] 1 W.L.R. 91

of two years immediately preceding the presentation of the petition.[43] However, for this purpose "continuous" does not mean continuous: the parties are allowed to resume living together for as long as six months without prejudicing their right to rely on this fact.[44] But the time they have spent together has to be deducted in calculating the overall period. For example, if H deserted W in January 1999, W could petition in July 2001 notwithstanding the fact that they had lived together from Christmas Eve 2000 until the beginning of May 2001; but on such facts W could not petition in January 2001.

(d) and (e) Living Apart

11–031 The two remaining "facts" are similar and can best be dealt with together. The first[45] is that *the parties to the marriage have lived apart for a continuous period of at least two years immediately preceding the presentation of the petition and the respondent consents to a decree being granted.* The second[46] is that *the parties to the marriage have lived apart for a continuous period of at least five years immediately preceding the presentation of the petition.*

These provisions permit divorce by consent after a period of separation, and divorce by repudiation after a longer period of separation; and they best justify the claim that the law is now based on the irretrievable breakdown of marriage. "Separation," it has been said,[47] "is undoubtedly the best evidence of breakdown, and the passing of time, the most reliable indication that it is irretrievable."

Computing the period

11–032 In relation to both "living apart" facts, the relevant period must have been completed when the petition is filed. A petition filed on the second or fifth anniversary of the commencement of separation will fail; the period has not been completed until the end of that day.[48] Moreover, the separation must have been for a period immediately preceding the presentation of the petition.

It is also necessary that the separation be "continuous"; but by continuous the Act does not necessarily mean continuous. This is because of the "provision designed to encourage reconciliation"[49] whereby no account is to be taken of any period or periods (not exceeding six months in all) during which the parties resumed living with each other. However, no period during which the parties lived with each other is to count as part of the period for which they lived apart. Hence it has been pointed out[50] that in cases based

---

[43] M.C.A. 1973, s.1(2)(c).
[44] M.C.A. 1973, s.2(5).
[45] M.C.A. 1973, s.1(2)(d).
[46] M.C.A. 1973, s.1(2)(e)
[47] *Per* Ormrod J., *Pheasant v. Pheasant* [1972] Fam. 202 at 207.
[48] *Warr v. Warr* [1975] Fam. 25.
[49] So described in the heading to s.3(5), D.R.A. 1969.
[50] *Santos v. Santos* [1972] Fam. 247 at 262.

on the two year period[51] the spouses could spend up to 20 per cent of their time together (i.e. six months in a period of thirty months) without interrupting the continuity of separation.

Meaning of "living apart"

11–033 It is the apparently simple requirement that the parties should have "lived apart" for the relevant period which requires most explanation. This is, partly at least, because the courts have held that living apart involves both (a) a physical and (b) a mental element.

First requirement: physical separation—two households, not two houses

11–034 In the typical case, the parties will have established separate households in different places, and there will be no doubt that they are physically "living apart". But even if they continue to live under the same roof it may still be possible to establish separation. This is because the Act provides[52] that "a husband and wife shall be treated as living apart unless they are living with each other in the same household, and references in this section to the parties to a marriage living with each other shall be construed as references to their living with each other in the same household."

Parliament's objective in enacting this provision has been said to be unclear,[53] but it is usually regarded as establishing for this "fact" the same test as was ultimately accepted for the "factum" of desertion under pre 1970 law.[54] Hence husband and wife can be treated as living apart, even if they are living under the same roof, unless it can be said that they are still living in the same household.[55] "Household" has an abstract meaning: it "essentially refers to people held together by a particular kind of tie".[56] The question therefore becomes: was there still any kind of community of life between the parties? The practical test applied in cases where the parties are still living under the same roof is usually whether one party continues to provide matrimonial services for the other, whether there is any sharing of domestic life. Thus if a husband shuts himself up in one or two rooms of the house and ceases to have anything to do with the wife there will be a sufficient separation of households.[57] If, on the other hand, although there is an estrangement (and even a refusal to have intercourse[58]) the parties still share the same living room, eat at the same table and sit by the same fire[59] (or perhaps watch television together) they are not to be regarded as living apart. They are still living in the same household, even if "they are living what

---

51 The same rule applies in petitions based on the five-year period; but the effect is less dramatic.
52 M.C.A. 1973, s.(6).
53 *Per* Sachs L.J., *Santos v. Santos* [1972] Fam. 247 at 262.
54 *Santos v. Santos* (above); *Mouncer v. Mouncer* [1972] 1 W.L.R. 321 at 323.
55 *Mouncer v. Mouncer* (above) at 324.
56 *Santos v. Santos* (above) at 262.
57 *Hopes v. Hopes* [1949] P. 227 at 235.
58 *Weatherley v. Weatherley* [1947] A.C. 268; *Mouncer v. Mouncer* (above).
59 *Hopes v. Hopes* (above) at 235.

only the most determined pessimist could regard as a normal married life."[60]

For example:

> In *Mouncer v. Mouncer*[61] the parties had for some time been on bad terms—to the extent that the wife petitioned for divorce on the ground of cruelty in 1969. Although that divorce suit did not go ahead, and the parties continued to live under the same roof, relations between them were strained and they occupied separate bedrooms. However, they usually took their meals together, and the wife did most of the household cleaning. In 1971 the husband left the house, and petitioned for divorce. Although the wife consented to divorce, the court held that the "fact" of living apart for two years had not been made out. There had been a single household between 1969 and 1971 and it made no difference to the result that the parties had acted "from the wholly admirable motive of caring properly for their children."

As husband and wife

There may be exceptional cases in which the parties live under the same roof and the one provides services for the other in some capacity other than that of a spouse. For example:

> In *Fuller v. Fuller*[62] husband and wife separated in 1964. The wife lived with another man as his wife, and took his name. In 1968 the husband had a serious heart attack. The medical advice was that he could not live on his own again. He therefore moved into the house in which the wife was living with her partner. The husband lived as a lodger, sleeping in a back bedroom, and was provided with food and laundry by the wife in return for a weekly payment. The Court of Appeal held that the parties were not living with each other in the same household. "Living with each other" connoted something more than living in the same household; the parties must also be living with each other as husband and wife, rather than as lodger and landlady.

Second requirement: the mental element

In *Santos v. Santos* the Court of Appeal[63] held that living apart only starts when one party recognises that the marriage is at an end—that is to say, when he and his spouse are, in common parlance, "separated" rather than simply living apart by force of circumstances:

> "living apart does not begin to exist until that day on which, if the spouse

---

[60] J.L. Barton (1970) 86 *L.Q.R.* 348 at 350.

[61] Above, approved in *Fuller v. Fuller* [1973] 1 W.L.R. 730.

[62] [1973] 1 W.L.R. 730.

[63] [1972] Fam. 247; see 88 *L.Q.R.* 328 (P.M. Bromley).

in question were compellingly asked to define his or her attitude to cohabitation, he (or she) would express and attitude averse to it. Until this state is reached, cohabitation is not . . . broken. When it is reached, living apart begins."[64]

However, strangely, the Court also held that it was not necessary for the one spouse to communicate the belief that the marriage was at an end to the other. If applied strictly these rules would have curious consequences:

H, with W's agreement, took up employment abroad in 1999. He has now met another woman whom he wishes to marry. W recognises that the marriage has irretrievably broken down, and is prepared to consent to a divorce. But she cannot petition under section 1(2)(d) until the end of two years from the date when H told her that he believed the marriage had broken down and that he wished to remarry. (Of course, if H admits adultery she will be able to petition under section 1(2)(a))

H has been a patient in a mental hospital for more than 10 years. W decided more than five years ago that she would never resume married live with H, but has not told him because she knew that to do so would upset him, and also because she did not wish to remarry. However, she has now met someone she does wish to marry; and there is no hope of H ever recovering sufficiently to leave hospital. W can immediately petition for divorce under section 1(2)(e) although H has had no ground to suspect that the marriage was in difficulties.

It is therefore not surprising that the *Santos* decision was controversial[65]; and the adoption of the "special procedure"[66] has undermined the assumption (on which the Court of Appeal's reasoning was founded) that consensual divorces based on separation require close judicial scrutiny. It is true that the Rules[67] require a petitioner to state the date when petitioner and respondent separated, to give "briefly the reason or main reason for the separation" and to state "the date when and the circumstances in which you came to the conclusion that the marriage was in fact at an end"; and the District Judge will need to be satisfied that the documentation has been correctly completed. But it is only in exceptional cases that there will be an opportunity for any probing of that evidence to take place; and accordingly in practice the only result of the *Santos* decision seems to be to complicate the law. The worst consequence of the *Santos* decision may therefore be that petitioners without access to legal advice, not realising the importance of stating that they had come to the conclusion that the marriage was over more than

[64] *Per* Turner J., *Sullivan v. Sullivan* (above) at 924.
[65] The arguments are summarised in the fifth edition of this work at pp. 126–127,
[66] See above.
[67] F.P.R. 1991, r. 2.24(3); Appendix 1, Form M7(e).

two or five years ago, will be denied for a time the divorce which a law truly based on irretrievable breakdown would have allowed them.

Differences between two and five year periods

11–035 There are two main differences between these two "facts". First, in two year cases the respondent must agree to the grant of the decree. Secondly, where the petition is founded solely on the five-year living apart "fact" the court has a statutory power[68] to refuse a decree if to do so would cause grave financial or other hardship to the respondent.

11–036 *Respondent's consent to divorce.* The Act requires a positive consent by the respondent to the grant of a decree and a mere failure to object is insufficient. Rules of Court seek to ensure that the respondent is given information necessary to understand the consequences (for example, relating to possible loss of pension and succession rights) of consenting to the grant of a decree.[69] The respondent will usually consent by answering in the affirmative the appropriate question in the form of acknowledgment of service, but until the pronouncement of decree nisi the respondent has an absolute right, for any or no reason, to withdraw any consent previously given.[70] Hence, a consent may be given conditionally (for example, on terms that the petitioner will not seek an order for costs against the respondent[71]). But even after decree nisi, the court may rescind the decree if it is satisfied that "the petitioner misled the respondent (whether intentionally or unintentionally) about any matter which the respondent took into account in deciding to give his consent."[72] The question appears to be entirely subjective: did this particular respondent in fact take the matter into account (not, would a reasonable respondent have done so). But the petitioner must have misled the respondent; the fact that the respondent was mistaken is not sufficient to justify recission.

Refusal of decree in cases of grave financial or other hardship, etc.

11–037 In the discussions leading up to the enactment of the Divorce Reform Act 1969 a great deal of anxiety was expressed about the plight of the "innocent" wife (that is to say, a wife could not have been divorced under the matrimonial offence doctrine), and it was thought necessary to provide special protection for wives (and husbands) threatened with divorce against their will.

The negotiations between the Law Commission and the Archbishop's group resulted in a proposal that the court be required to refuse a decree if satisfied that, having regard to the conduct and interests of the parties, the interest of

---

[68] M.C.A. 1973, s.5.

[69] M.C.A. 1973, s.2(7); Family Proceedings Rules 1991, Appendix 1 (Notice of Proceedings; Notes on Questions . . .).

[70] *Beales v. Beales* [1972] Fam. 210 at 221–2.

[71] *Beales v. Beales* [1972] Fam. 210 at 224.

[72] M.C.A. 1973, s.10(1).

the children and other persons affected, it would be wrong to dissolve the marriage, notwithstanding the public interest in dissolving marriages which have irretrievably broken down. But the corresponding provisions of the Act are far more restrictively drafted than the terms of the agreement would suggest, and the legislation has in turn been given a restrictive interpretation by the courts.

Section 5 of the Matrimonial Causes Act 1973 provides:

> "(1) The respondent to a petition for divorce in which the petitioner alleges five years' separation may oppose the grant of a decree on the ground that the dissolution of the marriage will result in grave financial or other hardship to him and that it would in all the circumstances be wrong to dissolve the marriage.
>
> (2) Where the grant of a decree is opposed by virtue of this section, then—
>
> (a) if the court finds that the petitioner is entitled to rely in support of his petition on the fact of five years' separation and makes no such finding as to any other fact mentioned in section 1(2) above, and
>
> (b) if apart from this section the court would grant a decree on the petition, the court shall consider all the circumstances, including the conduct of the parties to the marriage and the interests of those parties and of any children or other persons concerned, and if of opinion that the dissolution of the marriage will result in grave financial or other hardship to the respondent and that it would in all the circumstances be wrong to dissolve the marriage it shall dismiss the petition.
>
> (3) For the purposes of this section hardship shall include the loss of the chance of acquiring any benefit which the respondent might acquire if the marriage were not dissolved."

There are thus two elements: first, the hardship (whether financial or otherwise) must be "grave"; secondly that hardship must result from the dissolution of the marriage (rather than from the fact that it has broken down[73]).

"Grave hardship"

11–038 The word "grave" has its ordinary meaning of "important or very serious". It is not sufficient to show that a spouse will lose something and a spouse is not entitled to expect to be compensated pound for pound for everything that he or

---

[73] There is an extensive body of case-law on the interpretation of M.C.A. 1973, s.5. Although the threat of invoking the defence may be used in negotiating favourable financial settlements with a petitioner anxious to remarry, applications to the court are now rare and discussion has been abbreviated. For a full discussion, reference should be made to *Rayden & Jackson's Law and Practice in Divorce and Family Matters* (17th ed. N. Wall et al., ed., 1997); whilst much of the case-law is cited in the fifth edition of this book, at pp. 129–138.

she will lose in consequence of the divorce. This can be illustrated from two cases with contrasting facts:

> In *Reiterbund v. Reiterbund*[74] a 52-year-old wife would lose her entitlement to the state widows' pension if her 54-year-old husband died before she reached the age of 60. But the risk of her husband dying in the next eight years was not great, and even if he did, Mrs Reiterbund would receive exactly the same income from supplementary benefit from a state widow's pension. The court therefore rejected the defence and granted a decree.

> In *Archer v. Archer*[75] a 55 year old consultant orthopaedic surgeon had a large income but few substantial capital assets. His 53 year old wife claimed that she would suffer grave hardship because if (as was statistically probable) he pre-deceased her the £18,000 maintenance order against him would come to an end. But the wife had her own investments amounting to nearly £300,000 and she owned a house worth more than £200,000. The Court of Appeal agreed that the loss of the maintenance payments could not, in the circumstances, be regarded as "grave" hardship.

11–039 *Hardship other than financial hardship.* Although it is, in theory, open to a respondent to establish grave hardship which is not financial hardship there has been no reported case in which such a defence has succeeded. In particular the courts have taken a robust approach to pleas based on religious belief. It is not enough for the respondent to show that divorce is contrary to his or her religion and that divorce will cause unhappiness and a sense of shame; there must be evidence of some specific hardship flowing from the divorce:

> In *Banik v. Banik*[76] a Hindu wife's pleadings that she would be ostracised if divorced were held to establish a prima facie case of grave hardship; but the evidence was eventually held not to substantiate her claim and a decree was granted.[77]

11–040 *The hardship must result from the divorce, not from the breakdown.* The respondent must prove that her position as a divorced spouse is worse than it would be as a separated spouse. This is difficult to do. It is, for example, true that many divorced people suffer serious financial problems; but the court has wide powers to make financial orders on divorce, and the problems usually stem from the fact that the marriage has broken down and that there is insufficient money to keep two households, rather than from the fact that the marriage has been legally dissolved by divorce. Exceptionally, the divorce court for many years lacked adequate powers to reallocate contingent pension rights on divorce, and the "hardship" defence was sometimes successful where the wife could

---

[74] [1975] Fam. 99.
[75] [1999] 1 F.L.R. 327.
[76] [1973] 1 W.L.R. 860.
[77] *Banik v. Banik (No. 2)* (1973) 117 S.J: 874.

show that she would lose the substantial pension which would have been payable to her as the husband's widow—indeed in *Le Marchant v. Le Marchant*[78] the Court of Appeal held that the loss of a contingent right to an index-linked pension (*i.e.* one which gives a high degree of protection against the inflation then current) was prima facie grave financial hardship to a wife. But it seems that the powers which the court now has to make pension sharing orders on divorce will reduce the number of cases in which inability to deal with pension assets causes hardship.

11–041 *"Wrong in all the circumstances."* If, but only if, the court is satisfied that grave financial or other hardship would be caused by a divorce, it will proceed to the next stage, and consider whether it would "in all the circumstances"[79] be wrong to dissolve the marriage. This requires the court to put the hardship which divorce would cause the respondent into the scales against the policy embodied in the modern divorce law (which "aims, in all other than exceptional circumstances, to crush the empty shells of dead marriages"[80]). Case-law suggested the balance would often be in favour of termination. There have been very few cases in which a decree has been refused. *Julian v. Julian*[81] is one such:

> The husband was 61 and the wife 58. Neither was in good health. The wife was receiving periodical payments from the husband which would cease if the husband predeceased her and the wife would lose her right to a police widow's pension, leaving her with only a very small total income. The decision that it would be wrong to grant a divorce and thus (as the law then stood) deprive her of the pension was largely based on the belief that it was not particularly hard on the husband to deprive him of the chance to remarry.

11–042 *Other protection for respondents in separation cases.* The Act[82] contains a complex provision which is intended to secure the financial position of a spouse who is divorced on either of the two "living apart" facts. A respondent may apply to the court after the granting of a decree nisi for consideration of his or her financial position after the divorce. In such a case the court must not make the decree absolute unless it is satisfied that the financial arrangements are "reasonable and fair" or "the best that can be made in the circumstances." This provision was originally enacted when the court had less extensive financial powers than it now enjoys, and it is today rarely invoked. But there may be cases in which it is desirable for the court to ensure that all appropriate matters

---

[78] [1977] 1 W.L.R. 559; and see *K v. K (Financial Relief: Widow's Pension)* [1997] 1 F.L.R. 35 (which illustrates the utility of the grave hardship defence as a means of putting pressure on a petitioner unwilling to make a proper financial settlement).

[79] The Act specifically directs attention to the "conduct of the parties to the marriage and the interests of those parties and of any children or other persons concerned".

[80] *Reiterbund v. Reiterbund* [1974] 1 W.L.R. 788 at 798, *per* Finer J.

[81] (1972) 116 S.J. 763.

[82] M.C.A. 1973, s. 10(2).

have been properly dealt with before the marriage is finally terminated. For example:

> In *Garcia v. Garcia*[83] the wife alleged that her husband had failed to make the stipulated payments under a Spanish maintenance agreement. The court held that it had power to refuse to make absolute the decree nisi granted to the husband based on five years living apart.

V. THE FAMILY LAW ACT 1996: THE REFORM WHICH NEVER WAS

11–043 Although the reformed divorce law introduced by the Divorce Reform Act 1969 unquestionably allowed a large number of broken marriages to be legally terminated, it soon began to be questioned whether the Act had really achieved the objectives—defined by the Law Commission in 1965 as being to buttress rather than undermine the status of marriage but also allowing the "empty legal shell" of a broken marriage to be destroyed with "the maximum fairness and the minimum bitterness, distress and humiliation—of a good divorce law.[84] Some were concerned about the continued increase in the divorce rate, and suggested that the 1969 legislation (and the "special procedure" used for processing divorce petitions) had made divorce "too easy". Was the law was doing all that could be done to identify savable marriages and to facilitate the making of attempts to reconcile those whose marriages were in difficulty? From a different perspective, there was concern that—in spite of the optimism expressed by reformers in the 1960s—bitterness, distress and humiliation refused to go away. Why should someone who did not want a divorce, and believed that the marriage had broken down because of the other spouse's behaviour, have to be told that there was no point in seeking to resist divorce, perhaps founded on a petition alleging that it was the respondent who had been guilty of behaviour such that the petitioner could not reasonably be expected to go on living with him? What was the point of effectively depriving the parties of the right to have issues of responsibility adjudicated by a court when it still remained possible to consume so much time, money and emotional energy in deciding on the financial and other consequences of the breakdown?

Official inquiries

11–044 It was not long before these issues became the subject of official consideration; and in 1985 the *Report of the Matrimonial Causes Procedure Committee*[85] concluded that the bitterness and unhappiness of divorcing couples was frequently exacerbated and prolonged by the fault element in divorce, and that this was particularly so where the fact relied upon was behaviour, whether or not

---

[83] [1992] 1 FLR 256.

[84] *Field of Choice*, para. 15.

[85] Chairman: Mrs Justice Booth, D.B.E.

the suit was defended.[86] Then, in 1988, the Law Commission published a Report, *Facing the Future, A Discussion Paper on the Ground for Divorce*,[87] which whilst accepting that the modern law was a "considerable improvement on the previous position",[88] concluded that there was "no doubt" that the law fell far short of its original objectives.[89] In 1990, after consultation, the Commission reiterated its view that reform was needed. In 1993, the Government published its own Consultation Paper which, accepted that the law was not working well. In particular it was said[90] that:—

(a) the law allowed divorce to be obtained quickly[91] and easily without the parties being required to have regard to the consequences[92];

---

[86] para. 2.10.

[87] Law Com. No. 170, (1988).

[88] para. 3.47.

[89] para. 6.1. The Commission concluded (see paras 3.48–50): "The present law does not, nor could it reasonably be expected to, buttress the stability of marriage by preventing determined parties from obtaining a speedy divorce. Because of the compromise nature of the 1969 Act, the benefits referred to above have been bought at the price of incoherence and increased confusion for litigants. Thus the law is neither understandable nor respected and there is evidence of not inconsiderable consumer dissatisfaction. Attaining the aims of maximum fairness and minimum bitterness has been rendered impossible by the retention of the fault element. The necessity of making allegations in the petition 'draws the battle-lines' at the outset. The ensuing hostility makes the divorce more painful, not only for the parties but also for the children, and destroys any chance of reconciliation and may be detrimental to post-divorce relationships. Underlying all these defects is the fact that whether or not the marriage can be dissolved depends principally upon what parties have done in the past. In petitions relying on fault-based facts, the petitioner is encouraged to 'dwell on the past' and to recriminate.At the same time, the present divorce process may not allow sufficient opportunity for the parties to come to terms with what is happening in their lives. A recent study of the process of 'uncoupling' points out that one party has usually gone far down that path before the other one discovers this, by which time it may be too late. Once the divorce process has been started it may have a 'juggernaut' effect, providing insufficient opportunity for the parties to re-evaluate their positions. Thus, there is little or no scope for reconciliation, conciliation or renegotiation of the relationship. It is clear that both emotionally and financially it is much less costly if ancillary matters can be agreed between the parties. Where antagonism is created or exacerbated by the petition, or their respective bargaining power distorted, the atmosphere is not conducive to calm and sensible negotiations about the future needs of the parties and their children. Above all, the present law fails to recognise that divorce is not a final product but part of a massive transition for the parties and their children. It is crucial in the interests of the children (as well as the parties) that the transition is as smooth as possible, since it is clear that their short and long-term adjustment depends to a large extent on their parents' adjustment and in particular on the quality of their post-divorce relationship with each parent. Although divorce law itself can do little actively to this end, it can and should ensure that the divorce process is not positively adverse to this adjustment. As Lord Hailsham has said, 'though the law could not alter the facts of life, it need not unnecessarily exaggerate the hardship inevitably involved.' There seems little doubt that the present law is guilty of just this."

[90] *Looking to the future. Mediation and the ground for divorce* (Cm. 2424 (1993)), para. 5.1–24. The criticisms were repeated in the White Paper, *Looking to the future, mediation and the ground for divorce, the Government's Proposals* (Cm. 2799 (1995)), paras 2.12–2.20. (The White Paper is referred to subsequently as the 1995 *Divorce White Paper*).

[91] The process of dealing with a divorce case from the filing of a petition to the grant of the decree can take less than four months (save in the rare cases in which the petition is defended, in which case the average length of time to decree is seven months): *Fourth Annual Report* of the Advisory Board on Family Law, 2000/2001, para. 3.5.

[92] The parties may have remarried long before the consequences of the divorce have been worked out: *Looking to the future. Mediation and the ground for divorce* (Cm. 2424 (1993)), para. 5.5.

(b) it did nothing to save the marriage[93];
(c) it could make things worse for the children[94];
(d) it was unjust and exacerbated bitterness and hostility[95];
(e) it was confusing, misleading and open to abuse[96];
(f) it was discriminatory[97]; and
(g) it distorted the parties' bargaining positions.[98]

Finally in 1995, in the light of the extensive consultation process, the Government decided that there was indeed a strong case for reform of divorce law and procedures. In particular the Government "noted the failure of the current system to encourage reconciliation, and its tendency to exacerbate hostility and conflict and so the distress and harm caused to children". What form, then, might reform take?

Seeking something better

11–045 The Law Commission's 1990 Report[99] contained a remarkable and penetrating analysis of the realities of the divorce process. As already noted[1] the Commission believed the law failed to reflect the reality of the divorce process. There was still "overwhelming support" for irretrievable breakdown as the "fundamental basis" for divorce. Rather than returning to a wholly fault-based system or introducing some alternative ground (such as divorce based on living apart for a period of time, divorce by the mere fact of mutual consent, divorce by unilateral notice or—at the other extreme—allowing divorce only after a full inquiry into whether the relationship had indeed irretrievably broken down) the Commission believed that the law should concentrate on bringing parties to an understanding of the practical reality of divorce: what it would be like "to live

---

[93] The legal process will involve the initiator being asked to recount the worst things the other spouse has done; and couples are given a choice of either recrimating or separating. Solicitors are not trained to recognise that taking legal advice may be a cry for help: *Looking to the future. Mediation and the ground for divorce* (Cm. 2424 (1993)), paras 5.6–10.

[94] The parents either have to find fault with one another or live apart (thus engendering a period of uncertainty whilst things are sorted out): *Looking to the future. Mediation and the ground for divorce* (Cm. 2424 (1993)), paras 5.11–12.

[95] One of the remarkable features of the operation of the "irretrievable breakdown" divorce law in practice was that some 70per cent of divorce petitions were founded on "fault", *i.e.* either adultery or "behaviour": *Fourth Annual Report* of the Advisory Board on Family Law, 2000/2001, para. 3.5. Such petitions often do not reflect the reality of the couple's relationship, whilst the practical difficulties of defending a petition engender resentment: *Looking to the future. Mediation and the ground for divorce* (Cm. 2424 (1993)), paras 5.13–15.

[96] The "fact" relied on need have nothing to do with the breakdown; and it is difficult for the court to ascertain the truth: *Looking for the future. Mediation and the ground for divorce* (Cm. 2424 (1993)), paras 5.16–19.

[97] The law provides a "civilised" method of divorce for those whose resources allow them to live apart for two years, but not for others: *Looking to the future. Mediation and the ground for divorce* (Cm. 2424 (1993)), paras 5.20–24.

[98] Negotiations on such matters as the future care of children distribution of family assets, and financial provision may be distorted by the party who is in the stronger position in relation to the divorce—*e.g.* the threat of withholding consent to divorce can be used: *Looking to the future. Mediation and the ground for divorce* (Cm. 2424 (1993)), paras 5.22–24.

[99] *The Ground for Divorce,* Law Com. No. 192 (1990).

[1] See p. 318, n. 1, above.

apart, to break up the common home, to finance two households where before there was only one, and to have or to lose day to day responsibility for the children . . ."[2] and so on. The Commission thought that it was crucial that the "massive transition" involved in the ending of a marriage should be as smooth as possible if only to protect parents' post-divorce relationship with the children; and every opportunity was to be taken to divert the parties from recourse to hostile litigation. Divorce should no longer require proof of one of the "facts" specified in the 1969 Divorce Reform Act. Instead, breakdown would be inferred from the fact that a period of one year, intended for consideration of the practical consequences which would result from a divorce and reflection upon whether the breakdown in the marital relationship was irreparable had elapsed. It is difficult to deny that in consequence divorce would in principle be available if one party to the marriage insisted whatever the other thought about it; but the Law Commission evidently accepted the logical outcome of recognising that a partnership cannot survive if one party is implacably opposed. In this view, measures to promote reconciliation and support marriage would better uphold the institution of marriage than narrow definition of the ground for divorce.

The Politics of divorce law reform

11–046 After further consultation, the Conservative Government accepted the main thrust of the Law Commission's proposals for divorce "after a period for the consideration of future arrangements and for reflection"; and a Bill was introduced in November 1995. The Bill which became the Family Law Act 1996 did not have an easy passage through Parliament, in part because of the lack of enthusiasm of many (and opposition on the part of some) of the Government's own supporters.[3] In order to save the Bill from defeat[4] the Government had to accept many amendments.[5] Some of the amendments reflected concern about

---

[2] *The Ground for Divorce,* Law Com. No. 192 (1990), para. 2.

[3] Mrs Margaret Thatcher, in this as in other matters evidently reflecting the views of many members of the Conservative Party, has recorded that she "did not accept that we should follow the Law Commission's recommendation . . . that this should just become a process in which fault was not at issue. In some cases—for example, where there is violence—I considered that divorce was not just permissible but unavoidable, yet I also felt strongly that if all the remaining culpability was removed from marital desertion, divorce would be that much more common . . . "; See M. Thatcher, *The Downing Street Years* (1995, London), p. 630. Opposition to the Bill in the House of Lords was led by the Conservative former Cabinet Minister Baroness Young; and it seems that 112 Conservative members (including the Home Secretary and four other ministers) voted against the Government in the crucial free vote in the House of Commons on the retention of fault-based divorce: *Official Report* (H.C.) April 24, 1996, col. 543. Five cabinet ministers and 15 other ministers voted in favour of an extended period of reflection and consideration: *Official Report* (H.C.) June 17, 1996, col. 622. Some Conservative M.P.s who were not prepared to vote the Bill down lamented the fact that it had ever been brought forward: see, *e.g.* Mr P. Nicholls, *Official Report* (H.C.) April 24, 1996, col. 458; and Dame Elaine Kellet-Bowman who said in the course of the third reading debate that it would be best to "throw out the whole" of what she described as an appalling Bill "lock stock and barrel", but appears not to have voted in the crucial third reading division: *Official Report* (H.C.) June 17, 1996, cols 564, 565.

[4] The Bill was eventually given a third reading in the House of Commons by 427 votes to 9; but this final stage of the Bill's passage through the House of Commons was characterised by the Government's acceptance of amendments which it had previously rejected.

[5] 137 Amendments were made to the Bill in the course of its passage through the House of Commons; and many amendments had already been made in the House of Lords.

the need to uphold the institution of marriage, in practice by making it more difficult to obtain a divorce (whether by preserving some element of fault as a pre-requisite to divorce or at least by emphasising the relevance of the parties' conduct). Others were intended to ensure that the possibility of reconciliation be fully explored by increased use of counselling and marriage support services. Yet others reflected concern that the interests of children should be given greater protection. The result is that there is some lack of coherence in the detail of the legislation[6]; whilst what had been an essentially simple and elegant legislative scheme became exceedingly complex.

Divorce under the Family Law Act 1996: the legal process in outline

11–047 The Act would retain the general principle that the irretrievable breakdown of the marriage should be the only ground for divorce[7] but such breakdown would be inferred exclusively[8] from (a) the lodging of a statement of marital breakdown with the court (which can only be done after attendance at an information meeting[9]); (b) the expiration of a period after the making of the statement for "reflection and consideration"[10]; and (c) the making of an application for a divorce order which evidences compliance with the Act's requirements that the parties' arrangements for the future in respect of children and financial matters should first have been resolved[11] and which would be accompanied by a declaration that the applicant believed the marriage cannot be saved.[12] However, the court would have power (notwithstanding the fact that the marriage had irretrievably broken down and that the other requirements set out above had been satisfied) in some circumstances to make an order preventing divorce if it is satisfied that dissolution of the marriage would result in substantial financial or other hardship to a spouse or to a child of the family.[13]

Divorce under the Family Law Act 1996: other aspects of the divorce process

11–048 It will be apparent, even from the brief summary given above, that the Act is conceptually unusual. Why, for example, should a spouse be required to attend an information meeting before starting the divorce process? Why is the period which has to elapse between filing a statement of marital breakdown and being entitled to apply for a divorce order described as a "period for consideration and reflection"?

The answer to each of these questions is that the Act seeks to promote a remarkable collaboration between the legal process necessary to terminate the

---

[6] The Labour Party's spokesman on the Bill in the House of Commons, Mr Paul Boateng, is said to have described it as a "dog's breakfast": *Law Society Gazette*, May 30, 1996, p. 10.

[7] F.L.A. 1996, s.3(1)(a).

[8] "A marriage is to be taken to have broken down irretrievably if (but only if) . . . ": F.L.A. 1996, s.5(1).

[9] F.L.A. 1996, s.3(1)(a); s.8.

[10] *ibid.* s.7(1), (2).

[11] *ibid.* s.3(1)(c); s.9.

[12] *ibid.* s.5(1)(d).

[13] *ibid.* s.10.

legal status of marriage, and various applied social work measures intended to minimise the damage done to children and adults by marital breakdown and its consequences. As a former Conservative cabinet minister[14] put it:

> "For the first time in our history we are seeking to put on the statute book a process which must be gone through before divorce can be obtained; which is designed to question whether the divorce is necessary . . .; and, if that fails, at least to ensure that before the point of divorce is reached the parties have made arrangements as to how to provide for themselves and, above all, for their young children."

General principles underlying the divorce legislation

11–049 A fuller understanding of the policies to which the Act sought to give effect can be gathered by referring to the statement of "general principles underlying" the legislation which are set out in section 1 of the Act. These (it has been said) constitute an assertion of the framework within which the legislation was intended to operate.[15] Section 1 of the Act provides:

> The court and any person, in exercising functions under or in consequence of Parts II and III,[16] shall have regard to the following general principles—
>
> (a) that the institution of marriage is to be supported;
> (b) that the parties to a marriage which may have broken down are to be encouraged to take all practicable steps whether by marriage counselling or otherwise to save the marriage;
> (c) that a marriage which may have broken down and is being brought to an end should be brought to an end—
>
> (i) with minimum distress to the parties and to the children affected;
> (ii) with questions dealt with in a manner designed to promote as good a continuing relationship between the parties and any children affected as is possible in the circumstances[17];
> (iii) without costs being unreasonably incurred in connection with the procedures to be followed in bringing it to an end; and

---

[14] Lord Carr of Hadley (Home Secretary 1972–1974). See *Official Report* H.L. January 23, 1996, col. 942.

[15] *per* Lord Mackay of Clashfern, *Official Report* H.L. February 22, 1996, col. 1145, moving the insertion of the section at Report stage in the House of Lords. The fact that these general principles were only formulated at a comparatively late stage in the Bill's passage through Parliament is a telling indication of the unusual way in which the legislation evolved.

[16] *i.e.* the part of the Act dealing with divorce, separation, and with legal aid for mediation.

[17] s.1(c)(ii) was introduced by further Government Amendment on the third reading of the Bill in the House of Lords on March 11, 1996. The object of adding this specific reference to the desirability of promoting continuity was (according to the Lord Chancellor: *Official Report* H.L. March 11, 1996, col. 618) to underline the fact that children have *continuing* needs (for example, in relation to contact with parents) and to dispel any suggestion that the children's needs and problems can be disposed of when the marriage is terminated.

(d) that any risk to one of the parties to a marriage, and to any children, of violence from the other party should, so far as reasonably practicable, be removed or diminished.[18]

How then were these principles to be promoted? Support for the institution of marriage and encouragement to "save" particular marriages[19] was to be given by making marriage support available, particularly in seeking to promote prospects of reconciliation; whilst minimising distress, promoting continuing relationships and minimising cost was to be achieved by promoting what is generally called alternative dispute resolution (and, in the present context, a particular species of alternative dispute resolution now usually called mediation).

Promoting mediation

11–050 One of the major criticisms made of the divorce process under the Matrimonial Causes Act 1973 and the "special procedure" was that so-called "quicky" divorces, often based on adultery or behaviour, could be obtained (in most cases with little difficulty) within a few months of starting proceedings. Only then could the court deal with the parties' long term financial arrangements.[20] All too often, the parties worked out their emotions in the legal procedures—in theory of subsidiary importance[21]—for dealing with financial matters and in proceedings for resolving issues about the children's upbringing. These procedures are sometimes said to be adversarial[22] in nature; and certainly the processes of separate representation by different lawyers and the prospect of a full courtroom hearing with hostile cross-examination can engender a great deal of bitterness and distress. A great deal of voluntary effort was put into the development of facilities for conciliation or mediation ("the helping of parties to resolve their

[18] The case against the inclusion of s.1(d) in Part I of the Bill was powerfully urged by the Government spokesman (Mr Jonathan Evans) in the course of the fourth sitting of Standing Committee E: see *Official Report*, May 7, 1996. The Government evidently felt unable to carry this opposition to a division: see the Third Reading debate, and conceded that the potential for domestic violence would be present "for some at a number of points in the divorce and separation process, and that it is right for those exercising functions in connection with the process to take that into account": *Official Report* H.C., col. 601. However, the reader should bear in mind that the substantive provisions of the Famly Law Act dealing with domestic violence are to be found in Party IV (dealt with in Chap. 10 of this work).

[19] See the F.L.A. 1996, s.1(a), (b).

[20] As explained in more detail in Chap. 14, below, the court's powers to make financial provision and property adjustment orders only arose on or after a decree had been granted; and such orders generally only took effect when that decree was made absolute: M.C.A. 1973, s.23(1), (5); s.24(1), (3).

[21] It is for this reason that the court's powers to make financial orders were not exercisable until a decree has been granted. "Ever since divorce was introduced into our legal system in 1857, it has been an absolute requirement that no order for permanent (as opposed to interim) financial support can be made until the decree nisi has been pronounced. The purpose, no doubt, was to avoid any step that might hinder a reconciliation, for which the door would need to be kept open until the moment of decree": *Pounds v. Pounds* [1994] 1 F.L.R. 775, CA, *per* Waite L.J.

[22] In the interests of accuracy (or, as some would no doubt say, pedantry) it should be noted that in principle, the adversarial model has nothing to do with hostility, but merely reflects a dialectical approach to ascertaining the truth.

disputes"[23]). Expert help (it was suggested) might not save the marriage, but it could well help the parties to a marriage to resolve issues relating to finance and child custody with the minimum possible anxiety to themselves and their children. At the least, it might be possible to identify the issues on which the parties remained seriously at variance, and thus limit the scope of any litigation. There was for many years little Central Government help in providing these services; but in 1990 the Law Commission's Report[24] marked the beginning of a dramatic shift in official thinking. The Government came to believe that mediation should play a much greater part in the process of resolving the consequences of marital breakdown.[25] The Government defined the concept of mediation as follows[26]:

> ". . . a way of resolving disputes without resort to traditional adjudication through the courts. It describes different forms of negotiating agreements directly between parties concerning their children, finances and property with the minimum involvement of lawyers and courts . . ."

There are two distinctive characteristics of the process. First, the emphasis is on *agreement* rather than on *adjudication*. Secondly, reaching such agreement is to be faciliated by a third party, who will often not be a lawyer.

The Family Law Act 1996 was founded on the belief that mediation had "enormous potential[27]; and the Government believed that its use would help to achieve the general principle of bringing a failed marriage to an end with the minimum of distress and in such a way as to promote a good continuing relationship between the parties and children.[28]

The involvement of lawyers

11–051 Mediation tended to be contrasted with legal representation, and the temptation to suggest that mediation was a civilised process in which a disinterested mediator facilitates the shared purpose of reaching agreement, whilst legal representation involved hostile court-room duels between partisan lawyers paid to ignore all but their own client's interests was not always resisted. In reality, such a caricature misrepresents the role played by lawyers in general and solicitors in particular in the divorce process.[29] In reality the vast majority of divorce cases under the 1969 legislation were settled by negotiation between lawyers who

---

[23] See *Re H. (Conciliation: Welfare Reports)* [1986] 1 F.L.R. 476, *per* Ewbank J.

[24] *The Ground for Divorce* (Law Com. No. 192, 1990). The Law Commission considered that mediation and counselling could minimise the harmful emotional social and psychological effects of marital breakdown and divorce and thought that their proposals for reform of the ground for divorce would provide a more constructive and less damaging context for these services (para. 3.38).

[25] *Looking to the future, Mediation and the ground for divorce, the Government's Proposals* (Cm. 2799 (1995)) paras 5.21–5.25.

[26] *Looking to the future, Mediation and the ground for divorce* (Cm. 2424 (1993)), para. 7.6.

[27] *per* Lord Mackay of Clashfern. *Official Report* (H.L.), November 30, 1995, col. 700.

[28] F.L.A. 1996, s.1(c).

[29] See G. Davis, *Partisans and Mediators* (1988): R. Ingleby, *Solicitors and Divorce* (1992).

increasingly—following Codes of Practice laid down by the Solicitors' Family Law Association—sought to adopt a non-adversarial stance (whilst never forgetting that their duty lay to put forward to the best of their ability the client's case).[30] But legal services are undeniably costly; and the Government did not disguise its belief that diverting clients to mediation rather than allowing them legal representation would significantly save costs. Although research has subsequently demonstrated that this assumption may have been somewhat simplistic,[31] the Family Law Act was based on the belief that the role of lawyers acting as such in the divorce process should be significantly reduced. There was to be a definite encouragements to participate in mediation rather than having recourse to legal representation; and mediation was intended to be a pervasive factor in the new divorce process.[32]

Information for the families

11–052 The Law Commission had recommended[33] that the reformed divorce process should ensure so far as possible that husband and wife understood the "nature, purpose and requirements of the period upon which they are embarking and are fully acquainted with the various types of professional help which may be required" and how this could be obtained. This aim was to be achieved by the modest device of requiring the court to provide the spouses with a "comprehensive information pack". But the Government greatly extended the scope of the information-giving process. Anyone initiating the divorce process was to be required to attend a so-called information meeting at least three months before filing the necessary document, and delegated legislation was "in particular" to make provision "with respect to the giving of information about "(a) marriage counselling and other marriage support services; (b) the importance to be attached to the welfare, wishes and feelings of children; (c) how the parties may acquire a better understanding of the ways in which children can be helped to cope with the breakdown of a marriage; (d) the nature of the financial questions that may arise on divorce or separation, and services which are available to help the parties; (e) protection available against violence, and how to obtain support and assistance; (f) mediation; (g) the availability to each of the parties of independent legal advice and representation; (h) the principles of legal aid and where the parties can get advice about obtaining legal aid; (i) the divorce and separation process. These provisions were added to the Bill at a late stage in its passage

---

[30] See the Research Findings of the survey undertaken by G. Davis and others on behalf of the Legal Services Commission, and summarised in [2001] *Fam. Law* 110, 186, 265, 378.

[31] See G. Bevan and G. Davis [2001] *Fam. Law* 186.

[32] The Act provided that regulations would to make provision for the giving of information about mediation at the information meeting which a person seeking divorce had to attend: s.8(9)(f). Legal representatives would be required by regulations to inform a person making a "statement" about mediation, to give that person the names and addresses of persons qualified to help in connection with mediation, and to certify that they have done so: s.12(2). The court might give a direction requiring spouses to attend meetings about mediation: s.13. Finally, public funding was available in certain circumstances for mediation s.29. Curiously the Act contains no meaningful definition of what is mean by "mediation".

[33] *The Ground for Divorce* (Law Can. No. 192, 1990), para. 5.15.

through Parliament; and changes made in the course of debates reflect (amongst other things) the pressure exerted on the Government to shift the emphasis of the Act towards counselling marriage guidance and mediation. The uncertainty of the Government's concept of precisely what form the information meeting was to take is perhaps reflected by the decision to substitute the term "information meeting" in preference to the term "information session" (which appeared in the Bill originally introduced, but which it was feared might convey misleading connotations of "large, public communal events"[34]). A cloud of uncertainty and even confusion thus surrounded the concept of the information meeting, but the Government announced that the details would be settled in the light of the experience derived from pilot schemes to be conducted before the legislation came into force.[35]

Pilot schemes and research

11–053 Two distinct kinds of pilot scheme were established (one intended to assess the most effective way of implementing the provisions of the Act concerning Information Meetings and one intended to assess aspects of the effectiveness of publicly funded mediation). Research into both types of pilot scheme was commissioned from independent researchers.[36] The Lord Chancellor also established an Advisory Board on Family Law to provide independent advice on the implementation and operation of the Act.

Mediation pilot schemes

11–054 Although the provisions of the Family Law Act dealing with the substance of the divorce law were not brought into force, the Government did bring into force the provisions of Part III of the Act ("Legal Aid for Mediation in Family Matters") in March 1997.[37] This enabled the Legal Aid Board to secure the provision of mediation in disputes relating to family matters; and it was provided that a person should not be granted legal aid for representation unless he had first attended a meeting with a mediator to determine whether mediation was

---

[34] *Official Report* H.L. February 22, 1996, col. 1180. The 1995 *Divorce White Paper* had proposed that the information needed by those considering divorce should be dispensed at free-of-charge group sessions; but as eventually enacted the legislation provides (s.8(3)) that "different information meetings must be arranged with respect to different marriages"—a provision evidently intended to meant that the information meeting will be restricted to one couple's marriage. Government spokesmen have also made it clear that couples are not to be required to attend the same information session (thereby taking some account of concern about the plight of victims of domestic violence): see, *e.g. Official Report* H.L. November 30, 1996, col. 792.

[35] There are those who consider that the value of such pilots is reduced because (i) they will have to be conducted within the framework of the existing law, and (ii) it will be impossible to compel attendance at the meetings: see S.M. Cretney, "Family Law, A Bit of a Racket?" (1996) New L.J. 91.

[36] The research into Information Meetings was conducted by the Centre for Family Studies at the University of Newcastle upon Tyne under the direction of Professor Janet Walker. The Mediation research was directed by Professor Gwynn Davis of the Department of Law University of Bristol.

[37] The Family Law Act 1996 (Commencement No. 1) Order 1997, S.I. 1077 No. 1997.

suitable to the dispute, and, if so "to help the [applicant] to decide" whether to apply for funding of mediation rather than legal representation.[38]

The Research[39] demonstrated that the experience of people participating in mediation was on the whole positive; but it appears that many of those required to attend an "intake" meeting under the provisions set out above "seemed to accept that mediation was a good idea in principle" but "they were less sure that it would work in their case".[40] The Lord Chancellor's Advisory Board[41] noted that it was difficult to assess the impact of mediation so long as the substantive law of divorce relies heavily on "fault based facts", and that while mediation had a valuable part to play in the divorce process,[42] the Family Law Act "perhaps embodied unrealistic expectations" as to the extent to which mediation could properly "replace" legal services.

Information meeting pilot schemes

11–055 Fourteen information meeting pilots were established[43] but these schemes could not and did not replicate the conditions which would be experienced if the relevant provisions of the Act were implemented. This is because under the Act attendance would be obligatory; under the "pilot schemes" it was necessarily optional. However, the Research report (covering 957 pages of single-spaced typescript[44]) was based on a "thorough and detailed evaluation" of the pilots and (in the judgment of the Lord Chancellor's Advisory Board[45]) provided an "impressive analysis". The Report discussed many aspects of information giving; and made it clear that "information was valued and appreciated by those attending" the meetings,[46] and indeed that people "facing the ending of their marriage need and appreciate information which is clear and focussed". The research indicated that it was "unlikely that a rigidly structured information meeting would suit all circumstances and that people required a flexible format tailored to their personal needs".[47] The Research Team produced a new model for the Information Meeting which the Lord Chancellor's Advisory Board

---

[38] Family Law Act 1996, s.29. The provisions of Part III of the Act were repealed by the Access to Justice Act, but its effect is continued in the provisions of the Funding Code adopted by the Legal Services Commission (the body which has supplanted the Legal Aid Board in the administration of the public funding of legal services).

[39] The final research report by Professor Gwynn Davis, *Monitoring Publicly Funded Family Mediation,* was published by the Legal Services Commission in December 2000 and is available on the Internet. A summary is printed as Annex D to the *Fourth Annual Report* of the Advisory Board on Family Law, 2000/2001. A number of articles by Professor Davis and others summarise the findings and comment on relevant issues: see [2001] *Fam. Law* 110, 186, 265, 378.

[40] *Fourth Annual Report* of the Advisory Board on Family Law, 2000/2001, Annex D, para.6.2.

[41] See above.

[42] *Fourth Annual Report* of the Advisory Board on Family Law, 2000/2001, para.3.34.

[43] *ibid.*, 2000/2001, Annex C, p. 38.

[44] *Information Meetings and Associated Provisions within the Family Law Act 1996,* Lord Chancellor's Department, 2001. Key findings from the Research are summarised in Annex C to the *Fourth Annual Report* of the Advisory Board on Family Law, 2000/2001.

[45] *ibid.*, 2000/2001, para. 2.6.

[46] *ibid.* para. 2.1.

[47] *ibid.* para. 2.2

believed could, within the terms of the Act, "cope with the diversity of people's situations".[48]

The Advisory Board on Family Law

11–056 As already mentioned, the Government set up an Advisory Board to provide independent advice on issues arising from implementation of the Act; and in particular it was responsible for considering issues arising from the Mediation and Information Meetings Pilots.[49] On the basis of the emerging research findings, the Board formed the view that there were sufficient grounds for believing that full implementation of the Act could and should proceed[50]; and the Lord Chancellor's Officials continued to assert that the new divorce code would be brought fully into force in the year 2000. However, on June 17, 1999 the Lord Chancellor (apparently without prior consultation with the Board[51]) announced that implementation had been deferred. The Board thought it "particularly unfortunate" that the announcement was widely interpreted as a decision not to proceed further with implementation"[52] and it continued to monitor the research findings. In July 2000 the Board recommended that the shortcomings identified in the Act were not sufficiently serious to justify re-opening the whole discussion in Parliament and advised that there was no reason why the Lord Chancellor should not proceed to a decision to implement the new divorce code "in the near future".[53] But on January 16, 2001 the Lord Chancellor announced that the Government had decided not to proceed to implementation, and that Parliament would be invited to repeal the relevant sections of the Family Law Act once a suitable legislative opportunity arose.[54] Remarkably, no full explanation of the Government's decision has ever been given; but it has been suggested that the failure of couples to opt for mediation in preference to legal representation[55] on the scale apparently expected was significant; whilst the fact that many of those attending pilot information meetings chose a solicitor as their main path through divorce was manifestly not what the government wished to hear.[56]

Future uncertain

11–057 The outcome is therefore that the substantive law of divorce in England and Wales remains as set out in the Matrimonial Causes Act 1973, and that the "special procedure" with all its well substantiated imperfections continues to govern the divorce process. All that remains of the "radical new way" of organising divorce envisaged in the Family Law Act is that a measure of Gov-

---

[48] *ibid.* para. 3.15.
[49] *ibid.* paras 1.4–1.9
[50] *Third Annual Report* of the Advisory Board on Family Law, 1999/2000, para. 2.2.
[51] *Third Annual Report* of the Advisory Board on Family Law, 1999/2000, para. 2.3: Board "surprised and disappointed" by announcement.
[52] *ibid.* para. 2.3.
[53] *ibid.* para. 2. 11
[54] *Fourth Annual Report* of the Advisory Board on Family Law, 2000/2001, para. 2. 13.
[55] *ibid.* para. 3.19.
[56] *ibid.* Annex C, p. 42.

ernment funding has been made available for mediation rather than legal representation.[57] Section 1 of the Act remains in force as a statement of the general principles adopted by Parliament in 1996 as appropriate guides to the courts and others administering the divorce law, but has no legal substance as a part of the code of law governing divorce as a legal process.[58] The Advisory Board has stated that it does not believe that the section 1 objectives can be achieved under the law as it now stands.[59]

In these circumstances, it is not easy to predict further developments. A striking feature of the move for reform which culminated in the enactment of the Family Law Act 1996 is that pressure came from those with professional interests in the divorce process—whether as lawyers, mediators, or child welfare and social workers. In sharp contrast to the situation which had led to the reforms of divorce law in 1937 and 1969 (when strong and vocal pressure for change came from those who were unable to escape from the legal tie of a broken marriage) there seems to be no evidence of popular pressure for change. As the Lord Chancellor's Advisory Board point out,[60] the 1996 Act reflected the belief that the parties should themselves effectively take the decisions about the dissolution of their marriage; but the extremely complex structure of the Act as it emerged from Parliament seemed almost calculated to conceal the simple truth that dissolution of marriage was to be essentially a matter for private decision. The logic of the principle that the "divorce process should be seen as an administrative procedure"[61] rather than as litigation might indicate a more radical solution, perhaps simply allowing a couple to register the fact that their marriage has been dissolved in much the same way as they register the fact that a marriage has been created. But the debates on the Bill which became the 1996 Act made it abundantly clear that public opinion as reflected in the two Houses of Parliament was not yet ready to accept such a change. Lack of any popular enthusiasm for change, coupled with the fact that avowedly radical change would engender strong opposition not confined to any one political party, suggests that the prospects for new primary legislation are at best uncertain.

[57] See above.

[58] This is because the section applies only to "the court and any person . . . exercising functions under of in consequence of Parts II and III" of the Act. Part II contained the new substantive law governing divorce and separation, has never been brought into force, and is to be repealed. Part III applied to the provision of Legal Aid for Mediation which was also repealed: see above. However, the Legal Services Commission's Funding Code replicates the "general principles" which will therefore guide those concerned with the public funding of mediation.

[59] *Fourth Annual Report* of the Advisory Board on Family Law, 2000/2001, para. 2. 14.

[60] *ibid.* paras . 3.1, 3.7, 3.27 and 3.29.

[61] Albeit one supervised by the judiciary: see *Fourth Annual Report* of the Advisory Board on Family Law, 2000/2001, para.3.29

Chapter Twelve

JUDICIAL SEPARATION

INTRODUCTION

12–001 The Ecclesiastical Courts did not grant decrees of divorce dissolving marriage; but they did grant decrees of *divorce a mensa et thoro*[1] relieving the parties of the duty—at one time enforceable by an order for restitution of conjugal rights—to cohabit. The Matrimonial Causes Act 1857 renamed such decrees "judicial separation"[2]; and judicial separation remains available[3] after the enactment of the Divorce Reform Act 1969. However, the term "judicial separation is somewhat misleading since a decree does not in fact require a couple to separate, much less does it mean that the court will compel them to do so. This Chapter examines, first, the grounds upon which the decree is granted; secondly, the effect of the decree; and thirdly, the purposes which a decree may serve.

A. Grounds for Judicial Separation

12–002 The Divorce Reform Act 1969 amended the law so as to be consistent with the code of divorce introduced by that Act. A petition for judicial separation may[4] be presented to the court by either party to a marriage on the ground that one or more of the "facts" on which a divorce petition may be founded exists.[5] It is specifically provided that in the case of petitions for judicial separation the court is not to be concerned with the question whether the marriage has broken down irretrievably.[6] Hence, the court is bound[7] to grant a decree provided that one of the relevant facts—adultery, behaviour, desertion, or living apart—is proved.

---

[1] Which may be rather freely translated as "from bed and board".

[2] Such decrees—as equally their counterpart available from 1878 in magistrates' courts—were capable of causing great hardship since they denied the parties the possibility of remarriage.

[3] And was indeed frequently invoked, often apparently in order to give the parties the right to seek the financial orders (the court having powers similar to those exercisable in divorce).

[4] s.17(1), M.C.A. 1973.

[5] The "special procedure" applies to undefended judicial separation petitions in exactly the same way as to undefended divorce petitions: Family Proceedings Rules 1991, r. 2.24(3). However, there is no provision for a decree nisi in judicial separation; and the decree takes effect as soon as it is pronounced.

[6] s.17(2), M.C.A. 1973.

[7] The only exception to the rule that proof of a specified fact gives a right to a decree is that the court has power in exceptional circumstances to withhold the decree if it is concerned about arrangements for any children: M.C.A. 1973 (as substituted by Children Act 1989, Sched. 12, para. 31). The defence (M.C.A. 1973, s.5) to divorce based on grave financial or other hardship does not apply to judicial separation.

B. Effects of a Decree of Judicial Separation

12–003 A decree of judicial separation has two main legal consequences:

(i) Court may make orders relating to money and children

The court may, on or after granting a decree of judicial separation, exercise extensive ancillary financial powers; and it has power to make orders relating to the upbringing of the children of the family. The court may also grant injunctions in the course of judicial separation proceedings; and it may well be that this fact at one time explained why many judicial separation petitions were filed. However, the courts now have power (under the Part IV of the Family Law Act 1996) to make occupation and non-molestation orders without it being necessary to apply for any other relief.

(ii) Effect on succession rights

12–004 For the purposes of intestate succession, a decree of judicial separation has the same effect as a divorce[8]: neither spouse has thereafter any right to succeed to the property on the other's intestacy.[9] But judicial separation has no effect on entitlement under a will.[10]

C. The use made of Judicial Separation

12–005 Divorce can now be obtained on the basis of five years' separation. If either party wants the marriage dissolved, he or she will in time be able to get a divorce.[11] It is only in the very rare case where a bar to the granting of a divorce exists that the empty legal shell of a marriage can now be preserved at the instance of one party against the will of the other.[12] In consequence, judicial separation would seem to be appropriate in the following cases:

(a) Where the parties have religious or other objections to divorce; but nevertheless want the advantages of court orders regulating their affairs.

(b) Where a decree of divorce cannot yet be obtained because one year has not elapsed since the celebration of the marriage, and the petitioner

---

[8] s.18(2), M.C.A. 1973.

[9] This rule does not prevent a spouse applying to the court for reasonable provision under the Inheritance (Provision for Family and Dependants) Act 1975; see Chap. 8, above.

[10] Compare the effect of divorce: property given to former spouse passes as if he or she had died at date of divorce: see s.18A(1) Wills Act 1837, as inserted by Administration of Justice Act 1982 and amended by Law Reform (Succession) Act 1995.

[11] In effect, a decree of judicial separation can in due course be converted into a divorce; but procedurally it is still necessary to file a petition for divorce in the usual way: see *Butler v. Butler (The Queen's Proctor Intervening)* [1990] 1 F.L.R. 114.

[12] So long as divorce was only available on proof of a matrimonial offence, judicial separation allowed one party to a marriage to obtain financial orders against the other, whilst denying him the freedom to remarry: see, for example *Sansom v. Sansom* [1966] P. 52.

seeks the exercise of the court's ancillary powers to make financial orders and orders relating to the upbringing of the children of the family.

(c) Where the petitioner does not wish to obtain a divorce, but wants a formal recognition of the separation; and the respondent is not yet in a position to establish one of the "facts" necessary for a decree of divorce. For example, a wife may obtain a decree of judicial separation on the basis of her husband's adultery or behaviour; he may want a divorce, but not be able to obtain one until he can establish the five year living apart "fact."

In the year 1999 882 judicial separation petitions were filed, and the court granted 696 decrees.[13]

[13] *Marriage Divorce and Adoption Statistics 1999*, Table 4.23. The fact that in 1984 it became possible to petition for divorce after one year from the marriage (rather than three), and that the provisions of Family Law Act 1996 Part IV remove any advantage to obtaining a decree as a prelude to seeking injunctions probably account for the sharp fall—from 7,480 petitions in 1982 to 1,584 in 1996—in recourse to judicial separation.

CHAPTER THIRTEEN

TERMINATION OF MARRIAGE BY DEATH

13–001 In recent years, so much attention has been given to the increase in divorce that there is some danger of forgetting that the majority of marriages are still ended by the death of one of the spouses. A surviving spouse does, as we have seen, have important rights in relation to inheritance[1] and otherwise, and in order to establish entitlement to any of the rights to which a widow or a widower is entitled it is necessary to prove, first, that the applicant was married to the deceased at the date of the death; and, secondly, that the person said to be deceased is indeed dead. Normally these matters do not give rise to any difficulty both marriage and death can readily be proved by production of an official copy of the relevant entry in the appropriate register.[2] But this will not always be so. First, as we have seen, in some cases the validity of the survivor's marriage to the deceased will be put in issue, and secondly, there may be cases in which there is no conclusive evidence that the spouse concerned has in fact died.

What is the position if there is no positive proof that death has occurred? There are two possibilities. First—quite independently of any distinctive family law procedure—the court has jurisdiction to presume death for the purpose of distributing property and may presume it for other purposes.[3] Secondly, there is now a distinctive procedure which in some cases allows death to be presumed, but also dissolves the marriage if that presumption in fact turns out to be incorrect.

The presumption of death at common law

13–002 The court may presume death[4] if there is no affirmative evidence that for a continuous period of seven years or more the person concerned was alive, provided:

---

[1] See Chap. 8, above.

[2] Births and Deaths Registration Act 1953, s.34.

[3] See J. Jackson, *Formation and Annulment of Marriage* (2nd ed., 1969), pp. 150–155. For a recent exercise of this power, note that the death of the seventh Earl of Lucan who disappeared after the killing of his children's nurse, has been presumed to have occurred "on or since November 8, 1974": see *The Times*. February 15, 1995; and generally, Treitel (1954) 17 *M.L.R.* 530, and D. Stone, "The Presumption of Death: A Redundant Concept" (1981) 44 *M.L.R.* 516.

[4] *Chard v. Chard* [1956] P. 259; see also *Tweney v. Tweney* [1946] P. 180—presumption applied: first spouse absent for 12 years and exhaustive inquiries made; *Re Watkins* [1953] 1 W.L.R. 1323—presumption applied: 25 years' absence; *Taylor v. Taylor* [1967] P. 25. It should be noted that there is no "magic" for this purpose in seven years' absence; and that the three additional requirements referred to in the text must also be satisfied: per Harman J., *Re Watkins* [1953] 1 W.L.R. 1323 at 1327. If, for instance, there exist reasons why the missing spouse might have wished to disappear, or if he were a solitary person, the court might well refuse to presume death; on the other hand, death might more easily be presumed if he had been a gregarious man leading a public life, who had been in poor health or following a dangerous occupation.

(i) that there are persons who would be likely to have heard from the spouse during that period;
(ii) that those persons have not heard from him or her; and
(iii) that all due inquiries have been made appropriate to the period

Decree of presumption of death and dissolution

13–003 The shortcomings of the common law presumption can be seen by taking an example. Suppose that a man who has been married to W1 subsequently goes through a ceremony of marriage with W2. If the conditions governing the presumption of death set out above are satisfied, the marriage will be presumed to be valid; but if it subsequently transpires that W1 was alive at the date of the purported marriage to W2 that marriage will be void.

It was obviously unsatisfactory that a person whose spouse had disappeared should be unable to re-marry without the risk that the second marriage would be invalidated in this way by the reappearance of the absent party. The Matrimonial Causes Act 1937[5] accordingly made it possible to obtain a decree of presumption of death and dissolution of marriage. A decree absolute[6] under this procedure terminates the marriage even if the other party is in fact still alive[7]; and accordingly the petitioner can safely remarry.

The Matrimonial Causes Act now provides[8] that:—

> "Any married person who alleges that reasonable grounds exist for supposing that the other party to the marriage is dead may present a petition to the court to have it presumed that the other party is dead and to have the marriage dissolved, and the court may, if satisfied that such reasonable grounds exist, grant a decree of presumption of death and dissolution of the marriage."

The task of a petitioner[9] in satisfying the court that reasonable grounds exist for supposing that the other party to the marriage is dead is facilitated by the provision[10] that:—

> " . . . the fact that for a period of seven years or more the other party to the marriage has been continually absent from the petitioner and the petitioner has no reason to believe that the other party has been living within

---

[5] M.C.A. 1937, s.8.

[6] A decree of presumption of death and dissolution must in the first instance be a decree nisi which is not normally to be made absolute before the end of six weeks. M.C.A. 1973, s.19(4) If it is found, after the decree nisi but before the decree absolute, that the other party is still alive, the decree will be rescinded; *Manser v. Manser* [1940] P. 224.

[7] If the respondent subsequently appears, the court could exercise its powers to make financial provision and property adjustment orders: *Deacock v. Deacock* [1958] P. 230.

[8] M.C.A. 1973 s.19(1). There are no absolute or discretionary bars to a decree on this ground: *ibid.*, s.19(6); see Law Com. No. 33 (1970), p. 55.

[9] On whom the onus lies: *Parkinson v. Parkinson* [1939] P. 346.

[10] M.C.A. 1973, s.19(3).

> that time shall be evidence that the other party is dead until the contrary is proved."

It has been held[11] that the words "the petitioner has no reason to believe that the other party has been living within" the seven-year period should be read as: "if nothing has happened within that time to give the petitioner reason to believe that the other party was then living." The test of whether there is "reason to believe" relates to the standards of belief of a reasonable person: "pure speculation" is excluded.[12] If seven years' absence cannot be shown, the petitioner may still obtain a decree if reasonable grounds are shown for believing the spouse to be dead.[13] This must depend on the facts of the particular case.

---

[11] *Thompson v Thompson* [1956] P. 414.

[12] *ibid.*

[13] *MacDarmaid v. Att.-Gen.* [1950] P. 218. For example, a decree could no doubt be obtained in cases in which no trace was found of a person known to have been in the World Trade Centre New York on September 11, 2001.

CHAPTER FOURTEEN

FINANCIAL CONSEQUENCES OF MARITAL BREAKDOWN

INTRODUCTION

14–001 For many years, divorce law was primarily concerned with the question of whether or not the court would grant a divorce permitting remarriage. However, in recent years—and especially since the introduction of divorce for irretrievable breakdown[1]—attention has shifted from the change of status and increasingly focussed on the consequences of divorce[2] in terms of financial matters and the arrangements for the upbringing of children. In relation to children, section 41 of the Matrimonial Causes Act 1973 requires a petitioner to file a statement of arrangements proposed for the upbringing of children under 16, and the making absolute of the decree nisi of divorce may be delayed (although this rarely happens in practice) if the district judge considers the proposals unsatisfactory and that the court may need to exercise its power to make residence, contact and other orders under the Children Act 1989.[3] The reader should refer to Chapter 19 for an account of these matters.

Part II of the Matrimonial Causes Act 1973 is concerned with the court's powers to make financial relief orders—described[4] as its power to grant "ancillary relief" because the court's powers only arise[5] on or after the grant of a decree[6] (whether of divorce, nullity, or judicial separation in the case of financial provision and property adjustment orders, and of divorce or nullity in the case of pension sharing orders). The financial settlement is commonly a contentious issue for the parties, and the costs of protracted litigation either to those parties[7]

---

[1] Divorce Reform Act 1969, discussed in Chap. 11.

[2] An clear example of the remedial function of legal regulation: see J. Eekelaar *Family Law and Social Policy* (2nd ed., Weidenfeld & Nicholson, 1984) pp. 15–17; J. Dewar *Law and the Family* (2nd ed., Butterworths, 1992) pp. 3–5.

[3] A "section 8 order" as defined: Children Act 1989, s.8(2).

[4] The term "ancillary relief" is defined and used in the procedural code governing financial matters: Family Proceedings Rules 1991, r. 1.2(1), r. 2.51A-2.70.

[5] M.C.A. 1973, ss.23(1), 24(1, 24B(1) Orders made under the powers to make financial provision, property adjustment and pension sharing orders in favour of the spouses cannot take effect unless the decree had been made absolute: see *Dackham v. Dackham* [1987] 2 F.L.R. 358, CA. (where a decree was purportedly made absolute in defiance of the rules in order to allow the court to make a property adjustment order).

[6] This has sometimes given rise to difficulties in practice: see notably *Board (Board Intervening) v. Checkland* [1987] 2 F.L.R. 257, CA. (agreement reached on financial settlement and consent application filed—court indorsed papers "Back to Sandra for decree nisi"—order purportedly made before decree nisi—held: a nullity and husband could not be compelled to pay agreed lump sum after wife's death); *cf. Pounds v. Pounds* [1994] 1 F.L.R. 775, CA, where the court felt able to correct an order dated prior to the grant of the decree under the slip rule.

[7] For examples, see *F v. F (Ancillary Relief: Substantial Assets)* [1995] 2 F.L.R. 45, Thorpe J., *Piglowska v. Piglowski* [1999] 2 F.L.R. 763, HL.

or (through public funding) to the taxpayer can be very substantial. We consider below the contemporary "settlement culture" and the various policies and procedures which have been developed in recent years in order to promote settlement and curtail the costs of litigation.

For some years it has been the policy of the law to encourage parties to negotiate (with the assistance of both lawyers and mediators) and reach their own agreement about the financial consequences of divorce.[8] However, there is a certain tension between the policy of encouraging settlement and the traditional view that the state has a vital interest in ensuring that any settlement is fair and reasonable, in the interests both of the individuals concerned and of the community as a whole. The first part of this Chapter discusses the extent to which so-called "private ordering" is permitted. The text then analyses the legislative framework within which negotiations are conducted (both by lawyers and mediators) and which is applied to determine that small minority of cases proceeding to adjudication.

I. THE SETTLEMENT CULTURE

14–002 Reported cases may give the misleading impression that the majority of divorce financial settlements are achieved by a trial before a judge leading to a formal adjudication. Indeed, for many years, "collusion" was a bar to divorce (since it was not for individual citizens to decide for themselves whether their marriages should be terminated) and the fact that a divorcing couple had come to an agreement about the financial consequences of divorce might lead the court to suspect that they had done so as part of a collusive bargain.[9] Far from being a matter for satisfaction, the fact that a couple had come to an agreement between themselves about financial matters was for long regarded as something that should attract the court's vigilance; and it went almost without saying that the issue of whether there should be a divorce or not had to be decided before the court could turn its attention to the financial consequences. But since the Divorce Reform Act 1969 introduced divorce based on irretrievable breakdown it has been the policy of the law to encourage parties to settle their money and property

---

[8] *Gojkovic v. Gojkovic (No. 2)* [1991] 2 F.L.R. 233 at 238, *per* Butler-Sloss L.J. Less than a quarter of the cases studied at three court centres in Davis, Cretney and Collins, *Simple Quarrels* (1994) resulted in formal adjudication by the court. The study by a team at Cardiff University of the pre-settlement process found that only a minority of parties obtained court orders for ancillary relief: A. Perry, G. Douglas, M. Murch, K. Bader and M. Borkowski *How Parents Cope Financially on Marriage Breakdown* Report to the Joseph Rowntree Foundation (Cardiff Law School, November 1999). See also the reports of further research conducted at Bristol by Davis *et al.*: "Ancillary Relief Outcomes" (2000) *C.F.L.Q.* 43; D. Bird "Ancillary Relief Oucomes" (2000) *Fam. Law* 831. The National Centre for Social Research has recently conducted a study into the financial arrangements after separation and divorce: see S. Arthur, J. Lewis, S. Finch, M. MacLean and R. Fitzgerald "Settling Up: making financial arrangements after divorce or separation," National Centre for Social Research, 2002. The pro-settlement policy would have been even more overtly expressed had the relevant provisions of the Family Law Act 1996 (*e.g.* s.9) ever been enacted. See Chap. 11.

[9] At common law any agreement made between the parties to divorce proceedings was invalid if made collusively: *Hope v. Hope* (1856) 22 Beav. 35; (1857) 8 De GM and G 731.

affairs between themselves[10]; and what has been described[11] as the "settlement culture" came to pervade the divorce process. No fewer than 47,179 ancillary relief orders were made by consent in county courts in 2000.[12] The settlement ethos is now all-pervasive of lawyers' conduct of matrimonial proceedings,[13] and the Solicitors Family Law Association, the Family Law Bar Association and the Law Society have developed professional codes of conduct[14] which embody it.

A conflict of principle: ouster of court's jurisdiction contrary to public policy

14–003 The modern policy thus favours the making of private agreements, but traditionally the law has been reluctant to view the financial consequences of marriage breakdown as a purely private concern. Thus the common law did not enforce, and statute law[15] renders void, any provision in an agreement[16] purporting to restrict the right to apply to the court for an order for financial relief.[17] The result is that, however clear it may be that the parties intended an agreement to be conclusive and final it will be open to one of them, whether because of second thoughts or changed circumstances, to seek to reopen it if he or she becomes dissatisfied with the bargain.[18] In *Xyhdias v Xyhdias*[19] the Court of Appeal reasserted the fundamental principle that an agreement for the compromise of an ancillary relief application does not give rise to an agreement enforceable in law and is not governed by ordinary contractual principles; the award is always fixed by the court. The purpose of negotiation between the parties is not to determine financial liabilty (which can only be done by the court), but rather to reduce the length and expense of the legal process.

---

[10] Divorce Reform Act 1969, s.1(2)(d); collusion no longer invalidates an agreement not to defend a petition: *Sutton v. Sutton* [1984] Ch. 184.

[11] Davis, Cretney and Collins, *Simple Quarrels* (1994), p. 211.

[12] Judicial Statistics, Annual Report 2000, Table 5.7. Note the drop in numbers from the 63,385 reported for 1993 in the last edition of this book.

[13] Davis, Cretney and Collins, found that some practitioners regard a contested hearing as tantamount to an admission of professional failure: *Simple Quarrels* (1994), pp. 211–212; but the preference for a negotiated (as distinct from an adjudicated) outcome has not been without controversy: Davis *et al., supra*, pp. 211–227 and Chap. 11.

[14] See *e.g.* the *SFLA Code of Practice, Guide to Good Practice in Family Law on Disclosure, Guide to Good Practice on Correspondence, Guide to Family Cases with a Foreign Element,* Law Society's *Family Law Protocol,* 2002.

[15] M.C.A. 1973, s.34(1); see *e.g. Jessel v. Jessel* [1979] 1 W.L.R. 1148 at 1152, CA.

[16] The status of pre-nuptial agreements had been discussed in Chap. 4.

[17] *Pounds v. Pounds* [1994] 1 F.L.R. 775 at 776, *per* Waite L.J.; and see for the policies involved *Hyman v. Hyman* [1929] A.C. 601, HL; *Sutton v. Sutton* [1984] Ch. 184 (public policy consideration survived 1969 divorce reforms and abolition of collusion as bar to divorce). However, the precise scope of the principle is not clear; contrast *Sutton v. Sutton* [1984] Ch. 184 with *Amey v. Amey* [1992] 2 F.L.R. 89 and *Smallman v. Smallman* [1972] Fam. 25, CA.

[18] *Pounds v. Pounds* [1994] 1 F.L.R. 775 at 776, *per* Waite L.J. The procedure whereby such an attack can be made depends on the circumstances—sometimes, for example, there will be an application to the court under the provisions of the M.C.A. 1973, s.35; whilst in others it may be possible to pursue an application for financial relief in divorce proceedings: see *e.g. G v. G (Financial Provision: Separation Agreement)* [2000] 2 F.L.R. 472, FD; *Re X and X (Y and Z Intervening)* [2002] 1 F.L.R. 508, FD.

[19] [1999] 1 F.L.R. 683.

Reconciling the conflict of principle: the consent order

14–004 The law has developed a technique whereby these conflicting principles may be resolved in many cases. It came to be recognised that what could not be done by private agreement could be achieved by asking the court to embody the parties' agreement in a court order; and the parties' rights and duties and all other legal consequences would then flow from the order[20] just as would be the case if the order had been made in hostile litigation in which both parties had set out all the material they considered relevant. Under the consent order[21] procedure, the parties' agreement ceases to be a source of obligation or entitlement[22] and in this way court approval to the parties' agreement enables them to enjoy relative security and peace of mind.[23] Bad legal advice is not a ground on which a consent order incorporating a clean break can be re-opened.[24]

Procedure for obtaining a consent order: the court's role

14–005 The involvement of the court in the process gives rise to a number of difficult questions of legal principle, most of which stem from the essential difference between family litigation and other civil litigation. As Waite L.J. has said[25]:—

> "In most areas of our law, parties to litigation who are sui juris and independently advised can settle their differences on terms . . . with the authority of a judge who may not be aware of the terms of the deal at all (for example when they are endorsed on counsel's brief), still less be concerned with any question as to their suitability or fairness. That is not so in financial proceedings between husband and wife, where the court does not act, it has been said, as a rubber stamp . . . "

But this raises the question of what precisely is the court's role when dealing with an application for a consent order; and some understanding of the evolution of the law is necessary to answer that question.

In 1984[26] the House of Lords held that the court could not lawfully exercise its discretion to make orders relating to financial provision or property adjustment—whether by consent or otherwise—unless the court had before it information about all the circumstances of the case which was not only correct, but also complete and up-to-date. It was the duty of the court in every case, whether it was proceeding by consent of the parties or after a contested hearing, to be

---

[20] *De Lasala v. De Lasala* [1979] 2 All E.R. 1146.

[21] Defined in Matrimonial Causes Act 1973, s. 33A(3). On the stage at which a consent order comes into existence, see *Rose v. Rose* [2002] EWCA Civ. 208 [2002] 1 *F.L.R.* 978. There, the court had approved the agreement and it only remained for its detailed terms to be drafted by counsel. The court had made an unperfected order.

[22] *De Lasala v. De Lasala* [1980] A.C. 546; *Thwaite v. Thwaite* (1981) 2 F.L.R. 280, CA; *Xhydias v. Xhydias* [1999] 1 F.L.R. 683, CA; *Rose v. Rose* [2002] EWCA Civ. 208; [2002] 1 *F.L.R.* 978.

[23] *Pounds v. Pounds* [1994] 1 F.L.R. 775 at 779, *per* Waite L.J.

[24] *Harris v. Manahan* [1997] 1 F.L.R. 205.

[25] *Pounds v. Pounds* [1994] 1 F.L.R. 775 at 776–777, CA.

[26] *Livesey (formerly Jenkins) v. Livesey* [1985] A.C. 424.

satisfied that the provision of the order fulfilled the criteria laid down[27] by the Matrimonial Causes Act.[28]

This ruling caused concern, since it had apparently been common practice for district judges not to investigate the case at all but to rely on the fact that the parties were represented by competent solicitors who (it could be assumed) would carry out such investigations as were necessary to protect their clients' opposed interests. The possibility that many consent orders might be vulnerable to subsequent attack on the ground that the failure to investigate all the relevant facts had deprived the court of jurisdiction led to the insertion into the Matrimonial and Family Proceedings Act 1984 (then before Parliament) of a provision designed to achieve a workable compromise by minimising the risk that consent orders would be made without jurisdiction whilst at the same time seeking to ensure that the court would have all relevant information before it to enable it to perform its statutory duty of considering all relevant circumstances.

Legislation accordingly provides that the court may make a consent order for financial relief in agreed terms on the basis only of prescribed information furnished with the application[29]; and the rules[30] provide that every application for a consent order should be accompanied by two copies of the draft order sought and a statement of information, including such matters as the duration of the marriage, an estimate of the means of the parties, the arrangements to be made for the accommodation of the parties and any child, whether either party has any present intention to marry or to cohabit with another person, and also "any other especially significant matters.[31]"

It has been said[32] that the effect of these provisions is "to confine the paternal function of the court when approving financial consent orders to a broad appraisal of the parties' financial circumstances as disclosed to it in summary form, without descent into the valley of detail"; and that it is "only if that survey puts the court on inquiry as to whether there are other circumstances into which it ought to probe more deeply that any further investigation is required of the judge before approving the bargain that the spouses have made for themselves." The extent to which a court can sensibly discharge such a function—striking a balance between the role of rubber stamp on the one hand and "forensic ferret"

---

[27] *Pounds v. Pounds* [1994] 1 F.L.R. 775 at 779, CA, *per* Waite L.J.

[28] s.25; see below. A further consequence of the approach taken to the nature of consent orders by the House of Lords is that only terms which the court has jurisdiction to embody in an order can be included. Provisions about such matters as liability for outgoings will not usually be within the court's powers; and should accordingly be dealt with by undertakings given to the court. Difficult questions may arise in relation to enforcement of undertakings: see P. Moor and N. Mostyn [1992] *Fam. Law* 233; District Judge Price [1992] *Fam. Law* 371; and District Judge Bird [1990] *Fam. Law* 420; but it appears that undertakings to discharge financial obligations may in some cases be enforced by the judgment summons procedure: see *Symmons v. Symmons* [1993] 1 F.L.R. 317; *M v. M (Enforcement: Judgment Summons)* [1993] *Fam. Law* 469. On judgment summons procedure generally, see Chap. 16, below.

[29] M.C.A. 1973, s.33A(1), as inserted by Matrimonial and Family Proceedings Act 1984, s.7.

[30] Family Proceedings Rules 1991, r. 2.61.

[31] The information is prescribed as Form M1 in the Appendix to FPR 1991, and is limited. Information presented in Form M1 was considered in *X v. X (Y and Z Intervening)* [2002] 1 F.L.R. 508, FD.

[32] *Pounds v. Pounds* [1994] 1 F.L.R. 775 at 780, CA, *per* Waite L.J.

on the other[33]—is self-evidently difficult and there may well be diversity in judicial practice.[34] According to one district judge with great experience in this field, the court's role is limited to satisfying itself that the proposed order is within the band of reasonable discretion and does not offend any obvious principle.[35]

Agreements not embodied in a court order

14–006 What is the legal status of an agreement (in this context, commonly a separation agreement) which has not been embodied in a consent order? The existence of an agreement is an important factor for the court to consider in exercising its discretion to achieve a just and fair outcome under section 25[36] of the Matrimonial Causes Act 1925 in ancillary relief proceedings.[37] Since the court retains its discretion the agreement cannot *per se* be conclusive of outcome,[38] but in the end result may prove to be strongly persuasive.[39] According to Connell J. in *G v. G (Financial Provision: Separation Agreement)*[40] the most relevant questions for the court to ask are: how did the agreement come to be made? did the parties attach importance to it? have they acted upon it? In *X v. X (Y and Z Intervening)*[41] Munby J. emphasied[42] that the court must have regard to all the circumstances, judged in their totality; those surrounding the making of the agreement are important, but relevant circumstances also include social, personal, religious and cultural considerations.

That said, the court will not lightly permit parties who have made an agreement to depart from it. A solemn and freely negotiated bargain by which a party with competent legal advice[43] defines his own requirements ought to be adhered

---

[33] *B-T v. B-T (Divorce: Procedure)* [1990] 2 F.L.R. 1 at 17, *per* Waite L.J.

[34] For empirical studies, see "R. Ingleby, "Rhetoric and Reality: Regulation of out of court activity in matrimonial proceedings" [1989] *O.J.L.S.* 230; G. Davis, J. Pearce, R. Bird, H. Woodward and C. Wallace, "Ancillary Relief Outcomes" (2000) 12 *C.F.L.Q.* 43; R. Bird, "Ancillary Relief Outcomes" (2000) *Fam. Law* 831. For reported examples of courts expressing concern about the information provided in Form M31, see *B v. Miller & Co.* [1996] 2 F.L.R. 22, FD, and *X v. X (Y and Z Intervening)* [2002] 1 F.L.R. 508, FD.

[35] R. Bird, *Ancillary Relief Handbook* (Family Law, 3rd ed, 2002), p. 88.

[36] Either as one of the "circumstances" referred to in s. 25 (1) or as "conduct" under s. 25(2)(g): *Edgar v. Edgar* [1980] 1 W.L.R. 1410 at 1419; *Camm v. Camm* [1982] 4 F.L.R. 577; *G v. G (Financial Provision: Separation Agreement)* [2000] 2 F.L.R. 472, FD; *X v. X (Y and Z Intervening)* [2002] 1 F.L.R. 508.

[37] See *Hyman v. Hyman* [1929] A.C. 601 at 608–609, *per* Lord Hailsham; *X v. X (Y and Z Intervening)* [2002] 1 F.L.R. 508 *per* Munby J. at para. [103].

[38] The separation agreement in *Beach v. Beach* [1995] 2 F.L.R. 160 was not adhered to strictly but instead taken into account as part of the developing history.

[39] As in *G v. G (Financial Provision: Separation Agreement)* [2000] 2 F.L.R.18, FD.

[40] *G v. G (Financial Provision: Separation Agreement)* [2000] 2 F.L.R. 18, FD ("starting point for the order").

[41] [2002] 1 F.L.R. 508, FD.

[42] *ibid.* at para [103].

[43] *Camm v. Camm* (1983) 4 F.L.R. 577, CA. (where the quality of legal advice offered to the wife was a factor in allowing her to resile from an agreement), but note that in *Smith v. McInerney* [1994] 2 F.L.R. 1077, Thorpe J.—who had appeared as counsel for the unsuccessful husband in Camm—described it as a "truly exceptional case . . . the only case in the Court of Appeal post *Edgar v. Edgar* in which an applicant has been allowed more than he or she contracted for; *B. v. B. (Consent Order: Variation)* [1995] 1 F.L.R. 9; *B v. Miller & Co.* [1996] 2 F.L.R. 22.

to unless there are clear and compelling grounds for concluding that an injustice will be done if the parties are held to it.[44] A drastic and unforeseen (or overlooked) change of circumstances, or the presence of factors (such as undue pressure by one side, exploitation of a dominant position to secure an unreasonable advantage, inadequate knowledge, as well it seems as poor legal advice) which affected the conclusion of the agreement may be relevant,[45] and although the court must give first consideration to the welfare of children of the family,[46] there have been few cases in which a party has convinced the court that a formal agreement should be set aside. The leading case is still *Edgar v. Edgar*[47]:—

> The wife of a multi-millionaire entered into an agreement whereby she accepted property worth some £100,000 from her husband, and agreed not to seek any further capital or property provision from the husband whether by way of ancillary relief in divorce proceedings or otherwise. Three years later she petitioned for divorce, claimed a substantial capital sum, and at first instance was awarded a lump sum of £760,000. The Court of Appeal held that the wife had shown insufficient grounds to justify going behind the original agreement. It was immaterial that there may have been a disparity of bargaining power between the husband and the wife, since on the facts he had not exploited it in a way which was unfair to the wife (who had had the benefit of proper professional advice and had deliberately chosen to ignore it). In *X v. X (Y and Z Intervening)*[48] the parties were both Jewish and the wife's family very wealthy. The parties separated after five years of marriage, whereupon there was media gossip concerning the wife's alleged adultery. Following negotiations between the husband and the wife's family and between the parties' solicitors (who were highly experienced in the conduct of wealthy cosmopolitan divorces) minutes of a consent order for a clean break settlement were agreed between the parties, whereby *inter alia* the wife would petition for divorce on the ground of the husband's behaviour, the husband would receive £500,000 (to be paid by the wife's brother) and the husband would give a Get. The Get was duly given and a decree nisi subsequently granted. The district judge refused to approve the minutes of order: there were doubts about disclosure and an inadequate explanation of the basis of the husband's entitlement to receive the lump sum, given that the wife claimed she had no assets of her own and the husband admitted to £620,000 plus a £60,000 pension fund and £75,000 salary. The wife resiled from the agreement, on the basis that the essential condition of amicable, expeditious and discrete means of settling their affairs had not been met. The husband applied to require the wife to show

---

[44] *Edgar v. Edgar* [1980] 1 W.L.R. 1410 at 1424, *per* Oliver L.J.; *Benson v. Benson (dec'd)* [1996] 1 F.L.R. 692); *N v. N (Consent Order: Variation)* [1993] 2 F.L.R. 868 at 876, *per* Butler-Sloss L.J.; *H v. H (Financial Relief: Non-Disclosure)* [1994] 2 F.L.R. 94, Thorpe J.; *Smith v. McInerney* [1994] 2 F.L.R. 1077, Thorpe J; *X v. X (Y and Z Intervening)* [2002] 1 F.L.R. 508, Munby J.

[45] *Edgar v. Edgar; Camm v. Camm* (above).

[46] *N v. N (Consent Order: Variation)* [1993] 2 F.L.R. 868, CA (where it was held that the fact that the child's own periodical payments could be varied upwards was sufficient protection).

[47] [1980] 1 W.L.R. 1410, CA.

[48] [2002] 1 F.L.R. 508, FD.

> cause why the minutes of order should not be made an order of the court. The court granted the husband the summary order he sought. The wife should be held to the agreement, which she had willingly entered into with the benefit of expert advice. She had not established inequality of bargain power, or, even if it had existed, that it was the husband who had sought to exploit it. Far from the wife showing that she would suffer injustice if held to her agreement, it was the husband who would suffer serious injustice if she were not. He had faithfully performed his part of the bargain in circumstances where there could be no *restitutio in integrum*.

In contrast:—

> In *B v. B (Consent Order: Variation)*[49] a wife in a depressed and highly confused state accepted a settlement under which she would receive a lump sum and diminishing periodical payments over a specified term which was not to be capable of being extended. It was held that the wife had received such manifestly bad legal advice (given that it was most unlikely that she would be able to survive without lifetime periodical payments) that she should not be bound by the agreement; and an award of periodical payments at the rate of £25,000 for the parties' joint lives was made.

There may be a dispute as to whether an agreement has been concluded and, if so, what are its terms. In *Xydhias v. Xydhias*[50] there were intensive negotiations prior to trial; a number of draft consent orders were produced by counsel and the wife's solicitors asked the court to vacate the hearing date and substitute a short appointment. At that appointment it was stated that all offers made by the husband were withdrawn. The wife sought an order in the terms of the agreement reached by the parties at the end of their negotiations, and succeeded. The Court of Appeal held *inter alia* that the court has a discretion in determining whether an accord was reached, although it is to be hoped that the occasions on which it is required to exercise it will be rare. Ordinarily, heads of agreement (as distinct from a draft of the consent order) signed by the parties, or a clear exchange of solicitors' letters, will establish the necessary consensus. In *Rose v. Rose*[51] the judge had approved the agreement and it only remained for its detailed terms to be drafted by counsel. In these circumstances the Court of Appeal held that there was an unperfected order of the court.[52]

The law governing the setting aside of out-of-court agreements has been criticised unsatisfactory[53]; In the words of Hoffmann L.J. (as he then was):

---

[49] [1995] 1 F.L.R. 9, Thorpe J.

[50] [1999] 1 F.L.R. 683, CA.

[51] [2002] EWCA Civ. 208; [2002] *Fam. Law* 344; D.J. Davies "FDRs and the Unperfected Order" [2002] *Fam. Law*. 613.

[52] It was suggested that the considerations identified in *Stewart v. Engel* [2000] 1 W.L.R. 2268 were likely to be relevant where one party sought release between the making of an order in court and its subsequent perfection.

[53] See *Pounds v. Pounds* [1994] 1 F.L.R. 775 at 790, *per* Waite L.J and at 791, *per* Hoffmann L.J.

"If one of them changed his or her mind, they would have to go back to the negotiating table or litigate the matter de novo. This may be tiresome, as in the case of a house purchase where one party changes his or her mind before contracts are exchanged. But the parties would at least know where they stood. The result of the decision . . . in *Edgar v. Edgar* . . . is that we have . . . the worst of both worlds. The agreement may be held to be binding only after litigation, and may involve, as in this case, examining the quality of the advice which was given to the party who wishes to resile. It is then understandably a matter for surprise and resentment on the part of the other party that one should be able to repudiate an agreement on account of the inadequacy of one's own legal advisers, over whom the other party had no control and of whose advice he had no knowledge . . . We have created uncertainly and . . . added to the cost and pain of litigation."

Facilitating settlement

14–007 During the 1990s a number of developments contributed to reform of procedures with a view to facilitating settlement. Some of these originated from the courts themselves.[54] From 1992 a group of judges and practitioners met to consider procedural improvements, and this group later expanded into the Lord Chancellor's Advisory Group on Ancillary Relief.[55] The Group devised a pilot scheme seeking to encourage early definition of the matters in issue between the parties, and envisaging that in most cases financial issues would be referred to a Financial Dispute Resolution appointment, at which the parties would use their best endeavours to reach agreement, with assistance from the court. This scheme was introduced in selected courts in 1996[56] and after evaluation and amendment was implemented nationwide as standard procedure in 2000.[57] The overriding objective is to enable the courts to deal with cases justly and proportionately[58] through active case-management, including identification of issues, limiting disclosure, setting timetables and providing opportunities for settlement.[59] The details of the scheme are beyond the scope of a text of this nature,[60] but key elements[61] include a standard form in which evidence is given by each party, a statement of issues, a first appointment before a district judge designed to define

---

[54] See Davis, Cretney and Collins, *Simple Quarrels* (1994), pp. 162–202, on the experience of the Bristol County Court, including mediation appointments.

[55] R. Bird, *Ancillary Relief Handbook* (Family Law, 2nd ed., 2000), p. 166.

[56] See [1996] *Fam. Law* 197 at 230.

[57] The new procedure was implemented by the Family Proceedings (Amendment No 2) Rules 1999, which govern all applications for ancillary relief filed after June 5, 2000.

[58] F.P.R. 1991, r. 2.51B(1).

[59] *ibid.* r. 2.51B (5),(6).

[60] For a comprehensive account, see R. Bird *Ancillary Relief Handbook* (Family Law, 3rd ed., 2002), Chap 16; Thorpe L.J. "Procedural Reform in Ancillary Relief" [1996] *Fam. Law* 376; Coleridge *et al.*, "FDR—The Pilot Scheme" [1996] *Fam. Law* 746; on the consultation process, see [1999] *Fam. Law* 200; for a critical account, see D.J. Gerlis "Ancillary Relief—Progress or Decline?" [2001] *Fam. Law* 891; and for a response, see R. Bird "Ancillary Relief Procedure—A reply" [2002] *Fam. Law* 167.

[61] Family Proceeding Rules 1991, r. 2.61A–2.69F. On procedure under the 1999 Rules, see *Practice Direction of 25 May 2000 (Ancillary Relief Procedure)* [2000] 1 F.L.R. 997.

issues and save costs, and Financial Dispute Resolution Appointment. The latter (which is privileged) is squarely aimed at facilitating settlement; the parties are obliged to use their best endeavours to reach agreement on the matters in issue. At the Financial Dispute Resolution appointment, the judge may make a neutral evaluation of the likely outcome. The flexibility of judicial conduct of the Financial Dispute Resolution Appointment was emphasised by the Court of Appeal in *Rose v. Rose*[62] where it was also emphasised that in a finely balanced case the FDR is no substitute for a trial and should not be used as a discouragement to either party to go to trial in a case that can only properly be resolved by adjudication. If the case does proceed to a final hearing,[63] the district judge who has conducted the Financial Dispute Resolution Appointment can have no further involvement.

Incentives to settle: costs

14–008 The rules relating to liability to pay the legal costs incurred in resolving financial disputes have had a powerful influence in encouraging settlements in matrimonial cases. The starting point in civil litigation in England has for long been that costs "follow the event". The Civil Proceedings Rules 1998 state that the court has a discretion as to costs and then reiterate the general rule that the unsuccessful party will be ordered to pay the costs of the successful party.[64] In family proceedings the court has discretion as to costs,[65] but the general principle of civil litigation that costs follow the event does not in terms apply,[66] in part due to the difficulty of identifying "success" in family proceedings. Nevertheless, it is necessary to have some starting point for costs in family proceedings, and this—according to judicial interpretation of the Rules—is that costs prima facie follow the event, although that presumption is more easily displaced in family proceedings than in other civil proceedings.[67] In family proceedings courts make use of the costs sanction[68]

---

[62] [2002] EWCA Civ. 208 [2002] 1 F.L.R. 978.

[63] Note the comments by Wilson J. on the problems to which the limited evidence contained in Form E (F.P.R. 1991, Appendix 1A) may pose for the exercise of judicial discretion at a final hearing: *W. v. W. (Ancillary Relief: Practice)* [2000] *Fam. Law* 473. On procedure at the final hearing, see *Practice Direction of 10 March 2000 (Family Proceedings: Court Bundles)* [2000] 1 F.L.R. 536.

[64] Civil Proceedings Rules 1998, r. **44.**3(1),(2), (4)(5).

[65] Litigation misconduct in general sounds in costs and not in the substantive order: *Tavoulareas v. Tavoulareas* [1998] 2 F.L.R. 418; *Young v. Young* [1998] 2 F.L.R. 1131; but see *Clark v. Clark* [1999] 2 F.L.R. 498 where such misconduct was reflected in the quantum of the substantive award.

[66] Family Proceedings (Miscellaneous Amendments) Rules 1999, S.I. 1999 No. 1012, r. 4; *Practice Direction: Costs:* Civil Procedure Rules 1998 [2000] 2 F.L.R. 428.

[67] *Gojkioic v. Gojkovic (No. 2)* [1991] 2 F.L.R. 233, CA. On the current rules governing costs in ancillary relief proceedings, see Brasse, "The Sin of Costs is Death" [2000] *Fam. Law* 649 and Jones, "Ancillary Relief: The New Costs Rules" [2000] *Fam. Law* 850. On the relationship between the Civil Proceedings Rules 1998 and the Family Proceedings (Miscellaneous Amendment) Rules 199, see *M. v. M. (Costs in Children Proceedings)* [2000] *Fam. Law* 877, Singer J.

[68] Even in cases in which one or both parties are legally aided the effect of the statutory charge (as to which see below) will often be to deter an applicant from rejecting a settlement offer: see for a critical analysis of the operation of the charge S. Shute, "The Effect of the Statutory Charge

in a deliberate attempt to encourage parties to settle financial matters by agreement.[69] This is of particular importance where the costs run into six-figure sums, usually (although not invariably[70]) in "big money" cases.[71] The reduced availability of public funding has resulted in a number of devices to ensure continued legal representation particularly where there is a financial imbalance between the parties' resources.[72]

One highly significant manifestation of this policy was the development of the so-called *Calderbank*[73] offer (that is an offer to settle the case on specified terms "without prejudice save as to costs"). If the offer is accepted, the parties will seek a consent order[74] incorporating agreed terms about the allocation of liability for costs; but if the *Calderbank* offer is not accepted, the case will proceed to trial and no reference will be made at the trial to the offer until the court has announced its award. If that award is more than the amount of the *Calderbank* offer the successful party will normally be awarded his or her costs[75]; but if it is less—thus in effect implying that the applicant has incurred the costs of the hearing unnecessarily—the court will usually[76] make an order that the person who has rejected the offer should pay all the costs incurred by both sides after the time when the offer was made. The influence of the *Calderbank* doctrine will often be a very powerful factor in persuading an applicant to accept an offer.[77] The *Calderbank* principles have—with some changes of detail[78]—been codified in the Family Proceedings (Amendment No. 2) Rules 1999.

---

on legally aided matrimonial litigation" (1993) 109 *L.Q.R.* 636; and for its impact on settlements, Davis, Cretney and Collins, *Simple Quarrels* (1994), pp. 20–26. For an example of a costs order where both parties are legally aided, see *Chaggar v. Chaggar* [1997] 1 F.L.R. 566, CA, and on the procedure to enforce costs against a legally aided person, *Ager v. Ager* [1998] 1 F.L.R. 506. An order for costs can be made in favour of a party even where there is no substantive order: *Hurley v. Hurley (Davey Intervening)* [1998] 1 F.L.R. 213.

[69] "... a consciousness of a risk as to costs if reasonable offers are refused can only encourage settlement ... ": *Cutts v. Head* [1984] Ch. 290 at 306, *per* Oliver J.

[70] For examples of high costs in relation to modest assets, see *H v. H (Financial Relief: Costs)* [1997] 2 F.L.R. 57 and *Piglowska v. Piglowska* [1999] 2 F.L.R. 763; see R.Bailey-Harris and P. Coleridge, "Family Assets, Costs and Avenues of Appeal" [1999] 115 *L.Q.R.* 551.

[71] *F v. F (Duxbury Calculation)* [1996] 1 F.L.R. 833; *White v. White* [2000] 2 F.L.R. 981.

[72] *Sears Tooth (A Firm) v. Payne Hicks Beach. (A Firm)* 1997] 2 F.L.R. 116, FD (assignment of part of prospective ancillary relief award); *A v. A (Maintenance Pending Suit: Provision for Legal Fees)* 1 F.L.R. 377, FD (costs included in maintenance pending suit). See P. Rutter "Provision for Costs—A New Way to Get Paid?" [2001] *Fam. Law* 44.

[73] *Calderbank v. Calderbank* [1976] Fam. 93, CA.

[74] See above, pp. 322–324.

[75] *Gojkovic v. Gojkovic (No. 2)* [1991] 2 F.L.R. 233, CA ; *A. v. A. (Costs Appeal)* [1996] 1 F.L.R. 14; *Thompson v. Thompson* [1993] 2 F.L.R. 464, CA; *Butcher v. Wolfe and Wolfe* [1999] 1 F.L.R. 334.

[76] Subject to there being sufficient assets available: [1991] 2 F.L.R. 233 at 237, *per* Butler-Sloss L.J.

[77] Davis, Cretney and Collins, *Simple Quarrels* (1994) p. 18; *Singer v. Sharegin* [1984] F.L.R. 114 at 119, *per* Cumming-Bruce L.J.; but see S. Gerlis "Don't Bank on Calderbank" [1997] *Fam. Law* 624. For criticism of the Calderbank procedure where costs are high, see *H v. H (Financial Relief: Costs)* [1997] 2 F.L.R. 57.

[78] See R. Bird, *Ancillary Relief Handbook* (Family Law, 3nd ed., 2002), pp. 178–183 for a detailed discussion.

II. FINANCIAL RELIEF: THE LEGISLATIVE FRAMEWORK

14–009 The fact that the vast majority of financial disputes are settled rather than adjudicated at a final hearing does not render the statutory provisions and their interpretation in the case-law irrelevant. First, as we have just seen, final and conclusive agreements can only be made by means of a court order; and the court exercises a paternal jurisdiction (albeit now attenuated[79]) over the agreements submitted for its approval. The court can only assess the reasonableness of the parties' agreement by reference to what might have occurred had the case been fought out. Secondly, legal practitioners in negotiating inevitably have in mind what the outcome of a contest might be: the parties therefore negotiate (as it has been said[80]) in the shadow of the law. Even if the parties wish to reach an agreement by themselves, or with the aid solely of a mediator, they cannot rationally decide whether what emerges is fair unless they have some knowledge of the "going rate" for their situation. Finally, and inevitably, there are cases where the parties' approach is one of mutual hostility, inevitably leading to litigation.

The extent of the court's powers

14–010 English law is remarkable for the extent of the court's statutory[81] powers to make financial orders in divorce[82] proceedings. The policy of the law has been to put all economically valuable assets of the two spouses at the disposition of the court. As Waite L.J. observed in *Thomas v Thomas*[83]:

> "The discretionary powers conferred on the court by the amended ss 23–25A of the Matrimonial Causes Act 1973 to redistribute the assets are almost limitless."

The law reports are replete with illustrations of the court's willingness to exercise their ample powers. Moreover, the scope of the courts' powers have recently been extended in relation to pensions, often an asset of considerable significance.[84] Extensive as the court's powers are, they are not limitless. All the terms of the court's order must come within the statutory powers.[85]

---

[79] See *Pounds v. Pounds* [1994] 1 F.L.R. 775 at 780, CA, *per* Waite L.J.

[80] See R. Mnookin and L. Kornhauser, "Bargaining in the Shadow of the Law: The Case of Divorce" (1979) 88 *Yale L.J.* 950; an abbreviated version can be found in (1979) 32 *C.L.P.* 65.

[81] The powers are conferred only by statute: *Livesey (formerly Jenkins) v. Jenkins* [1985] F.L.R. 813 at 820, HL, *per* Lord Brandon of Oakbrook.

[82] Unless otherwise indicated, the powers are available in separation and nullity as well as in divorce proceedings.

[83] [1995] 2 F.L.R. 668 at 670D.

[84] Pensions Act 1995, inserting ss. 25B–25D into the Matrimonial Causes Act 1973; Welfare Reform and Pensions Act 1999, inserting ss. 21A and 24B into the Matrimonial Causes Act 1973 and amending ss. 24, 25, 25A, 25C, 25D. The range of the court's powers in relation to pensions are discussed below at p. 406.

[85] Thus there is no power to include in an order (even an order made by consent of the parties) a provision that one party should be solely responsible for a mortgage and outgoings in respect of a house, and for servicing and repayment of other loans. Such matters should be dealt with by

Finally, it should be noted that the exercise of the court's powers cannot prejudice the rights of third parties not before the court. Thus, if the matrimonial home is subject to a mortgage, a transfer of the house to the wife cannot affect the mortgagor spouse's contractual liability to pay the mortgage instalments,[86] nor the rights of the mortgagee to take action if the mortgage covenants are broken. In practice, mortgage deeds usually contain provisions prohibiting the mortgagor from transferring the property without the mortgagee's consent. Accordingly, rules provide for[87] the mortgagee to have notice of the application and be given an opportunity to be heard.

Almost as striking as the extent of the court's powers is the flexibility of the principles governing their exercise. The process has been graphically described by Lord Denning[88]:—

> The court (he said) "takes the rights and obligations of the parties all together and puts the pieces into a mixed bag. Such pieces are the right to occupy the matrimonial home or have a share in it, the obligation to maintain the wife and children, and so forth. The court then takes out the pieces and hands them to the two parties—some to one party and some to the other—so that each can provide for the future with the pieces allotted to him or to her. The court hands them out without paying any too nice a regard to their legal or equitable rights but simply according to what is the fairest provision for the future, for mother and father and the children."

The implicit over-arching objective of the section 25 exercise in seeking to achieve a fair outcome has been reiterated by the House of Lords in *Piglowska v. Piglowski*[89] and *White v. White*.[90]

Nevertheless, in recent years the width of discretion conferred by the statutory

---

undertaking: *Livesey (formerly Jenkins) v. Jenkins* [1985] F.L.R. 813 HL. It is, however, now common for the court to order one spouse to execute a charge for a proportion of the sale proceeds of the matrimonial home in favour of the other notwithstanding the absence of any statutory provision clearly authorising such a provision. Similarly, it might be questioned whether there is any power to include in an order a provision that one spouse be required to spend a lump sum in the purchase of substitute housing; but such an order was accepted without comment by the Court of Appeal in *Scallon v. Scallon* [1990] 1 F.L.R. 194. The court is in general bound by provisions restricting the transferability of property (*e.g.* a covenant against assignment in a lease); but note changes introduced by the Pensions Act 1995 and the Welfare Reform and Pensions Act 1999, discussed later in this Chap.

[86] In practice it is common for the party taking over the home to agree to indemnify the other party against liability under the mortgage, but such a provision will not be effective if for some reason (for example, bankruptcy) the indemnity ceases to be effective.

[87] F.P.R. 1991, r. 2. 59(4). For a case where the mortgagees were unwilling to consent to the proposed transfer, see *J. (H.D.) v. J. (A.M.)* [1980] 1 All E.R. 156 at 158F. If the property in question is a lease containing a covenant against assignment the landlord will invariably be given notice of the application: *Marsh v. Gilbert* (1980) 256 E.G. 715; and it will have to be decided whether he is in breach of the duty to give consent imposed by the Landlord and Tenant Act 1988. Under the law formerly in force it was held that the court would usually not make an order since that would have required it to decide whether the landlord was unreasonable in withholding consent: *ibid.*; *Regan v. Regan* [1977] 1 W.L.R. 84 at 85.

[88] *Hanlon v. The Law Society* [1981] A.C. 124 at 146, CA.

[89] [1999] 2 F.L.R. 763.

[90] [2000] 2 F.L.R. 981.

provisions in their current form has been called in question, since it leads to unpredictability and may produce high costs in cases which are the subject of protracted litigation.[91] Furthermore, to state the objective of a fair outcome in financial terms begs the question of what is the content of fairness[92] in the individual case, and whether there are agreed community values which can inform the judicial answer.[93] To date the formulation of more specific guidelines for the exercise of judicial discretion have been left to the appellate courts, but the question of whether Parliament should intervene remains open. These issues are discussed at the conclusion of this Chapter, when the advantages and disadvantages of the current system have been explored.

The text first discusses who can apply for orders; secondly[94] it analyses the powers of the court; thirdly, it outlines the statutory guidelines for the exercise of the court's discretion,[95] and thirdly deals with the court's powers to vary orders if, for example, there has been a change of circumstances, or if the original settlement was made under some misapprehension.[96]

A. The applicants

1. The spouses

14–011 All orders can be made in favour of either party to the marriage; and it has been said that husbands and wives "come to the judgment seat . . . upon a basis of complete equality."[97] Equality in that sense means procedural equality. That ancillary relief orders are more commonly made in favour of wives than husbands does no more than reflect economic and social realities in relation to income generation, asset acquisition and child care.[98] Nevertheless, as will be shown later in this Chapter, there is currently considerable controversy on whether equality of outcome between spouses—properly reflecting the different contribution of each to the marriage—is in fact achieved by court orders in ancillary relief proceedings, particularly in the context of "big money" cases.[99]

---

[91] *Piglowska v Piglowski* [1999] 2 F.L.R. 763, HL; *White v. White* [2000] 2 F.L.R. 981, HL; *Cowan v. Cowan* [2001] 2 F.L.R. 192, CA.

[92] R. Bailey-Harris, "Dividing the Assets on Family Breakdown: The Content of Fairness" [2001] *Current Legal Problems* 533.

[93] *Piglowska v Piglowski* [1999] 2 F.L.R. 763 at 785 *per* Lord Hoffmann; *White v. White* [2000] 2 F.L.R. 981 at 984 *per* Lord Nicholls.

[94] See "B. Orders that can be made", p. 333.

[95] See "C. The principles governing the exercise of the court's discretion", p. 340.

[96] See "D. Changed Circumstances, Variation of Orders and Related Matters", p. 386.

[97] *Calderbank v. Calderbank* [1976] Fam. 93 at 103.

[98] For examples of the exercise of the court's powers in favour of a husband, see, *e.g. Griffiths v. Griffiths* [1973] 1 W.L.R. 1454 (£7,000 lump sum); *B. v. B. (Financial Provision)* [1982] 3 F.L.R. 298, CA. (£50,000); *Browne v. Browne* [1989] 1 F.L.R. 291, CA. (£175,000); *Beach v. Beach* [1995] 2 F.L.R. 160 (£60,000); *A. v A. (Elderly Applicant: Lump Sum)* 2 F.L.R. 969 (£350,000); *Rampal v. Rampal (No 2)* [2001] EWCA Civ. 989; [2001] 2 F.L.R. 1179, CA (husband's claim reinstaed); *X v. X (Y and Z Intervening)* [2002] 1 F.L.R. 508 (£500,000). In *Wills v. Wills* [1984] F.L.R. 672 (a case under D.P. & M.C.A. 1978) it was accepted that an order for periodical payments might be made against a wife in favour of her disabled husband.

[99] See *e.g. White v. White* [2000] 2 F.L.R. 981, HL; *Cowan v. Cowan* [2001] 2 F.L.R. 192, CA; *L v. L (Financial Provision: Contributions)* [2002] 1 F.L.R. 642.

2. Other persons

14–012 There may be circumstances in which a third party wishes to seek a financial order—particularly an order in favour of a child for whom the applicant has assumed responsibility.[1] The Rules make provision for such applications by persons with appropriate interests.[2]

3. Orders for children

14–013 The court has power to make orders in respect of children of the family. These powers—which are now, by reason of the enactment of the Child Support Act 1991, of only limited relevance in practice—are considered in the Chapter dealing with Child Support.[3]

B. Orders that can be made

14–014 The orders available can usefully be divided into three main categories: those ordering periodical payments of an income nature, those concerned with the transfer of capital assets,[4] and pension-sharing orders.[5]

1. Income orders

14–015 The court has power to make (a) orders for periodical payments, secured or unsecured and (b) deferred orders.

(a) Periodical payments, secured or unsecured[6]

14–016 The court may order one spouse to make regular income payments to the other, and it may order that the payments be secured. If the order is unsecured, it simply directs a spouse to make payments (weekly, monthly, or annually). In the event of default, the payee may bring enforcement proceedings—for example, by seeking an order attaching the defaulting spouse's wages, or a

---

[1] Such a person may now apply for orders under the Children Act 1989, Sched. 1: see further Chap. 15, below.

[2] F.P.R. 1991, r. 2.54. An adult child may intervene with leave in the parents' divorce suit—perhaps many years after the making of the decree absolute—in order to apply for financial orders: see *Downing v. Downing, (Downing intervening)* [1976] Fam. 288, CA. See Chap. 15.

[3] See Chap. 15, below.

[4] Section 21 of the Matrimonial Causes Act 1973 draws a distinction between "financial provision orders" (*i.e.* periodical payment orders and lump sum orders) on the one hand, and "property adjustment orders" (*i.e.* transfers and settlements of property and variations of settlements) on the other. As Lord Diplock has said (see *De Lasala v. De Lasala* [1980] A.C. 546 at 559), "the difference between a lump sum order . . . and a property transfer order . . . is the difference between providing money and money's worth"; and a lump sum award (unless of a very small amount) is as much an order for the transfer of capital as any of the other orders.

[5] M.C.A., ss.21A and 24B, inserted by the Welfare Reform and Pensions Act 1999.

[6] M.C.A. 1973, s.21(1)(a),(b), s.23(1)(a)(b).

charging order which may lead to the defaulter's property being sold. In practice, however, enforcement procedures are often unsatisfactory, for example because the defaulter has no employer and no property which can be found. If, on the other hand, the order is secured, a fund of capital (usually[7] stocks and shares, and usually vested in trustees) has to be set aside; and that fund can then be resorted to if the payments are not made as they fall due. The main advantage of a secured order is that it remains enforceable even if a spouse disappears or ceases to earn.[8] A further advantage is that such orders may continue throughout the lifetime of the payee.

The court has an unfettered discretion as to whether to order security, and if it does so as to the proportion of the total payments which should be secured. Traditionally secured provision was regarded as a form of relief only suitable in cases in which a husband had substantial assets; and usually no more than one-third of a husband's free investments would be tied up in this way.[9] However, the courts have become increasingly prepared to order security if there is a special need for it.[10] In particular there seems no reason why the former matrimonial home should not be used as security in appropriate cases.[11]

(b) Deferred orders

14–017 As one means of dealing with pension entitlements on divorce, the court may make[12] a deferred order[13] giving one spouse the right to receive a share in the pension. Such orders, now known as attachment orders, are discussed later in this Chapter as part of the range of powers the court now possesses in relation to pension entitlements.

Duration of periodical payment orders

14–018 A periodical payment order in favour of a spouse will cease to have effect in certain circumstances:

---

[7] But not always: see, *e.g. F. v. F.* [1967] 1 W.L.R. 793 (former matrimonial home).

[8] *Shearn v. Shearn* [1931] P. 1 at 5 *per* Hill J.; and see *A v. A (A Minor: Financial Provision)* [1994] 1 F.L.R. 657 (application under Children Act 1989, Sched. 1 foreign resident, precarious life style).

[9] *Shorthouse v. Shorthouse* (1898) 78 L.T. 687; *Barker v. Barker* [1952] P. 184 at 194–195; *cf. Hulton v. Hulton* [1916] P. 57.

[10] See *Aggett v. Aggett* [1962] 1 W.L.R. 183 where maintenance was secured on the husband's only valuable asset (a house) in view of the fact that the wife had set up a guest-house in it which was her only means of earning a living, and that the husband (who had shown himself irresponsible and unconcerned for her welfare) might well go abroad leaving her without any other means of support.

[11] See Law Com. No. 25, para. 11; see *F. v. F.* [1967] 1 W.L.R. 793; *Parker v. Parker* [1972] Fam. 116 (second mortgage on husband's house).

[12] M.C.A. 1973, ss.25B, as inserted by the Pensions Act 1995, s.166 and amended by the Welfare Reform and Pensions Act 1999, s.21, Sched. 4, para. 1.

[13] *i.e.* by making an order under M.C.A. 1973, s.23 which deals with financial provision orders (*i.e.* periodical payment and lump sum orders).

(a) Death of either party

14–019 An unsecured order must terminate on the payer's death; a secured order need not.[14]

(b) Remarriage of the payee

14–020 The Matrimonial Causes Act 1973[15] gave effect to the recommendation of the Law Commission that periodical payment orders made in divorce or nullity proceedings should not extend beyond the remarriage of the party in whose favour the order was made.

It is submitted that the enactment of this rigid rule was, for several reasons, unfortunate. First, the application of the rule may mean that a divorced person loses substantially by remarriage; and this may have particularly unfortunate consequences if a mother with care of a child marries a man who is less affluent than her first husband. The child's right to maintenance will not be affected by the mother's remarriage; but the child may suffer disadvantages if the mother's own standard of living suddenly drops.[16] Secondly, the fact that remarriage will mean the end of entitlement to periodical payments may act as a disincentive to marriage. Cohabitation—even on a stable long-term basis—will only be taken into account to the extent that it has financial consequences; remarriage will automatically terminate the right to receive periodical payments.[17] The existence of cohabitation, in this context as in others, is a question of fact. It is impossible to produce a comprehensive list of criteria, but relevant considerations are living together in the same household, sharing daily life, stability and a degree of permanence, arrangements about finances and children, intention and motivation, and the opinion of reasonable others as to the nature of the parties' relationship.[18]

A lump sum or capital provision order once made cannot be varied or cancelled if the wife remarries. This is wholly justifiable on an entitlement (rather than dependency) analysis of the award.[19] This and other issues of policy are dealt with below.

---

[14] M.C.A. 1973, s.28(1)(a), (b).

[15] s.28(1)(a).

[16] See, *e.g. O'Regan (formerly Douglass) v. Douglass* [1969] 13 F.L.R. 417; and, for English cases in which the court recognised that a child would benefit from the preservation of the parent's standard of living, see *Cartwright v. Cartwright* [1982] 4 F.L.R. 463; and *E. v. E. (Financial Provision)* [1990] 2 F.L.R. 233 at 249 (not in child's interests that mother be in straitened circumstances).

[17] See *Duxbury v. Duxbury* [1987] 1 F.L.R. 7, CA; *Atkinson v. Atkinson* [1988] 7 F.L.R. 353, CA; *Hepburn v. Hepburn* [1989] 1 F.L.R. 373, CA; *Clutton v. Clutton* [1991] 1 F.L.R. 242; *Atkinson v. Atkinson* [1995] 2 F.L.R. 356; *Jessel v. Jessel* [1979] 1 W.L.R. 1148 at 1154 *per* Lord Denning M.R; *Frary v. Frary* [1993] 2 F.L.R. 696, CA.

[18] *Crake v. Supplementary Benefits Commission* [1982] 1 All E.R. 498; *Atkinson v. Atkinson* [1988] 2 F.L.R. 353; *Re J (Income Support: Cohabitation)* [1995] 1 F.L.R. 660; *Re Watson (dec'd)* [1999] 1 F.L.R. 878; *K v. K (Enforcement)* [2001] 1 F.L.R. 383. The last of these demonstrates the continuing utility of the inquiry agent in family proceedings.

[19] M. Hayes (1994) 110 *L.Q.R.* 124.

(c) The expiry of a specified term

14–021 The court is specifically required[20] to consider whether it would be appropriate to require periodical payments to be made "only for such term as would . . . be sufficient to enable the party in whose favour the order is made to adjust without undue hardship to the termination of his or her financial dependence on the other," and orders are now commonly made for specified terms—such as five years.[21] This provision is discussed below in the context of the court's general obligation under section 25A to consider making such orders as will effect a "clean break" between the parties. The circumstances in which such a term may be extended are also dealt with below.

2. Capital orders

14–022 The court has power, in the case of divorce,[22] separation and nullity proceedings to make lump-sum orders, orders for the transfer or settlement of property, and variation of settlement orders. It also has power[23] in certain circumstances to order the sale of property.

The Matrimonial Causes Act 1973 confers no power to make interim property adjustment orders.[24]

(a) Lump sum payments

14–023 The court may order payment of a lump sum in cash.[25] The Act also provides that the court may order payment by instalments, in which case payment may be secured,[26] and the court may order that the sums in question should carry interest.[27] The power to make an instalment order may be of use in cases where the parties are of modest means, and need time to pay; but it may also be of use

---

[20] M.C.A. 1973, s.25A(2).

[21] As in *Waterman v. Waterman* [1989] 1 F.L.R. 380; and see, *e.g. N v. N (Consent Order: Variation)* [1993] 2 F.L.R. 868 (five years); *Richardson v. Richardson (No. 2)* [1994] 2 F.L.R. 1051 (three years).

[22] The Family Law Act 1996, Sched. 2, para. 3 would if implemented have given the court power to make property adjustment orders prior to divorce if the circumstances were exceptional, but such orders will not normally have taken effect until the divorce or separation

[23] M.C.A. 1973, s.24A.

[24] In *Barry v. Barry* [1992] 2 F.L.R. 223 it was held that the court had an inherent jurisdiction to make administrative orders authorising purchase of house for wife's occupation from proceeds of sale of former matrimonial home on suitable undertakings being given to preserve the court's powers at the time. This was followed in *F v. F (Ancillary Relief: Substantial Assets)* [1995] 2 F.L.R. 25; but in *Wicks v. Wicks* [1998] 1 F.L.R. the Court of Appeal held that there was no source of jurisdiction enabling the court to make interim capital orders.

[25] M.C.A. 1973, s.21(1)(c), s.23(1)(c).

[26] M.C.A. 1973, s.23 (3)(c).

[27] M.C.A. 1973, s.23(6). The power order interest can only be exercised when the order is made: *L v. L (Lump Sum: Interest)* [1994] 2 F.L.R. 324. Subject to that, interest attaches to lump-sum orders as judgment debts from the date when the lump sum is due to be paid: Judgment Act 1838; but interest is only payable on lump-sum orders made in the County Court of £5,000 or more: County Courts Act 1984, s.74; County Court (Interest on Judgment Debts) Order 1991, S.I. 1991 No. 1184.

in cases where a spouse has substantial assets[28]—for example, farming land or a shareholding in a company—which it would be difficult, impracticable or undesirable to realise quickly.[29]

The power to order payment of a lump sum from a pension arrangement is discussed later in this Chapter in the context of the range of powers now available in respect of pensions.

(b) Transfer of property

14–024 The court may[30] order that specified property be transferred to the other spouse. This power may be used, for example, to order the transfer by one spouse to the other of specific shares, or very commonly the matrimonial home, or one spouse's interest in it.[31] It may be used in addition to a lump sum order where there is a special case for the transfer of a particular asset, or as an alternative to such an order. The power extends to reversionary property. For example, if one spouse's parent left property by will to X for life with remainder to the spouse, the court may during X's lifetime order that the spouse's reversionary interest be transferred to the other spouse. He or she could then either wait for it to fall into possession on X's death or sell the reversionary interest to a third party or use it as security for a loan.

(c) Settlements of property

14–025 The court may[32] direct that property to which a party to the marriage is entitled be settled for the benefit of the other party and/or the children of the family.

Traditionally, this power[33] was seen as a flexible way of using a fund of shares or other property for the family over a period of time—for example, by giving the other spouse a life interest, and preserving the capital for the children and their issue. In recent years, however, the power has most frequently been used in connection with the family home—often in an attempt to ensure that the parent who has day to day control will have a secure home for the children whilst preserving the investment interest of both spouses. This topic is considered below.

---

[28] See, *e.g. Penrose v. Penrose* [1994] 2 F.L.R. 621, CA (order for £500,000 by instalments).

[29] See *e.g. N v. N (Financial Provision: Sale of Company)* [2001] 2 F.L.R. 69 (£1million to be paid to the wife according to a detailed timetable). The court has power not only to re-timetable and adjust the amounts of individual instalments but also to vary, suspend or discharge the principal lump sum itself, although the last power is to be used very sparingly in exceptional circumstances: *Penrose v. Penrose* [1994] 2 F.L.R. 621, CA; *Tilley v. Tilley* (1980) *Fam. Law* 89; *Westbury v. Sampson* [2001] EWCA Civ. 407; [2002] 1 F.L.R. 166.

[30] M.C.A. 1973, ss.24(1)(a), 21(2)(a).

[31] See, *e.g. Mortimer v. Mortimer-Griffin* [1986] 2 F.L.R. 315, CA.

[32] M.C.A. 1973, ss 21(2)(a), 24(1)(b).

[33] Which originated in the court's power to order a wife guilty of adultery, cruelty or desertion to settle property in order to compensate the innocent parties for the pecuniary loss so caused to them: see *March v. March* (1867) L.R. 1 P. & D. 440; *Ulrich v. Ulrich* [1968] 1 W.L.R. 180: Law Com. No. 25, paras 50, 66.

(d) Variation of settlements

14–026 The court may make an order varying any "ante-nuptial or post-nuptial" settlement made on the parties to the marriage for the benefit of the parties and/or the children of the family.[34] The only restriction on the court's power to vary the settlement is that the variation must be "for the benefit" of the parties or children, and in an appropriate case the terms of the settlement may be completely re-written.[35]

The power to vary dates back to 1857; and was for long the only way in which the court could deal with capital on the breakdown of a marriage. The courts accordingly gave a broad interpretation to the word "settlement," so that (for example) it was held to extend to the case where a dwelling-house had been purchased in joint names[36] (or even in the name of one party provided that both had beneficial interests). The only qualification was that,[37] although the settlement did not have to be a marriage settlement in the strict sense, some "nuptial element" was required: the settlement must have been made on the parties as spouses,[38] and the effect of the transaction must have been to make some form of continuing provision[39] for both or either of the parties to the marriage.

This power for long seemed to be of little relevance in a world in which the traditional marriage settlement (designed primarily to protect a wife from the harsh effects of the common law rule whereby her property and earnings passed to her husband) seemed to be the stuff of legal history.[40] The power was however given some contemporary—albeit short-lived—impact by the decision of the House of Lords in *Brooks v. Brooks*,[41] which provided a limited solution in

---

[34] M.C.A. 1973, s.24 (1)(c), 21(2)(c).

[35] See *E. v. E. (Financial Provision)* [1990] 2 F.L.R. 233. The power's extend to replacing trustees: *E. v. E. (Financial Provision)* (above), not following *Compton v. Compton and Hussey* [1960] P. 201. The court's powers are not confined to varying the interests of the parties to the marriage, but extend to varying the interests of children and others under the settlement: *Brooks v. Brooks* [1995] 2 F.L.R. 13 at 20, *per* Lord Nicholls of Birkenhead. Note also that M.C.A. 1973, s.24(1)(d) empowers the court to reduce or extinguish the interest of either spouse under a nuptial settlement; and it seems that this power may be exercised notwithstanding the fact that to do so would not benefit the other spouse or children: *Cartwright v. Cartwright* [1982] 4 F.L.R. 463. Third parties such as trusteees may be joined as parties: *T v. Y (Joinder of Third Parties)* [1996] 2 F.L.R. 357, FD.

[36] *Brown v. Brown* [1959] P. 86.

[37] *Cook v. Cook* [1962] P. 235.

[38] *Young v. Young* [1962] P. 27; and see Law Com. No. 25, para. 66.

[39] Even a covenant securing an annuity to a spouse: *Bosworthick v. Bosworthick* [1927] P. 64. It was also held that a life policy effected under a trust for the wife's benefit fell within the definition of a settlement (see *Brown v. Brown* [1949] P. 91; *Lort-Williams v. Lort-Williams* [1951] P. 395.) In contrast, an outright gift by one party to the other falls outside the statutory definition of a settlement (see *Prescott (formerly Fellowes) v. Fellowes* [1958] P. 260).

[40] But notwithstanding this fact, and although the terminology of "ante-nuptial" and "post-nuptial" settlements may rightly be described as "archaic" (see *Brooks v. Brooks* [1995] 2 F.L.R. 13 at 19, *per* Lord Nicholls of Birkenhead) settlors remained concerned to make provision for their offspring and sometimes to seek to prevent family property passing to the wife and others, and settlements designed to achieve those objectives are still found: see *e.g. E v. E (Financial Provision)* [1990] 2 F.L.R. 223. Moreover, gifts in consideration of marriage have sometimes been favourably treated by tax legislation.

[41] [1995] 2 F.L.R. 13, HL. The first judicial suggestion that pension schemes might be susceptible to the exercise of this power was made by Ewbank J. in *Griffiths v. Dawson & Co.* [1993] 2 F.L.R. 315.

certain circumstances to the problem of dealing with pensions on divorce, in the absence at that time of the extensive powers subsequently conferred by legislation. *Brooks v. Brooks* laid down that in some circumstances a pension scheme fell within the definition of a nuptial settlement, and that accordingly the court could vary the terms of the settlement for the benefit of the wife or children. Since the husband had entered into the particular pension scheme in question with the intention of providing for the retirement of himself and his wife by the "highly tax efficient means afforded by" the scheme, it fell within the definition of a nuptial settlement. Accordingly, it would be appropriate to vary the terms of the pension scheme by directing that pensions be provided for the wife in priority to (and if need be in diminution of) the pension payable to the husband.

The decision in *Brooks v. Brooks* was always of limited scope[42] and now is of historical interest only. The scheme in question was comparatively unusual in having been created by the sole proprietor of a business, in which the wife was also employed; and it seems that the scheme could—without prejudicing the Inland Revenue's approval of the scheme—be converted into a multi-member scheme in which the wife could participate. Lord Nicholls of Birkenhead[43] observed that[44] "if the court is to be able to split pension rights on divorce in the more usual case of a multi-member scheme where the wife has no earnings of her own from the same employer, or to direct the taking out of life insurance, legislation will . . . be necessary". That power was given to the courts by the Welfare Reform and Pensions Act 1999, which abolished[45] the remedy created by *Brooks v. Brooks* in the context of pensions. The range of powers which the court now possesses is considered below.

(e) Power to order sale

14–027 The court has power on making an order for financial relief in divorce, nullity and separation proceedings, or at any time thereafter, to order the sale of any property in which, or in the proceeds of sale of which, either or both of the parties has or have a beneficial interest, either in possession or reversion; and an order may be made notwithstanding that a third party is also interested in the property.[46] But the court has no power under this provision to direct the payment

[42] It was applied in *W v. W (Periodic Payments)* [1996] 2 F.L.R. 480.

[43] Delivering a speech in which all the other Law Lords concurred.

[44] [1995] 2 F.L.R. 13 at 23.

[45] M.C.A. 1973, s. 24(1)(c) and (d), as amended by the Welfare Reform and Pensions Act 1999, Sched. 3, excluding a marriage settlement in the form of a pension arrangement from the categories of settlement which are variable.

[46] M.C.A. 1973, s.24A(1) Before making an order in such a case the court must give the third party an opportunity to make representations, and must consider those representations: M.C.A. 1973, s.25(6) as inserted by Matrimonial Homes and Property Act 1981, s.8(1). The provisions of s.24A were intended to give effect to the Law Commission Report on Orders for Sale of Property under the Matrimonial Causes Act 1973, Law Com. No. 99, 1980.

of the proceeds of sale to third parties[47]; in effect, the power is ancillary to or consequential upon the making of the other orders mentioned.[48]

3. Pension sharing orders

14–028 The Welfare Reform and Pensions Act 1999 gave the court power to make pension sharing orders in respect of petitions filed after December 1, 2000.[49] The full range of the court's powers in relation to pensions are discussed later in this Chapter.[50]

When orders can be made

14–029 An order for maintenance pending suit[51] can be made at any time after a petition for principal relief has been filed, but the courts' powers to make financial provision, property adjustment and pension attachment orders under section 23–24D of the Matrimonial Causes Act 1973 may be exercised only on or after the making of a decree of nullity, divorce or judicial separation.[52] Pension sharing orders may only be made on or after the making of a decree of divorce or nullity.[53]

C. The Principles governing the Exercise of the Court's Discretion

14–030 The Matrimonial Proceedings and Property Act 1970[54] was a comprehensive codification of the law,[55] setting out detailed guidelines to assist the court in the exercise of the extremely wide powers conferred on the court (for the first time) by that Act. However, the assumptions on which these guidelines had been

---

47 See *Burton v. Burton* [1986] 2 F.L.R. 419, following *Mullard v. Mullard* [1982] F.L.R. 330, CA. (no jurisdiction to make order that house be sold and part of proceeds paid to husband's creditors).

48 See *Norman v. Norman* [1983] 1 W.L.R. 295; *Thompson v. Thompson* [1985] F.L.R. 863, CA; *cf. R. v. Rushmoor B. C.* [1988] 2 F.L.R. 252, CA, *per* Sir Frederick Lawton. It is in any event clear that although there is a statutory power to vary orders for sale made under s.24A (see M.C.A. 1973, s.31(2)(f)) this power is not to be used so as to subvert the policy of the legislation that property adjustment orders should not be liable to be varied; see *Omielan v. Omielan* [1996] 2 F.L.R. 306, CA.

49 WRPA 1999, s. 19, Sched. 3, paras 1, 2 inserting ss. 21A and 24B into the M.C.A. 1973.

50 At p. 413.

51 Matrimonial Causes Act 1973, s. 22, discussed at p. 344.

52 The provisions of the Family Law Act 1996 which would have permitted financial provision orders to be made before a divorce or separation order (see Sched. 2) were never implemented.

53 M.C.A., s. 24B(1), inserted by the W.R.P.A. 1999, Sched. 3, para. 4.

54 Which was subsequently consolidated in the Matrimonial Causes Act 1973. After some initial hesitation, the radical nature of the change in the law effected by the 1970 Act came to be generally recognised, and it was described as "revolutionary" *per* Lord Denning M.R., *Trippas v. Trippas* [1973] Fam. 134 at 140, and at 144–145 *per* Scarman L.J.; see also *Griffiths v. Griffiths* [1974] 1 All E.R. 932 at 940, *per* Roskill L.J, "drastically reformed the law"; *Calderbank v. Calderbank* [1976] Fam. 93 at 101.

55 *Wachtel v. Wachtel* [1973] Fam. 72; *Trippas v. Trippas* [1973] Fam. 134; *Hunter v. Hunter* [1973] 1 W.L.R. 958 at 962, *per* Edmund Davies L.J.

formulated soon began to be questioned. The Law Commission undertook an examination of the issues and some changes—supposedly of an evolutionary rather than a revolutionary nature—were made to the law by the Matrimonial and Family Proceedings Act 1984. Since then, as we will show, the development of further guidelines has been undertaken by the judiciary rather than the legislature. It may be helpful in understanding the law to give a brief account of its historical development.

Historical evolution of the law

1. Financial relief under the offence-based divorce law

14–031 Until the coming into force of the Divorce Reform Act 1969,[56] a petitioner only had an unqualified right to divorce if he or she was an aggrieved and innocent victim of the other spouse's wrongdoing.[57] Marriage created a status, with reciprocal rights and duties; and so long as the parties remained married and the wife refrained from committing a matrimonial offence she had, as one of the incidents of that status, a legal right at common law[58] to be supported by her husband. It therefore seemed reasonable that the court's powers should be exercised in such a way as to keep the injured wife in the position in which she would have been had her husband properly discharged his marital obligations towards her. The principle applied was (as the Law Commission put it[59]) "very similar to that governing liability for breach of contract: a man who breaks a contract is liable to compensate the other party who is entitled to be put into the same position as if the contract had been carried out."

In practice, this contractual analogy was tempered over the years, particularly in a concern to ensure that a "guilty" wife (that is to say, one who had committed a matrimonial offence) should not necessarily forfeit all right to maintenance. However, the underlying principle of the law was at least clear. An "innocent" divorced wife was entitled to be kept in the same financial position as she would have enjoyed had the marriage continued; but the right and duty of maintenance was related to the performance of reciprocal matrimonial obligations, and the concept of a life-long right to and duty of support was "inextricably linked with the concept of divorce as a relief for wrongdoing."[60]

2. The implications for financial provision of a divorce law based on breakdown

14–032 How was financial provision to be regulated under a reformed divorce law, which sought to minimise reliance on guilt and innocence? Opponents of the

[56] Which came into force on January 1, 1971.

[57] The Law Commission's Discussion Paper, *The Financial Consequences of Divorce: The Basic Policy* (Law Com. No. 103 (1980)), para. 9.

[58] See Chap. 3, above.

[59] Law Com. No. 103, (1980), para. 11.

[60] *ibid.* para. 16.

Divorce Reform Act claimed that it would prove to be a "Casanovas' Charter" whereby blameless wives would be repudiated by their husbands and left destitute[61] and a powerful movement developed concerned to achieve financial protection for divorced women. In response to these pressures, the Lord Chancellor gave an undertaking that the Divorce Reform Act 1969 would not be brought into force until legislation had been brought in to deal comprehensively with the financial consequences of divorce.[62]

Unfortunately, the Law Commission's 1969 Report[63] on which the 1970 legislation was based[64] contained virtually no discussion[65] of the implications which the change in the basis of the ground for divorce might have for the determination of the financial consequences of divorce. Moreover, the Commission made assumptions—soon to be falsified—about other important matters (such as the effect of misconduct by one or both parties). The Matrimonial Proceedings and Property Act 1970 was brought into force on the same day as the Divorce Reform Act; and, on one view, was no more than the political price which had to be paid to secure the enactment of the reformed divorce law.[66]

3. Minimal loss: preservation of status quo, 1970–1984

14–033 The 1970 Act greatly extended the court's powers and firmly adopted what has been called[67] the minimal loss (or status quo) principle. This meant that, although the court was entitled to regard particular circumstances—for example the duration of the marriage—as being of such weight as to override the general direction to place the parties in the financial position in which they would have been had their marriage not broken down, nevertheless:—

> " ... the primary objective is that the financial position of the parties should so far as possible be unaffected by their divorce. In short, although

---

[61] *ibid.* para. 16.

[62] See *Hansard,* Vol. 794, col. 1560; and cols. 1597–1598; see further Law Com. No. 103, para. 19.

[63] *Financial Provision in Matrimonial-Proceedings* (Law Com. No. 25, (1969)).

[64] There was comparatively little discussion of the Bill in Parliament since debate in the House of Commons was much shortened by the decision to dissolve Parliament.

[65] Law Com. No. 25 contains little more than a single paragraph (see para. 81) on the question of principle: the paragraph states that it is desirable to introduce a "uniform and more detailed set of guidelines than under the old law" (when the only direction was to do what was thought reasonable, fit, or just). It does not advert to the objective of seeking to put the parties in the position in which they would have been had the marriage not broken down. The explanatory notes on the draft Bill annexed to the Report, however, made it clear that the Commission was apparently seeking to codify the principle enunciated by Lord Merrivale in *N. v. N.* (1928) 44 T.L.R. 324 at 328 with "some elaboration . . . to cover the possibility that, for example, both parties may have failed to discharge their marital obligations": draft cl. 5, n. 2.

[66] See *per* Mr Leo Abse M.P., *Hansard* (H.C.), Vol. 54, col. 416: " . . . we had to pay a price for the 1969 Act . . . In order to take take the House with us, we had to concede provisions relating to finance and conduct which were either inappropriate or which had a built-in obsolescence . . . Since, for the first time, it would be possible to divorce a wife without her consent even though the marriage might have broken down many years before, it was necessary to include in the Bill the provisions with which we are dealing today."

[67] See J. Eekelaar, *Family Law and Social Policy* (2nd ed., 1984), p. 109.

divorce terminates the legal status of marriage it will usually not terminate the financial ties of marriage which may remain life-long."[68]

In this respect it can be said that, although the English legislation was not based on any profound analysis of principle, it was at least alive to the risk that a shift to irretrievable breakdown as the ground for divorce would be what an American scholar has described as the "systematic impoverishment of divorced women and their children".[69] Indeed, in England criticism about the effect of the law came mostly from men who argued that it was they and their new families who were impoverished by the law.

4. Opposition to minimal loss principle: the law re-examined

14–034 This assumption that the parties to the marriage remained bound to provide for one another even after the marriage had been dissolved became the object of much criticism; and in 1980 the Law Commission undertook an examination of the underlying issues, and of the options for reform.[70] In the course of this examination, the Commission received an "overwhelming body of evidence that to direct the courts to seek to place the parties in the financial position in which they would have been if the marriage had not broken down is to impose a fundamentally mistaken objective, widely thought to be capable of producing unjust and inequitable results"[71] and it accordingly recommended "evolutionary" legislation,[72] to give effect to the following proposals:

(a) Statute should no longer impose on the court the duty so to exercise its powers as to place the parties in the financial position in which they would have been if the marriage had not broken down.[73]
(b) The law should seek to emphasise "as a priority" the necessity to make such financial provision as would safeguard the maintenance and welfare of the children.[74]
(c) Greater weight should be given to the importance of each party doing everything possible to become self-sufficient, so far as this would be

---

[68] Law Com. No. 103, para. 22.
[69] See L. Weitzman, *The Divorce Revolution* (1985) on the impact of no-fault divorce in the United States. Dr Weitzman's views are not universally shared: see, *e.g.* M. Garrison in S.D. Sugarman and H.H. Kay, *Divorce Reform at the Crossroads* (1991).
[70] The Law Commission's analysis of the principles underlying the law, and of various models for reform, was published as a Report: *The Financial Consequences of Divorce: The Basic Policy.* A Discussion Paper (Law Com. No. 103). This analysis (summarised in the 4th edition of this book at pp. 760–767) still repays study. Reference may also be made to the discussion of the objectives of financial provision in the Scottish Law Commission's Report on *Aliment and Financial Provision* (Scot. Law Com. No. 67, (1981)), Pt III.
[71] Law Com. No. 112, para. 6.
[72] The Report reported the tenor of the response to the earlier Discussion Paper and contained proposals, in general terms, for reform. For reasons set out in Law Com. No. 112, para. 3 and subsequently amplified in evidence to the House of Commons Special Committee, March 20, 1984, col. 63 (S.M. Cretney) it did not contain draft legislation.
[73] M.C.A. 1973, s.25(1).
[74] Law Com. No. 112, para. 24.

consistent with the interests of the children; and statute should positively assert this principle.

(d) Technical problems[75] which prevented the court from finally terminating a spouse's right to seek further support from the other should be removed, "so that in those comparatively few (and where there were infant children almost non-existent) cases" in which it would be appropriate to achieve a final once-for-all financial settlement at the time of the divorce the court would not lack the powers to do so.[76]

The statutory guidelines for the exercise of the court's discretion

14–035 The Matrimonial and Family Proceedings Act 1984 amended the law in accordance with the Law Commission's recommendations, and the statutory guidelines for the exercise of the court's discretion remain substantially unchanged. As will be explained, appellate courts have, within the broad discretionary framework and the implicit over-arching objective of achieving a fair outcome, from time to time provided guidelines in an attempt to structure the exercise of discretion.

1. Maintenance Pending Suit

14–036 The only guideline for exercise of the power to order maintenance pending suit is that the court shall make such order as it considers reasonable.[77] In practice this means the immediate needs of the applicant and children, assessed relatively with reference to prior standard of living. For example:—

> In *Peacock v. Peacock*[78] the wife was living on welfare benefits; the husband had take-home pay of some £82, out of which he had to meet travelling expenses of £10, and he also paid insurance premiums of £7. His board and lodging in his parents' home currently cost him £20, but he was about to set up in a new home which might cost as much as £35 weekly. In the circumstances, the court considered that a weekly payment of £15 would be appropriate for the three or four months before the financial position could be finalised. By contrast, in *F v. F (Ancillary Relief: Substantial Assets)*[79] the parties were immensely rich, and the wife claimed that she needed an annual income of £500,000 to meet her needs. Thorpe J. held that the question of what would be reasonable had, in such a case, to be determined by the standards of the ultra rich, and that it was not a defence to her claim that she "ought" to be able to manage on a quarter of a million pounds. Since some of the items which the wife claimed were clearly excessive—for example, £4,000 a year for the upkeep of her Labrador—

---

[75] *Dipper v. Dipper* [1981] Fam. 31.

[76] Law Com. No. 112, para. 29.

[77] M.C.A. s.22.

[78] [1984] 1 W.L.R. 532.

[79] [1995] 2 F.L.R. 45. The standard of living during the marriage is a very relevant factor but there are other considerations: *M v. M (Maintenance Pending Suit)* [2002] EWHC Fam. 317; [2002] 2 F.L.R. 123.

the court made an order for maintenance pending suit at the rate of £360,000 per annum. Other factors which have been taken into account in the case law include the availability of welfare benefits, the fact that the marriage has been very short, and that one party has admittedly been guilty of serious misconduct.[80]

Contests about the *quantum* of orders for maintenance pending suit are comparatively rare.[81] However, an issue of principle as to what items of expenditure can legitimately be included occasionally arises. In *A v. A (Maintenance Pending Suit): Provision of Legal Fees*[82] the question was whether an order for maintenance pending suit made against the petitioner husband could include the petitioner wife's legal fees for her applications for nullity and ancillary relief; her legal aid certificate had been discharged. Holman J. held that the words of section 22 of the Matrimonial Causes Act 1973 were wide enough to include an element of the payee's legal costs, provided it was reasonable to do so and provided that the court proceeded with caution. His Lordship's conclusion was fortified by Article 6 of the European Convention for the Protection of Human Rights and Fundamental Freedoms and by the concept of equality of arms in relation to legal representation.[83] The case was unusual in that at the stage of the application for maintenance pending suit, the availability of principal relief—and therefore of ancillary relief—was itself in issue.[84]

2. All other orders

The scheme of the legislation is, in outline, as follows:— **14–037**

(a) It is the duty of the court in deciding whether to exercise its powers and, if so, in what manner to have regard to all the circumstances of the case, first consideration being given to the welfare while a minor of any child of the family who has not attained the age of 18.[85]

(b) As regards the exercise of the powers to make financial provision orders, property adjustment orders, or orders for the sale of property in relation to a party to the marriage, it is provided that the court shall "in particular have regard to" certain specified matters[86] and the Act

---

[80] The court will not wish to prejudge any issues which are in issue between the parties and which are to be litigated: *Offord v. Offord* [1981] 3 F.L.R. 309.

[81] *per* Thorpe J. in *F v. F (Ancillary Relief: Substantial Assets)* [1995] 2 F.L.R. 45 at 49: "almost unknown".

[82] [2001] 1 F.L.R. 377; [2001] 1 W.L.R. 605, FD.

[83] In *Sears Tooth (A Firm) v. Payne Hicks Beach (A Firm)* [1997] 2 F.L.R. 116 at 11H-119A, Wilson J. drew attention to "a grave and widespread problem encountered increasingly in the Family Division: namely, how can a spouse, usually a wife, who is ineligible for legal aid but who has negligible capital, secure legal advice and legal representation in order to pursue her rights against her husband, particularly one who is rich, litigious or obstructive . . . ?"

[84] By reason of the Islamic marriage contracted by the parties in this country. For the resolution of the principal relief issues, see *A-M v. A-M (Divorce: Jurisdiction: Validity of Marriage)* [2001] 2 F.L.R. 6, FD discussed in Chap. 2 at p. 37.

[85] M.C.A. 1973, s.25(1).

[86] *ibid.* s.25(2).

also directs the court "in particular" to have regard to certain specified matters as regards the exercise of its powers to make such orders in relation to a child of the family.[87]

(c) Finally, the Act contains a number of provisions designed to direct the court's attention to the principle of self-sufficiency, and to facilitate the making of a "clean break" between the parties to the marriage in appropriate cases.[88]

The objective implicit in section 25

14–038 Section 25 of the Act since its amendment in 1984 expresses no objective, and the wide-ranging survey of "all the circumstances" which the court is required to undertake does not of itself give any clear guidance as to the principles on which the court should act. The absence of declared objective is particularly apparent where there are no minor children of the family and thus no "first" consideration. From time to time there have been attempts to gloss the statutory provisions with judicially formulated guidelines, in large part motivated by the desire to increase certainty of outcome and thereby to promote settlement and reduce the costs involved in protracted litigation.[89] Section 25 has been considered by the House of Lords on two occasions, in *Piglowska v. Piglowski*[90] and *White v. White*.[91] As we shall see, the current judicial formulation of the objective to be implied in section 25 is that of achieving a fair outcome, with fairness involving non-discrimination between husband and wife in the evaluation of their contributions to family welfare in their respective roles.[92] However, fairness is a very general concept; as Lord Nicholls observed in *White v. White*[93] " . . . fairness, like beauty, lies in the eye of the beholder". The current formulation of the statutory provisions limit the potential for judicially formulated principles (as opposed to guidelines[94]) even at the highest appellate level.[95] However, the dividing line between a principle or presumption and a mere guideline be difficult to draw.[96] Furthermore, in the absence of principles, the width of discretion leads inevitably to diversity in judicial approach,

---

[87] *ibid.* s.25(3).
[88] *ibid.* s.25A.
[89] *Piglowska v. Piglowski* [1999] 2 F.L.R. 763 at 785 *per* Lord Hoffmann.
[90] [1999] 2 F.L.R. 763.
[91] [2000] 2 F.L.R. 981.
[92] *per* Lord Nicholls in *White v. White* [2000] 2 F.L.R. 981 at 992; *per* Munby J. in *X v. X (Y and Z Intervening)* [2002] 1 F.L.R. 508 at para. [103].
[93] [2000] 2 F.L.R. 981 at 983.
[94] There have been numerous warnings about the limited precedent (as opposed to illustrative) value of decisions on the exercise of discretion under s. 25, particularly those at first instance: see *e.g. Martin v. Martin* [1978] Fam. 12 at 20 *per* Ormord J.; *Smith v. Smith* [1991] 2 F.L.R. 432 at 435 *per* Butler-Sloss L.J.; *Barry v. Barry* [1992] 2 W.L.R. 797; *Piglowska v. Piglowski* [1999] 2 F.L.R. 763.
[95] As Lord Nicholls explained in *White v. White* [2000] 2 F.L.R. 981 at 990, the formulation of further principles would be inconsistent with the current statutory provisions.
[96] Contrast for instance the approach of the Court of Appeal in *Smith v. Smith* [1991] 2 F.L.R. 432 with that in *Burgess v. Burgess* [1996] 2 F.L.R. 340; and see the remarks of Lord Cooke in *White v. White* [2000] 2 F.L.R. 981 at 997–999.

reflecting in turn a diversity of community views.[97] Whether the degree of diversity in judicial approach is currently too pronounced and whether it is to high a price to pay for the perceived advantages of tailor-made solutions in ancillary relief proceedings lies at the heart of the question—addressed at the end of this Chapter—of whether section 25 should be reformed.

The Decisions in Piglowska v. Piglowski and White v. White

14–039 No appeal on the interpretation of s. 25 reached the House of Lords until *Piglowska v. Piglowski*[98]; which, for a variety of reasons, focused more on costs and on the appellate process than on substantive issues. The assets totaled a modest £127,400: a London home, a flat in Spain and insurance policies. The wife had worked as a cleaner and dressmaker as well as homemaker and principal parent to the (now adult) children. The husband (an architectural assistant) had a new family and was living in Poland; they wished to move London. The district judge made a clean break order (upheld on appeal by the High Court) giving the husband 27 per cent of the assets (the Spanish flat and £10,000) and the wife the matrimonial home. The Court of Appeal varied this, ordering sale of both properties and dividing the proceeds 60 per cent to the wife and 40 per cent to the husband, to enable both to purchase modest accommodation in London. Ward L.J. considered that it was important to strike a fair balance between the needs of each party where assets are limited. The House of Lord's allowed the wife's appeal and restored the original order; the Court of Appeal had improperly substituted its own evaluation for that of the courts below. The costs (both parties were publicly funded) exceeded the value of the assets.

It was thus unsurprising that the leading speech of Lord Hoffmann was dominated by criticism of the appellate process and litigation costs. As to section 25 itself, the width of discretion conferred by the section was reiterated. The factors in section 25(2) are not as a matter of law ranked in any hierarchy, and their weight depends entirely on the facts of the case. Pronouncements in appellate decisions do not have the status of principle, and diversity in judicial approach is inevitable.

White v. White[99] provided a better opportunity for the House of Lords to give guidance on the substantive interpretation of section 25. Throughout a 33 year marriage the Whites in partnership operated a farming business on two farms. One farm belonged to the couple jointly, the other to the husband. The husband's father had provided an interest-free loan and some capital for the purchase of the first farm, and had purchased an estate from which the second farm, acquired on advantageous terms, was derived. On divorce both parties claimed ancillary relief. The assets were worth £4.6 million and all the surviving children were adults. Holman J. applying the then well-established "reasonable requirements"

---

[97] See *Piglowska v. Piglowski* [1999] 2 F.L.R. 763 at 785 *per* Lord Hoffmann.

[98] [1999] 2 F.L.R. 763; [1999] 1 W.L.R. 1360; R. Bailey-Harris and P. Coleridge "Family Assets, Costs and Avenues of Appeal" [2001] 117 *L.Q.R.* 1571.

[99] [2000] 3 W.L.R. 1571; [2000] 2 F.L.R. 98.

approach[1] awarded the wife £800,000 in addition to retention of her sole assets. The lump sum reflected her housing and capitalised income requirements, but her wish to farm in her own right (which would have required division of the enterprise) was rejected. The Court of Appeal increased the wife's award to £1.5 million. Thorpe L.J.[2] identified the farming partnership as the dominant feature of the case, with considerations of contributions and overall fairness also relevant to an increased award. According to Butler-Sloss L.J., the wife was entitled to more than was represented by her partnership share, since she had also contributed as wife and mother. An appeal and cross-appeal ensued, the husband seeking restoration of the trial judge's order, the wife an equal share in all the assets. The House of Lords dismissed both. The trial judge had misdirected himself in treating the parties "reasonable requirements" as the ceiling on the wife's award. The Court of Appeal's award was within the ambit of discretion and on the principles of *Piglowska v. Piglowski*[3] there was no basis for further appellate interference.

The decision has produced much academic and professional debate.[4] While it was welcomed as a step towards the recognition of marriage as an equal partnership, the capacity of judicially formulated guidelines to achieve a policy change and increased certainty in the law's operation have been questioned, and in practice the decision appears to have created increased opportunity for professional argument and to have made the task of advice more difficult.

The decision signalled the abandonment of the "reasonable requirements" ceiling on a wife's award in "big money" cases. The Court of Appeal in 1996 in *Dart v. Dart*[5] had considered this approach to be so well established that only Parliament could displace it. The reasonable requirements ceiling was subject to criticism for its injustice, connotations of dependency and failure to give proper recognition to contributions to family welfare.[6] As Lord Nicholls observed,[7] why should the assets built up during marriage become immaterial once the reasonable requirements of the wife are assessed, and the surplus remain with the husband? Since there is no hierarchy in the section 25(2) considerations,[8] needs (section 25(2)(b), from which the concept of reasonable requirements was

---

[1] *O'D v. O'D* [1976] Fam. 83; *Page v. Page* (1981) 2 F.L.R. 198; *Preston v. Preston* [1982] Fam. 17; *Gojkovic v. Gojkovic* [1990] L.R. 140; *R v. R (Financial Provision: Reasonable Needs)* [1994] 2 F.L.R. 1004; *F v. F (Ancillary Relief: Substantial Assets)* [1995] 2 F.L.R. 45; *Dart v. Dart* [1996] 2 F.L.R. 286. This approach is discussed below at p. 363.

[2] With whom Mantell L.J. agreed.

[3] [1999] 2 F.L.R. 763.

[4] S. Cretney [2001] *Fam. Law* 3; R. Bailey-Harris [2001] *Fam. Law* 12; P. Duckworth and D. Hodson "White - Bringing s 25 Back to the People" [2001] *Fam. Law* 24; J. Eekelaar "Back to Basics and Forward into the Unknown" [2001] *Fam. Law* 30; D.J. Brasse "White v. White—A return to Orthodoxy?" [2001] *Fam. Law* 191; R. Hayward-Smith "White v. White revisited" [2001] *Fam. Law* 682; D. Burrows, "Reform of s 25?" [2001] *Fam. Law* 698; R. Bailey-Harris, "Fairness in Financial Settlements on Divorce" (2001) 117 *L.Q.R.* 199; E. Cooke "A New Yardstick for the Marriage Partnership" (2001) 13 *C.F.L.Q.* 81.

[5] [1996] 2 F.L.R. 286 at 301, Thorpe L.J. said: "If a fundamental change is to be introduced it is for the legislature and not the judges to introduce it".

[6] See *e.g.* P. Singer, "Sexual Discrimination in Ancillary Relief" [2001] *Fam. Law* 115 (a paper delivered in 1992).

[7] [2000] 2 F.L.R. 981 at 992.

[8] [1999] 2 F.L.R. 763.

derived) cannot as a matter of law dominate the exercise. Thus the House of Lords in *White v. White* (as it had earlier done in *Piglowska v. Piglowski*) emphasised the width of discretion conferred by section 25.

However, in the later decision the House of Lords did not stop there. Lord Nicholls stated a principle of non-discrimination and equal value in respect of different contributions to the welfare of the family:

> " . . . there is one principle of universal application which can be stated with confidence. In seeking to achieve a fair outcome, there is no place for discrimination between husband and wife and their respective roles . . . If, in their different spheres, each contributed equally to the family, then in principle it matters not which of them earned the money and built up the assets. There should be no bias in favour of the money-earner and against the home-maker and child-carer."[9]

However, this principle arguably lacks the status of an overarching objective, since it is derived from a consideration of section 25(2)(f), namely "contributions to the welfare of the family". In *White v. White* the House of Lords followed its earlier approach in *Piglowska v. Piglowski* in stating that the implicit general objective of section 25 is to achieve a fair outcome.[10] Furthermore, if Lord Nicholl's principle of equal recognition and equal value of contributions was predicated on equality of effort ("*If,* in their different spheres, each contributed equally"[11]), then it could invite evaluation of the quality of the spouses' respective efforts in their different spheres. We shall show how the notion of "stellar", "exceptional" or "special" contribution has emerged in subsequent case-law,[12] resulting in an (arguably discriminatory) departure from equal division of assets.

As a means of translating the non-discrimination principle into practical outcome in ancillary relief proceedings, Lord Nicholls formulated the yardstick of equal division of assets against which a provisional award should be checked:

> "Sometimes, having carried out the statutory exercise, the judge's conclusion involves a more or less equal division of the available assets. More often, this is not so. More often, having looked at all the circumstances, the judge's decision means that one party will receive a bigger share than the other. Before reaching a firm decision along these lines, a judge would always be well advised to check his tentative views against the yardstick of equality of division. As a general guide, equality should be departed from only if, and to extent that, there are good reasons for doing so. The need to consider and articulate reasons for departing from equality would

---

9 Lord Nicholls at [2000] 1 F.L.R. 981 at 989: The principle may seem to have a somewhat old-fashioned flavour in that it suggests a dichotomy of roles, whereas most ordinary couples now mix them.

10 [2000] 2 F.L.R. 981 at 989.

11 *ibid.*, emphasis supplied.

12 *Cowan v. Cowan* [2001] 2 F.L.R. 192; [2001] 3 W.L.R. 684; *L v. L (Financial Provision: Contributions)* [2002] 1 F.L.R. 642.

> help the parties and the courts to focus on the need to ensure the absence of discrimination."

The nature of this yardstick is further considered below, after discussion of the section 25(2) factors.

The decisions in *Piglowska v. Piglowska*[13] and *White v. White*[14] establish that implicit in the section 25 consideration of "all the circumstances" are three components,[15] namely:

(i) the overall objective of achieving a fair outcome;
(ii) consideration of all the section 25(2) criteria relevant on the facts. As a matter of law there is no hierarchy among them. The interpretation of section 25(2)(f)—contributions to the welfare of the family—must be non-discriminatory;
(iii) at the end of the exercise, application of the yardstick of equal division of assets as a check on the provisional quantum of an award. Where equal division is departed from, reasons must be given.

As Thorpe L.J. encapsulated it in *Cordle v. Cordle*[16]:

> "The only universal rule is to apply the s 25(2) criteria to all the circumstances of the case (giving first consideration to the welfare of children) and to arrive at a fair result that avoids discrimination".

14–040 It is obvious that the court is left with considerable breadth of discretion. Fairness is a very general objective, and the decision in *White v. White* leaves much scope for diversity in outcomes, as in inevitable since the formulation of principles as opposed to guidelines (such as a presumption of equal shares) is outwith legitimate judicial interpretation of the provisions of Part II of the Matrimonial Causes Act in their current form. Even in cases involving a large surplus of assets after the parties' housing and income needs have been met, there are considerable opportunities for departure from equal division of assets. In the next sections of this Chapter we examine how the non-discrimination principle and the yardstick of equal division have been applied in subsequent case-law, with the proviso that at the time of writing it is early days for clear patterns to have emerged. In *W H-J v. H H-J*[17] Coleridge J. described this as "an area of jurisprudence . . . in a state of considerable flux and uncertainty."[18]

14–041 In *White v. White,* Lord Nicholls identified the issue before the House as the exercise of ancillary relief powers "in so-called big money cases, where the

---

[13] [1999] 2 F.L.R. 763.
[14] [2000] 2 F.L.R. 981.
[15] *D v. D (Lump Sum Order: Adjournment of Application)* [2001] 1 F.L.R. 633; *N v. N (Financial Provision: Sale of Company)* [2001] 2 F.L.R. 69; *S v. S (Financial Provision: Departing From Equality)* [2001] 2 F.L.R. 246; *Cowan v. Cowan* [2001] 2 F.L.R. 192; [2001] 3 W.L.R. 684; *L v. L (Financial Provision: Contributions)* [2002] 1 F.L.R. 642.
[16] [2001] EWCA Civ. 1791; [2002] 1 F.L.R. 207 at para. [34].
[17] [2002] 1 F.L.R. 415.
[18] *ibid.* at 417.

assets available exceed the parties' financial needs for housing and income".[19] An obvious question was the extent to which the principle of equality and the yardstick of equal division applied to cases other than those involving big money.[20] As we shall show later in this Chapter, the established judicial approach to limited means cases is to give priority to the housing needs of the parent with care of minor children, often by absolute transfer of the former matrimonial home. Would the decision in *White v. White* overturn this tradition and create an across-the-board entitlement (immediate or deferred[21]) to equal division of assets in the absence of good reasons to the contrary? There have been reports of "confusion and inconsistency" in county court practice around the country in ordinary cases involving limited assets,[22] and the case-law to date is limited. Some support for an "entitlement approach" even in limited means cases was allegedly derived from *Elliott v Elliott*.[23] There the orders were for the proceeds of sale of the matrimonial home to be used to provide another suitable home for the wife and children, subject to a charge back to the husband of 45 per cent of the former home's value. However, the message of more recent authorities is that the generality of the implicit over-arching objective of a fair outcome articulated in *White v. White*[24] leaves ample scope for the housing needs of the parent who is the primary carer to continue to dominate over other considerations.

In *B v. B (Financial Provision: Welfare of Child and Conduct)*[25] the only available asset was £124,000, the proceeds of sale of the matrimonial home in South London to which both parties had contributed financially The wife was currently in receipt of benefits but hoped in time to return to hairdressing; the husband's earning capacity was significantly higher. He was not supporting the child. The district judge ordered that the whole of the proceeds of sale be transferred to the wife. The husband appealed, arguing that *White v. White*[26] gave the husband an entitlement to receive some part of the equity in the former home, either immediately or on a deferred *Mesher v. Mesher*[27] basis. Connell J. dismissed the appeal. The correct approach, following *White*, was for the court to apply the section 25 criteria, considering each matter specified in section 25(2), giving first consideration to the child's welfare and with the over-arching objective of achieving a fair outcome in all the circumstances of the case. £124,000 was only sufficient properly to rehouse the wife and child, who had had a disturbed background and needed the security of a proper and satisfactory home. There was insufficient money to enable the husband to purchase a home.[28] Other relev-

---

19 [2000] 2 F.L.R. 981 at 984.

20 R. Bailey-Harris, "Dividing the Assets on Family Breakdown: The Content of Fairness" [2001] 54 *Current Legal Problems* 533. Connell J. deemed it unnecessary to decide the point in *D v. D (Lump Sum Order: Adjournment of Application)* [2001] 1 F.L.R. 633, which was characterized as a "big money case".

21 *Mesher v. Mesher* [1980] 1 All E.R. 126.

22 *Cordle v. Cordle* [2002] 1 F.L.R. 207 *per* Thorpe L.J. at para. [33].

23 [2001] 1 F.C.R. 477, CA.

24 [2000] 2 F.L.R. 981; [2001] 1 A.C. 596.

25 [2002] 1 F.L.R. 555, FD.

26 [2001] 1 A.C. 596; [2000] 2 F.L.R. 981.

27 [1980] 1 All E.R. 126.

28 *M v. B (Ancillary Provision: Lump Sum)* [1998] 1 F.L.E.R. 53 was distinguished on its facts.

ant considerations which were plainly good reasons for departing from equality were contributions and conduct. The principal feature of the parties' contributions was the care of the child, for which the wife had been and would remain responsible. Under section 25(2)(g) it would be inequitable to disregard the husband's conduct in relation to non-disclosure, removal of assets, failure to support the child, and abduction of the child.

Authoritative guidance on the impact of *White v. White*[29] for the "routine district judge case" was provided by the Court of Appeal in *Cordle v. Cordle*.[30] Thorpe L.J. stated:

> "The first point, that cannot be overemphasised, is that there is no rule in *White v. White* ... that district judges must produce equality of outcome unless there are good reasons to justify departure. The cross-check of equality of outcome is intended to be a safeguard against discrimination. What *White v. White* ... essentially decides (as this court has emphasised in the more recent decision of *Cowan v. Cowan* ...) is that it is the first duty of the court of trial to apply the s.25 criteria in search of the overarching objective of fairness. It seems to me that in search of that overarching objective of fairness in the typical ancillary relief case the district judge will always look first to the housing needs of the parties ... So in the ordinary case the court's first concern will be to provide a home for the primary carer and the children (whose welfare is the first consideration). Of course in many cases the satisfaction of that need may absorb all that is immediately available. But ... where there is sufficient to go beyond that, the court's concern will be to provide the means for the absent parent to re-house ... Another factor ... is butressing the ability of one or other of the parties to work ... Beyond that, if there be cash beyond that, then the judge has to look to what in his estimation is the fair result ... *The only universal rule is to apply the s 25(2) criteria to all the circumstances of the case (giving first consideration to the welfare of the children) and to arrive at a fair result that avoids discrimination*" (emphasis supplied).

According to these authorities, the section 25 exercise remains a broad discretionary one. In reality, while the notion of equality and the yardstick of equality division formulated by Lord Nicholls in *White* are in principle in point in smaller money cases, in practice they will have little impact on outcome, in respect of which little has altered outside the "big money" cases. The housing needs of the parent with care will continue to dominate, and only if sufficient funds are left over will the other spouse be able to purchase accommodation. Nevertheless, it remains to be seen whether these appellate pronouncements result in a standardisation of county court practice across the country.

We now examine the various stages in the section 25 exercise.

---

[29] [2000] 2 F.L.R. 981.

[30] [2001] EWCA Civ. 1791; [2002] 2 F.L.R. 207 at paras [33] and [34].

(a) The first consideration: children's welfare

14–042 The Act requires the court, in deciding whether to exercise its powers to make financial provision, property adjustment, or sale orders to "have regard to all the circumstances of the case, first consideration being given to the welfare while a minor of any child of the family who has not attained the age of 18."[31] It seeks thereby to give effect to the view of the Law Commission that the law should "emphasise as a priority" the need to make the financial provision necessary to safeguard the maintenance and welfare of the children, and thus refute the once widespread impression that the making of provision for children was a matter of secondary importance to the making of provision for the former spouse.[32] As mentioned above, the court have usually tried to ensure that the child has secure housing—for instance by ordering the transfer of the house to the parent with whom the child is to live, or division of proceeds of sale permitting her to purchase accommodation, or settling it on terms that it be not sold during the children's dependency.[33] As explained above, recent authorities[34] appear to confirm that this practice in smaller money cases is largely unaffected by the decision of the House of Lords in *White v. White*.[35] The particular accommodation needs of a child may justify a substantial capital award to the parent with care even where the marriage has been short.[36] Again, the court may think that the welfare of the children requires that the wife—notwithstanding the provisions encouraging self-sufficiency considered below—should have periodical payments at least until the children no longer need her full time attention.[37]

Where resources permit, in recent years the courts have emphasised the desirability[38] of the parent with whom the children do not have their principal home receiving an award sufficient to permit him to purchase accommodation suitable for staying contact, as in *M v. B (Ancillary Proceedings: Lump Sum)*.[39] However,

---

[31] M.C.A. 1973, s.25(1).

[32] Law Com. No. 112, para. 24.

[33] The courts have come increasingly to accept that children will in reality remain dependent on their parents beyond the age of majority: *Richardson v. Richardson (No. 2)* [1944] 2 F.L.R. 1051; *J v. C (Child: Financial Provision)* [1999] 1 F.L.R. 152.

[34] *B v. B (Financial Provision: Welfare of Child and Conduct)* [2002] 1 F.L.R. 555, FD; *Cordle v. Cordle* [2001] EWCA Civ. 1791; [2002] 2 F.LR. 207. See also *Elliott v. Elloitt* [2001] 2 F.C.R. 477, in which proceeds of sale were used to purchase a new home for the wife and children, but subject to a charge-back of 45% to the husband.

[35] [2001] 1 A.C. 596; [2000] 3 W.L.R. 1571; [2000] 2 F.L.R. 981.

[36] *C v. C (Financial Relief: Short Marriage)* [1997] 2 F.L.R. 26 (marriage of some nine months; mother needed to purchase a house in a clean air area suitable for the asthmatic child); *M v. M (Prenuptial Agreement)* [2002] 1 F.L.R. 654 (marriage of five years, lump sum of £575,000 to meet costs of a suitable home in London; in child's interests to reside there with mother and enjoy stability).

[37] *Waterman v. Waterman* [1979] 1 F.L.R. 380, CA; *E v. E. (Financial Provision)* [1990] 2 F.L.R. 233 at 249 (not in children's interests that mother be in straitened circumstances); *C v. C (Financial Relief: Short Marriage)* [1997] 2 F.L.R. 26.

[38] Although it is a "misuse of authority" to interpret such cases as laying down "some rule that both spouses invariably have a right to purchase accommodation": *Piglowska v. Piglowski* [1999] 2 F.L.R. 763 at 783, *per* Lord Hoffmann.

[39] [1998] 1 F.L.R. 5; see also *H v. H (Financial Provision: Conduct)* [1998] 1 F.L.R. 971 and *Cordle v. Cordle* [2001] EWCA Civ. 1791; [2002] 1 F.L.R. 207, CA.

it has equally been emphasised[40] that there is as matter of law no entitlement, where means are limited, that both spouses are entitled to purchase accommodation; everything turns on the particular facts, in particular the resources available.

The requirement that the court give first consideration to the welfare of children may also have an indirect effect on the orders which the court makes. Thus in *S v. S*[41] the court considered a "clean break" would be in the children's interests because ending the parents' financial relationship would remove the only remaining serious source of dispute between the parents, whilst in *M v. M (Sale of Property)*[42] the court considered that it would not be in the children's interests that the husband be burdened with the large debt involved in his retaining a "handsome and interesting" seventeenth-century country mansion (with the inevitable result that his concern for making the house an income-producing asset as a venue for such activities as university balls and civil war jousting events would dominate the family's lives).

The court has power to make property adjustment and financial provision orders to or for the benefit of any children of the family, but as a result of the enactment of the Child Support Act 1991, it is only in unusual circumstances that it will be able to exercise its powers to order periodical payments for children.[43]

Limitations on welfare principle

14–043 There are some significant limitations on the scope of the direction to give first consideration to children's welfare.

(i) First but not paramount

In deciding questions about the upbringing of a child, the court is directed[44] to regard the welfare of the child as the "paramount" consideration even if that means that the just claims of the child's parents or others affected have to be overridden. But in considering financial relief the court is not required to go so far. It need only give "first" consideration to the welfare of the child in question,

---

[40] *Piglowska v. Piglowski* [1999] 2 F.L.R. 763 at 783 *per* Lord Hoffmann; *B v. B (Financial Provision: Welfare of Child and Conduct)* [2002] 1 F.L.R. 555 *per* Connell J.; *Cordle v. Cordle* [2001] EWCA Civ. 1791; [2002] 1 F.L.R. 207 *per* Thorpe L.J. at paras [33] and [34].

[41] [1987] 1 F.L.R. 71, Waite J. (The decision of the Court of Appeal in this case (*S. v. S* (note) [1987] 1 W.L.R. 382) does not deal with or affect this matter).

[42] [1988] 1 F.L.R. 389, CA.

[43] These are discussed in Chap. 15, below. Even in cases where the court retains jurisdiction, it increasingly has regard to the Child Support Act's formulae in determining quantum: *E. v. C. (Child Maintenance)* [1996] 1 F.L.R. 472 at 476, *per* Douglas Brown J. This effect will be even more pronounced given the change introduced by the Child Support, Pensions and Social Security Act 2000, whereby the existence of a consent order no longer precludes, after one year, an application to the Child Support Agency for a child support maintenance determination: see s.4(10)(a) of the child Support Act 1991 as amended by the CSPASSA 2000, discussed in Chap. 15, below.

[44] Children Act 1989, s.1(1).

so that (it has been held[45]) the court must simply consider all the relevant circumstances, always bearing in mind the important consideration of the welfare of the children, and then try to attain a financial result which is just as between husband and wife. Thus:—

> In *Suter v. Suter*[46] the wife remained in the family home with the two children of the marriage. Her 21-year-old lover (a labourer in the Devonport dockyard earning £7,000 per annum) spent every night in the home with the wife. The judge ordered the husband to transfer his interest in the home to the wife, and to make periodical payments to her of an amount which would cover the whole of the mortgage interest. This was done to protect the children's housing needs; but the Court of Appeal held that the judge had been wrong to elevate the children's interests so as to control the outcome. The wife's lover could be expected to make a financial contribution; and the order was accordingly reduced. In *Akintola v. Akintola*[47] the Court of Appeal held that the judge, in considering that the son, who was at a fee-paying school, should not be housed either too far away or on an inappropriate housing estate, had not elevated the statutory duty to give first consideration to the boy's welfare to something unacceptably high. The case involved transfer of a housing association into the wife's sole name.

(ii) Applies only to children of the family

14–044 The expression child of the family is widely defined in the legislation[48] and extends to any child who has been treated by both of the parties to the marriage as a child of their family. But although this definition is wide, it does not extend to all those children who may, actually or prospectively, be affected by the orders made in the matrimonial proceedings in question. For example, the child born to a husband and his cohabitant[49] after the marriage breakdown is unlikely to be within the definition.

(iii) Applies only during infancy of children

14–045 The court is only required to give first consideration to the welfare while a minor of any child of the family who has not attained the age of 18. This has two particular consequences. First, the court is not obliged to give such consideration to the welfare of any child of the family who has at the date of the hearing already attained the age of 18, even if the child is undergoing

---

45 *Suter v. Suter* [1987] 2 F.L.R. 232 at 238, *per* Sir R. Cumming Bruce.
46 Above.
47 [2002] 1 F.L.R. 701, CA.
48 M.C.A. 1973, s.52(1).
49 Or a child born to the wife after the marriage has been dissolved: see, *e.g. Fisher v. Fisher* [1989] 1 F.L.R. 423, CA.

advanced education or training, or is disabled. Secondly, even in the case of children of the family who are, at the date of the hearing, under 18, the court is only obliged by this provision to give first consideration to their welfare whilst they remain minors. This provision does not require the court to take account of the fact that children in practice do often stay in their homes until a later age whether because they are undergoing education or training or because they are disabled or unemployed or simply because they prefer to do so, particularly during the early stages of their career. However, the courts have in fact shown an increasing readiness to recognise that children have needs which extend well beyond their attaining the age of 18,[50] but these needs do not have any priority.

(b) The court's duty to consider all the circumstances

14–046 Under the implied overarching objective of achieving a fair outcome,[51] the court is directed to have regard to "all the circumstances of the case," and "in particular" to have regard to an elaborate list of specific matters in section 25(2) covering almost "every conceivable factor."[52] The expression "all the circumstances" is a very wide one[53] and the court need not confine its attention to the specified matters but may also investigate other circumstances "past, present, and . . . future"[54] which arise on the facts of any particular case.

The matters specified in section 25(2) are in the text hereafter discussed in the order in which they appear in the statute, although, as the House of Lords has emphasised in *Piglowska v. Piglowska*[55] and in *White v. White,*[56] there is no hierarchy in law, and the weight to be accorded to each will depend on the exercise of judicial discretion on the particular facts. On those facts, one factor may be dominant.

(i) "the income, earning capacity, property and other financial resources which each of the parties to the marriage has or is likely to have in the foreseeable future, including in the case of earning capacity any increase in that capacity which it would in the opinion of the court be reasonable to expect a party to the marriage to take steps to acquire" (M.C.A. 1973, s.25(2)(a))

---

[50] *Richardson v. Richardson (No. 2)* [1994] 2 F.L.R. 105; *J v. C (Financial Provision)* [1999] 1 F.L.R. 152, FD.

[51] *Piglowska v. Piglowski* [1999] 2 F.L.R. 763, HL; *White v. White* [2000] 2 F.L.R. 981, HL; *Cordle v. Cordle* [2002] EWCA Civ. 1791; [2002] 2 F.L.R. 207.

[52] Matrimonial Causes Act 1972, s.25(2) *per* Sir J. Donaldson M.R., *Mortimer v. Mortimer-Griffin* [1986] 2 F.L.R. 315 at 318, CA.

[53] *Kokosinski v. Kokosinski* [1980] Fam. 72 at 183, *per* Wood J.

[54] *per* Scarman L.J., *Trippas v. Trippas* [1973] Fam. 134 at 144.

[55] [1999] 2 F.L.R. 763.

[56] [2000] 2 F.L.R. 981.

Ascertaining the facts

14–047 The first priority is to get at the truth about each party's financial resources. Following the Family Proceedings (Amendment No. 2) Rules 1999[57] the parties are required to provide and exchange evidence in standard form at an early stage of the proceedings prior to the first appointment.[58] The standard form[59] (which is a sworn document) requires full details of *inter alia* the parties' resources and their needs and obligations, and (in accordance with the spirit of the procedural reforms in reducing documentation and costs in the resolution of financial disputes[60]) is intended to be comprehensive for the vast majority of cases.[61] It replaced[62] the complex affidavit of means.

The parties are under an obligation to make a full, frank and clear disclosure of all relevant circumstances,[63] but in practice this is not always done.[64] A range of powers is available to compel an unwilling spouse to supply the information needed to assess his or her financial position, and a solicitor who fails to obtain proper evidence on these matters may be held to have been guilty of professional

---

[57] S.I. 1999 No. 3491.

[58] F.P.R. 1991, r. 2.6B(1) and (2).

[59] Form E, contained in Appendix 1A of the Rules. Where the parties apply for a consent order there is a different procedure prescribed by r. 2.61 and the relevant form is Form M1.

[60] Discussed *supra* at p. 327.

[61] The so-called "millionaires' defence" concedes that the wealth available is more than adequate to meet to meet any financial order the court might make: *Thyssen-Bornesmisza* [1985] 2 F.L.R. 670; *B. v. B (Discovery: Financial Provision)* [1990] 2 F.L.R. 180; but the court needs a minimum of information about the parties' assets and income, even in summary form, if it is to discharge it statutory duty: *Van G v. Van G (Financial Provision: Millionaires' Defence)* [1995] 1 F.L.R. 328; *F v. F (Financial Provision: Substantial Assets)* [1995] 2 F.L.R. 47; *Dart v. Dart* [1996] 2 F.L.R. 286, CA. *Sed quaere* the effect of *White v. White* [2000] 2 F.L.R. 981 on this defence, since the overall pool of assets on which the yardstick of equal division operates in "big money" cases has assumed greater importance.

[62] Nationwide for all applications for ancillary relief filed after June 5, 2000.

[63] *Livesey (formerly Jenkins) v. Jenkins* [1985] A.C. 424, H.L. This obligation underpins the whole basis of the exercise of the court's discretion to make financial orders (which is a paternal, and in an appropriate case, an inquisitorial jurisdiction: see *Hildebrand v. Hildebrand* [1992] 1 F.L.R. 244 at 247, *per* Waite J.). A striking consequence of the duty to disclose is that a party who has resorted to self-help (*e.g.* by secretly photocopying bank statements or other documents belonging to another party) is under a duty to disclose that he or she has those copies: see *T. v. T (Interception of Documents)* [1994] 2 F.L.R. 1083, Wilson J., where the judge ruled that a wife had been entitled to take such copies and to examine the contents of the husband's dustbins, but not to break the door and window of his office in order to get access to other documents. See generally N. Wilson, "Conduct of the Big Money Case" [1994] *Fam. Law* 504.

[64] See, *e.g. P v. P (Financial Relief: Non-Disclosure)* [1994] 2 F.L.R. 381 (where the wife's failure to give full disclosure was progressively revealed in the course of an extended cross-examination); *S v. S (Financial Provision) (Post-divorce Cohabitation)* [1994] 2 F.L.R. 228 (where a husband failed to reveal the existence of a number of bank accounts and had been deliberately deceitful over his financial affairs); *H v. H (Financial Relief: Non-Disclosure)* [1994] 2 F.L.R. 94 (where the husband, apparently by accident, produced at the hearing a cheque book relating to a previously undisclosed account). For an illustration of the complexities which can arise, see *Newton v. Newton* [1990] 1 F.L.R. 33 where the judge found that a property developer's income was quite uncertain and impossible on the evidence to ascertain, and that it was not safe to rely on anything the husband said regarding valuation of assets or of wealth generally.

negligence.[65] The Rules provide[66] for an investigation by the district judge of allegations, for the ordering attendance of any person, for the disclosure of any document, for further statements and for an inspection appointment. Ultimately the duty to disclose can be enforced by committal proceedings.[67]

The pool of available assets

14–048 Since the decision of the House of Lords in *White v. White*,[68] the ascertainment and valuation of the pool of assets on which the section 25 discretion operates appears to have assumed greater importance, at least in "big money" cases[69] involving marriages of some duration. This is the result both of an entitlement approach based on contributions over the length of the marriage and of the "yardstick" of equal division against which a provisional order must be checked. Another issue which has assumed importance is the liquidity or otherwise of assets: can they be realised in order to meet an order for ancillary relief, and if not, is this a valid reason for departure from the provisional yardstick of equal division[70]? In practice these questions can take up a considerable amount of court time in contested "big money" cases. Both the evaluation of contributions and the yardstick are discussed below.

Common issues

14–049 A number of issues arise frequently:

(i) *Reality not appearance*

The term "financial resources" has a meaning in section 25(2)(a) distinct from and wider than "income" or "property", as the following discussion will demonstrate. The court is concerned with the realities of the parties' financial

---

[65] See, *e.g. Dickinson v. Jones Alexander & Co.* [1993] 2 F.L.R. at 521 (where £330,238 in damages was awarded against a solicitor who had left the conduct of a case to an unsupervised articled clerk) and for a case in which a solicitor was held liable for failing to take action to protect the wife's pension expectancies, see *Griffiths v. Dawson & Co.* [1993] 2 F.L.R. 315. The argument that an action based on a solicitor's negligence in not securing adequate disclosure before seeking a consent order constituted a collateral challenge to the final order of a court of competent jurisdiction was rejected in *B. v. Miller & Co.* [1996] 2 F.L.R. 22. In contrast, solicitors who waste costs in excessive inquiry may be ordered to pay the costs involved: see, *e.g. Re a Solicitor (Wasted Costs Order)* [1993] 2 F.L.R. 959 (costs totalling £130,000 run up in case in which assets only justified lump-sum award of £20,000).

[66] F.P.R. 1991 as amended, r. 2.62.

[67] In appropriate (and exceptional) cases the High Court may make an *Anton Piller* order, in effect giving one party's representative the right to enter the other's premises without prior warning to inspect documents: see *Emmanuel v. Emmanuel* [1981] 3 F.L.R. 319; Practice Direction: *ex parte Mareva* and *Anton Piller* Orders [1994] 2 F.L.R. 704; *Burgess v. Burgess* [1996] 2 F.L.R. 33, CA. Such an order will be granted only in exceptional circumstances: *Araghinchi v. Araghinchi* [1997] 2 F.L.R. 142.

[68] [2000] 2 F.L.R. 981.

[69] *Cordle v. Cordle* [2001] EWCA Civ. 1791; [2002] 1 F.L.R. 207.

[70] See *e.g. N. v. N (Sale of Company)* [2001] 2 F.L.R. 69; *P v. P* [2002] EWHC Fam. 887; [2002] *Fam. Law.* GS6.

situation.[71] For example, if a spouse has an interest under a discretionary trust,[72] the court will not be deterred from making an order merely because a beneficiary under such a trust has no legal right to claim any part of the fund. The court may equally have regard to the realities of funds provided to a spouse by family members.[73] Furthermore, the realities include the ability to raise money by borrowing (particularly if that is the method the parties have used in the past to finance a particular life-style). Thus, in *Newton v. Newton*[74] the husband—a successful property developer—claimed that an order that he pay a lump sum of £750,000 to the wife would destroy his income-generating capacity; but the court held that the onus lay on him to show that he was unable to raise the sum which would be needed to meet the court's order. Adverse inferences may be drawn from non-disclosure and an order reflect the assumed realities of undisclosed assets.[75] A striking example is *Al-Khatib v. Masry*[76] where the award to the wife of £26.3 million was reputedly the largest ever; the husband denied the wife's claim that he was worth more than £140 million, but the order reflected very substantial undisclosed assets.

(ii) *Earning capacity and earning potential*

14–050 The court is concerned with what each spouse could reasonably have if the earning capacity were fully exploited. For example, in *Hardy v. Hardy*[77] the

---

[71] This is well explained by Waite L.J. in a passage in *Thomas v. Thomas* [1995] 2 F.L.R. 668 at 670–671, which merits extended citation: " . . . if justice is to be achieved between spouses at divorce the court must be equipped . . . to penetrate outer forms and get to the heart of ownership . . . [C]ertain principles emerge from the authorities. One is that the court is not obliged to limit its orders exclusively to resources of capital or income which are shown actually to exist. The availability of unidentified resources may, for example, be inferred from a spouse's expenditure or style of living, or from his inability or unwillingness to allow the complexity of his affairs to be penetrated with the precision necessary to ascertain his actual wealth or the degree of liquidity of his assets. Another is that where a spouse enjoys access to wealth but no absolute entitlement to it (as in the case . . . of a beneficiary under a discretionary trust or someone who is dependent on the generosity of a relative), the court will not act in direct invasion of the rights of, or usurp the discretion exercisable by, a third party. Nor will it put upon a third party undue pressure to act in a way which will enhance the means of the maintaining spouse. [But] . . . there will be occasions when it becomes permissible for a judge deliberately to frame his orders in a form which affords judicious encouragement to third parties to provide the maintaining spouse with the means to comply with the court's view of the justice of the case".

[72] As in *Browne v. Browne* [1989] 1 F.L.R. 291, CA, where the judge, in making a lump sum order against a wife of £175,000 had taken into account the fact that she had interests under substantial Swiss and Jersey trusts, and on the evidence had been able to obtain funds from those sources. But the court will not wish to exercise improper pressure on trustees of a discretionary trust: see *Howard v. Howard* [1945] P. 1, the passage from *Thomas v. Thomas* [1995] 2 F.L.R. 668 at 670, cited in n. 69, above and see also *J. v. J. (C. Intervening)* [1989] 1 F.L.R. 453.

[73] In *X v. X (Y and Z Intervening)* [2002] 1 F.L.R. 508 Munby J. did not need to find that the wife had very substantial resources available to her from her wealthy family, but would have been prepared to hold that they were more than sufficient to justify an order of £500,000 in favour of the husband.

[74] [1990] 1 F.L.R. 33; and see *J. v. J;* on appeal [1955] P. 236 where the husband (also a property developer) had a taxable income of only £70 per annum; and it was held that his expenditure was a better guide to his resources.

[75] *Baker v. Baker* [1995] 2 F.L.R. 829.

[76] [2002] EWHC Fam. 108; [2002] 1 F.L.R. 1053.

[77] [1981] 1 F.L.R. 321.

husband worked in his father's racing stables for much less than he could have earned elsewhere. The court saw no reason why he should enjoy this privilege at the expense of his wife and children; and made an order based on the earnings he could have obtained on the open market. Again, in *K v. K (Conduct)*[78] the husband had a drink problem and had been made redundant. The court found that he had not made adequate efforts to find work; and took that factor into account—albeit as "conduct" or as one of the surrounding circumstances rather than under the present head—in dividing the family assets between the spouses.

However, the court should only act on evidence that there is better paid work available. In *Williams (L.A.) v. Williams (E.M.)*[79] the trial court wrongly failed to take account of the telling fact that the welfare benefit authorities had accepted that the husband could not find work.

The Matrimonial and Family Proceedings Act 1984 added a specific reference to direct the court's attention to "any increase in earning capacity which it would be reasonable to expect" a spouse to take steps to acquire.[80] This requires proof of two separate matters: first, that a spouse could in fact increase his or her prospects of earning[81]; secondly, that it would be reasonable for him or her to be expected to do so. For example, if a wife had experience as a secretary before marriage there might be evidence that by retraining she could again find well-remunerated secretarial work. But even if that hurdle is surmounted the court must still be satisfied that it is reasonable to expect her to do so. This can be illustrated by comparing some outcomes. In *Leadbeater v. Leadbeater*[82] the wife, aged 47, had been a secretary, but earned only £1,608 per annum as a part-time receptionist. The judge thought she could, by working longer hours, reasonably earn somewhat more, but that it would not be reasonable to expect her at that age to familiarise herself with modern office technology. In *M v. M (Prenuptial Agreement)*[83] the court capitalised income provision for a wife aged 39 using a multiplier of five years. Her capacity to earn some limited income as a teacher in two years time was taken into account, but so was her probable return to a career in business in five years' time when the child in her care would be less dependent. In *M v. M (Financial Provision)*[84] the wife of a chartered accountant had worked as a secretary prior to her 20-year marriage, and had done some part-time work during the marriage. She tried valiantly and persistently to find some employment when the marriage broke down, but was unsuccessful. The judge held on the facts that she was unlikely at her age and with her job experience to achieve more than a fairly humble job in the secretarial field; and accordingly that her earning potential should not be assessed at more

---

78 [1990] 2 F.L.R. 225.

79 [1974] Fam. 55.

80 For a discussion of the background to this provision, see the 4th edition of this work at pp. 778–789.

81 It appears that expert re-employment consultants may be called on for evidence: see, *e.g. B v. B (Consent Order: Variation)* [1995] 1 F.L.R. 9 (where, however, their evidence was not found helpful).

82 [1985] F.L.R. 789.

83 [2002] 1 F.L.R. 654, FD.

84 [1987] 2 F.L.R. 1.

than £6,000 per annum.[85] In *A v. A (Financial Provision)*[86] it was held not to be reasonable to expect the wife of a wealthy man who has ongoing care of the children to seek full-time employment without previous work experience or to set up her own business.

(iii) *Resources of new partner*

14–051 The court has no power to order that a third party—for example, the husband's second wife or cohabitant—should provide for the applicant or the children of the family[87]; and it must not make an order which can only be satisfied by dipping into a third party's resources.[88] But the fact that such a person has means available may be relevant, because thereby the husband can more readily make appropriate provision.[89] As the Law Commission put it,[90] the husband is not allowed in such cases to say that he needs all or most of his income in order to provide for the needs of his new family. In effect the means of the cohabitant are taken into account at what is often the decisive stage of calculating the net effect of the proposed order.

(iv) *Derivation of the assets*

14–052 The discretion conferred by section 25 operates upon the totality of the parties' financial resources, and is not in principle confined itself to assets acquired during the marriage or with reference to the marriage. The derivation of an asset is nevertheless a factor relevant to the exercise of discretion as to the *quantum* of an award. The cases thus turn on their facts. In *Schuller v. Schuller*[91] a wife took a job as a housekeeper, and her employer left her his house in his will. The employer died before the ancillary relief application had been settled; and the court made an order on the basis that the wife's housing needs were now fully satisfied. Similarly, in *Daubney v. Daubney*[92] a flat which the wife had

[85] See also *Barrett v. Barrett* [1988] 2 F.L.R. 516, CA; and *Newton v. Newton* (above)—suggestion that 53 year old agoraphobic wife of millionaire should "pull herself together and get a job" very properly dropped before hearing. For a case where the wife's earning capacity was assessed at nil in an action for negligence against her former solicitors, see *Dickinson v. Jones Alexander & Co.* [1993] 2 F.L.R. 521.

[86] [1998] 2 F.L.R. 180, FD.

[87] *Macey v. Macey* (1981) 3 F.L.R. 7; *B v. B (Periodical Payments: Transitional Provisions)* [1995] 1 F.L.R. 459.

[88] *Re L. (Minors) (Financial Provision)* (1979) 1 F.L.R. 39; *Macey v. Macey* (1981) 3 F.L.R. 7; and see also *Fisher v. Fisher* [1989] 1 F.L.R. 423 at 430, CA; *B v. B (Periodical Payments: Transitional Provisions)* [1995] 1 F.L.R. 459. Nevertheless, funds in fact made available by a third party may legitimately be treated as the financial resource of a spouse: *X v. X (Y and Z Intervening)* [2002] 1 F.L.R. 508, FD (moneys made available by wife's wealthy family).

[89] *Macey v. Macey* (1981) 3 F.L.R. 7; *Suter v. Suter* [1987] Fam. 111, CA; *Atkinson v. Atkinson* [1995] 2 F.L.R. 356, FD.

[90] Law Com. No. 112, para. 4.

[91] [1990] 2 F.L.R. 193, CA.

[92] [1967] Fam. 267; and note *Wagstaff v. Wagstaff* [1992] 1 F.L.R. 333, CA, where the husband had received £325,000 in settlement of his claim for personal injuries. It was held that, although his needs were the first call on the family assets, yet the capital sum awarded was not sacrosanct and a lump sum payment of £32,000 should be made to the wife to redress the disparity between the parties' financial positions and do justice to the wife's claim; compare *C v. C (Financial Provision: Personal Damages)* [1995] 2 F.L.R. 171, below.

bought with personal injury damages was taken into account in working out the overall financial position.[93] Since the decision of the House of Lords in *White v. White*,[94] the derivation of funds (for example, from the parent of one spouse, an inheritance, or from the post-separation industry of one spouse) has assumed increased importance, both under section 25(2)(a) and as a reason for departing from the yardstick of equal division,[95] discussed below.

(v) *Expectations*

14–053 Financial resources may in appropriate circumstances include expectations. It has been held that the court may take account of financial expectations under a will or intestacy (for example, to inherit a house acquired from a local authority under the "right to buy" legislation) of a relative who is terminally ill—although in the normal case the uncertainties both as to the fact of the inheritance and as to the time when the death will occur makes the court reluctant to do so.[96]

(vi) *Pensions*

14–054 In many cases[97] entitlements under an occupational or personal pension scheme will be amongst the parties' most valuable assets; and the court must be provided[98] with evidence on the size of the fund and the parties' rights and expectation. The range of the court's powers in relation to pension entitlements is discussed below.[99]

---

93 *Morgan v. Morgan* [1977] Fam. 122. Contrast *C v. C (Financial Provision: Personal Damages)* [1995] 2 F.L.R. 171, where the husband was entitled to sums perhaps totalling £5 million under a "structured settlement", but it was held that in the light of the husband's needs there was no capital available for the wife. The court also refused to make a periodical payments order largely because it would not benefit the wife given her entitlement to welfare benefits (including benefits, such as free prescriptions, to which she was "passported"): see above.

94 [2000] 2 F.L.R. 981.

95 See *e.g. White v. White* [2001] 2 F.L.R. 981 (resources derived from husband's father); *Dharamshi v Dharamshi* [2001] 1 F.L.R. 736 (husband's family's contribution to business); *Cowan v. Cowan* [2001] 2 F.L.R. 192 (husband's contributions and increase in business value since separation).

96 *Michael v. Michael* [1986] 2 F.L.R. 389 ("The world is full of women in their eighties who had high blood pressure in their sixties", *per* Nourse L.J. at 397—no account to be taken of prospects of wife inheriting property from her 64-year-old mother notwithstanding poor health); but compare *MT v. MT (Financial Provision: Lump Sum)* [1992] 1 F.L.R. 362 where the husband was indefeasibly entitled under German law to share in the large estate of his 83-year-old father, and the parties financial behaviour throughout a 20 year marriage had been dominated by the knowledge that the "ship of inheritance" would come to port: *per* Bracewell J., at 364—wife's application adjourned until death of father-in-law).

97 A solicitor will be guilty of professional negligence if no adequate inquiry is made about a client's pension expectations: see *Griffiths v. Dawson & Co.* [1993] 2 F.L.R. 315; and this duty has been reinforced by the provisions of M.C.A. 1973 which states that the matters to be taken into account include any benefits under a pension scheme—which in this context has a wholly unrestricted meaning.

98 See Form M1 and Form E.

99 At p. 406.

(vii) *Other*

A spouse's statutory entitlement as primary carer to be rehoused by a housing association may be considered as a resource under s 25(2)(a).[1] **14–055**

(ii) "the financial needs, obligations and responsibilities which each of the parties to the marriage has or is likely to have in the foreseeable future" (M.C.A. 1973, s.25(2)(b))

(i) *"Needs"*

In practice needs assume crucial importance in cases where resources are limited. In that context, the housing needs of the parent with care will often be decisive, since first consideration must be given to minor children's welfare.[2] This approach appears to be undisturbed[3] by the decision of the House or Lords in *White v. White*.[4] Where assets permit, the court should attempt to meet the housing needs of the other parent, particularly if staying contact is envisaged.[5] Where there are no minor children, the needs of the spouses must be weighed in the balance.[6] Where resources are limited, it may not be possible to meet the needs of both spouses, and priority may have to be given to one of them.[7] **14–056**

In "big money" cases, for many years "needs" in section 25(2)(b) in practice assumed a dominance over the other considerations mentioned in the subsection, in the guise of the "reasonable requirements" ceiling which was imposed on the *quantum* of an award (usually to the wife).[8] In such cases it was accepted that the concept was a relative one; the wife of a wealthy man was entitled to maintain the high standard of living previously enjoyed. In contested cases much turned on arguments over the details of budgets[9] presented to the court. In *Dart v. Dart*,[10] the parties had enjoyed a lavish life style (spending £400,000 a year); and the husband's net worth was estimated at £400 million. The Court of Appeal refused to increase the judge's award to the wife of £9 million; but both Butler-Sloss and Peter Gibson L.JJ. expressed the view that the courts might have

---

[1] *Akintola v. Akintola* [2001] EWCA Civ. 1989 [2002] 1 F.L.R. 701.

[2] M.C.A. s. 25(1), discussed earlier in this Chapter.

[3] *Elliott v. Elloitt* [2001] 2 F.C.R. 477; *B v. B (Financial Provision: Welfare of Child)* [2002] 1 F.L.R. 555, FD; *Cordle v. Cordle* [2001] EWCA Civ. 1791; [2002] 2 F.L.R. 207, CA, discussed above.

[4] [2001] 1 A.C. 596; [2000] 3 W.L.R. 1571; [2000] 2 F.L.R. 981.

[5] *M v. B (Ancillary Proceedings: Lump Sum)* [1998] 1 F.L.R. 53, CA; *Cordle v. Cordle* [2001] EWCA Civ. 1791; [2002] 1 F.L.R. 207.

[6] *Scheeres v. Scheeres* [1999] 1 F.L.R. 241.

[7] As in *Piglowska v Piglowski* [1999] 2 F.L.R.763.

[8] *O'D v. O'D* [1976] Fam. 83; *Page v. Page* (1981) 2 F.L.R. 198; *Preston v. Preston* [1982] Fam. 17; *Gojkovic v. Gojkovic* [1990] F.L.R. 140, CA; *R v. R (Financial Provision: Reasonable Needs)* [1994] 2 F.L.R. 1044; *F v. F (Ancillary Relief: Substantial Assets)* [1995] 2 F.L.R. 45; *Dart v. Dart* [1996] 2 F.L.R. 286.

[9] The basis for the budget was the "Duxbury calculation": *Duxbury v. Duxbury* [1987] 1 F.L.R. 140.

[10] [1996] 2 F.L.R. 286, CA.

imposed too restrictive an interpretation upon the words of section 25 in their application to the wealthy; and that too great emphasis might have been placed on the requirement to have regard to the parties' reasonable requirements as against the other criteria set out in the section. However, although the "reasonable requirements" approach was not exclusive even in "big money" cases,[11] its domination was not removed until the decision of the House of Lords in *White v. White*.[12] As discussed above, Lord Nicholls highlighted the unfairness inherent in the "reasonable requirements" ceiling, which invariably left the surplus of assets in the hands of the entrepreneur.

In many cases, the parties' needs will be self evident—for example, the provision of housing and a modest income. In cases involving substantial assets, the court may decide that it should try to put the applicant in the position of having a certain spendable income each year; and a computer programme—the so-called *Duxbury* programme—has been devised[13] to calculate the lump sum needed to produce a given level of spending power allowing for inflation and a number of variables[14] and hypotheses—for example, the possibility that the applicant might obtain employment after a number of years' training. Such programmes provide a useful reference base, but cannot be more than a guide to the court, and may be wholly inappropriate in the particular circumstances, for instance where a spouse has a long life expectancy or alternatively a short one,[15] or where the marriage has been short.[16] The importance of the *Duxbury* calculation has diminished on the removal of the "reasonable requirements" ceiling on awards in big money cases; needs are now only one of the considerations in the section 25 exercise. It nevertheless remains a useful tool in calculating the income component of a lump sum.[17]

Two final points should be made about the orders that can be made on the basis of "need". First, it is not an objection that part of a lump sum computed so as to

---

[11] It was subject to an uplift for exceptional contributions: Conran v Conran [1997] 2 F.L.R. 615, FD and yielded to an entitlements approach recognising contributions over a very long marriage: *A v. A (Elderly Applicant: Lump Sum)* [1999] 2 F.L.R. 969.

[12] [2000] 2 F.L.R. 981.

[13] See T. Lawrence, "Duxbury Disclosure and Other Matters" [1989] *Fam. Law* 12; for judicial comment see *Gojkovic v. Gojkovic* [1990] F.L.R. 140; *B. v. B. (Financial Provision)* [1990] 1 F.L.R. 20; *Vicary v. Vicary* [1992] 2 F.L.R. 271; *F v. F (Ancillary Relief: Substantial Assets)* [1995] 2 F.L.R. 45; *F v. F (Duxbury Calculation: Rate of Return)* [1996] 1 F.L.R. 833. The Family Law Bar Association publish a guide, *At a Glance,* which contains a Table enabling a simplified calculation to be made; see also the computer programme *Capitalise* by Singer and Mostyn. For further discussion, see Lawrence, Mainz and Collinson [1996] *Fam. Law* 560; Posnansky [1998] *Fam. Law* 447; Singer *et al.* [1998] *Fam. Law* 741; Woelke [1999] *Fam. Law* 767; Woelke [1999] *Fam. Law* 52; Mostyn [2000] *Fam. Law* 52; Merron et al. [2001] *Fam. Law* 749; Marks [2002] *Fam. Law* 408.

[14] See *Gojkovic v. Gojkovic* [1990] 1 F.L.R. 140; *B. v. B. (Financial Provision)* [1990] 1 F.L.R. 20; *Vicary v. Vicary* [1992] 2 F.L.R. 271; *Fournier v. Fournier* [1998] 2 F.L.R. 662; *A v. A (Elderly Applicant: Lump Sum)* [1999] 2 F.L.R. 662; *W v. W (Ancillary Relief: Practice)* [2000] *Fam. Law* 493.

[15] See *Gojkovic v. Gojkovic* [1990] 1 F.L.R. 140; *B. v. B. (Financial Provision)* [1990] 1 F.L.R. 20; *Vicary v. Vicary* [1992] 2 F.L.R. 271; *Fournier v Fournier* [1998] 2 F.L.R. 662; *A v. A (Elderly Applicant: Lump Sum)* [1999] 2 F.L.R. 662; *W v. W (Ancillary Relief: Practice)* [2000] *Fam. Law* 493.

[16] *M v. M (Prenuptial Agreement)* [2002] 1 F.L.R. 654, FD.

[17] Marks [2002] *Fam. Law* 408. For a contrary view, see Merron *et al.*, "Is Duxbury Misleading? Yes it is" [2001] *Fam. Law* 747.

provide for needs may pass to a third party—such as the recipient's cohabitant. It is up to the recipient how he or she deals with the sum awarded.[18] Secondly, once the court has computed the sum which it regards as appropriate, the respondent is usually asked to make proposals as to the precise way in which that amount may be provided—for example, by way of a lump sum or transfer of property.

(iii) *Obligations and responsibilities*

14–057 The court is directed to consider the parties' financial "obligations and responsibilities"; and this requirement gives rise to a number of problems. For example, how far can a spouse claim that gross income should be reduced to take account of large travelling expenses, or the need to service a large mortgage on a house bought for the newly created family? The general answer—as is so often the case in the exercise of this highly discretionary jurisdiction—is that it depends on what is reasonable. In *Slater v. Slater*[19] the court thought the husband had been extravagant in deciding to live in a country house with consequent heavy transport and property maintenance expenses; and he was not allowed to deduct those expenses in working out his available income. But if the husband has reasonably decided to buy a new house with a heavy mortgage, leaving his divorced wife and family in the former matrimonial home, the court will not make an order against him such as would make it impossible for him to service the mortgage.[20]

The problem of supporting successive families raises difficult issues of policy. Where resources are limited, reality demands that account be taken of financial support of a second family.[21] But what of cases where there is surplus of assets after both parties needs have been satisfied, and the principle of equality and the yardstick of equal division formulated in *White v. White*[22] apply? Should the amount needed by one of the former spouses to support the child of a new relationship be notionally deducted from the pool of assets on which the yardstick operates, or at least be a valid reason for departure from equal division? To date the sparse case-law appears to be divided on the issue. In *S v. S (Financial Provision: Departing From Equality)*[23] a man's financial responsibility to his second family was one of the considerations justifying a departure from equal division of assets. However, in *W H-J v. W H-J*[24] Coleridge J. considered such an approach to be wrong in principle in a case involving sufficient resources: a man's responsibilities to a new child were his choice, and should be met from his own share of the assets after division with his wife. In Chapter 15 we discuss the recognition given by the Child Support Act 1991 to obligations towards children in second families.

---

[18] *Duxbury v. Duxbury* [1987] 1 F.L.R. 7; and see *Atkinson v. Atkinson* [1988] 2 F.L.R. 353. Note however that in *Al Khatib v. Masry* [2002] EWHC Fam. 108; [2002] 1 F.L.R. 1053, Munby J. awarded the wife £2.5 million specifically as a litigation-fighting fund.

[19] [1982] 3 F.L.R. 364; *Delaney v. Delaney* [1990] 2 F.L.R. 457.

[20] *Stockford v. Stockford* (1981) 3 F.L.R. 58, CA.

[21] *Barnes v. Barnes* [1972] 2 W.L.R. 1381; *Delaney v. Delaney* [1990] 2 F.L.R. 457.

[22] [2001] 1 A.C. 596; [2000] 2 F.L.R. 981, HL.

[23] [2001] 2 F.L.R. 246, FD.

[24] [2002] 1 F.L.R. 415.

(iii) "the standard of living enjoyed by the family before the breakdown of the marriage" (M.C.A. 1973, s.25(2)(c))

14–058 Under the "minimal loss" principle, standard of living was obviously an important factor since the court's objective was to ensure that the applicant's financial position remained unaltered. As the law now stands, a spouse is no longer absolutely entitled to expect to keep the standard of living enjoyed by the parties during the marriage, but "adequate recognition" should be given to it in deciding what is reasonable as between the parties; and where there has been a marriage of some duration the more vulnerable party is entitled to the security of a "reasonably decent" standard of living.[25] Thus:—

> In *Leadbeater v. Leadbeater*[26] the wife had been married for four years to a man worth £250,000, and had in consequence enjoyed a "much enhanced" life-style. That factor was taken into account, but so was the modest life-style she had previously enjoyed. In all the circumstances, a comparatively modest £37,500 lump sum was ordered.

> In *Attar v. Attar*[27] the wife (who had previously been an air-hostess with an Arab airline earning some £15,000 per annum net) was married for only six months to a man worth more than £2m. The court ordered a lump sum payment of £30,000 (based on an assessment of what she had lived on before the marriage) to enable her to adjust over a period of two years to the ending of the marriage.

The income required to support a post-divorce standard of living commensurate with that enjoyed during marriage is commonly taken into account under "needs" in section 25(2)(b), discussed above.

(iv) "the age of each party to the marriage and the duration of the marriage" (M.C.A. 1973, s.25(2)(d))

14–059 It is often not necessary to consider the parties' ages as a matter distinct from the court's assessment of their needs and resources: a young and healthy spouse will be able to get work; and if the applicant is elderly and infirm—or merely vulnerable and no longer young[28]—the needs will be that much greater.

The duration of the marriage is a matter of more importance in the exercise of the court's discretion under section 25. In enacting the current legislation,

---

[25] *M. v. M. (Financial Provision)* [1987] 2 F.L.R. 1; and see *Newton v. Newton* [1990] F.L.R. 33.

[26] [1985] F.L.R. 789.

[27] [1985] F.L.R. 649. Compare *R v. R (Financial Provision: Reasonable Needs)* [1994] 2 F.L.R. 1044 at 1049—wife entitled to continue living in "splendid mansion" and to lump sum of £550,000; and *F v. F (Ancillary Relief: Substantial Assets)* [1995] 2 F.L.R. 45 at 63, *per* Thorpe J: "The standard of living was undoubtedly opulent. But it was a rising and not a uniform standard of living. As the wife grew from a 25-year-old student to a 30-year-old inhabiting the beau-monde . . . both standard of living and expenditure inflated" to a figure of at least £1.75 million annually.

[28] *M. v. M. (Financial Provision)* [1987] 2 F.L.R. 1 at 10.

Parliament decisively repudiated the notion that one spouse is entitled solely by virtue of the status of marriage to be maintained on a scale appropriate to the other spouse's standard of life, exemplified in *Brett v. Brett*[29] decided on the old law. There the wife was a childless 23-year-old solicitor whose marriage had lasted for less than six months. She was awarded (in 1996 values) yearly periodical payments of some £16,000 and a lump sum of some £200,000.

Under the current law, the significance attached to the duration of the marriage will depend on the facts; it is only one of the factors in the section 25(2) equation.[30] It is generally agreed that the notion of equality and the yardstick of equal division formulated in *White v. White*[31] do not generally apply to short marriages,[32] although it is a matter of debate as to what constitutes a short marriage. In some short marriages, the basis of an award may be essentially rehabilitative: to permit adjustment to the post-marriage financial situation in the expectation that financial independence will be achieved. Thus in *Attar v. Attar*[33] the court thought a single capital payment of £30,000 was sufficient to enable the wife of an exceedingly wealthy man to retrain over a two-year period after a six-month marriage. In *Hobhouse v. Hobhouse*[34] the wife's award represented capitalisation of support for three to five years to permit her adjustment to a new life. In *M v. M (Prenuptial Agreement)*[35] where the marriage had lasted five years, the income component of the wife's lump sum was capitalised using a multiplier of five years, taking account of her plans to return to some paid employment after two years and further plans to resume a career in business in five years' time when the child in her care would be less dependent. An award based predominantly on needs may be appropriate, with adjustments for the brevity of the marriage. In *Leadbeater v. Leadbeater*[36] the court first of all calculated the wife's reasonable needs along the lines already explained, and held that they could be satisfied by a payment of £50,000. Since the marriage had only lasted four years, that figure was reduced by 25 per cent to £37,500, to be paid by way of once-for-all settlement of all her claims.[37] However, everything depends on the particular circumstances, and it is difficult to make generalisations. Where even a very short marriage has had a marked effect on a spouse's health and needs, a substantial lump sum and even continuing maintenance may be justified, as in *C v. C (Financial Relief: Short Marriage)*[38] a marriage of only nine and a half

---

[29] [1969] 1 W.L.R. 487.

[30] *G v. G (Financial Provision: Separation Agreement)* [2000] 2 F.L.R. 18, FD; on the facts, the most important consideration was the separation agreement.

[31] [2001] 1 A.C. 596; [2000] 2 F.L.R. 981.

[32] See the concession made on behalf of the wife in *M v. M (Prenuptial Agreement)* [2002 1 F.L.R. 654, FD.

[33] [1985] F.L.R. 649.

[34] [1999] 1 F.L.R. 961.

[35] [2002] 1 F.L.R. 654, FD.

[36] [1985] F.L.R. 789.

[37] See also *Hedges v. Hedges* [1991] 1 F.L.R. 196, CA (childless marriage between couple in late thirties lasted four years—lump sum order of £2,500—half of husband's disposal capital—in respect of loss of widow's pension and periodical payments of £250 monthly for 18 months upheld). The courts are reluctant to equate periods of extra-marital cohabitation with marriage for this purpose: see *Hewitson v. Hewitson* [1995] 1 F.L.R. 241, CA.

[38] [1997] 2 F.L.R. 27.

months' duration had produced child in poor health and had exacerbated the wife's past history of anxiety and depression into traumatic stress disorder.

Under an approach which focuses on entitlements built up though contributions to the family welfare, a long marriage may assume considerable significance. This approach was foreshadowed even prior to the decision in *White v. White.*[39] Thus in *A v. A (Elderly Applicant)*[40] the significant contributions[41] of the husband aged 79 over a marriage of some 43 years were held to have established his entitlement to an award higher than limited by the "reasonable requirements" approach then widely entrenched in practice. After *White v. White,* as has been explained earlier and will be further discussed in the next section, in marriages of a reasonable duration the contributions of the parties should be evaluated without discrimination and the yardstick of equal division of assets applied. This approach seems appropriate only where assets have been built up by joint efforts over a reasonable period of time.

(v) "any physical or mental disability of either of the parties to the marriage" (M.C.A. 1973, s.25(2)(e))

14–060 This provision was not included in the draft Bill originally put forward by the Law Commission, but was added as a result of parliamentary pressure during the passage of the original 1970 legislation. It adds little to the matters which are considered under other heads.[42]

(vi) "the contributions made by each of the parties to the welfare of the family, including any contribution made by looking after the home or caring for the family" (M.C.A. 1973, s.25(2)(f))

14–061 The law governing beneficial entitlement to matrimonial property was, as we have seen, widely felt not to give adequate recognition to the contributions which wives in particular often made towards the acquisition of so-called family assets—"those things which are acquired . . . with the intention that there should be continuing provision for [the parties] and their children during their joint lives, and used for the benefit of the family as a whole," as Lord Denning put it in *Wachtel v. Wachtel.*[43] That case made it quite clear that under the post-1969 divorce law such contributions would be taken fully into account. Nevertheless, over the last three decades the courts, in applying section 25(2)(f) of the Matrimonial Causes Act 1973, have struggled with the respective and relative values to be accorded, in terms of ancillary relief outcome, to financial and non-financial contributions to family welfare.

---

[39] [2000] 2 F.L.R. 981.

[40] [1999] 2 F.L.R. 969. See also *Smith v. Smith (Smith and Others Intervening)* [1992] 2 F.L.R. 432.

[41] See M.C.A. s. 25(2)(f), discussed below.

[42] Particularly the needs of the parties: see, *e.g. C v. C (Financial Provision: Personal Damages)* [1995] 2 F.L.R. 171; *C v. C (Financial Relief: Short Marriage)* [1997] 2 F.L.R. 969.

[43] [1973] Fam. 72, CA.

Prior to the decision of the House of Lords in *White v. White,*[44] there were signs of a growing recognition of a wife's indirect (as well, self-evidently, as direct[45]) contribution to the success of the business enterprise primarily generated by the husband. In *Vicary v. Vicary*[46] the Court of Appeal accepted that the wife of a millionaire businessman who had "supplied the infrastructure and support in the context of which [he was] able to work hard, prosper and accumulate his wealth" could properly be allowed credit for such indirect contributions. The decision of Wilson J. in *Conran v. Conran*[47] further liberalised the nexus between a range of different contributions and the creation of resources. In that case the wife of a successful businessman had acted as primary homemaker and parent and was energetic in making business contacts for the husband and in entertaining, as well as having her own career as a journalist. The award bringing her wealth up to £10.5 million (at the time reputedly the largest award ever made) recognised her outstanding contributions to the welfare of the family, in addition to her reasonable requirements.

We have already described the "reasonable requirements" ceiling imposed on awards in "big money" cases for several decades. While awards made on that basis may have appeared substantial, in fact they represented very small fractions of the total assets,[48] and thus tended to undervalue non-financial contributions to family welfare.[49] We have shown that the "reasonable requirements" approach was dominant but not wholly exclusive. Thus in *A v. A (Elderly Applicant: Lump Sum)*[50] it was recognised that the *Duxbury* technique would not meet the justice of the case where the husband had made full contributions over a marriage of more than 40 years, and an entitlement approach was adopted.

The highest appellate interpretation of section 25(2)(f) had to await *White v. White,*[51] which we have already discussed at some length. Both the non-discrimination principle and the yardstick of equal division expounded by their Lordships derive essentially from a construction of section 25(2)(f). The principle of non-discrimination would appear to go a considerable way towards the recognition of marriage as an equal partnership, in asserting that equal value is to be accorded on divorce (in the context of ancillary relief) to the different roles undertaken by the spouses during marriage. Non-entrepreneurial contributions to the family should in principle be of equal value in their own right, and there should no longer be any need to establish a causal link[52] the domestic contributions of one spouse and the business success of the other.

---

44 [2000] 2 F.L.R. 981.

45 *O'D v. O'D* [1976] Fam. 83; *Page v. Page* [1981] 2 F.L.R. 198. For another dramatic example of a husband and wife partnership, see *Gojkovic v. Gojkovic* [1990] 1 F.L.R. 140, above.

46 [1992] 2 F.L.R. 271, CA. But note that in *W v. W (Judicial Separation: Ancillary Relief)* [1995] 2 F.L.R. 259, Ewbank J. expressed the view that in a case in which wife had not made a direct contribution to the build-up of the family assets, the *Wachtel* principle should be limited to the division of the matrimonial home rather than the family assets as a whole.

47 [1997] 2 F.L.R. 615.

48 For example, 4.5% in *F v. F (Ancillary Relief: Substantial Asset)* [1995] 2 F.L.R. 47; 2.25% in *Dart v. Dart* [1996] 2 F.L.R. 286; 4.7% in *A v. A (Financial Provision)* [1998] 2 F.L.R. 180.

49 P. Singer, "Sexual Discrimination in Ancillary Relief" [2001] *Fam. Law* 115.

50 [1999] 2 F.L.R. 969.

51 [2000] 2 F.L.R. 981.

52 Even one liberally interpreted as in *Conran v. Conran* [1997] 2 F.L.R. 615.

One passage in Lord Nicholls' opinion in *White v. White*[53] may appear to suggest that this approach is predicated on equality of contribution in the spouses' respective spheres of activity, and thus permits an evaluation of their respective efforts and degrees of success. This opportunity has not been missed by practitioners, and the Court of Appeal in *Cowan v. Cowan*[54] endorsed the notion of exceptional contribution by one spouse, justifying departure from equal division of assets. The assets had been built up during the long marriage; the wife had made some initial contribution to the business, but the very substantial wealth had been generated by the husband's exceptional entrepreneurial skill in marketing plastic bin-liners. The Court of Appeal awarded the wife 38 per cent of the assets and the House of Lords dismissed her petition for leave to appeal.[55] This approach is open to the criticism that it is discriminatory in outcome and thus contrary to the spirit of *White v. White,* in that courts are more ready to draw the inference of exceptional performance in the entrepreneurial than in the domestic sphere.[56] The question of whether a contribution is special or exceptional is one of fact and is currently being further pursued in the case-law.[57] In *W H-J v. H H-J*[58] (where the assets totaled £2.7 million) Coleridge J. on the facts found nothing special or exceptional about the husband's contributions and was aware of the dangers of the thin end of the wedge going driven right into the heart of the principles underlying *White v. White*[59]; in the classic case of full contributions by each spouse over a long marriage the courts should be slow to "start nibbling at the edges" of cases where all other factors were equal and 50 per cent the natural and fair outcome. This was the first reported instance post-*White* of an equal division in a big money case. His Lordship further commented that even a small departure from equal division in a big money case leaves one party feeling that her efforts have been undervalued and warned against "the broad and sweeping reform underlying the speeches in *White* . . . [becoming] bogged down in a welter of zealous, over sophisticated and costly forensic analysis, or watered down by judicial reticence".[60]

(vii) "the conduct of each of the parties if that conduct is such that it would in the opinion of the court be inequitable to disregard it" (M.C.A. 1973, s.25(2)(g))[61]

14–062 The extent to which the conduct of the parties should be relevant in determining the financial outcome of divorce has been controversial; and a brief account of the historical evolution of the law is necessary.

---

[53] [2000] 3 W.L.R. 1571 at 1598: "If, in their different spheres, each contributed equally to the family . . . "

[54] [2001] 2 F.L.R. 192; [2001] 3 W.L.R. 684; J. Eekelaar "Asset Distribution on Divorce—The Durational Element" [2001] 117 *L.Q.R.* 552.

[55] [2001] 1 W.L.R. 2287.

[56] R. Bailey-Harris [2001] *Fam. Law* 499; J. Eekelaar (2001) 117 *L.Q.R.* 552.

[57] *L v. L (Financial Provision: Contributions)* [2002] 1 F.L.R. 642; permission to appeal has been given.

[58] [2002] 1 F.L.R. 415.

[59] [2000] 2 F.L.R. 981.

[60] [2002] 1 F.L.R. 415 at 430–431.

[61] Burles, "Conduct and Ancillary Relief" [1997] *Fam. Law* 804.

So long as divorce was based on the matrimonial offence doctrine the parties' conduct was of crucial importance: an "innocent" wife was entitled to full compensation for the loss of her status and the right to support flowing from it at common law; but a "guilty" wife would not in principle be entitled to maintenance at all. Over the years the harshness of this rule was mitigated. In the end it became accepted that a wife's misconduct would only be allowed to affect her right to maintenance if it could be described as really serious, disruptive, intolerable and unforgivable.[62]

The Divorce Reform Act 1969 was intended to allow the empty legal shell of a broken marriage to be destroyed with the minimum bitterness, distress and humiliation, but the legislation dealing with the financial consequences of divorce specifically required the court to have regard to the parties' conduct in determining how far it was just to place them in the financial position they would have been in had it not been for the breakdown. Did this mean—as was suggested in some of the early cases—that the courts would have to carry out an investigation into responsibility for the breakdown of the marriage? Did it mean that the judge had to hear the parties' "mutual recriminations and . . . go into their petty squabbles for days on end, as he used to do in the old days"?[63]

In 1973, in the leading case of *Wachtel v. Wachtel,*[64] the Court of Appeal refused to allow the policy of the divorce law to be subverted in this way. In the vast majority of cases (said Lord Denning) both parties would have contributed to the breakdown. In such cases the court should not reduce its order for financial provision merely because of what was formerly regarded as guilt or blame. Nevertheless, there would remain a "residue of cases" where the conduct of one of the parties had been (in the words of Ormrod J. at first instance) "both obvious and gross," so much so that to order one party to support another whose conduct fell into this category would be "repugnant to anyone's sense of justice." It was only in such cases that the financial order should be reduced.[65]

As a result of the acceptance of this decision, considerations of conduct were held rarely to be relevant; and it was evidently the intention of the draftsman of the Matrimonial and Family Proceedings Act 1984 to codify the practice of the Court of Appeal developed on the basis of *Wachtel,* whilst avoiding the use of the expression "obvious and gross" (which had become in danger of being used as if it were a statutory formula describing conduct which might be taken into account). Conduct was to be relevant only in those (exceptional) circumstances in which it would be "inequitable" to disregard it.[66]

Notwithstanding some early uncertainty, it came to be accepted[67] by the profession and by the judiciary that the 1984 Act confirmed but in no way affected the *Wachtel* interpretation of the law conduct would only rarely be relevant in

---

[62] *Ackerman v. Ackerman* [1972] Fam. 1, *per* Sir G. Baker, P.

[63] *Wachtel v. Wachtel* [1973] Fam. 72, CA.

[64] Above.

[65] [1973] Fam. 72 at 89–90.

[66] For a fuller discussion, see the 4th edition of this work at pp. 797–802 and (in particular) for a detailed summary of the case law, n. 13, p. 800.

[67] *K. v. K. (Financial Provision Conduct)* [1988] 1 F.L.R. 469 at 476, *per* Purchas L.J.

practice.[68] The test is "would a right thinking member of society say that the matters of conduct were such that it would be inequitable to disregard it?" There are a number of ways in which conduct is taken into account in the case-law.

"Conduct" is not a synonym for matrimonial misconduct and may involve financial dealings. Thus, in *Martin v. Martin*[69] it was held to be relevant that a man had during the marriage dissipated the family capital; because (as Cairns L.J. put it) a spouse "cannot be allowed to fritter away the assets by extravagant living or reckless speculation and then to claim as great a share of what was left as he would have been entitled to if he had behaved reasonably." In *Beach v. Beach*[70] the husband (who had been a millionaire dairy farmer) had "obstinately, unrealistically and selfishly trailed on to eventual disaster, dissipating in the process not only his money but his family's money, his friends' money, the money of commercial creditors unsecured and eventually his wife's money . . . "[71] Accordingly the husband should receive no more than was necessary to provide him with basic accommodation. In *Le Foe v. Le Foe and Woolwich plc*[72] the husband's deceptive mortagaging of the home was reflected in the *quantum* of the award. Furthermore, as we have seen, in Chapters 4 and 5 the existence and terms of a separation agreement[73] or a pre-nuptial agreement[74] may be taken into account as conduct under section 25(2)(g).

14–063 In one very limited category of case, conduct bars a claim to ancillary relief *in limine* on public policy grounds derived from the maxim "*ex turpi causa non oritur actio*". In *Whiston v. Whiston*[75] the husband obtained a decree of nullity on account of the wife's bigamy, of which she was well aware when she entered into her second "marriage". The Court of Appeal held that the crime of bigamy strikes at the heart of the institution of marriage, that her claim for ancillary relief derived from her crime, and that she should be prevented from proceeding further.[76] The Court of Appeal commented *obiter* that an innocent party to a bigamous marriage would be afforded relief and that a person entering a bigamous marriage in the genuine and reasonable belief that he was free to do so might also have an entitlement to ancillary relief. The narrow scope of the decision in *Whiston*—which has the drastic effect of barring the claim *in limine*—has been confirmed by subsequent case-law. The Court of Appeal has confirmed that the principle is confined to cases of bigamy involving conscious deception and does not apply in other cases of criminal conduct involving deception.[77] Furthermore,

---

[68] The fact that there is a contested issue of conduct is relevant in determining whether the complexity, difficulty or gravity of the case is such that it should be transferred to the High Court under the provisions of the President's Direction (Distribution and Transfer between the High Court and County Courts of Family Business and Family Proceedings) of April 6, 1988 [1988] 1 F.L.R. 540; but it is only if the issue (rather than the effect of admitted conduct) is contested that the matter arises: *Suter v. Suter* [1987] 2 F.L.R. 232 at 239, CA.

[69] [1976] Fam. 335 at 342.

[70] [1995] 2 F.L.R. 160.

[71] *per* Thorpe J. at 169.

[72] [2001] 2 F.L.R. 970, FD.

[73] *G v. G (Financial Provision: Separation Agreement)* [2000] 2 F.L.R. 18, FD.

[74] *M v. M (Pre-Nuptial Agreement)* [2002] 1 F.L.R. 654, FD.

[75] [1995] 2 F.L.R. 268.

[76] See the comments by J. Dewar in [1995] *Fam. Law* 549 and S. Cretney in (1996) 112 *L.Q.R.* 33.

[77] *J v. S-T (formerly J) (Transsexual: Ancillary Relief)* [1997] 1 F.L.R. 402 (CA *per* Sir Brian Neill and Potter L.J; Ward L.J. dissenting).

Whiston does not bar a claim by every culpable bigamist whatever the circumstances. It is legitimate for the court to have regard to the nature of the crime in its factual context of the case. Thus in *Rampal v. Rampal (No. 2)*[78] the husband's ancillary relief claim was not barred even though he knew the wife was married at the time he went through a ceremony with her; her culpability was greater than his, and the gravity of his offence was not such as to deny him his statutory rights on public policy grounds. Thus the *Whiston* principle will bar the claim of only the most culpable intentional bigamist.

The weight to be given to conduct under section 25(2)(g) is a matter for the court's discretion, of which the reported case-law merely provides illustrations. At one extreme, in rare cases conduct may be regarded as so extreme as to result in a nil entitlement—for practical purposes, the same outcome as if the claim had been held to be barred *in limine*. Thus is *J v. S-T (formerly J) (Transsexual: Ancillary Relief)*[79] the defendant a female-to-male transsexual, went through a ceremony of marriage with the plaintiff, a wealthy woman; their relationship lasted more than 12 years and with AID treatment produced two children. At no stage during courtship nor after marriage did the defendant reveal his true sexual identity. The Court of Appeal held that the defendant had been guilty of perjury and had deceived the plaintiff. She was granted a nullity decree, and the Court of Appeal dismissed the defendant's claim for ancillary relief.[80] In *Evans v. Evans*[81] a wife obtained a divorce from her husband, after a short marriage, in 1951. Over the next 35 years the husband meticulously complied with court orders for maintenance. However, in 1985 the wife was convicted of inciting others to murder the husband under a contract killing arrangement. She was sentenced to four years' imprisonment; and the husband then ceased to make the payments. In this case—so the Court of Appeal held—it had been right to discharge the order since otherwise the public "might think we had taken leave of our senses."[82]

On facts which are less extreme, the court having regard to conduct under section 25(2)(g) may reduce the *quantum* of an award to which an applicant would otherwise have been entitled by virtue of other considerations under that subsection. In *K v. K (Financial Provision: Conduct)*[83] the husband suffered from a depressive illness, which made his behaviour unpredictable and suicidal. The wife assisted the husband with suicide attempts not (so the judge found) from humanitarian principles but in order that she could set up home with her lover and get as much from the husband's estate as possible. In those circumstances (and also taking into account the wife's wholly deceitful conduct in relation to her association with her lover) it was held that it would be inequitable to disregard the wife's conduct, as one of the relevant circumstances. In the

---

78 [2001] EWCA Civ. 989; [2001] 3 W.L.R. 795; [2001] 2 F.L.R. 1179, CA.
79 [1997] 1 F.L.R. 402.
80 The majority (Sir Brian Neill and Potter L.J.) in the exercise of discretion having regard to s. 25(2)(g); Ward L.J. regared the claim as barred in limine in the application of *Whiston v. Whiston* [1995] 2 F.L.R. 268.
81 [1989] 1 F.L.R. 351, CA.
82 *per* Balcombe L.J. at 355.
83 [1988] 1 F.L.R. 469.

result, the lump sum awarded to the wife was reduced from £14,000 to £5,000.[84] In *Clark v. Clark*[85] a woman in straitened financial circumstances married a rich man some 36 years her senior. The marriage of five years duration was never consummated. Despite the husband's generosity in purchasing assets for the wife, she reduced him to the status of a virtual prisoner in the luxurious matrimonial home from which he was eventually rescued by relatives. The judge condemned the wife for matrimonial misconduct but nevertheless awarded her a lump sum of £552,500. The Court of Appeal reduced this to £125,000 taking account of her retention of other assets worth £50,000. One party's conduct may be a consideration leading to a more substantial award in favour of the other than might otherwise have been the case. In *B v. B (Financial Provision Welfare of Child and Conduct)*[86] the wife received the entire modest equity from the former matrimonial home; amongst several relevant considerations, it would have been inequitable to disregard the husband's conduct in respect of child abduction, non-disclosure and removal of assets, and failure to support the child. At the other end of the resource scale, in *Al-Khatib v. Masry*[87] Munby J. in awarding the wife £26.3 million took account *inter alia* of the husband's abduction of the children and the emotional effect on the wife and children. These examples graphically illustrate the breath of discretion conferred on the courts by the statutory provision.[88]

Litigation misconduct is now[89] normally[90] reflected by a penalty in costs rather than in the *quantum* of the substantive award in ancillary relief.[91]

Finally, in an appropriate case conduct will be regarded as a circumstance which should be taken into account as a positive factor influencing the provision. For example, in *Kokosinski v. Kokosinski*[92] the wife had (said the judge) "given the best years of her life to the husband. She had been faithful, loving and hard-working. She had helped the husband to build what was in every sense a family business. She had managed the husband's home and been a mother to and helped bring up a son of whom they were both justly proud." However, all this had occurred before the parties were able to marry; so that it could not be taken into account under a literal interpretation of section 25(2)(f) of the Act (which refers to contributions during the marriage). However, it would be inequitable not to take those matters into account as "conduct." The wife was held to have earned for herself some part of the value of the family business.[93]

---

[84] It should be noted that this was only a part of the provision ordered for the wife.

[85] [1999] 2 F.L.R. 498, CA.

[86] [2002] 1 F.L.R. 555, FD.

[87] [2002] EWHC Fam. 108; [2002] 1 F.L.R. 1053.

[88] See also, for a case near the line, *K v. K (Conduct)* [1990] 2 F.L.R. 225.

[89] For the earlier approach, see *B v. B (Real Property: Assessment of Interests)* [1988] 2 F.L.R. 490; *A v. A (Financial Provision)* [1998] 2 F.L.R. 393; *Tavoulareas v. Tavoulareas* [1998] 2 F.L.R. 418.

[90] But the principle is not absolute and litigation misconduct may be occasionally be reflected in: see *Clark v. Clark* [1999] 2 F.L.R. 498 and *B v. B (Financial Provision: Welfare of Child and Conduct)* [2002] 1 F.L.R. 555.

[91] *P v. P (Financial Relief: Non-Disclosure)* [1994] 2 F.L.R. 381, FD.

[92] [1980] Fam. 72.

[93] This case may be difficult to reconcile with the decision of the Court of Appeal in *Hewitson v. Hewitson* [1995] 1 F.L.R. 241, in which (on unusual facts) the court was unimpressed by matters which had occurred during extra-marital cohabitation.

(viii) "the value to each of the parties to the marriage of any benefit which by reason of the dissolution or annulment of the marriage of that party will lose the chance of acquiring" (M.C.A. 1973, s.25(2)(h))

14–064 This provision directs the court, in the exercise of its discretion, to consider the loss of benefits which will result from divorce. Marriage creates a status, which automatically confers certain legal rights and privileges For example, a surviving spouse has rights to succeed on the other's intestacy, and under a pension scheme connected with the deceased's employment. The court's extensive powers in relation to pension entitlements are discussed later in this Chapter.

The yardstick of equal division

14–065 In *White v. White,*[94] the House of Lords adopted the device of the yardstick of equal division of available assets against which the judge should check a provisional award in ancillary relief arrived at through consideration of the section 25 factors; the relevant passage from the speech of Lord Nicholls has been set out earlier in this Chapter.[95] Equal division as a staring point[96]—let alone a presumption[97] or principle[98]—was rejected by their Lordships as going "beyond the permissible bounds of interpretation of s 25"[99] and as an "impermissible judicial gloss on the statutory provision".[1] The distinction between a starting point or presumption and a yardstick is that the former operates *a priori* and the latter *a posteriore*. Lord Nicholls made it clear that the yardstick is to be applied as a check at the final stage of the section 25 exercise, and subsequent case law has confirmed this approach. It will be immediately apparent that the "equality" invoked by their Lordships is that of formal equality of division, and not that of substantive equality of outcome.[2] A major issue is the extent to which reasons for departure from equal division are accepted by the courts. Lord Nicholls himself indicated that unequal division would be common. As has been explained above, equal division is very unlikely to be outcome in cases where resources are limited, where the housing needs of the parent with care of the children will continue to dominate.[3] Hence most of the finer arguments about the operation of the yardstick and departure therefrom are likely to be confined

---

[94] [2000] 2 F.L.R. 981.

[95] At p. 406.

[96] See earlier *Burgess v. Burgess* [1996] 2 F.L.R. 34.

[97] In a context of child-parent contact "assumption" is now the preferred terminology: *Re L; Re V; Re M; Re H (Contact: Domestic Violence)* [2000] 2 F.L.R. 334.

[98] Though Lord Cooke doubted whether the attribution of these different "labels" would produce different results: [2000] 2 F.L.R. 981 at 999.

[99] For a recent exposition of the limitations of that role, see *Fitzpatrick v. Sterling Housing Association* [1999] 3 W.L.R. 1113.

[1] [2000] 2 F.L.R. 981 at 990.

[2] An important distinction well recognised in the literature: see for instance A. Diduck and H. Orton "Equality and Support for Spouses" (1994) 57 *M.L.R.* 681. But see the terminology used by Thorpe L.J. in *Cordle v. Cordle* [2001] EWCA Civ. 1791; [2002] 1 F.L.R. 207 at para. [33].

[3] *B v. B (Financial Provision: Welfare of Child and Conduct)* [2002] 1 F.L.R. 555, FD; *Cordle v. Cordle* [2001] EWCA Civ. 1971; [2002] 2 F.L.R 207, CA.

to "big money" cases. In that context there is also the question of the assets to which the yardstick applies: is it confined to assets built up by joint efforts?

Although at the time of writing the case-law is limited, it illustrates a number of factual situations in which departure from equal division has been held to be justified. One relevant consideration is the source of wealth: does it derive in part from a third party? In *White v. White*[4] itself, despite the finding of equality of contribution of which the reality of the business partnership between the spouses was a "notable aspect", equality of division was departed from, in that the order of the Court of Appeal with which the House of Lords declined to interfere gave Mrs White £1.5million out of £4.6million. The principal justification appeared to be the financial help provided by the husband's father, highlighted by Lord Nicholls as a "feature" of the case, albeit a less important "feature" than the equality of the spouses' own contributions. Lord Cooke expressed some unease with the outcome, given the length of the marriage which would tend to diminish the significance of the father's contribution.[5] In *Dharamshi v. Dharamshi*[6] where the assets totalled £4.7 million before tax and £2.9 million after tax, the wife who had contributed far less to the business than Mrs White received 35.2 per cent of the untaxed and 41.41 per cent of the taxed assets. One reasons for departure from equal division was the financial contribution of the husband's family to the business.

Another circumstance which has been held to justifying departure from equal division is that of inequality of contribution, *i.e.* where one spouse has made a contribution with special quality, discussed earlier in this Chapter.[7] Most commonly this will be entrepreneurial flair generating business success and the accumulation of substantial wealth. Thus in *Cowan v. Cowan*[8] and in *L v. L (Financial Provision: Contributions)*[9] the husbands received 62 per cent. However in *W H-J v. H H-J*[10] Coleridge J. warned against too ready a finding of unequal contribution in the "ordinary case"; that would be "the thin end of the wedge being driven right into the heart of the principles underlying White".[11] That case, in which the assets were valued at £2.7 million, appears to be the first reported example post-*White* of equal division in a case involving substantial assets. In his judgment, Coleridge J. expressed the view that equal division "goes to the core of the parties' understanding of fairness" and that (in a big money cases at least) any departure from equality however small leaves one party with a sense of grievance[12] from the undervaluing of efforts. In *B v. B (Financial Provision: Welfare of Child and Conduct)*[13]—a limited means case—the wife's responsibility past, present and future in caring for the child was regarded as one of the reasons plainly justifying departure from equal division.

[4] [2000] 2 F.L.R. 981.
[5] See *Haldane v. Haldane* [1977] A.C. 673 at 697.
[6] [2001] 2 F.L.R. 736.
[7] See p. 370.
[8] [2001] 2 F.L.R. 192.
[9] [2002] 1 F.L.R. 642.
[10] [2002] 1 F.L.R. 415.
[11] *ibid.* at 428.
[12] *ibid.* at 430.
[13] [2002] 1 F.L.R. 555, FD.

The limited case-law to date is divided[14] on whether new family obligations assumed post-marriage should in principle justify departure from equality of division in cases where there is a surplus of assets once needs have been satisfied.

Illiquidity of assets has for practical reasons been argued as a consideration justifying departure from equal division. In an appropriate case, a lump sum may be ordered to be paid in instalments in order to give the payor time to raise assets. In *N v. N (Financial Provision: Sale of Company)*[15] Coleridge J. observed that:

> " . . . the actual practicalities involved in valuing, dividing up and/or realising certain species of assets make the attaining of the White objective sometimes either impossible or only achievable at a cost which may not overall be in the family's best interests. . . . I am sure the House of Lords did not intend courts to exercise their far-reaching powers to achieve equality on paper if in so doing they, Samson-like, brought down or crippled the whole family's financial edifice to the ultimate detriment of the children (whose interests . . . remain the top priority) . . . the court must . . . be creative and sensitive to achieve an orderly redistribution of wealth . . . "[16]

In that case the main issue was liquidity: only £200,000 was immediately available. Coleridge J. awarded the wife £1 million (39 per cent of the assets), to be effected by the transfer of the home and three lump sums payable over two and a half years. It was accepted that "the goose may now have to go to market for sale . . . but it is essential that her condition be such that her egg-laying abilities are damages as little as possible".[17]

The very short duration of a marriage would seem to make equal division inappropriate.[18] However, the minimum duration of a marriage necessary to attract the operation of the *White v. White* yardstick is a matter for debate.

As we have discussed earlier,[19] equal division is unlikely to be the outcome in cases where resources are scarce. In that context, the accommodation needs of the parent with care continue to dominate the section 25 exercise.[20]

It has not yet been determined whether *White v. White*[21] has any implications for the division of income. The high income of one spouse could arguably be viewed as an asset built up by joint efforts, but the argument would be novel. In any event there would be serious practical problems of disincentive for the

---

14 *S v. S (Financial Provision: Departing from Equality)* [2001] 2 F.L.R. 246, FD (new family responsibility a reason for departure); *cf. W H-J v H H-J* [2002] 1 F.L.R. 415 (new family responsibility should be met from the husband's own share after division in the light of other considerations).

15 [2001] 2 F.L.R. 69; *P. v. P.* [2002] EWHC Fam. 887; [2002] *Fam. Law* 656.

16 *ibid.* at 71.

17 *ibid.* at 80.

18 See the concession made on behalf of the wife in *M v. M (Prenuptial Agreement)* [2002] 1 F.L.R. 654, FD.

19 At p. 351.

20 *B v. B (Financial Provision: Welfare of Child and Conduct)* [2002] 1 F.L.R. 555, FD; *Cordle v. Cordle* [2001] EWCA Civ. 1791; [2002] 2 F.L.R. 207, CA.

21 [2000] 2 F.L.R. 982.

payor to continue generating such income. A more likely eventuality is that the income of the high earner will be regarded as his or her resource under section 25(2)(a) in the broad judicial consideration of the section 25 factors. In *N v. N (Financial Provision: Sale of Company)*[22] Coleridge J. distinguished the husband's personal earning capacity from that generated by the partnerships in which he had an interest, and was prepared merely to "bear the latter in mind" as an asset in the overall consideration of section 25 factors.

(c) The court's duty to consider terminating financial obligations: the "clean break"[23]

14–066 Divorce severs the legal relationship of husband and wife and the common law duty on a husband to maintain his wife is terminated. But this does not mean that divorce ends the financial obligations imposed on them by court order. In particular, the court has wide powers to vary orders for periodical payments. Unfortunately, the right to apply to court for a variation gave further opportunity to reopen the wounds suffered in the breakdown of the marriage.[24] In 1984, the legislative guidelines contained in the Matrimonial Causes Act 1973 were amended on the recommendation of the Law Commission.[25] If the court decides to exercise its financial powers in favour of a party to the marriage, section 25A obliges it to consider "whether it would be appropriate so to exercise those powers that the financial obligations of each party towards the other will be terminated as soon after" the divorce as the court "considers just and reasonable". The policy of the law thus encourages parties to go their separate ways wherever fairness and practicalities allow.[26]

Nevertheless, the objective articulated in section 25A should not be elevated to the status of a principle,[27] nor is there a presumption in favour of a clean break.[28] The statute does not require courts to strive for a "clean break" regardless of all other considerations. The legislative structure is complex and requires careful analysis,[29] but ultimately the form of award remains a matter for the

---

[22] [2001] 2 F.L.R. 69.

[23] The term "clean break" originally referred to an arrangement whereby the wife abandoned her right to claim maintenance in return for a transfer by the husband of a capital asset, usually though not always, the matrimonial home: see *Clutton v. Clutton* [1991] 1 F.L.R. 242 at 245, *per* Lloyd L.J.

[24] For an illustration in the "big money" context, see *S v. S* [1986] Fam. 189; and in that of limited means, see *Ashley v. Blackman* [1988] 2 F.L.R. 278.

[25] Law Com. No. 112, para. 27. For the history of and background to the legislation, see *Whiting v. Whiting* [1988] 2 F.L.R. 189 at 194–197, *per* Balcombe L.J. The section was formally amended by the W.R.P.A. 1999, s.19, Sched. 3, paras 1 and 6.

[26] For judicial comments in the policy, see *e.g. per* Waite J., *Tandy v. Tandy*, October 24, 1986 as cited in *Whiting v. Whiting* [1988] 2 F.L.R. 189 at 199, *per* Balcombe L.J.; *S v. S* [1986] Fam. 189 at 193, *per* Waite J, (referring to *Minton v. Minton* [1979] A.C. 593, HL) *Morris v. Morris* [1985] F.L.R. 1176 at 1179; *C. v. C. (Financial Provision)* [1989] 1 F.L.R. 11 at 19, *per* Ewbank J.; *Mawson v. Mawson* [1994] 2 F.L.R. 985 at 990–991, *per* Thorpe J; *N v. N (Consent Order: Variation)* [1993] 2 F.L.R. 868 at 875, *per* Butler-Sloss L.J.

[27] *Clutton v. Clutton* [1991] 1 F.L.R. 242 at 245, *per* Lloyd L.J.

[28] *SRJ v. DWJ (Financial Provision)* [1999] 2 F.L.R. 176 at 181 *per* Hale J. *Phippen v. Palmers (A Firm)* [2002] 2 F.L.R. 408.

[29] For a dramatic illustration of the need to follow strictly the technical requirements laid down by statute, see *Richardson v. Richardson* [1994] 1 F.L.R. 286 (where all were agreed that the inten-

exercise of the court's discretion, which is very wide.[30] Opinion may reasonably differ,[31] from time to time and from judge to judge, over how that discretion should be exercised.[32] Provided that there has been a real and substantial consideration of the matters relevant to the exercise of the discretion, the appropriate statutory provisions have been referred to, and there has been no failure to take relevant facts into account or other misdirection, the Court of Appeal will not interfere with the exercise of the judge's discretion unless it is satisfied that the decision was "plainly wrong."[33] The same approach now applies to an appeal from a district judge to a circuit judge.[34] *Whiting v. Whiting*[35] illustrates the difficulty in the way of a successful appeal:—

> The wife had retrained as a teacher; and was in full-time employment earning in excess of £10,000 per annum, with pension entitlements. The husband had been made redundant, and earned some £4,000 per annum as a freelance management consultant. The husband asked the court to discharge the nominal order which had been made against him; but the judge refused on the ground that the wife should have the "last backstop" of a nominal order. The Court of Appeal, by a majority, held that the decision was not "plainly wrong." It is, however, perhaps significant that all three Lords Justice indicated that they would, if trying the case at first instance, have reached a different conclusion from that which they upheld. Against this background, decided cases can do little more than provide illustrations of how the statutory provisions have been applied.

Some recent developments may appear further to blunt the force of the clean break objective. One is a growing recognition that a spouse who has prejudiced her earning capacity through the domestic and parenting role may be entitled to compensation from the other spouse on divorce, effectively to equalise the economic effects of marriage; where capital is unavailable, this may have to take the form of maintenance payments.[36] Another is the increased emphasis on-

---

tion was to produce a "clean break" and that the wife would have no right to apply to extend the three-year term for which periodical payments had been ordered; but Thorpe J. held that, because the court had not made a direction under the provisions of M.C.A. 1973, s.28(1A) (the wife could make such an application and subsequently the prescribed term was extended: see *Richardson v. Richardson (No. 2)* [1994] 2 F.L.R. 1051).

[30] *per* Slade L.J., *Whiting v. Whiting* [1988] 2 F.L.R. 189 at 202.

[31] See for striking examples (involving the use of nominal maintenance orders) see *Whiting v. Whiting* [1988] 2 F.L.R. 189 and *SRJ v. DWJ (Financial Provisions)* [1999] 2 F.L.R. 176

[32] The fact that the court is exercising a discretion gives great weight to the decision of the trial judge since the Court of Appeal will not interfere with the properly directed exercise of a discretion unless the decision is "clearly wrong": see *G. v. G. (Minors: Custody Appeal)* [1985] F.L.R. 894, HL.

[33] *Whiting v. Whiting* [1988] 2 F.L.R. 189, CA; applying *G. v. G. (Minors: Custody Appeal)* [1985] F.L.R. 894, HL.

[34] *Cordle v. Cordle* [2001] EWCA Civ. 1791; [2002] 1 F.L.R. 207 *sed quaere*, given F.P.R., r.8.

[35] [1988] 2 F.L.R. 189 (again, a case on the slightly different variation provisions—see below—but it would appear that nothing turned on those differences).

[36] A. Didduck and H. Orton, "Equality and Support for Spouses" 57 *M.L.R.* 681; R Bailey-Harris, "The Role of Maintenance and Property Orders in Redressing Inequality" [1998] 12 *Australian Journal of Family Law* 3; *SRJ v. DWJ (Financial Provision)* [1999] 2 F.L.R. 176 *per* Hale L.J.

entitlement (built up by contribution) rather than need as the basis for the division of substantial assets on divorce, derived from the decision of the House of Lords in *White v. White*[37] and discussed earlier in this Chapter.

It is also important to bear in mind that the so-called clean break philosophy applies exclusively to the financial obligations of the spouses to support one another; and the courts have consistently emphasised that neither the court nor the parties can bring about a "clean break" between parent and child[38]: the ongoing responsibility of the parents is, and always has been, a basic factor. Effect will now usually be given to this ongoing responsibility primarily through the child support system; but it remains a fundamental principle of the law which continues to be applied in the divorce court, for example, in respect of a step-parent's obligations to a child of the family.

The text first considers the relevant statutory provisions. It then seeks to illustrate how they have been applied to different situations.

The relevant statutory provisions are:—

The general duty: the court's duty to consider the termination of financial obligations: s.25A(1)

14–067 The duty under section 25A(1) arises when the court decides to exercise its property adjustment or financial provision powers in favour of a party to the marriage on or after the grant of a decree of divorce or nullity of marriage. The duty imposed by this provision is entirely general, and there are other provisions of the Act which are relevant to its discharge.

(i) Court to consider potential increase in earning capacity: s.25(2)(a)

14–068 Self-sufficiency will often be based on an ability to earn a living. The matters to which the court's attention is particularly directed include a reference to any increase in earning capacity which it would in the opinion of the court be reasonable to expect a party to the marriage to take steps to acquire.[39] This will be particularly relevant to the duty imposed on the court to consider making a periodical payments order for a specified term, but it may also be relevant in a case where limited-term maintenance is capitalised.[40]

(ii) The duty to consider making a periodical payments order for a specified term: s.25A(2)

14–069 Where available funds permit, the court can discharge its duty to consider a termination of financial obligations by ordering a capital settlement, part of

---

[37] [2000] 2 F.L.R. 982.

[38] *Hulley v. Thompson* [1981] 1 W.L.R. 159; *Preston v. Preston* [1982] Fam. 17; *Crozier v. Crozier* [1994] 1 F.L.R. 126.

[39] Discussed earlier at 360.

[40] As in *M v. M (Prenuptial Agreement)* [2002] 1 F.L.R. 654, FD (wife able to earn a limited income after two years and an increased amount after five years).

which represents commutation of the right to be maintained on a periodic basis.[41] But there will be many cases in which such a once-for-all settlement is not possible; and the court will feel it appropriate to make an order for periodical payments. If it does decide to make such an order in favour of a party to the marriage, section 25A(2) of the Act then imposes on it a mandatory duty[42] "in particular" to:—

> " . . . consider whether it would be appropriate to require those payments to be made or secured only for such term as would in the opinion of the court be sufficient to enable the party in whose favour the order is made to adjust without undue hardship to the termination of his or her financial dependence on the other party."

It follows that in each case, the court must consider whether the order should be for a specified term (such as six months or five years)[43] and in making that decision the court must specifically ask[44] whether such a period would be sufficient for the applicant to adjust[45] without undue hardship[46] to the changed circumstances. There is no presumption that periodical payments are to cease as soon as possible unless the applicant can make out a case for continued support.[47]

The issue of whether to fix a term is one for the exercise of discretion, and the reported cases are no more than illustrative.

Where a parent has care of young children, a term order may be inappropriate on the particular facts.[48] In *C v. C (Financial Relief: Short Marriage)*[49] the short marriage had adversely affected the wife's health and she had care of the child who also had health problems; no term was fixed to the order for substantial periodic maintenance in favour of the wife. The Court of Appeal observed that it was not appropriate simply to presume the imposition of a term whenever there was a short marriage; it all depended on the particular circumstances, and

---

[41] Calculated according to the *Duxbury* formula, discussed earlier at p. 364.

[42] *Suter v. Suter* [1987] 2 F.L.R. 232 at 236, CA.

[43] Five years has been said to be "probably the longest term likely to be made": *N. v. N (Consent Order: Variation)* [1993] 2 F.L.R. 868 at 874, *per* Butler-Sloss L.J. For illustrations of five year terms, see *Waterman v. Waterman* [1989] 1 F.L.R. 380; *M v. M (Prenuptial Agreement)* [2002] 1 F.L.R. 654 (Connell J.).

[44] *Boylan v. Boylan* [1988] 1 F.L.R. 282, 290, *per* Booth J.

[45] *Suter v. Suter* [1987] 2 F.L.R. 232 at 236, CA.

[46] The words "undue hardship" are not to be regarded as referring solely to the needs of the spouse concerned: *Boylan v. Boylan* [1988] 1 F.L.R. 282 at 289, *per* Booth J.

[47] *Barrett v. Barrett* [1988] 2 F.L.R. 516, CA, *per* Butler-Sloss L.J; *Morris v Morris* [1985] F.L.R. 1176 (a case on variation governed by slightly different statutory provisions); *Flavell v. Flavell* [1997] 1 F.L.R. 353.

[48] *N v. N. (Consent Order: Variation)* [1993] 2 F.L.R. 868, *per* Butler-Sloss L.J. at 875 ("it is impossible to predict what may happen after five years where a child is concerned"); but contrast *Richardson v. Richardson (No. 2)* [1994] 2 F.L.R. 1051 where the wife's periodical payment order was extended to the time when her youngest child would have finished tertiary education, and it could confidently be predicted that the wife would by then be free of the responsibility for upbringing which had restricted her ability to earn; and see *Mawson v. Mawson* [1994] 2 F.L.R. 985, where the child's own maintenance was provided by a substantial child support assessment, and the wife's periodical payments were extended for a short period

[49] [1997] 2 F.L.R. 26.

here there was so much uncertainty in the wife's position that a term would have been inappropriate. In *Suter v. Suter*[50] the court held that, although it was likely that as the children grew up it would become progressively easier for the wife to organise and increase her earning capacity, and that she might expect to derive some financial support from her lover, yet there were too many uncertainties to predict the development of events over the next 10 years. The appropriate compromise was to make a nominal order, unrestricted as to time, which could be varied if the wife's financial position deteriorated. By contrast in *Waterman v. Waterman*[51] the 38-year-old wife had custody of the five-year-old child following breakdown of a short marriage. The judge made an order for periodical payments for the wife; and on the basis that she had an earning capacity, that it was in her interests "to get her life on its feet, to obtain an occupation and some source of income for herself," and that the difficulty of caring for a child would interfere less with her obtaining employment when he was 10 years old, directed that the periodical payments should terminate in five years time. The Court of Appeal held that he had not been wrong to do so.

It may be unrealistic to expect older women who have assumed a primarily domestic and parenting role during marriage to achieve economic self-sufficiency after divorce. Thus in *M v. M (Financial Provision)*[52] the court concluded that it would not be appropriate to terminate the wife's periodical payments order either in five years or at the end of any fixed period nor would it be just and reasonable so to do. Such a termination would cause undue hardship to a 47-year-old woman with only limited earning capacity whose marriage to a £60,000-a-year chartered accountant had broken down after 20 years, the more so since it would be unrealistic to suppose that the wife could become self-sufficient before or at the end of five years or any other period that the court might specify. In *Flavell v. Flavell*[53] the Court of Appeal observed *obiter* that it was not usually appropriate to provide for the termination of periodic payments in the case of a woman in her mid 50s; such orders would only be justified only where the wife had her own substantial capital or significant earning capacity. Moreover in *SRJ v. DWJ (Financial Provision)*[54] Hale J. suggested that in principle a wife who had made career sacrifices in order to care for the family over a long marriage should be entitled to be compensated by her husband on divorce for what she otherwise might have had in her own right.[55] On the particular facts of that case, a nominal maintenance order in the wife's favour (with no time limit) was considered appropriate, keeping alive the possibility of payments to her should the husband's financial situation improve in the future.

---

[50] [1987] 2 F.L.R. 232 at 236.
[51] [1989] 1 F.L.R. 380.
[52] [1987] 2 F.L.R. 1; and see *Boylan v. Boylan* [1988] 1 F.L.R. 282.
[53] [1997] 1 F.L.R. 353; for an example of no clean break for a woman of 60, see *Phippen v. Palmers (A Firm)* [2002] 2 F.L.R. 408.
[54] [1999] 2 F.L.R. 176.
[55] *ibid.* at 182.

(iii) Power to direct that no application be made to extend specified term: s.28(1A)[56]

14–070 It is important to bear in mind, first, that any periodical payments order may be varied at any time during the currency of the order[57] and, secondly, that the court also has power at any time before the end of a specified term to extend that term. The only way in which the parties can know that the order will under no circumstances be extended is to obtain a direction from the court that application for an extension of the term will not be entertained.[58] It has been said[59] that such a direction is "draconian", and is inappropriate in cases in which there is real uncertainty about the future, and particularly where young children are also involved.[60] The absence of a section 28(1A) direction was considered to be significant in itself in *Flavell v. Flavell*.[61] On the other hand, unless such a direction is made, the paying spouse is left at risk, with what appears to be no more than an indication from the trial judge that it would be appropriate to terminate the payments at the end of the specified term.

The power to dismiss a claim for periodical payments and to impose a clean break

14–071 The court has express power[62] to dismiss an application for periodical payments, and to make a direction that the applicant be not entitled to make any further application for a periodical payments order.[63] The court also power to direct that no application be permitted by a spouse for provision out of the other's estate under the provisions of the Inheritance (Provision for Family and Dependants) Act 1975.

Exercise of the discretion to impose a clean break

(i) The options available

14–072 In order to understand how the court is likely to carry out these duties and exercise its flexible powers it may be helpful to summarise the types of orders which may be made:

---

[56] Harcus, "Periodic Payments—End of Term?" [1997] *Fam. Law* 340.

[57] *Sandford v. Sandford* [1986] 1 F.L.R. 412, CA; *Flavell v. Flavell* [1997] 1 F.L.R. 353, CA.

[58] *Richardson v. Richardson* [1994] 1 F.L.R. 286; *N v. N (Consent Order: Variation)* [1993] 2 F.L.R. 868, CA.

[59] *Waterman v. Waterman* [1989] 1 F.L.R. 380, CA.

[60] "only in the most exceptional and unusual case" will such an order be made where a child under 18 remains in the care of the applicant: *N v. N (Consent Order: Variation)* [1993] 2 F.L.R. 868 at 883 *per* Roch J.

[61] [1997] 1 F.L.R. 353.

[62] M.C.A. 1973, s.25A(3) reversing the effect of *Dipper v. Dipper* [1981] Fam. 31, CA

[63] This power could be exercised to dismiss the claims of one party for periodical payments notwithstanding the fact that the claim of the other was left alive: *Thompson v. Thompson* [1988] 2 F.L.R. 170, Ewbank J.

(a) *Immediate clean break.* If the court considers that it would be appropriate to terminate the parties' financial obligations immediately, it may make a property adjustment order and it will dismiss any claim for periodical payments with a direction that neither party be entitled to make any further application for such an order.[64] It will also order that neither party be entitled to apply for provision under the Inheritance (Provision for Family and Dependants) Act 1975. This would be an example of the "clean break" in its purest form. Any omission (for example, a refusal to debar a spouse from the right to apply under the 1975 Act) leaves the other at some (albeit in that example restricted) risk that further financial obligations will be imposed in the future.

(b) *Periodical payment order—nominal or specified term?* If the court considers that it would not be appropriate to terminate the financial obligations of the parties to one another it will wish to make a periodical payments order (although this may only be for a nominal amount, with the consequences mentioned below). The court must then consider whether it would be appropriate to order the periodical payments for only a specified term.

(c) *Deferred clean break.* If the court decides that it would be appropriate to make a specified term order it must decide whether to direct that the applicant be debarred from applying for any extension of the term. Such an order may be called a "deferred clean break." In the absence of such a direction the applicant will be entitled at any time during the specified term to apply to have the term extended.[65]

(ii) The exercise of the discretion

14–073 Notwithstanding the width of discretion, the following patterns emerge.

(i) Wealthy parties

If there is substantial capital available it will often be possible to secure a "just and reasonable" settlement on a clean break basis. A lump sum order will reflect the parties' housing and income needs[66] and pension expectations, and (where there is a surplus) their entitlements built up by virtue of contributions to the marriage. Illustrations are provided by *White v. White*[67], *Cowan v. Cowan*[68] and *L v. L (Financial Provision: Contributions)*[69], all of which have been discussed above.

However, even in cases where the parties have ample means, there may be

---

[64] Under the M.C.A. 1973, s.25A(3).

[65] *Flavell v. Flavell* [1997] 2 F.L.R. 353.

[66] Using *Duxbury* calculation, which allows a large number of variables to be taken into account: see above.

[67] [2000] 2 F.L.R. 981.

[68] [2001] 2 F.L.R. 192.

[69] [2002] 1 F.L.R. 642.

factors which make it "inappropriate" to terminate the financial obligations between them. Thus in *M v. M (Property Adjustment: Impaired Life Expectancy)*[70] the district judge (whose decision was upheld on appeal) said that the fact that the wife had cancer and a life expectancy of only five to ten years meant that it was not, and never could be a clean-break case. The wife had only a limited earning capacity which would get less over the years, and substantial periodical payments would be needed from the husband.

Substantial periodic payments were held to be justified in *C v. C (Financial Provision: Short Marriage)*[71] where both the wife and child had health problems and there were uncertainties as to their future. Moreover, as we have seen, a lump sum order may be ordered to be paid in instalments in order to meet the practicalities of realising assets.[72]

(ii) Middle and lower range cases

14–074 The clean break philosophy has traditionally been of particular influential in those cases in which the only asset is there is a family home and the husband's income is limited. In such cases, the court may decide simply to transfer the matrimonial home (or the proceeds of sale[73]) to the wife and dismiss any claim for periodical payments for her.[74] In some cases of relatively modest means, fairness requires that a clean break order leaves one party with the majority of the assets but the other with some percentage.[75] The court may consider that fairness in all the circumstances requires a spouse to be able to realise his entitlement to a share in the home at a future date, and so a charge-back—preventing an immediate clean break—may be considered appropriate.[76] However, this is by no means an entitlement in principle,[77] and on appropriate facts it may be fair for one party to receive the whole equity outright.

Where no capital resources are available, fairness may in some circumstances demands a severance of the maintenance tie. *Seaton v. Seaton*[78] provides a dramatic illustration. The 42-year-old husband had suffered a heart attack and a stroke, as a result of which he could barely speak, and had only limited powers of concentration. After the breakdown of his 14-year marriage to a 36-year-old teacher (who earned some £8,000 per annum) he was cared for by his elderly parents, and they also contributed to his upkeep. He had no income apart from a state disability pension, and the prognosis was that he would in due course have to go into a state-provided home, where his needs would be provided for.

---

70 [1993] 2 F.L.R. 723, CA.

71 [1997] 2 F.L.R. 26.

72 *N v. N (Financial Provision: Sale of Company)* [2001] 2 F.L.R. 69.

73 *B v. B (Financial Provision: Welfare of Child and Conduct)* [2002] 1 F.L.R. 555 FD.

74 For illustrations, see *Liversey (formerly Jenkins) v. Jenkins* [1985] A.C. 424, HL and *Mawson v. Mawson* [1994] 2 F.L.R. 985.

75 For illustrations, see *Piglowska v. Piglowski* [1999] 2 F.L.R. 763, HL and *Cordle v. Cordle* [2001] EWCA Civ. 1791; [2002] 1 F.L.R. 207, CA.

76 *Elliott v. Elliott* [2001] 1 F.C.R. 477.

77 *B v. B (Financial Provision: Welfare of Child and Conduct)* [2002] 1 F.L.R. 555, FD; *Cordle v. Cordle* [2001] EWCA Civ. 1791; [2002] 1 F.L.R. 207, CA.

78 (1986) 16 *Fam. Law* 267, CA.

The Court of Appeal upheld a decision that there should be an immediate clean break, largely on the basis that he had no significant needs, and that no periodical payments by the wife could have any material effect in enhancing his life. However, everything turns on the court's assessment of what is a fair outcome in the particular circumstances. Thus in *SRJ v. DWJ*[79] the matrimonial home was repossessed by the mortgagees and the only significant asset was the husband's pension entitlement. The Court of Appeal held that a deferred lump sum order in respect of the pension would in the circumstances of indebtedness be incapable of benefiting the wife, but that a nominal periodical payments order was appropriate. Although there was no immediate alternative to the wife relying on state benefits, the nominal order (which was variable) would keep alive the possibility of the husband supporting the wife in future should his fortunes improve.

D. Changed circumstances: variation of orders, etc.

14–075 The court takes "all the circumstances" into account in deciding what orders to make in ancillary relief proceedings. But what is to happen if those circumstances change after the divorce? Such changes range from the mundane to the dramatic. An example of the latter is *Barder v. Barder (Caluori Intervening)*.[80]

The divorce court made a clean break order under which the husband was to transfer all his interest in the matrimonial home to the wife in full and final settlement of all claims made or capable of being made. Some five weeks later the wife killed the two children of the family and committed suicide. She left a will giving her property to her mother. Was the husband obliged to comply with the order and transfer the property (which had been intended to serve as a home for the wife and children) to the wife's executors?

In that case, it was not alleged that the wife had failed to disclose any material facts at the time of the making of the order; but in *Livesey (formerly Jenkins) v. Livesey*[81]:—

> The wife agreed with the husband that she would accept a transfer of the husband's interest in the matrimonial home in place of any periodical payments and in settlement of all financial claims against him. On the day before application was made for a consent order embodying those terms she became engaged to be married; and three weeks after the order was made she remarried. Had an order for periodical payments been made, it would have terminated; and the husband argued that he would not have agreed to the transfer of the family home to the wife had she disclosed her intentions.

The legal system provides three main procedures for dealing with such problems:

---

[79] [1999] 2 F.L.R. 176.
[80] [1988] A.C. 20, HL.
[81] [1985] A.C. 424, HL.

(i) The court has extensive powers to vary or discharge orders; or to suspend any provision of an order. However, in principle these variation powers do not extend to property adjustment or to lump sum orders,[82] save for lump sum attachment orders in respect of pensions.[83] A pension sharing order is variable if made before a decree is made absolute.[84]

(ii) There is a right to appeal against the terms of an order; and where the basis or fundamental assumption on which the order has been made has been invalidated by a change of circumstances the court has a discretion to give permission to appeal notwithstanding the fact that the prescribed period within which appeals can be brought as of right[85] has expired.

(iii) A party who alleges that an order has been obtained by fraud or non-disclosure may bring an action seeking to have the order set aside.

We consider these in turn.

1. Variation of orders

14–076 There is a difference in the policy towards maintenance orders on the one hand, and lump sum and property adjustment orders on the other (except lump sum attachment orders made in respect of pensions).

(a) Variation of maintenance orders

14–077 The Matrimonial Causes Act provides[86] that wherever a periodical payments order (or other order to which the section applies) has been made, the court has power to "vary or discharge the order or suspend any provision thereof temporarily and to revive the operation of any provision so suspended."

When the power to vary arises

14–078 The court's powers to vary arise whenever there is in force any order to which the legislation applies,[87] even if the order is for a nominal amount such as five pence yearly. For example, in *Jessel v. Jessel*[88] the wife had agreed to accept stipulated periodical payments "in settlement of all her claims to periodical payments," and had undertaken not to apply to increase the husband's liabilities.

---

[82] Except lump sum orders payable by instalments: *Tilley v. Tilley* (1980) *Fam. Law* 89; *Penrose v. Penrose* [1994] 2 F.L.R. 621; *Westbury v. Sampson* [2002] 2 F.L.R. 166.

[83] M.C.A. 1973, s. 31(2)(dd).

[84] M.C.A. 1973, s. 31(2)(g).

[85] For time limits, see F.P.R. 1991, r. 8.1; R.S.C. Ord. 58, r. 1; C.P.R. r. 52(4)(2).

[86] M.C.A. 1973, s.31(1).

[87] *i.e.* orders for maintenance pending suit, interim maintenance, periodical payments (secured or unsecured), any instalment provision of a lump sum order, and certain property adjustment orders made in judicial separation and orders relating to pensions: M.C.A. 1973 s.31(2).

[88] [1979] 1 W.L.R. 1148, CA.

Some six years later she applied to vary the payments, and the Court of Appeal held that the court had jurisdiction to entertain her application.

However, if a spouse's application has been dismissed there is no power to make a fresh order, and there is no existing order which could be varied. There is thus a crucial difference between the legal position of a spouse ordered to make nominal periodical payments and that of a spouse whose partner's claim for periodical payments has been dismissed, since in the former (but not in the latter) case the court may at any time vary the nominal order. The nominal order makes the husband the wife's insurer against a change of circumstances and preserves her entitlement should his fortunes improve[89]; to dismiss her claim achieves a clean break.

An application to vary an order for secured periodical payments may be made after the death of the person against whom it was made; in this case the court must consider the changed circumstances resulting from his death.[90]

Variation of specified term orders[91]

14–079 The court has jurisdiction to vary an order originally made for a specified term, so that it could (for example) extend an order made for three years for a further year, or for the joint lives of the parties, or without a termination date[92] Jurisdiction does not depend on an exceptional change in circumstances.[93] However, it will have no such power if the court, in making a periodical payments order (secured or unsecured), has directed that the party concerned shall not be entitled to apply for an extension of the order.[94] Moreover, once the term has expired, there is nothing to vary, but the court's jurisdiction is preserved provided the application for variation is issued during the life of the periodical payments order, even if the hearing does not occur till after its expiry.[95]

There is also power[96] to direct that a variation or discharge shall not take effect until the expiration of a specified period. This power could be exercised in effect to give the person entitled to the payments some time to adjust to the termination or reduction of the payment.

Exercise of the discretion to vary

14–080 In exercising the power to vary, the court is directed to have regard to all the circumstances of the case, first consideration being given to the welfare while a minor of any child of the family who has not attained the age of 18[97]; and it is

---

[89] *SRJ v. DWJ (Financial Provision)* [1999] 2 F.L.R. 176.

[90] M.C.A. 1973, s.31(7)(b).

[91] See Harcus, "Periodical Payments—End of Term" [1997] *Fam. Law* 340.

[92] *Flavell v. Flavell* [1997] 1 F.L.R. 353.

[93] *ibid.*

[94] *ibid.* s.28(1A); *Richardson v. Richardson* [1994] 1 F.L.R. 286.

[95] *Jones v. Jones* [2000] 2 F.L.R. 307, CA, disapproving *obiter* remarks of Ward L.J. in *G v. G (Periodical Payments: Jurisdiction)* [1997] 1 F.L.R. 368.

[96] *ibid.* s.31(10). The variation may be retrospective: *Macdonald v. Macdonald* [1964] P. 1; and as to the discretion to direct back-dating, see *S. v. S.* (Note) [1987] 1 W.L.R. 382, CA.

[97] *Flavell v. Flavell* [1997] 1 F.L.R. 353; *Jones v. Jones* [2000] 2 F.L.R. 307.

provided that the circumstances of the case shall include any change in any of the matters to which the court was required to have regard when making the order to which the application relates.[98] On hearing an application to vary, the court is not required to proceed from the starting point of the original order but considers the matter *de novo,* looking at all the relevant matters set out in section 25 of the Act afresh without being confined solely or essentially to matters of change.[99]

Imposing a clean break on a variation application

14–081 In furtherance of the policy of making a clean break in appropriate cases the court, in considering applications to vary periodical payment orders (secured or unsecured) made in divorce or nullity proceedings, is required[1] to:—

> "consider whether in all the circumstances and after having regard to any such change it would be appropriate to vary the order so that payments under the order are required to be made or secured only for such further period as will in the opinion of the court be sufficient . . . to enable the party in whose favour the order was made to adjust without undue hardship to the termination of those payments . . . "

The legislation therefore now applies to applications for variation and discharge principles similar to those which apply to original applications for financial relief: in particular, the variation legislation now picks out for mandatory consideration by the court not only the welfare of children but the possibility of terminating any periodical payments order.[2] There is no longer a sharp distinction between the factors relevant to the exercise of the discretion in making the original order and those relevant on variation.

Power to order capital provision on variation application

14–082 Originally, the court lacked power to require the making of a lump sum or property adjustment order in partial or total replacement for the periodical payments order which would be terminated by a clean break order. In some cases, the person liable to make payments would offer to make capital provision voluntarily in order to be rid of the burden of ongoing periodical payments, but the court would have to assess the adequacy of the offer, and there was no reported case in which an applicant's offer to commute the obligation to make continuing payments in this way had been accepted.[3] However, this was felt to be a gap in

---

[98] M.C.A. 1973, s.31(7).
[99] *Lewis v. Lewis* [1977] 1 W.L.R. 409, CA. *Garner v. Garner* [1992] 1 F.L.R. 573; *Flavell v. Flavell* [1997] 1 F.L.R. 353, CA.; *Cornick v. Cornick* (No. 3) [2001] 2 F.L.R. 1240, FD.
[1] M.C.A. 1973, s.31(7)(a).
[2] *S v. S* [1987] 1 F.L.R. 71 at 76, *per* Waite J.
[3] See *e.g. S v. S* [1987] 1 F.L.R. 71.

the legislation,[4] and the Family Law Act 1996[5] gave[6] the court power on discharging[7] a periodical payments order[8] to order the payment of a lump sum or to make a property adjustment order or one or more pension sharing orders.[9] The court may also debar the person entitled under the original order from making further applications for periodical payment orders or for extensions of the term.[10]

In *Harris v. Harris*[11] the Court of Appeal emphasised the width of discretion conferred by the new provisions. In many cases the appropriate approach will be a capitalisation of the wife's periodical payments on a joint life basis.[12] However, given the breadth of the discretion conferred, and the removal of the reasonable requirements ceiling by the decision of the House of Lords in *White v. White*,[13] there may be circumstances where the court is not bound by a capitalisation approach.[14]

(b) Variation of property adjustment and lump sum orders

General principle: no variation

14–083 Since one of the objects of property adjustment and lump sum orders is to achieve finality, the general principle embodied in the legislation is that no variation of such orders should subsequently be possible.[15] To this principle there are three exceptions:

(a) If orders for settlement of property or variation of an existing nuptial settlement[16] are made in respect of a separation, the court may vary them if the marriage is subsequently dissolved.[17]
(b) Where a lump sum is ordered to be paid in instalments, the court may vary the number and timing of the instalments or security for such an order[18]—*e.g.* if a husband is ordered to pay the wife £10,000 by 10

---

[4] *Harris v. Harris* [2001] 2 F.L.R. 955.
[5] Sched. 8, paras 16 (5)(a), (6)(b) and (7), inserting s.31(7A)–(7G) into M.C.A. 1973.
[6] The provision came into force on November 1, 1998.
[7] Or varying the order to provide for a fixed term: M.C.A. 1973, s.31(7A)(b).
[8] M.C.A. 1973, s.31(7B)(c), inserted by the F.L.A. 1996, Sched. 10, para. 6(2).
[9] M.C.A. 1973, s.31 (7B) (a)–(c). The power in respect of pension sharing was inserted by the W.R.P.A. 1999, s.19, Sched. 3, paras 1 and 7.
[10] M.C.A. 1973, s.31(7B)(c), as inserted by the F.L.A. 1996, Sched. 8, para. 16(7). On dismissal of an application, see Christy, "Dismissing the Right to Apply to Capitalise" [2001] *Fam. Law* 457 and R. Spon-Smith "The Other Side of the Argument" [2001] *Fam. Law* 693.
[11] [2001] 2 F.C.R. 68.
[12] *ibid.*
[13] [2000] 2 F.L.R. 981.
[14] *Cornick v. Cornick (No. 3)* [2001] 2 F.L.R. 1240, FD.
[15] Law Com. No. 25, paras 87–88.
[16] Lump sum orders and transfer of property orders are not included: s.31(2), M.C.A. 1973; *Omielan v. Omielan* [1996] 2 F.L.R. 306. If the separation is converted into a divorce, the court will be able to make further capital provision orders (under the general wording of ss.23 and 24 which s.31 does not cut down in this regard), and it was presumably thought undesirable that the court should be able to order repayment (although a new order could achieve this indirectly, *i.e.* by ordering payment of a compensating sum to the payer: Law Com. No. 25, para. 89).
[17] M.C.A. 1973, s.31(4).
[18] *ibid.* s.31(2)(d); see Law Com. No. 25, para. 89.

annual instalments of £1,000 secured on his shareholding in Abracadabra Ltd, the court could vary the order by providing that the money be paid in 15 instalments, and that the security be changed. Furthermore, it has been held that the court has power not only to discharge a particular instalment or even the whole outstanding balance,[19] but also to vary the *quantum* of the principal lump sum, although that power should be exercised sparingly in exceptional circumstances.[20]

(c) Where the court has made an order under the powers described later in this Chapter for a deferred lump sum to be paid by the trustees or managers of a pension arrangement.[21]

2. Appeals against orders: reopening clean break settlements

14–084 Although it is clear that the absence of a power to vary property adjustment and lump sum orders does have considerable potential for injustice, the principle of finality is nonetheless an important one, particularly in cases in which the order has been made as part of a clean break arrangement. The essence of a clean break settlement is that once the couple are divorced and their capital divided, they cannot normally expect to profit from (any more than they would expect to lose by) later changes in the other's fortune[22]; and each party (it has been said[23]) takes a clean break order for better or worse. Yet this principle must be made compatible with justice; so that the law "exceptionally, allows appeals out of time: so the law still more exceptionally, allows judgments to be attacked on the ground of fraud"; or in some other circumstances.[24] The text deals first with applications for leave to appeal founded on a change of circumstances. In such cases, the crucial question is whether the court in the exercise of its discretion will grant such leave.[25] If the court does grant leave, it will have to decide how to resolve matters. The text deals with these issues. It then discusses the circumstances in which an order will be set aside because of non-disclosure, or on any other ground.

(a) Appeals out of time: the grant of leave

14–085 The circumstances in which leave should be given to appeal out of time against a lump sum or property adjustment order in matrimonial proceedings

---

[19] *Penrose v. Penrose* [1994] 2 F.L.R. 621, CA; *Tilley v. Tilley* (1979) 10 *Fam. Law* 89 (where the wife could not meet an instalment without selling the family home and making herself and the children homeless).

[20] *Westbury v. Sampson* [2002] 1 F.L.R. 166.

[21] *i.e.* an order under M.C.A. 1973, s.25B(4), as inserted by the Pensions Act 1995, s.166(1). The power to vary extends to orders made in respect of deferred lump sums under s.25C (*i.e.* requiring the trustees or managers to pay to a specified beneficiary, or to the other spouse, or an order directing the pensioner to exercise a power of nomination: see M.C.A. 1973, s.31(dd) as inserted by the Pensions Act 1995, s.166(3)(a)).

[22] *Cornick v. Cornick* [1994] 2 F.L.R. 530 at 537, *per* Hale J.

[23] *Barder v. Barder* [1987] 1 F.L.R. 18 at 22, *per* Dillon L.J., CA.

[24] *per* Lord Wilberforce, *The Ampthill Peerage* [1977] A.C. 547 at 569, HL.

[25] *Greig Middleton & Co Ltd v. Denderowicz* [1998] 1 W.L.R. 1164.

were authoritatively stated by the House of Lords in the case of *Barder v. Barder (Caluori intervening)*,[26] the dramatic facts of which have been given above.[27]

The court may give such leave in cases in which there has been an unforeseen change of circumstances,[28] provided that four conditions are satisfied:

(a) the basis or fundamental assumption underlying the order had been falsified by a change of circumstances;
(b) such change had occurred within a relatively short time[29] of the making of the original order;
(c) the application for leave was made reasonably promptly[30]; and
(d) that the granting of leave would not prejudice unfairly third parties who had acquired interests for value in the property affected.

In *Barder* itself the court held that all these conditions had been satisfied; and that leave to appeal should be granted, and the appeal against the original order allowed.[31] There has been little conceptual analysis of what will suffice to falsify the basis or fundamental assumption underlying the order; but it has been suggested[32] that the test is essentially the same as applies in cases in which a court

---

26 [1988] A.C. 20, HL.

27 At p. 386.

28 There is no right to appeal against a decision granting leave to appeal out of time, but there is a right of appeal against a refusal of such leave: *Rickards v. Rickards* [1990] 1 F.L.R. 125, CA.

29 In *Barder v. Barder* [1988] A.C. 20, a maximum period of one year was suggested; and in *Cornick v. Cornick* [1994] 2 F.L.R. 530 at 538 the short-term share price movements—the price had doubled within five months and trebled within eight—would have satisfied this test. On the other hand, in *Worlock v. Worlock* [1994] 2 F.L.R. 689, CA, the relevant event—a transfer of shares to the husband, greatly increasing his wealth—had taken place two years after the original order (and four years before the hearing of the application for leave), and the Court of Appeal held that it was "far too late" for the *Barder* doctrine to apply: see *per* Stuart Smith L.J. at 696. See also *B v. B (Financial Provision: Leave to Appeal)* [1994] 1 F.L.R. 219 (husband lost job as pilot nearly two years after order—not sufficiently close to order to justify reopening). However, there is no inflexible rule imposing a time bar—the matter may perhaps be seen as an aspect of the public policy favouring finality in litigation: *Penrose v. Penrose* [1994] 2 F.L.R. 621 at 632, *per* Balcombe L.J.; and in *Hope-Smith v. Hope-Smith* [1989] 2 F.L.R. 56, CA, leave was granted two years after the making of the original order. In *Benson v. Benson* [1996] 1 F.L.R. 962 the wife died six months after the ancillary relief order; permission was refused.

30 See *Benson v. Benson (dec'd)* [1996] 1 F.L.R. 692 (application more than one year after event—dismissed). In *S v. S (Ancillary Relief: Consent Order)* [2002] EWHC 223; [2002] 1 F.L.R. 992, the wife's application more than eight months after the alleged supervening event was dismissed. The relevant date from which time begins to run is the date of the order (not the date when it had to be implemented): *B v. B (Financial Provision: Leave to Appeal)* [1994] 1 F.L.R. 219. In *S v. S (Financial Provision) (Post-Divorce Cohabitation)* [1994] 2 F.L.R. 228, leave was given to appeal 15 years after the order, but the facts of that case were (*per* Douglas Brown J.) unusual if not unique, in that the couple had resumed cohabitation after the decree; and note the critical comment of the Court of Appeal in *Hewitson v. Hewitson* [1995] 1 F.L.R. 241.

31 And note to the same effect *Smith v. Smith (Smith Intervening)* [1992] Fam. 69 (wife committed suicide six months after order—order based on her "needs" set aside). But the death of a party is not as such a sufficient change of circumstances to allow the matter to be re-opened: *Amey v. Amey* [1992] 2 F.L.R. 89; but compare *Benson v. Benson (dec'd)* [1996] 1 F.L.R. 692 (where a wife was thought to have a normal life expectancy, but was subsequently diagnosed as suffering from terminal cancer).

32 *Amey v. Amey* [1992] 2 F.L.R. 89 at 95, Scott Baker J.; and note *Benson v. Benson (dec'd)* [1996] 1 F.L.R. 692 (deterioration in business not sufficiently fundamental new event as husband had been aware of potential problem).

has to decide whether to intervene and set aside a contract for mutual mistake or frustration.

The case law gives some impression of the issues with which the courts have had to deal. For example, is the remarriage of one of the parties a sufficient change of circumstances in cases in which the family home has been transferred to that party? In such cases, the transferor—usually the husband—may have had a very bad bargain since any liability under a periodical payments order would have ceased on remarriage.[33] The answer is that it is a question of fact and degree as to whether the change of circumstances is sufficiently fundamental. Thus an appeal out of time was allowed in *Wells v. Wells*[34] where the wife remarried[35] and began living with her second husband in his house six months after the divorce court had ordered the husband to transfer his interest in the matrimonial home (the parties' sole asset) to the wife in order to provide a home for her and the children. The Court of Appeal accepted that this was a fundamental change of circumstances, and that the basis on which the order had been made[36] had been destroyed.[37] By contrast in *Hill v. Hill*[38] the wife's post-divorce cohabitation did not justify setting the order aside.

Many applications have been based on misvaluation of assets at the time of the order, or changes in the value of assets since the order was made. The essential question is always whether the fundamental assumption on which the order was made has been undermined. For example:

> In *Cornick v. Cornick*[39] an order was made giving the wife approximately half the couple's assets. The husband's investments subsequently rose dramatically in value—from £2.17 a share at the date of the hearing to a peak of £12.58 some 18 months later—and the wife's share of the assets was reduced to perhaps 20 per cent. But Hale J. pointed out that the shares had been correctly valued at the hearing[40] and that what had happened was a

---

[33] Compare *B v. B (Financial Provision: Leave to Appeal)* [1994] 1 F.L.R. 219 (wife's remarriage to Q.C. not basis for reopening property adjustment order founded on recompensing wife for her contributions during the marriage).

[34] [1992] 2 F.L.R. 66, CA.

[35] Note that this was not a case in which non-disclosure by the wife was alleged; *cf. Livesey (formerly Jenkins) v. Livesey*.

[36] Contrast *Chaudhuri v. Chaudhuri* [1992] 2 F.L.R. 73, CA, where the order against which it was sought to appeal expressly contemplated the wife's remarriage. Accordingly it could not be said that there had been a sufficient change of circumstances.

[37] Note also *S. v. S (Financial Provision) (Post-Divorce Cohabitation)* [1994] 2 F.L.R. 228 where the fact that the parties became reconciled and resumed cohabitation was held to destroy the fundamental assumption on which the order had been made.

[38] [1997] 1 F.L.R. 730. See also *Cook v. Cook* [1988] 1 F.L.R. 51.

[39] [1994] 2 F.L.R. 530. Subsequently the wife obtained an upward variation in the periodical payment order: *Cornick v. Cornick (No. 2)* [1995] 2 F.L.R., CA and eventually a lump sum order under M.C.A. s.31(7A): *Cornick v. Cornick (No. 3)* [2001] 2 F.L.R. 1240, FD.

[40] It may be that the difficulty of valuing house property will lead the court to look more sympathetically on the claim that a substantial difference in the realised value justifies the inference that the valuation was incorrect and that accordingly the basis of the order has been falsified by subsequent events: see, *e.g. Warren v. Warren* (1983) 4 F.L.R. 529, CA (where the matrimonial home was sold for £92,000 five months after a hearing at which it had been valued at £52,000); *Heard v. Heard* [1995] 1 F.L.R. 970, CA (house valued at £67,000; no purchase offer over £33,000 received); but contrast *Edmonds v. Edmonds* [1990] 2 F.L.R. 202, CA (where the fact that the house—valued at some £70,000 at the hearing—was sold for £110,000 was held not to destroy the basis on which an

natural, albeit dramatic, change in value.[41] The wife's case amounted in effect to no more than "saying that it is all terribly unfair"; and the court refused to intervene. In *Ritchie v. Ritchie*[42] the husband's receipt of a redundancy package subsequent to a clean break settlement was not considered to invalidate the fundamental assumptions on which the order had been based. In *Maskell v. Maskell*[43] the Court of Appeal held that the husband's redundancy was "a long way from a *Barder* situation".

In contrast:—

14–086 In *Thompson v. Thompson*[44] the parties had comparatively modest assets, amongst which was the former matrimonial home and the husband's, apparently failing, travel agency. The district judge was concerned to ensure that the wife and children had somewhere to live and he made an order under which the wife took £52,500 of the assets, and the husband £6,500. This was a "stern order from the husband's point of view"; but the district judge thought that it was the best that could be achieved in the circumstances. But less than two weeks after the hearing the husband sold the business for £40,000 (twice the value placed on it at the hearing). The Court of Appeal held that all concerned acted reasonably on the probably mistaken assumption that the correct value was that taken at the hearing; and that the subsequent sale was thus a new event. Accordingly, there was a discretion to grant leave to appeal out of time; and the interests of justice required that the matter be reopened.[45] In *Middleton v. Middleton*,[46] due to deliberate manipulation by the husband the principal asset was worth not £69,000 but after redemption of the mortgage only £652; permission was granted and the wife's appeal allowed.

---

order had been made, not least because the fact that the value was likely to increase had been known to all at the time of the hearing.) See also *Kean v. Kean* [2002] 2 F.L.R. 28, Fam. Div.

[41] See also *Worlock v. Worlock* [1994] 2 F.L.R. 689, CA, where the husband's family business had land which stood in its accounts at cost value (approximately £50,000). Subsequent to the hearing, the husband's mother transferred shares in the company to him; and the company obtained planning permission which increased the value of the land to some £3.5 million. The Court of Appeal refused the wife leave to appeal: it "is only the scale of events and the happening of those events which at the time of the order were unknown which have now come to pass" (*per* Stuart-Smith L.J. at 696). Similar considerations apply where property has fallen in value: see *B v. B (Financial Provision: Leave to Appeal)* [1994] 1 F.L.R. 219 (fall in value of house from £340,000 to £250,000 not sufficient to undermine basis of order).

[42] [1996] 1 F.L.R. 898.

[43] [2001] EWCA Civ. 858; [2001] 3 F.C.R. 296.

[44] [1991] 2 F.L.R. 530, CA.

[45] It may be that the distinction between *Thompson* and *Cornick* is that the *Cornick* valuation was unquestionably correct; whereas it would seem that the *Thompson* valuation was not correct. (But note that in *Heard v. Heard* [1995] 1 F.L.R. 970, CA, where a house sold for much less than had been estimated leave to appeal was granted although it is not clear that any valuation evidence was incorrect.) In any event, an application based on a mistaken valuation is likely to fail if the applicant has failed to probe material available at the trial: see *Edmonds v. Edmonds* [1990] 2 F.L.R. 202, CA; *Worlock v. Worlock* [1994] 2 F.L.R. 689. Similarly, the emergence of a substantial liability (*e.g.* for tax) will not be regarded as a sufficient supervening event if the person concerned could, with due diligence, have discovered the likely extent of the liability at the time of the hearing: *Penrose v. Penrose* [1994] 2 F.L.R. 621.

[46] [1998] 2 F.L.R. 821.

If one party's failure to comply with the terms of an order has frustrated the intention underlying the court order, the court will be more ready to allow the case to be reopened:—

In *Hope-Smith v. Hope-Smith*[47] the court ordered the husband to pay the wife £32,000 out of the proceeds of sale of the family home (the value of which was then estimated at £116,000). The assumption was that the house would be sold very soon; but the sale was delayed for nearly three years "by the husband's quite disgraceful behaviour".[48] The wife was given leave to appeal out of time[49]: the house was worth £200,000 by the time of the setting aside hearing and the fundamental assumptions underlying the order (in terms both of the husband's share of the assets and the kind of house which the wife could buy with the funds to be released to her from the sale) had been falsified. A further illustration is *Middleton v. Middleton*[50] in which the husband's unilateral actions in relation to a business rendered the consent order in effect a sham.

The courts have been confronted with the question whether a change in the law can constitute a "*Barder* event".[51] The introduction of the child support scheme was regarded by many as a fundamental change to the basis upon which divorce settlements (usually involving the transfer of the matrimonial home to the wife, and only a nominal periodical payment order for the children) were made; but in *Crozier v. Crozier*[52] Booth J. held that the creation of the Child Support Agency did not alter the basic principle—recognised for many years—that a parent could not get rid of responsibility to support children. All that had changed was the mechanism for enforcing that responsibility.

Outside the family law context, a change in the law was recognised by the Court of Appeal as capable of justifying permission to appeal out of time in *Greig Middleton & Co. v. Denderowicz*.[53] The question of whether the change in the law effected by *White v. White*[54] is sufficient to undermine the basis on which consent orders in ancillary relief were made was first raised in the literature[55] and subsequently in litigation. In *S v. S (Ancillary Relief: Consent Order)*[56] a consent order was made in September 2000, some six weeks before the delivery of the speeches of the House of Lords in *White v. White*. More than eight months later the wife sought permission to appeal, arguing *inter alia* that had the "reasonable requirements" ceiling not applied, she would have received considerably more. Bracewell J. dismissed the application. It was held that as a general proposition a change in the law may constitute a supervening *Barder* event, and that *White v. White* did constitute a new event, because although it

---

47 [1989] 2 F.L.R. 56, CA.
48 *Cornick v. Cornick* [1994] 2 F.L.R. 530 at 534, *per* Hale J.
49 Contrast *Rooker v. Rooker* [1988] 1 F.L.R. 219 where leave was refused because the applicant had had it in her power to apply to the court for enforcement of the order in question but had failed to do so.
50 [1998] 2 F.L.R. 821, CA.
51 E. Hamilton "Is White v White a 'Barder Event'?" [2001] *Fam. Law* 135.
52 [1994] 1 F.L.R. 126.
53 [1998] 1 W.L.R. 1164.
54 [2000] 2 F.L.R. 981
55 See n. 40 *supra*.
56 *S v. S (Ancillary Relief: Consent Order)* [2002] EWHC Fam. 223; [2002] 1 F.L.R. 992.

involved an exercise of discretion, the effect in big money cases was very significant, as demonstrated by the appeal in *Cowan v. Cowan*.[57] However, Bracewell J. held further that the new event must be unforseeable in the sense that it was not envisaged and could not reasonably have been envisaged at the time of making the order. Here, what happened in *White v. White* was foreseeable, and in the words of Balcombe L.J. in *Chaudhuri v. Chaudhuri*[58] an "obvious possibility"; within the legal profession, *White v. White* was anticipated to be a landmark decision, and the wife and her advisers knew or ought to have known that.[59]

The policy favouring finality in litigation requires that save in the most exceptional case of the cruellest injustice, bad legal advice should not be a ground for interfering with a consent order.[60] An aggrieved party may however wish to sue the legal adviser in negligence.[61]

(b) Principles to be applied in reopened cases

14–087 If the court does decide to grant leave to appeal,[62] it will decide what order should be made on the basis of all the facts as they are known at the time of the rehearing:—

> Thus, in *Smith v. Smith (Smith intervening)*[63] the judge made an order dividing the family assets between the parties equally on the basis that the needs of the parties, and especially the wife's housing needs, were the predominant consideration. Five months later the wife committed suicide; and under her will her estate would pass to her daughter. It was conceded that leave to appeal should be granted; and the judge hearing the appeal made an order on the basis that he should only look at the factors which had been taken into account in making the original order. Since the wife no longer had any housing needs, the order should be reduced to the very small sum necessary to pay her debts. The Court of Appeal held that such an approach was wrong, and that the court should start again from the beginning. What

---

[57] [2001] 2 F.L.R. 192.

[58] [1992] 2 F.L.R. 73.

[59] Bracewell J. further held that there was no reasonable excuse for the wife's delay of over eight months in making her application.

[60] *Harris v. Manahan* [1997] 1 F.L.R. 205; *P v. P (Consent Order: Appeal Out of Time)* [2002] 1 F.L.R. 743, FD; *S v. S (Ancillary Relief: Consent Order)* [2002] EWHC Fam. 223; [2002] 1 F.L.R. 992.

[61] *Channon v. Lindley Johnstone* [2000] 2 F.L.R. 734; Wagstaffe, "Bad Legal advice in Ancillary Relief Cases" [1999] *Fam. Law* 156; Denyer, "Professional Negligence Claims arising Out of Consent Orders Made in Family Proceedings" [1999] *Fam. Law* 773; *Hall and Co. v. Simms et als* [2000] 2 F.L.R. 545, HL; *Phippen v. Palmers (A Firm)* [2002] 2 F.L.R. 415.

[62] In many cases the application for leave and the hearing of the appeal will be combined: see *e.g. Middleton v. Middleton* [1998] 2 F.L.R. 821. However, if an applicant makes out a clear prima facie case the court will grant leave in order to allow the necessary detailed investigations to be carried out: see *Re C (Financial Provision: Leave to Appeal)* [1993] 2 F.L.R. 799 (and note the substantive hearing: *C v. C (Financial Provision: Non-Disclosure)* [1994] 2 F.L.R. 272).

[63] [1992] Fam. 69, CA.

would be the right order in a case in which the wife was known to have only six months to live?[64]

3. Non-disclosure: setting aside orders, etc.

14–088 So far, we have been concerned largely with the effect of a change of circumstances after the making of the order. But what is the position if it is claimed that facts material to the making of the order (or to the giving of consent to the making of the order) were not disclosed or were perhaps even concealed from the court and the other party? As a result of the decision of the House of Lords in *Livesey (formerly Jenkins) v. Livesey*[65]—the facts of which have been given above[66]—it is clear that the parties have a duty[67] to provide the court with all information relevant to the making of an order and to ensure that such information is correct, complete, and up-to-date. If there is a failure in this respect the matter may be reopened.[68] For example:—

> In *Vicary v. Vicary*[69] a consent order was made on the basis that the husband had assets amounting to some £430,000, including the shares in his private company. The husband knew, but the wife did not, that negotiations were taking place for the sale of the company; and shortly after the making of the consent order the husband's shareholding was sold for £2.8 million. The judge found that the husband, a dishonest witness, had by knowing non-disclosure of the true position about the value of his assets led the wife to agree to the terms of the consent order; and accordingly it was set aside. In *T v. T (Consent Order: Procedure to Set Aside)*[70] the husband had given his wife the impression that there was no free market in the shares of his company. A consent order was made on that basis. In fact he was negotiating a takeover by a public company and soon after the date of the consent order he received £1.6 million for his holding. The consent order was set

[64] An order to pay a lump sum of £25,000 to the wife was made; and the court stated that the question to whom this fund would pass under the wife's will was irrelevant.

[65] [1985] A.C. 424, HL.

[66] See p. 386, above.

[67] See the obligation to provide financial information in Form E (F.P.R. 1991, r. 2.61B(1) and (2), discussed at p. 357 above.

[68] The basic principle was stated by the Privy Council in *De Lasala v. De Lasala* [1980] A.C. 546 at 561: "where a party to an action seeks to challenge, on the ground that it was obtained by fraud or mistake, a judgment or order that finally disposes of the issues raised between the parties, the only ways of doing it . . . are by way of appeal from the judgment or order to a higher court or by bringing a fresh action to set it aside"; and a lump sum or property adjustment order is, for these purposes, a final order: *Thwaite v. Thwaite* [1982] Fam. 1, CA. There is unresolved uncertainty about the appropriate procedure for bringing the matter before the court—appeal, rehearing, fresh action—and whether the choice of procedure has substantive consequences: see *B-T v. B-T (Divorce: Procedure)* [1990] 2 F.L.R. 1 (Ward J.); *Re C (Financial Provision: Leave to Appeal)* [1993] 2 F.L.R. 799 (Thorpe J.); *Benson v. Benson (dec'd)* [1996] 1 F.L.R. 692; *T v. T* [1996] 2 F.L.R. 640 (Richard Anelay Q.C.); *Harris v. Manahan* [1997] 1 F.L.R. 205, CA; *P v. P (Consent Order: Appeal Out of Time)* [2002] 1 F.L.R. 743 (Bennett J.).

[69] [1992] 2 F.L.R. 271, CA. The leading case is *Livesey (formerly Jenkins) v. Livesey* [1985] A.C. 424 (failure to disclose intention to remarry—order for transfer of matrimonial home set aside).

[70] [1996] 2 F.L.R. 640.

aside. In *Middleton v. Middleton*[71] the husband failed to disclose his true plans with relation to a business and the consent order was set aside.

Not every failure of frank and full disclosure will justify the court in setting aside an order; and it has been said[72] that it will only be in cases when the absence of full and frank disclosure has led the court to make an order which is substantially different from the order which it would have made if disclosure had been made that a case for setting aside "can possibly be made good". Thus:—

In *Cook v. Cook*[73] it was alleged that a spouse had failed to disclose the extent of her emotional commitment to a third party; but the Court of Appeal held that the original order should remain unaltered. Even if the true facts had been known they would probably not have had any significant impact on the order made.

Are there any other grounds upon which an order may be set aside? The law is in a state of some uncertainty; but it would seem that orders obtained by fraud and possibly undue influence are vulnerable to attack.[74] An order made under a mistake of fact also appears vulnerable.[75] As to a mistake of law, in *S v. S (Ancillary Relief: Consent Order)*[76] Bracewell J. declined to extend to the field of ancillary relief the retrospective mistake of law doctrine expounded by a majority in the House of Lords in the context of a restitutionary remedy in *Kleinwort Benson v. Lincoln County Council*.[77] It was further held that there would be public policy considerations against setting aside a consent order on such a basis by reason of the floodgates opening.

III. WORKING OF THE LAW IN PRACTICE: HOUSING AND PENSIONS

14–089 Divorce settlements often fall into one of three categories.[78] First, there is the case involving large capital, where a clean break will be imposed in accordance with the principles set out above. At the opposite extreme, there is the case in which one or both parties will inevitably depend on welfare benefits; and the court's role is effectively restricted to determining how far one party should be

---

[71] [1998] 2 F.L.R. 821.

[72] *Livesey v. Jenkins* [1985] A.C. 424 at 445, *per* Lord Brandon. See also *P v. P (Consent Order: Appeal Out of Time)* [2002] 1 F.L.R. 743 (Bennett J.).

[73] [1988] 1 F.L.R. 521, CA.

[74] *De Lasala v. De Lasala* [1980] A.C. 546; *Thwaite v. Thwaite* [1982] Fam. 1; *cf. Tommey v. Tommey* [1983] Fam. 15. On the issue of mistake of law, see E. Hamilton, "White v. White—A 'Barder Event'?" [2001] *Fam. Law* 135. Mistake of law—as well as of fact—now gives rise to a restitutionary remedy on the principle of unjust enrichment: *Kleinwort Benson v. Lincoln County Council* [1999] 2 A.C. 349.

[75] *Maskell v. Maskell* [2001] 3 F.C.R. 296 (judge's mistake in valuation of pension).

[76] [2002] EHWC Fam. 223; [2002] 1 F.L.R. 992.

[77] [1999] 2 A.C. 349.

[78] See Davis et al., *Simple Quarrels* (1994).

required to relieve the taxpayer of the burden which would otherwise fall on the community. However, in a very large proportion of cases, the parties will have owned a house; and all the considerations referred to above—particularly the welfare of the children, the needs of the parties, and the desirability of terminating financial obligations—make the allocation of the house the central issue. Part A below therefore examines the options available. However, in recent years entitlements under pension arrangements have become an increasingly important component of family resources, and this has prompted legislation intended to facilitate the making of proper arrangements in that context. Part B seeks to explain those possibilities.

A. Housing

1. Factors influencing housing orders

14–090 There are two matters which have had a particular effect on the making of court orders relating to housing:

(a) Availability of income support and jobseekers allowance[79]

The rules governing the availability of income support and jobseekers allowance influence decisions on re-allocation of housing in two ways. First, the capital value of a house owned and occupied by the claimant is disregarded in determining whether the claimant has capital[80] in excess of the cut-off level for eligibility (the "means test"). Secondly, the applicable amount for income support and jobseekers allowance includes housing needs—including mortgage interest—but the amounts are now restricted, which has lessened their impact on divorce settlements.

(b) Impact of the statutory charge

14–091 Family litigation may be publicly funded[81]; and a party who obtains public funding does not in the first instance have to pay anything beyond his assessed (and usually modest) contribution towards the legal fees incurred on his behalf. But public funding makes out-and-out grants only to those who lose cases; it makes loans to those who win them.[82] If any property is "recovered or preserved"[83] for a funded individual in proceedings, the Legal Services Commission is entitled to a first charge on the property for the costs incurred on the litigant's behalf to the extent that these costs exceed the litigant's own contribu-

---

[79] On the system of Graduated Fees, see Walsh [2002] *Fam. Law* 582 and McFarlane [2002] *Fam. Law* 163.

[80] *Ellis v. Chief Adjudication Officer* [1998] 1 F.L.R. 184.

[81] Access to Justice Act 1999.

[82] *per* Sir J. Donaldson M.R., *Davies v. Ely Lilly & Co.* [1987] 1 W.L.R., CA.

[83] Access to Justice Act 1999, s. 10(7); *Hanlon v. The Law Society* [1981] A.C. 124; *Parkes v. Legal Aid Board* [1994] 2 F.L.R. 850; *Curling v. The Law Society* [1985] 1 W.L.R. 472.

tion and are not recovered from the other party to the litigation. "Property" is not defined in the Access to Justice Act 1999.[84]

The first £3000 of any money, or of the value of any property recovered or preserved by virtue of a property adjustment order or lump sum order is exempt from the charge.[85] However, there is power to defer the enforcement of the charge in cases where the property recovered or preserved is to be used as, or for the purchase of, a home for the assisted person or dependants.[86] If enforcement is postponed, simple interest is charged, but is not payable until the property comes to be sold. The courts will assume that the Legal Services Commission will exercise its discretion to postpone enforcement of the charge.

2. Types of housing orders often made by the court

14–092 As has been seen, the court's powers to make transfer of property and other property adjustment orders give it an almost total flexibility in the type of order it can make. In practice, however, the following seem to be the main types of order made:

(a) Outright transfer to one party: other compensated by reduction or extinction of periodical payments

14–093 This form of order can have the advantage of achieving a "clean break". Thus, in *Hanlon v. Hanlon*[87]:—

> Both the husband (a policeman earning £4,200 per annum) and the wife (a nurse earning approximately the same amount) were in full-time work. The husband was living rent-free in a police flat. The wife, after the separation in 1971, continued to live in the former matrimonial home with the children of the marriage (the youngest of whom was aged 12). The house was worth approximately £14,000, subject to a mortgage of some £4,000. The Court of Appeal allowed the wife's appeal against the order of Rees J. under which the matrimonial home had been ordered to be transferred into the joint names of husband and wife upon trust for sale (the sale to be postponed until the youngest child attained 17) and substituted an order transferring the home to the wife outright whilst reducing the periodical payments for the children from £14 weekly to a nominal sum.[88] The reason for this order was that if the house were sold under the terms of the original

---

[84] Nor was it defined in the Legal Aid Act 1988. The issue of the statutory charge and orders relating to pensions is discussed in the final section of this Chap.

[85] Community Legal Service (Financial) Regulations 2000 (S.I. 2000 No. 516), reg. 44(1)(d); Community Legal Service (Financial) (Amendment No. 3) Regulations (S.I. 2001 No. 3663).

[86] Comunity Legal Service (Financial) Regulations 2000, reg. 52(1).

[87] [1978] 1 W.L.R. 592. Note that the Child Support legislation would today make it impossible to fix the husband's maintenance obligation to the children at a nominal sum.

[88] It should be noted that a solution effectively exempting a parent from the liability to make a financial contribution to the child's welfare is, since the coming into force of the Child Support Act 1991, no longer available: see Chap. 15, below.

> order in five years' time (when the youngest child attained 17), the effect of the Legal Aid Charge would at that time have been that neither spouse would receive more than £2,500. The wife and children would then be homeless, and unable to house themselves with the result that the wife would have to be housed by the local authority (as would the husband when he left the police force). It was better that the parties should know where they stood, and the husband (with a larger income available than would otherwise be the case) enabled to make proper plans for his own future housing.

Outright transfer of the home or proceeds of sale thereof to the spouse with ongoing care of children of the marriage may be the only practicable solution where the equity is limited and there is no other capital available.[89]

The technique of outright transfer of the house with corresponding reduction or extinction of liability to make periodical payments has been found a satisfactory technique where the husband is unlikely to comply with a periodical payments order.[90]

(b) Outright transfer to one spouse: other compensated by immediate cash payment

14–094 This approach was again envisaged in *Wachtel v. Wachtel*,[91] where Lord Denning M.R. said that if the husband remained in the house it should be transferred to him (subject to liability for the mortgage payments), the wife being compensated by a lump sum of an amount the husband could raise by further mortgage on the house without financially crippling him. This technique has been adopted in a number of cases, and is particularly suitable when the wife has remarried, or is otherwise provided with housing, and the husband needs the house as a home for his own new family.[92] It is also used in cases in which the wife remains in the house. For example, in *Mortimer v. Mortimer-Griffin*[93]:—

> The court had made a settlement order under which the husband would be entitled to 20 per cent of the value of the house when sold. But the husband had in fact acquired another house, and his mortgage liabilities were covered by welfare benefits. Moreover, the Court of Appeal considered that the wife—who had retrained and made herself self-supporting—had shouldered a wholly disproportionate burden since the breakdown of the marriage. It therefore substituted an order under which the husband would receive an immediate lump sum of £2,500—the most which could be paid to him without it attracting the statutory charge—and the house would be

[89] See *e.g. B v. B (Financial Provision: Welfare of Child and Conduct)* [2002] 1 F.L.R. 555, FD.

[90] *Bryant v. Bryant, The Times*, November 7, 1973; see also *Jones (M.A.) v. Jones (W.)* [1976] Fam. 8.

[91] [1973] Fam. 72 at 96.

[92] See *Backhouse v. Backhouse* [1978] 1 W.L.R. 243.

[93] [1986] 2 F.L.R. 315, CA.

transferred to the wife outright. The court was particularly influenced by the possibility that the wife would find difficulty in rehousing herself when sale took place, and by the fact that the husband was unlikely to benefit from any larger lump sum. Orders for a postponed sale (said Sir John Donaldson M.R.) suffered from the defect that "chickens come home to roost" at an unpredictable time and in unpredictable circumstances; and that percentage allocations often gave rise to difficulties. In *Piglowska v. Piglowski,*[94] discussed earlier in this Chapter[95]; the house was transferred to the wife, the husband received a modest flat in Spain plus £10,000.

(c) Outright transfer to one spouse: other spouse compensated by deferred cash payment

14–095 Often it will be necessary to delay the payment of compensation to the spouse who leaves the matrimonial home until it is eventually sold. In such cases the courts will usually give the party affected a charge over the property for a share of the proceeds of sale. For example, in *Knibb v. Knibb*[96]:

> It was ordered that the former matrimonial home be vested in the wife subject to her obtaining the husband's release from any liability under the mortgage and to her executing a charge in his favour for 40 per cent of the sale proceeds of the property. The charge provided that the statutory power of sale and thus, in effect, the husband's right to enforce the charge[97] should arise only on certain events (including the wife's death, her remarriage or cohabitation with another man for a period exceeding three months, or her voluntarily leaving the property) specified in the order.

(d) Order for immediate sale[98] and division

14–096 Such an order may be appropriate if the proceeds will suffice to rehouse both parties, or if one or both of them is to be housed by a local authority. It is unlikely to be satisfactory where the equity is limited and there are children

---

[94] [1999] 2 F.L.R. 763

[95] At p. 347.

[96] [1987] 2 F.L.R. 396.

[97] In *Knibb v. Knibb* the order provided that the charge could be redeemed within four months by the wife paying the husband £3,500. The Court of Appeal held that the date for redemption was a vital term of the order, and that there was no jurisdiction to extend this time (but note that it is a fundamental term that a mortgagor may redeem the mortgage: and it does not seem entirely clear whether the wife could redeem the mortgage at any time on tendering 40 per cent of the sale proceeds, or only after the statutory powers of sale etc. had arisen, *i.e.* on her remarriage etc). See also *Kiely v. Kiely* [1988] 1 F.L.R. 248, CA (wrong to allow husband to enforce charge, *i.e.* in effect requiring that the property be sold, before events stipulated in order because to do so would constitute variation of order); but *cf. Ross v. Ross* [1989] 2 F.L.R. 257, CA, where leave to appeal against the terms of a charge was granted out of time (in part because the order as drawn up differed from the order pronounced by the judge); and *Masefield v. Alexander (Lump Sum: Extension of Time)* [1995] 1 F.L.R. 100, CA (time for payment of lump sum—in effect purchase price of house—extended.

[98] Under M.C.A. 1973, s.24A.

whose needs have to be considered. The fact that children may be disadvantaged by a move (perhaps involving a change of school) is a factor which has influenced the court against ordering an immediate sale, even in cases where the funds available would suffice to purchase a new house for the wife and children.

In many cases it is agreed that the home shall be sold, and the only real issue is the proportions of division of the proceeds.[99]

(e) Settlement orders[1]

14–097 Although the court's powers are extremely flexible, certain types of order have became common:

(i) The *Mesher* order: order for sale and division postponed during dependence of children

Such orders were at one time very popular, since they enabled the court to preserve each party's stake in what was then usually an appreciating capital asset, whilst at the same time preserving a home with their mother for the children.

In *Mesher v. Mesher*[2]:—

> The matrimonial home was in joint names and mortgaged (but there was a substantial equity). The husband intended to remarry and had already bought a new house; the wife intended to remarry but wished to stay in the former matrimonial home with the nine-year-old child of the family. The Court of Appeal held that it would be wrong to transfer the house outright to the wife since that would deprive the husband of the whole of his interest in the home; and that the right course was for the wife and child to have a home in which to live ("rather than that she should have a large sum of available capital"). Accordingly, it was ordered that the matrimonial home be held on trust for sale for the parties in equal shares, provided that the house be not sold so long as the child of the marriage was under the age of 17 (or until further order). The wife was to be at liberty to live there rent-free, paying and discharging all outgoings (except that repayments of the capital of the mortgage were to be borne equally).

After a time the dangers inherent in such orders became apparent. In particular, such an order would often leave the parties in a state of complete uncertainty as to the future, since they would not be able to predict what would happen when the property came to be sold. Would the money available to each party

---

[99] See *e.g. M v. B (Ancillary Proceedings)* [1998] 1 F.L.R. 53; *Cordle v. Cordle* [2001] EWCA Civ. 1791; [2002] 1 F.L.R. 207, CA.

[1] Note that the trust for sale has now been replaced by the trust of land: Trusts of Land and Appointment of Trustees Act 1996, discussed in Chap. 5.

[2] [1980] 1 All E.R. 126, CA.

suffice to rehouse him or her?[3] In some cases it was clear that after the period of postponement the wife would inevitably be homeless and in a very weak position to rehouse herself; and unless the sum she received were large enough to buy another house outright the wife might find great difficulty in obtaining a mortgage to finance the purchase.[4] Moreover, the use of a trust for sale might have the undesirable consequence that if the wife wished to move before the end of the period of postponement, she would not be entitled to have the husband's share of the proceeds applied towards the acquisition of a new house for herself and her family.[5] In the result, *Mesher* orders were no longer regarded as "the bible."[6]

A charge realisable on eventual sale may be the fair outcome.[7] However, recent authorities in small money cases emphasise that *White v. White*[8] did not create an in principle entitlement of each spouse to some part of the equity either immediately or on a deferred basis. The welfare of the child remains the first consideration, and thus in cases other than those involving big money the housing needs of the parent with care will continue to dominate.[9]

(ii) The *Martin* order: house settled on trust for one spouse for life

14–098 The difference between such an order and a *Mesher* order is that the wife's position is secured at least so long as she wishes to remain in occupation of the family home. For example:—

> In *Martin (B.H.) v. Martin (B.W.)*[10] the parties were childless. The court held that, since the husband enjoyed secure council housing, and the wife would not get sufficient money from a sale to rehouse herself, the right solution would be for the house to be settled on trust for the wife during her life or until her remarriage or such earlier date as she should cease to live there. Subject thereto it was to be held on trust for the parties in equal shares.[11]

> In *Bateman v. Bateman,*[12] the court ordered that the home be held on trust for sale, but the sale was to be postponed until the wife ceased to use the home as her main place of residence, remarried, or died, whichever should first occur. The wife was to receive one-quarter of the proceeds of sale if

---

[3] *Hanlon v. Hanlon* [1978] 1 W.L.R. 592 at 599, above.
[4] *Carson v. Carson* [1983] 1 W.L.R. 285, CA.
[5] See, *e.g. Thompson v. Thompson* [1985] F.L.R. 863, CA.
[6] *Mortimer v. Mortimer-Griffin* [1986] 2 F.L.R. 315 at 319, *per* Parker L.J.
[7] *Elliott v. Elliott* [2001] 1 F.C.R. 477.
[8] [2000] 2 F.L.R. 981.
[9] *B v. B (Financial Provision: Welfare of Child and Conduct)* [2002] 1 F.L.R. 555, FD; *Cordle v. Cordle* [2001] EWCA Civ. 1791; [2002] 1 F.L.R. 207, CA.
[10] [1978] Fam. 12, CA.
[11] It appears that there is power to require a spouse who is in occupation under a Martin order to pay an occupation rent: *Harvey v. Harvey* (1982) 3 F.L.R. 141, CA.
[12] [1979] Fam. 25.

still alive at the time of sale; subject thereto the proceeds were to be divided between the children.

Finally:—

In *Clutton v. Clutton*[13] the husband had a far greater earning capacity than the wife, and would have no difficulty in getting back "on the property ladder".[14] But the Court of Appeal felt that this was insufficient to justify depriving the husband forever of the sole capital asset of the marriage, when a *Martin* order would be equally effective in protecting the wife's housing needs. The fact that the wife had a stable relationship with a man was also relevant to the court's decision to make a *Martin* order under which the wife's occupation right would terminate on death, remarriage or cohabitation. Although the wife denied that she intended to marry or cohabit, the court considered that these were distinct possibilities, and that the bitterness which would be felt by the husband when he saw the former matrimonial home occupied by the wife's cohabitant would outweigh the bitterness caused to the wife by her feeling that her private life was under constant scrutiny.

3. Local authority and housing association housing[15]

14–099 At one time, it was considered doubtful whether the court had power under the Matrimonial Causes Act 1973 to make a property adjustment order in respect of a council house tenancy,[16] but it has now been settled that the court may make such an order[17] as well as one in respect of a housing association tenancy.[18] The court also has a statutory power under the Family Law Act 1996[19] to order the transfer of protected, statutory, secure, and assured tenancies.

The question whether such powers should in fact be exercised is a difficult one. It was at one time the conventional view that the allocation of public sector housing was primarily a matter for the local authority, and that the courts should not seek to put pressure on an authority to exercise its discretion in a particular way. In practice, local authorities were often able to resolve the couple's problems, either by rehousing the wife or by giving the husband notice to quit so that the wife could continue to occupy the matrimonial home. However, as a result of legislation[20] giving public sector tenants a degree of security of tenure,

---

[13] [1991] 1 F.L.R. 242, CA.
[14] *per* Lloyd L.J. at 247.
[15] S. Bridge, "Transferring Tenancies of the Family Home" [1998] *Fam. Law* 26; H. Conway, "Protecting Tenancies on Marriage Breakdown" [2001] *Fam. Law* 208.
[16] *Brent v. Brent* [1975] Fam. 1.
[17] *Thompson v. Thompson* [1976] Fam. 25; *Regan v. Regan* [1977] 1 W.L.R. 84; *Jones v. Jones* [1997] 1 F.L.R. 27; [1997] 2 W.L.R. 373. The power may also be exercised in respect of protected tenancies: *Church Commissioners v. El Emarah* [1996] 2 F.L.R. 544, *Newlon Housing Trust v. Alsulaimen* [1998] 2 F.L.R. 690, HL.
[18] *Akintola v. Akintola* [2001] EWCA Civ. 1989; [2002] 2 F.L.R. 701.
[19] s. 53 and Sched. 7.
[20] Housing Act 1980, Housing Act 1985; see Chap 7.

it may no longer be possible for authorities to act with the same freedom as they have done in the past. Accordingly, there may well be circumstances in which courts are prepared to exercise their powers to make orders in respect of public sector tenancies.[21] In *Jones v. Jones*[22] Morritt L.J. observed[23] that Parliament envisaged that the circumstances of security of tenure and the housing policy of local authorities should be matters which could be taken into account in determining whether to make an order under section 24 of the Matrimonial Causes Act 1973.[24] In *Akintola v. Akintola*[25] the Court of Appeal sensibly advised that rather than embarking on prolonged litigation at public expense, spouses who have occupied a secure housing association tenancy for many years should on separation approach the housing association to seek smaller separate accommodation for each.

B. Orders dealing with pensions

14–100 Rights under a pension scheme may be particularly significant, because for many married people their two single assets of greatest value—often indeed the only substantial assets—are the house in which they live and their expectations under a pension scheme.[26] Recent statistics show that a substantial proportion of family wealth is represented by pension entitlements.[27] A disparity between the accrued pension expectations of the two parties to a marriage is common, because (as Lord Nicholls of Birkenhead has put it) the "major responsibility for family care and home-making still remains with women" and the "consequent limitation on their earning power prevents them from building up pension entitlements comparable with those of men."[28] Pension entitlements represent future security in the light of which a couple plan their future together; they may also be viewed as a form of joint savings to which both have contributed during the marriage, whether directly or indirectly.[29]

The difficulties for many years experienced by courts in dealing with pension entitlements on divorce stemmed from the legal structure of pension arrange-

---

[21] *Jones v. Jones* [1997] 1 F.L.R. 27. In *Gay v. Sheeran* [1999] 2 F.L.R. 519, CA the woman failed in proceedings under the Family law Act 1996 to obtain a transfer of tenancy but obtained an occupation order. It was held that the court had no jurisdiction to transfer a tenancy held by one spouse or cohabitant jointly with a third party.

[22] [1997] 1 F.L.R. 27.

[23] *ibid.* at 33.

[24] See also *Beard v. Beard* [1981] 1 W.L.R. 369.

[25] [2002] 1 F.L.R. 701.

[26] *Brooks v. Brooks* [1995] 2 F.L.R. 13 at 15, *per* Lord Nicholls of Birkenhead.

[27] See Chap. 4, at pp. 101–102.

[28] *Brooks v. Brooks* [1995] 2 F.L.R. 13 at 16. See for research findings on this, H. Joshi and H. Davies, "Pensions, Divorce and Wives' Double Burden" (1992) 6 IJL&F 289; and generally J. Martin and C. Roberts, *Women and Employment, a lifetime perspective* (1984).

[29] On the nature of a claim in relation to a pension, see Hallam and Salter, "Pensions on Divorce: Compensation or Needs?" [1997] *Fam. Law* 608; Dnes [1998] *Fam. Law* 124; Meins "Valuing Pensions" [2000] *Fam. Law* 274; Brindley, "An Actuary's View of Pension-Sharing: Parts I and II" [2000] *Fam. Law* 845 and 914; Brindley, "Black and White in Pensions" [2001] *Fam. Law* 462.

ments. Although in some ways a typical occupational pension scheme[30] is merely a savings medium[31] in which assets are accumulated to provide benefits on retirement or death,[32] it is a savings medium which will (provided it is approved by the Inland Revenue[33]) benefit from exceedingly favourable tax treatment: the contributions made by the employer are not treated as the income of the employee, and the employee will not be charged to income tax on any contributions made out of his or her earnings to the scheme; while the fund will be invested by the trustees with virtual immunity from taxation. The price to be paid for this favourable treatment[34] is that—in order to comply with the Revenue's requirements—there will be severe restrictions on access to (and transfer

---

[30] This term is used here in a non-technical sense to mean any scheme under which an employee is entitled to receive a pension on retirement. Under a typical scheme, a company will transfer sums (perhaps including contributions from the employee) to trustees who will invest the funds—sometimes in life assurance policies—so as to provide resources to meet the stipulated benefits (which will usually include not only a retirement pension, but also death in service benefits and provision for dependants). For comprehensive information on the variety of pension schemes see Eversheds Pensions Law Team *Pensions Law Handbook 2002* (Eversheds, 2002); and see generally J. Masson, "A Poor and Lonely Old Age" in *Frontiers of Family Law* (A. Bainham and D. Pearl ed., 1993), p. 161.

[31] Although by no means all pension schemes are funded by the purchase of investments held on trust for the benefit of the members. In particular, pensions for the armed forces and civil service are simply paid out of tax revenue.

[32] For many years the problem was seen largely in terms of the pension payable to a surviving widow (or widower) and arose from the fact that divorce would prevent a spouse from qualifying as such; and the provisions of the M.C.A. 1973, s.25(2) (h) as originally enacted were specifically directed to this aspect of the matter. But in recent years—and particularly since the development of the concept of "portability" of pensions (*i.e.* the right to have the so-called "transfer value" transferred to another scheme under the Social Security Act 1985) the notion of a pension fund as a pool of investment capital has become more widely appreciated. The fact that this significant asset could not be effectively included in any divorce settlement came to be seen as more and more difficult to justify.

[33] See J. Masson, "Pensions, Dependency and Divorce" [1986] J.S.W.L. 343. The Revenue issue notes of guidance (IR No. 12) setting out the conditions normally required for approval; but these are frequently changed, and it is presumably not unreasonable to suppose that general guidance will, following the decision in *Brooks v. Brooks*, be given on how the Revenue's discretion will be exercised in cases in which a pension scheme can be varied under the court's power to vary settlements.

[34] Although, as stated in the text, the need to secure Inland Revenue approval may now be a dominant factor, the traditional rules governing pensions were influenced by the belief that a pensioner should be protected from losing his pension even by his own folly or misjudgment. Hence benefits were often provided under discretionary or protective trusts; and statute often made pensions exempt from attachment by legal process: see *Walker v. Walker* [1983] F.L.R. 779; *Roberts v. Roberts* [1986] 2 F.L.R. 152. The relevant provisions in respect of service pensions were Army Act 1955, s.203; Air Force Act 1955, s.203; Naval Discipline Act 1987, s.128G (inserted by Armed Forces Act 1991, s.16 to remedy the anomaly revealed by the decision of the Court of Appeal in *Cotgrave v. Cotgrave* [1992] 1 F.L.R. 10 whereby naval pensioners were treated less favourably than other service pensioners: see *Legrove v. Legrove* [1994] 2 F.L.R. 119, CA on transitional consequences). However these provisions protecting service pensions did not prevent a court from making an order once the pensioner had actually received the lump sum; they applied solely to anticipatory orders such as would prevent the pensioner from receiving in due course the pension for which the terms of engagement provided: *Happe v. Happe* [1990] 2 F.L.R. 212. The Pensions Act 1995, s.166(5) provides that nothing in the statutory provisions enumerated above (or indeed the general rule laid down by s.91 of the Act which generally prohibits assignment of pension rights or their attachment by court order or any provision "corresponding to any of those enactments" in a pension scheme) is to prevent the court exercising its powers to make financial provision orders under the Matrimonial Causes Act 1973 in respect of any benefits under a pension scheme which a party to the marriage has or is likely to have in the foreseeable future.

of) the assets in the fund. The underlying policy of the Revenue rules is to restrict the conversion of income which had escaped tax into tax free capital or other freely disposable resources; and accordingly in principle all except a lump sum not exceeding four times the final salary has to be taken from the fund in the form of income—effectively an annuity—which will itself be liable to tax.[35]

In recent years the powers of the courts to deal with pension entitlements and expectations in ancillary relief orders have been progressively and substantially increased by successive legislative enactments.[36] The text will outline[37] the range of powers available. However, some preliminary matters deserve mention. Before the court can decide whether to exercise its powers and if so, how, it will require detailed information about pension entitlements and professional advisers will need to become expert in assessing the parties' position. The subject is a complex one since pension arrangements take many different forms[38]; and the first and overriding principle is that the terms of the particular scheme must be analysed.[39] In the light of that analysis, an attempt must be made to value the parties' interests; and this is a matter on which expert evidence from an actuary is likely to be required. Valuation is not an exact science and the outcome depends on a number of assumptions, in part about economic factors—such as the anticipated yield on investments—and in part (at least in relation to some schemes, based on the employee's final salary) on personal matters—such as the employee's future earning pattern. However, regulations[40] stipulate that the so-called Cash Equivalent Transfer Value (CETV) be used for the purpose of calculating existing rights of members of pension schemes.[41] The value is to be determined on a date specified by the court between one year before the date of petition and the date of order.[42]

It is important to appreciate that the court's powers to make orders in respect of pensions are not discrete or self-contained, but merely part of the range of powers available in ancillary relief proceedings. Moreover, their exercise—as the exercise of other powers—is governed by section 25 of the Matrimonial Causes Act 1973 and the wide discretion thereby conferred. This was

---

[35] However, pensions schemes are still an effective tax shelter in part because the permissible lump sum is not insubstantial, while the entitlement to the periodical income payments will come at a time when the taxpayer is less likely to be subject to a high rate of income tax.

[36] Family Law Act 1996, s. 16; Pensions Act 1995; Welfare Reform and Pensions Act 1999.

[37] For detailed discussion, see R. Bird *Pension Sharing: The New Law* (Family Law, 1999); R. Ellison and M. Rae *Family Breakdown and Pensions* (2nd ed., Butterworths, 2001).

[38] See Eversheds, *Pensions Law Handbook 2002*. Some of the complexities were noted by Lord Nicholls of Birkenhead in *Brooks v. Brooks* [1995] 2 F.L.R. 13 at 16.

[39] Members of pension schemes (and their spouses) have statutory rights to certain information about the scheme and the benefits available under it: see Occupational Pensions (Disclosure of Information) Regulations 1986, S.I. 1986 No. 1046 and the Pensions on Divorce (Provision of Information) Regulations 2000, S.I. 2000 No. 1048 and the Pension Sharing (Valuation) Regulations 2000 (S.I. 2000, No. 1052). See *Griffiths v. Dawson & Co.* [1993] 2 F.L.R. 315, Ewbank J., for the professional duties of legal advisers.

[40] Made under M.C.A. s. 25D(2)(e): see Divorce etc (Pensions) Regulations 2000, S.I. 2000 No. 1123, reg. 3; Pensions on Divorce (Provision of Information) Regulations 2000, S.I. 2000 No. 1048, reg. 3; Pension Sharing (Valuation) Regulations 2000, S.I. 2000 No. 1052.

[41] For a critique, see Meins, "Valuing Pensions" [2000] *Fam. Law* 274. For judicial dicta on valuation in the context of ancillary relief, see *per* Thorpe L.J. in *Cowan v. Cowan* [2001] 2 F.L.R. 192 at [69] and in *Maskell v. Maskell* [2001] 3 F.C.R. 269 at para. [6].

[42] Divorce etc (Pensions) Regulations 2000, reg. 3(1)(a).

emphasised by Singer J. in *T v. T (Financial Relief: Pensions)*[43] in rejecting an argument that the earmarking provisions introduced into the Matrimonial Causes Act 1973 by the Pensions Act 1995 required a non-member spouse to be compensated for loss of pension benefits. The recent additions to the court's powers in relation to pension arrangements are not intended to overturn the general approach to the section 25 exercise.

Methods of re-allocation

The following techniques are available to the court: **14–101**

(a) Compensation from other assets: "Offsetting"

As we have seen, pension entitlements are relevant considerations under section 25(2)(a) and (h) of the Matrimonial Causes Act 1973 when the court is exercising its discretion in relation to ancillary relief. Under the approach now commonly known as "offsetting",[44] the pension scheme rights are left undisturbed, but their value is taken into account by the court ordering that the other party receive on divorce as compensation an appropriately enlarged share of the parties' other assets.[45] Thus:—

> In *Richardson v. Richardson*[46] the husband would, on retiring from the civil service some three years later, be entitled to a substantial pension and lump sum; and if the wife survived her husband she would have been entitled to a widow's pension. It was not possible to vary the terms of the pension; but the court decided to make an enhanced lump sum order in favour of the wife (which the husband could pay out of other capital) to compensate her for the loss of her expectations both in her own right and as a person who would have expected to share in the husband's assets.

Notwithstanding the availability of other statutory powers operating specifically upon pension arrangements, this remains an attractive option because of its simplicity and finality, and is likely to continue to be widely used. However, its crucial limitation is that it is wholly dependent on the availability of other free capital.[47]

---

[43] [1998] 1 F.L.R. 1072.

[44] See *Brooks v. Brooks* [1995] 2 F.L.R. 13 at 17, *per* Lord Nicholls of Birkenhead.

[45] "This compensatory approach suffers from the drawbacks that it is difficult to compare the value of pension rights, with their favourable tax treatment, and the value of non-pension rights subject to different tax treatment; unlike non-pension assets, pension values do not represent immediately available cash, so that typically a wife may finish up with the house and no pension, and the husband with a pension but no money for the time being; and this method cannot work if there are inadequate non-pension assets": *Brooks v. Brooks* [1995] 2 F.L.R. 13 at 17, *per* Lord Nicholls of Birkenhead.

[46] (1978) 9 *Fam. Law* 86.

[47] For an illustration of the previous limitations on the court's powers in this context, see *K v. K (Financial Relief: Widow's Pension)* [1997] 2 F.L.R. 35

(b) Attachment orders

14–102 Attachment (formerly known as "earmarking") was introduced[48] by the Pensions Act 1995[49] and elaborated by the Welfare Reform and Pensions Act 1999[50] and is governed by sections 25B to 25D of the Matrimonial Causes Act 1973 as amended. Attachment is an order made under the court's power conferred by section 23 on divorce or nullity and will take the form of an order for periodic payments (whether deferred or not) or a deferred lump sum. It is not a separate power, but rather a method of enforcing a periodic payments or lump sum order against the pension. In essence an attachment order requires the persons responsible for the pension arrangement (*i.e.* the fund manager or trustee), once the pension becomes payable, to pay the sums involved direct to the spouse concerned.[51] An attachment order must be specifically applied for.[52] Attachment and pension-sharing orders (discussed below) cannot be made in respect of the same pension arrangement.[53] The amount to be attached is to be expressed in percentage terms.[54] An attachment order is variable, and this includes an order for a deferred lump sum.[55] It remains to be seen how the power of variation will be exercised in relation to deferred lump sums.[56]

As Singer J. emphasised in *T v. T (Financial Relief: Pensions*[57]), the court is under no obligation to make an order relating to a pension arrangement, nor do the statutory provisions create an automatic entitlement to compensation for loss of benefit . The court has a discretion as to whether it is appropriate to make an order in respect of a pension and the power to make an attachment order is simply part of the ancillary relief exercise. The disadvantages of attachment orders (inconsistency with the "clean break" objective, and their highly specu-

---

[48] For earlier similar practice, see *Milne v. Milne* (1981) F.L.R. 286. Courts were formerly reluctant to make orders deferred for more than a comparatively short period such as two or three years: *Morris v. Morris* [1977] *Fam. Law* 244, CA; *Roberts v. Roberts* [1986] 2 F.L.R. 152; *Michael v. Michael* [1986] 2 F.L.R. 389; *Davies v. Davies* [1986] 1 F.L.R. 497; *Ranson v. Ranson* [1988] 1 F.L.R. 292. This reluctance was founded in the belief that any substantial deferral would be inconsistent with the "clean break" policy whereby financial matters were adjusted once and for all on divorce. Another objection to any substantial deferral was that such orders constituted a "hostage to fortune" since there might be dramatic unforseen changes of circumstance (perhaps one party's serious illness or long term disablement) which would make the terms of the order operate harshly: see *Legrove v. Legrove* [1994] 2 F.L.R. 119 at 120, *per* Waite L.J.

[49] s. 166.

[50] ss. 21 and 22 and Sched. 4.The power was made available where a petition for divorce or nullity was filed after July 1, 1996 and in respect of applications made on or after August 1, 1996.

[51] M.C.A. 1973, s.25B(4)–(6). The legislation also contains provisions empowering the court (i) to include in its order a direction to one spouse to commute all or part of the pension rights (for example, to provide a pension for the other spouse): see s.25B(7); (ii) power to include in a lump sum order a direction that trustees with a discretion as to the recipient of benefits should pay those benefits to the other spouse: s.25C(2)(a); (iii) power to require a pensioner to exercise any power to nominate the other spouse as beneficiary: s.25C(2)(b); and in other cases to pay a lump sum due under the scheme to one spouse to the other: s.25C(2)(c).

[52] Family Proceedings (Amendment No 2) Rules 1996, S.I. 1996 No. 1674, r. 3; F.P.R. 1991, r. 2.6(1A)(3).

[53] M.C.A. 1973, ss 24B(5), 25B(7B), inserted by W.R.P.A. 1999, Sched. 4, para. 1.

[54] M.C.A. 1973, s. 25B(5).

[55] Under M.C.A. 1973, s.31(2)(dd).

[56] R. Bird, *Ancillary Relief Handbook* (3rd ed., 2002) p. 108.

[57] [1998] 1 F.L.R. 1072.

lative nature) had earlier been cogently summarised by Lord Nicholls of Birkenhead in *Brooks v. Brooks*.[58] Since their introduction in 1996, attachment orders have not proved popular in practice (save where the spouse entitled to the pension is close to retirement or has already retired) and the case-law is very limited. In *T v. T (Financial Relief: Pensions)*[59] Singer J. declined to make an order in the wife's favour for deferred periodical payments from the husband's pension. Looking at all the section 25 considerations, she was immediately to receive by way of ancillary relief a substantial lump sum and, periodic payments which would be capable of variation. Retirement was a long way off and there were, consequently, uncertainties. However, an attachment order relating to the husband's death-in-service benefits was used to protect the wife against the termination of her maintenance stream in the event of his dying prior to retirement. In *Burrow v. Burrow*[60] Cazalet J. drew a distinction between the lump sum and annuity components of an attachment order made by a district judge; the former (whereby the wife was entitled to 50 per cent) but not the latter was upheld. Once again the future uncertainties inherent in the making of an attachment order in respect of the annuity component were highlighted. Cazalet J. appeared to apply an entitlement approach to the wife's claim to earmarking of the capital component of the pension, based on her contributions which were relevant under section 25(2)(f).

(c) Sharing the pension[61]

14–103 In many cases, the most equitable[62] method of dealing with a substantial pension fund is to "split" or "share" it between the spouses by court order at the time of divorce or nullity decree. Under the Conservative Government, the principle of pension-sharing was (albeit reluctantly[63]) first expressed in section 16 of the Family Law Act 1996, but that particular statutory provision was widely recognised as unsatisfactory[64] and was never brought into force.[65] Both Green[66] and White[67] Papers further explored and endorsed the principle of pension-sharing, and the Labour Government took up the consultation process in

---

[58] [1995] 2 F.L.R. 13 at 17.
[59] [1998] 1 F.L.R. 1073.
[60] [1999] 1 F.L.R. 508.
[61] For detailed discussions, see R. Ellison and M. Rae, *Family Breakdown and Pensions* (Butterworths, 2nd ed., 2001); R. Bird, "Pension Sharing" [2000] *Fam. Law* 455; R. Bird, *Pension-Sharing: The New Law* (Family Law, 1999); National Association of Pension Funds *Pension Sharing on Divorce* (2001); D. Salter, "A Practitioner's Guide to Pension-Sharing: Parts I, II and III" [2000] *Fam. Law* 489, 543 and 914; Brindley, "An Actuary's View of Pension-Sharing : Parts I and II" [2000] *Fam. Law* 845, 918; R. Bird, *Ancillary Relief Handbook* (Family Law, 3rd ed., 2002), Chap. 10; Salter, "The Pitfalls of Pension-Sharing" [2002] *Fam. Law* 598.
[62] For the administrative burdens involved, see *Brooks v. Brooks* [1995] 2 F.L.R. 13 at 17, *per* Lord Nicholls of Birkenhead.
[63] *Official Report* H.L. February 29, 1996.
[64] *Official Report* H.L. June 27, 1996, col 1090.
[65] It was eventually repealed by Sched. 13 of the W.R.P.A. 1999.
[66] *The Treatment of Pension Rights on Divorce* Cm. 3345 (1996).
[67] *The Treatment of Pension Rights on Divorce* Cm. 3564 (1996).

1998.[68] The result was the Welfare Reform and Pensions Act 1999, the relevant provisions (amending Part II of the Matrimonial Causes Act 1973) of which came into operation on December 1, 2000.[69] In addition there is a substantial body of detailed regulations.[70] The new provisions increase the range of the court's available powers in relation to pension arrangements (by adding pension-sharing to off-setting and attachment), but do not affect the existence or exercise of the broad discretion in relation to ancillary relief.[71] The courts no longer have power to make a *Brooks v. Brooks*[72] order under section 24(1)(c) of the Matrimonial Causes Act 1973.[73]

Orders that can be made

14–104 A pension-sharing order is defined in section 21A(1) of the Matrimonial Causes Act 1973[74] as an order which—

(a) provides that one party's—

(i) shareable rights under the specified pension arrangement, or
(ii) shareable state scheme rights,

be subject to pension-sharing for the benefit of the other party, and
(b) specifies the percentages to be transferred.

"Pension arrangement" is widely defined[75] so as to cover most private pensions: an occupational pension scheme, a personal pension scheme, a retirement annuity contract, an annuity or insurance policy transferred to give effects to rights under the abovementioned schemes, and an annuity to discharge liability under section 29 of the Welfare Reform and Pensions Reform Act 1999. The state scheme rights which may be shared are more limited[76]: the earnings-related

---

[68] *Pension Sharing on Divorce: Reforming Pensions for a Fairer Future* (1998).

[69] Welfare Reform and Pensions Act 1999, s. 85(2)(a); Welfare Reform and Pensions Act 1999 (Commencement No. 5) Order 2000 (S.I. 2000 No. 1116). The pension-sharing provisions were contained in Parts III and IV of and Scheds 3 to 6 of the W.R.P.A. 1999. See Bird [2000] *Fam. Law* 455; Salter [2000] *Fam. Law* 489; Brindley [2000] *Fam. Law* 918.

[70] Divorce etc (Pensions) Regulations 2000, S.I. 2000 No. 1123; Pensions on Divorce etc (Provision of Information) Regulations 2000, S.I. 2000 No. 1048; Pension Sharing (Implementation and Discharge of Liability) Regulations 2000, S.I. 2000 No. 1053; Pensions on Divorce etc (Charging) Regulations 2000, S.I. 2000 No. 1049; Pension Sharing (Valuation) Regulations 2000, S.I. 2000 No. 1052; Pension Sharing (Pension Credit Benefit) Regulations 2000, S.I. 2000 No. 1054; Pension Sharing (Consequential and Misc. Amendments) Regulations 2000, S.I. 2000 No. 2691; Welfare Reform and Pensions Act 1999 (Commencement Order No. 12) Order 2001, S.I. 2001 No. 4049.

[71] *T v. T (Financial Provision: Pensions)* [1998] 1 F.L.R. 1073.

[72] [1995] 2 F.L.R. 13, discussed at pp. 338–339 above.

[73] See M.C.A., s.24(1)(c) and (d) as amended by the W.R.P.A. 1999 s.19 and Sched. 3. It is still possible to apply for a *Brooks* order where the petition was issued before December 1, 2000: W.R.P.A. s.85(4).

[74] As inserted by W.R.P.A. s.19 and Sched. 3.

[75] W.R.P.A. 1996, s.26(1).

[76] *ibid.* s.47(2).

additional pension[77] and the shared additional pension.[78] The basic state pension cannot be shared. Pension sharing orders are available in respect of "shareable rights" in pension arrangements as defined[79] in section 27 of the 1999 Act. The public service pension entitlements of the Prime Minister, Treasurer and Speaker of the House of Commons are excepted.[80] In sum, most pension entitlements may be subject of an application for a pension-sharing order.

By virtue of the relevant rule,[81] most petitions will now as a matter of course include a claim for pension-sharing. A pension-sharing order can only be made on a decree of divorce[82] or nullity[83] (not on judicial separation[84]) and it does not take effect until the decree becomes absolute.[85] If an attachment order has already been made in relation to a pension arrangement, no pension-sharing order may be made.[86] More than one pension sharing order may be made in relation to a marriage,[87] but if a pension-sharing order has already been made in relation to a pension arrangement or state scheme, no further pension sharing order can be made in relation to that arrangement or scheme.[88]

The power to make a pension-sharing order is available only in respect of petitions filed after December 1, 2000. In *S v. S (Recission of Decree Nisi: Pension-Sharing Provision)*[89] Singer J. made an important ruling on a practical matter which had previously been controversial: could the time-bar be avoided by recission of a decree nisi, and if so in what circumstances, or would this be an abuse of process on public policy grounds? The court rescinded the decree nisi and gave leave to present another petition, in circumstances where the proposed step was by consent and both parties desired the one outcome in respect of pension-sharing, and where no issues involving children or the dismissal of maintenance claims were involved. This decision did not determine the issue where an application for recission is contested[90]; and the further of question whether the time bar can be avoided by issue of a second petition remains open.

---

[77] Social Security Contributions and Benefits Act 1992, s.44(3)

[78] *ibid.* s.55A.

[79] All rights under a pension arrangement, save those excluded by the Pension Sharing (Valuation) Regulations 2000 (S.I. 2000 No. 1052).

[80] Pension Sharing (Excepted Schemes) Order 2001 (S.I. 2001 No. 358)

[81] Family Proceedings Rules 1991 (S.I. 1991 No. 1247) as amended, r. 2.53(1)(d), prescribing Form A.

[82] Including an overseas divorce: W.R.P.A. 1999, s.22, amending the Matrimonial and Family Proceedings Act 1984.

[83] Where the petition was filed after December 1, 2000; see Glover, "Pension-Sharing Procedure" [2001] *Fam. Law* 691; *S v. S (Recission of Decree Nisi: Pension-Sharing Provision)* [2002] 1 F.L.R. 457.

[84] M.C.A., s.24B(1), as amended by the W.R.P.A. 1999, Sched. 3, para. 4.

[85] M.C.A., s.24B(2), similarly amended.

[86] M.C.A., s.24B(5) as similarly amended.

[87] M.C.A. 1973, s.24B(1).

[88] M.C.A. 1973, s.24B(3) and (4).

[89] [2002] 1 F.L.R. 457.

[90] D. Salter, "A Practitioner's Guide To Pension-Sharing, Part 3" [2000] *Fam. Law* 914; S. Glover, "Pension-Sharing Procedure" [2001] *Fam. Law* 691. In *H v. H (Pension Sharing: Recission of Decree Nisi)* [2002] EWHC Fam. 767; [2002] 2 F.L.R. 116, Bodey J. held that the *decree nisi* should not be rescinded where the issue is disputed.

The effect of a pension-sharing order

14–105 The essence of pension sharing is the system of pension credit and pension debit.[91] The effect of a pension sharing order is to credit the transferee with a percentage[92] of the transferor's pension arrangement, which is reduced accordingly.[93] For occupational and personal pensions, that percentage is a percentage of the CETV[94] of the transferor's benefit at the relevant date.[95] The transferee is thereby given not cash but an occupational or personal pension of her own. Putting the matter at its simplest,[96] the transferee normally has the choice whether to become a member of the original scheme or (subject to certain exceptions and modifications for unfunded public arrangements[97]) to have the fund transferred into a different arrangement[98] (which could be one in which she already has entitlements). There are Inland Revenue limitations on the extent to which the transferor can rebuild his pension fund. There is a four month[99] implementation period giving the trustees or fund managers time to make the necessary arrangements for transferring the funds. Where a state pension is shared, the effect of the pension credit is to give the transferee an additional pension.[1]

The exercise of the court's discretion

14–106 It is worth repeating that the exercise of court's power to make a pension-sharing order is governed by the broad discretion conferred by section 25 of the Matrimonial Causes Act 1973, and that pension entitlements are not to be seen in isolation from the overall pool of assets on which that discretion operates. The objective implicit in section 25 is that of achieving a fair outcome.[2]

The court is not obliged to make any order in relation to pensions,[3] and to do so may or may not be necessary or desirable, depending entirely on the circum-

---

[91] W.R.P.A. 1999, s.29.

[92] M.C.A. 1973, s.21A(1)(b).

[93] W.R.P.A. 1999, s.29(1) (private pensions); s 49(1) (state pension).

[94] W.R.P.A. 1999 s.30; Pension Sharing (Valuation) Regulations 2000, S.I. 2000 No. 1052.

[95] W.R.P.A. 1999, s.29(2), (4), (5); To be determined by the court, but no more than one year prior to the petition and no later than the date on which the court makes the order: Divorce etc (Pensions) Regulations 2000, reg. 3(1)(a) and (b). Benefits must be calculated as set out in reg. 3 of the Pensions on Divorce (Provision of Information) Regulations 2000.

[96] The details are contained in W.R.P.A. 1999, Sched. 5; for a full account, see R. Bird, *Ancillary Relief Handbook* (Family Law, 3rd ed., 2002) pp. 116–119.

[97] W.R.P.A. 1999, Sched. 5 paras 2, 3.

[98] W.R.P.A. 1999, Sched. 5, para. 1(3).

[99] W.R.P.A. 1999, s.34. It runs from the date when the order takes effect or that on which the prescribed information was received, whichever is later: Pensions on Divorce (Provision of Information) Regulations 2000, reg. 5. On failure to discharge liabilty in time, see W.R.P.A. s.33 and the Pension Sharing (Implementation and Discharge of Liabilty) Regulations 2000, S.I. 2000 No. 1053.

[1] W.R.P.A. 1999, s.49(1) and Sched. 6, inserting a new s.45B into the Social Security Contributions and Benefits Act 1992.

[2] *Piglowska v. Piglowski* [1999] 2 F.L.R. 763; *White v White* [2000] 2 F.L.R. 98; *Cowan v. Cowan* [2001] 2 F.L.R. 192; *Cordle v. Cordle* [2001] EWCA Civ. 1791 [2002] 1 F.L.R. 207.

[3] *T v. T (Financial Relief: Pensions)* [1998] 1 F.L.R. 1073.

stances and in the light of orders that can be made in respect of other assets.[4] Pension-sharing orders are likely to be most useful where there are few other assets or where there are liquidity problems. It is at the time of writing too early for any pattern to have emerged in the case-law. It may be that the "entitlement approach" derived from the decision in *White v. White*[5] may make claims to pension-sharing in big money cases somewhat easier to establish than if the reasonable requirements ceiling on awards had remained good law; a pension is to be treated as a capital asset (to which entitlement based on contribution may be claimed) and not as future income.[6] If the court decides to make a pension-sharing order, the percentage of the shares are entirely a matter for the court's discretion in the light of all the circumstances.

The Statutory Charge and Orders in Relation to Pensions

14–107 As we have seen, the statutory charge in favour of the Legal Services Commission operates on "property recovered or preserved" for a funded individual in ancillary relief proceedings.[7] There has been considerable debate and uncertainty concerning the effect of the statutory charge on orders in relation to pensions. The annuity component of an attachment order—unlike a capital(lump sum) component —does not attract the charge, being merely an order for periodical payments. Whether the rights divided between the parties under a pension sharing order come within the definition of "property" and attract the statutory charge, and if so, when, has been a matter of some debate.[8] The revised view of the Legal Services Commission is that any property recovered or preserved under a pension sharing or attachment order is exempt, apart from a lump sum payable under an attachment order.[9] If the charge can apply to a pension fund, the Legal Services Commission will apply it first to other assets of the client.[10]

IV. THE FINANCIAL CONSEQUENCES OF MARITAL BREAKDOWN: CONCLUSION

14–108 Few would argue that the law governing the financial consequences of marital breakdown is in a wholly satisfactory state, but it is not easy to identify solutions to the apparent problems. One of the major issues is the difficulty of steering between the Scylla of too wide a discretion (inevitably involving a degree of diversity in judicial application, unpredictability of outcome[11] and high costs in

---

[4] For a comparison of the various remedies available to the courts in relation to pensions, see R. Bird, *Ancillary Relief Handbook* (Family Law, 3rd ed., 2002), pp. 121–124.

[5] [2000] 2 F.L.R. 981.

[6] Brindley, "Black and White in Pensions" [2001] *Fam. Law* 462.

[7] Access to Justice Act 1999, s. 10(7).

[8] D. Burrows "Pension Orders and the Statutory Charge" [2001] *Fam. Law* 204; S. Wagstaffe, "Pension-Sharing and The Statutory Charge" [2001] *Fam. Law* 624.

[9] D. Salter, [2002] *Fam. Law* 598 at 602.

[10] Guidance on the effect of the statutory charge on pension attachment and pension sharing orders, para. 20.

[11] *Piglowska v. Piglowski* [1999] 2 F.L.R. 767 at 783 *per* Lord Hoffmann.

cases involving protracted litigation, as well as difficulties for practitioners in offering advice to clients) and the Charybdis of a too rigid a statutory formulation of principle (potentially productive both of injustice in the individual case and of increased litigation in rebuttal or by way of exception). But even if agreement could be reached on the desirability of legislative expression of clearer—and universally applicable—principles to govern ancillary relief, it would still be necessary to decide what the precise content of those principles should be.[12] This involves complex issues of social policy on which there is a plurality of views within the community.[13] What should replace the very general overarching objective of achieving a fair outcome[14]? Some possible grounds for an ancillary relief award are needs, expectations, compensation, entitlements built up by contributions to family welfare, and equalisation of the economic effects of the marriage.[15] Is the predominant community view that marriage is a truly equal partnership, different contributions to which should be given equal recognition on divorce in terms of ancillary relief outcome, or does a significant sector of the population still value the business entrepreneur above the home-maker and parent? If equality of recognition in terms of outcome is to be the goal, can it ever be realised outside the model of a community of property system familiar in civil law systems?

No clear views have emerged in response to these difficult questions in recent years. In 1998 the Lord Chancellor's Advisory Group on Ancillary Relief recommended[16] against introducing the principles of Scottish law[17] into the Matrimonial Causes Act 1973; the changes in social policy would have been far greater than perhaps contemplated by the Lord Chancellor when referring the question to the Group. Some recommendations for further structuring the exercise of judicial discretion through clearer articulation of objectives were made in the Green Paper *Supporting Families*[18] but a White Paper was never published[19] and the proposals (which in any event lacked rigour of analysis) have apparently now been dropped. The continuation of the status quo has received both support[20] and criticism.[21]

---

12 *Dividing the Assets on Family Breakdown,* R Bailey-Harris ed. (Family Law, 1998), Introduction.

13 *ibid.*

14 *Piglowska v. Piglowski* [1999] 2 F.L.R. 767, HL; *White v. White* [2001] 1 A.C. 596; HL; [2000] 2 F.L.R. 981; *Cowan v. Cowan* [2001] 2 F.L.R 192, CA; *C v. C* [2001] EWCA Civ. 1791; [2002] 1 F.L.R. 207.

15 R. Bailey-Harris "Dividing the Assets on Family Breakdown: the Content of Fairness" [2001] *Current Legal Problems* 533 at 535.

16 Report of the Lord Chancellor's Advisory Group on Ancillary Relief, L.C.D., July 1998.

17 For the law of Scotland, see the Family Law (Scotland) Act 1985, ss.9–10; E.M. Clive, *The Law of Husband and Wife in Scotland* (3rd ed., 1992), Chap. 24

18 H.M.S. 1998, paras 4.47–4.49.

19 The summary of responses to the Green Paper published in June 1999 reported at para. 4.19 that relatively few had responded on the ancillary relief question but that the majority who did were in favour of the Government's proposals.

20 S. Thorpe L.J. "The English System of Ancillary Relief", Chap. 1 in *Dividing the assets on Family Breakdown* R. Bailey-Harris, ed. (Family Law, 1998); S. Cretney, "Trusting the Judges: Money After Divorce" (1999) 52 *Current Legal Problems* 286.

21 J. Eekelaar "Should Section 25 Be Reformed?" [1998] *Fam. Law* 46; Cleverley, "An Opportunity Missed?" [1999] *Fam. Law* 326.

The decision of the House of Lords in *White v. White*[22] has, to judge by the ensuing case-law described earlier in this Chapter, singularly failed as yet to achieve the objectives either of injecting greater certainty into professional practice or of effecting a universal policy change towards recognition of marriage as an equal partnership. In *W H-J v. W H-J*[23]:

> "This is an area of jurisprudence which (as I am being polite) I will refer to as being in a state of considerable flux and uncertainty".

The unsatisfactory state of the present law has led commentators[24] to doubt the capacity of section 25 in its current form, and of judicial glosses thereon, to achieve the objectives of certainty and equality. The call for legislative reform has now been taken up by certain members of the judiciary.[25] But it seems unlikely that the Government will of its own initiative instigate a process of law reform, considered or otherwise, in the forseeable future. It thus seems inevitable that it will be left to the case-law to work out over time the implications of *White v. White*.[26] However, the substance of domestic law may eventually be changed by the European Commission if a third Brussels Convention dealing with harmonisation of financial provision laws throughout the European Community ever becomes a reality.[27]

---

22 [2001] 1 A.C. 596; [2000] 2 F.L.R. 981.

23 [2002] 1 F.L.R. 415 at 417

24 S. Cretney [2001] *Fam. Law* 3, R. Bailey-Harris [2001] *Fam. Law* 12; R. Bailey-Harris, "Dividing the Assets on Family Breakdown: The Content of Fairness" [2001] *Current Legal Problems* 533; J. Eekelaar, "Back to Basics and Forward into the Unknown" [2001 *Fam. Law* 30.

25 Thorpe L.J. and Robert Walker L.J. in *Cowan v. Cowan* [2001] 2 F.L.R. 192.

26 [2001] 1 A.C. 596; [2000] 2 F.L.R. 981.

27 D. Hodson, "Brussels III: Financial Provision. The Next Generation" [2002] *Fam. Law* 30.

Part IV

CHILD SUPPORT OBLIGATIONS

CHAPTER FIFTEEN

CHILD SUPPORT

I. INTRODUCTION

15–001 Child support raises "deeply complex issues of morality and social organisation".[1] Those issues include the origin of the parental responsibility (biological or social), priorities between first and second families and between children and adult dependants, and the respective responsibilities between individuals and the State. Not surprisingly, the law's response has varied over time according to the prevailing political, social and economic climate.[2]

Historically the law did little to ensure that children were properly maintained by their parents, in part because of the reluctance to pierce the veil of privacy surrounding the family. It is true that the common law imposed on the father a duty to maintain his legitimate[3] children, but the duty was unenforceable.[4] The only effective[5] procedure for compelling fathers to provide for their children was through the agency of the poor law[6] which required parents to reimburse the cost of providing relief for their offspring. However, financial orders were increasingly made available in divorce[7]; and legislation enacted in 1878[8] gave the magistrates' courts power to make a separation, custody and maintenance order. As part of the divorce reform package embodied in the Divorce Reform

---

[1] J. Eekelaar, *Regulating Divorce* (Oxford, Clarendon Press, 1986), p. 91.

[2] J. Eekelaar and M. Maclean, *Maintenance After Divorce* (Oxford, 1986) p. 107ff; J. Eekelaar, *Regulating Divorce* (Oxford, Clarendon Press, 1990), pp. 103–111.

[3] There was no duty on a father at common law to maintain an illegitimate child, but the Poor Law Amendment Act 1844 gave the mother a right to obtain a maintenance order against the father which could remain in force until the child was 13.

[4] "The strange state of our law is that there may be a so-called common law duty to maintain, but when one analyses what that duty is it seems effectively to come to nothing. Like so many rights, the right extends only so far as the remedy to enforce it extends . . . the common law has no remedy. The remedies to enforce a duty to maintain are the statutory remedies which are variously laid down in numerous statutes", *per* Ward J., *Re C (A Minor) (Contribution Notice)* [1994] 1 F.L.R. 111 at 116. For the scope of the common law duty, see *Mortimore v. Wright* (1840) 6 M. & W. 482; *Bazeley v. Forder* (1868) L.R. 3 Q.B. 559.

[5] At least in the sense of imposing a legal obligation. In practice, enforcement procedures often resulted in the defaulter's imprisonment rather than in his complying with his obligations: see "History of the Obligation to Maintain" by M. Finer and O.R. McGregor published as App. 5 to the Report of the Committee on One-Parent Families (Cmnd. 5629 (1974)) Table 2, p. 104.

[6] The Statute of Elizabeth 1601, s.6, imposed penalties for failure to maintain; and the authorities would seek to reclaim expenditure incurred. See generally (1955) 18 *M.L.R.* 114; and "The History of the Obligation to Maintain" by M. Finer and O.R. McGregor published as App. 5 to the Report of the Committee on One-Parent Families (Cmnd. 5629 (1974)).

[7] Matrimonial Causes Act 1857, s.45, conferred a restricted power to order settlements for children of the marriage; and the courts' powers were extended over the years.

[8] Matrimonial Causes Act 1878.

Act 1969[9] the divorce court's[10] powers were greatly extended and the court could make orders for financial provision and property adjustment in respect of children of the family.[11] Finally, the Matrimonial and Family Proceedings Act 1984[12] directed the court to give "first consideration" to the welfare while a minor of any child of the family who had not attained the age of 18 when considering whether and how to exercise those powers. The statute book thus provided machinery whereby the courts could make orders intended to ensure comprehensive financial support for children; yet in practice this machinery did not operate satisfactorily. Moreover, as has been seen, lawyers began to develop techniques to maximise the availability of welfare benefit support in cases of relationship breakdown; and the increasing burden became difficult to sustain—particularly for the Thatcher Government in power at the time, committed as it was to reducing reliance on state provision.

The 1990s brought a radical new approach[13] to child support, the essential conception of which has survived sustained criticisms over a decade, albeit with increasingly substantial modifications of its details. The genesis of the new system was the White Paper *Children Come First*[14] published in 1990, which offered the following diagnosis of the problems with the law as it then stood:

> "The present system of maintenance is unnecessarily fragmented, uncertain in its results, slow and ineffective. It is based largely on discretion . . . The cumulative effect is uncertainty and inconsistent decisions about how much maintenance should be paid. In a great many instances, the maintenance awarded is not paid or the payments fall into arrears and take weeks to re-establish."

15–002 The Government[15] considered that parents had a clear moral duty to maintain their children until they were old enough to look after themselves; and that although events might change the relationship between the parents they could

---

[9] The financial component of the "package" was the Matrimonial Proceedings and Property Act 1970. All relevant provisions were subsequently consolidated in the Matrimonial Causes Act 1973.

[10] The powers of magistrates' courts were extended by the Domestic Proceedings and Magistrates' Courts Act 1978, but remained comparatively restricted.

[11] The Family Law Reform Act 1987 gave comparable powers to make orders against parents and step-parents in proceedings instituted for that purpose; and those powers are now embodied in Children Act 1989, Sched. 1.

[12] See now M.C.A. 1973, s.25(1).

[13] Described as the most far-reaching social reforms to be made for 40 years by the House of Commons Social Security Committee, First Report, *The Operation of the Child Support Act*, First Report, Session 1993-4 H.C. 69.

[14] *Children Come First* (Cm. 1263).

[15] Under the forceful leadership of the Prime Minister, Margaret Thatcher, who subsequently wrote: "I was . . . appalled by the way in which men fathered a child and then absconded, leaving the single mother—and the taxpayer—to foot the bill for their irresponsibility and condemning the child to a lower standard of living. I thought it scandalous that only one in three children entitled to receive maintenance actually benefitted from regular payments. So—against considerable opposition from Tony Newton, the Social Security Secretary, and from the Lord Chancellor's department—I insisted that a new Child Support Agency be set up, and that maintenance be based not just on the cost of bringing up a child but on that child's right to share in its parents' rising living standards." (M. Thatcher, *The Downing Street Years*, 1995, p. 630)

not change the parents' responsibilities towards their children.[16] The emphasis was thus on individual responsibility, consistent with a predominant political culture[17] which has persisted into the present century, a change of government notwithstanding, and *Children Come First* was forceful in asserting the moral child support obligation of parents.[18] The Child Support Act 1991—which received all-party support[19]—was enacted in an attempt to give effect to this philosophy. At one level, the objective was to change a culture "in which it had become commonplace for maintenance to be regarded as optional and to ensure that regular and realistic maintenance was paid"[20]: but there was also a second objective which involved a major ideological shift. A corollary of the ideology of increased individual responsibility is a reduced role for the state in family matters. In the words of the House of Commons Social Security Committee,[21] the legislation "at long last challenged" what had become the common assumption—exemplified by the "welfare benefit divorce"—that the state (or taxpayers) should assume financial responsibility for the first family when a marriage or partnership broke down. Henceforth, the obligation of the state was to be limited to providing assistance in genuine cases where the natural parents' resources were insufficient to support their children.

The aims of the new system were clearly stated in *Children Come First*[22]; it is worth setting them out, as the yardstick against which the actual operation of the system may be evaluated:

— To enforce parents' support obligations effectively, cheaply and quickly
— To provide a scheme of universal application accessible to all
— To introduce certainty and predictability into the assessment of child support, reduce arbitrariness, and fix amounts which realistically reflect child-care costs
— To reduce the potential for inter-parental conflict
— To reduce dependency on social security and costs to the taxpayer.

To achieve these objectives, a fundamental change in technique was proposed. The legal system, dealing on a case by case discretionary basis with the assessment of child maintenance, was to be supplanted by an administrative system (originally intended to be, in time, of universal application) which would assess all maintenance according to uniform criteria. The Child Support Act 1991 lays

---

[16] *Children Come First,* foreword.

[17] Contrast the ethos of collective responsibility which some 15 years earlier underpinned the *Report of the Committee on One-Parent Families* (Cmnd. 5629), 1974 (the "Finer Report"); see D. Burrows "Anyone Remember Finer?" [1998] *Fam. Law* 699.

[18] *Children Come First,* para. 2.1.

[19] And the approval of the House of Commons Social Security Committee: see H.C. 277-I (1990-1991) and H.C. 277-II.

[20] Mrs R. Hepplewhite, then Chief Executive of the Child Support Agency, introducing the Agency's 1993/4 Annual Report and 1994/5 Business Plan, Child Support Agency, The First Two Years on July 4, 1994.

[21] House of Commons Social Security Committee, *The Operation of the Child Support Act,* First Report, Session 1993-4 H.C. 69, para. 3.

[22] *Children Come First,* para. 2.1

down a formula[23] whereby the liability of parents in respect of their children's maintenance is to be met. The Act imposes responsibilities and confers powers on the Secretary of State; a Minister is thus responsible to Parliament for the Act's administration. However, all decisions, determinations and calculations concerning child support under the Act can be made by officers acting under the Secretary of State's authority, namely officers of the Child Support Agency. Other key features of the legislation are the wide powers in respect of the obtaining of information[24] conferred on officials charged with the administration of the scheme, and wide powers of collection and enforcement.

15–003 From the outset the scheme proved deeply controversial and throughout its history has received sustained criticism from the public,[25] the media,[26] professional[27] and official sources[28] alike. It is not possible in a book of this nature to

---

23 The details of which have been substantially modified over time, as explained below.

24 The Child Support Act 1991 (see notably ss.4(4), 6(9) and 14) and Regulations (Child Support (Information, Evidence and Disclosure) Regulations 1992, S.I. 1992 No. 1812, as amended by the Child Support (Information, Evidence and Disclosure and Maintenance Arrangements and Jurisdiction) (Amendment) Regulations 2000, S.I. 2001 No 161) give the Secretary of State extensive power to require a non-resident parent and a person with care to provide information on a wide range of matters to enable the absent parent to be identified and the maintenance determination made. There are also powers to require employers, local authorities and others to give information. Non-compliance is a criminal offence: Child Support Act 1991, s. 14A, inserted by the CSPSSA 2000, s. 13. Inspectors may be appointed (they are CSA officers) who have power to enter at any reasonable time specified premises (other than premises used solely as a dwelling house) and which the inspector has reasonable grounds for suspecting are premises at which the non-resident parent is or has been employed or carries out a trade profession or business, or where another person holds information about the non-resident parent in the course of trade, profession or business. Under s. 15 (as amended by the Social Security Act 1998, s. 86(1), Sched. 7, para. 28 and the CSPSSA 2000, s. 14(2)–(4), any such person is required to furnish the inspector with all such documents as reasonably required, and it is a criminal offence intentionally to delay or obstruct any inspector exercising those powers, or (without reasonable excuse) to refuse or neglect to answer any question or furnish any information or produce any document which is required under the provisions of the Child Support Act. The child support authorities may obtain information from the Inland Revenue in order to trace the current address of an absent parent or the current employer of an absent parent.

25 R. Collier, "The Campaign Against the CSA" [1994] *Fam. Law* 384. Members of Parliament evidently received many complaints from constituents, and the Child Support Agency established a Parliamentary Business Unit expressly to deal with inquiries from Members of Parliament.

26 The headline "Child agency blamed after man's suicide" was not untypical of the more restrained broadsheet coverage following the Act's implementation: *The Times,* December 7, 1993.

27 Amongst the many commentaries critically assessing the objectives and operation of the legislation through successive amendments, the following may be found particularly helpful: C.S. Gibson, "The Future for Maintenance" [1991] C.J.Q. 330; M. Maclean and J. Eekelaar, "Child Support: the British Solution" (1993) 7 *IJL&F* 205; M. Maclean, "Child Support in the UK: Making the Move from Court to Agency" (1994) *Houston L. Rev.* 515; R. Cockfield and M. Mulholland, "Child Tax" in D. Lockton (ed.) *Children and the Law* (1994) discuss the relationship between child support and taxation and other policy; A. Garnham and E. Knights Putting the Treasury First, (C.P.A.G., 1994); M. Horton, "Improving Child Support—a missed opportunity" [1995] *C.F.L.Q.* 26. K Clarke, G. Craig and C. Glendinning, *Losing Support: Children and the Child Support Act* (The Children's Society, London, 1994); C. Glendinning, K. Clarke and G. Craig, "The Impact of the Child Support Act on lone mothers and their children" (1995) 7 *Journal of Child Law* No. 1, p. 18; Horton (1995) 7 CFLQ 26; Deas (1996) *Fam. Law* 112; Gillespie [1996] *Fam. Law* 274; J. Millar "Family Obligations and Social Policy: The Case of Child Support" (1996) 17 *Policy Studies* 181; J Priest, "Child Support and the Non-Standard Earner" (1997) 9 CFLQ 63; G. Davis, N. Wikeley and R. Young, *Child Support in Action* (Hart Publishing, 1998). For comparative material reference may be made to the material in Part IV of *Economic Consequences of Divorce, The International Perspective* L.J. Weitzman and M. Maclean (ed., 1992) (and in particular the paper by M. Harrison, "Child Maintenance in Australia,

provide a comprehensive analysis of the criticisms, but they may be summarised as follows. First, the process of policy formation was deeply flawed: successive governments have given little weight to the advice of those with knowledge of the working of the maintenance process on many of the problems inherent in the new system.[29] Secondly, the formula as originally conceived was over-complex and consequently difficult both to understand and to apply, with the result that there were long delays and inaccuracies in assessment. Moreover, the formula's rigidity was perceived as productive of injustice in individual cases, with lack of co-operation by parents[30] and damage to family relationships as the results.[31] Thirdly, the defects in the administration of the system led to the view that the performance of the Child Support Agency represented "a catastrophic administrative failure leading to the abandonment of many of the basic tenets of administrative justice".[32] The Government's confidence in improvements supposedly to be effected by managerial techniques and computer technology (as evidenced by the rhetoric of modern business management used in glossily

---

the New Era," Chap. 10); H. Krause, "Child Support Re-assessed: Limits of Private Responsibility and the Public Interests" (1989) 2 *U. Illinois L.R.* 367; S. Parker, "Child Support in Australia: Children's Rights or Public Interest?" (1991) 5 *IJL&F* 24; J. Pearson, N. Thomas and J. Anhalt, "Child Support in the United States: The Experience in Colorado" (1992) 6 *IJL&F* 321; J.T. Oldham, "Abating the Feminization of Poverty" (1994) 4 *Brigham Young U. L.R.* 841; N. Richardson, "The New Zealand Child Support Act" [1995] *C.F.L.Q.* 40; Rhoades, "Australia's child support scheme: is it working?" (1995) 7 *J.C.L.*, G. Reithmuller, "Amendments to the child support and social security schemes that increase the recognition of step-children" 15 *Australian Journal of Family Law* 178.

[28] .For official reviews, see the Reports by House of Commons Social Security Committee: First Report Session 1993–4, *The Operation of the Child Support Act* H.C. 69; Fifth Report Session 1993–4, *The Operation of the Child Support Act: Proposals for Change* H.C. 470; and (on the administration of the scheme) Second Report from the House of Commons Social Security Committee Session 1995–96, *The Performance and Operation of the Child Support Agency* H.C. 50; the Parliamentary Commissioner for Administration's Third Report Session 1994–5, *Investigation of complaints against the Child Support Agency*, H.C. 135 and the Parliamentary Commissioner for Administration's Third Report Session 1995–96, *Investigation of complaints against the Child Support Agency* H.C. 20. See The Child Support Agency Annual Reports 1994–5 onward (for 1996 see [1996] *Fam. Law* 457; The CSA's chief executive who resigned in 1994 herself admitted failings in the system: "Overall our standards of service did not reach acceptable levels and we did not achieve some of our key targets": Chief Executive's Foreword to the Agency's 1993/4 Annual Report and 1994/5 Business Plan, *Child Support Agency, The First Two Years* (1994). *Child Support Agency: National Client Satisfaction Survey* (DSS Research Report No. 39, M. Speed and J. Seddon, HMSO 1994. National Audit Office *Child Support Agency: Client Funds Account 1999–2000* (H.C. 658, 2000, TSO), para. 1.5.

[29] The Government promised consultation on the details of the scheme in its original form—much of which was left to delegated legislation—and around 100 organisations responded to a 158 page consultation document issued on November 1, 1991. However, neither the submissions nor even a summary was published, nor was any request made by the D.S.S. for further details or clarification of the scheme (see A. Garnham and E. Knights, *Putting the Treasury First* (C.P.A.G., 1994), p. 47); and there was little evidence that the Government had given serious consideration to the problems which the judiciary and practising lawyers had highlighted: see R. Bird, *Child Maintenance, The Child Support Act 1991* (Family Law, 2nd ed., 1993), para. 2.11.There has been continuing criticism of subsequent lack of consultation on proposed legislative change: see *e.g.* the Preface to R. Bird, *Child Support: The New Law* (4th ed., 2000); R. Bird, *Child Support: The New Law* (5th ed., 2002), para. 1.6.

[30] Mrs R. Hepplewhite (introducing the Agency's 1993/4 Annual Report and 1994/5 Business Plan, Child Support Agency, The First Two Years on July 4, 1994).

[31] See Glendinning *et al., supra* n. 27.

[32] Davis *et al., supra* n. 27, p. v.

produced successive Green and White Papers) proved to be sadly misplaced. The administrative machinery was wholly inadequate for the efficient introduction and sustaining of a scheme so ambitious in its original conception, and the Child Support Agency proved increasingly unable to cope with its intended case-load. The result was that the aim of achieving universality for the new system were shelved, and its operation was increasingly confined to cases where the parent in care was in receipt of welfare benefits. Those who were not obliged to use the system sidestepped it[33]; non-benefit cases continued to use the courts to settle child maintenance, and the interface between the two jurisdictions accordingly proved complex. Amongst those on benefits, many single mothers refused to co-operate with the Agency, therefore liable fathers were not identified and maintenance was not in practice collected, and many children in need failed to see increased levels of financial support. Where maintenance was collected by the Child Support Agency, families on benefits were no better off, due to the pound for pound deduction.[34] This in turn removed the incentive to comply with the system. Hence the creation of the Child Support Agency had a claim to be regarded as the worst failure of public administration[35] in this country in the twentieth century.

The response of successive governments to sustained criticisms of the child support system has been two-fold. On the one hand there has been a continuing and consistent assertion that the basic principles underlying the child support system are right and that a formula approach to the determination of child support is appropriate for the great majority of separated parents. On the other hand, changes of an increasingly substantial nature have been made to the details of the system's operation. Those of 1995 amounted essentially to a series of climb-downs as embarrassing for the Government as they have were confusing for professional advisers and for the public. The reforms effected by the Child Support, Pensions and Social Security Act 2000 are more radical in nature, but only time will tell whether official confidence in the modified system proves to be well placed.

Early changes to the original model of child support implemented by the Child Support Act 1991 were introduced by delegated legislation,[36] but more extensive reforms were soon to follow. In January 1995, the Government announced changes to the scheme[37] which were a reaction to criticisms of the rigidity of the formula. Some of the changes were introduced by delegated legislation with effect from April 1995[38]; others required the enactment of primary

---

33 S. Deas, "Family Lawyers Sidestep the CSA" (1998) *Fam. Law* 48.

34 Davis *et al., supra,* n. 27, pp. 220–201; Baroness Hollis, Parliamentary Under-Secretary of State, *Hansard,* H.L. Debate, Vol 612, col 461, April 17, 2001. The child maintenance bonus, introduced in 1995, of £5 per week became payable (as a lump sum) only when the parent with care ceased to receive benefit; it was abolished by s. 23 of the Child Support, Pensions and Social Security Act 2000, s. 23.

35 There are interesting analogies with the failure of the Community Charge (popularly known as the Poll Tax) regime: see D. Butler, A. Adonis, and T. Travers, *Failure in British Government* (1995).

36 The Child Support (Miscellaneous Amendments and Transitional Provisions) Regulations 1994, S.I. 1994 No. 227.

37 *Improving Child Support,* Cm. 2745.

38 The Child Support and Income Support (Amendment) Regulations 1995, S.I. 1995 No. 1045.

legislation.[39] The changes[40] demonstrated a loss of confidence in the capacity of a universally applicable formula to achieve justice for all. The formula was made even more complex by the inclusion of additional elements.[41] A departure system was introduced,[42] with the objective of meeting hardship in individual cases, albeit that the grounds for departure were strictly confined.[43] Arguably, the result of this tranche of reforms was the worst of both worlds: a formula of ever-increasing complexity, onto which was grafted a departure system which in itself was complex. In practice the departure system was little used.[44] The 1995 reforms were criticised as representing a missed opportunity to undertake more radical reform of the formula.[45] Empirical research played an important part in exposing the continuing flaws in the system's operation.[46] Following its election victory in May 1997, the Blair Government showed itself eager to make its mark on reform of the child support system, and embarked upon a process of consultation. A Green Paper *Children First: A New Approach to Child Support*[47] published in 1998 was followed in 1999 by the White Paper *A New Contract for Welfare: Children's Rights and Parents Responsibilities.*[48] The Government emphasised the need for the system to be fair to all three stake-holders: children, parents and the taxpayer. The White Paper set the proposed reforms to the child support system in the wider contexts of welfare reform and "active family policy" and reasserted that parental responsibility endures regardless of family separation,[49] and tersely articulated the stark failures of the child support system to that date:

> "Sadly, in practice child support has not improved the position of children living apart from their parents. The system has failed to deliver regular

---

[39] Child Support Act 1995.

[40] These changes were conveniently summarised in the Parliamentary Commissioner for Administration's Third Report Session 1995–96, *Investigation of Complaints against the Child Support Agency* (H.C. 20, App. 4).

[41] Housing costs for step-children, high travel-to-work costs, capital settlements made prior to the implementation of the Child Support Act 1991.

[42] Child Support Act 1995. The departure system was first piloted on a limited basis and subsequently introduced nationally in 1996. See R. Bird [1996] *Fam. Law* 112; Deas [1996] *Fam. Law* 759

[43] See the discussion later at p. 442 on the current system of variation, which has in name replaced that of departure.

[44] Deas [1996] *Fam. Law* 759; J. Priest, "Departure Directions Under the Child Support Scheme" (1998) 5 *Journal of Social Security Law* 104; N. Wikeley, "Child Support: The New Formula, Part 1" [2000] *Fam. Law* 820.

[45] M. Horton, "Improving Child Support—A Missed Opportunity" (1995) 7 CFLQ 26; J. Pirrie, "Child Support Act 1995" [1995] *Fam. Law* 610; R. Bird, "Child Support: Reform or Tinkering?" (1995) 25 *Fam. Law* 112.

[46] See principally Davis, *et al., Child Support in Action* (Hart Publishing, 1998).

[47] Cm. 3992 (DSS, The Stationery Office, 1998); Knights [1998] *Fam. Law* 606; C. Barton, "Third Time Lucky for Child Support?" [1998] *Fam. Law* 668; SFLA "'The Watery World of Child Support" [1999] *Fam. Law* 72; N. Mostyn [1999] *Fam. Law* 95.

[48] Cm. 4349 (DSS, The Stationery Office, 1999); C. Barton, "Child Support: Tony's Turn" [1999] *Fam. Law* 704; Pirrie, "Changes to Child Support—The SFLA View" [1999] *Fam. Law* 838; "The Social Security Select Committee's Report on the CSA 1998–9" (see [1999] *Fam. Law* 845) contained an evaluation of the White Paper.

[49] *Children's Rights and Parental Responsibilities,* Foreword by the Prime Minister Mr Tony Blair (vii) and (viii), Chap. 1, para. 1, and p. 57.

> maintenance and has become discredited. It has not in practice helped responsible parents—or forced those who had no intention of supporting their children to act responsibly . . . Fewer than half the children who gain from child support payments see the benefit of all the maintenance that the non-resident parents are assessed to pay . . . With hindsight, we can see that the problem lies with the way that the child support system was designed. The complex rules do not fit either with the lives of separated families or with other systems . . . So, we plan to abolish the current system and replace it with a simple and more deliverable system focussed on the needs of children and good, responsible parents. Parents who face up to their responsibilities will receive a better service. Irresponsible parents will face effective and speedy sanctions'.[50]

Three main problems[51] were identified in the White Paper: long delays in making assessments due to the formula's complexity; the very small proportion of the children on the Agency's books whose financial position was in fact improved; and the automatic deduction of child support from benefits resulted in no gain for the families concerned.

The reforms proposed were the most fundamental to date in the history of the child support system. While the formula approach was to be retained, the formula itself was to be radically simplified, to make it more comprehensible and accessible to parents and at the same time quicker and easier to administer.[52] Other key elements were a system of child maintenance premium for benefit cases,[53] a newly transparent, responsive, streamlined and customer-friendly Child Support Agency,[54] and enhanced powers to enforce compliance.[55] Comments were invited, but the ensuing Child Support, Pensions and Social Security Bill 1999[56] adhered closely to the original proposals. In the House of Lords the Government was forced to concede the imposition of a ceiling on payments where the non-resident parent has a very high income.[57]

The Child Support, Pensions and Social Security Act 2000[58] did not repeal the Child Support Act 1991,[59] but made substantial amendments and some specific repeals. The changes, operational in the first instance for new cases only[60]

---

[50] *ibid.* paras 2, 4 and 9.

[51] N. Wikeley, "Child Support: The New Formula" [2000] *Fam. Law* 820.

[52] *Children's Rights and Parents Responsibilities,* Chap 2.

[53] *ibid.* Chap. 3.

[54] *ibid.* Chap. 4.

[55] *ibid.* Chap. 8.

[56] Pirrie, "The Child Support, Pensions and Social Security Bill 1999" [1999] *Fam. Law* 199.

[57] Discussed later at p. 41.

[58] Which received Royal Assent on July 28, 2000.

[59] As amended by the Child Support Act 1995.

[60] "Existing cases will be brought in at a later date": *A New Contract for Welfare: Children's Rights and Parents' Responsibilities,* Chap. 1, para. 23; CSPSSA 2000 Notes For Guidance. The probable date is April 2003. N. Wikeley, "Child Support – The New Formula" [2000] *Fam. Law* 820, 821. The CSPSSA 2000 enables the Secretary of State to make transitional provisions: s. 29(2) J. Pirrie, "Child Support Update, Part 1" [2002] *Fam. Law* 195 at 202 estimates that there are a "million or so existing cases". Even in respect of "new" cases, the CSA has decided that changes will be phased in, in that "the CSA made the decision to protect parties against reductions in payments, as well as increases . . . Broadly, the increases and reductions are capped to £10 per week": Pirrie, *loc cit ibid.*

from April 2002, have been incorporated in the next section of this Chapter, under the following heads:

(1) The basis of liability under the Child Support Act 1991
(2) Meeting the responsibility for maintaining a child
(3) Quantifying child support: the formula
(4) Variations from the formula
(5) Revisions and appeals
(6) Collection and enforcement

Although existing cases will for a time continue to be dealt with by the unreformed system, and there will be a phasing in of the new rates in respect of new cases,[61] it is simply not practicable in a book of this nature to give a full description of the details of the old system[62] in parallel with the new one, nor of phasing in, nor of transitional arrangements.[63] Moreover, despite the reforms, the legislative framework of the scheme remains highly complex, with much of the detail contained in delegated[64] legislation. The objective of this Chapter is to explain the policy underlying the legislation and its main assumptions—matters which can easily be submerged by the mass of detail apparently inevitable in legislation of this kind.[65]

15–004 The last section of this Chapter gives an account of the court's residual powers under legislation other than the Child Support Act 1991[66] to make orders for the financial support of children.

---

[61] See n. 60, *supra.*

[62] Readers are referred to Chap. 16 of the 6th edition of this book, and to R. Bird, *Child Maintenance* (3rd ed., 1996, Family Law).

[63] See the Child Support (Transitional Provisions) Regulations, S.I. 2000 No. 3186.

[64] Of which the more significant are: Child Support (Maintenance Calculation and Special Cases) Regulations 2000 (S.I. 2001 No. 155); Child Support (Maintenance Calculation Procedure) Regulations 2000 (S.I. 2001 No. 157); Child Support (Maintenance Calculation and Special Cases) Regulations 2000 (S.I. 2001 No. 155); Social Security and Child Support (Decisions and Appeals) Regulations 1999 (S.I. 1999 No. 991); Child Support (Decisions and Appeals) (Amendment) Regulations 2000 (S.I. 2000 No. 3185); Child Support (Variation) Regulations 2000 (S.I. 2001 No. 156); Child Support (Information, Evidence and Disclosure) Regulations 1992 (S.I. 1992 No. 1812); Child Support (Information, Evidence and Disclosure and Maintenance Arrangements and Jurisdiction) (Amendment) Regulations 2000 (S.I. 2001 No. 161); Child Support (Collection and Enforcement) Regulations 1992 (S.I. 1992 No. 1989); Child Support (Collection and Enforcement and Miscellaneous Amendments) Regulations 2000 (S.I. 2001 No. 162); Child Support (Maintenance Arrangements and Jurisdiction) Regulations 1992 (S.I. 1992 No. 2645); Child Support Commissioners (Procedure) Regulations 1992 (S.I. 1992 No. 2640); Child Support Commissioners (Procedure) Regulations 1999 (S.I. 1999 No. 1305); Child Support (Collection and Enforcement of Other Forms of Maintenance) Regulations 1992 (S.I. 1992 No. 2643); Child Maintenance (Written Agreements) Order 1993 (S.I. 1993 No. 620); Child Support (Miscellaneous Amendments) Regulations 2002 (S.I. 2002 No. 1204).

[65] For more specialist coverage, the reader is referred to: R. Bird, *Child Support: The New Law* (Family Law, 2002); N. Mostyn *et al. Child's Pay* (3rd ed., Butterworths, 2002); E. Knights and C. Cox, *Child Support Handbook* (annual editions). Valuable updates on the state of the law and procedure at the time of writing can be found in J. Pirrie, "Child Support Update" [2002] *Fam. Law* 195 and "Child Support Process" [2002] *Fam. Law* 290.

[66] Matrimonial Causes Act 1973, Pt II; Sched. 1 to the Children Act 1989.

II. THE CHILD SUPPORT ACT

1. The basis of liability under the Child Support Act

Liability on parents

15–005 The underlying principle of the Child Support Act is that each parent of a qualifying child is responsible[67] for maintaining the child.[68] The model is one of "the partnership of equals and the joint enterprise models"[69]; we shall later discuss the way in which the legislation predicates that this joint liability is discharged by each parent. Parenthood for this purpose is primarily biological, but nevertheless "parent" receives an extended definition in section 54 of the Act , to mean any person who is in law the mother or father of the child. This includes an adoptive parent, and a person treated as a child's parent under the Human Fertilization and Embryology Act 1990.[70] The Act is thus based on the principle that children should look primarily to their natural parents (actual or presumed) for support.[71] The nature or even the existence of a relationship between the parents[72] is irrelevant to the coming into existence of the child support obligation, as is that between the parent and child; liability arises from procreation, not nurture. Thus liability under the Child Support Act 1991 arises even where the non-resident parent has no effective contact with the child; the view that it should not has been rejected.[73] However, the Child Support, Pensions and Welfare Reform Act 2000 (as will be explained below) permits an adjustment of the basic rate payable under the new formula where care of a child is shared between the

---

[67] There has been little discussion of the ideological basis for the parental support in government publications, which have tended instead simply to assert its existence: see *e.g. Children Come First,* (1990, Cm. 1263), para 2.1; *Children's Rights and Parental Responsibilities* (1999) Cm. 4349 pp. 1, 57. For academic discussions, see J. Eekelaar, *Regulating Divorce* (Clarendon Press, Oxford, 1990) pp. 91–120.; J. Eekelaar "Are Parents Morally Obliged to Support Their Children?" (1991) *Oxford Journal of Legal Studies* 340; S. Parker "Child Support in Australia: Children's Rights or Public Interest?" (1991) 5 *International Journal of Law and the Family* 24; S. Parker, "Child Support: Rights and Consequences" (1992) 6 *International Journal of Law, Policy and the Family* 148; R. Bailey-Harris, "Child Support: Is the Right the Wrong One?" 6 *International Journal of Law and the Family* 168; G. Barton and G. Douglas *Law and Parenthood* (Butterworths, 1995) pp. 28–29.

[68] Child Support Act 1991, s.1(1).

[69] G. Douglas *An Introduction to Family Law* (Clarendon Law Series, OUP, 2001), p. 187.

[70] Human Fertilisation and Embryology Act 1990, ss. 27,28. Children born prior to that Act's implementation are excluded: *Re M (Child Support: Parentage)* [1997] 2 F.L.R. 90.

[71] See *Children Come First,* paras 3.16–17; House of Commons Social Security Committee's First Report, *The Operation of the Child Support Act,* First Report, Session 1993–4, H.C. 69, para. 79.

[72] It has been observed that in recent years marriage has increasingly been replaced by parenthood as the key concept in family law: see J. Dewar *Law and Family* (2nd ed., 1992). The Child Support Act 1991 does not conform to a pattern of famililalism which privileges one form of relationship over another: see Dewar. The existence of child support liability does not depend on the existence of parental responsibility under the Children Act 1989, ss. 2, 3. The explanation lies partly in the emphasis given in to protection of the interests of the taxpayer.

[73] *Children's Rights and Parents' Responsibilities* Chap. 7, para. 8. Research has demonstrated a relationship in practice between contact and the payment of child maintenance: see generally M. MacLean and J. Eekelaar *The Parental Obligation* (1997).

two parents. The effect of this (if any) on negotiation and litigation under the Children Act 1989 remains to be seen.

Liability under the Child Support Act 1991 is based on an extended definition of natural parenthood. The Act does not does not directly impose a financial obligation on social parenthood, *i.e.* on a step-parent or other person who has treated the child as a child of the family. This can only be achieved through other legislation, namely the Matrimonial Causes Act 1973,[74] the Domestic Proceedings and Magistrates' Courts Act 1978[75] and the Children Act 1989.[76] In its original form, the Child Support Act did not allow a step-parent to take credit[77] for the fact that he or she was—notwithstanding the absence of any obligation under the Child Support Act—in fact maintaining the step-children.[78] The Government apparently believed that to make any such allowance would be to put step-children's interests before those of natural children.[79] This approach had the merit of logical consistency, but was inconsistent with the recognition increasingly given to factual as distinct from status relationships, and created real difficulties in practice.[80] One commentator observed[81] that to demand that money should "follow blood rather than affective ties" was a considerable culture shock.

In order to reflect a greater degree of social reality and not to ignore the needs of children living in a second family to whom the non-resident parent has responsibilities,[82] changes have now been introduced by the Child Support, Pensions and Welfare Reform Act 2000, whereby step-children (it has been said) "move centre stage".[83] The new formula permits allowance to be made for "relevant other children" of a non-resident parent.[84] These are defined[85] so as to include children living with the non-resident parent who are the children of that parent or his or her partner. As will be explained later in this Chapter, allowance takes the form of a percentage deduction from the income of the non-resident parent on which the basic rate operates under the formula.

---

[74] See the definition in M.C.A. 1973, s.52(1).
[75] Pt 1.
[76] Sched. 1.
[77] By way of adjustment to the person's "exempt income".
[78] The existence of stepchildren was however taken into account in the assessment of "protected income" which was intended to provide a safety net slightly above income support subsistence levels
[79] House of Commons Social Security Committee's First Report, *The Operation of the Child Support Act*, First Report, Session 1993–4, H.C. 69, para. 79.
[80] See the discussion in the Social Security Committee's Report, *op. cit.* above. It has been said that the Act created an "administrative nightmare" which operates as a "kind of domino effect, with each child in theory being entitled to support from its own biological" parent: G. Davis (1994) 31 *Houston L. Rev.* at 541.
[81] G. Davis (1994) 31 *Houston L. Rev.* at 541.
[82] *Children's Rights and Parents' Responsibilities*, p. 10.
[83] J. Pirrie, "Changes to Child Support—The SFLA View" [1999] *Fam. Law* 838 as 839.
[84] Child Support Act 1991, Sched. 1, para. 2(2).
[85] *ibid.* para. 10C(1), (2).

Liability only on parent who is habitually resident in United Kingdom or is a British public servant working overseas

15–006 Jurisdiction to make a maintenance calculation is confined to cases in which the non-resident parent parent[86] is habitually resident in the United Kingdom or who is not so habitually resident but is a member of the British civil service, naval, military or air forces, or an employee of certain prescribed companies or bodies, working overseas.[87]

The Child Support Act 1991 does not itself define "habitual residence", but there is ample authority on its interpretation elsewhere in the family law context.[88] It has been held[89] (in the context of jurisdiction for divorce proceedings[90]) that a person may be habitually resident in two countries at the same time.

Proof of parentage

15–007 The Child Support Act 1991 imposes child support liability primarily on the natural parent, and proof of parentage is therefore of central importance. For obvious reasons the issue of maternity almost never arises, but paternity issues are not uncommon. The Act provides that no maintenance calculation may be made against a person who denies that he is one of the child's parents, unless the case falls into certain defined categories.[91] Where it does so fall, the calculation will be made despite a denial of paternity: in other words, parentage is assumed, and child support can be calculated forthwith. Parentage will be assumed where[92]:

— the man was married to the child's mother between conception and birth;
— the man has been registered as father on the birth certificate;
— the alleged parent has refused to take a scientific test[93] or has taken such a test but refuses to accept its result;
— the child has been adopted by the alleged parent;

---

86 And the person with care and the qualifying child.

87 Child Support Act 1991 as amended, s. 44(1), (2A). For the prescribed bodies, see the Child Support (Maintenance Arrangements and Jurisdiction) Regulations 1992, as amended by the Child Support (Information, Evidence, Disclosure and Maintenance Arrangements and Jurisdiction) (Amendment) Regulations 2000.

88 *R. v. Barnet LBC, ex p.* Shah [1983] 2 A.C. 309, HL; *Re J (A Minor) (Abduction: Custody Rights)* [1990] 2 A.C. 562, HL; *Cruse v. Chittum* [1974] 2 All E.R. 940; *Re M (Minors) (Residence Order: Jurisdiction)* [1993] 1 F.L.R. 495, CA; see (1993) 109 *L.Q.R.* 538 (S.M. Cretney).

89 *Ikimi v. Ikimi* [2001] 2 F.L.R. 1288.

90 Domicile and Matrimonial Proceedings Act 1973.

91 Child Support Act 1991, s.26(1). It is to be noted that a finding that a child is a "child of the family" for the purposes of the M.C.A. 1973 is not sufficient.

92 .Child Support Act 1991 s. 26(2) (as amended by ss. 1(2), 15, Sched 3, para. 11(8), Sched 8, para. 12 of the CSPASSA 2000), brought into effect on January 31, 2001 by the Child Support, Pensions and Social Security (Commencement Order No. 5) Order 2000 (S.I. 2000 No. 3354). See N. Wikeley, "Child Support, Paternity and Parentage" [2001] *Fam. Law* 125.

93 Within the meaning of s.27A of the 1991 Act.

- — the alleged parent is the child's parent by virtue of an order under section 30 of the Human Fertilisation and Embryology Act 1990[94];
- — the alleged parent is a parent by virtue of sections 27 or 28 of the Human Fertilisation and Embryology Act (recognition of mother and father[95]);
- — a declaration of parentage under section 56 of the Family Law Act 1986 is in force[96];
- — in the case of a child resident in Scotland one or more of the presumptions set out in section 5(1) of the Law Reform (Parent and Child) (Scotland) Act 1986 applies;
- — paternity has been adjudged in earlier court proceedings.[97]

The second of these (added by the Child Support, Pensions and Social Security Act 2000) is likely to have significant impact, given that one-third of registered births occur outside marriage and in three quarters of such cases the man's name is registered.[98] It has however been suggested that this change in the law may lead in future to a decrease in the number of men permitting their name to be registered on the birth certificate of children born outside marriage.[99]

In cases involving disputed parentage which do not fall into any of the above categories, the Act provides[1] that the Secretary of State or the person with care[2] may apply to the court[3] for a declaration under section 55A of the Family Law Act 1986 as to whether or not the alleged parent is one of the child's parents. The court has power to direct (but not to order) that scientific tests be under taken.[4] A refusal by the alleged parent to submit to such tests will almost inevitably give rise to the inference that he is in fact the child's father.[5] In the case of a child, either the person with care and control may consent to a sample being taken, or where that parent objects, the court may do so if it considers that it is in the child's best interests.[6]

---

[94] See para. 18–003, below.
[95] *ibid.*
[96] *ibid.*
[97] *R. v. Secretary of State for Social Security ex p. West* [1999] 1 F.L.R. 1233; *R. v. Secretary of State for Social Security, ex p. W* [1999] 2 F.L.R. 604.
[98] N. Wikeley [2001] *Fam. Law* 125 at 126.
[99] Sharp, "Parental Responsibility—Where Next?" [2001] *Fam. Law* 607.
[1] Child Support Act 1991, ss.27, 27(1A).
[2] As defined: see below.
[3] There is no right of appeal in respect of a declaration made by magistrates under s.27: *T. v. Child Support Agency* [1997] 2 F.L.R. 275, FD.
[4] Family Law Reform Act 1969, s.20. Provision is made for the recovery of the costs incurred by the Secretary of State in relation to scientific tests from the alleged parent if parentage is established: Child Support Act 1991, s.27A as substituted by the Child Support, Pensions and Social Security Act 2000, s.1(2), Sched. 3, para. 11(9).
[5] *Re A (A Minor) (Paternity: Refusal of Blood Test)* [1994] 2 F.L.R. 463, CA; *Re H (Paternity: Blood Test)* [1996] 2 F.L.R. 65, CA; *F v. Child Support Agency* [1999] 2 F.L.R. 244, QBD.
[6] Family Law Reform Act, s.21(3) as amended by s.82(3) of the Child Support, Pensions and Social Security Act 2000, remedying the defect in the law exposed in *Re O and J (Paternity: Blood Tests)* [2000] 1 F.L.R. 418, FD, namely that the person with care and control of the child had an absolute statutory right of refusal. On the best interests test, see *S v. S; W v. Official Solicitor* [1972] A.C. 24; *Re E (A Minor) (Child Support: Blood Test)* [1994] 2 F.L.R. 548; *Re H (Paternity: Blood Test)* [1996] 2 F.L.R. 6; N. Wikeley "Child Support, Paternity and Parentage" [2001] *Fam. Law* 125 at 126–7. The power to order a blood test in a child's best interests was

Liability under Child Support Act only arises if parent "non-resident"

15–008 The Act states[7] a general principle that each parent of a "qualifying child" is responsible for maintaining the child; but a child will only fall within the definition[8] of a "qualifying child" if one or both of his parents is in relation to him a "non-resident parent".[9] For this purpose, a parent of any child is a non-resident parent in relation to him if that parent is not living in the same householdwith the child and the child has his home with a person who is, in relation to him, a "person with care".[10] The term "non-resident parent" was introduced by the Child Support, Pensions and Social Security Act 2000[11] to replace the earlier term "absent parent" which was criticised for its pejorative overtones.[12]

A "person with care" is defined[13] as a person with whom the child has his home and who "usually provides day-to-day care for the child, whether exclusively or in conjunction with any other person" and who does not fall within a prescribed category.[14]

It thus becomes clear that the Child Support Act is concerned with the situation in which a family relationship has broken down (or has never come into existence); and the Act follows the traditional pattern of English law which is to refuse to interfere in determining how a functioning family unit should allocate its resources. The Act is not concerned to define the level of support[15] appropriate to a child living under the same roof with the parents, that is, when a family is intact.

The relevance of the child's welfare

15–009 The Act provides[16] that where, in any case which falls to be dealt with under the Act, the Secretary of State is considering the exercise of any discretionary power conferred by the Act, he shall "have regard to the welfare of any child

exercised in *Re T (Paternity: Ordering Blood Tests)* [2001] 2 F.L.R. 1190, FD, in which Bodey J. weighed the child's interests against competing adult interests under Article 8, E.C.H.R.

[7] s.1(1).

[8] For these purposes, a child means (i) a person under the age of 16 (Child Support Act 1991, s.55(1)(a)) and (ii) in certain circumstances a person aged between 16 and 18 (ss.55(1)(b) and (c) and Child Support (Maintenance Assessment Procedure) Regulations 1992, (S.I. 1992 No. 1813, Sched. 1)). The conditions which have to be satisfied if persons aged 16 to 18 are to be regarded as children are modelled on those which govern eligibility for child benefit. See Chap. 7.

[9] s.3(1).

[10] s.3(2).

[11] s.1(2) and Sched. 3, para. 11(2).

[12] Second Report from the House of Commons Social Security Committee Session 1995–96, *The Performance and Operation of the Child Support Agency* (H.C. 50, para. 54); A. Diduck, "The Unmodified Family: The Child Support Act and the Construction of Legal Subjects" (1995) 22 *Journal of Law and Society* 527.

[13] s.3(3)(a),(b).

[14] s.3(3)(c) excludes categories of person prescribed by delegated legislation (see the Child Support (Maintenance Calculation Procedure) Regulations, 2000, S.I. 2001 No. 157, reg. 21(1), No. 1813, reg. 51): these are local authorities, and people (other than parents) with whom a child has been placed by a local authority. No child support maintenance is payable in such cases.

[15] For research on expenditure on children, see *Middleton et al. "Small Fortunes: spending on children, childhood poverty and parental sacrifice"* (1997); [1997] *Fam. Law* 531

[16] s.2. This provision did not appear in the original Bill as first presented to Parliament.

likely to be affected by his decision." The duty to have regard to welfare extends beyond the "qualifying children"[17] in respect of whom a maintenance calculation is likely to be sought so that (for example) a child support officer is obliged to have regard to the effect of relevant decisions on the non-resident parent's other children, on a non-resident parent's step-children—and even, perhaps, on a parent who is a "child".[18] What is the scope of the duty? The duty to have regard to children's welfare does not arise in those cases in which the legislation imposes a mandatory duty on the Secretary of State or officer acting under his authority.[19] Most importantly, it does not apply so as to give any discretion to depart from the formula laid down by the Act for the calculation of child support maintenance.[20] On the other hand, the range of discretionary powers to which the duty does apply is, perhaps surprisingly, wide: for example, the decision whether to arrange for the collection and enforcement of child support maintenance,[21] whether to revise or supersede an earlier decision,[22] whether to agree to a variation from the formula,[23] and whether to take certain kinds of enforcement action.[24] In general the appropriate procedure will be to seek judicial review[25] of the decision on the ground that the decision was one which could not properly have been reached had the Secretary of State or officer acting under his authority properly directed themselves in accordance with this statutory requirement.

15–010 The legislation on child support takes account of the interests of three "stakeholders", namely the child, the parents and the taxpayer. The child's interest does not predominate over all other interests under the Child Support Act 1991, in contrast to legislation dealing with children's upbringing[26] which requires courts and others to treat the child's welfare as the "paramount" consideration.[27]

---

[17] As defined in Child Support Act 1991, s.3; see above.

[18] This definition extends not only to teenage mothers (a group who may not have fully engaged the attention of those responsible for drafting the Children Act 1989: see *Birmingham C. C. v. H (No. 3)* [1994] 1 F.L.R. 224, HL but also an 18-year-old college student: see the definition of "child" in Children Act 199, s.55(1)(b).

[19] Child Support Act 1991, s.11(1).

[20] *R. v. Secretary of State for Social Security, ex p. Biggin* [1995] 1 F.L.R. 851, Div.Ct. Child Support Act 1991, s.11 imposes a mandatory requirement to fix the amount of child support maintenance in accordance with the provisions of the Act: but on the other hand, it would seem that the Secretary of State's extensive power to make regulations under the Act (see s.52) is a discretionary power in the exercise of which he is bound to take account of the welfare of all children likely to be affected.

[21] Child Support Act 1991, s.4(2)—"the Secretary of State may . . . ".

[22] Child Support Act 1991 ss.16,17.

[23] Child Support Act 1991, s.28F(2).

[24] *i.e.* whether to arrange the collection of child support maintenance (s.29) and other forms of maintenance (s.30), whether to make a deduction from earnings order (s.31) to apply to the magistrates for a liability order (s.33(2)), or to levy distress or seek a garnishee or charging order in support of a liability order (ss.35, 36) or to apply for a committal warrant (s.40). The requirement also applies to decisions whether to give a reduced benefit direction (s.46(5)) and on interim maintenance (s.12(1)).

[25] As was (unsuccessfully) done in *R. v. Secretary of State for Social Security, ex p. Lloyd* [1995] 1 F.L.R. 856, Div.Ct.; and see *R. v. Secretary of State for Social Security, ex p. Biggin* [1995] 1 F.L.R. 851, Div.Ct.

[26] Notably Children Act 1989, s.1.

[27] In considering applications for financial relief in divorce and similar proceedings, the court is required to give "first consideration" to the need to safeguard and protect the welfare of children: Matrimonial Causes Act 1973, s.25(1), as amended.

The child's interest does not even have the status of "first" consideration which it is given in relation to ancillary relief proceedings between husband and wife on divorce.[28] In *R. v. Secretary of State for Social Security, ex parte Biggin*[29] it was accepted that section 2 of the Child Support Act 1991 had no influence on the quantification of liability. However, in the same case, the judge refused to accept a submission by counsel for the Secretary of State that the agency's decisions (in those situations where the principle did apply) could not be attacked[30] if it were shown that the agency had merely taken note of the child's welfare in passing; and the judge suggested that the statute required "considerable weight" to be given to the welfare principle. In *R. v. Secretary of State for Social Security ex parte Lloyd*[31] the court dismissed as "fanciful, unrealistic and not supported by the Act" an argument that the parent with care should not be required to make application under section 6 for a maintenance application unless the Secretary of State had first made inquiries of the absent parent as to whether the welfare of children would be prejudiced if the application was required.

2. Meeting the responsibility for maintaining a child

15–011 For the purposes of the Child Support Act, a non-resident parent is to be taken to have met his responsibility to maintain any qualifying child of his by making periodical payments of maintenance with respect to the child in accordance with the provisions of the Act[32]—and it imposes a duty to make such payments on a non-resident parent in respect of whom a maintenance calculation has been made.[33] The Act itself is silent as to the way in which the parent with care meets her responsibility to maintain a qualifying child. However, the assumption that she does so by caring for the child in the home[34] emerges more clearly in the changes introduced to the formula by the Child Support, Pensions and Social Security Act 2000, explained below, whereby the income and other resources of the parent with care are of no relevance to the calculation of the child maintenance payable by the non-resident parent.

It is important to understand that the obligation to make payments under the Child Support Act arises on the making of a maintenance calculation, which will only be made where an application is made.[35] Either the person with care

---

[28] Matrimonial Causes Act 1973, s.25(1), as amended by the Matrimonial Proceedings and Property Act 1984, discussed in Chap. 14.

[29] [1995] 1 F.L.R. 851 at 1106, Div. Ct.

[30] The only procedure for challenging the exercise of the Secretary of State's discretionary power has traditionally by an application for judicial review in the High Court: *R. v. Secretary of State for Social Security, ex p. Biggin* [1995] 1 F.L.R. 851, Div. Ct. *Sed quaere* whether an action under ss.7 and 8 of the Human Rights Act 1998 could now be available in appropriate circumstances involving breach of a Convention right.

[31] [1995] 1 F.L.R. 856 at 857, QBD.

[32] Child Support Act 1991, s.1(2) as amended by the Child Support, Pensions and Social Security Act 2000, s.1(2), Sched. 3, para. 11(2).

[33] *ibid.* s.1(3).

[34] *Children's Rights and Parents' Responsibilities,* Chap 2, para. 32.

[35] Child Support Act 1991, s.4 (1).

or the non-resident parent may apply for a maintenance calculation.[36] There is nothing to stop a child's parents—so long as they are not in receipt of certain welfare benefits[37]—from making their own arrangements about child support; and indeed—subject to the same important proviso—there is nothing to stop them agreeing that one parent shall be exclusively responsible for a child's support. The Act specifically provides[38] that nothing in the Act should be taken to prevent any person from entering into a maintenance agreement. However, as we explain later in this Chapter, changes effected by the Child Support, Pensions and Social Security Act 2000 mean that the jurisdiction of the Child Support Agency to make a maintenance calculation can in future no longer be permanently excluded by the making of a consent order for child maintenance.[39]

The parents' freedom to agree is, however, subject to one important statutory qualification, and the Child Support Act 1991 draws a distinction between those parents who are in receipt of benefits and those who are not. For the former, non-compliance with the Act is subject to the ultimate sanction of a reduced benefit direction.[40] The Act—reflecting the settled policy of the law that child support is a matter of public concern which cannot be left to the free will of the parents and in which the interests of the taxpayer must be given regard[41]—provides[42] that the existence of a maintenance agreement shall not prevent any party to the agreement, or any other person, from applying for a maintenance calculation with respect to any child for whose benefit periodical payments were to be made under the agreement, and that any provision purporting to restrict such an application is void.[43]

The principle that it is a proper function of government to ensure that children are provided with adequate subsistence, but that the primary obligation to support a child must be placed on the parents rather than on the taxpayer, is reflected in section 6. Where income support, an income-based jobseeker's allowance or other prescribed benefit is paid[44] or claimed,[45] the person with care of a qualifying child will be treated as having applied for child support unless she requests the Secretary of State not to act.[46] A parent treated as having applied for child

---

36 *ibid.* ss.4, 11(1).

37 In which case the provisions of Child Support Act 1991, s.6, requiring the parent with care to authorise the making of an application, come into play: see below.

38 Child Support Act 1991, s.9(2).

39 See p. 453.

40 Child Support Act 1991, s.46 (5).

41 See *Hulley v. Thompson* [1981] 1 W.L.R. 159; *Crozier v. Crozier* [1994] 1 F.L.R. 126 at 135, *per* Booth J.

42 s.9(3).

43 s.9(4).

44 Where income support ceased, a calculation can still be made: *R v. Secretary of State for Social Security ex p. Harris* [1999] 1 F.L.R. 837.

45 The claim, not the calculation, brings s.6 into operation: *Secretary of State for Social Security v. Harmon; Secretary of State for Social Security v. Carter; Secretary of State for Social Security v. Cocks* [1998] 2 F.L.R. 598.

46 s.6 (3) and (5), as amended by the Child Support, Pensions and Social Security Act 2000, s.3. The amendment reverses the burden of proof, requiring benefit claimants to opt out of the scheme rather than to opt in as was the case under the earlier law: N. Wikeley, "Compliance, Enforcement and Child Support" [2000] *Fam. Law* 888 at 891.

support under this provision and who has not made such a request must[47] provide information needed to enable the absent parent to be traced, the appropriate amount of child support maintenance to be assessed. Where a parent has made a request that the Secretary of State not act, or (being treated as having applied for a maintenance calculation) refuses to provide the required information or to take a scientific test to determine paternity,[48] she will be given written notice requiring her to give reasons.[49] The Secretary of State must then consider whether there are reasonable grounds for believing that there would be a risk to the parent with care, or of any child living with her, "suffering harm or undue distress" as a result of his taking such action.[50] If he decides that no such grounds exist, he may (except in prescribed circumstances[51]) make a reduced benefit direction.[52] It has been suggested that the reversal of proof in section 6(3) may lead to an increase in the number of reduced benefit directions.[53]

It remains to be seen whether there will be a higher rate of compliance with the child support scheme as reformed from 2002 than there has been in the past, both amongst benefit cases and more generally.[54] For benefit cases, a (universally welcomed) incentive is the new child maintenance premium,[55] which came into operation after the implementation of the new formula in the amended Child Support Act 1991, namely in April 2002. This will mean a disregard, for those on income support or a jobseeker's allowance, of the (relatively modest) weekly sum of £10[56] child maintenance paid by the non-resident parent. More generally, the aspiration is that the simplified, comprehensible formula and the new customer-focussed child support service will make use of the Child Support Act 1991 more attractive to all parents.

3. Quantifying child support: the formula

15–012 In principle there are a number of possible theoretical models[57] available for determining the *quantum* of parental child support, of which the two most

[47] Child Support Act 1991, s.6(7). Section 14 gives the Secretary of State power to make regulations on the information required. Detailed regulations are contained in the Child Support (Information, Evidence and Disclosure) Regulations 1992, S.I. 1992 No. 1812 as amended by the Child Support (Information, Evidence and Disclosure and Maintenance and Jurisdiction (Amendment) (Regulations) 2000. There are sanctions for providing false information or refusing to provide information: Child Support Act 1991 s.14A, as amended by s.13 of the Child Support, Pensions and Social Security Act 2000.

[48] Child Support Act 1991, s.46(1)

[49] *ibid.* s.46(2).

[50] *ibid.* s.46(3).

[51] Child Support Act, s.46(5).

[52] Defined in s.46(10).

[53] N.Wikeley, "Compliance, Enforcement and Child Support" [2000] *Fam. Law* 888 at 891.

[54] Non-compliance in the past by benefit cases has been extensively documented, *e.g.* by G. Davis et al. *Child Support in Action;* and by the White Paper *Children's Rights and Parents' Responsibilities* (1999). For non-use of the system by non-benefit cases, see *e.g.* S. Deas, "Lawyers Sidestep the CSA" [1998] *Fam. Law* 48.

[55] *Children's Rights and Parents' Responsibilities* Chap. 1, paras 9–11, Chap. 2, and Chap. 4, paras 25–35.

[56] There is no provision for an inflation-linked increase.

[57] Discussed in J. Eekelaar and M. Maclean *Maintenance after Divorce* (Clarendon Press, 1986) p. 37ff; J. Eekelaar *Regulating Divorce,* (Clarendon Press, 1990) pp. 104–111; Parker, "Child Sup-

straightforward[58] are cost-sharing and resource-sharing. The cost-sharing model raises the question whether the relevant cost is that of the hypothetical "average" child in the community or is to be determined according to the income bracket of the family in question. The resource-sharing model looks to the standard of living the child could have expected had the family remained intact. Have the various versions of the formula which have been adopted in the legislation since the 1991 Act first came into operation conformed to any of the abovementioned models? The original formula appeared to adopt the cost-sharing model, albeit with child support costs calculated at a minimal basic level closely tied to benefit rates.[59] The new formula appears to follow in part a resource-sharing model, although the disregard of the income of one parent, plus the cap on the highest income level of a non-resident parent—both of which we explain below—seem inconsistent with a pure version of that model.

The complexity of the formula prior to[60] the reforms introduced by the Child Support, Pensions and Social Security Act 2000 was designed to achieve universality of application, but was of itself one of the major sources of criticism of the scheme in operation.[61] A High Court judge[62] described it as a "series of mathematically obtuse calculations in innumerable unintelligible Schedules[63] to the Act". It was unintelligible to many parents, and many legal practitioners needed assistance with its interpretation and application.[64] Staff of the Child Support Agency themselves found the formula difficult to apply, with consequent errors made in calculations. In brief outline,[65] the legislation prior to the amendments effected by the Child Support, Pensions and Social Security Act 2000 required a three-fold exercise.[66] The first step was to calculate the child maintenance requirement, a minimum necessary for any child's support, pegged to benefit rates payable to a parent in respect of children in her care, arrived at by an aggregate of a number of elements, including the income support payable in respect of a child and the carer's personal allowance, and family/lone parent premium . The second step was to calculate the parents' assessable incomes. In principle (if not in practice) in the majority of cases coming to the Agency's

---

port in Australia: Rights and Consequences" (1992) 6 *International Journal of Law and the Family* 140.

[58] Two more complex models are a normative standard and a derived level: see J. Eekelaar and M. Maclean, *Maintenance After Divorce, supra,* pp. 120–122; J. Eekelaar, *Regulating Divorce, supra,* pp. 109–111; Parker, "Child Support in Australia: Rights and Consequences", *supra,* p. 160.

[59] J. Eekelaar, *Regulating Divorce, supra,* pp. 116–117.

[60] The initial complexity of the formula was further compounded by the additional elements introduced by the Child Support and Income Support (Amendment) Regulations 1995.

[61] See in particular G. Davis, *et al. Child Support in Action* (Hart Publishing, 1998); *Children's Rights and Parents' Responsibilities,* Chap. 1, paras 4–8.

[62] Ward J. *Re C (A Minor) (Contribution Notice)* [1994] 1 F.L.R. 111 at 117.

[63] See, prior to the amendments effected by the Child Support, Pensions and Social Security Act 2000, the Child Support Act 1991, Sched. 1, and the Child Support (Maintenance Assessment and Special Cases) Regulations 1992, S.I. 1992 No. 1815.

[64] To this end, a number of professionally-targeted publications, in some cases supported by a computer package and updating bulletin, have been produced: N. Mostyn *et al., Child's Pay* (2nd ed., Butterworths, 2002); R. Bird, "Child Support Calculation Pack" (Family Law, 2002).

[65] For a detailed account see the 6th ed. of this book, pp. 512–520, and R. Bird, *Child Maintenance* (3rd ed., Family Law, 1996).

[66] "Old" cases will still be calculated according to this formula until taken into the new system; see CSPSSA 2000, s.29(2) and the Child Support (Transitional Provisions) Regulations 2000.

notice, both parents were expected to contribute according to their respective financial resources, and the income of each was taken into account. The absent parent's assessable income consisted of net income less exempt income, the latter taking account *inter alia* of a personal expenditure allowance at income support level, reasonable housing costs subject to a ceiling fixed by regulation, an allowance for his own children in his care, significant travel-to-work costs, and an allowance for property transfer made prior to April 1993. The legislation made no allowance for the living costs of the parent's spouse or partner, nor for the living costs of the parent's step-children: the principle was that children should look to their birth parents for support. The assessable income of the parent with care was to be calculated in the same way, but in practice was often irrelevant, since few parents with care had sufficient income to be taken into account. The two income sums were then added together and halved, the result being the sum available. The final stage was the maintenance assessment. If the sum available (under step two, *supra*) was less than the maintenance requirement (under step one, *supra*) the absent parent paid half his assessable income as child support. If however the sum available was more than the maintenance requirement, an additional element[67] was payable on top of the basic calculation, but at a lower rate up to a maximum ceiling fixed by regulation. An absent parent on income support with no assessable income still normally paid a small minimum amount. Every absent parent was guaranteed a minimum protected income to meet essential expenses, based on income support rates. The maximum payable under the maintenance assessment was 30 per cent of the absent parent's net income.

15–013 The White Paper *A New Contract for Welfare: Children's Rights and Parents' Responsibilities*[68] was highly critical of the formula's complexity and at the same time full of confidence in the capacity of a simplified formula both to restore public confidence and to improve its administration. Under the new formula[69] as introduced by the Child Support, Pensions and Social Security Act 2000, only the income of the non-resident parent is relevant. This proved controversial at the proposal stage,[70] but was defended by the Government of the day on several grounds.[71] The cost of supporting a child (approximately 30 per cent of family income) ought to be shared equally and the parent with care contributes financially by meeting housing and household costs; the child is entitled to financial support from the father just as if the parents were living together; and very few people would in practice be affected. However, the change is undoubtedly of symbolic and policy importance, and there is a risk of adverse publicity arising from even a statistically insignificant number of high-profile cases.[72]

The basic rate is the general rule[73] for the calculation of child support. Accord-

---

[67] Child Support Act 1991 prior to amendment by the CSPSSA 2000, Sched. 1, para. 2(3)(b).

[68] (1999) Cm. 4349, Chap. 1.

[69] Child Support Act 1991, s.11(6) and Sched. 1. The simplified formula draws on overseas models, *e.g.* The Child Support (Assessment) Act 1989 (Cth) in Australia.

[70] N. Mostyn, "The Green Paper on Child Support" [1999] *Fam. Law* 95 at 99.

[71] *Official Report* H.L. May 8, 2000, cols 1254, 1255, 1260, 1262 (Baroness Hollis).

[72] N. Wikeley, "Child Support—the New Formula" [2000] *Fam. Law* 820 at 822.

[73] Child Support Act 1991, Sched. 1, Pt 1, para. 1(1), as substituted by the CSPSSA 2000, s.1(3), Scheds 1, 3.

ing to the basic rate, the non-resident parent pays, of his weekly net income, 15 per cent for one qualifying child, 20 per cent for two and 25 per cent for three or more.[74] Net weekly income is to be determined "in such manner as is provided for in regulations".[75] The original proposal was that there should be no cap on the income on which the percentage was to operate, the principal rationale offered being that a child had the right to share in the income of the non-resident parent, however high.[76] However, widespread criticism[77]—principally directed to the fact that very high sums of child support would benefit the parent with care—led eventually to the government introducing a third reading amendment in the House of Lords shortly before Royal Assent, the effect of which was to impose a cap of £2000 on weekly earnings. The view officially offered was that the courts were in the best position to determine a range of financial matters in the case of family breakdown of those with very high incomes, and that a cap on child support would render the task of settling other financial arrangements easier.[78] The courts retain the power to make top-up orders in appropriate cases where income exceeds the cap.[79]

There are three rates additional to the basic rate. The reduced rate[80] applies where the non-resident parent's net weekly income is between £100 and £200. The flat rate[81] operates where the nil rate does not and where the non-resident parent's net weekly income is less than £100 or he is in receipt of a prescribed benefit, pension or allowance or has a partner who does so. The nil rate[82] applies where his net weekly income is less than £5 or he falls into a prescribed category: full-time student, under 16, on income support if 16 or 17, in hospital for at least a year, or in prison.

The reformed formula gives increased recognition to social parenthood, in that it makes allowance for relevant other (*i.e.* non-qualifying) children[83] living with the non-resident parent, such as step-children or his own children of a new relationship. The allowance takes the form of a deduction from his net weekly income on which the basic rate operates: 15 per cent for one relevant other child, 20 per cent for two, 25 per cent for three or more.[84] This gives a slight

---

[74] *ibid.* para. 2(1).

[75] *ibid.* para. 10(1). See Sched. to the Child Support (Maintenance Calculation and Special Cases) Regulations 2000. The Secretary of State has power to make regulations bringing back into account income of which a parent has intentionally deprived himself, and a parent may be treated as possessing income which he does not possess: Child Support Act 1991, Sched. 1, para. 10B, substituted by the Child Support, Pensions and Social Security Act 2000, Sched. 2 Cases of notional income are likely to be dealt with by variations, *sed quaere* how successful this will prove to be: N. Wikeley, "Child Support-The New Formula" [2000] *Fam. Law* 820 at 823.

[76] *Children's Rights and Parents' Responsibilities,* Chap. 2, para. 36; *Official Report* H.L. May 8 2000, cols 1251, 1252 (Baroness Hollis).

[77] See *e.g.* N. Mostyn, n. 70, p. 440.

[78] *Official Report* H.C. July 24, 2000, cols 793 and 794 (Angela Ellis MP).

[79] See p. 450 below.

[80] Child Support Act 1991, Sched. 1, para. 3; defined in the Child Support (Maintenance Calculations and Special Cases) Regulations 2000, reg. 3.

[81] *ibid.* para. 4; see the Child Support (Maintenance Calculations and Special Cases) Regulations 2000, reg. 4.

[82] *ibid.* para. 5; see the Child Support (Maintenance Calculation and Special Cases) Regulations 2000, reg. 5.

[83] *ibid.* para. 10C(2).

[84] *ibid.* para. 2(2).

preference to children in the first family; the alternative (rejected by the government[85]) of calculating support for all children and dividing by their number) would have introduced greater equality between "natural" and "social" children.

The child support rates are modified where both parents have substantial involvement in caring for their children, that is in cases of "shared care".[86] The Child Support, Pensions and Social Security Act 2000 has increased[87] the allowance made for the number of nights a child spends with the non-resident parent. Where the care of a qualifying child is shared between parents for a defined number of nights per year, the basic or reduced rate of liability is discounted.[88] The discount rates for the flat rate are: 52 to 103 nights, one-seventh; 104 to 155 nights, two-sevenths; 156 to 174 nights, three-sevenths; over 175 nights, one half. Parents who pay the flat rate may also be entitled to a discount for shared care, provided his net income is over £100 per week. It remains to be seen whether these rules will prove an incentive to parents to litigate over contact and shared residence under the Children Act 1989.

4. Variations from the formula

15–014 The original intention of the child support scheme was that the formula should be of universal application; its complexity was designed to achieve universality. However, this principle was compromised by the Child Support Act 1995 (and Regulations made under that Act[89]) which sought to give effect to the Government's view that—although the formula provides the best means for establishing maintenance liability in a fair and consistent way—there would always be a "small proportion of exceptional cases which cannot be fairly treated by any universal formula".[90] This was in essence an admission that the formula's rigidity could be productive of injustice. Under the system introduced by the Child Support Act 1995, either parent could apply for a "departure direction" (*i.e.* a variation of the formula) on the ground that the facts fell within one of three "cases" specified in the Act.[91] The provisions were complex and arguably the scheme as modified was the worst of both worlds, combining the least satisfactory features of a discretionary system with those depending on the application of a mathematical formula. It was the Government's intention that departure directions should not be common,[92] and in practice the scheme appeared to have been relatively little used.[93]

---

[85] *Children's Rights and Parents' Responsibilities,* Chap. 2 paras 9–15.

[86] *ibid.* Chap. 7, para. 11.

[87] Under the Child Support (Maintenance and Special Cases) Regulations 1992, reg. 20, maintenance liability was apportioned between parents where each cared for the child for 104 nights or more.

[88] Child Support Act 1991, Sched. 1, para. 7; see Child Support (Maintenance Calculations and Special Cases) Regulations 2000, reg. 7A.

[89] Child Support (Departure Directions and Consequential Amendments) Regulations 1996, S.I. 1996 No. 2907.

[90] *Improving Child Support,* Cm. 2745 (1995), para. 2.1.

[91] Child Support Act 1995, Sched. 2, the provisions of which were amplified by the Child Support (Departure Directions and Consequential Amendment) Regulations 1996, S.I. 1996 No. 2907.

[92] *Improving Child Support* (Cm. 2745, (1995)), para. 2.4.

[93] Deas [1999] *Fam. Law* 759; Priest (1998) 5 *J.S.S.L.* 104; N. Wikely [2000] *Fam. Law* 820.

In briefest outline,[94] the first category of specified case was "special expenses" on costs incurred in travelling to work, in maintaining contact with a child, debts incurred for the benefit of the family before breakdown, pre-1993 financial commitments,[95] costs incurred in supporting step-children, and certain costs incurred by reason of the long-term illness or disability of the applicant or a dependant. The second category was that of property or capital transfers made by court order or agreement before April 5, 1993 which effectively reduced the amount of the maintenance payable with respect to a child. Thirdly, there were prescribed additional cases in which a departure direction could be made: where the parent has income-producing assets, where income was diverted, a life-style inconsistent with declared income, unreasonably high housing costs, a partner's contribution to housing costs, and unreasonably high travel costs. If the case fell within one of the above categories, a departure direction was not automatic: there was a discretion whether to make one or not, and the ultimate question was whether it would be "just and equitable" to do so in the light of a number of specified considerations.

Departures are renamed "variations" by the Child Support, Pensions and Social Security Act 2000. The revised legislation continues to put its faith in the capacity of formula calculation (based on a newly simplified system of rates) to do justice in the vast majority of cases, and variations are intended to be available only for "clearly exceptional" cases.[96] The categories of case[97] under the new provisions, while similar in broad outline to their predecessors, are narrower in scope. Variations are to be permitted only in clearly defined circumstances; the intention was to strike a balance between making reasonable allowance for exceptional expenditure and re-introducing the undesirable complexities of the old formula.[98] The reasons for lowering the standard child support rates are strictly child-centred. Property and capital transfers effected prior to April 1993[99] to provide accommodation to help support a child are grounds for variations as they were formerly grounds for departure. The category of "special expenses"[1] of a non-resident parent is retained.[2] The enabling provision[3] sets out an exhaustive list of child-related costs: costs incurred in maintaining contact, costs attributable to a relevant other child's long-term illness or disability, certain debts incurred prior to separation for the joint benefit of both parents or a child, boarding school fees, and mortgage repayments on the former family home in which he no longer has an interest[4] but which is still the home of the

---

[94] For a detailed discussion, see pp. 533–536 of the 6th ed. of this work. The details were contained in the Child Support (Departure Direction and Consequential Amendments) Regulations 1996, S.I. 1996 No. 2907.

[95] Provided that a court order or maintenance agreement was in force at April 5, 1993 and at the date the commitment was contracted.

[96] *Children's Rights and Parents' Responsibilities,* Chap. 6, para. 3.

[97] Set out in Child Support Act 1991, Sched. 4B, Pt 1.

[98] *Children's Rights and Parents' Responsibilities,* Chap. 6, paras 4–7

[99] Child Support Act 1991, Sched. 4B, para. 3.

[1] *ibid.* Sched. 4B, para. 2(1). Special expenses are prescribed in the Child Support (Variation) Regulations 2000.

[2] *ibid.* Sched. 4B, para. 2(2).

[3] *ibid.* Sched. 4B, para. 2(3).

[4] It would appear that this is confined to the situation where the non-resident parent has divested himself of his entire interest.

qualifying child and parent with care. Finally, rates of child support may be raised in some exceptional circumstances. The Act as amended retains the category of "additional cases" in which a variation may be made. The enabling provision[5] lists examples of cases where the non-resident parent's weekly income is not an accurate reflection of his financial capacity, whether on account of capital assets, or otherwise; details are found in the Regulations.[6]

An application for a variation may be made either before or after a maintenance calculation has been made.[7] The original proposal in the Green Paper was that variation applications should be determined by a tribunal,[8] but this was reconsidered in the White Paper *Children's Rights and Parents' Responsibilities* which concluded that they "should be determined by officials."[9] It remains to be seen whether the officers of the Child Support Agency, acting under the authority of the Secretary of State, have the capacity to deal with variation applications with sufficient expedition. Variation is by no means automatic. The Secretary of State may reject the application on a preliminary consideration if there are no grounds on which he could agree, or there is insufficient information, or in other circumstances to be prescribed in regulations.[10] If the application proceeds further, not only must the Secretary of State be satisfied that the case falls within one of the clearly defined categories,[11] but he must in addition consider that it would be just and equitable in all the circumstances to agree to a variation.[12] In considering whether it would be just and equitable, the Secretary of State must have regard in particular to the welfare of any child likely to be affected if he did agree to a variation, and to any other relevant prescribed circumstances.[13] The Secretary of State may agree or not agree to the variation, or refer the application to an appeal tribunal for determination,[14] in which case the tribunal has the same powers.

5. Revisions and appeals

15–015 The Child Support Act 1991—reflecting in part a policy of keeping maintenance payments up to date with changed circumstances[15]—provided a system of several different types of review of child maintenance assessments[16]: by child support officers periodically, to correct errors of fact or law, on application of a parent on the ground of changed circumstances and as the first stage of an

---

[5] *ibid.* Sched. 4B, para. 4 (1).
[6] Child Support (Variation) Regulations 2000, regs 18, 19, 20.
[7] Child Support Act 1991 as amended, s. 28A(1), (3).
[8] Chap. 5, para. 27.
[9] *Children's Rights and Parents' Responsibilities* (1999), paras 15–18.
[10] *ibid.* s. 28B(2); Child Support (Variation) Regulations 2000, regs 6, 7.
[11] CSA 1991, Sched. 4B, Pt 1.
[12] Child Support Act 1991 s. 28F(1), (2), as amended by the Child Support, Pensions and Social Security Act 2000, s.5(5).
[13] *ibid.* s. 28F(2).
[14] *ibid.* s. 28D(1).
[15] *Children Come First,* Cm. 1263 (1990), para. 1.5; *ibid.* Summary, para. 3.
[16] Child Support Act 1991, ss. 16–19.

appeal. This system was modified by the Social Security Act 1998[17] and by the Child Support, Pensions and Social Security Act 2000.[18] Reviews have been renamed "revisions". The Secretary of State may[19] revise a decision which falls within section 16 of the Child Support Act,[20] either on application or on his own initiative. The relevant decisions are[21] those relating to maintenance calculations, default and interim calculations, those superceding earlier decisions,[22] a reduced benefit decision,[23] and a decision of an appeal tribunal on a referral.[24] The effect of the revision is backdated to the date of the original decision.[25] A wide range of decisions[26] may be superceded by a subsequent decision of the Secretary of State, either on application or on his own initiative. As one commentator has observed,[27] superceding means that the old decision is completely substituted by the new, rather than merely changed by revision.

The details of the appeal system from decisions[28] made under the Child Support Act 1991 as amended is beyond the scope of this work, save in briefest outline.[29] Substantial changes were effected by changes to all social security appeals in 1999[30] and later by the Child Support, Pensions and Social Security Act 2000. The first level of appeal is to a Child Support Appeal Tribunal, which (depending on the circumstances) comprises one legally qualified member or one legally and one financially qualified member.[31] Procedure and time limits are governed by regulation.[32] Hearings must generally be in public, unless the appellant requests a hearing in private or intimate personal or financial circumstances are involved.[33] Any party is entitled to be present and heard[34] and to call and test evidence.[35] The Tribunal may make a decision itself or remit the matter to the Secretary of State.[36] There is an appeal by a person aggrieved or the Secretary of State from a Child Support Appeal Tribunal on a question of law

---

[17] SSA 1998, s. 41

[18] CSPSSA 2000, ss. 8 and 9.

[19] Child Support Act 1991, s. 16(1).

[20] As amended by the Social Security Act 1998, s. 40 and the Child Support, Pensions and Social Security Act 2000, s. 8. Details are contained in the Child Support (Decisions and Appeals) (Amendment) Regulations 2000, amending the Social Security and Child Support (Decisions and Appeals) Regulations 1999.

[21] Child Support Act 1991 as amended s. 16(1A).

[22] *i.e.* under ss. 11, 12 or 17.

[23] Under s. 46.

[24] Under s. 28D(1)(b)

[25] Save in prescribed circumstances: s. 16(4).

[26] Listed in s. 17(1); the circumstances are set out in the Social Security and Child Support (Decisions and Appeals) Regulations 1999, reg. 6A.

[27] R. Bird, *Child Support: The New Law* (5th ed., 2002) p. 77

[28] Child Support Act 1991 as amended, s. 20(1).

[29] For a detailed discussion, see Bird, *op cit,* Chap. 8.

[30] Social Security and Child Support (Decisions and Appeals) Regulations 1999, S.I. 1999. 991.

[31] *ibid.* reg. 36(3).

[32] Child Support Act 1991, s. 20(4); Social Security and Child Support (Decisions and Appeals) Regulations 1991, regs 30–49.

[33] *ibid.* reg. 49(5).

[34] *ibid.* reg. 49(7).

[35] *ibid.* reg. 49(11).

[36] Child Support Act 1991, s. 20(8).

to a Child Support Commissioner,[37] and a further appeal on a question of law to the Court of Appeal.[38]

6. Collection and enforcement

15–016 There had traditionally been a low level of compliance with court orders for periodical maintenance[39]; and the Government believed that the Child Support Act 1991 would create an "efficient and effective service" to the public, ensuring that maintenance was paid regularly and on time, so that the "habit of payment" was established early and was not compromised by early arrears.[40] The Child Support Agency was also intended to take "appropriate enforcement action at an early date" when payments were not made.[41] Unfortunately the reality of the Agency's performance fell well short of expectations: the system failed to deliver regular maintenance without delay[42] and did not effectively enforce the responsibility of those unwilling to pay.[43] The White Paper *Children's Rights and Parents' Responsibilities*[44] put great store in reform of the CSA ("a new child support service"[45]) to improve the system of collection and also in a tougher sanctions regime "to make sure that non-resident parents cannot avoid their responsibilities."[46]

Arrangements for collection

15–017 The Child Support Agency, in addition to determining the amount of child support maintenance payable by the non-resident parent, also provides a collection service, which may involve direct payments between parents, or payments collected from the non-resident parent and passed on to the parent with care. If the parent with care is on benefit the Agency's collection service must be used,[47] whereas other parents may use the Agency's collection service or make private arrangements.[48] If the collection service is used, the Agency[49] will offer the non-resident parent two basic methods of payment[50] intended to be the norm in

---

[37] Child Support Act 1991 s. 24; Child Support Commissioners (Procedure) Regulations 1999.
[38] Child Support Act 1991, s.25.
[39] See *Children Come First* (Cm. 1263-1 (1990)) para. 5.1: "Only 30 per cent of all lone parents receive maintenance payments regularly; and the figure for those who receive Income Support is only 23 per cent".
[40] *ibid.* para. 2.1.
[41] *op. cit.,* para. 5.3.
[42] *Children's Rights and Parents' Responsibilities* (Cm. 4349, 1999), Chap. 1, paras 2, 18.
[43] *ibid.* para. 2.
[44] Cm. 4349 (1999).
[45] *ibid.* Chap. 1, paras 18, 19. See also Chap. 4, paras 25–32.
[46] *ibid.* Chap. 1, para. 16.
[47] Child Support Act 1991, s. 6(1).
[48] *ibid.* s. 4(1), (2); *Children's Rights and Parents' Responsibilities*, Chap 8, para 4.
[49] Exercising the functions of the Secretary of State: see s.29.
[50] Child Support Act 1991, s. 29(2) is the enabling provision; for details on how payments are made, see Child Support (Collection and Enforcement) Regulations 1992, as amended by the Child Support (Collection and Enforcement and Miscellaneous Amendment) Regulations 2000.

most cases: direct debit or standing order,[51] and will stipulate the intervals at which payment is to be made.[52] If these do not work effectively, a deductions from earning order will be set up, as discussed below.

The Child Support, Pensions and Social Security Act 2000 provides for the first time[53] for the recognition of voluntary payments made by a non-resident parent before a maintenance calculation is made, to avoid the accumulation of arrears before the exact amount of liability is determined and thus to provide an incentive for compliance; this is to be available in both benefit and private client cases.[54] The voluntary payment may be set off against arrears which may accumulate due to delay in the Agency making the calculation.[55]

Deduction from earnings orders

15–018 Traditionally, the law had been reluctant to allow a creditor direct access to a person's earnings (not least because of the strength of feeling on the part of organised labour to any interference with the sanctity of the pay packet[56]). But over the years restrictions on the powers of the courts to make orders for the attachment of earnings were removed[57]; and ultimately the Maintenance Enforcement Act 1991[58] made attachment of earnings freely available against those ordered to pay maintenance by court order.

The apparent acceptance of the principle that the court could order an employer to divert part of the employee's earnings direct to a spouse or other creditor, without it being necessary to show that the employee had ever defaulted in complying with the maintenance obligation, evidently encouraged the Government to vest similar powers in the Secretary of State. The Child Support Act 1991 provides that the Secretary of State may make a deduction from earnings order to secure the amount due under a maintenance calculation.[59] Such an order operates as an instruction to the employer to make a deduction from the liable

---

[51] *Children's Rights and Parents' Responsibilities,* Chap. 8, para 7; Child Support (Collection and Enforcement) Regulations 1992, S.I. 1992 No. 1989, reg.3. A liable person may be required to take "all reasonable steps" to open an account on which standing orders or direct debits may be operated: reg. 3(2).

[52] Child Support (Collection and Enforcement) Regulations 1992, S.I. 1992 No. 1989, reg. 4.

[53] Child Support Act s. 28J, inserted by the CSPPA 2000, s. 20.

[54] *ibid.* subs. (1).

[55] *ibid.* subs. (3).

[56] Successfully reflected in the Wages Attachment (Abolition) Act 1870 which protected the wages of "servants, labourers or workmen" from any form of attachment: see generally on the history of the Finer Report para. 4.140–9. Employers also opposed attachment for fear that it would not only involve a considerable burden of administrative work, but would also jeopardise good labour relations.

[57] Attachment was first introduced by Maintenance Orders Act 1958 in an attempt to provide an effective alternative to imprisonment as a means of dealing with maintenance defaulters; and experience of the operation of attachment in practice allayed many of the fears of employers and employees. The Administration of Justice Act 1970 extended the system to all civil debts and also removed a number of restrictions.

[58] Which abolished the principle that attachment could only be ordered against a spouse who had defaulted in making maintenance payment.

[59] Child Support Act 1991, s.31(2).

person's earnings[60] and pay over the amounts deducted to the Child Support Agency.[61] It is important to note that such an order is purely administrative, *i.e.* distinct from an attachment of earnings order made by a court.[62] It not necessary for payments to have fallen into arrears, and the distinction between collection and enforcement is therefore blurred. A deductions of earning order can however also be made to secure payment of arrears.[63] It appears that deduction of earnings orders are used in some 20 per cent of cases where the Agency collects child maintenance, essentially in cases where there is no other reliable method of collection, and this pattern is likely to continue under the reformed scheme, despite the unpopularity of such orders with many non-resident parents.[64] The Secretary of State is obliged in exercising this as other discretions under the Act to have regard to the welfare of any child likely to be affected; and there is a restricted right to appeal to the magistrates' court against the making of the order.[65]

Enforcement: liability orders

15–019 If a person who is liable to make payments of child support defaults and it appears to be "inappropriate" to make a deduction of earnings order—for example because the person concerned is not in employment, or if such an order has proved ineffective[66]—the Secretary of State may[67] apply to the magistrates for a liability order.[68] The magistrates' court is required to make such an order if the court is satisfied that the payments in question have become payable and have not been paid.[69] The making of a liability order is not an end in itself but rather gives the authorities recourse to a wide range of enforcement powers, including distress (sale and seizure of goods by bailiffs to pay a debt)[70] and recovery by means of a garnishee order (on funds in a bank or building society) or charging order (whereby property is sold to meet a debt) through the county court.[71] A late payment penalty rate has been introduced by the Child Support,

---

[60] The Child Support (Collection and Enforcement) Regulations 1992, as amended include complex rules governing the computation of the sums payable; and in particular the Regulations (reg.11) provide for a protected earnings rate below which the employer must not reduce the wages paid to the employee.

[61] Technically, to the Secretary of State: Child Support Act 1991, s.31(5).

[62] Attachment of Earnings Act 1972: see Chap. 16.

[63] Child Support Act 1991, s. 31(3).

[64] *Children's Rights and Parents' Responsibilities,* Chap. 8, para. 8.

[65] Child Support Act 1991, s.32(5).

[66] C.S.A. 1991, s.33 (1), as amended by the CSPSSA 2000, s. 1, Sched. 3, para. 11(17). For details, see Child Support (Collection and Enforcement) Regulations 1992 as amended, Pt IV.

[67] The duty to consider the welfare of children likely to be affected applies to this as to the exercise of other discretionary powers under the C.S.A. 1991; see s.2.

[68] C.S.A. 1991, s.33(2). In *The Queen on the Application of Denson v. CSA* [2002] EWHC Admin. 154, [2002] 1 F.L.R. 938, Munby J. held that a liability order was a necessary and proportionate part of the overall statutory scheme, and did not engage Art. 8 of the European Convention on Human Rights.

[69] *ibid.* s. 33(3).

[70] *ibid.* s.35; Child Support (Collection and Enforcement) Regulations 1992 as amended, reg. 30–32.

[71] *ibid.* s. 36. The Child Support (Collection and Enforcement) Regulations 1992, as amended Pt IV, make detailed provision.

Pensions and Social Security Act 2000.[72] The primary legislation[73] is laconic and provides simply that the amount of penalty payment may not exceed 25 per cent of the amount of child support payable for that week; as so often in this field, the details are governed by regulation.[74] The extra amount will not go to the parent with care but to the Consolidated Fund.[75]

If the above mentioned enforcement procedures fail, more draconian ones are available, the armoury having been augmented by the Child Support, Pensions and Social Security Act 2000, following the enthusiasm displayed in *Children's Rights and Parents' Responsibilities* for the potential effectiveness of novel tough sanctions for non-compliance.[76] Magistrates now have the option of disqualifying a non-resident parent from driving[77] where there is wilful refusal or culpable neglect.[78] This penalty has been criticised as *inter alia* "discriminatory and authoritarian"[79]; its fundamental objective seems as questionable as its proportionality.[80] As has been observed elsewhere,[81] the measure will no doubt affect a man's ability to go to night clubs or greyhound races but will, for the vast majority, also affect their ability to earn their living. As a very last resort,[82] the Secretary of State may apply to the magistrates' court for an order committing the liable person to prison; and the court may commit the defaulter to prison if, but again only if, there has been wilful refusal or culpable neglect.[83]

The enforcement scheme authorised by the Child Support Act 1991 is comprehensive and other remedies under the general law—such as a *Mareva* injunction—are not available in cases of non-payment under a child maintenance calculation.[84]

III. JURISDICTION OF THE COURTS IN RELATION TO CHILD SUPPORT

15–020 This part of the Chapter considers the residual role which courts exercise, notwithstanding the existence of the Child Support Act 1991, to make financial orders in respect of children, under legislation other than that Act.[85] The position

[72] s. 18.
[73] Child Support Act 1991, s. 41A.
[74] *ibid.* subs. (2),(4). Child Support (Collection and Enforcement) Regulations 1992, reg. 7A, as inserted by the Child Support (Collection, Enforcement and Miscellaneous Amendments) Regulations 2000.
[75] *ibid.* s. 41A(6).
[76] Chap. 8.
[77] CSA 1991, ss. 39A and 40B, as inserted by s. 16 of the CSPSSA 2000.
[78] *ibid.* subs. (3)(c).
[79] Lord Stoddart, *Hansard,* H.L., Vol. 612, col. 1347, May 8, 2000.
[80] An important consideration under the Human Rights Act 1998.
[81] S. Cretney, *Family Law* (Sweet and Maxwell, 2000), p. 180.
[82] For comments on the extreme nature of the power in the context of s. 76 of the Magistrates' Court Act 1980, see *per* Waite J. in *R. v. Luton Magistrates' Court, ex p. Sullivan* [1992] 2 F.L.R. 196.
[83] C.S.A. 1991, s.40(3). The maximum period of imprisonment is six weeks: *ibid.* s.40(6)(b).
[84] *Department of Social Security v. Butler* [1996] 1 W.L.R. 1528; [1996] 1 F.L.R. 65, CA.
[85] Namely, the Domestic Proceedings and Magistrates' Courts Act 1978, the Matrimonial Causes Act 1973 and the Children Act 1989, Sched. 1.

has been complicated by the failure over the years to make the Child Support Act system universal in its application.[86]

The General Principle

15–021 The original intention was that the Child Support Agency should assume full responsibility for assessing and reviewing child maintenance claims, and the courts would lose that responsibility.[87] The Act accordingly provides that where a child support officer would have jurisdiction to make a maintenance assessment with respect to a qualifying child and an absent parent, the court is debarred from exercising any power which it would otherwise have to make, vary or revive any maintenance order in relation to the child and non-resident concerned.[88]

Exceptions to the general principle

15–022 The general principle is not, however, as straightforward as might at first appear. The courts[89] retain their powers to make financial orders in respect of children in a number of situations.

(i) *Child support officer has no jurisdiction to make maintenance calculation*[90]

15–023 The child support officer has jurisdiction to make an assessment only if the parent with care, and the qualifying child are all habitually resident in the United Kingdom, and the non-resident parent is either resident in the United Kingdom or is a British public servant working overseas.[91] Accordingly, in any other case the court will be entitled to exercise its full range of powers.

(ii) *Topping-up orders*

15–024 We have already explained[92] that there is an upper limit on child maintenance payable under the formula; the non-resident parent's net weekly income in excess of £2000 is disregarded. However, above this "cap", if the maximum

---

[86] It was originally envisaged that this would be on April 6, 1997 at the end of a transitional period during which the Agency's work would gradually have been phased in. It was later decided to postpone full implementation: see Improving Child Support (Cm. 2745 (1995)), Chap. 4; Child Support Act 1995, s.18.

[87] *Children Come First,* Cm. 1263 (1990), para. 4.1.

[88] Child Support Act 1991, s.8(3). "Maintenance order" is defined in Child Support Act 1991, s.8(11).

[89] A. Clift-Matthews, "The Courts Versus the CSA" [1996] *Fam. Law* 474; S. Deas, "Family Lawyers Sidestep the CSA" [1998] *Fam. Law* 48; G. Davis *et al.* "Child Support and the Residual Role of Lawyers" [1998] *Fam. Law* 304.

[90] Child Support Act 1991, s.8(1).

[91] Child Support Act 1991, s.44, as amended by Social Security Act 1998, s. 86(1), Sched. 7, para. 41; CSPSSA 2000, ss. 1(2), 22, Sched. 3, para. 11(2). See the discussion at p. 432 above.

[92] See p. 441, *supra*.

child maintenance assessment is in force,[93] the court has power to make an order for periodical payments, whether secured or unsecured, provided that the court is satisfied that the circumstances of the case make it appropriate for the non-resident parent to make or secure the making of periodical payments in addition to the child support maintenance payable under the maintenance calculation.[94] The amount of a top-up order is determined in accordance with the relevant statutory criteria.[95] The resources of both parents will be considered in relation to a topping-up order, unlike a maintenance calculation under the Child Support Act 1991. Given the relatively high "cap", applications for top-up orders will be rare in practice.

(iii) *Education expenses orders*

15–025 The court may exercise its powers to make periodical payment orders in cases where the child[96] is, will be or (if the order were to be made) would be receiving instruction at an educational establishment (not defined[97]) or undergoing training for a trade, profession or vocation. It is, in this case, not necessary that any child support calculation should have been made; but the court order must be "made solely for the purpose of requiring" provision of some or all of the expenses incurred in connection with the provision of the instruction or training.[98] This provision covers *inter alia* school fees[99] and other school expenses and the educational expenses at college or university of those under 18.

(iv) *Disabled children*

15–026 The court may exercise its powers[1] to make maintenance orders in respect of a child who is disabled,[2] whether or not a child support calculation is in force. The order must be made solely to meet some or all of any expenses attributable to the child's disability, but a broad approach to the calculation of such expenses is adopted.[3]

---

[93] Child Support Act 1991, s.8(6). The court cannot exercise its powers under this provision unless a maintenance calculation is actually in force.

[94] In *A v. A (Minor: Financial Provision)* [1994] 1 F.L.R. 657, Ward J. made an order for secured periodical payments of £20,000 per annum (whereas the maximum Child Support assessment would at the time have been some £7,500).

[95] See the discussion below at p. 458.

[96] A person aged between 16 and 18 will only come within the definition of a "child" (Child Support Act 1991, s.55(1)) if he or she is attending a recognised educational establishment.

[97] *cf.* the definition of "recognised educational establishment" in CSA 1991, s. 55(3).

[98] Child Support Act 1991, s.8(7).

[99] *L v. L (School Fees: Maintenance Enforcement)* [1997] 2 F.L.R. 252.

[1] In *C v. F (Disabled Child: Maintenance Order)* [1998] 2 F.L.R. 1, the Court of Appeal held that s. 8(8) of the Child Support Act 1991 granted jurisdiction to make a free-standing order under Sched. 1 to the Children Act 1989, and therefore the age restriction in s. 55 of the Child Support Act 1991 (to those under 19) did not apply.

[2] Or in respect of whom a disability living allowance is paid. For the purpose of this provision a child is disabled if he is blind, deaf or dumb or is "substantially and permanently handicapped by illness, injury, mental disorder or congenital deformity" or any prescribed disability: Child Support Act 1991, s.8(9).

[3] .Thus in practice the approach under s. 8(8) is unlikely to be very different from that under Sched. 1 to the Children Act 1989 which permits consideration of all the circumstances: *C v. F (Disabled Child: Maintenance Order)* [1998] 2 F.L.R.1, CA.

(v) *Older children and young persons*

15–027 The court may exercise its powers[4] to make orders in the case of 17 and 18-year-olds who are not in full-time education, or if the education is advanced[5] (*i.e.* a degree course), or in the case of young persons who are over 18.[6] The support of young persons in tertiary education is discussed below in the context of the relevant statutory provisions.

(vi) *Orders against parent with care*

15–028 The Child Support Act provides[7] that the rules[8] restricting the court's powers shall not prevent a court from exercising any power which it has to make a maintenance order in relation to a child if the order is made against a person with care of the child. The policy underlying this provision is not altogether clear; but it may be that it was intended to fill the gap left by the inability of a child support officer to make a calculation against a parent with care notwithstanding the fact that both parents are equally responsible for the child's support. Instances of the exercise of this power will be rare.

(vii) *Written agreements and court orders*

15–029 If parents entered into a written maintenance agreement[9] before April 5, 1993 (the date on which the Child Support Act 1991 came into operation), the Child Support Agency's jurisdiction is ousted, provided the parent with care does not receive benefits.[10] Inevitably, the practical effect of this provision diminishes over time. However, more generally, notwithstanding section 8(3) of the Child Support Act 1991, the court has power in non-benefit cases to make an order in the same terms as a written agreement (a consent order) for the making or securing of periodical payments by a non-resident parent to or for the benefit of a child.[11] Once such a consent order has been made, the court may vary and

---

[4] See below for the definition of "child" in the legislation governing the courts' powers.

[5] See the definition of child in Child Support Act 1991, s. 55(1).

[6] The definition of "child" in s. 52 of the Matrimonial Causes Act 1973 makes no reference to age limits, but s. 29(1) and (3) impose conditions of education/training or special circumstances on the exercise of jurisdiction. The Children Act 1989, Sched. 1, para. 2(1) is to the same effect. It is increasingly recognised that dependency may outlast majority: see *e.g. Richardson v. Richardson (No. 2)* [1994] 2 F.L.R. 1051 *per* Thorpe J.; *J v. C (Child: Financial Provision)* [1999] 1 F.L.R. 152 (Hale J.). See generally M. Letts, "Children: The Continuing Duty To Maintain" [2001] *Fam. Law* 839.

[7] s.8(10).

[8] *i.e.* those contained in Child Support Act 1991, s.8.

[9] For the definition and effect of a maintenance agreement for these purposes, see Child Support Act 1991, s. 9.

[10] Child Support Act 1991, s. 4(10)(a); *B v. B (Periodical Payments: Transitional Provisions)* [1995] 1 F.L.R. 459. Once the parent with care is in receipt of benefits and an assessment is made (even a nil assessment) the court order for maintenance ceases to have effect for all time: *Askew-Page v. Page* [2001] *Fam. Law* 794.

[11] Child Support Act 1981, s.8(5); Child Maintenance (Written Agreements) Order 1993, S.I. 1993 No. 620. Where parties disagreed on the *quantum* of child maintenance, the Agency jurisdiction could nevertheless be avoided by the making of an nominal order at the start of proceedings, varied to an appropriate level at their conclusion: *per* Wilson J. in *V v. V (Child Maintenance)* [2001] 2 F.L.R. 799 at para. [19]; comment by G. Douglas in [1996] *Fam. Law* 649.

enforce its terms. This procedure was initially intended to be a temporary measure pending full implementation of the child support system, but for several years effectively made the Child Support Act optional for "private" cases. Prior to 2002, the making of a consent order permanently ousted the jurisdiction of the Child Support Agency, provided the parent with care was not in receipt of benefits, since no application for a maintenance assessment could subsequently be made. Use of consent orders in private cases proved popular in practice.[12] In addition, an order for spousal maintenance[13] may incorporate some of the costs of supporting children, subject to *pro tanto* reduction on a Child Support Agency calculation. It was held in *Dorney-Kingdom v. Dorney-Kingdom*[14] that such a mechanism is legitimate, since it does not purport to oust the Agency's jurisdiction but is essentially a holding device until the Agency could carry out its proper function; a substantial element of spousal maintenance is essential to its operation.

Changes effected by the Child Support, Pensions and Social Security Act 2000 will put an end (for "new" private law cases) to the permanent ousting of the Child Support Agency's jurisdiction. The change reflects proposals in *Children's Rights and Parents' Responsibilities,* to the effect that parents with court orders should be able in future to turn to the Agency, in the shadow of which private child maintenance arrangements should henceforth be made.[15] Notwithstanding professional[16] and official[17] controversy provoked by these proposals, the principal Act[18] has been amended[19] to permit applications for a maintenance assessment to be accepted provided that the consent order has been in force for a year (that period being one for reflection on the effect of the court order). The amount of child support payable will be determined at the new formula rates. This change will apply only prospectively to "new" cases, *i.e.* orders made after the implementation of the reforms, namely April 2002.[20] However, as a result of government concessions allowing parents a choice of variation avenues[21]—court or Child Support Agency—courts will retain power to vary post-April 2002 consent orders, provided no maintenance calculation has been made by the Child Support Agency.[22] If one is made, the court's power to vary ceases to exist. The finality of consent orders for "new" private cases thus having effectively been removed by the recent reforms, it remains to be seen in practice how many parents will in future opt for the Agency rather than the courts.[23]

---

[12] S. Deas, "Family Lawyers Sidestep the CSA" [1998] *Fam. Law* 48; J. Pirrie' "Periodical Payments by Consent Under the Children Act 1989" [1999] *Fam. Law* 680.

[13] Under s. 23(1)(a) of the Matrimonial Causes Act 1973.

[14] [2000] 2 F.L.R.855, CA.

[15] Chap. 8, paras 23–25.

[16] N. Mostyn, "The Green Paper on Child Support" [1999] *Fam. Law* 95 at 97; J. Pirrie, "Changes to Child Support" [1999] *Fam. Law* 838.

[17] House of Commons Social Security Committee, Tenth Report, *The 1999 Child Support White Paper*, H.C. 798, paras 54–63.

[18] CSA 1991, s. 4(10)(aa).

[19] By CSPSSA 2000, s. 2.

[20] CSA 1991, s. 4(10)(aa) "on or after the date prescribed".

[21] Baroness Hollis, *Official Report,* H.L. Vol. 615, col 1120, July 19, 2000.

[22] Child Support Act 1991, s. 8(3A).

[23] N Wikeley, "Private Cases and the Child Support Agency" [2001] *Fam. Law* 35 at 38.

(viii) *Child not a qualifying child: courts retain powers over children of the family*

15–030 As already pointed out, the Child Support Act only imposes liability on a parent[24]; whereas the Children Act 1989 and the divorce legislation empowers the court to make orders in respect of children of the family; and it follows that the court may still exercise its full range of powers to make financial orders against a child's step-parent. This is discussed in more detail below.

(ix) *Restriction on court's powers only extends to "maintenance orders"[25]: court retains power to make property adjustment and lump sum orders*

15–031 The Child Support Act is concerned only with periodical payments of maintenance; and child support officers have no power to make orders relating to capital. The court's jurisdiction to make such orders remains and is not directly[26] affected by the existence of the child support scheme. The exercise of this jurisdiction is discussed below.

Relationship with ancillary relief orders

15–032 From the outset the relationship between the Child Support Act 1991 and the ancillary relief jurisdiction under Part II of the Matrimonial Causes Act 1973 has been a troubled one.

The formula applied under the Child Support Act 1991 as originally enacted assessed the position of the parties as it was when the assessment was made[27]; and it took no direct account of the terms of settlements which the parties had made in the past. This was one of the most controversial features of the scheme.[28] The question of whether the court would be prepared to reopen a concluded settlement arose for decision in *Crozier v. Crozier*[29]:—

> A divorce court consent order required Mr Crozier to transfer his share in the matrimonial home to his former wife (who was on income support) in full and final settlement of all her financial claims against him; the wife was to be responsible for the mortgage payments, and a nominal order was

---

[24] See the definition of "qualifying child" in Child Support Act 1991, s.3.

[25] Defined by Child Support of Act 1991, s.8(11) to mean an order which requires the making or securing of periodical payments.

[26] The *quantum* of a child support assessment will, of course, affect the means of the absent parent and have an influence on the manner in which the court's discretion is exercised.

[27] See the evidence of the Minister, Mr Alistair Burt, to the House of Commons Social Security Committee, First Report, *The Operation of the Child Support Act,* Session 1993–4, H.C. 69, p. 156.

[28] See *e.g.* White Paper, *Children Come First* (Cm. 1263–1 (1990)), para. 4.12; House of Commons Social Security Committee (H.C. 1991, 277–1, para. 14); Reply by the Government to the . . . Social Security Committee, Cm. 1961 (1991), para. 14; House of Commons Social Security Committee First Report, *The Operation of the Child Support Act,* Session 1993–4 H.C., 69, para. 65.

[29] [1994] 1 F.L.R. 126, Booth J.

made in respect of periodical payments to the child. The result was intended to be that the wife and children would have secure housing (the mortgage interest being met as part of their income support entitlement), a modest but guaranteed income from state benefits, whilst the husband could make a fresh start free from financial obligation to his former wife. The child support assessment was likely to be £29 weekly[30]; and Mr Crozier's grievance was that he had already fulfilled his obligation to support the child by transferring his interest in the home. Since the child support assessment could not at that time make any allowance for the property settlement, Mr Crozier sought leave to appeal out of time against the original consent order made by the court[31] on the ground that the introduction of child support maintenance had destroyed the basis or fundamental assumption underlying the consent order. Specifically, he argued that if he were to be made to pay child maintenance at such a comparatively high level he should have part of the £20,000 received by the wife—who was living with the child and her intended husband in his house—from the sale of the home.

His application for leave was refused. The creation of an administrative procedure which by-passed the jurisdiction of the courts in order to compel a parent to contribute towards his child's maintenance did not fundamentally alter the position as it had been when the consent order had been made. The change related to the mechanism whereby the responsibility is enforced, rather than to the substance of that responsibility. It was true that the clean break principle formed part of the statutory code which governed the courts' approach to applications for ancillary relief; but different considerations had always applied to child maintenance where the ongoing responsibility of the parents had remained a basic factor to which the clean break had never applied.[32]

This judgment firmly closed the door on any attempt to reopen clean break settlements made before the enactment of the Child Support Act 1991[33]; but considerable pressure was exerted on the Government to introduce some modi-

---

[30] Since Mrs Crozier was in receipt of income support the Secretary of State could require her to authorise action under the Act: Child Support Act 1991, s.6.

[31] See *Barder v. Barder (Caluori Intervening)* [1988] A.C. 20, HL.

[32] See *Preston v. Preston* [1982] Fam. 17, CA. The judge also rejected an argument founded on contractual doctrine that the parties' agreement had been frustrated by the subsequent change in the law. Once a financial agreement has been made the subject of a court order its legal effect derives from that order and not from the parties' agreement: *De Lasala v. De Lasala* [1980] A.C. 546, PC; and see the discussion in Chap. 14 at p. 322.

[33] In *Smith v. McInerney* [1994] 2 F.L.R. 1077 Thorpe J. held that a husband who had entered into a separation agreement on the basis of his being released from any further obligation to maintain the wife and children could claim to be indemnified by the wife—by means of a property adjustment order in divorce proceedings—in respect of any Child Support assessment; see Miller, "The CSA and the Clean Break" (1995) 7 CFLQ 152. In *Mawson v. Mawson* [1994] 2 F.L.R. 985 the same judge was prepared, in deciding a wife's appeal against a periodical payments order made in her favour, to take account of the fact that legislative changes introduced into the child support scheme in February 1994 had reduced the husband's outgoings.

fication of the formula to take account of the perceived injustice[34] caused by the formula's failure to take account of property settlements intended to commute child support obligations. The response was to introduce two measures. The first, effected by delegated legislation,[35] was intended to give a measure of "broad-brush" relief where there had been a qualifying transfer of property before April 5, 1993, through inserting an additional consideration into the already complex formula.[36] The second was the departure system introduced by Child Support Act 1995 and continued—under the new terminology of "variation"—under amendments effected to the Child Support Act 1991 by the Child Support, Pensions and Social Security Act 2000, described earlier in this Chapter.[37]

The continuing "unsatisfactory interface" between the jurisdictions of the child support officer and of the courts in determining the level of child maintenance was commented on by Wilson J. in *V v. V (Child Maintenance),*[38] discussed below.[39] The essential problem is that the level of child maintenance bears upon the content of other orders the court makes in exercise of its ancillary relief jurisdiction,[40] yet the existence of two separate statutory schemes make a single, holistic resolution of all issues impossible.[41]

The reforms effected by the Child Support, Pensions and Social Security Act 2000 would appear to make the court's task in achieving a holistic result no easier, since henceforth a child maintenance calculation by the Child Support Agency will after one year override the *quantum* fixed by an order of the court.[42]

The exercise of the courts' statutory powers

15–033 We have explained above the circumstances in which the courts retain power to make financial orders for children, and a brief account of the relevant statutory provisions will therefore be given. For historical reasons, the law draws a distinction between divorce and other matrimonial proceedings on the one hand and applications by one parent against the other under the provisions of the Children Act 1989 on the other.

---

34 The White Paper *Improving Child Support* (Cm. 2745 (1995)) stated that the failure to take account of pre-1993 property settlements was perhaps the "biggest single criticism" of the Child Support Act: para. 3.2.

35 Child Support and Income Support (Amendment) Regulations 1995, S.I. 1995 No. 1045, regs. 45 and 46, and Sched. 3A.

36 By increasing the transferor's "exempt income"; *Improving Child Support,* Cm. 2745 (1995), para. 3.2. It was normally assumed that the partners were entitled to half of the equity in the property. No allowance was made if the applicant's transfer was less than £5,000; but for a transfer of £5,000 to £9,999 the transferor's "exempt income" was increased by £20 weekly, for a transfer of £10,000 to £24,999 by £40 weekly, and for a larger transfer £60 weekly. A transfer of only part of the beneficial interest qualified: *Secretary of State for Social Security v. Henderson* [1999] 1 F.L.R. 496.

37 p. 442 above.

38 [2001] 2 F.L.R. 799 at 800.

39 At p. 463.

40 Under Pt II of the Matrimonial Causes Act 1973, discussed in Chap. 14.

41 *V v. V (Child Maintenance)* [2001] 2 F.L.R. 799.

42 Child Support Act 1991, s. 4(10) (aa), discussed above at p. 453.

Powers exercisable in matrimonial proceedings

15–034 The principal source of power to make financial provision directly[43] in respect of children on divorce is the Matrimonial Causes Act 1973.[44]

The court's powers and duties in divorce proceedings[45] arise in respect of any child of the family[46]; and this broad definition—extending to any step-child brought up by a married couple[47]—reflects changing social patterns incidental to increasing divorce and remarriage.[48]

15–035 **(i) Orders that can be made.** The court's powers to make financial orders on divorce in respect of a child of the family are wide (but not limitless).[49] Thus the court has power to make periodical payment orders for the benefit of a child of the family direct to the child and to someone else on his behalf,[50] and such an order may be either secured or unsecured. The court may also order the payment of a lump sum or sums for the benefit of a child of the family to the child or to someone else on his or her behalf[51]; it may also order payment of a lump sum to meet liabilities or expenses incurred in maintaining or for the benefit of a child prior to the making of an application.[52] It may order the transfer[53] of specified property to a child, or to a third party on a child's behalf; it may order the settlement[54] of property for the benefit of children of the family; and it may make an order varying any "ante-nuptial or post-nuptial" settlement made on the parties to the marriage for the benefit of the parties to the marriage and/or of the children of the family.[55] If the court makes a secured periodical payments order, lump sum or property adjustment order, it may also order the

---

[43] Note that under s. 25(1) of the Matrimonial Causes Act 1973 the welfare of an minor child of the family is the first consideration in ancillary relief proceedings; see Chap. 14.

[44] A party to a marriage may apply to the Family Proceedings Court (on grounds which include failure to maintain a child of the family) for an order for periodical payments or a lump sum under the Domestic Proceedings and Magistrates' Courts Act 1978. In view of the limited relevance of this jurisdiction it is not separately discussed here.

[45] And in most of the other proceedings mentioned in this Chap.: see below.

[46] For the definition, see M.C.A. 1973, s.52(1).The question of whether the couple have treated the child as a child of their family is judged objectively: *Re A (Child of the Family)* [1998] 1 F.L.R. 347.

[47] But not a child of a cohabiting couple: *J v. J (A Minor: Property Transfer)* [1993] 2 F.L.R. 56.

[48] But an unborn child cannot be treated as a child of the family: if a man marries a woman who is pregnant by someone else the baby will be a child of their family if the husband treats it as such after birth—even if only for a very short time and even if the wife has deceived him into thinking that he is the father—but if the relationship breaks down before the birth the child will be outside the definition, whatever the husband may have said about his intentions to treat the baby as his own: *A v. A (Family: Unborn Child)* [1974] Fam 6.

[49] For a detailed consideration see the 5th ed. of this work, pp. 372–80.

[50] Both powers may be exercised simultaneously: *G v. G (Periodical Payments: Jurisdiction)* [1997] 1 F.L.R. 368.

[51] M.C.A. 1973, s. 23 (1)(f).

[52] M.C.A. 1973, s. 23(3)(a)(b); see *Askew-Page v. Page* [2001] *Fam. Law* 794.

[53] *Re B (Child: Property Transfer)* [1999] 2 F.L.R. 418; Webster [1999] *Fam. Law* 834.

[54] L. Cooke, "Children and Real Property—Trusts, Interests and Considerations" [1998] *Fam. Law* 349.

[55] The court may also make an order extinguishing or reducing the interest of either of the parties to the marriage under any such settlement: M.C.A. 1973, s.23(1)(b), (d), (e) and (f) and in s.24(1) (a), (b) and (c).

sale of any property in which one or both of the parties has a beneficial interest.[56] The exercise of discretion in respect of orders for capital provision is discussed at the conclusion of this Chapter.

15–036 **(ii) Exercise of the court's discretion.** In residual cases where the court's jurisdiction is retained, the formula applicable under the maintenance requirement calculated in accordance with the Child Support Act 1991 will, as we have explained above, exercise a powerful influence on the quantum of child maintenance.[57] The Matrimonial Causes Act 1973 provides that as regards the exercise of its powers to make periodical payment orders, transfer of property orders or orders for the sale of property in relation to a child of the family, the court should have regard to all the circumstances of the case, and in particular to:

> "(a) the financial needs of the child;
> (b) the income, earning capacity (if any), property and other financial resources of the child;
> (c) any physical or mental disability of the child;
> (d) the manner in which he was being and in which the parties to the marriage expected him to be educated or trained;
> (e) the spouses' financial resources and financial needs, the standard of living enjoyed by the family before the breakdown, and any disability of either party to the marriage.[58]

It has been held[59] that the court should not normally exercise the power to order a settlement of property so as to order life-long provision for a child who is under no disability and whose education is secured. Other restrictions on the making of capital provision orders are discussed at the conclusion of this Chapter.

A parent of a young person undertaking tertiary education, or the young person herself, may, where the parents are divorced or separated, bring an application against a parent for financial assistance with the expenses of that education. The court will consider all the circumstances in determining such an application and the general statutory criteria apply. It is difficult to discern general principles from the case-law in this context.[60]

The legislation seeks to structure the court's discretion by providing that, in regard to the exercise of its financial powers against the party to a marriage in favour of a child of the family who is not the child of that party, the court is also to have regard to the following specified matters[61]:—

---

[56] M.C.A. 1973, s. 24A.

[57] See p. 453 above; *E. v. C. (Child Maintenance)* [1996] 1 F.L.R. 472, *per* Douglas Brown J.

[58] 1973, s.25(3).

[59] *Lilford (Lord) v. Glynn* [1979] 1 W.L.R. 78; *Chamberlain v. Chamberlain* [1973] 1 W.L.R. 1557; *Kiely v. Kiely* [1988] 1 F.L.R. 248, CA; *Harnett v. Harnett* [1973] Fam. 156; and *A v. A (A Minor: Financial Provision)* [1994] 1 F.L.R. 657.

[60] *B v. B (Adult Student: Liability to Support)* [1998] 1 F.L.R. 373; Harte, "University Students and Financial Provision" [1998] *Fam. Law* 103; Silcock, "University Students and Financial Provision" [1998] *Fam. Law* 694; Costley-Evans, "Maintenance Liability for Students" [1999] *Fam. Law* 45; Snow, "Maintenance Liability for Students" [1999] *Fam. Law* 345.

[61] M.C.A. 1973, s.25(4).

"(a) to whether that party assumed any responsibility for the child's maintenance, and, if so, to the extent to which, and the basis upon which, that party assumed such responsibility and to the length of time for which that party discharged such responsibility;
(b) to whether in assuming and discharging such responsibility that party did so knowing that the child was not his or her own;
(c) to the liability of any other person to maintain the child."

(iii) Applications by a child in parents' divorce proceedings. The divorce legislation is primarily concerned with applications by one spouse for an order against the other, but a child of the family who has attained the age of 18 may make an application for financial relief by intervening in the parents' matrimonial proceedings.[62] Such a child may also intervene to seek a variation of an existing order.[63] **15–037**

(iv) Duration of orders and age limits **15–038**

(a) Financial provision orders and transfer of property orders cannot be made in respect of a child who has attained the age of 18.[64]
(b) Periodical financial provision (whether secured or unsecured, and whether in nullity, divorce, separation or failure to maintain proceedings) will not, in the first instance, be ordered beyond the child's attaining the upper limit of compulsory school age.[65] However, the court may extend the obligation to make the payments to a later date (but not beyond the age of 18) if it considers that in the circumstances of the case the welfare of the child so requires.[66]
(c) Periodical orders must determine when the child attains 18.[67]

However, these three restrictions do not apply if (a) the "child is, or will be or [if provision extending beyond 18 were made] would be, receiving instruction at an educational establishment or undergoing training for a trade, profession or vocation, whether or not he is also, or will also be in gainful employment"; or (b) there are "special circumstances which justify" the making of a different order.[68]

---

62 Family Proceeding Rules 1991 (S.I. 1999 No. 1247), r. 2.54; *Downing v. Downing (Downing Intervening)* [1976] Fam. 288 [1976] 3 W.L.R. 335, FD (even where the divorce was granted years earlier). The court can only make orders continuing after a child's 18th birthday if the child is receiving education or training or there are special circumstances: see below.
63 M.C.A. 1973, s.31.
64 MCA. 1973, s.29(2). A child attains a particular age at the commencement of the relevant anniversary of his birth: Family Law Reform Act 1969, s.9.
65 M.C.A. 1973, s.29(2).
66 s.29(2)(a).
67 s.29(1),(2)(b).
68 s.29(3).

Finally, it should be noted that periodical payments orders[69] in favour of a child terminate on the death of the payer, whether or not the order so provides.[70]

Financial orders for children under the Children Act 1989

15–039 Before the coming into force of the Children Act 1989 there were a number of unco-ordinated procedures governing the making of financial provision orders for children outside matrimonial proceedings—notably the provisions of the Affiliation Proceedings Act 1957 under which the court could make an affiliation order against the putative father of an illegitimate child, and provisions in the Guardianship of Minors Acts which allowed parents to seek orders about the upbringing of their children without making any order about their marriage. But the Children Act 1989 reformed and assimilated the various private law provisions relating to the courts' powers to order financial provisions in proceedings which are not connected with the marriage of a child's parents—in effect by generalising for all children the benefit of principles which had already been established in the context of particular proceedings.[71]

(a) Qualified applicants

15–040 The following persons may apply[72] for a financial order under the Children Act 1989 in respect of a child:—

(i) A parent. This expression extends to adoptive parents and to both parents of an illegitimate child. The ordinary meaning of the word is extended so as to "include any party to a marriage (whether or not subsisting) in relation to whom the child . . . is a child of the family." Hence, it will be possible for a child's biological parent to initiate proceedings claiming support for the child against the child's step-parent or for the step-parent to seek an order against the biological parent.

(ii) A guardian.

(iii) Any person in whose favour a residence order[73] is in force with respect to a child. Hence, anyone given the right to care for a child by court order can seek a financial order for the child's support.

(iv) An adult student or trainee or person who can show special circumstances may make an application for an order[74]; but in this case no

---

[69] But not a secured periodical payments order.

[70] M.C.A. 1973, s.29(4).

[71] Law Com. No. 172, para. 4.63.

[72] The court may also make a financial order whenever it makes, varies, or discharges a residence order—and a residence order may be made in any family proceedings, whether or not applied for, if the court considers that the order should be made. The court can also make financial orders if the child is a ward of court, whether or not any application has been made for such an order.

[73] *i.e.* an order which settles the arrangements to be made about where a child is to live.

[74] But the court's powers on such an application are limited to making periodical payment or lump sum orders.

order is to be made if the parents are living together in the same household.[75]

(b) Orders which may be made

15–041 The range of orders available is now very wide, on the pattern of the range of orders available for children in divorce proceedings. On an application under the Children Act 1989 the court may order the child's parent or parents[76]:

(i) To make periodical payments, secured or unsecured.
(ii) To pay a lump sum (and it is expressly provided[77] that such an order may be made to enable expenses in connection with the birth or maintenance of the child which were reasonably incurred before the making of the order to be met).
(iii) To make a transfer or settlement of specified property to which the parent is entitled either in possession or reversion. These latter two powers are discussed below.
(iv) To transfer a tenancy.[78]

15–042 **(v) Interim orders—variation of orders.** The court has wide powers[79] to make interim orders, and to vary periodical payment orders.

(c) The exercise of the discretion

15–043 The Children Act 1989[80] lays down guidelines for the exercise of the court's powers which largely follow the precedent of matrimonial law.[81] It is provided[82]:

> In deciding whether to exercise its powers, and if so in what manner, the court shall have regard to all the circumstances including—
>
> (a) the income, earning capacity, property and other financial

---

[75] The restriction thus gives effect to the settled policy of the law that a child cannot compel parents living together in a conventional relationship to provide support.

[76] Defined to include step-parents etc.

[77] Children Act 1989, Sched. 1, para. 5(1).

[78] *K. v. K. (Minors: Property Transfer)* [1992] 2 F.L.R. 220, CA (but note that the child's welfare is not the paramount consideration in determining such an application); *Pearson v. Franklin (Parental Home: Ouster)* [1994] 1 F.L.R. 246, CA (application under Children Act 1989, Sched. 1 is the appropriate procedure for dealing with occupation of family home). Under F.L.A. 1996, s. 53 and Sched. 7, the court has power to order the transfer of certain kinds of tenancy from one cohabitant to the other on the breakdown of their relationship. The use of this jurisdiction may have made applications for transfer of tenancies under the Children Act 1989, Sched 1. less frequent

[79] The powers of a (magistrates') Family Proceedings Court in relation to financial orders are limited: such a court cannot make orders for transfer or settlement of property, or for secured periodical payments, and its power to order a lump sum is restricted to a maximum payment of £1,000. Children Act 1989, Sched. 1, paras . 6 and 7 (variation) and 9 (interim orders).

[80] Children Act 1989, Sched. 1, para. 4(1).

[81] Law Com. No. 172, para. 4.64.

[82] Children Act 1989, Sched. 1, para. 4(1).

resources which the applicant, parents[83] and the person in whose favour the order would be made has or is likely to have in the foreseeable future;

(b) the financial needs, obligations and responsibilities which each of those persons has or is likely to have in the foreseeable future;

(c) the financial needs of the child;

(d) the income, earning capacity (if any), property and other financial resources of the child;

(e) any physical or mental disability of the child;

(f) the manner in which the child was being, or was expected to be, educated or trained.[84]

The legislation also contains a provision similar to that in the matrimonial legislation dealing with the factors to be taken into account where the "parent" against whom the order is sought is not the child's mother or father.[85]

The Children Act 1989 does not state that the child's welfare is to be the paramount or even the first consideration, but it is one of the circumstances to be taken into account.[86]

Orders for capital provision

15–044 Both the Matrimonial Causes Act 1973 and the Children Act 1989, as we have seen, confer powers to make capital orders.[87] The courts have been insistent—whether the application be made in divorce or in respect of an illegitimate child—that the question is whether provision is required for the child's maintenance during dependency,[88] and that it is not appropriate to make provision by way of capital endowment to create a legacy to be enjoyed after dependency has ceased.[89] Typical is the provision made for a home during the child's minority; an outright transfer to the parent with care is not normally ordered.[90] In *A*

---

[83] This states the broad effect of Children Act 1989, Sched. 1, para. 4(1)(b); but not the distinction drawn in the Act between applications for orders for persons over 18 and others.

[84] There are minor differences between the guidelines for the exercise of the discretion in proceedings instituted under the Children Act and those laid down in relation to divorce and other matrimonial proceedings. The divorce legislation requires the court to have regard to the contributions which each of the parties has made or is likely in the foreseeable future to make to the welfare of the family. In proceedings under the Children Act 1989 there is no reference to the standard of living enjoyed by the family before the breakdown of the marriage, there is no reference to the age of each party to the marriage or to the duration of the marriage.

[85] Children Act 1989, Sched. 1, para. 4(2).

[86] *J v. C (Child: Financial Provision)* [1999] 1 F.L.R. 152 at 156 *per* Hale J.

[87] For commentaries, see Wingert, "Capital Provision for Unmarried Parents" [1994] *Fam. Law* 194; Gifford, "Financial Provision for Children" [1996] *Fam. Law* 501; R. Spon-Smith, "Provision of a Home Under the Children Act 1989: A Suggested Trust Deed" [1999] *Fam. Law* 763. Note that the welfare of the child is the first consideration in proceedings under the M.C.A. 1973 (see s. 25(1)) but not under Sched. 1 to the Children Act 1989: *per* Wilson J. in *V v. V (Child Maintenance)* [2001] 2 F.L.R. 799 at 807.

[88] *Kiely v. Kiely* [1988] F.L.R. 248.

[89] Now realistically seen as continuing beyond the legal age of majority: *J v. C (Child: Financial Provision)* [1999] 1 F.L.R. 152 (age 21); *V v. V (Child Maintenance)* [2001] 2 F.L.R. 799 (age 21).

[90] *K v. K (Minors: Property Transfer)* [1992] 2 F.L.R. 220.

v. A (Minor) (Financial Provision)[91] Ward J. declined to order an outright transfer of the house in which the child was living even though the father was so rich that he could do so without even being aware of the fact.[92] The father's obligations were limited to providing for his child's maintenance and education (including tertiary education) until she reached independence. In the circumstances the house would be settled to provide her with a right to live there, and an order for secured periodical payments of £20,000 annually[93] was made.[94]

As a general principle, the powers should be exercised for the purposes of providing maintenance by way of specific expenditure on an item of capital, and not as means of capitalising periodic maintenance to circumvent the prohibition in section 8(3) of the Child Support Act 1991. In a number of cases the courts have held that it is legitimate to make a lump sum order. In *Phillips v. Peace*[95] the father's house was worth £2.6 million and he enjoyed a lavish lifestyle. He nevertheless obtained a nill child support assessment on the basis that he had no income. Johnson J. ordered him to pay £90,000 to provide a home and furniture,[96] holding that the court's powers under the Children Act should be exercised only to meet the child's needs for a particular item of capital expenditure, rather than a continuing future income. In *V v. V (Child Maintenance)*[97] where the parties were unable to agree the *quantum* of child maintenance either at the beginning or the conclusion of court proceedings and no nominal order capable of variation had been made at their outset, Wilson J. exercised jurisdiction[98] to order the payment of substantial lump sums for the benefit of two children, to make up the shortfall in their ongoing maintenance.[99]

A child has an entitlement to be brought up according to a standard of living commensurate with a parent's resources. Thus in *H v. P (Illegitimate Child: Capital Provision)*[1] the court held that the child of a man with annual earnings in excess of £30,000 was entitled to be brought up in circumstances commensurate with those earnings; and the court ordered that £30,000 be settled on terms that a home would be provided for the child during his minority or until he came to the end of his full-time education. In *J v. C (Child: Financial Provision)*[2] the child's father won £1.4 million on the national lottery, Hale J. ordered[3] settlement of £70,000 to provide housing and £12,000 for furniture, holding that the child was entitled to be brought up in circumstances which bore some relationship to the father's current resources.

---

[91] [1994] 1 F.L.R. 657.
[92] See [1994] 1 F.L.R. 657 at 662.
[93] And for school fees in addition.
[94] The father was a foreign resident who lived a precarious existence; and it seems the order was intended to survive his death.
[95] [1996] 2 F.L.R. 230; J. Priest, "Child Support and the Non-Standard Earner" (1996) 9 CFLQ 63.
[96] Plus some items of past expenditure: expenses associated with the birth, baby clothing and equipment, and school registration.
[97] [2001] 2 F.L.R. 799.
[98] Under the Matrimonial Causes Act 1973, s. 23(1)(d).
[99] On whether this exercise if jurisdiction was legitimate, see the comment by Professor G. Douglas in [2001] *Fam. Law* 649.
[1] [1993] *Fam. Law* 515, Wandsworth C. C., Collins J.
[2] [1999] 1 F.L.R. 152.
[3] Under Children Act 1989, s. 15 and Sched. 1.

That said, the court's powers to order capital provision for children are exercised sparingly, predominantly in cases where resources are ample and not in cases where parents are of limited means.[4]

The provisions[5] relating specifically to lump sum orders representing sums expended in the past on the maintenance of children, or otherwise attributable to their benefit, should not be overlooked. In *Askew-Page v. Page*[6] it was held to be legitimate for the court to make[7] a lump sum order in respect of debts attributable to the children which the mother had already incurred.

---

[4] *Kiely v. Kiely* [1988] 1 F.L.R. 248, CA. See also *Chamberlain v. Chamberlain* [1973] 1 W.L.R. 1557, CA; *Harnett v. Harnett* [1973] Fam. 156; and *Lilford (Lord) v. Glynn* [1979] 1 W.L.R. 78.

[5] M.C.A. 1973, s. 23(3); Children Act 1989, Sched. 1, para. 5.

[6] [2001] *Fam. Law* 794. See also *Phillips v. Peace* [1996] 2 F.L.R. 230 and *J v. C (Child: Financial Provision)* [1999] 1 F.L.R. 152.

[7] Under M.C.A. 1973 s. 23(3)(a).

CHAPTER SIXTEEN

ENFORCEMENT OF FINANCIAL OBLIGATIONS[1]

I. INTRODUCTION

16–001 It is one thing to obtain an order from a court; it is often quite another to make the person to whom the order is addressed comply. Many reasons are offered for non-compliance with orders for financial provision.[2] It may be difficult or impossible to trace the debtor.[3] Many debtors convince themselves that they lack the means to support their former partners.[4] Moreover, the obligation is connected with an intimate personal relationship; and divided loyalties may be involved. Even a debtor with ample means[5] may be angry, unreasonable[6] and determined not to pay.[7]

In Chapter 15 we have described both how the Government's lack of faith in a court-based system of child maintenance led to the creation of the Child Support Agency and the problems the Agency has encountered. It was originally envisaged that the Agency's collection service would extend also to spousal maintenance, but that proposal now appears finally to have been abandoned.[8] Thus there are many cases in which court orders dealing with financial matters[9]

---

[1] See *Report of the Committee on Statutory Maintenance Limits*, Cmnd. 3587, (1968); *Report of the Committee on the Enforcement of Judgment Debts*, Cmnd. 3909 (1969); *Report of the Committee on One-Parent Families*, Cmnd. 5629, (1974); *Children Come First, The Government's Proposals for the Maintenance of Children*, Cm. 1263 (1990) Vols I and II; McGregor, Blom-Cooper and Gibson, *Separated Spouses* (1970); Gibson [1982] 12 *Fam. Law* 138; Gibson, "The Future for Maintenance" [1991] C.J.Q. 330; S. Oliver and P. Clements *Enforcing Family Financial Orders* (Family Law, 1999); D. Levy, "Can't Pay Won't Pay: Enforcing Financial Orders in the UK" [2001] *Fam. Law* 48.

[2] See Chap. 14.

[3] For means of obtaining information for tracing a debtor, see D. Levy [2001] *Fam. Law* 48 at 49 and 50–51.

[4] The Committee on the *Enforcement of Judgment Debts*, Cmnd. 3587 (1969), saw the basic problem as "not a problem of enforcement but of economics, . . . we cannot too strongly or too often invite attention to the simple fact that no improvement which we can suggest in the machinery of the courts will put more money into pockets of husbands and debtors or enable them to meet commitments beyond their capacity to pay" (para. 1306).

[5] For a recent example, see *Mubarak v. Mubarak* [2001] 1 F.L.R. 673 [2001] 1 F.L.R. 698, FD, discussed later in this Chapter.

[6] See *Report of the Committee on One-Parent Families*, Cmnd. 5629 (1974), para. 4.172.

[7] The Maintenance Enforcement Act 1991 sought to make it less burdensome for those who were prepared in principle to pay maintenance by giving the courts power to make so-called "means of payment" orders. If a periodical payments order is made the court may also order the debtor to make payment by means of a standing order or direct debit; and it may make an attachment of earnings order: see s.1(4).

[8] No mention of spousal maintenance was made in Chap. 8 of *A New Contract for Welfare: Children's Rights and Parents' Responsibilities* (Cm. 4349, July 1999).

[9] The enforcement of child support through court orders has been discussed in Chap. 15.

have to be enforced by traditional court-focused methods, and this Chapter seeks to give a brief outline of the current law and practice.

II. RESTRICTIONS ON THE ENFORCEMENT OF MAINTENANCE ARREARS; REMITTING ARREARS

16–002 Historically, periodical payment orders were regarded as fundamentally different from other legal obligations. Whereas in the case of a contract debt it was no business of the courts whether the creditor needed the money owed or not, a maintenance order was seen to be justified only as a means of providing support for a dependant[10]; and the question of the parties' relative needs was therefore seen as highly relevant to the question whether the obligation should be enforced or not; and, in particular, the court would exercise a discretion over the extent to which enforcement of accrued arrears under such orders should be allowed.[11] If the creditor waited for a year or more to seek enforcement, it might be thought that she did not in reality need the money or at least had managed well enough without it; and to allow arrears to be enforced without limit might cause serious injustice to a debtor who might reasonably regard the liability as something he could forget about.[12]

For these reasons it became the practice not to allow the enforcement of more than one year's accumulation of arrears without leave of the court[13]; and statute[14] now provides that arrears which became due more than 12 months before the institution of the enforcement proceedings[15] are not to be enforced through the

[10] *Re Robinson* (1884) 27 Ch.D. 160; *Linton v. Linton* (1885) 15 Q.B.D. 239; *Watkins v. Watkins* [1896] P. 222 at 226–227; *H v. H (Financial Provision)* [1993] 2 F.L.R. 35; *B v. C (Enforcement: Arrears)* [1995] 1 F.L.R. 467; *Re Bradley-Hole (A Bankrupt)* [1995] 1 W.L.R. 1097. It followed from this doctrine that the right to receive payments under such an order cannot be assigned: *Re Robinson* (1884) 27 Ch.D. 160. The doctrine was originally developed by the Ecclesiastical Court in the context of alimony for a judicially separated wife. It was subsequently applied to an order for maintenance made on divorce (*Watkins v. Watkins* (*supra*)), and the same reasoning was held to be applicable to orders for maintenance made by magistrates: *Paquine v. Snary* [1909] 1 K.B. 688. The convention that "stale" arrears are not to be enforced was based on the view that a creditor who did not act speedily was probably not in need of support; but enforcement may now more readily be given if the order was part of a financial package and there is some reasonable explanation for the delay: *H v. H (Financial Provision)* [1993] 2 F.L.R. 35.

[11] *Robins v. Robins* [1907] 2 K.B. 13 at 17; *Campbell v. Campbell* [1922] P. 187 at 193; *Re Hedderwick* [1933] 1 Ch. 669 at 675; *Luscombe v. Luscombe (Westminster Bank Ltd Garnishee)* [1962] 1 All E.R. 668; *James v. James* [1964] P. 303 at 306-307; and n. 17, below.

[12] *Russell v. Russell* [1986] 1 F.L.R. 465 at 473, *per* Lord Donaldson of Lymington.

[13] For the factors which were considered relevant to the exercise of the court's discretion, see *Pilcher v. Pilcher (No. 2)* [1956] 1 All E.R. 463; *Luscombe v. Luscombe (Westminster Bank Ltd Garnishee)* [1962] 1 All E.R. 668; *Purba v. Purba* [2001] 1 F.L.R. 444.

[14] Matrimonial Causes Act 1973, s.32 and Domestic Proceedings and Magistrates' Courts Act 1978, s.32(4) apply to enforcement in the High Court and county court; and there is no statutory prohibition on the enforcement of arrears by proceedings in a magistrates' court: see *Pilcher v. Pilcher (No. 2)* [1956] 1 All E.R. 463; *Ross v. Pearson* [1976] 1 W.L.R. 224; *Fowler v. Fowler* (1981) 2 F.L.R. 141; *Dickens v. Pattison* [1985] F.L.R 610; *B v. C (Enforcement of Arrears)* [1995] 1 F.L.R. 467 from which it appears that the usual practice is to refuse enforcement of arrears in accordance with the practice of the superior courts.

[15] The rule applies not only to arrears under unsecured periodical payment orders, but also to arrears under other financial provision orders and interim orders for maintenance: M.C.A. 1973, s.32(1).

High Court or any county court without the leave of the court.[16] If the court is asked to allow enforcement of arrears over one year old, the starting point is that the arrears should not be enforced unless there are special circumstances.

The court also has a statutory power to remit the payment of the arrears or of any part thereof[17]; and the exercise of this discretion is governed by a rule of practice—which is not, however, inflexible—that arrears accrued more than 12 months before the enforcement proceedings were started will be remitted.[18]

III. DIFFERENT COURTS; DIFFERENT REMEDIES

16–003 It is necessary to distinguish between enforcement of financial orders in the county court and the High Court ("the superior courts") on the one hand and enforcement of maintenance orders in the magistrates' courts on the other. An important link between the two systems exists to the extent that a High Court or a county court maintenance order may be registered in a magistrates' court for enforcement and will be treated as a magistrates' court order for so long as the order is so registered.[19] In 1998 the Lord Chancellor's Advisory Group on Ancillary Relief submitted a *Report on Enforcement of Orders* in which it observed that one of the defects of the present system is its fragmented nature and that there should be one originating process for enforcement.[20] To date the recommendations have not been acted upon and it appears that the reform of enforcement remedies in family proceedings may have been subjugated to a wider review of enforcement procedures in civil justice.[21] At the time of going to press, the Group's recommendations are once again under consideration.

IV. THE SUPERIOR COURTS

Enforcement in the superior courts

16–004 The following enforcement procedures may be relevant:

(i) Bankruptcy;

---

[16] If an application for leave to enforce such an order is made, the court may refuse leave, or grant leave subject to such restrictions and conditions (including conditions as to the allowing of time for payment or the making of payment by instalments) as the court thinks proper: M.C.A. 1973, s.32.

[17] *B v. C (Enforcement of Arrears)* [1995] 1 F.L.R. 467, *per* Johnson J. (relying on *Russell v. Russell* [1986] 1 F.L.R. 465, CA).

[18] Magistrates' Courts Act 1980, s.95; M.C.A. 1973, s.31(2A).

[19] *Russell v. Russell* [1986] 1 F.L.R. 465, CA; *Bernstein v. O'Neill* [1989] 2 F.L.R. 1; *R v. Bristol Magistrates' Court ex p. Hedge* [1997] 1 F.L.R. 88; *R. v. Cardiff Magistrates Court ex p. Czech* [1999] 1 F.L.R. 95. But the underlying principle is that the discretion is a discretion whether to enforce stale arrears, not whether there is a discretion to remit them: *B v. C (Enforcement: Arrears)* [1995] 1 F.L.R. 467.

[20] *Report on Enforcement of Orders*, LCD, 1998, para 5.1

[21] *per* Thorpe L.J. in *Mubarak v. Mubarak* [2001] 1 F.L.R. 698 at para [42]. Note that the new enforcement regime of the Civil Procedure Rules 1998, Pts 70–73 (in force March 25, 2002) does not currently apply to family proceedings, which continue to be governed by the "old" Rules of the Supreme Court and County Court Rules: FPR 1991, r. 1.3(1); CPR 1998, r. 2.1(2).

(ii) Execution against goods;
(iii) Garnishee order;
(iv) Charging order;
(v) Appointment of a receiver;
(vi) Sequestration;
(vii) Committal to prison: the judgment summons;
(viii) Attachment of earnings;
(ix) Registration in the magistrates' court.

of the coverage given to them.

1. Bankruptcy[22]

16–005 The making of a bankruptcy order[23] has a dramatic effect: in principle, the bankrupt is debarred from dealing with his property,[24] and the bankrupt's estate will vest in a trustee[25] who is obliged to distribute the property amongst the creditors in respect of the "bankruptcy debts".[26] Bankruptcy also involves certain civic and other penalties.[27] In due course,[28] the debtor will usually be discharged from bankruptcy, and that discharge releases him from all bankruptcy debts.[29]

It has never been possible to found a bankruptcy petition on a failure to make periodical payments of maintenance[30]; and, although at one time a lump sum order was enforceable as a bankruptcy debt,[31] it is now provided[32] that obligations arising under an order made in family or domestic proceedings are not provable.[33] In *Levy v. Legal Services Commission*[34] the Court of Appeal held

[22] Miller, "The Effect of Insolvency on applications for Financial Provision" (1998) 10 CFLQ 29; Costley-White, "Bankruptcy—Back to Basics" [2000] *Fam. Law* 181.

[23] Under Insolvency Act 1986.

[24] Insolvency Act 1986, s.284; see *Re Flint (A Bankrupt)* [1993] 1 F.L.R. 763 (divorce court consent order for transfer of bankrupt's interest in matrimonial home void). As to whether a court order constitutes a disposition for the purposes of this provision, *cf. Burton v. Burton* [1986] 2 F.L.R. 419 at 425, *per* Butler-Sloss J.; and *Re Mordant, Mordant v. Halls* [1996] 1 F.L.R. 334 at 343, *per* Sir D. Nicholls V.-C. The court has power to give its consent to (or subsequently ratify) a disposition by the bankrupt; but the factors relevant to the exercise of that discretionary power are not discussed in *Re Mordant, Mordant v. Halls* (above) notwithstanding the fact that it was an application by a wife to review the District Judge's refusal to consent to a payment made to her.

[25] Insolvency Act 1986, s.306.

[26] *ibid.* s.324.

[27] A bankrupt may not sit as a Member of Parliament, nor may a bankrupt practise any of a large number of professions.

[28] Usually not more than three years after the commencement of the bankruptcy: Insolvency Act 1986, s.279.

[29] Insolvency Act 1986, s.281.

[30] *Linton v. Linton* (1885) 15 Q.B.D. 239; *Re Henderson* (1888) 20 Q.B.D. 509; *Re Hawkins* [1894] 1 Q.B. 25; *Kerr v. Kerr* [1897] 2 Q.B. 439.

[31] *Curtis v. Curtis* [1969] 1 W.L.R. 422.

[32] Insolvency Rules 1986, S.I. 1986 No. 1925, r. 12(3). The suggestion that this rule may be *ultra vires* (see *Woodley v. Woodley* [1992] 2 F.L.R. 417) has not been accepted by the Court of Appeal: *Woodley v. Woodley (No. 2)* [1993] 2 F.L.R. 477.

[33] *Re A Debtor; JP v. A Debtor* [1997] 1 F.L.R. 926. On whether a foreign order (or components thereof) is capable of constituting a provable debt, see *Cartwright v. Cartwright* [2002] EWCA Civ. 931 (unreported), July 3, 2002, CA.

[34] [2001] 1 F.L.R. 435. See also *Wehmeyer v. Wehmeyer* [2001] 2 F.L.R. 84. See G. Miller, "Bankruptcy as a Means of Enforcement in Family Proceedings" [2002] *Fam. Law* 21.

that a costs order was not a provable debt. The Court went on to hold that the court had jurisdiction[35] to make a bankruptcy order on the petition of a creditor with a non-provable debt,[36] but that it was difficult to envisage the exceptional circumstances in which the jurisdiction would be exercised.[37]

Hence bankruptcy is not generally[38] available as a means of enforcing a lump sum or property transfer order made in ancillary relief proceedings. The trustee in bankruptcy cannot pay any of the bankrupt's estate to a wife seeking enforcement of an ancillary relief order, who is left to pursue other methods of enforcement described below, after the other creditors have been satisfied

2. Execution against goods

16–006 In default of payment of any sum due, a creditor may[39] obtain a writ of *fieri facias*[40] which authorises the sheriff or bailiff to seize sufficient of the defaulter's goods[41] to pay the debt, and (unless the sum is paid off) sell them to pay off the debt and costs. A substantial number of debtors pay under the threat of sale. However, although this process is relatively common in debt collecting[42] it now seems to be little used in family proceedings.

3. Garnishee orders[43]

16–006A A garnishee order directs a person who owes money to the debtor to pay it to the creditor[44]—so that, for example, a spouse who has an unsatisfied order may obtain a garnishee order directed to the other spouse's bank, which must then (if the account is sufficiently in credit) pay the sum due direct to the wife.[45]

---

35 Under Insolvency Act 1986, s. 264

36 *Russell v. Russell* [1998] 1 F.L.R. 936, ChD.

37 [2001] 1 F.L.R. 435 at 445 *per* Jonathan Parker L.J.

38 The question of whether a spouse with a property adjustment order in her favour is a creditor within the meaning of ss. 382 and 383 of the Insolvency Act 1986 so that a transaction in her favour might be a preference within s. 340 is shortly to be considered at appellate level; see *Jackson v. Bell* [2001] EWCA Civ. 387 [2001] BPIR 612 [2001] *Fam. Law* 879. On foreign orders, see *Cartwright v. Cartwright*, n. 33 above.

39 Subject to compliance with the relevant Rules: R.S.C. Ord. 47; C.C.R. Ord. 26.

40 The county court equivalent is called a warrant of execution: see F.P.R. 1991, Pt VII; and C.C.R. Ord. 25, Ord. 26. In the High Court the procedure is governed by R.S.C. Ord. 46.

41 But certain items (notably "such clothing, bedding, furniture, household equipment and provisions as are necessary for satisfying the basic domestic needs" of the debtor and his family) are now exempt from seizure: Supreme Court Act 1981, s.138(3A) as inserted by Courts and Legal Services Act 1990, s.15(1).

42 In 2001, 394,611 warrants of execution were issued in county courts and 53,248 writs of *fieri facias* were issued in the High Court: Judicial Statistics, Annual Report 2001, Cm. 5551, Tables 3.11 and 4.19.

43 The Government intends that this remain a means of enforcing a child support calculation: see *A New Contract for Welfare: Children's Rights and Parents' Responsibilities* (Cm. 4349, 1999), Chap. 8 para. 11.

44 The procedures are laid down by R.S.C. Ord. 49, and C.C.R. Ord. 30. In the Civil Procedure Rules 1998, Pt. 72, the term "garnishee order" is replaced with "third party debt order"; but those Rules do not apply to family proceedings.

45 For a case in which a wife successfully used garnishee proceedings against a bank account and solicitor's client account to enforce orders against her husband (who had left the country) see

4. Charging orders[46]

16–007 The court has power[47] to make a charging order over certain specified interests in property to which the debtor is entitled. Such an order has the like effect,[48] and is enforceable in the same way as an equitable charge "created by the debtor by writing under his hand"[49]; and the creditor accordingly gains a measure of priority and a right to resort to specific property of the debtor (for example, his house, or shares which he owns). A creditor who has obtained a charging order over the debtor's interest in the family home or other property is a "person interested" in the property[50]; and may in consequence seek an order that the property be sold if the default continues.[51] There were 581 applications for charging orders in the High Court and 22,098 in the county court in 2001.[52] It is understood that very few charging orders in fact result in a sale; and that creditors attach most importance to securing a degree of priority.

5. Appointment of receiver

16–008 The court has power,[53] in all cases in which it appears just and convenient to do so, to appoint a receiver[54] who is entitled to receive rents, profits, and other

---

Cohen v. Cohen [1982] 4 F.L.R. 451. In 2001 a total of 169 garnishee orders were made in the High Court and 4,139 in the county court: Judicial Statistics, Annual Report (2001), Tables 3.11 and 4.19.

[46] The Government intends that this remain a means of enforcing a child support calculation: *supra* n. 41.

[47] Under Charging Orders Act 1979, s.1. The Act is based on recommendations made by the Law Commission: see *Report on Charging Orders* (Law Com. No. 74 (1976)); and the procedure (which involves a two stage process of order nisi and order absolute) is governed by R.S.C. Ord. 50 and C.C.R. Ord. 31. The power to make an order is discretionary; and in deciding whether to make an order the court is required to consider all the circumstances of the case, and, in particular, any evidence before it as to (a) the personal circumstances of the debtor and (b) whether any other creditor of the debtor would be likely to be unduly prejudiced by the making of the order: s.1(5). Difficult questions have arisen where a commercial creditor of one spouse seeks a charging order in respect of that spouse's interest in property (often the former matrimonial home) which might be subject to a property adjustment order on the application of the other: see *First National Securities Ltd v. Hegerty* [1985] Q.B. 850; [1985] F.L.R. 80, CA; *Harman v. Glencross* [1986] Fam. 81, CA; *Austin-Fell v. Austin-Fell* [1989] 2 F.L.R. 497, CA.

[48] The property capable of being the subject matter of a charging order is specified in Charging Orders Act 1979, s.2, and includes the debtor's interest in land, most English stocks and shares and unit trusts and the debtor's beneficial interest under trusts, including *e.g.* the debtor's beneficial interest in the proceeds of sale of land held under a trust for sale: *National Westminster Bank Ltd v. Stockman* [1981] 1 W.L.R. 67. In certain circumstances, the court also has power to make a charging order in respect of the land held under a trust for sale: Charging Orders Act 1979, s.2(1)(b); see *Clark v. Chief Land Registrar* [1993] 2 F.L.R. 500. The charge may in appropriate cases be protected under the Land Charges Act 1972 and the Land Registration Act 2002: see *Parkash v. Irani Finance* [1970] Ch. 101; *Barclays Bank Ltd v. Taylor* [1974] Ch. 137, CA; *Clark v. Chief Land Registrar* [1993] 2 F.L.R. 500.

[49] Charging Orders Act 1979, s.3(5).

[50] *Lloyds Bank plc v. Byrne* [1993] 1 F.L.R. 369, CA.

[51] The court will normally order a sale unless there are exceptional circumstances: *Lloyds Bank plc v. Byrne* [1993] 1 F.L.R. 369, CA; *Barclays Bank plc v. Hendricks* [1996] 1 F.L.R. 258. The court also has power to appoint a receiver: see below.

[52] Judicial Statistics, Annual Report 2001, Tables 3.11 and 4.19.

[53] The procedure is governed by R.S.C. Ord. 51; and C.C.R. Ord. 32.

[54] Supreme Court Act 1981, s.37; and see County Courts Act 1984, ss.38 and 107.

proceeds of property belonging to the debtor, or of a business carried on by him. The order may be supplemented by an injunction restraining the debtor from dealing with the property,[55] so that in effect, the receiver intercepts the debtor's income before it reaches him, and accounts for it to the creditor. The remedy is, however, an exceptional one, and will only be granted in exceptional cases.[56]

6. Sequestration

16–009 A writ of sequestration is a coercive measure primarily designed to prevent the defaulter from dealing with the property until he has made good his default.[57] The writ[58] is available when periodical payment[59] and other financial provision and property adjustment orders are not complied with, and is issued on the basis that the defaulter, by reason of failure to comply with the court order, is in contempt of court.[60] The procedure is very rarely invoked in financial cases,[61] but may be effective in coercing a debtor who is outside the jurisdiction, but has property here.[62]

7. Committal to prison—the judgment summons

16–010 The Debtors Act 1869 gave the court power to commit any person who made default in payment of a debt due in pursuance of any court order or judgment[63]

[55] *Levermore v. Levermore* [1979] 1 W.L.R. 1277.

[56] *S v. S* (1973) 117 S.J. 649 (where the husband owed a substantial sum of money in respect of maintenance arrears; and a receiver was appointed to receive the profits of a proprietary club in which the husband had an interest until the arrears were discharged); *Levermore v. Levermore* [1979] 1 W.L.R. 1277 (where a receiver was appointed in respect of the husband's interest in a house which he owned jointly with his brother, the receiver being given liberty to take such proceedings in the name of the husband as were necessary to enforce a sale of the property. N.B. since the coming into force of the Charging Orders Act 1979 the making of a charging order would have been the appropriate remedy).

[57] See *Romilly v. Romilly* [1964] P. 22 at 23. The procedure in the High Court (which is normally considered the appropriate forum, notwithstanding the fact that the county court now also has jurisdiction: *Rose v. Laskinkton Ltd* [1990] Q.B. 562) is governed by R.S.C. Ord. 46, r. 5.

[58] Which takes the form of a command from the sovereign to not less than four commissioners chosen by the applicant, and authorises them "to enter upon the messuages, lands, tenements and real estate whatsoever of the [debtor] and to collect receive and sequester into [their] hands not only all the rents and profits of his said messuages, lands, tenements and real estate, but also all his goods, chattels and personal estate whatsoever". The sequestrators are commanded to "detain and keep the same under sequestration" in their hands until the defaulter pays the sums outstanding and thus clears his contempt: *Bucknell v. Bucknell* [1969] 1 W.L.R. 1204 at 1206.

[59] *Capron v. Capron* [1927] P. 243.

[60] *Pratt v. Inman* (1889) 43 Ch.D. 175 at 179; *Coles v. Coles* [1957] P. 68; *Bucknell v. Bucknell* [1969] 1 W.L.R. 1204 at 1206.

[61] Sequestration may be used in an attempt to coerce a person who has removed a child from the jurisdiction: *Richardson v. Richardson* [1989] Fam. 95; *Mir v. Mir* [1992] 1 F.L.R. 624.

[62] As in *Romilly v. Romilly* [1964] P. 22. It has been held that the court may authorise the sale of the property: *Mir v. Mir* [1992] 1 F.L.R. 624; and see *Richardson v. Richardson* [1990] 1 F.L.R. 186. However, sequestration is an expensive remedy (see *Clark v. Clark* [1989] 1 F.L.R. 174, and *Clark v. Clark (No. 2)* [1991] 1 F.L.R. 179, where the sequestrator raised some £17,000 from the husband's assets, but all of this went to meet costs incurred).

[63] It has been held that an undertaking as to periodical payments to pay school fees was an integral and indivisible part of the court's order, and thus enforceable by way of judgment summons: *Symmons v. Symmons* [1993] 1 F.L.R. 317; and in *M v. M (Enforcement: Judgment Summons)*

to prison for a term not exceeding six weeks, or until payment of the sum due; and the Administration of Justice Act 1970 preserved this power in respect of orders for matrimonial, periodical or other payments.[64] However the 1869 Act also provides[65] that the power to commit "shall only be exercised where it is proved to the satisfaction of the court that the person making default either has or has had since the date of the order . . . the means to pay the sum in respect of which he has made default, and has refused or neglected, or refuses or neglects, to pay the same"; and the power is thus in effect a power to punish for dishonesty[66] or contempt of a court order, which should accordingly only be exercised if the court is satisfied beyond reasonable doubt that the debtor has or has had the means to pay.[67]

The judgment summons requires the debtor to appear and be orally examined on whether he has property or means of satisfying the judgment against him.[68] In practice the making of a suspended committal order (in which the committal order is made but suspended on terms that the arrears be paid off by specified instalments) has traditionally proved the most effective, particularly the man in business on his own account (against whom no attachment of earnings order can be made[69]) and generally against those of means and social status who refuse to comply with an ancillary relief order.[70]

The Human Rights Act 1996 has challenged the traditional use of the judgment summons as a means of enforcement of ancillary relief orders. In *Mubarak v. Mubarak*[71] the husband, a successful international jeweller, failed to comply with an order that he pay the wife £5 million. The wife sought enforcement by

---

[1993] *Fam. Law* 469 a circuit judge held that an undertaking to pay an unquantified capital sum is enforceable in this way. Note also that in *Graham v. Graham* [1992] 2 F.L.R. 406, CA, it was held that an order to bring a sum of money into court as security against the final determination of an ancillary application was an order for the payment of maintenance within the meaning of the 1970 Act. The question of whether an undertaking can be enforced by the judgment summons procedure is of great practical importance because *Livesey v. Jenkins* [1985] A.C. 424, HL, requires many financial matters (*e.g.* a requirement to make mortgage or insurance payments) to be dealt with by way of undertaking; and the law is not altogether clear: for a range of views, see compare the views of P. Moor and N. Mostyn [1992] *Fam. Law* 371; District Judge Price [1989] *Fam. Law* 120; District Judge Bird [1990] *Fam. Law* 420; D. Burrows [1998] *Fam. Law* 158.

64 See Administration of Justice Act 1970, s.11, and Sched. 8, para. 2A. The Act partially implemented the recommendations of the Payne Committee on the Enforcement of Judgment Debts (Cmnd. 3909 (1969)).

65 s.5(2).

66 *Stonor v. Fowle* (1887) 13 App. Cas. 20.

67 See *Woodley v. Woodley* [1992] 2 F.L.R. 417, CA. In that case it was held that the power to commit could be exercised notwithstanding the fact that the debtor had been made bankrupt (and all his assets had vested in his trustee because he had had the means to satisfy the court order for a period of two months between the date of the order and the bankruptcy. The legislation was both coercive and punitive in intention.

68 R.S.C. Ord. 48, r. 1(1); F.P.R., r.7.4 for civil proceedings, see now CPR 1998, Pt. 71.

69 Because he is not in employment.

70 Payne, *Committee on the Enforcement of Judgment Debts*: views of 3 members favouring retention of imprisonment for maintenance defaulters (Cmnd. 3909 (1969)), para. 1967. See, *e.g. J v. J* [1955] P. 215; *Ette v. Ette* [1964] 1 W.L.R. 1433.

71 [2001] 1 F.L.R. 698

judgment summons in accordance with current procedural requirements.[72] In support of the judgment summons the wife relied—as had become usual practice—on the evidence adduced at the trial of her ancillary relief application, the judge's findings, the judgment of the Court of Appeal in refusing permission to appeal, and affirmations by the husband. The husband was committed to prison for six weeks and the order suspended on condition that he made payments by specified dates.[73] The Court of Appeal set the committal order aside and formulated procedural requirements necessary to make the judgment summons process compatible with Article 6 of the European Convention for the Protection of Human Rights and Fundamental Freedoms, which is engaged because the judgment summons procedure even when originating in family proceedings is properly characterised as a criminal proceeding. Thus the respondent has a right to the presumption of innocence, precise articulation of the charge, adequate time to prepare a defence, and examination of evidence. The procedures under the Debtors Act 1869 and the rules were not compatible with Article 6, but the defect was capable of correction by practice direction.[74] It is too early to test Thorpe L.J.'s prediction[75] that this re-evaluation of the judgment summons procedure in the light of the Human Rights Act 1998 is likely to render it a largely obsolete method of enforcement.

8. Attachment of earnings

16–011 An attachment of earnings order is an order directed to a person who appears to the court to have the debtor in his employment which operates as an instruction to the employer to make periodical deductions from the debtor's earnings,[76] and to pay over the sums deducted to the collecting officer of the court.[77] Restrictions on the availability of attachment (reflecting long-standing opposition on the part of organised labour to any interference with the sanctity of the wage packet[78]) have been gradually removed, and, as a result of a significant change of policy embodied in the Maintenance Enforcement Act 1991,[79] attachment is now freely available against those ordered to pay maintenance.

The legislation[80] is complex; but its main features are as follows:

---

[72] Family Proceedings Rules 1991 (S.I. 1991 No. 1247), r.7; Form M17 effectively reversed the burden of proof.

[73] *Mubarak v. Mubarak* [2001] 1 F.L.R. 763, FD.

[74] *Practice Direction: Committal Proceedings* May 28, 1999; expressly applied to family proceedings by *President's Direction: Committal Proceedings* March 16, 2001[2001] *Fam. Law* 333.

[75] [2001] 1 F.L.R. 698 at para. [41].

[76] In accordance with the provisions of Attachment of Earnings Act 1971, Sched. 3, Pt I.

[77] Attachment of Earnings Act 1971, s.6(1).

[78] Successfully reflected in the Wages Attachment (Abolition) Act 1870.

[79] Which abolished the principle that attachment could only be ordered against a spouse who had defaulted in making maintenance payments.

[80] Embodied in the Attachment of Earnings Act 1971, as amended (notably by the Maintenance Enforcement Act 1991). The relevant court rules are to be found in C.C.R. Ord. 27.

(a) The court[81] may[82] make an attachment of earnings order[83]—either on the application of an interested party[84] or of its own motion—whenever it makes a qualifying periodical maintenance order.[85] This provision completely destroys the principle that attachment is an exceptional procedure, and that interference with the relationship between an employer and employee can only be justified in cases in which the employee is shown to be in default in respect of maintenance obligations.[86]

(b) The court may also make an order at any later time on an application by an interested party[87] or of its own motion in the course of any proceedings (*e.g.* a variation application) concerning the order.[88]

(c) Amount to be attached. The legislation seeks to ensure that the debtor is always left with an adequate level of income to support himself and his family. To this end, it is provided[89] that the order shall specify two rates of deduction:

(i) The "normal deduction rate" is the rate at which the court thinks it reasonable for the debtor's earnings to be applied in

---

[81] *i.e.* the High Court and the county court: Maintenance Enforcement Act 1991, s.1(1). (As to attachment in the magistrates' court see below).

[82] In deciding whether to exercise its powers the court must, if practicable, give every interested party an opportunity to make representations and must have regard to any representations made by any such party: s.1(8).

[83] Maintenance Enforcement Act 1991 also empowers the court to make a means of payment order (*e.g.* to make payments by standing order): s.1(1), (4), (5).

[84] As defined: s.1(10).

[85] Maintenance order is widely defined by reference to the definition in Administration of Justice Act 1970, Sched. 8 (see Maintenance Enforcement Act 1991, s.1(10)) and extends to most orders made in matrimonial proceedings and to financial orders made under Children Act 1989, Sched. 1. An order is only a "qualifying" order if the debtor is ordinarily resident in England and Wales at the time the order is made: Maintenance Enforcement Act 1991, s.1(2).

[86] *i.e.* the principle of the sanctity of the wage packet. Until the coming into force of the Maintenance Enforcement Act 1991, an attachment order could only be made on a creditor's application if (i) at least 15 days had elapsed since the making of the order; (ii) the debtor failed to make one or more of the payments due under the order; and the court was satisfied that the debtor's failure to make payments was due to the debtor's wilful refusal or culpable neglect: Attachment of Earnings Act 1971, s.3. The principle that default must first be established if an attachment order is to be made has been retained in respect of an order other than a maintenance order: Attachment of Earnings Act 1971, s.3, (3A).

[87] *i.e.* the person required to make the periodical payments, the person to whom those payments are to be made, and any other person who applied for the periodical payments order (*e.g.* the parent of a child): Maintenance Enforcement Act 1991, s.1(10), (2).

[88] Maintenance Enforcement Act 1991, s.1(3).

[89] Attachment of Earnings Act 1971, s.6(5). In order that the court should be in possession of the information relevant to the exercise of these powers, the court may order the debtor to provide a signed statement giving (i) the name and address of any person by whom earnings are paid; (ii) specified particulars as to the debtor's earnings and anticipated earnings, and resources and needs; and specified particulars (such as a payroll number) for the purpose of enabling the debtor to be identified by an employer: s.14(1); and any person appearing to the court to have the debtor in his employment may be ordered to give a signed statement of the debtor's earnings and anticipated earnings: s.14(1)(b). If an attachment order has been made, the court may at any time order the debtor to provide the information set out above; it may also order the debtor to attend the court to give that information: s.14(2) as amended by Administration of Justice Act 1982, s.53.

meeting the liabilities under the order.[90] It is provided[91] that this is not to exceed the rate which appears to the court necessary for the purpose of meeting the payments under the order as they fall due and payment within a reasonable period of any accrued arrears.

(ii) The "protected earnings rate" is the rate below which, having regard to the debtor's resources and needs, the court thinks it reasonable that the earnings actually paid to him should not be reduced.[92] The expression "the debtor's needs" extends to the needs of any person for whom the debtor must, or reasonably may, provide.[93] The court will thus be able to consider the needs of the debtor's second spouse or of the debtor's cohabitant.

If on any pay day the debtor's attachable earnings[94] are equal to or less than the protected earnings, no deduction is to be made[95]; but otherwise the employer must[96] pay over a sum equal to the normal deduction[97] to the collecting officer of the court[98] who must then pay the monies over to the creditor.[99]

The legislation leaves the fixing of the normal and protected earnings rates to the court's discretion[1]; and it has been held that there is no rule of law under which the protected earnings rate must not be less than the appropriate income support scale rate,[2] and that there may be exceptional circumstances in which it would be appropriate to assess the debtor's needs at a lower

---

[90] s.6(5)(a).

[91] Attachment of Earnings Act 1971, s.6(6)(b), applied in *Billington v. Billington* [1974] Fam. 24 (normal deduction rate fixed at £1.50, being £1 in respect of the weekly sum due under the order, and £0.50 in respect of outstanding arrears).

[92] s.6(5)(b).

[93] s.25(3).

[94] As defined in Sched. 3, para. 3, as amended.

[95] Attachment of Earnings Act 1971, Sched. 3, para. 6(4).

[96] The Act contains complex rules to cover the case where several attachment orders are in force against the same person: the basic principle is that orders rank for priority according to the date on which they were made; but maintenance orders and certain other orders (*e.g.* those made in respect of fines) are given priority as against simple judgment debts: Attachment of Earnings Act 1971, Sched. 3, Pt. II.

[97] *ibid.* para. 6(2). If the attachable earnings exceed the protected earnings, but do not amount to the normal deduction, the employer will pay over the amount by which the protected earnings are exceeded; and the shortfall will in effect be carried forward and deducted from future attachable earnings: *ibid.* para. 6(3). The employer may also deduct and retain a prescribed sum (currently £1) towards the employer's administrative and clerical costs: s.7(4)(a); Attachment of Earnings (Employer's Deduction) Order 1991, S.I. 1991 No. 356.

[98] s.6(1)(b). The term "collecting officer" is defined by s.6(7); and power has been taken (but not yet exercised) to remove this function from the courts in favour of other officers: s.6(9) as inserted by Courts and Legal Services Act 1990, s.125(2).

[99] s.13.

[1] Compare the rigid formula for the assessment of support obligations under the Child Support Act 1991: Chap. 15, above.

[2] See Chap. 7, above.

figure.[3] But the court may only take account of the debtor's actual earnings[4]; and it must not consider the potential earnings of the debtor in some other occupation.[5]

16–012 The attachment of earnings procedure is irrelevant in cases where the debtor is either unemployed or self-employed.[6] The introduction of wage attachment had an immediate effect in reducing the number of persons imprisoned[7] for non-payment of maintenance orders.

9. Registration in magistrates' court

16–013 The Maintenance Orders Act 1958 introduced a procedure whereby a periodical payments order made by the county court or the High Court may[8] be registered in a magistrates' courts (and an order made by a magistrates' court may be registered in the High Court).[9] The main effects of registration are, first, that the order becomes enforceable in the court of registration as if it had originally been made by that court[10]; and secondly that only the court of registration has power to vary the order.[11] In 2001, 226 county court orders were registered[12]; and it

[3] *e.g.*, if the debtor is living with his parents: *Billington v. Billington* [1974] Fam. 24.

[4] This expression is widely defined by Attachment of Earnings Act 1971, s.24(1) and extends to cover, *e.g.* overtime pay and bonus payments (see *Billington v. Billington* [1974] Fam. 24, at 30) as well as discretionary payments made by the trustees of a pension fund: *Edmonds v. Edmonds* [1965] 1 W.L.R. 58. Certain categories of earnings (*e.g.* disablement pension and the pay of members of the Armed Forces) are not to be treated as earnings: s.24(2).

[5] *Pepper v. Pepper* [1960] 1 W.L.R. 131 at 136.

[6] The court may, however, vary an order by redirecting it to any other person "who appears to have the debtor in his employment": Attachment of Earnings Act 1971, s.9(4); and the court can and should do this of its own motion if it has the necessary information: C.C.R., Ord. 27, r. 13; Lord Chancellor's Practice Direction (September 2, 1981) para. 7. A debtor is required to notify the court whenever he changes his employment, and at the same time give particulars of his earnings, actual or anticipated; and a person who becomes the employer of the debtor, knowing that an attachment order has been made, and by what court, must notify the court that he is the employer, stating the debtor's actual and anticipated earnings: Attachment of Earnings Act 1971, s.15.

[7] In 1958 (before attachment was available) 4,910 maintenance defaulters were received in prison, and maintenance defaulters constituted 52 per cent of all non-criminal prisoners; in 1961 4,929 attachment orders were made, and the number of receptions into prison was only 2,867 (*i.e.* 30 per cent of all non-criminal prisoners).

[8] The procedure is governed by F.P.R. 7.22–2.29. The court which made the order has a discretion whether to grant an application for registration: Maintenance Orders Act 1958, s.2(1); and it has been said that the general practice is that an interim order will not normally be registered; and that even in the case of a final order it will usually be necessary to show some good reason for the application, *e.g.* that there are arrears or that the benefit of the order has been diverted to the D.S.S. under the procedure explained above: R. Bird, *Sweet & Maxwell's Family Law Manual*, p. 439. Guidance has been issued: see Notes for Guidance September 1985 issued by the Lord Chancellor's Department: *ibid.*, para. 11–022.

[9] Maintenance Orders Act 1958, s.1.

[10] *ibid.*

[11] *ibid.*, s.4(2); *Hackshaw v. Hackshaw* [1999] 2 F.L.R. 876. It has been pointed out that the result of this provision is that the matrimonial jurisdiction of magistrates remains of greater significance than would appear from the number of financial applications originally made to magistrates under the Domestic Proceedings and Magistrates' Courts Act 1978 (see Chap. 3, above): see C. Gibson [1982] *Fam. Law* 138–141.

[12] See Judicial Statistics Annual Report 2001, Table 5.8.

has been officially recognised that the magistrates' procedures are those usually invoked in cases of maintenance default.[13] It appears that the efficient administrative procedure[14] available in the magistrates' courts for the collection of payments is the main factor influencing applications for registration; since (as will be seen) the actual enforcement procedures available in respect of periodical payment orders[15] are not now notably different.

V. MAGISTRATES' COURT

Enforcement in the magistrates' court

16–014 A magistrates' court maintenance order[16] may be enforced by the following procedures[17]:

(i) Distress;
(ii) Attachment of earnings;
(iii) Committal to prison;
(iv) Fine for non-payment.

In addition, the Maintenance Enforcement Act 1991 empowered the court to make "means of payment" orders, under which payments are to be made by standing order or direct debit.[18] Before discussing the enforcement procedures, something should be said about the administrative support provided by the magistrates' clerks' service, since this has come to make a major contribution to the enforcement process.

The role of the magistrates' clerk in the enforcement process

16–015 Until the coming into force of the Maintenance Enforcement Act 1991 periodical payments had to be made to the justice's clerk, rather than direct to the creditor[19]; and there were a number of advantages to this procedure. First, the clerk's office kept proper accounts, so that it was easy to establish whether or not payments were in arrears. Secondly, the parties were kept at arm's length,

---

[13] See Judicial Statistics Annual Report 1993, p. 54.

[14] *i.e.* through the Clerk of the Court acting as Collecting Officer, above.

[15] Procedures such as charging orders and garnishee orders have, of course, a part to play in the enforcement of capital orders.

[16] *i.e.* a maintenance order (as defined in Administration of Justice Act 1970, Sched. 8) which has been made by or has been registered for enforcement in a magistrates' court: see Magistrates' Courts Act 1980, s.150.

[17] The court also has power to make a means of payment order under the Maintenance Enforcement Act 1991 in certain circumstances.

[18] Magistrates' Courts Act 1980, s.59(3)(c) as substituted by Maintenance Enforcement Act 1991, s.2. It appears that the magistrates lack the power given to the High Court and county courts by Maintenance Enforcement Act 1991, s.1(6) to order a maintenance debtor to open a bank account from which such payments may be made.

[19] "unless upon representations expressly made in that behalf . . . it is satisfied that it is undesirable to do so": see Magistrates' Courts Act 1980, s.59.

but the clerk's office remained in touch with both. Finally, all matters relating to the making, variation, and collection of orders were centralised in a single building, under the supervision of responsible officials.

The position has been somewhat complicated by provisions of the 1991 Act, which seem to reflect the policy that the state should not be involved in such matters unless its involvement can be shown to be necessary. The position now is that (a) if a magistrates' court itself makes a qualifying maintenance order[20] it must either order payment to the clerk, or order payment directly by the debtor to the creditor, or make an attachment of earnings order, or make a means of payment order for payment by standing order etc[21]; (b) if a superior court order is registered[22] in the magistrates' court, the court must order payment to be made to a magistrates' clerk unless a means of payment order is in force.[23]

The clerk still plays a central role in cases of default, since he is required,[24] if requested in writing and unless it appears unreasonable so to do, to proceed in his own name for the enforcement of arrears.[25]

1. Distress

16–016 A magistrates' court has power to issue[26] a warrant of distress for the purpose of levying a sum due under an order. Such a warrant[27] authorises the seizure[28] of money or goods[29] belonging to the debtor[30]; and goods seized are to be sold by public auction[31] if the sum due is not paid within six days. In 1974,

---

[20] Defined by Magistrates' Courts Act 1980, s.59(2) (This, and subsequent references to the Magistrates' Courts Act 1980 and other legislation, are to the legislation as amended.)

[21] Magistrates' Courts Act 1980, s.59(3), (6).

[22] Under Maintenance Orders Act 1958, Pt I.

[23] Maintenance Orders Act 1958, s.2(6ZA)(a). The court has power to vary, revoke, etc., such orders: Maintenance Orders Act 1958, s.2(6ZB).

[24] In cases in which there is a means of payment order or payment has been ordered to be made through the clerk: Magistrates' Courts Act 1980, s.59A(1).

[25] Magistrates' Courts Act 1980, s.59A(1). If payments are to be made to the clerk, the creditor may give authority for the clerk to take enforcement proceedings in the clerk's name for the recovery of any arrears, and the clerk then has a duty to proceed unless it appears to him unreasonable in the circumstances: Magistrates' Courts Act 1980, s.59A(3).

[26] There is power to postpone the issue of a warrant until such time and on such conditions as the court thinks just: Magistrates' Courts Act 1980, s.77(1); but once the warrant has been issued the magistrates have no jurisdiction to suspend the operation of the warrant: *Crossland v. Crossland* [1993] 1 F.L.R. 175.

[27] Issued under Magistrates' Courts Act, 1980, s.76(1).

[28] The warrant is directed to the constables of the police area or others authorised: Magistrates' Courts Rules 1981, r.54(1)(b) and (c).

[29] The wearing apparel or bedding of the debtor or the debtor's family or the tools and implements of the debtor's trade up to a value of £150 are exempt from seizure: Magistrates' Court Rules 1981, r.54(4). Note that this exemption is considerably narrower in scope than that applicable when distress is levied under an order of the superior courts: see n. 41 above.

[30] Magistrates' Courts Rules 1981, S.I. 1981 No. 1552, r. 54(2). Subject to any direction to the contrary in the warrant, where the distress is levied on household goods, those goods are not without the written consent of the person concerned to be removed from the house until the day of sale: and in the meantime the goods are marked and impounded: *ibid.*, r. 54(8).

[31] Or in such other manner as the debtor in writing allows.

the Finer Committee[32] said that the remedy had fallen into desuetude and recommended its abolition; but it is to be noted that distress continues to be the first option considered when a liability order is made in respect of a child support calculation.[33]

2. Committal to prison[34]

16–017 It is provided[35] that where default is made in making payments due under an order[36] the court may issue a warrant committing the defaulter to prison.[37] But imprisonment is not to be ordered unless the court has inquired, in the presence of the defendant,[38] whether the default was due to the defendant's wilful refusal or culpable neglect[39]; and a committal order is not to be made in any case in which the court has power to make an attachment of earnings order or an order for payment by standing order, etc. if the court considers that it is appropriate to make such an order.[40] Even if the court has power to make a committal order it has been said that the court will seek for methods of enforcing its orders which will avoid where possible the necessity to imprison a debtor (particularly where there are children)[41]: the power to make a committal order is one of extreme severity which should be exercised sparingly and only as a last resort.[42] The court has power to fix a term of imprisonment but to postpone the issue of a warrant, subject to the defendant satisfying certain conditions[43]—*e.g.* that the arrears be paid off.[44] Although it is often claimed that the power to threaten imprisonment is effective in

---

[32] *Report of the Committee on One-Parent Families*, Cmnd. 5629 (1974), para. 4.135.

[33] See Chap. 15, *supra*.

[34] For a historical survey, see the *Report of the Committee on One-Parent Families*, Cmnd. 5629 (1974), paras 4.135–9; see also O.R. McGregor, *Social History and Law Reform* (1981), Chap. 5 ("The Case of Imprisonment for Debt").

[35] Magistrates' Courts Act 1980, s.76.

[36] But proceedings cannot be started earlier than 15 days after the making of the order: *ibid.* s.93(2). Imprisonment cannot be ordered in respect of a failure to pay interest on arrears: *ibid.* s.93(6)(c).

[37] Either when it has been established that the defaulter's money and goods are insufficient to satisfy a distress warrant, or instead of granting a distress warrant: *ibid.* s.76(2). The term of imprisonment must be not less than five days, and the maximum (which depends on the amount of the arrears) must not exceed six weeks: Magistrates' Courts Act 1980, ss.76(3), 93(7), 132, and Sched. 4, para. 3. Imprisonment does not discharge the debtor from liability for the arrears (s.93(8)) but (unless the court otherwise directs) no arrears accrue whilst the defaulter is in custody, and he cannot be imprisoned twice for failure to pay the same sum: s.94.

[38] If the defendant fails to appear, a warrant for his arrest may be issued: *ibid.* s.93(5).

[39] Magistrates' Courts Act 1980, s.93(6). These are words which "set the degree of blameworthiness . . . at a very high level. It is not just a matter of improvidence or dilatoriness. Something in the nature of a deliberate defiance or reckless disregard of the court's order is required": see *R. v. Luton Magistrates' Court, ex p. Sullivan* [1992] 2 F.L.R. 196 at 197, *per* Waite J. But note also *R. v. Cardiff Justices, ex p. Salter* [1986] 1 F.L.R. 162 (fact that debtor on income support not conclusive of question whether there is wilful default).

[40] Magistrates' Courts Act 1980, s.93(6)(b); and see *R v. Birmingham Justices, ex p. Bennett* [1983] 1 W.L.R. 114 (distress should be resorted to in preference to imprisonment).

[41] *Levermore v. Levermore* [1979] 1 W.L.R. 1277 at 1278–1279, *per* Balcombe J.

[42] *R v. Luton Magistrates' Court, ex p. Sullivan* [1992] 2 F.L.R 196; *R v. Slough Magistrates Court ex p. Lindsay* [1997] 1 F.L.R. 695.

[43] *ibid.* s.77(2); and see, *e.g. Fowler v. Fowler* (1981) F.L.R. 141.

[44] *e.g.* £100 at the rate of £0.25 per week: *Pilcher v. Pilcher (No. 2)* [1965] 1 All E.R. 463.

securing compliance with court orders, it can also be argued that the existence of a power to commit to prison for non-payment of maintenance in a society which long ago closed the Marshalsea prison and abandoned imprisonment as a primary remedy for the enforcement of civil debts is anomalous[45]; and on one view "imprisonment of maintenance defaulters . . . is morally capricious, economically wasteful, socially harmful, administratively burdensome and juridically wrong."[46] For whatever reason, there has in recent years been a dramatic reduction in the number of persons serving sentences of imprisonment for non-payment of maintenance.[47]

3. Attachment of earnings

16–018 The procedure is similar to that already described in relation to the superior courts. It is not necessary that the debtor should be in default: as a result of amendments made by the Maintenance Enforcement Act 1991 a magistrates' court making a qualifying maintenance order[48] must exercise its powers relating to the method whereby payment is to be made, and these methods now include the making of an attachment of earnings order.[49] Moreover, the court may make an attachment order in proceedings for enforcement of a qualifying maintenance payment. It seems that the making of an attachment of earnings order is the most common outcome of enforcement action in the magistrates' court.

4. Fine for non-payment

16–019 The Maintenance Enforcement Act 1991 provides that a debtor who fails to comply with a provision requiring payments to be made through the justices' clerk or by standing order, etc., may be fined up to £1,000.[50]

VI. INTERNATIONAL ENFORCEMENT OF MAINTENANCE ORDERS

16–020 In a world of ever-increasing trans-national mobility of individuals, it is essential to have effective arrangements for the reciprocal enforcement of orders made in family proceedings. A number of statutes provide for reciprocal enforcement of maintenance orders between England and Wales and

---

45 *per* Waite J. *R v. Luton Magistrates' Court, ex p. Sullivan* [1992] 2 F.L.R. 196 at 201. The question whether the sanction should be retained divided the Committee on the Enforcement of Judgment Debts (The Payne Committee) (Cmnd. 3909 (1969) but the Finer Committee reached a strongly abolitionist conclusion

46 Views of the six members of the Committee on the Enforcement of Judgment Debts (The Payne Committee) (Cmnd. 3909 (1969)) who favoured the abolition of imprisonment for maintenance defaulters: para. 1099.

47 See n. 7, above.

48 As defined: Magistrates' Courts Act 1980, s.59(2).

49 *ibid.* s.59(1), (3)(d).

50 *ibid.* s.59B.

other countries. The law is complex and a detailed discussion[51] is outside the scope of a text such as this. What follows is the briefest outline of the schemes currently in operation.

The Maintenance Orders (Reciprocal Enforcement) Act 1972 provides for the enforcement in this country of orders made in reciprocating countries[52] and Hague Convention countries.[53] Jurisdiction is based on the payer's residence or existence of assets in this country[54] and an order is enforced as it is a magistrates' court maintenance order.[55]

The Civil Jurisdiction and Judgments Act 1982 applies to civil matters generally and is not specific to family matters. It gives effect in this country to the Brussels Convention on Jurisdiction and the Enforcement of Judgments in Civil and Commercial Matters 1968 ("Brussels I"[56]) and the Lugano Convention. An order made in one contracting state and registered in a court of another contracting state has the same effect as if it had been made by the court which registers it.[57] Jurisdiction for enforcement generally is based on the payer's domicile in a contracting state; in relation to maintenance, the payer may be sued *inter alia* in the courts of the creditor's domicile or habitual residence.[58] It has been held that a maintenance creditor for the purposes of Brussels I includes a person applying for maintenance for the first time.[59] Brussels I does not apply to matrimonial property rights,[60] but an order is characterised as a maintenance order if it is "designed to enable one spouse to provide for him or herself or if the needs and resources of each spouse are taken into consideration . . . in the determination of its amount".[61] This can include a lump sum order made in ancillary relief proceedings under Part II of the Matrimonial Causes Act 1973,[62] provided that section 25(2)(a) and (b) are taken into consideration in determining *quantum*.

---

51 See *Rayden and Jackson on Divorce* (Butterworths, 17th ed., 1999) Chap. 34, Section 5; S. Oliver and P. Clements, *Enforcing Family Financial Orders* (Family Law, 1999).

52 UN Convention for the Recovery Abroad of Maintenance 1956; Recovery Abroad of Maintenance (Convention Countries) Order 1975 (S.I. 1975 No. 423); Reciprocal Enforcement of Maintenance Orders (Designation of Reciprocating Countries) Order 2001, S.I. 2001 No. 3992; Reciprocal Enforcement of Maintenance Orders (Designation of Reciprocating Countries) Order 2002 (S.I. 2002, No. 788).

53 Reciprocal Enforcement of Maintenance (Hague Convention Countries) Order 1993 (S.I. 1993 No. 593).

54 Maintenance Orders (Reciprocal Enforcement) Act 1972, s. 6(2).

55 *ibid.* s. 8(1)(4). On some implications of this, see *K v. M M and L* [1998] 2 F.L.R. 59.

56 See also Council Regulation 44/2001/E.C. of December 22, 2000, in operation March 1, 2002 (Brussels I Regulation). Note that "Brussels II" (Brussels Convention (E.C.) on Jurisdiction and the Recognition and Enforcement of Judgments in Matrimonial Matters 1998; Regulation 1347/2000; European Communities (Matrimonial Jurisdiction and Judgments) Regulations 2001, S.I. 2001 No. 310, in force March 1, 2001) has no direct effect in relation to the recognition or enforcement of maintenance or property adjustment orders within the European Community; see D. Truex, "Brussels II– It's here" [2001] 1 I.F.L. 7.

57 Civil Jurisdiction and Judgments Act 1982, s. 5(4).

58 Art. 5(2).

59 *Farrell v. Long* [1998] 1 F.L.R. 559, E.C.H.R.

60 Brussels Convention, Art. 1.

61 *ibid.* Art. 5.

62 *Van den Boogard v. Lauman* [1997] 2 F.L.R. 399, E.C.H.R.; *Al Khatib v. Masry* [2002] EWHC (Fam), [2002] 1 F.L.R. 1053, F.D.

Two other statutes deserve mention. The Maintenance Orders (Facilities for Enforcement) Act 1920 extends reciprocation to Commonwealth countries which are not reciprocating countries for the purposes of the Maintenance Orders (Reciprocal Enforcement) Act 1972; its overall scheme is very similar to the later Act. The Maintenance Orders Act 1920 provides for reciprocal enforcement in component parts of the United Kingdom.

Part V

CHILDREN AND FAMILY LAW

CHAPTER SEVENTEEN

CHILDREN

I. INTRODUCTION

17–001 "The modern tendency of the law is to recognise that children are indeed people."[1] The Children Act 1989 defines a child as "a person under the age of eighteen"[2] but neither all its provisions[3] nor other laws relating to children are linked to the age of majority.[4] Indeed, there is little consistency in the age below which legislation concerning children applies. Children under 18 may not be tattooed,[5] or enter betting shops,[6] those under 17 may not buy crossbows[7] and those under 16 may buy National Lottery tickets,[8] seek a paternity test[9] or obtain the "morning-after" pill without a prescription.[10] At common law[11] and by statute[12] a child's capacity to act may depend not on age[13] but maturity so that there is no simple way adults can know what adolescents may lawfully do.

Much of the law relating to children is based on paternalism or control.[14] Children are viewed as potential victims; Parliament has sought to protect the young from the exploitation of unscrupulous adults and from their presumed

---

[1] *Kingston upon Thames B.C. v. Prince* [1999] 1 F.L.R. 593, CA *per* Hale J. at 603. For a discussion of earlier approaches see below, para 17–002.

[2] s.105(1); similarly U.N. Convention on the Rights of the Child, Art. 1 "unless . . . majority is attained earlier." The age of majority is 18 years: Family Law Reform Act 1969, s.1(1).

[3] Care and supervision orders may not be made in respect of children over the age of 17 years: s.31(3); but any existing order may last until age 18: s.91(10); s.8 orders may only be made in respect of children over the age of 16 in exceptional circumstances: s.9(7); *e.g. Re M. (Contact: Parental Responsibility)* [2001] 2 F.L.R. 342.

[4] C Hamilton and A Fiddy, "At what age can I?" (2001) 180 *Childright* 9.

[5] Tattooing of Minors Act 1969, s.1.

[6] Betting, Gaming and Lotteries Act 1963, s.21.

[7] Crossbows Act 1987, s.1.

[8] National Lottery Act 1993, s.12; National Lottery Regulations 1994, S.I. 1994 No. 189, r. 3. Raising the age to 18 has been recommended: *Report of the Gaming Board for Great Britain* (1994-5 H.C. 587) and a third of pupils aged 13–15 have bought lottery tickets: National Lottery Commission, *Under 16s and the National Lottery* (2000).

[9] A *Gillick* competent child ought to be able to consent to such a procedure but the D.H. *Code of practice and guidance on genetic and paternity testing services* (2001), p. 7 states services should not be provided solely on their request.

[10] Prescription Only Medicines (Home Use) Amendment (No. 3) Order 2000 S.I. 2000 No. 3231; hormonal emergency contraception is available to under 16's on prescription.

[11] *Gillick v. W. Norfolk and Wisbech A.H.A.* [1986] A.C. 112 discussed below.

[12] *e.g.* Children Act 1989, s.10(8) (obtain leave to bring proceedings), ss.43(8), 44(7) (refuse a medical examination ordered by the court).

[13] But the Children (Scotland) Act 1995 provides that children aged 12 are presumed to be competent to form a view (s.6(1)).

[14] H. Hendrick, *Child welfare, England 1872–1989* (1994); J. Eekelaar *et al.* "Victims or threats? children in care proceedings" [1982] J.S.W.L. 68; L. Fox-Harding, *Perspectives in child care policy* (1991).

inability to make wise decisions.[15] There are many statutes which deny children access to substances and services[16] which may be equally damaging for adults but it is unacceptable (or impracticable) to restrict the liberty of adults in a democratic society. In recognition of the investment children represent for society, paternalistic provisions have been enacted which are intended to help young people reach their full potential[17] and to protect them from the worst consequences of their own failings.[18] Young people are also seen as threats and controlled for the good of society in the belief that they must be made to take responsibility[19] or because their labour might reduce of adult wage rates or employment.

Most children[20] live for at least part of their childhood with their parents; parents are able to control the actions and determine the experiences at least of young children. The relationship between parents and the state, *i.e.* the extent to which the law allows parents freedom to choose how their children grow up is important. Originally parents' control of young children was recognised by the common law, subject only to criminal penalties for abuse.[21] However, parental failure to protect children from harsh employment conditions in the nineteenth century led to the introduction of legislation which protected children and consequently limited parental action.[22] Later statutes enabled children to be removed from parents who ill-treated them.[23] The European Convention on Human Rights, particularly Article 8 which imposes obligations to respect private and family life,[24] has influenced state/family relationships for half a century.[25] The Children Act 1989 now provides that the state may intervene to protect children

---

[15] There is considerable evidence that older children are not less capable, at least if they are able to obtain decision-making experience: see G. Melton, G. Koocher and M. Saks, *Children's Competence to Consent* (1982), pp. 14–16. Even young children can display considerable competence: P. Alderson, *Young children's rights* (2000), pp. 56–61; consulting children develops their capacity towards autonomy: J. Fortin, *Children's rights and the developing law* (1998), p. 21.

[16] *e.g.* alcohol, tobacco, gambling.

[17] Particularly compulsory education, although the intention may be merely to produce adults trained in the way society or the parents choose, see below. Also, local authority duties to children in need, see: Children Act 1989, Pt III and Chap. 22, below.

[18] *e.g.* the introduction of the juvenile court: see A. Platt, *The Child Savers: the Invention of Delinquency* (1969); P. Parsloe, *Juvenile Justice in Britain and the United States* (1978). The Beijing rules (1985) set out internationally agreed standards for juvenile justice see Van Bueren (1995) p. 170.

[19] "Children above the age of criminal responsibility are generally mature enough to account for their actions and the law should recognise this." *No more excuses—a new approach to tackling youth crime in England and Wales* (Cm. 3809, 1997) Introduction; C. Piper, "The Crime and Disorder Act 1998: Child and community 'safety' " [1999] *M.L.R.* 397.

[20] For a statistical account of the child population see: J. Church & C. Summerfield (eds.), *Social Focus on Children* (1994); J. Matheson and C. Summerfield (eds.), *Social focus on young people* (2000); NCH *Factfile* (2001).

[21] See L. Pollock, *Forgotten children: parent child relations from 1500–1900* (1983), pp. 92–95 for examples of newspaper reports of parents' trials.

[22] J. Eekelaar, "The emergence of children's rights" (1986) 6 Ox. J.L.S. 161 at 167.

[23] Prevention of Cruelty to Children Act 1889; see: R. Cooter (ed.), *In the name of the child: health and welfare 1880–1940* (1992).

[24] This includes positive obligations not just preventing interference: *Marckx v. Belgium* (1979) 2 E.H.R.R. 330; J. Fortin, *Children's rights and the developing law* (1999).

[25] The U.K. ratified the Convention in 1951 and recognised the right of the Court of Human Rights to hear individual petitions in 1966. There were important decisions about child law from the late 1970's and the Children Act 1989 was drafted to comply with the obligations in the Convention.

where they are suffering (or likely to suffer) significant harm.[26] The development of the welfare state improved access to health and social care.[27] Changes in the economy have impacted severely on children.[28] Children are targeted and exploited as consumers[29]; more children than ever before are now experiencing the consequences of the breakdown of their parents' relationship and the poverty and disruption this often brings.[30] The Government's attempts at ending child poverty have been focused on improving education and increasing employment amongst lone parents rather than making direct provision for families.[31] Changes in education have brought children into formal schooling earlier and sought to raise the proportion continuing in education beyond age 18.[32] Children's lives are thus shaped by their parents, by the state which controls and supports them and their parents and by the commercial world. The law sets the balance between the state and the family, within the family between the parents and the child and may regulate the markets in services aimed at children.[33]

17–002 The extent to which children have been recognised and treated as different from adults has varied over time and between social classes.[34] In medieval times, children beyond infancy worked and socialised alongside adults; childhood was less distinct and special than it is now.[35] Later, changes associated with the Renaissance and the Reformation led to children being placed in "a sort of quarantine"[36] for education and indoctrination before they were considered fit to join adult society. Industrialisation initially brought children into factories working alongside their parents but the danger to their health and the threat they posed to adult employment lead to legislation[37] to exclude children from the

---

[26] Children Act 1989, s.31(2).

[27] See generally, H. Hendrick, *Child welfare in England 1872–1989* (1994); R. Rogers, *Crowther to Warnock* (1980).

[28] S. Hewlett, *Child neglect in rich nations* (1993); V. Kumar, *Poverty and inequality in the U.K.: the Effects on Children* (1993).

[29] D. Piachaud, "Child poverty, opportunities and the quality of life' [2001] *Political Quarterly* 446; H. Sleaford, "Children and childhood: perceptions and realities" [2001] *Political Quarterly* 454.

[30] ONS, *Social Trends 32* (2002) 18; see also Church and Summerfield *op. cit.* Tables 1.9 and 3.11 and G. Jones, *Family support for young people* (1995). For a discussion of the effect of family breakdown on children and their relationships see: B. Rodgers and J. Pryor, *Divorce and separa. tion: the outcomes for children* (1998).

[31] Home Office, *Supporting Families* (1998); D. Piachaud, *op. cit.*

[32] DFES, *Tomorrow's future: building a strategy for children and young people* (2000) the government has set National Learning Targets for 16, 19 and 21 year-olds; by 2002 it wants 60% of 21 year-olds to obtain NVQ level 3 or its equivalent.

[33] For example, by restricting advertising during children's television programmes as in Sweden.

[34] P. Aries, *Centuries of Childhood* (1979); I. Pinchbeck and M. Hewitt, *Children in English Society, Vol. I* (1969), *Vol. II* (1973); F. Pollock and F. Maitland, *The History of English Law before the time of Edward I Vol. 2* (1923); L. Pollock, *A lasting relationship: parents and children over three centuries* (1987); C. Heywood, *A history of children and childhood in the west medieval to modern times* (2001).

[35] C. Heywood *op. cit.*, pp.18, 171 *cf.* Aries *op. cit.*, p. 125 who suggested that there was no concept of childhood.

[36] Aries *op. cit.*, p. 396.

[37] Children and Young Persons Act 1933, ss.18–21 as amended by the Children (Protection at Work) Regulations 1998; S.I. 1998 No. 276 to implement E.C. 94/33; Children (Protection at Work) (No. 2) Regulations 2000; S.I. 2000 No. 2548. The U.K. has also ratified ILO Convention No. 182 on the elimination of the most hazardous forms of child labour.

workforce. Despite controls many children work.[38] The complexity of modern life and society's expectations of young people increased the period of education needed to prepare for it.[39] In recent years, the lack of employment opportunities for those without skills, the removal of social security benefits[40] and the shortage of affordable housing have together extended the period during which young people live with their families.[41]

Three separate but interwoven threads may be identified in the treatment of childhood by the law: minority, parental rights[42] and emancipation. In early English society the age when a child reached his majority depended on the position of his family within the feudal system.[43] Only boys from the knightly class had to wait until they were 21; before that age they were considered physically too weak to take an adult role by wearing armour.[44] Gradually the age of 21 came to be regarded as the age of majority for all children. However, the lack of clear or relevant reasons for that age encouraged the Latey Committee on the Age of Majority[45] to recommend the reduction to age 18.[46] This was enacted in the Family Law Reform Act 1969.[47] The United Nations Convention on the Rights of the Child applies to all young people below the age of 18 unless they achieve full civil rights at an earlier age.[48] Below the age of majority a person's participation in civic life is restricted. Under 18s may not vote,[49] sit on a jury[50] nor hold public office. This was used to justify the abolition of pupil governors for schools.[51] Minors cannot hold a legal estate in land[52] nor can they make a valid will.[53] However, minority was never viewed as a time when a

---

[38] For a discussion of the importance of child labour to families P. Mizen *et al.* (eds.), *Hidden hands* (2001) and B. Pettitt (ed.), *Children and work in the U.K.* (1998).

[39] Aries noted that childhood lengthened more rapidly for boys than girls who might be married and running a household in their early teens. This was reflected in Scots law; "pupils" *i.e.* girls below 12 and boys below 14 had more limited capacity but now the Age of Legal Capacity (Scotland) Act 1991 applies the same age to both boys and girls. The English common law took a contrary view, girls reached the age of discretion at 16 but boys at 14. This protective approach to girls is reflected in current attitudes to girls' sexuality.

[40] Social Security Act 1988, s.4(1); lower rates of benefit are also payable to single people under the age of 25 without children; see generally N. Harris, *Social security for young people,* (1989) and G. Jones & C. Wallace, *Youth, family and citizenship* (1992).

[41] Nearly half those aged under 24 continue to live with a parent; the age of leaving home has risen since 1991: J. Matheson and C. Summerfield, *op. cit.*, p. 12; see also: I. Rauta, *Who would Prefer Separate Accommodation?* (O.P.C.S., Social Survey Division, 1986), pp. 68, 86–87.

[42] Part of parental responsibility: see Children Act 1989, s.3.

[43] Pollock and Maitland (1923), p. 438.

[44] *ibid.*

[45] Cmnd. 3342 (1967).

[46] "That most young people mature today earlier than in the past; at 18 most young people are ready for these responsibilities and would greatly profit by them as would . . . the community as a whole." para.134.

[47] s.1.

[48] Art. 1.

[49] Representation of the People Act 1949, s.1(1)(c) and Sched. 2.

[50] Juries Act 1974, s.7(2)(a).

[51] Education (No. 2) Act 1986, s.15(4); see *Hansard* H.C. Vol. 93, col. 207 and D. Pannick (1986) 25 *Childright* 15.

[52] Law of Property Act 1925, s.1(6). They may hold an equitable estate under a trust: Trust in Land and Appointment of Trustees Act 1996, Sched.1; *Kingston upon Thames B.C. v. Prince* [1999] 1 F.L.R. 593, CA.

[53] Wills Act 1837, ss.7, 11. The effect is that children die intestate see: *Bouette v. Rose* [2000] 1 F.L.R. 363 CA.

person lacked all legal capacity. Minors of any age can be liable in tort for their actions[54] and those beyond 10[55] under the criminal law. At common law, contracts entered into by minors are enforceable by them but not against them, with the exception of contracts for necessaries or for certain lasting property rights and contracts of employment.[56] The position in Scotland is different. Children aged 16 have the capacity to enter into any transaction; any child may enter into transactions "of a kind commonly entered into by persons of the child's age and circumstances and on terms which are not unreasonable."[57]

The nature and extent of a parent's right to control a child's life has been the subject of considerable controversy.[58] In Victorian times, it appears that the father was viewed as having near absolute rights over his children and could exercise these without consideration for their welfare. This approach to parental rights can be likened to treating the child as property.[59] However, there is authority for the propositions that parents had rights merely so that they could protect their children, that the proprietary right protected by the law was not the right to the child's custody but the right to determine the marriage of an heir[60] and that parents' rights are not capable of founding an action in tort for the benefit of the parents.[61]

17–003 Where the law gave a parent control over the child's action, this did not make the child legally incapable nor the parent liable for the child's torts,[62] but put those who dealt with the child at risk of an action by the parent. Thus, a minor could contract a valid marriage but the spouse might be liable to the parent for

---

[54] W. Rogers, *Winfield and Jolowicz on Tort* (15th ed., 1998), p. 832; liability in negligence depends on the reasonable foresight of a child of the defendant's age: *Mullin v. Richards* [1998] 1 All E.R. 920 CA.

[55] Children and Young Persons Act 1933, s.50 as amended by Children and Young Persons Act 1963, s.16. The presumption of *doli incapax* which applied to those between ages 10 and 13 has been abolished: Crime and Disorder Act 1998, s.34; S. Bandali, "Abolition of the presumption of *doli incapax* and the criminalisation of children" (1998) 37(2) *Howard Journal* 114.

[56] The Infants Relief Act 1874 made minors' contracts for loans and non-necessaries "absolutely void" but following recommendations in Law Commission Report No. 134 (1984 H.C.P 494) it was repealed by the Minors' Contracts Act 1987.

[57] Age of Legal Capacity (Scotland) Act 1991, s.2 (1). Children of 12 may also make their will, s.2(2).

[58] A modern example of the different views can be seen in the different views of the Court of Appeal and House of Lords in *Gillick v. W. Norfolk and Wisbech A.H.A.* [1986] A.C. 112, HL which is discussed fully below. See also J. Hall, "The waning of parental rights" [1972B] *C.L.J.* 248; J. Eekelaar "What are parental rights?" (1973) 89 *L.Q.R.* 210; S. Maidment, "The fragmentation of parental rights" [1981] *C.L.J.* 135; B. Dickens, "The modern function and limits of parental rights" (1981) 97 *L.Q.R.* 462; F. Zimring, *The Changing Legal World of Adolescence* (1982).

[59] J. Montgomery, "Children as property?" (1988) 51 *M.L.R.* 323; Eekelaar suggests that children were viewed as agents for the devolution of property within the family, J. Eekelaar "The emergence of children's rights" (1986) 6 Ox. J.L.S. 161 at 163.

[60] Pollock & Maitland (1923), p. 444; W. Holdsworth, *A History of English Law* (3rd ed., 1923), Vol. III, p. 512. Holdsworth refers to a conflict in the Middle Ages between the older view that guardianship was for the benefit of the guardian and the newer view that it was for the child, but notes that the common law had no machinery to enforce the guardian's responsibilities.

[61] *F. v Wirral M.B.C.* [1991] Fam. 69, CA. But in *TP and KM v. U.K.* [2001] 2 F.L.R. 549 both the mother and daughter obtained compensation for breach of their rights of respect for family life after the improper removal of the daughter by the local authority.

[62] Unless these were the result of the parent's negligent control of the child, *Winfield & Jolowicz* (1998), p. 833.

loss of the child's services.[63] A similar action could be brought by the parent when the child had been injured or killed. These actions were abolished by the Law Reform (Miscellaneous) Provisions Act 1970 and parents were left with no obvious way to enforce their control against third parties.

The modern conception of parental power is one of responsibilities rather than rights.[64] The Children Act 1989 defines "parental responsibility" in terms of "rights, duties and powers."[65] Parental responsibility is also seen as diminishing as the child grows in maturity—"it starts with a right of control and ends with little more than advice."[66] It thus leaves older children with an ever increasing sphere within which to make their own decisions.

The concept of emancipation—which enables a child to gain the right to be free from parental control—has not yet been fully developed in English law. Children beyond the age of discretion, which was 14 for boys and 16 for girls,[67] were not subject to complete parental control; the courts would refuse a parent's action for *habeas corpus* in respect of a child who did not wish to return to the parents and might apply the same rule to younger children who were mature.[68] There was, however, no general rule that minors acquired increased capacity at 16.[69] Mature children under 16 may bring proceedings under the Children Act 1989 if they wish to live separately from their parents,[70] but the court does not remove the parents' parental responsibility. A residence order which determines where the child lives also confers parental responsibility on the person with the order.[71] Under Scots law children acquire full legal capacity (but not civil rights) at age 16.[72] In the United States, the judiciary allowed the termination of obligations which arose from the parent/child relationship; emancipation statutes removed the disabilities of minors. Emancipation was intended to assist mature minors by recognising their independence but is frequently sought by parents seeking to end their obligations.[73]

---

[63] J. Fleming, *Law of Torts* (9th ed., 1998), p. 721. Originally there was no action where a child had merely been abducted because a parent had no proprietary right in his child: *Barham v. Dennis* (1600) Cro. Eliz. 770, but a more general remedy was sanctioned probably in the seventeenth century.

[64] Law Com. No. 118 *Illegitimacy* (1982), para. 4.19; Law Com. No. 172 *Guardianship & Custody* (1988), para.2.4.

[65] s.3.

[66] *per* Lord Denning M.R., *Hewer v. Bryant* [1970] 1 Q.B. 357 at 369; see also *Gillick v. W. Norfolk and Wisbech A.H.A.* [1986] A.C. 112, below.

[67] *R. v. Howes, ex p. Barford* (1860) 3 E. & E. 332; see also *Re Agar-Ellis* (1883) 24 Ch. D. 317.

[68] *R. v. Gyngall* [1893] 2 Q.B. 232 at 245.

[69] H. Bevan, *Child Law* (1989), para.1.12.

[70] The child must obtain leave: Children Act 1989, s.10(8); and may be permitted to bring proceedings without a guardian *ad litem* or next friend: F.P.R. 1991, r. 9.2A; *Re S. (A Minor) (Child Representation)* [1993] Fam. 263, CA; *Re T. (A Minor) (Child Representation)* [1994] Fam. 49, CA; see also H. Houghton-James, "Children divorcing their parents" [1994] J.S.W.F.L 185 and below.

[71] Children Act 1989, ss.8(1), 12(2) and below.

[72] Age of Legal Capacity Scotland Act 199, s.1; see Scottish Law Commission *Consultative Memo No. 65, Legal Capacity and Responsibility of Minors and Pupils* (1985) for the background to this Act. Parental power is consequently limited in relation to over 16 year olds; Children (Scotland) Act 1995, ss.1, 2.

[73] R. Mnookin, *Child, Family & State* (1978), Chap. 6; C. Sanger and E Willemsen "Minor changes: emancipating children in modern times" (1992) 25 *U. Mich. J. L. Ref* 239.

The interrelation of these three concepts—minority, parental responsibilities and emancipation—is not clear. The Latey Committee's confusion is evident from their acknowledgement that minors had legal capacity to act without parental consent but their acceptance that rigid disciplinary rules in colleges could be justified by reference to the concept of *in loco parentis*.[74] The law relating to contract developed separately from that relating to parental rights; whatever powers parents had it appears that minors were able to enter into contracts of employment without parental consent.[75]

A fourth strand, social citizenship,[76] is beginning to influence public and private relationships with children and the common law[77] but only has limited recognition in English law.[78] Social citizenship acknowledges children's capacity to influence[79] their own lives and moral right to participate in decisions affecting them[80] by supporting children's consultation within and beyond the family. It reflects both the development of more democratic relationships within families[81] and the recognition by international law that children have rights.[82] There has been a major growth in advocacy and children's rights services[83] particularly for children in public care. A Children's Commissioner for Wales has been established to safeguard and promote the welfare of children in public care there and to make representations to the Welsh Assembly about the rights and welfare of children in Wales.[84] Children's commisioners or ombudsmen have been established in many countries to promote children's rights and the implementation of the Children's Rights Convention.[85]

---

[74] *i.e.* that college authorities were in the position of the parents.

[75] Eekelaar *op. cit.* citing *Doyle v. White City Stadium Ltd* [1935] 1 K.B. 110 where a minor was held bound by his contract as a professional boxer.

[76] J. Roche, "Children's rights, participation and citizenship" (1999) *Childhood* 6(4) 475; B. Neale and C. Smart, *Good the talk?* (2001).

[77] *Gillick v. W. Norfolk and Wisbech A.H.A.* [1986] A.C. 112.

[78] The Children Act 1989, s.22(4)(5) requires local authorities to consult looked after children in relation to their care and s.1(3) requires the courts to consider the child's wishes and feelings when making decisions about upbringing. But there is no comparable obligation on parents *cf.* Children (Scotland) Act 1995, s. 6 where those exercising parental power to make major decisions are required to have regard to the child's views and children aged 12 years are presumed to have sufficient maturity to form a view.

[79] Referred to by sociologists as their "agency" and the subject of many of the studies in the ESRC's 5–16 programme: www.hull.ac.uk/children5to16programme/.

[80] D.H. *Children Act Now* (2001); children's participation is one of the key themes in the D.H. *Quality Protects* programme for enhancing the lives of looked after children: LAC(98)28.

[81] Neale and Smart, *op cit*, pp. 6, 22.

[82] U.N. Convention on the Rights of the Child, Art. 12 sets out children's right to express views, and have them given due weight, in matters affecting them, see below, para. 17–006.

[83] *e.g.* NYAS (the National Youth Advocacy Service); NCH Action for Children runs children's rights services for many local authorities. There is to be a Children's Rights Director with responsibilities for children's services regulated by the Care Standards Commission (children in the public care and in regulated care facilities such as nursing homes).

[84] Care Standards Act 2000, ss 72A and 73A and Children's Commissioner for Wales Act 2001 see: K. Hollingsworth and G. Douglas, "Creating a children's champion for Wales" [2002] *M.L.R.* 58.

[85] For a discussion of the role of such services see: *Independent institutions protecting children's rights* Innocenti Digest No. 8 (2001).

II. CHILDREN'S RIGHTS

Theoretical perspectives

17–004 A discussion of children's rights requires a consideration of the nature of rights[86] and of the problems in applying theories of rights to children. It is necessary to determine which rights children should be recognised as holding and whether rights provide an adequate framework for handling ethical issues relating to children. The phrase "children's rights" has been called a slogan in search of a definition and has been used in many different ways.[87] "Rights" has been used in the Hohfeldian sense of something which another person has a duty to permit,[88] for example the right to express a view to a decision-maker, the right to education or the right to leave home. The word "right" has also been applied to indicate moral or social goals. Thus the United Nations Declaration of the Rights of the Child, a forerunner of the 1989 Convention[89] set out the rights which were intended to produce a "happy childhood"[90] but established no enforcement mechanism.

There are two broadly competing theories of the nature of rights—the "will" and the "interest" theory. The "will" theory is based on the notion that to have a right involves being able to make a choice about the enforcement of duties imposed on others. It has been used to deny the possibility of young children having rights because they lack the physical and intellectual capacity to exercise choice over most aspects of their lives.[91] The "interest" theory does not require an autonomous claimant only an identifiable interest and a corresponding duty. It allows the recognition of rights for children and has been relied on widely. Development of children's rights from this theory requires consideration of which of children's interests should give rise to rights.[92] Two approaches have been identified: the "Nurturance orientation" and the "self-determination orientation".[93] Both have sought to improve children's lives, the former by protecting them, the latter by permitting them greater autonomy. Taking children's rights more seriously requires policies, practices, structures and laws which both protect children and their rights.[94] For this reason Freeman, adapting Rawls'

---

[86] For a discussion of this issue see W. Lucy, "Controversy about children's rights" in D. Freestone, *Children and the Law* (1990).

[87] See M.D.A. Freeman, (a) "The rights of children in the International Year of the Child" [1980] C.L.P. 1, 16, and (b), *The Rights and Wrongs of Children* (1983), Chaps 1, 2; M. Freeman and P. Veerman (eds.), *Ideologies of children's rights* (1992).

[88] W.N. Hohfield, *Fundamental Legal Conceptions* (1919).

[89] United Nations Convention on the Rights of the Child, see G. Van Bueren, *The International Law on the Rights of the Child* (1994) Chap. 1 and below.

[90] United National Declaration of the Rights of the Child 1959, Preamble.

[91] N. MacCormick "Children's rights: a test case for theories of right" (1976) 62 *Fur Rechts und Sozialphilosophie* 305 (reprinted in N. MacCormick, *Legal right and social democracy* (1982) Chap. 8); see also T. Campbell, "The rights of the minor" (1992) 6 Int. J. Law & Fam. 1, 2.

[92] Campbell, *op. cit.*, p. 7.

[93] C. Rogers and L. Wrightsman, "Attitudes towards Children's Rights—Nurturance or Self-determination" (1978) 34 *Journal of Social Issues* No. 2, p. 59.

[94] M. Freeman, "Taking children's rights more seriously" (1992) 6. Int. J. Law & Fam. 52 at 69.

theory of justice,[95] has argued for "liberal paternalism",[96] a middle way which acknowledges both autonomy and protection. The first two of Freeman's categories, rights to welfare and rights to protection are paternalistic—rights which the adult world would consider appropriate whether or not children claimed them for themselves. The third and fourth categories, the right to be treated like adults and rights against adults, belong to a more liberalist school.[97] Freeman recognises that these rights may conflict with each other and with parents' rights. He argues that children's rights to be treated like adults should depend on their capacity, assessed on a case by case basis.[98] Parents should be able to impose their decisions where these are consistent with an objective evaluation of Rawls' "primary social goods", for example liberty, health and opportunity. In other cases disputes between parents and children should be referred to the courts.[99] This approach largely reflects that taken under English law. But where a dispute about a child's upbringing is referred to the courts the decision is made according to what is in the child's best interests. Thus the court may refuse any order if this would enshrine a state of affairs which could be better resolved by discussion[1]; and it may make orders which conflict with a child's wishes.[2]

John Eekelaar has examined the status of the concept of children's rights within English law.[3] Using Joseph Raz's definition of rights and interests,[4] he has identified three interests which merit protection as rights and which might plausibly be claimed by children. According to Eekelaar, children have a "basic interest" in receiving physical and emotional care within the social capabilities of their immediate care-givers, which is recognised by child protection legislation. They also have a "developmental interest" in having an equal opportunity to have their capacities developed to their best advantage.[5] The third interest, the "autonomy interest," which may only be a version of the developmental interest, is the child's interest in taking action freely without adult control. Since this interest might conflict with basic interest and the developmental interest (without some protective control a child might lose the opportunity to become a rational adult) Eekelaar ranks it as subordinate to the other two. He concludes that both the developmental interest and the autonomy interest have been recognised to some extent by English law[6] and that the emphasis on decision-making capacity in the *Gillick* case[7] allows the conflicts between them to be reconciled.

---

[95] J. Rawls, *Theory of Justice* (1972).

[96] M. Freeman, *The Rights and Wrongs of Children* (1983); M. Freeman, *The moral status of children* (1997)

[97] Freeman (1983), pp. 45–49; A. Bainham, *Children the modern law* (2nd ed., 1998), p. 87.

[98] Freeman, p. 46.

[99] *ibid.* pp. 51–2.

[1] *Re C. (A Minor) (Leave to Seek Section 8 Orders)* [1994] 1 F.L.R. 26.

[2] *Re C. (A Minor) (Care: Child's Wishes)* [1993] 1 F.L.R. 832; *Re M (Minors) (Care Proceedings: Child's Wishes)* [1994] 1 F.L.R. 749; even refusing permission for a change of name for children aged 12, 14 and 16: *Re B. (Change of Surname)* [1996] 1 F.L.R. 79.

[3] J. Eekelaar, "The emergence of children's rights" (1986) 6 Ox J.L.S. 161.

[4] J. Raz, "Legal rights" (1984) 4 Ox J.L.S. 1.

[5] *op. cit.*, p. 170.

[6] *op. cit.*, p. 176.

[7] See below.

Bainham notes that there is much common ground between these theories.[8] Although all the theories accept the legitimacy of some paternalistic interventions there is disagreement about the basis of decisions which can be imposed on children.[9] Freeman and Eekelaar require adult decision-makers to follow what children would ideally want for themselves, but others suggest that they should form an objective view of what might be best for the child.[10]

Despite the predominance of rights talk O'Neill has argued for the development of theories based on fundamental obligations because these can give a more complete view of the ethical aspects of children's lives.[11] Whereas rights theories were developed in relation to adults from the rejection of paternalism, O'Neill considers that paternalism may be what is required of those whose actions impact on children's lives.[12] She asserts that theories of rights are inadequate for dealing with "imperfect obligations", such as to help children or be kind and considerate to them, because they are neither owed to all children, nor to identifiable individuals, so no one can claim or waive performance of the corresponding right.[13] These obligations are crucial to children's experience of childhood and their development[14]; focusing on the agent's perspective may deliver more for children.[15] But this view has been criticised by Freeman and others who consider that O'Neill has not sufficiently considered the reality of childhood, the developing capacities of children and the similarities between children's and adults' needs.[16]

17–005 Even if rights theories do not adequately deal with all aspects of children's experience, Eekelaar argues that it remains important to recognise that children have rights. For Eekelaar, defining what should be included in the list of rights involves a consideration of what is, or might plausibly be, claimed by children. This is an empirical task which relies on what children say and demands that children are heard.[17] Recognising that children have rights places them in a central and powerful place where the value of being the subject and not merely the object of concern is acknowledged. Thus, although Eekelaar accepts that the United Nations Convention on the Rights of the Child could have been formu-

---

[8] Bainham (1998), p. 91.

[9] *ibid.*

[10] See R. Adler, *Taking Juvenile Justice Seriously* (1985), pp. 73 at 141. Children Act 1989, s.1 requires the court to give para. mount consideration to the child's welfare which includes wishes and needs. Bainham suggests that this accords more with allowing the decision-maker to impose a view than relying on the child's substituted judgement.

[11] O. O'Neill, "Children's rights and Children's lives" (1992) 6. Int. J. Law & Fam. 24 (reprinted in P. Alston, *et al., Children's rights and the law* (1992)).

[12] *ibid.* p. 40. But other modern writers generally agree that paternalism should be kept to a minimum: J. Fortin (1998) p. 28

[13] *ibid.* pp. 26–27, but these might as easily be analysed in terms of rights: see C. Coady, 6. Int. J. Law & Fam. 43 at 45.

[14] *ibid.* p. 37.

[15] *ibid.* p. 34.

[16] C. Coady, "Theory, rights and children: a comment on O'Neill and Campbell" 6 Int. J. Law and Fam. 43 at 49; Freeman, (1992) 6 Int. J. Law & Fam. 52 at 56–59. Eekelaar has also developed thinking about obligations: J. Eekelaar, "Are parents morally obliged to care for their children" (1991) 11 Ox J.L.S. 340.

[17] J. Eekelaar, "The importance of thinking that children have rights" (1992) 6 Int. J. Law & Fam. 221 at 228–230. Children's right to be consulted is therefore crucial.

lated as a list of duties owed by adults to children, he thinks that it would not have the same potential.[18]

Children's rights in international law

17–006 In 1989 the United Nations adopted the Convention on the Rights of the Child.[19] To date this Convention has been ratified[20] by 192 countries, including the United Kingdom[21] making it the most successful international instrument.[22] This broad support for children's rights suggests that some of the Convention's provisions may acquire the status of customary international law and have universal application.

The idea for the Convention was suggested in 1979[23] by the Polish Government who proposed that the principles in the United Nations Declaration of the Rights of the Child 1959 be translated into international law. The Polish draft was rejected but work began to develop a new Convention on children's rights. The Convention brings a new approach to the rights of children; they are not to be seen as in opposition to the rights of adults or as an alternative to the rights of parents but as an integral part of human rights.[24] The general aims of the Convention have been referred to as the "4 P's"—prevention, protection, provision and participation[25] each with equal importance in a holistic approach to the rights of the child.

The Convention applies to all persons below the age of 18 unless majority is achieved at an earlier age.[26] It avoids the conflict between states which accept contraception and abortion and those that do not by not defining the beginning of childhood.[27] The rights in the Convention are provided for all children without

---

[18] *ibid.* p. 234.

[19] 28 ILM 1448; see generally, G. Van Bueren, *The International Law on the Rights of the Child* (1994); P. Newell, *The UN Convention and children's rights in the UK* (1991); S. Detrick (ed.), *The United Nations Convention on the Rights of the Child* (1990); D. Hodgson, "The historical development and internationalisation of the Children's Rights movement" 6 Aust. J. *Fam. Law* 252; B. Walsh, "The United Nations Convention on the Rights of the Child: a British view" (1991) 5 Int. J. Law & Fam. 170; and for a more sceptical view, M. King, "Children's rights as communication: reflections on autopoietic theory and the United Nations Convention" [1994] *M.L.R.* 385 and L. LeBlanc, *The Convention on the Rights of the Child* (1995).

[20] Ratifying states may enter reservations in relation to parts of the Convention so long as these are not incompatible with the principles of the Convention: Art. 51(2) see: A. Bissett-Johnson "Qualifications of signatories to the United Nations Convention on the Rights of the Child—what did States Parties really agree to?" in N. Lowe and G. Douglas (eds) *Families across frontiers* (1996) p.115.

[21] The Convention was ratified by the U.K. on December 16, 1991 and came into force in the U.K. on January 15, 1992.

[22] The United States of America, Somalia and Taiwan have not ratified. For an explanation of the USA's position see: S. Kilbourne, "The wayward Americans—why the USA has not ratified the U.N. Convention on the Rights of the Child" [1998] *C.F.L.Q.* 243.

[23] The International Year of the Child.

[24] M. Santos Pais, "General introduction to the Convention on the Rights of the Child: from its origin to its implementation" Defence for Children International, *Selected essays on international children's rights* (1993), vol. 1, p. 1.

[25] G. Van Bueren, "The U.N. Convention on the Rights of the Child" (1991) 3 J.C.L. 63.

[26] Art. 1.

[27] But States Parties recognise that every child has the inherent right to life: Art. 6(1).

discrimination of any kind.[28] The Convention lists basic human rights—rights to name, nationality, identity, privacy and liberty[29]; civil and political rights—freedom of expression, thought, conscience, religion and of assembly[30]; economic and social rights—health care, standard of living and social security[31]; cultural rights—rights to education to develop the child's full potential, play and leisure[32]; and protective rights for children deprived of their families,[33] refugees,[34] those placed in care[35] and to protect all children from violence, drugs, abduction,[36] and all forms of exploitation.[37] Two optional protocols adopted by the U.N. General Assembly in 2000 seek to provide further protection against sexual exploitation and for child soldiers.[38]

The Convention adopts the best interest standard as "a primary consideration" for all action concerning children by public and private institutions and administrative bodies.[39] However, children who are capable of forming their own views are recognised as having the right to express those views freely in matters affecting them. Children's views should be given due weight in accordance with the child's age and maturity; children should have an opportunity to be heard in judicial and administrative proceedings affecting them.[40] Also, the fundamental importance to children of their parents is recognised.[41] Parents[42] have the primary responsibility for their child's upbringing. States must respect the responsibilities, rights and duties of parents and the wider family in a manner consistent with the child's evolving capacities[43] and should render appropriate assistance to parents.[44] Children should not be separated from parents against their will; where separation occurs they should be enabled to maintain relationships.[45]

The correlative duties in the Convention are addressed to states but the responsibility to ensure that children's rights are recognised lies with everyone. States are required to undertake all legislative, administrative and other measures for the implementation of the Convention. With regard to economic, social and cultural rights they must undertake such measure to the maximum

---

[28] Art. 2(1). Perhaps the most important principle given the divisions imposed on childhood within many countries based on gender, religion or ethnic background.
[29] Arts 7, 8, 16 and 37.
[30] Arts 13, 14 and 15.
[31] Arts 24, 26 and 27.
[32] Arts 28, 29, 30 and 31.
[33] Art. 20.
[34] Art. 21.
[35] Art. 25.
[36] Arts 19, 33 and 35.
[37] Arts 32, 34 and 36.
[38] General Assembly Resolution A/RES/54/263 opened for signature May 25th, 2000.
[39] Art 3. Note this is not the same as the duty in Children Act 1989, s.1, see below.
[40] Art. 12. But this is rarely the case in divorce proceedings.
[41] As far as possible the child should have a right to know and be cared for by his or her parents (Art. 7(1)).
[42] "States parties shall use their best effort to ensure recognition of the principle that both parents have common responsibilities for the upbringing and development of the child." (Art. 18(1)).
[43] Art. 5.
[44] Art. 18.
[45] Art. 9. Art. 10 provides for family reunification.

of their available resources.[46] They must publicise the Convention to adults and children.[47]

The Convention is not incorporated into English law; individual children cannot rely on its provisions in the English courts.[48] Enforcement in the international arena is by political not legal processes. The Convention establishes the Committee of the Rights of the Child; each state must report regularly to the Committee on its progress in implementing the Convention.[49] The Committee has issued guidance about how States compile their reports[50]; non-governmental organisations may also submit reports.[51] The United Kingdom's First Report, completed with little consultation, provided a rosy picture of childhood in Britain[52] but a more realistic review was submitted following wide discussions by voluntary organisations and children's groups.[53] The Committee's response was critical, notably about the lack of provision for considering children's views especially in education law, and of a co-ordinating mechanism to implement the Convention.[54] The United Kingdom's Second Report emphasised the involvement of young people in its preparation and stressed the benefits of the Human Rights Act 1998 to promote a judicial human rights culture and directly support compliance with the Convention.[55]

The Convention is an important document. It establishes that the signatories accept (or wish to be seen as accepting) that children are persons with the human rights already recognised for adults. It is evidence that the international community has reached a consensus about the rights of children and the obligations of the family, the state and the international community.[56] Ratification by many countries and regular reporting promote and disseminate the idea of children's rights. It is hoped that it will enable a more

---

[46] Art. 4.

[47] Art. 42.

[48] Some jurisdictions, notably the Netherlands and Germany have made such provision. An optional protocol is currently under consideration which will give a right of individual petition to those who claim their Convention rights have been infringed.

[49] Arts 43 and 44. Reports must be submitted within two years of the entry into force of the convention and then every five years (Art. 44(1)). For a discussion of the work of the Committee see: C. Price Cohen and S. Kilbourne "Jurisprudence of the Committee on the Rights of the Child: a guide for research and analysis" (1998) Mich. J. Int. L. 633; U. Kilkelly "The U.N. Committee on the Rights of the Child an evaluation in the light of recent U.K. experience" [1996] *C.F.L.Q.* 105. It has been said that the Committee has a western bias in its approach: S. Harris-Short [2001] Melb. J. Int. Law 305.

[50] U.N. Doc. CRC/C/5 (1991).

[51] Country reports are available on the U.N. website www,unhchr.ch and those from NGOs on www.crin.org

[52] The U.K.'s *First Report to the U.N. Committee on the Rights of the Child* (1994).

[53] Children's Rights Development Unit, *U.K. Agenda for Children* (1994); see CRC/C 115 (Centre for Human Rights, Geneva 1995), G. Lansdown [1995] *C.F.L.Q.* 122 and U. Kilkelly [1996] *C.F.L.Q.* 105.

[54] U.N. Doc. CRC/C/15/Add.34 (1995), paras 8 and 14.

[55] *The U.K.'s Second Report to the U.N. Committee on the Rights of the Child* (1999) CRC/C/83/Add.3, paras 1.6 and 5.1.5. The substantial backlog in the work of the Committee means that the report will only be considered in October 2002.

[56] D. McGoldrick, "The United Nations Convention on the Rights of the Child" (1991) Int. J. Law & Fam. 132 at 158.

child-centred jurisprudence of human rights to develop.[57] It has the potential to transform adulthood as well as childhood and lay the foundations for a better world[58] not only because the rights in the Convention will enable children to reach their potential but because fulfilling these obligations to children will improve the lives of adults. However, converting social goals into law cannot automatically improve children's lives but it may avoid the complexities of the problems posed and give a false impression that something is being done.[59] The Convention needs major world-wide changes to implement its principles fully. It remains to be seen whether it is able to improve children's lives.

17–007 The Convention has yet to have an impact on law reform in England and Wales. Apart from the reports to the Children's Rights Committee, there is little acknowledgement of the Convention in government publications or the family courts on the basis that the Children Act 1989 encapsulates it.[60] The government seems more willing to recognise children's rights in relation to its aid programmes than at home.[61] However, there is growing awareness of the Convention's principles amongst those working with children in health and social services, even though negative attitudes to the concept of children having rights have not been dispelled.[62]

III. CHILDREN'S RIGHTS AND ENGLISH LAW

17–008 The extent to which children have rights as individuals which they can exercise without the permission of their parents depends on both case and statute law. During the 1980s there were two quite contradictory developments. The courts recognised the increased independence of young people by accepting that if they could establish their maturity they could make many decisions free from parental control. In contrast Parliament, facing a weak economy and a reduction in employment opportunities for young people with few qualifications, legislated to remove social security rights so that young people's dependency on their families increased.[63]

---

[57] Bainham (1998), p. 66.

[58] J. Eekelaar "The importance of thinking that children have rights" (1992) 6 Int. J. Law & Fam. 221 at 234.

[59] M. King, "Children's rights as communication: some reflections on Autopoetic Theory and the United Nations Convention" [1994] *M.L.R.* 385, 401.

[60] The Government regarded the Children Act 1989 as implementing many of the obligations under the Convention (Cm. 2144, para. 1.13) despite no mention of the Convention during Parliamentary debates. *Re C (HIV Test)* [1999] 2 F.L.R. 1004, 1021E "Wilson J set out various Articles of the U.N Convention on the Rights of the Child 1989. We do not in a sense need that. It is all encapsulated in s. 1 of the Children Act . . . " *per* Butler-Sloss L.J.

[61] *U.K.'s Second Report to the U.N. Committee on the Rights of the Child* (1999) para. 5.5.1.

[62] W. Utting, *People like us* (1997), para.10.1.

[63] J. Masson, "The Children Act 1989 and young people: dependence and rights to independence" in D. Lockton, *Children and the Law* (1993), pp. 1, 10.

A. The *Gillick*[64] case

17–009 In December 1980 the DHSS issued a notice[65] which contained advice to doctors about the provision of contraceptive services to children under 16. It stated that it would be "most unusual" for a doctor to provide advice about contraception without parental consent, but acknowledged that, in some circumstances, unless children were treated in confidence, they might not seek treatment and suffer in consequence. Doctors should seek to persuade children to involve parents, but the decision whether to treat was a matter for clinical judgement. Mrs Victoria Gillick, the mother of five girls under the age of 16, sought an assurance from the local health authority that the girls would not be given contraceptive treatment without her consent. When she did not receive a reply which she regarded as satisfactory she sought a declaration that the DHSS notice had no authority in law and gave advice which adversely affected the welfare of the Gillick children, her rights as a parent and her ability to discharge her parental duties. At first instance Woolf J., refused the application.[66] The Court of Appeal unanimously reversed the decision. The House of Lords by a majority of three to two allowed the appeal and provided the foundation for the development of a distinctive concept of children's rights.

Three separate arguments were put forward on behalf of Mrs Gillick: on criminal law, on the age of consent to treatment and on parental rights. These will now be considered.

First, the Sexual Offences Act 1956 makes it unlawful for anyone to have sexual intercourse with a girl under the age of 16[67] or to encourage anyone to do so.[68] It was, therefore, argued that a doctor, who prescribed contraceptives for a girl without the parent's consent, committed a crime even though he or she only sought to act in her best interests. The DHSS notice was consequently unlawful because it amounted to advice to commit the offence of encouraging unlawful sexual intercourse or of being an accessory to unlawful sexual intercourse.[69] Woolf J., accepted that a doctor who provided contraceptives to a girl under 16, or her partner, with the intention of encouraging them to have sexual intercourse, would commit an offence but rejected the view that a doctor could necessarily commit an offence by following DHSS guidelines.[70] This latter point was conceded by both sides.[71] In the Court of Appeal, Parker L.J., considered the protection against sexual

---

[64] [1986] A.C. 112; [1984] Q.B. 581; see Glanville Williams, "The Gillick Saga" (1985) New L.J. 1156 and 1179; J. Eekelaar, "The eclipse of parental rights" (1986) 102 *L.Q.R.* 4; S. Cretney, "Gillick and the concept of legal capacity" (1989) 105 *L.Q.R.* 356; A. Bainham, "The balance of power in family decisions" [1986] *C.L.J.* 262; J. Eekelaar, "The emergence of children's rights" (1986) 6 Ox. J.L.S. 161; J. Montgomery, "Children as property" (1988) 51 *M.L.R.* 323.

[65] H.N. (80) 46 now replaced by LAC (86) 3 which is due for review in 2002; see also D.H. *Consent - what you have a right to expect: a guide for children and young people* (2001).

[66] [1984] Q.B. 581.

[67] ss.5, 6(1) no offence is committed by the girl.

[68] s.28(1).

[69] Contrary to ss.5, 6(1), 28(1).

[70] [1984] Q.B. 581 at 593–595, 599.

[71] [1986] A.C. 112 at 134.

intercourse provided to young girls by the criminal law but based his reasoning on the fact that an internal examination would normally be carried out before contraceptives were prescribed,[72] and that this would amount to an indecent assault[73] by the doctor because the 1956 Act precluded a girl under 16 giving a valid consent to it. In the House of Lords only Lord Brandon, considered the criminal law in detail; and Woolf J.'s analysis was accepted by the other Law Lords. Lord Brandon concluded that to provide advice about contraception, to examine with a view to providing contraceptive services and their prescription promoted, encouraged or facilitated sexual intercourse and were contrary to public policy whether or not they amounted to an offence.[74] The only answer the law should give to a girl who threatened to have unprotected intercourse was "Wait till you are 16."[75] He rejected the view that the DHSS had a duty to provide contraceptive services to girls under 16 on the basis that either they were not "persons" within the meaning of the National Health Service Act 1977 or that their requirements were not reasonable.[76]

Although counsel for Mrs Gillick and Parker L.J., both linked criminal liability with the absence of parental consent, Woolf J. clearly stated that if the doctor, or anyone else, commits an offence by or in the course of providing contraceptive services the parent's consent is immaterial.[77] Indeed if an offence were committed, a parent who consented might also be liable.[78] The arguments based on criminal law prompted an interesting discussion of public policy and adolescent sexual behaviour, but are not relevant to other areas. Had they been accepted, a further distinction between adolescent boys and girls would have been enshrined in law.

In relation to the second issue (the age of consent to treatment) the position is that if a valid consent[79] is not given, medical examination or treatment constitutes an assault and the doctor is liable in tort. The Family Law Reform Act 1969, s.8(1) provides that a person of 16 may consent to medical treatment and that "nothing in this section shall be construed as making ineffective any consent which would have been effective" under the general law.[80] Thus, the courts had to consider in what circumstances, if any, a younger child could consent to treatment. Woolf J., relying on the decision

---

[72] *ibid.* at 136–137. Fox and Everleigh LJJ. did not examine the criminal law.

[73] Contrary to Sexual Offences Act 1956, s.14.

[74] Williams criticised this reasoning (1985) 135 New L.J. 1156 at 1159.

[75] [1986] A.C. 112 at 197F.

[76] There is a statutory duty on the Secretary of State to provide a service which meets all reasonable requirements for contraception in England and Wales, s.5(1)(b).

[77] [1984] Q.B. 581 at 594. Although a parent's consent may prevent treatment being an assault, if the doctor were behaving indecently the agreement of the parent could not remove his liability.

[78] Sexual Offences Act 1956, s.14.

[79] The doctrine of informed consent has no part in English Law: *Sidaway v. Bethlem Royal Hospital Governors* [1985] A.C. 871 (Lord Scarman dissenting).

[80] Enacted following the recommendations of the Latey Committee which was concerned that some minors would have to wait for treatment if parental consent was required. The Committee did not specifically consider children under 16 but acknowledged that it was customary to accept the consent of those over 16, *op. cit.* para.179.

in a Canadian case,[81] held that a child who was capable of making a reasonable assessment of the advantages and disadvantages of the treatment proposed could give a valid consent. This would depend on the child's age and intelligence and the nature and implications of the treatment.[82] Parker and Fox L.JJ., adopting a different view of parental power, interpreted the section as requiring parental consent for any treatment of a child under 16.[83] The majority[84] of the House of Lords rejecting this view agreed with Woolf J.'s interpretation.

17–010 However, the importance of the case derives from their Lordship's opinions on the third issue, namely the nature and extent of parental power and their acceptance that children could act independently. The Court of Appeal's view of parental rights and duties has been described as traditional and simplistic and contrasted with the radical view of the House of Lords.[85] Parker and Fox L. JJ., concluded that the right to legal custody which included the right to decide "the place and manner in which [the child's] time is spent"[86] gave parents complete control over the child's actions until he or she reached the age of discretion.[87] These rights could only be abridged by statute or by the courts in proceedings where the decision had to be based on the paramountcy of the child's welfare.[88] There was no discussion in the Court of Appeal of the purpose of parental rights but some indication that parents were in the best position to make judgments in the child's welfare.[89]

In the House of Lords, in contrast, Lord Fraser, relying on Blackstone, stated that parental rights "exist for the benefit of the child and are justified only in so far as they enable a parent to perform his duties towards the child."[90] Lord Scarman was also clear that they exist for the child's protection[91] and consequently "yield to the child's right to make his own decisions when he reaches sufficient understanding and intelligence to be capable of making up his mind on the matter in question."[92] Thus, there was no parental right to forbid an action within a mature minor's capacity unless this was specifically provided by statute—"[T]he right to determine whether or not their minor child below the age of 16 will have medical treatment terminates if and when the child achieves sufficient understanding".[93] It is less clear that Lord Fraser accepted that parental rights were terminated in these circum-

---

81 *Johnston v. Wellesley Hospital* (1970) 17 D.L.R. (3d) 139.
82 [1984] Q.B. 581 at 596.
83 [1986] A.C. 112 at 123, 138, 145; Everleigh L.J. did not consider the general issue.
84 Lord Fraser, Lord Scarman, with whom Lord Bridge agreed. Lord Templeman agreed on this point although he did not consider that girls under 16 had the maturity to consent to decisions about contraception.
85 Cretney [1985] All E.R. Rev. 171 at 172.
86 Children Act 1975, s.86 (repealed by Children Act 1989).
87 [1986] A.C. 112 at 124, 143.
88 *ibid.* 125–127, 140, a parent's decision could always be challenged in wardship: see below.
89 *ibid. per* Everleigh L.J. at 146–147.
90 *ibid.* 170.
91 "[P]arental rights are derived from parental duty and exist only so long as they are needed for the protection and property of the child" *per* Lord Scarman at 184.
92 At 186.
93 *per* Lord Scarman at 188.

stances. His speech may be interpreted as accepting the retention of parental control which could only be disregarded if it were in the child's best interests so to do.[94] Alternatively, he may have intended that consultation with a mature minor's parents was relevant only to good professional practice. Lord Bridge agreed with both Lord Scarman and Lord Fraser. Lord Templeman appears to have agreed with Lord Scarman although on the issue of contraception he viewed all girls under 16 as insufficiently mature to make a valid decision.[95]

Although a test based on maturity rather than age created difficulties for those dealing with young people and for young people themselves,[96] the majority of the House of Lords considered that age-related limits should not be imposed on the process of growing up. Whether a child was sufficiently mature was a question of fact. Both Lord Scarman and Lord Fraser gave guidance about what a child had to understand to establish that he or she had capacity, but there is, arguably, substantial difference between them. Lord Scarman stated that:

> "She must also have a sufficient maturity to understand what is involved. There are moral and family questions, especially her relationship with her parents; long term problems associated with the emotional impact of pregnancy and its termination; and there are risks to health of sexual intercourse at her age, risks which contraception cannot eliminate."[97]

Lord Fraser merely said that the girl must understand the doctor's advice. However, in the conclusion to his opinion he set out, without reasons, five points which would justify a doctor providing contraceptive treatment without parental consent:

> "(1) that the girl (although under 16 years of age) will understand his advice;
> (2) that he cannot persuade her to inform her parents or allow him to inform the parents that she is seeking contraceptive advice;
> (3) that she is likely to begin or continue having sexual intercourse without contraceptive treatment;

---

[94] Eekelaar (1986) 102 *L.Q.R.* 4 at 5–6; the parent may have a duty to act reasonably: see Bainham [1986] *C.L.J.* 262 at 280.

[95] "[A]ny decision on the part of a girl to practise sex and contraception requires not only knowledge of the facts of life and of the dangers of pregnancy and disease but also an understanding of the emotional consequences to her family, her male partner and to herself. I doubt whether a girl under the age of 16 is capable of [the necessary] balanced judgement . . . there are many things which a girl under 16 needs to practise but sex is not one of them." at 201.

[96] See Bainham *op. cit.* p. 277 and *R. v. D.* [1984] 1 All E.R. 574, at 581, where the Court of Appeal decided that a child could not be kidnapped by a parent because of difficulties of establishing the child's consent. The House of Lords, reversing the decision, considered this could safely be left to the jury: [1984] 2 All E.R. 449 at 457; for criticism see G. Williams, "Can babies be kidnapped?" [1989] Crim. L.R. 473.

[97] at 186.

(4) that unless she receives contraceptive advice or treatment her physical or mental health or both are likely to suffer;
(5) that her best interests require him to give her contraceptive advice, treatment or both without parental consent."[98]

This would seem to subject the child to professional control in place of parental authority. Such control is more likely to be based on the doctor's attitude to sexual activity in young people than on knowledge of the child concerned.[99] Moreover, on either formulation, it may be possible for a person who disagrees with the child to conclude that the child's decision is an immature one and thus one which he or she has no right to take.[1]

The House of Lords decision is rightly regarded as a milestone in the development of adolescent's rights. The concept of "*Gillick* competence" has been applied to decisions about medical treatment, requests for access to personal records,[2] children's participation in civil proceedings[3] and is reflected in some of the provisions of the Children Act 1989.[4]

The concept of "*Gillick* competence" or maturity has advantages. It is flexible recognising children's capacity to make simpler decisions at younger ages and can protect children[5] by ensuring that they understand fully the implications of what they propose. The general test of capacity to make decisions applies; children must be able to comprehend and retain information relevant to the decision; believe it; and weigh it in the balance to arrive at a choice.[6] But it has been suggested that, in the case of children who may be influenced by their carers, understanding may not be a sufficient basis for accepting that a decision is autonomous.[7] It is also vague allowing professionals to deny children competence because of the complexity of the **17–011** decision,[8] by withholding information from them,[9] or if they appear child-

---

[98] At 174; Eekelaar (1986) 102 *L.Q.R.* 4 at 7; Montgomery (1988) 51 *M.L.R.* 323 at 339. The formulation has been incorporated in LAC 86(3).

[99] Family planning clinics and some G.Ps provide contraceptive services for young people. approximately 7% of girls aged 13–15 attend family planning clinics: D.H., *N.H.S. Contraceptive services, England 1999–2000* (2000).

[1] Eekelaar (1986) *op. cit.*, p. 9.

[2] D.H., *Data Protection Act (1998) Guidance for local authorities* (2000), para. 5.8; the Data Protection Act 1998 makes no special reference to access by children except in relation to Scotland (s. 67).

[3] *Re T. (A Minor) (Child: Representation)* [1994] Fam. 49, CA; *Re S. (A Minor) (Representation)* [1993] Fam. 263 CA; see below, para. 17–015.

[4] See below.

[5] *Re R. (A Minor) (Wardship: Consent to Treatment)* [1992] Fam. 11 at 26, *per* Lord Donaldson M.R.

[6] *Re C. (Adult: Refusal of Medical Treatment)* [1994] 1 F.L.R. 31 at 33 *per* Thorpe J. applied by Wall J. to children in *Re C. (Detention: Medical Treatment)* [1997] 2 F.L.R. 180.

[7] M. Brazier and C. Bridge, "Coercion or caring: analysing adolescent autonomy" (1996) L.S. 84 at 91.

[8] Lord Scarman set a high standard for understanding sexual activity and contraception in *Gillick* at 189. In *Re S. (A Minor) (Representation)* [1993] Fam. 263 an 11-year-old boy was said to lack sufficient understanding to participate in an emotionally fraught residence dispute between his parents. The boy finally succeeded in establishing his maturity when he was 13.

[9] *Re L. (Medical Treatment: Gillick Competency)* [1998] 2 F.L.R. 810 (a 14 year-old girl's refusal of a blood transfusion was overridden because she was unaware that she faced a painful death from gangrene if she did not have an operation); see Bridge [1999] *M.L.R.* 585.

like,[10] are mentally disturbed[11] or make unacceptable decisions.[12] Thus in *Re E* a 15-year-old leukaemia patient's refusal of treatment was rejected because he did not have sufficient comprehension of the pain he would suffer or the distress to his family of watching him die.[13] Similarly, a 15-year-old girl with a potentially fatal condition was regarded as immature because she hoped for a miracle cure.[14] Also, it has been said that children who are mentally ill are not "*Gillick* competent" even at times when their symptoms are not apparent.[15]

B. The retreat from *Gillick*

17–012 If young people have the right to consent to medical treatment, logically they should also have the right to refuse treatment.[16] However, the Court of Appeal, lead by Lord Donaldson M.R., has held that the court exercising its inherent jurisdiction, or a person with parental responsibility, may override the child's refusal and give the doctor the necessary consent to treatment[17]:—

> In *Re R.*[18] a 15-year-old girl in care[19] with florid psychotic behaviour was placed by the local authority in an adolescent psychiatric unit. When she refused treatment the local authority made her a ward of court and sought the court's permission for treatment. The Court of Appeal held that her mental condition meant that she was not "*Gillick* competent"[20] but proceeded to discuss whether a valid refusal could veto all treatment.

Lord Donaldson interpreted Lord Scarman's dictum that "the parental right to determine whether their child will have medical treatment terminates if and when the child achieves sufficient understanding" as only preventing a

---

[10] *Re S. (A Minor) (Consent to Medical Treatment)* [1994] 2 F.L.R. 1065 at 1076, *per* Johnson J. (the child's growth was stunted because of her medical condition).

[11] *Re R. (A Minor) (Wardship: Consent to Treatment)* [1992] Fam. 11; in *Re W. (A Minor) (Medical Treatment: Court's Jurisdiction)* [1993] Fam. 64 at 80, Lord Donaldson, M.R. doubted the correctness of Thorpe, J.'s view that a 16-year-old anorexia nervosa patient was *Gillick* competent.

[12] *Re E. (A Minor) (Wardship: Medical Treatment)* [1993] 1 F.L.R. 386.

[13] *per* Ward J. at 391. The young man died after refusing further treatment when he reached age 18.

[14] *Re S. (A Minor) (Consent to Medical Treatment)* [1994] 2 F.L.R. 1065 at 1076, *per* Johnson J. But irrationality has been said not to indicate incompetence: *per* Lord Donaldson, M.R. in *Re W. (A Minor) (Medical Treatment: Court's Jurisdiction)* [1993] Fam. 64 at 76.

[15] *Re R. (A Minor) (Wardship: Consent to Treatment)* [1992] Fam. 11 at 26, *per* Lord Donaldson M.R.

[16] Bainham (1992) 108 *L.Q.R.* 194, 198; M. Brazier, *Medicine patients and the law* (2nd ed., 1992), p. 345; I. Kennedy and A. Grubb, *Medical Law* (3rd ed., 2000), pp. 971, 985.

[17] *Re R. (A Minor) (Wardship: Consent to Treatment)* [1992] Fam. 11; *Re. W. (A Minor) (Medical Treatment: Court's Jurisdiction)* [1993] Fam. 64. But the discussion of the power of the court was *obiter:* see *S. Glamorgan C.C. v. W. and B.* [1993] 1 F.L.R. 574 at 584, *per* Douglas Brown J.

[18] [1992] Fam. 11.

[19] *i.e.* the girl was subject to a care order: Children Act 1989, s.33. The local authority had parental responsibility as a result of the order, see Chap. 22, below.

[20] [1992] Fam. 11 at 26.

parental veto of treatment consented to by the child.[21] Each parent retained an independent right to consent which was sufficient to enable the doctor to treat their child without incurring liability for trespass to the person.[22] Similarly, the court could override the decisions of "*Gillick* competent" children either by exercising its inherent jurisdiction[23] or by making an order under section 8 of the Children Act 1989.[24]

This decision was followed in *Re W.*[25]:—

> A 16-year-old orphan in the care of the local authority was suffering from anorexia nervosa. She had been treated for some time in a local hospital but her condition had not improved. A place had been found for her at a specialist unit but she refused to go there. The local authority applied for leave to seek an order under the inherent jurisdiction so that the girl could be moved without her consent.[26] The order was granted and the girl appealed unsuccessfully.

Lord Donaldson M.R. took the opportunity to apply his reasoning where the young person was "*Gillick* competent." He held that Family Law Reform Act 1969, s.8(3) which states that "Nothing in this section shall be construed as making ineffective any consent . . ." preserved the parental right to consent to examination and treatment of children over 16. Those with parental responsibility therefore had a "flak jacket" which they could use to defend the doctor from a claim of assault by a child over 16 or any "*Gillick* competent" child.[27] Once a child had given a valid consent only the court exercising its inherent jurisdiction could override the child's decision, but doctors could not be required to treat except in accordance with their clinical judgement.[28] Lord Donaldson also suggested that the court could make a prohibited steps or specific issue order.[29]

Although this allows the court and those with parental responsibility to disregard a child's refusal of treatment, the importance of giving young people progressively more responsibility whilst protecting them from unac-

---

[21] *ibid.* at 23. Staughton L.J. clearly did not agree and confined his decision to the powers of the High Court under the inherent jurisdiction (at 27) as did Farquharson L.J.

[22] *ibid.* at 22. A person with parental responsibility is a "keyholder" who can unlock the legal door to treatment. Where the patient objects the doctor may have ethical problems.

[23] For an explanation of this High Court jurisdiction see para. 19–045 below.

[24] *ibid.* at 25. A specific issue order has been held to be sufficient to override the refusal of a parent to given consent: *Re R. (A Minor) (Blood Transfusion)* [1993] 2 F.L.R. 757. But a local authority may not apply for a specific issue order if the child is in care: s.9(1).

[25] [1993] Fam. 64.

[26] Such an order is only available to a local authority if there is no other way for it to proceed: s.100(4), (5). But if parental responsibility enables the child's decision to be overridden leave cannot be given where there is a care order.

[27] [1993] Fam. 64 at 78.

[28] *ibid.* at 83.

[29] *ibid.* at 82. But these orders under the Children Act 1989, s.8 can only be available if parental responsibility continues. If a parent is unable to veto the child's decision it would appear that the court cannot exercise its statutory powers in this way.

ceptable risks was affirmed.[30] The court must have regard to the child's wishes and feelings[31]; and Nolan L.J., suggested that the question of whether major surgery or abortion should be carried out against a competent child's consent should always be referred to the court.[32] However, the recognition that some aspects of parental power endure when children have become competent means that children who refuse treatment are reliant on medical ethics or the court's exercise of its welfare jurisdiction rather than rights.[33] Given the deference to medical opinion it is most unlikely that a request for authority to treat an objecting child will be refused by the courts.[34]

There are further reasons for criticising these decisions. Young people with mental illness, who are treated as voluntary patients with the consent of their parents or under care orders, do not have the safeguards of the Mental Health Act 1983.[35] Also, the court's power to override the refusal of treatment conflicts with the provisions in the Children Act 1989 which uphold the refusal of assessments ordered in child protection proceedings[36] and require consent for assessments and treatment where the child is subject to a supervision order.[37] Moreover, if the child is in care there appears to be no way the local authority's decision to authorise treatment can be challenged except by applying for discharge of the care order.[38] Although the courts purport to base decisions on the child's understanding, they are actually reacting to the potential results of children's choices.[39]

C. Children's rights under the European Convention of Human Rights[40]

17–013 This Convention was drafted in the immediate post-war period when protection from oppression by fascist states was a major concern and the concept of children's rights remained undeveloped. Consequently, it is "adult ori-

---

[30] "[G]ood parenting involves giving minors so much rope as they can handle without an unacceptable risk that they will hang themselves." *per* Lord Donaldson M.R. at 81.

[31] *per* Balcombe at 88; *per* Nolan L.J. at 93.

[32] at 94.

[33] But the child's co-operation my be essential for successful treatment, see P. Alderson, *Children's consent to surgery* (1993).

[34] A doctor who has consent from a person with parental responsibility has no need to bring legal proceedings: *Re K., W. and H. (Minors) (Medical Treatment)* [1993] 1 F.L.R. 854 at 859, *per* Thorpe J. nevertheless applications continue to be made in extreme cases: *Re M. (Medical Treatment: Consent)* [1999] 2 F.L.R. 1096 (heart transplant). It is unlikely that compulsory medical treatment would breach E.C.H.R., Art. 3 see Swindells *et al.* (1999) para. 3.12.

[35] For example second opinions and review of the treatment, see Masson [1992] *Fam. Law* 528.

[36] Children Act 1989, s.38(6) (interim care or supervision orders); s.43(8) (child assessment order); s.44(7) (emergency protection order).

[37] Children Act 1989, Sched.3, paras 4(4), 5(5).

[38] A prohibited steps order could not be made: s.9(1); the inherent jurisdiction is not available: *A. v. Liverpool C.C.* [1982] A.C. 363.

[39] Bridge and Brazier, *op. cit.*, p. 109.

[40] see generally: J. Fortin, *op. cit.* (1998); U. Kilkelly, *The child and the European Convention on Human Rights* (1999); J. Fortin, "Rights brought home for children" [1999] *M.L.R.* 350; H. Swindells *et al.* (1999); C. Forder, *Legal establishment of the parent child relationship* Ph.D. thesis, Maastricht University (1995).

ented" focusing on protecting civil and political rights, does not explicitly recognise the specific requirements of children and provides no clear guidance on reconciling parents' rights to freedom from state interference with children's rights to develop independence from their parents.[41] However, in balancing parents' and children's rights to family life, the European Court of Human Rights has attached particular importance to the best interests of the child.[42] Although there have been few applications to the European Court of Human Rights by children, the Convention has had considerable impact children's rights throughout Europe. The incorporation of the Convention into U.K. domestic law has raised its importance by requiring public bodies to act in accordance with it[43] and facilitating enforcement of the rights it guarantees.[44] There is growing recognition that children may sometimes have stronger claims than adults under the Convention.[45]

Although the whole of the Convention can apply to children, it is Article 8, the right to respect for private and family life, which has had the greatest influence on children's lives.[46] The state's responsibility is not limited to restricting interference with rights but includes taking positive action to promote family relationships.[47] The Convention led to major changes in child care law, particularly restricting local authority discretion and requiring local authorities to consult parents and to promote contact between children and their families.[48] Corporal punishment was ended in all schools[49] following decisions that it could infringe a parent's rights in relation to their child's education[50] or a child's right to be protected from degrading treatment.[51]

---

[41] J. Eekelaar and R. Dingwall, *Human Rights: Report on the replies of Governments to the Enquiry under art 57* (Council of Europe 1987) p. 21; Fortin [1999] *M.L.R.* 350, 354; Fortin (1998), *op. cit.*, pp. 51–56.

[42] "[A] fair balance must be struck between the interests of the child and those of the parent . . . the best interests of the child . . . depending on their nature and seriousness, may override those of the parent." *Sahin v. Germany* [2002] 1 F.L.R. 119 at para. 42; see also *Johansen v. Norway* (1996) 23 E.H.R.R. 33 at para.78.

[43] Human Rights Act 1998, ss.6(1).

[44] *ibid.* s.7; *Re W. and B., Re W.* [2001] 2 F.L.R. 582 CA; *sub nom. Re S. (minors) (care order: implementation of care plan)* [2000] 1 F.L.R. 815, HL. It will no longer be necessary to go to the European Court of Human Rights to obtain a remedy, although this will provide a last resort see Masson [2002] *C.F.L.Q.* 77.

[45] Swindells, *et al.* (1999), para. 6.14, citing *Berrehab v. The Netherlands* (1988) 11 E.H.R.R. 322.

[46] See J. Fortin, "The HRA's impact on litigation involving children and their families" [1999] *C.F.L.Q.* 237 at 247.

[47] *Marckx v. Belgium* (1979) 1 E.H.R.R. 330; *Hokkanen v. Finland* [1996] 1 F.L.R. 289.

[48] *TP and KM v. U.K.* [2001] 2 F.L.R. 549; *W. v. U.K.* (1987) 10 E.H.R.R. 29. The parents' inability to challenge local authority decisions on contact breached their rights under Arts 6 and 8 and was remedied by legislation: Health and Social Services and Social Security Adjudications Act 1983. Further obligations were imposed on local authorities by the Children Act 1989, ss.22(4)(5), 34 and Sched. 2, para. 15.

[49] Education (No. 2) Act 1986, ss.47 and 48; Education Act 1993; see now Education Act 1996, ss.548, 549; and see Fortin (1998), *op. cit.*, pp. 235–8.

[50] Contrary to Protocol 1, Art. 2; *Campbell and Cosans v. U.K.* (1982) 4 E.H.R.R. 293.

[51] Contrary to Art. 3; *Tyrer v. U.K.* (1978) 2 E.H.R.R. 175 (the Manx birching case); *Costello-Roberts v. U.K.* (1993) 19 E.H.R.R. 112 (7 year-old slippered at prep school). The court, by a majority, found no breach of Art. 3 in *Costello-Roberts* but regarded it as a borderline case. The commission (but not the court) considered there had been a breach of the right to private life (Art. 8).

Failure to protect children from corporal punishment at home has also been held to breach children's rights:—

> In *A. v. U.K.*[52] a 9 year-old boy was beaten with a garden cane by his step-father on a number of occasions, leaving obvious bruises. The step-father was prosecuted for assault but acquitted. From this is could be inferred that the jury regarded the beating as "reasonable chastisement".[53] In Strasbourg, the government accepted there had been a violation of the boy's Article 3 rights; the court unanimously found a violation because English law did not provide adequate protection against such punishment. Following the decision, the Government consulted on reform but appears loathed to legislate against physical punishment of children.[54]

Article 3 has also provided the basis for a claim where a local authority social services department failed protect children from severe abuse and neglect.[55] Changes have also been made to the way children are tried for serious offences.[56] Not all decisions have promoted children's rights:—

> In *Neilson v. Denmark*[57] the European Court of Human Rights held that there had been no violation of the rights of a 12 year-old boy, caught up in a residence dispute between his parents, who was committed to a psychiatric unit at the request of his mother. The placement did not amount to detention[58] but was a responsible exercise by his mother of her rights.

Overall, Fortin concludes the European Court of Human Rights has affected children in a variety of unpredictable ways. Through applications by children and parents it has recognised important rights—protection from corporal punishment and contact with parents—but has emphasised parental autonomy and family privacy which has the potential to damage children's rights.[59] Nevertheless, the incorporation of the Convention has potential to change the way children are viewed and treated by the law. Public bodies must exercise their powers in ways which are not incompatible with the Convention, and

---

[52] [1998] 2 F.L.R. 959; for the effect of this case on the common law see: *R. v. H. (Assault of Child: Reasonable Chastisement)* [2001] 2 F.L.R. 431, CA.

[53] Children and Young Persons Act 1933, s.1(1)(e).

[54] D.H. *Protecting children, supporting parents: a consultation document on the physical punishment of children* (2000); J. Fortin, "Children's rights and the use of physical force" [2001] *C.F.L.Q.* 243.

[55] *Z. v. U.K.* [2001] 2 F.L.R. 612. The House of Lords in *X. (Minors) v. Bedfordshire C.C.* [1995] 2 A.C. 633 that the local authority was immune from liability in negligence for failing to remove the children from their parents, see Chap. 22, below.

[56] *T. v. U.K.; V v. U.K.* [2000] All E.R.1024 (note).

[57] (1988) 11 E.H.R.R. 175.

[58] Contrary to Art 5. In *Re K (Secure Accommodation Order: Right to Liberty)* [2001] 1 F.L.R. 526 CA Thorpe L.J. (dissenting) applied this same reasoning to use of secure accommodation under Children Act 1989, s.25; see Masson [2002] *C.F.L.Q.* 77.

[59] Fortin (1999), *op. cit.*, pp. 369–370.

the courts must consider children's issues in terms of human rights and in the light of decisions of the European Court in Strasbourg.

D. Children's rights and the Children Act 1989

17–014 It has been stated that the Children Act 1989 does nothing to change the underlying principle of the *Gillick* decision.[60] However, the Act neither recognises that mature children necessarily have legal capacity nor attempts the impossible task of defining how parental responsibility and children's rights interrelate.[61] Where there is a dispute between parents or between the parents and the child, the court's decision is to be made applying the welfare principle[62] rather than on the basis of the child's rights. The child will not necessarily be a party to those proceedings.[63] The child's consent is not required for a parent to arrange the child's emigration or for a change of name[64] nor for the imposition of a family assistance order.[65] A child who objects to a parent's decision may seek leave to apply for a prohibited steps order,[66] but leave will only be granted where the court is satisfied that the child has sufficient understanding[67] and the court's decision on the substantive issue will be made applying the welfare principle. Children who were not parties to the original proceedings may not apply to have a contact order varied and must rely on their carer or direct action to avoid contact.[68] Where the child is looked after by the local authority, or is the subject of child protection proceedings, the Act recognises the child's right to be consulted[69] but it removed the rights[70] of mature children under 16 to refer themselves to local authority accommodation or to remain there against their parents' wishes.[71] However, the consent of a mature child is required for a medical or psychiatric examination even where this has been ordered in court proceed-

---

[60] *per* Lord Mackay, Lord Chancellor, Children Bill Committee stage, *Hansard* H.L. Vol. 502, col. 1351.

[61] L.C. No 172, para. 2.2.

[62] Children Act 1989, s.1; the welfare checklist in s.1(3) includes "(a) the ascertainable wishes and feelings of the child concerned (considered in the light of his age and understanding)": see Chap. 20, below.

[63] Party status is discussed below at para. 17–015.

[64] Children Act 1989, s.13(1) *Practice Direction (Child) (Change of Surname)* [1995] 1 F.L.R. 548; for a discussion of children's participation in migration decisions see: Ackers [2000] *C.F.L.Q.* 167.

[65] s.16. The consent of all other people named in the order must be obtained: s.16(3).

[66] s.8. For details of court powers, see Chap. 19 below.

[67] s.10(8); *Re T. (A Minor) (Child: Representation)* [1994] Fam. 49, CA; *Re H. (Residence Order)* [2000] 1 F.L.R. 780, FD.

[68] Despite the clear wording the child is not apparently "named in the order" for the purpose of s.10(6), *Re H. (Residence Order)* [2000] 1 F.L.R. 780 at 784 *per* Johnson J.

[69] Children Act 1989, s.22(4)(b), (5)(a).

[70] The D.H.S.S. considered that children of 16 had such a right and stated that it might be appropriate to grant this to younger children "provided that this did not interfere with the competing interest of the parents" *Review of the Child Care Law*, Discussion Paper 2, para. 72. The discussion paper was written before the House of Lords decision in *Gillick* which can be interpreted as providing this right for all mature children.

[71] Children Act 1989, s.20(8), (11).

ings,[72] for emigration arrangements[73] and for the provision of an independent visitor.[74] Also the power of the courts to make orders is curtailed; section 8 orders[75] will only be made, or remain in force, in respect of children over the age of 16 in exceptional circumstances.[76] Thus, the Children Act 1989 takes a narrow view of *Gillick*, mature children may make some decisions which are essentially personal, but where others are involved the decision is left to the carers whose actions may be challenged in the courts.[77]

E. Children as parties in legal proceedings[78]

17–015 Children have the same rights to bring or defend ordinary civil proceedings as do adults but they are regarded as "legal incompetents" and subject to procedural protections and controls like those applied to mental patients.[79] Also, their access to the courts in private law family proceedings is restricted. A child who wishes to seek a section 8 order, for example a contact order to require a parent to allow contact with a sibling,[80] or a residence order to enable the child to live with a relative,[81] must first obtain leave.[82] The application must be made in the High Court[83]; this limits decisions to a small number of judges and may discourage applications. The court must find that the child has sufficient understanding to make the application[84] and

---

72 s.44 and Sched.3, para. 4(4). But not under the inherent jurisdiction: *Re R. (A Minor) (Wardship: Consent to Treatment)* [1992] Fam. 11; *Re W. (A Minor) (Medical Treatment: Court's Jurisdiction)* [1993] Fam. 64; *S. Glamorgan C.C. v. W. and B.* [1993] 1 F.L.R. 574; and below.

73 Sched.2, para. 19(3); this only applies where there is a care order.

74 Sched.2, para. 17; independent visitors are appointed to befriend children looked after by a local authority who have little or no contact with their families see M. Winn Oakley and J. Masson, *Official friends or friendly officials* (1999).

75 For an explanation of these orders, see Chap. 19 below.

76 ss. 9(6), 91(10), *e.g.* if the child had limited intellectual capacity or is irresponsible: *Re M. (Contact: Parental Responsibility)* [2001] 2 F.L.R. 342, FD. Residence orders in favour of people other than parents and guardians can last until the child is 18: s.12(5) to be added by Adoption of Children Bill 2002.

77 If a child under 16 wants to remain in local authority accommodation against the wishes of the parent the court may not be able to intervene. Neither the inherent jurisdiction nor a s.8 order can be used to "achieve a result which could be achieved by a residence order" or to "require a child to be accommodated by the local authority": ss.9(5), 100(2). Residence orders may not be made in favour of the local authority: s.9(2). The child could complain about the failure to take care proceedings but judicial review is likely to be refused: *R. v. E. Sussex C.C., ex p. W.* [1998] 2 F.L.R. 1082.

78 See J. Masson, "Representations of children" [1996] C.L.P. 245. For a review of the nature and extent of litigation by children see: J. Masson and A. Orchard, *Children and civil litigation* LCD Research Report No. 10 (1999). The Australian Law Reform Commission has conducted an extensive review of children's involvement in litigation: ALRC, Report No. 84, *Seen and Heard: Priority for children in the legal process* (1997).

79 Civil Procedure Rules 1998; S.I. 1998 No. 3132, r. 21; see below.

80 *Re F. (Contact Child in Care)* [1995] 1 F.L.R. 510, FD; *Re S. (Contact: Application by a Sibling)* [1998] 2 F.L.R. 897, FD (application for contact with adopted sibling).

81 *Re T. (A Minor) (Child Representation)* [1994] Fam. 49.

82 Children Act 1989, s.10(8)(9); s.10(9) applies to contact but not to residence applications: *Re S. (Contact: Application by a Sibling)* [1998] 2 F.L.R. 897 at 904–7 *per* Charles J.

83 *Practice Direction* [1993] 1 F.L.R. 668. This direction was intended to ensure that child applicants were not acting on behalf of adults.

84 s.10(8) and where s.10(9) applies *Re S. (Contact: Application by a Sibling)* [1998] 2 F.L.R. 897, 906B *per* Charles J.

that the issue could not properly be considered without this application.[85] The views of other potential parties may be heard.[86]

17–016 Courts have tended to regard children's involvement in these disputes negatively. There is a fear that it could "drive a wedge between parents and children" and make proceedings more acrimonious.[87] Judges have been haunted by the "spectre" of parents being cross-examined on behalf of their children[88] and also concerned to protect children from the stresses of litigation.[89] However, it is increasingly being recognised that children have a right to a voice in proceedings,[90] can benefit from participation[91] and may sometimes need represention in proceedings between their parents.[92] Article 6 of the European Convention on Human Rights is likely to encourage this trend.[93] The court has wide powers to permit children to be made parties to and be represented in family proceedings.[94] Where this will assist the court, for example by enabling expert evidence to be obtained rather than relying on the views of a court appointed officer, the court may be willing to permit the child to be a party to litigation between parents.[95]

17–017 In *Re A.*[96] the mother made allegations of sexual abuse against the father when he applied for staying contact. The judge ordered psychiatric reports on both parents and made a contact order. The mother refused to allow contact and failed to attend any further hearings. She was at risk of imprisonment for disobeying the orders. The mother approached the National Youth Advocacy Service (a voluntary organisation) who sought leave for the child to be made a party to the proceedings and to act as her guardian *ad litem*. This application was refused but the Court of Appeal appointed the Official Solicitor[97] as the child's guardian

---

[85] *Re H. (Residence Order)* [2000] 1 F.L.R. 780 at 783 *per* Johnson J. A similar approach applies to making adults parties to proceedings: *North Yorkshire C.C. v. G.* [1993] 2 F.L.R. 732.

[86] F.P.R. 1991, r. 4.3. Leave may be granted without a hearing: r. 4.3(2)(a).

[87] Advisory Board on Family Law, *First Annual Report* (1998), para. 4.12.

[88] *Re H. (Residence Order)* [2000] 1 F.L.R. 780 at 783 *per* Johnson J.

[89] *Re C.(A Minor)(Care: Child's wishes)* [1993] 1 F.L.R. 832, 841, *per* Waite J.; *Re W. (Secure Accommodation Order: attendance at court)* [1994] 2 F.L.R. 1092 at 1096 *per* Ewbank J.

[90] A. O' Quigley, *Listening to children's views: the findings and recommendations of recent research* (2000); B. Neale and C. Smart, *Good to talk?* (2001).

[91] *Re K. (Secure Accommodation: Right to Liberty)* [2001] 2 F.L.R. 526 at 541 *per* Butler-Sloss P.

[92] *Re A. (Contact: Separate Representation)* [2001] 1 F.L.R. 715 at 719 *per* Butler-Sloss P. and 721 *per* Hale L.J.

[93] The termination of contact between a child and a parent infringes both their civil rights and so hearing must satisfy Art. 6(1)in respect of the parent and the child; see Fortin [1999] *C.F.L.Q.* 237, 244 and *Sommerfield v. Germany* [2002] 1 F.L.R. 119.

[94] F.P.R. 1991, r. 9(5). The implementation of Family Law Act 1996, s.64 would not allow for any greater participation except in the family proceedings court. The existing provisions are "broadly satisfactory": Advisory Board on Family Law, *Second Annual Report* (1999) para. 3.14.

[95] *Re A.(Contact: Separate Representation)* [2001] 1 F.L.R. 715 CA; *Re N. (Residence: Appointment of solicitor: Placement with extended family)* [2001] 1 F.L.R. 1028.

[96] [2001] 1 F.L.R. 715, CA.

[97] Representation would now be provided through CAFCASS: *CAFCASS Practice Note* [2001] 1 F.L.R. 151 and see Chap. 19, below. If CAFCASS officers are able to conduct their own extensive

> *ad litem* so that there could be a proper investigation of the abuse allegations.[98]

As a general rule children may only bring or defend civil proceedings if they are represented by a litigation friend.[99] This person then serves and accepts service of any documents,[1] instructs the solicitor and determines how the proceedings should be conducted. However, a radical departure from long-established practice, introduced with apparently little consideration of its potential effects,[2] enables children who have "sufficient understanding" to bring or continue private law proceedings[3] under the Children Act 1989 or the inherent jurisdiction of the High Court[4] without a next friend or guardian *ad litem*.[5] Nevertheless, it has been said that a balance must be struck between recognising that children are individuals with rights and views to express and protecting them from the pressures of responsibility and decision making in the proceedings.[6]

A child who wishes to proceed independently must seek leave from the court.[7] Although the rules provide for a solicitor to accept the instructions of a child who has sufficient understanding,[8] it has been held that in such cases the court still has power to determine whether the child can proceed.[9]

> In *Re S.*[10] the Court of Appeal refused to allow an 11-year-old to intervene without a guardian *ad litem* in acrimonious litigation between his parents over his residence, education and contact because the case cried out for objective and experienced judgment.

---

inquiries these might satisfy the court's (but not the child's) needs for representation. Where the child's own welfare is not in issue he or she can be represented by the Official Solicitor: *Practice Note* [2001] 2 F.L.R. 155.

[98] CAFCASS Legal may alternatively be appointed as *amicus curiae* (friend of the court) but this does not give party status nor allow an appeal: *Re H. (A Minor) (Guardian ad litem requirement)* [1994] Fam. 11, 17.

[99] C.P.R. r. 21.2(3) (the court has the power to make an order allowing a child to proceed without a litigation friend); F.P.R. 1991, r. 9.2 (next friend or guardian *ad litem*); Johnston [2001] *Fam. Law* 515. Parents can act as the child's next friend unless they have interests which conflict with those of the child. A solicitor cannot be retained by a client incapable of giving instructions: Law Society, *Guide to professional conduct of solicitors* (8th ed. 1999), para. 24.04.

[1] F.P.R. 1991, rr.9(2), 9(3).

[2] M. Thorpe, "Independent representation of minors" [1993] *Fam. Law* 20.

[3] *i.e.* proceedings which do not involve a local authority. A local authority may take action to protect the child in public law proceedings under the Act. The child's position in public law proceedings is discussed below.

[4] For an explanation of this jurisdiction see Chap. 19, below.

[5] F.P.R. 1991, r. 9.2A added by Family Proceedings (Amendment) Rules 1992, S.I. 1992 No. 456, r. 9.

[6] *Re S. (A Minor) (Independent Representation)* [1993] Fam. 263 at 276, *per* Sir Thomas Bingham M.R.

[7] F.P.R. 1991, r. 9.2A(1)(a).

[8] F.P.R. 1991, r. 9.2A(1)(b).

[9] *Re T. (A Minor) (Child: Representation)* [1994] Fam. 49, C.A.; *Re S. (A Minor) (Independent Representation)* [1993] Fam. 263, CA.

[10] [1993] Fam. 263. The boy subsequently obtained leave to proceed without the Official Solicitor when he was 13.

But the court cannot impose a guardian *ad litem* on a competent child[11]—

> In *Re T.*[12] a 13-year-old girl who had become estranged from her adoptive parents obtained leave to apply for a residence order to enable her to live with her natural aunt. The adoptive parents, who opposed contact with the natural family, made the girl a ward of court so that the Official Solicitor could act as her guardian *ad litem*. The girl appealed successfully against the order. The Court of Appeal held that wardship should not be invoked where issues could be resolved under the Children Act 1989[13] and did not provide a means of imposing a guardian *ad litem* on a child with sufficient understanding to proceed without one.[14]

There is no definition of "sufficient understanding" in relation to an application for leave to proceed independently, but this is a test of "*Gillick* competence" which must be "assessed relatively to the issues in the proceedings".[15] Although Lord Scarman in *Gillick* referred to the ability "to exercise a wise choice in one's own interests"[16] it has been accepted that a child with sufficient rationality to give consistent and coherent instructions could instruct their own solicitor.[17] Guidance has been prepared to help solicitors[18] assess whether children have sufficient understanding, "Maturity can be assessed on the child's ability to understand the nature of the proceedings and to have an appreciation of the possible consequences of the applications to the court both in the long and short term."[19] Leave may be revoked and a guardian *ad litem* imposed if it becomes clear that the child lacks the necessary understanding.[20] And it has been said that the court is unlikely to permit a child who proposes not to be legally represented to proceed independently unless the guardian *ad litem* agreed.[21] Solicitors should act scrupulously and conscientiously when assessing children's ability to give instructions and risk withdrawal of legal aid if they do not.[22] Participating as a

---

[11] F.P.R. 1991, r. 9.2A(6).
[12] [1994] Fam. 49.
[13] p. 65.
[14] p. 67.
[15] *Re S. (A Minor) (Independent Representation)* [1993] Fam. 263 at 276, *per* Sir Thomas Bingham M.R.
[16] [1988] A.C. 112 at 188.
[17] *Re H. (A Minor) (Care Proceedings: Child's wishes)* [1993] 1 F.L.R. 440 at 449.
[18] Solicitors Family Law Association, *Guide to good practice for solicitors acting for children* (5th. ed., 2000); Law Society, *Guidance on acting for children in private law proceedings under the Children Act 1989* (1994); see Ray [1994] *Fam. Law* 529. Examples are also discussed in C. Liddle, *Acting for children* (1992) and P. King and I. Young, *The child as client* (1992) and in *Re S.* (above) at 278. In the past solicitors have approached this task in different ways: C. Sawyer, *The rise and fall of the third party* (1995).
[19] Solicitors Family Law Association, *op. cit.*, p. 6.
[20] F.P.R. 1991, r. 9.2A(8), (10).
[21] *Re S. (A Minor) (Independent Representation)* [1993] Fam.263 at 276.
[22] *Re S. (A Minor) (Independent Representation)* [1993] Fam.263 at 276, *per* Sir Thomas Bingham M.R. But in borderline cases solicitors should be given the benefit of the doubt: *Re T.* (above) at 67, *per* Waite, L.J.

party requires more than instructing a solicitor about one's views; a party must be able to follow the evidence and given instructions on issues as the case proceeds.[23] Children who are parties may need to give instructions relating to psychiatric reports[24] or want their lawyer to advocate that they should live with an abuser.[25] But as parties they cannot be required to give evidence and therefore could only be called to give evidence if they chose to do so. The level of understanding required to participate in legal proceedings has been regarded as less than that required to refuse a psychiatric examination.[26]

The rules make very different provision for the representation of children in "specified proceedings", *i.e.* certain proceedings involving a local authority exercising its powers to protect children.[27] The child is represented by a children's guardian from CAFCASS[28] and a solicitor.[29] The guardian's duties include investigating the case, explaining matters to the child and advising the court on the child's best interests and wishes.[30] The children's guardian instructs the solicitor unless the child is competent,[31] wants to do so and has instructions which conflict with those of the children's guardian.[32] In such a case the solicitor must follow the child's instructions and consequently may have to advocate that a child not receive professional help for disturbance which is ruining his educational prospects[33] or be allowed to live with a sibling he is thought to have abused.[34] Where there is a conflict the court should be informed and may direct that the children's guardian is separately represented.[35] This procedure should enable the court to hear full arguments relating both to the child's wishes and the child's welfare.

Children do not have the right to attend proceedings brought under the

---

[23] *Re H. (A Minor) (Guardian ad litem requirement)* [1994] Fam.11 at 13, *per* Booth J. The extent to which a child party may be protected by being excluded from proceedings is unclear: see below.

[24] *Re M. (Minors) (Care proceedings: Child's wishes)* [1994] 1 F.L.R. 749 (psychiatric reports about parents); *Re H. (A Minor) (Care proceedings: Child's wishes)* [1993] 1 F.L.R. 440 (psychiatric report on child).

[25] *Re H. (A Minor) (Guardian ad litem requirement)* [1994] Fam.11.

[26] *Re H. (A Minor) (Care proceedings: Child's wishes)* [1993] 1 F.L.R. 440 at 449, *per* Thorpe J.

[27] Children Act 1989, s.41; F.P.R. 1991, r.4.2(2); F.P.C. 1991, r.2(2). For a detailed analysis of representation in public law proceedings see: J. Masson and M. Winn Oakley, *Out of Hearing* (1999) and J. Masson, "Representation of children in England" [2000] F.L.Q. 467.

[28] Children Act 1989, s.41; Criminal Justice and Court Services Act 2000, s.12. The children's guardian is normally a qualified social worker with substantial child care experience.

[29] F.P.R. 1991, rr. 4.10–4.12; F.P.C. 1991, rr.10–12. But it has been held that this does not entitle the child to public funding where the merits test applies: *W. v. Legal Services Commission* [2000] 2 F.L.R. 821, CA.

[30] F.P.R. 1991, rr. 4.11, 4.11A; F.P.C. 1991, rr.11, 11A.

[31] Disputes about the child's competence should be referred to the court: *Re H. (A Minor) (Care proceedings: Child's wishes)* [1993] 1 F.L.R. 440. In practice children's guardians and solicitors work to avoid conflict: Masson and Winn Oakley, *op. cit.*, pp. 77–79.

[32] F.P.R. 1991, rr.4.11A(1)(b), 4.12(1)(a); F.P.C. 1991, rr.11A(1)(b), 12(1)(a).

[33] *Re H. (A Minor) (Care proceedings: Child's wishes)* [1993] 1 F.L.R. 440.

[34] *Re M. (Minors) (Care proceedings: Child's wishes)* [1994] 1 F.L.R. 749. But if the child's instructions are wholly unreasonable the solicitor must report the matter to the Legal Services Commission: *Funding Code* Pt 2, para. C44(i) and funding will be withdrawn: Pt 1, para.14.5(vi).

[35] *Re M. (Minors) (Care proceedings: Child's wishes)* [1994] 1 F.L.R. 749. The costs of the children's guardian's representation fall on CAFCASS.

Children Act 1989 even where they are parties, but a party may not be excluded unless they are represented by a children's guardian or a solicitor.[36] Attending court is considered by some to be damaging to children because it may make them feel responsible for the decisions and increase their anxiety.[37] It is not an experience which should be wished on a child as young as 13.[38] The trial judge should balance the rights of children to participate and be heard in litigation, and the need to protect children from exposure to material which might be damaging.[39] Children subject to secure accommodation proceedings must be afforded the protection the European Convention of Human Rights, Art. 6(3) and should feel they have been treated fairly.[40]

Despite growing acceptance of children as individuals with rights, the courts remain most concerned to protect what they consider to be children's interests.[41] The ability of children to make an application and represent themselves does not lie easily with the adversarial procedures of the court.[42] Allowing children to appear without a next friend or guardian *ad litem* puts them at risk of being manipulated by parents or by solicitors.[43] However, rather than seeking change to legal proceedings to make it easier for children to participate, the judiciary has exercised its power to limit children's direct involvement.[44] If the power to appoint children's guardians were extended to all family proceedings so that greater emphasis could be given to children's interests, the courts might be more willing to hear children's views.

F. Rights in other legislation

17–018 Education law takes even less notice of children's rights.[45] Choice of school is regarded as a parental right[46] and children have no right to express

---

[36] F.P.R. 1991, r. 4. 16(2); F.P.C. 1991, r. 16(2). But a child may be ordered to attend proceedings for an order under Pt IV and V of the Children Act 1989 (s.95(1)).

[37] The argument put by the Official Solicitor in *Re W. (Secure Accommodation Order: Attendance at Court)* [1994] 2 F.L.R. 1092.

[38] *Re C. (A Minor) (Care: Child's wishes)* [1993] 1 F.L.R. 832 at 841, *per* Waite J.

[39] *Re A. (Care: Discharge Application by Child)* [1995] 1 F.L.R. 599 at 601, *per* Thorpe J.

[40] *Re C. (Secure Accommodation Order: Representation)* [2001] 2 F.L.R. 169, paras 34 and 41 *per* Brooke L.J.

[41] C. Sawyer, *Rules, roles and relationships: the structure and function of child representation and welfare in family proceedings* Centre for socio-legal studies, Oxford University (1999); C. Sawyer, "Conflicting rights for children: implementing welfare autonomy and justice in family proceedings" [1999] *J.S.W.F.L.* 99.

[42] M. Booth, Address to Lawyers for Children Conference 1993 [1993] *Fam. Law* 652 at 653.

[43] M. Thorpe [1994] *Fam. Law* 20. The Solicitors Family Law Association Guide (2000) recognises that solicitors may effectively take over the litigation and reminds them to be prepared to allow the child to withdraw their action: p. 8.

[44] See J. Masson, "Representations of children" [1996] C.L.P. 245 and J. Roche, "Children's rights: in the name of the child" [1995] *J.S.W.F.L.* 281 at 285.

[45] See: C. Hamilton, "Rights of the child: a right to education and a right in education" in C. Bridge (ed.) *Family law towards the millennium* (1997) 201; Bainham (1998) Chap. 16 and N. Harris, *Law and education* (1993). The State has obligations relating to education under UNCRC, Arts. 28 and 29. The right to education is guaranteed under E.C.H.R., First Protocol, Art. 2.

[46] Education Act 1996, s.9 imposes a qualified duty on the Secretary of State and Local Education Authorities to provide education which accords with the parents' wishes; School Standards and

preferences or make representations to the local education authority.[47] The parent (not the child) may withdraw the child from religious education[48] or some sex education.[49] Thus a parent may interfere with a mature child's decision to seek religious instruction or contraceptive advice during school hours but not at other times.[50] Only parents and pupils over the age of 18 have rights to appeal following a pupil's permanent exclusion.[51] Only a parent may appeal a decision about a child's special educational needs.[52] Parental duties to ensure their children are educated while they are between 5 and 16[53] and to maintain them while they are under 16[54] would not seem sufficient justification for giving parents control which they would not have at common law. Such control may also be against the state's interest in achieving a healthy and well qualified workforce.

Children's economic dependence on their families has not been reduced following *Gillick*. Reductions in social security provision have been made on the basis that they could (and should) reside with their parents.[55] State benefits are not generally available to enable children under 18 to live independently from their parents and benefit for under 18s and those aged between 18 and 25 is set at lower rates.[56] Only limited recognition is given to the fact that there are children who have no family to live with or whose welfare demands that they live elsewhere.[57] Mature children who wish to leave their families must thus be more self-reliant than adults who can obtain state benefits when they are unemployed and seeking work. Children's

---

Framework Act 1998, s.86 obliges the L.E.A. to make arrangements for parents to express a preference with which it may be bound to comply unless one of the exceptions applies: see Harris (1993), pp. 19–21 and Chap. 5.

[47] School Standards and Framework Act 1998, s.94.

[48] School Standards and Framework Act 1998, s.71(1).

[49] Education Act 1996, s.405, but not sex education which forms part of the National Curriculum in secondary schools. Parental control of sex education was criticised by the Committee on the Rights of the Child. Although the government has set out a national programme to reduce the teenage conception rate it has not removed parental control: *Second Report to the U.N. Committee on the Rights of the Child by the U.K.* (1999), paras 1.3.3e and 8.21.7.

[50] There is some support for the existence of a parental right to determine a child's religion: see J. Eekelaar, "What are parental rights?" (1973) 89 *L.Q.R.* 210, 221 and *Re J. (Specific Issue Order: Muslim Upbringing and Circumcision)* [1999] 2 F.L.R. 678, 693; but this was not accepted as existing when the child reached maturity: *Stourton v. Stourton* (1857) 8 De G.M. & G. 760.

[51] School Standards and Framework Act 1998, s.67(1).

[52] Education Act 1996, s.442; Disability Discrimination Act 1995, s.28K(2); *S. v. Special Educational Needs Tribunal and the City of Westminster* [1996] 1 F.L.R. 663 CA. This is the case even if the education concerns an adult *per* Leggatt L.J. at 665.

[53] Education Act 1996, s.7; it is perhaps odd that there is no duty on the child who may be removed by the police from a public place for truanting (Crime and Disorder Act 1998, s.16) and subjected to an education supervision order (Children Act 1989, s.36).

[54] A duty which is enforceable in public law but not by the child.

[55] N. Harris, *Social security in context* (2000), p. 185.

[56] Social Security Contributions and Benefits Act 1992, s.124(1); Income Support (General) Regulations 1987, S.I. 1987 No. 1967, Sched.2 (as amended for annual uprating). See generally, A. Ogus and E. Barendt, *The Law of Social Security* (4th ed., 1995), pp. 461–466.

[57] Jobseekers Act 1995, s.16; Jobseekers Allowance Regulations S.I. 1996 No. 207 Pt IV. Local authorities remain financially responsible for young people under 18 who have left care: Children (Leaving Care) Act 2000, s.6.

economic dependence gives parents power that they could not claim as part of parental responsibility.

G. Children of unmarried parents[58]

17–019 Discrimination on the grounds of parents' status conflicts with both the United Nations Convention on the Rights of the Child[59] and the European Convention on Human Rights.[60] At common law children were only "legitimate" if the parents were married when they were born or conceived.[61] A child born to unmarried parents was a *filius nullius* or *filius populi*; no legal relationship was recognised with the mother or father nor with any other "relatives." Hence the child had no legal right to succeed to their property, nor to receive maintenance[62] and other benefits deriving from the status of parent and child.

Legal intervention was originally primarily concerned to protect against the financial consequences of children becoming a charge on the community; and thus the Poor Law began the formal association between birth outside marriage and criminality, relics of which lingered on for many years. In the twentieth century two separate developments mitigated the harshness of the common law. First, the definition of "illegitimate" was narrowed by allowing children whose parents married after their birth to be legitimated.[63] and by recognising as legitimate some children born of void marriages.[64] Secondly, rights accorded to children born within marriage were extended to all children. For example, the Fatal Accidents legislation[65] virtually eliminated the distinction for the purposes of "dependency" claims brought under it, and

---

[58] For a more detailed analysis of the history and social policy, see the 4th edition of this work, Chap. 20.

[59] The anti-discrimination principle in Art. 2. Art. 18 requires States' Parties to use their best efforts to ensure the recognition of the principle that both parents have common responsibilities for the upbringing and development of the child.

[60] Art. 14. In *Marckx v. Belgium* (1979) 2 E.H.R.R. 330 and *Inze v. Austria* (1987) 10 E.H.R.R. the European Court of Human Rights held that discrimination against illegitimate children in relation to inheritance rights breached their Art. 14 rights. But the inheritance of a title is not protected: *Re Moynihan* [2000] 1 F.L.R. 113 HL and *X. v. U.K.* (1978) 2 E.H.R.R. 63.

[61] Blackstone, *Commentaries,* p. 454. A child born after the husband's death or divorce was also legitimate: *Knowles v. Knowles* [1962] P. 161.

[62] Note, however, according to R.H. Helmholz, "Support Orders, Church Courts and the rule of Filius Nullius. A Reassessment of the Common Law" (1977) 63 Va L. Rev. 431 the church courts gave a right of support.

[63] The Legitimacy Act 1926 allowed legitimation if the father was domiciled in England at the date of the marriage and neither party was married to anyone else at the date of the child's birth. The Legitimacy Act 1959 allowed a child born of an adulterous relationship to be legitimated. The Children Act 1975, Sched.1 made changes to the status conferred by legitimation. These provisions were consolidated in the Legitimacy Act 1976, s.8 which provides that a legitimated person should have all the same rights as a legitimate one but it did not affect titles, nor dispositions made before January 1, 1976.

[64] The Legitimacy Act 1959, consolidated in the Legitimacy Act 1976, s.1 treated such children as legitimate provided the father was domiciled in England at the time of birth and at least one parent believed at the time of marriage that the marriage was valid.

[65] See Fatal Accidents Act 1976, (as substituted by Administration of Justice Act 1982) s. 1(5)(b).

the law of inheritance was changed to enable a child born outside marriage to claim under a will,[66] the father's intestacy[67] and to seek family provision.[68] This process culminated in the Family Law Reform Act 1987 which has, with two major exceptions,[69] ended the distinction between children based on their parent's marriage.

The Family Law Reform Act 1987, s.1(1) provides that for all legislation and instruments made after April 4, 1988[70]:—

> "references (however expressed) to any relationship between two persons shall, unless the contrary intention appears, be construed without regard to whether or not the father and mother of either of them, or the father and mother of any person through whom the relationship is deduced, have or had been married to each other at any time."[71]

This rule of construction is also applied to some existing statutes.[72] Where the rule does not apply it is still necessary to determine whether the child was or is legitimate; and the provisions of the Legitimacy Act 1976 defining legitimate, legitimated children and children treated as legitimate although their parents' marriage was void are still relevant.[73] Thus all children's inheritance rights[74] and rights of support are now the same, but where the parents are not married the child does not automatically[75] have a father with legally recognised rights, nor qualify for British citizenship where only the father is British. The Law Commission's terms of reference for the review which led to the 1987 Act precluded it making definitive proposals about the citizenship of children born to unmarried parents[76] but it accepted that differential treatment amounted to unjustified discrimination[77] and provisionally recommended reform.[78] However, the government rejected this apparently because there were no adequate legal procedures for determining paternity.[79]

---

[66] Family Law Reform Act 1969, s.16.

[67] Family Law Reform Act 1969, s.14; (the Legitimacy Act 1926 allowed succession under the mother's intestacy).

[68] Family Law Reform Act 1969, s.18; Inheritance (Provision for Family and Dependants) Act 1975, ss.1, 25(1).

[69] *i.e.* the status of the father and the child's citizenship (which affects the child's rights to enter and remain in the U.K.).

[70] For a full discussion see *Current Law Annotated Statutes*.

[71] s.1(3) defines a person "whose father and mother were married to each other at the time of his birth" to include all legitimate, legitimated and adopted children. See also, D. Pearl, "Recent changes in the law relating to children of unmarried parents" (1989) 1 J.C.L. 126 and N. Lowe, "The Family Law Reform Act 1987—Useful reform but an unhappy compromise" [1988] Denning L.J. 77.

[72] Family Law Reform Act 1987, s.2.

[73] s.1(3) the definition of children treated as legitimate is amended by Family Law Reform Act 1987, s.28; see below.

[74] Family Law Reform Act 1987, ss.18–20; but inheritance of titles of honour and succession to the throne are generally not affected.

[75] Financial support for all children is now provided under the Children Act 1989, Sched.1.

[76] Law Com. No. 118, *Illegitimacy* (1982–3 H.C.P. 98), paras 11.1, 11.20.

[77] *ibid.* para.11.6

[78] W.P. 74, *Illegitimacy* (1979), para.7.12.

[79] Law Com. 118, para. 11.8. It was not appropriate to devise such procedures just for citizenship claims.

The Commission did not think that proof of parentage was an insuperable problem and suggested that British or overseas birth certificates or declarations could be used.[80] The advent of DNA testing, which is capable of proving a child's parentage[81] and is used for this in immigration disputes,[82] removes objections based on problems of proof but there have been no further developments in relation to citizenship.

The British Nationality Act 1981 abolished the so-called *ius soli,* the rule by which everyone born in the United Kingdom automatically acquired British citizenship. Entitlement to citizenship depends on the citizenship and marital relationship of the child's parents.[83] Children whose parents are not married are at a disadvantage in two main factual circumstances. A child born in this country to a British father and a foreign mother will not be entitled to British citizenship if the parents are not married.[84] Similarly, a child born abroad to a father who is a British citizen, otherwise than by descent and a mother who is either foreign or a British citizen by descent only, will not be entitled.[85] In each circumstance the child would have been entitled if the parents had been married.[86] However, a child born in the United Kingdom who spends the first 10 years of life here will be entitled to registration as a British citizen provided that he or she has not been absent for more than 90 days each year during this time.[87] Also a child whose mother is a British citizen only by descent may be entitled to registration as a British citizen[88] and the Secretary of State has discretionary powers to register any child as a British citizen.[89]

Children who are not British citizens but are born here do not require leave to remain but it is advisable if the child is to travel and seek readmission.[90] Leave to enter is granted to coincide with that of the parent, defined in the Immigration Rules to include the father of a non-marital child.[91] Although the rules emphasise family reunification, the admission of children of one parent families is only granted in restricted circumstances. It is thus extremely difficult for a child born overseas, whose parents were not married,

---

[80] *ibid.* para.11.21.

[81] D. Webb, "The use of Blood grouping and D.N.A. fingerprinting tests in Immigration proceedings" [1986] Immig. & Nat. L. & P. 53; R. White and J. Greenwood "D.N.A. fingerprinting and the law" (1988) 51 *M.L.R.* 145.

[82] See *Hansard,* H.C., Vol. 154, col. 464 written answers, June 14, 1989.

[83] British Nationality Act 1981, s.1. For further explanation, see Law Com. No. 118, paras 11.3 *et seq.*; I. Macdonald, *Immigration Law and Practice* (5th ed., 2001).

[84] The Immigration and Nationality Directorate's policy is to register the child as a British citizen where there are no doubts about paternity, no reasonable objections from the parents or those with parental responsibility and no good character objections: Macdonald, *op. cit.*, para.2.37.

[85] British Nationality Act 1981, ss.1(1), 2(1), 50(9)(b).

[86] This is contrary to the non-discrimination principle in the U.N. Convention on the Rights of the Child, Art. 2, but the U.K. Government made a reservation relating to nationality and immigration see: *Second Report to the U.N. Committee on the Rights of the Child by the U.K.* (1999), para.7.31.

[87] British Nationality Act 1981, s.1(4); Macdonald (2001), para.2.43.

[88] s.3(2), see Macdonald (2001), para. 2.47.

[89] s.3(1). The discretion will not be exercised if one parent objects and the child's links with the U.K are limited. This policy is not unlawful: *R. on app. Montana v. Secretary of State for Home Department* [2001] 1 F.L.R. 449, CA.

[90] Macdonald (2001), para. 11.67.

[91] Immigration Rules (1994–5 H.C. 395), para. 6; Macdonald (2001), paras . 11.61 *et seq.*

to enter this country to live with one parent while the other is alive and capable of looking after the child elsewhere.[92]

Although citizenship and immigration laws may mean that a child does not have the right to live with both parents in the United Kingdom this may not breach the child's right for respect for family life under Article 8.[93] States have a wide margin of appreciation; the legitimate aims of immigration policy are weighed against rights to family life,[94] and the interests of the child are not paramount.[95] In this area of law children's rights depend on their parents' rights and status and are not moderated by considerations for their welfare.[96]

---

[92] *ibid.* para. 297(e), (f). The parent must have had "sole responsibility for the child's upbringing" and "there are serious and compelling family or other considerations which make exclusion of the child undesirable and suitable arrangements have been made for the child's care."

[93] *Ahmut v. The Netherlands* (1997) 24 E.H.R.R. 62 (Art. 8 does not guarantee that a family can choose between possible countries of residence); *Berrehab v. The Netherlands* (1988) 11 E.H.R.R. 322 (breach of the child's and the father's Art. 8 rights where he was deported after marriage breakdown and only allowed visas to visit his child); *Ciliz v. The Netherlands* [2000] 2 F.L.R. 469 (breach of the father's Art. 8 rights by deportation whilst child contact was being assessed).

[94] *R. on app. Mahmood v. Secretary of State for Home Department* [2001] 1 F.L.R. 757, CA; *R. v. Secretary of State for the Home Department, ex p. Isiko* [2001] 1 F.L.R. 930, CA.

[95] *R. v. Secretary of State for Home Department, ex p. Gangadeen* [1998] 1 F.L.R. 762 at 774 *per* Hirst L.J.

[96] See: "The status of immigrant children in the UK and conflicts between immigration law and procedure and the welfare of the child" in Society for Advanced Legal Studies, Family law Working Group, *Report on the cross border movement of children* (1999), p.19.

CHAPTER EIGHTEEN

PARENTS

I. INTRODUCTION—NEW CONCEPTS

18–001 Modern child law has been shaped by a number of guiding principles, chief of which is that the primary responsibility for the upbringing of children rests with their parents.[1] The Children Act made parenthood not guardianship the primary concept; "parental responsibility" replaced parental rights and duties and the courts now make decisions about a child's "residence" not "custody".[2] To some extent this may only be "cosmetic renaming"; those with parental responsibility have "rights".[3] However, these and not the former concepts influence judicial thinking and are being adopted elsewhere.[4]

Guardianship was rooted in the feudal system: guardians were largely concerned with the property of the child heir.[5] The Court of Chancery developed the concept of the Crown as *parens patriae* for infants who needed protection. Guardians were also appointed by the ecclesiastical courts, by custom and under statute. Guardianship became the instrument for maintaining the father's authority over the children. Natural or parental guardianship was originally confined to the father of a legitimate child but the Guardianship of Infants Act 1925[6] gave the mother[7] "like powers" to apply to the court. The Guardianship Act 1973[8] provided that the mother's rights and authority were the same as the father's but neither Act expressly made her a guardian. The Law Commission considered that parenthood should be regarded as the primary concept and be distinguished from guardianship to remove anomalies in the law and any doubts that mothers and fathers had equal status.[9] Their scheme also enabled the powers

---

[1] See *The Law on Child Care and Family Services*, Cm. 62 (1987), para. 5a and Law Com. No. 172, *Review of Child Law Guardianship and Custody* (1988) H.C.P. 594, para. 2.1; C. Barton and G. Douglas, *Law and Parenthood* (1995).

[2] For the background to these reforms see: Law Com. W.P. 91 *Guardianship* (1985); W.P. 96 *Custody* (1986); W.P. 100 *Care, supervision and interim orders in custody proceedings* (1987); W.P. 101 *Wards of Court* (1987); J. Priest and J. Whybrow, *Custody law in practice in the divorce and domestic courts (supplement to W.P. 96)* (1986); Report No. 172, *Review of Child Law Guardianship and Custody.*

[3] *Re P. (A Minor) (Parental Responsibility)* [1994] 1 F.L.R. 578 at 585 *per* Wilson J.

[4] Scotland and Australia.

[5] F. Pollock and F. Maitland, *The History of English Law* (1923), Vol. II, p. 443.

[6] Guardianship of Infants Act 1925, s.2. The mother was not even the guardian of her illegitimate child who thus had no guardian during her lifetime.

[7] See S. Cretney, "What will the women want next?" [1996] *L.Q.R.* 110.

[8] Guardianship Act 1973, s.1(1).

[9] Law Com. No. 172, para. 2.3; Law Com. Working Party 91, paras 3.2–4. The Commission rejected the notion that the Crown's power as *parens patria* made guardianship the primary concept.

of guardians and others acting in the place of parents[10] to be defined by reference to the powers and responsibilities of parents.[11]

The Children Act 1975 used the phrase "the parental rights and duties" to describe all the rights and duties a mother and father had in relation to a legitimate child and his property.[12] This was "not only inaccurate as a matter of juristic analysis but also a misleading use of ordinary language."[13] The decision of the House of Lords in *Gillick v. West Norfolk and Wisbech A.H.A*[14] underlined this by acknowledging that the powers parents have over their children exist only to enable them to perform their responsibilities.[15] Consequently, although it would make little difference in substance, the Law Commission recommended that "parental responsibility" a phrase which recognised the everyday reality of being a parent should replace parental rights and duties.[16]

The concept of parental responsibility performs two distinct but interrelated functions.[17] It describes the power of a parent in terms of responsibility not rights, and locates the obligation to care for children with the parents not with the state.[18] The change in terminology was intended to change perceptions about the parent child relationship[19] and its use appears to have made it easier to impose legal obligations on parents whose children commit offences or who fail to maintain their children adequately.[20]

The term "custody" was used variously to describe a state of fact, the child being under the adult's physical control (actual custody)[21] and a state of law, the right to control the child physically or, in a wider sense (legal custody)[22] the "bundle of powers" relating to the child's person.[23] The courts had wide but inconsistent powers to reallocate legal custody and could, in some circumstances, make orders in respect of actual custody, care and control[24] and access (contact).[25] The Law Commission considered that it was a "mistake to see custody, care and control and access as differently sized bundles of powers and responsibilities in a descending hierarchy of importance".[26] Rather, the law

---

[10] *in loco parentis.*
[11] See Children Act 1989, ss.3(5), 5(6), 12(2).
[12] See Children Act 1975, s.85(1). Other phrases were used in other statutes: Child Care Act 1980, s.10(2), "powers and duties"; Guardianship Act 1973, s.1(1), "rights and authority".
[13] Law Com. No. 118, *Illegitimacy* (1982), para. 4.18.
[14] [1986] A.C. 112, see above.
[15] The Scottish Law Commission has proposed that this should be made clear by statute: S.L.C. No. 135, paras 2.14, 2.35; Children (Scotland) Act 1995, s.2(1).
[16] Law Com. No. 172, para. 2.4.
[17] J. Eekelaar, "Parental responsibility: state of nature or nature of the state" [1991] *J.S.W.F.L.* 37.
[18] *ibid.*
[19] Bainham (1993), p. 63.
[20] S. Edwards and A. Halpern "Parental responsibility an instrument of social policy" [1992] *Fam. Law* 113 discussing the Child Support Act 1991 and the Criminal Justice Act 1991; Gelsthorpe, "Youth crime and parental responsibility" in A. Bainham *et al.* (eds) *What is a parent?* (1999), p. 217.
[21] Children Act 1975, s.87(1).
[22] Children Act 1975 s.86(1); legal custody is now encompassed with "parental responsibility"; see Children Act 1989, s.3(1).
[23] Law Com. W.P. 96, para. 2.34.
[24] *ibid.* paras 2.5, 2.34–2.51.
[25] *ibid.* paras 2.55–6, 4.27–4.34.
[26] *ibid.* para. 4.31.

should recognise that a parent caring for a child needed to take responsibility for the duration of that care. The courts should determine the duration of care rather than the status of the person undertaking it. Under the Children Act 1989, the courts determine disputes about the child's residence, arrangements for child contact and any restrictions on the exercise of parental responsibility.[27] They can also make orders granting or removing parental responsibility from parents and others.[28]

II. WHO ARE THE CHILD'S PARENTS?

Mother

18–002 Motherhood has traditionally been established through birth[29] although there is evidence that any child could be considered the couple's child and the father's legitimate child if he accepted the child as such.[30] Modern developments in assisted reproduction and the treatment of infertility[31] mean that the definition of mother must be re-examined. If a child is born following the donation of an egg or embryo and implantation, the law must decide whether the genetic mother or the gestational/birth mother, is the legal mother.[32] The Warnock Committee recommended that the birth mother should be the legal mother.[33] They gave no reasons for this view but considered it in the context of donation to an infertile woman rather than the needs of a woman who could not carry a pregnancy for someone to do this for her. However, the Family Law Reform Act 1987[34] provided for parentage to be determined by scientific tests indicating that the genetic

---

[27] Children Act 1989, s.8 ; private law disputes between persons with parental responsibility are dealt with applying the welfare principle: s.1. For details of the court's powers see Chap. 19, below.

[28] Children Act 1989, ss.4,4A, 12(1)(2) and 14C(1)(a); for revocation see para. 18–046, below. Parental responsibility can only be removed from married parents or mothers by adoption although its exercise may be restricted by a court order: Children Act 1989, ss.2(8),33(3)(4). Parental responsibility is retained even when another person acquires it.

[29] "Motherhood, although also a legal relationship is based on fact, being proved demonstrably by parturition" *per* Lord Simon *Ampthill Peerage Case* [1977] A.C. 547 at 577. A procedure was established in Roman Law for the examination of women who claimed to be pregnant and the witnessing of births to prevent fraudulent claims and substitution of babies: Justinian XXV, iv i 10. Similar procedures existed in early England.

[30] Pollock and Maitland (1923), p. 399. The willingness to accept this sort of informal adoption at the instigation of the mother may reflect the very limited effect motherhood had on a woman's legal rights.

[31] For a description of these, see Report of the Committee of Inquiry into Human Fertilisation and Embryology (*The Warnock Report*) Cmnd. 9314 (1984), Chaps 5–7; *Human Fertilisation and Embryology, A framework for legislation* Cm. 257 (1987) and R. Deech, "The legal regulation of infertility in Britain" in *Cross Currents* (S. Katz *et al.* eds., 2000) pp. 165, 175.

[32] If the birth follows a surrogacy agreement a third person, the requesting mother, who may be the sperm donor's wife, may also have a claim but English law does not consider surrogacy arrangements enforceable and any claim would seem to be defeated by the status provisions of the Human Fertilisation and Embryology Act 1990, s.27, see below.

[33] Cmnd. 9314 (1984), para. 6.8. The same view has generally been taken in the USA; see D. Vetri, "Reproduction technologies and US Law" (1988) 37 I.C.L.Q. 505 at 527.

[34] s.23(1) amending Family Law Reform Act 1969, s.20(1), (2). This may not have been intended but results from replacing references to "paternity" with "parentage".

contribution determined motherhood. The Government, subsequently accepted the view of the Warnock Committee[35]; the Human Fertilisation and Embryology Act 1990 provides that where a woman gives birth following egg or embryo donation she alone is to be treated as the child's mother.[36] Thus the law discourages surrogacy by refusing automatic recognition to the commissioning woman even if the child developed from her genetic material.[37] However, where a woman or her husband provide genetic material for implantation in a surrogate and a child is born, the couple can apply to the court for a parental order which gives the woman the status of an adoptive mother.[38]

Father

18–003 With four exceptions, the law recognises the child's biological father as his legal father. First, if the parents are married[39] any child born to the wife is presumed to be the child of the couple.[40] At common law the presumption could only be rebutted where evidence put the matter beyond reasonable doubt; now the matter is determined on the balance of probabilities using scientific tests which can clearly establish parentage.[41] However, where the mother's husband does not dispute paternity and no other man claims it the husband will be the legal father, although his status could be overturned later in proceedings.[42] Secondly, following the recommendations of the Law Commission and the Warnock Committee,[43] a child born in England or Wales as a result of AID or embryo donation to the wife, "shall be treated in law as the child of the parties to the marriage" and no one else, unless it is proved that the husband did not consent to the

---

[35] The effect of s.23 was not acknowledged in the White Paper on Human Fertilisation (1987) Cm. 259, para. 88.

[36] s.27; see generally G. Douglas, *Law, fertility and reproduction* (1991); S. McLean, *Law reform and human reproduction* (1992).

[37] Douglas (1994) 57 *M.L.R.* 636 at 637. But in California the genetic mother has been accepted as the legal mother because she intended to become a parent whereas the gestational mother intended to give birth and then hand over the child: *Johnson v. Calvert* 5 Cal 4th 84 (1993); see: G. Annas in *Cross Currents, op cit.*, p.153 and *Re W. and W. v. IT. (Abduction surrogacy)* [2002] 1 F.L.R. 1008, FD.

[38] Human Fertilisation and Embryology Act 1990, s.30; Parental Orders (Human Fertilisation and Embryology) Regulations 1994, S.I. 1994 No. 2767. Family Proceedings (Amendment)(No. 2) Rules 1994, S.I. 1994 No. 2165; Family Proceedings Courts (Children Act 1989) Rules 1994, S.I. 1994 No. 2166. But the order cannot be sought by an unmarried couple. For further discussion see Chap. 23.

[39] But not if they are judicially separated: *Ettenfield v. Ettenfield* [1940] P. 96.

[40] *Pater est quem nuptiae demonstrant* see Bromley (1998), p. 272. Child Support Act 1991, s.26(2) case A1 amended by Child Support and Pensions Act 2000, s.15.

[41] Family Law Reform Act 1969, s.26 following recommendations of the Law Commission: Law Com. No. 16, *Blood tests and the proof of paternity in civil proceedings*, para. 15. Where tests are carried out the point may be only academic, but s.23 allows the court to "draw such inferences, if any, as appear proper" from a person's failure to comply with a test direction: *Re A. (A Minor) (Paternity: Refusal of Blood Test)* [1994] 2 F.L.R. 463 and cases discussed below. Also paternity may be in dispute after the death of the "parents" as in the *Ampthill Peerage Case* [1977] A.C. 547.

[42] Family Law Act 1986, s.55A.

[43] *Warnock Report*, para. 4.17; Law Com. No. 118, *Illegitimacy* (1982) para. 12.2.

wife's treatment.[44] There is no formal means of establishing consent and the civil standard of proof applies.[45] Where the couple is unmarried there is a similar provision but the woman must receive treatment services "provided for her and a man together" in a licensed clinic.[46]

> In *U. v. W*[47] an unmarried woman sought to conceive using her partner's sperm. When treatment in England was unsuccessful they visited a clinic in Rome and were persuaded to use donated sperm. The man signed a document produced by the clinic accepting paternity but, following the breakdown of the relationship, was unwilling to support the disabled twins who had been born as a result of the procedure. The woman sought a declaration that the man was the children's father so that she could obtain child support. The clinic in Rome was not licensed by the HFEA, consequently the declaration was refused.[48]

A test based on "treatment together" is a problematic concept since the male partner receives no treatment.[49] The fact that both the mother and the man are willing to accept the man as the father is not sufficient for him to acquire this status if the test is not satisfied.[50] A female to male transsexual is not a man and therefore cannot be the father of a child born to his partner after donor insemination.[51] However, if the gender reassignment occurs after the child's birth, the biological father does not lose right to be recognised as the child's father.[52] Thirdly, where treatment at a licensed clinic involves the use of donated sperm, the donor, despite being the genetic father, does not have this legal status.[53] This facilitates licensed infertility treatment by protecting sperm donors from the responsibilities of parenthood.[54] Fourthly, where a child is conceived using gen-

---

[44] Human Fertilisation and Embryology Act 1990, s.28(2). But not where the child was born before April 4, 1988 when the Family Law Reform 1987 was implemented: *Re M. (Child Support: Parentage)* [1997] 2 F.L.R. 90.

[45] The Law Commission canvassed views on formal procedures for consent but rejected them because of the disadvantages of complexity and the possibility of hardship to the child where the formalities were not met: Law Com. No. 118, para. 12.16. The Human Fertilisation and Embryology Authority *Code of Practice* (2001) states that centres should take "all practicable steps" to obtain [the man's] written consent (para. 7.28).

[46] Human Fertilisation and Embryology Act 1990, s.28(3).

[47] [1997] 2 F.L.R. 282.

[48] Wilson J. rejected arguments that this breached either Treaty of Rome, Art. 59 or E.C.H.R., Art. 8. If the sperm donor gave consent for the donation the child would legally be fatherless: H.F.E.A. 1990, s.28(6)(a).

[49] He may receive counselling although this may take place separately. Being the woman's partner is not sufficient to satisfy the test: *Re Q. (Parental Order)* [1996] 1 F.L.R. 369 at 372, *per* Johnson J. But where the couple planned a child together and the man provided the sperm used by the licensed clinic after the couple had separated the man was held to be the father: *Re B. (Parentage)* [1996] 2 F.L.R. 15.

[50] *Re D. (Parental Responsibility: IVF baby)* [2001] 1 F.L.R. 972, 979 *per* Hale L.J.

[51] *X., Y. and Z. v. U.K.* [1997] 2 F.L.R. 892. This decision is not sustainable following *Goodwin v. UK* app. no. 28957/95.

[52] *Re L. (Contact: Transsexual Applicant)* [1995] 2 F.L.R. 438, the father's application for parental responsibility was granted.

[53] Human Fertilisation and Embryology Act 1990, s.28(6)(a).

[54] The donor is also guaranteed confidentiality, Human Fertilisation and Embryology Act 1990, s.31(5); see also, H.F.E.A. *Code of Practice* (2001), para. 12.3.

etic material from a man who has already died that man is not recognised in law as the child's father.[55] The child is legally fatherless.

These provisions have been criticised as flawed, inconsistent and difficult to operate, and it has been suggested that parentage in cases involving infertility treatment should instead be based on assumption of responsibility for the child.[56] Such a test would be more stringent than consent to the woman's treatment, delaying the man's commitment until birth.[57] It would exclude parentage (and financial responsibility) from men who were willing to donate sperm directly who do not benefit from the protection given to clinic donors.[58] It would also be inconsistent and difficult to justify; the social father of a child born following donor insemination could be the legal father but a man who took responsibility from birth for a naturally conceived child would not.

Determination of parentage

18–004 There is a rebuttable presumption that the mother's husband is her child's father.[59] Registration of the birth also creates a presumption about the child's parentage so that the Child Support Agency (and others)[60] are entitled to regard a man named on the birth certificate as the father.[61] In practice, the development of genetic screening or DNA profiling has made it easier to resolve most disputes about parentage. We first of all give an outline of the part played by scientific test evidence in establishing parentage, then birth registration and finally, the judicial procedures available for determining parentage.

1. Scientific tests

18–005 DNA profiling can establish parentage with virtual certainty.[62] DNA profiling compares the pattern produced by sequences of nucleotide bases known as mini

---

[55] Human Fertilisation and Embryology Act 1990, s.28(6)(b) as in the case of the child born to Mrs Blood: *R. v. Human Fertilisation and Embryology Authority ex p. Blood* [1997] 2 F.L.R. 742, CA.

[56] S. Bridge, "Assisted reproduction and the legal definition of parentage" in *What is a parent?* (Bainham *et al.* ed., 2000), p. 87.

[57] Legally parental responsibility only arises at birth but the social commitment to the child exists much earlier.

[58] Given the evidential difficulties of establishing whether a pregnancy arose from intercourse or artificial insemination this would increase the uncertainty about the parentage of children born outside marriage.

[59] Child Support Act 1991, s.26(2) as amended by Child Support, Pensions and Social Security Act 2000, s.15; see Bromley (1998) 272–276.

[60] Child Support Act 1991, s.26(2) as amended by Child Support, Pensions and Social Security Act 2000, s.15; *Brierley v. Brierley and Willliams* [1918] P. 257. The Lord Chancellor has proposed reform whereby joint registration of birth will automatically give the unmarried father parental responsibility: Lord Chancellor's Department, *Procedures for the determination of paternity and the law on parental responsibility for unmarried fathers* (1998) and para. 18–036, below.

[61] In some Commonwealth jurisdictions cohabitation creates prima facie evidence of paternity, see: Law Com. W.P. 74, para. 9.12. The Law Commission opposed such a presumption for English Law, see: Law Com. No. 118, para. 10.54.

[62] K. Kelly, J. Rankin and R. Wink, "Method and application of DNA fingerprinting: a guide for the non-scientist" [1987] Crim. L.R. 105; R. White and J. Greenwood, "DNA fingerprinting and

satellites which can be obtained by subjecting body samples: blood, semen, saliva, hair-roots, etc., to series of complex processes which enable the pattern to be read like a bar code.[63] A child obtains half its genetic material from each parent but is a unique individual. Thus the child's DNA will include patterns identical to those found in each parent's DNA. DNA profiling where parentage is disputed requires samples from the child and both alleged parents. However, sufficient information may be available from testing one parent and two siblings so long as the parentage of the second child is undisputed.[64] Although the validity of the test is not in doubt, its accuracy relies on the skill of the tester handling the samples and reading the results. The cost of these tests is much higher than for simple blood tests[65] and this may determine the choice of test for some litigants.

The testing of a child raises questions of welfare and rights of children, and the rights of adults. A person with parental responsibility can arrange for a child's genetic parentage to be tested[66] but will need access to genetic samples from at least one of the biological parents and the child. Tests are available by post using mouth swabs (saliva) or hair samples but the D.H. Code advises service providers not to undertake "motherless tests" *i.e.* tests where no sample is provided by the mother, without her consent. Also, despite procedures for authentication, if the sample has been taken by the applicant the tester cannot be sure it came from any named person.[67] Unauthorised tests can provide the basis for bringing proceedings but the court may require further proof.

In any civil proceedings in which parentage is in question the court may direct the use of scientific tests[68] with or without an application by any party.[69] There are no statutory guidelines as to when tests should be ordered. Where the case concerns only adults a direction should be made if scientific

---

the law" (1988) 51 *M.L.R.* 145 and A. Hall, "DNA fingerprinting—black box or black hole" [1990] N.L.J. 203; A. Jefferys *et al.*, "The efficiency of multilocus DNA finger print probes for individualisation and the establishment of family relationships" (1991) 48 Am. J. Hum. Genet. 824.

[63] *ibid.* The chance of two non-related individuals having the same pattern is less than one in five thousand million million; see White and Greenwood at 147.

[64] *ibid.* at 150. Testing the child and one alleged parent may establish the absence of a parental relationship.

[65] These compare the antigens in the separate samples of blood; where the antigens present are uncommon the probability of a relationship between those from whom the samples were taken is high, see: B. Dodd, "Where blood is the argument" (1980) Med. Sci. Law 231.

[66] Children Act 1989, s.2(7); D.H. *Code of Practice and guidance on genetic paternity testing* (2001) section 2. This code does not have statutory force [2001] *Fam. Law* 573.

[67] D.H. *Code*(2001) section 3 suggests the retention of signed photographs of applicants by the tester so that there is a reliable audit trail. The Advisory Board on Family Law *Second Annual Report* (1999), Annex CIII noted the need for "stringent security" when non-invasive bodily samples were used.

[68] Originally only blood tests could be used but it is possible to use other "bodily samples" *e.g.* saliva or cranial hair: Family Law Reform Act 1987, s.23; Blood tests (Evidence of Paternity) Amendment Regulations 2001, S.I. 2001 No. 773. These non-invasive samples avoid problems and objections to the use of blood samples.

[69] Family Law Reform Act 1969, s.20(1). This includes an application for contact: *Re E. (Parental Responsibility: Blood Tests)* [1995] 1 F.L.R. 392. Anyone named in the application may be subject to tests in proceedings under Family Law Act 1986, ss.55A and 56, (s.20(2A)).

evidence can promote a fairer trial[70]; the extent to which this may be so will depend on the availability of the relevant samples. The child's welfare is not the paramount consideration[71] but the court it must see that "the interests of the child are not neglected."[72] Tests may be refused where one party is merely engaged in a "fishing exercise,"[73] or where the outcome would be the same with or without blood tests.[74] Striking examples can be found in the Law Reports of the utility of blood testing[75]; more weight has been given to the virtue of discovering the truth than preserving legal presumptions or the *status quo*.[76] It has been said that a child's long-term interests are better served by knowing the truth and securing that adults found their lives on fact rather than wish.[77] Current emphasis on rights[78] and genetic heritage is likely to strengthen this trend.

> In *Re H. (Paternity: Blood Test)*[79] the mother's former lover sought blood tests in proceedings for leave to apply for contact and a parental responsibility order. The mother had become reconciled with her husband after the extra marital affair and the court accepted that a contact order was unlikely to be made. Nevertheless, the mother's desire to conceal her past relationship could not be given priority over the child's welfare.[80] The child had a right to know the truth unless his welfare clearly justified a cover-up. The child was bound to discover that there were doubts about his paternity; the sooner the child was told the better. The tests were ordered.

---

[70] A. Bradney, "Blood tests, paternity and the double helix" (1986) 16 *Fam. Law* 378.

[71] Unless the child's upbringing is at issue, Children Act 1989, s.1.

[72] *S. v. McC., W. v. Official Solicitor* [1972] A.C. 24 at 44, *per* Lord Reid.

[73] *S. v. McC., W. v. Official Solicitor* [1972] A.C. 24 at 48, *per* Lord MacDemott. If paternity is not at issue, tests may not be ordered: see *Hodgkiss v. Hodgkiss* [1985] *Fam. Law* 87. The husband had conceded the children were "children of the family" but wanted to satisfy his curiosity.

[74] *Re F. (A Minor) (Blood Tests: Parental Rights)* [1993] Fam. 314. But where the right to respect for family life is in issue the court would need to show that refusing a blood test was proportional: *MB v. U.K.* App No. 22920/93 (the Commission found no violation of Art. 8 where blood test refused to man who was not seeking custody).

[75] See, *e.g. R. v. R.* [1968] P. 414; *B. v. Att-Gen.* [1967] 1 W.L.R. 776; *Dixon v. Dixon* (1983) 4 F.L.R. 99; *Re Moynihan* [2000] 1 F.L.R. 113, H L.

[76] *H. v. H. (H. by his Guardian Intervening)* [1966] 1 All E.R.356 at 357 *per* Ormrod J. "there are graver wrongs [than to bastardise a child]." A similar approach has been taken by the European Court of Human Rights in *Kroon v. The Netherlands* (1994) 19 E.H.R.R. 263 para. 40 "respect for family life requires that biological and social reality should prevail over legal presumption which flies in the face of both established fact and the wishes of those concerned."

[77] *Re. G. (A Minor) (Blood Test)* [1994] 1 F.L.R. 495 at 502, *per* M. Horowitz Q.C.; *Re H. (Paternity: Blood Test)* [1996] 2 F.L.R. 65; *cf. Re CB. (A Minor) (Blood Tests)* [1994] 2 F.L.R. 762; *Re F. (A Minor) (Blood Tests: Paternity Rights)* [1993] Fam. 314.

[78] Compliance with the UN Convention on the Rights of the Child, Arts 7(1) and 8(2) which requires States' Parties to provide assistance to children deprived of elements of the identity may justify requiring blood tests.

[79] [1996] 2 F.L.R. 65; and see *Re H. and A. (Paternity: Blood Tests)* [2002] 1 F.L.R. 1145, CA; see also *K. v. M.* [1996] 1 F.L.R. 312, where the lover's application was unsuccessful.

[80] The issue of respect for family life would also have to be considered, nor may the court make distinctions on the basis of the marital status of the parties see: Arts 8, 14 and *Sahin v. Germany* [2002] 1 F.L.R. 119.

However the contrary view has also been expressed by the Court of Appeal:

> In *O. v. L.*[81] the child was conceived whilst the mother was having an extra marital affair. She continued to live with her husband until the child was three years old and only suggested that he was not the father when she separated to live with and marry her lover. She sought an order for blood tests in her former husband's proceedings for contact but this was denied. The court thought she would undermine the child's beneficial relationship with her first husband and it was better to postpone establishing the truth of the child's paternity.

The choice between the alternative types of tests is for the applicant; the court directs tests by an accredited provider.[82] The court may not order that a party provides a sample; consent must be obtained before samples are taken.[83] Where the person with care and control of a child under 16 refuses consent, a sample may be taken if the court considers it would be in the best interests of the child.[84] Those who decline to comply with orders must expect adverse inferences to be drawn against them.[85] Thus where the presumption of legitimacy operates and a party fails to follow a direction, the court may dismiss the claim even though there is no evidence to rebut the presumption. However, avoiding decisions based on inference rather than fact by compulsory testing might be preferable.[86]

2. Birth registration

The significance of entries in the register

18–006 Entry of the name of a particular man as the child's father in the register is prima facie evidence that he is the father[87]; the onus of proof is on anyone who

[81] [1995] 2 F.L.R. 930, CA, but testing was favoured in *Re H. and A. (Paternity: Blood Tests* [2002] 1 F.L.R. 1145, CA.

[82] Family Law Reform Act 1969, s.20(1A) amended by the Child Support, Pensions and Social Security Act 2000, s.82(2). Conditions for accreditation are set out in Blood Tests (Evidence of Paternity) (Amendment) Regulations 2001, S.I. 2001 No. 773, those accredited should also comply with the D.H. *Code of practice and guidance on genetic paternity testing* (2001).

[83] Family Law Reform Act 1969, s.21. The consent of a child over 16 but younger *Gillick competent* children cannot consent; there is no power to take a sample from a child over 16 who refuses. The D.H. *Code of practice and guidance on genetic paternity testing* (2001) requires testing services to provide information so that they can give informed consent.

[84] Family Law Reform Act 1969, s.21(3) as amended by Child Support, Pensions and Social Security Act 2000, s.82. Where the court has already exercised its discretion to order tests it is unlikely to find testing against the child's interests but if an older child objected strongly the court might need to reconsider. In effect this produces compulsory testing of the child.

[85] Family Law Reform Act 1969, s.23(1); *F. v. Child Support Agency* [1999] 2 F.L.R. 244, 248 *per* Scott Baker J.; "The court should only uphold an objection that is objectively valid" *Re G. (Parentage: Blood Sample)* [1997] 1 F.L.R. 360 C A. *per* Thorpe L.J. at 366H.

[86] Bromley and Lowe (1992), p. 276. A system which ensured that paternity was established for all children would be more in keeping with U.N. Convention on the Rights of the Child, Art 8(1); see also M-T. Meulders-Klein, "The position of the father in European legislation" (1990) 4 Int. J. Law & Fam. 131, 141.

[87] Births and Deaths Registration Act 1953, s.34(2); *Brierley v. Brierley and Williams* [1918] P. 257.

wishes to dispute the matter. Thus birth registration constitutes an important method of establishing parentage. A brief account of it is given here.

Registration

18–007 The Births and Deaths Registration Act 1953 provides[88] that the mother and father of every child born in this country must, within 42 days of the birth, give the Registrar of Births the required information.[89] A father who is not married to the child's mother is not under this duty.[90]

Registration is an administrative process, thus no inquiry is usually made into the truth of the informant's statements. The informant is asked to state the name of the child's father and that name will be recorded without further evidence if he is the mother's husband. If the couple are not married the father's name can only appear on the register where the statute permits.[91] The circumstances were considerably extended following the recommendations of the Law Commission[92] but basically require either the agreement of both parties or a court order establishing that the man is the father. The father's name can be included where the parties jointly request registration either by personal attendance before the registrar or by providing statutory declarations of paternity and the mother's acknowledgement of it,[93] or if the parties have made a parental responsibility agreement, by providing evidence of that agreement.[94] Alternatively, where the court has made a parental responsibility order or certain other orders which involve determining parentage, by providing evidence of that order.[95] The father need not be the child's biological father[96] but the Registrar-General has refused to register as father a female to male transsexual whose partner gave birth to a child following artificial insemination.[97] If the father's name is not known a line is drawn in the relevant space; this also occurs if he dies without making a declaration or agreement even though paternity was acknowledged or proved.[98] However, where the father's name was not originally included on the register, the birth may be re-registered later subject to the same conditions about evidence and also the agreement of the child if he or she is 16 or over.[99] Re-registration may

---

[88] s.2; where the parents are incapable this may be done by a "qualified informant": ss.1(2) and 2(b). It is an offence not to do so: s.36.

[89] Registration of Births, and Deaths Regulations 1987, S.I. 1987 No. 2088, as amended by S.I. 1994 No. 1948.

[90] s.10(1).

[91] Births and Deaths Registration Act 1953, s.10, as amended by Children Act 1989, Sched. 12, para. 6. Many fathers are not aware of this: R. Pickford, *Fathers marriage and the law* (1999), p.25.

[92] Law Com. No. 118, *Illegitimacy* (1982), para. 10.59.

[93] s.10(1)(a), (b), (c).

[94] s.10(1)(d) added by Children Act 1989, Sched. 12, para. 6(2).

[95] ss.10(1A), 10A(1A) added by Children Act 1989, Sched. 12, para. 6(3); or a maintenance order under Children Act 1989, Sched. 1: ss.10(1)(f), 10A(1)(f).

[96] Human Fertilisation and Embryology Act 1990, s.28, see above.

[97] *X., Y. and Z. v. U.K.* [1997] 2 F.L.R. 892 the European Court of Human Rights accepted that this was an area where there was no consensus and a wide margin of appreciation should be given (para. 44). But see now *Goodwin v. UK*, app. no. 28957/75.

[98] DNA testing does not require fresh samples.

[99] Births and Deaths Registration Act 1953, s.10A(1).

also occur where a declaration of parentage has been made under the Family Law Act 1986[1] or the parents have married.[2]

Birth certificates

18–008 A birth certificate is simply a certified copy of the entry made in the register, and is thus evidence of the birth to which it relates.[3] Birth certificates can be used to establish the date and place of birth as well as parentage. The fact that there will be joint registration of the father's name, or worse, no name at all means that it may often be possible to tell whether a child's parents were married from the long form of birth certificate. In 1947 when considerable stigma attached to the child because of illegitimacy,[4] provision was made for a short form of birth certificate to be issued.[5] This does not contain any particulars of parentage or adoption but only the child's name, sex, date and place of birth. It is still possible to obtain a full birth certificate but the short form is issued free on registration and will be provided unless the long form is specifically requested. However the full form may be required, for example in adoption proceedings.[6] Although its contents may be embarrassing they may provide the only information recorded about the parents and thus assist a child tracing them and other relatives.[7]

3. Judicial procedures for determining parentage

18–009 Findings of parentage may be required for many purposes. A person may need to establish that he is a "child of A" to inherit property or a "father of B" to have standing to seek a parental responsibility order under the Children Act 1989. In divorce proceedings the issue may arise because proof that the husband is not the father of his wife's child may be proof of her adultery.[8] In all these cases the court will have to adjudicate on parentage; its findings will bind the

---

[1] s.56; Births and Deaths Registration Act 1953, s.14A added by Family Law Reform Act 1987, s.26. It could therefore occur after the death of a parent.

[2] s.14. It is an offence for parents not to provide the necessary information: Legitimacy Act 1976, s.9.

[3] Births and Deaths Registration Act 1953, s.34(6). A birth certificate does not establish that an individual is the person named but have been used most notoriously in F. Forsyth, *The Day of the Jackal* to obtain passports, etc.

[4] Vivid illustrations of the embarrassment of this were given in the parliamentary debates on the Births and Deaths Registration Bill—see particularly, *Hansard*, H.C., Vol. 432, col. 2107; *Hansard*, H.L., Vol. 145, col. 851.

[5] See Births and Deaths Registration Act 1953, s.33; Birth Certificate (Shortened Form) Regulations 1968, S.I. 1968 No. 2050.

[6] Because it is essential to know whether the application concerns a child of married parents; see Chap. 23.

[7] This is of particular relevance to children who have been adopted but may apply in other cases of family estrangement; for an explanation of family searching using birth records see A. Pavlovic, in J. Masson *et al.* (eds) *Lost and Found* (1999), Chap. 10.

[8] See above, para. 11–013, *et seq.*

parties.[9] A finding of paternity will provide prima facie evidence which would need to be rebutted in any subsequent proceedings.[10]

The law also provides procedures solely for the conclusive resolution of disputes about legitimacy or the validity of a marriage. In 1988, following recommendations of the Law Commission a more consistent legislative code was introduced[11] but the law still failed to provide a simple and coherent scheme for determining paternity disputes. Declarations of parentage had to be sought by the child[12] but a person with care or the Secretary of State could obtain a declaration solely for the purposes of child support.[13] In 1998, the Lord Chancellor's Department reviewed these provisions to ensure that the law adequately reflected modern social attitudes[14]; the results of the review have now been incorporated in legislation.

The Family Law Act 1986 (as amended) enables the family courts[15] to grant declarations of parentage, marital status or legitimacy.[16] Any person may apply to the court for a declaration as to whether or not a named person is or was the parent of another named person.[17] The court only has jurisdiction if at least one of the named persons is or was domiciled or habitually resident in England and Wales at the time of the application or their death.[18] Unless the applicant is a parent or child of a named person, the court can only hear the application if it considers that he or she has sufficient personal interest in the issue[19]; a parent with care (who may wish to seek child support) is treated as having a sufficient interest.[20] This precludes vexatious applications and mud-raking by the media but should not prevent family members who want to establish a right to inheritance from doing so.[21] Also, where one of the named persons is a child, the court

---

9 Although the rights of non-parties would not be affected *Re J.S.* [1981] Fam. 22. For this reason it has been argued inappropriate for the child to be made a party: *Re O. and J. (Paternity: Blood Test)* [2000] 1 F.L.R. 418, F D at 433F. But a declaration under the Family Law Act 1986 binds everyone: s.58(2).

10 Civil Evidence Act 1968, s.12 as amended. If there was no finding the matter is not treated as *res judicata* and a further application could be made: *Hager v. Osborne* [1992] Fam. 94, F D. (where a mother sought financial provision and wanted DNA testing although she had failed to obtain an affiliation order after inconclusive blood testing).

11 Law Com. No. 132, *Declarations in Family Matters* (1984); Family Law Act 1986 Pt III. Section 56 which concerns parentage and legitimacy was replaced by F.L.R.A. 1987, s.22 and came into force on April 22, 1988.

12 Family Law Act 1986, s.56, the family proceedings court had no jurisdiction; but see below for the amended provision.

13 Child Support Act 1991, s.27.

14 Lord Chancellor's Department, *Procedures for the determination of paternity and the law on parental responsibility for unmarried fathers* (1998) and Advisory Board on Family Law, *Second Annual Report* (1999) Annex C para. 2. The parental responsibility proposals are discussed below.

15 Family Proceedings Courts (Family Law Act 1986) Rules 2001 S.I. 2001 No. 778. Proceedings for declarations of marital status or legitimacy must still be brought in the High Court or the county court.

16 ss.55, 55A and 56 as added and amended by Child Support, Pensions and Social Security Act 2000, s.83.

17 Family Law Act 1986, s.55A. Similarly a declaration can be sought about the validity of a marriage, divorce or annulment, s.55(1).

18 s.55A(2), or s.55(2) for declarations of marital status.

19 s.55A(3)(4); s.55(3) makes similar provision for declarations of marital status.

20 Child Support Act 1991, s.27 as amended by Child Support, Pensions and Social Security Act 2000, Sched. 8, para. 18.

21 Advisory Board on Family Law, *op. cit.* para. C2iv.

may refuse to hear the case if the determination would not be in the best interests of the child.[22] Since a declaration will concern the private or even the family life of the applicant and those named, decisions to refuse a hearing must comply with the European Convention on Human Rights. Declarations may also be made regarding legitimacy or legitimation but only the person concerned may apply.[23] These declarations cannot put in question the status of anyone else, although the validity of the parents' marriage may be in issue. Where the truth of the proposition is proved to the satisfaction of the court[24] it must make the declaration unless this would manifestly be contrary to public policy. The declaration granted is binding on everyone[25] unless it has been obtained by fraud.[26] Where a declaration of parentage, legitimacy or legitimation is made the birth may be re-registered.[27]

III. WHAT IS PARENTAL RESPONSIBILITY?

18–010 The Children Act 1989, s.3(1) provides that:

> "In this Act parental responsibility means all the rights, duties, powers, responsibilities and authority which by law a parent of a child has in relation to the child and his property."

This non-definition has been linked to respect for family privacy—a reluctance to state what parental responsibilities are or should be.[28] However, the Law Commission considered that it was not possible to provide a statutory list of parental obligations because this would need to change to meet differing needs and circumstances, and to vary with the maturity of the child.[29] In contrast, the Children (Scotland) Act 1995, following recommendations of the Scottish Law Commission, provides clear statutory statements of both parental responsibilities

---

[22] s. 55A(5); the Advisory Board on Family Law suggested that it could be appropriate to refuse a hearing where the child was settled in an adoptive family or, where the child had been conceived as the result of rape, the mother opposed the application, *op. cit.* para. C2vi.Where a hearing is refused the court may impose a leave requirement on the applicant, s.55A(6).

[23] s.56(1), (2). The provision precluding declarations of illegitimacy has been repealed: Child Support, Pensions and Social Security Act 2000, s.83(3).

[24] s.58(1). "This formulation is intended to make it clear that the standard of proof is high and that the court should only grant the declaration when the evidence . . . is clear and convincing." Law Com. No. 132, p. 37, n. 365. But the Advisory Board on Family law thought that a simple test of balance of probabilities should be adequate given the certainty provided by DNA evidence *op. cit.* para. C2ix. The Attorney-General has power to protect third parties, s.59.

[25] s.58(2).

[26] "T]here must be conscious and deliberate dishonesty and the declaration must be obtained by it", *per* Lord Wilberforce *The Ampthill Peerage* [1977] A.C. 547 at 571.

[27] ss.55A(7), 56(4) and Births and Deaths Registration Act 1953, s.14A. The Registrar-General contacts the person named in the application for a declaration to establish whether the court's findings are in dispute, allowing 28 days for a reply before re-registering the birth: Lord Chancellor's Department, *op. cit.* para. 18.

[28] W. Utting, *People like us?* (1997), para. 6.1.

[29] Law Com. No. 172, para. 2.6.

and rights.[30] Without this assistance some attempt must be made to define what actions can be taken on the basis of parental responsibility.[31] This would seem to include the following:

A. Rights and powers

1. The right to physical possession

18–011 At common law a parent has the right to possession of his child.[32] This right was in the past enforced by means of the writ of *habeas corpus*.[33] A person who had parental responsibility could require any other person who had possession of the child to hand him or her back.[34] Whilst the child remained in another's care, the parent could also rely on this right to control the child's movements.[35]

The parental right to possession is a good illustration of the significance of the concept of parental rights today. On the one hand, it can be argued for two reasons that the legal right to possession is of no importance. First, even at common law the courts would not enforce the right against the wishes of the child who had reached the age of discretion.[36] Secondly, if a dispute about the child's upbringing is brought to court the matter will be decided by reference to the child's best interests, not necessarily by ordering the return of the child to those with parental responsibility.[37]

On the other hand, it should be noted that these arguments apply primarily to cases where a person with parental responsibility seeks to enforce it against

---

[30] ss.1(1), 2(1) following Scottish Law Com. No. 135, paras 2.2, 2.26.

[31] See generally for discussions of the common law Bainham (1993), pp. 9–20; Bromley (1998), pp. 350–375; Bevan, Chap 1; Craffe, *La Puissance Paternelle en Droit Anglais* (1971); J. Hall, "The waning of parental rights" [1972B] *C.L.J.* 248; J. Eekelaar, "What are parental rights?" (1973) 89 *L.Q.R.* 210; S. Maidment, "The fragmentation of parental rights" (1981) 40 *C.L.J.* 135; B. Dickens, "The modern function and limits of parental rights" (1981) 97 *L.Q.R.* 462 and Chap. 17.

[32] *Re Agar-Ellis* (1883) 24 Ch.D. 317. Lord Scarman described this decision as horrendous in *Gillick v. West Norfolk A.H.A.* [1986] A.C. 112 at 183.

[33] *e.g. Barnardo v. Ford* [1892] A.C. 326. For an illuminating account of the background to this litigation, see G. Wagner, *Barnardo* (1979), Chap. 13.

[34] See *R. v. Barnardo* (1889) 23 Q.B.D. 305, particularly at 310–311, *per* Lord Esher M.R. *Habeas corpus* is no longer regarded as an appropriate remedy in the Family Division: *Re K. (A Minor)* (1978) 122 S.J. 626. Wardship proceedings, proceedings for a residence order or to enforce a residence order under Children Act 1989, ss.8, 14 should be started if possession of the child is in issue. Where the child is in care, etc., a recovery order under Children Act 1989, s.50 may be made. However, in *Re G. (Wardship) (Jurisdiction: Power of Arrest)* (1983) 4 F.L.R. 538, *habeas corpus* proceedings do seem to have been issued.

[35] *Flemming v. Pratt* (1823) 1 L.J. (O.S.) K.B. 195: guardians of child directed her governess not to permit her to visit a tavern kept by a relative, held: guardians justified in sending police officers to remove her.

[36] It is not clear that a mature child under the age of 16 has a right to choose not to live with a person with parental responsibility against their wishes. However, where one person has a residence order, another person who takes the child against the child's will may be guilty of the offence of kidnapping even if he or she has parental responsibility, and may also commit offences under the Child Abduction Act 1984. Where the child seeks refuge in a "safe house" those assisting him are exempt from prosecution but a child in care may still be recovered: see Children Act 1989, ss.50, 51.

[37] Children Act 1989, s.1; see, *e.g. J. v. C.* [1970] A.C. 668.

another by legal process. In contrast, where those seeking to detain the child have no parental responsibility, the significance of entitlement to physical possession is very clear. They have no right to keep the child against parental demands.[38] They could commence wardship proceedings, apply to adopt[39] or (with leave, if necessary) seek a residence order, but if they do not do so there will be nothing to stop the parent simply taking the child back.[40]

> In *Re B. (Adoption: Child's Welfare)*[41] the parents who were African arranged that their daughter should go to England and stay for a prolonged holiday with an English couple they had met. After 18 months the English couple applied to adopt the girl who had become very attached to them. The parents objected, but made no application to the court arguing that, if the order was rejected, as parents they had the right to the child without having to establish that return was in her best interests.[42] Wall, J. accepted their argument and the girl's return was ordered but the order was disobeyed.[43]

Those detaining the child may be criminally liable.[44] Although a parent may effectively lose the right to the child to an individual who cares for him or her for a prolonged period,[45] the parent will retain the right to reclaim the child from a local authority unless a care order is made on proof of significant harm or adoption is planneed and an order sought.[46] Indeed, it is fundamental to the system for providing local authority accommodation for children that parents should retain the right to remove their child at any time.[47] The parent's right to physical possession of their child is also reflected in the regime of the Hague Convention on International Child Abduction. Where a child has been taken in

---

[38] The police may keep children for short periods for their protection, despite parental objections: Children Act 1989, s.46 and J. Masson, "Police protection, protection whom?" [2002] *J.S.W.F.L.* 157.

[39] But there are restrictions on adoption where the child is not placed by an adoption agency.

[40] *Re F. (A Minor) (Wardship: Appeal)* [1976] Fam. 238. Although Children Act 1989, s.3(5) may, according to the Lord Chancellor, justify the child's retention if the parent is unfit: *Hansard* H.L. Vol. 505, col. 370–1 Children Bill, 3rd Reading.

[41] [1995] 1 F.L.R. 895.

[42] Under the Adoption Act 1976, s.6 the court only gives first consideration to the child's welfare, other factors like the parents' wishes can be given weight. Adoption orders can only be made if the parents consent or the court dispenses with their agreement, s.16(2). See also Chap. 22, below.

[43] The prospective adoptive father was subsequently apprehended and committed to prison for contempt of court: *Re B. (Contempt: Evidence)* [1996] 1 F.L.R. 239.

[44] Child Abduction Act 1984, s.2, but not if they provide a certificated refuge: Children Act 1989, s.50; see below.

[45] A person who has cared for the child for three years will not need to seek leave to commence proceedings for a residence order and may seek such an order even after the child has been removed: Children Act 1989, s.10(5), (10). Where a residence order is sought the court will apply the welfare checklist and may favour the person who has been caring for the child. If the proposals in the Adoption of Children Bill are enacted the court will be able to make an adoption order which will end the birth parents' parental responsibility despite parental objections where the child's welfare requires it (cl. 52(1)(b)).

[46] Children Act 1989, ss.20(8), (9), 31; Adoption of Children Bill 2002, cl. 30 and Chap. 23, below.

[47] *per* Lord Mackay, Lord Chancellor, *Hansard* H.L., Vol. 512 col. 737; *per* David Mellor, Secretary of State for Health, Standing Committee B, col. 146–152 (Children Bill Committee Stage, Thursday, May 18, 1989).

breach of "rights of custody" from their country of habitual residence, the court must order their return.[48]

2. The right to control or direct the child's upbringing[49]

18–012 This right above all others depends on the child's stage of development. The recognition by the majority of the House of Lords in *Gillick*[50] that children acquire the right to make decisions as they gain the capacity to do so[51] clearly establishes that the parental right is a diminishing one.[52] Parents do not have a right to control mature children's access to information or advice[53]; their status gives them strong entitlement to information about their child but this does not override rights to confidentiality.[54] Parents are not legally obliged to consult children about their views[55] or, in most cases, the other parent.[56] Parental decision-making is always potentially subject to court review on welfare grounds[57] and no one may exercise parental responsibility in a way which conflicts with a court order.[58] The state may not intervene unless the child is suffering or likely to suffer significant harm.[59] But in *F. v. Wirral M.B.C.*,[60] the Court of Appeal held that interference with a parent's right to take care of a child's welfare did not give rise to a cause of action.[61] There was therefore no redress for a mother whose relationship with her children was ended by the local authority placing the children with a couple who expected to be able to adopt them. The European Court of Human Rights has awarded compensation where a mother's right to respect for family

---

[48] For a detailed discussion of these provisions see: Chap. 21, below.

[49] The Scottish Law Commission preferred the enactment of a statutory right in these general terms to more specific rights relating to education, medical treatment and religion: Scottish Law Com. No. 135, para. 2.21; Children (Scotland) Act 1995, s.2(1)(b).

[50] [1986] 1 A.C. 112.

[51] See above, Chap. 17.

[52] The Scottish Law Commission used the phrase "control, direct or guide" for this reason, Scottish Law Com. No. 135, para. 2.30. The UN Convention on the Rights of the Child, Art. 5 requires States' Parties to respect parental responsibilities "in a manner consistent with the evolving capacities of the child".

[53] Children have the right to use confidential services: see above, Chap. 17. The Scottish Law Commission considered it would be contrary to children's interests to oblige doctors to pass on information to parents and that to require others to do so would be an excessive interference with their legitimate interests: *ibid.* para. 2.33.

[54] *Re C. (Disclosure)* [1996] 1 F.L.R. 797 at 803 *per* Johnson J.

[55] *cf.* Children (Scotland) Act 1995, s.6 following the recommendations of the Scottish Law Commission: S.L.C. No. 135, paras 2.60–2.66. The UN Convention the Rights of the Child, Art. 12(1) requires States' Parties to assure to the child who is capable of forming his or her own view the right to express a view and have it taken into account.

[56] S. Maidment, "Parental responsibility?—is there a duty to consult" [2001] *Fam. Law* 518.

[57] Children Act 1989, s.1.

[58] Children Act 1989, s.2(8).

[59] Children Act 1989, Pt IV especially s.31; see Chap. 22 below.

[60] [1991] Fam. 69; Bainham (1993) 517. *cf.* Children (Scotland) Act 1995, s.2(4) which confirms that parents and others have title to sue in any action for the infringement of parental responsibilities.

[61] The interference was a result of the local authority's exercise of its child care functions. To recognise responsibilities to the parents could adversely affect the carrying out of these functions; there were public law remedies, *per* Ralph Gibson L.J.

life was breached by the local authority removing her daughter following a negligent investigation.[62]

Parents may publicise aspects of their children's lives by giving agreement for the making of a film or speaking to reporters[63] but giving interviews will not always amount to an exercise of parental responsibility.[64] Young children cannot participate in media activities without parental consent.[65] Parental power is limited; parents are not entitled to surrender their child's right to confidentiality in respect of medical treatment unless this is in the interests of the child.[66] Any profit obtained by selling the child's story should belong to the child.[67]

3. Power to control education

18–013 At common law, the person with parental rights could determine what education (if any) the child received. The old books contain striking cases where this right was enforced. In *Tremain's* case[68] the child:

> "... being [under 21] ... went to Oxford, contrary to the orders of his guardian, who would have him go to Cambridge. And the court sent a messenger to carry him from Oxford to Cambridge. And upon his returning to Oxford, there went another tam to carry him to Cambridge, quam to keep him there."

A parent's rights in relation to education is protected by the European Convention on Human Rights[69] but parental power is now very much affected by legislation and the parents' powers under the Education Act 1996 can be exercised by

---

[62] *TP and KM v. U.K.* [2001] 2 F.L.R. 549. The court also found breaches of Arts. 6 and 13 because the mother had been unable to challenge the local authority's evidence and could not obtain a remedy under English law.

[63] *Re Z. (A Minor) (Freedom of Publication)* [1996] 1 F.L.R. 191 at 210, *per* Ward L.J.; *Re W. (Wardship: Discharge: Publicity)* [1995] 2 F.L.R. 466, *per* Hobhouse L.J. at 476G. Where the information relates to legal proceedings there are controls on publicity, see Chap. 19 below.

[64] *Oxfordshire County Council v. L. and F.* [1997] 1 F.L.R.235 at 254 *per* Stuart-White J. Where it does not, the parent cannot be restrained by a prohibited steps order.

[65] But the suggestion by Stephen Brown P. in *Nottingham City Council v. October Films* [1999] 2 F.L.R. 347 at 358 that any approach by the media requires parental consent may go too far.

[66] *Re Z. (A Minor) (Freedom of Publication)* [1996] 1 F.L.R. 191 at 214, *per* Ward L. J. See also Palmer, *The Spectator,* October 21, 1995. When she reached 18, the young woman concerned, Flora Keyes, and her mother complained bitterly about the effect of the restrictions on normal childhood, for example not being photographed in a school play.

[67] *Douglas and others v. Hello! Ltd* [2001] 1 F.L.R. 982, C.A. Children have no lesser rights to privacy under E.C.H.R., Art. 8 than adults.

[68] (1719) 1 Strange 167. Parental disputes about education are determined applying the welfare principle: *Re A. (Specific Issue Order: Parental Dispute)* [2001] 1 F.L.R. 121, CA (appeal against order that child attend Lycee Francaise rather than an English language school refused); *Re P. (A Minor) (Education)* [1992] 1 F.L.R. 316, CA (father's appeal against decision that child attend boarding school allowed because the child, age 14, did not want to board).

[69] Protocol No. 1, Art. 2 "[T]he State shall respect the right of parents to ensure such education and teaching [is] in conformity with their religious and philosophical convictions." The government entered a reservation limiting its acceptance of the protocol in line with the duty in Education Act 1996, s.9. This reservation is preserved by the H.R.A. 1998, s.15.

anyone with care of the child.[70] A parent[71] is, by law, obliged to ensure that his or her child, being of compulsory school age, receives efficient full-time education suitable to age, ability and aptitude, either by regular attendance at school or otherwise.[72] Education authorities must comply with parental preferences where this does not prejudice efficient education or efficient use of resources, and is not incompatible with the character of the school.[73] Where their child is refused a place at the chosen school parents may appeal to a local appeals committee.[74] In order to enable parents to make a choice they must be given information about the schools available[75] and specified information about their curricula, discipline, pastoral care, examination policies and results.[76] The introduction of the National Curriculum in state schools means that parents who object to its ethos or content must seek an independent school[77] or arrange for their child to be educated at home.[78] A person with parental responsibility or the care of a child who fails to ensure that the child is educated may be guilty of a criminal offence[79] and the child may be subject to an education supervision order.[80] Parents are thus effectively deprived of their right not to educate their children[81] but may exercise such choice as their social and economic circumstances permit about the type of schooling.

4. Discipline

18–014 A person with parental responsibility has the right to inflict moderate and reasonable corporal punishment[82] and this right may apparently be dele-

[70] s. 576(1)(b); *Fairpo v. Humberside C. C.* [1997] 1 F.L.R. 339. Parental responsibility is not required.

[71] The definition of parent includes anyone with care of the child, Education Act 1996, s.576.

[72] Education Act 1996, s.7.

[73] Education Act 1996, s.9; School Standards and Framework Act 1998, s.86.

[74] School Standards and Framework Act 1998, s.94. Nearly 90,000 appeals were lodged in 2000, of these 21,000 were decided in the parents' favour DfES, SFR 27/2001. If a statement of special educational needs is maintained in respect of the child appeal is to the Special Educational Needs Tribunal: Education Act 1996, ss.325, 326 and Sched. 27, para. 8(3).

[75] School Standards and Framework Act 1998, s.92.

[76] Education Act 1996, s.537 and the regulations made thereunder.

[77] The National Curriculum does not apply to independent schools although some adhere to it, Education Act 1996, s.352. Parents may require their children to be excused from any religious education and sex education which does not form part of the National Curriculum, School Standards and Framework Act 1998, s.71; Education Act 1996, s.405.

[78] Such education must be "efficient full-time education": Education Act 1996, s.7. Where the education authority is satisfied that the duty to educate the child is not being complied with it must serve a school attendance order: Education Act 1996, s.437.

[79] Education Act 1996, ss.443 and 444. Parents may no longer be imprisoned for breach of a school attendance order but may be fined or made subject to a parenting order: Crime and Disorder Act 1998, s.8(1)(d). Imprisonment could follow breach of an injunction requiring the parents not to interfere with the child's attendance: *Re P. (Care Orders: Injunctive Relief)* [2000] 2 F.L.R. 385, FD.

[80] Children Act 1989, s.36; or a care order but only if the "significant harm" test in s.31 is satisfied: see *Re O. (Care Proceedings: Education)* [1992] 1 W.L.R. 912 and Chap. 22, below.

[81] B. Hoggett, *Parents & Children* (4th ed., 1993), p. 21.

[82] *R. v. Hopley* (1860) 2 F. & F. 202; C.Y.P.A. 1933, s.1(7); *R. v. H. (Assault of Child: Reasonable Chastisement)* [2001] 2 F.L.R. 431, CA. The right does not extend to a person not *in loco parentis*, *R. v. Woods* (1921) 85 S.J. 272. For a wider discussion see, P. Newell, *Children are people too* (1989) and J. Fortin, "Children's rights and the use of physical force" [2001] *C.F.L.Q.* 243.

gated.[83] In response to *A. v. U.K.*[84] the British Government initially proposed to clarify what amounts to "reasonable chastisement" and indicated that it did not intend to make physical punishment by parents illegal.[85] Despite a decision by the Scottish Executive to legislate to ban hitting children under the age of three years,[86] no change is to be made for the law of England and Wales on the basis that the Human Rights Act 1998 now ensures that children are adequately protected.[87]

Nine out of 10 children have experienced smacking[88] and the majority of parents believe that parents should be allowed to smack (but not use canes etc.) on naughty children over two years old.[89] However, corporal punishment may no longer be administered, even if the parents approve, in schools[90] or community homes[91] or by foster parents.[92] The continued acceptance of a right to hit children is controversial; a number of states including Sweden, Denmark and Austria have outlawed it.[93] Attempts at reform are continuing.[94] Parents may

[83] Children Act 1989, s.2(9); Children and Young Person Act 1933, s.1(7). In *London Borough of Sutton v. Davis* [1994] 1 F.L.R. 737 the local authority refused to register a child minder who would not comply with the authority's no smacking policy. The child minder appealed to the magistrates' court (Children Act 1989, s.77(6)) who overturned the authority's decision on the basis that the authority was not bound by the Department of Health, Guidance Vol. 2, para. 6.22 and that parents had both a right to smack and to delegate their power. The magistrates' decision was upheld by Wilson J. who accepted that the application to the court required the magistrates to determine the appropriateness of the refusal of registration for themselves in the light of the Guidance. The Department of Health has responded by issuing guidance which permits smacking by child minders if a parent consents: LAC (94) 23 and this has been incorporated in DFEE, *National Standards for Day Care* (2000).

[84] [1998] 2 F.L.R. 959 (caning of a boy by his step-father was held to breach the boy's Art. 3 rights), see above p. 502.

[85] D.H. *Protecting children, supporting parents* (2000), p. 13. An attempt during the passage of the Children Bill to repeal C.Y.P.A. 1933, s.1(7) was unsuccessful: *Hansard* H.L., Vol. 504, col. 344–352.

[86] Amendments are proposed for the Criminal Justice Bill to outlaw smacking of children under three, all blows to the head and use of implements in Scotland: Scottish Executive, *News release*, September 6, 2001.

[87] D.H., *Analysis of the responses to the protecting children supporting parents consultation document* (2001) para. 74.

[88] M. Smith *et al.*, "Parental Control within the family the nature & extent of parental violence to children" in D.H., *Child protection messages from research* (1995), pp. 83–85.

[89] ONS Survey (1998) quoted in *Protecting children* (2000) *op. cit.* annex A. There were similar findings in Scotland in a survey for the Scottish Law Commission: S.L.C. No. 135, paras 2.72–2.105.

[90] Education Act 1996, s.458 as substituted by School Standards and Framework Act 1998, s. 131. Teachers may use physical restraint: Education Act 1996, s. 550A added by Education Act 1997, s.4.

[91] Corporal punishment is banned in community homes under the Children's Homes Regulations 1991, S.I. 1991 No. 1508, reg. 8; guidance is provided on permissible forms of control LAC (93) 13.

[92] It is a term of the foster care agreement, Fostering Services Regulations 2002 (S.I. 2002 No. 57, Sched. 5, para. 8. Restrictions could be imposed on private foster parents by the local authority: Children Act 1989, Sched. 8, para. 6(1)(d) but might not be accepted on appeal to the court, see *London Borough of Sutton v. Davis* [1994] 1 F.L.R. 737.

[93] Sweden (1979), Denmark (1986), Austria (1989), Italy (1996), Israel (2000); see P. Newell, *Children are people too* (1989); Scottish Law Com. No. 135, para. 2.68.

[94] The organisations Children are Unbeatable and EPOCH (end physical punishment of children) have been campaigning vigorously, particularly since the decision in *A. v. U.K.* (above).

also restrict the liberty of their children and may permit others to do so.[95] But if the child is looked after by a local authority or in hospital or a residential school, detention in secure accommodation must be authorised by the court.[96]

5. Choice of religion

18–015 A person with parental responsibility has a common law right to determine the child's religious education[97] and may by statute require the child's exclusion from religious studies lessons and school assembly.[98] Freedom of religion is protected by the European Convention on Human Rights, Art. 9 but where there is a dispute about a child's religious upbringing the court balances competing rights by applying the welfare principle.[99] The practical impossibility of a carer bringing up a child in a faith other than their own is now recognised by the courts.[1] In relation to older children, sensitivity to traditional or religious influences is likely to give way to the integrity of the child concerned.[2] The power to determine the child's religion is not acquired by a local authority which has parental responsibility under a care order, and where a child is to be adopted the adoption agency must give due consideration to the child's religious persuasion.[3]

6. Right to services

18–016 The person with parental responsibility has at common law the right to the domestic service of his or her unmarried minor children.[4] It is not possible to

[95] *Re K. (Secure Accommodation: Right to Liberty)* [2001] 1 F.L.R. 526, CA but the majority (Thorpe L.J. dissenting) held that the restrictions of secure accommodation could not be justified on the basis of parental authority. The European Court of Human Rights has accepted that parental power is limited but held, by a majority of nine to seven that a parent's decision to commit a 12-year-old son to a mental hospital did not breach the child's right to liberty under Art. 5(1), (4) of the European Convention of Human Rights because it was "a responsible exercise by the mother of her custodial rights in the interests of the child" see: *Neilsen v. Denmark* (1989) 11 E.C.H.R. 175 and Masson [2002] *C.F.L.Q.* 77.

[96] Children Act 1989, s.25; Children (Secure Accommodation) Regulations 1991, S.I. 1991 No. 1505; Children (Secure Accommodation) (No. 2) Regulations 1991, S.I. 1991 No. 2034. Detention is also permitted under the Mental Health Act 1983 and even perhaps under the inherent jurisdiction: *Re C. (Detention: Medical Treatment)* [1997] 2 F.L.R. 180, FD.

[97] *Andrews v. Salt* (1873) 8 Ch. App. 622; Bevan, paras 11.02–16; St J Robilliard, *Religion and the Law* (1984), Chap. 12; C. Hamilton, *Family Law and Religion* (1995); A Bradney, *Religion, rights and laws* (1993), p. 46.

[98] School Standards and Framework Act 1998, s.71.

[99] *Re J. (Specific Issue Orders: Muslim Upbringing and Circumcision)* [1999] 2 F.L.R. 678 at 685 *per* Wall J. approved by the Court of Appeal at [2000] 1 F.L.R. 571, 575; *Re P. (s.91(14) Guidelines and Religious Heritage)* [1999] 2 F.L.R. 573, CA (the benefits to a rabbi's daughter of being brought up within her family were not sufficient to balance the detriment of moving her from non Jewish foster carers to whom she was strongly attached).

[1] *Re S. (Change of Names: Cultural Factors)* [2001] 2 F.L.R 1005, FD at 1015 (the Sikh father also accepted that the child should be brought up as a Muslim by his Muslim mother); *Re P. (s.91(14) Guidelines and Religious Heritage)* [1999] 2 F.L.R. 573, CA (when the foster parents obtained a residence order they were permitted to determine all questions of education, religion and upbringing and were no longer expected to maintain Jewish dietary laws for the child).

[2] *Re KR. (Abduction)* [1999] 2 F.L.R. 542 at 548 *per* Singer J.

[3] Adoption and Children Bill 2002, cl.1(5).

[4] For an account of the varying importance of children as economic assets, see V. Zelizer, *Pricing the priceless child* (1994); P. Mizen *et al.* (eds) *Hidden Hands* (2001) pp. 24–36, 59–68.

enforce this right directly, but it was of some indirect practical importance since it was an actionable tort to do an act[5] wrongfully depriving a parent of a child's services. Hence a parent could have an independent cause of action against someone who negligently injured the child. However, this cause of action was abolished by the Administration of Justice Act 1982.[6] The right to services does not appear to fit with the view that rights exist so that parents can perform their responsibilities. It may alternatively be seen as part of a mutual moral obligation which is necessary for communal living.[7]

What is the position if a child takes paid employment? Can the parents insist on having wages paid over to them? Can they at least insist on receiving some contribution to the child's upkeep?[8] There is almost no modern English authority on these issues[9] but in some circumstances, where a parent is claiming income support, the amount allowable for a child will be reduced on the basis that the child has an adequate income.[10]

7. Administration of property

18–017 Parental responsibility includes the parent's right at common law over the child's property together with such rights as a guardian of the child's estate would have.[11] Since minors (unless they are on actual military service[12]) cannot make a valid will, parents (but not others with parental responsibility) also have the right to inherit their unmarried children's property.[13]

---

[5] Provided the act was not rape, seduction or enticement: see s.5, Law Reform (Miscellaneous Provisions) Act 1970 (implementing the recommendations in Law Com. No. 25, paras 101, 102). In *Lough v. Ward* [1945] 2 All E.R. 338 the father obtained damages of £500 against a couple who ran a religious house where his daughter, aged 16, was living against his wishes. Such an action would seem to be precluded by the 1970 Act.

[6] s.2(b). This was one of the reasons the court was unwilling to accept that parents had the broader right claimed in *F. v. Wirral M.B.C* [1991] Fam. 69: see *Winfield and Jolowicz* (1994), p.510.

[7] It is not mentioned by the Scottish Law Commission.

[8] See the discussion in the *International Encyclopaedia of Comparative Law*, Vol. IV, Chap. 7 by S. J. Stoljar; and Jenk's *English Civil Law* (4th ed., 1947), para. 1939 and the authorities there referred to.

[9] See, however, *Hewer v. Bryant* [1970] 1 Q.B. 357.

[10] If a child has under £3,000 capital his or her income is treated as the parents for the purposes of income-related benefits, but income above the child's personal allowance plus any disabled child premium is ignored: Social Security Contributions and Benefits Act 1992, s.136(1); S.I. 1987 No. 1967, reg. 44(5), 47. Similar provision is made in regulations relating to other benefits see; A. Ogus and E. Barendt, *The Law of Social Security* (4th ed., 1995), pp. 474–476. and N. Harris, *Social Security in context* (2000), p. 185.

[11] Children Act 1989, s.3(2); before the Act the position was confused, see Law Com. W.P. 91 *Guardianship*, paras 2.32–34. The High Court may appoint a separate guardian of the child's estate: s.5(11).

[12] Wills (Soldiers and Sailors) Act 1918.

[13] Administration of Estates Act 1925, s.46(i), (iii); and Family Law Reform Act 1987, s.18(2). See Chap. 8, above.

8. Right to represent the child in legal proceedings

18–018 Except in the case of "family proceedings"[14] a child can generally only bring or defend legal proceedings by a "litigation friend".[15] A person with parental responsibility is prima facie entitled to act in this capacity[16] (unless he or she has an interest adverse to the child), but the court may remove a "litigation friend" if a proper case is made out.[17] There appears to be no right to continue proceedings which are not for the benefit of the particular child.[18] Nor may an action be settled without the court's approval.[19]

9. Right to consent to medical treatment

18–019 A person with parental responsibility has some rights to consent to the treatment of his or her children[20] but treatment may be given or refused against such a person's wishes.[21] Although children over the age of 16 have a statutory right to consent to treatment,[22] a person with parental responsibility may give a valid consent overriding the child's refusal.[23] It has been said that parental responsibility is not sufficient to authorise sterilisation and the matter should be referred to the court.[24] Also, that it may not be ethical to treat where only one of three people holding parental responsibility consents.[25] Where a child is at risk of suffering significant harm because of lack of treatment, a care order or an emergency protection order can be made and the parent's refusal overridden.[26] In

---

[14] Family Proceedings Rules 1991, r. 9.2A. A child with sufficient understanding may "begin, prosecute or defend" any family proceedings (except "specified proceedings") with leave of the court; see above, para. 17–015.

[15] C.P.R. 1998, r. 21. The court has a discretion to allow a child to proceed alone: r. 21.2(3).

[16] *Woolf v. Pemberton* (1877) 6 Ch.D. 19. In practice mothers take this role in the majority of cases: J. Masson and A. Orchard, *Children and civil litigation* LCD research series No. 10 (1999).

[17] *Re Taylor's Application* [1972] 2 Q.B. 369 (successful application to remove parent who refused to accept compromise of thalidomide litigation, reversed on appeal); *Re A. (Conjoined Twins: Medical Treatment)(No. 2)* [2001] 1 F.L.R. 267, CA (unsuccessful attempt by Pro-life Alliance to remove Official Solicitor and appeal against decision to allow separation of conjoined twins).

[18] *Kinnear v. DHSS* (1989) 19 *Fam. Law* 146.

[19] C.P.R. r. 21.10(1).

[20] *Gillick v. W. Norfolk and Wisbech A.H.A.* [1986] A.C. 112; *Re W. (A Minor) (Medical Treatment: Court's Jurisdiction)* [1993] Fam. 64; see Chap. 17, above.

[21] A doctor cannot be required to treat against his clinical judgment: *Re J. (A Minor) (Child in Care) (Medical Treatment)* [1993] Fam. 15; *Re C. (A Minor)(Medical Treatment)* [1998] 1 F.L.R. 384, FD where the court accepted the Royal College of Paediatrics and Child Health, *Withholding or withdrawing lifesaving treatment for children* (1997). Parents cannot obtain declarations about future treatment: *R. v. Portsmouth NHS Trust ex p. Glass* [1999] 2 F.L.R. 905.

[22] Family Law Reform Act 1969, s.8.

[23] *Re W. (A Minor) (Medical Treatment: Court's Jurisdiction)* [1993] Fam. 64. Carers may incur criminal liability if they withhold consent: see A. Bainham (1993), p. 252; M. Brazier and C. Bridge (1996) 16 L.S. 84.

[24] *Re D. (Sterilisation)* [1976] Fam. 185; *Re B. (A Minor) (Wardship Sterilisation)* [1988] A.C. 199. *cf. Re H.G. (Specific Issue Order: Sterilisation)* [1993] 1 F.L.R. 587, it was held that sterilisation could be authorised by a specific issue order, indicating a decision within parental responsibility. In such cases the child is represented by CAFCASS Legal Services: *CAFCASS Practice Note* [2001] 2 F.L.R. 151, para. 5.

[25] *Re O. (A Minor) (Medical Treatment)* [1993] 2 F.L.R. 149 at 154, *per* Johnson J.

[26] Children Act 1989, ss.31, 33, 44. If the child is subject to an interim care order or emergency protection order the court may make directions about medical treatment, ss.38(6), 44(6).

other cases a specific issue order may be obtained.[27] However, if a treatment such as a blood transfusion is essential to save the child's life, doctors have been advised by the Department of Health that they are unlikely to be held liable for assault and should treat without waiting for a court order.[28] Also a decision about the child's treatment can always be over-turned by the court in exercise of its inherent jurisdiction.[29]

10. Right to consent to marriage

18–020 This right is governed by statute.[30] Parental refusal may be overridden by the court.[31]

11. Right to contact with the child

18–021 It has been has been asserted that a parent has a common law right to contact.[32] The Children Act 1989 makes no specific reference to contact as a right but where a child is in care, the local authority is under a duty to promote contact and can only restrict it with permission of the court.[33] The courts are also empowered to make various orders concerning contact between adults[34] and the child and have interpreted these to establish a presumption of parental contact.[35] In contrast, the Children (Scotland) Act 1995 specifically provides that parents have a right to maintain personal relations and direct contact with their children on a regular basis.[36] The right to respect for family life in Article 8 includes the right to maintain contact with children living separately[37] but is subject to the considerations of the rights of others and, particularly the welfare of the child.[38]

---

[27] *Re R. (A Minor) (Blood Transfusion)* [1993] 2 F.L.R. 757.

[28] Ministry of Health circular F/P9/1B, April 14, 1967. But it seems that it is more common to seek a court order, see: *Re R. (A Minor) (Blood Transfusion)* [1993] 2 F.L.R. 757 and *Re O. (A Minor) (Medical Treatment)* [1993] 2 F.L.R. 149.

[29] *Re D. (Sterilisation)* [1976] Fam. 185, *Re W. (A Minor) (Medical Treatment: Court's Jurisdiction)* [1993] Fam. 64, *Re O. (A Minor) (Medical Treatment)* [1993] 2 F.L.R. 149. Statutory powers in the Children Act 1989 may be sufficient; the court could make a specific issue or prohibited steps order on the application of any person who has obtained leave: ss.8, 10.

[30] Marriage Act 1949, Sched. 2 as amended by Children Act 1989, Sched. 12, para. 5; see Chap. 1, above.

[31] Marriage Act 1949, s.3(1)(b), (5).

[32] *Re C. (Mental Patient: Contact)* [1993] 1 F.L.R. 940. Under the Children Act 1975, s.85(1) the right to legal custody included "a right of access" to the child.

[33] Children Act 1989, Sched. 2, para. 15(1) and s.34; see Chap. 22, below.

[34] Children Act 1989, ss.8, 34. A child can also obtain an order to allow contact with another child, *Re F. (Contact: Child in Care)* [1995] 1 F.L.R. 510 where the order was refused because siblings did not want to see the applicant.

[35] *Re O. (Contact: Imposition of Conditions)* [1995] 2 F.L.R. 124.

[36] s. 2(1)(c) following Scottish Law Com. No. 135, paras 2.31–35. But there is no presumption of contact under Scots Law: *S v. M (Access Order)* [1997] 1 F.L.R. 980, HL(S.)

[37] *R. v U.K., O. v U.K., W. v U.K.* [1988] 2 F.L.R. 445 where the failure to provide a remedy where contact was terminated by a local authority amounted to breach of Arts. 8 and 13 of the Convention. Failure by the state to enforce a parent's right of access was held to breach Art 8, *Hokkanen v. Finland* (1995) 19 E.H.R.R. 134.

[38] *Johansen v. Norway* (1996) 23 E.H.R.R. 33 at para. 77. The court applies a stricter scrutiny to restrictions on contact: *Sahin v. Germany* [2002] 1 F.L.R. 119, para. 41.

Similarly, the House of Lords held in the case of *Re K.D.* that a parent has no fundamental right to contact with a child[39]; the parent's claim will always yield to the child's welfare.[40] Contact relates to social relationships rather than the parental responsibility; consequently the court need not establish the legal relationship before ordering contact.[41] However, only parents, step-parents and (former) long-term carers[42] can apply for contact without first seeking the leave of the court. Where leave is required there is no presumption of contact.[43]

12. Choice of name

18–022 Previous editions of this work regarded naming a child largely as a matter of usage and custom but this is an area where rules have developed.[44] The courts no longer regard names as relatively unimportant but consider that they provide crucial recognition of the link between a child and the father.[45]

> In *Re S.*[46] a boy was born after his Muslim mother eloped to Gretna Green with a Sikh man with whom she had become infatuated. The woman was ostracised by her family and community. The marriage failed and the woman sought to re-establish relationships with her family. The boy had been given Sikh names but his mother used a Muslim first name for him. She applied to change all his names and presented expert evidence that the Sikh names were a barrier to his acceptance in the Muslim community. She wanted a different first name because the current one was similar to the father's nickname. The court permitted the boy to be given Muslim middle and last names but refused a formal change by deed poll because this would comprehensively eliminate the Sikh identity. The first name had to be retained so that the boy had an enduring sense of his identity.

Formally, a child is named when the birth is registered; only a parent with parental responsibility may effect the registration alone, although two unmarried parents may do this jointly.[47] The name given at birth is not conclusive but any

---

[39] [1988] A.C. 806; J. Eekelaar (1988) 51 *M.L.R.* 629.

[40] Children Act 1989, s.1: see Chap. 20; *Re L.; Re V.; Re M.; Re H. (Contact: Domestic Violence)* [2000] 2 F.L.R. 334, CA; *Re M. (Contact: Welfare Test)* [1995] 1 F.L.R. 274, CA; *Re CH. (Contact Parentage)* [1996] 1 F.L.R. 569.

[41] *Re D. (Parental Responsibility: IVF baby)* [2001] 1 F.L.R. 972, CA (parental responsibility refused but indirect contact ordered to man claiming to be father following IVF to his former partner). *O. v. L.* [1995] 2 F.L.R. 930, CA (application by ex husband granted); *K. v. M.* [1996] 1 F.L.R. 312 (application by former lover refused).

[42] Children Act 1989, s.10(4),(5).

[43] *Re A. (Section 8 Order: Grandparent's Application)* [1995] 2 F.L.R. 153, CA.

[44] See A. Bond, "Reconstructing families—changing children's surnames" [1998] *C.F.L.Q.* 17 and Hayes [1999] *C.F.L.Q.* 423.

[45] *Dawson v. Wearmouth* [1999] 1 F.L.R. 1167 at 1174 *per* Lord Jauncey; *Re B. (Change of Surname)* [1996] 1 F.L.R. 791 at 795 *per* Wilson J.

[46] *Re S.(Change of Name Cultural Factors)* [2001] 2 F.L.R. 1005, FD.

[47] Births and Deaths Registration 1953, s.10; Registration of Births and Death Regulations 1987 S.I. 1097 No. 2088. Where the married father and mother each registered the birth separately, the second registration (the mother's) was cancelled but the mother was permitted to use the given names she had chosen for the child: *Re H (Child's Name: First Name)* [2002] EWCA Civ. 190; [2002] 1 F.L.R. 973, CA.

subsequent formal change[48] is a serious issue[49] and will be permitted by the court only if it is in the interests of the child.[50] Where both parents have parental responsibility, neither may change the child's name without the consent of the other.[51] A father without parental responsibility may use section 8 orders to prevent a name change or require a return to the former name.[52] Also where the child is subject to a residence order the consent of everyone with parental responsibility or leave of the court is required.[53] No one may change the name of a child who is in the care of the local authority but the courts have permitted such changes in the child's interests.[54]

13. Miscellaneous rights

18–023 A number of miscellaneous rights follow from those discussed above—for example a person with parental responsibility has certain powers to enter into contracts on the child's behalf[55]; and, as an incident to the parental right to have possession of a child a parent may sometimes prohibit the child's emigration.[56] Consent of a person with parental responsibility is required before a child can obtain a passport; a parent may also veto the issue of a passport.[57] The right to administer the child's estate carries with it duties to arrange the child's funeral.[58]

---

[48] The Enrolment of Deeds (Change of Name) Regulations 1994, S.I. 1994 No. 604; *Practice Direction* [1995] 1 F.L.R. 46. It has been suggested that the court cannot control informal action: *Re B. (Change of Surname)* [1996] 1 F.L.R. 791, CA *per* Wilson J. at 795 but it may direct that a parent takes no steps to cause the child to be known by a new name.

[49] *Re PC. (Change of Surname)* [1997] 2 F.L.R. 730 F.D. In *Dawson v. Wearmouth* [1999] 1 F.L.R. 1167 the House of Lords rejected the suggestion that refusal to order that a child had the father's name breached the father's rights under E.C.H.R., Art 8.

[50] *Dawson v. Wearmouth* [1999] 1 F.L.R. 1167, HL; *Re. W, Re A., Re B. (Change of Name)* [1999] 2 F.L.R. 930 C.A. the decision of the court of first instance will only be overturned where the principles in *G. v. G. (Minors: Custody Appeal)* [1985] 2 All E.R. 225, HL apply.

[51] *Re PC. (Change of Surname)* [1997] 2 F.L.R. 730, FD. Despite the wording in Children Act 1989, s.13(1)(a) a residence order is not required. The Law Commission took the view that a parent should not be able to take unilateral action to change the name: Law Com. 172, para. 4.14. *Re T. (Change of Surname)* [1998] 2 F.L.R. 620, CA.

[52] But Hayes suggests that the courts should not interfere with the unmarried mother's statutory right to choose the child's name and that Children Act 1989, s.1 may not apply: Hayes, *op. cit.*, p. 428.

[53] Children Act 1989, s.13.

[54] *Re M., T., P., K. and B. (Care: Change of Name)* [2000] 2 F.L.R. 645, FD (name changes required to protect children who had been abused and required a witness protection programme); *Re S.(Change of Name)* [1999] 2 F.L.R. 672, CA (name change allowed on appeal for 15 year old whose father was acquitted of abusing her).

[55] See *Mills v. I.R.C.* [1973] Ch. 225. However, the tax advantages of arrangements whereby child maintenance was paid to a school with whom the child had a contract were removed by the Finance Act 1988.

[56] Children Act 1989, s.13, Sched. 2, para. 19. If the child is in care or subject to a residence order the court may give approval but a child who is accommodated by the local authority may not go to live outside England and Wales without the agreement of everyone with parental responsibility. In other cases the court will determine an application to remove a child applying the welfare test see: Chap. 19, below.

[57] There must be a court order preventing the child's removal or the request must come from the only person with parental responsibility see Passport Agency website: www.ukpa.gov.uk

[58] *Williams v. Williams* (1881) 20 Ch.D. 659; the court may appoint another administrator: Supreme Court Act 1981, s.116; *Buchanan v. Milton* [1999] 2 F.L.R. 846, FD. The position of a special

Where the child was looked after by the local authority it may arrange the funeral but must, so far as practicable, obtain the consent of everyone with parental responsibility.[59] In cases of dispute the court may determine the matter.[60]

B. Duties

1. To care

18–024 It is clear that parents are expected to care for their children but the standard of that care is uncertain. Article 18 of the United Nations Convention refers to the parental responsibility "for the upbringing and development of the child." The Children (Scotland) Act 1995 requires parents to "safeguard and promote the child's health development and welfare."[61] A similar duty is imposed by the Children Act 1989 but only on local authorities in respect of the children they look after and those in need.[62] A parent's duties can be discerned from the consequence of their failure. Those who neglect their children may be liable to criminal prosecution under various statutes.[63] Failure to provide reasonable care or to protect the child from abuse by the other parent may justify a local authority bringing care proceedings if it leads or is likely to lead to "significant harm".[64] Thus parents who refused to show affection might find their child subject to a care order.[65] Parents are not immune from liability in tort[66] for harm to their children but expectations of parental care must make allowance for the rough and tumble of family life.[67] The obligation to care for a child has been viewed as a trust[68]; and abuse of the child a breach of trust.[69]

Although contact is termed a right of the child there does not appear to be a

---

guardian is unclear but he or she has a duty to inform the parents of the child's death: Children Act 1989, s.14C(5) (to be added by Adoption and Children Bill 2002, cl.113).

59 Children Act 1989, Sched. 2, para. 20.

60 *Fessi v. Whitmore* [1999] 1 F.L.R. 769, Ch.D.

61 s.1(1)(a) following recommendations in Scottish Law Com. No. 135, para. 2.6.

62 Children Act 1989, ss.17(1)(a), 22(3).

63 Bevan (1989), paras 9.37–9.41. For a chilling example of neglect, see The Bridge Child Care Consultancy, *Paul, death through neglect* (1995).

64 Children Act 1989, s.31; see below, Chap. 22.

65 *M. v. Wigan M.B.C.* [1980] Fam. 36 where parental rights were assumed under the Child Care Act 1980, s.3(1)(b)(v) because of the parents' failure to discharge the obligations of a parent.

66 *J. Eastham v. B. Eastham and I. Eastham* [1982] C.L.Y. 2141; *Pereira v Keleman* [1995] 1 F.L.R. 428; *S. v. W. and another (Child Abuse Damages)* [1995] 1 F.L.R. 862. *Roller v. Roller* 37 Wash. 242; 79 P. 788 (1905). Parental immunity exists in most states of the USA and in England for pre-natal injury caused by the mother other than by driving: Congenital Disability (Civil Liability) Act 1976, ss.1(1), 2; see Wright (1994) 6 J.C.L. 104.

67 *Surtees v. Kingston-upon-Thames R.B.C.* [1991] 2 F.L.R. 559; liability of others *in loco parentis* rests on the standard of reasonable care: see *Carmarthenshire C. C. v. Lewis* [1955] A.C. 549.

68 L. Blom Cooper, *A Child in trust* (1985); Blom Cooper was particularly concerned with a child subject to a care order living at home: p. 21; O'Donovan (1993), pp. 102–104; Barton & Douglas (1995), p. 22.

69 *M. (K.) v. M. (H.)* (1992) 96 D.L.R. 596. The victim could sue her abusive father many years after the event because breach of trust was not subject to a limitation period *cf. Stubbings v. Webb* [1993] A.C. 498 but there is discretion to extend the limitation period if the tort is not assault but breach of duty: *S. v. W (Child Abuse Damages)* [1995] 1 F.L.R. 862.

corresponding legal duty on parents to maintain personal relations and direct contact.[70] Failure to exercise contact may lead to the conclusion that it would not be in the child's interests to re-establish it[71] and justify an order for its termination.[72] Rejection of a child may impair emotional development and mental health and justify a care order.

Parents whose children commit offences are required to attend their child's court proceedings.[73] They are responsible for paying any financial penalties[74] and may be bound over or fined to ensure that their children do not commit further offences.[75]

Parental responsibility continues until the child is aged 18[76] but a court may only exceptionally make orders relating to parental reponsibility for a child over the age of 16.[77] Under Scots law parental duties end at different ages; the duties to maintain contact and administer the child's property end when the child reaches 16[78] but other duties continue throughout childhood although the way they are exercised varies with the child's age.[79]

2. To maintain

18–025 The Child Support Act 1991, s.1 provides that for the purposes of the Act each parent shall be responsible for maintaining a qualifying child. Where a maintenance assessment has been made the duty is satisfied by paying the sum assessed.[80] A wide range of penalties may be imposed on those who do not pay, including removal of a driving licence or imprisonment.[81] If income support is paid in respect of the child it can be recovered from a parent who may also be liable to prosecution.[82] The Child Support Act 1991 has suspended the jurisdic-

---

[70] *Cf.* Children (Scotland) Act 1995, s.1(1)(c) and see: Scottish Law Com. No. 135, para. 2.6.

[71] *Re. M. (A Minor) (Access Application)* [1988] 1 F.L.R. 35. *Cf. Re P. (A Minor) (Contact)* [1994] 2 F.L.R. 374. But it has not been suggested that a parent failing to maintain contact (unlike one refusing contact) should have to undergo counselling or education: Advisory Board on Family Law: Children Act sub-committee, *Making contact work* (2002).

[72] Children Act 1989, ss.8, 34. In *Re D. (Parental Responsibility: IVF baby)* [2001] 1 F.L.R. 951, CA consideration of the father's application for parental responsibility was deferred for two and a half years to see whether he maintained his commitment to the child.

[73] Children and Young Persons Act 1933, s.34A but only if the child is under 16 years of age.

[74] Powers of Criminal Courts (Sentencing) Act 2000, s.137. Orders will not be made against parents (or local authorities) if it is unreasonable to do so, for example where they have done all that could be reasonably expected to control their child: *D. v. DPP* [1995] 2 F.L.R. 502 or if the offence is entirely outside their control: *TA v. DPP* [1997] 2 F.L.R. 887, CA.

[75] Powers of Criminal Courts (Sentencing) Act 2000, s.150.

[76] Children Act 1989, ss.2, 3, 105(1).

[77] Children Act 1989, s.9(6), (7); new s.12(5)(6) (to be added by the Adoption and Children Bill 2002 will empower the court to make residence orders in favour of non-parents which last to age 18. Care orders cannot be made in relation to those over 17, s.31(3).

[78] Under Scots law children have full legal capacity at 16 but the court may ratify or set aside transactions by those under 18: Age of Legal Capacity (Scotland) Act 1991, ss.1, 3, 4.

[79] Children (Scotland) Act 1995, ss.1(2)(b), 2(7) and see: Scottish Law Com. No. 135, paras 2.7–2.12

[80] Child Support Act 1991, s.1(2)(3) and see Chap. 15, above.

[81] Child Support Act 1991, ss.39A, 40, 40B but only where there has been wilful refusal or culpable neglect.

[82] Social Security Administration Act 1992, ss.78, 105 and 106.

tion of the courts to make or vary maintenance orders against a parent who could be subject to a maintenance assessment.[83] But there are circumstances where a child (or young adult) can obtain financial support from a parent[84] via the courts.[85] A child of any age may intervene in the parents' divorce proceedings and seek a financial order[86]; with leave a child can apply for a residence order to be made or discharged and the court may make a financial order.[87] Where a young person who is receiving education or training, or there are special circumstances (for example disability) which justify this,[88] maintenance orders may be made or extended beyond the age of 18.[89] However, there is no power to order a parent to maintain a child who is looked after by the local authority after the age of 16.[90] There is no general obligation to support adult children, nor to provide for them from the parent's estate.

Parents can be required to pay financial support but this does not depend on their having parental responsibility—unmarried fathers without parental responsibility also have to pay. This is also the case for step-parents where the child is a "child of the family".[91] In contrast, maintenance cannot be ordered from non-parents who have parental responsibility, but in the absence of other sources of financial support,[92] such people do have to support children living with them because they could be held liable for neglect if they failed to do so.

The importance of parental responsibility

18–026 Parental responsibility is not a unitary concept; the Children Act 1989 draws distinctions between the parental responsibility of parents and guardians and that of other people. Those who acquire parental responsibility by an agreement or court order can have it removed by the revocation or discharge of that order. Also, despite the wording of Children Act 1989, s.3, parental responsibility does not provide all the important attributes of parenthood.[93] Fathers without parental

---

[83] Child Support Act 1991, s.8(1).

[84] For these purposes parent is defined in the Children Act 1989, Sched.1, para. 16 to include "any party to a marriage (whether or not subsisting) in relation to whom the child concerned is a child of the family." It does not encompass all people with parental responsibility.

[85] A court may make an order against a parent to pay an additional amount or expenses relating to education, training or a disabled child's disabilities; orders can also be made against a parent with care: s.8. A former step-parent may also be requested to support a "child of the family": M.C.A. 1973, s.25 (3),(4).

[86] *Downing v. Downing (Downing Intervening)* [1976] Fam. 288; but see para. 15–037 above.

[87] Children Act 1989, Sched. 1, paras 1, 6.

[88] *C. v. F. (Disabled Child: Maintenance Orders)* [1998] 2 F.L.R. 1, CA.

[89] Children Act 1989, Sched. 1, paras . 2(1), 3(2). The policy of encouraging students to depend on loans is not relevant to the court: *B. v. B. (Adult Student: Liability to Support)* [1998] 1 F.L.R. 373.

[90] Children Act 1989, Sched. 2, para. 21(3).

[91] M.C.A. 1973, ss.25(3),(4) and 52(1); S. Ramsey and J. Masson, "Stepparent support of stepchildren: a comparative analysis of policies and problems in the American and English experience" (1985) 36 Syracuse L.R. 659.

[92] Guardians, special guardians and those with residence orders may seek orders from the parent: Children Act 1989, Sched. 1, para. 1 and can receive support from the local authority (para. 15). In some circumstances they will be entitled to state benefits.

[93] J. Eekelaar, "Re-thinking parental responsibility" ' [2001] *Fam. Law* 426.

responsibility must maintain their children[94] and non-parents with parental responsibility cannot make decisions about adoption,[95] nor unless they are guardians or special guardians, appoint a guardian to take responsibility in the event of their death.[96] The absence of parental responsibility does not mean that even a non-parent has no rights or responsibilities in relation to the child. A person whose parental responsibility was removed by the making of a care order must be allowed contact with the child.[97] Non-parents without parental responsibility can apply for section 8 orders without leave if they are married to a parent or have had care of the child for three years.[98] The above discussion of rights and duties makes clear that anyone with care of a child has some responsibility to ensure that the child attends school and is properly looked after. Also, where a person has a relationship which amounts to family life within Article 8, public authorities must respect their rights.[99] Indeed having Convention rights may become more important than parental responsibility.

IV. WHO HAS PARENTAL RESPONSIBILITY?

A. Married parents

18–027 At common law the relationship between parent and child was only recognised if the child was "legitimate", that is, either born or conceived at a time when the parents were validly married. The ordinary case of birth to married parents involves both conception and birth during the parents' marriage; but under the common law a child born after a marriage had been ended by death or divorce[1] is also legitimate. Despite the increase in births outside marriage some couples marry during the pregnancy.[2] Originally, the father had the legal power over his legitimate child exclusively but the father's power waned and mothers were given greater legal recognition until equality was achieved.[3] The Children Act 1989 now provides that where a child's mother and father were married to each

---

94 See above.

95 Adoption Act 1976, s.16 (Adoption and Children Bill 2002, cl.52(6)); Children Act 1989, s.5 (amendments relating to special guardianship in Adoption and Children Bill 2002, cl.113(4)).

96 Children Act 1989, s.5(3),(4). Provisions relating to special guardians are to be found in the Adoption and Children Bill 2002, cl.113.

97 Children Act 1989, s. 34(1) and see Chap. 22, below.

98 Children Act 1989, s. 10(5) and Chap. 19, below.

99 H.R.A. 1998, s.6, *K. and T. v. Finland* [2001] 2 F.L.R. 707 and above, para. 17–013.

1 *Knowles v. Knowles* [1962] P. 161.

2 The percentage of conceptions outside marriage which result in births within marriage has declined from 8.1 per cent in 1971 to 3.2 per cent in 1995 see C. Smart and P. Stevens, *Cohabitation breakdown* (2000) p.17 and K.E. Kiernan and V. Estough, *Cohabitating extra-marital child bearing and social policy* Family Policy Studies Centre, Occasional Paper 17 (1993), Chap. 2.

3 See S. Maidment, *Child Custody* (1984), Chap. 5 and J. Brophy, "Parental rights and children's welfare. Some problems of feminist strategy in the 1920s" (1982) 10 Int. J. of Soc. L. 149 and S. Cretney, "What will the women want next?" (1996) *L.Q.R.* 110.

other at the time of the birth,[4] they shall each have parental responsibility for their child, including a child born as a result of assisted reproduction.[5]

The rigours of the common law were mitigated by allowing a child whose parents married later to be legitimated and treating as legitimate some children of invalid marriages.[6] These notions were preserved when the Family Law Reform Act 1987 removed the remaining legal consequences of birth outside marriage so far as children are concerned.[7]

In addition to the simple case of birth to married parents both parents have parental responsibility in the following circumstances:

1. Void marriage

18–028 All children of void marriages were illegitimate until the Legitimacy Act 1959 adopted the civil law principle of "putative marriage,"[8] under which children of such unions are treated as legitimate provided that the defect rendering the marriage void was not known to one or both parties.[9] The Legitimacy Act 1976 now provides that[10]:

> "The child of a void marriage, whenever born shall . . . be treated as the legitimate child of his parents if at the time of the insemination resulting in the birth or, if there was no such insemination, the child's conception (or at the time of the celebration of the marriage, if later) both or either of the parties reasonably believed that the marriage was valid."

The rule applies only if the child's father was domiciled in England or Wales at the time of birth.[11]

It is only necessary for one party to have believed the marriage was valid. Thus, where the wife alone knows that she is under 16 or the husband that he is already legally married[12] both parents will automatically gain parental responsibility. It is understandable that the law should be drafted generously to protect a child but less clear why a father who knows that his marriage is invalid

---

[4] s.2(1). The phrase "married to each other at the time of [the child's] birth" is given a wide meaning by s.1(3) of the F.L.R.A. 1987 and includes certain children born of void marriages, legitimated and adopted children and those treated as legitimate.

[5] Human Fertilisation and Embryology Act 1990, s.29(1).

[6] For a historical account, see the 4th edition of this book at pp. 581–584.

[7] Family Law Reform Act 1987, s.1.

[8] See E.J. Cohn (1948) 64 *L.Q.R.* 324; J. Jackson, *The Formation and Annulment of Marriage* (2nd ed., 1969), pp. 50–53.

[9] The Act implemented the recommendation of the Morton Commission, Royal Commission on Marriage & Divorce 1951–5, Cmd. 9678 (1956), para. 1186.

[10] s.1 as amended by Family Law Reform Act 1987, s.28(1) to take account of new methods of fertilisation.

[11] Or if he died before the birth, was so domiciled immediately before his death: s.1(2). For this reason Daniel was not legitimate and could not succeed to his father's title see: *Re Moynihan* [2000] 1 F.L.R. 113 at 128 *per* Lord Slynn.

[12] See M.C.A. 1973, s.11.

should nevertheless be able to rely on it to gain parental responsibility.[13] The belief must continue until the insemination, conception or, if later, the marriage, but a child may not apparently be treated as legitimate if he or she was born before the void marriage.[14]

The requirement of reasonable belief caused difficulty because doubts were expressed whether a mistake of law could ever be reasonable.[15] Also, it could be impossible to prove the parent's state of mind at the time of conception. However, following the recommendations of the Law Commission[16] both these problems were resolved by the Family Law Reform Act 1987. A belief may be reasonable even though it was due to a mistake of law[17]; in relation to children born after April 4, 1988 and unless the contrary is shown, the Act presumes that one parent did have such a belief at the relevant time.[18] Where the father is claiming parental responsibility relying on a void marriage his claim would only be defeated by establishing that neither parent reasonably believed in the validity of the marriage at the relevant time. It has been suggested that reasonableness should be assessed objectively[19] but an honest belief, it is submitted, should be sufficient. However the further the belief diverges from the reasonable the more difficult it will be to establish that it was honestly held. If the marriage is voidable rather than void no problems arise for the parents because decrees of nullity do not have retrospective effect.[20]

2. Marriage after birth

18–029 The concept of legitimation by subsequent marriage was introduced into English law in 1926 and is now governed by the Legitimacy Act 1976. Providing that the father is domiciled in England or Wales at the date of their valid marriage,[21] both parents will from that date have parental responsibility for any child of theirs born prior to the marriage.[22]

3. Adoption

18–030 An adoption order gives parental responsibility to the adoptive parents and ends parental responsibility held by the natural parents and anyone else under a court

[13] The Law Commission's reasons for not extending parental responsibility to all fathers would seem to apply equally to the circumstance of a man who gets his wife pregnant knowing that their marriage is invalid: Law Com. No. 118, paras 4.46 and 4.31–36.

[14] *Re Spence (dec'd)* [1990] Ch. 652, CA.

[15] P. Bromley, *Family Law* (6th ed., 1981), p. 267.

[16] Law Com. No. 118, *Illegitimacy* (1982), para. 10.51–2.

[17] Legitimacy Act 1976, s.1(3) added by Family Law Reform Act 1987, s.28.

[18] s.1(4).

[19] *Hawkins v. Att.-Gen.* [1966] 1 W.L.R. 978.

[20] M.C.A. 1973, s.16 (for decrees granted after July 31, 1971); see above.

[21] *Re Spence (dec'd)* [1990] Ch. 652 where the marriage was void.

[22] Legitimacy Act 1976, s.2. This includes a child of the parties who had been adopted by one of them as a single parent; see s.4.

order.[23] Only adoption (or an order freeing a child for adoption) ends a mother's or married father's parental responsibility.[24] The provisions of the Adoption and Children Bill, if enacted, will allow a step-parent to adopt a child alone without changing the status of his or her spouse, the child's parent. The couple will then both have parental responsibility for the child.[25] Orders freeing a child for adoption will be abolished; parental consent to placement and placement orders will both give parental responsibility to the adoption agency and, if the child is placed for adoption, the prospective adopters.[26] Placement will not remove the parents' parental responsibility but will prevent them from exercising it except in ways agreed by the adoption agency.[27]

4. Surrogacy

18–031 A parental order[28] gives parental responsibility to the commissioning couple who must be married. It also destroys the parental responsibility held by anyone else by birth or a court order but only for the period after the order was made.

B. Unmarried parents

18–032 Where the parents are unmarried at the time of the child's birth[29] only the mother has parental responsibility as of right; the father may obtain it by a court order, a formal agreement with the mother or if the Adoption and Children Bill is enacted, registering the child's birth jointly with the mother.

Differential treatment for children dependent on their parent's marital status is contrary to the anti-discrimination principle of the United Nations Convention on the Rights of the Child.[30] The European Convention on Human Rights protects family life[31] and this requires states to take positive steps to enable family

---

23 Adoption Act 1976, s.12 as amended by Children Act 1989, Sched. 10, para. 3; Adoption and Children Bill 2002, cl. 46(2) A child who has been adopted cannot make a claim against a birth parent under the Inheritance (Provision for Family and Dependants) Act 1975, s.1(1)(c): *Re Collins (dec'd)* [1990] Fam. 56. For further details, see Chap. 23, below.

24 A freeing order makes a parent a "former parent" who thus requires leave to seek an order under the Children Act 1989, s.8: *Re C. (Minors) (Adoption: Residence Order)* [1994] Fam. 1. Freeing orders are revocable: Adoption Act 1976, s.20 and *Re C. (Adoption: Freeing Order)* [1999] 1 F.L.R. 348 FD.

25 Adoption and Children Bill 2002, cl. 46(3)(b).

26 Adoption and Children Bill 2002, cl. 25.

27 cl. 25(4); this restriction applies to the exercise of parental responsibility by the prospective adopters.

28 Adoption Act 1976, s.12 as modified by the Parental Orders Regulations 1994, S.I. 1994 No. 2767; see Chap. 23.

29 This phrase is given a wide meaning by F.L.R.A. 1987, s.1(3); see also A. Bainham, "When is a parent not a parent? Reflections on the unmarried father and his child in English Law" (1989) 3 Int. J. Law & Fam. 208.

30 Art. 2. States Parties are required to take all appropriate measures to ensure that the child is protected against "all forms of discrimination . . . on the basis of the status . . . of the child's parents . . . " (Art. 2(2)).

31 Art. 8(1).

life to develop normally.[32] The Convention protects family life not bare rights but very weighty reasons must be advanced before a difference in treatment between children based on birth status could be justified.[33] In *B. v. U.K.*[34] a claim based on the treatment of unmarried fathers with regard to the acquisition of parental responsibility was declared inadmissible. Given that relationships between unmarried fathers and their children ranged from "indifference and ignorance to close stable relationships" it was reasonable for parental responsibility not to be automatic.[35] However, Irish legislation which precluded any involvement of an unmarried father in his child's adoption has been held to breach the Convention: because the pregnancy had been planned the father had a right to family life with a child he had seen only once.[36] Although arguably the current English law provides a satisfactory balance between the unmarried father and the family of the mother and child,[37] promoting family life may necessitate taking further action to recognise fully the father child relationship in the large number of unmarried families.[38]

Over the last 25 years there has been a substantial increase in the number of children born to unmarried parents and repeated re-assessment of the position of unmarried fathers. In 1979, the Law Commission suggested total the abolition of illegitimacy so that unmarried fathers were in the same position as mothers and married fathers.[39] However, this caused serious anxiety to a significant body of commentators[40] and was therefore replaced by a more limited scheme whereby fathers could apply to the court to obtain parental rights and duties jointly with the mother. The infinite variety of relationships, the need to protect single mothers and children and the belief that court scrutiny was justified where rights were conferred outside marriage, meant private agreements should not be allowed.[41] However, this view was criticised because it undervalued natural fathers, required unnecessary court proceedings in consensual cases and could

---

[32] *Marcx v. Belgium* (1979) 2 E.H.R.R. 330; *Johnstone v. Ireland* (1987) 9 E.H.R.R. 203. See J. Davidson, "The European Convention on Human Rights and the illegitimate child" in D. Freestone (ed.), *Children and the Law* (1990), p. 75 at p. 104 and C. Forder, (1993) 7 Int. J. Law & Fam. 40.

[33] *Inze v. Austria* (1987) 10 E.H.R.R. 394; *Sahin v. Germany* [2002] 1 F.L.R. 119, para. 57. But see the strong dissenting judgment by Judges Mifsud and Bonnici in *Kroon v Netherlands* [1995] 2 F.C.R. 28 at 44.

[34] [2000] 1 F.L.R. 1 (the father had been unable to obtain a declaration that the removal of his child by the mother was unlawful for the purposes of the Hague Convention on Child Abduction). But note following the decision in *Re H. (Abduction: Rights of Custody)* [2000] 1 F.L.R. 374 HL the father may have been able to get the child returned to the U.K. and see Chap. 21 below.

[35] *B. v. U.K.* [2000] 1 F.L.R. 1 at 5.

[36] *Keegan v. Ireland* (1994) 18 E.H.R.R. 342. The Irish provision is comparable to that under the Adoption Act 1976; see also *McMichael v. U.K.* (1995) 20 E.H.R.R. 205 where proceedings under the Social Work (Scotland) Act 1968 breached Art. 8(1).

[37] C. Forder (1993) 7 Int. J. Law & Fam. 40, 97; *cf.* Deech (1992) 4 J.C.L. 3 who strongly criticises the view that protecting family life requires automatic parental responsibility for unmarried fathers.

[38] ONS, *Birth Statistics 1999*, FM1 No. 28 Table 1.1 almost 40 per cent of births were to unmarried parents.

[39] Law Com. W.P. 74, *Illegitimacy* (1979), paras 3.17–3.22.

[40] Law Com. No. 118, *Illegitimacy* (1982), para. 4.46; M. Hayes (1980) 43 *M.L.R.* 299; R. Deech (1980) 10 *Fam. Law* 101.

[41] Law Com. No. 118, para. 4.39.

discourage couples from legally sharing rights.[42] In 1985, in their working paper on Guardianship the Law Commission noted that "[J]udicial proceedings, however, may be unduly elaborate, expensive and perhaps unnecessary, unless the child's mother objects . . . " and recommended a form of guardianship which would give the father parental responsibility alongside the mother.[43] It saw no inconsistency between extending guardianship and the earlier proposals but acknowledged the resource implications of requiring proceedings.[44] Subsequently, the Law Commission issued a *Second Report on Illegitimacy* reaffirming the need for court proceedings, but expressing the hope that such orders would frequently be sought and granted.[45] The Family Law Reform Act 1987[46] gave the court power to grant parental responsibility to unmarried fathers; the proposal for agreements was widely supported[47] and was included in the Children Act 1989.[48]

18–033 In 1992, the Scottish Law Commission accepted that the balance had swung in favour of treating all parents as parents.[49] It rejected the notion that a casual relationship or even rape[50] justified a presumption that the man's acquisition of parental responsibility was contrary to the child's interests. The existing law was sufficient to deal with fathers who abandoned their children or acted contrary to their welfare.[51] Nevertheless, the provisions in the Children (Scotland) Act 1995 on parental responsibility for unmarried fathers mirror those in the Children Act 1989.[52]

In 1998 the Lord Chancellor's Department sought views on reform to make obtaining parental responsibility easier for unmarried fathers.[53] It noted that over a third of all births were outside marriage[54] and because of ignorance of the law and assumptions about their rights[55] only a small number of the fathers obtained parental responsibility.[56] The consultation paper considered three alternatives for acquisition of parental responsibility:—automatically for all fathers, for fathers

---

[42] J. Eekelaar, "Second thoughts on illegitimacy reform" (1985) 15 *Fam. Law* 261 at 262–3; R. Ingleby [1984] J.S.W.L. 170 at 172; A. Bainham [1985] J.S.W.L. 50 at 52.

[43] Law Com. W.P. No. 91, *Guardianship* (1985), para. 4.21.

[44] *ibid.* para. 4.24.

[45] Law Com. No 157 *Illegitimacy* (Second Report) (1986).

[46] s.4. This provision is now included in Children Act 1989, s.4(1)(a).

[47] Law Com. No. 172, para. 2.18.

[48] s.4(1)(b). Minor changes were necessary so that the father's position was identical following an agreement or with an order.

[49] Scottish Law Com. No. 135 *Report on Family Law,* para. 2.48 citing UN Convention on the Rights of the Child, Art. 18(1).

[50] The Scottish Law Commission noted that rape in marriage would not prevent the husband having parental responsibility (para. 2.47).

[51] *ibid.* paras 2.41–2.47; consultees were fairly evenly balanced in their views on the proposals.

[52] s.4 in each Act.

[53] Lord Chancellor's Department, *The procedures for the determination of paternity and on the law on parental responsibility for unmarried father* (1998). The Scottish Executive has also consulted on this issue: *Improving Scottish Family Law* (1999); *Consultation Paper on Scottish Family Law* (2000).

[54] *ibid.* para. 52. The figure is now almost 40 per cent: ONS, *Birth Statistics 1999,* FM1 No. 28, Table 1.1.

[55] *ibid.* para. 53 and see R. Pickford, *Fathers, marriage and the law* (1999).

[56] *ibid.* In 1996 the courts made 5,587 parental responsibility orders and approximately 3,000 parental responsibility agreements were registered.

who jointly register the birth, or for fathers cohabiting with the mother at the time of birth.[57] None of these mechanisms is without difficulty. Parental responsibility acquired automatically or via cohabitation would not necessarily be marked by any document identifying the father or showing his relationship to the child. This could cause difficulties where the father's consent is required; mothers and adoption agencies could be involved in further investigations to locate him and in paternity proceedings.[58] Cohabitation could not be taken to reflect commitment; housing difficulties might prevent couples establishing a common home.[59] Although joint registration could be a proxy for agreement, it took place shortly after the birth when mothers might be easily pressured to agree.[60] If mothers registered the birth alone in order to preclude fathers obtaining parental responsibility,[61] there could be negative consequences for children who would be denied a record of their paternity, and for mothers because of the need to prove paternity for child support claims.[62] However, the expectations and beliefs of large numbers of unmarried parents provided the strongest reasons for extending parental responsibility to jointly registering fathers.[63] The Department announced that it proposed to base reform on joint registration of birth; a provision to this effect is included in the Adoption and Children Bill 2002. When this is enacted there will be three ways for an unmarried father to obtain parental responsibility: birth registration, agreement and court order.

1. Court orders

18–034 An order under Children Act 1989, s.4 effectively places the father in the same legal position as a married father so that he holds parental responsibility alongside all others and can exercise it without consent[64] but the order can be revoked.[65] If the court makes a residence order in favour of a father without parental responsibility it must make this order.[66] On an application for a section 4 order, the court considers the degree of commitment which the father has shown towards the child; the degree of attachment which exists between them;

---

[57] *ibid.* paras 56–61.

[58] *ibid.* para. 57; R. Pickford, "Unmarried fathers and the law" in A. Bainham *et al.* (eds) *What is a parent?* (1999) 143, 154–7; *cf.* J. Eekelaar [2001] *Fam. Law* 426, 430 who argues that parental responsibility makes very little difference to the position of unmarried fathers.

[59] Pickford, *op. cit.* (1999), p. 154.

[60] SFLA evidence to Select Committee on the Adoption and Children Bill 2001, (2001 H.C. 431-iv) app. 20.

[61] Pickford, *op. cit.*, p. 153; approximately 194,000, 72 per cent of births outside marriage were jointly registered, and of these 77 per cent of parents gave the same address: ONS, *Birth Statistics 1999*, FM1 No. 28, Table 3.10. See also: J. Ashley 1999] *Fam. Law* 175.

[62] For this reason Eekelaar argues that registration should merely be a recording exercise and all fathers should have parental responsibility: Eekelaar, *op. cit.*, p. 430.

[63] Pickford, *op. cit.*, p.157; C. Smart and P. Stevens, *Cohabitation breakdown* (2000), p. 48; Eekelaar, *op. cit.*, p. 426.

[64] Children Act 1989, s.2(6)(7).

[65] see below para. 19–014.

[66] Children Act 1989, s.12(4).

and the reasons the father has for applying for the order.[67] The welfare test applies to these proceedings.[68] It has been said that it is overwhelmingly in the child's interests for both parents to have parental responsibility.[69] Where the father has had regular contact and provided financial support, cogent evidence is required to establish that an order should not be made.[70] Abuse of power can be controlled by court orders[71] but where the father could not exercise parental responsibility[72] or was highly likely to misuse it[73] an order should not be made. Orders may be made even though the denial of contact[74] or adoption plans[75] makes it impractical for the father to exercise parental responsibility:—

> In *Re. H*[76] the mother left the father when the child was three months old and married. The father continued to see his son until he was one year old when the mother and step-father moved to Scotland. The step-father threatened to leave the mother if the father continued to see his son. The father's application for contact was rejected and he was banned from any contact until further order but his appeal against refusal of a parental responsibility order was allowed. By maintaining contact and writing appreciatively to the mother about her care the father had shown commitment and attachment to his son.

Or where the child is in care, the father lacks insight into the child's needs and is unable to get on with social workers.[77] Parental responsibility has been granted despite the fact that the father has undergone an operation to acquire female characteristics[78]; or there is hostility and lack of respect between the parents[79]; and where the father's commitment to the children has not extended to providing regular maintenance.[80] However, where a father has not established commitment

---

[67] *Re H. (Minors) (Local Authority: Parental Rights) (No. 3)* [1991] Fam. 151 at 158, CA; *Re. C. (Minors) (Parental Rights)* [1992] 1 F.L.R. 1, CA. Other matters can also be considered such as the father's violence: *Re H. (Parental Responsibility)* [1998] 1 F.L.R. 855, CA.

[68] This appears to have been assumed rather than decided; see *Re. F. (A Minor) (Parental Responsibility Order)* [1994] 1 F.L.R. 504, CA; *Re E. (Parental Responsibility: Blood Tests)* [1995] 1 F.L.R. 392.

[69] *Re P. (A Minor) (Parental Responsibility Order)* [1994] 1 F.L.R. 578 at 586, *per* Wilson J.

[70] *Re E. (Parental Responsibility: Blood Tests)* [1995] 1 F.L.R. 392, CA.

[71] *Re S. (Parental Responsibility)* [1995] 2 F.L.R. 648 at 657, *per* Ward L.J. It does not necessarily justify refusing the order.

[72] *M. v. M.(Parental Responsibility)* [1999] 2 F.L.R. 737, FD (father had brain damage).

[73] *Re P. (Parental Responsibility)* [1998] 2 F.L.R. 96, CA; *Re M. (Contact: Parental Responsibility)* [2001] 2 F.L.R. 342, FD.

[74] *Re C. and V. (Contact and Parental Responsibility)* [1998] 1 F.L.R. 392; *Re P. (A Minor) (Parental Responsibility Order)* [1994] 1 F.L.R. 578; *Re H. (A Minor) (Parental Responsibility)* [1993] 1 F.L.R. 484.

[75] *Re H. (Minors) (Local Authority: Parental Rights) (No. 3)* [1991] Fam. 151. The child was freed for adoption thus the order gave him the status of a "former parent" who could apply for the revocation of the freeing order, see below. Under the Adoption and Children Bill 2002, cl.52(10) if the father acquires parental responsibility after the mother has consented to the child's placement he is treated as having given consent. He could withdraw his consent, see Chap. 23.

[76] *Re H. (A Minor) (Parental Responsibility: Blood Tests)* [1993] 1 F.L.R. 484.

[77] *Re G. (A Minor) (Parental Responsibility Order)* [1994] 1 F.L.R. 504, CA.

[78] *Re L. (Contact: Transsexual Applicant)* [1995] 2 F.L.R. 438.

[79] *D. v. S.* [1995] 3 F.C.R. 783; *Re A.* (1996) 160 JPN 84.

[80] *Re H. (Parental Responsibility: Maintenance)* [1996] 1 F.L.R. 867, CA.

because of limited contact,[81] spending long periods in prison,[82] or had no insight about the impact of his violence on the children[83] the court has been prepared to refuse it.

The order confers status and should not be denied under section 1(5) because the parents agree about the child's care. A study in 1992 indicated that 50 per cent of applications were not contested[84] but a substantial proportion of applications do not lead to orders.[85] This may reflect a strategic use of applications as bargaining chips alongside applications for residence or contact.[86] When joint registration provides parental responsibility, the courts will be faced with applications where the man's relationship with the mother had ended before the birth of the child, the father refused to register the birth jointly, or the mother did not want his name to appear on the birth certificate. They may be less willing to grant orders.

2. Formal agreements

18–035 Parents may make an agreement for the father to have parental responsibility but it is only effective if in the prescribed form[87] and registered with the court.[88] The court's role is administrative and not judicial; there is no investigation of the child's welfare when an agreement is registered[89] nor can a local authority preclude parents agreeing to share parental responsibility for a child in care.[90] A court order is necessary to terminate an agreement. Few cohabiting parents make agreements; ignorance about the father's legal position and a disinclination to seek formality which might indicate lack of trust appear to be the main reasons for this.[91] This has not been a successful mechanism; in 1996 only about 3000 agreements were registered.[92]

3. Registration of birth

18–036 The Adoption and Children Bill 2002, if enacted, will provide that a man whose name is entered on the birth certificate by joint registration or joint re-

---

[81] *Re D. (Parental Responsibility: IVF baby)* [2001] F.L.R. 230 CA (consideration of application delayed so that father could show he maintained commitment); *Re J. (Parental Responsibility)* [1999] 1 F.L.R. 784 (limited contact over 11 years inadequate).

[82] *S. v. P. (Contact Application: Family Assistance)* [1997] 2 F.L.R. 277; *Re P. (Parental Responsibility)* [1997] 2 F.L.R. 722, CA.

[83] *Re G. (Domestic Violence)* [2000] 1 F.L.R. 865, FD.

[84] I. Butler *et al.*, "The Children Act 1989 and the unmarried father" (1993) 5 J.C.L. 157 (data based on a survey of 511 private law applications by fathers without parental responsibility).

[85] *Judicial Statistics 2000* Table 5.3. Approximately 25 per cent of the 10,000 applications made did not lead to orders.

[86] I. Butler *et al., op cit.* p. 158.

[87] Parental Responsibility Agreement (Amendment) Regulations 2001, S.I. 2001 No. 2261.

[88] Children Act 1989, s.4(2). Informal agreements may have limited effect: see ss.2(9) and 3(5), discussed below.

[89] S. Cretney [1989] *Fam. Law* 375. "The object is to ensure that, as far as possible, both parents understand the importance and effects of their agreement." Law Com. No. 172, para. 2.19.

[90] *Re X. (Parental Responsibility Agreement: Children in Care)* [2000] 1 F.L.R. 517, FD.

[91] R. Pickford, *Fathers, marriage and the law* (1999) pp. 25, 34.

[92] Lord Chancellor's Department *op. cit.*, para. 53. In 1993 4,500 agreements were registered: CAAC Report 1992/3, Table 5.

registration will have parental responsibility for his child.[93] In effect the act of registration is treated as an agreement between the parents. The provision will not operate retrospectively[94] and the court will have the power to remove parental responsibility. Considerable publicity will be required to ensure that the new significance of joint registration is properly understood.[95]

C. Guardians

18–037 The term "guardian of the child" has had a wide variety of meanings but in modern times has been limited in law to a parent or a person who took over a parent's responsibilities after their death.[96]

Until 1991, parents and guardians had similar but not identical powers[97]; the Law Commission recommended that the distinctions should be abolished so that guardians could be brought fully within the scheme for parental responsibility,[98] and that the term guardian should be restricted to non-parents.[99] This was enacted in the Children Act 1989; under the Act guardians have parental responsibility.[1] Guardians can be appointed by parents and special guardians,[2] or failing them by the court.[3]

1. Appointments by parents, guardians and special guardians[4]

18–038 A parent with parental responsibility, a guardian or special guardian[5] may appoint a person to be the child's guardian in the event of their death. The appointment takes effect immediately on death.[6] But where there is a surviving parent with parental responsibility, an appointment by the other parent only

---

93 cl. 109(2) amending Children Act 1989, s.4; similar provision is made for Scotland and Northern Ireland. It follows that if the man's name is included following proceedings which establish paternity he will not have parental responsibility. A short birth certificate does not include the names of parents and will not (unless redesigned) indicate whether the father has parental responsibility.

94 This was not discussed by the Lord Chancellor's Department but the Scottish Executive paper *op. cit.* considered that this was required to avoid interference with the child's and the mother's life (para. 2.16). This contradicts the main reason for the change, that it accords with current beliefs about the law.

95 Advisory Board on Family Law, *Second Annual Report* (1999) Annex C para. 3iii, iv.

96 Law Com. W.P. 91, *Guardianship* (1985), paras 2.4–6. A child may also have a guardian *ad litem* and a "children's guardian" whose powers are quite different, see above, Chap. 17, and below, Chap. 22.

97 Law Com. W.P. 91, para. 2.26.

98 Law Com. No. 172, paras 2.23–5.

99 *ibid.* para. 2.3.

1 s. 5(6): a guardian is not liable to maintain the child: see Sched. 1.

2 Adoption and Children Bill 2002, cl. 113(4) amending Children Act 1989, s. 5(1),(4) and (7).

3 Children Act 1989, s.5(1)–(5). For the earlier law see: Guardianship of Minors Act 1971 (as amended) and the 4th edition of this book at pp. 316–320.

4 The provisions relating to special guardians depend on the enactment of the Adoption and Children Bill 2002, cl.113.

5 Children Act 1989, s.5(3), (4); two people may make an appointment jointly s.5(10).

6 Children Act 1989, s. 5(7). Similarly it will take effect on the death of the last surviving special guardian even if there is a parent with parental responsibility still living.

takes effect after the death of both parents.[7] A parent only has parental responsibility alongside a guardian if the deceased parent had a residence order and the surviving parent did not.[8]

The Law Commission wanted to simplify appointments.[9] Appointments only need be in writing and signed by the person making them, or signed and witnessed at his or her direction.[10] Appointments are revoked by written revocation, by intentional destruction of the document,[11] or by making another appointment unless it is clear that the intention is to add a guardian.[12] If the appointment is made by will, it is revoked if the will is revoked.[13] The appointment of a spouse is revoked by divorce or a decree of nullity unless a contrary intention appears.[14] A person appointed may disclaim the appointment but must do so within a reasonable time and in writing.[15] The court may also revoke an appointment.[16]

2. Appointments by the court

18–039 The court's powers mirrored those of parents and the Law Commission recommended that this should continue.[17] The court may appoint a person to be a child's guardian whether or not an application has been made.[18] A local authority may not be the child's guardian but may support an individual making an application.[19] A court may only appoint a guardian if the child has no parent with parental responsibility, a parent, guardian or special guardian with a residence order in his favour dies while the order is in force, or the last surviving special guardian dies.[20] The court may exercise its power to appoint even though the deceased made a valid and effective appointment, and may do so either to

---

[7] Children Act 1989, s.5(8). An appointment by a guardian may take effect while the child has a guardian with a residence order but a court may not make an appointment at such a time s.5(1).

[8] Children Act 1989, s.5(1), (7), (8), or the child had a special guardian. The Law Commission thought that requiring a parent who was caring for a child to share parental responsibility with a guardian presented the parent with "individious choice" and that there was little reason to require such sharing.

[9] Law Com. W.P. 91, paras 1.31 and 3.43. So that more appointments would be made. Only a small minority of people make wills but death rates for people with young children are low. Relatives and friends may care for children without formally being appointed guardians. Figures for court appointments are so low as not to be recorded separately in the *Judicial Statistics*.

[10] Children Act 1989, s.5(5).

[11] s.6(2), (3).

[12] s.6(1).

[13] s.6(4): if the testator marries: see Wills Acts 1837, ss.18, 18A.

[14] Children Act 1989, s.5(3A) added by Law Reform (Succession) Act 1995, s.4(1) and amended by the F.L.A. 1996, Sched. 8, para. 41 and operative for deaths after January 1, 1996.

[15] s.6(5), (6). The power to make regulations has not been exercised.

[16] Children Act 1989, s. 5(1),(2); see below para. 18–046.

[17] Law Com. No. 172, para. 2.31

[18] s.5(1), (2).

[19] *Guidance*, Vol. 1, paras 2.14–2.16; *Re SH. (Care Order: Orphan)* [1995] 1 F.L.R. 746. Where the lack of any person with parental responsibility placed the child at risk of significant harm a care order could be obtained: *Re M.(Care Order: Parental Responsibility)* [1996] 2 F.L.R. 84, FD.

[20] s.5(1): even if another person (who cannot be a parent) still has a residence order which is in force.

add or to substitute a new guardian. Decisions about guardians are made applying the welfare test in section 1.

The Law Commission considered whether there should be a power to supervise or disqualify persons acting as guardians but decided that it was difficult to justify the resources that this would require.[21] However, a court considering the appointment or discharge of a guardian may call for reports[22] and a family assistance order may be made to provide short-term assistance for a guardian and the family.[23]

A guardian of the estate of any child may also be appointed under the inherent jurisdiction of the High Court in accordance with rules of court.[24]

D. Other persons

18–040 Other people, most frequently step-parents but also relatives[25] and foster carers may take on the role of parent but these "social parents" do not automatically acquire parental responsibility by marrying a parent or looking after the child. Some step-parents and relatives adopt[26] but this use of adoption was criticised for disrupting or confusing relationships.[27] The Children Act 1975 restricted adoption by step-parents[28] and made it possible for some carers to apply for custody or custodianship.[29] These orders never became popular and few carers formalised their relationships.[30] The Law Commission criticised the restrictive and inconsistent custody law but their proposal for guardianship for carers whilst parents were alive received little support.[31] They also suggested that all non-parents should be able to apply for custody with leave of the court as a filter to prevent "unwarranted interference" and further controls on foster carers to protect the local authority's plan for the child.[32] Orders in favour of non-parents

---

[21] Law Com. W.P. 91, paras 3.23 *et seq.;* Law Com. No. 172, para. 2.32.

[22] Children Act 1989, s.7 discussed in Chap. 19, below.

[23] Children Act 1989, s.16 discussed in Chap. 19, below.

[24] Children Act 1989, s.5(11), (12); C.P.R. 1998, r.20.12. Only the Official Solicitor may be appointed.

[25] J. Haskey, "Stepfamilies and stepchildren in Great Britain" (1994) 76 *Population Trends* 18, over a million children are estimated to live in stepfamilies. In 2000 there were 6,300 children fostered by local authorities with friends or relatives: *Children Act Report 2000,* para. 1.40. Many other children are cared for by relatives, privately.

[26] In 2000, 1551 of the 4438 adoption orders were in favour of a parent and step-parent: *Judicial Statistics 2000*, Table 5.4. There were far more adoption orders in favour of step-parents in the past: see J. Masson *et al., Mine, yours or ours?* (1983), fig. 2.1a.

[27] Report of the Departmental Committee on Adoption of Children, Cmnd. 5107 (1972) (*The Houghton Report*), paras 105, 108, 111.

[28] ss.10(3) and 11(4); Adoption Act 1976, ss.14(3) and 15(4). These restrictions were removed by the Children Act 1989, Sched. 15.

[29] A form of custody. For details fo the various provisions see 6th edition of this book p.645.

[30] E. Bullard and E. Malos, *Custodianship* (1991); 491 orders were made in 1991: Cm. 1990, Table 5.11.

[31] Law Com. W.P. 96, paras 5.21–5.25; "*Inter-vivos* guardians" Law Com. W.P. 91, paras 4.9 *et seq.;* Law Com. No. 172, para. 2.2.

[32] Law Com. W.P. 96, paras 5.37–5.39; Law Com. No. 172, paras 4.40–4.48. For a the law and practice relating to leave for residence order applications see Chap 19, below.

should be very similar to those for parents[33]; non-parents caring for a children needed the same responsibilities as a parent and should not have a separate status.[34]

1. Non-parents with residence orders

18–041 The Children Act 1989 enacted the Law Commission's proposals with only minor changes. A residence order may be made in favour of anyone in any family proceedings.[35] Non-parents require leave of the court for an application unless they are a step-parent, have cared for the child for three years or have the relevant consents.[36] Foster parents, except those who are relatives of the child or have cared for him or her for more than three years,[37] require the consent of the local authority before they can apply for leave.[38] A residence order confers parental responsibility for the child for the duration of the order, normally until the child is 16.[39] In exceptional circumstances, the order may be extended until the age of 18.[40] A residence order discharges a care order and therefore enables a foster carer to end the involvement of the local authority. The local authority may continue to provide financial support[41] (but authorities are rarely generous in this respect); any other assistance would depend on the authority accepting that the child required services.[42]

Although the Children Act 1989 has introduced a coherent scheme for the acquisition of parental responsibility by court order, few step-parents or carers have made use of this.[43] Ignorance of the law, feelings that formal status is irrelevant to the practice of parenting or concerns about the cost and complexity

---

[33] "Some of the statutory provisions which equate guardians with parents would not be appropriate, in particular the power to appoint a testamentary guardian or to consent to adoption or to freeing the child for adoption. The child is not 'theirs' to dispose of in this way; indeed, they may wish to adopt him against the parent's will." Law Com. No. 172, para. 4.27.

[34] *ibid.* paras 4.26, 4.28.

[35] Children Act 1989, s.10(1). A residence discharges a care order and may be used to secure the child lives with relatives who have not previously had care: see s.91(1).

[36] Children Act 1989, s.10(2), (5), see Chap. 19 and below.

[37] This period will be reduced to one year if the Adoption and Children Bill 2002, cl.111 is enacted. This will bring it in line with the restrictions on adoption applications.

[38] s.9(3). This also applies to people who have fostered the child in the previous six months. This further restriction was not recommended by the Law Commission but thought necessary to avoid discouraging parents from placing their children in local authority accommodation. It also removes local authority decisions from court review in this respect.

[39] Children Act 1989, s.12(2).

[40] Children Act 1989, ss.9(6), 91(10); *Re M. (Contact: Parental Responsibility)* [2001] 2 F.L.R. 342, FD. The Adoption and Children Bill 2002, cl.112 (adding Children Act 1989, s.12(5),(6)) extends the power to make residence orders lasting to age 18 in favour of people who are neither parents nor guardians. This was originally recommended by the *Interdepartmental Review of Adoption Law* (1992), para. 6.5.

[41] Children Act 1989, Sched. 1, para. 15.

[42] Children Act 1989, s.17 and see Chap. 22, below. Those who obtain special guardianship or adoption orders may have a right to an assessment but the level of service will depend on the local authority's view of their needs.

[43] In a study in the south-west of England in 1996–7, only 10 per cent of applications for residence are made by non parents and 8 out of 10 of these are grandparents: J. Pearce *et al.* [1999] *Fam. Law* 22, 23.

of legal proceedings are all likely to be factors.[44] Proposals have been made for agreements whereby step-parents can acquire a parental responsibility, and for a new legal status for carers, "special guardianship" to provide them with more security without terminating the child's relationship with the birth family.

2. Step-parents

18–042 The Interdepartmental Review of Adoption Law proposed that step-parents should be able to obtain parental responsibility by agreement with both the child's parents, or if this was not forthcoming, a court order.[45] The Adoption and Children Bill 2002 makes provision for this.[46] The married[47] partner of each parent can acquire parental responsibility by an agreement or a court order. The requirement that both the parents consent to any agreement gives the parent who is not the step-parent's partner bargaining chips, an effect which the Law Commission sought to avoid in disputes between parents, and may make agreements unattractive. It is unclear why this parent's agreement is thought necessary; granting parental responsibility to a person does not involve the reduction of the power of others holding it, nor would it be possible to stop the other parent sharing responsibility informally, unless this placed the child at risk. Where the other parent refuses agreement or cannot be found a court order will be required. However, it remains possible for the parent (or anyone else with parental responsibility) to delegate this informally without any consent.[48]

3. Special guardians

18–043 In 1993, the Government proposed a status termed "*inter-vivos* guardianship" or "foster-plus" as an addition to a residence order and an alternative to adoption, for relatives and foster parents.[49] Concern about the instability of arrangements and the lack of family life for children looked after by local authorities[50] led to the resurrection of these proposals, updated and renamed "special guardianship."[51] However, there has been no reconsideration of fundamental questions whether a new order is required, or carers want to formalise their relationships and, in the case of foster carers, they wish to take on more responsibility and

---

[44] All these views have been expressed by relatives caring for children and unmarried parents: see Bullard and Malos, *op. cit.* and Pickford, *op. cit.*

[45] *Interdepartmental Review of Adoption Law* (1992), para. 19.8. Step-parent adoption would also be available but the existence of a simple alternative way of obtaining parental responsibility was intended to discourage unsuitable applications for adoption. The parental responsibility order would not effect inheritance rights: *Adoption: the future* Cm. 2288 (1993), para. 5.21. The Scottish executive has also considered such as scheme *op. cit.* paras 2.25–2.42.

[46] cl. 110 adding Children Act 1989, s.4A.

[47] An unmarried partner could apply jointly with the parent for a residence order.

[48] Children Act 1989, s. 2(9).

[49] *Adoption: the future,* Cm. 2288 (1993), paras 5.24 *et seq.* No provision was made for this in the Draft Adoption Bill 1996.

[50] Select Committee on Health, Second Report on Health, Session 1997–8, *Children looked after by local authorities* (1998 H.C. 247); Performance and Innovation Unit, *Adoption Review* (2000).

[51] *Adoption—a new approach* (2000 Cm. 5017) paras 5.8–5.11.

exclude the local authority. The Adoption and Children Bill makes provision for special guardianship.[52] The order can be sought by anyone (except a parent or step-parent) over the age of 18 years who is a guardian, has a residence order, is entitled to apply for a residence without leave or has fostered the child for one year.[53] Others will be able to apply with leave or be granted the order without an application.[54] Couples seeking the order will not need to be married.[55] Despite the terminology there is little which a special guardian can do which is not available to a person with a residence order; special guardians may appoint a guardian, and can take the child abroad for up to three months without consulting others with parental responsibility.[56] The order may be revoked.[57] The attractiveness or otherwise of this order to foster carers is likely to depend on the provision local authorities make for financial and other support[58]; the Bill makes similar provision as for adoption support services but only creates rights to assessments, not to services.[59]

E. Local authorities

18–044 Before the implementation of the Children Act 1989, local authorities could obtain control over children either by obtaining a care order in court proceedings or administratively, by passing a "parental rights resolution" in relation to a child in voluntary care. The effects of these procedures were not identical and were, in some respects, obscure[60] but most aspects of a parent's parental responsibility were suspended. The Children Act 1989 abolished parental rights resolutions; it provides that a care order grants the local authority parental responsibility for the child without removing the parent's parental responsibility.[61] Local authorities can control parent's exercise of their parental responsibility but only to the extent necessary to safeguard and promote the child's welfare.[62] Similarly,

---

[52] cl. 113 adding new sections 14A–14G to the Children Act 1989.

[53] s. 14A(2)–(5).

[54] s. 143(b) and 6(b).

[55] Children are said to be confused by arrangements whereby one foster carer adopts them and this person's partner obtains a residence order: BAAF evidence to the Select Committee on the Adoption and Children Bill, May 1, 2001 (2001 H.C 431 ii), p. 43. Adoption by unmarried couples is being debated, see Chap. 22, below.

[56] s. 14C. If the child is of school age such a trip would exceed the permissible period of holiday absence. They cannot change the child's name or agree to adoption. For a comparison of the two arrangements see the discussion parental responsibility held by more than one person.

[57] s.14D and see below.

[58] Evidence to the Select Committee on the Adoption and Children Bill, (2001 H.C 431) April 24, 2001 p.22 (BASW); May 1, 2001, p. 35 (BAAF).

[59] Adoption and Children Bill 2002, cl.113 adding Children Act 1989, ss.14F and 14G.

[60] Review of Child Care Law: Discussion Paper 4, *Compulsory admissions to care and parental rights resolutions* (1985); Child Care Act 1980, ss.4, 10. There was no clear provision regarding the child's intestacy, change of name or consent to marriage after a resolution. The procedure was heavily criticised: Second Report of Social Services Committee (1983–4), *Children in Care* (H.C.P. 360), paras 131–143.

[61] s.33(3). Existing parental rights resolutions and orders committing children to care under the inherent jurisdiction became deemed care orders; Sched. 14, para. 15.

[62] s.33(3)(b),(4); the local authority cannot prevent the parents making a parental responsibility agreement: *Re X. (Parental Responsibility Agreement: Children in Care)* [2000] 1 F.L.R. 517, FD.

an emergency protection order grants the applicant parental responsibility, although its exercise is restricted by statute and regulations.[63]

V. WHERE PARENTAL RESPONSIBILITY IS HELD BY MORE THAN ONE PERSON

18–045 None of the methods of acquiring parental responsibility outlined above, except adoption and parental orders, automatically removes parental responsibility but care orders discharge residence orders.[64] It therefore follows that parental responsibility may be held simultaneously by a number of people. Where this is so, the Act provides some guidance about what each may do and permits any dispute, except some involving children in care or awaiting adoption,[65] to be determined by the court, applying the welfare principle.

The Law Commission thought that it was essential for individuals with parental responsibility to be able to act independently in order to prevent one person from making it more difficult for another to care for a child.[66] A legal duty to consult was undesirable and unworkable; the child could suffer if decisions were delayed or inhibited by the need to obtain consent. The Children Act 1989 provides that where more than one person has parental responsibility each of them may act alone except where the consent of all is specifically required.[67] But this approach was criticised for undermining the parental responsibility of parents who do not have care of the child.[68] It has been emphasised that parents should not be seeking to interfere while they do not have care of the child.[69] However, the courts have begun to identify a small group of important decisions which require the agreement of both parents or the court.[70] Also, it has been asserted that parental responsibility confers a right to be consulted or informed about important steps such as sending a child to boarding school.[71]

---

[63] Children Act 1989, s.44(4)(c). The local authority may take over the order: Emergency Protection Order (Transfer of Responsibility) Regulations 1991, S.I. 1991 No. 1414.

[64] Children Act 1989, s. 91(2); residence orders discharge care orders, s.91(1).

[65] The court may not make any s.8 order, other than a residence order in respect of a child who is in care. Contact can be dealt with under s.34 but other disputes must be brought within the complaints system under s.26. Similarly under the Adoption and Children Bill 2002 where an adoption agency is authorised to place a child for adoption only disputes about contact can be referred to the court, cl. 26.

[66] See Law Com. No. 172, para. 2.10. The former law was unclear and inconsistent: the Guardianship Act 1973, s.1(1) allowed married parents to do so but the Children Act 1975, s.85(3) only permitted one of "joint" holders of a parental right to act alone if the other had not signified disapproval.

[67] s.2(7).

[68] Bainham (1990) 53 *M.L.R.* 206 at 217–218.

[69] *D. v. D. (Shared Residence Order)* [2001] 1 F.L.R. 495, CA *per* Hale L.J. at para. 23.

[70] *Re J. (Specific Issue Orders: Child's Religious Upbringing and Circumcision)* [2000] 1 F.L.R. 571, CA *per* Butler Sloss P. at 577. These include name change and non-therapeutic circumcision; and see Maidment [2001] *Fam. Law* 518. But Eekelaar [2001] *Fam. Law* 426, 430 argues strongly that there should be no duty to consult on any matter.

[71] *Re G. (Parental Responsibility: Education)* [1994] 2 F.L.R 964, CA, *per* Glidewell L.J. but no authority or reasoning was given.

In contrast, where the local authority looks after[72] a child, it has a duty to consult parents and people with parental responsibility about all decisions unless this is not reasonably practicable.[73] The local authority has power to determine how the parents may exercise their parental responsibility in relation to a child in care[74] which it may use to avoid consultation that would be contrary to the child's welfare.[75] Given that the European Court of Human Rights applies strict scrutiny to restrictions on family life which go beyond the removal of the child from the parent's care[76] such a decision must be exceptional.

Placement for adoption, freeing and adoption require the agreement of all parents and guardians but not other people with parental responsibility or a local authority.[77] A special guardian will be entitled to exercise parental responsibility to the exclusion of all others (except the other special guardian) unless the decision requires the consent of more than one person with parental responsibility.[78] Children who wish to marry under the age of 18 require the consent of all parents and guardians and the local authority if it has parental responsibility. But if there is a residence order, the consent required is that of the person with whom the child lives under the order.[79] Both changing a child's name and removing a child from the United Kingdom for more than four weeks require the consent of all persons with parental responsibility.[80] Where consent is not forthcoming the court may approve the proposed action.[81] The Act also restricts decisions where there is a court order; no one may act incompatibly with an order even though they have parental responsibility.[82] However, it is not clear whether limitations on behaviour have to be explicit or can be inferred from the circumstances.[83] But there is a power to impose detailed conditions in section 8

---

[72] Children Act 1989, s.22(1), the local authority duty applies both where it has a care order and where it only accommodates the child.

[73] Children Act 1989, s.22(4), see below, Chap. 22.

[74] Children Act 1989, s.33(3); Eekelaar was highly critical of the decision to allow parents to retain parental responsibility when there was a care order [1989] New L.J. 217 at 760, and Chap. 22, below.

[75] *Re P. (Children Act 1989, ss.22 and 26: Local Authority Compliance)* [2000] 2 F.L.R. 910, FD.

[76] *Johansen v. Norway* (1996) 23 E.H.R.R. 33, para. 64. Where the child is disturbed by the an abusive parent being consulted it should be possible for the local authority to show that its actions are necessary.

[77] Adoption Act 1976, s.16(1) (Adoption and Children Bill 2002, cll. 19 and 47); Children Act 1989, ss.12(3), 33(6). But the Bill provides that where one parent has given consent for the child's placement, the other parent is treated as having also given consent if he only acquired parental responsibility at a later date, cl.52(10).

[78] Children Act 1989, s. 14C to be added by Adoption and Children Bill 2002, cl.113(1).

[79] Marriage Act 1949, s.3(1A) added by Children Act 1989, Sched. 12. This provision is to be further amended: see Adoption and Children Bill 2002, Sched. 3, paras 1–5. Even if the residence order expired when the child reached the age of 16, s.3(1A)(d). Special guardians will also be able to consent to marriage without reference to others unless there is a care order, residence order or placement order.

[80] Children Act 1989, s.13(1); (the period is three months if the removal is by a special guardian, s.14C(4). This applies to name change even where there is no residence order: *Re PC. (Change of Name)* [1997] 2 F.L.R. 730 FD.

[81] Children Act 1989, s.13(1), (3); the welfare test applies; see below, Chap. 20.

[82] Children Act 1989, s.2(8). There are penalties for breach of a residence order under the Magistrates' Courts Act 1980, s.63(3); Children Act 1989, s.14. See Chap. 19, below.

[83] The Law Commission gave the example of a non-residential father arranging to have the child's hair done in a way which would lead to the child's exclusion from the school selected by the

orders on parents and persons with parental responsibility.[84] Where the residential parent dies and appoints a guardian the Act gives no indication whether the guardian or the surviving parent is entitled to care for the child. Either may wish to impose new arrangements.[85] Despite these provisions the fact that two or more estranged parties have parental responsibility for the child is likely to increase the opportunities for dispute rather than resolve problems.

VI. REVOCATION OF PARENTAL RESPONBSIBILITY

18–046 The parental responsibility of mothers and married fathers is only terminated by adoption[86] but in all other cases the court may remove parental responsibility on application of a person with parental responsibility or, with leave, the child.[87] In order to enhance their security, there are further restrictions on the revocation of special guardianship. Parents and guardians need leave to apply for revocation and cannot seek leave within an year of the order; leave can only be granted if there has been a significant change of circumstances.[88] The court may also terminate guardianship and special guardianship of its own motion.[89] Parental responsibility is only brought to an end in extreme cases:—

> In *Re P. (Terminating Parental Responsibility)*[90] the parents made a section 4 agreement after the baby had been removed by the local authority because of severe injuries. Subsequently it became clear that the father had caused the injuries. The mother successfully applied for the agreement to be ended. The father had forfeited responsibility[91]; a court would not have granted a section 4 order had it been aware of the facts, and to allow the father to retain parental responsibility could be unsettling for the mother and foster carers.

---

mother: Law Com. No. 172, para. 2.11. Unless there is a detailed order the court may be unwilling to hold that there is a breach.

[84] Children Act 1989, s.11(7)(b); *Re O. (A Minor) (Contact: Imposition of Conditions)* [1995] 2 F.L.R. 124; *Re T. (A Minor) (Care Order: Conditions)* [1994] 2 F.L.R. 423 where a condition was included that the father should not share a bed with the child.

[85] The Law Commission thought that the onus should be on "the person wishing to challenge existing arrangements" *ibid.* para. 2.28. Bainham argues that this does not make sense and is predicated on an assumption that the non-residential parent should not resume care, see [1990] *Fam. Law* 192, 195. It would also seem contrary to the parental preference expressed by the Court of Appeal in *Re K. (A Minor)(Ward: Care and Control)* [1990] 1 W.L.R. 431.

[86] Adoption Act 1976, s.12(3); Adoption and Children Bill 2002, cl.46(2).

[87] Children Act 1989, ss.4(3), 4A(3) (to be added by the Adoption and Children Bill 2002, cl.110), 5(7), 91(1),(2). A power to revoke was recommended by the Law Commission which thought that the ability to remove the father's powers might make the courts less reluctant to grant orders: Law Com. No. 157, para. 3.3.

[88] Children Act 1989, s.14D(5),(6).

[89] ss.5(1), (2), 14D(2). A local authority with a care order could seek the removal of the child's guardian: *Guidance,* Vol. 1, para. 2.21 or the court could do this when making a care order in relation to the child.

[90] [1995] 1 F.L.R. 1048.

[91] at 1053, *per* Singer J.

VII. RIGHTS OF THOSE WITHOUT PARENTAL RESPONSIBILITY

A. Delegation

18–047 A parent cannot transfer or surrender parental responsibility by private agreement,[92] but it is common for parents to arrange with others, such as child minders or teachers, for some parental responsibilities to be exercised by them. The Law Commission thought that such arrangements should be recognised in order to encourage separated parents to make agreements and to assist those who looked after children during parental absence. Such agreements should not be irrevocable; no court would uphold an agreement which was contrary to the child's welfare and the onus of bringing a case to court should not be with the parents.[93] The Children Act 1989 enacted these proposals. People with parental responsibility may arrange for all or some of their responsibilities to be met by others, but such agreements do not affect liability for failure to discharge parental responsibility.[94]

B. De facto carers

18–048 The Law Commission also sought to clarify the position of those without parental responsibility who were actually caring for a child.[95] The Children Act 1989, s.3(5) now provides that any person with care of the child but without parental responsibility may "do what is reasonable in all the circumstances of the case for the purpose of safeguarding or promoting the child's welfare." What is reasonable will depend on the circumstances. Where parents have indicated the course of action they approve: a haircut, dental treatment or participation in an adventure holiday, there should be little difficulty; similarly where the child needs immediate (and non-controversial) treatment because of an accident. Problems are likely to arise where the parents oppose action which, objectively, could be seen to be in the child's interests—for example a child accommodated by the local authority remaining with foster parents.[96] Even if it is unlawful for the foster parent to refuse to hand over the child until the following morning, it is not clear that the parents would have any redress.[97] Also, it may be difficult for carers to convince a doctor that they have sufficient authority to consent to medical treatment which may be desirable but is not essential, such as vaccina-

---

92 Originally a common law rule; see now Children Act 1989, s.2(9).

93 Law Com. No. 172, paras 2.13, 2.14.

94 s.2(9), (10), (11).

95 Law Com. No. 172, para. 2.16. Such a person could be liable under the general law of crime or tort but their powers were unclear: Bevan, paras 9.48–9.55, 10.25.

96 The Children Act 1989 removed the former requirement to give notice and the Government resisted all attempts of reintroduction because this would undermine the voluntary nature of local authority accommodation. However, the Lord Chancellor asserted that s.3(5) could justify the refusal to hand over a child late at night or to an incapable parent, *per* Lord Mackay, Lord Chancellor, *Hansard,* H.L., Vol. 502, col. 1337.

97 The foster parent might commit an offence under the Child Abduction Act 1984, s.2 but the parent has apparently no cause of action in damages see *F. v. Wirral M.B.C* [1991] Fam. 69. A limited interference to protect a child would probably not breach the parents' Art. 8 rights.

tion.[98] Those caring for children may have Article 8 rights even if they have no formal relationship with them[99] and therefore must be consulted in plans that any public authority makes in relation to the child.[1]

C. Unmarried fathers

18–049 Where an unmarried father does not have parental responsibility the law does not treat him as a stranger to his child; he is a parent within the meaning of any post 1987 statute. Thus, he does not require leave to seek an order giving him parental responsibility or any section 8 order.[2] Where his child is looked after by the local authority he has some rights to be involved. There is a qualified duty to ascertain every father's wishes and feelings,[3] if there are care proceedings he must be notified unless the court directs otherwise[4] and where his child is subject to a care order the authority must allow him reasonable contact.[5] However, his consent is not required for adoption arrangements[6] and he has no statutory right be notified of the adoption proceedings unless he is maintaining the child.[7] Nevertheless, the adoption agency must record the father's wishes and feelings about the adoption unless this is not practicable,[8] and courts have ruled that fathers who might be able to claim Article 8 rights[9] in respect of their child should be notified of the adoption.[10] Fathers should only be excluded if they could not claim rights to family life or where this extreme measure is proportionate to the risk to the mother or child posed by informing them.

---

[98] Home Office Circular 54/1991 advises the police that s.3(5) can be used to authorise a medical examination for a child in police protection under Children Act 1989, s. 46.

[99] *K. and T. v. Finland* [2001] 2 F.L.R. 707 at para. 150 (a man who was the unmarried partner of the mother and father of her younger child was held to have Art. 8 rights also in relation to her older child).

[1] Children Act 1989, s.22(4)(d) can be interpreted to allow this.

[2] Children Act 1989, s.10(4)(a).

[3] Children Act 1989, s.22(4)(b); see below, Chap. 22.

[4] Family Proceedings Rules 1991, rr. 4.4(3), 4.8(8); *Re X. (Care: Notice of Proceedings)* [1996] 1 F.L.R. 186. He need not be made a party to those proceedings: *Re P. (Care Proceedings: Father's Application to be Joined as a Party)* [2001] 1 F.L.R. 781, FD.

[5] Children Act 1989, s.34(1) unless there is a court order limiting his contact, see Chap 22, below.

[6] Adoption Act 1976, ss.16, 18 and 72; Adoption and Children Bill 2002, cl. 52(6).

[7] Adoption Rules 1984 (1984 S.I. No 265), rr.2(2), 15(2)(a)(h); *Re C. (Adoption: Parties)* [1995] 2 F.L.R. 483, CA.

[8] Adoption Rules 1984 (1984 S.I. No 265), rr.4(4) 22 and Sched. 2.

[9] This requires more than a genetic link: *Keegan v. Ireland* (1994) 18 E.H.R.R. 342 and above para. 17–013.

[10] *Re R. (Adoption: Father's Involvement)* [2001] 1 F.L.R. 302, CA; *Re M. (Adoption: Rights of Natural Father)* [2001] 1 F.L.R. 745, FD (notification not required); *Re H.; Re G. (Adoption: Consultation of Unmarried Fathers)* [2001] 1 F.L.R. 646, FD (notification for H but not G).

CHAPTER NINETEEN

COURT PROCEEDINGS

I. INTRODUCTION

19–001 Before 1989 incremental statutory and case-law developments produced a complex system where three separate levels of court (magistrates' courts, county courts and the High Court) had jurisdiction over various issues concerning children, and sometimes were required to apply different criteria. Most of the desired remedies were available but a single court might not be able to hear all relevant issues together; court procedures differed between the three levels of court and the effect of the orders depended on the powers under which they were made.[1] Particularly, the powers to make and the effects of orders in "public law" cases involving local authorities exercising their responsibilities to protect children and in "private law" cases where family members disputed the upbringing of a child did not correspond even though individual cases might involve both sets of issues. These problems were widely recognised; a number of organisations and committees had called for the creation of a unified Family Court,[2] which would have jurisdiction over all matters concerning children. Proposals had also been made to simplify procedure in matrimonial cases with a view to reducing disputes and cutting costs.[3]

The *Review of Child Care Law*[4] focused on changes in the care system including so called "public law" proceedings through which children might be committed to the care of a local authority by the courts.[5] It wanted to make these more like ordinary civil proceedings in which parents had the right to play a full part and evidence was disclosed in advance.[6] If a family court were not introduced there needed to be a system for transferring complex cases from the magistrates' court to the higher courts, powers to enable local authorities to intervene in "private law" disputes and jurisdicton to make "private law" orders, (such as custody orders) in care proceedings.[7] The Law Commission considered the reform of the "private law" relating to children. It wanted to create a framework which would recognise and encourage the continuation of beneficial relationships between the child, the parents and other significant adults; to ensure that where parental responsibility was divided or shared the people concerned could understand their position; and to see that the allocation

---

[1] For a detailed account of the problems see the 4th edition of this book, Chaps. 14–17.

[2] See below, para. 19–005.

[3] Report of the Matrimonial Causes Procedure Committee (1985) (Booth Report), p. 2.

[4] (1985). For a discussion of the role of the Review in the reform of child law see below.

[5] For a detailed discussion see Chap. 22, below.

[6] Review of Child Care Law (1985), paras 3.23, 3.33.

[7] Review of Child Care Law (1985), Chap. 23.

of power by the law reflected a state of affairs which was workable and sensible.[8] The Commission was also concerned that[9] orders relating to children should have the same effect irrespective of the court making them and the proceedings in which they were made.[10]

The Children Act 1989 did not create a unified Family Court but it reformed the magistrates court, giving the "family proceedings court"[11] jurisdiction over all civil matters concerning the upbringing of children[12] with the exception of matters such as sterilisation which could only be determined under the inherent jurisdiction of the High Court.[13] It also established a system whereby cases could be transferred between courts to make better use of court resources, so that higher courts dealt with more complex disputes and to allow all proceedings concerning a child to be heard together.[14] The Act created four orders relating to children. These are the residence order which states where the child should live; the contact order which requires a carer to allow someone to have contact with the child; the prohibited steps order which restricts the exercise of parental responsibility; and the specific issue order which determines how parental responsibility is to be exercised.[15] Together these are known as "section 8" orders. It also provides for any of these orders to be made in any family proceedings.[16] Orders may be made with or without an application[17] but the court should not impose the responsibility for children on individuals who have not sought it.[18] The power to make these orders can be exercised in the family proceedings courts, county courts or the High Court either alongside other matters such as domestic violence injunctions or divorce proceedings or alone. The High Court's inherent jurisdiction (which includes wardship) now has a residual role.[19]

In the decade since the implementation of the Children Act 1989 there have been some further changes. Although the Civil Procedure Rules do not generally apply to family proceedings, the principles behind them—court control and reducing delay—were entrenched in the procedure introduced by the Act.[20] The

---

[8] Law Com. W.P. 96, paras 3.7–3.8.
[9] Law Com. No. 172, paras 1.7–1.9.
[10] Law Com. No. 172, paras 6.2–6.13.
[11] Children Act 1989, s.92.
[12] Children (Allocation of Proceedings) Order 1991, S.I. 1991 No. 1677.
[13] *Re B. (A Minor) (Sterilisation)* [1988] A.C. 199.
[14] Children Act 1989, s.92 and Sched.11; Children (Allocation of Proceedings) Order 1991, S.I. 1991 No. 1677 as amended by S.I. 1994 No. 2164; S.I. 1994 No. 3138; S.I. 1995 No. 1649; S.I. 1997 No. 1897; S.I. 2001 No. 775. For a list of courts with jurisdiction in Children Act cases see Hershman and McFarlane *Handbook*.
[15] Children Act 1989, s.8, see below.
[16] Children Act 1989, s.8(3), (4); see below.
[17] Children Act 1989, s.10(1) (2). But there must be proceedings: *Re C. (Contact: Jurisdiction)* [1995] 1 F.L.R. 777, CA. An order for contact made when a child was freed for adoption could not be varied by the court using the power under s.10(1) but the High Court could do so under its inherent powers.
[18] *Re K. (Care Order or Residence Order)* [1995] 1 F.L.R. 675.
[19] See below, paras 19–045 *et seq.* Wardship has a number of advantages: *Re W. (Wardship: Discharge: Publicity)* [1995] 2 F.L.R. 466, CA; J. Mitchell [2001] *Fam. Law* 130–134, 212–216.
[20] Civil Procedure Rules 1998, S.I. 1998 No. 3132; they apply subject to modification to committal applications arising out of family proceedings: *President's Direction* [2001] 1 F.L.R. 949; *Practice Direction (Case Management)* [1995] 1 F.L.R. 456.

work of the family courts was originally overseen by the Children Act Advisory Committee; in 1997 this body was replaced by the Advisory Board on Family Law whose main function was to promote a multi-disciplinary approach to the implementation of the Family Law Act.[21] The decision not to implement the 1996 Act lead to the closure of the Board and discussions about an inter-disciplinary structure for the family justice system.[22] In April 2001, the Children and Family Court Advisory and Support Service (CAFCASS) was established by bringing together the the staff and responsibilities of the probation service in private law proceedings, guardian *ad litem* panels for public law proceedings and the child section of the Official Solicitor's Department, to provide welfare reporting and other support services for family proceedings.[23]

II. COURT PROCEEDINGS—THE PRINCIPLES

19–002 Three guiding principles, introduced to make the operation of the law consistent and intelligible[24] apply to proceedings under the Children Act 1989.

A. The welfare principle

This is discussed in detail in the following Chapter.

B. The "no order" principle

19–003 The Law Commission took the view that orders were not always necessary and should only be used where they were the most effective way of helping the child not just as "part of the package." Orders could polarise parent's roles and alienate them; "joint custody" arrangements appeared to provide the maximum opportunity for maintaining the child's relationship with both parents and could be achieved without an order.[25] Removing the need for an order could encourage the parties to reach agreement and make it clear that where they do so the court is not free to impose its view on them.[26] It would also reflect the belief that compulsory intervention by local authorities should not be used where services would be accepted voluntarily.[27] The Government was also concerned to reduce

---

[21] Responsibility for a strategic overview of Children Act matters was given to the Children Act Sub-Committee of the Advisory Board: Advisory Board on Family Law, *First Annual Report 1997–8*, para. 1.10.

[22] Lord Chancellor's Department, *Promoting inter-agency working in the family justice system* (2002).

[23] See below para. 19–008.

[24] *An Introduction to the Children Act 1989* (1990), paras 3.1, 3.13.

[25] Law Com. No. 172, para. 3.2; Law Com. W.P. 96, paras 4.35–4.43.

[26] Law Com. No. 172, paras 3.3–4. Where there are "family proceedings" the court may make orders relating to children even though no applications have been made, Children Act 1989, s.10.

[27] It was not the intention of the legislation to require local authorities to demonstrate that voluntary agreements had failed: D.H., *Children Act Report 1992*, paras 2.20–21.

the number of applications concerning children after divorce because of the cost to the public purse.[28]

The Children Act 1989 provides that the court "shall not make the order or any of the orders unless it considers that doing so would be better for the child than making no order at all."[29] There are three[30] elements to this:— It is wrong in principle to make unnecessary orders;[31] no order is necessary if the parties can reach agreement;[32] and the court should begin with a preference for the least interventionist response.[33] Where the parents are not disputing the arrangements for children at divorce, the court will almost certainly take the view that there it should not make orders.[34] Guidance states that it is likely to be better to make an order where the court has had to resolve a dispute[35] but there is a strong preference in the courts for settlement over adjudication, consequently an order may be refused.[36]

Where there is no order between married parents the effect nearly equates to that under a shared residence order, both parents retain parental responsibility but their exercise of it is unrestricted.[37] In practice, because the parents are now living apart, they will need to agree on arrangements. If they can do so an order may be unnecessary.[38] But, in many cases, the confirmation of arrangements for

---

[28] See J. Eekelaar, *Regulating Divorce* (1991); *Funding Code* (2000) section 11; public funding is only available for litigation in family disputes where it has become clear that the matter cannot be resolved either through mediation or negotiation, see: Legal Services Commission, *The Funding Code Decision Making Guidance* (2001), para. 20.6.

[29] s.1(5). This does not apply to applications under Sched.1: *K. v. H. (Child Maintenance)* [1993] 2 F.L.R. 61.

[30] A fourth, the burden lies on the person seeking the order was stressed by Munby J. in *Re X. and Y. (leave to remove from the jurisdiction: no order principle)* [2001] 2 F.L.R. 118 but rejected by the Court of Appeal in *Re H. (Children: Residence Order: Condition)* [2001] 2 F.L.R. 1277, CA.

[31] A. Bainham, "Changing families and changing concepts—reforming the language of family law" [1998] *C.F.L.Q.* 1 stresses that the "no order" principle is about no unnecessary orders but it has been reconfigured by commentators (including himself) as the basis for a policy of non-intervention. Whether an order is necessary is not purely a matter of its legal effect: in *Royal Wolverhampton Hospitals NHS Trust v. B.* [2000] 1 F.L.R. 953 (following a breakdown of trust with her parents, the clarity of an order relating to treatment was in the child's best interests).

[32] But where an agreement has been achieved after difficult negotiations it may be counter productive for this not to be ratified by the court, see Phillimore and Drane [1999] *Fam. Law* 40.

[33] This fits with the notion of proportionality in E.C.H.R., Art. 8(2) see: *Re O. (Supervision Order)* [2001] 1 F.L.R. 923, 929, *per* Hale L.J.

[34] G. Douglas *et al.*, "Safeguarding children's welfare in non-contentious divorce: towards a new conception of legal process?" [2000] 63 *M.L.R.* 177.

[35] Guidance Vol. 1, para. 2.56. *cf. Re C. (A Minor) (Leave to Seek Section 8 Orders)* [1994] 1 F.L.R. 26. The specific effects of orders may be required, see below.

[36] Davis and Pearce [1999] *Fam. Law* 457; R. Bailey-Harris *et al.*, "Settlement culture and the use of the 'no order' principle" [1999] *C.F.L.Q.* 53 and see below, p. 567.

[37] Even where there is no residence order one parent may not change the child's name unilaterally: *Re PC. (Change of Surname)* [1997] 2 F.L.R. 730, 739 *per* Holman J. It is an offence under the Child Abduction Act 1984, s.1(1)–(3) for a parent to remove the child from the U.K. without the permission of the other. The fact that there is no order will affect the right to remove the child from local authority accommodation: s.20(8), (9); the right to consent to applications for residence and contact orders: s.10(5) (c); the effect of an appointment as guardian: s.5(7)–(9); the right to consent to marriage: Marriage Act 1949, s.3(1A) (b); and preclude action for enforcement.

[38] There is no general duty on one parent to consult the other: Children Act 1989, s.2(7); S. Maidment [2001] *Fam. Law* 518; A. Bainham, "The privatisation of the public interest in children" (1990) 53 *M.L.R.* 206 at 208–214. *Cf. Re G. (Parental Responsibility: Education)* [1994] 2 F.L.R. 964, CA.

public authorities responsible for housing or income support, and the clarification of the parties' respective roles may make an order desirable in the interests of the children.[39] Where the carer is not a parent a residence order is required to confer parental responsibility.[40]

There is a degree of tension between the "no order" principle and the welfare principle[41]; focussing on section 1(5) may mean that insufficient attention is paid to children's interests. Interpreted as a principle of "non-intervention" it is used to avoid adjudication by coercing disputing parties to achieve settlement on the basis that agreements promote parental autonomy. This is quite different from what was originally intended[42] and fails to recognise the positive effect the authority of the court can have.[43] It is generally accepted that most children adjust best when they maintain contact with both their parents, but the "no order" principle may not help achieve this. The coercion of orders may be ineffective or counter-productive,[44] but the court's refusal to ratify agreements with orders may increase the likelihood of breakdown and delay the re-introduction of contact.[45] Initially the number of residence orders was far lower than that for the comparable orders before the Children Act 1989 because the courts no longer routinely made orders on parental divorce. Whether or not section 1(5) discouraged resort to the courts, there has been a steady rise in private law disputes about children over the last decade.[46]

C. The principle of no delay

19–004 The paramountcy of the child's welfare and the speed with which young children develop attachments mean that delay can determine the outcome of the dispute to the detriment of one of the parties[47]; protracted proceedings

---

[39] Law Com. No. 172, para. 3.2.

[40] *B. v. B. (A Minor) (Residence Order)* [1992] 2 F.L.R. 327. Johnson J. was prepared to overturn the magistrates' decision to refuse the order because the Education Authorities had been unwilling to accept the grandmother's signature and if medical treatment were necessary the grandmother could not give consent. Additionally he referred to the child's concern about the lack of stability and the mother's impulsive nature.

[41] A. Bainham, "Welfare & non-interventionism" [1990] *Fam. Law* 143, 145.

[42] Bailey-Harris *et al., op cit.*; A. Bainham, "Changing families and changing concepts" [1998] *C.F.L.Q.* 1.

[43] Drane and Phillimore [1999] *Fam. Law* 40. Some courts continue to make consent orders see Bailey Harris *et al.*, above n.36.

[44] In *M. v. M. (Defined Contact Application)* [1998] 2 F.L.R. 244, FD the court made an order of no order but recorded in it the parents' joint expectations about contact.

[45] In *S v. E (A Minor) (Contact)* [1993] *Fam. Law* 406 the magistrates refused a contact order because the parties had reached agreement but the mother failed to comply. It was 20 months before the father's appeal against the no order was heard.

[46] Davis and Pearce [1998] *Fam. Law* 614.

[47] See, *e.g. Stockport M.B.C. v. B. & L.* [1986] 1 F.L.R. 80 where the local authority took two years to bring the case to court by which time the child was settled with foster-carers; *Re C. (Change of Surname)* [1998] 2 F.L.R. 656, CA where the father was unable to obtain a specific issue order to change the child's name back to that on her birth registration because she was used to the new name.

mean uncertainty for the child and delay permanent placement.[48] It had long been argued that decision-making processes should take account of the child's sense of time.[49] The damage the uncertainty of litigation could do to children[50] and the existence of a legal culture where delay was acceptable[51] led the Law Commission to proposed that legislation should include a duty to minimise delay.

The law acknowledges that any delay is likely to prejudice the welfare of the child[52] and Article 6(1) of the European Convention on Human Rights protects the right to "a fair hearing within a reasonable time." Public authorities must exercise "exceptional diligence"[53] where delay may lead to the loss of family relationships. Solicitors who fail to take prompt action may be liable in negligence:—

> In *LR v. Witherspoon, Sanders and Bostridge*[54] when her baby was removed from her and placed with foster carers, the mother instructed her solicitors to "do anything to get my son back." The solicitors did nothing for a year during which time the local authority placed the child with prospective adopters. When the court heard the mother's applications for residence and contact it dismissed them because the child had spent 14 months (half his life) with prospective adopters. The judge described the solicitors' inaction as a "tragedy" and the mother brought an action in negligence.

The court is required to set a timetable for proceedings and set a return date at each hearing.[55] Legal representatives have a duty to ensure that cases are resolved with the minimum of delay.[56] But hearing a case where a party is unprepared can lead to unfairness.[57] Purposeful delay, for example to allow the completion of an assessment is to be encouraged[58] but where a care order is inevitable the court should not defer making its decision in order to supervise the local authority.[59] The lack of court and other resources particularly for long

---

[48] The practice of concurrent planning involves working simultaneously for rehabilitation and adoption: *Re D. & K. (Care Plan: Twin Track Planning)* [1999] 2 F.L.R. 872 but is not widely available.

[49] J. Goldstein *et al., Beyond the best interests of the Child* (1973), p. 40.

[50] Law Com. No. 172, paras 4.54–58; see also Booth Committee Report (1985), para. 4.133.

[51] M. Murch and L. Mills, *The Length of Care Proceedings,* Bristol University Centre for Socio-legal and Family Studies (1987), para. 3.3.6.

[52] Children Act 1989, s.1(2).

[53] *H. v. UK* (1987) 10 E.H.R.R. 95, para. 85.

[54] [2000] 1 F.L.R. 82, CA.

[55] F.P.R. 1991, rr. 4.14(2)(a), 4.15(2); F.P.C. 1991, rr. 14(2)(a), 15(2); Children Act 1989, s.32 for proceedings under Pt IV of the Act.

[56] CAAC, *Handbook of best practice in Children Act cases* (1997), p. 22–3.

[57] *Re B. and T.(Care Proceedings: Legal Representation)* [2001] 1 F.L.R. 485, CA. (It was not unfair to parents to proceed with a hearing after their lawyers had withdrawn *cf. P., C. and S. v. UK* delay was unfair to the children) app. no. 56547/00.

[58] *C. v. Solihull M.B.C.* [1993] 1 F.L.R. 290 at 304, *per* Ward J.

[59] *Re S (Case Order: Implementation of Case Plan) and others* [2002] 1 F.L.R. 815, HL on appeal from [2001] 2 F.L.R. 582, CA. The local authority's care plan must be appropriately specific to be tested by the parties *per* Lord Nicholls at para. 99.

hearings,[60] the arrangements for transferring cases to higher courts,[61] the complexity of cases, and the need to obtain expert evidence all contribute to the time taken to complete cases.[62] The emphasis on settlement is also a factor in delay; private law cases are repeatedly adjourned to provide opportunities for settlement, if this fails there will be a further wait for a welfare report.[63] On average public law cases take seven months in the family proceedings court and over 11 months in the county court or the High Court.[64] Firm judicial control and case management are required; there needs to be sufficient time allocated for the hearing and realistic timetabling, clear instructions should be given to experts and late requests for assessments should not be allowed to derail the timetable.[65]

Although it is accepted that there may be grave disadvantages for parents if a full care order is made while they are awaiting criminal proceedings on substantially the same facts,[66] the fact that there are criminal proceedings is not a reason to adjourn care proceedings. The court dealing with the care proceedings must consider the particular circumstances, recognise the danger of delay for the child and treat the child's welfare as paramount.[67]

III. THE FAMILY COURT SYSTEM

19–005 Although the shortcomings of the court system were well recognised and there was a powerful and prolonged campaign to create a unified family court,[68] such a court has not been established.[69] Instead, the existing resources of triple jurisdiction in the family proceedings court,[70] county courts and the High Court have

[60] Particularly judges and court accommodation: CAAC Report 1992/3, pp. 51–53, 83. Advocates should co-operate to produce accurate time estimates: *Practice Direction* [1994] 1 F.L.R. 108; *Re M.D. & T.D. (Minors) (Time Estimates)* [1994] 2 F.L.R. 336.

[61] Children (Allocation of Proceedings) Order 1991, S.I. 1991 No. 1677 as amended by S.I. 1994 No. 2164; S.I. 1994 No. 3138; S.I. 1995 No. 1649; S.I. 1997 No. 1897; S.I. 2001 No. 775. There appears to be little scope for lateral transfer to avoid delay: CAAC Report 1992/3, p. 48.

[62] Booth J., *Avoiding delay in Children Act cases* (1996); LCD, *Scoping Study on Delay* (2002).

[63] Bailey-Harris *et al.*, above n. 36, p. 57–8.

[64] CAAC Final Report 1997, Tables 5A and 5B. There has been a steady increase in the duration of proceedings in the higher courts since the Act was implemented.

[65] Following Dame Margaret Booth's report on delay the President issued guidance to Family Court Business Committees, see: CAAC Final Report 1997, Chap 2, annex A.

[66] *Re S. (Care Order: Criminal Proceedings)* [1995] 1 F.L.R. 151 at 153 *per* Butler-Sloss L.J., CA.

[67] *Re TB. (Care Proceedings: Criminal Trial)* [1995] 2 F.L.R. 801, CA; *R. v. Exeter Juvenile Court ex p. H. and H.* [1988] 2 F.L.R. 214 at 222B *per* Stephen Brown P.

[68] See Finer Report, Chaps. 13 & 14; B. Hoggett, "Family courts and family law reform—which should come first" (1986), 6 *Legal Studies* 1. Such courts were introduced in Australia and New Zealand in the 1970's. Apart from the question of resources, the lack of agreement about the form of a family court inhibited its development: see M. Murch, *Justice and Welfare in Divorce* (1980), p. 235.

[69] The Lord Chancellor stated that he hoped his speech introducing the Children Bill "redeemed his pledge to make a statement about the Family Court" but also that the Bill was not a "substitute for the Family Court . . . or . . . laying foundations for it" *per* Lord Mackay, *Hansard* H.L. Vol. 502, cols. 495 and 537–538 (Children Bill, Second Reading).

[70] A part of the magistrates' court, Children Act 1989, s.92(1).

been developed to provide a system of concurrent jurisdiction. Comparable procedures operate for all Children Act proceedings.[71] The courts have similar powers.[72]

There is not only a specialist division of the High Court, the Family Division, all family courts are specialist courts. Those who preside over them have been specially selected[73] and given training in matters such as child development and social work practice to ensure that they have "a firm commitment to the ideals and philosophy" of the Act.[74] County courts are divided into four categories: non-divorce county courts, divorce county courts, family hearing centres and care centres. Of these only care centres can hear all types of case and family hearing centres can hear contested private law cases.[75]

A system of allocating and transferring cases between the three tiers of court was devised to make full use of existing resources rather than reflect the gravity of the issue, and to leave as many cases as possible to the lower courts. It was expected that about 75 per cent of public law cases would be heard in the family proceedings court.[76] This appears to be the case although proportions vary widely.[77] Public law applications must usually be made to the family proceedings court.[78] However, the right of the applicant to select the tier of court for a private law application remains. Cases can be transferred to the tier most

---

[71] Family Proceedings Rules 1991, S.I. 1991 No. 1247, as amended by S.I. 1992 No. 2067; S.I. 1994 Nos 808, 2165 and 3155; S.I. 1997 No. 1893; S.I. 2001 No. 821 for the High Court and County Court; Family Proceedings Courts (Children Act 1989) Rules 1991, S.I. 1991 No. 1395, as amended by S.I. 1992 No. 2068; S.I. 1994 Nos 809, 2166 and 3156; S.I. 1997 No. 1895; S.I. Nos 615 and 818 for the family proceedings court. These rules are not identical but the Children Act Advisory Committee stated that procedure between the various tiers of courts should be consistent: CAAC Report 1992/3, p. 36. The same forms are used in all courts. For the current wording of the rules see Hershman and McFarlane, *Handbook,* Pt II.

[72] The President of the Family Division has indicated that certain matters should only be dealt with in the High Court: *Practice Direction* [1993] 1 W.L.R. 313 (applications by children for leave); *Re H.I.V. (Tests) (note)* [1994] 2 F.L.R. 116 (AIDS tests); *Re S. (A Minor) (Contact: Contact Order)* [1993] 2 F.C.R. 234 (contact after adoption); *Re L. (A Minor) (Removal from the Jurisdiction)* [1993] *Fam. Law* 280; *Re G. (Adoption: Illegal Placement)* [1995] 1 F.L.R. 403; *Practice Direction* [1994] 1 F.L.R. 110 (adoption of children from overseas); *Practice Direction* [2000] 2 F.L.R. 429 (proceedings seeking a declaration of incompatibility under the Human Rights Act 1998).

[73] Under the Courts and Legal Services Act 1990, s.9 the Lord Chancellor has power to "nominate" judges for public and private family proceedings; see also: *Practice Direction Family Proceedings (Allocation to judiciary directions)* [1999] 2 F.L.R. 799. The non-availability of a judge with the relevant standing and ticket is one reason for delay, Booth Report (1996), paras 2.2 *et seq.*

[74] CAAC Report 1991/2, pp. 10–11.

[75] CAAC Report 1991/2, p. 12. This rationalisation means that parties may have to travel a considerable distance to court. For the distribution of care centres and family hearing centres see: CAAC Final Report 1997, pp. 10–11. From October 2001 only county courts which are adoption centres can hear county court adoption applications: President of the Family Division, *Adoption proceedings—a new approach* (2001). This guidance does not apply to family proceedings courts.

[76] CAAC Report 1992/3, p. 46.

[77] For statistics on the distribution between levels of court see: CAAC Final Report 1997, App. 2. In 1996 over 80% of public law but only about 30% of private law applications were made to the family proceedings court, just over 20% of public law cases were transferred to county court care centres.

[78] Children (Allocation of Proceedings) Order 1991, S.I. 1991 No. 1677, arts. 3, 4.

suited to their complexity,[79] or to enable matters to be consolidated[80] either on the application of a party or by the court itself.[81] Thus a mother's application to discharge a care order and a father's for a parental responsibility order can be heard at the same time as the local authority's application to terminate contact. Where these cases involved contested medical evidence or other complicating factors they are likely to be heard in the county court. If the court refuses the transfer the applicant may appeal.[82] There have been some difficulties determining which cases should be transferred; transfer contributes to delay.[83]

The family courts are expected to play an active part in the proceedings, not merely act as umpires between the parties.[84] They must control their proceedings by setting timetables and giving directions about matters such as the assessment of the child,[85] the appointment of experts[86] and the filing of witness statements. They may make orders without any application from a party.[87] The court has the power to determine the form of the hearing, including whether there is an oral hearing[88] but the process must be fair within the European Convention on Human Rights, Art. 6(1). The fact that there is a presumption that proceedings will be held in private does not conflict with Article 6(1)[89]; nothing must be done in secret.[90]

19–006 Proceedings under the Children Act 1989 are said not to be adversarial[91] but it is less clear what this means. The parties and their representatives often treat proceedings as a contest regarding cases and even children as won or lost.[92] In most[93] public law proceedings the child is represented by a children's guardian,

---

[79] Children (Allocation of Proceedings) Order 1991, art. 7(1) (a) (from magistrates' to county court), art. 11 (from county court to magistrates' court), art. 12 (from county court to the High Court), art. 13 (from High Court to county court); *Practice Direction* [1992] 1 W.L.R. 586 (other family proceedings). Hearings of up to three days can take place in the family proceedings court: CAAC Final Report 1997, p. 44

[80] Children (Allocation of Proceedings) Order 1991, art. 7(1) (b).

[81] *ibid.* arts. 7(1), 11,12, 13. In a small study of transfers in 1993 43% occurred on the court's motion; 6% were opposed: CAAC Report 1992/3, p. 105.

[82] S.I. 1991 No. 1677, art. 9 and Children (Allocation of Proceedings) (Appeals) Order 1991, S.I. 1991 No. 1801, art. 2.

[83] J. Brophy, C. Wale and P. Bates, *Myths and Practices* (1999).

[84] *An Introduction to the Children Act 1989* (1990), para. 1.51.

[85] F.P.R. 1991, rr. 4.14(2), 4.18; F.P.C. 1991, rr. 14(2), 18; for guidance see: CAAC Final Report 1997 Chap. 2, App. A.

[86] F.P.R. 1991, r. 4.14(2) (f); F.P.C. 1991, r. 14(2) (f); *Re CB and JB (Care Proceedings: Guidelines)* [1998] 2 F.L.R. 211, FD; experts should be told that the court has permitted their instruction, *Re A. (Family Proceedings: Expert Witnesses)* [2001] 1 F.L.R. 723, FD.

[87] Children Act 1989, s.10(1) even if no application could be made, *Gloucestershire C.C. v. P.* [1999] 2 F.L.R. 61, CA; but not without proceedings: *Re C. (Contact: Jurisdiction)* [1995] 1 F.L.R. 777 (children had been freed for adoption).

[88] *Re B. (Minors) (Contact)* [1994] 2 F.L.R. 1, CA; *Re B. (Contact: Stepfather's Opposition)* [1997] 2 F.L.R. 579, CA.

[89] F.P.R. 1991, r. 4.16(7); F.P.C. 1991, r. 16(7); *B. v. U.K.; P. v. U.K.* [2001] 2 F.L.R. 261.

[90] *Re CB and JB (Care Proceedings: Guidelines)* [1998] 2 F.L.R.211 at 224 *per* Wall J.

[91] *Oxfordshire C.C. v. M.* [1994] 1 F.L.R. 175 at 184, *per* Sir Stephen Brown P.; similar statements were made about care proceedings even in the 1970s: *Humberside C.C. v. D.P.R.* [1977] 1 W.L.R. 1251 at 1255, *per* Lord Widgery C.J.; see also *Re L. (Police Investigation: Privilege)* [1996] F.L.R. 731, HL at 738 and 743.

[92] See R. Ingleby, *Solicitors and Divorce* (1992), p. 99 and B. Lindley, *Families in Court* (1994) Family Rights Group. The practical effects of orders may make this inevitable.

[93] A children's guardian should be appointed in "specified proceedings": Children Act 1989, s.41(6) as extended by F.P.R. 1991, r. 4.2(2) and F.P.C. 1991, r. 2(2).

appointed by the court, whose duty it is to investigate the case, to advise the court about the available options and to safeguard the child's welfare in the proceedings.[94] In private law proceedings the court may appoint a children and family reporter from CAFCASS to investigate the circumstances and make recommendations.[95] Where a more thorough investigation is necessary the child can be joined as a party and represented by a guardian *ad litem*.[96] The court may order the disclosure of reports commissioned by a party,[97] call evidence,[98] obtain reports on any matter relevant to the welfare of the child,[99] and make orders of its own motion, but in practice, it remains essentially dependent on the parties.

The implementation of the Children Act 1989 was marked by a programme of training for social workers, the judiciary, medical professionals and others.[1] It was also recognised that the operation of the legislation would need monitoring so that difficulties arising from the changes could be tackled. The Children Act Advisory Committee was therefore established to advise the relevant government ministers and the President of the Family Division whether the Act's guiding principles were being achieved and the court system was operating satisfactorily.[2] Local committees were established at each care centre to deal with local issues and provide information to the centre. In 1997, this work was passed to the Advisory Board on Family Law but this body was wound up at the end of 2001 although a new interdisciplinary structure is being considered.[3]

IV. WELFARE SERVICES FOR THE COURTS

19–007 There are a number of reasons why courts dealing with disputes about the care of children need access to welfare services. The inquisitorial nature of the jurisdiction and particularly the duty to give paramount consideration to the welfare of children may require a wider understanding of family functioning and independent assessments of the child's needs or the carers' capacities which the parties have not provided and the court cannot obtain in the course of the hear-

---

[94] F.P.R. 1991, r. 4.11; F.P.C. 1991, r. 11 and see para. 22–051, below.

[95] Children Act 1989, s.7; F.P.R. 1991, r. 4.13; F.P.C. 1991, r. 13. These persons were formerly known as welfare officers.

[96] *Re N. (Residence: Appointment of a Solicitor: Placement with Extended Family)* [2001] 1 F.L.R. 1028, CA; *Re A. (Contact: Separate Representation)* [2001] 1 F.L.R. 715, CA. CAFCASS Legal should initially be approached in such cases: *CAFCASS Practice Note* [2001] 2 F.L.R. 151.

[97] *Oxfordshire C.C. v. M.* [1994] 1 F.L.R. 175; *Re L. (Police Investigation: Privilege)* [1996] 1 F.L.R. 731, HL. The court may also compel discovery of documents from the police or local authorities: *Re A. & B. (No. 2)* [1995] 1 F.L.R. 351, *per* Wall J.

[98] *Re A. & B. (Minors) (No. 2)* [1995] 1 F.L.R. 351; *Re DH. (A Minor) (Child Abuse)* [1994] 1 F.L.R. 679, this process enables all parties to cross-examine the witness.

[99] Children Act 1989, s.7(1); R.S.C. Ord. 40, *Re K. (Contact: Psychiatric Report)* [1995] 2 F.L.R. 432.

[1] J. Masson, "Implementing change for children: Action at the centre and local reaction" (1992) 19 J. Law and Society 320, the Department of Health budget for training material exceeded £500,000. See also CAAC Report 1993/4, p. 34.

[2] CAAC Report 1991/2, p. 5.

[3] CAAC Final Report 1997, p.7; LCD, *Promoting inter-agency working* (2002).

ing. The emphasis on settlement[4] necessitates services to assist the parties to negotiate and reduce conflict. The emotional, economic and social problems which family breakdown produces mean that those using the family courts may need advice and counselling.

Nevertheless until the establishment of CAFCASS (the Children and Family Court Advisory and Support Service) in April 2001 there was no single body dedicated to providing welfare services for the courts. In private law cases, reports, mediation and advice were provided by court welfare officers, employed by the Probation Service and jointly funded by local authorities and the Home Office. Family court work fitted poorly with the criminal justice functions of the Probation Service[5]; the proportion of resources for civil court work was limited and declining.[6] Specialist workers were often seconded from probation work and in some areas facilities were shared.[7] In public law cases, and in adoption, reports and representation were the responsibility of guardians *ad litem* and reporting officers who were members of local GALRO panels. Panels were funded by local authorities and the Department of Health, administered by local authorities or voluntary organisations,[8] and comprised of specialist child care social workers contracted to undertake the work.[9] There were concerns about the independence of the service because of funding and administration by local authorities who were parties to the proceedings in which guardians operated.[10] Advice for the court and representation for children in complex, public or private law cases in the High Court or county courts, was provided by the Official Solicitor's office under the Direction of the Lord Chancellor's Department.[11] Solicitors, and civil servants who were generally not qualified social workers, undertook these difficult cases.[12] This work was conducted alongside representa-

---

[4] R. Bailey-Harris *et al.* "Settlement culture and the use of the 'no order' principle" [1999] *C.F.L.Q.* 53; G. Davis and J. Pearce "A view from the trenches—practice and procedure in section 8 applications" [1999] *Fam. Law* 457.

[5] Home Office, *Joining forces to protect the public—consultation paper* (1998).

[6] *Thematic Inspection* (1997), p. 81; in 1995–6 family court welfare work received between 5.5% and 8.9% of the Probation Service budget. Financial restriction hampered development: Murch and Hooper (1992), p. 67.

[7] H.M. Inspectorate of Probation, *Family court welfare work—report of a thematic inspection* (1997), pp. 83–86. From 1996 new court welfare officers were required to attend six days of induction training relating to their work.

[8] Guardians *ad litem* and Reporting Officers (Panels) Regulations 1991, S.I. 1991 No. 2051; *Guidance* Vol. 7; D.H., *The guardian ad litem and reporting officer service annual reports 1994–5 (an overview)* (1995); J. Masson, "Representation of children in England" [2000] F.L.Q. 467. In 2000, there were 57 panels in England and Wales.

[9] Of the 860 guardians in 2000, only 113 were employed; *R. on application of Nagalro v. CAFCASS* [2002]1 F.L.R. 255, QBD.

[10] *R. v. Cornwall C.C., ex p. Cornwall guardians ad litem and reporting officers panel* [1992] 1 W.L.R. 427; CAAC Report 1992/3, p. 65. See also J. Masson and M. Shaw "The work of guardians ad litem" [1988] J.S.W.L. 164 at 180 and B. Lindley, *Families in Court* (1994), pp. 34–40.

[11] Supreme Court Act 1981, s.90; For a more detailed account of the work of the Official Solicitor see: 6th edition of this work, pp. 667–8.

[12] There were 4 solicitors and 57 other staff in the children section in 1998: D.H., H.O., L.C.D. and W.O., *Support services in family proceedings—future organisation of court welfare services—consultation paper* (1998), para. 1.17. Lack of social work qualification led to reliance on experts, particularly psychiatrists: J. Masson, "The Official Solicitor as the child's guardian ad litem under the Children Act 1989" (1992) 4 J.C.L. 58.

tion for mentally incapable adults, the administration of estates where there was no one else to do this, and the operation of the Child Abduction Unit.[13]

A. CAFCASS

19–008 In 1997, a joint review by the three government departments concluded that integrating services could improve provision and efficiency in welfare services for the courts. A consultation paper was issued[14]; the Advisory Board on Family Law welcomed the introduction of a unified service with a clear vision beyond the administrative "tidying-up" of existing services.[15] However, the extent to which practices would be aligned and staff would work in both public and private law remained unclear. Legislation[16] was introduced and a project team was established to prepare for the operation of the Children and Family Court Advisory and Support Service as a non-departmental public body accountable to the Lord Chancellor. Delays in the parliamentary process left too little time to complete the arrangements for CAFCASS. Consequently, many of the tasks essential to the smooth running of the new services had not been completed by April 2001. The organisations trubulations have been only too public[17]; permanent accommodation had not been found for staff, contractual arrangements had not been agreed with self-employed guardians *ad litem*[18] and new policies were not in place. Workers, particularly guardians, decided not to join CAFCASS leaving it with insufficient experienced workers to continue as before.

The functions of CAFCASS include to safeguard and promote the welfare of children in family proceedings, to give advice to the court about applications, to provide representation for children and to provide information, advice and other support services for children and their families.[19] These responsibilities are not limited to current proceedings and would allow it to provide advice to parents contemplating separation,[20] mediation services or contact centres.[21] To develop this work it needs further funding.[22] CAFCASS officers with new titles[23]

---

[13] Official Solicitor's Office, *Annual Report 1999–2000* (2000), p. 4; only about 20% of O.S. cases concern representation of children in family proceedings but this accounts for about half the workload, pp. 6–7.

[14] D.H., H.O., L.C.D. and W.O., *Support services in family proceedings—future organisation of court welfare services—consultation paper* (1998).

[15] Advisory Board on Family Law, *Second Annual Report* (1999), para. 3.6 and annex D; *Third Annual Report* (2000), para. 3.31.

[16] Criminal Justice and Court Services Act 2000, ss.11–17 and Sched. 2.

[17] Advisory Board on Family Law: Children Act Sub-committee, *Making contact work report* (2002), para. 1.17.

[18] Concerns were expressed by the Advisory Board on Family Law: *Fourth Annual Report* (2001), para. 2.76 *et seq.; R. on application of Nagalro v. CAFCASS* [2002] 1 F.L.R 255, QBD (the withdrawal of the self-employed contract held to be unlawful).

[19] Criminal Justice and Court Services Act 2000, s.12(1).

[20] For example running information meetings similar to those which were required under Family Law Act 1996, s.8: *Thematic Inspection* (1997), p. 77.

[21] Alternatively CAFCASS could make grants to organisations running such services under s.12(1). The Advisory Board on Family Law considered that contact centres would be integral to CAFCASS work: *Fourth Annual Report* (2001), para. 2.75.

[22] *Making contact work report* (2002), Chap. 6.

[23] Family Proceedings (Amendment) Rules 2001 (2001 S.I. No 821), r.15; *CAFCASS Practice Note* [2001] 2 F.L.R. 151. CAFCASS legal only accepts cases which are "exceptionally difficult,

now carry out the work previously undertaken by the three services; children and family reporters act in private law cases, children's guardians in public law cases and CAFCASS Legal Services has taken over the Official Solicitor's work for children in family proceedings. In practice, work has not been integrated, with separate public and private law teams in each of the 10 regions and CAF-CASS Legal Services based in London.

During private law proceedings, CAFCASS officers undertake two distinct functions at the request of the court. They meet the parties at the first directions hearing[24] to clarify issues in dispute, and where parties agree to this, mediate[25]; in cases which are not resolved, children and family reporters who have not been involved in mediation provide reports to the court.[26] Also they may be appointed to undertake Family Assistance Orders.[27] The role and function of children's guardians is discussed in Chapter 22. The Act enables CAFCASS officers to conduct litigation but only lawyers from CAFCASS Legal do so.[28] There is considerable scope for CAFCASS to develop a service that operates equally and to a consistently high standard throughout the country.[29]

B. Local authorities

19–009 Although CAFCASS undertakes the majority of work in family proceedings, the courts may request reports and seek assistance from local authorities.[30] They do this where there are child protection concerns or the local social services depart-

---

unusual or sensitive", where the O.S. acted previously. Private law cases where the child needs to be made a party are also taken: *Re A. (Contact: Separate Representation)* [2001] 1 F.L.R. 715, CA.

[24] Home Office, *National Standards for Probation Service Family Court Welfare Work* (1994), para. 2.1; *Thematic Inspection* (1997), p. 23 *et seq*.; Davis and Pearce [1999] *Fam. Law* 457 at 458.

[25] This is "other support" within Criminal Justice and Court Services Act 2000, s.12(1) (d). There was a statutory duty to undertake this work: Probation Rules 1984, S.I. 1984 No. 647, r. 35(1). The term mediation is preferred to conciliation: *National Standards* (1994), para. 3.2. The officer has roughly an hour to see if the parties can reach an agreement: M. Murch *et al., Safeguarding children's welfare in uncontentious divorce—report to the Lord Chancellor's Department* (1998), p. 162.

[26] Criminal Justice and Court Services Act 2000, s.12(1) (b); *National Standards* (1994), para. 1.9; Probation Rules 1984, S.I. 1984 No. 647, r. 35. Reports were requested in over 36,000 reports in 1997: D.H., H.O., L.C.D. and W.O., *Support services in family proceedings—future organisation of court welfare services—consultation paper* (1998), para. 1.14.

[27] Children Act 1989, s.16; *National Standards,* Chap. 5; and below para. 19–025.

[28] Criminal Justice and Court Services Act 2000, s.15; this provision was controversial; guardians and solicitors were concerned that it would be used to abolish the tandem system of representation where children's guardians appoint solicitors who act for the child in public law proceedings: Family Proceedings Rules 1991, r. 4.11A(1), 4.12(1) and see Chap. 22, below.

[29] The *Thematic Inspection* (1997) identified considerable differences in private law work. There is wide variation in practice in public law work see: J. Masson (2000) *op. cit.* CAFCASS must determine its own policies, policy issues are the responsibility of the CAFCASS Board. New draft National Standards have been prepared and are on www.cafcass.gov.uk

[30] Children Act 1989, ss.7, 16 and 37. There are no statistics about the number of cases handled by local authorities where they are not party to the proceedings. Family disputes which do not raise child protection concerns have low priority; local authorities are reluctant to take on work such as supervising contact see below para. 19–016. There is guidance relating to s.37 appointments: CAAC, *Handbook of best practice in Children Act cases* (1997) App. A.

ment is known to be working with the family.[31] Local authority social workers who provide court reports are termed "welfare officers".[32] This work forms only a small part of the work of local authority social services departments whose functions are discussed in Chapter 22.

Welfare reports

19–010 The court has complete discretion whether or not to call for a welfare report.[33] It must weigh the benefits of further information against the detriment of delaying the decision.[34] The decision to appoint a welfare officer should not be grounds for an appeal[35] but refusal to make an apointment might preclude a fair hearing.[36] In practice, extensive use is made of the power.[37] Reports are most likely to be ordered in contested cases.[38] When making the appointment the court may specify particular matters to be covered[39] but this does not preclude the inclusion of other issues. The officer preparing the report may pursue opportunities to help the parties to reach agreement but the role does not extend to dispute resolution.[40]

The section 7 reporter is "the eyes and ears of the judge"[41] and is required to inquire professionally and impartially into the circumstances.[42] Their role is to help the judge decide what is best for the child.[43] Children and family

---

[31] CAAC, *Handbook* (1997) App. AI, para. 10.

[32] Family Proceedings Rules 1991, r. 4.13. The duties are similar to those imposed on children and family reporters under r. 4.11B but there is no duty to inform the child of the content of the report.

[33] Children Act 1989, s.7; *Re W. (Welfare Reports)* [1995] 2 F.L.R. 142, C.A. Reports should not be ordered unless there is a live issue before the court, and only exceptionally following a written request from the parties: CAAC, *Handbook* (1997), App. AVI, para. 3.

[34] *Re H. (Minors) (Welfare Reports)* [1990] 2 F.L.R. 172; *Re C. (Section 8 Order: Court Welfare Officer)* [1995] 1 F.L.R. 617, CA. The *National Standards* require reports normally to be completed within 10 weeks (para. 4.28). Some courts allow longer but only half reports meet the 10 week deadline: *Thematic Inspection* (1997), Table 19.

[35] *Re W. (Welfare Reports)* [1995] 2 F.L.R. 142, CA.

[36] *Elsholz v. Germany* [2000] 2 F.L.R. 486 (a decision to dismiss an application for contact without seeking a report or holding a hearing has been held to breach E.C.H.R., Arts. 6(1) and 8).

[37] See above, n. 26.

[38] The Lord Chancellor stated at Committee Stage of the Children Bill that some sort of report would be required in "most contested cases" *Hansard,* H.L., Vol. 502, col. 1203. Criteria for ordering reports should be agreed between courts, local authorities and the probation service: *National Standards,* para. 4.1.

[39] F.P.R. 1991, r. 4.14(3) (g); F.P.C. 1991, r. 14(3) (g); *Practice Direction* [1981] 2 All E.R. 1056; *National Standards,* para. 4.5. The judge may not specify how the inquiry is to be conducted: *Re A.* (1979) 10 *Fam. Law* 114 nor require the local authority to refer the child to a psychiatrist: *Re K. (Contact: Psychiatric Report)* [1995] 2 F.L.R. 432, CA.

[40] *National Standards,* para. 4.3. Mediation should be considered before a report is ordered: CAAC *Handbook* (1997) App. AVI, para. 2. A report based on a conciliation meeting is not admissible in evidence unless it includes statements which indicate the maker has harmed or is a serious risk to the children: *Re D. (Minors) (Conciliation: Privilege)* [1993] 1 F.L.R. 932; *Practice Direction* [1986] 2 F.L.R. 171.

[41] M. Wilkinson, *Children & Divorce* (1981), p. 26; CAAC *Handbook* (1997) App. AI, para. 9.

[42] *National Standards,* para. 4.4. The probation service received more complaints about its family court work than its other work: *Thematic Inspection* (1997), para. 6.51; most were unsubstantiated.

[43] *Re C. (Section 8 Order: Court Welfare Officer)* [1995] 1 F.L.R. 617 at 619, *per* Hale J.

reporters and welfare officers have the power to inspect the court file[44] and will usually interview the parties[45] and contact relevant agencies such as the school. No confidentiality should be promised to anyone who provides information.[46] Although children's welfare is the focus of the inquiry, children were seen alone for less than half of reports, and are not seen at all for nearly a sixth. In only a third of cases were children seen with both parties separately.[47] The report, should contain a summary of the investigation process, consideration of the welfare checklist, a reasoned assessment of the options available and, where appropriate, a specific, reasoned recommendation.[48] On average, reports take 13 hours to complete.[49]

The report is confidential[50]; it must be served on the parties before the hearing[51] but can only be disclosed to others with the court's permission.[52] Reports inevitably contain some hearsay and have been excluded because of this.[53] Further information about the report or the way it was prepared can be obtained by cross-examining the person who prepared it.[54] A properly prepared report is invaluable[55] but the court is not bound by any recommendation contained in it[56]; the decision should be made by the judge not the report writer.[57] However, if the court wishes to depart from a firm conclusion in a welfare report they should hear evidence from the reporter[58] and reasons should be given if the report is

---

[44] F.P.R. 1991, r. 4.23(1); F.C.R. 1991, r. 23.

[45] It is the practice in some areas to interview the parties together but they should be informed of their right to choose to be seen separately: *National Standards*, paras 4.12–13. Most parties were only seen once: *Thematic Inspection* (1997), para. 4.10.

[46] *Re G. (Minors) (Welfare Report)* [1993] 2 F.L.R. 293. The welfare officer may not provide other information to the judge in confidence.

[47] *Thematic Inspection* (1997), paras 4.12–4.14.

[48] *National Standards*, paras 4.20 *et seq.*; *Practice Direction* [1986] 2 F.L.R. 171. See also A. James and W. Hay *et al.*, *Court welfare work: research practice and development* (1992). A third of reports examined in the *Thematic Inspection* (1997) did not include a reasoned assessment (Table 16).

[49] Home Office, *The work of the probation service in serving the needs of children involved in separation or divorce* (1991), p. 55. Each welfare officer completes over 50 reports a year.

[50] F.P.R. 1991, r. 4.23(1); F.P.C. 1991, r. 23(1). This should be explained to the parties by the district judge or justices' clerk: CAAC *Handbook* (1997), App. AVI, para. 5.

[51] F.P.R. 1991, rr. 4.11B(2), 4.13(1); F.P.C. 1991, rr. 11B(2), 13(1). Service is by the reporter at least 14 days before the hearing.

[52] F.P.R. 1991, r. 4.23(1); F.P.C. 1991, r. 23(1). It can be used in connection with an application for legal aid or shown to an expert appointed by the court.

[53] Children Act 1989, s.7(4) (b); Children (Admissibility of Hearsay Evidence) Order 1993, S.I. 1993 No. 621. The report may be considered despite the hearsay rule but "Where a judge has to arrive at crucial findings of fact he should found them upon sworn evidence rather than unsworn report." *per* Buckley L.J., *Thompson v. Thompson* [1986] 1 F.L.R. 212 at 217

[54] *Re I. and H. (Contact)* [1998] 1 F.L.R. 876, CA. But officers need only attend court if so directed: F.P.R. 1991, rr. 4.11B(3), 4.13(3); F.P.C. 1991, rr. 11B(3), 13(3). Where attendance is directed, the court release the officer after their evidence is complete: CAAC *Handbook* (1997), App. AVI, para. 10.

[55] *per* Ewbank J., *Re H. (Conciliation: Welfare Reports)* [1986] 1 F.L.R. 476.

[56] *Leete v. Leete and Stevens* (1984) 14 *Fam. Law* 21, CA; *Dimino v. Dimino* [1989] 2 All E.R.280, CA. (The judge should not notify the parties of the order he intends to make on the basis of the report before he has heard the evidence.)

[57] *Mnguni v. Mnguni* (1979) 1 F.L.R. 184; *S. v. S.* (1978) 1 F.L.R. 143.

[58] *Re A. (Children: 1959 UN Declaration)* [1998] 1 F.L.R. 354, CA; *Re C. (Section 8 Order: Court Welfare Officer)* [1995] 1 F.L.R. 617, CA; *Re CB. (Access: Attendance of Court Welfare Officer)* [1995] 1 F.L.R. 622, CA.

not followed.[59] Failure to give reasons or to consider the evidence in the welfare report is a ground for appeal.[60]

V. FAMILY PROCEEDINGS

19–011 In family proceedings the court may make any section 8 orders[61] and exercise its other powers under the Children Act 1989 for example order a report or an investigation into the child's circumstances[62] and, in exceptional cases, make a family assistance order.[63]

A. The meaning of "family proceedings"

19–012 "Family proceedings" are defined as proceedings under the inherent jurisdiction of the High Court (except an application by a local authority for leave to bring such proceedings) and any proceeding under the following provisions:—

(a) Parts I, II and IV of [the Children Act 1989];
(b) the Matrimonial Causes Act 1973;
(d) the Adoption Act 1976 (the Adoption and Children Act 2002);
(e) the Domestic Proceedings and Magistrates' Courts Act 1978;
(f) Part III of the Matrimonial and Family Proceedings Act 1984;
(g) the Family Law Act 1996;
(h) sections 11 and 12 of the Crime and Disorder Act 1998.[64]

In addition the Human Fertilization and Embryology Act provides that proceedings for a parental order are "family proceedings".[65]

So long as there are family proceedings before the court it can grant any private law orders under the Children Act.[66] The inclusion of the inherent jurisdiction of the High Court has facilitated the decline in that jurisdiction which now only needs to be used if the statutory powers are inadequate.[67] The inclusion of the Matrimonial Causes Act 1973 widens the court's powers in respect of children in proceedings for divorce, nullity or separation or for financial relief. The court may make such orders where financial relief is sought after an over-

---

[59] *W v. W (A Minor: Custody Appeal)* [1988] 2 F.L.R. 505, CA; *Re W. (Residence)* [1999] 2 F.L.R. 390, CA.
[60] *W v. W (A Minor: Custody Appeal)* [1988] 2 F.L.R. 505, CA: *Re CB. (Access: Attendance of Court Welfare Officers)* [1995] 1 F.L.R. 622, CA.
[61] See below.
[62] Children Act 1989, ss.7, 37, see above and below.
[63] Children Act 1989, s.16, see below.
[64] s.8(4).
[65] Human Fertilization and Embryology Act 1990, s.30(8) (a).
[66] Children Act 1989, ss.10(1), 16(1) But an order in favour of someone *e.g.* a foster carer who was precluded from applying under s.9(3) would be exceptional: *Gloucestershire C.C. v. P.* [1999] 2 F.L.R. 61, CA.
[67] Law Com. No. 172, para. 4.35. For a discussion of the use of the inherent jurisdiction, see below, paras 19–045 *et seq.*

seas divorce. However, the restrictions on the court's jurisdiction over maintenance for children where the Child Support Act 1991 applies[68] means that the court cannot resolve all matters. Where there are adoption proceedings the court can make additional or alternative orders.[69] In cases of domestic violence, the family proceedings court, the county court and the High Court can make orders relating to children when considering applications for occupation or non-molestation orders. It may be essential to determine who will be caring for the children and what contact the parents should have. Similarly, where a court makes or enforces a child safety order under the Crime and Disorder Act 1998, it may be necessary to clarify the child's residence. Whether or not there is an application, the court must be clear that it has the necessary information about the child; orders for children should not be made in favour of those unwilling to accept this responsibility.[70] Not all proceedings brought under the Children Act 1989 are "family proceedings": applications to place children in secure accommodation[71] and orders under Part V are excluded.[72]

B. Orders that can be made

19–013 The Law Commission's scheme sought to focus the court's attention on issues which needed resolution.[73] Parents should retain their parental responsibility and power to act independently unless this was incompatible with a court order.[74] Since most parental responsibility can be exercised only while a parent is caring for a child, the court's powers should be directed to allocating the child's time between the parents rather than setting out differently sized bundles of powers and responsibilities.[75] This could help to "lower the stakes" in disputed cases because neither parent would lose their status nor responsibilities[76] and might also encourage co-operation between separated parents. Orders should normally be cast in general terms to leave the parties maximum flexibility when circumstances changed, but there should be power to attach conditions to end or prevent further difficulties.[77] The same orders (with largely the same effects) should be available in disputes between parents and between parents and third

---

[68] Child Support Act 1991, s.8(3) and above, Chap. 15.

[69] For example, a residence order could be made instead of an adoption order. In *Re M. (Adoption or Residence Order)* [1998] 1 F.L.R. 570 the adoption was refused and residence granted even though the prospective adopters said they would reject the child unless they could adopt, a threat which they reputedly carried out.

[70] *Re K. (Care Order or Residence Order)* [1995] 1 F.L.R. 675.

[71] Facilities where disturbed children may be locked up, Children Act 1989, s.25; see below Chap. 22.

[72] *i.e.* child assessment orders, s.43; emergency protection orders, s.44; recovery orders, s.50. No consideration to the making of private law orders in emergency proceedings was given by the *Review of Child Care Law*, see para. 19.10. In most cases, emergency proceedings would not provide the court with a sufficient basis for making a s.8 order but an interim order for residence could secure care by a relative or friend and avoid the need for public law proceedings.

[73] Law Com. No. 172, paras 4.2–5, 4.8.

[74] *ibid.* para.4.6.

[75] *ibid.* para. 4.8. The Booth Committee took a very different view, see *Report of the Matrimonial Causes Procedure Committee* (1985), para. 2.27.

[76] *ibid.* paras 4.5, 4.9.

[77] Law Com. No. 172, para. 4.10.

parties.[78] Also, key powers under the inherent jurisdiction should be included in the statutory scheme to avoid resort to that jurisdiction.[79]

The Children Act 1989 enacted the substance of the Law Commission's proposals. A person with parental responsibility may not act incompatibly with a court order[80]; no general duty was imposed on parents to consult one another.[81] Nevertheless, the courts have held that there are a few important and exceptional decisions which cannot be taken without the agreement of the other parent.[82] Requiring consent places the burden on the parent wishing to take the decision to obtain the agreement of the other parent or apply to the court. Where communication is good between them, this should not cause difficulties but there are cases where locating the other parent or getting agreement would make it oppressive. Where consent is not required, the objecting parent must apply for the court for the action to be prevented or over-turned.[83]

In family proceedings the courts may make four types of private law order: a residence order, a contact order, a prohibited steps order and a specific issue order.[84] These are known collectively as "section 8 orders" and often described as the "menu" of orders. In addition the court has power to make interim orders, to impose conditions in orders, to allow change of name or removal from the jurisdiction and to make family assistance orders. The use,[85] effects of and limitations on these orders will be considered in turn.

1. Residence order

19–014 A residence order is an order "settling the arrangements to be made as to the person with whom the child is to live".[86] It does not connote possession nor exclude the other parent.[87] Where a residence order is made in favour of an unmarried father without parental responsibility the court must also make a parental responsibility order under section 4.[88] Non-parents obtain parental responsibility by virtue of a residence order but they have no power to consent

---

[78] *ibid.* paras 4.24–28.

[79] *ibid.* para. 4.1; Law Com. W.P. 101, *Wards of Court* (1987), paras 4.6, 4.21–5.

[80] s.2(8).

[81] s.2(7); *cf. Re G. (Parental Responsibility: Education)* [1994] 2 F.L.R. 964 at 967, *per* Glidewell L.J. where it was suggested that the non-residential parent should be consulted over major decisions. See also Maidment [2001] *Fam. Law* 518. A duty to consult existed prior to the Children Act 1989: *Dipper v. Dipper* [1980] 3 W.L.R. 626, CA. There is a duty on local authorities to consult: s.22(4) (5) and below para. 22–063.

[82] *Re J. (Specific Issue Orders: Child's Religious Upbringing and Circumcision)* [2000] 1 F.L.R. 571, CA; *Re C. (Change of Surname)* [1998] 2 F.L.R. 656, CA. Permission would have been required for the change of name if there had been a residence order, s.13.

[83] See prohibited steps orders, below.

[84] Children Act 1989, s.8(1). The "public law" orders listed in Pt IV require an application (by a local authority or the N.S.P.C.C.) and proof of the grounds in s. 31.

[85] In a study of 400 applications for s.8 orders conducted in the South-west of England in 1996–7 only 10% of applications were made by non-parents, over half of these by grandparents. Almost 20% of cases the oldest child was under two years; in 10% he or she was over 11 years: J. Pearce *et al.* [1999] *Fam. Law* 22, 23.

[86] Children Act 1989, s.8(1).

[87] *Re W. (Minors) (Residence Order)* [1992] 2 F.L.R. 332, CA.

[88] Children Act 1989, s.12(1) (4).

to the child's placement for adoption or an adoption order, or appoint a guardian for the child.[89] The residence order automatically debars anyone from changing the child's surname or removing the child from the United Kingdom for a period of more than one month without the written consent of everyone with parental responsibility or the court.[90] In addition, no one may act incompatibly with the order.[91] But this does not preclude the deportation of an adult with a residence order in respect of a child who has a right to remain in the United Kingdom.[92] The appointment of a guardian[93] by a parent with a residence order takes effect immediately on the death of the parent unless the residence order was made jointly with the surviving parent.[94]

In its simplest form a residence order need do no more than name the person with whom the child will live, but the phrase "settling the arrangements" gives the court considerable scope to impose detailed directions or conditions on parents, people with parental responsibility and carers but not on others.[95] For example, the limited right of the person with a residence order to remove the child from the United Kingdom may be unacceptable to the non-residential parent who fears that the child may not be returned, will be taken overseas without proper arrangements for vaccination or medical insurance, or that travel may disrupt schooling. Orders may also prohibit a move to another town,[96] a change of school, allowing the child to meet a friend of the residential parent,[97] or even sharing a bed with the child.[98] Broader injunctions may be granted under the inherent jurisdiction.[99] Conditions may also be included to ensure that a child

---

[89] Adoption and Children Bill 2002, cll. 19, 52; Children Act 1989, s.5(3) (4).

[90] Children Act 1989, s.13(1) (2). Comparable restrictions applied under the Matrimonial Causes Rules 1977, rr.92(3), 94(2); but the position in other proceedings was not clear, particularly short-term removal from England and Wales was not controlled unless specific provisions was made in the order: see Law Com. No. 172, para. 4.14–15.

[91] Children Act 1989, ss.2(8), 3(5). Action which is forbidden by the order would prima facie not be reasonable. The Law Commission suggested that if the order resulted in the child going to a school with a strict dress code the other parent could not arrange for the child to have their hair done in a way which led to exclusion from the school (Law Com. No. 172, para. 2.11). But unless the order were specific enforcement action for breach would be problematic, see below.

[92] *R v. Secretary of State for Home Department, ex p. T.* [1995] 1 F.L.R. 293; *R. v. Secretary of State for the Home Department, ex p. Isiko* [2001] 1 F.L.R. 930, CA. Similarly the court will not allow wardship to be used to fetter or influence the decision of the Secretary of State: *Re F. (A Minor) (Immigration: Wardship)* [1990] Fam. 125.

[93] See above Chap. 18.

[94] Children Act 1989, s.5(7) (b), (9).

[95] *ibid.* s.11(7); *Leeds C.C. v C.* [1993] 1 F.L.R. 269.

[96] Restrictions on the placed where the carer lived should only be included in exceptional cases: *Re E. (Minors) (Residence Orders)* [1997] 2 F.L.R. 638, CA; *Re D. (Residence: Imposition of Conditions)* [1996] 2 F.L.R. 281; *Re H. (Children) (Residence Order: Condition)* [2001] 2 F.L.R. 1277, CA (the test for relocation within the U.K. is less strict than for emigration). The adverse effect of similar orders on mothers in California has been noted, see C. Bruch, "And how are the children? The effects of ideology and mediation on child custody law and children's well-being in the United States" (1988) 2 Int. J. Law & Fam. 106 at 113.

[97] Restrictions preventing a parent from allowing a child contact with a third party were sometimes included in access orders: *G. v. G.* (1981) 1 *Fam. Law* 148 (transsexual not to be accompanied by his male friend) and see *Plant v. Plant* (1982) 4 F.L.R. 305 and D. Bradley, "Homosexuality and Child Custody in English Law" (1987) 1 Int. J. of Law & Fam. 155.

[98] *Re T. (A Minor (Care Order: Conditions)* [1994] 2 F.L.R. 423.

[99] *D. v. N. (Contact Order: Conditions)* [1997] 2 F.L.R. 797. An order could also be made under the Family Law Act 1996 or the Protection from Harassment Act 1997.

receives necessary medical treatment despite the objection of the carer[1]; to allow a child's move to a new carer to be phased over a period[2]; or to require the parents to co-operate over their assessment.[3]

A residence order may be made in favour of two or more persons even though they do not live together.[4] Whether a shared order is more appropriate than a residence order to one person and a contact order to the other will depend on the amount of time spent in each household and the carers' legal relationship with the child and with each other. The order must be in the interests of the child but the court has been willing to make such orders where there is considerable distrust between the parties.[5] Where it reflects the reality of the parents' involvement, a shared residence order should be granted:

> In *Re H. (Shared Residence: Parental Responsibility)*[6] the applicant was the father of one child and the step-father of the other. The parties originally planned to share the care of the children but the mother was looking after them full-time and the applicant had weekend contact. Nevertheless the court rejected her application for variation to sole residence. A shared residence order was appropriate because it enabled the man to have a status and be involved in the lives of both children.

The order may specify the periods spent in each household or leave this to the parties.[7] Although good communication between separated parents is important,[8] there is no duty on parents to consult with each other but neither parent may take action which is incompatible with the order.[9] Consequently, the order

---

1 But in *Re S. (A Minor) (Blood Transfusion: Adoption Order Condition)* [1994] 2 F.L.R. 416 the Court of Appeal upheld the adopters' appeal against the requirement that they give an undertaking because the need for transfusion was speculative. See also *Jane v. Jane* [1983] 4 F.L.R. 712.

2 For example, to allow a relationship to be built up between the child and the carer: Children Act 1989, ss.9(1), (2), 91(1). There is no specific provision for phased return in the Act which previously could be arranged through wardship: *Re E. (S.A.) (A Minor) (Wardship)* [1984] 1 All E.R. 289.

3 *C. v. Solihull M.B.C.* [1993] 1 F.L.R. 290.

4 Children Act 1989, s.11(4). In *G. v. F. (Contact and Shared Residence: Applications for Leave)* [1998] 2 F.L.R. 799, FD leave was granted to the mother's lesbian, former partner who had been a co-parent to the child.

5 *D. v. D. (Shared Residence Order)* [2001] 1 F.L.R. 495, CA; *Guidance*, Vol. 1, para. 2.28. Such orders should not be made if they confuse the children: *Re WB. (Residence Order)* [1995] 2 F.L.R. 1023.

6 [1995] 2 F.L.R. 883, CA; similarly *Re R. (Residence Order: Finance)* [1995] 2 F.L.R. 612, CA where the mother was refused sole residence which would have brought to an end a sharing arrangement.

7 Children Act 1989, s.11(4); *D. v. D. (Shared Residence Order)* [2001] 1 F.L.R. 495, CA. The court may need to set or approve detailed schedules.

8 The Children Act 1989 supports parallel rather than co-operative parenting after separation see B. Hoggett "Joint parenting systems: the English experiment" (1994) J.C.L. 8; C. Smart and B. Neale, *Family fragments?* (1999).

9 Children Act 1989, s.2(7); S. Maidment [2001] *Fam. Law* 518; A. Bainham, "The privatization of the public interest in children" (1990) 53 *M.L.R.* 206 at 208–214. *Cf. Re G. (Parental Responsibility: Education)* [1994] 2 F.L.R. 964 at 967 *per* Glidewell L.J. Some consultation was required prior to the Children Act 1989: *Dipper v. Dipper* [1981] Fam. 31. The Law Commission considered that making one party do what the other had decided was contrary to the tenor of modern law: see Law Com. No. 172, para. 4.18.

should be specific on points such as schooling which are fundamental to the success of the arrangement. Where the child alternates between two parents, a shared residence order places them both in the same position but, unless specific conditions or the restrictions relating to name change or emigration are required, this could be achieved by making no order at all.[10] A residence order made in favour of both parents ceases to have effect if they live together for a continuous period of more than six months.[11]

19–015 Residence orders can only be made or continue in respect of children over the age of 16 if there are "exceptional circumstances".[12] This may reflect the reality of limited parental power but has the disadvantage of leaving non-parents caring for young people without any status. For this reason the Adoption and Children Bill provides that courts should have the power to extend their residence orders to age 18 at their request.[13]

Residence orders were sought in approximately 31,800 cases in 2000. 27,000 orders were made, including 1,200 in public law proceedings 3,200 applications were withdrawn, 500 applications refused and no order was made in 1,000.[14] It appears that orders are not obtained in the majority of divorces.[15]

2. Contact order

19–016 A contact order requires "the person with whom the child lives or is to live to allow the child to visit or stay with the person named in the order or for that person and the child otherwise to have contact with each other."[16] It imposes a duty on the carer to allow contact, but does not oblige the person with the order to make any visits.[17] An order is necessary where a satisfactory agreement cannot be reached and the carer is restricting or preventing contact, or where the child's welfare demands the control or termination of contact.

The language of judges explaining contact decisions has shifted over time; contact has been claimed as a parental right but also described as a right of

---

[10] See para. 19–003, above for a discussion of whether an order should be made A residence order will provide parental responsibility for a person who does not have it.

[11] Children Act 1989, s.11(5); *Re P. (Abduction Declaration)* [1995] 1 F.L.R. 831. The unmarried father will retain parental responsibility; cohabitation has no effect on the s.4 order made by virtue of s.12(1).

[12] Children Act 1989, s.9(6) (7) *e.g.* where the carer would not otherwise have parental responsibility: *Re B. (Adoption by One Parent to the Exclusion of Other)* [2001] 1 F.L.R. 589 at 595 *per* Hale L.J. or where the child has major disabilities: *Re M. (Contact: Parental Responsibility)* [2001] 2 F.L.R. 342, FD.

[13] cl. 112 (amending Children Act 1989, s.12). Such orders will only be able to be varied with leave of the court. This is intended to make residence orders more attractive to carers.

[14] *Judicial Statistics 2000*, Tables 5.2 and 5.3.

[15] Custody orders were made in 88,488 cases in 1991: *Judicial Statistics 1991*, Cm. 1990, Table 5.4.

[16] Children Act 1989, s.8(1).

[17] J. Masson, "Thinking about contact—a social or a legal problem" [2000] *C.F.L.Q.* 15 consequently there can be no legal right in the child to maintain contact, see also *Re K.D. (A Minor) (Ward: Termination of Access)* [1988] A.C. 806, 825 *per* Lord Oliver and Advisory Board on Family Law: Children Act sub-committee, *Making contact work report* (2002), paras 14.53–14.56.

the child.[18] These issues are both sidestepped by addressing the order to the carer.[19] The Law Commission considered that contact was generally beneficial to children and sought to encourage it.[20] They saw positive attitudes to contact as more important than legally enforceable rights and discussed ways of achieving these,[21] proposing guidance as to what constitutes "reasonable contact" and emphasising the continuing responsibility of parents which could be exercised during visits.[22] The Act took the second point on board but set no standards for contact in the area of private law.[23] There is no statutory presumption of contact and no duty on the carer to permit it[24] unless there is a court order, but the courts have repeatedly stated that maintaining contact with the non-residential parent is almost always in a child's interests.[25]

Contact orders usually permit "reasonable" contact but may define the duration, frequency, times and location of visits.[26] In an unusual case it may be appropriate for a third party, for example a local authority or a child psychiatrist, to have the power to determine when contact occurs.[27] Contact may be supervised[28] or ordered to take place at a contact centre.[29] A family

[18] *Re L.; Re V.; Re M. and Re H. (Contact: Domestic Violence)* [2000] 2 F.L.R. 334 at 360 *per* Thorpe L.J. and see *Re K.D.* [1988] A.C. 806 (parent's right) where the House of Lords held that court decisions about access must nevertheless be subject to the welfare principle; *M. v. M.* [1973] 2 All E.R. 81, *per* Wrangham J. (right of the child).

[19] This fits better with provisions which impose no limit on the individuals who could be named in the order.

[20] Law Com. W.P. 96, paras 4.27–4.34.

[21] *ibid.* para. 4.33–4. The Law Commission apparently dismissed the possibility that a non-residential parent might be required to maintain contact as he is to provide financial support.

[22] *ibid.* para. 4.34. Unfortunately the Law Commission had no empirical evidence against which it could test its theory.

[23] *Cf.* in relation to public law: Children Act 1989, s.34(1) and Sched.2, para. 15(1) which require the local authority to permit reasonable contact and to endeavour to promote contact between the child and his family and friends. Reasonable contact is contact which is agreed between the parties or contact "which is objectively reasonable", *per* Ewbank J. in *Re P. (Minors) (Contact with Children in Care)* [1993] 2 F.L.R. 156 at 161C.

[24] Although it could be argued that parental responsibility must be exercised for the child's benefit and thus contact which is beneficial must be allowed: see *Gillick v. W. Norfolk and Wisbech A.H.A.* [1986] A.C. 112, *per* Lord Scarman at 184. The Family Law Act 1996, s.11(4) (c) included a "general principle" that regular contact was in the child's interests.

[25] *Re O.(Contact: Imposition of Conditions)* [1995] 2 F.L.R. 124 at 128 *per* Sir Thomas Bingham M.R.; *Re B. (Contact: Step-father's Opposition)* [1997] 2 F.L.R. 579 at 584 *per* Lord Woolf M.R.; *Re L.: Re V.; Re M.; Re H.; (Contact: Domestic Violence)* [2000] 2 F.L.R. 334 at 365 *per* Thorpe L.J; C. Sturge and D. Glaser [2000] *Fam. Law* 615. This amounts to "judge-made presumption" R. Bailey-Harris *et al.*, "From utility to rights? The presumption of contact in practice" (1999) 13 Int. J. Law, Pol. and Fam. 111 at 114. For a critical view see: Smart and Neale [1997] *Fam. Law* 332.

[26] Children Act 1989, ss.8(1), 11(7). Orders may be very detailed including, for example the content of messages in cards and the cost of gifts: *A. v. L. (Contact)* [1998] 1 F.L.R. 361, FD.

[27] *Re O. (Transracial Adoption: Contact)* [1995] 2 F.L.R. 597.

[28] *Practice Direction (Access: Supervised Access)* [1980] 1 W.L.R. 334 every effort should be made to enlist the help of individuals acceptable to both parties; only where this is unsuccessful should CAFCASS officers be involved. Where no relative is prepared to take a child to visit a parent in prison only indirect contact can be ordered: *A. v. L. (Contact)* [1998] 1 F.L.R. 361, FD. Supervision by the local authority cannot be required unless there are child protection issues: *Leeds C.C. v. C.* [1993] 1 F.L.R. 269; *Re DH.* [1994] 1 F.L.R. 697.

[29] See below, para. 19–042; most contact centres only provide supported contact. Courts must ensure that the centre will accept the referral before making an order see: "Protocol for the referral of families by judges and magistrates to child contact centres" [2001] *Fam. Law* 616.

assistance order may be made to help establish contact.[30] Where direct contact is not possible the court will usually order indirect contact:—

> In *Re K. (Contact Mother's Anxiety)*[31] the father and paternal grandfather had brutally kidnapped the child from the mother's care in the early hours of the morning and taken him abroad. The father was imprisoned for contempt and later for kidnapping but proceeded with his application for contact on his release. A child psychologist advised that the child would benefit from contact. A consent order was made for supervised contact which the mother applied to be varied. Although the father had behaved well at the contact sessions and the child related well to him, he totally failed to recognise the impact his violence had on the mother. Contact created intolerable anxiety for her and led to unmanageable stress for the child. Indirect contact was ordered, including school reports anonymised to protect against a further abduction.

When ordering indirect contact the court may include conditions requiring the parent with care to read and keep letters and encourage a reply.[32]

19–017 The courts have taken the view that contact with the non-residential parent is crucial for the child's well being[33] and should be permitted unless there are cogent reasons for refusing it[34] such as the child's refusal[35] or the risk of serious harm to the child.[36] The fact that a child has no relationship with a parent is not a reason for denying contact.[37] Nor is the carer's implacable opposition unless contact would have such an affect as to undermine the

---

[30] Children Act 1989, s.16 and see below para. 19–025.

[31] [1999] 2 F.L.R. 203, FD; see also, *Re H.(Contact Order) (No. 2)* [2002] 1 F.L.R. 22, FD.

[32] *Re O. (Contact: Imposition of Conditions)* [1995] 2 F.L.R. 124, CA (the mother was permitted to censor unsuitable material); *Re D. (Contact: Reasons for Refusal)* [1997] 2 F.L.R. 48, CA (mother required to provide progress report). In *Re S. (Violent Parent: Indirect Contact)* [2000] 1 F.L.R. 481, FD contact was to be by pre-arranged phone call to the father. It was unclear how it would occur as the 6 year-old was frightened of the father and the three year old could not have made such a call unaided.

[33] *cf.* the views of Goldstein, Freud and Solnit (1973), p. 38, and note in particular the comments thereon of M. Richards and M. Dyson, *Separation, Divorce & the Development of Children* (1982), p. 64.

[34] *Re H. (Contact Principles)* [1994] 2 F.L.R. 969, CA; *Re W. (A Minor) (Contact)* [1994] 2 F.L.R 441, CA *Re CH. (Contact: Parentage)* [1996] 1 F.L.R. 569, FD (contact order granted in favour of a legal father who was not the biological father); *Re D. (Parental Responsibility: IVF baby)* [2001] 1 F.L.R 972, CA (indirect contact in favour of legal father who was not the genetic father).

[35] *Re M. (Contact: Welfare Test)* [1995] 1 F.L.R 274; *Re F. (Contact: Child in Care)* [1995] 1 F.L.R. 510; *Re F. (Minors) (Denial of Contact)* [1993] 2 F.L.R. 677, CA.

[36] See the views expressed by the welfare officer in *Re C.B. (Access: Attendance of Court Welfare Officer)* [1995] 1 F.L.R. 622; *Re T. (A Minor) (Parental Responsibility: Contact)* [1993] 2 F.L.R. 450 where the father behaved with callous cruelty detaining the child for 9 days after a two hour contact visit; *Re C. and V. (Contact and Parental Responsibility)* [1998] 1 F.L.R. 392 (where the father was unable to manage the child's serious health condition); *M. v. M. (Parental Responsibility)* [1999] 2 F.L.R. 737, FD (father suffering brain damage, unpredictable and violent behaviour).

[37] *Re M. (Contact: Supervision)* [1998] 1 F.L.R. 727, CA and see C. Sturge and D. Glaser [2000] *Fam. Law* 615.

stability of the child's home.[38] The courts have been prepared to allow some contact between a sexually abused child and the abuser.[39] A parent who makes malicious allegations of abuse against another risks their own contact with the child being seen as potentially damaging.[40] Orders for direct contact are not made if children strongly object to seeing a parent or are disturbed by the experience.[41] The courts have been prepared to determine contact without deciding questions of paternity.[42] Contact decisions should not be linked with the provision of financial support.[43]

Increasing concern has been expressed about the court's failure to take account of the impact violence against the parent with care could have on children. Violence often continues despite parental separation; both parent's and child's physical safety and emotional well being are at risk.[44] The Advisory Board on Family Law's Children Act Sub-committee prepared good practice guidelines and issued a consultation paper seeking views about the court's approach and the need for legislation or guidance.[45] The responses indicated broard agreement that, in the absence of evidence to the contrary, children's welfare is generally served by maintaining contact with family members, but a powerful public perception, accepted by many professionals, is that courts did not adequately address the issue of domestic violence in contact cases.[46] Although there was some support for a statutory presumption

---

[38] *Re D. (A Minor) (Contact: Mother's Hostility)* [1993] 2 F.L.R. 1, CA where a violent father who separated from the mother before the child's birth was refused contact; cogent evidence will be required for the "draconian order" of no contact: *Re F. (Minors) (Contact Mother's Anxiety)* [1993] 2 F.L.R. 830, CA; *Re W. (A Minor) (Contact)* [1994] 2 F.L.R. 441, CA.

[39] *L. v. L. (Child Abuse: Access)* [1989] 2 F.L.R. 16, CA (supervised access); *S v. S (Child Abuse: Access)* [1988] 1 F.L.R. 213, CA (contact to siblings who were not abused).

[40] *Re M. (Contact: Welfare Test)* [1995] 1 F.L.R. 274; *Re F. (Minors) Denial of Contact)* [1993] 2 F.L.R. 677; *Re L. (Contact: Transsexual Applicant)* [1995] 2 F.L.R. 438, FD (the father's application for face to face contact was adjourned whilst he underwent a sex change).

[41] *Re M. (Contact: Welfare Test)* [1995] 1 F.L.R. 274; *Re L. (Contact: Transsexual Applicant)* [1995] 2 F.L.R. 438, FD (father's direct contact adjourned whilst he underwent a sex change); *cf. Re W. (Contact: Parent's Delusional Beliefs)* [1999] 1 F.L.R. 1263, CA (contact cut from fortnightly to short visits, monthly pending rehearing because children aged 10 and 11 found it boring and disturbing.)

[42] *K. v. M. (Paternity: Contact)* [1996] 1 F.L.R. 312 (contact to former lover refused); *O. v. L. (Blood Tests)* [1995] 2 F.L.R. 930, CA (contact to husband who had lived with child for four years granted). Where the person claiming contact has had no involvement with the child he may not have a right to family life which would be protected under the E.C.H.R. see: *Keegan v. Ireland* (1994) 18 E.H.R.R. 342.

[43] *cf.* A. Kitch, "Conditioning child support payments on visitation access: a proposal" (1991) 5 Int. J. Law & Fam. 318. In practice there are links between finance and contact—parents who see their children are more likely to support them: see Maclean and Eekelaar (1997), p. 127. Under the Child Support regime the obligation of an absent parent who has contact for at least 52 nights a year is reduced: Child Support, Pensions and Social Security Act 2000, Sched.1, para. 7; N. Wikeley [2000] *Fam. Law* 820 at 822.

[44] M. Hester and L. Radford, *Domestic violence and child contact in England and Denmark* (1996); A. Mullender and R. Morley, *Children living with domestic violence* (1994); R. Bailey-Harris *et al.*, "From utility to rights? The presumption of contact in practice" (1999) 13 Int. J. Law Pol. and Fam. 111; Smart and Neale [1997] *Fam. Law* 332.

[45] Advisory Board on Family Law, *Second Annual Report* (1999) para. 3.29; Advisory Board on Family Law: Children Act Sub-committee, *Consultation paper on Contact between children and violent parents* (1999).

[46] Advisory Board on Family Law: Children Act Sub-committee, *A report to the Lord Chancellor on the question of parental contact in cases of domestic violence* (2000), paras 3.1.1 and 4.2. The

against contact[47] where there was domestic violence, the Sub-committee proposed the introduction of a Practice Direction and training for judges and CAFCASS officers.[48]

Shortly after the report was published, the Court of Appeal decided *Re L.; Re V.; Re M.; Re H. (Contact: Domestic Violence)*.[49] It upheld decisions refusing direct contact to all four fathers who had attacked the children's mothers. The court relied heavily on an expert report, commissioned by the Official Solicitor, which explored the benefits and risks of contact where there was family violence.[50] This tentatively suggested the onus of establishing the value of contact should be on the violent parent—a view rejected by the court.[51] The President accepted that the courts had not previously regarded domestic violence as relevant to children and that allegations should be adjudicated. She alluded to many aspects of the Sub-committee's guidance but stressed that these cases, like all others, required individual assessment. There was no presumption against contact; the court had to balance the seriousness of violence and risks to the child against any positive factors in favour of contact.[52] Thorpe L.J. agreed and doubted the need for specific guidelines.[53] Both judges denied that earlier decisions were inconsistent with the court's approach and warned of a pendulum swing against contact where there has been domestic violence.[54] However, an applicant who has been violent may need to make genuine efforts to change and demonstrate that he is a fit person to exercise contact.[55]

19–018 A child who wants to see siblings against the wishes of the children's parent or carer can, with leave, apply for a section 8 contact order.[56] This is the case even if the child applicant is in care unless it is the local authority which is restricting contact.[57] A contact order may be sought to require foster parents or

---

Chairman of the Sub-committee Wall J. had also made this point in *Re M. (Contact: Violent Parent)* [1999] 2 F.L.R. 321.

47 Under New Zealand legislation the court is required to refuse contact unless it is satisfied that the child will be safe during contact: Guardianship Act 1968, s.5(4) (b). The Family Homes and Domestic Violence (Northern Ireland) Order 1997 requires consideration of safety but only where an injunction has been granted see: Advisory Board on Family Law: Children Act Sub-committee, *Consultation paper on contact between children and violent parents* (1999), Apps 2 and 4.

48 Advisory Board on Family Law: Children Act Sub-committee *Report* (2000), paras 4.4–4.7; Advisory Board on Family Law, *Third Annual Report* (2000), paras 3.2–3.25.

49 [2000] 2 F.L.R. 334.

50 C. Sturge and D. Glaser, "Contact and domestic violence—the experts' court report" [2000] *Fam. Law* 615. The experts agreed with the view in the Sub-committee's report that more consideration should be given to the impact of domestic violence on children, *Re L. (Contact Domestic Violence)* [2000] 2 F.L.R. 334, 337–8. Both Butler-Sloss P. and Thorpe L.J. drew extensively on the report.

51 [2000] *Fam. Law* 615, 623, at 341 and 370

52 at 336, 341–4.

53 at 370. Guidelines have not been formally issued.

54 at 342 and 370. Amendments to formalise the consideration of domestic violence in contact proceedings were tabled during the Adoption and Children Bill (NC 10) but did not receive government support: *Hansard* H.C. May 16, 2002, col. 948; Lords Grand Committee col. CWH 331.

55 *Re L.; Re V.; Re M.; Re H. (Contact: Domestic Violence)* [2000] 2 F.L.R. 334 at 342 *per* Butler-Sloss P.; *Re M. (Contact: Violent Parent)* [1999] 2 F.L.R. 221 at 333 *per* Wall J.

56 Children Act 1989, s.10(9); *Re S. (Contact: Application by Sibling)* [1998] 2 F.L.R. 897, FD.

57 *Re F. (Contact: Child in Care)* [1995] 1 F.L.R. 510. Disputes with local authorities about contact to children in care are governed by Children Act 1989, s.34, see Chap. 22, below.

residential home staff to allow visits to a child accommodated by the local authority but not one who is in care.[58] The order cannot be directed to the local authority and thus a separate application is necessary for each placement where difficulties arise. Grandparents, relatives and friends seeking contact orders must first apply for leave.[59] There is no presumption in favour of contact by grandparents who have obtained leave.[60]

Contact may be terminated by making an order for "no contact"[61] or a prohibited steps order—

> In *Re H. (Prohibited Steps Order)*[62] a mother cohabited with a man who abused one of her children. The local authority obtained supervision orders in relation to her remaining children and also sought to control the man's contact with the children. The Court of Appeal held that a prohibited steps order could not be made to prevent the mother allowing the man contact because section 9(5) required an order for no contact to be used. A prohibited steps order could be used to stop the man contacting the children even though he was not a party to the proceedings. The "no contact" order alone would not have protected the children against an approach by the man unknown to the mother.

A contact order which requires one parent to allow the other to visit or otherwise have contact with the child ceases to have effect if the parents live together for a continuous period of at least six months.[63] All contact orders cease to have effect if an adoption agency is authorised to place the child for adoption or a placement order is made.[64]

In 2000, there were nearly 55,000 applications for contact in private law proceedings. Approximately 5,500 applications were withdrawn, 1,200 were refused and 2,000 resulted in an order of no order. Overall there were about 46,000 orders made.[65] In a study of legally aided contact cases 14 per cent resulted in supervised contact and six per cent in indirect contact.[66]

---

[58] Children Act 1989, s.9(1), orders under s.34 are available in such cases, see Chap. 22 below. Contact should not be ordered at the foster carer's home without their informed consent: CAAC Final Report 1997, p. 31. A s.8 order may be made requiring a parent to let a child in care have contact with siblings living at home: *Re F. (Contact: Child in Care)* [1995] 1 F.L.R. 510, FD.

[59] Children Act 1989, s.10(9) these criteria are also apposite if the child is in care: *Re M. (Contact Care Grandmother's Application)* [1995] 2 F.L.R. 86. In disputed cases evidence should be heard: *Re F. & R. (s.8 Orders: Grandparent's Application)* [1995] 1 F.L.R. 524.

[60] *Re A. (A Minor) (Section 8 Order: Grandparent's Application)* [1995] 2 F.L.R. 153, CA; but this view may need to be revised following the Human Rights Act 1998: *Re W. (Contact Application: Procedure)* [2000] 1 F.L.R. 263, FD; see also F. Kanagas and C. Piper, "Grandparents' contact: rights v. welfare revisited" (2001) 15 Int. J. Law, Pol. and Fam. 250.

[61] *Nottinghamshire C. C. v. P.* [1994] Fam. 18, CA. But this order cannot prevent parents having contact with each other: *Croydon L.B.C. v. A. (No. 1)* [1992] 2 F.L.R. 341.

[62] [1995] 1 F.L.R. 638, CA. A condition controlling the man's contact could not be included in the supervision order, Children Act 1989, Sched. 3, Pts I and II.

[63] Children Act 1989, s.11(6). This does not apply where anyone else is named in the contact order.

[64] Adoption and Children Bill 2002, cll. 26(1), 29(2). Contact orders will be available under cl. 26.

[65] *Judicial Statistics 2000*, Table 5.3.

[66] S. Maclean, *Legal aid and the family justice system, research paper 2* (1998) there were 178 cases in the sample.

3. Prohibited steps order

19–019 This order prevents any person taking "a step which could be taken by a parent in meeting his parental responsibility for a child" without the consent of the court.[67] The order cannot be used to control matters which do not relate to parental responsibility such as contact between the parents or the occupation of the matrimonial home.[68] But the order may be made against any person, even if they are not a party to the proceedings, and restrict that person's contact with the child.[69] The Law Commission proposed this order to incorporate the most valuable features of wardship into the statutory scheme and because it was sometimes necessary for the court to play a continuing role.[70]

When a child is warded "no important step" may be taken without the leave of the court[71]; a prohibited steps order is more precise, the issues to be referred to the court must be specified. Where there is a residence or contact order, the bar on name change[72] and the power to impose conditions may avoid the need for this order.[73] If no order is made initially, it will still be open for a parent or guardian[74] to seek one when a particular problem arises. Neither this order nor the specific issue order is intended to substitute for residence, contact, care or supervision orders.[75] In 2000, approximately 5,500 orders were made, 650 applications were withdrawn, 120 orders were refused and no order was made in 180 cases.[76]

4. Specific issue order

19–020 This order gives directions "for the purpose of determining a specific question which has arisen, or may arise, in connection with any aspect of parental responsibility for a child."[77] For example, the court may consent to medical

---

[67] Children Act 1989, s.8(1). Thus it will not be effective to stop a child from making a decision which he is mature enough to make, see *Gillick v. W. Norfolk & Wisbech A.H.A.* [1986] A.C. 112. The order can be used to prevent a parent publicising the child's activities, *Re Z. (A Minor) (Freedom of Publication)* [1996] 1 F.L.R. 191, CA.

[68] *Croydon L.B.C. v. A. (No. 1)* [1992] Fam. 169; *Nottinghamshire C.C. v. P.* [1993] 2 F.L.R. 134.

[69] *Re H. (Prohibited Steps Order)* [1995] 1 F.L.R. 638, CA. see above p. 588.

[70] Law Com. No. 172, para. 4.20.

[71] See below for an explanation of the wardship jurisdiction.

[72] Children Act 1989, s.13(1); where there is no residence order a prohibited steps order can be used: *Re B. (Change of Surname)* [1996] 1 F.L.R. 791, CA.

[73] *ibid.* s.11(7); *Re WB. (Residence Orders)* [1995] 2 F.L.R. 1023. A prohibited steps order may be valuable to assist proceedings overseas even after a child has been removed, see: *Re D. (A Minor) (Child: Removal from the Jurisdiction)* [1992] 1 F.L.R. 637.

[74] Children Act 1989, s.10(4), other people (except those with a residence order) need leave of the court. An order can be made to underline the refusal of a specific issue order: *Re J. (Specific Issue Orders: Muslim Upbringing)* [1999] 2 F.L.R. 678, FD (order barring father arranging child's circumcision).

[75] Law Com. No. 172, paras 4.19–4.20; Children Act 1989, s.9(5) (a); *Nottinghamshire C.C. v. P.* [1993] 2 F.L.R. 134.

[76] *Judicial Statistics 2000*, Tables 5.2, 5.3.

[77] Children Act 1989, s.8(1). Where the order sought goes beyond parental responsibility the inherent jurisdiction can be used: *Re W. (A Minor) (Medical Treatment: Court's Jurisdiction)* [1993] Fam. 64.

examination or treatment,[78] determine where a child is educated,[79] approve a change of the child's name,[80] authorise the interview of a child for legal proceedings[81] or require the child is told of the father's identity.[82] Previously such matters were dealt with in wardship.[83] A determination that a child is "in need" and thus able to seek services from a local authority cannot be made by a specific issue order[84] nor may the order may be used to exclude parents from the family home.[85] The court, applying the welfare principle, may impose its own view but could refer the issue to an appropriate third party such as a doctor[86] or even order that one of the parties should be free to make the decision. In 2000 approximately 2,500 orders were made.[87]

5. Order of "no order"

19–021 This order records a finding that it is not appropriate to make an order, for example where the threshold conditions for a care order are satisfied but an order is not required for the child's protection. In private law proceedings this order allows the court to disengage from the dispute[88] and leaves the matter in the hands of the parties (or one of them).[89]

6. "Interim orders"

19–022 There is no longer any distinction between interim and final section 8 orders.[90] All orders may be subject to specific time limits[91] and can be varied at any time

---

78 *Re R. (A Minor) (Blood Transfusion)* [1993] 2 F.L.R. 757; *Re C. (HIV Test)* [1999] 2 F.L.R. 1004, CA. The availability of a specific issue order would seem to preclude the use of the inherent jurisdiction by a local authority, s.100(4): *cf. Re O. (A Minor) (Medical Treatment)* [1993] 2 F.L.R. 149.

79 *Re A. (Specific Issue Order: Parental Dispute)* [2001] 1 F.L.R. 121, CA.

80 *Re W., Re A., Re B. (Change of Name)* [1999] 2 F.L.R. 930, CA; *Dawson v. Wearmouth* [1999] 1 F.L.R. 1167, HL. Where there is a residence order the application is made for permission under Children Act 1989, s.13(1).

81 *Re F. (Specific Issue: Child Interview)* [1995] 1 F.L.R. 819, CA.

82 *Re K. (Specific Issue Order)* [1999] 2 F.L.R. 280, FD (order refused).

83 Law Com. No. 172, para. 4.18. There was also a power under the Guardianship Act 1973, s.1(3).

84 Children Act 1989, s.17; *Re J. (Specific Issue Order: Leave to Apply)* [1995] 1 F.L.R. 669.

85 *Pearson v. Franklin* [1994] 1 F.L.R. 246, at least if the parent has rights of occupation. The court may be able to order a transfer of the property under Sched.1, para. 1(2)(e)(i) and then exclude the non-owning parent or exercise its powers under the Family Law Act 1996, Pt IV.

86 The effect of the order in *Re C. (A Minor) (Wardship Medical Treatment)* [1989] 3 W.L.R. 240, CA, was to permit the medical staff to determine the treatment the child should have. But in *Orford v. Orford* (1979) 1 F.L.R. 260, CA *per* Orr J. leaving a decision about access to a welfare officer was said to be "wrong in principle".

87 *Judicial Statistics 2000,* Tables 5.2, 5.3.

88 Before the Children Act 1989 courts adjourned cases *sine die* (without fixing any date for a further hearing).

89 *M. v. M. (Defined Contact Application)* [1998] 2 F.L.R. 244, FD where the parents' joint wishes were recorded but a defined contact order was not made; *Re H. (Contact Order) (No. 2)* [2002] 1 F.L.R. 22 (appropriate to leave contact decisions to mother).

90 *S v. S (Custody: Jurisdiction)* [1995] 1 F.L.R. 153. Under some previous law interim orders could only last for three months maximum; the Law Commission saw no value in such rigid limits: Law Com. No. 172, para. 4.24.

91 Children Act 1989, s.11(7) (c).

before the child reaches the age of 16.[92] Where it is necessary to make an order on limited information, for example to ensure that the carer has parental responsibility, the court can set a timetable for a full hearing and specify the further material that it wants by that date.[93] However, the courts are advised to be cautious when making orders without a full understanding of the facts[94]; where the principle of contact is genuinely in dispute, interim contact may be ordered so the potential for contact can be assessed, but not to establish a pattern of visits.[95]

7. Permission to change the child's name

19–023 This is considered in Chapter 18, above.

8. Permission to remove the child from the jurisdiction[96]

19–024 The question of the child's removal from the jurisdiction may arise in connection with visits with the non-residential parent[97] or permanent emigration. The court's control over visits allows it to impose mechanisms such as the requirement for "mirror orders"[98] or bonds[99] to secure the child's return. This is particularly important if the visit is to a country which has not ratified the Hague Convention on Abduction.[1] Emigration cases raise more complex issues; the court must balance the benefits to the child of living with the parent with care in a place she wants to live and often has family support, against the detriment of attenuating the relationship with the other parent and his family:—

> In *Payne v. Payne*[2] the mother applied for leave so that she could return to New Zealand with her four year-old daughter. The father cross-applied for residence; when permission was given to the mother he appealed. The parents were not happy in London, the mother returned to New Zealand and the father went to Malaysia for work and then to New Zealand. The parents

---

[92] *ibid.* s.9(7). A variation after age 16 is only permitted in exceptional circumstances.

[93] *ibid.* s.11(1), (7) (d); F.P.R. 1991, r. 4.14; F.P.C. 1991, r. 14. Without notice residence orders should only be made for the shortest possible time: *Re G. (Minors) (ex p. Interim Residence Order)* [1993] 1 F.L.R. 910, CA; *Re P. (A Minor) (ex p. Interim Residence Order)* [1993] 1 F.L.R. 915, CA.

[94] *Re D. (Contact: Interim Order)* [1995] 1 F.L.R. 495.

[95] *Re M. (Interim Contact: Domestic Violence)* [2000] 2 F.L.R. 377, CA.

[96] See generally: The Society for Advanced Legal Studies Family Law Working Group, *Report on the Cross Border Movement of Children* (1999).

[97] Unless a prohibited steps order has been made, the residential parent may take the child out of the jurisdiction without permission for up to one month: Children Act 1989, s. 13(2). Where the residential parent needs permission, the court should consider the application thoroughly: *Re K. (Removal from Jurisdiction: Practice)* [1999] 2 F.L.R. 1084, CA.

[98] See para. 21–006.

[99] *Re L. (Removal from the Jurisdiction: Holiday)* [2001] 1 F.L.R. 241, FD. Bonds may also be used to ensure that contact continues after emigration. *Re S. (Removal from Jurisdiction)* [1999] 1 F.L.R. 850, FD.

[1] See Chap. 21, below for an explanation of the effects of this Convention.

[2] [2001] 1 F.L.R.1052, CA.

separated and the father obtained an order under the Hague Convention on Abduction for the child's return to England. The mother brought her back and obtained a residence order. The father had regular staying contact amounting to about two-fifths of each month. The mother was isolated and unhappy and this could impact on her child. The move would reduce the father's contact but he could afford to visit three times a year. The court was satisfied that the judge had applied the welfare test appropriately and refused the appeal.

There is no presumption in favour of the applicant parent but the reasonable proposals of a residential parent who wishes to live abroad carry great weight.[3] The conditions in the new country[4] and the arrangements that will be made if permission is refused are relevant.[5] Although permission to take a child abroad impinges on the right to family life, it has been stated that a decision which gives primacy to the child's welfare does not conflict with Article 8.[6]

9. Family assistance order[7]

19–025 The court may order the short-term involvement of a social worker[8] to assist a family resolve conflicts arising from family breakdown by making a family assistance order.[9] This order may be made whether or not section 8 orders are made[10] but the court must be satisfied that the circumstances are exceptional. The order cannot be imposed on any adult party; everyone named in the order

---

[3] *Payne v. Payne* [2001] 1 F.L.R.1052 at 1079 *per* Butler-Sloss P. Even speculative plans may be acceptable: *Re M. (Leave to Remove from Jurisdiction)* [1999] 2 F.L.R. 334, FD (mother given conditional leave so that she could apply to emigrate to Canada; both parents were asylum seekers and neither had permission to remain in the U.K.).

[4] *Re K. (Application to Remove from the Jurisdiction)* [1998] 2 F.L.R. 1006, FD. Despite the difficult conditions in Nigeria the court granted permission for the mother to take the children there. Both parents were from Nigeria and had family there.

[5] *Re C. (Leave to Remove from the Jurisdiction)* [2000] 2 F.L.R. 457, CA (mother's appeal against refusal of permission rejected; she had given evidence that she would remain in this country rather than join her new husband).

[6] *Payne v. Payne* [2001] 1 F.L.R. 1052 at 1064 *per* Thorpe L. J. referring to *Johansen v. Norway* (1996) 23 E.H.R.R. 33. But it has been suggested that the restriction conflicts with the Treaty of Rome, Art. 48 see The Society for Advanced Legal Studies Family Law Working Group, *op. cit.* p. 18.

[7] A. James and L. Sturgeon-Adams, *Helping families after divorce: assistance by order* (1999); L. Sturgeon-Adams and A. James [1999] *Fam. Law* 471; L. Trinder and N. Stone, "Family assistance orders: professional aspiration and party frustration" [1998] *C.F.L.Q.* 291; J. Sedden, "Family assistance orders and promoting welfare" (2001) 15 Int J. Law, Pol. and Fam. 226.

[8] The court may appoint an officer from either CAFCASS or the local authority: Children Act 1989, s.16(1). The local authority may only be appointed if it agrees or the child lives in its area: s.16(7). Where the local authority is unwilling to allocate resources enforcement proceedings against it are inappropriate: *Re C. (Family Assistance Order)* [1996] 1 F.L.R. 424, FD.

[9] *Guidance*, Vol. 1, para. 2.50.

[10] Children Act 1989, s.16(1). The Law Commission intended that orders should not be available where the child was in care but this is not expressly provided by the Act: see Law Com. No. 172, para. 5.15.

(except the child) must consent to it.[11] The persons who may be named are the child, the parents or guardians, anyone with whom the child is living and anyone in whose favour a contact order has been made.[12] Named persons are required to keep the appointed officer informed of relevant addresses and to permit visits.[13] The officer is required to advise, assist and befriend any person named in the order[14] but has no powers other than to refer the question of variation or discharge of a section 8 order to the court.[15] Work under this order needs to be clearly focused if problems are to be resolved.[16] The court should make plain why family assistance is needed and what is hoped to be achieved by it.[17] Concerns over child abuse or neglect should be referred to the local authority for investigation.[18] Family assistance orders are mainly used in relation to difficulties over contact.[19] They provide the only specific mechanism for the professional supervision of contact.[20] It was right to make an order against a reluctant local authority where this is the only way to ensure that a child continues to have contact ordered in her best interests.[21] The order is not intended to provide long-term support; it lasts for up to six months but can be renewed.[22]

Although family assistance orders were considered to have considerable potential for helping families, they have been little used. Only 864 orders were made in 1998[23] and there are wide variations in use between areas.[24] Lack of resources discouraged their recommendation in court reports and judges made half of the orders without a formal recommendation.[25] Thus the low level of

---

[11] Children Act 1989, s.16(3); *National Standards*, para. 5.8. In *Re M. (Contact: Family Assistance: McKenzie friend)* [1999] 1 F.L.R. 75, CA the court sought to encourage the mother's consent by preventing further applications by the father for six months if she did so.

[12] Children Act 1989, s.16(2).

[13] Children Act 1989, s.16(4). The obligations of the named persons are thus much more limited than those of the "responsible person" for a supervised child: see Sched. 3, Pts I and II, and Chap. 22, below.

[14] Children Act 1989, s.16(1); see *National Standards*, Chap. 5 for a statement of the role as undertaken by family court welfare officers before the creation of CAFCASS.

[15] Children Act 1989, s.16(6).

[16] *National Standards*, paras 5.9 *et seq.* required probation officers to visit within three weeks of receiving the order and provide information to the family.

[17] *Guidance*, Vol. 1, para. 2.52, following Law Com. No. 172, para. 5.20 and Booth Committee, para. 4.140.

[18] The local authority has a duty to investigate by virtue of s.47(1) (b), if the case were still being heard the court could order investigation under s.37 and make an order under s.38. Truancy should be referred to the local education authority: *National Standards*, para. 5.14.

[19] L. Trinder and N. Stone, *op. cit.*; J. Sedden, *op. cit.*

[20] Lord Chancellor's Department, *Making contact work: consultation paper* (2001), p. 23.

[21] *Re E. (Family Assistance Order)* [1999] 1 F.L.R. 512, FD (family assistance order granted to escort child and supervise contact with mother who was detained mental patient; this contact was established when the child was in local authority care); *cf. S v. P (Contact Application)* [1997] 2 F.L.R. 277, FD (family assistance order refused to escort children to prison to see violent father).

[22] Children Act 1989, s.16(5); *Re L. (Contact: Transsexual Applicant)* [1995] 2 F.L.R. 438; *Re E. (Family Assistance Order)* [1999] 1 F.L.R. 512, FD.

[23] Lord Chancellor's Department, *Making contact work: consultation paper* (2001), p. 24. But this figure cannot be regarded as accurate given the variations in recording practice identified by Sturgeon-Adams and James.

[24] Sturgeon Adams and James, *op. cit.*, p. 471; Trinder and Stone, *op. cit.* p. 302.

[25] Sturgeon-Adams and James, *op. cit.*, p. 473.

orders also reflects judicial uncertainty about their value.[26] Where orders are made the type of work undertaken and the affects achieved also vary with researchers identifying no change in over two-thirds of cases.[27] The Advisory Board on Family Law has proposed that local authority responsibility for these orders ends and CAFCASS develops specific programmes for them; orders should not require consent and the court should set their duration in accordance with the needs of the case.[28]

10. Orders restricting further applications, s.91(14)

19–026 The court has the power to preclude a party to proceedings making any further applications relating to the child without first obtaining the leave of the court.[29] The Act imposes no limits on the use of the power but the Court of Appeal has given guidance.[30] The judge must decide whether the best interests of the child require interference with the right of access to the court.[31] The power is a useful weapon to control those who have harassed a family through litigation,[32] or seek to pursue a hopeless case.[33] The order may also be imposed where the parent's fragility or the child's need for stability[34] mean that further proceedings are contrary to the child's welfare.[35] However, this is a draconian order which should be used sparingly and not where there is no history of unreasonable applications or no suggestion that applications have imposed unacceptable strain

---

[26] Their shortcomings were described by Thorpe L.J as "manifest" *Re L.; Re V.; Re M.; Re H. (Contact: Domestic Violence)* [2000] 2 F.L.R. 334 at 367B.

[27] Sturgeon-Adams and James, *op. cit.*, p. 473; Sedden, *op. cit.*, p. 236; Trinder and Stone, *op. cit.*, pp. 295–7. Sturgeon-Adams and James noted that in some areas similar work was undertaken as part of preparing a court report instead of under a FAO.

[28] Advisory Board on Family Law: Children Act Sub-committee, *Making contact work report* (2002), paras 11.9 *et seq.*

[29] Children Act 1989, s.91(14); before the Act these orders were made under the inherent jurisdiction: *Re H. (Child Orders: Restricting Applications)* [1991] F.C.R. 896, FD. The order may be made for a limited period: *Re M. (Section 91(14) Order)* [1999] 2 F.L.R. 553, CA.

[30] *Re P.(Section 91(14) Guidelines) (Residence and Religious Heritage)* [1999] 2 F.L.R. 573, CA *per* Butler-Sloss L.J. at p. 952–3. Butler-Sloss L.J. rejected the argument that imposing a leave requirement breached E.C.H.R., Art. 6(1) and in *Graeme v. U.K.* [2000] I.F.L. 188 an application by a person barred was declared inadmissible

[31] *B. v. B. (Residence Order: Restricting Applications)* [1997] 1 F.L.R. 139, CA *per* Waite L.J. at 146F–147A, the power must be exercised with great care, at 145 *per* Butler-Sloss L.J. Despite the fact that a decision to control access to the court does not relate directly to the child's upbringing s.91(14) should be read in conjunction with s.1(1) see Butler-Sloss L.J. in *Re P.* [1999] 2 F.L.R. 573 at 592. The power to declare a person a vexatious litigant is more restrictive: Supreme Court Act 1981, s.42.

[32] *Re C. (Contact: No Order for Contact)* [2000] 2 F.L.R. 723, CA (two applications in five years, appeal against s.91(14) order allowed); *Re R. (Residence: Contact: Restricting Applications)* [1998] 1 F.L.R. 749, CA (three unsuccessful applications for residence in three years, appeal against order dismissed).

[33] *Re Y. (Child Orders: Restricting Applications)* [1994] 2 F.L.R. 699, FD; *Re H. (Child Orders: Restricting Applications)* [1991] F.C.R. 896, FD.

[34] Making such an order alongside a residence order gave the father the security he sought through adoption: *Re B. (Adoption by one natural parent to exclusion of other)* [2001] 1 F.L.R. 589 at 595 *per* Hale L.J.

[35] *Re M. (Adoption or Residence Order)* [1998] 1 F.L.R. 570; *Re P.(Section 91(14) Guidelines) (Residence and Religious Heritage)* [1999] 2 F.L.R. 573, CA.

on the child.[36] The degree of restriction must be proportionate.[37] It may be difficult to decide when a litigant is acting so unreasonably that access to the court should be restricted.[38] Public funding may be withdrawn from those with weak cases and unreasonable litigants[39] but this may only remove the moderating influence of the solicitor.[40] Where the restriction applies, leave should be sought without notice[41]; the applicant must persuade the judge that he or she has an arguable case with some chance of success.[42] Leave will be granted if the applicant demonstrates a need for further judicial investigation.[43]

C. Restrictions on making orders

19–027 Although both the Law Commission and the *Review of Child Care Law* recommended that the effects of residence and care orders should be comparable, they also accepted that the boundaries between public and private law and the different roles of the courts and local authority social services departments should be clearly defined. Local authorities should not be able to intervene in family life without satisfying the "significant harm" test.[44] Only a local authority's major decisions about a child in care such as contact or discharge of a care order should be subject to scrutiny by the courts.[45] Consequently, the power to make section 8 orders is restricted in the Act.[46] A local authority's decision to place a child with foster parents or in another county is not subject to court review.[47] Residence and contact orders may not be made in favour of a local authority; nor may prohibited steps or specific issue orders be made to have a comparable

---

[36] *Re P.(Section 91(14) Guidelines) (Residence and Religious Heritage)* [1999] 2 F.L.R. 573, CA *per* Butler-Sloss L.J. at 952 3; *Re C. (Contact: No Order for Contact)* [2000] 2 F.L.R. 723.

[37] *Re P. (Section 91(14): Residence and Religious Heritage)* [1999] 2 F.L.R. 573, CA *per* Butler-Sloss L.J at 593. For example, the restriction could be for a limited time: *Re T. (A Minor) (Parental Responsibility: Contact)* [1993] 2 F.L.R. 450 but note the restriction in in that case precluded an application for leave and was made under the inherent jurisdiction.

[38] CAAC Final Report 1997, p. 72: "Children who are the subject of repeated applications are almost always detrimentally affected."

[39] *Funding Code decision making guidance* (2001), para. 20.22.

[40] See M. Maclean and J. Eekelaar, *Family Lawyers* (2000), pp.103, 109, 185.

[41] A hearing is only required if the court is considering allowing the application: *Re N. (s.91(14) Order)* [1996] 1 F.L.R. 356.

[42] *Re P.(Section 91(14) Guidelines) (Residence and Religious Heritage)* [1999] 2 F.L.R. 573, CA *per* Butler-Sloss L.J. at 953H.

[43] *Re A. (Application for Leave)* [1998] 1 F.L.R. 1, FD.

[44] Law Com. No. 172, paras 5.2–5.8; *Review of Child Care Law*, Chap. 15. For a detailed discussion of this issue see Chap 22, below.

[45] Law Com. No. 172, paras 4.51–4.52; *Review of Child Care Law*, paras 2.20–2.21. The ways of challenging local authority decisions are discussed in Chap. 22, below. Decisions about contact with children in care can be made by the courts, s.34 not s.8: see below.

[46] Children Act 1989, s.9(1)–(3). But the court could exceptionally make a residence order in favour of a foster carer who was not entitled to apply for leave to make an application: *Gloucestershire C. C. v. P.* [1999] 2 F.L.R. 61, CA.

[47] But where there is a departure from the care plan which threatens a parent's or child's human rights a challenge may be made under the Human Rights Act 1998, ss. 7,8: *Re M. (Care: Challenging decisions by local authority)* [2001] 2 F.L.R. 1300, FD approved in *Re S. (Minors) (Care Order: Implementation of Care Plan* [2002] 1 F.L.R. 815, HL, para. 62.

effect.[48] Thus the court may not restrict a parent's right to remove a child who is accommodated by the local authority,[49] require a parent to allow a child to have contact with a social worker or give the local authority a right to exercise parental responsibility unless the "significant harm" test[50] is satisfied and a care or supervision order is made[51]:—

> In *Nottinghamshire C. C. v. P.*[52] the local authority did not wish to take financial responsibility for the treatment of the father, a sexual abuser, in a specialist clinic for abusers. Therefore it chose not to apply for care orders in respect of his children but to seek a prohibited steps order requiring the father not to reside with his children nor to have contact with them. The Court of Appeal rejected the local authority's appeal against the refusal of prohibited steps order and criticised the local authority for failing to use its powers under Part IV of the Children Act 1989.[53]

However, a prohibited steps order may be used to end the contact of a non-parent who does not live with the child.[54] A local authority could therefore seek a prohibited steps order to keep an undesirable person away from a child who is not in care. Only residence orders may be made in respect of a child in care and the making of such an order has the effect of discharging the care order.[55]

D. Children in respect of whom orders can be made

19–028 The court's powers can be exercised over "any child" about whose welfare a question arises in family proceedings.[56] The child need not be a "child of the family"[57] but this definition remains important for determining whether an adult who is not a parent or guardian may seek an order without first obtaining leave.[58] The phrase "any child" is wider and may permit the court to make orders in respect of children who are not treated by the parties as a child of their family including children fostered with them by a local authority. There are no statutory limitations on the making of orders (rather than applications)[59] in favour of

---

[48] Children Act 1989, s.9(5) (a). This could confuse rather than clarify the position as to parental responsibility: see Law Com. No. 172, para. 4.19.

[49] Children Act 1989, s.9(5) (b), 20(7)–(9), 100(2) (a), (b), (d). *Re S. and D. (Children: Powers of the Court)* [1995] 2 F.L.R. 456, CA. The existence of a residence order restricts removal but not by a person with sole residence: s.20(9) (10).

[50] Children Act 1989, ss.31(2), 33, 35.

[51] Children Act 1989, ss.9(5) (b), 100(2) (a),(d).

[52] [1993] 1 F.L.R. 513, FD; [1993] 2 F.L.R. 134, CA.

[53] The Part concerned with care proceedings, see below, Chap. 22.

[54] *Re H. (Prohibited Steps Order)* [1995] 1 F.L.R. 638, CA.

[55] Children Act 1989, ss.9(1), 91(1). An order for contact between a child in care and siblings not in care is made in respect of the siblings so it does not conflict with this provision: *Re F. (Contact Child in Care)* [1995] 1 F.L.R. 510, FD.

[56] Children Act 1989, s.10(1). But the Adoption and Children Bill 2002, cl. 29(3) will, if enacted, preclude making s.8 orders in respect of children subject to placement orders.

[57] *ibid.* s.105(1); see below.

[58] Children Act 1989, s.10(5) (a).

[59] Children Act 1989, s.10(1) (b). Certain people may only apply for an order after obtaining the leave of the court, s.10(2) (b), (8),(9).

individuals in respect of accommodated children[60] but it has been held that orders in favour of those who could not apply for them would be most exceptional.[61]

There is generally no jurisdiction to make section 8 orders in respect of children who are not either habitually resident[62] in England and Wales, or present in England and Wales and not habitually resident in any other part of the United Kingdom.[63] Jurisdiction is also excluded under Brussels II where there are divorce proceedings pending elsewhere in the E.U.[64] It follows that section 8 orders cannot be made in preparation for a child's visit for contact in this country.[65] Even when a child resident overseas is in England, the court may refuse to make an order on the basis that the courts in the child's home country should make any decisions.[66]

Section 8 orders may only be made in exceptional circumstances in respect of children[67] over the age of 16.[68] Custody orders endured until a child reached 18 but the Law Commission was concerned about the practicality and justice of enforcing orders against older children and thus recommended the change.[69] Orders may be necessary in respect of over 16s with learning difficulties[70] and others who are immature,[71] particularly if they are cared for by people who would not otherwise have parental responsibility for them. Where orders are made in respect of older children they should be made parties to the proceedings.[72]

---

[60] A child who is looked after by the local authority by agreement with a person with parental responsibility or an orphan who is not subject to a care order: see below, Chap. 22. There are restrictions on making orders in favour of local authorities and in respect of children in care, s. 9(1) (2).

[61] *Gloucestershire C.C. v. P.* [1999] 2 F.L.R. 61, CA at 73 *per* Butler-Sloss L.J. (order in favour of foster carers who could not apply because they had looked after the child for only two and a half years, see s.9(3)).

[62] For an explanation of this concept see para. 21–014, below.

[63] Family Law Act 1986, ss. 1(1) (a), 2(1), 2A, 3. These restrictions do not apply to s.4 orders which can be made in relation to children overseas, *Re S. (Parental Responsibility: Jurisdiction)* [1998] 2 F.L.R. 921, CA.

[64] Council Regulation 1347/2000 and the European Communities (Matrimonial Jurisdiction and Judgment) Regulations 2001 (2001 S.I. No. 310) and para. 21–021 below.

[65] "Mirror" orders may be made under the inherent jurisdiction to support orders of courts in the state of habitual residence: *Re P. (A Child: Mirror Orders)* [2000] 1 F.L.R. 435, FD.

[66] *Re F. (Residence Order: Jurisdiction)* [1995] 2 F.L.R. 518. This is in keeping with the spirit of the Hague Convention on Abduction, see below, Chap. 21.

[67] There is no Children Act 1989 jurisdiction in relation to adults but the High Court may exercise its inherent jurisdiction to grant declarations in the best interests of those with limited mental capacity: *Re F. (Adult Court's Jurisdiction)* [2000] 2 F.L.R. 513, FD.

[68] Children Act 1989, s.9(7). In *Re M. (Contact: Parental Responsibility)* [2001] 2 F.L.R. 342 (a severely disabled 17 year old woman). The Adoption and Children Bill, 2002, cl. 112 proposes the extension to age 18 of some residence orders in favour of non-parents.

[69] Children over the age of 16 may apparently live away from their family home without parental consent: Law Com. No. 172, para. 3.25 "The older the child becomes, the less just it is even to attempt to enforce against him an order to which he has never been a party."

[70] Major issues such as the child's sterilisation would still need to be referred to the court: *Re B. (A Minor) (Sterilisation)* [1988] A.C. 199, *per* Lord Templeman at 205-6 see *Practice Note* [2001] 2 F.L.R. 158. Most other medical decisions will be able to be made by those with the residence order, Children Act 1989, s.2(7) and above para. 18–019.

[71] *Re S.W. (A Minor)* [1986] 1 F.L.R. 24 was cited by the Law Commission as a case where the jurisdiction was required. But the label of immaturity may merely be used to justify control.

[72] But this is not mandated by the rules: see F.P.R. 1991, r. 4.7; F.P.C. 1991, r. 7.

E. Who may apply for orders?

19–029 The Law Commission sought to create a logical scheme to protect the family from unwarranted interference and reduce recourse to the inherent jurisdiction of the High Court. It therefore developed a three-tier scheme which allows direct access to some applicants whilst requiring others to obtain the leave of the court.[73] The Children Act 1989 enacts this scheme which is modified by the Adoption and Children Bill 2002.[74]

1. All applications without leave

19–030 There are three categories of person who may apply for any section 8 order as of right[75]—

(i) parents (including fathers who do not have parental responsibility)[76];
(ii) guardians[77];
(iii) those in whose favour there is a residence order.

2. Contact and residence applications without leave

19–031 A wide range of people can seek residence or contact orders without leave.[78] These are:—

(iv) any party to a marriage (whether or not subsisting) in relation to whom the child is a child of the family[79];
(v) any person with whom the child has lived for a period of at least three years within the previous five years[80];
(vi) any person who has obtained the relevant[81] consents.

Where such applicants are seeking to care for or have contact with the child (but not orders to restrict other's exercise of parental responsibility), their close

---

[73] Law Com. No. 172, para. 4.41. For a detailed exposition of the old law, see the 4th edition of this work, pp. 363–364, 377–379, 386, 410–412.

[74] It requires leave for any application for residence where there is a special guardianship order—Children Act 1989, s.10(7A); for a parental application for residence where the child is placed or subject to a placement order, cl.28(1); and precludes any application for contact under the Children Act 1989, cl.26(2)(a).

[75] Children Act 1989, s.10(4).

[76] Step-parents who acquire parental responsibility under Children Act 1989, s.4A added by Adoption of Children Bill, 2002, cl 107 are not apparently included.

[77] Under the Adoption and Children Bill 2002, Sched. 3, para. 55 this includes a "special guardian" appointed under Children Act 1989, s.14A.

[78] Children Act 1989, s.10(5).

[79] Children Act 1989, ss.10(5) (a), 105(1) and see below.

[80] Children Act 1989, s.10(5) (b), (10). A similar provision existed for custodianship.

[81] The following consents are required "(i) where a residence order is in force . . . each of the persons in whose favour the order was made; (ii) where the child is in care . . . the local authority; (iii) in any other case the consent of each person with parental responsibility." Children Act 1989, s.10(5) (c).

relationship with the child or support from those with parental responsibility means that leave would be a meaningless formality.[82] Orders may be varied or discharged on the application of:—

(vii) any person who applied for the order or who is named in a contact order.[83]

The Act only removed the automatic right of application from some grandparents[84]; there is power to restore this by rules.[85]

Meaning of "child of the family"

A child of the family is now defined in relation to parties to a marriage as:— **19–032**

"(a) a child of both those parties;
(b) any other child, not being a child who is placed with those parties as foster parents by a local authority or voluntary organisation who has been treated by both those parties as a child of their family."[86]

All children of both parties to the marriage are included, but the Act goes much further, reflecting the reality of family relationships[87] and making the existence of a biological or formal legal relationship (such as adoption) between the carers and child irrelevant so long as the child has been "treated as a child of the family" by both parties.[88] A child who is being looked after long-term by relatives[89] is likely to fall within the definition, as is a child who is being privately fostered.[90]

---

[82] Law Com. No. 172, para. 4.48.

[83] Children Act 1989, s.10(6).

[84] Only some grandparents had an automatic right to apply: G.M.A. 1971, s.14A; D.P.M.C.A. 1978, s.14; Children Act 1975, s.34(1) (a). Considerable concern was expressed about the treatment of grandparents in the debates on the Children Bill: *Hansard*, H.L., Vol. 503, col. 1342 (Report Stage); *Hansard*, H.C., Vol. 158, cols. 1288–1306. See also F. Kaganas and C. Piper, "Grandparents and the limits of the law" (1990) 4 Int. J. Law & Fam. 27; G. Douglas and N. Lowe, "Grandparents and the legal process" [1990] J.S.W.L. 89 and F. Kaganas and C. Piper, "Grandparents and contact: 'rights v welfare' revisited" (2001) 15 Int. J. Law & Fam. 250.

[85] Children Act 1989, s.10(7). No rules have been made.

[86] *ibid.* s.105(1). For earlier definitions, see M.C.A. 1973, s.52(1) and D.P.M.C.A. 1978, s.88(1).

[87] A child who is a child of the family should be recognised as having a right to respect for their family life with the carers under ECHR, Art. 8. and *vice versa* see: *K and T. v. Finland* [2001] 2 F.L.R. 707 (step-father held to have right to family life with step-child). Where a same sex couple share care the child ought to be considered as a child of their family so that either party may apply for an order: *Re W. (Adoption: Homosexual Adopter)* [1998] Fam. 58 at 59 where Singer J. described a lesbian couple as a family and *Fitzpatrick v. Sterling Housing Association* [2000] 1 F.L.R. 271.

[88] *W. (R.J.) v. W. (S.J.)* [1972] Fam. 152. There must have been a family: *Re M. (A Minor)* [1980] 2 F.L.R. 184, CA (child born after couple separated not a child of the family even though husband visited and signed cards "Dad"); *Teeling v. Teeling* [1984] F.L.R. 808, CA.

[89] *Re A. (Child of the Family)* [1998] 1 F.L.R. 347, CA. A child whose grandparents had taken over her care and refused to allow the mother to reclaim her was a child of their family. Temporary helping out by relatives may not be sufficient *per* Butler-Sloss L.J.

[90] Children placed by a local authority or voluntary organisation are specifically outside the definition but only while the fostering arrangement lasts: see Law Com. No. 172 para. 4.46.

Indeed, it may be practically impossible for a step-parent with whom a child lives[91] to avoid treating the child as a child of the family. The test of "treatment" is objective and it is immaterial that the wife has deceived her husband about the child's paternity.[92] But an unborn child cannot be treated by the husband as a member of his family.[93]

3. Applications only with leave

19–033 All other applicants, including parents whose children have been adopted and "former parents" whose children have been freed for adoption[94] require leave. Applications for leave can be considered without notice but only refused following a hearing.[95] The "welfare test" does not apply; instead the court must consider the criteria in the Act[96] and the likelihood of success of the substantive application.[97]

Restriction of access to the courts will not breach the European Convention of Human Rights, Article 6(1) unless the applicant can show that their civil rights, for example their right to family life, are at issue. Whether a relationship with a child amounts to "family life" is a question of fact[98]; and the state may impose a requirement of leave in order to pursue a legitimate aim such as family privacy.[99] Refusal of leave in accordance with the Act may be a proportionate response even where the applicant has family life with the child, for example where further litigation would disrupt other relationships or harm the child.[1]

---

[91] See *D. v. D. (Child of the Family)* (1980) 2 F.L.R. 93, *per* Templeman L.J. at 98. Unless of course the parties separate all responsibility for the child. Where the child merely has staying visits he may not become a child of that family, *per* Orr L.J. at 96.

[92] *W. (R.J.) v. W. (S.J.)* [1972] Fam. 152 although this would be relevant to the quantification of maintenance see M.C.A. 1973, s.25(3) and might give rise to an action for deceit: *P. v. B. (Paternity: Damages for Deceit)* [2001] 1 F.L.R. 1041.

[93] *A. v. A. (Family: Unborn Child)* [1974] Fam. 6, approved in *W. v. W. (Child of the Family)* [1984] F.L.R. 796 at 802, *per* Sheldon J.

[94] *M. v. C. and Calderdale M.B.C.* [1993] 1 F.L.R. 505, CA.

[95] F.P.R. 1991, r. 4.3; F.P.C. 1991, r. 3 but unless a very clear case is put forward a hearing will be required: *Re W. (Contact Application: Procedure)* [2000] 1 F.L.R. 263 F.D. *Ex parte* applications are undesirable where leave is required because of an order under s.91(14): *Re N. (Section 91(14) Order)* [1996] 1 F.L.R. 356, CA. All persons with parental responsibility should be notified of an application by the child concerned see: *Re SC. (A Minor) (Leave to Seek Residence Order)* [1994] 1 F.L.R. 96. Where the applicant is a parent seeking contact with an adopted child the Official Solicitor and the adoption agency should be notified: see *Re. C. (A Minor) (Adopted Child Contact)* [1993] 2 F.L.R. 431; *cf. Re T. (Adopted Children: Contact)* [1995] 2 F.L.R. 792, CA.

[96] Children Act 1989, ss.10(8), (9) and below.

[97] *Re A. and W. (Minors) (Residence Order: Leave to Apply)* [1992] Fam. 182, CA; *C. v. Salford C. C.* [1994] 2 F.L.R. 926; *Re J. (Specific Issue Order: Leave to Apply)* [1995] 1 F.L.R. 669; *cf. Re C. (A Minor) (Leave to Seek section 8 Order)* [1994] 1 F.L.R. 26.

[98] Swindells *et al.* p. 44 citing *X., Y. and Z. v. U.K.* [1997] 2 F.L.R. 892; in *K. and T. v. Finland* [2001] 2 F.L.R. 707, para. 150 the court drew no distinction between the mother and the stepfather because they jointly enjoyed "family life" with the children.

[99] See *Ashingdane v. UK* (1985) 7 E.H.R.R. 528 at para. 57; the restriction must be proportionate.

[1] By analogy with *Soderback v. Sweden* [1999] 1 F.L.R. 250 where an adoption order in favour of a step-parent and without the permission of the natural father struck a "fair balance" between the competing interests and was within the state's margin of appreciation. Kanagas and Piper, *op. cit.* argue that both granting and refusing leave can be regarded as proportional, at p. 262.

Applicants who require leave can be divided into four categories:

(i) local authority foster parents and former foster parents;
(ii) children concerned in the proceedings;
(iii) other persons with no right to apply (for example, grandparents and other relatives);
(iv) persons on whom a leave requirement has been imposed under s. 91(14).[2]

The need to seek leave can be avoided by an application to ward the child except where the child is being looked after by a local authority.[3]

Local authority foster parents

19–034 Unless they are the child's relatives, local authority foster parents and those who have fostered a child within the last six months require the permission of the authority before they may apply for leave for a section 8 order.[4] The Law Commission considered that such people should be in a special category to avoid undermining parents' confidence in the provision of accommodation[5] by local authorities. Parents should be no more "at risk of losing their children" than they would by making a private arrangement, and local authorities should feel confident of their responsibility to make plans for all the children they look after.[6] Originally the period of restriction was three years but after one year foster carers could apply to adopt without risking the child's removal by the local authority.[7] The Adoption and Children Bill 2002, will remove this anomaly[8] but reduce the protection to parents who place children in accommodation. The need to obtain permission protects the interests of the authority but not those of the natural parents:—

In *C. v. Salford City Council*[9] Jewish parents requested adoption for their child who suffered from Down's Syndrome. The child was placed with non-Jewish carers while a suitable adoptive family was sought. The foster

---

[2] Applications by those subject to a restriction under s. 91(14) are considered above, para. 19–026.
[3] *A. v. Liverpool C.C.* [1982] A.C. 363. In *C. v. Salford* [1994] 2 F.L.R. 926 Hale J. said (*obiter*) it would have been "a very bold decision" to permit an application in wardship where leave was refused.
[4] Children Act 1989, s.9(3) (4). The local authority must consider this decision applying s.22(3)–(5), see below.
[5] For an explanation of local authority accommodation, see Children Act 1989, s.20 in Chap. 22, below.
[6] Law Com. No. 172, para. 4.43; L.C.W.P. 96, paras 5.41–5.48.
[7] Adoption Act 1976, ss.30(2), 31(1). A similar provision is found in the Adoption and Children Bill 2002, cl. 42(4). Leave to remove will not be given if the adoption application has a realistic prospect of success: *Re C. (A Minor) (Adoption)* [1994] 2 F.L.R. 513 at 520–523, *per* Butler-Sloss L.J.
[8] cl. 111 amends s. 9(3) and repeals s. 9(4); *Re C. (A Minor) (Adoption)* [1994] 2 F.L.R. 513 at 515.
[9] [1994] 2 F.L.R. 926. The residence order was made. This case has been the subject of further litigation: *Re P. (s.91(14)) (Residence and Religious Heritage)* [1999] 2 F.L.R. 573, CA and see below para. 20–015.

carers wanted to continue to look after the child and obtained permission from the local authority to seek leave for a residence order. Leave was granted despite the parents' objections and the fact that an adoptive family had been found. The child's life and the adoption plan would be disrupted if she had to move from the applicants but the delay of a few months whilst the application for a residence order was considered would not cause any further harm.

Where the child is in care, the authority's permission enables a residence order to be obtained without leave. If the child is only accommodated, leave of the court or of everyone with parental responsibility will also be required but support from the local authority is likely to be influential.[10]

In *Re A. and W. (Minors) (Residence Order: Leave to Apply)*[11] a foster carer used judicial review to challenge the decision of the local authority to remove four children placed with her. Before the hearing the local authority agreed to the foster carer applying for leave to seek residence orders. However, leave was refused because it was unlikely that a court would make such orders against the wishes of the children who were aged between 13 and 9 years.

Foster carers who obtain residence orders may be supported financially by the local authority[12] but are not subject to regulatory controls.[13] Where the local authority refuses permission, a mature child could apply for a residence order in favour of the foster carers.

Criteria for leave—the child concerned[14]

19–035 The requirement that children should obtain leave before initiating applications is designed to ensure that the application is the child's, not that of any adult[15] and the matter is serious enough to justify court proceedings. Children seeking leave will need to establish that they "have sufficient understanding to

---

[10] The court must have regard to both the authority's plans and the parent's wishes and feelings: Children Act 1989, s.10(9) (d); see *C. v. Salford City Council* [1994] 2 F.L.R. 926 for an example of how these matters are considered.

[11] [1992] Fam. 182.

[12] Children Act 1989, Sched.1, para. 15; payments are frequently lower than to foster carers but this may be subject to challenge.

[13] People who were disqualified from being foster carers following a change in the regulations could continue to look after a child under a residence order: *Re RJ. (Fostering: Person Disqualified)* [1999] 1 F.L.R. 605, CA, at 610 *per* Butler-Sloss L.J. In the event wardship was used: *Re RJ. (Wardship)* [1999] 1 F.L.R. 619. The local authority supported the foster carers in their applications.

[14] s.10(8) applies where the person seeking leave is "the child concerned." Where a child wishes to obtain contact with another the criteria in s.10(9) apply: *Re S. (Contact: Application by Sibling)* [1998] 2 F.L.R. 897 at 905 *per* Charles J.

[15] Law Com. No. 172, para. 4.44; *Re H. (Residence Order)* [2000] 1 F.L.R. 780, FD (leave refused because the child had no separate issue). The *Funding Code decision making guidance* (2001), paras 20.4.3, 20.22.11(c) states, "It is unlikely that Legal Representation would be granted to a child to apply for a residence order."

make the proposed application",[16] but competence does not qualify them for leave.[17] The court also considers the impact the child's presence may have on the proceedings, their impact on the child and the likelihood of success of the application.[18] The application must be made in the High Court[19]; the child may appear without a next friend or guardian *ad litem* only if the court accepts that he or she is capable of instructing a solicitor[20]:—

> In *Re C. (Leave to Seek Section 8 Orders)*[21] a 14-year-old girl sought leave for a residence order and a specific issue order so that she could live with friends and go on holiday to Bulgaria with them. Leave was refused. Granting an order would formalise the arrangements which would be better resolved by discussion within the family; granting leave might indicate a willingness in the court to side with children who disagree with their parents.

> But in *Re S C. (A Minor) (Leave to Seek a Residence Order)*[22] leave was granted to allow a 14-year-old girl living in a children's home and subject to a care order to apply for a residence order in favour of a friend who had agreed to care for her. Although the mother opposed the application and the local authority had previously rejected the friend as the girl's foster carer, the application had a reasonable prospect of success.

A child who objects to parental plans for his name change or emigration may seek leave to apply for a prohibited steps order.[23] A child who cannot seek leave may still be joined as a party to any proceedings[24]; but most children are dependent on the adult parties and the court to ensure that their interests are considered.

Criteria for leave—other persons

19–036 In all cases, including applications by local authority foster parents, the court must have regard to the nature of the proposed application[25]; the applicant's

---

[16] Children Act 1989, s.10(8): see *Re S. (A Minor) (Independent Representation)* [1993] Fam. 263. see also Chap. 17, above.

[17] *Re SC. (A Minor) (Leave to Seek Residence Order)* [1994] 1 F.L.R. 96; *Re C. (A Minor) (Leave to Seek section 8 orders)* [1994] 1 F.L.R. 26, where the court emphasised the disadvantage that orders would enshrine the dispute between a 15-year old girl and her parents.

[18] *Re C. (Residence: Child's Application for Leave)* [1995] 1 F.L.R. 927 at 931.

[19] *Practice Direction* [1993] 1 F.L.R. 668.

[20] F.P.R. 1991, r. 9.2A; *Re T. (A Minor) (Wardship Representation)* [1994] Fam. 49; see also J. Masson, "Representations of Children" [1996] C.L.P. 245.

[21] [1994] 1 F.L.R. 26. Johnson J. has now accepted that the child's welfare is not the paramount consideration in these cases: *Re H. (Residence Order)* [2000] 1 F.L.R. 780, FD.

[22] [1994] 1 F.L.R. 96.

[23] Alternatively the child could seek to enforce their rights by applying for an injunction or make themself a ward of court.

[24] *L. v. L. (Minors) (Separate Representation)* [1994] 1 F.L.R. 156; *Re N. (Residence Appointment of Solicitor: Placement with Extended Family)* [2001] 1 F.L.R. 1028, CA.

[25] Children Act 1989, s.10(9) (a); successful applications for specific issue or prohibited steps orders by people who are not caring for the child are likely to be rare unless the child's welfare is seriously at risk: see Law Com. No. 172, para. 4.41.

connection with the child; and the risk that the child's life might be disrupted to a harmful extent by the proposed application.[26] Leave should scarcely be a hurdle to close relatives such as grandparents, uncles and aunts or brothers and sisters who wish to care for or visit the child[27]:—

> In *Re F. and R. (Section 8 Order: Grandparents Application)*[28] the parents opposed an application for contact by a grandmother who interfered and swore in front of the grandchildren. The application was refused but the appeal was successful.

But parents whose children have been adopted,[29] adopted children[30] and a children's guardian[31] whose professional involvement in a case had ended have been unsuccessful in persuading the courts to let them bring an issue before them:—

> In *Re E. (Adopted Child: Contact Leave)*[32] the natural parents were promised photographs of their child by the adopter's social worker at a hearing the adopters did not attend. No condition was put in the adoption order and the adopters refused to provide the photographs. Although the court recognised the real injustice to the natural parents it did not give them leave because contact was fundamentally inconsistent with an unconditional adoption order.

It has been said that the test for leave should not be applied in a restrictive way but the granting of leave does not create any presumption that the substantive application will succeed.[33]

F. Procedure under the Children Act

19–037 Applications for orders under the Children Act 1989 are made by completing the appropriate application form and sending it to the court.[34] Where leave is

---

[26] Children Act 1989, s.10(9) (c). The criteria are also relevant when leave is sought for a s.34 contact order: *Re M. (Care: Contact: Grandmother's Application)* [1995] 2 F.L.R. 86, CA.

[27] In *Re O. (Minors) (Leave to Seek Residence Orders)* [1994] 1 F.L.R. 172 the father's cousin who had cared for the children for only three days was granted leave and an interim residence order on an oral application. On appeal the decision to grant leave was upheld but the order was said to be too long.

[28] [1995] 1 F.L.R. 524.

[29] *Re C. (A Minor) (Adopted Child: Contact)* [1993] 2 F.L.R. 431.

[30] *Re S. (Contact: Application by Sibling)* [1998] 2 F.L.R. 898, FD.

[31] *Re M. (Prohibited Steps Order: Application for Leave to Apply)* [1993] 1 F.L.R. 275.

[32] [1995] 1 F.L.R. 57. But in *Re T. (Adopted Children: Contact)* [1995] 2 F.L.R. 792, CA leave was given so that the adopters of the applicant's siblings could explain why they had reneged on their agreement to provide her with annual reports.

[33] *Re M. (Care: Contact: Grandmother's Application)* [1995] 2 F.L.R. 86, CA; *G v. F (Contact and Shared Residence)* [1998] 2 F.L.R. 799 at 802 *per* Bracewell J. (leave granted to a lesbian co-parent after separation from the child's mother).

[34] F.P.R. 1991, r. 4.4; F.P.C. 1991, r. 4.

required a written request must be made.[35] The application must be served on all the parties; in private law proceedings this includes everyone with parental responsibility but not the child.[36] The child can be made a party in private law proceedings; representation is usually by an officer of CAFCASS who has the same duties as a children's guardian and can therefore undertake substantial investigations.[37] The parties and those caring for the child must usually be notified of the application but the court may give leave to proceed *ex parte* and make orders without notifying anyone.[38] Thus a specific issue order for medical treatment,[39] or a prohibited steps order to prevent the child's removal from the country may be granted with great speed. Residence orders should only be granted without notice for the shortest time necessary.[40] There are systems for court decisions to be made out of hours in emergencies.[41]

The parties attend a directions hearing before a district judge or clerk to the justices.[42] The timetable for the proceedings is set[43] and further directions are given about the submission of evidence, preparation of reports, the form of the hearing, to add or remove parties,[44] or to transfer the proceedings.[45] The court may be asked to give directions on other matters as the case proceeds. Although directions hearings enable the court to keep a hold on the litigation,[46] and should shorten final hearings, they require considerable resources and limit court time for substantive hearings.[47] Where directions are not complied with a penalty of costs may be imposed.[48]

---

[35] F.P.R. 1991, r. 4.3; F.P.C. 1991, r. 3; *cf. Re. O. (Minors) (Leave to Seek Residence Order)* [1994] 1 F.L.R. 172.

[36] F.P.R. 1991, rr. 4.7, 4.8 and App. 2; F.P.C. 1991, rr.7, 8 and App. 2. The child is a party in specified proceedings and service is to the children's guardian or the child's solicitor, F.P.R. 1991, rr. 4.11A(8), 4.12(2); F.P.C. 1991, rr. 11(8), 12(2).

[37] *Re A.(Contact: Separate Representation)* [2001] 1 F.L.R. 715, CA; *L. v. L. (Separate Representation)* [1994] 1 F.L.R. 156, CA; F.P.R. r. 9.5.

[38] F.P.R. 1991, r. 4.4(4); F.P.C. 1991, r. 4(4) but not if this breached common law principles of fairness: *Re C. (Secure Accommodation Order: Representation)* [2001] 2 F.L.R. 169, CA or E.C.H.R. Art. 6(1).

[39] *e.g. Re R. (A Minor) (Blood Transfusion)* [1993] 2 F.L.R. 157.

[40] *Re G. (Minors) (ex parte Interim Residence Order)* [1993] 1 F.L.R. 910; *Re P. (A Minor) (ex parte Interim Residence Order)* [1993] 1 F.L.R. 915.

[41] CAAC Report 1992/3, pp. 50, 62; CAAC Report 1993/4, pp. 38, 51.

[42] F.P.R. 1991, rr. 4.14, 4.16; F.P.C. 1991, rr. 14, 16.

[43] CAAC *Handbook* (1997), p.17 gives guidance for judges dealing with directions in public law cases. The parties and their advocates should co-operate to discuss the likely length of hearing: *Re M.D. and T.D. (Minors) (Time Estimates)* [1994] 2 F.L.R. 336.

[44] F.P.R. 1991, r. 4.7(2); F.P.R. 1991, r. 7(2). Concern has been expressed about the proliferation of parties: CAAC Report 1992/3, p. 27. Where the interests of those who wish to intervene are identical to those of a party intervention should not be allowed: *Re M. (Minors) (Sexual Abuse Evidence)* [1993] 1 F.L.R. 822; applicants must have a reasonable chance of succeeding with their substantive application: *G. v Kirklees M.B.C.* [1993] 1 F.L.R. 805. A party who has no constructive part to play in proceedings may be discharged: *Re W. (Discharge of Party to Proceedings)* [1997] 1 F.L.R. 128.

[45] F.P.R. 1991, r. 4.14; F.P.C. 1991, r. 14. See also CAAC Report 1992/3, p. 59 for a list of specimen directions.

[46] See: *Practice Direction (Case Management)* [1995] 1 F.L.R. 456; *Guidance from the President to Family Court Business Committees*, CAAC Final Report 1997, Chap. 2, App. A.

[47] CAAC Report 1992/3, p. 51.

[48] Family Proceedings (Costs) Rules 1991, S.I. 1991 No. 1832, r. 15; *Practice Direction* [1999] 1 F.L.R. 1295. But it has been held that it would be wrong to exclude evidence where a direction is not complied with: *R. v. Nottinghamshire C.C.* [1993] *Fam. Law* 543.

Advance disclosure of evidence is required[49]; witnesses prepare signed statements for the lawyers and the court to read before the hearing.[50] Witness statements replace evidence-in-chief so that hearings are not prolonged.[51] Justice precludes the court from relying on confidential material unless real harm would come to the children from disclosure.[52] In care proceedings, the positive obligation on the State to protect the interests of the family requires material to be given even though no request has been made.[53] Areas of conflict should be identified and focused on at the hearing. The parties must conduct the litigation reasonably. Where one party acts oppressively, increasing costs by making unrealistic applications and false allegations, a penalty of costs can be imposed:—

> In *M. v. H. (Costs Residence Proceedings)*[54] the father agreed during mediation that shared residence was unrealistic. Later, during negotiations about contact arrangements, he applied for residence and refused to mediate unless the mother agreed to shared residence. He persisted with this application, knowing that it was causing the mother financial hardship, even after it was clear that he had no prospects of success. The judge ordered him to pay 75 per cent of the mother's costs, £42,628.

Costs can be ordered against lawyers who fail in their duties to the court.[55]

19–038 Hearings take place in private[56]; the privacy of the child and the parties, and the interests of justice justify this despite the general right to a public hearing.[57] The right to a fair trial demands that a person whose civil rights are at issue has an opportunity to be heard.[58] The interests of the children must also be consid-

---

[49] F.P.R. 1991, r. 14.17; F.P.C. 1991, r. 17. Sworn statements (affidavits) are used in proceedings under the inherent jurisdiction, see below.

[50] F.P.C. 1991, r. 21(1); *Hampshire C.C. v. S.* [1993] 1 F.L.R. 559; CAAC Report 1992/3, p. 2. The advocates are expected to prepare a complete file of papers for the judge: *Practice Direction (Family Proceedings: Court Bundles)* [2000] 1 F.L.R. 536.

[51] *Practice Direction* [1995] 1 F.L.R. 456.

[52] *Official Solicitor v. K.* [1965] A.C. 201; *Re D. (Adoption Reports: Confidentiality)* [1995] 2 F.L.R. 687, HL; *Re M. (Disclosure)* [1998] 2 F.L.R. 1028 an opportunity should be given to the party affected to make representations. Lack of disclosure may amount to a breach of E.C.H.R., Art. 6(1): *McMichael v. U.K.* (1995) 20 E.H.R.R. 205.

[53] *TP and KM v. U.K.* [2001] 2 F.L.R. 549 at para. 82. It may still be possible for the local authority to resist disclosure by claiming public interest immunity and leaving the question of disclosure to the court: *Re C. (Expert Evidence: Disclosure Practice)* [1995] 1 F.L.R. 204.

[54] [2000] 1 F.L.R 52.

[55] C.P.R. 1998, r. 48.7; *Re G., S. and M. (Wasted Costs)* [2000] 1 F.L.R. 52 (failure to ensure that expert witness had the necessary information).

[56] F.P.R. 1991, r. 4.16(7); F.P.C. 1991, r. 16(7).

[57] *B. v. U.K.; P. v. U.K.* [2001] 2 F.L.R. 261 an appeal to the European Court following *Re PB. (Hearings in Open Court)* [1996] 2 F.L.R. 765, CA.

[58] Art. 6(1); *Re I. and H. (Contact: Right to Give Evidence)* [1998] 1 F.L.R. 876; *H. v. West Sussex C.C.* [1998] 1 F.L.R. 863, 864 *per* Johnson J. The court may permit adoption proceedings without notification to the biological father who could not claim "family life" with his child: *Re M. (Adoption: Rights of Natural Father)* [2001] 1 F.L.R. 745; *Re H.; Re G. (Adoption: Consultation of Unmarried Fathers)* [2001] 1 F.L.R. 646, CA.

ered.[59] The form of hearing is a matter for the judge.[60] There is a spectrum of procedure from without notice application on minimal evidence to full and detailed oral hearings.[61] There may be no need for further evidence where an issue has already been considered by the court[62] but the practice of dismissing apparently weak cases without considering any evidence does not satisfy the Convention.[63]

The court also determines whether a child party can attend the proceedings. Child parties who are represented may be excluded if this is in their interests[64] and does not prevent effective representation.[65] Attending court has been considered potentially damaging for children and appropriate only in exceptional cases.[66] Consequently, arrangements have not been made to include children and they have often not been asked whether they would like to attend.[67]

The child may be a witness for any of the parties but the family courts are deeply reluctant to allow children to give evidence.[68] A child's statement may be given to the court by a third party; evidence given in connection with the upbringing, maintenance or welfare of a child is admissible despite the rules relating to hearsay.[69] But hearsay may not be allowed where the proceedings primarily affect the parents.[70] The admissibility of hearsay avoids the need for the child to repeat statements made to a teacher or other confidant (which would be impossible in the case of a young child) and protects children from court attendance and cross examination. A welfare report is the usual way to obtain

---

59 *Re B. and T.(Care Proceedings: Legal Representation)* [2001] 1 F.L.R. 485 *per* Buxton L.J. at para. 21 (an adjournment would have delayed unacceptably providing security for the children).

60 F.P.R. 1991, r. 4.21; F.P.C. 1991, r. 4.21; Hershman [1994] *Fam. Law.* 449; *Practice Direction* [1995] 1 F.L.R. 456.

61 *per* Butler-Sloss, L.J. *Re. B. (Minors) (Contact)* [1994] 2 F.L.R. 1 at 5. For a discussion of the obligations of the applicant in without notice cases see: *Re S. (Ex parte Orders)* [2001] 1 F.L.R. 308.

62 *Re F. (Contact: Enforcement: Representation of the Child)* [1998] 1 F.L.R. 691, CA.

63 For example in *Cheshire C. C. v. M.* [1993] 1 F.L.R. 463 and *Re B. (Contact: Step-father's Opposition)* [1997] 2 F.L.R. 579, CA; see Swindells *et al.* 8.118–9.

64 Children Act 1989, s.95; F.P.R. 1991, r. 4.16(2); F.P.C. 1991 r. 16(2). The issue of attendance at appeals is uncertain: *Re. C. (A Minor) (Care: Child's Wishes)* [1993] 1 F.L.R. 832 at 841. In *Re. W. (Secure Accommodation Order: Attendance at Court)* [1994] 2 F.L.R. 1092 the child's appeal against the order on the grounds that he had been excluded from the proceedings was rejected. The fact that the child would have been physically restrained if he had attended was sufficient to justify his exclusion, *per* Ewbank J. at 1096.

65 A child party who is separately represented must have the opportunity to instruct their lawyer: *Re AS. (Secure Accommodation Order)* [1999] 1 F.L.R. 103.

66 CAAC Report 1992/3, p. 71–2 citing *J. v. Lancashire C.C.* (unreported) May 25, 1993; *Re. C. (A Minor) (Care: Child's Wishes)* [1993] 1 F.L.R. 832 at 841; CAAC *Handbook* (1997), p.21.

67 Masson and Winn Oakley (1999), p. 109. Young people involved in care proceedings are now informed that they can ask to attend see *Powerpack* (2001). There is some recognition of the benefits to children of participation: *Re K.(Secure Accommodation Order: Right to Liberty)* [2001] 1 F.L.R. 526 at para. 44.

68 Advisory Board on Family Law: Children Act Sub-Committee, *Making contact work* (2002) para. 3.46. The practice of a child swearing an affidavit in favour of one parent in a residence dispute is deprecated: *Re M. (family proceedings: affidavits)* [1995] 2 F.L.R. 100 *per* Butler-Sloss L.J.

69 Children Act 1989, s.96(3) and Children (Admissibility of Hearsay Evidence) Order 1993, S.I. 1993 No. 621.

70 *C. v. C. (Contempt: Evidence)* [1993] 1 F.L.R. 220.

evidence of the child's views[71] but some children write direct to the judge. Judges and magistrates should only interview children if there are unusual circumstances and only exceptionally if there is a children's guardian or welfare reporter.[72] Such meetings are a complete departure from the normal forensic process[73] and may be more for the judge's benefit than the child's.[74] Where the child is interviewed and the judge relies on something said without giving the parties the opportunity to question it, the order may be set aside.[75] Consequently, the child should not be offered confidentiality.[76]

Where matters are in dispute the court should make findings of fact[77]; the case may be heard in two parts to establish the facts before consideration of proposals for the child's future.[78] The parties may give evidence or call witnesses on relevant matters.[79] The court has power to control access to court papers and assessments of the child.[80]

> In *Re A. (Family Proceedings: Expert Witnesses)*[81] the parents were involved in a very contentious contact dispute. During contact at a contact centre, the father made a secret video. His solicitors sent this to a psychologist with anonymised information about the family and instructions to prepare a report. The father then applied for residence attaching the report to his evidence. Although the rules about disclosure of papers and examination of children had not been broken, Wall J. strongly condemned the father, his solicitor and the expert who should not have accepted instructions anonymously.

19–039 Evidence about children from a review of documents is rarely as persuasive as that from assessments[82] but the court's desire to restrict examinations of chil-

---

[71] Children Act 1989, s.7 . In specified proceedings the children's guardian provides a report, s.41.

[72] *Re M. (Child) (Ascertaining Wishes and Feelings)* [1993] 2 F.C.R. 721; *B. v. B. (Minors) (Interviews and Listing Arrangements)* [1994] 2 F.L.R. 489, CA.

[73] CAAC Report 1993/4, p. 45.

[74] J. Masson, "The role of the judge in children's cases" (1988) 7 C.J.Q. 141 at 145. There are no recent statistics on judges' use of this power but in 1966 Hall found that half of the judges he contacted used it but only one-fifth did so where custody was contested, L.C.W.P. 15 (1966), para. 7.

[75] *Elder v. Elder* [1986] 1 F.L.R. 610, CA.

[76] *H. v. H.* [1974] 1 All E.R. 1145; *Elder v. Elder* [1986] 1 F.L.R. 610; *Re D. (Adoption Reports: Confidentiality)* [1995] 2 F.L.R. 687, HL; see also: *Re C. (Disclosure)* [1996] 1 F.L.R. 797.

[77] *Re L.; Re V.; Re M.; Re H. (Contact Domestic Violence)* [2000] 2 F.L.R. 334, CA at 341H *per* Butler-Sloss P.; *Re G. (A Minor) (Care Proceedings)* [1995] Fam. 16, 20. There is no strict rule of issue estoppel but the court is reluctant to rehear a matter already determined by a court: *Re B. (Children Act Proceedings) (Issues Estoppel)* [1997] 1 F.L.R. 285. Researchers in the 1990's noted a reluctance in the courts to adjudicate in private law matters: Pearce *et al.* [1999] *Fam. Law* 22; Davis and Pearce [1999] *Fam. Law* 237.

[78] *Re G. (Care Proceedings: Split Trials)* [2001] 1 F.L.R. 872, CA. The same judge should take both hearings if possible. Any appeal should be heard before the second stage: *Re B. (Split Hearing: Jurisdiction)* [2000] 1 F.L.R. 334, CA.

[79] The parties may subpoena those who have relevant information: *D. v. M. (A Minor) (Custody: Appeal)* [1983] Fam. 33 at 37 (health visitor).

[80] F.P.R. 1991, rr. 4.18, 4.23; F.P.C. 1991, rr. 18, 23. Where permission is not obtained to seek an expert report its cost will not be paid out of public funds.

[81] [2001] 1 F.L.R. 723.

[82] CAAC, *Handbook of best practice* (1997), p. 26.

dren and avoid delays means it may limit the quality of evidence submitted by parents in care proceedings.[83] Expert witnesses must have the necessary knowledge and expertise[84]; general permission to instruct should not be given.[85] Experts must be given full instructions so they are clear about the issues before the court and the questions on which their opinion is sought.[86] Their duty is to give opinions on the matters within their expertise not to assist one party.[87] Where there is more than one expert they should meet to identify areas of agreement and the issues which need to be resolved[88]; where there is no arguable case, the proceedings should not continue.[89] Where leave has been given for expert evidence to be obtained the court can require its disclosure. Litigation privilege which would protect a party from having to disclose a report on which he or she chose not to rely does not apply[90]:—

> In *Re L. (Police Investigation: Privilege)*[91] the House of Lords upheld a decision ordering the disclosure to the police of a pathologist's report commissioned by the mother for care proceedings. The parents were heroin addicts and their child had been poisoned by methadone, accidentally according to the mother. The report indicated that the mother's story was improbable. Lord Jauncey, delivering the majority opinion, stated that litigation privilege had no place in Children Act proceedings. Communication between solicitor and client remains privileged.[92]

Before giving the decision, magistrates must record any findings of fact and the reasons for their decision.[93] Reasons should relate to the welfare checklist

---

[83] J. Brophy and P. Bates, "The position of parents using experts in care proceedings: a failure of 'partnership' " [1998] *J.S.W.F.L.* 23.

[84] Those without recognised expertise may not be permitted to give evidence: *Re X. (Non-Accidental Injury: Expert Evidence)* [2001] 2 F.L.R. 90 (court rejected the existence of temporary brittle bone disease) .

[85] *Re G. (Minors) (Expert Witnesses)* [1994] 2 F.L.R. 291; CAAC *Handbook of best practice* (1997), p. 25.

[86] The letter of instruction should be disclosed: *Re M. (Minors) (Care Proceedings: Child's Wishes)* [1994] 1 F.L.R. 749; CAAC *Handbook of best practice* (1997), p.26. Lawyers must ensure that the expert has all the relevant information: *Re G., S. and M. (Wasted Costs)* [2000] 1 F.L.R. 52.

[87] *Vernon v. Bosley (No. 2)* [1998] 1 F.L.R. 304, CA.

[88] *Re R. (Child Abuse Video Evidence)* [1995] 1 F.L.R. 451; *Re C. (Expert Evidence: Disclosure Practice)* [1995] 1 F.L.R. 204; CAAC, *Handbook of best practice* (1997), p. 26.

[89] *Re N. (Contested Care Application)* [1994] 2 F.L.R. 992. Where all the experts concluded that the children should not be placed with the parents.

[90] *Oxfordshire C.C. v. M.* [1994] 1 F.L.R. 175, CA; *Re L. (Police Investigation: Privilege)* [1996] 1 F.L.R. 731, HL; [1996] 1 F.L.R. 731, HL. But the court will not order a party to disclose details of experts instructed in criminal proceedings: *S. County Council v. B.* [2000] 2 F.L.R. 161.

[91] [1996] 1 F.L.R. 731 H.L. Lord Nicholls delivered a strong dissenting opinion and expressly rejected the argument that there was a duty to disclose information (at p. 747) but the E.C.H.R. declared inadmissible the Art. 6(1) complaint that requiring disclosure breached Art. 6(1): *L. v. U.K.* [2000] 2 F.L.R. 322.

[92] This does not apply to criminal communication such as obscene and menacing statements: *C. v. C. (Evidence Privilege)* [2001] 2 F.L.R, 184, CA

[93] F.P.C. 1991, r. 21(5); the wording of the comparable r. 4.21(4) for the higher courts allows the decision to be given and the judgment to be delivered later. Failure of magistrates to abide by r. 21(5) has justified a considerable number of appeals, see, *e.g.* *Re W. (A Minor) (Contact)* [1994] 1 F.L.R. 843.

and other statutory criteria.[94] An order of no order should be made if this is the appropriate outcome.[95] Judgments are not generally given in public but anyone with an interest may be given leave to obtain a copy.[96]

VI. THE COURT AS A WELFARE AGENCY

19–040 The courts dealing with family matters are not primarily therapeutic agencies and those who use them seek justice not welfare.[97] However divorce proceedings and disputes about children have provided both the opportunity and the justification for entrusting the courts with welfare responsibilities. But facilities and resources have not reflected the level of concern expressed, nor even the needs of families.[98]

The court's role as a welfare agency developed from the recommendations of the Morton Commission.[99] They thought it essential that everything possible should be done to mitigate the effect on children of the disruption of family life.[1] Parents were not always the best judges of their children's interests. Therefore the Commission suggested that the obligation to submit a "statement of arrangements" for the children with the divorce petition[2] should be strengthened and enforced by requiring the court's approval of arrangements before a decree of divorce could be made absolute.[3] In addition, the Commission believed that there would be a few cases where the family could not make satisfactory arrangements; in these the court should have the power to require the local authority to receive the children into care.[4] Both these recommendations were first enacted in the Matrimonial Proceedings (Children) Act 1958 and were incorporated, largely unaltered, in the Matrimonial Causes Act 1973.[5] However, both run counter to the fundamental principles of non-intervention in the Chil-

---

[94] *R. v. Oxfordshire C.C. (Secure Accommodation Order)* [1992] Fam. 150. Reasons should enable the parties to understand how the magistrates approached their task and their main findings: *Re L. (Residence: Justices Reasons)* [1995] 2 F.L.R. 445 at 451; general guidance is available: CAAC *Handbook of best practice* (1997), App. X but is not mandatory: *Re C. (Contact: No Order for Contact)* [2000] 2 F.L.R. 728

[95] Children Act 1989, s.1(5); *S. v. R.* [1993] *Fam. Law* 339.

[96] The E.C.H.R. has accepted that this does not amount to a breach of Art. 6(1) see *B. v. U.K.; P. v. U.K.* [2001] 2 F.L.R. 261 at para. 48.

[97] S. Cretney, "Defining the limits of State intervention: the child and the courts" in D. Freestone (ed.), *Children and the Law* (1990), pp. 59–60.

[98] See: Murch and Hooper (1992), Chap. 7. The establishment of CAFCASS provides the courts with an agency dedicated to advising and supporting the courts whereas it previously relied in private law cases on local authorities and the Probation Service, both of which had other priorities.

[99] Royal Commission on Marriage and Divorce 1951–1955, Cmd. 9678 (the *Morton Report*).

[1] *Morton Report,* para. 362.

[2] This had been embodied in the Matrimonial Causes Rules 1947 following the recommendation in the Final Report of the Committee on Procedure in Matrimonial Causes (1947), Cmd. 7024 (the Denning Committee).

[3] *Morton Report,* paras 366, 373.

[4] *ibid.* paras . 395–6.

[5] ss.41, 43. Children could also be committed to care or placed under supervision under the D.P.M.C.A. 1978, s.10(1); Guardianship Act 1973, s.2(2) (b); the Children Act 1975, s.34(5); or the Adoption Act 1976, s.26(1).

dren Act 1989 and have consequently been reformed. Nevertheless, the courts retain some residual functions as a welfare agency.

Mediation services[6]

19–041 Mediation is a process whereby the parties are encouraged to reach agreement on some or all matters in dispute. The mediator, unlike the court has no power to impose a settlement and may be unable to redress power imbalances between the parties.[7] However mediation can help the parties to re-establish a lasting co-operative relationship.[8] Mediation is available through CAFCASS, a variety of local voluntary organisations and from solicitors who are qualified mediators.[9] There are approximately 10,000 family mediations each year.[10]

In an attempt to encourage mediation and reduce litigation, the Family Law Act 1996 introduced a requirement that those seeking public funding for litigation would first co-operate with an assessment of the suitability of the dispute for mediation.[11] Public funding was made available for mediation.[12] Mediation was seen as a better and cheaper alternative to lawyers who were suspected of aggravating family disputes.[13] Requiring attendance at mediation was controversial[14]; it changed what mediators were expected to do, demanded major development of mediation services and restricted access to legal advice, without evidence that mediation could deliver fair settlements in the interests of children. Compulsion can also be inefficient; requiring one party to attend cannot encourage mediation unless the other party is also willing.[15] Research was commissioned to establish the cost-effectiveness of mediation compared with legal services.[16] Although quite high levels of consumer satisfaction with mediation were found, there were higher levels of approval for solicitors. Solicitors facilitated negotiation; there was no

---

6 See generally R. Dingwall and J. Eekelaar (eds.) *Divorce mediation and the legal process* (1988); G. Davis, *Partisans and mediators* (1988); C. Piper, *The responsible parent* (1993); Murch and Hooper (1992); J. Walker *et al.*, *Mediation: the making and remaking of co-operative relationships* (1994).

7 Davis (1988), p. 51.

8 In Walker's study over half the clients were satisfied with the outcome of comprehensive mediation; the figure for child-focused mediation was 38 per cent. Settlement rates were higher for child-focused mediation: Walker *et al.* (1994), pp. 71, 78.

9 For a recent account of what mediators do see: R. Dingwall and D. Greatbatch [2001] *Fam. Law* 378.

10 LSC press release January 2001 reported by Fisher [2001] *Fam. Law* 272.

11 Family Law Act 1996, s.29, amending Legal Aid Act 1988, s.15. Information about mediation was also to be provided in the information meetings which were to be mandatory for all those applying to divorce: Family Law Act 1996, Pt II. For the background to these provisions see: Lord Mackay, *Looking to the future,* Cm. 2799 (1995), Foreword.

12 This is now provided through the Legal Services Commission.

13 Maclean and Eekelaar (2000) Chaps. 1 and 9; G. Davis *et al.* [2001] *Fam. Law* 265.

14 G. Davis *et al.* [20001] *Fam. Law* 265. Concern was expressed that victims of domestic violence would not be identified and would be required to enter mediation despite the duty of mediation services to screen for domestic violence: C. Piper and F. Kanagas, "Family Law Act 1996, s.1(d): How will 'they' know there is a risk of violence?" [1997] *C.F.L.Q.* 279–289.

15 Following the implementation of s.29 there were approximately four intake appointments for every mediation started: G. Davis *et al.* [2001] *Fam. Law* 265, 267.

16 G. Davis *et al.* [2001] *Fam. Law* 110, 186, 265; The full report is available on the Legal Services Commission web-site www.legalservices.gov.uk

evidence that they inflamed disputes.[17] Mediation did not appear to reduce recourse to publicly funded legal services, or to reduce legal costs.[18]

Following the research, the Legal Services Commission revised the criteria in the Funding Code in relation to attendance at mediation. A person seeking public funding for legal services in family cases only has to go to a meeting with a mediator if the other party indicates that they are willing to mediate.[19] This largely abandons section 29 and leaves mediation to create its own market.[20] Mediators who receive public funding are required to comply with the Legal Service Commission's Code of Practice.[21] They must inform clients that sessions are privileged and cannot be disclosed, and ensure that clients are not forced into mediation by fear of violence. Mediators must assess whether children should be included in the process and ensure that clients consider the welfare, wishes and feelings of their children.[22] Unlike solicitors, mediators should remain impartial between clients and neutral as to the outcome. Nevertheless, they do appear to have views about what arrangements for children are unacceptable and to impose pressure where, for example, a residential parent refuses any contact.[23]

Contact centres

19–042 Contact centres provide a "neutral venue", often a church hall, where children who would not otherwise have contact can meet their non-residential parent or other family members.[24] The development of contact centres has been very significant for the management of contact disputes,[25] they are an integral part of court-based welfare services[26] but most are run by voluntary organisations. Their aim is to establish sufficient trust for contact to take place away from a centre. Most centres provide only "supported" contact and do not monitor it, but a few provide supervised contact.[27] Centres may allow visits to be observed for court reports but they will generally not provide reports themselves. Courts may refer families to

---

[17] G. Davis *et al.* [2001] *Fam. Law* 110, 112–4; Maclean and Eekelaar (2000), p.195.

[18] G. Davis *et al.* [2001] *Fam. Law* 186, 188. The authors acknowledge considerable limitations to this research, notably it takes no account of whether mediated agreements last longer than court imposed ones. Davis *et al.'s* findings are the subject of critical comment by T. Fisher and D. Hodson [2001] *Fam. Law* 271.

[19] Willingness to mediate remains a condition for public funding for most family cases see: *Funding Code Decision making guidance* (2001) 20.11.

[20] Legal Services Commission, *Funding Code Procedures,* rr. C27–C29, referral to family mediation; G. Davis *et al.* [2001] *Fam. Law* 268.

[21] The requirement was originally inserted by Family Law Act 1996, s.27 adding Legal Aid Act 1988, s.13B.

[22] No children were included in the cases in a recent study see: R. Dingwall and D. Greatbatch [2001] *Fam. Law* 378 at 381.

[23] R. Dingwall and D. Greatbatch [2001] *Fam. Law* 378, 380.

[24] E. Halliday, " The role and function of child contact centres" [1997] *J.S.W.F.L.* 53–60; B. Kroll, "Not intruding, not colluding: process and practice in a contact centre" (2000) *Children and Society* 14, 182J. Mitchell [2001] *Fam. Law* 613.

[25] Association of circuit judges evidence to consultation on contact and domestic violence: Advisory Board on Family Law: Children Act Sub-Committee, *Report* (2000), para. 3.14.7.

[26] Advisory Board on Family Law, *Third Annual Report 1999/2000,* para. 3.43. The Children Act Sub-committee stressed the importance of CAFCASS developing close links with contact centres.

[27] For a detailed explanation of these terms see National Association of Contact Centres, *Manual* (2000), para. 8.1 reproduced in Advisory Board on Family Law: Children Act Sub-Committee, *Making contact work: consultation paper* (2001), para. 3.18–9.

contact centres but must first establish that resources are available and the referral is suitable.[28] Supported contact centres are not suitable where there is a danger of a parent misbehaving.[29] In 1998, approximately 19,000 children used a contact centre.

A. Arrangements for children on divorce

19–043 Before the introduction of the Children Act 1989 the procedure under Matrimonial Causes Act 1973, s.41 required the applicant for divorce to file "statement of arrangements" to be approved by a judge in chambers at a "children appointment"— a brief hearing usually attended only by the parent with care. If the judge was satisfied with the arrangements he granted a "certificate of satisfaction" which allowed the divorce to be made absolute. Certificates were rarely refused.[30] This power and its operation were criticised on a number of grounds.[31] It failed to support families when they needed help, did not identify problems effectively and took up scarce judicial and social work resources. Even if problems were identified, the power to withhold the decree was inappropriate where parents needed positive encouragement and assistance.

The Children Act 1989 amended section 41 in line with its philosophy of placing responsibility for children's interests primarily on their parents and reducing state intervention. Children's appointments were abolished and the statement of arrangements revised to require more information.[32] However, it is examined only after the district judge has determined that the petition is made out.[33] The court no longer has to approve arrangements, only "consider . . . whether it should exercise any of its powers under the Children Act 1989 with respect to . . . " any children of the family.[34] Only if the court may need to exercise its powers, is unable to do so without giving further consideration to the case and there are exceptional circumstances, may it delay the divorce.[35] District judges consider statements of arrangements only briefly and rarely seek further information by requiring the parties to attend or ordering a welfare report.[36] The procedure remains largely ineffective at identifying cases where children's welfare may be at risk or making sup-

---

[28] Protocol for the referral of families by judges and magistrates to child contact centres [2001] *Fam. Law* 616.

[29] E. Butler-Sloss [2001] *Fam. Law* 355.

[30] For a discussion of the principle findings of the research into s.41 see G. Douglas *et al.*, "Safeguarding children's welfare in non-contentious divorce: towards a new conception of the legal process?" (2000) 63 *M.L.R.* 177, 181.

[31] See generally, Davis, Macleod and Murch, *op. cit.;* G. Davis, "Public issues and private troubles: the case of divorce" (1987) 17 *Fam. Law* 299; Maidment (1984); Booth Committee Report (1985) and Law Com. W.P. 96, paras 4.8–4.10.

[32] Form M4.

[33] F.P.R. 1991, r. 2.39. There is no scrutiny where the parties are in dispute and an application has been made for a s.8 order, rr.2.39(1), 2.40. The Law Commission had recommended that scrutiny should take place early in the proceedings.

[34] s.41(1).

[35] s.41(2).

[36] Douglas *et al. op cit.* pp. 189–90. Out of 353 cases studied, the district judge sought additional information in 18; in only one was the divorce delayed. The fact that parents had not separated led district judges to exercise their powers but the lack of contact did not.

port available for parents at a stressful time; judges have neither the time nor the inclination to look at cases more closely.

Although the child's wishes and feelings are included in the welfare checklist which the court applies when making a decision about a child's upbringing,[37] the process for dealing with these undefended divorces makes no provision for involving children.[38] Consequently, it does not appear to satisfy the requirements of the U.N. Convention on the Rights of the Child, Art. 12.[39] Family Law Act 1996 emphasised children's welfare by requiring courts to treat this as paramount and to consider the checklist when handling undefended divorces but did not include any process to involve children.[40] The Lord Chancellor commissioned a further review of section 41 which has suggested that the parties should be encouraged to file a Parenting Plan,[41] the respondent should be required to comment on the arrangements, the court should obtain independent information from the child's school and that district judges should be more proactive in referring parents to other agencies.[42] What and how children are told about parental divorce remains a matter for parents; the Lord Chancellor's Department does encourage parents to tell their children and provide leaflets to assist them.[43]

B. Court ordered investigation

19–044 Before the introduction of the Children Act 1989, a court could commit a child into the care of the local authority in exceptional circumstances.[44] However, this conflicted fundamentally with the reform[45] because it allowed the court to intervene in the family without proof of significant harm and to impose its standards on the local authority. The Law Commission recommended[46] that the courts should be able to order the local authority to investigate and, where the "significant harm" test is satisfied, to make an interim care or supervision order. In

---

[37] See Chap. 20, below.

[38] Parents are not required to discuss arrangements with children, nor do children sign the statement of arrangements. The Children (Scotland) Act 1995, s.6, imposes a duty on parents to have regard to the children's views when making decisions. Lack of information about what is happening and of involvement in arrangements is a source of concern to children: B. Neale and C. Smart, *Good to talk?* (2001).

[39] Douglas *et al.* have suggested that this, taken with Arts 6 and 8 of the E.C.H.R., could possibly form the basis of a challenge that uncontentious divorce process fails to protect children's rights to respect for family life and for due process, *op. cit.*, p.195.

[40] Family Law Act 1996, s.11. The provision was never implemented.

[41] Parenting plans were introduced from Australia for the information meeting pilots under the Family Law Act 1996 to encourage parents to discuss arrangements for children and involve them in their discussions.

[42] Family Law Board Report 2000–2001, para. 2.37–8.

[43] Leaflets A1 to A4 available on the Lord Chancellor's Department web-site: www.lcd.gov.uk

[44] Matrimonial Causes Act 1973, s.43. Similar powers existed in guardianship and other proceedings relating to children. The effect of the order was similar to a care order. Few orders were made see 6th edition of this work p.701.

[45] *Review of Child Care Law,* paras 2.23, 15.11, 15.35–37; Law Com. W.P. 100, paras 2.70–11, 2.52; *The Law on Child Care & Family Services* (1987) Cm. 62, paras . 5c, 59; Law Com. No. 172, para. 5.1. See also Chap. 22, below.

[46] It provisionally proposed that the court should be able to treat a case as if a care order had been sought but concluded that there were "obvious disadvantages" in making the local authority

addition, the local authority should be able to intervene in any family proceedings and request a care order.[47] The Children Act 1989 implemented these proposals.[48] Also, if family proceedings are started whilst care proceedings are pending, the court has power to transfer so that cases can be heard together.[49]

The court may direct an investigation in any family proceedings relating to a child where it appears that it "may be appropriate for a care or supervision order to be made."[50] Where the court makes such a direction it may also appoint a children's guardian.[51] The appointment is not automatic; if an interim care or supervision order is not being made the court must be satisfied that an appointment is necessary and that the guardian will have a useful role.[52] The local authority must investigate the case; consider whether to apply for a care or supervision order, to provide services or to take any other action with respect to the child[53]; and report their decisions, reasons and actions to the court within eight weeks or such other period as the court directs.[54] Where the local authority decides not to apply for a care or supervision order it must also decide whether and when to review its decision.[55] The court ordering an investigation may make an interim[56] care or supervision order.[57] If the local authority thinks this unnecessary it may apply for the order to be discharged but cannot merely send the child home.[58]

Concern has been expressed about the misuse of section 37 in order to appoint children's guardians in private law proceedings[59] or to avoid delays in obtaining a court report.[60] That the court has no power to compel the

---

apply for an order it did not want: Law Com. W.P. 100, para. 2.52(i); Law Com. No. 172, para. 5.4.

47 *ibid.* paras . 5.3, 5.5–6.

48 ss.31(4), 37, 38.

49 Children (Allocation of Proceedings) Order 1991, S.I. 1991, No. 1677, art. 7(1) (b).

50 Children Act 1989, s.37(1); *Re H. (A Minor) (Section 37 Direction)* [1993] 2 F.L.R. 541 where the court was considering an application for a residence order for an unrelated child by a lesbian couple; *F. v. Cambridgeshire C.C.* [1995] 1 F.L.R. 516, where an investigation was ordered in relation to a step-father's application for contact where sexual abuse was an issue.

51 Children Act 1989, s.41(6). The guardian's role is not to supervise the local authority's assessment: *Re M. (Official Solicitor's Role)* [1998] 2 F.L.R. 815, CA.

52 *Re CE. (s.37 Direction)* [1995] 1 F.L.R. 26, *per* Wall J. at 41.

53 Children Act 1989, s.37(2), *e.g.* the local authority could refer the case to the education department to consider an application for an education supervision order. There is no requirement to see the child: *cf.* Children Act 1989, s.47(4).

54 Children Act 1989, s.37(3), (4). A letter from the local authority should normally be sufficient; there is no provision in the rules for attendance by the local authority but it is unlikely that an invitation would be refused: *per* Wall J. in *Re CE. (s.37 Direction)* [1995] 1 F.L.R. 26 at 48.

55 Children Act 1989, s.37(5).

56 A full order requires an application from the local authority or the N.S.P.C.C.: s.31(1). The local authority thus retains control over the use of its resources.

57 Children Act 1989, s.38(1) (b), (2).

58 Children Act 1989, s.39(1) (c), (2) (c). The Placement with Parents etc. Regulations 1991, S.I. 1991 No. 893 apply.

59 Directions should not be made unless it appeared that a public law order might be appropriate see: *Re CE. (s.37 Direction)* [1995] 1 F.L.R. 26 at 41 *per* Wall J.; *Re L. (Section 37 Direction)* [1999] 1 F.L.R. 984, CA.

60 1890 directions were made between January and June 1993: CAAC Report 1992/3, p. 32.

local authority to take action is a matter of deep concern[61] as is the focusing of social work resources on investigations.[62]

VII. WARDSHIP AND THE INHERENT JURISDICTION OF THE HIGH COURT

19–045 Before the Children Act 1989 the inherent jurisdiction of the High Court was usually exercised through the machinery of wardship[63] which gives the court a continuing responsibility for the child.[64] But it is not necessary to make a child a "ward of court"[65]—the court's powers are equally exercisable outside wardship.[66] Proceedings under this jurisdiction are "family proceedings"[67] but the High Court, exercising its inherent jurisdiction, is not limited to making orders under the Act.[68] The main use is to supplement the statutory powers[69]; injunctions may be granted.[70] Many of the circumstances where the

---

[61] *Nottinghamshire C.C. v. P.* [1993] 2 F.L.R. 134 at 148. Sir Stephen Brown P. regretting the absence of wardship considered that the authority might lay itself open to judicial review. Actions for negligence or breach of statutory duty have been ruled out by the House of Lords: *X. v. Bedfordshire C.C.* [1995] 2 A.C. 633 and Chap. 22, below.

[62] D.H., *Child protection messages from research* (1995).

[63] *Re W. (A Minor) (Medical Treatment: Court's Jurisdiction)* [1993] Fam. 64 at 85, *per* Balcombe L.J.

[64] Where the child is a ward no important decision may be made without the leave of the court. For a list see: see *Kelly v. BBC* [2001]1 F.L.R 197 at 218 or Hershman and MacFarlane (1999) Vol. 1, paras C1060–1062. The court cannot control a ward's application to the E.C.H.R.: *Re M. (Petition to European Commission of Human Rights)* [1997] 1 F.L.R. 755 (a further step in the "Zulu boy" case: *Re M. (Child's Upbringing)* [1996] 2 F.L.R. 441).

[65] The law and practice is comprehensively discussed in N. Lowe and R. White, *Wards of Court* (2nd ed., 1986). See also *Latey Report,* paras 192–214; Cross (1967) 83 *L.Q.R.* 200; Balcombe (1982) 1 Lit. 223; Law Com. W.P. No. 101, *Wards of Court* (1987); J. Masson and S. Morton, "The use of wardship by local authorities" (1989) 52 *M.L.R.* 762 and J. Hunt, *Local authority wardships before the Children Act: The baby or the bathwater?* (1993).

[66] *Re W. (A Minor) (Medical Treatment: Court's Jurisdiction)* [1993] Fam. 64 at 73, *per* Donaldson M.R.; *Re Z. (A Minor) (Identification: Restrictions on Publication)* [1997] Fam. 1, 14. "For all practical purposes the jurisdiction . . . is one and the same." *per* Ward L.J. *cf.* M. Parry, "The Children Act 1989: local authorities, wardship and the inherent jurisdiction" (1992) *J.S.W.F.L.* 212 at 214.

[67] Children Act 1989, s.8(3) (a).

[68] It may make section 8 orders but not care orders or residence orders in favour of local authorities: Children Act 1989, s.100(1) (2); *Re C. (Contact Jurisdiction)* [1995] 1 F.L.R. 777, CA (variation of contact for child freed for adoption).

[69] See for example *Re M. (Care: Leave to Interview Child)* [1995] 1 F.L.R. 825; *Re C. (Contact: Jurisdiction)* [1995] 1 F.L.R. 777; *S. Glamorgan C.C. v. W. and B.* [1993] 1 F.L.R. 574; *Re X. (A Minor) (Adoption Details: Disclosure)* [1994] 2 F.L.R. 450, CA.

[70] *Cambridge C.C. v. D.* [1999] 2 F.L.R. 42 (application by a local authority to prevent a boyfriend harassing a girl in care; the power for third parties to make applications under the Family Law Act 1996, s.60 is not yet implemented). *Re G. (Celebrities: Publicity)* [1999] 1 F.L.R. 409, CA (to prevent parents speaking to the press about each other following their divorce); *Re. O. (Minors) (Adoption: Injunction)* [1993] 2 F.L.R. 737 (to prevent the birth parents approaching the children after adoption). *Re S. (Minors) (Inherent Jurisdiction: Ouster)* [1994] 1 F.L.R. 623 (to exclude an alleged abuser, but the use of ouster by local authorities would appear to be against the spirit of *Nottinghamshire C.C. v. P.* [1993] 2 F.L.R. 134).

jurisdiction was used are now dealt with by statute[71] but it continues to have a role in complex cases, particularly relating to medical treatment.[72] The welfare principle applies.

1. The rise and fall of wardship

19–046 The inherent jurisdiction of which wardship is a part has its roots in the feudal system and originates in the Crown's special duty as *parens patriae*[73] to protect minors against injury of any kind. Between 1875 and 1971 wardship was exercised in the Chancery Division but the Administration of Justice Act 1970 transferred it to the Family Division[74] and certain powers can now be exercised in the county courts.[75] The main function of the court was originally to protect the property[76] of a minor whose parents were dead or unable to act, and in practice it was only the concern of the wealthy.[77] In 1950 public funding (legal aid) was made available for wardship; transfer to the Family Division increased its availability[78] and its use. Wardship came to be seen by judges,[79] lawyers and particularly local authorities[80] as the appropriate forum for complex cases concerning children.[81]

---

[71] Disclosure of the child's whereabouts, recovery and the surrender of a passport may all be achieved under the Family Law Act 1986, ss.33, 34 and 37. The Family Law Act 1996 provides for injunctions to protect children and the Adoption and Children Bill 2002, cll. 24, 26 will give the court power to revoke placement orders and regulate contact pending adoption.

[72] *Re A. (Conjoined Twins: Medical Treatment)* [2001] 1 F.L.R. 1; *Re M. (Medical Treatment: Consent)* [1999] 2 F.L.R. 1097 (heart transplant for 15 year old, parental consent given); *Royal Wolverhampton Hospital NHS Trust v. B.* [2000] 1 F.L.R. 953 F.D. (declaration that child should be treated in accordance with advice of paediatrician *i.e.* not be ventilated if she collapsed). There may be advantages in bringing controversial medical decisions into the public domain but a specific issue order could be used to order treatment where both parents and child objected, no order is required if there is consent for treatment, and doctors cannot be required to treat against their medical judgement.

[73] "Father of the nation"; in *Re Gault* 387 U.S. 1 (1967) at 16, it was noted that the meaning of this expression is "murky and its historic credentials are of dubious relevance" to questions of the right of the state to intervene in a minor's life. See also, J. Seymour, "Parens patriae and wardship powers: their nature and origins" (1994) 14 Ox. J.L.S. 159.

[74] s.1(2); see now Supreme Court Act 1981, s.61 and Sched.1.

[75] Matrimonial and Family Proceedings Act 1984, s.38(2) (b),(5).

[76] *Re F. (Orse A.) (A Minor) (Publication of Information)* [1977] Fam. 58 at 88, *per* Lord Denning M.R.

[77] The court had no means of acting except where it had property to be used for the child's maintenance: see *Wellesley v. Beaufort* (1827) 2 Russ 1 at 21; *Wellesley v. Wellesley* (1828) 2 Bligh (N.S.) 124 at 132; *Re Brown's W.T.* (1881) 18 Ch. D. 61. If the ward was a girl the court considered (and if appropriate approved) the arrangements for her marriage: see *Latey Report*, para. 200.

[78] Applications could be made to the district registries.

[79] *Re D. (A Minor) (Justices' Decision: Review)* [1977] Fam. 158, *per* Dunn J. at 164; *Re B. (Wardship: Child in Care)* [1975] Fam. 36, *per* Lane J. at 44; *R. v. N. Yorkshire C. C., ex p. M. (No. 3)* [1989] 2 F.L.R. 82, *per* Ewbank J. at 84, *Cleveland Report* (Butler-Sloss J.), p. 253.

[80] See Masson and Morton, *op. cit.*, pp. 769–773.

[81] But not before birth, *Re F. (In Utero)* [1988] Fam. 122. There is no *parens patriae* jurisdiction with regard to mentally handicapped adults but the court may declare that a sterilisation operation would not be unlawful, *Re. F. (Mental Parent: Sterilisation)* [1990] 2 A.C. 1; by analogy it can also regulate contact: *Re C. (Mental Patient: Contact)* [1993] 1 F.L.R. 940, FD; *Re D-R (Adult: Contact)* [1999] 1 F.L.R. 1161, CA.

Wardship increased dramatically in the 1980's, there were nearly 4,961 applications in 1991, over 55 per cent by local authorities.[82] Not everyone favoured the development of wardship.[83] The *Review of Child Care Law* made no proposals for changes to wardship but thought reform would reduce the need to use it.[84] However, its scheme for compulsory intervention would have been severely undermined had local authorities continued to use wardship extensively. The Law Commission considered that the objective of a comprehensive code necessitated review of wardship. Wardship could operate as an alternative jurisdiction to achieve results which could also be achieved under the code; an independent jurisdiction to fill any gaps left by the code; a supportive jurisdiction to achieve more effectively results which could be achieved under the code; and to review decisions taken under the code. It suggested that the alternative and review uses of wardship should be removed because they "made nonsense" of the careful consideration which had gone into framing the new statutory code. The independent use might also be inconsistent with the spirit of the code but would allow defects in the new scheme to be remedied as they arose. The supportive role merely pointed to ways in which the statutory scheme should be improved.[85] The Law Commission recommended incorporating elements of wardship into the statutory scheme[86]; the Children Act 1989 went further, restricting local authorities' use of wardship and the High Court's exercise of the inherent jurisdiction in respect of children in care.[87] The Court of Appeal also stressed that wardship should be restricted to cases where the case could not be resolved under the Act or the child needed the court's protection.[88] Wardship has a residual role; only about 400 applications are made annually but its importance lies in the ways it can be used.[89]

---

[82] The reasons for local authority use are discussed in Masson and Morton, *op. cit.* and include difficulties in satisfying the statutory test, the lack of a right of appeal, dislike of magistrates' court procedure and party status for parents.

[83] R. Dingwall, J. Eekelaar and T. Murray, *The Protection of Children* (1983); *Care or control?* (1983) were concerned about the extension of state intervention; Second Report from the Social Services Committee 1983–84. H.C. 360, (the *Short Report*) suggested that judges should exercise "self-denial" (para.82).

[84] *Review of Child Care Law* (1985), para. 15.38.

[85] Law Com. W.P. 101, paras 3.53, 4.4–4.9.

[86] Law Com. No. 172, para.1.4.

[87] Children Act 1989, s.100, a controversial measure: see N. Lowe [1989] New L.J. 87; Bainham (1990), paras 8.53–8.55; *cf.* J. Eekelaar and R. Dingwall [1989] New L.J. 217. Its inclusion relates partly to cost, indeed savings, through ending use of wardship by local authorities are expressly referred to in the Financial Memorandum attached to the Bill. Wards in care became subject to care orders: Children Act 1989, Sched. 14, paras . 15(1) (h), 16A.

[88] *Re T.(A Minor) (Wardship: Representation)* [1994] Fam. 49, *per* Waite L.J at 60.

[89] J. Mitchell [2001] *Fam. Law* 130–4, 212–6.

2. Proceedings under the inherent jurisdiction[90]

19–047 Only unmarried[91] minors[92] may be warded; the child need not be a British subject nor present in England and Wales.[93] Under the Family Law Act 1986 a court only has jurisdiction to make Part I orders[94] which include orders under the inherent jurisdiction for care, contact or education if (a) the child is habitually resident in England and Wales or (b) is present in England and Wales and not habitually resident elsewhere in the United Kingdom.[95] In addition, jurisdiction cannot be exercised if divorce, nullity or judicial separation proceedings are continuing in another part of the United Kingdom[96] or elsewhere in the EC.[97] But, where the child is present in England and Wales when the proceedings are commenced, the inherent jurisdiction may be exercised if the court considers that this is immediately necessary for the child's protection.[98]

Any individual[99] who has a sufficient interest[1] may start proceedings. There is no requirement to obtain the court's leave. Although people with a professional interest[2] in a child's welfare may start proceedings they do so in a personal capacity and are consequently unlikely to act unless their professional association or another organisation supports them. In practice, the availability

---

[90] See N. Lowe, "The limits of the wardship jurisdiction: who can be made a ward?" (1988) 1 J.C.L. 6.

[91] There is no authority on this point: see Bevan, para. 8.08, but wardship was held not to terminate on the ward's marriage: *Re Elwes (No. 2) The Times*, July 30, 1958.

[92] *Re F. (In Utero)* [1988] Fam. 122 (no jurisdiction over a foetus); *Re F.* [1990] 2 A.C. 1 (no jurisdiction over mentally incapable adults). If the child has diplomatic immunity there is immunity from suit: *Re C. (An Infant)* [1959] Ch. 363; *Re P. (Children Act: Diplomatic Immunity)* [1998] 1 F.L.R. 624, FD.

[93] *Re B-M. (Wardship: Jurisdiction)* [1993] 1 F.L.R. 979. But a jurisdictional claim founded solely on nationality was "exorbitant": *Al Habtoor v. Fotheringham* [2001] 1 F.L.R. 951 at 968 *per* Ward L.J. consequently the English court could not make an order to assist the mother to recover her child from the natural father who had obtained custody overseas by giving false evidence in *ex parte* proceedings. The mother subsequently sought to abduct her child back to England but was imprisoned.

[94] Family Law Act 1986, s.1. as amended by Children Act 1989, Sched.13, para. 62. Consequently a finding of habitual residence may be crucial if the court is to order the child's return from overseas: *Re V. (Jurisdiction: Habitual Residence)* [2001] 1 F.L.R. 253, FD; *B. v. H. (Habitual Residence: Wardship)* [2000] 1 F.L.R. 388, F.D. (baby born overseas).

[95] Family Law Act 1986, s.3(1).

[96] *ibid.* ss.2A, 3(2).

[97] So long as the children are children of both the spouses, the issue relates to parental responsibility and there is no urgent requirement for protective measures: Council Regulation 1347/2000 (Brussels II): European Communities (Matrimonial Jurisdiction and Judgements) Regulations 2001 S.I. 2001 No. 310; see M. Nicholls [2001] *Fam. Law* 368 and [1998] O.J. C221/27 (Explanatory Report by Prof. Borras). Denmark is not a party to this Convention.

[98] Family Law Act 1986, s.2(3) (b); Brussels II, Art. 12; *A. v. L. (Jurisdiction: Brussels II)* [2002] 1 F.L.R. 1042, FD.

[99] Including the child, who may appear without a guardian *ad litem; Re T. (A Minor) (Wardship: Representation)* [1994] Fam. 49; F.P.R. 1991 r. 9.2A.

[1] *cf. Re Dunhill* (1967) 111 S.J. 113, where a night-club owner made a girl a ward largely for publicity purposes. Applicants must now state their relationship to the minor.

[2] *Re D. (A Minor) (Wardship Sterilisation)* [1976] Fam. 185; (education psychologist); *Re B. (A Minor) (Wardship: Medical Treatment)* [1981] 1 W.L.R. 1421 (doctor); *A. v. Berkshire C. C.* [1989] 1 F.L.R. 273, CA (guardian *ad litem*). Alternatively the court may recommend that a parent does so: *R. v. Portsmouth Hospitals NHS Trust ex p. Glass* [1999] 2 F.L.R. 905, CA at 910 (following a recommendation by the Official Solicitor).

of the new statutory scheme to anyone with leave makes this aspect of wardship less important. Moreover, it has been said that it would be a "bold decision" to allow an application to proceed under the inherent jurisdiction after refusal of leave under the Children Act 1989.[3]

Unless it has the support of another party,[4] a local authority wishing to use the court's inherent jurisdiction must seek leave and satisfy the court that the result desired by the authority could not be achieved without these powers[5] and that the child is likely to suffer significant harm if the jurisdiction is not exercised[6]:—

> In *Cambridge County Council v. D.*[7] a disturbed young man with a history of violence formed a relationship with a troubled young woman who was accommodated by the local authority. The local authority obtained leave from the High Court to obtain injunctions to prevent the man molesting or harassing the girl. The man continued to write her love letters and accompanied her to the antenatal clinic when she was pregnant with their child. He was sentenced to 12 months imprisonment for breach of the injunctions but this was reduced to three months on appeal.

3. Powers under the inherent jurisdiction

19–048 Although the court's powers have been described as "limitless"[8] this is clearly no longer true. Apart from restrictions in the Children Act 1989,[9] the courts have also recognised that it is inappropriate to make a wide range of orders.[10] The High Court will not exercise its jurisdiction where Parliament has provided

---

[3] *C. v. Salford C. C.* [1994] 2 F.L.R. 926, 933, *per* Hale J.

[4] Wilson J.'s pragmatic view: *Medway Council v. B.B.C.* [2002] 1 F.L.R. 104 at 107.

[5] Questions relating to medical treatment for children incapable of consenting can be dealt with by s.8 orders: *Re R. (A Minor) (Blood Transfusion)* [1993] 2 F.L.R. 757 at 760, *per* Booth J. Wardship has the advantage of independent representation compared with guardianship under the Mental Health Act 1983, and family proceedings relating to siblings could be heard together: *Re F. (Mental Health Act: Guardianship)* [2000] 1 F.L.R. 192, CA.

[6] Children Act 1989, s.100(3)–(5); F.P.R. (1991), r. 4.3 applies see r. 5.1(2). If harm is not likely leave must be refused: *Essex C.C. v. Mirror Group Newspapers* [1996] 1 F.L.R. 585; *Medway Council v. B.B.C.* [2002] 1 F.L.R. 104, FD.

[7] [1999] 2 F.L.R. 42, CA.

[8] *Re J. (A Minor)* [1984] F.L.R. 535 at 539, *per* Wood J.; see also Fricker [1993] *Fam. Law* 226.

[9] Children Act 1989, s.100(1), (2); care orders discharge wardship, s.91(4).

[10] *Re J.S. (A Minor) (Declaration of Paternity)* [1981] Fam. 22 (bare declaration of paternity); *Re G. (Wardship) (Jurisdiction: Power of Arrest)* (1983) 4 F.L.R. 538 (power of arrest attached to an injunction); *Re G. (A Minor) (Witness Summons)* [1988] 2 F.L.R. 396 (to set aside a witness summons requiring a three-and-a-half-year-old to appear at a court martial conducted by the U.S. Army); *Re Manda* [1993] Fam. 183 (to restrict the access of a former ward to documents relating to the proceedings for use in a negligence action); *Re G., Re R. (Wards) (Police Interviews)* [1990] 2 F.L.R. 347 (in ways which inhibit police investigations); *Medway Council v. B.B.C.* [2002] 1 F.L.R. 104 (to prevent the broadcast of an interview with the child obtained with consent); *Re O. and J. (Paternity: Blood Tests)* [2000] 1 F.L.R. 418 (to take a blood sample from a child despite the carer's objection. Such orders are now provided by Child Support, Pensions and Social Security Act 2000, s.82(3) amending F.L.R.A. 1969, s.21(3)).

a statutory code.[11] Consequently, in *A. v. Liverpool City Council*[12] the mother was unable to challenge the local authority's decision to refuse contact with her child. Where there are gaps in a code, wardship has sometimes been used to provide a solution, a response that has been criticised as judicial legislation.[13] Orders under the inherent jurisdiction are not limited to controlling the exercise of parental responsibility but may cover the actions of third parties for the child's protection.[14] Orders may be very detailed[15] and bind the child as well as the adults.

There are other special features if the child is a ward of court. The court in effect becomes in law the ward's parent and takes control of the child[16] and the child's property. The court has the power to protect wards from decisions, even their own, which undermine their welfare[17] but this does not place the ward above the law.[18] The court must exercise its powers in accordance with the Human Rights Act 1998; restrictions on parents or children must be proportionate and those whose rights are restricted must have a fair hearing.[19] Orders do not have extra-territorial effect but have been known to encourage co-operation authorities overseas:—

In *Re KR (Abduction)*[20] Sikh parents planned an arranged marriage for their

---

[11] *Re Mohammed Arif* [1968] Ch. 643 (immigration decisions); but note in *Re F. (A Minor) (Immigration: Wardship)* [1990] Fam. 125 the court continued the wardship to prevent the child being concealed pending the Secretary of State's decision and in *Re K. & S. (Wardship: Immigration)* [1992] 1 F.L.R. 432 wardship was continued to ensure the children's care pending the carer's deportation. The Children Act 1989 should be used where its powers are adequate: *Re T. (A Minor) (Wardship: Representation)* [1994] Fam. 49, CA. But in *Re RJ. (Wardship)* [1999] 1 F.L.R. 618, FD the court gave care and control in wardship to carers who were forbidden from acting as foster carers following a change in regulations and who were refused residence orders because this was contrary to public policy. The court emphasised the exceptional nature of the case and the negative impact on the children's welfare.

[12] [1982] A.C. 363; the court accepted that Parliament had intended that local authorities should have complete discretion over contact. Where local authorities act improperly judicial review can be used: *W. v. Hertfordshire C. C.* [1985] A.C. 791 at 793 *per* Lord Scarman.

[13] For a recent example see R. Spon-Smith, "The inherent jurisdiction and the revocation of freeing orders" [2000] *Fam. Law* 43.

[14] To prevent the Registrar General disclosing details of the child's adoption during her minority: *Re X. (A Minor) (Adoption Details: Disclosure)* [1994] 3 All E.R. 372; to exclude a step-parent or son-in-law who poses a risk to the child from the home; *Re S. (Minors) (Inherent Jurisdiction: Ouster)* [1994] 1 F.L.R. 623; *Devon C.C. v. S.* [1994] 1 F.L.R. 355 (restricting access to a family by a convicted sex abuser). See also N. Lowe, "The limits of the wardship jurisdiction the extent of the court's powers" (1989) 1 J.C.L. 44; Lowe and White (1986), Chap. 6.

[15] *Re R. (P.M.) (An Infant)* [1968] 1 W.L.R. 385 (the number of letters and the collection of luggage). Conditions in s.8 orders may achieve this: *Re M. (A Minor) (Contact Conditions)* [1994] 1 F.L.R. 272; *Re O. (Contact: Imposition of Conditions)* [1995] 2 F.L.R. 124, CA.

[16] *R. v. Gyngall* [1893] 2 Q.B. 232 at 239, *per* Lord Esher M.R.; *Re E. (S.A.) (A Minor)* [1984] 1 All E.R. 289 at 290, *per* Lord Scarman.

[17] *Re R. (A Minor) (Wardship: Consent to Treatment)* [1992] Fam. 11 at 25, *per* Donaldson M.R.

[18] *Re A. (A Minor) (Wardship: Police Caution)* [1989] Fam. 103.

[19] On this basis some injunctions granted in the past might breach Art. 8 *e.g. Cambridge C.C. v. D.* [1999] 2 F.L.R. 42 (see above p. 620) and *Devon C. C. v. B.* [1997] 1 F.L.R. 591 where the judge at first instance had barred the mother from going within 10 miles of a named town until the child was 16. In *Re C. (Detention: Medical Treatment)* [1997] 2 F.L.R. 180 the court provided the same protection as would have applied in secure accommodation proceedings.

[20] [1999] 2 F.L.R. 542, FD.

daughter who had been born and brought up in England. They took her to India and left her with an aunt. Her elder sister made her a ward of court. The court made orders for her return to England, inviting the co-operation of judicial and administrative bodies in India to put her in contact with the British High Commission. KR managed to convince her family that she was willing to stay in India, they took her to the High Commission and she was returned to England.

The jurisdiction is a continuing one and the court retains its overall responsibility to supervise the child's welfare. No major decision may be taken without the permission of the court[21]; action taken improperly without leave constitutes contempt of the court.[22] The person with care and control must look after the child in accordance with the court's directions[23]:—

In *Re K (Adoption and Wardship)*[24] a Bosnian Muslim child was brought to England for medical treatment and adopted although the Bosnian Government had not given its agreement and some relatives had been traced. The adoption order was subsequently revoked because the procedure was severely flawed. However, the child's attachment to her carers made return to her family inappropriate. With the consent of all parties K. was made a ward of court. The carers continued to look after her; detailed orders were made in relation to contact with her relatives in Switzerland and instruction in Islam and the Bosnian language. The Official Solicitor remained involved to provide reports for the grandfather and for review hearings.

An officer of CAFCASS may be appointed to assist the court and act as a buffer between disputing parties.[25]

19–049 All these powers must be exercised applying section 1 of the Children Act 1989. But where the issue is the publication of articles about the child or their parents other considerations apply, particularly European Convention on Human Rights, Arts. 8 and 10.[26] The inherent jurisdiction cannot be used solely to protect a family's privacy[27]:—

---

[21] See Lowe and White (1986) Chap. 5.

[22] A party prejudiced may apply for a committal order under R.S.C. Ord. 52 and *Practice Direction* [2001] 1 F.L.R. 949 or sequestration of assets: *Re F. (Orse A.) (A Minor) (Publication of Information)* [1977] Fam. 58. The court may use the penalty of costs: *Havering L.B.C. v. S.* [1986] 1 F.L.R. 489.

[23] They may be given discretion over some matters: see *Re RJ. (Wardship)* [1999] 1 F.L.R. 618 F.D. where the carers were allowed to arrange medical treatment and remove the children from the jurisdiction for up to 30 days. They would have had these powers if the court had made a residence order.

[24] [1997] 2 F.L.R. 221, FD and CA.

[25] *CAFCASS Practice Note* [2001] 2 F.L.R. 151 (this role was formerly undertaken by the Official Solicitor); *Re W. (Wardship Discharge: Publicity)* [1995] 2 F.L.R. 466, CA *per* Balcombe L.J. but the personal supervision envisaged can only be available to a small number of cases.

[26] For a succinct analysis of the case law see *Kelly v. BBC* [2001] 1 F.L.R. 197 at 216 *per* Munby J. For a discussion of the effect of the E.C.H.R. see: *Douglas, Zeta-Jones, Northern & Shell plc v. Hello! Ltd* [2001] 1 F.L.R. 982 and *Thompson and Venables v. News Group Newspapers et al.* [2001] 1 F.L.R. 791, FD.

[27] *Re W. (Wardship: Publication of Information)* [1992] 1 F.L.R. 99 at 102, *per* Neill L.J. This will usually be possible without any identification of the ward other than to people who already know the facts.

In *Mrs R. v. Central Independent Television plc.*[28] a mother was not able to obtain an injunction restraining the broadcast of a television programme about her former husband, the father of her child who was a convicted paedophile. The programme had nothing to do with the upbringing of the child and thus there was nothing to balance against freedom to publish.

However, if the publication touches on the matters of direct concern to the court in its supervisory role[29] or directly about a child[30] a balancing exercise is required. The court must strike a balance between protecting the child and freedom of speech.[31] In most cases the public interest in favour of publication can be satisfied without identification of the ward; for example comment may be made about local authority action or medical decisions without identifying children, their parents or their current carers.[32] A convincing case of harm must be established before an injunction will be granted.[33] It is not a contempt for the media to interview a ward[34]; only if the media activities are essentially bound up with the child's care, has the court claimed the power to control them in exercise of its parental responsibility.[35]

The Administration of Justice Act 1960, s.12 makes it contempt of court to publish details of proceedings brought under the inherent jurisdiction or the Children Act 1989 but other material can be published unless an injunction has been made and notified to the press.[36] The court will not use its powers to prevent the disclosure of evidence to the police[37] nor for use by the minor in litigation.[38]

---

[28] [1994] 2 F.L.R. 151.

[29] *Kelly v. BBC* [2001] 1 F.L.R. 197; *Mrs R. v. Central Television plc.* [1994] 2 F.L.R. 151 at 160, *per* Neill L.J. Publicity may be allowed even of wardship proceedings if confidentiality is harmful to the ward: *Re H. (Publication of Judgement)* [1995] 2 F.L.R. 542.

[30] *X. County Council v. A.* [1984] 1 W.L.R. 1422 (a story about the child of Mary Bell, the child killer).

[31] E.C.H.R., Art. 10; *Cleveland C.C. v. F.* [1995] 1 F.L.R. 797 at 802–3 *per* Hale J.; *Oxford C.C. v. L. and F.* [1997] 1 F.L.R. 235 at 252 *per* Stuart-White J. Inevitably family judges may give too much weight to welfare: *Re G. (Celebrities: Publicity)* [1999] 1 F.L.R. 409 at 418 *per* Thorpe L.J. But freedom of speech does not automatically override other Convention rights: *Douglas, Zeta-Jones, Northern & Shell plc v. Hello! Ltd* [2001] 1 F.L.R. 982 at para. 137 *per* Sedley L.J.

[32] *Re M. and N. (Minors)* [1990] Fam. 211, CA; *Re C.(A Minor) (Wardship: Medical Treatment) (No. 2)* [1990] Fam. 39, CA.

[33] *Kelly v. BBC* [2001] 1 F.L.R. 197 at 228–9 *per* Munby J; *Thompson and Venables v. News Group Newspapers et al.* [2001] 1 F.L.R. 791, FD *per* Butler-Sloss P. at para. 44. Injunctions against publication are inevitably granted without notice to all the media; those effected should be given a clear indication of the basis on which injunctions were made. H.R.A. 1998, s. 12(3) (4) must be satisfied. For proforma injunctions see [2001] *Fam. Law* 644.

[34] *Kelly v. BBC* [2001] 1 F.L.R. 197 at 212, 218; providing there is no injunction forbidding this. A media interview is not "a major step" requiring court permission.

[35] *Re Z. (A Minor) (Freedom of Publication)* [1996] 1 F.L.R. 191 where the court refused leave for a child to be filmed for a programme about her treatment at a therapeutic institute.

[36] *Re L. (A Minor) (Wardship: Freedom of Publication)* [1988] 1 All E.R. 418; *Kelly v. BBC* [2001] 1 F.L.R. 197; *Re G. (Celebrities: Publicity)* [1999] 1 F.L.R. 409. There is a statutory bar on the identification of children involved in proceedings: Children Act 1989, s.97(2) which appears to impose greater restrictions see: J. Dixon [2001] *Fam. Law* 757. For a comprehensive survey, see Lord Chancellor's Department consultation paper, *Review of Access to and Reporting of Family Proceedings* (1993).

[37] *Re F. (Minors) (Wardship: Police Investigation)* [1989] Fam. 18, CA.

[38] *Re Manda* [1993] Fam. 183, where a young man who had been taken into care following a diagnosis of sexual abuse sought to sue the doctor in negligence. Restricting disclosure could breach Art. 6(1).

4. Procedure under wardship and the inherent jurisdiction

19–050 The reforms introduced by the Children Act 1989[39] mean that there are few advantages in terms of procedure or evidence in using the inherent rather than the statutory jurisdiction of the High Court. Wardship is "instantly available."[40] As soon as the originating summons is issued the child becomes a ward, but wardship lapses if the applicant fails to make an appointment for a hearing within 21 days.[41] Where immediate action is required the court can give directions or grant injunctions without notice.[42] The first appointment is usually before a district judge who may make agreed orders[43] and determine what should be referred to the judge. The main hearing takes place before a judge but, outside London, this may be a Circuit judge, Deputy Circuit judge, Recorder or Assistant recorder, nominated by the Lord Chancellor to do family work.[44] The Matrimonial and Family Proceedings Act 1984[45] allows wardship proceedings, but not orders warding or dewarding children, to be transferred to the county court but more complex matters are kept in the High Court.[46] All proceedings take place in chambers but judgment is occasionally given in open court.[47] Children are not necessarily parties to these proceedings.[48] If they are they may be represented by the a CAFCASS officer or (rarely) by the Official Solicitor.[49]

VIII. ENFORCEMENT OF ORDERS

19–051 Increasing concern has been expressed in the courts about the non-compliance with court orders. This is not just a private matter between the parties; the right to respect for family life means that the State has a positive obligation to enable parents and children to maintain relationships and must provide effective remed-

---

39 Without notice orders may be made under the Children Act 1989: see F.P.R. 1991, r. 4.4(4); F.P.C. 1991, r. 4(4) and above, para. 19–037. F.P.R. 1991, r. 9(2A) applies. Wardship does not provide a means of imposing a guardian *ad litem* on a competent but unwilling child: *Re T. (A Minor) (Wardship: Representation)* [1994] Fam. 49. Evidence is given by affidavit and oral testimony is required *cf.* F.P.R. 1991, r. 4.17; hearsay evidence is admissible under both jurisdictions: S.I. 1993 No. 621.

40 Law Com. W.P. 101, para. 2.8. Supreme Court Act 1981, s.41(2).

41 R.S.C. Ord. 90, rr. 3, 4; see Lowe and White (1986), paras 4.6–4.15.

42 Duty judges are available to deal with emergency applications: see Lowe and White (1986), paras 4.24 *et seq.; Re O. (A Minor) (Medical Treatment)* [1993] 2 F.L.R. 149 at 154.

43 R.S.C. Ord. 90, r. 12 allows district judges to make orders on any matter which could be dealt with by a judge in chambers and has not been reserved by the judge. See also *Practice Direction* [1999] 2 F.L.R. 799 and Lowe and White (1986), paras 6.67–6.71.

44 *Practice Direction* [1999] 2 F.L.R. 799.

45 s.38(2) (b).

46 *Practice Direction* [1992] 2 F.L.R. 87.

47 A solicitor who conducted the case in chambers may appear in open court with leave of the judge in an emergency or where judgement is given: Courts and Legal Services Act 1990, s.32(1) (a).

48 Lowe and White (1986), paras 3.4, 3.8; Masson and Morton, *op. cit.*, pp. 777–8.

49 F.P.R. 1991 r. 9.5(1); *CAFCASS Practice Note* [2001] 1 F.L.R.151; *Practice Note (Official Solicitor appointment)* [2001] 1 F.L.R. 155. See above for a discussion of CAFCASS and the Official Solicitor.

ies.[50] Orders are only effective if they are obeyed; sanctions exist to force compliance.[51] In cases concerning children, orders require personal actions and impact on relationships. These cases have no easy answer; high levels of emotion and obsessional behaviour[52] may not respond to judicial reasoning or the powers of the court. Both attempts at enforcement and failure to enforce may enrage disputes, undermine the welfare of children and breach human rights.

Powers of the court

19–052 Section 8 orders[53] made by a family proceedings court can be enforced by fining[54] persons in default or committing them to custody until the default is remedied but for no longer than two months.[55] The court may act on its own motion or by complaint.[56] But it has been said that courts should be inhibited by specific procedural safeguards from moving to committal without careful consideration of the consequences.[57] Considerable care must be taken that the correct procedures are followed; for example a residence order may only be enforced where a copy of the order has been served on the other person[58]; an order for contact must state the date and time of the handover.[59] Breach of the order must be wilful; the act or omission must be carried out with knowledge of the terms of the order.[60]

In the county court and the High Court, breach of an order may be treated as contempt of court but declaratory orders such as those for reasonable contact cannot be enforced.[61] Contemnors may be imprisoned for up to two years for breach of a High Court order, their property may be sequestered or they may be fined.[62] Sequestered property may be sold to raise money to pay for the enforce-

---

[50] *Hokkanen v. Finland* [1996] 1 F.L.R. 289; *Ignaccolo-Zenide v. Romania* E.C.H.R. App. 31679/96; *cf. Glaser v. U.K* [2001] 1 F.L.R. 153 where initiating enforcement was seen as the responsibility of the applicant not the State.

[51] Pressure to comply may also come from a party's solicitor see: C. Smart and B. Neale [1997] *Fam. Law* 332.

[52] *e.g. Harris v. Harris; A-G. v. Harris* [2001] 2 F.L.R. 895, FD where the father "a man devoid of all moral scruple" harassed his family, the lawyers and the judges and destroyed his relationship with his children by his "obstinacy".

[53] Children Act 1989, s.14 mentions only residence orders but it was held in *P. v. W.* [1984] Fam. 32 that Magistrates' Courts Act 1980, s.63(3) applied to access orders because these were orders "to do anything other than the payment of money or to abstain from doing anything." This applies equally to all s.8 orders so long as they are made by a court not a single justice. It may not apply to directions; see CAAC Report 1992/3, p. 42.

[54] £50 per day up to a maximum of £5000; see also CAAC Report 1993/4, p. 52.

[55] Magistrates Courts' Act 1980 s.63(3); Contempt of Court Act 1981, s.17(2) and Sched. 3.

[56] Contempt of Court Act 1981, s.17, Sched. 3.

[57] CAAC Report 1993/4, p. 53.

[58] Children Act 1989, s.14(2).

[59] *Re H. (Contact: Enforcement)* [1996] 1 F.L.R. 614.

[60] *P. v. W.* [1984] Fam. 32 at 38, *per* Wood J.

[61] *D. v. D. (Access: Committal)* [1991] 2 F.L.R. 34. The order would need to specify when, where and by whom contact was to be allowed.

[62] Contempt of Court Act 1981, s.14. The duration of the committal must be fixed: *Re C. (A Minor) (Contempt)* [1986] 1 F.L.R. 578. Credit should be given for admissions: *Re R. (A Minor) (Contempt)* [1994] 2 F.L.R. 185. There is no power to suspended sentences for contempt: *Harris v. Harris* [2002] 1 F.L.R. 248, CA.

ment of the order.[63] Breach of the order must be established using the criminal standard of proof,[64] before a person may be committed and cumbersome procedural rules must be followed.[65] Breach of a court order may also give rise to criminal proceedings for offences such as child abduction;[66] contempt proceedings should be dealt with swiftly and not be delayed, pending the criminal trial.[67]

Where an order made in England or Wales which requires a child to be handed to another is disobeyed, the court may authorise an officer of the court (or in the case of a magistrates' court, a constable) to enter premises (with force if necessary), search, take charge of and deliver the child to the person concerned.[68] In practice, the courts appear reluctant to use these enforcement powers except to ensure that children are returned to their residential carer. Where a child is wrongfully kept following contact[69] the court may order their return but may refuse to do so pending a hearing if the parent with care has a good relationship with the child, can provide adequately and has made serious allegations about the care of the residential parent.[70] There is no question that the courts disapprove of parents who "snatch" children and that this is a powerful factor in the consideration of the child's future care, but the welfare test applies.[71] Where a child is settled temporarily, a further move may be undesirable but delay undermines the position of the other parent and may lead the court to sanction the arrangement.

Contact orders pose even more severe enforcement problems.[72] A residential parent who refuses to permit contact may be imprisoned—two very different approaches have been taken to this power. In *Churchard v. Churchard*[73] the court, applying the welfare test, refused the father's applications for residence and to commit the mother for refusing contact. Ormrod L.J. referred to commit-

---

[63] *Richardson v. Richardson* [1990] 1 F.L.R. 186. Money raised by mortgaging the wife's house was used by the husband to bring proceedings in Eire for the return of the children taken there in breach of an order in wardship. In *Mir v. Mir* [1992] 1 F.L.R. 624 the husband's house was sold following a variation of the sequestration order: *Re S. (Abduction: Sequestration)* [1995] 1 F.L.R. 858.

[64] *Dean v. Dean* [1987] 1 F.L.R. 517; *Cleveland C.C. v. W. et al.* [1989] F.C.R. 625; *Re M. (A Minor) (Contempt of Court: Committal of Court's Own Motion)* [1999] Fam. 263. Procedures may need to satisfy E.C.H.R. Art. 6((3) see Swindells *et al.* 262–4 and *Mubarak v. Mubarak* [2001] 1 F.L.R. 698, CA.

[65] *President's Direction* [2001] 1 F.L.R. 949 applying the Civil Procedure *Practice Direction* and modifying Ord. 52 and C.C.R. 1981, Ord. 29. The requirements for information specified in the CPR *Direction* must be satisfied: *President's Direction* [2001] 1 F.L.R. 949, para.1.1(c).

[66] Child Abduction Act 1984, see below.

[67] *Szczepanski v. Szczepanski* [1985] F.L.R. 468; *Keeber v. Keeber* [1995] 2 F.L.R. 748, CA.

[68] Family Law Act 1986, s.34 as amended. *cf. R. v. Chief Constable of Cheshire, ex p. K.* [1990] 1 F.L.R. 70. Unless there is an order directed at them the police should not give the impression that they are enforcing civil court orders: *Re J.(Children: Ex parte Orders)* [1992] 1 F.L.R. 606.

[69] *W. v. D.* [1980] 1 F.L.R. 393; *Jenkins v. Jenkins* (1978) 9 *Fam. Law* 215, CA.

[70] *Re J. (A Minor) (Interim Custody)* [1989] 2 F.L.R. 304, CA.

[71] *Re J. (A Minor) (Interim Custody)* [1989] 2 F.L.R. 304 at 307, *per* Butler-Sloss L.J. This is not necessarily the case in "International cases" where the child is moved from one country to another, see below Chap. 21.

[72] Advisory Board on Family Law: Children Act Sub-committee, *Making contact work report* (2002); see also C. Smart and B. Neale [1997] *Fam. Law* 332 who view the emphasis on contact and enforcement as contrary to the welfare of carers and children.

[73] [1984] F.L.R. 635, CA.

tal as a "futile remedy", "the last hope of the destitute" which would only damage the father's relationship with his children. The court should not be concerned about its dignity.[74] In contrast, in *A. v. N.*[75] Ward L.J. doubted whether the child's welfare was paramount in proceedings for enforcement.[76] He refused an appeal against committal by a mother of a four-year-old child for preventing the father's contact, even though the mother's imprisonment would have "a grievous effect" on the child. The distress of separation had to be balanced against the long-term damage of not knowing the father. Courts should not tolerate the flouting of their orders.[77] But it has been said that a court that puts enforcement above harm to the child must be very clear about the correctness of the orders being enforced.[78] Committal is a weapon of last resort[79] but the court may order it without an application.[80]

Before enforcing contact the court may attempt to make it more acceptable by defining or reducing it, but a parent who is implacably opposed cannot expect the court to agree that this makes contact undesirable.[81] The court may make a family assistance order in the hope that a welfare officer can produce an acceptable arrangement[82] and may even threaten a change in the child's residence[83] or restrict some other aspect of parental responsibility.[84] The court's actions must be proportionate and balance the harm to the child of lack of contact with the impact to the child of parental imprisonment. A substantial impact on the child's

---

[74] at 638 *per* Ormrod L.J.

[75] [1997] 1 F.L.R. 533, CA and see *Making contact work report* (2002), App. 4

[76] at 540; in *Re M. (A Minor) (Contempt of Court: Committal of Court's Own Motion)* [1999] Fam. 263 at 281 he referred to "giving proper weight" to the interests of children even if their welfare was not strictly paramount.

[77] at 540–541. The father had a history of violence but Ward L.J. placed the blame firmly on the mother, "This little child suffers because the mother chooses to make her suffer." Beldam L.J delivered a concurring judgment. But Ward L.J has said that there is no danger in a parent's defiance becoming public knowledge and demeaning the court's authority because these proceedings are heard in private: *Re M. (A Minor) (Contempt of Court: Committal of Court's Own Motion)* [1999] Fam. 263 at 282.

[78] *Re F. (Contact: Enforcement)* [1998] 1 F.L.R. 691, CA at 696 *per* Hale J.

[79] *A. v. N.* [1997] 1 F.L.R. 533 at 542 *per* Beldam L.J.; *Re N. (A Minor) (Access: Penal Notice)* [1992] 1 F.L.R. 134, *per* Waite L.J. at 137, the Court of Appeal upheld a refusal to grant a specific access order incorporating a penal notice when the child was unwilling to see the father. Rather than suspending sentence, the court may adjourn to establish whether there will be compliance: *A. v. Y. (Child's Surname)* [1999] 2 F.L.R. 5. See also, CAAC Report 1993/4, p. 53.

[80] *Re M. (A Minor) (Contempt of Court: Committal of Court's Own Motion)* [1999] Fam. 263. The judge should not initiate committal proceedings and then sit in judgment on them.

[81] *Re E. (A Minor) (Access)* [1987] 1 F.L.R. 368, CA; *cf. Re D. (A Minor) (Contact: Mother's Hostility)* [1993] 2 F.L.R. 1 where hostility justified not ordering contact.

[82] Children Act 1989, s.16, above. A family assistance order is generally not appropriate where an escort service is required because there is no relative who will transport the child to see a father in prison: *S. v. P. (Contact Application: Family Assistance Order)* [1997] 2 F.L.R. 277. Contact difficulties are the main reason for making these orders: L. Trinder and N. Stone, "Family assistance orders: professional aspiration and party frustration" [1998] *C.F.L.Q.* 291–302.

[83] *Re K. (Residence Order: Securing Contact)* [1999] 1 F.L.R. 582, CA; but transfer of residence is unlikely to be appropriate where children are well settled: *Re B.(Residence Order: Status Quo)* [1998] 1 F.L.R. 368, CA and see *Making contact work report* (2002), paras 14.26–7.

[84] N. Fricker, CAAC Report 1994/5 p. 45. Judge Fricker has also suggested that the court's powers under Family Law Act 1986, s.34 to take charge of and deliver a child should be used to enforce contact see: Advisory Board on Family Law : Children Act Sub-committee, *Making contact work* consultation paper (2001), p.42 but this was not supported, *Report* (2002), p. 92.

well-being, for example resulting from entering the care system,[85] or a failure to consider the child's views could mean that enforcement by committal breached the child's Article 8 rights.

In their report, *Making contact work,* the Advisory Board on Family Law favoured a structured approach to enforcing contact similar to that operating in Australia.[86] It proposed that the court should have much wider powers and proposed a range of measures to advise and educate parents about the importance of contact, to make provision to support contact and to punish defaulters. The court would be able to direct resident parents to parenting programmes or require them to seek psychiatric advice—if they still disobeyed the contact order they could be required to undertake community service or attend parenting classes; imprisonment would be a last resort.[87] Although these proposals are creative and well-meaning it is difficult to ignore the illogicality of seeking to educate parents with care about their children's needs whilst large numbers of non-residential parents fail to maintain contact or pay child support and some continue to abuse former partners. Parents and children need far more support, but there is no evidence that compulsory counselling for parents who refuse contact will promote children's well-being or improve compliance with court orders.

---

[85] The power of the court in exceptional circumstances to commit children to care without an application from the local authority was removed by the Children Act 1989.
[86] *op. cit.* paras 14.23 and 14.55.
[87] *op. cit.* paras 14.50–14.57.

Chapter Twenty

EXERCISE OF THE COURT'S DISCRETION: THE WELFARE PRINCIPLE

CHILD'S WELFARE PARAMOUNT

Section 1 of the Children Act 1989 provides:— **20–001**

> "When a court determines any question with respect to—
>
> (a) the upbringing of a child; or
> (b) the administration of the child's property or the application of any income arising from it,
>
> the child's welfare shall be the court's paramount consideration."

The principle that the child's welfare should determine the outcome of disputes originates from the practice of the Chancery Court in wardship and guardianship cases in the late eighteenth and nineteenth centuries.[1] The Guardianship of Infants Act 1886 first prescribed the child's welfare as a relevant consideration together with the conduct and wishes of the parents. Although there was growing concern for the welfare of children during the early part of the last century,[2] the Guardianship Infants Act 1925 would not have been passed if feminists had not been claiming equality for mothers during marriage.[3] The 1925 Act made the child's welfare the "first and paramount consideration"[4] when a court determined a relevant issue and declared that neither parent had a superior claim.[5] It was subsequently held to be declaratory of the then existing law and also to apply equally to disputes between the parents and other people.[6] The word "first" was thought by the Law Commission to suggest that the child's welfare

---

[1] Law Com. W.P. 96; *Custody*, para. 6.2.

[2] Concern for children developed the work of the great Victorian reformers, Barnardo, Shaftesbury, Carpenter *et al.*, see I. Pinchbeck and Hewitt, *Children in English Society* (1973), Vol. II; H. Hendrick, *Child Welfare England 1872–1989* (1994).

[3] For a full account drawing on unpublished official and other material, see S. Cretney, "What will the women want next? The struggle for power within the family 1925–1975" (1996) 112 *L.Q.R.* 110 (reprinted in Cretney (1998) 155); S. Maidment, *Child Custody and Divorce* (1984), p. 139; J. Brophy, "Parental rights and children's welfare: some problems of feminists strategy in the 1920s" (1982) 10 *International Journal of the Sociology of Law* 149–168.

[4] Guardianship of Infants Act 1925, s.1; the provision was re-enacted in the Guardianship of Minors Act 1971, s.1.

[5] Mothers did not have equality of parental rights: the child's father remained the sole legal guardian. Mothers only acquired guardianship rights by the Guardianship Act 1973 and even then were not described as the child's guardian; see Guardianship Act 1973, s.1; Law Com. W.P. 91, *Guardianship*, para. 2.8.

[6] *J. v. C.* [1970] A.C. 668, *per* Lord Guest at 697. Both these claims seem at odds with the origins of the provision: see Cretney (1998), pp. 176–179.

should be balanced with other factors[7] consequently, it was not retained in the Children Act 1989.

The welfare of the child who is the subject of the proceedings[8] has been said to be the "only" consideration in cases where section 1 applies[9] but it has been argued that the "no-order" principle undermines the paramountcy rule.[10] Despite a recommendation from the Law Commission that the welfare of no one child in the family should prevail,[11] there is no statutory requirement to balance the interests of all children involved in the proceedings. Courts have avoided considering the conflicting interests of a parent below the age of 18 and her child,[12] and of siblings[13] by focussing legalistically[14] on the application:—

> In *Re T. and E. (Proceedings: Conflicting Interests)*[15] two children with the same mother were in care following sexual abuse to the older child, T, by her stepfather who was her uncle and father of the younger child, E. T's father applied to discharge her care order and for residence. No Children Act application was made in respect of E. The application was granted because it was in T's best interests although it was in E's interests for T to be placed for adoption with her.

Where two or more children involved in the same proceedings have conflicting interests, it has been suggested that[16] the court should strike a balance between their interests and seek to find the least detrimental alternative.

All arguments must focus on the impact on the child of the behaviour or arrangements. Thus parental conduct is relevant to the extent that it affects par-

---

7 Law Com. 96, para. 6.9; Law Com. No. 172 *Review of Child Law Guardianship and Custody* (1988) H.C. 594, para. 3.13.

8 *Birmingham C.C. v. H. (No. 3)* [1994] 1 F.L.R. 224, HL.

9 *S. (B.D.) v. S. (D.J.)* [1977] Fam. 109; but Hall [1977] *C.L.J.* 252 considered there may still be room for considerations of justice in evenly balanced cases.

10 A. Bainham, "The privatisation of the public interest in children" (1990) 53 *M.L.R.* 206. In *Re J. (A Minor) (Contact)* [1994] 1 F.L.R. 729, CA the Court of Appeal refused to overturn a decision to make no order even though they recognised this was unjust, because it was clear that an order would be ineffective but in *Re R. (A Minor) (Contact)* [1994] 2 F.L.R. 441 the order was made despite threats of disobedience from the mother.

11 Law Com. No. 172, para. 3.13, Draft Bill, cl. 1(2).

12 *Birmingham C.C. v. H. (No. 3)* [1994] 1 F.L.R. 224, HL. The application was made under Children Act 1989, s. 34(4) but could as easily have been made under s.34(2) by the mother who was in care.

13 *Re T and E. (Proceedings: Conflicting Interests)* [1995] 1 F.L.R. 581; *Re S. (Contact: Application by Sibling)* [1998] 2 F.L.R. 897.

14 The approved approach involves considering which child is subject to the application: *F. v. Leeds C.C.* [1994] 2 F.L.R. 60 at 63, *per* Ward, J; in *Re F. (Contact: Child in Care)* [1995] 1 F.L.R. 510, this was the child living with the parents not the applicant child in care who would be named in the s.8 order. Consequently, leave was refused despite the adverse effect on an applicant child where the adoptive parents' attitude made pursuing contact potentially disruptive for the other child: *Re S. (Contact: Application by Sibling)* [1998] 2 F.L.R. 897.

15 [1995] 1 F.L.R. 581.

16 *Re A. (Conjoined Twins: Medical Treatment)* [2001] 1 F.L.R. 1 at 49 *per* Ward L.J., at 102 *per* Robert Walker L.J.

enting capacity,[17] the child's relationship with the parent,[18] or the child's safety[19] or development.[20] Violent behaviour may threaten the child's well-being by undermining the parent with care, damaging the child's emotional development and placing him or her at physical risk.[21] Doing justice between the parents, or the notion that parents have rights over their children,[22] has been said to play no part in the application of the welfare test. However, "the right to family life"[23] can only be restricted to the extent permitted by the European Convention on Human Rights.

20–002 The Children Act 1989 applies the "welfare principle" to cases concerning the upbringing of children, including care proceedings where the court must also be satisfied that the threshold conditions for an order exist.[24] Maintenance is specifically excluded[25]; decisions about the emigration of children in care require additional considerations.[26] Where the child has been abducted, return will be ordered unless this poses a grave risk.[27] Also the decision to make a secure accommodation order is not one to which section 1 applies.[28] Other statutes,

---

[17] *Re R. (Minors) (Custody)* [1986] 1 F.L.R. 6: the father had a criminal record and a drink problem.

[18] *Re F. (Minors) (Denial of Contact)* [1993] 2 F.L.R. 677, CA where the children were upset by their father's transsexualism. It might be argued that a child who sees one parent behaving badly towards the other will not be able to respect him and this will lead to a poor relationship. There are *dicta* in *Richards v. Richards* [1984] A.C. 174 that it is not good for a child to see one parent "get away" with behaving badly.

[19] *Re D.* [1977] A.C. 602; the father's homosexuality (which the court appears to have confused with paedophilia) was said to endanger the child because of possible approaches from other men who visited the child's home; *cf. Re C. (Residence Order: Lesbian Co-parents)* [1994] *Fam. Law* 468. If the issue is contact the child may be protected by arranging for direct contact take place at a contact centre or be supervised, or for indirect contact: *Re S. (Violent Parent: Indirect Contact)* [2000] 1 F.L.R. 481 but not if the child rejects the non-residential parent: *Re C. (Contact: No Order for Contact)* [2000] 2 F.L.R. 723.

[20] *S v. S (Custody of Children)* (1978) 1 F.L.R. 143 the children were thought to be at risk of embarrassment and "serious harm" because their mother was a lesbian. In *Re V. (Residence: Review)* [1995] 2 F.L.R. 1010, CA, the father's negative attitude to the mother and to women generally was thought damaging to the boy's emotional development.

[21] *Re L., Re V., Re M., Re H. (Contact: Domestic Violence)* [2000] 2 F.L.R. 334, CA; Sturge and Glaser [2000] Fam. L. 615; H. Cleaver *et al., Children's needs—parenting capacity* (1999). Continued conflict can also undermine the carer: *Re M.(Contact: Parental Responsibility)* [2001] 2 F.L.R. 342, FD.

[22] *Re K.D. (A Minor) (Ward. Termination of Access)* [1988] A.C. 806.

[23] E.C.H.R., Art. 8.

[24] Children Act 1989, s.31(2); the DHSS *Review of Child Care Law* (1985) rejected the welfare test as a basis for intervention in family life: para. 15.10; see para. 22–016, below.

[25] Children Act 1989, s.105(1); in maintenance cases under that Act the court must consider the matters in Sched.1, para. 4; and see *K. v. K. (Minors: Property Transfer)* [1992] 2 F.L.R. 220. Under the Matrimonial Causes Act 1973, s.25(1) the court must give "first consideration" to the child's welfare; see *Suter v. Suter and Jones* [1987] Fam. 111 but note that this has become irrelevant in most cases because of the Child Support Act 1991.

[26] Children Act 1989, Sched. 2, para. 19; *Re G. (Minors) (Care: Leave to Place Outside the Jurisdiction)* [1994] 2 F.L.R. 301; *MH. v. GP. (Child: Emigration)* [1995] 2 F.L.R. 106, CA.

[27] Child Abduction and Custody Act 1985, Sched.1, Hague Convention on the Civil Aspects of Child Abduction, Arts 12, 13(b); the court is not permitted to conduct an examination of the child's welfare, see Chap. 21, below.

[28] Children Act 1989, s.25; *M. v. Birmingham C.C.* [1994] 2 F.L.R. 141; *Re M. (Secure Accommodation Order)* [1995] 1 F.L.R. 418, CA. *cf. Guidance,* Vol. 4, para. 8.9.

notably the Adoption Act 1976 and the Child Support Act 1991, apply other welfare formulations.[29]

Where Parliament has provided a different standard the courts may not apply the welfare test by considering the matter under the inherent jurisdiction.[30] Moreover, the rule of paramountcy does not apply where upbringing is only incidental to some other dispute.[31] The child's welfare is not paramount in a dispute concerning the occupation of the family home.[32] But where a decision about a child impinges upon a decision about the matrimonial home, and vice versa, it is desirable for them to be dealt with together so that the judge can look at matters in the round.[33] Under the Family Law Act 1996[34] the court must consider whether the applicant or any "relevant child"[35] is likely to suffer "significant harm" attributable to the respondent's conduct and balance this against the harm to the respondent or any relevant child. In the case of married or formerly married couples, the court must make the order unless the balance favours the respondent.[36] Welfare has been said to yield to considerations of public policy.[37] Freedom of speech is guaranteed in the E.C.H.R. and must take precedence over the interests of individual children so, where there are no proceedings relating to the upbringing of a child the court will not control publicity about a family even though this might be damaging for the children.[38] Where there is litigation about children, press freedom may be balanced against a child's welfare and restrictions imposed on publication which allow comment on matters of public interest but do not pander to curiosity[39]:—

---

[29] s.6 welfare is only the "first consideration" but the Adoption and Children Bill 2002, s.1(2) states that the child's welfare "throughout his life" must be the paramount consideration in adoption decisions. The Child Support Act 1991, s.2 only requires the Secretary of State and child support officers "to have regard" to welfare when exercising discretion. CYPA 1933, s.44 courts must "have regard" to the welfare of a child brought before them.

[30] *A. v. Liverpool C.C.* [1982] A.C. 363. *cf. Re N. (A Minor) (Adoption)* [1990] 1 F.L.R. 58.

[31] See *Re X. (A Minor) (Wardship Jurisdiction)* [1975] Fam. 47 at 62, *per* Pennycuick J., a case concerning the publication of a book about the ward's father. Or where the issue is the parent's deportation: *R. v. S.S. for Home Department, ex p. Gangadeen* [1998] 1 F.L.R. 762, CA.

[32] *Richards v. Richards* [1984] A.C. 174; The Children Act 1989 did not overrule this decision: *Gibson v. Austin* [1992] 2 F.L.R. 437.

[33] *Re B. (A Minor: Custody)* [1991] 2 F.L.R. 405, *per* Butler-Sloss L.J. at 409.

[34] F.L.A. 1996, Pt IV; see generally Chap. 10, above.

[35] F.L.A. 1996, s.62(2).

[36] ss.33(7), 35(8), 36(8); *B. v. B. (Occupation Order)* [1999] 1 F.L.R. 715.

[37] 4th edition of this book, p. 325 citing *Re Mohamed Arif* [1968] 1 Ch. 643 particularly *per* Russell L.J. at 662–663. However, this case is an early example of the ousting of wardship where the situation is within a statutory code (see *A. v. Liverpool C.C.* [1982] A.C. 363) and may be explained without this further rule.

[38] *Mrs R. v. Central Independent Television plc* [1994] 2 F.L.R. 151 where the Court of Appeal overturned the decision to ban a programme which identified the child's paedophile father. Pictures of child, her mother and their home were removed by the company by agreement. The action sought was beyond the scope of the inherent jurisdiction: *Re Z. (A Minor) (Freedom of Publication)* [1996] 1 F.L.R. 191 at 212, *per* Ward L.J.; *Kelly v. B.B.C.* [2001] 1 F.L.R. 197 at 216 *per* Munby J.

[39] *Re W. (Wardship: Publication of Information)* [1992] 1 F.L.R. 99; *Re Z. (A Minor) (Freedom of Publication)* [1996] 1 F.L.R. 191 at 213, CA, *per* Ward L.J.; *Re G. (Celebrities: Publicity)* [1999] 1 F.L.R. 409 the publicity in this exceptional case justified restrictions beyond those in the Administration of Justice Act 1960, s.12. In rare cases publicity may be in the child's interests: *Re H. (Publication of Judgment)* [1995] 2 F.L.R. 542.

In *Re H. (Minors) (Injunction: Public Interest),*[40] a transsexual parent wished to publish a book about his life. The court permitted the publication subject to removal of details of his children's names, address or schools.

A balance also must be held between the child's welfare and the disclosure of information in confidential reports.[41]

The welfare principle in section 1 applies to courts,[42] but parents, local authorities and children themselves must also have regard to children's welfare. Decisions by parents which conflict with welfare may be reviewed by the courts[43] and thus it has been said that parents must apply the welfare principle.[44] The same could be said of decisions by children.[45] Local authority decisions which do not require court approval, are generally immune from review on the merits[46] but local authorities are under a duty to safeguard and promote the welfare of children in need and those they are looking after.[47]

Presumptions and assumptions

20–003 It is said that there are no presumptions in the Children Act 1989 which can displace the paramountcy of the welfare principle.[48] However, judges have suggested principles or assumptions[49] which should guide the application of the welfare test, and even used these to preclude the "balancing exercise" which welfare decisions normally require.[50] It has been assumed that being brought up

---

[40] [1994] 1 F.L.R. 519, CA.

[41] *Official Solicitor v. K.* [1965] A.C. 201; *Re D. (Adoption Reports: Confidentiality)* [1995] 2 F.L.R. 687, HL; *A County Council v. W. (Disclosure)* [1997] 1 F.L.R. 574.

[42] CAFCASS officers must have regard to the welfare checklist in s.1(3): F.P.R. 1991, r.4.11(1); F.P.C. 1991, r.11(1); the welfare test in the Adoption and Children Bill 2002, s.1 also applies to adoption agencies.

[43] Under the inherent jurisdiction or by seeking a section 8 order under the Children Act 1989. A child or third party who sought to bring proceedings would require leave: s.10(1) (a) (ii); and welfare is not paramount in proceedings for leave: see s.10(9): *Re A. and W. (Minors) (Residence Order: Leave to Apply)* [1992] Fam. 182.

[44] *Gillick v. W. Norfolk and Wisbech Health Authority* [1986] A.C. 112, *per* Lord Scarman at 184. However, parents' statutory duties require considerably less: see Children and Young Persons Act 1933, ss.1, 3, 4, 11 and Children Act 1989, s.31(2). Amendments to the Children Act 1989 which would have required local authorities to act "as a good parent" to children leaving care were rejected because the notion was too vague, see Lord Mackay, Lord Chancellor, *Hansard,* H.L., Vol. 503, col. 144 (January 17, 1989, Children Bill, Lords, Committee Stage).

[45] *Re W. (A Minor) (Medical Treatment: Court's Jurisdiction)* [1993] Fam. 64.

[46] *A. v. Liverpool City Council* [1982] A.C. 363. Compulsory admission to care, contact and some other decisions require court sanction, if the local authority's plan for the child is contrary to the child's welfare the court may refuse the order requested: *Berkshire C.C. v. B.* [1997] 1 F.L.R. 171. Judicial Review is available for decisions which are *ultra vires* or irrational: *R. v. Harrow LBC ex p. D.* [1990] Fam. 133.

[47] Children Act 1989, ss.17(1) (a), 22(3) (a); welfare may defer to the need to protect members of the public from serious injury: see s. 22(6).

[48] *Re P. (Section 91(14) Guidelines) (Residence and Religious Heritage)* [1999] 2 F.L.R.573 at 585 *per* Butler-Sloss L.J.

[49] For a discussion see: C. Piper, "Assumptions about children's best interests" [2000] *J.S.W.F.L.* 261. Similarly more prescriptive "rules of thumb" have been used but "there are no rules of thumb" *per* Wood J. *Edwards v. Edwards* [1986] 1 F.L.R. 187 at 203.

[50] See for example *Re K.(A Minor) (Ward: Care and Control)* [1990] 2 F.L.R. 64, CA; *Re D. (Care: Natural Parent Presumption)* [1999] 1 F.L.R. 135, CA.

by a parent,[51] maintaining current arrangements (the *status quo*) and contact with the non-residential parent are each in children's best interests.[52] These assumptions are derived from research into child development, the beliefs of child welfare professionals[53] and notions about how children should be brought up after parental separation.[54] Although assumptions cannot provide precedents for individual cases, they influence lawyers and their clients to settle on the basis of the court's likely approach. Where assumptions by professionals or courts replace the individual assessment of a case, they distort the balancing exercise required by section1(1).

Welfare and the Human Rights Act 1998

20–004 The implementation of the Human Rights Act 1998 demands consideration of whether court's approach to disputes about relationships with children complies with the E.C.H.R. The welfare principle must be interpreted and applied in accordance with the Convention.[55] The right to respect for family life imposes positive obligations on the state including to provide a framework for adjudication and enforcement for disputes between individuals[56]; and the state can only interfere with private and family life to the extent permitted by Article 8(2).

It has been argued that Article 8 and the welfare principle are not compatible because more evidence is necessary to show that interference with a right is "necessary" and the judgments required are qualitatively different.[57] Similarly it has been suggested that there is a danger that the welfare principle will be diluted in the face of parents' claims to their rights.[58] However, in *Re KD. (A Minor) (Ward: Termination of Access)*[59] Lord Oliver concluded that there was nothing in Convention case-law which undermined the welfare principle. Subsequently, the case-law of the European Court has emphasised the importance

---

[51] *Re D. (Care: Natural Parent Presumption)* [1999] 1.F.L.R. 135, CA; *Re N. (Residence: Appointment of a Solicitor: Placement with Extended Family)* [2001] 1 F.L.R. 1028 J. Fortin [1999] *C.F.L.Q.* 435.

[52] *Re O. (Contact: Imposition of Conditions)* [1995] 2 F.L.R. 124 at 128 *per* Bingham M.R; R. Bailey-Harris *et al.*, "From utility to rights? The presumption of contact in practice" [1999] Int. J Law, Pol. and Fam. 111. In *Re M. (Contact: Parental Responsibility)* [2001] 2 F.L.R. 342, FD the benefit of the contact for a severely disabled young woman amounted to maintaining the interest of the paternal family so they might remain involved if something happened to the mother.

[53] *Re L., Re V., Re M. and Re H. (Contact: Domestic Violence)* [2000] 2 F.L.R. 334 at 365 *per* Thorpe L.J.

[54] The (unimplemented) Family Law Act 1996, s.11(4) (c) included a rebuttable presumption that the child's welfare will be best served by regular contact with family members and those who have parental responsibility, and maintaining relationships with both parents. Similarly the Protection of Children Act 1999 operates on the presumption that those convicted of offences against children continue to pose a danger to children.

[55] Human Rights Act 1998, s.3; if this is not possible the High Court should make a declaration of incompatibility, s.4.

[56] *X. and Y. v. The Netherlands* (1986) 8 E.H.R.R. 235; *Glaser v. U.K.* [2001] 1 F.L.R. 153, ECtHR.

[57] J. Herring, "The Human Rights Act and the welfare principle in family law—conflicting or complementary?" [1999] *C.F.L.Q.* 223 at 231.

[58] J. Fortin "The HRA's impact on litigation involving children and their families" [1999] *C.F.L.Q.* 237 at 251.

[59] [1988] A.C. 806 at 825, 828.

of the child's welfare.[60] Applying Article 8, the Court has stated that the interests, freedoms and rights of all concerned must be taken into account, particularly the best interests of the child[61]; that a parent cannot be entitled to measures from the state which would harm the child's health or development[62]; and that where parental contact appears to threaten the child's interests, it is for the national authorities to strike a fair balance between them.[63] Moreover, most disputes about a child's upbringing involve competing claims from adults who have incompatible rights to privacy and family life. In using the child's welfare as the balancing factor the courts are making a decision "in accordance with the law and one which is "necessary"[64] to protect the interests of the child. Only if the restriction on a parent's right was disproportionate to what was required could it be impugned.[65]

When determining disputes about children's upbringing, courts should be mindful that they are also adjudicating on rights to family life and ensure that their decisions are based on facts and professional assessments[66] and not merely on presumptions or prejudice.[67] This may have the effect of injecting far greater rigour into judicial decision-making[68] and placing greater emphasis on facts and on expert evidence.

The meaning of the principle

20–005 The leading modern case on the welfare principle is *J. v. C.*[69] where the courts considered whether a 10-year-old boy should be returned to his parents (Spanish nationals resident in Spain) or remain with English foster parents who had looked after him for all, except 18 months, of his life. The House of Lords upheld the decision of the trial judge and the Court of Appeal that he should stay in England. Lord MacDermott stated that paramountcy of welfare means:

> "more than that the child's welfare is to be treated as the top item in a list of items relevant to the matter in question. [The words] connote a process

---

[60] *Scott v. U.K.* [2000] 1 F.L.R. 958 at 968

[61] *Glaser v. U.K.* [2001] 1 F.L.R. 153 at 168, para. 66.

[62] *Johansen v. Norway* (1996) 23 E.H.R.R. 33 at 72-3.

[63] *Hokkanen v. Finland* [1996] 1 F.L.R. 289 at 305; *Olsson v. Sweden (No. 2)* (1994) 17 E.H.R.R. 134 at 181–2. The "margin of appreciation" which the Court allows to national authorities varies in the light of the nature and seriousness of the issues at stake: *K. and T. v. Finland* [2001] 2 F.L.R. 707, para. 155.

[64] In terms of protecting rights or interests allowed under Art. 8(2) and being the only way of so doing see: J. Fortin, *op. cit.* p.247.

[65] "Proportionality . . . is the key" *per* Hale L.J. *Re O. (Supervision Order)* [2001] 1 F.L.R.923, CA at para. 28.

[66] *Elsholz v. Germany* [2000] 2 F.L.R. 486. The dismissal of the father's application for contact without a hearing or an independent psychological report breached the father's rights under Arts 6 and 8.

[67] See *Hoffman v. Austria* (1993) 17 E.H.R.R. 293 where the transfer of custody from the mother who had become a Jehovah's Witness to the father breached Arts 8 and 14; *Salgueiro da Silva Mouta v. Portugal* (1999), App. 00033290/96 where transfer of legal custody from the father, a homosexual, to the mother breached Arts 8 and 14.

[68] Fortin, *op. cit.*, p.255.

[69] [1970] A.C. 668.

> whereby, when all the relevant facts, relationships claims and wishes of parents, risks choices and other circumstances are taken into account and weighed the course to be followed will be that which is most in the interests of the child's welfare as that term is now understood . . . [It is] the paramount consideration because it rules upon or determines the course to be followed."[70]

The boy's welfare necessitated that he remain with the parent figures he was attached to, the more so since his natural parents would have been unable to cope with his consequent maladjustment. Against these considerations the claims of "unimpeachable"[71] natural parents could not prevail. The court came to a different conclusion in a similar case in 1996:—

> In *Re M.*,[72] a Zulu boy, aged six, was brought by an Afrikaner widow to England after her maid, the child's single mother, had signed papers (which she later claimed she thought related to insurance) agreeing to his adoption. He lived in London for four years, obtained a scholarship to attend public school and lost his ability to speak his mother tongue. Thorpe J. acknowledged that the child had "two psychological mothers" and favoured his return to South Africa after a series of visits to be paid for by the Afrikaner woman. The woman was unable to keep her undertaking to pay for visits and appealed. The Court of Appeal held, despite the boy's protests, that it was in his interests to return to live with his parents in South Africa immediately. However, after six months the boy had not settled and was returned by his mother to live with the Afrikaner woman.

Applying the welfare test requires an individual assessment in each case. Consequently, precedent has little value,[73] except perhaps to indicate the approaches which currently find favour with the judiciary. Indeterminancy, the lack of any precise meaning to the notion of welfare[74] has enabled judges (and social workers) to use it to justify their own subjective decisions.[75] Thus the Court of Appeal has upheld a decision which granted custody to a disciplinarian

---

[70] *ibid.* at 710–711.

[71] Before *J. v. C.* conduct might determine the outcome of a dispute, see, *e.g. Re L.* [1962] 3 All E.R. 1 where the mother's adultery and the father's lack of bad behaviour or "unimpeachability" justified awarding custody to him. It has been said that the "umimpeachable parent" is in "forensic limbo" *Re R. (Minors) (Wardship Jurisdiction)* (1981) 2 F.L.R. 416 at 425.

[72] [1996] 2 F.L.R. 441, CA. Despite the obvious similarities, *J. v. C.* was not cited in the judgment but considerable emphasis was placed on the child's right to be brought up in his homeland by his natural parents.

[73] *Re K.* [1977] Fam. 179 at 183, *per* Stamp L.J.; *Lonslow v. Hennig* [1986] 2 F.L.R. 378 at 381.

[74] R. Mnookin, "Bargaining in the shadow of the law: The case of divorce" [1979] C.L.P. 65; D. Chambers, "Rethinking the substantive rules for custody disputes in divorce" [1984–85] Michigan Law Rev. 477.

[75] M. King, "Playing the symbols—Custody and the Law Commission" (1987) 17 *Fam. Law* 186, 189; H. Reece, "The paramountcy principle consensus or contruct?" [1996] C.L.P. 267 at 272–5. For a discussion of different ideological approaches affecting social work decision-making, see L. Fox-Harding, *Perspectives in child care policy* (2nd ed., 1997), and "The Children Act 1989 in context: Four perspectives in child care law and policy" [1991] *J.S.W.F.L.* 179 at 285.

father rather than an easy-going mother[76]; refused to disturb a decision which denied custody to an unemployed father because it was his duty to work and support the family,[77] refused custody to a mother who was a Jehovah's Witness because the children would not celebrate Christmas,[78] and favoured placement for adoption over custody to a teenage father who had yet to face the stresses of reaching maturity.[79]

20–006 The growth of child welfare professions and the desire to reach better and more justifiable decisions has shifted the reasoning in cases towards arguments based on child development theory.[80] The emphasis on evidence-based practice in medicine and social work has highlighted the importance of research, but this can only identify (and sometimes quantify) issues, risks and protective factors not future outcomes for particular individuals. Research does not necessarily permit firm conclusions.[81] Welfare assessments need to be grounded in research and reflect the realities of the care which can be provided for the child in the family or elsewhere.[82] They will also reflect the values of those undertaking the assessment.[83] Judges are hugely dependent on the assessments of CAFCASS officers[84] and expert witnesses[85] (whose views may conflict).[86] But it has been suggested that "child welfare knowledge" is captured and reconstructed by the legal process.[87]

Bowlby's work on attachment and separation[88] was for long most influential

---

[76] *May v. May* [1986] 1 F.L.R. 325; both parents were apparently equally capable of caring for the children. A decision against a parent and step-parent who had a liberal approach to nudity was over turned: *Re W. (Residence Order)* [1999] 1 F.L.R. 869, CA.

[77] *B. v. B. (Custody of Child)* [1985] F.L.R. 166.

[78] *T. v. T.* (1974) 4 *Fam. Law* 190. They would be deprived of the "wholesome joys of life . . . the charms of crackers and paper hats" *per* Stamp L.J. at p. 191. The mother's mental condition also gave rise to anxiety. Reasoning of this sort appears to breach E.C.H.R., Arts 8 and 14 see *Hoffman v. Austria* (1993) 17 E.H.R.R. 293 and *Salgueiro da Silva Mouta v. Portugal* (1999), App. 00033290/96.

[79] *Re M. (A Minor: Custody Appeal)* [1990] 1 F.L.R. 291.

[80] See generally S. Maidment (1984).

[81] See, for example, D. Quinton *et al.*, "Contact between children placed away from home and their birth parents: research issues and evidence" (1997) Clinical Child Psychol. and Psychiat. 393.

[82] See: D.H., *A framework for assessing children and families* (1999), 15.

[83] These may be set out in service standards, see, for example, D.H., *National Standards for Adoption for England* (2001).

[84] *Re W. (Residence)* [1999] 2 F.L.R. 390 at 395 *per* Thorpe L.J. The judge is not required to follow such a recommendation but must give reasons for not doing so: *Re CB. (Access: Court Welfare Report)* [1995] 1 F.L.R. 622; *Re A. (Children 1959 UN Declaration)* [1998]1 F.L.R. 354, CA; *Re D. (Grant of Care Order: Refusal of Freeing Order)* [2001] 1 F.L.R. 862, CA.

[85] Particularly from the Child and Adolescent Mental Health Service: J. Brophy *et al, Myths and practices: a national survey in the use of expert evidence in child care proceedings* (1999).

[86] Because they have made different observations or because they have made assessments from a different ideological standpoint, see Fox-Harding (1997). The courts are attempting to limit the number of experts and the conflicts between them: *Re G. (Minors) (Expert Witnesses)* [1994] 2 F.L.R. 291 and CAAC, *Handbook of best practice in Children Act cases* (1997), Chap. 5.

[87] M. King and C. Piper, *How the law thinks about children* (2nd ed., 1995), p. 43. King and Piper base their arguments on a development of Teubner's autopoietic theory. The model of family law which King and Piper use has been criticised for failing to reflect the discretionary and therapeutic mode for decisions about children: K. O'Donovan, *Family law matters* (1993), p. 28.

[88] J. Bowlby, *Child Care and the Growth of Love* (2nd ed., 1953); J. Bowlby, *Attachment and Loss*, Vols. I–III (1969, 1973 and 1980).

but more recent re-assessments of it by Rutter[89] and others[90] mean, particularly in disputes between parents, that such theories may offer no solution. Attachment theory suggests that for healthy psychological (and physical) development a child needs to have a close relationship with a limited number of adults who will relate closely to him or her, preferably in a warm and nurturing way. Bowlby, whose original work was done with institutionalised children, stressed the value of a single mother figure, but Rutter has shown that children can relate to more than one such figure and that gender is not important. Children become attached to these "psychological parents"[91]; separation from them produces anxiety and prolonged separation leads to depression and disturbed behaviour. Younger children may regress, losing skills they had already mastered; older children may become aggressive or withdrawn. Attachment can occur at any age although it develops more quickly with young children. Children who do not become attached, or whose attachments are disrupted, may successfully be attached to others[92] but adoption does not necessarily provide a better outcome for abused children.[93] Attachment is not the sole determinant; children may become attached to dangerous or disturbed parent figures[94] and may also be attached to both[95] or neither[96] of the parties involved in a dispute.

The term resilience is used to identify the capacity to function well despite adversity.[97] Understanding what makes children resilient may help prevent harm and the development of programmes for those who have suffered trauma. Resilience is not innate nor merely a product of development but involves the interplay of psycho-social processes which support health development. There is considerable agreement about the attributes of resilient children, their psychological functioning and important protective factors but, as yet, far less understanding about the processes through which resilience is achieved. Resilient children are generally healthier, of higher socio-economic status, younger when they experience trauma but have not suffered early separations of losses. They have good self-esteem, self-control and a sense of humour. Resilient children have a warm relationship with at least one carer, receive competent parenting and have good friendship networks and educational experiences.

20–007 An awareness of individual's family, racial and cultural heritage is an aspect

---

[89] M. Rutter, *Maternal Deprivation Reassessed* (1972) (2nd ed., 1981).

[90] W. Sluckin, M. Herbert and A. Sluckin, *Maternal Bonding* (1983).

[91] This phrase is used by J. Goldstein, A. Freud and A. Solnit in *Beyond the Best Interests of the Child* (1973) (revised ed., 1996). For a recent reassessment of this work see M.D.A. Freeman, "The best interests of the child?"(1997) 11 Int J. Law, Pol. and Fam. 360.

[92] B. Tizard, *Adoption, a Second Chance* (1977). A. Rushton and J. Treseder, "Developmental recovery" (1986) Vol. 10 No. 3 *Adoption & Fostering* 54.

[93] D.H., *Child protection: messages from research* (1995), p. 67, citing J. Gibbons *et al., Development after physical abuse in early childhood: a follow-up study of children on protection registers* (1995).

[94] *e.g.* where the child is abused see D. Jones, J. Pickett, M. Oates, P. Barbor, *Understanding Child Abuse* (2nd ed., 1987).

[95] *e.g. Re M. (Child's Upbringing)* [1996] 2 F.L.R. 441 or in a dispute between parents at separation.

[96] *e.g. Re D. (Care: Natural Parent Presumption)* [1999] 1 F.L.R.134 or where members of a child's family are seeking residence in care proceedings but the local authority favours adoption

[97] P. Fonagy *et al.,* "The theory and practice of resilience" (1994) 35 J. Child Pyschol. Psychiat. 231; E. Hetherington and M. Stanley-Hagan "The adjustment of children and divorced parents: a risk and resiliency perspective" (1999) 40 J. Child Pyschol. Psychiat. 129.

of development which has, perhaps, not been given sufficient prominence.[98] A well-developed sense of identity is important for children's adjustment. Identity has been said to be a sense of psycho-social well-being and a feeling of being at home in one's own body.[99] Although there are many theories about the development of identity it is agreed that a child's identity is neither predetermined nor free from outside influence. The most influencial theorist, Erikson, emphasised intra-psychic processes and the continual reworking of earlier life experiences.[1] Later writers have drawn attention to the ways institutions, including the law, shape identity by permitting or restricting individual expression.[2]

Issues of identity and attachment are interlinked. A child with a poor sense of identity may not be able to make attachments.[3] Attachment may also affect the identity which develops. The identity of children of mixed parentage has been seen to be distinct, reflecting elements from each parent and culture[4] and children placed transracially may not identify with either community.[5] Identity and attachment theories may lead to conflicting responses to maintaining links for children living away from their birth family. It has been asserted that contact may undermine security[6] but if contact is terminated or a "closed" adoption arranged, this may have a damaging effect on the child's identity.

It is not clear that the court system ensures that the assessments necessary to make welfare decisions are available[7] or that judges, magistrates or practising lawyers always understand child development sufficiently.[8] Decisions about welfare involve an element of prediction and can require fine judgments; experts' opinions cannot remove the responsibility of the judge to reach a conclusion on all the evidence. Neither experts nor judges are free from subjectivity. The

---

98 D.H., *Manual of Practice Guidance for Guardians ad litem and Reporting Officers* (1992), p. 68. But see *Re M. (Section 94 Appeals)* [1995] 1 F.L.R. 546; *Re O. (Transracial Adoption: Contact)* [1995] 2 F.L.R. 597 and D.H. Circular LAC (99)29.

99 E. Erikson, "The problem of ego identity" (1956) *Journal of the American Psychological Association* 74.

1 E. Erikson, *Identity, youth and crisis* (1968); *Identity and the life cycle* (1959), (1979).

2 J. Shotter and K. J. Gergen, *Texts of Identity* (1989).

3 H. R. Schaffer, *Making decisions about children* (1990).

4 B. Tizard and A. Phoenix, *Black, white or mixed race?* (1993).

5 O. Gill and B. Jackson, *Adoption and race* (1983); D. Kirton, *Ethnicity and Adoption* (2000); see also *Re B. (Adoption Setting Aside)* [1995] 1 F.L.R. 1 for an account of the experience of the child of English Catholic and Kuwaiti Muslim parents adopted by Jewish parents.

6 For a discussion of the research on the effect of parental visits on foster-home breakdown see: J. Masson, "Contacts between parents and children in long term care" (1990) 4 Int. J. Law and Fam. 97, 104; D. Quinton *et al., op cit.* In *Re O. (Transracial Adoption: Contact)* [1995] 2 F.L.R. 693, the court (unusually) accepted that adoption provided the security for contact which could develop the child's racial identity.

7 J. Brophy and P. Bates, "The position of parents using experts in care proceedings: a failure of 'partnership' "? (1998) *J.S.W.F.L.* 23; J. Brophy, *Expert evidence in child protection litigation* (1999) Resource limitations and concerns about delay mean that welfare reports are only available in approximately half of contested cases. In the study by R. Bailey Harris and colleagues welfare reports were ordered in 49% of cases: [1999] *C.F.L.Q.* 53, 58.

8 *cf.* Maidment (1984), p. 205. Far greater efforts are now made to inform the judiciary. Understanding has certainly developed since the decision in *Re Thain* [1926] Ch. 676 where it was said that the effect of moving a seven year-old child from an aunt and uncle to the father after six years would be "mercifully transient." But the legal system may reconstruct and misuse scientific knowledge about children, King and Piper, (2nd ed., 1995), p. 52; M. King and J. Trowell, *Children's welfare and the law* (1992), Chap. 6.

approach taken can be inconsistent. For example, although contact has been regarded as essential after parental separation, views that contact between children in state care and absent parents is unsettling are sometimes expressed[9] and contact after adoption is rarely ordered. The importance of identity is becoming recognised[10] as is the damage that is done by continued contact with a violent parent.[11]

Application of the welfare principle

20–008 Studies[12] of the outcomes of cases in the divorce and family proceedings courts indicate that, in the past, courts almost always made orders which confirmed the current arrangement or *status quo* as far as the child's residence was concerned. In Eekelaar's study of 652 cases there were only 13 where the child's residence had changed by the end of the proceedings and in only six was this due to the court order.[13] However, the majority of cases were not contested—one parent was merely seeking an order to confirm his or her position.[14] Orders most frequently granted custody to the mother but this was not because the courts were favouring her care but because they were confirming the arrangements which had been made by the parties.[15] Siblings were apparently rarely split.[16] This reflected the view that, following divorce, children would be cared for by one parent possibly with a step-parent.[17] However this approach has gradually been replaced by preference for co-parenting, the continued involvement of both biological parents in separate households. Arrangements following separation are fluid so that agreements or court orders are varied or cease to

---

9 *Re W. (A Minor) (Access)* [1989] 1 F.L.R. 163, *cf. Re E. (A Minor: Access)* [1987] 1 F.L.R. 368. Priest and Whybrow also noted a reluctance in magistrates to value contact with an unmarried father, see J. Priest and J. Whybrow, *Custody Law in Practice in the Divorce and Domestic Court,* Law Com. W.P. 96 *Supplement* (1986), para. 6.6.

10 *Re W. (A Minor) (Contact)* [1994] 2 F.L.R. 441, CA; *Re P. (A Minor) (Contact)* [1994] 2 F.L.R. 374 at 379; *cf. Re F. (A Minor: Paternity Test)* [1993] 1 F.L.R. 598 at 604. The welfare test does not apply to the decision to order blood tests but is relevant to the application for a parental responsibility order. Indirect contact may be used to maintain links where direct contact is impracticable or inappropriate: *Re S. (Violent Parent: Indirect Contact)* [2000] 1 F.L.R. 481; *Re K. (Contact: Mother's Anxiety)* [1999] 2 F.L.R. 703.

11 Sturge and Glaser *op. cit.; Re L., Re V., Re M. and Re H. (Contact: Domestic Violence)* [2000] 2 F.L.R. 334.

12 S. Maidment, "A study in child custody" (1976) 6 *Fam. Law* 200; J. Eekelaar, E. Clive with K. Clarke and S. Raikes, *Custody after Divorce,* SSRC (1977); J. Eekelaar, "Children and divorce: some further data" [1982] Ox. J.L.S. 63 and Priest and Whybrow (1986). For a more detailed study in the USA see E. Maccoby and R. Mnookin, *Dividing the child* (1992).

13 Eekelaar and Clive (1977), para. 5.3.

14 Eekelaar's study included 39 contested cases; Priest and Whybrow's six contested cases in the Domestic Court, see Priest and Whybrow (1986) at para. 4.5. Despite s.1(5) consent orders continue to be granted: R. Bailey-Harris *et al.,* "Settlement culture and the use of the 'no order' principle under the Children Act 1989" [1999] *C.F.L.Q.* 53, 59.

15 Eekelaar and Clive (1977), paras 5.2 *et seq.* See also S. Maidment, *Child custody: what chance for fathers* (National Council for One-parent Families, 1981); Priest and Whybrow (1986), Tables 7 & 9.

16 Eekelaar and Clive (1977), para. 5.2; Priest and Whybrow (1986), give no information about this which perhaps calls into question the analysis in Table 7.

17 The "clean break", the transfer of financial responsibility from fathers to the state, the acceptance of the end to contact and the practice of step-parent adoption re-inforced this approach.

reflect what is happening. Good relationships may promote co-operative parenting; in contrast, imposing co-parenting may create opportunities for parents to undermine each other and the welfare of the child.[18]

Recent research by Bailey-Harris and colleagues suggests that courts are now putting considerable emphasis on the parents reaching their own agreement, even in contested cases, on the assumption that there is more likely to be compliance. Parents are said to know their children best and have responsibility for working out arrangements. Where settlements are not reached quickly there are repeated directions appointments and delay.[19] Only two-thirds of applications resulted in a substantive order.[20] The notion that the parents' agreed solution necessarily best serves the child's welfare does not sit easily with the court's responsibility to consider cases individually, nor with divorce legislation which requires court oversight of arrangements. Moreover, there is no evidence that agreements reached under pressure last.

Disputes over contact are more common than residence disputes.[21] Although there is wide agreement about the value of maintaining contact between children and their parents after relationship breakdown, there are differences in the use of court orders to achieve this. Some judges apparently consider that it is better to make no order and leave the parties to agree between themselves, others make orders for reasonable contact. Orders defining the frequency, duration and location of meetings are made in only a minority of cases.[22] This may reflect the view that disputes over contact are intractable and that there is little judges can do to make arrangements work in the face of parental opposition.[23] It is the quality of contact rather than the quantity that appears to be important,[24] a matter over which the court can have little influence. Contact is often infrequent and diminishes over time.[25] Despite duties to promote contact, children a third of children looked after by a local authority have no parental contact.[26] Any dispute

[18] B. Neale and C. Smart, "In whose best interests? Theorising family life following parental separation" in S. Sclater and C. Piper (eds) *Undercurrents of divorce* (1999), pp. 33, 37, 43–4; C. Smart and B. Neale, *Family fragments?* (1999).

[19] R. Bailey-Harris *et al.*, (1999) *op. cit.*, pp. 57–59.

[20] 27% resulted in no order and 5% in an order of 'no order'; see *ibid.*, p. 59

[21] The courts deal with more applications for contact than for residence: *Judicial Statistics 2000*, Table 5.3. Although there were slightly fewer initial applications for contact than residence in the recent Bristol study over 70% included contact issues at the directions hearing: J.Pearce *et al.* [1999] Fam. L. 21,22.

[22] Eekelaar and Clive (1977), paras 5.7 *et seq.;* Priest and Whybrow (1986), Pt VI. See also the discussion of s.1(5) and *Re S. (Contact: Grandparent)* [1996] 1 F.L.R. 158, CA above, Chap. 19.

[23] A. James and K. Wilson, "The trouble with access: a study of divorcing families" (1984) 14 *Brit. J. Soc. Wk.* 487; see the discussion of contact enforcement para. 19–051, above. In *Re A. (Section 8 Order: Grandparent's Application)* [1995] 2 F.L.R. 153, the judgment, although refusing the application, was expressed in conciliatory language.

[24] Rodgers and Pryor (1998) p. 7.

[25] Rodgers and Pryor (1998) p. 17; Eekelaar and Clive (1977), paras 5.8 *et seq.* and Table 35; J. Gregory & K. Foster, *The consequences of divorce* (1990), Tables 10.17, 10.18, J. Walker and J. Hornick, *Communication in marriage and divorce* (1996), p. 24. The decline in contact may be very rapid: see A. Leeming *et al., Lone Mothers,* DSS Research Report No. 30 (1994), p. 51. Where parents have never cohabited contact is less likely to occur: Maclean and Eekelaar (1997) p.94.

[26] H. Cleaver, *Fostering family contact* (2000). There are a variety of barriers to contact in such circumstances: see S. Millham, R. Bullock, K. Hosie and M. Little, *Access disputes in child-care* (1989)—a study applying to pre-Children Act 1989 law; J. Masson, C. Harrison and A. Pavlovic,

about contact can be referred to the court but judicial attitudes have been less favourable to contact where the child is likely to remain in care long-term.[27]

Problems with the welfare principle

20–009 The welfare principle itself has been criticised on a number of grounds. The move from easily applicable rules of thumb[28] to a broad undefined approach to welfare demands sophisticated, individual assessments which judges are unable to make alone.[29] The lack of consensus on what children's welfare demands and of adequate scientific information about what ensures healthy psychological development enables those who take the decisions to impose subjective and value-laden views.[30] Without further rules or guidelines the use of the welfare principle simply creates unexaminable discretion.[31] Such apparently arbitrary decisions undermine the authority of judges and the legal system. But indeterminancy may be reduced through the influence of community standards.[32] In addition, the lack of a comprehensible and predictable standard makes it more difficult for couples to reach settlements by negotiation. This may increase the number and intensity of disputed cases. It may also assist the stronger party to impose their preferred solution on the weaker one.[33] The effect on private ordering is particularly important because of the influence existing arrangements have on court orders.

> In *Re V. (Residence Order: Finance),*[34] the mother left the child, aged two years, and the father in the matrimonial home and moved to a house nearby. Both parents worked full time, the paternal grandmother cared for the child during the day and he spent three out of four weekends and some holidays with his mother. Nine months later the mother applied for a residence order. The judge made an order confirming the existing arrangement and the mother's appeal seeking a transfer of the child's care to her was dismissed.

Lost and Found (1999). Contact arrangements in care plans often remain unimplemented: Health Select Committee 2nd Report (1997–8 H.C. 247), para. 81 or are short term J. Harwin *et al., Making care orders work* (2002).

[27] Children Act 1989, ss.8, 34; *Re B. (A Minor) (Care Contact: Local Authority's Plans)* [1993] 1 F.L.R. 543; *Re T. (Minors) (Termination of Contact)* [1997] 1 All E.R 65, CA; Masson, *op. cit.* and see para. 22–065, below.

[28] For example, that girls and young children should live with their mother, and older boys with their father, see above para. 20–003.

[29] M. Fineman, "The politics of custody and gender" in C. Smart and S. Sevenhuijsen (eds.), *Child Custody and the Politics of Gender* (1989), pp. 27, 30, 32. The *status quo* approach may have replaced the old rules of thumb, see Maidment (1984), p. 212. But this can also be viewed as an honest response to the collapse of a hierarchy of values in the community, S. Parker, "The best interests of the child principle and problems" (1994) 8 Int. J. Law & Fam 36.

[30] H. Reece, "The paramountcy principle consensus or construct" [1996] C.L.P. 267, 272–3; Chambers *op. cit.* 481; King, *op. cit.* 189; Law Com. W.P. 96, para. 6.25. "There is always the danger that stereotyped, culturally conditioned judgments . . . will lead to decisions . . . which do not benefit children." J. Montgomery, "Children as property" (1988) 51 *M.L.R.* 323, 328.

[31] S. Parker, *op. cit.*

[32] C. Schneider, "Discretion, rules & Law: Child custody decisions and the best interest standard" in K. Hawkins (ed.), *The uses of discretion* (1993).

[33] Mnookin, *op. cit.* pp. 86 *et seq.*

[34] [1995] 2 F.L.R. 612, CA.

Despite this criticism the welfare principle is widely supported because it represents an important social and moral value, that children who are are necessarily vulnerable and dependent must be protected from harm and given every opportunity to become healthy and well-adjusted adults.[35] Any change in the criteria could put children's welfare at risk because it would inevitably reduce the emphasis given to welfare.[36] Alternative rules may be no less indeterminate.[37] However, Goldstein, Freud and Solnit, while supporting the welfare principle, suggested that the phraseology be changed to "the least detrimental alternative" to remind decision-makers that they can only do their humble best.[38]

Various proposals have been made to improve the operation of the welfare principle by changing the decision-making process, removing the need to make certain decisions or assigning weight to particular factors.[39] It has been argued that decision-making would be improved if children had representatives who could challenge the views of the parties.[40] However, there is general reluctance to allow children to participate in proceedings.[41] Alternatively, lawyer judges and lay magistrates could be replaced with people qualified in assessing children's welfare.[42] Again, this is likely to change biases in the system rather than remove them.

20–010 Lack of confidence in the welfare principle is one reason for the current emphasis on settlement. Mediation[43] and negotiation are encouraged because judges, CAFCASS officers and lawyers recognise the problems of adjudication and wish to avoid them. Any solution chosen by the parties is considered more likely to be kept and therefore better because it will reduce disputes and the uncertainties of litigation which are both thought contrary to children's wel-

---

[35] King, *op. cit.* 189; *cf.* Reece *op. cit.* 276–281 at 302 who argues that adults' rights should not be subordinated to children's needs. However Neale and Smart, *op. cit.* pp. 46–9 argue that fathers who claim a right to a relationship with their child after separation do not work at maintaining their relationship and impose arrangements which may undermine the other parent.

[36] Law Com. W.P. 96, paras 6.17, 6.22; Law Com. No. 172, para. 3.13. The entrenchment of a best interest standard in the United Nations Convention on the Rights of the Child, Art. 3(1) makes formal departures from the welfare principle unthinkable for countries which have ratified the Convention. See also P. Alston, "The best interests principle towards a reconciliation of culture and human rights" (1994) 8 Int. J. Law & Fam. 1.

[37] Parker, *op. cit.* pp. 29–36. Decisions may be indeterminate because the possibilities of all the alternative outcomes are unknown.

[38] Goldstein, Freud & Solnit, *Beyond*, p. 62.

[39] For a theoretical analysis of the reasons for the failure of the Anglo-American system to make welfare based decisions, see King and Piper (1995).

[40] R. Hansen, "The role and rights of children in divorce actions" (1966) 6 J. Fam. L. 1; Mnookin, *op. cit.* p. 95; M. Murch *et al., The Representation of the Child in Civil Proceeding Research Project 1985–89* (1990), p. 52; C. Lyon *et al., Effective support systems for children and young people when parental relationships break down* (1998); B. Neal and C. Smart, *Good to talk?* (2001). Inclusion of the child's views may be required: *Sahin v. Germany* [2002] 1 F.L.R. 119.

[41] C. Piper, "The wishes and feelings of the child" in Piper and Sclater, *op. cit.;* J. Masson and M. Winn Oakley, *Out of Hearing* (1999), p. 107.

[42] J. Masson, "The role of the judge in children's cases" (1988) 7 C.J.Q. 141; King and Piper (1995), p. 158; Fineman has commented that "[t]he resort to non judicial decision-making in order to apply the best interests standard masks the severe problem with the substantive test." Fineman, *op. cit.* 31.

[43] L. Parkinson, *Conciliation in Separation and Divorce* (1986); M. Roberts, *Mediation in family disputes* (1997). Just over half of the clients of mediation services in Walker's study thought that mediation had helped to protect the best interest of the children, J. Walker *et al., Mediation: the making and remaking of co-operative relationships* (1994), Table 5.4.

fare.[44] However, it is unclear that agreed solutions produce better outcomes for children[45] and they may leave adults dissatisfied.[46]

The Law Commission sought to "lower the stakes" in disputes over children following divorce by removing the notion that "winner takes all." Its scheme for retention of parental responsibility after divorce was intended to reduce the opportunities for litigation.[47] Under the Children Act 1989 parental responsibility is unaffected by divorce.[48] The principal matters which concern the court are issues of the child's residence and continued contact. The retention of parental responsibility is intended to encourage involvement of the non-residential parent and thus promote the child's well-being.[49] However, this approach is not uncontroversial and it is argued that it increases opportunities for dispute and for interference with decisions of the person caring for the child.[50] Indeed, disputes about children appear to have increased.[51]

Weighting of specific factors could clarify the likely outcome in most disputes over children, reducing the problem of indeterminancy and assisting the judges as well as parties who negotiate their own agreements.[52] Guidelines in the form of presumptions for maternal care (later replaced by the gender-neutral "primary carer" care) and for joint custody have operated in some American States[53] and elsewhere.[54] Chambers has argued that the effect of loss of care on the primary carer, combined with the advantages of an easily applicable test, justify a primary carer preference for children under five years.[55] However, it has been argued that this standard fails to value a mother's special role and to recognise the interest a mother has in the care of children she gave birth to,[56] and that there should be a return to a maternal preference.[57] In contrast, it has also been suggested that preference should be given to arrangements where the care of the

---

[44] Bailey-Harris *et al., op. cit.*, p. 54.

[45] See generally Piper (1993), pp. 186 *et seq.*; Walker *et al.* (1994), Chap. 5.

[46] Bailey-Harris *et al., op. cit.*, p. 60.

[47] Law Com. No. 172, para. 4.5.

[48] Children Act 1989, ss.2, 8: see above, and A. Bainham [1990] *Fam. Law* 192, 195. In practice carers bear most of the responsibility; A. Leeming *et al.*, p. 54.

[49] Neale and Smart *op. cit.*, pp. 37–9 consider that this reflects a new formulation of welfare which stresses the importance of fathers and the equality of their rights. See also Law Com. No. 172, para. 4.5; Maidment (1984), p. 279.

[50] J. Brophy, "Custody Law, child care and inequality in Britain" in *Child Custody and the Politics of Gender* (C. Smart and S. Sevenhuijsen ed., 1989), Chap. 9; Booth Report, para. 2.27.

[51] G. Davis and J. Pearce, "Privatising the family?" [1998] *Fam. Law* 614 at 616–7.

[52] Chambers, above, *op. cit.* p. 48; Law Com. W.P. 96, para. 6.29; Mnookin, *op. cit.* pp. 85 *et seq.*

[53] Law Com. W.P. 96, para. 6.28; Chambers, *op. cit.* Fineman, *op. cit.* But the effect of the two standards may be substantially the same: Maccoby and Mnookin (1992), p. 284. Presumptions of same race placements have also been enacted for some care and adoption cases, see Indian Child Welfare Act 1978, U.S. Public Law 95,608 and J. Hollinger, "Beyond the best interests of the tribe: The Indian Welfare Act and the Adoption of Indian Children" (1989) 66 U. Detroit L.R. 451.

[54] Law Com. W.P. 96, paras 6.28, 6.33.

[55] *op. cit.* p. 561. Chambers argues for a presumption not a rule which would exclude demonstrably unfit parents but this may shift the focus of the litigation to the caretaker's conduct.

[56] The nature of this interest in discussed by Chambers, *op. cit.* pp. 499–503.

[57] Fineman, *op. cit.* p. 34; K. Sandberg, "Best interests and justice" and S. Boyd, "From gender specifity to gender neutrality" in Smart and Sevenhuijsen, *op. cit.* p. 152.

child is shared but this is hotly contested.[58] Such changes in approach can be accommodated by reinterpreting the notion of welfare, but the advantages claimed for rules are that they facilitate decision-making and limit the cases where the dispute must be determined by the courts.[59]

The use of rules or guidelines was rejected by the Law Commission. It was difficult to frame guidelines which did not undermine the paramountcy rule.[60] The only guidelines which the Law Commission considered justified by current knowledge would not assist in the most typical disputes where the child was attached to both parents who could provide adequately.[61] Guidelines which could help in such a case were arbitrary because they could not be shown necessarily to promote the welfare of children.[62] Instead, the Law Commission favoured listing those matters which the court should consider without allocating weight to any of them.[63] This has been done by including a checklist in the Children Act 1989, s.1(3).[64]

The statutory checklist

20–011 In the Law Commission's view a checklist could assist the courts to operate the welfare principle and make clear to all concerned the factors which the courts considered. It would thus help the parties to understand how judicial decisions are made and to focus their private discussions on relevant issues. It should enable advisors to prepare relevant evidence and thus avoid prolonged hearings or delays caused by adjournments.[65] A checklist which does not ascribe weight to particular aspects of a case would be flexible. Its application can change as understanding of child welfare develops.[66] It is an aide-memoire designed to ensure that no relevant factors are forgotten.[67] However, it is not clear what assistance a checklist can provide if it merely lists the factors to be considered and does not indicate how they should be viewed. In children's cases the courts perform a "balancing exercise" which is different from that undertaken for the re-allocation of resources. Cases reaching the appellate courts typically involve decisions by the lower courts which give inappropriate weight to relevant factors but rarely fail to consider them completely.

The Law Commission stated that a checklist would only be practicable if it were confined to major points.[68] A detailed list could not be applicable in all cases and could increase opportunities for an appeal where the judge's reasons

---

[58] California has a preference for joint legal custody which creates a legal arrangement similar to that under the Children Act 1989, s.2(8) but this proposal goes much further: see Maccoby and Mnookin (1992), p. 284.

[59] This has been a key factor in the approach to appeals: see below.

[60] Law Com. W.P. 96, paras 6.30–6.34.

[61] *ibid.* para. 6.31.

[62] *ibid.* para. 6.32; see also Chambers *op. cit.*

[63] *ibid.* paras 6.34–6.39; Law Com. No. 172, paras 3.17–3.21.

[64] A similar checklist is applied to adoption cases: Adoption and Children Act 2002, s.1(4).

[65] Law Com. No. 172, paras 3.17 and 3.18.

[66] *ibid.* para. 3.19.

[67] *Southwark LBC v. B.* [1993] 2 F.L.R. 559 at 573, *per* Waite L.J.

[68] Law Com. No. 172, para. 3.19.

omitted an item from the list.[69] Working through the list is is a useful and important discipline but judges are not required to reflect on every item[70]; magistrates have pro formas for their reasons which itemise the considerations in the checklist.[71] But nevertheless there continue to be cases where the reasons given are inadequate.[72]

Although the Law Commission thought that a checklist could provide a clear statement of "what society considers the most important factors in the welfare of children",[73] its own selection of factors appears to have been determined by the practice of the courts.[74] It did review the social science evidence on the well-being of children after divorce when considering the objectives of custody law[75] but based its list, with one exception, on the current approach of the English courts. Only the "wishes and feelings of the child" received any broader consideration.[76]

During the passage of the Children Bill through Parliament some attempts were made to change the content of the checklist but these were rejected by the Government either on the basis that they would "upset the careful balance"[77] which had been achieved or because they were already implied by the general words used. Thus, although there is no reference to keeping siblings together in this part of the Act,[78] this is one aspect of the child's emotional needs. The checklist also makes no reference to either short- or long-term needs so both must be considered.[79] The order of the items has no special significance; factors should be weighted according to the circumstances.[80]

The Law Commission was concerned that the checklist should not lead to more intervention by the courts where the parties have reached their own agreement.[81] This approach was endorsed by Parliament and consequently, it only applies as a matter of strict law to contested applications to make, vary or discharge section 8 orders and any applications in relation to orders under Part IV of the Children Act 1989.[82] It need not be used for other applications, for

---

69 Law Com. No. 172, para. 3.19. The rules relating to appeals are considered below.

70 *H. v. H. (Residence Order: Leave to Remove from the Jurisdiction)* [1995] 1 F.L.R. 529, CA; *Oldham M.B.C. v. E.* [1994] 1 F.L.R. 568, CA; *B. v. B. (Residence Order: Reason for Decision)* [1997] 2 F.L.R. 602 at 608 *per* Holman J.

71 Magistrates must give written reasons before their decision: F.P.C. 1991, r. 21(5); *Handbook of best practice in Children Act cases* (1997) App. A x, guidance prepared by Cazalet J.

72 See *e.g. Croydon LBC v. R.* [1997] 2 F.L.R. 675; *Re P. (Contact: Supervision)* [1996] 2 F.L.R. 314; *R. v. Oxfordshire C.C. (Secure Accommodation Order)* [1992] Fam. 150.

73 Law Com. No. 172, para. 3.19.

74 Law Com. W.P. 96, para. 6.38. The only references in this paragraph are to decided cases.

75 Law Com. W.P. 96, Pt. III.

76 Law Com. W.P. 96, paras 6.40–6.44; Law Com. No. 172, paras 3.22-5.

77 *per* Sir Nicholas Lyell (Solicitor General) Children Bill, Committee Stage, *Hansard,* Standing Committee B, col. 5, May 9, 1989.

78 It is mentioned in relation to placement of children in care: Children Act 1989, s.23(7) (b).

79 *Re H. (Minors) (Access)* [1992] 1 F.L.R. 148. Short-term interests may prevail on the basis that a variation can be made later, see *Thompson v. Thompson* (1987) 17 *Fam. Law* 89, CA or because plans to meet of long-term needs are speculative: *Berkshire C.C. v. B.* [1997] 1 F.L.R. 171. Long-term welfare may prevail if trauma is thought to be short lived: *Re B. (Residence Order: Leave to Appeal)* [1998] 1 F.L.R. 520.

80 *Re W. (Minors) (Residence Order)* [1992] 2 F.C.R. 461.

81 Law Com. No. 172, para. 3.19.

82 Children Act 1989, s.1(4).

example, in relation to parental responsibility, guardianship and emergency protection orders. But this does not mean that there are two potentially conflicting views of welfare.[83]

CAFCASS officers carrying out their functions representing children in "specified" proceedings or preparing reports for the court are required to consider the checklist when carrying out their duties.[84] Children's guardians are also directed to a further list of principles which are particularly relevant to children looked after by local authorities.[85]

The provisions of the checklist will now be considered in turn.

(a) The ascertainable wishes and feelings of the child concerned (considered in the light of his age and understanding)

20–012 The right of mature children to express their views and of all children to be heard in legal proceedings concerning them is protected by the United Nations Convention on the Rights of the Child.[86] In the nineteenth century, children's wishes could be the determining factor in court decisions.[87] The Law Commission noted that welfare checklists from other jurisdictions included a consideration of children's views and stated that these views should be taken into account not just as an aspect of welfare.[88] The checklist defines the child's views as an aspect of welfare[89] but does not require a child to be *Gillick* competent[90] before his or her views are considered. In some cases the child's views are decisive[91]:—

> In *Re M. (Contact: Welfare Test)*[92] two children aged seven and eight had lived with their father for over five years following the separation of their parents. Contact with their mother broke down but 18 months later she sought a contact order. Contact was refused and the decision upheld on

---

[83] *Southwark L.B.C. v. B.* [1993] 2 F.L.R. 559 at 573, *per* Waite L.J.

[84] F.P.R. 1991, r. 4.11(1); F.P.C. 1991, r. 11(1). For further explanations of these roles see above Chap. 19 and below, Chap. 22.

[85] D.H. *Manual of Guidance for Guardians ad litem and Reporting Officers* (1992), p. 6 referring to the list in D.H., *The care of children, principles and practice in regulations and guidance* (1989), p. 18.

[86] Art. 12; Fortin (1998), Chap. 8. The European Convention on the Exercise of Children's Rights (1997) which has not been ratified by the U.K. grants children the right to receive information, to be consulted, to express their views and to be represented in family proceedings. The right is limited to those considered to have sufficient understanding: Arts 3, 4.

[87] Custody of Children Act 1891, s.4; *R. v. Clarke* (1857) 7 El. & Bl. 186; see J. Roche, "Children and Divorce: a private affair" in Sclater and Piper (1999), pp. 55, 70.

[88] Law Com. W.P. 96, paras . 6.40 *et seq.;* Law Com. 172, para. 3.23; C. Piper "The wishes and feelings of the child" in Sclater and Piper (1999), pp. 77, 79.

[89] J. Roche *op. cit.* Similarly the Adoption and Children Bill 2002 contains no provision other than s.1(4) through which the child's attitude to adoption is considered.

[90] *Gillick v. West Norfolk and Wisbech A.H.A.* [1986] A.C. 112. The views of a *Gillick* competent child should be given greater weight: *Re S. (Change of Name)* [1999] 1 F.L.R. 672 at 674 *per* Thorpe L.J.

[91] *e.g. Re P. (A Minor) (Education)* [1992] 1 F.L.R. 316 where a 14-year-old boy's preference for a day school determined the dispute although Butler-Sloss L.J. recognised there were undoubted advantages of boarding-school education and would have imposed that choice on a younger child.

[92] [1995] 1 F.L.R. 274, CA.

appeal. The children did not wish to see their mother, ordering contact against their wishes would be harmful.[93]

In other cases the child's needs will be given more weight:—

> In *Re V. (Residence: Review)*[94] the father sought residence of one of his three children, a twin boy. Some years earlier the parents had witnessed the drowning of their other children. The father had suffered post-traumatic stress disorder. He was a damaged person, unemployable and vulnerable. The boy ran away to his father's home with his elder brother but was returned pending a full hearing. Although the child wanted to live with his father and two of the three experts involved recommended this, the judge accepted that the mother was better able to deal with the boy's physical needs and also the view of a child psychiatrist that the boy's emotional welfare would suffer if he lived with the father. The mother's residence was confirmed but with a review after six months.

The attitude of the courts to giving weight to children's views varies, in part reflecting the age of the child, the issue before the court and the views expressed. More weight is given to the views of adolescents, at least in relation to matters carrying little risk so that orders, except in relation to medical treatment,[95] which contradict "the wishes of normal children aged 16, 14 and 12 are virtually unknown to family law."[96] The views of children below the age of 10 years appear to be conclusive only rarely. Between ages 10 and 14 there is a "grey area where there is little consistency in judicial approach."[97] Judges have been hesitant to let children's antipathy dissuade them from the view that contact with a parent is in their best interests.[98] But where the child's wishes are rational and in accordance with views about their welfare, courts are more willing to comply with them.[99] The fervence and persistence of the child's views may also be influential.[1]

Many concerns have been expressed about stressing the importance of chil-

---

[93] A similar view as expressed in relation to contact between two boys aged 9 and 12 and their transsexual father: *Re F. (Minors) (Denial of Contact)* [1993] 2 F.L.R. 677, CA. But there may be an obligation on the state to provide counselling to support the re-establishment of a parent child relationship: *Ignaccolo-Zenide v. Romania* E.C.H.R. App. 31679/96.

[94] [1995] 2 F.L.R. 1010, CA. The tort action arising out of the original tragedy is reported as *Vernon v. Bosley (No 1)* [1997] 1 All E.R.577. For subsequent litigation concerning the disclosure of evidence from family proceedings see: *Vernon v. Bosley (No. 2)* [1998] 1 F.L.R. 304.

[95] *Re E. (A Minor) (Wardship: Medical Treatment)* [1993] 1 F.L.R. 386; *Re W.(Medical Treatment: Court's Jurisdiction)* [1993] Fam. 64 where the court decided in favour of medically advised treatment.

[96] *Re B. (Change of Surname)* [1996] 1 F.L.R. 791 at 794 *per* Wilson J. The judge declined to hold that the refusal to allow the change of the children's surname was wrong.

[97] Fortin (1998), p. 213.

[98] *Re K. (Contact: Psychiatric Report)* [1995] 2 F.L.R. 432, CA but where the child's objection is against a background of domestic violence the court is becoming more sensitive: *Re L; Re V; Re M.; Re H. (Contact: Domestic Violence)* [2000] 2 F.L.R. 334, CA.

[99] *Re M., T., P., K. and B. (Change of Name)* [2000] 2 F.L.R. 645.

[1] *Re T. (Abduction: Child's Objections to Return)* [2000] 2 F.L.R. 192 where the 11 year-old child ("mature beyond her years") wrote a series of letters objecting to return to her alcoholic mother.

dren's wishes. This places too great a burden on the child[2] and may enable them to manipulate the parents. It is unreliable because what children say may be inconsistent,[3] may not reflect what they really want or be only a passing feeling.[4] Children are frequently seen as poor decision-makers, over influenced by material considerations or short-term gains.[5] Children may have been conditioned by the views of a carer,[6] bribery or the desire to care for their parents or live with them.[7] The circumstances in which the views were obtained may have influenced them.[8] Ultimately, what children want may not be accepted as in their best interests.[9]

20–013 However, ignoring children's views risks endangering their welfare further. Children may resort to self-help, conducting relationships secretly or running away.[10] Imposing decisions on unwilling children may be ineffective.[11] There is considerable evidence that some children do want to have a say in decisions which directly affect them, including with which of two disputing parties they should live[12] and that parents do not always consult them.[13]

The phrase "wishes and feelings" encompasses not only what the child expresses directly but also information which may be obtained by a third party. There is no single procedure for ascertaining the child's views.[14] Judges and magistrates[15] may interview the child in private, although it is questionable how

---

[2] T. Campbell, "The rights of the minor" in Alston, Parker and Seymour (1992) pp. 21–2; *M. v. M.* (1977) 7 *Fam. Law* 17; *Adams v. Adams* [1984] F.L.R. 768.

[3] *Re M. (Medical Treatment: Consent)* [1999] 2 F.L.R.1097 where the girl did not want a heart transplant but did not want to die.

[4] B. Cantwell and S. Scott "Children's wishes, children's burdens" (1995) *J.S.W.F.L.* 337.

[5] See comments of Lord Templeman in the *Gillick* case [1986] A.C. 112; Wallerstein and Kelly (1980), pp. 314–315. *Re C. (A Minor) (Care: Child's Wishes)* [1993] 1 F.L.R. 832.

[6] But "parental alienation syndrome" is not recognised condition: C. Sturge and D. Glaser, "Contact and domestic violence—the experts' court report" [2000] *Fam. Law* 615 at 622; *Re R. (A Minor) (Residence: Religion)* [1993] 2 F.L.R. 163 where the views of a 10-year-old who wanted to remain with members of the Exclusive Brethren after his mother's death were not decisive.

[7] B. Neale and A Wade, *Parent problems! Children's views on life when parents split up* (2000); *B. v B. (Minors) (Interviews and Listing Arrangements)* [1994] 2 F.L.R. 489, CA, at 495 (the children refused to state a preference); Wallerstein and Kelly (1980), p. 70.

[8] Younger and more dependent children are inevitably more prone to influence from their carers: C. Sturge and D. Glaser, *op. cit.*, p.621.

[9] *Re C. (A Minor) (Leave to Seek Section 8 Order)* [1994] 1 F.L.R. 26 where a 14-year-old's wish for a residence order in favour of friends was overridden because it could prevent conciliation with her parents.

[10] *Re P. (Abduction: Minor's Views)* [1998] 2 F.L.R. 825, CA.

[11] *Re B. (Residence Order: Leave to Appeal)* [1998] 1 F.L.R. 520 where the boys' behaviour at contact with their mother made transfer of residence to her impracticable; *Re HB (Abduction: Child's Objections)* [1998] 1 F.L.R. 422 and see B. Hale [1999] *C.F.L.Q.* 377, 378 where a girl's refusal to take the plane prevented her return to Denmark under the Hague Abduction Convention.

[12] A Children's Legal Centre survey of 600 teenagers in 1989 indicated that 90 per cent wanted to be consulted on this: see (1989) 60 *Childright* 6; Lyon *et al.*, *op cit.*; Neale and Smart *op. cit.*

[13] M. Murch *et al.*, *Safeguarding children's welfare in uncontentious divorce: a study of s. 41 of the Matrimonial Causes Act 1973* (1998) pp. 156–8; C. Thomas, *Listening to children's views* (1999).

[14] For a review of the approaches, see H. Bevan, *Child Law* (1989), para. 3.11 and Masson (1988), *op. cit.* Older children may seek party status and have their wishes advocated directly: *Re T. (A Minor) (Wardship: Representation)* [1994] Fam. 49 but this may not be allowed: *Re H. (Residence Order: Application for Leave)* [2000] 1 F.L.R.780; Bainham (1993), p. 447.

[15] *Re W. (A Minor) (Contact)* [1994] 1 F.L.R. 843; *Re M. (A Minor) (Justices' Discretion)* [1993] 2 F.L.R. 706. But it is unnecessary or undesirable for magistrates to see the child if a CAFCASS

far this is likely to produce reliable information. They cannot offer children confidentiality although this may make children more willing to express their views.[16] In care proceedings there will normally be a children's guardian who has a duty to make the child's wishes known to the court[17]; in other cases this may be done by a children and family reporter appointed to provide a report.[18] CAFCASS officers frequently consult very young children[19]; some are very experienced in communicating with children and may seek to ascertain their feelings through play or by interpreting drawings.[20] But children are not always given sufficient information about the options.[21] Also there are disputed cases where no one independent of the parties attempts to establish the child's views[22]; in such cases the court still has to consider them. In *Sahin v. Germany*[22a] the court's failure to establish the views of the child (aged five) about contact with her father breached E.C.H.R., Art. 8.

(b) His physical, emotional and educational needs

20–014 In the past the concept of need relied heavily on subjective assessment, often informed by subjective views about what is good for children[23] and bias in favour of the dominant culture.[24] Far greater emphasis is now placed on formal assessments informed by research.[25] There is considerable research evidence on

---

officer is involved; *B. v. B. (Minors) (Interviews and Listing Arrangements)* [1994] 2 F.L.R. 489, CA and CAAC Report 1993/4, p. 45.

[16] *B. v. B. (Minors) (Interviews and Listing Arrangements)* [1994] 2 F.L.R. 489 at 495, *per* Wall J.; those reporting about children's views should not promise confidentiality: *Re D. (Adoption Reports: Confidentiality)* [1995] 2 F.L.R. 687, HL.

[17] F.P.R. 1991, r. 4.11(4) (b); F.P.C. 1991, r. 11(4) (b); J. Masson, "Representation of children in England" [2000] F.L.Q. 467.

[18] Children Act 1989, s. 7; "all children should be seen by the court welfare officer unless there are strong grounds for not doing so" Home Office, *National Standards for Probation Service Family Court Welfare Work* (1994), para. 4.17 but welfare reports are not available in all contested cases.

[19] For a discussion of the practices of children's guardians see: J. Masson, (2000) *op. cit.* Information for s.7 welfare reports is not always obtained directly from the child or out of the presence of the parent: M. Hester and L. Radford, *Domestic violence and child contact arrangements in England and Denmark* (1996); and half the children in a recent study of private law proceedings felt that their voices had not been heard either by the court process or their parents: A. Buchanan *et al., Families in conflict* (2001).

[20] Careful interpretation is necessary: see D.H., *Manual of Practice for guardians ad litem and reporting officers* (1992) pp. 69–70. Solicitors have also been advised to use these techniques: Law Society, *Acting for children* (1992), Chap. 3 but some are reluctant even to talk to children: Masson (2000) *op. cit.*, p.480.

[21] Children have no specific rights to information in either private law or public law proceedings, nor are their parents required to inform them; *cf.* Children (Scotland) Act 1995, s.6(1).

[22] For solicitors' approaches to their role in ascertaining children's views (as required by the Legal Services Commission, *Family Transaction Criteria*) see Piper (1999) *op. cit.* pp. 85–8.

[22a] [2002] 1 F.L.R. 119.

[23] See *May v. May* [1986] 1 F.L.R. 325 (judicial preference for firm discipline); *Re W. (Residence Order)* [1999] 1 F.L.R 869, CA (attitude of judges to nudity in the home).

[24] For example, bias against homosexual parents see Reece *op. cit.* p. 286.

[25] D.H. *A framework for assessing children and families* (1999) known as the purple book is a basic text for assessments of "children in need"—Children Act 1989, s.17 and under s.47. Assessments may also be undertaken by other professionals.

children's needs at various stages of their development.[26] Research also suggests that long-term problems occur when the parenting style is generally low on warmth and high on criticism.[27] Parental separation and divorce have been shown to affect children's life chances adversely[28] but there is no clear understanding of what processes are occurring or the steps which should be taken to mitigate these. Considerable emphasis is placed on children's need to maintain a relationship with each parent and on the negative effects of conflict.[29] And for these reasons permission to change a child's surname has been refused.[30] In disputes about medical treatment, courts place great weight on medical opinion about its likely outcome.[31] Where the child has special educational needs there is provision for assessment (statementing) under the Education Act 1996.[32] Mothers may be favoured over fathers on the basis of a young child's physical[33] or emotional needs, particularly if the father is not going to care for the child himself.[34] In any particular case the child's various needs may conflict:—

> In *Re R. (A Minor) (Residence Order Religion)*[35] the court was faced with competing applications for residence and contact orders in respect of a 10-year-old boy whose mother had died, by an aunt, by some friends who were all members of the Exclusive Brethren sect and by the boy's father who had been excluded from the sect. The boy had been brought up within the sect and identified strongly with its teaching but he also wanted to be with his father. These spiritual and emotional needs were incompatible; there was no middle way. The Court of Appeal upheld a decision to grant a residence order to the father and to allow supervised contact with the aunt upon her undertaking not to speak to the child about religious matters.

Material factors, matters which have commonly been considered but are not specifically included in the checklist, may also be introduced under this heading.[36] Accommodation is clearly important but its availability may depend on

---

[26] H. Cleaver *et al.*, *Children's needs—parenting capacity* (1999), Pt. 4.

[27] D.H., *Child Protection messages from research* (1995), p. 19.

[28] B. Rodgers and J. Pryor, *Divorce and separation the outcomes for children* (1998).

[29] J. Pryor and F. Seymour, "Making decisions about children after parental separation" [1996] *C.F.L.Q.* 229; Rodgers and Pryor (1998) pp. 16, 42; Sturge and Glaser *op. cit.*

[30] *Re B. (Change of Surname)* [1996] 1 F.L.R. 791, CA. See also *Dawson v. Wearmouth* [1999] 1 F.L.R. 1167 at 1175 *per* Lord Jauncey (dissenting).

[31] *Re C. (HIV)* [1999] 2 F.L.R. 1004; *Royal Wolverhampton Hospitals NHS Trust v. B.* [2000] 1 F.L.R. 953; *Re MM. (Medical Treatment)* [2000] 1 F.L.R. 224; *cf. Re T (Wardship Medical Treatment)* [1997] 1 F.L.R. 502 (emphasis on the reasonable views of caring parents).

[32] The poor levels of educational attainment for children looked after by local authorities is a matter of concern: Select Committee on Health, Second Report (1997–8) para. 289.

[33] *Re W. (A Minor) (Residence Order)* [1992] 2 F.L.R. 332, (breast feeding); *cf. Re D. (Minors)* [1995] 1 F.C.R. 301, CA.

[34] *Re W. (A Minor) (Residence Order)* [1993] 2 F.L.R. 625 at 635 (step-mother); *Plant v. Plant* [1983] 4 F.L.R. 305 (child minder).

[35] [1993] 2 F.L.R. 163, CA.

[36] Welfare is not to be equated with material advantages but unwillingness to support one's children may indicate a failure to understand their needs *Re S. (Contact: Evidence)* [1998] 1 F.L.R.798 at 802 *per* Hale J; differences in the resources available to spouses should be dealt with by reallocating assets using the powers in Children Act 1989, Sched.1 and realistic levels of child support.

having care of a child.[37] There is evidence that poverty is linked with poor health, poor physical development and lower educational attainment.[38] However emphasis on material standards is likely disproportionately to affect mothers because of women's lower wages.

(c) The likely effect of any change in circumstances

20–015 The emphasis put on maintaining current arrangements in disputes between parents has been discussed.[39] Arrangements which are working satisfactorily are also likely to be highly influential in applications for residence orders by relatives or foster parents who are caring for the child and in the variation applications:—

> In *Re P. (s.91(14)) (Residence and Religious Heritage)*[40] the parents, a rabbi and his wife were unable to care for their daughter, who was born with Down's syndrome. At the age of 17 months the girl was placed by the local authority with a non Jewish family where she thrived. A residence order was granted in favour of the foster carers when she was four years old. Four years later, her parents applied for variation of residence arguing the crucial importance of her Jewish heritage. The court rejected the application and reduced their contact. Although her heritage was important, her welfare demanded that she remain with those she regarded as her parents; visits by parents who retained the hope that she would return to them might undermine the placement.

This factor is less helpful in disputes between parents at the time of separation.[41] Research has highlighted the fluidity of arrangements at the time of breakdown and emphasised the importance of adjustment to new roles and relationships.[42] This factor is also relevant to disputes over contact where relationships have ended or never developed because of lack of contact. Re-introduction of a parent will help to meet the child's identity needs but needs careful planning.[43] The courts have sometimes justified refusing orders on the basis that it would be too

---

[37] A homeless person caring for a child has a priority need and some rights to rehousing, as amended by the Homelessness Act 2002, ss. 6–8: Housing Act 1996, s.193.

[38] See the findings of the National Child Development Study, especially P. Wedge and H. Prosser, *Born to Fail?* (1974) and E. Ferri, *Growing up in a One-parent Family* (1976).

[39] Above, para. 20–008.

[40] [1999] 2 F.L.R. 573, CA; the earlier history of this case is reported as *C. v. Salford* [1994] 2 F.L.R. 926; see also *Re B. (Residence Order Status Quo)* [1998] 1 F.L.R. 368, CA where the decision to transfer a child to the mother after three years with the father was reversed on appeal.

[41] If the child's return home is being sought under the Hague Convention on International Child Abduction the *status quo* is immaterial until one year has elapsed: see Art. 12 (Child Abduction and Custody Act 1985, Sched. 1) and Chap. 21, below.

[42] Wallerstein and Kelly (1980); Maccoby and Mnookin (1992).

[43] Sturge and Glaser *op. cit.*, pp. 621–2, 625; *Re W. (A Minor) (Contact)* [1994] 2 F.L.R. 441; *Re L. (Contact: Transsexual Applicant)* [1995] 2 F.L.R. 438; *Re K. (Adoption and Wardship)* [1997] 2 F.L.R. 221.

disruptive to the child to re-introduce the parent,[44] although the research evidence on this is equivocal.[45] Adjustment to new roles is also crucial to a child's successful return after a period being looked after by a local authority.[46]

It is also recognised that emphasising the *status quo* may encourage one party to delay.[47] Delay in court proceedings can allow one party to establish a settled arrangement before the matter is considered by the court. The Children Act 1989 specifically draws the attention of the courts to the fact that any delay is "likely to prejudice the welfare of the child."[48] Delay prolongs the uncertainty for the child and carers, makes it more difficult for the court to reach a decision which is in the child's best interests,[49] and may amount to a breach of human rights.[50]

(d) His age, sex, background and any characteristic of his which the court considers relevant

20–016 There is some research evidence that parental separation affects children differently according to their age[51] and also that new "parental" relationships may be established successfully for children beyond infancy.[52] Consideration of age is also linked with other factors such as the child's needs,[53] wishes and education. The relevance of the child's sex was reflected in the old rules of thumb but research does not appear to support the view that children do better living with a lone parent of the same gender.[54] There is no evidence that mothers are necessarily better carers.[55] However, in a society where men and women engage in different activities on the basis of their gender, girls may prefer activities with mothers and boys with fathers. A parent of the same gender may also be better able to understand the problems experienced as the child grows up.

The Children Act 1989 lists four factors which must be considered by local authorities when making decisions about children they are looking after which may also be relevant to this paragraph. These are: religious persuasion, racial

---

[44] *Re M. (A Minor) (Access Application)* [1988] F.L.R. 35, CA (child in local authority care); *Re W. (A Minor: Access)* [1989] 1 F.L.R. 163.

[45] See J. Masson, "Contact between parents and children in the long-term care of others: the unresolved dispute" (1990) 3 Int. J. of Law & Fam. 97. A substantial proportion of children who return home from care have had little contact with their families whilst in care, see S. Millham *et al., Lost in Care* (1986).

[46] R. Bullock *et al., Going Home* (1993), pp. 177, 206.

[47] Law Com. W.P. 96, para. 6.32.

[48] Children Act 1989, s.1(2); the Adoption and Children Bill 2002, s.1(3), see Chap. 19, above. The courts are required to set a timetable for the litigation: Children Act 1989, ss.11(1), 32; F.P.R. 1991, r. 4.15; F.P.C 1991, r. 15.

[49] *R. v. Bolton M.B.C., ex p. B.* [1985] F.L.R. 346, *per* Wood J. at 348; *Re R. (No. 1) (Intercountry Adoption)* [1999] 1 F.L.R. 1014.

[50] E.C.H.R., Art. 6(1); *H. v. U.K.* (1987) 10 E.H.R.R. 95.

[51] Rogers and Pryor (1998), p. 38.

[52] See B. Tizard, *Adoption: a second chance* (1977).

[53] See H. Cleaver *et al., Children's needs—parenting capacity* (1999), Pt. 4.

[54] Rodgers and Pryor (1998), p. 39.

[55] See Chambers, *op. cit.*, pp. 515–524. Mothers are more likely to have experience of caring for children but there is no presumption that they should have care: *Re W. (A Minor) (Residence Order)* [1992] 2 F.L.R. 332, CA.

origin, cultural background and linguistic background.[56] Guidance has been provided for local authorities which states that placement with a family of similar ethnic origin and religion is likely to safeguard a child's welfare most effectively because it will provide continuity and a familiar environment.[57] But all factors must be considered, for example half siblings with different ethnic origins may need to be placed together. A local authority's long term plans should not exclude placement with a family who does not share the child's heritage.[58] The courts must not pass judgment on beliefs of parents but only be concerned with the social or emotional effects of the parent's adherence to any particular sect.[59] It has been said that religious and cultural heritage cannot be an overwhelming factor.[60]—

> In *Re J. (Specific Issue Orders: Child's Religious Upbringing and Circumcision)*[61] the father sought an order that his son, aged five years, be circumcised in accordance with Muslim practice. The boy was living with his mother, a non-practising Christian, his only contact with Islam was through his father, a non-practising Muslim. Although the boy was recognised as a Muslim under Muslim religious law, this was not sufficient to establish that circumcision which carried a small risk of physical and psychological damage and would cause pain should be imposed against the wishes of the mother who was caring for him.

Issues of race are highly contentious and should not be ignored.[62] The courts recognise the special value of care by the natural parents which necessarily provides links with the child's culture and heritage.[63] There is some evidence that being brought up in a family which does not reflect racial, cultural and religious background negatively impacts on a child's identity and self-esteem;

---

[56] Children Act 1989, s.22(5) (c).

[57] *Guidance* Vol. 3, paras 2.40–2.42 and D.H. Circular LAC (98)20, paras 11–18.

[58] SSI letter CI (96)4 Adoption, para. 15; LAC(98)20, pp. 3–4. Private foster carers who did not recognise the child's racial and cultural needs were inappropriate carers: *H. v Trafford B.C.* [1997] 3 F.C.R 113.

[59] This would be discrimination contrary to E.C.H.R., Art. 14; see *Hoffman v. Austria* (1993) 17 E.H.R.R. 293. Concerns have been expressed about social isolation, see *Hewison v. Hewison* (1977) 7 *Fam. Law* 207, CA (Exclusive Brethren); about psychological damage from indoctrination *Wright v. Wright* (1980) 2 F.L.R. 276 (Jehovah's Witness); about separation from the only surviving parent *Re R. (A Minor) (Residence: Religion)* [1993] 2 F.L.R. 163; and about health risks where the parent would not agree to a blood transfusion. However, health may be protected by making a specific issue order (Children Act 1989, s.8(1)) or accepting an undertaking from the parent, see *Re H. (A Minor) (Custody: Religious Upbringing)* (1980) 2 F.L.R. 253; *Re S. (A Minor) (Blood Transfusion: Adoption Order Condition)* [1994] 2 F.L.R. 416, CA. See generally, A Bradney, *Religion, rights and laws* (1993).

[60] *Re P. (s.91(14)) (Residence and Religious Heritage)* [1999] 2 F.L.R. 573 at 586 *per* Butler-Sloss L.J. Issues of race must not be ignored for a child of mixed parentage, *Re. M. (Section 94 Appeals)* [1995] 1 F.L.R. 546.

[61] [1999] 2 F.L.R. 678; [2000] 1 F.L.R. 571, CA; see also *Re T. and M.* [1995] 1 E.L.R. where a mother who converted to Islam was permitted to introduce the children to Islam but prevented from moving them from a Church of England school or withdrawing them from religious education classes.

[62] *Re M. (Section 94 Appeals)* [1995] 1 F.L.R. 546 at 550, CA.

[63] *Re M. (Child's Upbringing)* [1996] 2 F.L.R. 441, CA (the Zulu boy case); *Re B. (Adoption: Child's Welfare)* [1995] 2 F.L.R. 895 (Gambian child).

children from minority ethnic groups may not be equipped to deal with the racism by carers from the dominant community.[64] This has justified a decision to move a mixed race child from a white family where he had lived for 18 months from birth, to a black family[65] but was insufficient to require a white surrogate mother to hand over twins to their Asian father when they were five months old.[66]

Where a child has lost or not acquired the language of their family this is a factor which may prevent return to them but carers may be required to ensure that a child receives appropriate instruction.[67] Cultural and linguistic factors may be relevant in adoption and care proceedings where the risk to the child living with the parents must be balanced with the risks of going into care.[68] The only limit on considering something under this paragraph is that it must not be such that no reasonable judge would consider it.[69]

(e) Any harm which he has suffered or is at risk of suffering

20–017 A care order may only be made where the harm, or likely harm is significant[70] and is proved on the balance of probabilities.[71] Similarly, in private law cases, the courts require evidence that the child is at risk of harm[72] but the risk need not be attributable to the parent seeking the order.[73]

Harm may arise from granting or denying contact. Witnessing a parent being abused is damaging to children.[74] There is no automatic assumption against contact where there has been domestic violence but physical and emotional

---

[64] B. Prevatt Goldstein and M. Spencer, *"Race" and ethnicity* (2000); see also Inter-departmental Review of Adoption Law, *Background paper 2* (1990), pp. 50–59. *Adoption, the future* (Cm. 2288, 1993) urged common sense professional assessment and the avoidance of ideology (para. 4.28). Contact may be beneficial in transracial adoptions: *Re O. (Transracial Adoption: Contact)* [1995] 2 F.L.R. 597.

[65] *Re P. (A Minor) (Adoption)* [1990] 1 F.L.R. 96; see also *Re N. (A Minor) (Adoption)* [1990] 1 F.L.R. 58.

[66] *Re P. (Minors) (Wardship: Surrogacy)* [1987] 2 F.L.R. 421.

[67] *Re K. (Adoption and Wardship)* [1997] 2 F.L.R. 221.

[68] Special weight cannot be given to the child's culture if this would leave him with unacceptably poor care, *Re H. (Minors) (Wardship: Cultural Background)* [1987] 2 F.L.R. 12.

[69] *G v. G (Minors: Custody Appeal)* [1985] 1 W.L.R. 647, see the discussion of appeals, below.

[70] Children Act 1989, s.31(2); "harm" is defined for the purposes of care proceedings as "ill-treatment or the impairment of health or development". s.31(9), and see n.74, below.

[71] *Re H. and R. (Child Sexual Abuse: Standard of Proof)* [1996] 1 F.L.R. 80, HL.

[72] The courts have not specifically applied *Re H. and R.* [1996] 1 F.L.R. 80; see: *Re N. (Residence: Hopeless Appeals)* [1995] 2 F.L.R. 230 at 233 *per* Butler-Sloss L.J.; *Re P. (Sexual Abuse: Standard of Proof)* [1996] 2 F.L.R. 333 at 342, *per* Wall J. but have rejected evidence because it was not obtained appropriately: *Re B. (Sexual Abuse: Expert's Report)* [2000] 1 F.L.R. 871, CA. For a chilling example of this see J. Groner, *Hilary's trial: The Elizabeth Morgan case* (1991).

[73] *Re K.(Specific Issue Order)* [1999] 2 F.L.R. 280 where the mother had told the child that the father was dead and would undermine any attempt to tell the child the truth. *Re B. (Contact: Stepfather's Opposition)* [1997] 1 F.L.R. 579, CA where the risk arose from the step-father's threat to reject the child and the mother if the proceedings continued.

[74] D.H., *Child protection messages from research* (1995), p. 18 citing L. Waterhouse *et al.*, "Evaluating parenting in child physical abuse" in L. Waterhouse, *Child abuse and child abusers* (1993). This is recognised by an amendment to s.31(9) in the Adoption and Children Bill 2002, cl. 117.

safety need proper consideration.[75] The ability of the violent parent to recognise the effects of their past conduct and the need to change are important considerations.[76] The seriousness of the parental problem (mental illness, domestic violence or substance abuse) is less relevant than the level to which the child is directly involved.[77]

The research evidence on the impact of abuse on children and their experiences in different forms of substitute care is complex.[78] Comparisons between children who have been abused and other children indicate more behaviour problems and greater difficulty with friendships amongst the abused group but one in five abused children were said to have faired well at home.[79] Persistent abuse and a combination of abuse and neglect tended to make the outcome worse; a fifth[80] of children living at home were re-abused but there was no link between this and the long-term outcome. Substitute care improved abused children's social status, physical growth and vocabulary but not their behaviour or mental well-being. Children who had been adopted had as many behaviour and friendship problems as those who remained with their parents after abuse, but children in foster care faired better.[81]

(f) How capable each of his parents and any other person in relation to whom the court considers the question to be relevant is of meeting his needs

20–018 Capacity to parent should not be seen as predetermined[82]; carers may learn to parent but the courts will not expect children to wait until deficient parents have gained the necessary skills.[83] Parental problems (mental illness, substance abuse and domestic violence) impact on parenting capacity, particularly where they exist in combination.[84] A carer may simply demonstrate their ability to care; it may be harder for the other parent, particularly a father who has had little

---

[75] *Re L., Re V., Re M. and Re H. (Contact: Domestic Violence)* [2000] 2 F.L.R. 334, CA; Sturge and Glaser, *op. cit.*

[76] *Re L., Re V., Re M. and Re H. (Contact: Domestic Violence)* [2000] 2 F.L.R. 334 at 344 *per* Butler-Sloss P.; *Re M. (Contact: Violent Parent)* [1999] 2 F.L.R. 321 at 333 *per* Wall J.

[77] Cleaver *et al., op cit.* p. 42.

[78] D.H., *Caring for children away from home* (1998); D.H., *Child protection messages from research* (1995); D.H., *Patterns and Outcomes in child placement* (1991); Cleaver *et al., op cit.* (1999), Pt 3.

[79] J. Gibbons *et al., Development after physical abuse in early childhood* (1995) in D.H., *Child protection messages from research* (1995), p. 66

[80] This figure is comparable with those in other studies: see D.H., *Child protection messages from research* (1995).

[81] J. Gibbons *et al., op cit.*, p. 67. But these findings are in contradiction to the weight of evidence in other studies where adopted children have faired well and foster care has been associated with poor outcomes: see B. Tizard, *Adoption: a second chance* (1977) and D.H., *Patterns and Outcomes in Child placement* (1991). Gibbons suggests that poorer outcomes may relate to parenting styles.

[82] See Chambers, *op. cit.* pp. 515–524. Research indicates that non-custodial fathers can acquire caring skills but mothers are still seen as the natural carers for very young children: *Brixey v. Lynas* [1995] 2 F.L.R. 499, HL (S), *per* Lord. Jauncey at 504–5.

[83] *Re D.(Grant of Care Order: Refusal of Freeing Order)* [2001] 1 F.L.R. 862, CA; *Scott v. U.K.* [2000] 1 F.L.R. 958 at 970.

[84] Cleaver *et al., op cit.* Pt 2.

involvement to do so.[85] Capable parents need not care for their children full-time but must show that they understand their children's needs when making alternative arrangements.[86] The courts have sometimes favoured care by a parent and step-parent over care in a one-parent family.[87] Parental remarriage is likely to improve the child's economic circumstances[88] but may impose greater emotional stress.[89]

This paragraph is also relevant to consideration of the effect of an order on the parent caring for the child. Where contact will undermine the ability to care the court may refuse an order, although this would not be done lightly[90]:—

> In *Re H. (Contact: Domestic Violence)*[91] the father had assaulted the mother and made threats to kill her, apparently because of her failure to conform strictly to the Muslim faith. The mother ran away with the children, changing her name and those of the children to avoid detection and brought them up in a secular, westernised way. Three years later the father applied for contact. The judge accepted that the mother remained fearful that the father would abduct the children and that his influence would undermine her. Indirect contact was ordered and the father's appeal was dismissed.

(g) The range of powers available to the court under this Act in the proceedings in question

20–019 There are wide powers in the Children Act 1989 to make orders and the terms of the orders themselves provide considerable scope[92] to the court. Where there is no statutory power, the inherent jurisdiction may still be available.[93] The court has power to make orders other than those applied for[94] but can only commit

[85] This will be highly relevant where an unmarried father seeks a residence order and the mother wants the child placed for adoption because the father will not be in dispute with anyone caring for the child, see *Re O. (A Minor) (Custody: Adoption)* [1992] 1 F.L.R. 77, CA; *cf. Re M. (A Minor: Custody Appeal)* [1990] 1 F.L.R. 291, CA where the father was only 17 years old. A positive assessment from the local authority can be crucial: *B. v. P. (Adoption by Unmarried Father)* [2000] 2 F.L.R. 717.

[86] *Re K. (Minors) (Children: Care and Control)* [1977] Fam. 179. The father's arrangements which involved a rota of childminders indicated that he did not or could not give sufficient attention to the children's needs for continuity and consistency.

[87] *Re D.W. (A Minor) (Custody)* (1984) 14 *Fam. Law* 17. The Court of Appeal upheld the decision to move a child aged 10 from his step-mother to his mother and step-father although he had lived with his step-mother (and his father who had now left) for over eight years. Such decisions are difficult to justify except on the basis of expert assessments of the individuals involved.

[88] J. Eekelaar and M. Maclean, *Maintenance after Divorce* (1986), p. 69.

[89] M. Maclean and M. Wadsworth, "The interests of children after parental divorce: a long-term perspective" (1988) 2 Int. J. Law & Fam. 155, 160–161; Wallerstein and Kelly (1980), p. 301; Rodgers and Pryor Chap. 5.

[90] *Re D. (A Minor) (Contact: Mother's Hostility)* [1993] 2 F.L.R. 1; *Re L., Re V., Re M. and Re H. (Contact: Domestic Violence)* [2000] 2 F.L.R. 334; *Re K. (Contact: Mother's Anxiety)* [1999] 2 F.L.R. 703.

[91] [2000] 2 F.L.R. 334, CA.

[92] Children Act 1989, ss.8, 11(7); above.

[93] *A. v. Liverpool C.C.* [1982] A.C. 363; *Re J. (Freeing for Adoption)* [2000] 2 F.L.R. 58; but not where the limitations in Children Act 1989, s.100 apply.

[94] Children Act 1989, ss.10(1), 31(2); orders in favour of those who cannot apply for them are exceptional: *Gloucestershire C.C. v. P.* [1999] 2 F.L.R. 61, CA.

the child to local authority care when the grounds for a care order have been proved.[95] But an individual who has not applied for a residence order and who does not want the responsibility conferred by it should not be required to accept it:—

> In *Re K. (Care Order or Residence Order)*[96] the local authority started care proceedings in respect of a child who had been injured by his schizophrenic mother. The child and his older brother were placed with their maternal grandparents. The grandparents were willing to care for the children but preferred to do this as foster carers so that they would have the financial and professional support of the social services department because both the children had muscular dystrophy which would make them increasingly disabled as they grew up. The local authority wished to withdraw its application for care orders but the court made care orders.

Before making any order the court must also be satisfied that "doing so would be better for the child than making no order at all."[97] The court may thus decide that it should make no order because it would only engender further conflict or, alternatively, because the parties are now able to make their own arrangements. It should be noted, however, that informal agreements do not have the same effect as orders.[98]

Review of the court's decisions on welfare

20–020 The appellate courts have long been concerned not to become involved in the reconsideration of the very many cases which have been determined applying the welfare test. These cases which involve the exercise of discretion, have "no right answer" and there may be two possible decisions which are "both equally right."[99] Consequently it would be wrong for the Appeal Court to substitute its view for that of the judge. Judges and magistrates hearing children cases are specifically trained and appointed for this work.[1] Where the judge has formed views by assessing the parties, the appellate court is in a poor position to gainsay him or her and would not be able to determine the case, only remit it for rehearing.[2] Moreover, the child's need for a final outcome without delay encourages policies which prevent prolonged litigation.[3] A requirement of leave for

---

[95] Children Act 1989, ss.9(5) 31; see below.
[96] [1995] 1 F.L.R. 675.
[97] Children Act 1989, s.1(5); see above.
[98] Children Act 1989, ss.2(8), 5(6), 12, 13; *Re W. (A Minor) (Contact)* [1994] 2 F.L.R. 441; see above.
[99] *per* Lord Fraser *G v. G* [1985] 1 W.L.R. 647 at 651. *cf.* R. Ormrod [1978] C.L.P. 123 at 135–136 who states that he never had any difficulty distinguishing between right, plainly wrong and doubtful decisions; both disagreements and successful appeals were rare.
[1] *Re L. (Contact: Domestic Violence)* [2000] 2 F.L.R. 334 at 366 *per* Thorpe L.J.
[2] *per* Bridge L.J. *Re F. (A Minor) (Wardship Appeal)* [1976] Fam. 238 at 266; see J. Eekelaar (1985) 48 *M.L.R.* 704 at 705.
[3] *ibid.*

appeals is used to restrict appeals.[4] The more difficult the case, the more difficult it is said to be to mount an appeal.[5] Appeals can only be expedited if "extraordinary prejudice" to children is likely or the case is brought under the Hague Abduction Convention.[6] Counsel should take care not to encourage hopeless appeals.[7]

In *G v. G*[8] the House of Lords explained the role of the appellate court in welfare cases and set out the principles on which an appeal should be allowed:

> "[T]he appellate court should only interfere when it considers that the judge of first instance has not merely preferred an imperfect solution which is different from an alternative imperfect solution which the Court of Appeal might or would have adopted, but has exceeded the generous ambit within which a reasonable disagreement is possible."[9]

Thus appeals should be allowed where the decision is "plainly wrong". For example, where the judge has preferred lay evidence to that of medical experts but given no reasons[10]; or made no reference to the special position of the father in a dispute with relatives who were caring for the child[11]; or ordered staying contact pending an assessment of a child who was disturbed after contact[12]; or magistrates have dismissed a care application while an assessment is being carried out[13]; or decided only to make a supervision order despite reasons indicating grave concern for a child's safety[14]; or where the judge has imposed a condition on adopters in the face of express opposition from their advocate.[15] But quite comparable decisions have been held to be within the "generous ambit of the court's reasonable discretion." So a father whose application for contact was dismissed in the face of the mother's objections failed in his appeal[16]; and a mother's appeal against the imposition of shared residence was refused.[17]

20–021 Lord Fraser, with whom the other members of the House agreed, expressly rejected the view that the court should approach these cases like judicial review of administrative action and only consider whether the judge had followed a

[4] Appeals to the Court of Appeal, except those in relation to habeas corpus or secure accommodation require leave from the Court of Appeal: R.S.C. Ord, 59, r. 1B(1) (a)–(c); *Practice Direction (Court of Appeal procedure)* [1999] 2 All E.R.490; P. Gallagher [2001] Fam. L. 459. A survey for the Lord Chancellor's Department found that in 1997/8 63% of appeals were successful where there was a leave filter but only 29% where there was no filter.

[5] *Re D. (Parental Responsibility: IVF baby)* [2001] 1 F.L.R. 972, CA *per* Butler-Sloss P. at para. 27.

[6] *Practice Direction (Court of Appeal procedure)* [1999] 2 All E.R. 490, para. 6.7.3.

[7] *Re N. (Residence: Hopeless Appeals)* [1995] 2 F.L.R. 230 at 231, *per* Butler-Sloss L.J.

[8] [1985] 1 W.L.R. 647.

[9] *per* Lord Fraser at 652.

[10] *Re B. (Split Hearing: Jurisdiction)* [2000] 1 F.L.R. 334 (appeal allowed against finding even though no decision or order had been made).

[11] *Re N. (Residence: Appointment of Solicitor: Placement with Extended Family)* [2001] 1 F.L.R. 1028.

[12] *Re W. (Staying Contact)* [1998] 2 F.L.R. 450, CA.

[13] *C. v. Solihull M.B.C.* [1993] 1 F.L.R. 290.

[14] *Leicestershire C.C. v. G.* [1994] 2 F.L.R. 329.

[15] *Re S. (A Minor) (Blood Transfusion: Adoption Order Condition)* [1994] 2 F.L.R. 416.

[16] *Re J. (A Minor) (Contact)* [1994] 1 F.L.R. 729.

[17] *A. v. A. (Minors) (Shared Residence)* [1994] 1 F.L.R. 669.

course which "no reasonable judge having taken into account all the relevant circumstances could have adopted."[18] However, the distinction between these two tests (if any) is a very fine one.[19] A judge who has exceeded the generous ambit has reached a decision which no reasonable judge would have reached. The same approach is also applied where a judge hears an appeal from the family proceedings court.[20] Where magistrates' reasons omit important factors, fail to explain a departure from a welfare officer's recommendation or are unclear on crucial matters, the appellate court is justified in looking to see that the magistrates have correctly carried out the balancing exercise.[21] This narrow approach to appeals has been criticised because it does not provide what litigants want[22] or what, in the interest of the child, a difficult case may require[23]—the opinion of a bench of senior judges. Also, because it may limit the guidance on matters of principle, which would improve decision making in the lower courts and remove the need for appeals.[24] It has been suggested that the appeal court should at least be able to direct a rehearing in other circumstances.[25]

Although the decision in *G v. G* seems to require the judge of first instance to have been "plainly wrong," the Court of Appeal has also allowed appeals where subsequent events have indicated that the original decision was ill-founded[26] or inoperable[27] and where the judge's reasons indicate he or she carried out the balancing exercise incorrectly.[28] The court has complete discretion whether to admit new evidence but is in no position to evaluate conflicting testimony about the child's relationship with a parent.[29] The Court of Appeal

[18] *per* Stamp L.J. *Re F. (A Minor) (Wardship Appeal)* [1976] Fam. 238 at 254 quoted by Lord Fraser at 653.

[19] See Lord Bridge [1985] 1 W.L.R. 647 at 656.

[20] Children Act 1989, s.94; *Re M. (Section 94 Appeals)* [1995] 1 F.L.R. 546. Also where there is an appeal from a district judge at the Principal Registry: *Re S. (Appeal from Principal Registry: Procedure)* [1998] 2 F.L.R. 856.

[21] *Re M. (Section 94 Appeals)* [1995] 1 F.L.R. 546 at 549, *per* Butler-Sloss L.J.

[22] Maidment (1984), p. 58 argued that appeals are being used to rectify the inadequacies of the decision-making process at trial level and recommended a specialised panel of judges which has now been provided see above, Chap. 19.

[23] H. Bevan, *Child Law* (1989) 3.81.

[24] Eekelaar (1985) *op. cit.*, pp. 706–707. "[C]lear guidance from this court simplifies the task of the trial judge and helps to limit the volume of appeals." *Payne v. Payne* [2001] 1 F.L.R. 1052 at 1061 *per* Thorpe L.J.

[25] Sir John Latey, letter to *The Times*, August 31, 1989.

[26] *Re W. (A Minor) (Residence Order)* [1993] 2 F.L.R. 625. Similarly decisions have been upheld when new evidence has justified them: *M. v. M. (Minor: Custody Appeal)* [1987] 1 W.L.R. 404.

[27] *Re B. (Residence Order: Leave to Appeal)* [1998] 1 F.L.R. 502; *Re HB. (Abduction: Child's Objections)* [1998] 1 F.L.R. 422 both cases where children's behaviour made the implementation of the original order impossible.

[28] *W. v. P. (Justices Reasons)* [1988] 1 F.L.R. 508, the magistrates described the child's welfare as the top item on their list; *Re M. (Section 94 Appeals)* [1995] 1 F.L.R. 546 where the magistrates, amongst other errors, failed to refer to the issue of race; *Re L. (Residence: Justices Reasons)* [1995] 2 F.L.R. 445 where the magistrates failed to make any finding on the central issue of the mother's alcohol problem; *Re P. (Contact: Supervision)* [1996] 2 F.L.R. 314 where the court had given too much weight to the effect of contact on the mother's health; *Re T.(Wardship: Medical Treatment)* [1997]1 F.L.R. 502 where the judge emphasised the mother's unreasonableness and focused narrowly on the medical aspects of the transplant decision; *Re W.(Residence Order)* [1999] 1 F.L.R. 869 where the judge allowed his aversion to nudity to override all other factors.

[29] *Re M. (A Minor) (Appeal) (No. 2)* [1994] 1 F.L.R. 59 at 66, *per* Waite L.J. The appellate court is not a forum for testing fresh evidence: *Re V. (Residence Review)* [1995] 2 F.L.R. 1010 at 1021, *per* Russell L.J.

has also warned that costs may be awarded against the appellant if it considers the appeal unjustified.[30]

G v. G does not preclude an appeal if the judge has applied the wrong test[31] nor if procedural requirements such as the giving of reasons have been ignored.[32] But an appeal may be denied where reasons are incomplete if the appellate court is satisfied that the same decision would have been reached.[33]

---

[30] *Re G. (A Minor) (Role of Appellate Court)* [1987] 1 F.L.R. 164; *R. v. R. (Costs: Child Case)* [1997] 2 F.L.R. 92.

[31] *Re H. (Minors: Access)* [1992] 1 F.L.R. 148; *Re D. (Natural Parent Presumption)* [1999] 1 F.L.R. 135 C.A.

[32] F.P.C. 1991, r. 21(5); *W. v. Hertfordshire C.C.* [1993] 1 F.L.R. 118. Also where a judge has failed to make clear the basis for the decision: *B. v. B. (Residence Order: Reasons for Decision)* [1997] 2 F.L.R. 602

[33] *Re M. (Section 94 Appeals)* [1995] 1 F.L.R. 546 at 550 *per* Butler-Sloss L.J.; *H. v. H. (Residence Order: Leave to Remove from the Jurisdiction)* [1995] 1 F.L.R. 529, CA.

CHAPTER TWENTY-ONE

CHILD ABDUCTION[1]

I. INTRODUCTION

21–001 Children are taken by strangers for abuse or for ransom; by both parents for forced marriage[2]; by non-residential parents from the parent with care; by the parent with care; and children are not returned after contact visits. All these are forms of child abduction. There are various reasons why parents abduct their children.[3] Some cannot bear to be parted from them or hope that abduction will force their former partner to return; others are motivated by a desire to hurt the other parent or to protect the child from abuse.[4] After the breakdown of a relationship, parents who have previously emigrated may wish to return with their child to their former home country, for support from family and friends. Unless such a relocation is agreed,[5] it may amount to an abduction of the child.

Abduction can be used to gain advantage or avoid disadvantage in proceedings. Custody laws and court practices have encouraged parental abduction by exercising jurisdiction on the basis of mere presence in the country[6]; by giving great weight to the status quo without providing for speedy decisions; by favouring care by fathers rather than mothers (or vice versa); by making it difficult for a parent with care to relocate lawfully; and by failing to enforce decisions about contact. Although abduction has long-term adverse effects on children's welfare,[7] courts, applying the best interests standard, have been willing to make orders in the abductor's favour taking a nationalistic approach to welfare.[8]

---

[1] P. Beaumont and P. McEleavy, *The Hague Convention on International Child Abduction* (1999); A. Hutchinson, R. Roberts and H. Setright, *International parental child abduction* (1998); A. Anton, "The Hague Convention on International Child Abduction" (1981) 30 I.C.L.Q. 537; C. Bruch, "International Child Abduction Cases: Experiences under the 1980 Hague Convention" in *Parenthood and Modern Society: legal and social issues for the Twenty-first Century* (J. Eekelaar and P. Sarcevic ed., 1994); G. Van Bueren, *The best interests of the child—international co-operation in child abduction* (1993). Information is also available from Reunite, the National Council for abducted children, P.O. Box 24875, London E1 6FR or at www.reunite.org

[2] *Re KR. (Abduction: Forcible Removal by Parents)* [1999] 2 F.L.R. 542; Home Office, *Choice by right* (2000).

[3] See G. L. Grief and R.L. Hegar, *When parents kidnap* (1993), p. 8.

[4] J. Groner, *Hilary's trial—The Elizabeth Morgan case—a child's ordeal in the American legal system* (1991). Elizabeth Morgan spent two years in custody for refusing to give information about her daughter whom she alleged had been sexually abused. The child's grandparents took her to New Zealand.

[5] By the other parent and/or the court. For a discussion of the law and practice in relocation cases see Chap. 19, above.

[6] As was the case under the inherent jurisdiction, see above, Chap. 19.

[7] Greif and Hegar (1993), p. 209.

[8] A. Dyer, "The Hague Convention—towards global co-operation, its successes and failures" (1993) 1 Int. J. of Children's Rights 273.

Abduction potentially interferes with the right to family life of the left-behind parent and the child; where the law or the courts fail to protect these rights effectively they breach the European Convention on Human Rights.[9] The legal system has been hard pressed to find a satisfactory solution to child abduction but is developing a range of strategies in criminal, civil, domestic and international law. These are based on the principle that the interests of children will be best served by preventing abduction. The aim is to make it more difficult for parents to succeed in abducting their children and to facilitate return so that disputes are heard in the courts of the child's home state. Ensuring that the abductor does not benefit from the abduction should deter others, but will only do so if the rules relating to return are strictly adhered to.

II. PREVENTING ABDUCTION

21–002 The Child Abduction Act 1984 was passed following the conclusion of the Criminal Law Revision Committee that the law on child stealing was inadequate.[10] Under this Act it is an offence for a person connected with the child[11] to remove a child under 16 years from the United Kingdom without the appropriate consent.[12] Anyone who does not have parental responsibility also commits an offence if he or she removes or keeps a child under 16 from any person with lawful control.[13] In 1991 there were 89 prosecutions and 45 convictions for offences under the Child Abduction Act 1984.[14] Moreover, the common law offence of kidnapping is committed by anyone, even a parent, who takes a child who does not consent[15] but prosecution for this offence is rare.

The criminalisation of child abduction by a parent gives the police a role in what otherwise would be considered as a civil matter, and enables enforcement action to be taken where there is no court order.[16] Where there is reasonable suspicion that an offence will be committed, the police have the power to arrest a parent and can prevent the child's removal from the country.[17] It may even be possible for the abductor to be extradited from a country where civil action to

[9] N. Mole, "The Hague Convention and art. 8 of the European Convention on Human Rights" [2000] I.F.L. 121; Swindells *et al.*, para. 7.46 *et seq.* and see para. 21–024, below.

[10] Criminal Law Revision Committee, 14th Report, *Offences against the Person,* Cmnd. 7844 (1980).

[11] Child Abduction Act 1984, s.1(2).

[12] The consent of all those listed in s.1(3) of the Child Abduction Act 1984 is required: the mother, the father if he has parental responsibility, any guardian, any person in whose favour there is a residence order, any person with custody, and following amendment in the Adoption and Children Bill 2002, Sched. 3, any special guardian. Where there is a court order, leave of the court will be sufficient.

[13] Child Abduction Act 1984, s.2. The offence requires intentional removal from someone known to have lawful control: *O. v. Governor of Holloway Prison and Government of USA* [2000] 1 F.L.R. 147. A person who is or reasonably believes himself to be the child's (non-marital) father has a defence: s.2(3) (a).

[14] *Hansard* H.C. Vol. 221, col. 249.

[15] *R. v. D.* [1984] A.C. 778 and G. Williams, "Can babies be kidnapped?" [1989] Crim. L.R. 473.

[16] Home Office Circular 21/1986, para. 3; where there is at risk of significant harm the police may use their power under Children Act 1989, s.46 to take the child into police protection.

[17] Home Office Circular 75/1984, para. 6.

reclaim the child would be difficult.[18] However, enforcement of the criminal law in this area requires sensitivity[19]; it has been argued that it may be counter-productive.[20] Although the possibility of conviction may deter some parents, it is also important to examine other ways of preventing abduction and of securing the child's return if it occurs.

Where abduction is suspected, perhaps because of threats or because one parent has strong links with another country, section 8 orders should be sought and granted.[21] A residence order allows the residential parent to remove the child from the United Kingdom for up to one month[22]; further restrictions may be desirable[23] so that any removal without consent is prohibited.[24] The parent with care also needs to be vigilant in preventing opportunities for taking the child and to ensure that those looking after the child, for example teachers or childminders, are aware of the risk. Any contact the suspect (or their family) has with the child may need to be supervised. A solicitor who is aware of plans to abduct a child is not required to maintain the confidentiality of a client seeking advice to plan a criminal offence[25]; the court may order a solicitor to disclose a client's whereabouts.[26] A solicitor who encourages the breach of a court order is in contempt of court and could also be liable for "wasted costs" incurred in proceedings.[27]

If the child is likely to be taken overseas the following action should be considered.[28]

1. Passport control

21–003 After October 1998 it was no longer possible for children to be included on their parent's passport.[29] Passports are normally granted to children on the application of a parent with parental responsibility.[30] Where there is a court order restricting the child's removal from the jurisdiction, a person who objects

---

[18] *Re O.(Child Abduction: Re-abduction)* [1997] 2 F.L.R. 712.

[19] Home Office Circular 75/1984, para. 5.

[20] A. Dyer, "Childhood rights in international law" (1991) 5 Australia J. *Fam. Law* 103.

[21] Lord Mackay [1991] *Fam. Law* 457. A real risk of abduction is a reason for granting residence to the other parent: *Re K.(Residence Order: Securing Contact)* [1999] 1 F.L.R. 583, CA (residence of the two year-old child granted to father).

[22] s.13(2).

[23] Either by a prohibited steps order, *Re D. (A Minor) (Child: Removal from the Jurisdiction)* [1992] 1 F.L.R. 637, or a condition under s.11(7) (b).

[24] Removal would then be an offence: Child Abduction Act 1984, s.1(4A); it would also be "wrongful" under the Hague Convention, see below.

[25] Law Society, *Guide to professional conduct of solicitors* (8th ed., 1999.) para. 16.02.

[26] *Re B. (Abduction: Disclosure)* [1995] 1 F.L.R. 774, CA; *Re H. (Abduction: Whereabouts Order to Solicitors)* [2000] 1 F.L.R. 766.

[27] *Re. K. (Minors) (Incitement to Breach of Contact Order)* [1992] 2 F.L.R. 108 advice to parent to take children away to avoid contact; Supreme Court Act 1981, s.51.

[28] Further details of practical steps are set out in Reunite, *Child Abduction Prevention Pack*, see, n.1, above.

[29] This facility was removed to make international abduction more difficult. Passports including children continue to be valid for travel with a child under 16 years.

[30] Guidance from the United Kingdom Passport Agency see: www.ukpa.gov.uk

to the child travelling can ask the Passport Agency not to issue a passport.[31] Where the child already has a United Kingdom passport (or has been included on a parent's) the court may require its surrender if there is an order prohibiting or otherwise restricting the child's removal from the United Kingdom.[32] A parent who holds a foreign passport may be required to deposit it with solicitors as a precondition of contact[33] but there is no way of preventing a foreign country from issuing a passport to one of its nationals.

2. All ports warning[34]

21–004 Since removal of a child from the United Kingdom may be an offence under the Child Abduction Act 1984, the police may be asked to assist by instituting a port-alert. The police must be satisfied that the danger of removal is "real and imminent," *i.e.*, that it is not merely sought for insurance and may occur within the next 48 hours.[35] No court order is required unless the child is over 16.[36] The request should provide as much relevant information as possible about the child, the suspected abductor, their likely travel plans and the grounds for seeking a port-alert. Particulars of the child are circulated to all ports through the Police National Computer and receiving forces are asked to make arrangements with the local Immigration Service. The child's name remains on the port-stop list for four weeks but further applications may be made. An immigration officer has no right to detain the child or the abductor but could make a citizen's arrest.

3. Security for the child's return

21–005 A person permitted to remove a child for a visit may be required to give an undertaking,[37] to enter into a bond or to provide surety for the child's safe return,[38] but this may provide insufficient incentive where they are determined to abduct. However, such action should not be required routinely.[39] The property of someone who knows of a court order for return of the children and aids a

---

[31] The court will not do so: Clarke Hall and Morrison, Vol. 2, para. 5; *Practice Direction* [1986] 1 All E.R. 983.

[32] Family Law Act 1986, s.37; *e.g.* a residence order.

[33] See *Al Kandari v. Brown* [1988] Q.B. 665. The solicitor owes a duty of care to the other parent not merely to the client and may be liable if the children are abducted after the client has obtained the passport; *Re A-K. (Foreign Passport: Jurisdiction)* [1997] 2 F.L.R. 569, CA.

[34] See generally *Practice Direction* [1986] 1 All E.R. 983 and Home Office Circular 21/1986.

[35] See Home Office Circular 21/1986, para. 9 for relevant factors.

[36] It is not an offence under the Act to remove a child over 16 although it could still amount to kidnap.

[37] *Re S. (Leave to Remove from the Jurisdiction: Securing Return from Holiday)* [2001] 2 F.L.R. 507, FD there was insufficient time to obtain mirror orders but the court made the children wards and declared their state of habitual residence to be England.

[38] *Re L.(Removal from the Jurisdiction: Holiday)* [2001] 1 F.L.R. 241 (£50,000 bond required where mother wished to take child to United Arab Emirates for a holiday).

[39] See *Practice Note* (1987) 17 *Fam. Law* 263; *Re H. (Minors) (Wardship: Surety)* [1991] 1 F.L.R. 40.

parent to conceal them may also be sequestered.[40] The sale of sequestered property can be ordered to finance legal proceedings.[41]

4. "Mirror" orders

21–006 A parent who wishes to remove a child overseas for contact may sometimes be expected first to obtain orders in that jurisdiction, equivalent to the order of the U.K. court. Orders are preferable to undertakings given to the court here which are likely to have no effect abroad. Where such "mirror" orders are obtained and the child is not returned, enforcement action can be taken in the country of contact.[42]

III. TRACING CHILDREN

21–007 In any proceedings relating to a section 8 order or an order under the inherent jurisdiction of the High Court, the court may order any person who has relevant information about the child's whereabouts to disclose it.[43] A person may not refuse to answer on the grounds of self-incrimination.[44] Assistance may be obtained via the court from various government departments in connection with proceedings under the Child Abduction and Custody Act 1985 or the enforcement of a "Part I order" (which includes any section 8 order or order for custody, access or care and control)[45] under the Family Law Act 1986.[46] The Department of Social Security can trace people in employment (through their National Insurance number) and benefit claimants; the Office of National Statistics holds the National Health Service Central Register and can trace a person who registers with a G.P.; the Passport Agency holds details of all applicants for passports; service personnel and those who have recently left the services may be traced through the Ministry of Defence. Government Departments are geared to react speedily to requests for help.[47] However, in some cases, particu-

---

[40] *Re. S (Abduction: Sequestration)* [1995] 1 F.L.R. 858; *Re W. (Ex parte Orders)* [2000] 2 F.L.R. 927. In *Al-Khatib v. Masry* [2002] 1 F.L.R. 1053, FD, the court increased the wife's ancillary relief to enable her to bring proceedings.

[41] *Mir v. Mir* [1992] Fam 79; *Richardson v. Richardson* [1989] Fam. 95.

[42] *Re T. (Staying Contact in Non-Convention Country)* [1999] 1 F.L.R. 262 (Egypt); *Re A.(Security for Return to Jurisdiction)* [1999] 2 F.L.R. 1 (Saudi Arabia). Mirror orders can also be obtained (exceptionally) in England to ensure a child returns home after staying contact here even where the child is neither habitually resident nor present here: *Re P. (A Child: Mirror Orders)* [2000] 1 F.L.R. 435.

[43] Family Law Act 1986, s.33(1) as amended. Such orders should only be made against the police in exceptional circumstances: *Chief Constable of W. Yorkshire Police v. S.* [1998] 2 F.L.R. 973, CA. There is a comparable power in relation to proceedings brought under the Child Abduction and Custody Act 1985, s.24A where a child has been abducted to the U.K.

[44] Family Law Act 1986, s.33(2). Orders may be made against solicitors overriding their duty of confidentiality to their client: *Re B. (Abduction: Disclosure)* [1995] 1 F.L.R. 774, CA; *Re H. (Abduction: Whereabouts Order to Solicitors)* [2000] 1 F.L.R. 766.

[45] *ibid.*, s.1 as amended.

[46] *Practice Direction* [1989] 1 F.L.R. 307, amended by *Practice Direction* [1995] 2 F.L.R. 813.

[47] Lord Chancellor's Department, *Child Abduction* (1997), p. 17.

larly where the child has been taken abroad, it may be necessary to instruct a private investigator.

IV. RECOVERY OF THE CHILD

21–008 Recovery of children is never simple but the difficulties posed, the procedures that must be used, and the principles that apply depend on the country to which the child has been taken. Within the United Kingdom cases are dealt with under the Children Act 1989 and the Family Law Act 1986.[48]

A. Abduction within England and Wales

21–009 Where a parent takes a child without consent of a person with parental responsibility the courts may grant a residence order *ex parte*,[49] or on short notice[50] so that the child retains their settled home pending a decision about residence. However, there is no general rule which requires summary return.[51] The court may make a recovery order for the production, removal and return of any child in care, in police protection or subject to an emergency protection order, who has been unlawfully removed, has run away or is missing.[52]

B. Abduction from one part of the United Kingdom to another

21–010 The Family Law Act 1986 is designed to ensure that jurisdiction relating to a child's residence can generally be exercised only[53] by the courts in one part of the United Kingdom[54] at any one time and that "Part 1" orders[55] relating to

---

[48] See Law Com. No. 138 Custody of Children—jurisdiction and enforcement within the United Kingdom, Cmnd. 9419 (1984). The Act has been amended to fit within the Brussels II regime see Council Regulation 1347/2000 and European Communities (Matrimonial jurisdiction and judgments) Regulations 2001 (S.I. 2001 No. 310), arts 6–9. Brussels II provides for the mutual enforcement of "parental responsibility" orders relating to the spouses' children made in matrimonial proceedings in E.U. States (excluding Denmark), its extension to other parental responsibility cases is under discussion (Brussels IIBis).

[49] *Re B. (A Minor) (Residence Order: Ex parte)* [1992] 2 F.L.R. 1 where a 20-month-old boy was returned to live with his father and sisters; *Re G. (Minors) (Ex parte Interim Residence Order)* [1993] 1 F.L.R. 910 where return was not ordered because of "compelling reasons relating to drugs"—allegations relating to cannabis use.

[50] F.P.R. 1991, r.4.8(8) (b); F.P.C. 1991, r.8(8) (b).

[51] *Ex parte* orders should no be made without good reason: *Re J. (Children: Ex parte Orders)* [1997] 1 F.L.R. 606, Hale J.

[52] Children Act 1989, s.50; *Re R. (Recovery Orders)* [1998] 2 F.L.R. 401; *Guidance,* Vol. 1, paras 4, 90 *et seq.*

[53] The inherent jurisdiction of the High Court is restricted to cases where the child is present in England or Wales and needs immediate protection. The restrictions apply if the child is not habitually resident in England and Wales, is habitually resident in another part of the U.K. or there are matrimonial proceedings in Scotland or Northern Ireland: Family Law Act 1986, ss.2(3), 3.

[54] *i.e.* England and Wales, Scotland or Northern Ireland, Family Law Act 1986, s. 42(1). The Act also applies to the Isle of Man: see Family Law Act 1986 (Dependent Territories) Order, S.I. 1991 No. 1723.

[55] F.L.A. 1986, s.1.

children are enforceable throughout the United Kingdom.[56] Consequently, abductors should not be able to strengthen their position by obtaining an order after taking the child and those with court orders should be able to recover[57] abducted children.

However, the provisions do not always operate to achieve this:—

> In *S v. S (Custody: Jurisdiction)*[58] the father and mother both applied for custody in Scotland and the father was successful. The mother failed to return the child at the end of the contact visit, went to England with the child and could not be found. Over a year later she applied for and obtained an interim order for residence. The father applied to have the English proceedings stayed and his Scottish order enforced. However it was held that the Scottish order had ceased to have effect when the English order was made.[59]

If there are matrimonial proceedings[60] in England and Wales, a court in England and Wales can make a section 8 order only if it has jurisdiction under either the Family Law Act 1986 or Brussels II.[61] Where Brussels II does not apply, the courts for the country where the child is habitually resident[62] have jurisdiction to determine residence.[63] Where the child has no country of habitual residence within the United Kingdom, jurisdiction can be exercised only where the child is or where divorce proceedings are pending or have taken place.[64]

> In *Re M. (Minors) (Residence Order Jurisdiction)*[65] two children of unmarried parents were living with the mother's agreement with paternal grandparents in Scotland. The children visited their mother for a two week holiday and she decided that they should not return to Scotland. The grandparents obtained, *ex parte,* an order for custody in Scotland. On the day it was served on the mother she applied for a residence order in England. The grandparents appealed against the decision that the English court

---

[56] F.L.A. 1986, s.25.

[57] Family Law Act 1986, s.34. Orders for recovery are discretionary and should not be made *ex parte* because of the risk of additional moves for children: *A. v. A. (Forum Conveniens)* [1999] 1 F.L.R. 1.

[58] [1995] 1 F.L.R. 153; see also *D. v. D. (Custody: Jurisdiction)* [1996] 1 F.L.R. 574, when courts in England and Scotland were seised of the same custody dispute because the parties failed to raise the jurisdictional issue.

[59] F.L.A. 1986, s.15. the new order had to be competently made. The child had presumably lost her habitual residence in Scotland and even possibly gained habitual residence in England after 18 months living there.

[60] Brussels II and the Domicile and Matrimonial Proceedings Act 1973 set out the principles for determining which court has jurisdiction for these proceedings.

[61] F.L.A. 1986, ss.1(1) (a), 2(1), 2A(1), (2), 13 (Scotland), 21 (Northern Ireland); S.I. 2001 No. 310. Brussels II only applies where the child is the child of the spouses. Matrimonial proceedings are treated as continuing until the child reaches 18 (16 in Scotland): s.42(2) (3).

[62] For a discussion of this concept see below para. 21–014.

[63] F.L.A. 1986, ss.2(2), 3 (England and Wales); ss.8, 9, 10, 12, 15(2) (Scotland); ss.19, 20 (Northern Ireland).

[64] Family Law Act 1986, ss.2A 3(1) (b), 10, 20(1) (b); *D. v. D. (Custody: Jurisdiction)* [1996] 1 F.L.R. 574.

[65] [1993] 1 F.L.R. 495; Cretney (1993) 109 *L.Q.R.* 538.

had jurisdiction to decide the mother's applications. Whilst the children were in Scotland with the mother's agreement they were habitually resident there. They had lost this habitual residence when they came to England but had not yet gained habitual residence there. Even though it might appear unfair that a two week holiday visit should be decisive the English court had jurisdiction because the children were present in England and not habitually resident elsewhere.[66]

Proceedings taken in conflict with these provisions are stayed.[67] Furthermore, a child who has been removed from the country of habitual residence without the necessary consents cannot acquire a new habitual residence for a year.[68]

Part I orders granted in one part of the United Kingdom are recognised and enforceable in any other part as if they had been made there.[69] The person in whose favour the order was made requests the court which made the order to send a certified copy of it to the appropriate court[70] for the country where the child has been taken.[71] The order is then registered in that country and an application to enforce it may be made.[72] Any person interested may apply to have the application stayed or dismissed but only on grounds that proceedings are being taken elsewhere or the order has ceased to have effect.[73]

V. INTERNATIONAL ABDUCTION

21–011 Article 11 of the United Nations Convention on the Rights of the Child requires States Parties to take measures to combat the illicit transfer and non-return of children and promote the conclusion of bilateral and multilateral agreements or accession to existing agreements.[74] It has been successful as a catalyst for such agreements; over 70 countries have joined the Hague Convention on the Civil Aspects of International Child Abduction.[75] The United Kingdom is a party to this Convention, the European Convention on the Recognition and Enforcement of Decisions Concerning the Custody of Children[76] and Brussels II.[77] These treaties therefore determine the treatment

---

[66] *per* Balcombe L.J. at 502; F.L.A. 1986, s.3(1) (b).

[67] F.L.A. 1986, ss.5, 14, 22; Brussels II, Art. 11; *Re S. (A Minor) (Stay of Proceedings)* [1993] 2 F.L.R. 912, CA.

[68] F.L.A. 1986, s.41.

[69] *ibid.* s.5.

[70] *ibid.* s.32(1)—the High Court in England and Wales or Northern Ireland, the Court of Session in Scotland.

[71] Family Law Act 1986, s.27.

[72] *ibid.* s.29.

[73] *ibid.* ss.30, 31.

[74] UN Convention on Rights of the Child, Art. 11(2).

[75] By ratification or accession. A current list of countries who are parties to this Convention can be found in on the Hague Conference web site: www.hcch.net

[76] Child Abduction and Custody Act 1985.

[77] Council Regulation 1347/2000 and S.I. 2001 No. 310. Courts exercising jurisdiction under Brussels II must do so in conformity with the Hague Convention, Art. 4 but Brussels II takes precedence over the European Convention, Art.37.

of children abducted to (or from) the United Kingdom to other Convention countries. The United Kingdom has not yet concluded any bilateral agreements, so no special provisions apply to assist the return of a child taken to or from other (non-Convention) countries. Consequently, two distinct regimes are operated by the U.K. courts—the Hague scheme for Convention countries and the common law for everywhere else.

As the freedom of movement between countries increases so does the number of international child custody disputes. World travel is easy and border controls have been reduced between many countries. Many abducted children have dual nationality and are nationals of the state to which they have been taken. The Foreign Office operates a policy of non-interference in such cases because of the general international law principle of comity. This may create an insurmountable obstacle to securing the child's return from a non-Convention country.[78] International child abduction appears to be rising.[79] In 1999 there were approximately 1250 Hague Convention cases world wide[80]; in England and Wales in 1996, 206 applications for return were received and 166 were made.[81] The number of abductions to non-Convention countries is unknown.[82]

Role of the Central Authority[83]

21–012 In every Convention country a designated Central Authority provides direct assistance to parties and their lawyers.[84] The Central Authority for England and Wales is the Lord Chancellor's Department; the work is undertaken in the Child Abduction Unit.[85] Central Authorities are required to co-operate with each other to achieve the objectives of the Convention and secure the return of the child. Their role includes discovering the whereabouts of the child, preventing further harm, securing voluntary return, initiating proceedings[86] and making the administrative arrangements for return.[87] The cost of the child's return falls on the parents. The Central Authority may refuse to handle a case which is manifestly not well founded.[88] Individuals whose

---

78 Van Bueren (1993), p. 6.
79 Beaumont and McEleavy (1999), pp. 14–15.
80 N. Lowe and A. Perry, (a) *Statistical Analysis* Hague Conference, 4th Special Commission (2001) pre doc 3 and (b) "International abduction—the English experience" [1999] I.C.L.Q. 127 (1996 data).
81 Lowe and Perry (a), *op. cit.* p. 129.
82 Reunite received reports of approximately 100 such cases in 1999 see: Carter [2000] I.F.L. 102.
83 C. Bruch, "The Central Authority's role under the Hague Child Abduction Convention: a friend in deed" (1994) 28 Fam. L.Q. 35; Carter [1999] I.F.L. 102.
84 Hague Convention, Art. 6; European Convention, Arts 4, 5; Child Custody and Abduction Act. 1985, ss.3, 14.
85 This is part of the Official Solicitor's Office. Details of this work and links to related sites can be found on the Lord Chancellor's Department web-site: www.lcd.gov.uk
86 Approximately 20% of applications are resolved by agreement. The Child Abduction Unit in London forwards applications to specialist solicitors within 24 hours: Lowe and Perry (1999), p.138.
87 Hague Convention, Art. 7.
88 *ibid.* Art. 27.

children have been abducted are advised to contact any Central Authority.[89] The Central Authority in the home state deals directly with the Central Authority in the country where the child has been taken. It has been said that palpable advantages result from experience and the history of trustworthy professional relationships between staff in the various Central Authorities.[90] Also that the successful operation depends on the mutual confidence of the parties which may be difficult to maintain as the number of members grows.[91]

A. Abduction to a country which has ratified or acceded[92] to the Hague Convention

21–013 The Convention is based on the premise that children's best interests demand that they are not the subject of unilateral removals or retentions.[93] By strictly enforcing return, the Convention seeks to deter abduction, enable the courts in the child's home state to determine disputes and ensure that their orders are respected by other parties to the Convention.[94] Strict enforcement also encourages voluntary return. However, there is a danger that in an individual case the child's welfare will not be furthered by return.[95]

The Child Abduction and Custody Act 1985, Pt I implements the Hague Convention on Civil Aspects of Child Abduction but the key concepts which determine the scope of the Convention are not dependent on their meaning in any single legal system.[96] The Convention applies where a child under 16[97] who is habitually resident in one contracting state is wrongfully removed to, or retained in, another.[98]

---

[89] Lord Chancellor's Department, *Child Abduction* (1997), pp. 8,13.

[90] Bruch, *op. cit.*, p. 48.

[91] *Re E. (Abduction: Non-Convention Country)* [1999] 2 F.L.R. 642 at 646 *per* Thorpe L.J.

[92] In cases of accession the Convention only operates between countries who have accepted the accession.

[93] Beaumont and McEleavy (1999), p. 21.

[94] D. Harris, "Is the strength of the Hague Convention on Child Abduction being diluted by the Courts? The English perspective." [1999] I.L.M. 35; Beaumont and McEleavy (1999), Chap. 4.

[95] For example, if the home state court would agree to their relocation overseas, if the abducting parent is unable or unwilling to return or if the conditions there are adverse, see: M. Kaye, "The Hague Convention and the flight from domestic violence: how women and children are being returned by coach and four." [1999] Int. J. Law Policy and Fam. 191 and para. 21–019, below.

[96] Conclusion of the Second meeting of the Special Commission to discuss the operation of the Convention (1994) The conclusions of the Third (1997) and Fourth Special Commissions (2001) are on the Hague Convention web-site: www.hcch.net and a database of case-law under the convention is available at www.incadat.com

[97] *Re H. (Abduction: Child of 16)* [2000] 2 F.L.R. 930. When implemented, the 1996 Hague Convention on the Protection of Children will apply to those aged 16–18 see: L. Silberman [2000] Fam. L.Q. 239.

[98] Child Abduction and Custody Act 1984, s.13; An order can be obtained even though children are not in England or Wales if there is good reason to think that they will be brought here: *A. v A. (Abduction: Jurisdiction)* [1995] 1 F.L.R. 341.

Habitual residence[99]

21–014 Habitual residence requires voluntary presence in a country for some time,[1] with a settled purpose of remaining there[2]; it is a question of fact whether and when habitual residence is established.[3] A child's habitual residence follows that of the carers but where both parents have parental responsibility the child's habitual residence cannot be changed by one parent acting unilaterally.[4] Where the family divide their time between two homes the child cannot be habitually resident in both places simultaneously but may be habitually resident in either in accordance with the parents' arrangements.[5] Habitual residence may be ended by leaving with the intention not to return. Consequently, the unmarried father in *C. v. S. (Minor) (Abduction: Illegitimate Child)*[6] could not rely on the Convention because the child was no longer habitually resident in Australia after her removal to England but a Swedish mother whose absence from Sweden occurred whilst she studied could reclaim her child from the care of his father in England.[7] There is a fine balance to be struck between denying a child the protection of the Convention by failing to recognise that he or she has established habitual residence, and applying the Convention to return a child to a state with which there is little real connection. For this reason Beaumont and McEleavy have suggested that six months should be treated as a guideline figure for establishing habitual residence.[8]

---

[99] For a detailed analysis of this concept see Beaumont and McEleavy (1999), Chap. 7 and R. Schuz, "Habitual residence under the Hague Abduction Convention—theory and practice" [2001] 1 *C.F.L.Q.* 1.

[1] *C. v S. (Minor: Abduction: Illegitimate Child)* [1990] A.C. 562 at 578 *per* Lord Brandon; the period required may be quite short: *Re F.(A Minor) (Child Abduction)* [1992] 1 F.L.R. 548 (three months); a child may have little real connection with the jurisdiction where any dispute will be heard: see Beaumont and McEleavy (1999), p. 108.

[2] Permanent residence is not required, *Re F. (A Minor) (Child Abduction)* [1992] 1 F.L.R. 548. where the parents had shipped 19 packing cases to Australia they had acquired habitual residence there even though they held return tickets. In *D. v. D. (Custody: Jurisdiction)* [1996] 1 F.L.R. 574, renting a flat, acquiring furniture and buying school uniforms together suggested the parties were habitually resident. A young child, sent to live with relatives in Ghana, did not acquire habitual residence there because the mother had not established that she intended this residence to be long-term: *Re V. (Jurisdiction: Habitual Residence)* [2001] 1 F.L.R. 253, FD.

[3] *Nessa v. Chief Adjudication Officer* [1999] 2 F.L.R. 1116, HL.

[4] *D. v. D. (Custody: Jurisdiction)* [1996] 1 F.L.R. 574 at 581, *per* Hale J. Where parents move abroad but only one becomes habitually resident the children retain their original habitual residence: *Re N. (Abduction: Habitual Residence)* [2000] 2 F.L.R. 899, FD. If the only parent with parental responsibility dies, the child retains their habitual residence: *Re S. (Custody: Habitual Residence)* [1998] 1 F.L.R. 122, HL. A parent with a residence order who removes the child permanently in breach of the Children Act 1989, s.13(2) should not be able to end the child's habitual residence; see Bruch (1993), p. 66.

[5] *Re V. (Abduction: Habitual Residence)* [1995] 2 F.L.R. 992. But a child who never lives in the parents' new state of habitual residence does not acquire habitual residence there: *Al Habtoor v. Fotheringham* [2001] 1 F.L.R. 951; *cf. B. v. H. (Habitual Residence: Wardship)* [2002] 1 F.L.R. 388, *per* Charles J. where the youngest child, who had not entered the U.K. was held to have habitual residence here because his mother had retained her U.K. habitual residence; *cf. W. and B. v. H. (Child Abduction: Surrogacy)* [2002] 1 F.L.R. 1008, FD, where Hedley J. held that a baby had no habitual residence.

[6] [1990] A.C. 562 at 578.

[7] *Re H. (Abduction: Habitual Residence: Consent)* [2000] 2 F.L.R. 294.

[8] *op. cit.*, p. 112.

Wrongful removal or retention

21–015 Removal or retention is wrongful where it is in breach of "rights of custody" attributed to a person, an institution or any other body[9] and actually exercised by them.[10] Thus the unilateral removal of a child by one parent was wrongful because it precluded the other parent who (had equal rights) exercising them.[11] Where a child has staying contact, his or her retention beyond an agreed period is wrongful.[12] Where there is doubt about the legality of the child's removal or retention a declaration of wrongfulness may be sought in the state of habitual residence.[13] It has been said that a declaration of wrongfulness obtained in the state of habitual residence is generally more useful than any *ex parte* order for custody there.[14]

In *Re P. (Abduction: Declaration)*[15] the parents married in Las Vegas in 1990 and came to England where their child was born. After an unsuccessful attempt to remove the child, the mother obtained the court's permission for a visit to California. She then returned to live with the father. In 1992, following contested proceedings, the mother obtained a residence order and permission to remove the child permanently to the USA but she again resumed cohabitation with the father. In January 1994, the parents left the child with her paternal grandparents in London and went to Hawaii to place a second child for adoption and to Egypt for a holiday; the mother then returned to California alone. The mother's sister tricked the grandmother into handing the child to her and took the child to California where the mother sought guardianship.

The father made an application under the Convention but the Californian authorities were unwilling to accept it because of the 1992 order. The Lord Chancellor's Department suggested that the father seek a declaration under the Family Law Act 1985, s.8[16] that the child's removal was wrongful. The declaration was granted. The 1992 residence order had ceased to have effect because of the parents' cohabitation. The Court of Appeal rejected the mother's appeal; even though the declaration involved considering matters

---

9 Art. 3(a); *Re H. (Abduction: Rights of Custody)* [2000] 1 F.L.R. 374, HL. (rights of an Irish court seised of a guardianship application). Where a court has rights of custody the application for return should be made by the person whose application gave rise to the court's rights *per* Lord Mackay at 381H. *Re W, Re B. (Abduction: Unmarried Father)* [1998] 2 F.L.R. 146, Hale J. (English court seised of parental responsibility application); *Re JS. (Private International Adoption)* [2000] 2 F.L.R. 638 (overseas adoption agency).

10 Art. 3.

11 *Re F. (Child Abduction: Risk if Returned)* [1995] 2 F.L.R. 31 at 36, *per* Butler-Sloss L.J. Removal would be an offence under the Child Abduction Act 1984.

12 Retention becomes wrongful when the decision not to return is made even though the period has not expired: *Re S. (Minors) (Abduction: Wrongful Retention)* [1994] Fam. 70.

13 Art. 15.

14 Bruch (1993), p. 60; *cf.* Beaumont and McEleavy (1999), p. 64 who are concerned about delay and suggest that proof of foreign law under Arts 8f and 14 provides a better approach.

15 [1995] 1 F.L.R. 831.

16 Declarations may be made "for the purposes of Art. 15". A declaration could also be granted under the inherent jurisdiction: *Re J. (Abduction: Ward of Court)* [1989] Fam. 85.

which were to be determined by the Californian court, the English court could not refuse to exercise a power given by statute.

A declaration of wrongful removal obtained in the requesting state will not determine the matter because the requested state is free to take its own view of whether the child was habitually resident at the time of removal and whether removal was in breach of custody rights.[17]

Rights of custody

21–016 "Rights of custody" include rights relating to the care of a person and the right to determine a child's place of residence.[18] The existence of "rights of custody" is determined under the law of the country of the child's habitual residence but the question whether rights were breached by bringing a child to England is answered applying English law.[19]

In *Re V-B. (Abduction: Custody Right)*[20] on divorce, a Dutch court had awarded the father contact. Without consulting the father the mother brought the children to Wales. The father sought their return under the Hague Convention but this was refused. Although he had a right to be informed about any matters of importance relating to his children, Dutch law (unlike English law) gave him no rights to object to a move and thus no rights of custody.

Under English law, removal of a child from England and Wales without permission of a person with parental responsibility or in contravention of a residence order[21] is wrongful. It might be thought that a mother who had not married the child's father would be able to move without constraint, and that a father without parental responsibility could not prevent his child being taken abroad.[22] This is not the case if the court has rights of custody because an application for parental responsibility or residence is pending.[23] The English court have taken an even broader view, recognising that person without parental responsibility but involved in caring for a child may have "inchoate rights" which amount to rights of custody.[24]

---

[17] *Re P. (Abduction: Declaration)* [1995] 1 F.L.R. 831 at 838, *per* Millett L.J. Difficulties arise with Art. 15 where the place of habitual residence is disputed.

[18] Art. 5.

[19] *Re F. (Child Abduction: Risk if Returned)* [1995] 2 F.L.R. 31, CA.

[20] [1999] 2 F.L.R. 192, CA.

[21] Children Act 1989, s.13(1) (b) (2). Similarly, if the child is a ward or there is a prohibited steps order.

[22] This was the basis of the claim under E.C.H.R., Art. 14 by the father in *B. v. U.K.* [2000] 1 F.L.R. 1 which was held inadmissible.

[23] *Re H. (Abduction: Rights of Custody)* [2000] 1 F.L.R. 374, HL. The court gains rights of custody when the relevant application is served *per* Lord Mackay at 380F. The view of the Child Abduction Unit reported in *Practice Note* [1998] 1 F.L.R. 491 is no longer tenable.

[24] *Re B. (A Minor) (Abduction)* [1994] 2 F.L.R. 249, CA *per* Waite L.J. Staunton L.J. held that an agreement between the parents for the child's care gave the father "rights of custody". Peter Gibson L.J. dissented. *Re O. (Child Abduction: Custody Rights)* [1997] 2 F.L.R. 702 (grand parents). This development is criticised by Beaumont and McEleavy (1999), p.60 but it ensures

Proceedings

21–017 A person whose rights have been breached may apply via the Central Authority in their country. Central Authority will arrange for the necessary proceedings and also seek to negotiate voluntary return.[25] In England and Wales legal aid is provided[26] but the Convention does not require states to provide legal aid unless it is available to nationals.[27] Proceedings are peremptory; the courts are forbidden to investigate the merits of the case[28] and are required to return the child unless one of the conditions in Articles 12 or 13 applies.[29] The High Court has a good record in processing cases speedily.[30] Judges have been known to make arrangements with judges overseas to facilitate return.[31] Some children are interviewed by welfare officers at the Royal Courts of Justice.[32] There is no right to give oral evidence and it is rarely heard.[33] Strict limits on the use of oral evidence may make procedures more expeditious and fairer for the left behind parent but doubts have been expressed about the ability of English courts to assess claims under Art. 13b from affidavits alone.[34]

Return is mandatory if the child was taken less than 12 months before,[35] unless, at the time of the removal, the applicant was not exercising custody rights or consented to it, or subsequently acquiesced; there is grave risk of physical or psychological harm if the child is returned; or a mature child objects.[36] If the abduction has lasted for longer, the child must be returned unless settled in the new environment.[37] Where the court has a discretion to order return it must

---

that there is no discrimination against those without parental responsibility who have E.C.H.R., Art. 8 rights.

25 As required by Art. 10. Reunite is piloting a mediation scheme.

26 Non-means, non merit-tested Legal Representation is available to the applicant for return under the Hague or European Conventions see: Legal Services Commission, *Funding Code* (1999) para. 11.13 and *The Funding Code—decision-making guidance* (2001) para. 20.24. Public funding is only available to defend proceedings under the criteria in section 11 of the code (means and merit testing).

27 Art. 26. In the USA no legal aid is available but some inter bar agreements have been made for the provision of a pro bono counsel.

28 Art. 19.

29 The Convention is "draconian" in its adherence to summary return: *Re M. (Abduction: Psychological Harm)* [1997] 2 F.L.R. 690 at 694 *per* Butler-Sloss L.J.

30 see Lowe and Perry (1999), pp. 138–9.

31 *Re M. and J. (Abduction: International Judicial Co-operation)* [2000] 1 F.L.R. 803, Singer J. Hague Conference, *Best practices* (2000) para. 1e emphasises the value of direct communication between judges.

32 *Re T. (Abduction: Child's Objections to Return)* [2000] 2 F.L.R. 192, CA (the 11 year-old girl also wrote letters to the court).

33 *Re E. (A Minor) (Abduction)* [1989] 1 F.L.R. 135, CA; *Re F. (A Minor) (Child Abduction)* [1992] 1 F.L.R. 548, CA.

34 Harris (1999), p. 44.

35 Art. 12. Judicial refusals to return occurred in only about 5% of Lowe and Perry's sample, *op. cit.*, p.143.

36 Art. 13. Art 13 provides a limited mechanism through which the courts can take a more traditional child-oriented approach: J. Caldwell "Child welfare defences in child abduction cases—some recent developments" [2001] *C.F.L.Q.* 121.

37 Art. 12; *Re N. (Minors) (Abduction)* [1991] 1 F.L.R. 413 Bracewell J. A parent who has concealed the child's whereabouts cannot rely on this to argue that the child is settled: *Re L. (Abduction: Pending Criminal Proceedings)* [1999] 1 F.L.R.433 at 441.

balance the welfare of the child against the fundamental purpose of the Convention.[38] The normal expectation is that the court will order the child's return even where one of the exceptions applies[39] unless the applicant was seeking a tactical advantage or return would lead to children yo-yoing between countries.[40] But where the applicant fails to pursue the application for return it may be struck out.[41] The English courts are regarded as thoughtful and sophisticated in their interpretation of the Hague Convention.[42]

Article 13a—consent or acquiescence

21–018 A parent who has agreed to the relocation of a child cannot subsequently claim their peremptory return. The concept of acquiescence is potentially broad; but the courts have been careful not to discourage amicable settlements by including negotiation within the definition. Except where the action is unequivocal, acquiescence depends on the subjective intentions of the wronged parent; it must be established by the parent resisting return.[43] The following have been held to amount to acquiescence: failing to object when the wife gave up her job and cancelled the child's nursery place[44]; taking the wife and the children to the airport knowing they were making a one-way trip[45]; writing to the abductor that the father was not going to fight for custody[46] and taking no action to oppose an application for residence.[47] Acquiescence requires some knowledge that action could be taken but a full understanding of the position under the Convention was not necessary[48]:—

> In *Re. S. (Minors) (Acquiescence)*[49] the mother removed three boys from Australia to England. The father immediately consulted solicitors who told him (incorrectly) that they required $5000 before they could take any action. He consulted another firm and was told it would be difficult to obtain an order in respect of the older children because they were British. Subsequently a law student who joined the firm advised him to apply to the Central Authority. He did so and began proceedings under the Convention.

---

[38] *Re D. (Abduction: Discretionary Return)* [2000] 1 F.L.R. 24 (return ordered); *Re D. (Abduction: Acquiescence)* [1999] 1 F.L.R. 53 (return refused).

[39] Clarke Hall and Morrison, Vol. 2, para. 61.

[40] *Re A. (Minors) (Abduction: Acquiescence) (No. 2)* [1993] Fam. 1; *cf.* C. Bruch, "International child abduction: the experience under the 1980 Hague Convention" in Eekelaar and Sarcevic (eds.) (1994), pp. 353, 356.

[41] *Re G. (Abduction: Striking Out Application)* [1995] 2 F.L.R. 410.

[42] Bruch (1993) 78.

[43] *Re H. (Abduction: Acquiescence)* [1998] A.C. 72 *per* Lord Browne-Wilkinson at 88F.

[44] *Re M. (Abduction) (Consent: Acquiescence)* [1999] 1 F.L.R 171.

[45] *Re R. (Abduction: Acquiescence)* [1999] 2 F.L.R. 818.

[46] *Re A. (Minors) (Abduction: Custody Rights)* [1992] Fam. 106, CA. But a statement that the father would not take "heroic action" did not amount to acquiescence: *Re R. (Child Abduction: Acquiescence)* [1995] 1 F.L.R. 716, CA.

[47] *Re AZ. (A Minor) (Abduction: Acquiescence)* [1993] 1 F.L.R. 682, CA.

[48] *Re A. (A Minor) (Abduction: Custody Rights)* [1992] Fam. 106 at 119–120, *per* Stuart-Smith L.J.

[49] [1994] 1 F.L.R. 819, CA.

Despite the passage of eight months[50] (and fortunately for the firms' insurers) the father was held not to have acquiesced in the boys' removal.

Article 13b—grave risk of harm or an intolerable situation

21–019 The court requires clear and compelling evidence of grave risk or harm or intolerability; this must be substantial and more severe than would necessarily result from an unwelcome return.[51] In *N v. N (Abduction: Article 13 Defence)*[52] the father's mental illness, some evidence of sexual abuse and the children's disturbance were insufficient to justify refusal to return. But in *Re F. (Child Abduction: Risk of Return)*[53] return was refused because the four-year-old who had been abused and observed violence by his father to his mother and grandmother exhibited fear and disturbance (bedwetting and aggression) at the suggestion of return to the place where the violence had occurred. Some harm is inevitable, the abductor cannot rely on harm which results from their behaviour.[54] But where siblings have refused to return[55] or the caring abductor's mental health will seriously deteriorate on return,[56] the risk to the child may be sufficiently grave.

The power of the court in the state of return to grant injunctions[57] and undertakings, for example to provide a home and financial support for the abductor, are accepted by the English courts as mitigating the potential harm of return.[58] However, in some states these may be disregarded with impunity with dire consequences for the returning parent and children.[59] The narrow approach of the court to Article 13a and its willingness to accept undertakings has been criticised, particularly for failing to recognise the impact of domestic violence.[60]

---

[50] But in *W. v. W. (Child Abduction: Acquiescence)* [1993] 2 F.L.R. 211 the father's failure to take action for 10 months after hearing of his wife's refusal to return the children amounted to acquiescence.

[51] *Re C. (Abduction: Grave Risk of Psychological Harm)* [1999] 1 F.L.R. 1145 *per* Ward L.J. at 1154.

[52] [1995] 1 F.L.R. 107. Similarly in *Re S. (Abduction: Return into Care)* [1999] 1 F.L.R. 845 where the mother had separated from the abuser and there would be a social services assessment.

[53] [1995] 2 F.L.R. 31, CA.

[54] *Re L. (Child Abduction) (Psychological Harm)* [1993] 2 F.L.R. 401 (return of the child alone); *Re C. (Abduction: Grave Risk of Physical or Psychological Harm)* [1999] 2 F.L.R. 479 (separation of siblings).

[55] *B. v. K. (Child Abduction)* [1993] 1 F.C.R. 382.

[56] *Re G. (Abduction: Psychological Harm)* [1995] 1 F.L.R. 64.

[57] *TB. v. JB. (Abduction: Grave Risk of Harm)* [2001] 2 F.L.R. 515, CA the majority of the Court of Appeal were satisfied that a woman who had been terrorised by her husband's violence would be protected by a court order.

[58] *Re O. (Child Abduction: Undertakings)* [1994] 2 F.L.R. 349; *Re M. (Abduction; Non-Convention Country)* [1995] 1 F.L.R. 89, CA.

[59] M. Kaye, "The Hague Convention and the flight from domestic violence: how women and children are being returned by coach and four." [1999] Int. J. Law Policy and Fam. 191; in a small study by Reunite undertakings were breached in 11 of the 14 cases where they were given: Reunite, *Information document March 2001* (2001). Undertakings may be regarded as undermining the exclusive jurisdiction of the court of habitual residence: Society for Advanced Legal Study, Family Law Working Group, *Report on the cross border movement of children* (1999), p. 75.

[60] *ibid.*

The child's objections

21–020 A child's objections will only be sufficient where they are strongly held and relate to the return to be ordered.[61] Children are not usually separately represented in these proceedings.[62] Although the court has respected the views of children as young as seven[63] it has not accepted that the child's objections determine the matter.[64] Rational objections from a child are more likely to be persuasive[65] and where a mature child objects on their own behalf and for a younger sibling, the court has held that neither should be returned.[66] The court is "rightly sceptical of attempts by parents to invoke art 13 to try to stave off the almost inevitable requirement to return the child."[67] However, cases where return has been ordered but children's behaviour has convinced airline staff not to take them indicates that the courts cannot always assess the strength of children's feelings.[68]

In terms of numbers of ratifications and the operation of its provisions, the Hague Convention must be regarded as successful. In terms of promoting the welfare of children, it is unclear the extent to which it has deterred abduction. However, the narrow approach to Article 13 and the lack of mechanisms to secure the well-being of those who have been returned means that it has adversely impacted on some children. There is a danger that unless these concerns are addressed the Convention will not retain the high regard that it has achieved.

Abduction within Europe

21–021 The Hague Convention applies within Europe but there are two further regimes for the recognition and enforcement of decision relating to children.[69] The Hague Convention takes precedence over both Brussels II and the earlier European Convention.[70] Proceedings under these regimes are only important where Hague proceedings have been completed or the issue is the enforcement of contact.

---

[61] *Re S. (Minors) (Abduction: Custody Rights)* [1993] Fam. 242; *Re R. (A Minor: Abduction)* [1992] F.L.R. 105 at 107.

[62] *Re S. (Abduction: Separate Representation)* [1997 1 F.L.R. 486 is a rare exception.

[63] *B. v. K. (Child Abduction)* [1993] 1 F.C.R. 382; see also *Re R. (Child Abduction: Acquiescence)* [1995] 1 F.L.R. 716 at 729–30.

[64] *Re S. (Minors) (Abduction; Custody Rights)* [1993] Fam. 242.

[65] See *Re B. (Abduction: Children's Objections)* [1999] 1 F.L.R. 667.

[66] *Re T. (Abduction: Child's Objections to Return)* [2000] 2 F.L.R. 192, CA.

[67] *Re P. (Abduction: Minor's Views)* [1998] 2 F.L.R. 825, CA *per* Butler-Sloss L.J. at 827. Here the 13 year-old boy had run away and lived rough after return had been ordered. The child's appeal was allowed and the case remitted.

[68] *TB. v. JB. (Abduction: Grave Risk of Harm)* [2001] 2 F.L.R. 515, CA; *Re HB. (Abduction: Children's Objection) (No. 2)* [1998] 1 F.L.R. 654 (11 year-old girl) and for the subsequent outcome see: B. Hale, "The view from court 45" [1999] *C.F.L.Q.* 377 at 378.

[69] All the States which have ratified the European Convention have also ratified the Hague Convention; all but Denmark are also subject to Brussels II.

[70] Hague Convention Art 16; Child Abduction and Custody Act 1985, s.9(b); *Re R. (Abduction: Hague and European Conventions)* [1997] 1 F.L.R. 663, CA. Council Regulation 1347/2000, Art. 37.

The European Convention on Recognition and Enforcement of Decisions Concerning the Custody of Children[71] is implemented by Part II of the Child Abduction and Custody Act 1985. It seeks to spare children the unsettling effect of a potential conflict of orders for custody or contact in different jurisdictions.[72] It enables a person who has obtained an order, relating to the custody of or access to a child under 16[73] in a contracting state[74] to have that decision recognised and enforced in another contracting state.[75] This includes an order made prior to the ratification of the Convention[76] or after the child has been improperly removed.[77] For further details of this Convention see the sixth edition of this work.

Brussels II similarly seeks to ensure that only one court can make matrimonial orders, including orders in relation to the spouses' children when a court in a Member State is seised of proceedings for divorce, nullity or legal separation.[78] The jurisdictional rules are strict but non-recognition of "parental responsibility"[79] judgments is permitted in limited circumstances. Recognition may be refused where recognition is manifestly contrary to public policy because for example it fails to take account of the child's best interests, if procedurally flawed because of defects in the service of the parties or it was made without giving the child or other person with parental responsibility an opportunity to be heard, or because it is irreconcilable with a later, recognised order. Applications for enforcement are made to the relevant court of the State where enforcement is sought, no special procedures apply.[80]

B. Abduction under the common law (from or to a country which has not ratified the Hague Convention)

21–022 The welfare principle governs applications for return of children abducted from non-Convention countries.[81] These cases are also dealt with by peremptory return because the child's welfare is usually best served by decisions being made

---

[71] Also known as the Luxembourg Convention. For a list of States Parties see the Lord Chancellor's Department web-site: www.lcd.gov.uk

[72] *Re A. (Foreign Access Order: Enforcement)* [1996] 1 F.L.R. 561 at 567, *per* Waite L.J.

[73] Arts. 4 and 11. This includes residence and contact orders; see Child Abduction and Custody Act 1985, s.27(1), Sched. 3.

[74] Child Abduction and Custody Act 1985, s.13.

[75] *ibid.* s.15 and Arts. 4 and 7.

[76] *Re L. (Child Abduction: European Convention)* [1992] 2 F.L.R. 178.

[77] Arts 1, 12; *Re S. (Custody: Habitual Residence)* [1998] 1 F.L.R. 122, HL. Such orders are referred to a "chasing orders". But such orders cannot be made if the court's jurisdiction has been suspended under Brussels II, for example because one parent has commenced divorce proceedings in another E.U. Member State: Child Abduction and Custody Act 1985, s.12(3), added by S.I. 2001 No. 310.

[78] For the background to the regulation see: [1998] O.J. C221/27 Explanatory Report by Dr A. Borras. The limitations of this regulation have been recognised; a new draft regulation (Brussels IIBis) which will apply to all orders relating to parental responsibility (guardianship, residence and contact) is under discussion see: I. Karsten [2001] *Fam. Law* 885 at 914.

[79] Art. 3; this is a wide term covering such matters as residence and contact: see D. Truex [2001] I.F.L. 7.

[80] Arts 21–23.

[81] *Re JA. (Abduction: Non-Convention Country)* [1998] 1 F.L.R. 231, CA. (U.A.E.) return refused; *Re E. (Abduction: Non-Convention Country)* [1999] 2 F.L.R. 642, CA (Sudan) return ordered.

in a court which has direct knowledge of the prevailing conditions in the child's home state.[82] A full investigation on the merits precludes the speedy return necessary to minimise disruption to the child's relationships with family and culture.[83] Underlying peremptory return is the principle of international comity, the assumption that judges in the state of habitual residence will provide a fair hearing for the dispute.[84] The courts in England and Wales will not reject an application for return merely because the requesting parent resides in a country which applies the very different notions of welfare of Muslim Law.[85]

> In *Re E. (Abduction: Non-Convention Country)* the mother and father, both Sudanese, divorced. The mother remarried and sought custody of her three children but an order was made for them to live with her family and later with the father's family. Remarriage disqualified her from custody but the mother retained contact. The mother and her second husband came to England with the children and claimed asylum.[86] The father's application for peremptory return was successful and the mother's appeal was dismissed. The future of these Sudanese children should be determined by the Sudanese courts.

However, peremptory return to a non-Convention country should not be ordered merely by analogy with the Hague Convention.[87] Agreement or acquiescence should be taken into account but without automatically applying the Hague approach.[88]

A parent wishing to use legal means to obtain the child's return from a non-contracting state may seek an order directing the child's return,[89] try to have the

---

[82] But other matters such as the availability of legal aid to both parties may justify a merits hearing in England rather than overseas, at least if the child has a substantial connection here: *H. v. H. (forum conveniens)* [1993] 1 F.L.R. 959.

[83] *Re L. (Minors) (Wardship: Jurisdiction)* [1974] 1 All E.R.913 at 926 *per* Buckley L.J.

[84] *Re M. (Abduction: Peremptory Return Order)* [1996] 1 F.L.R. 478 at 480 *per* Waite L.J. Behind this is the hope that courts overseas will take the same approach if children are abducted from England, see: Setright [2000] I.F.L. 125 at 127.

[85] *Re E. (Abduction: Non-Convention Country)* [1999] 2 F.L.R. 642 at 650 *per* Thorpe L.J. Thorpe L.J. apparently thought that there should be no inquiry into the family justice standards applying in the state of habitual residence because no such inquiry was made in Convention countries. However, in *Re JA.* [1998] 1 F.L.R. 231, CA the mother's inability to obtain an order for relocation to the U.K. justified a finding that return was contrary to the child's welfare.

[86] The asylum application had not been determined when the children's return was ordered. The mother's treatment as a remarried woman might possibly enable her to satisfy the test of "well founded fear of persecution for reasons of membership of a particular social group" (Convention relating to the Status of Refugees, Art. 1A(2) see: *R. v. Immigration Appeal Tribunal ex p. Shah* [1999] 2 All E.R. 545, HL where women victims of domestic violence in Pakistan had arguable claims for asylum.

[87] *Re JA. (Abduction: Non-Convention Country)* [1998] 1 F.L.R. 231 at 234 *per* Ward L.J.

[88] *Re Z. (Abduction: Non-Convention Country)* [1999] 1 F.L.R. 1270.

[89] A residence order or an order in wardship: *Re V. (Jurisdiction: Habitual Residence)* [2001] 1 F.L.R. 253, FD (the child must be habitually resident in the U.K.). But wardship cannot be exercised to punish a person unless they are in contempt of court: *Re B. (Child Abduction: Wardship: Power to Detain)* [1994] 2 F.L.R. 479. The father who had abducted the children to Algeria could not be imprisoned to secure return of the children who had been warded by their mother. A bench warrant could be used to bring a person before the court.

abductor extradited[90] for abduction and reclaim the child, or bring proceedings in the country where the child is now living. Limited help may be available through the Foreign and Commonwealth Office.[91] Despite the wide-scale ratification of the Convention on the Rights of the Child many countries remain where foreign orders are not recognised and action by a non-national is almost bound to fail.

VI. ENFORCING CONTACT DECISIONS

21–023 The Hague Convention contains no mandatory provisions to enforce contact comparable with its provisions relating to custody.[92] It imposes no duties whatever on the courts and creates no rights which parents can directly enforce.[93] However, Central Authorities are bound to promote the peaceful enjoyment of access rights and to remove obstacles to their enforcement.[94] Unless they have obtained an order which is enforceable under Brussels II,[95] those wishing to enforce contact in England and Wales must apply for a section 8 contact order.[96] The Central Authority arranges for a solicitor but there is no special provision of legal aid.[97] It is accepted that satisfactory contact may reduce abduction, that the desire to enforce contact may lead to an application for the child's peremptory return and that the existing provisions are weak. The development of better mechanisms for the enforcement of contact is under active consideration.[98]

Orders relating to contact[99] can be registered and enforced under Brussels II

---

[90] See: Home Office, *The law of extradition* (2001), App. D for a list of countries with whom the U.K. has extradition treaties.

[91] See *Practice Direction* [1984] 3 All E.R. 640 and Lord Chancellor's Department, *Child Abduction* (1997), p.10–12. *Re KR. (Abduction: Forcible removal by Parents)* [1999] 2 F.L.R. 542 is a striking example of co-operation (following proceedings instituted by her sister) to facilitate the return of a child abducted to India.

[92] A. Anton, "The Hague Convention on International Child Abduction" (1981) 30 I.C.L.Q. 537 at 554 and N. Lowe, "Problems relating to access disputes under the Hague Convention on International Child Abduction" (1994) 8 Int. J. Law and Fam. 374: Beaumont and McEleavy (1999), Chap.12. Abduction which interferes with access does not give rise to summary return if the wronged person does not have rights of custody: *S. v. H. (Abduction: Access Rights)* [1997] 1 F.L.R. 971.

[93] *per* Hoffman L.J. in *Re G. (A Minor) (Enforcement of Access Abroad)* [1993] Fam. 216 at 229.

[94] Hague Convention, Art. 21. But this does not require the enforcement of a contact order against the wishes of a 13-year-old girl: *Re H. (A Minor) (Foreign Custody Order)* [1994] Fam. 105, CA.

[95] Council Regulation 1347/2000. Contact orders made in one part of the U.K. can be enforced in another under Family Law Act 1986, s.25.

[96] *Re G. (A Minor) (Enforcement of Access Abroad)* [1993] Fam. 216 at 229. A foreign order would be entitled to "grave consideration" but the child's welfare is the paramount consideration: *McKee v. McKee* [1951] A.C. 352 at 365.

[97] *Re T. and others (Minors) (Hague Convention: Access)* [1993] 2 F.L.R. 617 at 622–3.

[98] Using the Hague Convention on the Protection of Children (1996), Brussels IIBis or (draft) Council of Europe Convention on Contact concerning children, see: W. Duncan, *Transfrontier access/contact* Hague Conference 4th Special Commission Prel doc 4 (2001).

[99] Child Abduction and Custody Act 1985, s.27(4); A-M. Hutchinson, "Enforcement of contact orders and the Luxembourg Convention" [2000] I.F.L. 106.

or the European Convention; the basis for enforcement is the same as for custody orders.[1] Orders may not be varied under the Convention but the court may fix conditions for their implementation.[2]

VII. ABDUCTION AND HUMAN RIGHTS

21–024 The European Convention on Human Rights should not be interpreted so as to undermine the objectives of the Hague Convention.[3] Article 20 of the Hague Convention permits refusal of return where return would breach fundamental principles of human rights in the requested state but was not included in the U.K. implementing legislation.[4] The fact that unmarried fathers do not automatically have "rights of custody" does not necessarily amount to discrimination against them under the E.C.H.R.[5] Parents' right to relocate are not absolute[6]; nor can the E.C.H.R. justify precluding relocation which is in the child's best interests. Peremptory return can be justified in terms of E.C.H.R., Art. 8(2) in order to protect the child's relationship with the other parent.[7] Similarly, the emphasis on peremptory return and the absence of the wronged parent may justify a more limited hearing than of an ordinary residence dispute. Speed is of the essence so that delay may mean that the trial is unfair.[8] Where return had been ordered, the failure of the requested state to take action to enforce the order has amounted to a breach of the mother's rights under Article 8.[9] However, the European Court has accepted, at least in cases relating to contact, that those seeking to enforce orders bear substantial responsibility for the conduct and direction of the proceedings.[10]

---

[1] See above para. 21–021.

[2] European Convention, Art. 11. It was therefore wrong to allow staying access in England when a father sought recognition and enforcement for the order of a French court granting staying access in France see: *Re A. (Foreign Access Order: Enforcement)* [1996] 1 F.L.R. 561, CA. Enforcement does not necessarily follow registration: *Re H. (A Minor) (Foreign Custody Order)* [1994] Fam. 105.

[3] E.C.H.R., Art 53; Mole [2000] I.F.L. 121, 123.

[4] Regard may be had to Art. 20 on the interpretation of the other exceptions to return: *Re K. (Abduction: Psychological Harm)* [1995] 2 F.L.R. 550 at 557E *per* Leggatt L.J.

[5] Art. 14; *B. v. U.K.* [2000] 1 F.L.R. 1; the E.C.H.R. declared the father's application inadmissible but in *Sahin v. Germany, Sommerfield v. Germany* [2002] 1 F.L.R. 119 provisions in German law which made it more difficult for unmarried fathers to obtain contact were held to breach Arts. 6,8 and 14.

[6] Art. 2 of the Fourth Protocol (which has not been ratified by the U.K.) guarantees freedom of movement but does not prevent a restrictive residence order being made in relation to children see: Beaumont and McEleavy (1999), p. 175.

[7] *Payne v. Payne* [2001] 1 F.L.R. 1052, CA.

[8] In *Larson v. Sweden* App 33250/96 the Commission held that a delay of one year (six months of which was due to a request to delay from the applicant) was not excessive.

[9] *Ignaccolo-Zenide v. Romania* E.C.H.R. App. 31679/96.

[10] *Glaser v. U.K.* [2001] 1 F.L.R. 153 (no violation of the father's Art. 6 or 8 rights arising from delays and inability to enforce English contact order in Scotland) *cf. Hokkanen v. Finland* [1996] 1 F.L.R. 289.

VIII. CONCLUSION

21–025 The number of countries which have ratified the Conventions continues to increase but major parts of the world remain beyond its reach. Although implementation is considered generally to be good there have been difficulties with some countries,[11] and proceedings are slow.[12] Despite provisions for mandatory return, the Lord Chancellor's Department succeeded in obtaining return in only half the cases where children were taken to Convention countries.[13] In contrast, two-thirds of parents bringing proceedings in England and Wales were successful.[14] Courts may be expanding the use of the defences and refusing return more readily.[15] Low success rates undermine the deterrent effects of the Conventions; lack of provision for repatriation and legal costs limit their effectiveness, and the changing nature of abduction calls into question the broad application of summary return.

---

[11] Beaumont and McEleavy (1999), p.241; *Ignaccolo-Zenide v. Romania* E.C.H.R. App. 31679/96.

[12] A. Dyer, "The Hague Convention—towards global co-operation, its successes and failures" (1993) 1 Int. J. of Children's Rights 273, 275, 284. England and Wales have a good record for handling cases speedily see: Lowe and Perry (1999) *op. cit.* pp.138–143.

[13] Lowe and Perry (1999) *op. cit.* p. 145. Half these cases were unresolved at the end of the study.

[14] *ibid.*

[15] L. Silberman, "The Hague Children's Conventions" in *Cross Currents* (S. Katz *et al.*, ed., 2000) 589 at 596; J. Caldwell [2001] *C.F.L.Q.* 121 at 136. The authors disagree whether this development is good or bad.

CHAPTER TWENTY-TWO

LOCAL AUTHORITIES

I. INTRODUCTION

22–001 In this Chapter we consider questions about the state's role in supporting children and their carers, the proper limits of state interference in family life and the allocation of decision-making responsibility between the state (courts or local authorities) and individual members of the family. These are human rights issues; the state has obligations to protect children from abuse which may amount to inhuman treatment[1] and to respect family life. Action taken to safeguard children, for example their removal from parents disrupts family life, and must be limited to protect their Article 8 rights and those of their parents.[2]

Despite "the most comprehensive and far reaching reform of child law in living memory"[3] intended to bring "clarity and consistency"[4] this remains an area of legal complexity but one where decisions may be made by social workers[5] without legal advice and by lay magistrates rather than professional judges. Social workers are central but legal agencies play a crucial role in defining problems,[6] determining disputes and ensuring the accountability of public authorities. The Children Act 1989 brought increased legalism, the Human Rights Act 1998 has added a further layer, the caselaw of the European Court of Human Rights.[7] Public child law has become a specialist area of practice.

The development of the social services[8]

22–002 In 1889, following campaigns from voluntary organisations particularly the NSPCC, the first child protection legislation was enacted; parents could be pro-

---

1 Art. 3; *Z. v. U.K.* [2001] 2 F.L.R. 612. The failure of the local authority to take action to protect children from abuse in their family amounted to a breach of Arts 3 and 13. Compensation was awarded. And see discussion of *X. v. Bedfordshire C. C.* [1995] 2 A.C. 633, HL, below.

2 Arts 6 and 8; *W., R., O., B., H. v. United Kingdom* (1988) 10 E.H.R.R. 29 also reported as *R. v. U. K.* [1988] 2 F.L.R. 445 (restriction on contact which could not be challenged violated Arts 6 and 8); *K. and T. v. Finland* [2001] 2 F.L.R. 707 (emergency removal of child for his protection violated Art. 8); *Olsson v Sweden* (1988) 11 E.H.R.R. 259 (separate placement and distant placement of children violated Art. 8)

3 *per* Lord Mackay, Lord Chancellor Children Bill, Second Reading, *Hansard* H.L. Vol. 502, col. 488.

4 *The law on child care and family services* (Cm. 62, 1987), para. 4.

5 Social workers are required to register with the General Social Care Council (or its equivalent for Wales): Care Standards Act 2000, ss.58, 58 and 61.

6 C. Grace, *Social Workers, Children and the Law* (1994); N. Parton, *Governing the family* (1991).

7 H.R.A. 1998, s.2.

8 See generally, H. Hendrick, *Child welfare England 1972–1989* (1994); R. Parker "The Gestation of reform: the Children Act 1948" in P. Bean and S. MacPherson, *Approaches to Welfare* (1983); J. Masson "From Curtis to Waterhouse: State care and child protection in the U.K. 1945–20" in *Cross Currents* (S. Katz *et al.* eds 2000).

secuted for child cruelty and their children could be removed.[9] Although the guardians, and subsequently local authorities, had responsibilities for poor children in need of relief under the Poor Law and could be appointed as "fit persons" for children removed under the child protection legislation,[10] there was no comprehensive child care service until the welfare state was established in 1948. Many children were cared for by voluntary organisations such as Dr Barnardo's in homes which had been set up by philanthropists in the nineteenth century. The accommodation provided for children ranged from gloomy, unmodernised workhouses which also housed the elderly and disturbed, and spartan, barrack type buildings, to bright purpose-built cottages[11]; children were also boarded out with families.[12] The quality of care also varied enormously. There were few trained social workers, and welfare work in the community was largely provided by the clergy, family doctors, their wives and other volunteers.

Child care became part of the Welfare State. The Children Act 1948 gave local authorities responsibility for orphans and children whose parents were unable to look after them but voluntary organisations continued to play a major role. Local authorities were required to establish Children's Committees and appoint a specialist Children's Officer.[13] In 1968 the policy of specialisation was rejected by the Seebohm Committee which considered that integrated social services, staffed by generic social workers, would permit a more comprehensive response to problems.[14] This re-organisation was implemented in 1970. In consequence, child care became one of the services provided by teams of social workers acting under a Director of Social Services responsible to the Social Services Committee.[15] However, the legal knowledge and skills required for child care work were increasingly seen as demanding specialists; local authorities re-introduced "children and families teams" and now experience difficulties in providing integrated services where parents have problems (mental ill-health

---

[9] Prevention of Cruelty to Children Act 1889; Hendrick, *op. cit.* pp. 49–64; H. Ferguson, "Cleveland in history" in R. Cooter (ed.) *In the name of the child* (1992).

[10] For a contemporary account of child care before the Children Act 1948, see *Report of the Care of Children Committee,* Cmd.6922 (1945) (*Curtis Report*). This report was one of the factors leading to the passing of the Children Act 1948, see: S. Cretney "The State as Parent: the Children Act 1948 in retrospect" (1998) 114 *L.Q.R.* 419.

[11] *ibid.* paras 140, 234, 236. Those who believe in progress should read accounts of residential care in A. Levy and B. Kahan, *The Pindown Experience and the Protection of Children* (1991).

[12] The death of one such child, Dennis O'Neill, was the subject of an inquiry in 1945. Report on the circumstances which led to the Boarding out of Dennis and Terence O'Neill at Bank Farm Minsterley, and the steps taken to supervise their welfare, (Cmd. 6636, 1945) (*Monckton Report*).

[13] Children Act 1948, ss.39, 41. On the important role of this official, see J. Packman, *The child's generation* (1981), pp. 9–12.

[14] Committee on Local Authority and Allied Personal Services, (Cmnd. 3703, 1968). For a discussion of the evolution of social policy over this period, see J. Cooper, *The Creation of the British Personal Social Services 1962–1974* (1983).

[15] Local Authority Social Services Act 1970, ss.2, 3, 6. The Committee may establish sub-committees and may delegate: s.4. Not all members of the committees need be members of the local authority, but a majority of the members of the Social Services Committee must be so, and at least one member of a sub-committee must be so. Although the local authority delegates its functions to the Committee, the duties remain those of the local authority itself: *R v. Birmingham C. C., ex p. O.* [1983] A.C. 578. For accounts of the characteristics of social services departments, see reports from the Social Services Inspectorate and reports of inquiries into child deaths *e.g.* Haringey: *Inquiry into the death of Victoria Climbie* (forthcoming).

or disability) which require support from an "adult team."[16] Many local authorities have established adoption units so that they can develop adoption services; specialist youth offending teams have been convened to work with young offenders. Local authority re-organisation, particularly the creation of unitary authorities, has meant that social services functions are exercised by far more authorities some of which are too small to provide a range of specialist services.[17]

Not all state social services for children were the responsibility of the Social Services Committee. The National Health Service provided respite care for handicapped children and long-term care in hospitals for some who were severely disabled.[18] The Children Act 1989 gave local authorities powers to provide such care and responsibilities towards all children living away from home other than those cared for by close relatives.[19] Social services staff still need to work in conjunction with other welfare workers, particularly health visitors who have special responsibilities for the under fives, educational welfare officers who handle problems of non-attendance at school, and voluntary organisations which still perform an important role providing specialist services, for example supporting young people leaving care.[20] The private sector has also grown, running fostering and residential services, and providing placements to local authorities. A mixed economy of care has developed.[21]

There have been major changes in the demands on social services and the services provided. The re-discovery of child abuse in the 1960's led to increasing social work attention being given to child protection. Procedures were introduced to formalise response and substantial amounts of staff time became devoted to child protection investigations.[22] "Abuse and neglect" is now the main reason for children entering the public care system, and more than a quarter of children receiving services in the community do so because of such concerns.[23] Poverty and substance abuse have also increased, undermining parents' abilities to care for children adequately. Children's departments initially focussed on looking after children and made considerable use of residential homes. From the early 1960's they were given powers to provide services to

---

[16] D.H., *Children Act Now: messages from research* (2001), p.110 and see *Re W. and B. (Care Plan)* [2001] 2 F.L.R. 582.

[17] G. Craig and J. Manthorpe, *Unfinished business? Local government re-organisation and social services* (1999).

[18] Under National Assistance Act 1948, s.21.

[19] Children Act 1989, ss.17, 24, 62, 64, 67 and 85–87. Services for under 18s do not come within the National Health Service and Community Care Act 1990, s.42(1). Regulation and inspection of children's homes is now a matter for the National Care Standards Commission established under the Care Standards Act 2000.

[20] "The Government believes that voluntary organisations can offer a flexible and innovative approach, extending choice and variety of provision particularly in experimental or specialised services." *Children in Care* (1988–89) H.C. 67, para. 22.

[21] Cm. 2584 (1994), para. 2.16. Local authorities are required to facilitate the provision of services by voluntary or private organisations and may subcontract service provision: Children Act 1989, s.17(5).

[22] N. Parton, *The politics of child abuse* (1985) The DHSS issued its first guidance on such matters in 1974; D.H. *Child protection: messages from research* (1995).

[23] D.H. *Children Act Report 2000* (2001), para. 3.5. Child protection concerns are a key gateway to services, D.H., *Children Act Now* (2001), p. 44.

prevent the need to accommodate children. These powers were substantially extended in the Children Act 1989 with the aim of refocusing provision to support families. In any week, almost a quarter of a million children receive social services, of these only a quarter are looked after by the local authority, the rest are living with their families.[24] The number of children who are looked after has declined from over 100,000 in the 1980's to under 60,000.[25] The residential care service has shrunk; the high cost of provision and the recognition that many residents had been physically or sexually abused led to voluntary organisations and local authorities closing very many children's homes.[26] Two-thirds of looked-after children live in foster families.

Despite changes in legislation, organisation and services, there continue to be substantial problems with the quality of provision which are obvious in the negative outcomes for looked after children.[27] The system has been under performing and the failure to provide adequate educational opportunities for looked-after children is scandalous.[28] There is "striking variability" in the quality of services provided by local councils.[29] Responsibilities for regulation and inspection of residential care services, including children's homes, have been removed from local authorities and placed in the hands of the National Care Standards Commission.[30] This organisation has also acquired responsibility for inspecting local authorities' adoption and fostering services and residential homes. Inspection of childminding and day-care has been transferred from local authorities to OfSted so that that body now has responsibility for all early years education.[31]

The reform of child care law[32]

22–003 In the 41 years between the two great Children Acts[33] Parliament did not neglect the welfare of children. A series of statutes together with judicial decisions produced a system which was complex, confusing and unsatisfactory with far-reaching (and often adverse) consequences for the welfare of children.[34] There were more than a dozen ways in which children could enter local authority care, each one with different conditions and powers and giving rise to different

---

[24] D.H., *Children Act Report 2000* (2001), para. 3.5.

[25] D.H., *Children looked after by local authorities A/F 12* (published annually).

[26] W. Utting, *People like us* (1997), p. 21; *Lost in care* (2000 H.C. 201); C. Wolmar, *Forgotten children* (2000).

[27] Select Committee on Health, Second Report of the Select Committee on Health Session 1997–8, *Children Looked after by Local Authorities,* H.C. 247 (1998); W. Utting *op cit.;* D.H. *Response to the children's safeguards review* (1998).

[28] Select Committee on Health *op. cit.* para. 50.

[29] S.S.I., *Developing quality to protect children* (2001), para. 1.7.

[30] Care Standards Act 2000 following the proposals in *Modernising Social Services* (Cm. 4169, 1998).

[31] Care Standards Act 2000, s.79 adding Children Act 1989, Pt. XA. Such a transfer also re-orients the services from social care to education.

[32] For a more wide ranging discussion of the background to reform, see N. Parton and N. Martin, "Public inquiries, legislation and child care in England & Wales" (1989) 3 Int. J. Law & Fam. 21 and J. Eekelaar and R. Dingwall, *The Reform of Child Care Law* (1990).

[33] 1948 and 1989.

[34] Second Report of the House of Commons Social Services Committee 1983–4, *Children in Care* H.C. 360 (*Short Report*), para. 118.

rights of appeal.[35] The problems were exacerbated by overlapping and conflicting jurisdictions as between courts and the lack of a system which allowed all the issues relating to a child to be heard by a single court.[36] Many of the provisions were far from satisfactory; parents were not parties to care proceedings to remove their children, emergency powers allowed children to be removed from home for 28 days, and parents' rights could be removed without court proceedings.[37] The Children Act 1975 had weakened the position of parents in order to provide security for children in foster care. Pressure groups such as the Family Rights Group, the Children's Legal Centre and the National Association for Young People in Care were established in the late 1970s and early 1980s and began to campaign for improved services for children and their families and increased regulation of the social services. Cases were also taken to the European Court of Human Rights challenging the removal of parental rights and the termination of parental contact without court proceedings,[38] and highlighting the importance of making any new law compliant with the Convention.[39]

The House of Commons Select Committee on the Social Services began an inquiry into Children in Care in July 1982. It recommended a thorough review of the statute law[40] and an inter-departmental working party was set up which issued discussion papers and a report, *The Review of Child Care Law* in 1985.[41] The Review adopted many of the ideas and recommendations of the Select Committee with a view to the production of a clearer and more consistent body of law, comprehensible not only to those operating the system but also to those affected by it.[42] The Lord Chancellor and the Home Secretary established a separate official working party to review the case for a unified family court.[43] In addition, the Law Commission commenced its work on the private law of children which provided the opportunity to develop public and private child law so that they did not conflict.

The Government's response to the Review which largely endorsed the recommendations was published in 1987[44] and Law Commission Report No. 172 the following year.[45] Over the same period the deaths of a number of

---

[35] *ibid.* paras 118–119. See also S. Maidment, "The fragmentation of parental rights of children in care" [1981] J.S.W.L. 21.

[36] This could occur in wardship cases, but the High Court was not able to handle a large number of cases, and the principle applied, "the welfare principle" was not appropriate; see below.

[37] The Short Committee recommended 25 changes to the law, see p. 143 and Social Services Committee Second Report 1988–9, Children Bill H.C. 178, para. 4.

[38] *W., R., O., B., H. v. United Kingdom* (1988) 10 E.H.R.R. 29 also reported as *R. v. U. K.* [1988] 2 F.L.R. 445.

[39] "The Children Act anticipated the introduction into English Law of the European Convention" *per* Scott Baker J. in *Re S. (Sexual Abuse Allegations: Local Authority Response)* [2001] 2 F.L.R. 776 at 794; see also *Re F. (Care Termination of Contact)* [2000] 2 F.C.R. 481.

[40] *Short Report,* para.119.

[41] DHSS, Review of Child Care Law Discussion papers 1–12 (1985); *Review of Child Care Law* (1985).

[42] *ibid.* Foreword, para. 2.

[43] Lord Chancellor's Department, *Interdepartmental Review of Family and Domestic Jurisdiction* (1986).

[44] *The Law on Child Care and Family Services,* (Cm. 62, 1987)

[45] Law Com. No. 172 *The Review of Child Law Guardianship and Custody* H.C. 594 (1988). Hale L. J., then Prof. Brenda Hoggett Q.C., a Law Commissioner, was also a member of the Review of Child Care Law.

children who were subject to care orders or about whose care a local authority had grave concern were the subject of detailed inquiries.[46] These approved the Government's proposals and also made further recommendations. The publicity given to these cases and, particularly, that surrounding child sexual abuse in Cleveland[47] increased pressure for reform. The public was dissatisfied with the operation of the child protection service—social workers seemed unable to protect children at risk or to respect the privacy and authority of innocent families. Greater control of social worker's power and increased recognition of parent's rights were seen as essential for a better framework for child care practice.[48]

The Children Bill was incomplete when it was introduced into the Lords in December 1988 and proceeded to the Commons before the Government had devised a scheme for allocating cases between courts and before provisions relating to appeals, for reforming the system of regulation for day care and some other matters had been drafted. The Government tabled hundreds of amendments most of which received little detailed consideration because of the timetabling and guillotining of debate. No amendments opposed by the Government were successful but some were taken into account.[49] Much was left to Regulations and Rules of Court. In the last 10 years, the Children Act has been subject to amendment particularly to supervise local authorities' care plans, to widen their responsibilities to care leavers and to remove functions relating to the registration and inspection of daycare and residential care.[50] A review of research on practice concluded that the integrity of the Act had not been undermined[51] but that it needed remedial attention in specific areas.[52]

The philosophy of the Children Act 1989[53]

22–004 Child care policy has operated like a pendulum, swinging between the various competing interests and favouring different approaches as social work styles

---

[46] *e.g.* Tyra Henry, Kimberley Carlile and Jasmine Beckford, see D.H., *A Study of Inquiry Reports 1980–1989* (1991) and P. Reder *et al., Beyond blame, child abuse tragedies revisited* (1993).

[47] *The Report of the Inquiry into Child Abuse in Cleveland 1987,* (Cm. 412, 1988).

[48] For a criticism of this legalism, see Parton (1991); Parton and Martin, *op. cit.,* pp. 26, 36.

[49] *e.g.* the words "or complaints" were added to the provision dealing with procedures for making representations to the local authority, see now s.26(3). The definition of "specified proceedings" in s.41(6) was extended in the court rules although an amendment with this aim was rejected.

[50] Adoption and Children Bill, cl. 118; Children (Leaving Care) Act 2000; Care Standards Act 2000.

[51] *Children Act now* (2001), p.10. This is difficult to maintain in relation to the Crime and Disorder Act 1998, s.12(5) (a) which allows a care order to be made without the "significant harm" test being satisfied.

[52] *Children Act now* (2001), p.149, notably in ensuring that services are provided to children in need and securing that legal proceedings are not subject to delay.

[53] See B. Hoggett, "The Children Bill: the aim" (1989) 19 *Fam. Law* 217; M. Ryan, "The Children Bill 1989: the philosophy and the reality" [1989] 1 J.C.L. 102 (Cm. 62, 1987) and HMSO, *Guide to the Children Act 1989* (1989); B. Jordan, "Social Work, Justice and the Common Good" in *Social Work and Social Welfare Year Book (3)* (1992), p. 17; J. Roche, "The Children Act and children's rights: a critical; reassessment" in *The New handbook of children's rights* (B. Franklin ed., 2001).

changed and more became known of their effects on children in care and their families.[54] Concern for the plight of children in "voluntary care"[55] who had lost contact with their families but lacked a permanent substitute family led to emphasis being placed on obtaining control and planning. The Children Act 1975 facilitated this by extending the grounds on which "parental rights" could be removed, strengthening the position of foster parents and introducing a procedure whereby children could be freed for adoption.[56] The phrase "permanency planning"[57] was coined to connote the work done to enable a child to return to his or her family or move to an adoptive home, but was most frequently associated with adoption rather than rehabilitation. Studies in the 1980s raised awareness of the damage which state care could do to family links and also indicated that local policies and practices had enormous impact on the numbers of children in care, their length of stay and the care provided for them. The emotional and financial costs of care encouraged local authorities to operate strong gate-keeping techniques to prevent children entering the system. But providing care only as a last resort left both families and social workers feeling that they had failed if a child came into care.[58] The repeated reports of child abuse and the need to satisfy the public that everything possible was being done for such children also focused social work attention on taking control and not taking risks. Social work thus became something which was done to clients rather than a way of helping families to help themselves.

Against this background the changes in policy underlying the 1989 Act were quite dramatic. Central to the philosophy of the Act is the belief that children are best looked after within their family with both parents playing a full part and without recourse to legal proceedings.[59] Services to families who need help should, where possible, be arranged in partnership with parents.[60] The care of children away from home should be a collaborative effort with the local authority involving, consulting and valuing parents.[61] Supporting families and preventing the need for state care should be emphasised, but care is not to be viewed negatively. Local authorities should gain greater control of cases only following proof of risk of significant harm; an order must be sought in court proceedings where parents are represented. Even after a care order has been made, partnership should continue and links with family members be main-

---

[54] See Grace (1994), pp. 14, 32; Hendricks (1994), Chap. 11.

[55] *i.e.* children accommodated by local authorities in respect of whom the authorities did not have parental responsibility (Child Care Act 1980, s.2).

[56] Children Act 1975, ss.14, 33, 57 (Child Care Act 1980, s.3); Adoption Act 1976, s.18. For a discussion of the 1980 Act, see the 4th edition of this work at pp. 487–523; for freeing for adoption, see the 6th edition of this work pp. 908–911.

[57] See especially A.N. Maluccio, E. Fein and K.A. Olmstead, *Permanency Planning for Children: Concepts and Methods* (1986).

[58] See M. Fisher, P. Marsh *et al.*, *In and Out of Care* (1986).

[59] Children Act Report 1992, (Cm. 2144, 1993), para. 1.8.

[60] Partnership is not a term in the legislation. *Guidance,* Vol. 3, para. 2.10 states: "Partnership will only be achieved if parents are advised about and given explanations of the local authority's power and duties . . . " Family Group Conferences which are arranged by some local authorities enable families to have greater influence on the services provided for their children, see: Family Rights Group, *Family Group Conferences in the U.K.* (1995).

[61] Even if they have harmed their children, see: D.H., *The challenge of partnership in child protection: Practice guide* (1995).

tained. The Act repositioned the court, in some instances making it the key decision-making forum, in others withdrawing judicial scrutiny.[62] It is also a "charter for children"[63] allowing the child's views to be heard when decisions are taken about his or her care. The Act sought to strike a balance between the rights of children to express their views, the rights of parents to exercise their responsibilities and the duty of the state to intervene to protect children.[64] The Act meets many of the main obligations in the U.N. Convention on the Rights of the Child.[65]

The Act did not merely provide the framework for practices which were already well-established. Rather it required major changes in professional attitudes and service delivery[66] in order to establish a new balance between the family and the State,[67] and between child protection and family support services.[68] It drew on four distinct approaches to child welfare: laissez-faire, state paternalism, parents' rights and children's rights.[69] These approaches necessarily conflict; greater rights for social workers to protect children mean that parents lose some of their rights.[70] Emphasis on balance does not necessarily deny this conflict, but recognises the need to take account of conflicting objectives in order to prevent both over and under reaction. The Children Act brought about major positive changes in the provision of social services for children and families but still left a system where there is wide variation in the availability of services and, too frequently, poor outcomes for children.[71]

The role of central government

22–005 There is no Ministry for Children; the Department of Health deals centrally with issues relating to care and adoption in England and these are the responsibility of the National Assembly in Wales.[72] Other government departments, notably the Home Office, the Department for Education and Skills, the Lord Chancellor's Department and the Department of Environment, Transport and the Regions all have responsibilities which impinge on local authority care for children. The Children Act 1989 gave the Secretary of State considerable power to issue regulations which can extend or restrict the ambit of the Act or the way it

---

[62] J. Roche *op. cit.* p. 63.
[63] Cm. 2144, para. 1.6 although it removed some rights from children whilst recognising others, see above, Chap. 17.
[64] Cm. 2144, para. 1.7.
[65] Cm. 2144, para. 1.13; for a less optimistic view see Children's Rights Development Unit, *U.K. Agenda for Children* (1994).
[66] Cm. 2144, para. 1.15.
[67] D.H., *Introduction to the Children Act 1989* (1989), p. iii; Cm. 2144, para. 1.7.
[68] D.H., *Child protection messages from research* (1995), foreword.
[69] L. Fox-Harding, *Perspectives in child care policy* (1991); L. Fox-Harding, "The Children Act 1989 in context: Four perspectives in child care law and policy" [1991] *J.S.W.F.L.* 179 at 285.
[70] Fox-Harding (1991), p. 230.
[71] *Children Act now* (2001), pp. 117, 124 and 145;
[72] These functions were undertaken by the DHSS before 1989 and by the Welsh Office before devolution.

is operated.[73] Under the Local Authority Social Services Act 1970[74] the Secretary of State for Health has power to issue guidance to local authorities. This power has been repeatedly exercised—at least 11 volumes have been published relating specifically to the Children Act 1989[75] and guidance is also issued as circulars.[76] Local authorities are required to carry out their social services functions in accordance with directions given by the Secretary of State[77] and the courts should have regard to such guidance.[78] Guidance may give rise to expectations about the way cases will be dealt with so that departure from it provides a basis for judicial review. It may be seen as a form of tertiary legislation.

The Department of Health also carries out other functions relating to child care. In conjunction with the Social Services Inspectorate it develops policy and standards,[79] and advises ministers. It publishes statistics including an annual report to Parliament,[80] funds research and ensures the wide dissemination of its findings.[81] It is empowered to undertake inquiries.[82] Most services are financed by local authorities with the assistance of block grants from central government but the Department of Health supports the work of some voluntary organisations and pays for specific training initiatives.[83] In order to secure the effective operation of the Children Act 1989, the Department of Health commissioned an extensive implementation programme.[84] The Social Services Inspectorate provides advice to local authorities and voluntary organisations, undertakes inspections of social services, and carries out practice studies on issues causing concern.[85] Reports from these activities and performance indicators developed from

---

[73] Children Act 1989, s.104. For example under s.17(4) the Secretary of State may effectively rewrite Sched. 2 of the Act.

[74] ss.7, 7A.

[75] The 10 volumes of Children Act 1989 Guidance and Regulations, referred to here as *Guidance*, and *Working Together to safeguard children* (1999).

[76] Details of many current circulars can be found in *Clarke, Hall and Morrison On Children* or on the Department of Health web-site: www.doh.gov.uk

[77] Local Authority Social Services Act 1970, ss.7, 7A; *R. v. Islington LBC, ex p. Rixon* [1997] E.L.R. 66, but it is not binding on education authorities: *Essex C.C. v. B.* [1993] 1 F.L.R. 866 at 879.

[78] *Oxfordshire C.C. v. R.* [1992] 1 F.L.R. 648 at 654, *per* Douglas Brown J. The magistrates' failure to consider the guidance was a ground for appeal; see also: *Re J. (Minors) (Care: Care Plan)* [1994] 1 F.L.R. 253 and *R. v. Tameside M.B.C., ex p. J.* [2000] 1 F.L.R. 942.

[79] It has been the practice of the Department to consult widely with local authorities and child care organisations. In future minimum standards will be published: Care Standards Act 2000, s.23.

[80] Children Act 1989, s.83(6); Children Act Report 1995–1999 (Cm. 4579) was only produced after the Health Select Committee noticed the failure to produce reports for five years: Children Act Report 2000 (2001).

[81] Notably, *Children Act now* (2001) and *Child Protection messages from research* (1995). Major earlier research overviews are: *Social Work Decisions in Child Care* (1985); *Patterns and Outcomes in Child Care* (1990).

[82] Children Act 1989, s.81. Most inquiries are undertaken by local authorities but the Cleveland Inquiry was set up by the Secretary of State.

[83] Children Act 1989, s.82.

[84] J. Masson, "Implementing the Children Act 1989: Action at the Centre and Local Reaction" (1992) 19 J. Law & Society 320; Cm. 2144, paras 1.19–1.28. From 1983 to 1994 Rupert Hughes, Assistant Secretary in the Department played a key role in furthering child care reform.

[85] See *e.g.* inspections: S.S.I., *Someone else's children* (1998); *Getting family support right* (1999); *Developing quality to protect children* (2001), practice studies: S.S.I. *Residence orders study* (1995); *Care planning and court orders study* (1998).

them provide a basis for determining what is considered to be good practice in social work. The Department also has responsibility for maintaining lists of people who are unsuitable to work with children or vulnerable adults.[86] The Secretary of State has a default power which can be used where a local authority fails to carry out its functions.[87]

In 1998 with the aim of transforming children's social services, in a major new initiative, *Quality protects*,[88] the Department of Health, set objectives and required local authorities to produce management action plans to show how they would develop services to meet these. Grants were provided when plans were submitted, and the quality of services was measured against specific targets. It is too early to tell whether this will produce long-term improvement[89] but it has made local authorities more aware of the services they manage. Although the objectives have wide support, the targets, such as no more that 16 per cent of looked after children to have more than three placements in one year, and a least 75% of those leaving care at age 16 in 2003 having one GCSE, are unambitious.[90]

The balance of power between court and social services departments

22–006 Before the Children Act the courts could commit children to the care in custody and wardship proceedings without an application from a local authority and could also direct the authority how the child should be cared for.[91] But if the child was in care under other provisions the courts had no power to review the care arrangements. Both the *Short Report* and the *Review of Child Care Law* emphatically rejected the notion that the courts should have a role beyond determining whether an order should be made.[92] The *Review* sought to create a coherent scheme; the local authority had control over day to day decisions about the care of children including placement and could manage their resources but major decisions such as making or discharging care orders, and adoption were subject to court review.[93] This dichotomy is not without difficulty; placement

---

[86] Under the Protection of Children Act 1999 and the Care Standards Act 2000, s.81 and see *R. v. Secretary of State for Health, ex p. C.* [2000] 1 F.L.R. 627, CA. Appeals against inclusion are now to the Care Standards Tribunal.

[87] Children Act 1989, s.84 and below.

[88] Cm. 4169, paras 3.25–3.29; Circular LAC 98(20). The programme was initially for three years but has been extended to five years with total funding of £885 million. A comparable programme is operating in Wales: Welsh Office, *The Children First programme in Wales: Transforming children's services* (1999) Circular 20/99.

[89] See D.H. *Transforming children's services—an evaluation of the Quality Protects programme year 3* (2001). Progress in improvement has been slower than local authorities had hoped or predicted, para. 11.

[90] Unambitious because they reflect poor outcomes compared with the rest of the population and because many authorities already achieve them see *Children Act Report 2000*, paras 1.36 and 4.19.

[91] In practice the power to commit a child to care was rarely used without an application by the authority and the courts had no system for monitoring compliance with directions.

[92] *Short Report*, para. 71; *Review of Child Care Law*, paras 2.20 *et seq*. Where wardship was used the court could consider and continue to oversee the arrangements for the child.

[93] *Review of Child Care Law*, para. 2.21.

decisions are crucial to the long-term outcome of care and also affect contact which in turn affects rehabilitation and discharge from care. The Act drew a clear line between the responsibility of the court and the local authority,[94] restricting the court's control to the period before the care order is made and the issues of contact, emigration and adoption.[95] This was controversial; the courts were uneasy about trusting the local authority and in some cases attempted to retain control by delaying final care orders or imposing conditions.[96] Nevertheless the House of Lords refused to endorse a Court of Appeal decision which would have enabled more supervision of local authority decisions.[97] Lord Nicholls noted that the Children Act contained no effective machinery to allow a young child to challenge care decisions in the courts after the order had been made but that this reflected the scheme of the Act.[98] However, he did not find it necessary to hold that the Act was incompatible with Article 6(1).[99]

II. MODERN CHILD CARE LAW—SERVICES FOR CHILDREN IN NEED

Family support and prevention[1]

22–007 Children's services were originally focussed on looking after children whose parents were prevented from doing so, but services were developed to support children in their families, where this diminished the need for them to be received into or kept in state care.[2] In 1983, the Social Services Select Committee acknowledged the importance of preventive work but noted a lack of commitment to it within local authorities, and recommended that the power was extended.[3] The *Review of Child Care Law* considered that the emphasis on keeping children out of care placed insufficient stress on general family support and also undermined the role of short-term care as a positive means of helping families.[4] It wanted the duty to be a general one and not owed to individual families and children. There could thus be no conflict between an authority's duty to take action to protect individual

---

[94] *Re S. (F.C.)* [2002] U.K.H.L. 10 at para. 25 *per* Lord Nicholls.

[95] s. 34, Sched. 2, para. 19; Adoption Act 1976.

[96] See J. Dewar, "The courts and local authority autonomy" [1995] *C.F.L.Q.* 15; M. Hayes, "The proper role of the court in child care cases" [1996] *C.F.L.Q.* 20; M. Thorpe and E. Cooke, *Divided duties* (1998).

[97] *Re S. (Minors) (Care order: Implementation of Care Plan)* [2002] 1 F.L.R. 815 overruling the decision in *Re W. and B.; Re W. (Care Plan)* [2001] 2 F.L.R. 582, CA.

[98] at paras 86–88. The Adoption and Children Bill 2002, cl. 116 remedies this by amending s. 26.

[99] Even if the scheme of the act were incompatible a declaration would only be granted to a victim of an actual or proposed breach of a Convention right. The mother's Art. 6 rights had been met through her appeal, at para. 88.

[1] See D. Bedingfield, *The child in need* (1998).

[2] Child Care Act 1980, ss.1, 2, replacing the Children Act 1948. The original duty to provide preventive services was added by the Children and Young Persons Act 1963 following the recommendations of the Ingelby Committee (Cmnd.1191, 1960).

[3] *Short Report*, paras 30, 40.

[4] *Review of Child Care Law*, paras 5.7–5.17.

children and its duty to provide family support,[5] nor should it be possible for the courts to review a local authority's policy decisions on allocation of resources to preventive work. Emphasis on preventive work reinforced the notion that the family had the primary responsibility for the care of children and portrayed the local authority positively as a resource for families in difficulty. The Government accepted this.[6] Part III of and Schedule 2 to the Children Act 1989 now set out the duties of local authorities; these are more clearly targeted and owed only to "children in need" and their families.

Local authorities' duties to provide family support

22–008 The Children Act 1989, s.17(1) imposes general duties on local authorities to provide an appropriate range and level of services to "safeguard and promote the welfare of children within their area who are in need; and so far as is consistent with that duty, to promote the upbringing of such children by their families . . ." Section 17(2) imposes specific duties to: provide information about services; maintain a register of disabled children; assess children's needs; take reasonable steps to prevent neglect, abuse and the need to bring children before the courts. These duties must be considered whenever local authorities exercise powers which affect children in need.[7] Local authorities must in consultation with other agencies prepare and publish plans for children's services.[8] Local authorities are required to take account of the needs of different racial groups (but only specifically in relation to day care and fostering) and to make it easier for all separated children to live with or have contact with their families.[9] Social services departments are not expected to meet every need,[10] to provide services free of charge where families can pay,[11] or to take over the responsibilities of housing authorities:—

In *R. ota A. v. Lambeth LBC*[12] a lone mother of two autistic sons sought

---

[5] General duties "cannot be tested on a child-by-child basis": *R. v. Barnet LBC, ex p. B.* [1994] 1 F.L.R. 592 at 611 *per* Auld J.; *R. ota A. v. London Borough of Lambeth* [2002] 1 F.L.R. 353, CA. It is for the local authority not the court to look at what weight should be given to the circumstances of individual children.

[6] *The Law on child care and family services* (Cm. 62, 1987), paras 15–17; *Review of Child Care Law* (1985), Chap. 4.

[7] *R. v. Wealden D. C. ex. p. Wales* [1995] N.P.C. 145, a decision to direct removal of new age travellers under the Criminal Justice and Public Order Act 1994 was quashed because of failure to consider the children's welfare.

[8] Children Act 1989, Sched. 2, para. 1A, added by Children Act 1989 (Amendment) (Children's Services Planning) Order 1996, S.I. 1996 No. 785.

[9] Sched. 2, Pt I.

[10] *Guidance,* Vol. 2, para. 2.11. The local authority can therefore take account of the cost of providing a service as in the case of community care: *R. v. Gloucester C. C., ex p. Barry* [1997] 2 All E.R. 1, HL but must take account of the impact of its decisions on the child's needs: *R. v. Hammersmith and Fulham LBC, ex p. D.* [1999] 1 F.L.R. 642.

[11] Children Act 1989, s.17(7)–(9); *Guidance,* Vol. 2, paras 2.38–2.41. Those on income support, working families tax credit or other means-tested benefits cannot be charged. There is a regime for levying and enforcing charges for looking after children: Children Act 1989, Sched. 2, Pt 3. For a discussion of policy issues relating to charging see: K. Judge and J. Matthews, *Charging for Social Care* (1980).

[12] [2002] 1 F.L.R. 353, CA. The Court of Appeal subsequently held this was decided *per incuriam: R. ota W. v. Lambeth LBC* [2002] 2 F.L.R. 327, CA.

rehousing so her children would have somewhere to play. When the housing department placed her on a waiting list she approached social services who assessed the family as requiring rehousing and support in the home. No new home was found for the family and the mother sought judicial review. Her application was refused at first instance and she appealed. The Court of Appeal upheld the decision. The Children Act had not transferred responsibility for housing families to social services departments nor altered the scheme in the Housing Act 1996 for establishing priorities for rehousing. Both Otton J. and Chadwick L.J. held that there was no power to provide accommodation under section 17 but Laws L.J. considered that accommodation could be "assistance in kind" under section 17(6). The majority's view would have prevented social services departments assisting intentionally homeless families with accommodation but a government amendment to section 17[13] clarifies that this can be done and thus should ensure that parents and children are not separated purely because of failure to pay rent.[14] In addition, section 2 of the Local Government Act 2000 permits expenditure to benefit any resident.[14a]

Services must be provided where a child would otherwise be homeless or destitute:—

In *R. ota G. v. Barnet LBC*[15] the mother came with her child to London from Holland. She did not qualify for social security or housing benefits and sought assistance from the social services department under the Children Act. The local authority provided temporary hotel accommodation, offered to pay for their return to Holland and, failing that, to accommodate the child alone. The mother obtained judicial review of the decision not to provide long-term accommodation for her with her child. The Court of Appeal allowed the local authority's appeal. It accepted that the local authority had complied with its duties by offering to aid their return to Holland. This was the best way of meeting the child's needs. The local authority could not be expected to accommodate the mother but had a duty to accommodate the child under section 20 where the mother was unable to do so.

In addition to accommodating children in foster or residential homes, a wide range of services is provided by local authorities. There are family centres offering advice to parents, practical training in child care and budgeting, social

---

[13] Adoption and Children Bill 2002, NC 7.

[14] The duties to homeless families (now the Housing Act 1996, Pt VII) were introduced to avoid breaking up families through homelessness which had been graphically portrayed in the play *Cathy Come Home* (1967). The *Code of Guidance on parts 6 and 7 of the Housing Act 1996* (2001) para. 14.4f states "Children should not normally be provided with accommodation by social services as a result purely of family homelessness."

[14a] *R. ota A. v. Enfield LBC* [2002] 2 F.L.R. 1 (services for a mother so that child could remain with her in accordance with Art. 8).

[15] [2001] 2 F.L.R. 877, CA. But in *R. v. Hammersmith and Fulham LBC ex p. D.* [1999]1 F.L.R. 642 the authority's refusal to make any further offer after the mother refused her fare to return to Sweden judicial review was granted.

activities for parents and play-groups for children. Some family centres also provide residential facilities to improve the parenting of parents who have had a child removed or are at risk of such action. Some provide play schemes or toy libraries to cater for the needs of children with disabilities.[16] Local authorities need not provide all these services themselves and should liaise with voluntary organisations.[17] They may make payments to families in exceptional circumstances[18] and may provide direct payments to parents of disabled children, or disabled children aged 16 years or over, so that they can purchase their own services.[19]

"Children in need"

22–009 A child who requires local authority services to maintain or achieve a reasonable standard of health or development; or whose health or development will be significantly or further impaired without services or who is disabled is a "child in need".[20] No indication is given in the statute as to what constitutes a "reasonable standard" of health and development but it cannot mean merely freedom from significant harm. Whether or not a child is "in need" is a matter for the local authority alone; but a decision that a child is not "in need" is plainly susceptible to judicial review.[21] Services can be provided for the child's family or any member of it if they are provided with a view to safeguarding or promoting the child's welfare.[22] "Family" includes anyone who has parental responsibility for the child or with whom the child has been living.[23] The definition is "deliberately wide" to reinforce the emphasis on preventative services for families[24] and recognise the part played in caring for children by significant others[25] but does not expressly include relatives who are willing to look after a child in the future.[26] In contrast to the position relating to adults, local authorities have

---

16 For a discussion of the range of services, see *Guidance,* Vol. 2, Chap. 3. Each local authority is required to publicise its services: Sched. 2, para. 1(2).

17 s.17(5).

18 s.17(6) but are under no duty to do so; *Re K. and A. (Local Authority: Child Maintenance)* [1995] 1 F.L.R. 688. There may be advantages for the child of approving carers as foster parents rather than making a payment because the child will be entitled to aftercare support: *Re T. (Accommodation by Local Authority)* [1995] 1 F.L.R. 159; Children Act 1989, ss.24A, 24B.

19 Children Act 1989, s.17A (the adult who receives payment for a child must have parental responsibility); similar provision is made for adults under the Community Care (Direct Payments) Act 1996.

20 Children Act 1989, s.17(10). Disabled is defined in s.17(11) so the same groups are included as are within the National Assistance Act 1948, s.29.

21 *Re J. (Specific Issue Order: Leave to Apply)* [1995] 1 F.L.R. 669 at 673, *per* Wall J.; see para. 22–074. A specific issue order could not be used to determine whether a child was "in need".

22 s.17(3).

23 Children Act 1989, s.17(10); *Re T. (Accommodation by Local Authority)* [1995] 1 F.L.R. 159—friends who were looking after the child were within the definition.

24 *Guidance,* Vol. 2, para. 2.7. A statement which conflicts with that in the Financial Statement issued with the Children Bill which estimated that the new responsibilities in Pt III would only cost 1.7 million and require 150 extra staff in England and Wales.

25 *Children Act Now* (2001), p.64.

26 Once the relative obtained a residence order the child would form part of his family but relatives may prefer informal arrangements. It may be possible for the local authority to assist the relative under s.17(3) if "family" is used there in the more usual sense of a group of related individuals.

only powers, not duties, to assess children's needs.[27] The Department of Health research indicates that assessment practices have been inadequate with clients matched to existing services and little attention being paid to their particular needs.[28] Detailed guidance on conducting assessments has now been produced.[29] Where families are dissatisfied because of services provided or refused they have a right to complain and may be able to obtain a review by the courts.[30]

Most local authorities operate a priority system[31]; in practice this means that services are focussed on families where issues of child maltreatment are evident. The Department of Health has sought to re-orient social work away from child protection investigations towards family support by proposing a single approach to assessment for all children rather than separate systems for those in need (section 17) and those requiring protection (section 47).[32] The Department's overview of research on the Children Act, *Children Act Now,* notes that section 17 has been poorly understood, resulting in many problems in its implementation.[33] The emphasis has been on rationing rather than service development.[34] Local authorities have continued to use eligibility criteria based on risk and to restrict services to cases of abuse and neglect.[35] Fear of floods of families seeking services which would over-stretch resources has meant social workers acting as gatekeepers to services with high thresholds, and local authorities not publicising services adequately. Families in contact with social services were frequently not informed about what services could be provided.[36] Local authorities need to obtain more information about the numbers of children in need and the needs they have so that they can allocate sufficient resources and plan services.[37] The inadequate implementation of the preventative provisions provides an object lesson in how a rational and humane policy can be undermined by a failure to provide adequate funding.[38]

---

[27] Children Act 1989, Sched. 2, para. 3; *cf.* NHS and Community Care Act 1990, s.47(1) (a).

[28] *Children Act now* (2001), pp. 118–122.

[29] D. H, *et al., Framework for the assessment of children in need and their families* (2000) (a comparable document has been published by the National Assembly for Wales); D.H., *Assessing children in need and their families: practice guidance* (2000).

[30] The complaints service may be available: Children Act 1989, s.26(3). It should be used before seeking judicial review: *R. v. Kingston upon Thames R.B.C., ex p. T.* [1994] 1 F.L.R. 798; see below, para. 22–071.

[31] Cm. 2144, Chap. 3; Audit Commission, *Seen but not heard* (1994), para. 44.

[32] W. Rose, Deputy Chief, Social Services Inspector, *Children Act News* No. 16, p. 1 (1994); D.H., *Child protection messages from research* (1995), p. 55. These ideas have been taken forward in the *Framework for assessment* (2000) *op. cit.*

[33] *Children Act Now* (2001), p. 22.

[34] Audit Commission, *Seen but not heard* (1994), p. 19. The Department of Health recognises that lack of resources (staff and funding) has contributed to this: *Children Act Now* (2001), p. 127.

[35] *Children Act Now* (2001), pp. 22 and 117.

[36] *Children Act Now* (2001), pp. 74, 115. Despite clear obligations to publicise service provision: Children Act 1989, Sched. 2, para. 1(2).

[37] Audit Commission, *Seen but not heard* (1994). Considerable efforts are being devoted to assessing the range and volume of need in the community through the development of the CiN census see: *Children Act Report 2000* (2001), Chap. 3.

[38] Second Report of Select Committee on Health 1997-8 H.C. 247, para. 68. Even the Department of Health has recognised that inadequate resources have been a problem: *Children Act Now* (2001), p. 127.

Duty to provide accommodation

22–010 Children who enter the care system come from the most disadvantaged sections of society. This reflects not only the problems their parents face in caring for them but the fact that such families are subject to closer scrutiny, and social work practices.[39] Although their parents retain parental responsibility for looked after children, the local authority has responsibility for their day to day care, and often for planning their futures. The local authority is their corporate parent.

The Children Act 1948 imposed a duty on local authorities to receive into their care orphans and children whose parents were incapable of caring for them.[40] Care was used both for short-term needs, for example during a mother's illness or imprisonment and cases of more intractable difficulty where parents were unable or unwilling to provide a home for their children because of their own problems, the children's difficult behaviour or a combination of the two.[41] These children were not subject to court orders and could be removed by their parents at any time until the Children Act 1975 gave local authorities greater control over "voluntary care."[42] Changes in child-care policy and attitudes generally[43] affected the use made of reception into care. Social workers became more aware of the problems of rehabilitating children in care with their parents,[44] of the inadequacy of the care provided (particularly the frequent breakdown of foster placements and consequent lack of consistent care) and of the high cost of residential care. The number of children received into voluntary care declined but the use of compulsory measures of care increased.

The *Review of Child Care Law* considered that the existing framework for caring for children away from home was unsatisfactory for four reasons. The respective powers of parents and local authorities were unclear and this could lead to disputes; some parents were reluctant to use care because they feared that they would not get their child back; there was stigma associated with care, and participation by parents which was crucial to rehabilitation was too low. The *Review* therefore recommended the replacement of voluntary care with

---

[39] Details of the child care population can be found in the D.H., *Children in care statistics* series A/F/12 for the relevant year and below. See also A. Bebbington and J. Miles, "The background of children who enter local authority care" (1989) 19 Brit. J. Soc. Wk. 349, H. Cleaver *et al., Children's needs—parenting capacity* (1999) and D. Thorpe, "Career patterns in child care—implications for service" (1988) 18 Brit. J. Soc. Wk. 137.

[40] Children Act 1948, s.1, repeated in Child Care Act 1980, s.2.

[41] Such children were "victims, villains and the volunteered" see: J. Packman, L. Randall and N. Jacques, *Who Needs Care?* (1986). This study has been repeated following the implementation of the Children Act: J. Packman and C. Hall, *From care to accommodation* (1998).

[42] Children Act 1975, s.56 (Child Care Act 1980, s.13) parents could be required to give 28 days notice before removing their child and the local authority could pass a resolution or use wardship to prevent removal, see 5th edition of this work, p.597.

[43] Until 1975 fathers who were caring for young children alone were not able to claim income support without registering for work. Rather they were expected to place their children in local authority care and work to support them. Single mothers were expected to care not work, see Finer Report (1974), para. 5.33. See also N. Parton, "Children in care: recent changes & debates" (1985) 13 Crit Soc. Pol. 107.

[44] In 1984 Millham and his colleagues concluded that the first six weeks of care were crucial to achieving rehabilitation. S. Millham *et al., Lost in Care* (1986); and D.H., *Patterns and outcomes in child placement* (1991).

"shared care" which provided more clearly for a genuine and voluntary partnership between parents and the local authority.[45] The Government accepted that care should be a service to families, provided so far as possible on a basis of partnership with parent.[46] Agreements should be made to cover such matters as the initial placement, schooling, access and notice prior to return home; changes in arrangements should also be settled by agreement.

22–011 The Children Act 1989, s.20(1) imposes a duty on local authorities to provide accommodation for children in need who require it as a result of—

"(a) there being no person who has parental responsibility for him;
(b) his being lost or having been abandoned; or
(c) the person who has been caring for him being prevented (whether or not permanently, and for whatever reason) from providing him with suitable accommodation or care."

Accommodation is used in a broad range of circumstances, but many children who are accommodated would probably have been the subject of care proceedings under the previous system.[47] Local authorities try to avoid single, short-term admissions by supporting care by relatives or friends. Respite care, regular planned admissions for children with disabilities and some others, has developed to be a major form of family support.[48] However, accommodation continues to be an unplanned response to crises, and families sometimes create a crisis in order to force reluctant social workers to agree to accommodation.[49] The courts have been reluctant to force local authorities to provide accommodation:—

In *R. v. Birmingham City Council, ex p. A.*[50] a girl with educational and psychiatric problems was admitted to an adolescent psychiatric unit following the death of her adoptive father. The girl's relationship with her adoptive mother had broken down and she could not return home. The consultant recommended that she be placed in specialist foster care but the local authority was unable or unwilling to find a placement and the girl remained in the clinic for a year after the assessment. The girl applied via her mother for judicial review and sought an order requiring the local authority to accommodate her. The court refused the order because it considered that judicial review was not appropriate; instead a complaint should have been made to the local authority.[51]

---

[45] *Review of Child Care Law*, paras 7.3–4. In addition the Review proposed a system of "respite care" which would provide substitute care for up to one month but leave the primary responsibility for the child with the parents (Chap. 6).

[46] Cm. 62 (1987), paras 21 *et seq.*

[47] *Children Act now* (2001), p. 210 citing Packman and Hall *op. cit.*

[48] J. Aldgate and M. Bradley, *Supporting families through short-term fostering* (1999). There is a special regime for such placements: Arrangement for Placement of Children (General Regulations 1991 (S.I. 1991 No. 890), r. 13; Fostering Services Regulations 2002 (S.I. 2002 No. 57), r. 37.

[49] *Children Act now* (2001), p. 211 citing Packman and Hall *op. cit.*

[50] [1997] 2 F.L.R. 841; *cf. Re T. (Accommodation by Local Authority)* [1995] 1 F.L.R. 159.

[51] Children Act 1989, s.26 and see below para. 22–071.

Although this duty applies to all children under age 18 it is further qualified in relation to children in need over the age of 16. The local authority has a duty to provide accommodation for such children if it considers that the child's welfare is likely to be "seriously prejudiced" if accommodation is not provided.[52] It is not clear that parents have a duty to maintain children over 16, and over 16s may apparently leave home. Thus their need for local authority care and accommodation does not fit easily within the words of section 20(1). Young people aged 16 and 17 may request services on their own behalf.[53] Although the requirement of serious prejudice to welfare may provide a basis for refusal of section 20 accommodation by the social services department, under the Housing Act 1996[54] homeless[55] young people[56] have a priority need and right to accommodation for up to two years. Social services departments should agree a division of responsibilities with the local housing authority and make arrangements to ensure that young people receive ongoing support so that they can maintain their tenancy.[57] Local authorities also have a power to provide any child with accommodation if it would safeguard or promote his or her welfare. For the same reasons they may provide accommodation in a community home for anyone aged between 16 and 21.[58] However few young people are provided for in this way.[59]

During the 1990's it became common for young people who were looked after by local authorities to leave the care system when they reached the age of 16. Pressures on resources and the availability of social security benefits to care leavers led local authorities to favour this in order to cut expenditure and not to develop residential services attractive to young people.[60] Despite the duty to provide aftercare services[61] there was "deplorably little support" for care leavers; many failed to continue in education or find employment and became homeless after

---

[52] s.20(3). The possibility of support under s.17 is unlikely to justify refusal of accommodation for a child in need over 16: *Re T. (Accommodation by Local Authority)* [1995] 1 F.L.R. 159 at 162.

[53] This is not explicitly stated in the Act but the DHSS, *Review of Child Care Law* Discussion paper 2 (1985), paras 38–72 concluded that there was such a right and the House of Lord's decision in *Gillick v. W. Norfolk and Wisbech A.H.A.* [1986] A.C. 112 would seem to support this. It is clear that children over 16 cannot be removed from local authority accommodation by their parents against their will, see s.20(11).

[54] ss.189, 193; see also the Government's housing policy statement, *The way forward for housing* (2000) and Homelessness Act 2002.

[55] "For some young homeless applicants the most appropriate solution may be reconciliation between them and their families so they can return home. However, in some cases . . . it may not be safe . . . to return home. [S]ocial services should be involved in such cases . . . ." *Code of Guidance on Parts 6 and 7 of the Housing Act 1996* (2001), para.14.4e.

[56] This includes those aged 16 and 17 who are not eligible for aftercare services as local authority care leavers, care leavers aged 18–21, those vulnerable because they have an institutional background and people under the age of 25 years who are vulnerable for any reason see: *Code of Guidance* (2001), paras 14.4b,14.10–14.17 and the DETR, *Supplementary guidance on determining vulnerablity* (2001).

[57] *Code of Guidance* (2001), paras 14.4c and 14.4d; DETR, *Supplementary guidance on effective joint working for young people who are homeless* (2001).

[58] s.20(4), (5). Children accommodated under s.20(5) cannot be placed in secure accommodation: Children (secure accommodation) Regulations 1991, S.I. 1991 No. 1505, r.5(1), other accommodated children over 16 could choose to leave at any time s.20(11).

[59] See Children in care statistics series A/F/12 and *Children Act Report 1995–1999* (2001), para. 6.5.

[60] *Children Act Report 1995–1999* (2000), Chap. 6.

[61] Children Act 1989, s.24; see also SSI, *When leaving care is leaving home* (1997).

leaving care.[62] The Department of Health proposed increasing local authorities' responsibilities to older care leavers and removing rights to benefits for care leavers under age 18[63]; this was enacted in the Children (Leaving Care) Act 2000 and implemented on October 1, 2001.[64] Other responsibilities owed by local authorities to children they look after are discussed at para. 22–059, below.

Voluntary agreement

22–012 The Children Act, Pt III does not give local authorities any power to impose services; families have a right to receive sympathetic support and cannot be required to co-operate.[65] Children under 16[66] may not be provided with accommodation if a person with parental responsibility who is able or willing to accommodate them objects, nor can parents who have agreed to residential care be forced to accept foster care for their child:—

> In *R.v. Tameside M.B.C. ex p. J.*[67] the local authority had accommodated a severely disabled girl in a residential home with her parents' agreement. The plan was for the girl to remain in residential care, with regular contact with her family who lived locally. The local authority then planned a move to a foster home; the parents, who objected, sought judicial review. The court held that the local authority's power to look after the child did not extend to making a placement[68] against parents' wishes and endorsed the partnership approach set out in *Guidance*.[69]

Children who are accommodated may be removed by anyone with parental responsibility who will arrange for their care.[70] Court orders may not be made preventing removal of a child from local authority accommodation, nor may parents be required to give undertakings to this effect.[71] If there is a residence order the child may enter or remain in local authority accommodation providing all of the people with the order agree to this.[72] Notice of removal is no longer

---

[62] Select Committee on Health, Second Report session 1997–8, H.C. 247 *Children looked after by local authorities*, para. 313.
[63] D.H., *Me, Survive, Out there?* (1999).
[64] The Act adds ss.24A and 24B to the Children Act 1989. It is expected to lead to an increase in the care population: *Children Act Report 2000* (2001), para. 1.3.
[65] *Guidance*, Vol. 2, para. 2.7.
[66] s.20(11) this apparently applies irrespective of the child's maturity.
[67] [2000] 1 F.L.R. 942.
[68] Counsel for the parents accepted that the local authority could substitute one residential home and another, at 949D; Scott Baker J. suggested that the local authority could discharge its duty by offering a service even if this was rejected by the parent and could seek a care order if the significant harm threshold was crossed, at 949F.
[69] *Guidance*, Vol. 2, paras 2.10–2.14, 2.50.
[70] s.20(7) (10)) unless another person with a residence order, special guardianship or care and control under the inherent jurisdiction agrees to accommodation, s.20(9). The objection of someone with parental responsibility who is unable or unwilling to care for the child may be discounted: s.20(7).
[71] Children Act 1989, ss. 9(5), 100(2) (b): *Re S. and D. (Children: Powers of the Court)* [1995] 2 F.L.R. 456, CA; *Re B. (Supervision Order: Parental Undertaking)* [1996] 1 F.L.R. 676, CA.
[72] s.20(9).

required nor can written agreements which impose it be enforced.[73] Several attempts were made during the passage of the bill to add such a provision, but all were rejected by the Government because a notice requirement would undermine the voluntary nature of the arrangement and discourage those who needed the service from using it.[74] The Government accepted that it was good practice to prepare a child for any move but this should not be forced on an unwilling parent. Nevertheless, the Lord Chancellor suggested that foster parents were entitled by section 3(5) to refuse to hand over a child late at night or to a drunken parent and that this provided adequate protection for the child.[75] This interpretation probably cannot be sustained. In *Lewisham London Borough v. Lewisham Juvenile Court*[76] the House of Lords held that the comparable duty in the 1980 Act did not compel the child's return to an unfit parent because the local authority had a duty to keep the child so long as his or her welfare required.[77] Also, the Court of Appeal held that the 1948 Act imposed no absolute duty on the local authority to return the child[78] and a mandatory injunction was refused because both the foster parents and the child (who was almost 18 at the hearing of the appeal) were unwilling for her to return home. However, the Children Act 1989 appears to give person with parental responsibility an unqualified right to remove the child[79] and must be interpreted compatibly with Article 8 rights.

Where the child is at risk of suffering significant harm unless a service is accepted, the local authority may seek a care or supervision order to impose its plan.[80] Where refusal to accept, or removal from, accommodation, places the child at immediate risk, the local authority may seek an emergency protection order or request the use of police protection powers.[81] Alternatively, a foster carer may make the child a ward of court or seek a residence order but might jeopardize their financial support from the local authority.[82] Although emphasis

---

[73] A fact which may not be apparent to parents, particularly if they are informed that a court order will be sought if they attempt to remove the child. There is evidence that pressure is put on some parents to agree to accommodation or face care proceedings: *Children Act now* (2001), p.51 citing J. Hunt *et al., The last resort* (1999).

[74] See *Hansard,* H.L., Vol. 502, cols. 1337, 1342–4, Children Bill, Committee Stage; Vol. 503, cols. 1411–3, Report Stage; Vol. 512, cols. 737–9, Consideration of Commons Amendments.

[75] *Hansard,* H.L., Vol. 505, cols. 370–1, Children Bill, Third Reading. *Guidance,* Vol. 3 is silent on this but advises of the use of emergency protection orders where removal could be harmful (para. 2.66).

[76] [1980] A.C. 273.

[77] Child Care Act 1980, s.1(2). Lords Salmon and Keith suggested that the local authority had no right to retain the child even though the parent demanding his return was incapable, at 290H, 301F.

[78] *Krishnan v. Sutton LBC* [1970] Ch. 181.

[79] Foster parents are required to sign an undertaking to allow the local authority to remove the child, Fostering Services Regulations 2002 (S.I. 2002 No. 57), r. 36 and Sched. 5, para. 15. Where they breach their undertaking the local authority may remove the child without permission or take proceedings.

[80] Children Act 1989, s.31: see below para. 22–027.

[81] ss.44, 46 see below. Foster carers could also seek an EPO but applications not from local authorities are exceptionally rare.

[82] The local authority may not ward the child nor may the court require the child to be accommodated by the authority if he is a ward or commit him to care: s.100. Unless the child has lived with the foster parents for three years, leave of the court (or those with parental responsibility)

on parents' wishes and on voluntary arrangements may improve the service offered by local authorities, it may be detrimental to the welfare of some children, particularly those who have been accommodated by the local authority for long periods, and may add to the insecurity felt by foster carers.[83] Initially it was suggested that the Children Act made planning for children more difficult but there is little evidence to support this.[84]

Given that child protection concerns are the main trigger for local authorities offering services, questions arise about the extent to which parents are freely accepting services. Although there is evidence that agreements with parents have enabled local authorities to avoid lengthy court proceedings, research also raises concerns about pressure on parents to accept accommodation for their children,[85] inappropriate resort to court and delay in bringing proceedings.[86] Overall, the balance between voluntary accommodation and compulsory care has again swung in favour of compulsion with almost two-thirds of looked after children being subject to court orders.[87] Accommodation has diminished as a family support service, except where a series of short-term placements (respite) is provided.[88]

Co-operation between authorities

22–013 Services for children in need cannot be met by one agency, but demand the pooling of skills and resources from many areas[89] such as housing, special education and health. The local authority carries the principal responsibility for co-ordinating and providing services for children in need[90] but may request help from another local authority and education, housing or health authorities.[91] Joint working has been strengthened by duties to develop and review plans for children's services with other local agencies[92] and the power to pool budgets[93] but there has been wasteful litigation between local authorities in an attempt to avoid responsibility for children and families with connections elsewhere.[94] Any authority whose help is sought must comply with the request if it is compatible with their own statutory duties and obligations and does not unduly prejudice

---

is required: s.10(5) (b). Local authorities are permitted to pay allowances to foster parents who obtain residence orders: Children Act 1989, Sched. 1, para. 15.

[83] J. Rowe, H. Cain, M. Hundleby and A. Keane, *Long-term foster care* (1984), p. 199.

[84] J. Gibbons in D.H., *Child protection messages from research* (1995) p. 15; *Children Act now* (2001), p. 55.

[85] J. Hunt *et al., The last resort* (1999); *Children Act now* (2001), p. 51.

[86] *Children Act now* (2001), p. 52; J. Hunt *et al., op cit.;* J. Packman and C. Hall, *From care to accommodation* (1998); *Children Act now* (2001), p. 51.

[87] *Children Act now* (2001), p. 49. The Departement of Health has expressed concern that proceedings should not be used indiscriminately, p.143.

[88] *Children Act Report 2000* (2001), para. 1.21 *et seq.*

[89] *Children Act now* (2001), p. 96.

[90] *Guidance,* Vol. 2, para. 1.14.

[91] s.27(3); help can also be requested from Health Authorities, NHS Trusts and the NSPCC.

[92] Children Act 1989, Sched. 2, para. 1A.

[93] Health Act 1999, s.27 and 31.

[94] *R. ota Stewart v. London Borough of Wandsworth and others* [2001] EWHC Admin. 709 (s.17); *Northamptonshire C. C. v. Islington L.B.C.* [2000] 2 W.L.R. 193, CA (care order); *R. v. Lambeth LBC, ex p. Caddell* [1998] 1 F.L.R. 253, QBD (s.24).

the discharge of any of their functions.[95] Local authorities have been enjoined to establish policies and procedures[96] to ensure good co-operation and it has been stressed that the "game of pass the parcel" has no place in this field.[97] However, in *R. v. Northavon District Council., ex p. Smith*[98] the House of Lords refused judicial review where a housing authority rejected a request from social services to rehouse an intentionally homeless family.[99] The court could not decide the form co-operation between authorities should take.[1] Each authority may make its own decision whether the request to assist social services prejudices the discharge of its functions. Where a housing authority fails to co-operate the social services department will have to make provision by accommodating the children, assisting the family to obtain a tenancy in the private sector, or in the case of those from overseas, assisting return to their home country.[2]

III. THE CHILD PROTECTION SYSTEM

A. Child abuse and neglect[3]

22–014 It is widely accepted that child maltreatment is a socially constructed phenomenon which reflects the values and opinions of a particular culture at a particular time.[4] Ill-treatment of children by their parents was recognised as a social problem in the nineteenth century. A number of voluntary organisations, including the National Society for the Prevention of Cruelty to Children (NSPCC), were established to improve the lot of abandoned, neglected and ill-treated children by rescuing them from the streets, by encouraging and cajoling their parents to act responsibly and by campaigning for legislation which would enable them to be protected.[5] However, it was not until the early 1960s that the extent and nature of the problem of child abuse began to be recognised in Britain.[6] Amer-

---

95 s.27(2) but it has been held that this does not require one department within a unitary authority to comply with a request from the social services department: *R. v. Tower Hamlets LBC, ex p. Byas* (1992) 25 H.L.R. 109.

96 *Guidance,* Vol. 2, para. 1.13; As far as disabled children are concerned and despite considerable progress there continue to be barriers to good co-operation: SSI, *Removing the barriers for disabled children* (1998).

97 *per* Lord Donaldson M.R., *R. v Tower Hamlets LBC, ex p. Begum* [1993] 1 All E.R. 447 at 456.

98 [1994] 2 F.L.R. 671, HL.

99 Housing authorities owe only limited duties to those who are intentionally homeless but have a priority need for housing: Housing Act 1996, s.190. They must secure temporary accommodation and provide assistance.

1 *R. v. Northavon D.C., ex p. Smith* [1994] 2 F.L.R. 671 at 677, *per* Lord Templeman.

2 *R. ota G. v. Barnet LBC* [2001] 2 F.L.R. 877, CA; *R. v. Hammersmith and Fulham LBC, ex p. D.* [1999] 1 F.L.R. 642 and above para. 22–008.

3 See B. Corby, *Child abuse towards a knowledge base* (2000); NSPCC, *Child maltreatment in the United Kingdom a study of the prevalence of child abuse and neglect* (2000); N. Parton, *The politics of child abuse* (1985).

4 See: M. Brandon *et al., Safeguarding children with the Children Act 1989* (1999), p. 2; D.H., *Child protection messages from research* (1995); Parton (1985).

5 See Pinchbeck and Hewitt (1973), p. 622; Hendrick (1994) pp. 49–67.

6 For an account of developments up to 1969, see J. Eekelaar, R. Dingwall and T. Murray, "Victims or threats? Children in care proceedings" [1982] J.S.W.L. 67 and Hendrick, pp. 242–246.

ican paediatricians had identified injuries commonly found together in young children—fractures of different ages to the long bones and subdural haematoma (a collection of blood immediately below the skull) and suggested that these were caused by violent parents.[7] Henry Kempe, now recognised as a leading authority on child abuse, termed this the "battered child syndrome."[8]

Child abuse is not limited to such injuries, indeed such multiply-injured children are now rare amongst those recognised as abused.[9] Burns, bruising, particularly as a result of shaking, squeezing or gripping, and bite marks are frequently associated with child abuse but what is abusive parenting cannot simply be determined from the occurrence of individual incidents. Behaviour needs to be seen in context before it can be thought of as maltreatment.[10] An understanding of normal patterns of parenting,[11] children's needs and of the impact of styles of parenting on children is important for those making decisions about whether action should be taken to intervene in a family.[12] Children are still neglected: insufficient attention to physical care, hygiene and feeding leads to stunted growth and poor general development, a condition termed "failure to thrive". Children who receive adequate physical care may fail to develop normally where they are emotionally neglected or abused.[13] Parenting styles which are low on warmth and high on criticism are associated with poor outcomes for children.[14] A few parents fabricate symptoms so that their children are subject to repeated medical intervention.[15] Neglected children are sometimes also victims of physical or sexual abuse; some suffer injury because they are inadequately supervised. Sexual abuse has been defined as "the involvement of dependent, developmentally immature children and adolescents in sexual activities that they do not fully comprehend and to which they are unable to give informed consent or that violate the social taboos of family roles."[16] It includes molestation, sexual

---

[7] J. Caffey, "Multiple fractures of the long bones of infants suffering chronic subdural haematoma" (1945) 55 *American Journal of Roentgenology* 1; Caffey did not identify parents as causing the injuries but his work led to further investigations and articles which did, see Parton (1985), pp. 49–54.

[8] See C.H. Kempe *et al*, "The Battered Child Syndrome" (1962) 181 Journal of the American Medical Association 17; R. Kempe and C.H. Kempe, *Child Abuse* (1978); R. Helfer and R. Kempe (eds.), *The Battered Child* (4th. ed., 1987).

[9] D. Jones, J. Pickett *et al., Understanding Child Abuse* (2nd ed., 1987), p. 69, (for a description of the main physical manifestations of abuse and neglect see pp. 70–88).

[10] D.H., *Child Protection messages from research* (1995), p. 14.

[11] D.H., *Child Protection messages from research* (1995), p. 12; M. Smith and M. Grocke, *Normal family sexuality and sexual knowledge in children* (1995); M. Smith *et al., Parental Control within the family: the nature and extent of parental violence to children* (1995).

[12] D.H., *Child Protection messages from research* (1995), p. 15; H. Cleaver *et al., Children's needs—parenting capacity* (1999), p. 45.

[13] For examples of emotional abuse, see J. Furnell, P. Dutton and J. Harris, "Emotional abuse: References to a Scottish Children's panel reporter over 5 years" (1988) 28 *Medicine, Science & Law* 219.

[14] D.H., *Child Protection messages from research* (1995), p. 19.

[15] The term Munchausen syndrome by proxy is sometimes used for this condition. The Department of Health has issued a supplement to *Working Together to safguard children* relating to these cases.

[16] M. Schechter and L. Roberge, "Sexual exploitation" in *Child abuse and neglect: the family and the community* (R. Helfer & C.H. Kempe eds., 1976). This definition was adopted in the *Cleveland Report* (1988), para. 4.

intercourse (oral, vaginal or anal), rape[17] and the involvement of children into prostitution and the creation of pornography.[18] It is sometimes perpetrated by organised groups who prey on children of members and others.

Child maltreatment is not confined to particular classes or family types. However, families whose children are dealt with by the child protection system differ from the population as a whole.[19] Over a third of them are headed by a lone parent, and in less than a third do both natural parents reside with the children. Nearly three-fifths lack a wage earner and over half are dependent on income support. At least a quarter of the women are victims of domestic violence and the lives of nearly a sixth of families are disrupted by mental illness. Many of the parents have been abused or in care as children.[20]

The British public's awareness of child abuse was heightened following the death of Maria Colwell in 1971. Maria had been removed from her mother as a baby by a court order and fostered with an aunt and uncle. Her mother subsequently re-ordered her life, remarried and sought Maria's return. The care order was discharged but Maria was neglected and finally died of multiple injuries aged seven and a half despite the existence of a supervision order and a number of calls to the social services department and NSPCC about her. The DHSS set up an inquiry which received wide publicity and set the tone for media coverage of child abuse.[21]

Over 100 inquiries into child deaths have taken place since 1973,[22] most have identified failures by the agencies involved to co-operate with each other to identify signs of abuse, assess the quality of parental care and monitor the child's progress. Although frequently social workers have been blamed, prior to the Children Act 1989, the law was also seen as providing an inadequate framework for child protection because it was too difficult for social workers to understand, did not help to secure long-term placements and failed to ensure that the court had a complete picture of the child's situation.[23] The response of the Department of Health has been to issue detailed guidance on the organisation of the child protection system and the handling of individual cases,[24] and on assessment.[25]

Social work involvement with child sexual abuse began to increase in the mid-1980s following similar developments in the USA in the 1970s. Public

---

[17] See generally, J. La Fontaine, *Child sexual abuse* (1990); *Cleveland Report* (1988), Chap. 11 and Apps. F & L; J. La Fontaine, *The extent and nature of organised and ritual sexual abuse* (1994).

[18] W. Utting, *People like us* (1997), pp. 97–104; D.H. *et al., Safeguarding children involved in prostitution* (2000). Young prostitutes should therefore be regarded as victims not offenders.

[19] D.H., *Child protection messages from research* (1995), p. 25. Mental illness, substance abuse and domestic violence were even more frequent amongst parents whose children were the subject of care proceedings, see: H. Cleaver *et al.* (1999), p.21.

[20] J. Gibbons *et al., Operating the child protection system* (1995), Chap. 4.

[21] DHSS, *Report of the Committee of Inquiry into the care and supervision provided in relation to Maria Colwell* (1974); see also Parton (1985), Chap. 4.

[22] DHSS, *Child Abuse: A Study of Inquiry Reports* (1982); D.H., *Child abuse: a study of Inquiry reports 1980–1989* (1991).

[23] The Children Act 1975 remedied some of these defects but piecemeal reform added to the problems caused by the complexity and volume of legislation.

[24] D.H. *et al., Working Together* (1988) and (1991) now replaced by D.H. *et al., Working Together to Safeguard Children* (1999). The original circular on child protection was issued in 1974, see Parton (1985) 102–9.

[25] D.H. *et al., A Framework for the Assessment of children in need and their families* (2000).

consciousness was also raised by an inquiry.[26] In the spring of 1987, in Cleveland, there was a dramatic rise in the number of cases in which child sexual abuse was diagnosed. Over a hundred children were admitted to hospital following such diagnosis and their siblings were also removed for examination and protection under emergency court orders. The health service, the courts, and the social services department could not deal adequately with the number of cases. Co-operation between the police and the social services department broke down so that it became difficult to investigate cases and prepare further action. There was widespread disbelief that child sexual abuse could have been identified in so many cases and considerable scepticism, particularly amongst the medical profession and the police, about one method of diagnosis (reflex anal dilatation)[27] which was given considerable prominence in the press. Aggrieved parents brought the matter to public attention and a statutory inquiry[28] was held under the chairmanship of Dame Elizabeth Butler-Sloss, then a High Court Judge.

22–015 The Cleveland Report acknowledged that child sexual abuse was widespread[29] and that more information was needed about its incidence and identification, but gave the impression that the diagnosis had been incorrect in a large proportion of cases.[30] The report attributed the crisis to lack of communication and understanding amongst the agencies involved but also criticised individuals and recommended changes to child protection law and practice.[31] Many of the changes in practice were accepted by the DHSS and incorporated in departmental guidance.[32] Legal changes which followed earlier government proposals were incorporated in the Children Act 1989.[33]

---

[26] *Report of the Inquiry into Child Abuse in Cleveland 1987,* Cm. 412 (1988) (*Cleveland Report*); a brief account is contained in the short version of the report, Cm. 413 (1988). For alternative accounts, see B. Campbell, *Unofficial Secrets* (1988); S. Bell, *When Salem came to the Boro'* (1988). For a Scottish parallel see the *Report of the Inquiry into the removal of children from Orkney February 1991* (1992 H.C. 195).

[27] C. Hobbs and J. Wynne, "Buggery in childhood—a common syndrome of child abuse"[1986] *The Lancet* 792: "Child sexual abuse—an increasing rate of diagnosis" [1987] *The Lancet* 842. Hobbs and Wynne described their findings and publicised the test but did not develop it. RAD has been known to forensic physicians for many years, see DHSS, *Diagnosis of Child Sexual Abuse: Guidance for Doctors* (1988), para. 12.18. Failure to conduct a thorough physical examination may mean that signs of abuse are missed, see *Cleveland Report,* App. L.

[28] Under National Health Service Act 1977, s.84 and Child Care Act 1980, s.76. Children Act 1989, s.81 now makes provision for inquiries.

[29] *Cleveland Report* (1988), p. 243, para. 1.

[30] The report was written in such a way that it was impossible to determine whether individual cases had been confirmed, but p. 244, para. 13, recorded that "Most of the 121 children diagnosed by Drs Higgs and Wyatt as sexually abused, were separated from their parents and their home by place of safety orders. The majority have now returned home some with all proceedings dismissed, others on conditions of medical examinations and supervision orders." The fact that children returned home does not necessarily mean that abuse did not occur.

[31] *ibid.* Pt. 3, paras 2, 17; pp. 245–253.

[32] DHSS, *Working Together* (1988); D.H., *Diagnosis of Child Sexual Abuse: Guidance for Doctors* (1994).

[33] The Report "strongly endorsed" the proposals in Cm. 62 (1987) and recommended that courts should have more control over contact and medical examinations in child protection proceedings. pp. 252–253. See now Children Act 1989, ss.38(1), (6) and 44(6). The Report also recommended the continuation of wardship for care cases and a Family Court but these proposals were not accepted.

More recent inquiries have alerted the public to the vulnerability of children who are looked after away from home. These have made local authorities aware of the need to vet staff and inspect homes,[34] and led to the establishment of stronger safeguards against unsuitable people working with or caring for children.[35]

B. Intervention in family life

22–016 The limits of parental freedom to determine how their children should be raised and the role of the state in protecting children have been the subject of considerable debate.[36] The appropriate standard or threshold for state intervention in family life and how this should be determined are central to this debate. The placing of the threshold is influenced by moral and legal questions and pragmatic concerns such as whether the local authority will be able to provide adequate care.[37] Evidence of outcomes and of parents' and children's concerns should contribute decisions about what is and what is not abusive.[38]

Before the implementation of the Children Act 1989 there were a large number of ways in which a child could be made the subject of local authority care compulsorily.[39] The DHSS noted that the statutory code had both strengths and weaknesses. The grounds were sufficiently widely drawn and had become familiar to those working with them, but there were variations in interpretation, some technical difficulties and a general problem of complexity.[40] Changes were essential to simplify the law to provide a coherent basis for intervention[41] and restore faith in the system.[42]

The *Review of Child Care Law* examined proposals for committal to care based on a welfare test but rejected them because this would lead to "widely varying and subjective interpretations . . . and fail to offer (the family) the degree

---

[34] A. Levy and B. Kahan, *The pindown experience and the protection of children* (1991); A. Kirkwood, *The Leicestershire Inquiry* (1992) (into the management of children's homes following the conviction of Frank Beck for buggery); *Lost in care* 2000 H.C. 201 (the *Waterhouse Report*); W. Utting *op. cit.* and C. Wolmar, *Forgotten children* (2000).

[35] D.H., *Choosing with care* (1992) (*Warner Report*); Protection of Children Act 1999; Care Standards Act 2000, s.22.

[36] M. Wald, "State intervention on behalf of "neglected" children: a search for realistic standards" (1975) 27 *Standford Law Review* 985–1040; J. Goldstein, A. Freud and A. Solnit, *Before the Best interests of the Child* (1979); and E. Szwed, "The best interests syndrome and the allocation of power in child care" in *Providing Civil Justice for Children* (H. Geach & E. Szwed ed., 1983); R. Dingwall, J. Eekelaar and T. Murray, *The Protection of Children* (1983), Chap. 10; D.H., *Child Protection: messages from research* (1995), p. 15; R. Hetherington, *Protecting children messages from Europe* (1997).

[37] D.H., *Child Protection messages from research* (1995), p. 15.

[38] *ibid.*, p. 17; H. Cleaver *et al.* (1999).

[39] M.D.A. Freeman, "The legal battlefield of 'care' " (1982) 35 C.L.P. 117 at 118 and see 6th edition of this work at p.790.

[40] *Review of Child Care Law, Discussion paper 3, op. cit.*, paras 19, 66–115; *Review of Child Care Law*, paras 15.6–15.9.

[41] *Short Report*, para. 117.

[42] *Review of Child Care Law, Discussion paper 3, op. cit.*, paras 19, 66–115; *Review of Child Care supported by evidence: R. Dingwall and J. Eekelaar, T. Murray, The Protection of Children* (1983), p. 225. There were wide variations between authorities in the extent that protection proceedings, see: J. Packman *et al.* (1986) and Packman and Hall (1998).

of statutory protection against unwarranted interference" which was essential.[43] For the same reason it rejected an "exceptional circumstances" criterion.[44] The court's power to commit a child to care in matrimonial, domestic and guardianship proceedings (but not in wardship) should be abolished[45]; changing the grounds for care proceedings and other improvements would reduce the need to resort to the High Court but it should be retained as a safety net. The Law Commission disagreed; the existence of this broad jurisdiction "made nonsense" of carefully devised checks and balances in the statutory codes.[46] The *Review* proposed a standard for intervention based on actual or likely harm, where "harm" connoted a substantial deficit and rejected any grounds based on specific incidents or conditions. The court would be expressly required to find that parental care fell below an objectively acceptable level.[47]

The Government accepted the threshold for intervention proposed by the *Review of Child Care Law* and agreed that exceptions should not be permitted Although there was a danger that the new grounds might not cover all cases, other jurisdictions managed without a safety net like wardship. The Lord Chancellor reasoned that "The integrity and independence of the family is a basic building block of a free and democratic society and the need to defend it should be clearly perceivable in law."[48] Retaining wardship would give the courts, not local authorities, control over care. Also the proposed system for concurrent jurisdiction required that all courts applied the same principles. The Lord Chancellor commented that the new test for intervention in the Children Act should not be regarded as grounds for an order but as "the minimum circumstances which the government considers should always be found to exist before . . . the state should be enabled to intervene compulsorily in family life."[49]

A single route for child protection proceedings does not mean that there is a uniform standard for intervention. Child protection is a process which involves a number of stages where social workers and other professionals have to decide whether they should take further action.[50] Thresholds vary over time and between authorities[51]; different professionals have different views.[52] The Children Act 1989 intends that only the most extreme cases require adjudication by

---

[43] *Review of Child Care Law*, para. 15.10. Judges of the Family Division were reported to have said that such a test, if applied literally, would lead to "a substantial proportion of the child population . . . [being] taken into care . . . [because] they would be better off with foster parents." However, it is now proposed that the child's welfare should be the main ground for dispensing with parental consent to adoption see: Adoption and Children Bill 2002, cl.52(1) (b).

[44] *ibid.* para. 15.11.

[45] *Review of the Child Care Law*, para. 15.35–8.

[46] Law Com. W.P., *Wards of Court* (1987), paras 4.9–10. This view was supported by research: J. Masson and S. Morton, "The use of wardship by local authorities" (1989) 52 *M.L.R.* 762. No proposals to abolish local authority use of wardship were included in the report, see: Law Com. No. 172, para. 1.4.

[47] *Review of Child Care Law*, paras 15.23, 15.20.

[48] Lord Mackay, "Perceptions of the Children Bill and beyond" [1989] New L.J. 505 at 507.

[49] *ibid.* at 506.

[50] D.H., *Child Protection messages from research* (1995), pp. 15, 25.

[51] *ibid.* pp. 15, 33. The overview concludes that thresholds have generally been lowered, see also J. Gibbons, *et al.*, *Operating the Child Protection System* (1995).

[52] J. Thoburn, *et al.*, *Paternalism or Partnership? Family involvement in the Child Protection process* (1995).

the courts[53]; research indicates that it has achieved its purpose of raising thresholds for court intervention.[54] Where parents accept the need for support to improve child care, the local authority can provide services under Children Act 1989, Pt III, including accommodation without court proceedings.

C. The Child Protection Service

22–017 The child protection system is interdisciplinary, involving the participation of the police, educational bodies, doctors and others.[55] Although the agencies involved have statutory responsibilities, the framework for their co-operation is set out in Department of Health guidance, *Working Together to Safeguard Children*[56] and local procedures. The primary responsibility for child protection, the prevention of abuse and neglect, its investigation, the bringing of care proceedings and the care of children who have been removed from their families lies with local authorities.[57] The police play a major role, conducting joint investigations with social services in cases of suspected abuse and removing children in emergencies for their protection.[58] Protecting children almost always involves the co-operation of other agencies with responsibilities for health and education who have contact with families and information about individual children. In order to facilitate this, Area Child Protection Committees have been established.[59] The ACPC has a senior representative from each agency and has responsibility for reviewing arrangements for inter-agency co-operation including joint training.

D. Investigation of child abuse and neglect

(a) Duty to investigate

22–018 Local authorities have a statutory duty to make inquiries in all cases where they have reasonable cause to suspect that a child in their area is suffering or likely to suffer significant harm[60] They may start or continue inquiries after an

---

[53] D.H., *Child Protection messages from research* (1995), p. 32.

[54] D.H., *Children Act now* (2001), p. 55, citing Brandon *et al.* (1999), Hunt *et al.* (1999) and J. Thoburn *et al.*, *Family support in cases of emotional maltreatment and neglect* (2000).

[55] *X. v. Bedfordshire C. C.* [1995] 2 F.L.R. 276 at 301 *per* Lord Browne-Wilkinson.

[56] (1999), referred to here as *Working Together* (1999). Previous editions were published in 1988 and 1991.

[57] Local Authority Social Services Act 1970, Sched. 1 (as amended); Children Act 1989; ss.21, 23, Pts IV and V, and Sched. 2, para. 4. The NSPCC is authorised to bring proceedings under the Children Act 1989, s.31(9) but no longer does so, see: B. Joel-Esam, "The NSPCC in the 1990s" in A. Levy, *Refocus on child abuse* (1994), p. 157.

[58] All but one force has a dedicated unit handling child protection matters see: Her Majesty's Inspector of Constabulary, *Child Abuse, Thematic Inspection* (1998) and below para. 22–019.

[59] See D.H. *et al.*, *Working Together* (1999), Chap. 4.

[60] s.47(1); *Working Together* (1999), paras 5.13–5.19. Aspects of the inquiry may be delegated, *e.g.* to a health visitor. The Department of Health has produced a good practice guide, D.H., *The challenge of partnership* (1995); each ACPC has its own procedural manual.

alleged perpetrator has been acquitted.[61] Initial inquiries must enable the authority to determine whether they should exercise any of their powers, for example, to bring proceedings or provide services. They must ensure that access to the child is obtained unless they are satisfied that they already have sufficient information.[62]

Although local authorities monitor the care of children they have contact with, they rely on other agencies—the medical services,[63] the police, school teachers and members of the public[64]—to refer concerns about abused and neglected children.[65] Children, particularly those counselled through ChildLine[66] may request help from teachers or other adults who then contact social services[67]; some parents seek help from social services because of fears that they or their partner will harm a child.

Doctors, general practitioners, casualty officers and paediatricians may all identify[68] child abuse in the course of examining or treating children. Although doctors have a legal and ethical duty to maintain confidentiality, the General Medical Council has advised that disclosures may be necessary to prevent risk of death or serious harm to the patient or others, for example to protect a child from abuse.[69] Children's health is also monitored by community based nurses. Health visitors are primarily concerned with the healthy development of children under the age of five. They have no statutory powers but provide a service which typically involves visiting pre-school children at home and running clinics where babies are weighed, their development assessed and mothers are given advice

---

[61] *Re S. (Sexual Abuse Allegations: Local Authority Response)* [2001] 2 F.L.R. 776, QBD. Similarly it need only have reasonable cause to suspect that abuse has occurred.

[62] Children Act 1989, s.47(4). The statutory duty makes it plain to social workers what is expected of them and provides a lever where families are reluctant to allow access. The social worker who investigated allegations of abuse to Kimberley Carlile told the inquiry into her death that he had only been allowed to see her through a glazed bedroom door. London Borough of Greenwich, *A Child In Mind* (1987), p. 115.

[63] See J. Gibbons *et al.*, *Operating the child protection system* (1995), p. 41.

[64] Half of child protection referrals come via the child or a member of the family, see D.H., *Child Protection messages from research* (1995), p. 26 and H. Cleaver and P. Freeman, *Parental Perspectives in cases of suspected child abuse* (1995).

[65] See generally, C. Wattam, *Making a case in child protection* (1992). The need for referral should be discussed with the family unless this places the child at increased risk of significant harm: *Working Together* (1999), paras 5.6, 5.11.

[66] A confidential telephone counselling service.

[67] Solicitors may breach client confidentiality where there is a serious threat to a child's life or health: Law Society, *Guide to professional conduct of solicitors* (8th ed.), para. 16.02.4; Solicitors Family Law Association, *Guide to good practice for solicitors acting for children* (5th ed., 2000) para. J.

[68] Identification, even in cases of physical abuse or neglect, may not be a simple matter. The doctor needs to examine the child for clinical signs and also consider whether any explanation offered for the injuries is consistent with what has been found. In cases of failure to thrive the doctor will also need to establish whether there is any organic reason for the child's condition. Diagnosis may be contested: *Re A. (Non-accidental Injury: Medical Evidence)* [2001] 2 F.L.R. 657, FD or missed: R. Dingwall, J. Eekelaar and T. Murray, *The Protection of Children* (1983), Chap. 2.

[69] *Working Together* (1999), para. 7.29 *et seq.*; General Medical Council, *Confidentiality* (1995) paras 11 and 18. There is no statutory duty on doctors to report child abuse only to co-operate with inquiries of the local authority: Children Act 1989, s.47(9)–(11). *cf.* Many states of the United States of America where various professionals are legally required to report suspicions of abuse, see L. Bell and P. Tooman, "Mandatory reporting laws a critical overview" (1994) 8 Int. J Law & Fam. 337.

about parenting.[70] Health visitors aim to maintain the confidence and co-operation of the families they visit so that they may continue to offer assistance and check children's progress.

School teachers' daily involvement with older children puts them in a position to identify cases and make referrals. They may see signs of ill-treatment when children prepare for P.E. lessons, observe disturbed behaviour or changes in behaviour which lead them to suspect abuse, or be told of incidents by a child. Each school should make a senior member of staff responsible for co-ordinating the school's response to child abuse and for referring cases to a named person in the social services department.[71]

When the local authority receives a referral it must make an initial assessment and determine whether to protect for the child's immediately.[72] The social services department, the police and other relevant agencies should hold a strategy discussion to share information, plan further inquiries and agree a course of action.[73] Typically the initial investigation involves visiting the person making the allegation (unless it is anonymous) to verify details, and seeing the child,[74] the parents with care, other significant adults and other children in the household.[75] The NSPCC provides a specialist child protection service to investigate allegations where children have been abused in care.[76]

The local authority may call on the assistance of other local authorities, a local education authority, local housing authority, health authority and the NSPCC who must comply unless it would be unreasonable in all the circumstances of the case.[77] Obligations of confidentiality to clients may not justify refusing to provide information but it has been said that a local authority has no duty to disclose the identity of perpetrators to other local authorities in whose area they are now residing.[78]

Too many investigations are undertaken and resources expended with little

---

70 The expectations of health visitors are clarified in *Working Together* (1999), paras 3.34–3.38. The U.K. Central Council for Nursing, Midwifery and Health Visiting, *Guidelines for professional practice* (1996) supports the disclosure of information without the clients consent in cases of child abuse (paras 55, 56).

71 *Working Together* (1999), paras 3.10–3.15.

72 *ibid.* paras 5.13–5.27. D.H., *The Challenge of Partnership* (1995), paras 5.2, 5.10 *et seq.*

73 *Working Together* (1999), paras 5.28–5.32. Each A.C.P.C. should have a protocol for joint police and social services investigations (para. 5.32).

74 s.47(4) (a). Research has identified common pitfalls in the conduct of initial child protection visits see *Working Together* (1999), p.44 and H. Cleaver *et al.*, "Children living at home: the initial child protection enquiry. Ten pitfalls and how to avoid them" in *Assessing risk in child protection* (H. Cleaver *et al.* ed., 1998).

75 *Working Together* (1999), para. 5.13; D.H., *Framework for assessment of children in need and their families* (2000); D.H., *The challenge of partnership* (1995), paras . 4.8, 6.15 *et seq.*

76 B. Joel-Esam, "The NSPCC in the 1990s" in *Re-focus on Child Abuse* (A. Levy ed., 1994), pp. 157, 161 *et seq.*

77 Children Act 1989, s.47(9)–(11).

78 *Re V. (Sexual Abuse: Disclosure)* [1999] 1 F.L.R. 267 at 272 *per* Butler-Sloss L.J. This refers to findings in civil proceedings. Where a person has been convicted or cautioned for an offence against children an inter-agency case conference should be arranged to manage the risk they pose: *Working Together* (1999), paras 3.66, 7.37. Information may be disclosed by the police: Crime and Disorder Act 1998, s.115; Home Office, *Guidance on Statutory Crime and Disorder Partnerships* (1999) and below, para. 22–024.

apparent benefit.[79] 160,000 referrals are made to the child protection system each year.[80] Of these 40,000 are closed after inquiries of other agencies and a check of the child protection register.[81] 120,000 children are visited by child protection workers and one third of these become subject to a child protection conference.[82] Three thousand children enter the care system as a result of these processes and another 3,000 are accommodated. In 96 per cent of cases the children remain at home with relatives.[83] The Department of Health has reported that the failure to follow through interventions with much needed services has prevented professionals from meeting the needs of children and families.[84] Families generally experience child protection inquiries negatively, they do not find the process helpful nor do they feel involved in it.[85]

(b) The role of the police

22–019 The police have general responsibility for the protection of life and limb, the prevention and investigation of crime and the submission of cases for criminal proceedings.[86] The police also have a power remove or detain children who would otherwise be likely to suffer significant harm.[87] The *Cleveland Report* identified failure of police co-operation as a contributory factor in the crisis and recommended that police should recognise and develop their responsibility for child protection but the Children Act 1989 imposed no obligation on the police to assist local authority inquiries.[88] Nevertheless, close working relationships between the police and social services have been developed.[89] The increased emphasis on the prosecution of child abusers, the establishment of specialist police units and the introduction of the *Memorandum of Good Practice on Video-recorded Evidence*[90] led to the police becoming more involved in child abuse investigation. There are dangers that families may find this even more threatening, that their wider needs will be missed and that it will be difficult for

[79] D.H., *Child Protection messages from research* (1995), pp. 54–5.
[80] *ibid.* p. 28.
[81] See below, para. 22–021.
[82] Where a local authority finds that concerns are substantiated but decides not to call a child protection conference the decision should be endorsed by "a suitably qualified and designated person within the social services department": *Working Together* (1999), para. 5.51.
[83] D.H., *Child Protection messages from research* (1995), p. 31; *Children Act now* (2001) p. 68 *et seq.*
[84] *ibid.* p. 55; *Children Act now* (2001), pp. 45–46.
[85] P. Freeman and J. Hunt, *Parental perspectives on care proceedings* (1998); D.H., *Child Protection messages from research* (1995), p. 43; J. Thoburn *et al.*, *Paternalism or partnership: Family involvement in the child protection process* (1995).
[86] *Working Together* (1991), paras 4.11–4.15; Police and Criminal Evidence Act 1984, s.17(1) (e).
[87] Children Act 1989, s.46(1); J. Masson, "Police Protection—protecting whom?" [2002] *J.S.W.F.L.* 157 and below, para. 22–045.
[88] David Mellor, Secretary of State for Health, explained these omissions on the basis that "police refusal to co-operate on any matter would be indefensible" Children Bill, Committee Stage (Standing Committee B, col. 342, June 6, 1989), see also *Cleveland Report* (1988), Chap. 6.
[89] C. Hallett and E. Birchall, *Working Together in child protection* (1995); E. Farmer and M. Owen, *Child protection practice: private risks and public remedies* (1995), pp. 123–7; HMIC, *Child Abuse, Thematic Inspection* (1998).
[90] Home Office with the Department of Health (1992). This has now been replaced by Home Office, *Achieving best evidence in criminal proceedings* (2002), see below.

social workers to establish co-operative relationships with them subsequently. The Department of Health has suggested that video-recorded interviews should only be used when thay are really necessary and should not be allowed to eclipse other aspects of the work with the family.[91]

(c) Child protection conferences

22–020 Inquiring into child abuse involves more than receiving referrals and visiting the child. All relevant information must be collated; this is usually done by calling a child protection or case conference[92] and inviting the parents or carers and all professionals involved with the child to attend.[93] The purpose of the conference is to share and analyse information about the child and parents; to make judgments about the likelihood of significant harm in the future; and to decide what action should be taken to safeguard the child.[94] Conferences reduce professional anxiety by sharing the responsibility and also develop an official view within agencies about a family.[95] Formally, the conference draws up an outline child protection plan where the child is at risk and enters the child's name on the child protection register. Parents should be involved in the formulation of the plan and be given a copy of it.[96] The conference must also appoint a key worker[97] and set a date for the first review conference.[98] Review conferences are reconvened at intervals[99] and decide whether to remove the child's name from the register.[1] The conference may recommend that care proceedings are taken, but the local authority decides whether to do so. Where a child is in need the conference should ensure, subject to parental agreement, that services will be considered.[2]

Child protection conferences are part of the child protection system which

---

[91] D.H., *The challenge of partnership* (1995), para. 5.19–20.

[92] This should occur within 15 days of the strategy discussion: *Working Together* (1999), paras 5.23–7, 5.90 and 5.98.

[93] The child may also be invited if this is appropriate: *Working Together* (1999) para. 5.53. In practice children attend where parents are unable to make babysitting arrangements: E. Farmer and M. Owen, *Child protection practice: private risks and public remedies* (1995), p.108. Where court permission is required for disclosure of material to the conference there should be the utmost co-operation between the court and the conference: *Re M. (Disclosure)* [1998] 1 F.L.R. 734, CA. (decision to preclude disclosure of material to health authority overturned).

[94] *Working Together* (1999), para. 5.53; see also: D.H., *Child Protection messages from research* (1995) p. 29.

[95] Farmer and Owen, *op. cit.* pp. 90, 100.

[96] *Working Together* (1999), para. 5.83. The parents' copy should be written in their first language.

[97] This person who must be employed by either the social services department or the NSPCC is responsible for developing the child protection plan, completing the core assessment and co-ordinating the implementation of the plan: *Working Together* (1999), paras 5.75–6.

[98] *Working Together* (1999), paras 5.64–5.70.

[99] Where the child is looked after by a local authority this review should be integrated with that required under the Review of children's cases regulations 1991 S.I. 1991 No. 895; *Working Together* (1999), paras 5.96–7.

[1] *Working Together* (1999), paras 5.93–5. This is known as deregistration.

[2] The conference can act as a gateway to services but it may be necessary for the local authority to complete the core assessment before determining what services to offer: *Working Together* (1999), para. 5.67.

can lead to children being removed from the family. Parents must be involved in the decision-making process in order to protect their interests and respect their right to family life.[3] *Working Together* advises that parents and involved family members should normally be invited to conferences but accepts that "exceptionally, it may be necessary to exclude one or more family members" for example because of violence or intimidation.[4] Parents who are excluded or who are unwilling to attend should be given the opportunity to present their views. Parents may bring "an advocate, friend or supporter"[5] to the conference and this could include a lawyer.[6] But a case conference is a discussion not a court hearing. Complaints about case conferences should be dealt with according to local authority procedures.[7] The courts have been reluctant to subject case conference procedures and decisions to judicial review. It has been said that in balancing child protection against fairness to an adult, the interest of an adult may have to be placed second, and that the authorities should be allowed to perform this delicate task without constant supervision from the courts.[8]

Third parties, particularly those working with children, may also be effected by the recommendation of a case conference. Where a person's occupation is threatened it has been held that sufficient details of the allegations and an opportunity to meet them must be given before action is taken.[9]

Family Group Conferences have been developed in a number of authorities to reduce the power imbalance between the family and the professionals. They are based on an idea from New Zealand which prevents compulsory measures of care being imposed before the family have been informed in a formal meeting with child protection services of the concerns about the child, and had an opportunity for private discussion to formulate their own protection plan.[10] They have not replaced the more formal child protection conference in England and Wales but are used to develop child protection plans with family co-operation.[11]

---

[3] *W. v. U.K.* (1988) 10 EH.R.R. 29; *Scott v. U.K.* [2000] 1 F.L.R. 958; and see: S. Choudry [2001] *Fam. Law* 531.

[4] para. 5.58. The decision to exclude must be made by the Chair of the conference.

[5] para. 5.57 but suitable services may not be available see: B. Lindley *et al.*, "Advice and advocacy for parent in child protection cases—what is happening in current practice" [2001] *C.F.L.Q.* 167.

[6] *R. v. Cornwall C. C., ex p. LH.* [2000] 1 F.L.R. 236, QBD (policies to refuse permission for solicitors to attend case conferences and not to provide copies of the minutes to parents declared unlawful). The Law Society's Family Law Committee has issued guidance for solicitors attending case conferences (1997), see: Clarke Hall and Morrison 1, para. 1900U.

[7] *Working Together* (1999) paras 5.71–3; Complaints Directions issued under Local Authority Social Services Act 1970, s.7B;

[8] *R. v. Harrow LBC, ex p. D.* [1990] Fam. 133 at 138 *per* Butler-Sloss L.J.; *R. v. Hampshire C. C., ex p. H.* [1999] 2 F.L.R. 359, CA.

[9] *R. v. Wandsworth LBC, ex p. P.* [1989] C.O.D. 262; a foster mother removed from the list of approved foster parents following an allegation; *cf. R. v. Avon C.C. ex p. Crabtree* [1996] 1 F.L.R. 502, CA where it was accepted that the decision to de-register a foster parent was fair where there had been a lengthy discussion of issues but no charge sheet; see also *Working Together* (1999) para. 6.13–6.22.

[10] Children, Young Persons and their Families Act 1989 (N.Z.), ss. 31, 70. Care proceedings can only be started if the family have failed to agree a satisfactory plan.

[11] *Working Together* (1999), paras 7.13–7.18; see also K. Morris *et al.*, *Family Group conferences—a training pack* (1998).

(d) The child protection register

22–021 This is a central point of inquiry which enables professionals to establish the existence and nature of current concerns about significant harm to a child. Children are registered under one or more of the categories—physical, emotional, sexual abuse or neglect.[12] It has been held that that a decision to register a child must be based on evidence of harm in the relevant category.[13] Approximately 30,000 children have their names included on the register; each year the number of new registrations equals the number of de-registrations.[14] Registration rates differ widely between authorities and do not merely reflect differences in the incidence of abuse.[15] The former practice of including the names of alleged abusers on the register has been discontinued; separate registers are held by the police and by the Department of Health under the Protection of Children Act 1999.

(e) Negligent investigations

22–022 Incompetent investigation can lead to children being separated from their families unnecessarily,[16] or sustaining long periods of abuse or neglect. Inquiries into child deaths have identified numerous failures in the child protection system.[17] However, child protection legislation is not treated as existing for the benefit of abused children but for society in general. Thus a local authority's failure to carry out its duties under the Children Act 1989, ss.17 and 47[18] does not give rise to an action for breach of statutory duty.[19] Also, the House of Lords has held that a local authority is not liable in negligence for failing to use its powers to protect children:—

> In *X. v. Bedfordshire County Council*[20] the local authority received numerous reports from professionals, relatives and neighbours that the children, aged five and under, were severely neglected[21] and abused. Their home was

---

[12] *Working Together* (1999), para. 5.101.

[13] *R. v. Hampshire C. C., ex p. H.* [1999] 2 F.L.R. 359, CA but a psychologist's report is not necessary to establish emotional harm.

[14] *Children Act Report 2000,* paras 2.5–2.7. In 1997 re-registrations accounted for almost 20 per cent of all registrations; the Department of Health wishes to reduce this by 10 percent (*i.e.* to under 18 per cent) by 2002: see *Children Act Report 1995–9,* Chap. 3.

[15] J. Gibbons *et al., Operating the child protection system* (1995), p. 8.

[16] *M. v. Newham LBC* [1995] A.C. 648, HL reported in the E.C.H.R as *TP. and KM. v. U.K.* [2001] 2 F.L.R 549 (removal of child from mother's care); *L. and P. v. Reading B.C. and the Chief Constable of Thames Valley Police* [2001] 2 F.L.R. 50, CA (exclusion of father).

[17] The Lord Laming's Inquiry into the death of Victoria Climbié is a recent example; the system cannot be expected to prevent all such deaths.

[18] The same conclusion was reached in respect of the earlier legislation, Children and Young Persons Act 1969, s.2 and Child Care Act 1980, ss.1,18.

[19] *X. v. Bedfordshire C.C.* [1995] 2 A.C. 633; see also R. Bailey-Harris and M. Harris, "The immunity of local authorities in child protection functions—Is the door now ajar" [1998] *C.F.L.Q.* 227, 228.

[20] [1995] 2 A.C. 633.

[21] Research commissioned by the Department of Health indicates that neglect cases are less likely than abuse cases to be subject to thorough inquiries but that the progress for children neglected long term is poor, D.H., *Child Protection messages from research* (1995), pp. 33–5, 42.

filthy with faeces and urine, the children were dishevelled, smelly and hungry, and were frequently locked out of the home. No child protection conference was held for four years; when a conference was held it was decided not to place the children's names on the register and not to take court proceedings. Eventually, following repeated requests from the parents, the children were removed. The children brought proceedings for negligence and the local authority applied to have the action struck out. The local authority's application was granted and this decision was upheld on appeal.

Although the local authority could foresee damage to the children if statutory duties were carried out negligently and the relationship between the plaintiffs and the local authority was sufficiently proximate, it was not "fair, just and reasonable"[22] to impose a common law duty of care. First, such a duty would cut across the whole interagency system. It would be manifestly unfair to hold liable only one agency within multidisciplinary group; imposing liability on all participant bodies would lead to impossible problems of determining the extent to which any one was negligent.[23] Secondly, these decisions are "extraordinarily delicate". Imposition of liability might make local authorities unwilling to take risks and encourage further, defensive investigations which would delay response and reduce the resources available for other social services activities. Thirdly, the nature of child protection work means the risk that local authorities would have to respond to many vexatious claims is too high to ignore.[24] Moreover, the development of a tort of in this area does not follow incrementally from any existing category of negligence.[25]

22–023 This decision does not mean that a local authority can never be held liable in negligence in respect of actions in connection with child protection and child care. The House of Lords has held that a local authority can be liable for negligently failing to safeguard the welfare of a child in care, and refused to strike out claims for negligently causing psychiatric injury to children and their parents resulting from sexual abuse to the children by a foster child, placed without warnings about his behaviour.[26] These cases make it possible to argue for negligence liability in relation to some aspects of child protection work providing the general requirements of the tort are satisfied. Such cases require a full examination of the facts and application of the *Caparo* tests; summary dismissal by striking out the application is not appropriate.[27] The decision which is challenged

[22] *per* Lord Browne-Wilkinson at 749, applying the test in *Caparo Industries Plc. v. Dickman* [1990] 2 A.C. 605.

[23] *ibid.* at 750. Although this may be the effect of a Part 8 Review into a child's death, see *Working Together* (1999) or a Public Inquiry.

[24] *ibid.* at 751.

[25] *ibid.* at 751 as required by *Caparo Industries Plc. v. Dickman* [1990] 2 A.C. 605.

[26] *Barrett v. London Borough of Enfield* [1999] 2 F.L.R. 426, HL; *W. v. Essex C. C.* [2000] 1 F.L.R. 657, HL and see Bailey-Harris and Harris, *op. cit.*

[27] *Barrett v. London Borough of Enfield* [1999] 2 F.L.R. 426 at 430 *per* Lord Browne-Wilkinson; *L. and P. v. Reading B. C. and the Chief Constable of Thames Valley Police* [2001] 2 F.L.R. 50, CA.

must be "operational" rather than one of policy[28] and any discretion exercised unreasonably. This might include the convening and conduct of a child protection conference, failing to report part of an assessment or misrecording an interview.[29] Local authorities can be vicariously liable for the negligence of their staff[30] but in *M. v. Newham London Borough Council*[31] it was held that the psychiatrist and social worker who made an incorrect assessment that the child was at risk leading to her removal from home, owed no duties to the mother and child for which their employers could be vicariously liable. These professionals were retained by the local authority and their duty was to the local authority alone.[32] The House of Lords also held, overruling the Court of Appeal on this point,[33] that the psychiatrist had witness immunity because her examination had an immediate link with possible proceedings.[34] Immunity is not available to a witness who undermines justice by intentionally misleading the court.[35]

The European Convention on Human Rights is an important influence on this area of law:—

> In *Z. v. U.K.*[36] the Official Solicitor, acting on behalf of the children in the Bedfordshire case sought redress under the European Convention of Human Rights, arguing breach of their rights under Articles 3, 6, 8 and 13.[37] The Commission unanimously found that the children had been subject to inhuman and degrading treatment. The Government did not dispute this; the State had failed in its positive obligation under Article 3 to protect the children.[38] Although there was no mechanism for redress, the Human

---

[28] See Lord Browne-Wilkinson in *X. v. Bedfordshire C.C.* [1995] A.C. 633 at 737 *et seq.* and Bailey-Harris and Harris, *op. cit.* p. 231–3. This is a difficult decision which requires a full assessment of the facts: *Barrett v. London Borough of Enfield* [1999] 2 F.L.R. 426, HL at 429–430 *per* Lord Browne-Wilkinson, at 445–6 *per* Lord Slynn, at 461 *per* Lord Hutton.

[29] See Bailey-Harris and Harris *op. cit.* p. 241. *Barrett v. London Borough of Enfield* [1997] 2 F.L.R. 167 at 175 *per* Lord Woolf and *L. and P. v. Reading B. C. and the Chief Constable of Thames Valley Police* [2001] 2 F.L.R. 50, CA (where the claim relates to an interview which was conducted oppressively and misreported).

[30] *Christmas v. Hampshire C. C.* [1995] 2 A.C. 633, a case heard with *X. v. Bedfordshire* but based on failure by the educational psychology service; Bailey-Harris and Harris, *op. cit.*, p.242.

[31] [1995] A.C. 648, HL; *TP. and KM. v. U.K.* [2001] 2 F.L.R 549, E.C.H.R.

[32] *ibid.* at 753. The court's analogy with a doctor who provides a medical report for an insurance company has been criticised: Bailey-Harris and Harris, *op. cit.* p. 237; Cretney [1994] *Fam. Law* 435.

[33] [1994] 1 F.L.R. 431 at 460, 468. The decision of the Court of Appeal was apparently based on a misapprehension that the psychiatrist's opinion never formed part of the evidence.

[34] [1995] 2 A.C. 633 at 755 *per* Lord Browne-Wilkinson.

[35] *L. and P. v. Reading B. C. and the Chief Constable of Thames Valley Police* [2001] 2 F.L.R. 50 at 67 *per* Otton J. In this case the applicant father's and child's claims, which remain to be considered at a full hearing, are based on misfeasance in public office and conspiracy to injure as well as negligence.

[36] [2000] 2 F.C.R. 245 (Commission Decision); [2001] 2 F.L.R. 612 E.Ct.H.R.

[37] *ibid.* The Court held that no separate issue arose in relation to Art. 8, paras 76, 77 but liability based on a breach of the procedural safeguards in Art 8. was considered in *TP. v. KM. v. U.K.* [2001] 2 F.L.R. 549 at paras 57–83 (the *M. v. Newham* case). There was a positive duty to give the mother information about the interview; had this been done the mistake would have been discovered and the child returned. Both mother and daughter were awarded compensation. Disclosure is now required in such cases: *Re C. (Expert Evidence: Disclosure)* [1995] 1 F.L.R. 204, FD; *Re JC. (Care Proceedings: Procedure)* [1995] 2 F.L.R. 77, FD.

[38] [2001] 2 F.L.R. 612, paras 70–73.

Rights Act 1998 now provides a remedy.[39] The children were awarded substantial compensation to cover psychotherapy, future loss of earnings and for their suffering.[40] However, the Court accepted the Government's argument that, as a matter of law, the children had no case in negligence against the local authority. Consequently, there could be no breach of Article 6 when the claims were struck out.[41]

Despite the apparent closure of this issue by the House of Lords in 1995 and the upholding of that decision in Strasbourg it seems that there will be cases where negligence actions by children and even parents will succeed against social workers, doctors, police officers, and their employers, where investigations have failed to match accepted standards.[42]

(f) Registers of offenders and community notification[43]

22–024 Concern that those who have abused children may repeat their actions, and particularly seek positions with access to children have led to the establishment of various registers. These are preventative, alerting prospective employers of the person's unsuitability, and can also assist the police investigating offences against children. Under the Sex Offenders Act 1997, those who are convicted or cautioned for certain offences are required to notify the police of their current address for a period related to the length of their sentence.[44] This information is stored in the police national computer system and is accessible to all forces. A separate register of individuals who are considered unsuitable to work with children has been created under the Protection of Children Act 1999.[45] Information may be included without a conviction, for example where there have been disciplinary proceedings by an employer or a child protection investigation relating to a foster carer.[46] The Care Standards Tribunal hears disputes about an individual's inclusion. Child care organisations are required to check this register and may not employ a person in a child care position who is listed.[47] The

[39] *ibid.* paras 105–111; Art. 13 had been breached but see H.R.A. 1998, ss.7(1) (a), 8. The Government accepted that the Criminal Injuries Compensation Scheme, the Local Government Ombudsman and the Children Act 1989 complaints system did not satisfy Art. 13 in this case.

[40] But the awards may be low compared with damages in negligence, See: R. Bailey-Harris [2001] *Fam. Law* 583, 585.

[41] *ibid.* paras 87–104. In doing so the court accepted that it had misunderstood negligence law in *Osman v. U.K.* [1999] 1 F.L.R. 193. The treatment of the claim did not amount to an exclusionary rule or an immunity which prevented access to the courts, paras 96, 100.

[42] Applying the test in *Bolam v. Friern Hospital Management Committee* [1957] 1 W.L.R. 118.

[43] For a more detailed discussion see: C. Cobley, *Sex Offenders* (2000), Chap. 7 and *Exercising constant vigilance: the role of the Probation Service in Protecting the public from sex offenders* (1998).

[44] s.1(4). It is an offence to fail to notify or provide false information, s.3(1).

[45] This combines and puts on a statutory basis the "consultancy index" held by the Department of Health and "list 99" held by the Department for Education.

[46] Protection of Children Act 1999, ss.2–2C, 3.

[47] Protection of Children Act 1999, s.7. These checks are made at the same time as criminal records checks under the Police Act 1997, s.113. Poor practices in the employment of care staff have been a concern for some time see: N. Warner, *Choosing with care* (1992), the *Warner Report* and W. Utting, *People like us* (1997).

information held in registers is used primarily by the police and social services but may be disclosed to others where there is a "pressing need" to protect children. Each case must be considered on its own facts[48]; disclosure is the exception not the rule:—

> LM[49] had a contract to transport children for the local education authority. He agreed to a police check and his contract was terminated; the police and social services had disclosed that, more than seven years before, there had been two separate investigations into indecent assaults of children by him. LM successfully obtained judicial review of the decision to disclose this information to the education authority, and of the refusal to give assurances that it would not be disclosed in future.

In contrast with many parts of the United States where community notification statutes have been enacted, there is no provision for informing the public.[50] The risks of encouraging vigilante attacks and of offenders refusing to co-operate with registration are considered by professionals to make such provisions counter-productive; general notification also conflicts with the right to privacy.

E. Compulsory measures of care

22–025 In this section we consider the role of the court in child protection particularly, the tests which must be satisfied if a child is to be committed to the care of the local authority, the orders the court can make, their discharge and appeal.

Care proceedings

22–026 Court orders should only be sought where there appears to be no better way to safeguard the child.[51] Only a local authority or the NSPCC may initiate care proceedings[52] in respect of a child under 17.[53] Proceedings are in two stages which may involve separate hearings.[54] The court must first be satisfied that the threshold criteria in section 31 are met; then it must consider the local authority's

---

[48] *R. v. Local Authority and Police Authority in the Midlands, ex p. LM.* [2000] 1 F.L.R. 612, QBD; *R. v. Chief Constable of North Wales Police, ex p. Thorpe* [1999] Q.B. 396, CA; Home Office Circular 39/1997.

[49] *R. v. Local Authority and Police Authority in the Midlands, ex p. LM.* [2000] 1 F.L.R. 612, QBD.

[50] U.S.C. 14071(d) known as Megan's law after Megan Kanka who was murdered by her neighbour, a convicted sex offender; see B. Hebenton and T. Thomas, *Keeping Track? Observations on Sex Offender Registers in the U.S.* Home Office Crime Detection and Prevention Series No. 83 (1997); C. Cobley *op. cit.* 7.74 *et seq.;* ChildLine *et al., Protecting children, managing sex offenders in the community* (1998).

[51] *Guidance,* Vol.1, para. 3.2.

[52] Children Act 1989, ss.31(1), (7), (9), 92. The NSPCC now rarely brings proceedings see Joel-Esam *op. cit.*

[53] No order may be obtained in respect of a married child over 16 or any child over 17: Children Act 1989, s.31(3) previously such children could be warded see *Re S.W.* [1986] 1 F.L.R. 24.

[54] *Re B. (Split Hearing: Jurisdiction)* [2000] 1 F.L.R. 334, CA; *Re G. (Care Proceedings: Split Trials)* [2001] 1 F.L.R. 872, CA. The two hearings should be before the same judge.

care plan applying the welfare test, using the checklist[55] and the "no order" principle,[56] and decide whether to make an order.[57]

(a) Threshold criteria[58]

22–027 The Children Act 1989, s.31(2) provides that a care or supervision order may only be made if the court is satisfied:—

> "(a) that the child is suffering or is likely to suffer significant harm; and
> (b) that the harm or likelihood of harm is attributable to—
>
> (i) the care given to the child or likely to be given to him if the order were not made, not being what it would be reasonable to expect a parent to give to him; or
> (ii) the child's being beyond parental control."

Significant harm

22–028 "Harm" means "ill-treatment or the impairment of health or development."[59] This broad definition allows intervention both because of what carers do and where the care given to the child has a substantially deleterious effect on the child. It may allow intervention where the parents have adopted a life-style which has a damaging effect on their child's health or development, for example isolating their children from the community, continuously travelling, or forcing a marriage[60] as well as more obvious cases of abuse or neglect.[61] The harm must be significant but there is no clear indication of what this means in cases of ill-treatment. It has been held that depriving a child of parental care by murdering his mother amounts to significant harm but this may be questioned.[62] A minor injury may be significant because of the child's age[63] or disabilities already suffered. For example, minor burns to the hands could prevent a blind

---

[55] Children Act 1989, s.1(3), (4).

[56] s.1(5); see above, para. 19–003.

[57] *Re J. (Minors) (Care: Care Plan)* [1994] 1 F.L.R. 253 at 258, *per* Wall, J; cross applications for residence orders do not have to be considered first, *Oldham M.B.C. v. E.* [1994] 1 F.L.R. 568 at 576, *per* Waite L.J.

[58] See generally M. Freeman, "Care after 1991" in *Children and the law* (D. Freestone ed., 1990); A. Bainham, "Care after 1991—a reply" [1991] J.C.L. 99; M. Freeman, "Legislating for child abuse" in *Re-focus on child abuse* (A. Levy ed., 1994), p. 18 and M. Brandon *et al.*, *Safeguarding children with the Children Act 1989* (1999), Chap. 1.

[59] s.31(9) "ill-treatment," "health" and "development" are all defined in s.31(9) and include physical, emotional and sexual abuse and neglect. An amendment added by the Adoption and Children Bill 2002 recognises that seeing or hearing the ill-treatment of another can lead to impairment.

[60] *Re KR. (Abduction)* [1999] 2 F.L.R. 542 at 548 *per* Singer J. (*obiter*).

[61] The *Review of Child Care Law*, para. 15.16 stated that "the concept of substantial detriment will adequately distinguish between cases of real harm and cases of acceptable variation in parenting standards."

[62] *Re M. (A Minor) (Care Order: Threshold Conditions)* [1994] 3 W.L.R. 558 at 562, Bracewell J. The House of Lords upheld the decision but Whybrow [1994] J.C.L. 88, 89 points out that the ill-treatment was of the mother. The baby was present (but possibly asleep); the impact on the child may thus have been from its consequences rather than the event itself.

[63] *Humberside C.C. v. B.* [1993] 1 F.L.R. 257.

child learning to read Braille. Also minor injuries such as bruises may suggest that more serious harm is likely in the future. Where sexual abuse produces serious psychological disturbance or is likely to do so in the future, it clearly causes significant harm but, arguably, any such ill-treatment is significant because of the way it is handled in the community.[64] Harm may be significant because of the way it was caused; cigarette burns are usually deliberate. Behaviour which may not be recognised as serious such as shaking a young baby may produce serious brain damage.[65] Similarly, inattention to the diet of a child with diabetes may have significant consequences for the child's health and development. Over protection may amount to harm.[66] Although it is possible for a local authority to bring proceedings on the basis of a single act of ill-treatment this rarely occurs.[67] A few children who have been grossly abused need to be removed from the homes for that reason but in the majority of cases the general family context is more important to the outcome for the child than an abusive event.[68]

In cases involving consideration of the child's health or development (but not ill-treatment) "significant" requires a comparison between the child and what "could reasonably be expected of a similar child."[69] This is intended to require comparison of children's attributes to take account of the fact that the child might ordinarily achieve more or less than an average child[70] but not to enable lower standards to be applied in respect of disadvantaged children.[71] *Guidance* states that it may be necessary "to take account of environmental, social and cultural characteristics of the child".[72]

Truancy was the reason for approximately 10 per cent of the care orders under the 1969 Act.[73] However the *Review of Child Care Law* considered that care proceedings were inappropriate for most cases of truancy.[74] Nevertheless, in *Re O. (A Minor) (Care Proceedings: Education)*[75] the court recognised that failure to receive education can amount to significant harm even to a child approaching

---

[64] *cf. Review of Child Care Law,* para. 15.16. The Review recommended the inclusion of the word "well-being" in the definition of harm to cover cases of sexual abuse to older children.

[65] *Re A. and D. (Non-accidental Injury: Subdural Haematomas)* [2002] 1 F.L.R. 357; Geddes *et al.* "Neuropathology of inflicted head injury in children" (2001) 124 Brain 1290.

[66] *Re V. (Care or Supervision Order)* [1996] 1 F.L.R. 776, CA.

[67] D.H., *Child Protection messages from research* (1995), p. 18. For a discussion of the range of cases in which proceedings are used see J. Hunt *et al., The last Resort* (1999); M. Brandon *et al., op cit.* Chap 8.

[68] D.H., *Child Protection messages from research* (1995), p. 54.

[69] s.31(10). In *Re O. (A Minor) (Care Proceedings: Education)* [1992] 1 W.L.R. 912 the court compared a truanting child with "a child of equivalent intellectual and social development who had gone to school."

[70] B. Hoggett, "The Children Bill: the aim" (1989) 19 *Fam. Law* 217, 221.

[71] See Lord Mackay, Lord Chancellor, *Hansard,* H.L., Vol. 503, cols. 354–355, Children Bill, Committee Stage; Vol. 503, col. 1525, Report Stage.

[72] *Guidance,* Vol. 1, para. 3.20.

[73] CYPA 1969, s.1(2) (e); DHSS, *Children in Care* (1986) A/F/12/86, Table 1.

[74] paras 12.22–3, 15.26.

[75] *Re O. (A Minor) (Care Proceedings: Education)* [1992] 1 W.L.R. 912 ; for a more recent example see: *Re P. (Care Orders: Injunctive Relief)* [2000] 2 F.L.R. 385, FD.

the end of compulsory schooling.[76] Local education authorities may enforce school attendance by prosecuting the parents or seeking an education supervision order.[77]

The commission of an offence is no longer a ground as such for a care order.[78] Criminal activity may indicate significant harm to a child's social development and can place a child who steals and "joy rides" cars at physical risk. Care proceedings could therefore be brought and might be appropriate for offenders who need treatment such as victims of sexual abuse who abuse others.[79] The fact that a member of the child's household had committed specified offences was also grounds for an order.[80] It is now necessary to establish that the previous incident makes it likely that the child will suffer significant harm.[81]

"Is suffering"

22–029 In *Re M. (A Minor) (Care Orders: Threshold Conditions)*[82] a baby was accommodated after his father murdered his mother. The local authority started care proceedings and almost immediately a relative, who was caring for the boy's half-siblings, applied for a residence order. The House of Lords held, reversing the decision of the Court of Appeal,[83] that the relevant time for applying the "is suffering" test is when the local authority "initiated protective arrangements," not the date of the hearing, provided that the arrangements had remained continuously in place.[84] Thus a care order could be made despite the relative's offer. But because the child had been placed with her following the Court of Appeal's decision, he stayed with her.[85]

Arrangements the family makes for the child's protection after the initial local authority intervention are not privileged and only have to be accepted where the

---

[76] This analysis could justify the removal of children to police protection (Children Act 1989, s.46) by truancy patrols but under the Crime and Disorder Act 1998, s.16 there is a separate system for removing truants which does not depend on belief that the child is at risk of significant harm.

[77] Education Act 1996, ss.443–4; Children Act 1989, s.36 and Sched. 3, Pt III. An education supervision order lasts for one year but can be extended for up to three years. Successive orders may theoretically be made in respect of a child but the court must be satisfied that the order will be effective (s.1(5)). The child's stated intention not to comply with the order is not determinative but force would not be used: *Essex C.C. v. B.* [1993] 1 F.L.R. 866.

[78] *cf.* Children and Young Persons Act 1969, s.1(2) (f) but cautioning and prosecution had become the main ways of dealing with young offenders.

[79] See generally, NCH, *The report of the committee of enquiry into children and young people who sexually abuse other children* (1992).

[80] Children and Young Persons Act 1933, Sched. 1; Children and Young Persons Act 1969, s.1(2) (b), (bb).

[81] *Re S., S. and A. (Care Proceedings: Issue Estoppel)* [1995] 2 F.L.R. 244 a previous finding of abuse is relevant.

[82] [1994] 2 A.C. 424, approving *Northampton C.C. v. S.* [1993] Fam. 136.

[83] [1994] Fam. 95.

[84] [1994] 2 A.C. 424 *per* Lord Mackay at 433G. The local authority can rely on assessments which it obtained after this date if they indicate a state of affairs at the time of intervention: *Re G. (Care Proceedings: Threshold Conditions)* [2001] 2 F.L.R. 1111, CA.

[85] The order was made on the understanding that he should do so, a rare example of the court imposing its view of a social services responsibility on the local authority.

child's welfare demands this.[86] Where the child suffered significant harm in the past but has made a complete recovery it is doubtful whether the threshold criteria would be satisfied.[87]

"Attributable to the care given to the child"

22–030 To form the basis of an order, significant harm must be attributable to care given to the child or the child being beyond parental control. This may not require the identification of the person who injured the child:—

> In *Lancashire County Council v. B.*[88] a baby sustained shaking injuries from two separate incidents whilst in the care of her parents or child-minder. The local authority began care proceedings in respect of the girl and the child-minder's baby. The judge dismissed both applications on the basis that the harm could not be attributed to any of the adults. The local authority appealed; the Court of Appeal granted the order in respect of the injured baby, but not the child-minder's child.[89] The parents appealed. The House of Lords, stressing the difficulties in establishing the facts in such cases and the need to protect children from abuse, dismissed the appeal. Where the care of the child was shared, the "care given to the child" covered the care from any of the carers. The threshold condition could therefore be satisfied even when there was only a possibility that a parent had caused the injuries.[90]

"Care" includes catering for a child's total needs.[91] It is judged objectively in relation to the particular child concerned. Thus a parent is expected to take account of their child's particular needs[92] for example, providing reasonable emotional care such listening to and monitoring the behaviour of a child who has been abused.[93] Consequently, parents who fail to co-operate with a social services assessment of children with serious problems may be failing to provide reasonable care. Concern was expressed that the drafting of the Bill would lead to impoverished parents and those from minority ethnic backgrounds being

---

[86] See Masson [1994] J.C.L. 170 and Whybrow [1994] J.C.L. 88, 177; competing residence and care applications should be heard together with the court considering s.31(2) first, *per* Lord Mackay at 437C. However, current practice favours placements with suitable relatives because they appear more stable: *Children Act Report 2000*, para. 1.41.

[87] *cf. Guidance*, Vol. 1, para. 3.19; but note that the wording of the Bill was amended to replace the words "has suffered" with "is suffering": *Hansard*, Standing Committee B, col. 221, May 23, 1989.

[88] [2000] 1 F.L.R. 583, HL; reported as *Re B. and W. (Threshold Criteria)* [1999] 2 F.L.R. 833, CA.

[89] This case concerned only risk of future harm see below the discussion of *Re H. and R. (Minors) (Sexual Abuse Standard of Proof)* [1996] A.C. 563. The local authority did not appeal this decision.

[90] *per* Lord Nicholls at 589D-G. This did not mean that a care order would be made but unless it is clear that a person was not responsible for the child's injuries it may be difficult to assess their ability to provide care in the future.

[91] Freeman (1994), *op. cit.*, p. 27.

[92] The court may need expert evidence, *Guidance*, Vol. 1, para. 3.23.

[93] *Re B. (A Minor) (Interim Care Order: Criteria)* [1993] 1 F.L.R. 815.

judged by the standards of the white middle class.[94] The wording of the Act does not prevent this.

Where the harm has been caused by a third party for example a relative or baby-sitter, the test is satisfied if the parents bear responsibility because, for example they knew of that person's unsuitability.[95] An order may apparently be granted to prevent the removal of children whose relationship with their carers is such that removal would cause significant harm even though the care offered by the parents would be adequate for other children. This interpretation invites the conclusion that there is no care which would be reasonable for these parents to give this child. It also calls into question the need for para. (ii); the parents of a child who is beyond control may similarly be seen as providing inappropriate care despite their best endeavours. Para.(ii) refers to a state of affairs which may be in the past, present or future according to the context.[96] So in *M. v. Birmingham City Council*[97] an order could be made in respect of a "wayward, uncontrollable, disturbed and periodically violent" teenage girl who was accommodated by the local authority despite the claim by her mother that she and her partner could control her.

Likelihood of harm

22–031 An order may also be made where the child is likely to suffer significant harm. A risk of future harm may relate to the carers' inability to meet a child's needs because of their limitations or the child's condition. The Act does not indicate when the harm should occur but it has been suggested that the test "would probably" be satisfied if carers were unable to meet the child's emotional needs years in the future.[98] Nor does the Act indicate how likely the harm should be; it has been said that a comparatively small risk of really serious harm can justify action while even the virtual certainty of slight harm may not.[99] There must be a "real possibility" of significant harm which cannot "sensibly be ignored" having regard to the nature and gravity of the feared harm.[1]

> In *Re C. and B.*[2] both parents had had a difficult childhood and their relationship was marked by repeated separation; the mother had learning diffi-

---

[94] *per* Lord Banks, *Hansard,* H.L., Vol. 503, col. 1525, Children Bill, Report Stage.

[95] See *Guidance,* Vol. 1, para. 3.23; but note that mothers are sometimes accused of failing to protect their children when they too are victims of abuse. In such cases support and protection for the mother may be more appropriate.

[96] *M. v. Birmingham C.C.* [1994] 2 F.L.R. 141 at 147, *per* Stuart-White J.; see also *Re K. (Secure Accommodation: Right to Liberty)* [2001] 1 F.L.R. 526, CA where care proceedings were brought because the parents were no longer willing for their son (who had abused others) to remain in secure accommodation.

[97] [1994] 2. F.L.R. 141.

[98] *Re H. (A Minor) (s.37 Direction)* [1993] 2 F.L.R. 541 at 548, *per* Scott Baker J. In that case the child had been placed in an arrangement akin to surrogacy with a lesbian couple. One of the carers had a history of mental health problems and broken relationships.

[99] *Re C. and B. (Care Order: Future Harm)* [2001] 1 F.L.R. 611, CA at para. 28 *per* Hale L.J.

[1] *Re H. and R. (Child Sexual Abuse: Standard of Proof)* [1996] 1 F.L.R. 80, HL, *per* Lord Nicholls at 95.

[2] [2001] 1 F.L.R. 611, CA.

culties and had suffered from mental ill health in the past. Care orders were imposed in relation to the oldest child, then aged nine years, on the basis of emotional and intellectual impairment and the second oldest because she was likely to suffer similarly. Two years later the local authority removed two children who had been born after the original proceedings, despite evidence that they were well cared for, on the basis that they were at risk. Care orders were granted by the county court and the parents appealed. The Court of Appeal accepted that there had been evidence which satisfied the threshold condition but considered that a care order was not a proportionate response[3] and remitted the case for rehearing.

Where children have been orphaned the local authority's powers to accommodate them may be sufficient but if the local authority wishes to place the child for adoption it will be necesary to establish that the threshold test could be satisfied.[4]

(b) Evidence in care proceedings

22–032 The civil rules of evidence and standard of proof govern care proceedings[5]; the burden of proof lies on the applicant for the care order. In *Re H. and R.*[6] Lord Nicholls, expressing the opinion of the majority, rejected the notion that a higher standard had to be applied to more serious allegations.[7] Nevertheless he asserted that the "inherent improbability of an event" should be taken into account and "the more serious the event the less likely it is that the event occurred." Consequently, stronger evidence should be required.[8] The logic of this argument is questionable; the probability of a possible event cannot help one to know whether it has occurred in a particular instance and the incidence of sexual abuse and other causes of harm to children is uncertain.[9] Where the matter to be proved is whether the child is at risk of harm, Lord Nicholls held that there must be proven facts from which the court can properly conclude that

---

[3] See below, para. 22–035 both considering the risks involved and E.C.H.R., Art. 8.

[4] So that a placement order could be obtained: Adoption and Children Bill 2002, cll. 18, 21(2) In *Re S.H. (Care Order Orphan)* [1995] 1 F.L.R. 746 (prior child protection concerns) and *Re M. (Care Order: Parental Responsibility)* [1996] 2 F.L.R. 84 (abandoned baby) care orders were made *cf. Birmingham C. C. v. D. and M.* [1994] 2 F.L.R. 502 where Thorpe J. considered that Pt III of the Act provided all the necessary safeguards. The CAAC expressed concern that local authorities may not be able to acquire parental responsibility for orphans: CAAC Report 1994/5, p. 32.

[5] Evidence from covert video surveillance is admissible: *Re D.H. (A Minor) (Child Abuse)* [1994] 1 F.L.R. 679 at 709, *per* Wall J. but see now Regulation of Investigatory Powers Act 2000 and D.H., *Safeguarding children in whom illness is induced* (2001).

[6] [1996] 1 F.L.R. 80, HL.

[7] [1996] 1 F.L.R. 80 at 96–7 disapproving *Re G. (No. 2) (A Minor) (Child Abuse: Evidence)* [1988] 1 F.L.R. 314 and *Re W. (Sexual Abuse: Standard of Proof)* [1994] 1 F.L.R. 314. All the judges agreed on this point although Lords Browne-Wilkinson and Lloyd dissented on other points, see below.

[8] [1996] 1 F.L.R. 80 at 96.

[9] White [1996] N.L.J. 51; information about the incidence of various forms of abuse is discussed in D.H., *Child protection: messages from research* (1995) and on the basis of reports from adults about their childhood: NSPCC, *Child maltreatment in the United Kingdom* (2000).

harm is likely. Thus a care order could not be made in respect of siblings because of risk of sexual abuse when the court was not satisfied that their sister (who had alleged rape by their father) was telling the truth. Suspicion of abuse is insufficient.[10] Strong dissenting opinions were given by Lords Browne-Wilkinson and Lloyd who were both prepared to accept that a finding of likely harm could be made without proof of any specific incident.[11] There should be no unnecessary litigation, so where parents accept that the threshold test is satisfied, the court may not need to make findings of fact.[12] Where a court has made a finding of fact, the matter may be reconsidered in subsequent proceedings.[13] Criminal allegations may be re-investigated despite an acquittal.[14] The facts can be crucial to the children's future care, for example the safety of contact or rehabilitation.

The same rules of evidence apply to all care cases wherever they are heard. Witnesses may be compelled to give evidence[15] but they are given some protection against self-incrimination. Evidence in care proceedings is not admissible in criminal proceedings (except for perjury) but a witness could be cross-examined on the basis of earlier statements.[16] Nevertheless, the courts are reluctant to delay care proceedings until criminal proceedings have been completed.[17]

It has been said that parents have a duty to give a full and frank explanation to the court[18] but this statement may be too sweeping.[19] However, in *Re L. (Police Investigation: Privilege)*,[20] the House of Lords held, Lords Nicholls and Mustill dissenting, that litigation privilege does not apply in proceedings where the child's welfare is paramount. Consequently, the court could order disclosure[21] of a report prepared for proceedings on behalf of a parent who did not

---

[10] [1996] 1 F.L.R. 80 at 99, 101. But in some cases there will be ample evidence of poor parenting so that significant harm may be proved even if allegations of sexual abuse cannot be made out see: *Re G. and R. (Child Sexual Abuse: Standard of Proof)* [1995] 2 F.L.R. 867, CA.

[11] 1996] 1 F.L.R. 80 at 83, 92. Lord Browne-Wilkinson noted that the reasoning of the majority would make the law unworkable and make it more difficult to protect children in cases of sexual abuse.

[12] *Re B. (Agreed Findings of Fact)* [1998] 1 F.L.R. 968, CA; *Re M. (Threshold Criteria: Parents' Concessions)* [1999] 2 F.L.R. 728, CA.

[13] *Re D. (Child: Threshold Critera)* [2001] 1 F.L.R. 274, CA; *K. v. P. (Children Act Proceedings: Estoppel)* [1995] 1 F.L.R. 248; *Re S., S. and A. (Care Proceedings: Issue Estoppel)* [1995] 2 F.L.R. 242 at 248. Estoppel *per rem judicatam* has a place in Children Act proceedings but the court may refuse to be bound by it.

[14] *Re S. (Sexual Abuse Allegation: Local Authority Response)* [2001] 2 F.L.R. 776, QBD.

[15] Magistrates' Court Act 1980, s.97. The court may refuse to issue a witness summons if this would be oppressive: *Re P.(Witness Summons)* [1997] 2 F.L.R. 447, CA.

[16] s.98 following a recommendation of the *Review of Child Care Law*, para. 17.27; It is unclear what s.98 covers, it may not include statements made during investigations see: *Re G. (Social Worker: Disclosure)* [1996] 1 F.L.R. 276 at 285 *per* Butler Sloss L.J., *cf Cleveland C.C. v. F.* [1995] 1 F.L.R. 797.

[17] *Re L. (Care: Confidentiality)* [1999] 1 F.L.R. 165 at 169 "[I]f the parents tell the truth in both proceedings there is no risk to them." *per* Johnson J.

[18] *Oxfordshire C.C. v. P.* [1995] 1 F.L.R. 552 at 558, *per* Ward J.

[19] *Re L. (Police Investigation: Privilege)* [1996] 1 F.L.R. 731 at 747 *per* Lord Nicholls. Lord Jauncey preferred not to comment on the existence or scope of this duty: at 740.

[20] [1996] 1 F.L.R. 731, HL and see C. Tapper, "Evidential privilege in cases involving children" [1997] *C.F.L.Q.* 1. Requiring disclosure does not breach Art. 6: *L. v. U.K.* [2000] 2 F.L.R. 322 (application found inadmissible).

[21] Preparation of the report had required the permission of the court under F.P.R. 1991, r. 4.23(1). Lord Jauncey held that a condition of disclosure could be imposed and that in so doing the judge

wish to rely on it because it was adverse to her case. Legal professional privilege remains; it is not possible to order a solicitor to disclose the client's instructions[22] but instructions to experts must be disclosed. The local authority also has a duty to disclose all relevant information which could assist parents, except any covered by public interest immunity.[23] Failure to disclose to the parent details of the child's allegation has been held to breach Article 8. The local authority should have made the material available to the parent without waiting for an order for its disclosure.[24] The right to a fair trial does not require access to all documents; the court could withhold information if its disclosure would breach the privacy right of a party.[25] Children's guardians have a statutory right of access to the social services department's records concerning the child and can therefore bring material to the court's attention without disclosure.[26]

The evidence of experts plays a major part in care proceedings.[27] Various medical experts may be able to determine how and when injuries were caused, and whether they were accidental; mental health experts assess children's needs and development, and the capacity of the adults to meet these.[28] It is crucial that experts of the right calibre and with appropriate experience are instructed, and given clear instructions.[29] Where possible this should be agreed by the parties.[30] The court controls the use of experts[31] and may refuse to admit evidence from assessments of the child, undertaken without its permission.[32] In practice, the first application to instruct experts usually comes from the local authority, until

---

had acted correctly by balancing issues of welfare and the administration of justice, at 741. Lord Nicholls disagreed, "The rule ought not to be used as a means of preventing a party from obtaining advice in confidence from an expert." at 747.

[22] *R. v. Derby Magistrates Court, ex p. B.* [1996] 1 F.L.R. 513; *S. County Council v. B.* [2000] 2 F.L.R. 161, FD (father could not be required to disclose names of experts he had instructed solely for criminal proceedings).

[23] *R. v. Hampshire C. C., ex p. K.* [1990] 2 Q.B. 71.

[24] *TP. and KM. v. U.K.* [2001] 2 F.L.R. 549.

[25] *Re B. (Disclosure to Other Parties)* [2001] 2 F.L.R. 1017, FD (disclosure refused to father of some information about mother and step-children on the basis that the harm would be disproportionate to any forensic purpose served by disclosure).

[26] Children Act 1989, s.42; *Re R.(Care Proceedings; Disclosure)* [2000] 2 F.L.R. 751, FD and CA (disclosure of Pt 8 report concerning death of child's sibling).

[27] a) J. Brophy *et al., Expert evidence in child protection litigation* (1999); b) J. Brophy *et al., Myths and Practices* (1999).

[28] Child and adolescent psychiatrists provide the majority of expert evidence. A child and family psychiatric assessment appeared in 41% of cases: Brophy (1999a) *op. cit.* p. 12.

[29] See *Handbook of Best Practice* (1997), Chap. 5.

[30] *Re M. (Minors) (Care Proceedings: Child's Wishes)* [1994] 1 F.L.R. 749; *Re T. and E. (Proceedings: Conflicting Interests)* [1995] 1 F.L.R. 581. Experts should meet in advance of the hearing to identify areas of conflict: *Manchester C.C. v. B.* [1996] 1 F.L.R. 324; *Re C. (Expert Evidence: Disclosure Practice)* [1995] 1 F.L.R. 204; CAAC Report 1994/5 p. 24. In practice joint instruction is problematic see Brophy (1999a), p. 90.

[31] Detailed principles have been set out for leave and directions to experts: *Re G. (Minors) (Expert Witnesses)* [1994] 2 F.L.R. 291 at 290, *per* Wall J.; about the role of experts: *Re A.B. (Child Abuse: Expert Witnesses)* [1995] 1 F.L.R. 181; about instructions to experts and preliminary meetings: *Re T. and E. (Proceedings: Conflicting Interests)* [1995] 1 F.L.R. 581 and *Handbook of Best Practice* (1997), Chap. 5.

[32] F.P.R. 1991, r. 4.18; F.P.C. 1991, r. 18. See above Chap. 19. *Re L. (Police Investigation: Privilege)* [1996] 1 F.L.R. 731, HL; *R. v. Derby Magistrates' Court, ex p. B.* [1996] 1 F.L.R. 513, HL.

this is filed the case is unclear so parents may be unable to identify suitable experts. Parents are also limited in their choice of experts and the types of reports they can obtain. Courts are unwilling to allow further examinations of children and some experts are unwilling to provide evidence without this, consequently parents are not equal parties in proceedings.[33] Changes to procedure and evidence in relation to the use of experts may be required to ensure compliance with Article 6.[34]

The Children Act 1989 abolished the competency requirement in respect of children's evidence in all civil proceedings; a child's evidence may be heard if he or she understands the duty to speak the truth and has sufficient understanding of the events.[35] It is unusual for children to give evidence directly because hearsay given in connection with the welfare of a child, for example a statement a child makes to a social worker or a video-recorded interview[36] is admissible.[37] Similarly, the children's guardian's report and evidence given about matters in it is admissible.[38]

22–033 Concerns for the privacy of children and families involved in care proceedings and the public interest in encouraging frankness in these proceedings make it important to maintain confidentiality.[39] The court's permission is required to disclose documents prepared for court outside the proceedings.[40] This does not prevent a social worker repeating to the police a parent's admission, made during investigations[41] but the information collected by a children's guardian is confidential to the proceedings.[42] Disclosure has been permitted to the police to facilitate a criminal investigation,[43] to bodies with responsibility for professional

---

[33] Brophy (1999a), p. 97; J. Brophy and P. Bates "The position of parents using experts in care proceedings: a failure of partnership" [1998] *J.S.W.F.L.* 23. Brophy notes that the poor quality of representation for parents contributes to this.

[34] *Children Act Now* (2001), p. 175.

[35] s.96(1), (2). See generally, J. Spencer and R. Flin, *The evidence of children* (2nd ed., 1993).

[36] See H.O. *et al., Achieving best evidence in criminal proceedings* (2002), Vol. 3; *B v. B (Court Bundles: Video Evidence)* [1994] 1 F.L.R. 323, and see below.

[37] Children Act 1989, s.96(3); The Children (Admissibility of Hearsay Evidence) Order 1993, S.I. 1993 No. 621. Care must be taken to ensure that the interviews produce reliable material: see *Re A-M. (Minors) (Wardship: Child Abuse: Guidelines to Social Workers)* [1991] 1 W.L.R. 1026.

[38] Children Act 1989, s.41(11).

[39] *Re X. (Disclosure of Information)* [2001] 2 F.L.R. 440 at 447 *per* Munby J.

[40] F.P.R. 1991, r. 4.23; F.P.C. 1991, r. 23; *Re C. (A Minor) (Care Proceedings: Disclosure)* [1997] Fam. 76.

[41] *Re G. (Social Worker: Disclosure)* [1996] 1 F.L.R. 276, CA; *Re W. (Disclosure to Police)* [1998] 2 F.L.R. 135, CA. Interagency disclosure of material not controlled by the court is subject to the guidance in *Working Together* (1999), see above para. 22–017 *et seq.*

[42] *Oxfordshire C.C. v. P.* [1995] 1 F.L.R. 552 at 555 *per* Ward J. In *Re G. (Social Worker: Disclosure)* [1996] 1 F.L.R. 276, CA. Butler-Sloss L.J. disapproved part of the Oxfordshire case, accepted that the judge had been right to dismiss a children's guardian who had given a witness statement to the police repeating the mother's admission and expressed no opinion about the scope of the guardian's duty, at 281–2.

[43] *Re C. (A Minor) (Care Proceedings: Disclosure)* [1997] Fam. 76. *cf. Re M. (Care Proceedings: Disclosure: Human Rights)* [2001] 2 F.L.R. 1316, FD. (where prosecution would prevent the parents from engaging in therapy and therefore preclude rehabilitation of a shaken baby, disclosure of mother's confession was refused).

discipline[44] and to child witnesses to confirm that their evidence has been believed and to assist with therapy and compensation.[45] Although this facilitates interagency co-operation, there is a danger that it may inhibit parents from speaking to social workers and thus make it more difficult to protect children.[46]

(c) Care plans

22–034 The local authority must produce a care plan for the court to scrutinise.[47] This should identify the overall aim of the plan, the child's needs, the views of others such as parents[48] and carers, details of the child's placement[49] and other services to be provided, and the responsibility for implementing and reviewing the plan.[50] Plans should be sufficiently specific, make clear why a course of action has been chosen and give realistic time-scales for achieving key aspects[51] so the court can assess its suitability and viability.[52] If the plan does not meet the child's needs the court may refuse the order unless it represents the only practical course of action.[53] The court does not to oversee the plan but entrusts its execution to the local authority.[54] Where assessments are incomplete the court may make an interim order but this power must not be abused to prevent control passing to the local authority.[55]

Research[56] indicates, care plans have often not included clear time-scales or contingency plans. More worryingly, in a substantial minority of cases children

---

[44] *Re W. (Disclosure to Police)* [1998] 2 F.L.R. 135, CA; *Re L. (Care Proceedings Disclosure to Third Party)* [2000] 1 F.L.R. 913, FD (UKCC); *Re A. (Disclosure of Medical Records to GMC)* [1998] 2 F.L.R. 641, FD.

[45] *Re X. (Disclosure of Information)* [2001] 2 F.L.R. 440, FD.

[46] Wells [1996] Fam Law 137; White [1995] N.L.J. 1649; see also J. Masson, "Introducing non-punitive approaches to child protection" in *Child protection and family support* (N. Parton ed., 1997).

[47] Circular LAC (99)29. The Adoption and Children Bill 2002, cl. 118 adds Children Act 1989, ss.31(3A) and 31A which creates a statutory duty on the local authority to prepare and file a careplan; the court must consider the plan before making a care order.

[48] There is a duty to involve the parents and the child: s.22(4) (5) and E.C.H.R., Art. 8: *Scott v. U.K.* [2000] 1 F.L.R. 958.

[49] The children's guardian may examine confidential reports on proposed placements and advise the court on their suitability: *Manchester C.C. v. T.* [1994] Fam. 181. Children Act 1989, s.42 overrides the duty of confidentiality (Adoption Agency Regulations 1983, S.I. 1986 No. 1964, r. 14) but would not allow access to records not held by the local authority.

[50] Circular LAC (99)29, paras 12–13.

[51] *ibid.* para. 14, *e.g.* for rehabilitation or the identification of a permanent placement.

[52] *Re S (F.C.) and others* 1 F.L.R. 815, HL, para. 99.

[53] *Re B. (Supervision Order: Parental Undertaking)* [1996] 1 F.L.R. 676, CA (decision to refuse a care order upheld); *Re S. (Care or Supervision Order)* [1996] 1 F.L.R. 753, CA (decision to refuse a care order overturned). The court applies the welfare and the no order tests on the basis that the plan will be achieved.

[54] *Re J. (Minors) (Care: Care Plan)* [1994] 1 F.L.R. 253 at 265, *per* Wall J.

[55] *Re S (F.C.) and others* [2002] 1 F.L.R. 815, HL, para. 100; *C. v. Solihull M.B.C.* [1993] 1 F.L.R. 290; *Re B. (Minors) (Termination of Contact: Paramount Consideration)* [1993] Fam. 301; see below.

[56] J. Hunt and A. Macleod, *The best-laid plans* (1999); J. Harwin, *et al., A study to investigate the implementation of care orders under the Children Act 1989* (2002) both summarised in D.H., *Children Act Now* (2001).

were not placed as specified in the plan.[57] The shortage of specialist placements prevented adoptive, foster and residential placements; child protection concerns lead to the failure or non implementation of plans to place children with their parents.[58] Non-implementation or change of care plans is a cause of concern. Although there is no evidence that local authorities intentionally mislead the courts, questions of justice to parents and children are raised where the court makes an order on the basis of a plan which is ignored or soon abandoned.[59] Also, a change made without full consultation may breach Article 8.[60] Nevertheless, in *Re S.(F.C)*[61] the House of Lords rejected an innovative scheme which would have required the court to identify essential milestones in the care plan and forced the local authority to inform the children's guardian if these were not met.[62] However, the Human Rights Act, s.7 provides a remedy and an amendment to the Children Act 1989 requires the review of care plans by Independent Reviewing Officers who can refer cases to children's guardians who may bring proceedings.[63]

(d) Orders in care proceedings

22–035 The applicant indicates which type of order is being sought; the court, taking account of the children's guardian's recommendation, decides what orders, if any, to make.[64] Where there are competing applications from the local authority for a care order and from relatives for a residence order, the court is not bound to consider the residence application first.[65] The court may make a care or supervision order only if it is satisfied that the significant harm test is proved.[66] Alternatively, it may make a section 8 order[67] or no order whether or not there is proof of significant harm. The choice between these depends on the best way of secur-

---

[57] Harwin *op. cit.* 58% for adoption, 68% for fostering, 60% for residential care, 78% for kinship care and only 41% for parental care (data relates to 21 months after the care order was made); Hunt and Macleod, Chap. 7. There were considerable variation between areas in Hunt and Macleod's study, Table 7.9.

[58] *ibid.*, Hunt and Macleod pp. 196 *et seq.* and Table 8.7.

[59] *Re F., F. v. Lambeth LBC* [2002] 1 F.L.R. 217, FD. If the change of plan breaches rights to family life the court may exercise its powers under the H.R.A. 1998, see *Re M. (Care: Challenging Decisions by Local Authority)* [2001] 2 F.L.R. 1300, FD, below para. 22–075.

[60] *R. v. U.K.* [1988] 2 F.L.R. 445 at para. 63; *Re M. (Care Proceedings)* [2001] 2 F.L.R. 1300, FD; para. 22–075.

[61] [2002] 1 F.L.R. 815, HL.

[62] *Re W. and B. (Care Plan)* [2001] 2 F.L.R. 757, CA at para. 31 *per* Thorpe L.J, at para. 48 *per* Sedley L.J. and at para. 79 *per* Hale L.J. The original idea of starred care plans was based on a paper to a judicial conference by A Poysner see M. Thorpe and E. Clarke, *Divided duties* (1998).

[63] s.26(2A)–(2C) added by Adoption and Children Bill 2002, cl. 116.

[64] The children's guardian's report should identify the alternative courses of action and their advantages and disadvantages for the child: D.H., *Manual of Practice Guidance for Guardians ad Litem and Reporting Officers* (1992), pp. 42, 46.

[65] *Oldham M.B.C. v. E.* [1994] 1 F.L.R. 568 at 576, *per* Waite L.J. This part of the decision was not overruled by *Re M. (A Minor) (Care Orders: Threshold Conditions)* [1994] 2 A.C. 424.

[66] Children Act 1989, s.31(1).

[67] ss.8(1), (3), (4) (a), 10(1). S.8 orders except residence order, may not be made in respect of children in care, s.9(1); a residence order discharges a care order: s.91(1). A s.8 order may not require a child to be accommodated: s.9(2), (5); *Re S. and D. (Children: Powers of Court)* [1995] 2 F.L.R. 456.

ing the child's welfare but the court's response must be proportionate to the risk presented.[68] The effects of the order[69] are relevant:—

> In *Re C.*[70] the mother had been repeatedly assaulted by the father. When the baby was two weeks old the mother left him in his father's care so that she could register the birth. Whilst she was out the father attacked the child causing serious brain damage. The local authority started care proceedings. The mother and child went to a residential unit, and the mother showed a strong bond with her child, co-operated fully with all the professionals and was allowed to take him home. Nevertheless the local authority, supported by the children's guardian, sought a care order because of the mother's lack of judgment in leaving the baby with his father and the risk she might form a relationship with another violent man. The court granted a supervision order.
>
> In *Re M.*[71] a girl, aged four, was admitted to hospital underweight, emaciated and severely dehydrated. She had bruises on many parts of her body and internal injuries caused either by a punch or a heavy fall. The local authority obtained an interim care order and the girl was placed in foster care. She made allegations of physical and sexual abuse by her mother and step-father. The local authority sought a care order, the mother and the maternal grandparents applied separately for a residence order. The allegations of abuse were not proved but the judge found that the child had suffered significant harm because the mother had failed to seek medical assistance promptly. A residence order was granted to the mother on condition that she resided with the child at the step-father's parents' house. The local authority's appeal was refused.

Care and supervision orders are fundamentally different. A care order gives the local authority parental responsibility, the power to control the parents' exercise of it and the right to remove the child without a court order.[72] Under a supervision order the child's safety depends on the parents.[73] Either order may be used where the child is placed with the parents at home or in a residential family centre.[74] A care order may be more appropriate if the parental care is

---

[68] *Re O. (Supervision Order)* [2001] 1 F.L.R. 923, CA; *Re C. and B. (Care Order: Future Harm)* [2001] 1 F.L.R. 611, CA; *Re C. (Care Order or Supervision Order)* [2001] 2 F.L.R.466, FD.

[69] *Re V. (Care or Supervision Order)* [1996] 1 F.L.R. 776, CA; *Re O. (Supervision Order)* [2001] 1 F.L.R. 923 at paras 24–28 *per* Hale L.J.

[70] [2001] 2 F.L.R.466, FD.

[71] *Re. M. (A Minor) (Appeal) (No. 2)* [1994] 1 F.L.R. 59, see also *Re M. (Appeal: Interim Order) (No.1)* [1994] 1 F.L.R. 54. The child later died from further injuries.

[72] *Re O. (Supervision Order)* [2001] 1 F.L.R. 923 at paras 24–25 *per* Hale L.J. Hunt and colleagues have suggested that there should be a form of care order without this power see: J. Hunt *et al., The last resort* (1999).

[73] *Re S.(J.) (A Minor) (Care or Supervision Order)* [1993] 2 F.L.R. 919 at 950 *per* Judge Coningsby Q.C.

[74] *Re D. (A Minor) (Care or Supervision Order)* [1993] 2 F.L.R. 423; *Re T. (A Minor) (Care or Supervision Order)* [1994] 1 F.L.R. 103, CA; *Re R. and G. (Minors) (Interim Care or Supervision Orders)* [1994] 1 F.L.R. 793. If the child is at home under a care order the Placement of Children with Parents etc. Regulations 1991, S.I. 1991 No. 893, must be complied with.

declining[75] or there is a high risk of parents leaving the family centre because it can be used to remove the child. In contrast, where the local authority's past decision-making has been flawed leading to inappropriate removal of the children, only a supervision order should be made to prevent further removal without court approval.[76]

The effects of care orders and supervision orders will now be considered.

(i) Care order

22–036 A care order gives the local authority parental responsibility for the child and the power to determine the extent to which parents may exercise their parental responsibility. It does not remove the parents' parental responsibility[77]; Eekelaar argued that this is inappropriate because the order follows from parental failure,[78] but this view ignores the fact that most children return to their families, a process which is facilitated by parents remaining involved in their children's lives.[79] A care order discharges any section 8 order in respect of the child thus ending the parental responsibility of non-parents.[80]

Although the local authority acquires parental responsibility it lacks the power to take certain major decisions. It may not cause the child to be brought up in a different religion[81]; agree to the child's adoption[82]; or appoint a guardian (but it may apply to the court to have an existing guardian removed).[83] If it wishes to change the child's surname[84] or arrange for the child to stay outside the United Kingdom for more than one month,[85] it must obtain the written consent of everyone with parental responsibility or permission from the court. If the local authority wishes to arrange the child's emigration (even to Scotland) it must obtain the court's approval.[86] The court also has control over contact between children in care and their parents.[87] No other conditions may be

---

75 *Re T. (A Minor) (Care or Supervision Order)* [1994] 1 F.L.R. 103, CA.

76 *Re O. (Care: Discharge of Care Order)* [1999] 2 F.L.R. 119, FD.

77 s.33(3) (4). A mother retains the right to make a s.4 agreement with the father to share parental responsibility: *Re X. (Parental Responsibility Agreement: Children in Care)* [2000] 1 F.L.R. 517, FD.

78 J. Eekelaar and R. Dingwall [1989] New L.J. 217 at 238; J. Eekelaar [1989] New L.J. 760.

79 R. Bullock *et al., Going Home* (1993); E. Farmer and R. Parker, *Trials and Tribulations* (1991).

80 ss.12(2), 91(2).

81 s.33(6) (a). But foster carers need not be of the same religious persuasion as the child nor give an undertaking to bring the children up in their own religion: the Fostering Services Regulations 2002 (S.I. 2002 No. 57). Where the child is in residential care the Children's Homes Regulations 1991, S.I. 1991 No. 1506, reg. 11 apply; see also *Guidance*, vol. 4, paras 1.121–1.124.

82 s.33(6) (b) (i), (ii). Under the Adoption and Children Bill 2002, a local authority seeking to arrange adoption without parental consent will need to apply for a placement order, cll. 19, 21.

83 ss.6(7) (a), 33(6) (b) (iii).

84 s.33(7). An application can be made *ex parte*, a children's guardian may be appointed: *Re J. (A Minor) (Change of Name)* [1993] 1 F.L.R. 699.

85 s.33(8).

86 Sched. 2, para. 19; court approval can only be given where the conditions in para. 19(3) are satisfied. The consent of everyone with parental responsibility is required except where para. 19(4) or (5) applies: *Re G. (Minors) (Care: Leave to Place outside the Jurisdiction)* [1994] 2 F.L.R. 301.

87 s.34, see below, para. 22–065 *et seq.*

imposed by the court.[88] The local authority must also comply with any regulations made by the Secretary of State concerning the treatment of children in care.[89] Care orders last until the child is 18 unless they are discharged earlier.[90]

The number of applications for care orders has increased steadily since the Children Act was implemented. In a study of care application made in the first two years of the Children Act 1989, 57 per cent resulted in care orders, 17 per cent in supervision orders, 13 per cent in residence orders and 14 per cent with no order. In over half the cases where a care order was obtained the local authority's plan was adoption or long-term care.[91] There are approximately 38,000 children subject to care orders. In 2000, there were 7,000 applications for care orders; 6,300 care orders and 1,400 residence orders were made in public law proceedings.[92]

(ii) Supervision order

22–037 This order places the child under the supervision of a social worker[93] who is under a duty "to advise, assist and befriend" the child.[94] The local authority cannot be required to make facilities available but there is no point making the order if the local authority will not provide the services required. This order lasts for one year, or for any shorter period specified,[95] but may be extended for up to three years.[96]

The Short Committee noted that supervision orders were considered ineffective and infrequently made and recommended that supervisors should have greater powers to impose conditions on children and parents.[97] The *Review of Child Care Law* agreed and proposed a list of conditions which have been incorporated in the Act.[98] Supervision orders are used to monitor the care given to the child and to require the family to accept services, for example, to improve socialisation through the child's participation in activities or care through the parents' attendance at courses.[99] They may enable the local authority to super-

---

[88] *Re T. (A Minor) (Care Order: Conditions)* [1994] 2 F.L.R. 423, CA. But the court has been prepared to grant injunctions to stop parents preventing their child, living at home under a care order, attending college: *Re P. (Care Orders: Injunctive Relief)* [2000] 2 F.L.R. 385.

[89] See *Guidance,* Vols. 3 and 4 and the regulations included therein. The child may not be placed with a parent or with other specified people unless certain checks have been made: Placement of children with parents etc. Regulations 1991, (S.I. 1991 No. 893). Other placements with relatives must be approved as foster placements under S.I. 2002 No. 57.

[90] s.91(12). The local authority has aftercare responsibilities until the young person is 21: ss.23A–24D, as amended by the Children (Leaving Care) Act 2000.

[91] J. Hunt and A. Macleod, *The best-laid plans* (1999), p. 16.

[92] *Judicial Statistics 2000,* Table 5.2; Statistical Bulletin, *Children Looked after by local authorities* 2000/ 2001, Table 2.

[93] Children Act 1989, Sched. 3, para. 9.

[94] Children Act 1989, s.35(1) (a).

[95] *M. v. Warwickshire C. C.* [1994] 2 F.L.R. 593.

[96] Children Act 1989, Sched. 3, para. 6.

[97] *Short Report,* para. 150.

[98] paras 18.6–18.12; Children Act 1989, Sched. 3, paras 2–5.

[99] *Croydon LBC v. A. (No. 3)* [1992] 2 F.L.R. 350; conditions should be apparent on the face of the order: *Re T. (A Minor) (Care Order: Conditions)* [1994] 2 F.L.R. 423.

vise parental contact with a child.[1] But the county court and the family proceedings court have no power to accept undertakings so other conditions, such medical treatment for a parent, cannot be required.[2] Directions are imposed by the supervisor not the court.[3] The supervisor may enter into a written agreement with the child and any person who has parental responsibility or care of the child (responsible persons)[4] which states what they must achieve and what the supervisor will provide. The consent of responsible persons is required to any conditions[5] but they may have little choice if the supervisor considers this essential for the working of the order.

The supervisor is required to take such steps as are reasonably necessary to give effect to the order.[6] The supervisor may require the responsible persons, with their consent, to take reasonable steps to ensure that the child complies with directions to participate in activities, and to keep the supervisor informed of their address.[7] The child may be required to submit to such medical or psychiatric examinations or treatment as the court thinks fit, but such conditions may not be imposed on a mature child who does not consent.[8] There is no direct way of enforcing a supervision order[9]; the supervisor has no right of entry to the child's home and no right to remove the child. No penalties are prescribed for breach of a supervision order but the supervisor may seek its variation and the magistrates could impose penalties.[10] In variation or extension proceedings the court can only impose a care order if the significant harm test is re-proved.[11] In practice, lack of co-operation from parents or the failure of the local authority to provide resources, particularly to allocate a social worker, renders a supervision order in effective. In Hunt and Macleod's study only half of the families subject to supervision co-operated fully with the local authority, and a third of these placements failed. None of the local authorities allocated a supervisor to all cases for the duration of the order. Overall, the researchers concluded that

---

1 *Re Z. and A. (Contact: Supervision Order)* [2000] 2 F.L.R. 406; *Re D.H. (A Minor) (Child Abuse)* [1994] 1 F.L.R. 679 at 700. Alternative means of ensuring supervision beyond the six months of a family assistance order do not exist but supervision orders are only suitable for more serious cases with a child protection element.

2 *Re B. (Supervision Order: Parental Undertaking)* [1996] 1 F.L.R. 676, CA, Neill L.J. did suggest that the mother's agreement to seek treatment could be recorded in the preamble to the order. Despite their unenforceability undertakings are used.

3 Sched. 3, para. 3; *Re H.* (1994) 158 J.P.N. 211.

4 Children Act 1989, Sched. 3, para. 1.

5 *ibid.*, para. 3(1).

6 s.35(1) (b).

7 Sched. 3, paras 1, 3, 7. The child must also keep the supervisor notified of his address: para. 8.

8 Sched. 3, paras 4, 5; *Re W. (A Minor) (Medical Treatment: Court's Jurisdiction)* [1992] Fam. 64.

9 *Re R. and G. (Minors) (Interim Care or Supervision Order)* [1994] 1 F.L.R. 793. The supervisor can only refer it back to the court, s.35(1) (c). Consequently, it was inappropriate to make a supervision order in relation to a child just before his seventeenth birthday because the ultimate sanction of a care order would be lost then: *Re V. (Care or Supervision Order)* [1996] 1 F.L.R. 776, CA.

10 Magistrates' Courts Act 1980, s.63. However the *Review of Child Care Law* considered that this would rarely be appropriate.

11 Children Act 1989, s.39; *Re R. and G. (Minors) (Interim Care or Supervision Orders)* [1994] 1 F.L.R. 793; *Re A. (Supervision Order: Extension)* [1995] 1 F.L.R. 335, CA. An extension beyond three years also necessitates re-proving the threshold conditions but this does not justify using a care order where long term supervision is required: *Re O. (Supervision Order)* [2001] 1 F.L.R. 923, CA.

an unreservedly good outcome was only achieved for one in six of the children, and a more powerful order might have been helpful for half them. Care orders were made subsequently in respect of a third of the children and two were adopted.[12]

Despite the increase in powers supervision orders have not become more widely used. It has been suggested that the emphasis on voluntariness means that cases suitable for supervision orders are managed without any order.[13] Supervision orders were made in 1,300 cases in 2000[14]; it is likely that approximately a quarter of these were made to support residence orders granted in care proceedings.[15]

(iii) Interim care and supervision orders

22–038 The *Review of Child Care Law* was concerned that care proceedings should be dealt with as quickly as possible but recognised that it took time for the children's guardian to prepare the report.

They recommended that interim orders should last eight weeks with extensions only in exceptional circumstances for up to 14 days.[16] These proposals were accepted but the Act is less restrictive; interim orders may be made for up to eight weeks with extensions of four weeks.[17] It has not proved possible to hear care cases within 12 weeks; most interim orders are renewed by consent, but any party may contest this and the court must always consider whether an order should be renewed.[18]

The Children Act 1989 permits the court to make an interim care or supervision order when proceedings are adjourned or a section 37(1) investigation is ordered if it is satisfied that there are reasonable grounds for believing that the case passes the significant harm test.[19] The child can be protected until the court is able to decide whether or not an order should be made.[20] If a residence order is made in care proceedings, the court must make an interim supervision order unless it is satisfied that the child's welfare does not require it.[21] Interim orders should not be used to keep a case under review by the court.[22] Care plans inevitably involve some uncertainties; it is for the judge to decide whether to approve the plan and make the final order or to allow a limited period of "pur-

---

[12] J. Hunt and A. Macleod, *The Best-laid Plans* (1999), p. 201–203 and Table 8.8. The study was based on 133 children involved in care proceedings in three local authorities. Supervision orders were made in 23 cases.

[13] *Children Act Now* (2001), p. 62.

[14] *Judicial Statistics 2000,* Table 5.2.

[15] J. Hunt and A. Macleod, *op. cit.,* Table 1.10.

[16] *Review of Child Care Law,* paras 17.4, 17.16–18.

[17] s.38(4), (5); Cm. 62 (1987), para. 61.

[18] See *Handbook of Best Practice* (1997), Chap. 2

[19] s.38(1),(2); *Humberside C.C. v. B.* [1993] 1 F.L.R. 257. The efficacy test in s.1(5) also applies.

[20] *Re S. (F.C.)* 1 F.L.R. 815, HL at para. 90; *Re B. (Care: Expert Witnesses)* [1996] 1 F.L.R. 667, CA.

[21] s.38(3).

[22] *Re S. (F.C.)* 1 F.L.R. 815, HL at para. 90; *cf. Buckingham C.C. v. M.* [1994] 2 F.L.R. 506 (full order not appropriate during rehabilitation); *C. v. Solihull M.B.C.* (interim order pending parental assessment).

poseful delay" so issues can be clarified.[23] The court has power to order assessments (but not treatment) and can therefore explore the potential for care by a particular person but it cannot require mature children[24] or adults to participate.[25] The high cost of residential assessments, the shortage of places and the lack of alternatives for assessing some parents makes the decision whether to order such an assessment particularly difficult.

A residential assessment is ordered if it is in the child's best interests, required for a proper decision and not unreasonable to expect the local authority to fund it[26]:—

> In *Re JN. and others (Care: Assessment)*[27] the local authority brought proceedings in respect of five children of a single parent who had had an extremely damaging upbringing in care. The NSPCC was asked to investigate the possibility of rehabilitating the children and suggested a residential placement for the whole family with psychotherapeutic treatment. The judge ordered a preliminary report to assess the suitability of the treatment (which was favourable) but the local authority announced that it would not fund an initial six week assessment. The judge ordered the local authority to explain this decision. There was further delay. By the time the mother's application for a direction for this assessment was heard there was no longer a vacancy. The application was therefore refused.

Figures are not available for the total number of interim orders made or the average number of interim orders per case. The average duration of proceedings suggests that repeated interim orders are necessary in most cases unless children are protected by agreement with the parents.[28] In March 2001, 8,000 looked after children were subject to interim care orders, approximately one-fifth of those subject to care orders.[29]

(iv) Domestic violence injunctions

22–039 The Law Commission proposed that the courts should have the additional power to exclude a suspected abuser from the family home so that the child

---

[23] *Re S. (F.C.)* [2002] U.K.H.L. 10 at para. 95.

[24] The objection could be overridden by the High Court: *Re W. (A Minor) (Medical Treatment: Court's Jurisdiction)* [1992] Fam. 64.

[25] s.38(6); *Re W. (Assessment of Child)* [1998] 2 F.L.R. 130, CA. Co-operation will often provide parents with the only chance of rehabilitation.

[26] *Re C.(Interim Care Order: Residential Assessment)* [1997] 1 F.L.R. 1, HL; *Re M. (Residential Assessment Directions)* [1998] 2 F.L.R. 371, FD; *Re B. (Psychiatric Therapy for Parents)* [1999] 1 F.L.R. 701, CA (order for assessment over turned and care order made).

[27] 1996] 1 F.L.R. 203. The decision to refuse funding was "a gross error that displays a fundamental misunderstanding of the respective roles of social worker, consultant child psychiatrist and judge" *per* Thorpe J. at 209.

[28] See CAAC *Final Report 1997*, Tables 5A, 5B.

[29] Statistical Bulletin, *Children looked after by local authorities* 2000/ 2001, Table 2. Some of these children were placed with a parent or relative.

could be protected without removal from home.[30] The Family Law Act 1996 amended the Children Act 1989 to enable a court making an interim care order[31] to include an exclusion requirement or accept undertakings.[32] This requirement can only be imposed where there is reasonable cause for believing that if a person is excluded from the child's home,[33] or prevented from entering it, the child will cease to suffer, or cease to be likely to suffer, significant harm.[34] In addition, another person living in the home must be able and willing to care for the child and consent to the requirement.[35] But in contrast to exclusion injunctions, the court is not required to balance potential hardship to the excluded parent and the child. The order cannot last longer than the interim care order; a power of arrest may be attached to allow a constable to arrest, without warrant, any person reasonably believe to be in breach.[36] Breach of an undertaking is enforced through proceedings for contempt of court.[37] Exclusion requirements and undertakings cease to be enforceable if the child is removed by the local authority for more than 24 hours.[38] It has been suggested that the wide powers to exclude a person without a full trial of the allegations are unfair and will encourage false allegation[39] but few orders have apparently been made.

These powers are additional to those under the Family Law Act 1996 to make occupation orders relating to the family home on application[40] and non-molestation orders in any family proceedings where the respondent is a party.[41] The complex conditions which apply to occupation orders may make it impossible to continue the exclusion after the end of the interim order. The Law Commission found no support for long-term exclusion as an alternative to a care

---

[30] Law Com. No. 207, *Domestic Violence and Occupation of the Family Home* (1992), paras 6.15 *et seq.*

[31] This provision was originally in the Family Homes and Domestic Violence Bill 1995. The Association of Directors of Social Services and the Family Rights Group both supported adding the power to interim supervision orders. Without such a power there is a risk that the court would make an interim care order solely for this purpose, see: Proceedings of the Special Public Committee on the Family Homes and Domestic Violence Bill, H.L. 55 (1994–5). A prohibited steps order could be made to prevent contact by an abuser without an interim care order: *Re H. (Prohibited Steps Order)* [1995] 1 F.L.R. 638, CA.

[32] Children Act 1989, ss.38A, 38B; F.P.R. 1991, r. 4.24A; F.P.C. 1991, r.25A. The local authority has a power to provide accommodation for an alleged perpetrator who leaves but no duty to do so: Children Act 1989, Sched. 2, para. 5.

[33] s.38A(3) or from a defined area where the home is, but not from the child's school etc.

[34] s.38A(2) (a). By agreeing to the order the local authority is accepting that the carer is not likely to cause significant harm, but in many cases there will be residual concerns: A. Pack [2001] *Fam. Law* 216, 219.

[35] s.38A(2) (b); F.P.R. 1991, r. 4.24; F.P.C. 1991, r. 24. D.H. Circular LAC (97)15 recognises that social workers undertaking a child protection investigation may feel a conflict of interest if they have to advise a carer about these provisions, and suggests that the carer should have access to independent advice, para. 22.

[36] s.38A(5). Note this contrasts with the duty to include a power of arrest in certain circumstances under the F.L.A. 1996, s.47(2), see above. In relation to enforcement see: *President's Direction* [1998] 1 F.L.R. 495; *Re W. (Exclusion Requirement: Statement of Evidence)* [2000] 2 F.L.R. 666.

[37] s.38B(3) and see below.

[38] s.38A(10), 38B(3) and see below.

[39] Proceedings of the Special Public Committee on the Family Homes and Domestic Violence Bill, H.L. 55 (1994–5) memorandum of Dr Susan Edwards and Ms Ann Halpern.

[40] F.L.A. 1996, ss.3–41. The provision for third party applications for domestic violence injunctions has not been implemented (s.60) and see 6th edition of this book p. 826 and Chap. 10, above.

[41] F.L.A. 1996, s.42(2).

order.[42] This could be tantamount to imposing particular family relationships which might be unsustainable in the long term. Also, it was not appropriate to give the child's needs precedence without considering the balance of hardship between the adults.[43]

(e) Discharge of care and supervision orders

22–040 The child, any person with parental responsibility, the supervisor in the case of a supervision order and the local authority may apply for discharge of a care or supervision order.[44] Any other person who seeks discharge of a care order must apply for a residence order which ends the care order and grants them parental responsibility.[45] The court may only discharge the order if it is in the child's best interests to do so[46]; it is not sufficient that the parents are fit and able to care for their child. Although the *Review* considered that state intervention in family life should not be permitted by reference to a welfare test, this was the appropriate standard for discharge proceedings. It would be illogical to require parents to establish more than in private law proceedings; an alternative test could result in the court continuing an order which it knew was not in the child's best interests.[47] However, this approach may not accord with Article 8. The Strasbourg Court has repeatedly emphasised that care should be seen as a temporary measure with the aim of family reunification. It has accepted that a child's interests in maintaining family relations with a foster carer may preclude return home[48] but this argument would not prevent discharging an order in relation to a child who has lacked a stable home in care.

The local authority is required to review the case of a child regularly and must consider whether the order should be discharged.[49] Most applications for discharge of care orders are made by local authorities,[50] usually after the child has returned home.[51] It is to the local authority's advantage to have the order discharged—a child who ceases to be looked after before age 16 is not owed

---

[42] Law Com. No. 207, para. 17.

[43] *ibid.*

[44] Children Act 1989, s.39. A child does not require the leave of the court: *Re A. (Care Discharge Application by Child)* [1995] 1 F.L.R. 599.

[45] ss.8(1), 10, 91(1). Leave may be required, see above. A special guardianship order will have the same effect, s. 91(5A) to be introduced by the Adoption and Children Bill 2002, Sched. 3.

[46] s.1, the checklist applies: s.1(4) (b); the burden of proof rests with the person making the application: *Re M.D. and T.D. (Minors) (No. 2)* [1994] *Fam. Law* 489

[47] paras 20.11–21. See also *Review of Child Care Law Discussion Paper No. 9* (1985).

[48] *Johansen v. Norway* (1996) 23 E.H.R.R. 33.

[49] Review of Children's Cases Regulations 1991, S.I. 1991 No. 895, reg. 3 and Sched. 2. There is a positive obligation to work for reunification of the family: *Eriksson v. Sweden* (1989) 12 E.H.R.R. 183, para.71.

[50] See E. Farmer and R. Parker, *A Study of the Discharge of Care Orders*, (University of Bristol, 1985), Table 4. Out of a sample of 186 applications for discharge 144 were made by the local authority, 31 by parents and nine by children. The success rate of L.As. was 88 %, that of parents 32 %.

[51] See generally R. Bullock *et al.*, *Going Home* (1993); E. Farmer and R. Parker, *Trials and tribulations* (1991).

aftercare duties.[52] Parents or a child who seek discharge may have difficulty establishing that this is in the child's best interests, particularly where they have had little contact. The inability of the magistrates' court to order the child's phased return to the family was seen as a significant defect by the judiciary, but despite support in the *Review*, the Children Act 1989 made no specific provision for this.[53]

(f) Appeals

22–041 Before the introduction of the Children Act 1989 there was no coherent scheme for appeals in child care cases and appeal rights were restricted.[54] The *Review* recommended that parents and local authorities should be able to appeal; the Act gives all parties to the original decision a right to appeal.[55] But no appeal may be made against the making or refusal of an emergency protection order.[56] Appeals against decisions by a magistrates' court are heard in the High Court by a Family Division judge sitting in open court; other appeals go to the Court of Appeal.[57] The appeal is not a full re-hearing; the principles in *G. v. G.* apply.[58]

The Act provides for the child's protection pending an appeal. If there is an interim care or supervision order and a full order is refused, the court may nevertheless make an order for "the appeal period" subject to such conditions as it thinks fit.[59] This period expires with the time-limit for appealing unless an appeal is made, and continues until the case is determined by court.[60]

F. Protection of children in emergencies

22–042 From the first introduction of child protection legislation, it was general practice to remove or "rescue" children before proving the case for their committal to care.[61] A magistrate could authorise a child's removal to a "place of safety" on

---

[52] Children Act 1989, ss.24–24D. It is government policy not to end care prematurely see: *Children Act Report 1995–99*, para. 6.2.

[53] *Short Report,* Vol. III, evidence, p. 588. Parents could use wardship: *Re J. (Wardship: Jurisdiction)* [1984] 1 W.L.R. 81; *Review of Child Care Law,* para. 20.26. For possible mechanisms see 6th edition of this work, p.819.

[54] See 5th edition of this work, p. 625.

[55] *Review of Child Care Law,* Chap. 19; Cm. 62 (1987), para. 66; F.P.R. 1991, r. 4.22.

[56] s.46(10); *Essex C.C. v. F.* [1993] 1 F.L.R. 847, theoretically judicial review is available, alternatively an application for an interim care order could be made see: *Re P. (Emergency Protection Order)* [1996] 1 F.L.R. 482 at 484, *per* Johnson J.

[57] s.94(1); F.P.R. 1991, r. 4.22; R.S.C. Ords 55 and 59 (CPR 1998, Sched.1); *Practice Direction* [1992] 1 W.L.R. 261.

[58] [1985] 1 W.L.R. 647, see above, para. 20–020.

[59] s.40; *Re M. (A Minor) (Appeal: Interim Order)* [1994] 1 F.L.R. 54. There are comparable provisions for cases of discharge. The appellate court cannot make an order under s.40(1) but may make an interim order under s.38: *Croydon LBC v. A. (No. 2)* [1994] 2 F.L.R. 348.

[60] s.40(6); the magistrates may specify a different time (s.40(4)) but this may be extended by the appellate court (s.40(5)).

[61] H. Ferguson, "Cleveland in history: the abused child and child protection 1880–1914" in R. Cooter (ed.) *In the name of the child: health and welfare 1880–1940* (1992) and H. Ferguson "Re-thinking child protection practice: a case for history" in Violence against children study group, *Taking child abuse seriously* (1990).

the application of any person with reasonable cause to suspect that the child was being ill-treated.[62] The police also had the power to detain children on similar grounds.[63] Place of safety orders were the subject of considerable criticism: they lasted too long, were used too readily and were not subject to review; the grounds were not sufficiently focused on emergencies; the applicant had no clear responsibility for the child's welfare; the powers to obtain medical examinations were unclear; and orders could result in long periods without contact with the family.[64] The Government accepted proposals from the Short Committee and the *Review of Child Care Law* to limit emergency powers.[65] Immediate separation of the child was not necessary and could be harmful to the child; compulsory separation could make it more difficult to work with the family for the child's rehabilitation.[66]

(a) Emergency protection orders[67]

22–043 The purpose of the order is to enable a child to be provided with immediate short-term protection in a genuine emergency.[68] Anyone[69] may apply to the court for an emergency protection order which empowers them to remove (or prevent the removal of) the child concerned. The application may be heard *ex parte* by a single magistrate.[70] Consequently, it may not be appropriate for a dispute about medical treatment.[71] A Children's Guardian should be appointed but only very limited inquiries are possible.[72]

The court may only grant the order if it is satisfied that there is reasonable cause to believe that the child is likely to suffer significant harm if he is not

---

[62] Prevention of Cruelty to Children Act 1894, s.10; Children and Young Persons Act 1969, s.28. see J. Masson *et al.*, *Working in the dark* (2001), Chap. 1. Under the 1969 Act detention was limited to 28 days.

[63] Prevention of Cruelty to and Protection of Children Act 1889, s. 4; Children and Young Persons Act 1933, s.40; Children and Young Persons Act 1969, s.28(2). Detention without warrant was limited to eight days by the 1933 Act but the police could also obtain a warrant to search and detain a child for 28 days.

[64] *Short Report,* paras 122–130; *Review of Child Care Law,* Chap. 13; *Cleveland Report,* p. 306–7; Cm. 62, paras 45–47; T. Norris and N. Parton, "The administration of place of safety orders" [1987] J.S.W.L. 1. Approximately 5,000 place of safety orders (POSO's) were made in 1990: Cm. 2584, para. 3.10.

[65] Cm. 62 (1987), para. 46; *Short Report,* paras 122–130; *Review of Child Care Law,* Chap. 13.

[66] Packman *et al.* (1986). Many of these points were re iterated in the *Cleveland Report* (1988).

[67] Children Act 1989, ss.44, 45.

[68] *Guidance,* Vol. 1, para. 4.28.

[69] But the local authority may take over the case: Emergency Protection Order (Transfer of Responsibilities) Regulations 1991, S.I. 1991 No. 1414. Use of an EPO in a family dispute is rarely appropriate and likely to lead to a child protection investigation.

[70] F.P.C. 1991, r. 2(5) (a). Leave is required, rr. 3, 4(4). Alternatively the court may allow the case to proceed with less than one days notice: *Essex C.C. v. F.* [1993] 1 F.L.R. 847.

[71] *Re O. (A Minor) (Medical Treatment)* [1993] 2 F.L.R. 149 at 152 in such cases a specific issue order could be sought, preferably on notice, see above.

[72] *Guidance,* Vol. 7, paras 2.69–2.71; D.H., *Manual of Practice Guidance for Guardians ad litem and Reporting Officers* (1992), pp. 54–56.

removed or detained[73]—or, in the case of applications by a local authority or the NSPCC, the applicant has reasonable cause to suspect actual or likely significant harm and their inquiries are being frustrated by unreasonable refusal of access to the child.[74] Where access to the child is being refused the court is unlikely to refuse the order. The introduction of this ground, late in the passage of the Bill, was controversial. It was argued that a weak ground should only justify ordering assessment not removal, but this was rejected by the Government on the basis that a local authority with a duty to see a child needed a right of access.[75]

An emergency protection order directs the child's production to the applicant; empowers the applicant to remove the child or to prevent this; and gives the applicant parental responsibility for the child.[76] It may authorise entry and search of specific premises, also a warrant may be obtained to permit forcible entry by the police.[77] The applicant may not remove or detain the child unless this is necessary to safeguard the child's welfare and may return the child and remove him or her on more than one occasion while the order is in force.[78] In exercise of parental responsibility the applicant may only do what is reasonably required to safeguard or promote the child's welfare. This would include consenting to required medical treatment, making arrangements for the child's care and maintaining links with the family.[79] The court may direct that either contact or assessment may or may not be allowed.[80]

Following the recommendation of the Law Commission,[81] where the court makes an EPO it may include an exclusion requirement or accept undertakings[82] on the same basis and with the same effect as when granting an interim care order.[83] This exclusion ceases to be enforceable if the applicant removes the

---

[73] s.44(1) (a). This test appears stricter than the previous law because the court must be satisfied that the condition exists.

[74] s.44(1) (b), (c); a parent who refuses access at night to a sleeping child or who offers to take a child to the clinic in the morning may not be unreasonable: *Guidance,* Vol. 1, para. 4.39.

[75] s.47(4), see Children Bill Committee Stage (*Hansard,* Standing Committee B, cols. 276–321 May 25, 1989) especially *per* David Mellor, Secretary of State for Health, *Hansard,* H.C., cols. 316–321. Report Stage, *Hansard,* H.L. Vol. 158, cols. 593–594; Consideration of Commons Amendments, Vol. 512, cols. 782–784, "The emphasis on urgency, court scrutiny of applications, making orders only where this is necessary and removing the child only when this is necessary will ensure that the balance we seek is achieved in practice . . . ." *per* Lord Mackay, Lord Chancellor.

[76] s.44(4). It is an offence intentionally to obstruct exercise of the power in s.44(4) (b): s.44(15).

[77] s.48. The police may also enter premises to save life or limb without a warrant: Police and Criminal Evidence Act 1984, s.17(1) (e).

[78] s.44(5) (a), (10), (12). The child must be returned if it is safe to do so.

[79] s.44(5) (b); the applicant must allow the child reasonable contact with the persons listed in s.44(13). The local authority has a duty to provide accommodation under s.21(1).

[80] s.44(6)–(9).

[81] Law Com. No. 207, *Domestic Violence and the Occupation of the Family Home* (1992) paras 6.15 *et seq.* The possibility of including such powers was considered during the debates on the Children Bill but shelved pending the report from the Law Commission.

[82] Originally there were no provisions relating to undertakings. The Law Commission considered that adjourning proceedings to enable the respondent to attend to give undertakings could be dangerous to the child. Also the person with care might have little incentive to report the breach (Law Com. No. 207, para. 6.15). But the views of the Association of District Judges that undertakings would be a valuable addition to the court's powers was accepted: see Proceedings of the Special Public Committee (H.L. 55, 1994–5).

[83] See above p. 739; Children Act 1989, ss.44A, 44B added by F.L.A. 1996, s.52 and Sched. 6,

child for more than 24 hours[84]; the Law Commission was concerned that families might otherwise "lose both ways" by having both the suspected abuser excluded and the child removed.[85] Despite the considerable thought given to these provisions, exclusion of the perpetrator rarely provides adequate protection for children when an EPO is sought.[86] In EPO proceedings the court may make a non-molestation order against any respondent if this would benefit any other party to the proceedings or the child.[87]

The emergency protection order may last for up to eight days and may be extended once for up to seven days,[88] but only where the court has reasonable cause to suspect that the child will suffer significant harm if the order is not extended.[89] No challenge is allowed during the first 72 hours of an EPO but the child, a parent, a person with parental responsibility or anyone with whom the child was living prior to the order may seek its discharge unless either they had notice of the original hearing and were present, or the order has been extended.[90] Any person excluded may apply for the variation or discharge of an exclusion requirement.[91] There is no appeal.[92]

22–044 The sudden separation of a parent and child breaches the rights to family life of both unless it is a necessary response to an immediate crisis. The European Court of Human Rights has stated that "extraordinarily compelling reasons"[93] are needed to justify removal of a baby at birth but has been less than clear in explaining the circumstances in which emergency action is and is not justified:—

> In *K. and T. v. Finland*[94] the mother, *K*, who suffered from serious mental illness and was hospitalised from time to time, agreed to her son's accommodation by the welfare authorities. A few months later she gave birth to a daughter who was removed from her in the hospital delivery suite, under a court order. Shortly afterwards her son was also made subject to an emergency order so he could not be removed from the children's home. There was no prior discussion with the parents; the welfare authorities apparently rejected any possibility that *T*, the father, could a care for his baby. The parents were allowed only supervised contact. Although the father demonstrated he could care for the baby the authorities decided to place her in

[84] Children Act 1989, ss.44A(10), 44B(3).
[85] Law Com. No. 207, para. 6.19.
[86] A. Pack [2001] *Fam. Law* 217.
[87] F.L.A. 1996, s.42(2) (3).
[88] s.45(1), (2), (5).
[89] s.45(5). In practice it is more usual to proceed direct to an interim care order. The *Review of Child Care Law* recommended that there should be no extension: paras 13.23–4.
[90] s.45(8)–(11).
[91] s.45(8A), (8B) added by F.L.A. 1996, Sched. 6.
[92] s.45(10); *Essex C.C. v. F.* [1993] 1 F.L.R. 847; judicial review is theoretically available. The lack of a mechanism for speedy review has been criticised see: *Re P. (Emergency Protection Order)* [1996] 1 F.L.R. 482 at 485, *per* Johnson J.
[93] *K. and T. v. Finland* [2001] 2 F.L.R. 707 at para. 168
[94] [2001] 2 F.L.R. 707 (Grand Chamber); *K. and T. v. Finland* [2000] 2 F.L.R. 79; *P.C. and S v. UK* app. no. 56547/00.

foster care with her brother. After unsuccessfully challenging the decisions, the parents applied to the European Court of Human Rights. The court found a breach of Article 8. The State's action has been "arbitrary and unjustified." The mother did not appear ill or irrational when the baby was removed, no other measures of protection were tried, and despite pre-planning, no attempt was made to inform the parents.[95] Finland requested the case be referred to the Grand Chamber. There the majority accepted that Article 8 had been breached in removing the baby, but not in detaining the son. There were strong dissenting opinions from three judges who considered that there had been no violation in relation to the baby[96] and four judges who found a breach in the detention of the son. Underlying the reasoning was concern for the proper use of these extreme powers. The judges who found a breach of Article 8 considered that intervention without notice should be confined to unforeseen emergencies and imminent danger.[97] However, this conflicts with the decision of the majority in relation to the son who was made subject to an order without any parental threat to remove him. The minority were more sympathetic to the dilemmas child protection emergencies create for the authorities.[98]

The reforms in the Children Act have reduced the use of emergency orders[99]; care proceedings are no longer routinely started by ordering the child's removal. In many courts *ex parte* orders are a rarity.[1] Following the decision in *K. and T. v Finland* court clerks may become more reluctant to allow applications to be heard without notice to the parents, at least where the local authority intends to remove the child. In 2000, approximately 2,500 EPOs were sought, 90 per cent of which were made.[2] However, 40 per cent of children were separated from their parents before care proceedings were started, and there is some evidence that parents are forced to agree to their child's accommodation to avoid the use of EPOs and care orders.[3]

(b) Police protection[4]

22–045 Little was known about how the police used their powers to detain children for their protection when the Children Act was passed. The *Review of Child*

---

[95] [2000] 2 F.L.R. 79 at paras 144–146.

[96] In addition Pellonpaa J. and Sir Nicholas Bratza found a violation only because of the manner in which the order was implemented. They would apparently have accepted an order to prevent the removal of the baby from the hospital.

[97] paras 166–170 and the dissenting judgement of Rees, Fuhrmann, Pantiru and Kovler JJ. The majority appeared less concerned about the order relating to the son because he was already separated from his mother and step-father, but that made the risk of harm from their retaining rights far less.

[98] Bonnello J. favoured rescuing children over protecting the mother's rights.

[99] *Children Act Now* (2001) p. 56; *Children Act Report 1995–1999,* Table 10.2. In 1990 about 5,000 place of safety orders were made each year: Cm. 2584, para. 3.10.

[1] Research currently being undertaken by J. Masson and colleagues indicates wide variations in the use of *ex parte* EPOs.

[2] *Judicial Statistics 2000,* Table 5.2.

[3] Brandon *et al.* (1999), pp. 136–138 and Table 8.1; *Children Act Now* (2001), p. 51.

[4] s.46.

Care Law accepted that the police needed power to act without a court order, but recommended that detention should be limited to 72 hours.[5] Children Act 1989, s.46 implements this and imposes obligations on the police to safeguard children and their families.

A constable who has reasonable cause to believe that a child would otherwise be likely to suffer significant harm may remove a child or prevent removal from hospital or elsewhere. The child is under police protection.[6] The constable must, as soon as practicable,[7] inform the local authority, the parents and the child; secure investigation by a designated officer and suitable accommodation for the child.[8] These powers mean the police should not merely take a runaway child home but must investigate the incident. The police do not acquire parental responsibility, but the designated officer has a duty to act reasonably to safeguard and promote the child's welfare. The family must be allowed reasonable contact with the child provided it is in the child's best interests. The child must be released after 72 hours or sooner if there is no longer cause for concern. Where the child remains at risk the designated officer may seek an EPO on behalf of the local authority without consultation.[9]

Police protection is used in two distinct ways.[10] Officers remove or detain children they find at risk following calls from parents, children, and the public, or in the course of ordinary policing. In addition they receive requests from social services to take action. Child protection outside normal working hours is frequently arranged through police protection instead of emergency protection orders.[11] Although it has been suggested that its use breaches Article 5[12] police protection appears permissible within Article 5(1) (d).[13] National statistics are not kept on the use of police protection but it has been estimated that police forces outside London use the power in respect of about 6,000 children each year, and that London forces use it more frequently.[14]

---

[5] paras 13.32–3.

[6] s.46(1), (2). Although officers and others refer to "police protection orders" the action requires no proceedings, nor the approval of a senior officer.

[7] s.46(3) (4). The constable must also take steps to discover the child's wishes and feelings but not specifically in relation to contact. If it were clear the child objected to seeing someone, arguably it would not be reasonable to allow it, s.46(10).

[8] Home Office Circular 54/1991 advises that police premises are not suitable except for a short period in exceptional circumstances, para. 15.

[9] s.46(7), (8). Local child protection procedures should provide for consultation: *Working Together* (1991), para. 4.17.

[10] J. Masson *et al., Working in the dark* (2001); J. Masson "Police protection- protecting whom" [2002] *J.S.W.F.L.* 157.

[11] *ibid.*; Dame M. Booth, *Delay in Public Law Children Act cases second report* (1996), para. 8.15.

[12] Aire Centre Quarterly review, "Secure accommodation orders etc." March 2001, p. 4.

[13] Police protection is a preliminary to local authority investigation; the police are required to notify the local authority and ensure etc. Being looked after would amount to "educational supervision" *Bouamar v. Belgium* (1988) 11 E.H.R.R. 1; *Re K. (Secure Accommodation Order: Right to Liberty)* [2001] 1 F.L.R. 526, CA. It is also arguable that the child is not detained.

[14] J. Masson "Police protection—protecting whom" [2002] *J.S.W.F.L.* 157, 159.

(c) Child assessment orders

22–046 The idea for this order came from an inquiry into the death of an abused child.[15] The Government initially resisted its introduction on the basis that assessment could be achieved under an EPO and the existence of two similar orders might confuse social workers and magistrates.[16] Pressure from voluntary organisations, notably the NSPCC, and support from the Association of Directors of Social Services led to a Government amendment.[17] Concern then shifted to the grounds for the order and its duration. Originally the Government proposed the child's removal for up to 28 days to allow for comprehensive assessment,[18] but following objections and to fit with the more restrictive EPO, the order was limited to seven days.

The court may grant this evidence-seeking order[19] if the applicant[20] has reasonable cause to suspect that the child is suffering (or likely to suffer) significant harm, an assessment of the child is necessary to determine this and is unlikely to be made without a court order. This order may not be made where there are grounds for an emergency protection order.[21] Notice of the application must be given[22]; the child should be represented by a children's guardian.[23] The order requires the persons named to produce the child and comply with directions relating to assessment; it authorises the child's assessment and removal from home but only for the purposes of assessment.[24] A child assessment order lasts for seven days; it is clearly impossible to complete the assessment process[25] within such a period. Orders are rarely made.[26] It would seem that the order provides a framework for negotiation and is only obtained where this fails.[27]

---

[15] London Borough of Greenwich, *A Child in Mind, Report of the committee of inquiry into the circumstances surrounding the death of Kimberley Carlile* (1987), pp. 153–156: see also (1989) 55 *Childright* 12.

[16] Lord Mackay, *Hansard* H.L. Vol. 503, cols. 430–431, Children Bill Committee Stage; Vol. 504, col. 315, Report Stage.

[17] See *per* David Mellor, *Hansard* H.C. Vol. 158, col. 593, Children Bill Report Stage; (1989) 55 *Childright* 12.

[18] See Standing Committee B, cols. 276–329, May 25, 1989 especially *per* David Mellor, Secretary of State for Health at col. 295.

[19] *per* David Hinchcliffe M.P., *Hansard* H.C., Vol. 158, col. 604, Children Bill Report Stage.

[20] Only the local authority or an authorised person (NSPCC) may apply.

[21] s.43(1), (4), s.43(3). Where a ground in s.45(1) is satisfied an EPO may be made, s.43(3). This limitation is intended to prevent magistrates deciding in favour of the weaker order but it does not require them to make an EPO.

[22] s.43(11); seven days notice: F.P.R. 1991, Sched. 2; F.P.C. 1991, Sched. 2.

[23] D.H., *Manual of Practice Guidance for Guardians ad litem and Reporting Officers* (1992), pp. 56–7.

[24] s.43(5)–(7) (9).

[25] See generally, D.H., *A framework for assessing children and families* (2000). In *Re B. (A Minor) (Care Order: Criteria)* [1993] 1 F.L.R. 815, Douglas Brown J. granted an interim care order because the assessment would take three months.

[26] In 1993 Less than 100 applications, a quarter of these were withdrawn and only 55 orders were made: Cm. 2584 (1994), Table 3.1. Statistics are no longer published.

[27] See J. Dickens, "Assessment and control in social work: An analysis for the reasons for the non-use of the child assessment order" [1993] *J.S.W.F.L.* 88. Negotiation may produce a longer period of assessment for the local authority and enable the parent to have a say in the process. It has been suggested that there should be a more general assessment order so that the court could control investigative assessments see: R. Lavery, "The child assessment order—a reassessment" [1996] *C.F.L.Q.* 41.

G. Child protection proceedings

(a) The nature of care proceedings

22–047 Care proceedings developed from criminal proceedings; care cases were conceptualised as disputes between the local authority and the child, parents were not parties.[28] Concern for justice for parents led some local authorities to use wardship instead of care proceedings.[29] Pressure for reform of care proceedings came from many quarters and favoured moves towards inquisitorial procedure.[30] Justice could not be done unless parents were full parties; the courts could only make the right decisions if cases were fully aired before them and they had access to independent sources of information.[31]

Proceedings under the Children Act 1989 are not adversarial although an adversarial approach is adopted by some parties; the court has a responsibility to investigate and to seek to achieve a result which promotes the child's welfare.[32] Substantial use is made of written statements rather than oral evidence; where there is a dispute about the source of harm to the child the hearing can be split so that the facts are determined before any consideration of the care plan.[33] Such cases are unusual and few cases end with contested final hearings.[34] Proceedings are confidential.[35]

---

[28] Parents were only permitted to rebut allegations made against them; they could not obtain legal aid for representation before 1984. There was apparently no attempt to challenge this state of affairs under the European Convention on Human Rights. For further details see 5th edition of this work, pp. 626–74.

[29] J. Masson and S. Morton, "The use of wardship by local authorities" (1989) 52 *M.L.R.* 762. There was a major increase in wardship during the 1980s and over half of cases were started by local authorities.

[30] See *Short Report*, paras 94–100 (the views of relevant organisation can be seen in the minutes of evidence); A. Morris *et al., Justice for Children* (1980), p. 99, A. Macleod and E. Malos, *Representation of children and parents in care proceedings*, (University of Bristol, 1984) and *R. v. Hampshire CC, ex p. K.* [1990] 1 F.L.R. 330.

[31] The lack of information to the court was a contributing factor in the deaths of Maria Colwell and Wayne Brewer; see A. Morris *et al.* (1980), p. 100. *cf.* Dingwall, Eekelaar and Murray (1983) 45 who thought that care proceedings "ought properly to be conceptualised as a dispute between parents and state agencies over the care of the child."

[32] *Oxfordshire C.C. v. M.* [1994] Fam. 151 at 161, *per* Sir Stephen Brown P. During debates on the Bill the Solicitor General said "The Children Bill is only the beginning of a rolling programme to renew the substantive law and the arrangements for its application. The wider programme, which involves more than provisions for children, will be informed by the need for legal consistency, the desirability of all proceedings for one family being heard together, and the need to move away from advensarial to inquisitorial procedures": *Hansard,* Standing Committee B. col. 456, June 8, 1989.

[33] *Re B. (Split Hearing: Jurisdiction)* [2000] 1 F.L.R. 334, CA; *Re G. (Care Proceedings: Split Trials)* [2001] 1 F.L.R. 872, CA. The two hearings should be before the same judge.

[34] In Hunt and Macleod's sample only six out of 82 proceedings had a contested final hearing, and in only one of these did the local authority fail to establish its case: J. Hunt and A. Macleod (1999), p. 39.

[35] See above, para. 22–033.

(b) Care proceedings

22–048 Care proceedings are started by filing an application[36] in the family proceedings court[37] and serving it on the parties at least three days[38] before the hearing. The respondents are the child and anyone with parental responsibility.[39] Other people must be notified[40] and can be made parties if they have a separate interest.[41] Public funding is available.[42] These are "specified proceedings"[43] and the court must appoint a children's guardian to represent the child unless this is not necessary to safeguard the child's interests.[44] The court is required to set a timetable for the proceedings.[45] It has wide powers to issue directions to control the conduct of the proceedings.[46] Proceedings may only be withdrawn with the consent of the court.[47]

(c) Representation of the parties

22–049 In care and other "specified" proceedings the child is represented by a children's guardian and a solicitor.[48] Children are represented so that the court has

---

36 F.P.R. 1991, r. 4.4; F.P.C. 1991, r. 4 (Form C1 with C13).

37 Children (Allocation of Proceedings) Order 1991, S.I. 1991 No. 1677, art. 3(1) (b) proceedings may be transferred to the higher courts: art. 7(1).

38 F.P.R. 1991, r. 4.8 and App. 3; F.P.C. 1991, r. 8 and App. 2.

39 F.P.R. 1991, App. 3; F.P.C. 1991, App. 2.

40 All parties in relevant pending proceedings and parents without parental responsibility: F.P.R. 1991, F.P.C. 1991, rr. 4.8(8), 8(8) confers a general discretion allowing the court to dispense with notice, the child's welfare is not paramount for this decision: *Re X. (Care: Notice of Proceedings)* [1996] 1 F.L.R. 186. Since the implementation of the H.R.A. 1998 the courts have been less willing to dispense with notice in adoption cases: *Re R. (Adoption: Father's Involvement)* [2001] 1 F.L.R. 302, CA and *Re H., Re G. (Adoption: Consultation of Unmarried Fathers)* [2001] 1 F.L.R. 646, FD.

41 *Re M. (Minors) (Sexual Abuse: Evidence)* [1993] 1 F.L.R. 822 at 825, *per* Butler-Sloss L.J.; the courts are reluctant to join parties if this will delay proceedings: *Re H. (Care Proceedings: Intervener)* [2000] 1 F.L.R. 775, CA (older sibling, refused); *Re P.(Care Proceedings: Father's Application to be Joined as a Party)* [2001] 1 F.L.R. 781, FD (father refused).

42 *Funding Code* (1999), paras 11.7–11.9; Public funding is granted "without reference to means, prospects of success or reasonableness" *Funding Code decision-making guidance,* para. 20.12.

43 s.41(6) includes applications for (and variation or discharge of) care or supervision orders; applications for residence orders or contact in respect of children in care; cases were the court had directed an investigation and is considering making an interim order; proceedings under Pt V of the Act; the corresponding appeals; and proceedings listed in F.P.R. 1991, r. 4.2(2)—secure accommodation applications, change of name or emigration for children in care and the extension of supervision orders.

44 s.41(1); F.P.R. 1991, r. 4.10(1); F.P.C. 1991, r. 10(1); s.4(1). In *Re J. (A Minor) (Change of Name)* [1993] 1 F.L.R. 699 the court was satisfied that all the relevant issues had been brought out by counsel for the local authority.

45 s.32; *Handbook of Best Practice* (1997), Chap. 1 and App. A5. Solicitors and advocates are expected to co-operate and the local authority should present its case objectively: *Re JC. (Care Proceedings: Procedure)* [1995] 2 F.L.R. 77.

46 F.P.R. 1991, r. 4.14; F.P.C. 1991, r. 14 and Chap. 19, above.

47 F.P.R. 1991, r. 4.5; F.P.C. 1991, r. 5; cogent reasons should be provided for withdrawal: *Re N. (Leave to Withdraw Care Proceedings)* [2000] 1 F.L.R. 134, FD.

48 Children Act 1989, s. 41; F.P.R. 1991, rr. 4.10, 4.12; F.P.C. 1991, r. 10, 12; *cf. W. v. Legal Services Commission* [2000] 1 F.L.R. 821, CA. In cases of exceptional difficulty in the High Court or the county court, CAFCASS Legal (which has taken over this work from the Official Solicitor) may be appointed for the child: *CAFCASS Practice Note* [2001] 2 F.L.R. 151.

information about their welfare, their wishes and any relevant information, not to enable them to participate in the proceedings.[49] Children are rarely given access to documents but the guardian's recommendations "should be shared with them."[50] Despite being a party, the child has no right to attend the proceedings; this is a matter for the court,[51] even where the order will result in the child's detention in secure accommodation.[52] Although *Guidance* encourages the attendance of children at case conferences,[53] it has been said that there would need to be exceptional circumstances for a 15-year-old girl to attend her care proceedings because of the risk of emotional damage and the inhibition of submissions to the court.[54] Also that it is clearly undesirable for a child to hear critical cross-examination of a parent.[55] These paternalistic ideas rest on the belief that participation in court proceedings may cause further harm and ignore the abusive effect of being excluded.[56]

Concerns have been expressed about the quality of representation for parents, which is frequently by solicitors who lack specific expertise. Parents were generally satisfied with their representatives and the fairness of the judiciary but found the proceedings highly stressful and wanted an opportunity to put their views directly to the judge.[57] Representation is important: the European Court of Human Rights in *P., C. and S. v. UK* held that the assistance of a lawyer was an "indispensable requirement" in proceedings which would lead to the end of the parents' relationship with their child. The hearing is only part of the process which must be fair overall, parents must be sufficiently involved in decisions concerning the care of their children.[58]

(i) Provision of children's guardians

22–050 In April 2001, responsibility for the provision of children's guardians (guardians *ad litem*) was transferred from local authorities to CAFCASS (the Children and Family Court Advisory and Support Service), a non-departmental

---

[49] J. Masson and M. Winn Oakley, *Out of Hearing* (1999) pp. 21–26 and Chap. 7; J. Masson, "Representation of children in England" [2000] F.L.Q. 467 at 488.

[50] *ibid.*; CAFCASS, *Draft National Standards* (2001), para. 19.

[51] s.95; F.P.R. 1991, r. 4.16(2); F.P.C. 1991, r. 16(2). Masson and Winn Oakley 109–116.

[52] *Re. W. (Secure Accommodation Order: Attendance at Court)* [1994] 2 F.L.R. 1092 but fairness requires that the child has a proper opportunity to give instructions: *Re C. (Secure Accommodation Order: Representation)* [2001] 1 F.L.R. 857, FD.

[53] *Working Together* (1999), para. 5.57.

[54] *J. v. Lancashire C.C.* (unreported) May 25, 1993; CAAC Report 1992/3, p. 72 see also *Re C. (A Minor) (Care: Child's Wishes)* [1993] 1 F.L.R. 832 at 841.

[55] CAAC Report 1993/4, p. 45.

[56] For a discussion of this issue see: J. Masson, "Representations of the child" [1996] C.L.P. 245. At least half of the children in recent studies of care proceedings said they would have liked to be able to attend Masson (2000), p.490.

[57] P. Freeman and J. Hunt, *Parental perspectives on care proceedings* (1998); Masson and Winn Oakley (1999), p.150.

[58] *Re B. and T. (Care Proceedings: Legal Representation)* [2001] 1 F.L.R. 485, CA, App. No. 56547/00 at paras 100, 138: there was a breach of both Arts 6 and 8, *cf* where the Court of Appeal sought to balance justice to the parents against the rights of the children to an early determination of their future.

Public Body under the direction of the Lord Chancellor.[59] Disagreements over the new contractual arrangements for the 900 children's guardians "hijacked" management attention from other urgent issues and left CAFCASS in disarray.[60] It has prepared draft *National Standards*[61] and issued new materials for children who are the subject of proceedings[62] but substantial work is required to ensure that an equivalent service is offered to all children and that high quality representation is maintained.

(ii) Role of the children's guardian

22–051 The children's guardian is the lynchpin in care proceedings.[63] Guardians are experts in child care social work practice,[64] and their duties are set out in court rules.[65] The guardian must regard as paramount the need to safeguard and promote the child's best interests, investigate all the circumstances of the case, represent the child, provide a report to the court and consider whether there should be an appeal. The children's guardian usually appoints the child's solicitor.[66] The relationship between the guardian and the solicitor should be one of partnership and mutual professional respect.[67] The guardian is the link between the solicitor and the child, forming a view about what outcome is in the child's interests, establishing the child's wishes, instructing the solicitor and accepting documents on behalf of the child.[68] The solicitor must follow the guardian's instructions[69] unless the child is capable of giving coherent and consistent instructions[70] and gives conflicting instructions. Public Funding is not available to the children's guardian where the solicitor accepts the child's instructions[71]; CAFCASS is responsible for their legal representation. The guardian has substantial responsibility for case management, advising the court about timetabling, transfer of proceedings and the joinder of additional parties.[72] Guardians

---

[59] Criminal Justice and Court Services Act 2000, ss.11–23 and Sched. 2; for background to this change see: D.H. *et al. Support services in family proceedings—future organisation of court welfare services* (1998) and above, Chap. 19, and for a description of the previous organisation see 6th edition of this work, p.830.

[60] Magistrates' Court Service Inspectorate, *Setting up* (2002), p. 36. There was litigation about the contractual dispute: *R. ota NAGALRO v. CAFCASS* [2002] 1 F.L.R. 255, FD.

[61] These will replace the D.H., *National Standards for the Guardian ad litem and Reporting Officer Service* (1995), see www.CAFCASS.gov.uk

[62] *Powerpack* (2001) available at www.nspcc.org.uk/inform

[63] J. Brophy, *Expert evidence in child protection litigation* (1999), p. 82.

[64] *ibid.* p. 39; *Re R. (Care Proceedings: Disclosure)* [2000] 2 F.L.R. 751 at 761 *per* Butler-Sloss P.

[65] F.P.R. 1991, rr. 4.11, 4.11A; F.P.C. 1991, rr. 11,11A. See also D.H., *Manual of Practice Guidance for Guardians ad litem and Reporting Officers* (1992); *Guidance*, Vol. 7.

[66] F.P.R. 1991, rr.4. 11(1),(2), 4.11A(1) (a),(6); F.P.C. 1991, r. 11(1) (2), 11A((1) (a),(6). Guardians *ad litem* may appoint solicitors who are not members of the Law Society Children Panel, D.H., *Manual of Practice Guidance for Guardians ad litem and Reporting officers* (1992), p. 26.

[67] D.H., *Guide* (1995), p. 53; "each should curb the excesses and irrelevancies of the other": *Re CB. and JB. (Care Proceedings: Guidelines)* [1998] 2 F.L.R. 211 at 230 *per* Wall J.

[68] F.P.R. 1991, r. 4.11A(4) (b) (e), (8); F.P.C. 1991 r. 11(4) (b), (8).

[69] F.P.R. 1991, r 4.12(1) (a); F.P.C. 1991, r. 12(1) (a).

[70] *ibid.*; *Re H. (A Minor) (Care Proceedings: Child's Wishes)* [1993] 1 F.L.R. 440.

[71] *Funding Code*, para. 2.2.

[72] F.P.R. 1991, r. 4.11A(4), (6); F.P.C. 1991, r. 11A(4), (6); D.H., *Manual* (1992), p. 23; D.H., *Guide* (1995), Chap. 9; Brophy (1999).

advise about the choice of expert witnesses and convene meetings between experts to identify areas of agreement and dispute.[73] The guardian prepares a report for the court, informing it about the child's wishes and advising on the child's welfare.[74] Not all these roles are necessarily compatible. Although guardians should be independent of the parents and local authority they find themselves taking action to alleviate shortcomings in the representation of other parties.[75]

The children's guardian has a statutory right of access to records held by the local authority, including confidential adoption reports.[76] If the local authority obtains disclosure of witness statements held by the police or the CPS, the guardian may also see them.[77] The court may give directions if the children's guardian wishes to observe meetings between the child and the parents or to have the child medically examined.[78] In addition, it has been held that while proceedings are pending the local authority must consult the guardian before making a significant change in the child's placement.[79]

The children's guardian's appointment continues for such time as is specified or until terminated by the court.[80] Where proceedings are continuing, the appointment can only be ended by a court order.[81] Even after proceedings have been ended the children's guardian may have a role if the care plan is not implemented. The Independent Reviewing Officer is empowered to refer the case to CAFCASS so that a failure which breeches the child's human rights can be brought before the court on behalf of the child.[82] If proceedings cease to be "specified" because the local authority conducting a section 37 inquiry decides not to seek an order, a county court or the High Court may, with the guardian's agreement, continue the appointment but this should not be used as a back door method of getting a children's guardian for private law proceedings.[83] However,

---

[73] CAAC *Final Report* (1997), p. 31; D.H., *Guide* (1995), p. 57; J. Brophy (1999); *Re R. (Child Abuse: Video Evidence)* [1995] 1 F.L.R. 451; *Re M. (Minors) (Care Proceedings: Child's Wishes)* [1994]1 F.L.R. 749.

[74] F.P.R. 1991, r. 4.11A(7); F.P.C. 1991, r. 11A(7).

[75] J. Brophy (1999), p. 77; J. Brophy and P. Bates, *The guardian ad litem, complex cases and the use of experts following the Children Act 1989* (1999).

[76] s.42(1) (including NSPCC records); *Manchester C.C. v. T.* [1994] Fam. 181 but not necessarily to disclose them further: *Re R. (Care Proceedings: Disclosure)* [2000] 2 F.L.R. 751, CA.

[77] In *Nottingham C.C. v. H.* [1995] 1 F.L.R. 115 the order restricted disclosure to "those social workers or other member of [the director of social services] staff who are directly concerned in the care of [the children]."

[78] ss.38(6), 44(6); F.P.R. 1991, rr.4.14, 4.18; F.P.C. 1991, rr.4, 18.

[79] *R. v. N. Yorkshire C.C., ex p. M.* [1989] 1 All E.R. 143, but the decision as to the form of representation to the adoption panel is for the panel: *R. v. N. Yorkshire C.C. ex p. M. (No. 2)* [1989] 2 F.L.R. 79.

[80] F.P.R. 1991, r. 4.10(9); F.P.C. 1991, r. 10(9); *Re M. (Terminating Appointment of Guardian ad litem)* [1999] 2 F.L.R. 717, FD. Where there are fresh proceedings involving the same child it is usual to appoint the same guardian: *Re J. (Adoption: Appointment of Guardian ad litem)* [1999] 2 F.L.R. 86, CA.

[81] *Re CE. (s. 37 Direction)* [1995] 1 F.L.R. 26 at 44, *per* Wall J.

[82] Children Act 1989, s.26(2A)(c), added by Adoption and Children Bill 2002, cl. 116. Sched. 3 of the bill repeals Criminal Justice and Court Services Act 2000, s.12(5)(b). This Scheme seeks to solve the difficulties of failure in care plans identified in *Re S. (F.C.)* [2002] 1 F.L.R. 815, HL.

[83] F.P.R. 1991, r. 9.5; *Re CE. (s. 37 Direction)* [1995] 1 F.L.R. 26 at 45 *per* Wall J. There are no set criteria for deciding whether to appoint a children's guardian where there is a s.37 direction but matters to be considered were set out by Wall J. at 41.

the status of children's guardian gives no right to make children wards of court nor to apply for section 8 orders.[84]

(iii) The practice of children's guardians

22–052 There are considerable variations in the ways children's guardians approach their work and the number of hours they spend on each case.[85] Their work is time-limited and task-centred; they have to acquire enough knowledge and understanding to present the court with a coherent view of the child's situation, the options available and a clear recommendation of the appropriate outcome for the child.[86] On average each care inquiry takes 100 hours.[87] Direct work with the child occupies only a small proportion of the guardian's time; many hours are spent seeing other family members, reading social services files, seeking experts' opinions, attending directions appointments and writing the report. Cases are frequently quite fluid during the proceedings; the guardian's involvement can influence the approach of the local authority and the attitudes of parents, assisting agreement rather than changing the orders made.[88] The children's guardian must file a report at least 14 days before the hearing and serve it on the parties[89] The report must give a clear statement of the child's views and interests.[90] The court is free to reject these proposals but must give reasons for so doing.[91] The guardian's report is confidential to the proceedings; the court's permission is required even for the local authority to disclose it to its social workers providing therapy for the child.[92] The children's guardian has responsibility for ensuring that, where appropriate, the decision is explained to the child.

(iv) The child's solicitor

22–053 In 1983 the Law Society established a specialist panel of solicitors to act for children in care proceedings. Solicitors with the necessary experience and train-

---

[84] *A. v. Berkshire C.C.* [1989] 1 F.L.R. 273; *Re M. (Prohibited Steps Order: Application for Leave)* [1993] 1 F.L.R. 275. But a former children's guardian, acting as a litigation friend has obtained judicial review to quash a local authority's decision about funding placements with relatives: *R. ota L. v. Manchester C. C.* [2002] 1 F.L.R. 43. CAFCASS may not agree to such action.

[85] J. Masson, "Representation of children in England" [2000] F.L.Q. 467; A. Clark and R. Sinclair, *The child in focus* (1999); J. McCausland, *Guarding children's interests* (2000); M. Ruegger, "Seen and Heard but how well informed" (2001) *Children and Society* 15 at 133.

[86] D.H., *Manual of Practice Guidance for Guardians ad litem and Reporting Officers* (1992), p. 35.

[87] D.H., *Panel Managers Annual Workshop* (1999) p. 33.

[88] Masson *op. cit.*, p. 478; D.H., *Manual* (1992), p. 88.

[89] F.P.R. 1991, r. 4.11A(7); F.P.C. 1991, r. 11A(7), the court may specify a different period and may grant leave to withhold confidential information where there are compelling reasons: *Re C. (Disclosure)* [1996] 1 F.L.R. 797.

[90] D.H., *Manual* (1992), p. 42.

[91] *S. v. Oxfordshire C.C.* [1993] 1 F.L.R. 452 at 461, *per* Connell, J. Failure to do so is grounds for an appeal.

[92] *Re C. (Guardian ad litem: Disclosure of Report)* [1996] 1 F.L.R. 61. The use of national rather than local experts also poses difficulty for ensuring children receive the services they are assessed to need: J. Brophy and P. Bates *op. cit.*(1999).

ing can become members of the Children Panel.[93] Guidance is available to solicitors about acting for children; child clients should always be afforded the same respect as adult clients.[94] Solicitors should always meet their child clients and assess their ability to give instructions.[95] Where a child has sufficient maturity to give instructions and these differ from those of the children's guardian, the solicitor must follow the child's instructions.[96] In practice these principles are not always applied; solicitors rely heavily on children's guardians and do not involve child clients in the legal process.[97]

H. Child protection and the criminal law

(a) Historical background

22–054 The earliest child protection laws in England and Wales required criminal proceedings to be taken against the parent.[98] The NSPCC prosecuted thousands of parents in an attempt to coerce them and others to provide adequate care.[99] The development of separate civil proceedings in 1952 and the difficulty of proving cases at the criminal standard led to a decline in the use of prosecution. Before the 1990's there was little co-operation between the police and social services in relation to child protection.[1] The interagency system now requires this and police Child Protection Unit officers work closely with social workers.[2]

In recent years there have been a large number of investigations of "historic" child abuse following allegations by former residents, now adults, of children's homes and boarding schools. In some cases there has been evidence that earlier complaints made by children were not believed.[3] These scandals indicate how little regard was taken of children and their statements in the past, and how easy it was for abusers to infiltrate child welfare

[93] J. Ellison, "The child's solicitor in child protection proceedings" in *Re-focus on child abuse* (A. Levy ed., 1994). Enhanced rates of remuneration are paid by the Legal Services Commission.

[94] C. Liddle, *Acting for Children* (1992); Law Society's Family Law Committee, Attendance of solicitors at child protection conferences (1994); Solicitors' Family Law Association, *Guide to good practice for solicitors acting for children* (5th. ed., 2000), p. 5.

[95] *ibid.*

[96] F.P.R. 1991, r. 4.12(1) (a); F.P.C. 1991, r. 12(1) (a); Liddle (1992), pp. 77, 81, 89; SFLA, *Guide to good practice* (2000), pp. 3–5. *Re P. (Representation)* [1996] 1 F.L.R. 486, CA.

[97] Masson and Winn Oakley (1999), Chap. 7; Masson *op. cit.* p.488.

[98] The Prevention of Cruelty of Children Act 1889 allowed the court to commit a child to the care of a fit person if the carer had been bound over, convicted or committed for trial for ill-treating the child. For a consideration of offences relating to sexual abuse see: V. Bailey and S. Blacktown, "The Punishment of Incest Act 1908: A case study in law creation" [1979] Crim. L.R. 708 and L. Zedner, "Regulating sexual offences within the home" in *Frontiers of criminality* (I. Loveland ed., 1995).

[99] L. Housden *The Prevention of Cruelty to Children* (1955), Chap. 4.

[1] See the discussion in C. Hallet and E. Birchall, *Co-ordination and child protection* (1992), pp. 133 *et seq.*

[2] See D.H., *Working Together* (1999), paras 3.57–3.64; H.M.I.C., *Child protection: thematic inspection report* (1998).

[3] See C. Wolmar, *Forgotten children* (2000); *Lost in care* (2000), Chaps 50 and 51. Most police forces have been engaged in such inquiries *Hansard* H.C. November 1, 2001 col. 856W.

services.[4] They also raise concerns about the difficulties of testing evidence and providing a fair trial, long after alleged offences took place.

(b) The importance of prosecution

22–055 Although prosecution rates are low and have apparently declined since the Cleveland crisis,[5] the prosecution of those who commit offences against children plays an important role in the protection of all children and may have enormous impact on individual children. A conviction for an offence against a child[6] is no longer grounds for a care order but is likely to prevent a person working in any position with responsibility for children and preclude him and anyone he lives with being registered as a childminder or foster carer.[7] The conviction of an abuser may prevent the need for care proceedings; the victim may also be helped by knowing that he or she has been believed.[8] There is evidence that those who sexually abuse children frequently commit offences against many children and target vulnerable children.[9] Those convicted of sexual offences are required to register with the police[10]; this information is used to prevent and detect offences, but labelling can have limited effect whilst conviction rates remain very low.

The criminal justice system is ineffective in deterring offenders and in securing convictions of those who are guilty. Its failings are most marked in relation to the most vulnerable—the very young and the disabled.[11] Conviction rates are low[12] and acquittals can undermine care proceedings.[13] Criminal proceedings can also have damaging effects on child victims of abuse. Prosecution of a parent may lead to children being blamed (or blaming themselves) for the

---

[4] W. Utting (1997), p. 1 and paras 1.40 *et seq.*

[5] W. Utting (1997), paras 20.4–20.10; C. Wattam, *Making a case in child protection* (1992); T. Frothingham *et al.*, "Child sexual abuse in Leeds before and after Cleveland" (1993) 23 Child Abuse Rev. 23.

[6] Criminal Justice and Court Services Act 2000, s.26 and Sched. 4 These were formerly known as "schedule 1 offences" Children and Young Persons Act 1933, Sched.1.

[7] Criminal Justice and Court Services Act 2000, s.28; Children Act 1989, s.68, 71(2); Disqualification for Caring for Children (England) Regulations 2002. Rehabilitation of Offenders Act 1974 (Exceptions) Order 1975 S.I. 1975 No. 1023, r. 3, and Sched.1, Pt II, para. 14 exempts from its provisions those who care for children; enhanced criminal records certificates can be obtained by prospective employers: Police Act 1997, ss.113 and 114. Staff and volunteers working with social services departments must be vetted: Protection of Children Act 1999; the Department of Health runs a register of those considered unsuitable to work with children.

[8] L. Berliner, "Treating the effects of sexual assault" in *Intervening in sexual abuse* (K. Murray and D. Gough eds., 1991); J. Fontaine, *Child sexual abuse* (1990), pp. 222 *et seq.*

[9] C. Cobley, *Sex Offenders* (2000); J. La Fontaine, *op. cit.* Chap. 5.

[10] Sex Offenders Act 1997; C. Cobley *op. cit.* p. 323–332.

[11] W. Utting (1997) *op. cit.* p. 189; the Government rejected proposals to modify the standard of proof in these cases: *The Government's Response to the Children's Safeguards Review* (Cm. 4105, 1998), paras 10.8–10.9.

[12] Approximately half the defendants were acquitted in a recent study of cases involving child witnesses see: G. Davies *et al., Videotaping children's evidence and evaluation* (1995), p. 34; Utting cites figures of 14% for indecent assault against a female and 11% for rape but these do not relate only to children, *op. cit.* para. 20.8.

[13] This appears to have been a major reason that the judge in *Re H. and R. (Sexual Abuse: Standard of Proof)* [1996] 1 F.L.R. 80 regarded the girl's evidence as inadequate.

imprisonment and the break-up of the family, rather than being supported.[14] Where the abuser is acquitted the consequences may be very severe; the child suffers the abuse and the proceedings, the perpetrator's claim of innocence appears vindicated, and the child goes into care. Despite a policy of ensuring their speedy progress, the prosecution of child abuse cases takes a long time.[15] Conviction may enable the perpetrator to receive treatment so that he does not re-offend but there is no guarantee that this will be available and success rates are apparently low.[16] Many convicted abusers are detained in isolation[17] for their own protection so that they mix only with others with similar convictions. Sentences often seem short when the harm to the child is considered.[18] But it has been argued that the emphasis on custodial sentences discourages perpetrators from accepting responsibility.[19]

(c) The decision to prosecute[20]

22–056 The decision to prosecute is made by the Crown Prosecution Service guided by the Code for Crown Prosecutors. There must be a "realistic prospect of conviction" and therefore sufficient reliable, evidence.[21] The strength of the complainant child's account and the existence of supporting evidence are crucial to the decision to prosecute.[22] The prosecution must be in the public interest. The interests of the victim are an important matter but the Crown Prosecution Service acts in the public interest not for individuals.[23] The Crown Prosecution Service appears concerned to protect children from court proceedings but negotiation of charges and pleas operate to reduce the severity of sentences, delay proceedings and deny justice to children.[24]

---

14 J. La Fontaine (1990) p. 230, cites a study of victims referred to Great Ormond Street Hospital for therapy, only 14% remained with both parents.

15 J. Plotnikoff and R. Woolfson, *Prosecution of child abuse: an evaluation of the Government's speedy progress policy* (1995).

16 See A. Horton, *The Incest Perpetrator—the family member no one wants to treat* (1990) and C. Cobley (2000), pp.254 *et seq.*

17 Under Prison Rules 1964 (S.I. 1964 No. 388), r. 43. This may encourage more offending, K. Murray and D. Gough "Implications and prospects" in K. Murray and D. Gough, *Intervening in Child Sexual Abuse* (1991).

18 For a discussion of the principles applied to sex offences see generally C. Cobley (2000), Chap 4; *Attorney General's Reference No. 1 of 1989* (1989) 11 Cr. App. R. (S.) 409 (incest): *No. 35 of 1994* (1995) 16 Cr. App. R. (S) 635 (indecent asault).

19 D. Glaser and J. Spencer, "Sentencing, children's evidence and children's trauma" [1990] Crim. L.R. 371. *cf.* S. Viinikka, "Child sexual abuse and the law" in E. Driver and A. Droisen, *Child sexual abuse: feminist perspectives* (1989), p. 153.

20 See C. Wattam, *Making a case in Child Protection* (1992); C. Keenan and L. Maitland, "There ought to be a law against it—police evaluation of the efficacy of prosecution in a case of child abuse" [1999] *C.F.L.Q.* 379.

21 Crown Prosecution Service, *Code of Practice for Crown Prosecutors* (2000), paras 5.1, 5.3.

22 G. Davis *et al.*, *An assessment of the admissibility and sufficiency of evidence in child abuse prosecutions, Report to the Home Office* (1999).

23 *ibid.* paras 4.2, 6, 6.7. The impact on the child and family are factors considered by the police when deciding whether to refer the case to the CPS: C. Keenan and L. Maitland (1999) *op. cit.* p.408.

24 C. Wattam (1992), p. 146; CPS, *The Inspector's Report of cases involving child witnesses* (1998), para. 2.1.

(d) Children's evidence[25]

22–057 In many cases of child abuse only the child's evidence links the incident to the perpetrator; unless the child can give credible evidence there can be no prosecution. Rules of evidence applying to child witnesses and procedures which can help children to give evidence are therefore crucial. Until recently English culture and law served children poorly in both respects. Children were not regarded as reliable informants; young children who could not understand the oath were not competent witnesses,[26] and children's evidence had to be corroborated.[27] The oral adversarial process required children to give evidence like adults in open court and face cross-examination,[28] which they often experienced as confusing and distressing,[29] and this did not assist the court to establish the truth.[30]

A campaign for reform by academics, the NSPCC and others during the passage of the Criminal Justice Bill 1988 lead to the setting up of the Pigot Committee[31] and the introduction of a scheme whereby some children could give evidence by live link video from an adjacent room. The Pigot Committee recommended a system which would have enabled children's evidence to be obtained at an early stage and avoided the need for them to attend the trial[32] but this was rejected by the Government despite support from the judiciary.[33] Instead, the Criminal Justice Act 1991 introduced a package of measures which, although designed to facilitate prosecution by making it easier for children to give evidence, appears to have made the investigation of child abuse cases more difficult. Pressure for further reform continued[34] and eventually led to the Youth Justice and Criminal Evidence Act 1999 which allows the court to apply "special measures" to assist and protect children and other vulnerable witnesses.[35]

---

[25] For a detailed and authoritative account, see J. Spencer and R. Flin, *The Evidence of Children* (2nd ed., 1993); Home Office, *Speaking up for Justice* (1998) and for a discussion of recent reforms: P. Bates "The Youth Justice and Criminal Evidence Act—the evidence of children and vulnerable adults" [1999] *C.F.L.Q.* 289. For a comparative analysis, see J. Spencer *et al.* (eds.), *Children's evidence in legal proceedings* (1990).

[26] *R. v. Wallwork* (1958) 42 Cr. App. R. 153; children were presumed incompetent.

[27] See J. Spencer and R. Flin (1993), pp. 212 *et seq.*

[28] C.Y.P.A. 1933, ss. 42,43 enabled evidence to be given on deposition but was almost never used: Spencer and Flin (1993) p. 85.

[29] G. Davies and E. Noon, *An evaluation of the live link for child witnesses* (1991). Utting considered it harmful, *op. cit.* para. 20.31.

[30] J. Spencer and R. Flin (1993).

[31] The Advisory Group on Video Evidence.

[32] Home Office, *Report of the Advisory Group on Video Evidence* (1989), rec. 4.

[33] *Hansard,* H.L., Vol. 527, col. 127, Criminal Justice Bill (2nd Reading, May 21, 1991) reported by Lord Ackner.

[34] CAAC Report 1993/4, p.40; W. Utting (1997), para. 20.19; Home Office, *Speaking up for justice* (1998); ChildLine conference (1999).

[35] ss. 18–30. Special measures include screening the witness box, giving evidence in private or by live link, using pre-recorded video evidence and questioning through an intermediary. These provisions replace those introduced by the Criminal Justice Act 1991, put on a statutory basis other practices to protect child witnesses, add to the protection for children and extend it to other vulnerable witnesses. See also, Home Office, *Achieving best evidence in criminal proceedings* (2002).

Children, whatever their age, are competent to give evidence if they can understand questions put to them and give comprehensible answers.[36] Children's evidence does not have to be corroborated.[37] Competent child witnesses, like adults, can be compelled to give evidence. The child may give evidence in chief by pre-recorded video provided that this "is in the interests of justice"[38] and cross-examination may use the live link or a pre-recorded video.[39] Provision has also been made for children to be questioned by an intermediary rather than by counsel.[40] The accused may not cross-examine the child in person.[41]

The Home Office issued detailed guidance on how children should be interviewed[42]; *Memorandum* interviews are usually video-recorded; the recording is both the witness statement and the evidence for court. Police officers and social workers have been trained to undertake these interviews and interview suites have been established. Although children are compellable witnesses, they cannot be required to provide a statement for the police and their consent should be sought[43] Parental consent is not required but the guidance recognises that interviewing children without informing parents can create problems for any subsequent social services involvement.[44] Despite the submission of thousands of videos prosecution rates have remained low.[45] Some children do not, apparently, find it easy to talk about their abuse with

---

[36] Youth Justice and Criminal Evidence Act 1999, s.53; children under 14 years cannot give evidence on oath, s.55

[37] Criminal Justice Act 1988, s.34(2); Criminal Justice and Public Order Act 1994, s.32 abolished the requirement for a warning against convicting for sexual offences on uncorroborated evidence.

[38] Youth Justice and Criminal Evidence Act 1999, s.27(2); Home Office *Achieving best evidence* (2002)

[39] Youth Justice and Criminal Evidence Act 1999, ss.24; 28. Live link was originally introduced by the Criminal Justice Act 1988.

[40] Youth Justice and Criminal Evidence Act 1999, s.29; Home Office, *Guidance for the use of an intermediary under s.29 of the Youth Justice and Criminal Evidence Act 1999* (2002). Intermediaries should be used where children are very young, very traumatised or use idiosyncratic or specialised systems of communication: Home Office, *Achieving best evidence* (2002), para. 2.39.

[41] Youth Justice and Criminal Evidence Act 1999, s.35

[42] Home Office, *Achieving best evidence in criminal proceedings* (2002) this guidance replaces Home Office, *Memorandum of good practice on video-recorded interviews with child witnesses* (1992); and see: G. Davies and H. Westcott, *Interviewing children under the Memorandum of Good Practice* Home Office Police Research Series No. 115 (1999). The video provides the CPS with information about the child's demeanour at the time of interview which is important to their decision to prosecute, Davis *et al.*, (1999) *op. cit.*

[43] Home Office, *Achieving best evidence* (2002) paras 2.17–2.25, 2.68 *et seq. cf.* if there is a direction for recorded cross-examination.

[44] *ibid.* para. 2.71; *Working Together,* para. 5.3.7; D.H., *The challenge of partnership* (1995), para. 5.19. If a parent refuses to consent to their child being interviewed a specific issue order may be sought: *Re F. (Specific Issue Order: Child Interview)* [1995] 1 F.L.R. 819, CA or under the court's inherent jurisdiction if the child is in care: *Re M. (Care Leave to Interview Child)* [1995] 1 F.L.R. 825.

[45] D.H., *The child, the court and the video* (1994), p. 43; G. Davies *et al., Video taping children's evidence: an evaluation* (1995), p.17. There were 15,000 videos made in the first nine months, of these 24% were submitted to be CPS but up to June 1994 only 640 applications were made to show a video, of these 470 were granted, p. 26.

the constraints of a *Memorandum* interview.[46] If children are required to attend court for cross-examination they remain vulnerable to the most stressful part of the proceedings without the preparation of giving evidence in chief.[47] Videoing interviews should ensure good practice by interviewers[48] but there is no evidence that the availability of video-taped interviews increases either guilty pleas or convictions.[49] Practices necessary for working in partnership with parents and children may conflict with models of investigation developed to satisfy the requirements of a criminal trial.[50] Despite the rarity of prosecutions for abuse, the criminal model now dominates child abuse investigations.

Attempts have been made to safeguard the welfare of child victims within the criminal justice process. Courts have child liaison officers, the NSPCC has made a video explaining to children the process of being a witness and the Witness Service arranges familiarisation visits to courts.[51] The CPS has issued guidance which states that the best interests of the child are the paramount consideration in deciding whether to provide therapy for a child witness before the trial.[52] Although the prosecution of parents should not delay care proceedings,[53] delay may be the inevitable consequence if the parents are involved in two sets of complex and contested proceedings. Where there are both civil and criminal proceedings, joint directions hearings may be held to cover such matters as timetables, medical examination of the child and the disclosure of evidence and unused material.[54] Guidance has been issued on the disclosure of local authority records[55] but disclosure of social services documents for criminal proceedings may undermine the trust between children and their carers. The CPS should instruct counsel with experience in these cases.[56]

---

[46] This is unsurprising given what is known about the way children disclose sexual abuse, see Wattam (1992), pp. 49 *et seq.* But Davies *et al.* (1995) *op. cit.* p. 22 found 70% to be articulate.

[47] The child may not give evidence in chief on matters included in the recording or without the permission of the court: Youth Justice and Criminal Evidence Act 1999, s.27(5) (b),(7).

[48] The same approach should be applied to interviews used in civil proceedings: *Re B (Sexual Abuse: Expert's Report)* [2000] 1 F.L.R. 871 at 873 *per* Thorpe L.J.

[49] Davies *et al.* (1995), p. 42.

[50] H. Wescott, *One year on: professionals' concerns about the Memorandum of Good Practice* (1994); Wattam (1992), pp. 187 *et seq.*; J. Masson, "Developing legal issues in child protection" in *Protecting children from abuse* (T. David ed., 1994), pp. 15, 23.

[51] NSPCC, *Being a witness, what its really like* (2000); NSPCC, *Child witness pack* (2000); Davies *et al.* (1995), p. 29 found that 30% of children had no preparation for giving evidence.

[52] CPS, *The provision of therapy for child witnesses prior to a criminal trial* (2000), para. 4.4. The guidance also expresses concerns that therapy may undermine the child's evidence and notes that records of therapy may be have to be disclosed, para. 3.6 *et seq.*

[53] *Re TB. (Care Proceedings: Criminal Trial)* [1995] 2 F.L.R. 801, CA; Home Office Circular 84/1982; *cf. Re S. (Care Order: Criminal Proceedings)* [1995] 1 F.L.R. 151, CA and see above.

[54] CAAC *Final Report* (1997), p. 35 see also *Re A. and B. (Minors) (No. 2)* [1995] 1 F.L.R. 351.

[55] *Handbook of Best Practice* (1997), p. 33.

[56] CPS, *The Inspector's Report of cases involving child witnesses* (1998)—cases were frequently returned at the last moment and alternative counsel instructed.

(e) Compensation for child abuse victims

22–058 In most cases child abuse amounts to a tort so the victim could claim damages from the perpetrator.[57] Rules on the limitation of actions require negligence claims to be brought within three years of the date when the claimant knew the relevant facts, but trespass to the person claims must be brought within six years.[58] In *Stubbings v. Webb*[59] this prevented a successful claim by woman who had been abused by her adoptive father and brother because she only realised after she had received therapy, that her psychological illness resulted from the abuse. The Law Commission has proposed a new limitation regime with no special rules for sexual abuse cases. A three year primary period of limitation will apply to all personal injury cases and start when the claimant knows, or ought to have known, he or she could make a claim. The court would have a discretion to disapply the limitation period but have to consider prejudice to the defence. Where an adult claimant is disabled, including where the abuse causes mental illness, the limitation period would be suspended for at least 10 years from the onset of the disability.[60]

Child abuse is frequently an "offence of violence" so that a claim may be made to the Criminal Injuries Compensation Authority. It is not necessary that the offender be convicted[61] but the victim should have informed an appropriate authority who could be a parent or a social worker.[62] Claims must be made within two years of the last incident, but in exceptional circumstances this requirement is waived.[63] An award will not be made if the perpetrator would benefit from it or if it is thought to be against a minor's interests.[64] Substantial awards should be placed in trust for the child. Where the child is in care the application should be made by the local authority, in other cases it should be made by someone with parental responsibility.[65] Awards are low.[66] However,

---

[57] In *Pereira v. Keleman* [1995] 1 F.L.R. 428 damages of between £16,500 and £10,500 were awarded to three sisters; children abused by care staff have received compensation from local authorities (or their insurers) see: C. Wolmar *op. cit.* pp. 189 *et seq.* The managers of care homes can be vicariously liable for abuse of residents by staff: *Lister v. Hesley Hall Ltd* [2001] 2 F.L.R. 307, HL.

[58] Limitation Act 1980, ss.2,11. The limitation period does not start to run when the claimant is under age 18, s. 28.

[59] *Stubbings v. Webb* [1993] A.C. 498; the European Court of Human Rights held that this did not breach the Convention: *Stubbings v. U.K.* (1997) 23 E.H.R.R. 213. *Cf. M. (K.) v. M. (H.)* (1992) 96 D.L.R. 596 (Canadian Supreme Ct.) where intrafamilial abuse was analysed as a breach of trust for which there was no limitation period.

[60] Law Com. No 270, *Limitation of Actions* (2001 H.C. 23) paras 4.23–4.33. The Law Commission considered that "dissociative amnesia" would amount to a disability, para. 4.27.

[61] A full explanation of the reasons for the failure to prosecute is required: C.I.C.A., *The Criminal Injuries Compensation Scheme 2001* (2001), para. 10.

[62] *ibid.* para. 13(a).

[63] *ibid.* para. 18. The time limit is normally waived for claimants under 21.

[64] *ibid.* para. 16.

[65] The Official Solicitor acts for children who cannot otherwise make a claim.

[66] Under the tariff scheme the maximum payment for repeated rape or buggery over a period of more than three years is £22,000. Compare the awards from the C.I.C.A. and the E.C.H.R. to the children in *Z. v. U.K.* [2001] 2 F.L.R. 612 at paras 49, 127 and 131.

concerns have been expressed that compensation motivates those who make complaints, especially in cases of historic abuse.[67]

IV. MODERN CHILD CARE LAW—THE LOOKED-AFTER SYSTEM

A. Local authorities' powers and duties

22–059 In general the local authority owes the same duties to all children it is looking after[68] irrespective of their legal status, but has substantially more power over children in care for whom it has parental responsibility. Where a child is only accommodated, the local authority may take the same action as would be permitted if done by any other *de facto* carer. It may "do what is reasonable for the purpose of safeguarding and promoting the child's welfare."[69] It may thus take day-to-day decisions and act in emergencies. If the parents will not agree to the local authority's proposals for the child's placement or education, the authority must obtain a care order.[70] Where the dispute relates to arrangements for contact the parents may refer the matter to court by seeking a contact order.[71] However, it is unlikely that the courts would interfere with other aspects of local authority discretion unless there was a breach of the Human Rights Convention.[72]

The local authority must safeguard and promote the welfare of each child, make reasonable use of services which are available to children cared for by their own parents and provide advice, assistance and friendship with a view to promoting the child's welfare afterwards.[73] It must review each case regularly so that it is fully aware of the child's current situation when making decisions.[74] In effect, the authority must act as a good parent[75] towards such children and, like other parents, may be constrained through lack of resources and other priorities. Failure of a local authority to provide a reasonable level of care may give rise to an action in negligence.[76] A detailed consideration of the local authority's specific duties is beyond the scope of this work, but a brief indication of the main areas is given here because

---

[67] R. Webster, *The great children's homes panic* (1998) discussed in C. Wolmar *op. cit.* pp. 161–6.

[68] Children Act 1989, s.22(1); this includes children accommodated under s.20.

[69] *ibid.* s.3(5).

[70] *R. v. Tameside M.B.C., ex p. J.* [2000] 1 F.L.R. 942, QBD and above para. 22–012.

[71] Children Act 1989, s.8; see Chap. 19 above.

[72] *A. v. Liverpool C.C.* [1982] A.C. 363; the House of Lords upheld the High Court's refusal to exercise its discretion in wardship to interfere with *intra vires* decisions of a local authority relating to children in compulsory care. There is no authority relating to accommodated children but the basis for the decision—that Parliament had given discretion over a matter to the local authority and not to the courts—would seem to apply to prevent the courts making specific issue orders about the way a child is looked after.

[73] ss.22(3), 24(1).

[74] s.26; Review of Children's Cases Regulations 1991, S.I. 1991 No. 895; *Guidance,* Vol. 3, Chap. 8; R. Grimshaw and R. Sinclair, *Planning to care: regulation procedure and practice under the Children Act 1989* (1997).

[75] 1987, Cm. 62, para. 29; *Review of Child Care Law,* para. 9.6. An amendment which would have required local authorities specifically to act as good parents when providing aftercare was rejected in the Lords: *Hansard,* H.L., Vol. 503, cols. 144–148, Children Bill Committee Stage.

[76] *Barrett v. Enfield LBC* [1999] 2 F.L.R. 426, HL (the court refused to strike out a claim by a young man who had been brought up in the care system who alleged that his psychiatric condition

of their relevance to legal proceedings (for example the decision to grant a residence order rather than a care order or to discharge a care order).

(a) Maintenance and accommodation

22–060 The local authority must maintain all children they are looking after and provide accommodation for them.[77] There are two main ways in which this is discharged[78]: either the child is boarded out (*i.e.* placed with foster carers who agree to provide a home indefinitely or for a specific period)[79]; or alternatively, placed in a residential establishment (a "community home" run by the authority, a "voluntary home" run by a voluntary organisation, or a "registered children's home" run privately).[80] Children in care may also be placed at home.[81] In planning the placement the local authority must consider the views of the child and family[82] and the child's religion, race, culture and language.[83] The accommodation provided should be near the child's home,[84] with siblings if they are looked after by the authority,[85] and not unsuitable for the disabled child.[86] The child's welfare may only be discounted where this is necessary to protect the public from serious injury.[87] However, the lower cost,[88] the emphasis on the provision of a substitute family, and concerns about abuse and poor care in residential homes has increased the use made of foster care so that on March 31, 2001, 65 per cent of children looked after by local authorities in England and Wales were in this type of placement. Only 10 per cent were in children's homes, 12 per cent were with their families and the remainder lived in lodgings, hostels and

---

resulted from the negligent way the local authority looked after him). The local authority has been held not to be vicariously liable for the actions of foster carers: *S. v. Walsall M.B.C.* [1985] 1 W.L.R. 1150 but may be liable for negligently placing or leaving the child with foster parents who harm him or her: *S. v. Gloucestershire C.C.* [2000] 1 F.L.R. 825, CA.

77 s.23(1).

78 Children Act 1989, s.23; see J. Rowe, M. Hundleby and L. Garnett, *Child Care Now—a survey of placement patterns* (1989) and Cm. 2584, Table 4.2.

79 *Guidance,* Vol. 3 and Arrangements for Placement of Children (General) Regulations 1991, S.I. 1991 No. 890; Fostering Services Regulations 2002 (S.I. 2002 No. 57).

80 Children Act 1989, Pt VI-VIII; Children's Homes Regulations 1991, S.I. 1991 No. 1505; *Guidance,* vol. 4; D.H., *Caring for children away from home: messages from research* (1998). All children's homes are now subject to regulation by the Care Standards Commission established under the Care Standards Act 2000.

81 s.23(5); Placement with Parents etc. Regulations 1991, S.I. 1991 No. 893; *Guidance,* Vol. 3, Chap. 5. See generally, J. Thoburn, *Captive Clients* (1980); E. Farmer and R. Parker, *Trials and Tribulations* (1991).

82 s.22(4) (5), see below.

83 s.22(5) (c); *Guidance,* Vol. 3, para. 2.40–2.42.

84 s.23(7) (a). Children frequently return to their home area on discharge from care; rehabilitation is more likely where links with the family have been maintained, see S. Millham, *et al., Lost in Care* (1986); R. Bullock *et al., Going Home* (1993).

85 s.23(7) (b); this provision was added at the instigation of the National Association for Young People in Care (NAYPIC).

86 s.23(8); *R. v. Brent LBC, ex p. S.* [1994] 1 F.L.R. 203. This wording was chosen to avoid putting an unrealistically heavy burden on local authorities: *per* Gibson L.J. at 215.

87 s.22(6).

88 Average costs calculated in 1997–8 were £1,378 per week for residential placement sand £191 per week in foster care: D.H., *Children Act Report 1995–1999,* Table 9.4 .

boarding schools, or were placed for adoption.[89] Fostering is more common for those under the age of 10 years and increasingly local authorities are fostering children with their relatives.[90] In practice, local authorities distinguish between respite, short-term, temporary or bridging[91] placements, long-term fostering and fostering with a view to adoption. There are detailed regulations governing the selection of foster carers, medical examination of children and so on.[92] The regulations also require foster carers to sign undertakings in specified form, to care for and bring, the child up as a member of their own family (but not administer corporal punishment), to look after the child's health and permit the child to be visited. Foster carers are required to allow children to be removed from their care.[93]

There is a crisis in foster-care[94] with a shortage of placements and a lack of placement choice. Private agencies have been established to identify and support foster carers for local authorities.[95] Many children experience a succession of unsatisfactory placements and repeated moves. Breakdown rates as high as 50 per cent occur.[96] These have been attributed to the instability of fostering arrangements and unsettling interference from the natural family,[97] but recent research implicates failure by local authorities to provide adequate support.[98] The government standard is that no more than 16 per cent of looked after children should have more than three placements in any year.[99]

(b) Permanency: rehabilitation and adoption

22–061 The European Court of Human Rights regards state care as a temporary measure; the right to family life requires states to work towards the reunification of families where children are in care.[1] It applies stricter scrutiny to further limitations on parent child relationships but accepts that there are circumstances where

---

[89] D.H., *Children looked after in England 2000/2001 Statistical Bulletin,* Table 3.

[90] These placements appear more durable: B. Broad *et al., Kith and kin; kinship care for vulnerable young people* (2001); D.H., *Children Act Report 2000* (2001), Table 1.9. Local authorities may not as a matter of policy pay lower allowances to relative carers: *R. ota L. v. Manchester C.C.* [2002] 1 F.L.R. 43.

[91] Placements which prepare children for permanent family placement.

[92] Fostering Services Regulations 2002 (S.I. 2002 No. 57).

[93] *ibid.* Sched. 5. Despite National Standards for the service there are considerable variations in planning and decision-making in foster care: SSI, *Someone else's children* (1998); D.H., *Children Act Report 1995–1999* (2000), fig. 2.3.

[94] Select Committee on Health, *Second Report 1997–8: Children looked after by local authorities* (H.C. 247), para. 118.

[95] Local authorities still have to approve the carers and visit children placed. In practice carers move to private agencies and receive higher payments, and local authorities pay additional charges to the private sector.

[96] Berridge and Cleaver (1987), p. 55; J. Fratter *et al., Permanent Family Placement* (1991), Chap. 3.

[97] R. Parker, *Caring for Separated Children* (1980), p. 75; *cf.* Fratter *et al.* (1991) whose survey shows comparable breakdown rates in adoption and fostering for children aged five or more at placement.

[98] Berridge and Cleaver (1987) found wide differences in breakdown rates in different authorities; see also Fratter *et al.* (1991), p. 55.

[99] see D.H., *Children Act Report 1995–1999* (2000), para. 2.36.

[1] *Andersson v. Sweden* (1992) 14 E.H.R.R. 615; *Johansen v. Norway* (1996) 23 E.H.R.R. 33; *Olsson v. Sweden (No. 2)* (1992) 17 E.H.R.R. 134 at para. 81.

children should not be returned.[2] There has been concern to ensure that children in care have a secure, family upbringing since at least the 1970s[3]; local authorities developed policies and practices designed to promote permanency, particularly through adoption, but it was also recognised that long-term fostering with family contact or returning children to their families fulfilled this aim.[4] Although the Children Act 1989 promoted partnership with families, local authorities continued to seek adoptive placements for children whose families could not provide adequate care. In 2000, the *Prime Minister's Review of Adoption* stressed the importance of family care and gave a new impetus to adoption.[5]

In 2000, 24,700 children left the care system, many returned to their families, 3000 were adopted and about 25 per cent were discharged from care because of their age.[6] A child who does not return home within six weeks is statistically likely to remain in care for at least two years; the longer the period of care the less likely links with the family will be preserved.[7] Working with the parents and preparation for independence are crucial.

(c) Leaving care and aftercare

22–062 Following recommendations from the *Review of Child Care Law,* the Children Act 1989 extended the local authority's duty to make arrangements for children to live with their families to cover all children it looks after[8] and imposed a new duty to prepare children for a life outside care.[9] Nevertheless in 1998, the Select Committee on Health concluded in that the current system did "deplorably little" for care leavers and endorsed proposals to impose further duties on local authorities.[10] The Children (Leaving Care) Act 2000 imposes duties on local authorities in relation to those leaving care over the age of 16 years. The local authority which last looked after the young person must plan for their independence, keep in touch and provide support until at least age 21.

B. The position of parents

22–063 The Children Act intended to encourage partnership between parents and the local authority so that arrangements to provide substitute care would equate with those made within the family. Parents retain parental responsibility; they have a right

---

[2] *Olsson v. Sweden (No. 2)* (1992) 17 E.H.R.R. 134 at para. 90; *L. v. Finland* [2000] 2 F.L.R. 118 at paras 122–125.

[3] The extent of drift became clear in J. Rowe and L. Lambert, *Children who wait* (1972).

[4] J. Thoburn, "What kind of permanence?" (1985) 9 *Adoption and Fostering* 29.

[5] Performance and Innovation Unit, *The Prime Minister's Review of Adoption* (2000); set a target of increasing the number of children adopted from care by 40%, see also *Adoption: a new approach* (Cm 5017, 2000) and Chap. 23.

[6] D.H. *Children looked after in England 2000/20001 Statistical Bulletin,* Table 6. Half of these were aged 18, the rest 16 or 17 years old.

[7] S. Millham (1986) pp. 196 *et seq.*; D.H., *Patterns and Outcomes* (1991).

[8] *Review of Child Care Law,* paras 10.2–10.5; Children Act 1989, s.23(6). If the child is in care the Placement of Children with Parents, etc., Regulations 1991, S.I. 1991 No. 893, must be complied with unless the placement is a foster placement.

[9] s.24(1); *Guidance,* vol. 3, Chap. 9.

[10] Select Committee on Health Second Report 1997–8, *Children looked after by local authorities* (H.C. 247), para. 313; W. Utting (1997) paras 8.54 *et seq.*

to be consulted before any decision is made about their child's care where this is reasonably practicable, and their views must be given due consideration.[11] If there is a care order the local authority may determine how parental responsibility is exercised so far as this is necessary to safeguard the child's welfare[12]—

> In *Re P. (Children Act 1989, ss. 22 and 26: Local Authority Compliance)*[13] the father was in prison for serious sexual assault on the mother and child. The mother was unable to look after the children, care proceedings were started and plans were made for their future care. Neither the mother nor the children wanted any further involvement with the father. The local authority proposed not to consult the father nor provide him with information about the children but only give him a brief annual report about their well-being. The court accepted that the local authority's power to control the exercise of parental responsibility permitted this and made an order under section 91(14) precluding the father applying to the court without leave.

Parents enter written agreements which set out the child's address, the services to be provided and the responsibilities of those concerned. Such agreements may delegate to the carer the right to consent to medical treatment, give permission for the child to participate in various activities, and settle arrangements for the child's education.[14] Parents should be involved in the review of their child's case, notified of the results and informed of decisions.[15] But unless parents have access to independent advice they may be unaware of their rights. Parents may complain about the services provided[16] but may have little alternative to accepting what is offered. Parents remain financially responsible for their children aged under 16 years but cannot be required to pay if they are in receipt of means-tested benefits or tax credits.[17]

C. Rights of children

22–064 A local authority with parental responsibility has no more authority over a child in care than parents have in respect of other children.[18] All children being looked

[11] s.22(4) (b), (c), (5) (b); Arrangements for Placement of Children Regulations 1991, S.I. 1991 No. 895, reg. 7; *Guidance,* Vol. 3, paras 2.45–2.53; failure to involve parents may amount to a breach of their Art. 8 rights: *Scott v. U.K.* [2000] 1 F.L.R. 958. Parents and people with parental responsibility are required to keep the authority informed of their address, Sched. 2, paras 15(2) (b).

[12] Children Act 1989, s.33(3) (b), (4). The local authority may only control the parents' exercise of parental responsibility where the child's welfare demands this.

[13] [2000] 2 F.L.R. 910, FD.

[14] Arrangements for Placement of Children (General) Regulations 1991, S.I. 1991 No. 890, reg. 3 and Sched. 4; *Guidance,* Vol. 3, paras 2.30–2.39.

[15] Review of Children's Cases Regulations 1991, S.I. 1991 No. 895, reg. 7. In practice parents, particularly those who have no contact with their children are not consulted: J. Masson *et al.* eds, *Lost and Found* (1999).

[16] s.26(3) (b). For a full discussion, see below.

[17] Children Act 1989, Sched. 2, Pt III; where there is no agreement about contributions the matter may be referred to the court: *Re C. (Contribution Notice)* [1994] 1 F.L.R. 111.

[18] See above. "The Bill does nothing to change the underlying principle of Gillick which has to be taken into account by all who exercise parental responsibility over a child mature and intelligent

after by the local authority have a right to be consulted about decisions which affect them where this is reasonably practicable; children's views must be given due consideration having regard to their age and understanding.[19] Many local authorities have established Children's Rights Services. Looked-after children have a statutory right to complain about the care provided for them,[20] and those who are refused contact may bring proceedings.[21] Unless they are subject to a court order they may leave local authority accommodation once they are 16[22]; children in care may seek the discharge of a care order at any age.[23]

There is a "very worrying difference" between the lives of children looked after by local authorities and those of other children which led the Select Committee on Health to conclude that the system was "under-performing."[24] Particular concern has been expressed about high rates of school exclusion, poor educational attainment and high rates of teenage pregnancy. The Department of Health has issued guidance and set targets to raise standards and improve life chances for these young people.[25] The Children Act has increased children's participation in decisions but many remain poorly informed about plans for their care and their rights.[26] Shortages of social workers mean that cases are frequently unallocated, and many children also experience repeated changes of worker.

V. MODERN CHILD CARE LAW—JUDICIAL CONTROL OVER LOCAL AUTHORITY DECISION-MAKING

1. Decisions requiring court approval

(a) Contact with children in care

22–065 The mutual enjoyment by parent and child of each other's company is fundamental to family life which continues despite the child's entry to the care system.

---

enough to make decisions for himself." *per* Lord Chancellor, *Hansard*, H.L., Vol. 502, col. 1351, Children Bill Committee Stage.

[19] s.22(4) (a), (5) (a); *Guidance*, Vol. 3, paras 2.47–2.48. In *R. v. Devon C.C., ex p. O.* [1997] 2 F.L.R. 388 a decision to remove a child from prospective adopters was quashed because the child's wishes had not been ascertained.

[20] s.26(3) (a). For a full discussion, see below.

[21] ss. 8 or 34, see below para. 22–065.

[22] s.20(11) gives children a right to remain against parental wishes after age 16. If they can do this then arguably they may also leave.

[23] s.39(1) (b). In practice they can only do this effectively if they have sufficient understanding to instruct a solicitor and have alternative accommodation but they do not require leave from the court: *Re A. (Care: Discharge Application by Child)* [1995] 1 F.L.R. 599.

[24] 1997–8 H.C. 247 Summary, para. 3. Particular concern was expressed about school exclusion, poor educational attainment ane poor health education.

[25] See D.H., *Children Act Report 1995–1999* (2000), Chap. 5 and *Children Act Report 2000* (2001) Chap. 4.

[26] *Children Act Now* (2001), pp. 92–93 citing R. Grimshaw and R. Sinclair, *Planning to care* (1997); Children with sufficient understanding can exercise rights of access to their personal records held by social services: D.H., *Data Protection Act 1998 Guidance for local authorities* (2001), para. 5.8.

Unless the child's welfare demands otherwise, state care should be regarded as temporary and provided with a view to reuniting the family.[27] Interference with parental contact must be justified under Article 8(2) and be proportionate to legitimate aims of safeguarding the child. The Strasbourg Court applies strict scrutiny to restrictions of contact.[28] Contact is not only a matter of rights but also of welfare. Contact increases the likelihood of the child's return home and the success of rehabilitation.[29] It gives children the sense that their parents love them, helps to preserve children's sense of identity and contributes to their well-being in care.[30] Contacts, however occasional, may continue to have value for the child even when there is no question of return to the family.[31] Contact is more likely to be maintained where the social worker sees the parents regularly.[32] However, visits to children in care by their parents cause problems for carers, and supporting contact demands substantial social work resources; lack of contact is associated with chronic parenting difficulties and poor attachment.[33] Ending parental contact has been regarded as facilitating planning, particularly adoption, and consequently in the interests of looked-after children who cannot return home.[34] Where parental contact is ended social workers frequently lose touch with parents who become excluded from their children's lives.[35]

Until 1983 local authorities had complete discretion in relation to contact,[36] but following pressure from the Family Rights Group and applications to the European Court of Human Rights, legislation was introduced which enabled parents to challenge the termination of contact.[37] Few parents pursued their objections, courts were concerned not to undermine local authority plans and were reluctant to order contact.[38] *The Review of Child Care Law* accepted that the courts should have a wider role in public law contact disputes. Care orders

---

[27] *Olsson v. Sweden* (1988) 11 E.H.R.R. 259; *Andersson v. Sweden* (1992) 14 E.H.R.R. 615; *Johansen v. Norway* (1996) 23 E.H.R.R. 33; *Olsson v. Sweden (No. 2)* (1992) 17 E.H.R.R. 134 para. 81.

[28] *Andersson v. Sweden* (1992) 14 E.H.R.R. 615; *Johansen v. Norway* (1996) 23 E.H.R.R. 33 para. 64. Contact is a civil right and a hearing which satisfies Art. 6(1) must be available: *W. v. U.K.*(1987) 10 E.H.R.R. 29.

[29] S. Millham *et al.* (1986); D.H., *Patterns and outcomes of child placement* (1991); R. Bullock *et al., Going Home* (1993); D.H., *Children Act Now* (2001), p.133.

[30] Berridge and Cleaver (1987) a view endorsed by Simon Brown L.J. in *Re E. (A Minor) (Care Order Contact)* [1994] 1 F.L.R. 146 at 155; H. Cleaver, *Fostering family contact* (2000).

[31] *Guidance,* Vol. 3, para. 6.9.

[32] A. Bilson and R. Barker, "Parental contact with children fostered and in residential care after the 1989 Children Act" (1995) 25 Brit. J. Soc. Wk. 367; D.H., *Children Act Now* (2001), p.133.

[33] H. Cleaver, *Fostering family contact* (2000).

[34] S. Millham *et al., Lost in Care* (1986); J. Masson, "Contact between parents and children in the long-term care of others: the unresolved dispute" (1990) 4 Int. J. of Law & Fam. 97; S. Jolly, "Cutting the ties—the termination of contact in care" [1994] *J.S.W.F.L.* 229.

[35] J. Masson *et al.* ed., *Lost and found* (1999). In most cases this was not because parents posed a danger to their children.

[36] Parents had no rights under the Child Care Act 1980 until it was amended by the Health and Social Services and Social Security Adjudications Act 1983. In *A. v. Liverpool C.C.* [1982] A.C. 363 the House of Lords held that the inherent jurisdiction of the High Court could not be used to override the control given by Parliament to local authorities, see above Chap. 19.

[37] Health and Social Services and Social Security Adjudications Act 1983 adding Child Care Act 1980, ss.12A–12F.

[38] See 6th edition of this book at p.852; S. Millham *et al., Access disputes in child care* (1990) and J. Masson (1990) *op. cit.*

should include a presumption of reasonable contact and that the court's permission should be required to vary or end arrangements under an order.[39]

The Children Act 1989 largely adopted the *Review*'s recommendations; new duties were imposed on local authorities and the court was given wider powers to determine contact issues. Local authorities must endeavour to promote contact between children they are looking after and their families and friends unless this is not reasonably practicable or consistent with the children's welfare.[40] Contributions may be made towards the cost of visits.[41] Before making a care order, section 34 requires the court to consider the local authority's arrangements for contact and invite the parties to comment on them.[42] Where the child is subject to a care order, the local authority must allow the child reasonable contact[43] with parents, guardians and anyone who had a residence order or care under the inherent jurisdiction immediately before the care order was made.[44] These people, the child and anyone else with leave of the court[45] may seek orders for contact. The local authority (and the child) may also apply to have contact ended but, without an order, it may only refuse contact for up to seven days where this is necessary, as a matter of urgency, for the child's welfare.[46] Orders may be made when a care order is made or afterwards in any family proceedings, with or without an application.[47] The welfare test in Children Act 1989, s.1 applies and the court may impose such conditions as it thinks fit. Orders may define the frequency, duration and location of meetings or leave this for the parties to agree; any order may be varied by agreement.[48] Where reasonable contact is appropriate there is no need to make an order.[49] If the local authority wants to terminate contact an order may be made that there should be no contact, but this does not preclude it re-introducing contact.[50] The local authority thus retains discretion over contact subject only to the right of others to refer the matter to the court.

---

[39] paras 21.1, 21.12–16. In contrast the Short Committee considered that Child Care Act 1980, ss. 12A–12F had gone too far, paras 73, 324.

[40] Sched. 2, para. 15.

[41] Sched. 2, para. 16.

[42] Details of contact should be in the care plan: *F. v. Manchester C.C.* [1993] 1 F.L.R. 419; *Guidance,* Vol. 3, para. 2.62; LAC 99(29) para. 13, section 2.5.

[43] Contact is reasonable if the parties agree or it is "objectively reasonable": *Re P. (Minors) (Contact: Children in Care)* [1993] 2 F.L.R. 156, *per* Ewbank J.

[44] Disputes about contact with children accommodated by the local authority can be dealt with by a contact order under s.8.

[45] The test for leave is not that in s.10(9) although those criteria are apposite. The applicant must satisfy the court that there is a good arguable case: *Re M. (Care: Contact: Grandmother's Application for Leave)* [1995] 2 F.L.R. 86, CA.

[46] s.34(6); Contact with Children Regulations 1991, S.I. 1991 No. 891, reg. 2.

[47] It was therefore immaterial whether a child in care who was also a parent was applying under s.34(2) or s.34(3): *Birmingham C.C. v. H.* [1994] 2 A.C. 212 at 223 *per* Lord Slynn.

[48] Contact with Children Regulations 1991, S.I. 1991 No. 891, reg. 3. The child's agreement is required to any change if he or she has sufficient understanding but there is no provision for representation of children.

[49] *Re S. (A Minor) (Care: Contact Order)* [1994] 2 F.L.R. 222. "Contact at the local authority's discretion" also requires the authority to provide reasonable contact: *L. v. London Borough of Bromley* [1998] 1 F.L.R. 709, FD.

[50] *Re W. (Section 34(2) Orders)* [2000] 1 F.L.R. 502, CA, *Kent C.C. v. C.* [1993] 1 F.L.R. 308, FD.

22–066 The courts have been reluctant to challenge local authorities about contact. The Court of Appeal has stated that the local authority's proposals "command the greatest respect", that the presumption of contact should be considered against the long-term plan for the child, and that contact which endangers this will not be allowed.[51] Also, where the nature and extent of contact is an integral part of the local authority's care plan, review by the court would amount to straying into the forbidden territory of supervising the implementation of the authority's arrangements.[52] However, the local authority must justify the ending of contact[53] and, where there are serious doubts that a plan of adoption will be achieved, the judge may order contact which conflicts with it.[54] The courts have been willing to make orders giving the local authority discretion to terminate contact in the future, permitted termination on the basis that there is a plan for adoption and refused to reconsider such decisions without a change in circumstances:—

> In *Re T. (Minors) (Termination of Contact)*[55] the court granted orders permitting the local authority to end contact on the basis that two seriously disturbed boys, S and B, would be adopted. Neither boy was adopted; S was with his third set of foster carers and B was in a therapeutic residential placement. The mother was allowed contact for one hour each month with the boys at a family centre. She applied to discharge the orders permitting termination of contact, and S requested increased contact. The mother's contact with B was suspended during the proceedings. The judge refused the application and the mother appealed. The Court of Appeal discharged the order in relation to S because the local authority had abandoned its plan for his adoption but refused to do so in relation to B. It accepted that contact could be terminated where there was a probable need in the foreseeable future to end contact, and that such decisions could only be challenged by appeal or if there were a change in circumstances.[56]

Such decisions may not withstand a challenged under the Convention. This court-imposed restriction is not supported by the Act which only precludes applications within six months of a refusal by the court.[57] Also, restricting con-

---

[51] *Re B. (Minors) (Termination of Contact: Paramount Consideration)* [1993] Fam. 301, *per* Butler-Sloss L.J. at 311.

[52] *Re S. (A Minor) (Care: Contact Order)* [1994] 2 F.L.R. 222 at 226, *per* Simon Brown L.J.

[53] *Re B. (Minors) (Termination of Contact: Paramount Consideration)* [1993] Fam. 301, *per* Butler-Sloss L.J. at 311; Contact between a child and their family will be assumed to be beneficial and the local authority must justify their wish to terminate it, *Re M. (Care: Contact: Grandmother's Application for Leave)* [1995] 2 F.L.R. 86, CA *per* Ward L.J. at 95.

[54] *Berkshire C.C. v. B.* [1997] 1 F.L.R. 171, FD. The local authority could apply to reduce contact in the future.

[55] [1997] 1 F.L.R. 517, CA. In *Re L. (Sexual Abuse: Standard of Proof)* [1996] 1 F.L.R. 116 at 127 Butler-Sloss L.J. stated (*obiter*) that termination of contact was appropriate if there was no prospect of rehabilitation and the child was to be placed for adoption.

[56] Contact may be re-established if the child's social worker recognises the value of this but may have no redress where the social worker opposes contact see: J. Masson "Thinking about contact—a social or a legal problem" [2000] *C.F.L.Q.* 15.

[57] s.91(17). There is nothing in the statute which justifies imposing a test of change of circumstance. If the court considers there should be no further applications it has power to impose a condition

tact is not a proportionate response to an adoption plan where no placement has been identified. Nor can it be necessary to terminate contact unless this can be shown to be damaging the child when the willingness of the adoptive carers to accept this remains unknown.

The implementation of the Children Act 1989 has had a fundamental impact on contact. Four times as many children in foster care now see their parents weekly, but a third still have no parental contact.[58] However, where contact is in dispute, the courts remain more willing to accept arguments that contact disrupts placements or deters adopters than that it aids well-being and provides continuity.[59] The need to support fostering and the lack of a legal framework for open adoption[60] means that contact is seen as conflicting with the child's needs despite evidence of the success of more inclusive substitute care arrangements.[61] Where the plan is for the child's adoption there are good reasons for continuing contact until the adoption order is made; adopters may not be found[62] or may be willing to continue contact.[63]

Although there is a duty to place siblings together[64] there is no presumption of contact between siblings. For most people relationships with their siblings are the most enduring; the loss of such relationships may be felt acutely by children in care. A child in care who wishes to see another child against the wishes of the local authority may make an application under section 34; the welfare of the child applicant is paramount.[65] But in other cases where a looked-after child wants to have contact with another child, leave must be obtained.[66] The application is made under section 8 and the welfare of the child named (not the applicant) is given paramount consideration.[67]

---

under s.91(14) this should not be used routinely: *F. v. Kent C.C.* [1993] 1 F.L.R. 432 but can be used in extreme circumstances: *Re Y. (Child Orders: Restricting Applications)* [1994] 2 F.L.R. 699; or to provide stability: *Re P. (s.91(14) Guidance)* [1999] 2 F.L.R. 573, CA.

[58] H. Cleaver (2000) *op cit.; Children Act Now* (2001), p. 179. Two-thirds of looked-after children are in contact with mothers and half with siblings, but one-sixth have no family contact.

[59] S. Jolly *op. cit.*; J. Masson (1990) *op. cit.* and see *Children Act Now* (2001), p.181.

[60] See Chap. 23.

[61] J. Triseliotis, "Foster care outcomes" (1989) *Adoption & Fostering* 5. When allowance is made for the age of the child permanent placements with contact are no less stable than those without: J. Fratter *et al.* (1991), p. 50.

[62] Only six out of 10 children in Harwin and Owen's study of care plans were placed according to their plan see *Children Act Now* (2001), p. 125 and J. Harwin and M. Owen, "A study of care plans and their implementation" in *Delight and Dole* (M. Thorpe and C. Cowton, eds, 2002), p. 63.

[63] *cf. Re A. (Adoption: Contact)* [1993] 2 F.L.R. 645 at 649–650 where Butler-Sloss L.J. noted that monthly contact was incompatible with adoption and that "the view of open adoption embraced by experts does not seem to be shared by prospective adopters." Also, *Re S. (Contact: Application by Sibling)* [1998] 2 F.L.R. 897 where the adoptive parents refused to allow contact with the child's sibling who had been placed separately.

[64] s.23(7) (b) and see A. Mullender (ed.) *We are family* (1999).

[65] *Re F. (Contact: Child in Care)* [1995] 1 F.L.R. 510 at 513–4 *per* Wilson J. The order does not oblige the other child to have contact: *Birmingham C.C. v H. (No. 3)* [1994] 2 A.C. 212.

[66] s.10(8) (9). The "child concerned" means the subject of the application not the applicant: *Re S. (Contact: Application by Sibling)* [1998] 1 F.L.R. 897, FD therefore a child applicant need not establish competence to make the application.

[67] *Re F. (Contact with Child in Care)* [1995] 1 F.L.R. 510.

In 2000, there were over 1,300 applications under section 34; nearly three-quarters resulted in orders but it is not clear whether these were granting or refusing contact.[68]

(b) Secure accommodation[69]

22–067 This is "accommodation provided for the purpose of restricting liberty"[70] where young people are looked after and receive education etc. in a secure facility. Any accommodation used to restrict liberty is secure accommodation.[71] Confining a child to part of a building or otherwise preventing free movement is within the definition but normal household security is allowed.[72] Regimes vary but have been likened to boarding school or a medium to high security prison.[73] Parental responsibility alone does not empower carers to impose this degree of restriction on children, except possibly for a very limited period.[74] Breach of the regulations amounts to false imprisonment.[75]

Until 1983 children looked after by local authorities could be placed in secure accommodation by social workers without any court proceedings.[76] However, claims by the Children's Legal Centre that this breached Article 5(4) of the European Convention on Human Rights[77] led the Government to introduce legislation providing for court hearings.[78] Applications for secure accommodation

---

[68] *Judicial Statistics 2000,* Table 5.2.

[69] For a detailed discussion of the issues, see R. Harris and N. Timms, *Between Hospital & Prison or thereabouts* (1993); R. Bullock *et al., Secure treatment outcomes—the care careers of very difficult adolescents* (1998); M. Parry, "Secure accommodation—the Cinderella of family law" [2000] *C.F.L.Q.* 101, and *Guidance,* Vol. 4, Chap. 8.

[70] Children Act 1989, s.25(1).

[71] *A Metropolitan Borough Council v. DB* [1997] 1 F.L.R. 767, FD (locked ward in a maternity hospital); *cf. Re C. (Detention: Medical Treatment)* [1997] 2 F.L.R. 180, FD (special residential clinic treating anorexic girls); A. Downie [1998] *C.F.L.Q.* 101. Department of Health approval is required for the provision of secure accommodation in a community home; voluntary homes and registered children's homes are no longer prohibited from providing secure accommodation, Children (Secure Accommodation) Amendment Regulations 1995, S.I. 1995 No. 139.

[72] *Guidance,* Vol. 4, paras 1.91(vi), 8.10; D.H., *Guidance on permissible forms of control in children's residential care* (1993), section IV.

[73] *Re K.(Secure Accommodation: Right to Liberty)* [2001] 1 F.L.R. 526 at 542 *per* Thorpe L.J.; *Koniarska v. U.K.* E.C.H.R. Application No. 33670/96, hearing 10 December, 2000.

[74] *Re K.(Secure Accommodation: Right to Liberty)* [2001] 1 F.L.R. 526 *per* Butler-Sloss P. at para. 29 and *per* Judge L.J. at para. 101. Thorpe L.J. disagreed, see paras 49–61; see also J. Fortin, "Children's rights and physical force' [2001] *C.F.L.Q.* 243.

[75] The pindown regime was considered to have breached the regulations, A. Levy and B. Kahan, *The pindown experience and the protection of children* (1991), para. 12.60. Substantial compensation was paid to the children.

[76] Under the Child Care Act 1980, s.10(2). The power to make such placements is no longer expressly granted by statute. The basis for detention is somewhat obscure. In *Re M. (Secure Accommodation Order)* [1995] 1 F.L.R. 418 at 425 Hoffmann L.J. said it derived from the local authority's parental responsibility or the parent's request for the child to be looked after but this analysis was not accepted by the majority in *Re K.(Secure Accommodation: Right to Liberty)* [2001] 1 F.L.R. 526, paras 29, 97–101 who saw it as dependent on authorisation by the court.

[77] In *X. v. U.K.*, November 5, 1981 the European Court of Human Rights held that the compulsory detention of mentally disturbed patients breached Art. 5.4.

[78] Child Care Act 1980, s.21A, added by the Criminal Justice Act 1982, s.25.

orders are now made under the Children Act 1989, s.25, which largely repeats the earlier provisions but most of the detailed rules are found in regulations.[79]

Any child[80] over the age of 13[81] may only be placed or kept in secure accommodation if it appears:

> "(a) that
>
> (i) he has a history of absconding and is likely to abscond from any other description of accommodation; and
>
> (ii) if he absconds he is likely to suffer significant harm; or
>
> (b) that if he is kept in any other description of accommodation he is likely to injure himself or other persons."[82]

Detention for more than 72 hours within any 28-day period requires court approval. This is a draconian order; children facing secure accommodation proceedings should be afforded the same Article 6(3) rights as those charged with criminal offences.[83] If the criteria are satisfied the court must make the order; the child's welfare is not the paramount consideration.[84] The court's powers are limited to testing the evidence[85] and fixing the duration of the order[86]; orders may last for up to three months with extensions of up to six months.[87] The court authorises the use of secure accommodation; the local authority must continually review whether the child should be kept there.[88] Children who are only accom-

---

[79] Children (Secure Accommodation) Regulations 1991, S.I. 1991 No. 1505; Children (Secure Accommodation) (No. 2) Regulations 1991, S.I. 1991 No. 2034; Children (Secure Accommodation) Amendment Regulations 1992, S.I. 1992 No. 2117; Children (Secure Accommodation) Amendment Regulations 1995, S.I. 1995 No. 1378; Children (Homes and Secure Accommodation) (Miscellaneous Amendments) Regulations 1996, S.I 1996 No. 692.

[80] Children may be detained under the Mental Health Act 1983, the Powers of Criminal Courts (Sentencing) Act 2000 (conviction for grave offences), or the Crime and Disorder Act 1998 without a secure accommodation order: S.I. 1991 No. 1505, reg. 5(1). The regulations apply subject to modification to children remanded to local authority accommodation, reg. 6: *Re G. (Secure Accommodation Order)* [2001] 1 F.L.R. 884. Children bailed with a condition that they reside in local authority accommodation are subject to s.25: *Re C. (Secure Accommodation: Bail)* [1994] 2 F.L.R. 922. Children accommodated under s.20(5) or s.43 may not be held in secure accommodation, reg. 5(2).

[81] S.I. 1991 No. 1505, reg. 4; the Secretary of State's permission is required if the child is under 13.

[82] s.25(1); there are two alternative conditions: *Re D. (No. 1)* (1996) J.P.N. 286.

[83] *Re C. (Secure Accommodation Order: Representation)* [2001] 2 F.L.R. 169, CA at paras 25 and 34. These are "specified proceedings". A children's guardian should be appointed; see D.H., *Manual of practice guidance for guardians ad litem etc.* (1992), pp. 57–61.

[84] s. 25(4); *Re M. (Secure Accommodation Order)* [1995] 1 F.L.R. 418, CA *Cf. Guidance,* Vol. 4, para. 8.9, which suggests that the court has a discretion. An interim order can be made even if full evidence has not been heard: s.25(5); *Re C.(Secure Accommodation Order: Representation)* [2001] 2 F.L.R. 169, CA *per* Thorpe L.J. at para. 31.

[85] Hearsay evidence is admissible: *R. v. Oxfordshire C.C. (Secure Accommodation Order)* [1992] Fam. 150.

[86] *Re W. (A Minor) (Secure Accommodation Order)* [1993] 1 F.L.R. 692. The order should last no longer than necessary; overlong orders effectively delegate the court's responsibility to the local authority:, *per* Booth J. at 679.

[87] S.I. 1991 No. 1505, rr. 11, 12. The time periods run from the date of authorisation, *Re B. (A Minor) (Secure Accommodation)* [1994] 2 F.L.R. 707.

[88] *Re K.(Secure Accommodation: Right to Liberty)* [2001] 1 F.L.R. 526 at paras 22 and 101; regs 15 and 16.

modated by the authority may be removed at any time by those with parental responsibility.[89]

Despite the restrictive nature of secure accommodation, the Court of Appeal held in *Re K. (Secure Accommodation: Right to Liberty)*[90] that detention authorised under section 25 did not breach Article 5. Under the Convention, detention "for the purpose of educational supervision" is lawful. Classroom teaching is not required, life skills and social skills training could be sufficient, but there must be "educational supervision" even where the child was over compulsory school age.[91] Even though the Act made no mention of education, section 25 was not incompatible with the Convention.[92]

Court proceedings have not operated as an effective check on the use of secure accommodation[93] but (largely for reasons of cost) local authorities have developed procedures intended to limit its use. Secure accommodation should be seen as a "last resort" and not used merely because of lack of suitable alternatives, nor as a form of punishment.[94] Running away may indicate abuse or unhappiness which locking up will not remedy. Use of secure accommodation has increased because of the poor facilities (particularly low level of staffing) in open units, the problems of caring for young sex abusers and children involved in prostitution, and the desire to keep boys awaiting trial or convicted of grave crimes out of penal establishments.[95] There are just over 420 secure places available in community homes and youth treatment centres but over half are used by the Youth Justice Board for young people convicted or on remand[96]; only 25 per cent of residents were looked after by a local authority.[97] Some young people benefit from placements in secure units, for others they amount to little more than prison.[98]

(c) Placement outside England and Wales

22–068 Until the 1960s, arrangements were made by voluntary organisations and local authorities for thousands of children in their care to emigrate.[99] Children were

[89] s.25(9). This is also relevant to children placed by health or education authorities. In *M. v. Birmingham C.C.* [1994] 2 F.L.R. 141 the local authority obtained a care order because of the mother's refusal to agree to a secure placement.

[90] [2001] 1 F.L.R. 526 ; J. Masson [2002] *C.F.L.Q.* 77 Thorpe L.J. rejected the notion that this was a deprivation of liberty, relying on *Neilsen v. Denmark* (1989) 11 E.H.R.R. 175 and viewing it as within the parental power to control children.

[91] Art. 5(1) (d); *Bouamar v. Belgium* (1989) 11 E.H.R.R. 1; *Koniarska v. U.K.* E.C.H.R. Application No. 33670/96, hearing 10 December, 2000.

[92] *Re K. (Secure Accommodation: Right to Liberty)* [2001] 1 F.L.R. 526 at para. 43 *per* Butler-Sloss P. and at para. 116 *per* Judge L.J. The attention of the Court was not drawn to Education Act 1996, s.562 which disapplies the education duties to those detained under a court order.

[93] Timms and Harris, p. 49.

[94] *Guidance,* Vol. 4, para. 8.6.

[95] The Department of Health has rejected claims that use is determined by supply rather than need: *Children Act Report 1995–9,* para. 9.35.

[96] D.H., *Statistical Bulletin* 2001/17, Table A(1).

[97] *ibid.* On March 31, 2001 6% of residents were accommodated under s.20, 11% under care orders and 8% placed following remand to local authority accommodation.

[98] See D. Simpson, "My experience in secure units" Evidence to Short Committee: Vol. III, pp. 364–365; W. Utting (1997) *op. cit.* paras 2.18–2.10.

[99] See G. Wagner, *Children of the Empire* (1981); P. Bean and J. Melville, *Lost Children of the Empire* (1989); M. Humphreys, *Empty cradles* (1994).

placed overseas with families and in institutions to save costs and populate the colonies, with the hope that they would have a better life. However, "child migration was bad and, in human terms, a costly mistake."[1] Changes in Britain and in the receiving countries —Australia, Canada and elsewhere—brought an end to this practice; children are now only placed overseas with relatives or if their foster carer emigrates.

Under the Children Act 1989, the agreement of all people with parental responsibility is required if an accommodated child is to leave England and Wales, for example to move to Scotland with foster carers.[2] If agreement is refused there is no way of overriding this decision unless the foster carers obtain parental responsibility.[3] The emigration of children in care requires the court's permission.[4] The court may only give this where the move is in the child's best interests, suitable arrangements have been made for the child's welfare in the receiving country and the child and every person with parental responsibility has consented. The court may act without the consent of an immature child or of a person with parental responsibility who cannot be found, is incapable of giving consent or is withholding it unreasonably.[5] Parents retain their parental responsibility, consequently it is more difficult than in adoption to establish that refusal is reasonable, particularly where contact is to be maintained.[6] Where the child has no relationship with the parents or no chance of living with them the court will usually permit emigration.[7] Where permission has been granted the child may also be adopted overseas.[8]

(d) Other decisions

22–069 Children in care sometimes want to change their names, either to identify with foster carers or to cut links with abusive parents. It is provided that no person may cause a child in care to be known by a new surname without the written consent of all those with parental responsibility or leave of the court.[9]

---

[1] Select Committee on Health, *The welfare of former British child migrants*, Third Report Session 1997–8 H.C. 755, paras 15–19 and 98.

[2] Children Act 1989, Sched. 2, para. 9(2); *Guidance*, Vol. 8, Chap. 6, see below.

[3] By a residence or special guardianship order, Children Act 1989, ss.8, 13(1) (b), 14C(3); such a person could go to Scotland permanently without consent; the court's leave may be sought for the child's emigration outside the U.K. if permission is refused.

[4] Children Act 1989, Sched. 2, para. 19; permission is not needed for visits of one month or less: s.33(7) (b). In *Flintshire v. K.* [2001] 2 F.L.R 476, FD the court approved a care plan so that the "internet twins" could be returned to the U.S.A. and cared for permanently there.

[5] Sched. 2, para. 19(4)(5); *Re G. (Minors) (Care: Leave to Place outside the Jurisdiction)* [1994] 2 F.L.R. 301. Children must give consent in writing, a deep level of understanding is therefore required: *Re J. (Freeing For Adoption)* [2000] 2 F.L.R. 58 at 67 *per* Black J.

[6] *Re G. (Minors) (Care: Leave to Place outside the Jurisdiction)* [1994] 2 F.L.R. 301 at 306, *per* Thorpe J. The children were placed with an aunt in the USA with their parents' (reluctant) consent.

[7] *Payne v. Payne* [2001] 1 F.L.R. 1052 (a private law case where the father was able to maintain good contact.) Placement at a distance which undermined contact could breach Art. 8, particularly if there were viable alternatives: *Olsson v. Sweden* (1988) 11 E.H.R.R. 259 (children placed in three separate foster homes far from parents' home).

[8] Sched. 2, para. 19(6) (as amended) disapplies Adoption and Children Bill 2002, cl.85.

[9] s.33(7) (a).

Children may apply[10]; foster carers without a residence order are unlikely to take proceedings or be granted permission.[11] These cases raise many of the same issues as other cases on name but the objectives of the applicant, the motives and objections of parents and the views of the children's guardian are also relevant.[12] A child in care who wishes to marry must obtain the consent of the local authority and any parent with parental responsibility or their guardian, but may obtain consent from the court if this is refused.[13] The local authority's parental responsibility avoids the need for court permission and prevents review of other decisions.[14] For issues such as sterilisation[15] which go beyond parental responsibility, the inherent jurisdiction of the High Court may be invoked, but only if the child would otherwise be at risk of significant harm.[16] Where the child is accommodated the court may review relevant decisions in proceedings for a section 8 order.[17]

B. Challenging local authority decisions

22–070 Theoretically, services provided by social services departments are the responsibility of locally elected council members who are accountable through the ballot box for the quality of services. However, political accountability is inadequate for minority concerns such as social services for poor families which are rarely issues in local elections, and does not give a means of redress to individual complainants. The courts have only taken a limited role in supervising local authorities through actions for judicial review, breach of statutory duty[18] or under the Human Rights Act 1998. The concentration of professional expertise and political, administrative and institutional authority in the social services department means that the power in relationships with clients rests with departments.[19] Partnership with parents requires the development of procedures and practices to shift that balance, empower clients, provide them with real oppor-

---

[10] These are specified proceedings but children's guardian may not be required: *Re J. (A Minor) (Change of Name)* [1993] 1 F.L.R. 699.

[11] See para. 19–024, above.

[12] *Re M., T., P., K., and B. (Care: Change of Name)* [2000] 2 F.L.R. 645, FD *cf. Re S. (Change of Surname)* [1998] 1 F.L.R. 672, CA.

[13] Marriage Act 1949, s.3(1) (b), (1A).

[14] *A. v. Liverpool C. C.* [1982] A.C. 363; but the court may determine disputes about the scope of parental responsibility: *Re M. (Care: Leave to Interview Child)* [1995] 1 F.L.R. 825.

[15] *Re F. (Wardship: Sterilisation)* [1990] 2 A.C. 1; *Re B. (A Minor) (Wardship Sterilisation)* [1988] A.C. 199.

[16] s.100(4), (5); *Re X. (A Minor) (Adoption)* [1994] 2 F.L.R. 450, where an order was granted restricting disclosure of details in the adoption register; see also above.

[17] s.9(2), (5); see the discussion of s.100 above.

[18] See B. Markesinis and S. Deakin, *Tort Law* (4th ed., 1999); statutory duties relating to child care will rarely give rise to a private law cause of action: *X. v. Bedfordshire C.C.* [1995] 2 A.C. 633; *O'Rouke v. Camden LBC* [1998] A.C. 189; *cf. Guevara v. London Borough of Hounslow, The Times,* April 17, 1987 and [1987] J.S.W.L. 374

[19] National Consumer Council & National Institute for Social Work, *Open to Complaints* (1988), p. 6; *Children Act Now* (2001), p. 70; see also S. Braye and M. Preston-Shoot, "Accountability, administrative law and social work practice: redressing or re-inforcing the power imbalance?" [1999] *J.S.W.F.L.* 235.

tunities to influence decisions made about them, and to challenge those they disagree with. A complaints system was required to make social services departments and social workers more accountable for their actions and responsive to clients' needs. Opening the door to complaints provides valuable feedback about social work action and helps make services more responsive.[20]

Procedures must be able to handle a wide range and possibly a large number[21] of different complaints. Clients may be dissatisfied with the professionalism of staff or the quality of the service they provide; the availability of a service, *i.e.* the resources committed by the authority to it and the criteria used for rationing; or the appropriateness of the services offered in their case. A disagreement with a local authority may contain all these elements, as well as disputes about the factual basis on which assessments were made and the law. Different types of complaint may require different consideration and different action; the source of the problem may affect the chances of reaching a satisfactory solution. For example, where the lack of a local service results from a decision not to resource it, the matter is essentially a political one unless there is a duty to provide it. Irrespective of the strength of complaint, provision can only be made if the service is available privately or from another authority and money can be found to purchase it. In contrast, where the complaint concerns a professional issue such as the assessment of the client's needs and thus the priority of their claim for a service or its appropriateness, a review may reveal the justice of the complaint and lead to redress. In practice, it may be difficult for clients to distinguish between professional and political decisions and to know where their complaint should be directed. Most complaints about services will reflect, in some measure, the limitations of resources. But this should not justify poor quality or inappropriate provision.

(a) Complaints procedures

22–071 Complaints procedures have an essential protective function[22]; a lack of complaints systems contributed to the failure to identify and stop the widespread abuse in children's homes in the 1970s and 1980s.[23] Before the Children Act 1989 only a minority of social services departments had mechanisms for handling complaints, publicity for services was often limited and procedures were

---

[20] *Guidance*, Vol. 3, para. 10.11. The complaints system must be monitored and any annual report provided for the Social Services Committee: Representations Procedure (Children) Regulations 1991, 1991 S.I. No. 894, reg. 10; *Guidance*, Vol. 3, paras 10.52 *et seq.*

[21] The ability to attract and deal with complaints may be seen as a mark of success. Schemes which receive few complaints may be insufficiently accessible. A D.H. survey during the first 9 months of the Children Act 1989 revealed under 4,000 complaints, 542 from children: Cm. 2144, Table 3.12.

[22] W. Utting (1997), para. 18.12. But the existence of a complaints system was one of the justifications for not imposing a duty of care on the local authority: *X. v. Bedfordshire C.C.* [1995] 2 A.C. 633.

[23] *Lost in Care* (2000 H.C.201), pp. 829 and 834. Sympathetic responses to residents' complaints were also crucial to the discovery of abusive regimes in North Wales, Staffordshire and elsewhere.

woefully inadequate.[24] Both the *Short Report* and the *Review* recommended the introduction of a complaints system.[25]

There are two sets of statutory obligations governing different types of complaints. The Children Act 1989, s.26(3) makes provision for complaints about Part III services[26]; other complaints for example about child protection investigations or care for the elderly are handled under the Local Authority Social Services Act 1970, s.7B[27] but the main differences between these schemes have been removed following consultation.[28] Complaints under the Children Act scheme may be made by children looked after by the local authority and other "children in need", their parents, those with parental responsibility for them, other people whom the authority considers have sufficient interest in the child's welfare to warrant their representations being considered,[29] local authority foster parents[30] and by some people in connection with adoption services.[31] Currently there are no time limits for making complaints but new regulations are proposed to require them to be made within 12 months of the incident.[32] An informal resolution stage will also be added which must be completed within 14 days and the time periods for considering complaints by adults will be relaxed. The Children Act requires a two-stage process; complaints unresolved at the first stage are considered by a panel.[33] An independent person who is neither a member nor an officer of the authority must take part in the consideration of the complaint at both stages. It has also been proposed that a children's complaints officer should be employed to protect children's interests in the handling of their complaints.[34] Complaints may be linked to other action by the applicant, for

---

[24] National Consumer Council, *Complaints Procedures in Social Services Departments—a survey report* (1986), N. Lewis, M. Seneviratne and S. Cracknell, *Complaints Procedures in Local Government Report to ESRC* (1987).

[25] *Short Report* paras 361 *et seq.*; *Review* paras 9.10–12. The idea that clients should have a right to complain was accepted by the British Association of Social Workers: BASW, *Clients are fellow citizens* (1980).

[26] s.26(3); Representations Procedure (Children) Regulations 1991, S.I. 1991 No. 894. (The Adoption and Children Bill 2002, cl. 115 amends s.26 and new regulations will follow implementing D.H., *Listening to people a consultation on improving social services complaints procedures* (2000). See also SSI, *Third overview report of complaints procedures in local authority social services departments* (1996). The Children's Rights Director in the Care Standards Commission should help ensure that young people's complaints about these facilities are properly dealt with: D.H. (2000) *op. cit.* para. 11.21.

[27] Local authority social services (complaints procedure) Order 1990; S.I. 1990 No. 2244; Complaints Procedure Directions 1990 (new directions will be issued following the transfer of responsibilities for registration and inspection to the National Care Standards Commission); *Working Together* (1999), para. 5.72.

[28] D.H., *Listening to people* (2000), paras 3.2 and 3.5.

[29] s.26(3) (a)-(c), (e); *Guidance,* Vol. 3, para. 10.7, including complaints by groups, para. 10.9.

[30] s.26(3) (d) including complaints about the number of children who may be fostered: Sched. 7, para. 5.

[31] s.26(3B) to be added by Adoption and Children Bill 2002, cl. 115(4).

[32] s.26(4A) to be added by Adoption and Children Bill 2002, cl. 115(6); D.H., *Listening to people* (2000), para. 4.4.

[33] This is more onerous than the system required by for community care, requiring an independent person at both stages: S.I. 1991 No. 894, rr. 5, 8(3).

[34] It has been suggested that local authorities employ a Children's Complaints Officer to protect children's interests in the handling of their complaints: *Lost in care* (2000 H.C. 201) recommendations 3–7; *Learning the Lessons* (2000) - the Government's response agreed this "in principle" p.19. Most authorities now have children's rights officers.

example a claim for compensation, or by the authority, for example child protection inquiries or disciplinary procedures. Priorities must be established in each case but the need to protect the child must come first.[35] Practice guidance recommends that the complaints officer should be given a power to halt decisions which are the subject of complaint,[36] but this is not formally part of the system. The authority is only required to give due consideration to the findings and to notify those involved; it need not act on them.[37] But it has been said that it will be unusual for the authority not to follow the panel's recommendations.[38] Judicial review is available if complaints are not properly considered.[39] Poor handling of complaints may amount to mal-administration. Where the complaints system fails to comply with the regulations the remedy is the Secretary of State's default power.[40]

(b) The local Commissioner for administration

22–072 The role of the Commissioner or local ombudsman is limited to complaints by those who claim to have suffered injustice as a result of mal-administration where there is no remedy by way of court proceedings, or it would be unreasonable to expect the claimant to pursue it.[41] Not every improper act may give rise to an injustice and injustices may occur without impropriety. The Commissioner investigates complaints,[42] makes findings of mal-administration and injustice as appropriate, issues a report and may recommend compensation.[43] The authority must consider the report, but in cases concerning children the passage of time may mean that the local authority is not able both to give redress and to comply with its duty to safeguard the child's welfare.

(c) The power of the Secretary of State

22–073 Although decisions about social services for children are within the control of local government, central government retains some power to deal with complaints. The Secretary of State may establish an inquiry into a local authority's actions, the results of which may influence individual decisions and future policy.[44] Where a local authority is not meeting the Government's "best value"

---

[35] *Guidance*, Vol. 3, para. 10.26.

[36] S.S.I., *The right to complain* (1991); D.H., *Listening to people* (2000), para. 9.2.

[37] s.26(4), (7).

[38] *R. v. Brent LBC, ex p. S.* [1994] 1 F.L.R. 203 at 211, *per* Ralph Gibson L.J.

[39] *R. v. Kingston upon Thames R.B.C., ex p. T.* [1994] 1 F.L.R. 798.

[40] s.84; *R. v. Barnet LBC, ex p. B.* [1994] 1 F.L.R. 592.

[41] Local Government Act 1974, s.26; see generally M. Seneviratne, *Ombudsmen: public services and administrative justice* (2002) and www.lgo.org.uk

[42] Where confidential information is required for the investigation disclosure will be ordered: *Re a Subpoena (Adoption: Commissioner for Local Administration)* [1996] 2 F.L.R. 629, QBD.

[43] For examples see Local Government Ombudsman Annual Reports and M. Seneviratne [2000] *J.S.W.F.L.* 209. In 2001 approximately 6% of complaints concerned social services but not all these related to children's services.

[44] Children Act 1989, s.81 *e.g.* the Victoria Climbie Inquiry. The Inquiry into child abuse in North Wales was established by the Secretary of State for Wales.

requirements, the Secretary of State may direct it to take action.[45] In addition, where the local authority has defaulted on its duties, for example by failing to provide any services for children in need, an order with directions enforceable by mandamus may be issued.[46] Default powers in other legislation have rarely been used[47] but the Government has declared its willingness to intervene where councils are failing.[48] Local authorities whose standards have been found unacceptable by the Social Services Inspectorate have been put under "special measures" involving target-setting and monitoring; a Taskforce has been established to tackle poor performance and spread best practice in adoption, and where a Director of Social Services has resigned the Department of Health has identified an experienced Director for appointment. The existence of a default power has been held to preclude the use of other judicial remedies[49] but section 84 does not prevent the use of judicial review.[50] However, the court hearing an application by a person aggrieved may refuse to exercise its discretion where this might conflict with the minister's decision.[51] Thus the default power may be a hindrance to individuals as well as a lever against local authorities. Also, it has been said that where the minister has a default power this will generally be a better remedy, particularly if the merits of the decision are at issue. The minister, unlike the court, has the department's expertise, can conduct an inquiry and can direct the solution to be applied.[52] Where judicial review is refused the minister may still be willing to investigate the case.[53]

(d) Under the inherent jurisdiction of the High Court, by judicial review[54] or under the Human Rights Act 1998, s.7

22–074 In 1981 in *A. v. Liverpool City Council*[55] the House of Lords confirmed the view that the High Court should not exercise its wardship jurisdiction to review decisions relating to children in care. Parliament had by statute entrusted the power and duty to make decisions to local authorities without reserving a power of review to the courts and thus marked out an area where decisions about children are removed from both parents and the courts.[56] The Children Act 1989, s.100 extended the restrictions; local authorities cannot refer any matter which could be dealt with under statutory powers to the High Court's inherent jurisdic-

---

45 Local Government Act 1999, s.15. The direction may be enforced by court order.
46 Children Act 1989, s.84. This could be in response to a SSI investigation or to a complaint.
47 J. Logie, "Enforcing statutory duties: the court and default powers" [1988] J.S.W.L. 185, 186, 196.
48 *Modernising Social Services* (Cm. 4169, 1998), para. 7.21.
49 *Pasmore v. Oswaldtwistle U.D.C.* [1898] A.C. 387.
50 *R. v. Brent LBC, ex p. S.* [1994] 1 F.L.R. 203 at 214, *per* Peter Gibson L. J.
51 *R. v. Secretary of State for the Environment, ex p. Ward* [1984] 1 W.L.R. 834; but see Logie, *op. cit.* at 194—the matter has only been considered by the High Court.
52 *R. v. Devon C.C., ex p. Baker and Johns* (1992) 11 B.*M.L.R.* 141, *per* Simon Brown L. J. at 160.
53 *R. v. Brent LBC, ex p. S.* [1994] 1 F.L.R. 203 at 214.
54 De Smith *et al.*, *Judicial Review of Administrative Action* (5th ed., 1995) and M. Fordham, *Judicial Review Handbook* (3rd ed., 2001).
55 [1982] A.C. 363 the approach dates back to the decision in *Re M.* [1961] Ch. 328. Law Com. W.P. 101, *Wards of Court,* paras 3.39 *et seq.*
56 *per* Lord Wilberforce at 372.

tion. Although the statutory restrictions do not apply to individuals and the local authority may accept the jurisdiction, the High Court is unwilling to allow its powers to be used to circumvent the Children Act.[57]

Where impropriety is alleged the matter should be dealt with by judicial review.[58] An application for judicial review may only be made with permission[59] by someone with sufficient interest in the matter; this might preclude relatives initiating proceedings but not parents or children.[60] The applicant must have exhausted other more suitable remedies.[61] The grounds for judicial review have developed through case-law; local authorities must not act unlawfully,[62] unreasonably,[63] in breach of reasonable expectations[64] or without following the proper procedure, and must comply with the rules of natural justice.[65] The courts have been willing to review decisions taken where the authority has failed to consider issues required by statute or guidance,[66] where it has fettered its discretion[67] or acted without adequate inquiry[68]:—

> In *R. v. Devon County Council, ex p. O.*[69] a local authority placed a disturbed seven year-old boy with prospective adopters. Social workers monitored his progress but remained concerned about his welfare. Two and a

---

[57] *C. v. Salford C.C.* [1994] 2 F.L.R. 926 and see above para. 19–047.

[58] *per* Lord Scarman in *W. v. Hertfordshire C. C.* [1985] A.C. 791 at 793; *Re D.M. (A Minor) (Wardship Jurisdiction)* [1986] 2 F.L.R. 122. Where the action is unlawful under the H.R.A. 1998 and application could be made under s.7(1).

[59] C.P.R. 1998, r.54; R. Spon-Smith [2001] *Fam. Law* 143.

[60] D. Oliver [1989] J.C.L. 58. The test for *locus standi* is set out in *R. v. I.R.C., ex p. National Federation of Self Employed and Small Businesses Ltd* [1982] A.C. 617.

[61] The complaints procedure should have been used: *R. v. Kingston upon Thames R.B.C.; ex p. T.* [1994] 1 F.L.R. 798; *R. v. East Sussex C. C., ex p. W.* [1998] 2 F.L.R. 1082, 1092; *cf. R. v. Wokingham D. C., ex p. J.* [1999] 2 F.L.R. 1136, 1147 (only a discretionary bar); but it is not necessary to have complained to the Secretary of State under s.84: *R. v. Brent LBC, ex p. S.* [1994] 1 F.L.R. 203, CA.

[62] *R. v. Cornwall C.C., ex p. Cornwall Guardians ad litem Panel* [1992] 1 W.L.R. 427, where the director of social services' attempt to limit investigations by children's guardians was quashed.

[63] The narrow approach to unreasonableness established in *Associated Provincial Picture Houses Ltd v. Wednesbury Corporation* [1948] 1 K.B. 223 has been superseded in *R. v. Secretary of State ex p. Daly* [2001] 3 All E.R. 433, HL. A public authority must show that any decision which interferes with human rights is proportionate. A decision which conflicts with the recommendation of the complaints panel may be unreasonable: *R. v. Kingston upon Thames R.B.C., ex p. T.* [1994] 1 F.L.R. 798 at 815.

[64] *R. on app Nagalro v. CAFCASS* [2002] 1 F.L.R. 225; *R. v. Cornwall County Council, ex p. LH.* [2000] 1 F.L.R. 236, QBD.

[65] See *R. v. Harrow L.B.C., ex p. D.* [1990] 1 F.L.R. 70; the requirements of natural justice are not rigid: *R. v. Avon C.C., ex p. Crabtree* [1996] 1 F.L.R. 502, CA.

[66] *R. v. Wealden D.C. ex p. Wales* [1995] N.P.C. 145 exercise of powers to remove campers without consideration of duties to children in need in the Children Act 1989; *R. v. Devon C. C., ex p. O.* [1997] 2 F.L.R. 388 (removal of child from long-term foster carers without consulting carer or finding out child's wishes; *R. v. Cornwall County Council, ex p. LH.* [2000] 1 F.L.R. 236, QBD (disregard of the *Working Together* guidance on involvement of parents in case conferences).

[67] *R. v. Hammersmith and Fulham LBC, ex p. D.*[1999] 1 F.L.R. 642, QBD (decision not to offer any alternative services if parent refused assistance to return to her own country).

[68] *R. v. Local Authority and Police Authority in the Midlands, ex p. LM.* [2000] 1 F.L.R. 612, QBD (decision to disclose offences of bus operator to neighbouring local authority); *Re T. (Accommodation by Local Authority)* [1995] 1 F.L.R. 159 (decision not to accommodate orphan under s.20(3) but only to make s.17 payment).

[69] [1997] 2 F.L.R. 388, QBD.

half years after the placement, following a strategy meeting, the authority served notice for the boy's return within seven days. The prospective adopters had not been invited to the meeting nor consulted about a possible removal, and the boy, who expected to be adopted, had not been asked for his views. The court quashed the decision finding that the local authority had acted improperly by failing to consult the carers, had breached Children Act 1989, s.22 by not consulting the child, and had acted unreasonably by seeking removal so precipitously.

The courts have refused to review decisions requiring a housing authority to co-operate with the social services department[70] or a social services department to find a placement for a child in hospital.[71] Where the local authority refuses to accept that a child is "in need" redress is by judicial review.[72] But the duty in section 17 is only a "target duty".[73] The court considers financial constraints on the local authority and does not investigate its priorities.[74] It cannot decide that a specific service should be provided.[75] Courts have stressed the value of the complaints system on the basis that they have no investigatory powers[76] and emphasised the importance of local authorities being able to exercise their child protection functions without fear of challenge by judicial review.[77]

22–075 The remedies for judicial review are discretionary; the court may make mandatory, prohibiting or quashing orders alongside other civil remedies including damages, and can issue declarations of incompatibility.[78] Unlike the High Court in wardship, it may not substitute its own view of the merits of a decision. Remedies may be illusory if the local authority reaches the same conclusion when it reconsiders the decision, but the granting of permission to seek judicial review may precipitate the necessary change of view.

Where a local authority acts (or proposes to act)[79] in breach of the European Convention on Human Rights a victim may bring proceedings against the authority.[80] Leave is not required but it has been said that applications should not be made under section 7 until other appropriate remedies have been

---

[70] *R. v. Northavon D.C., ex p. Smith* [1994] 2 F.L.R. 671, HL; Children Act 1989, s.27(2).

[71] *R. v. Birmingham C. C., ex p. A.* [1997] 2 F.L.R. 841, QBD.

[72] Sunkin (1992) 4 J.C.L. 109, 111

[73] *R. v. Kingston upon Thames R.B.C., ex p. T.* [1994] 1 F.L.R. 798 at 810, *per* Ward J.; *R. on app G. v. Barnet LBC* [2001] 2 F.L.R. 877, CA; *R. on app. A. v. Lambeth LBC* [2002] 1 F.L.R. 353, CA.

[74] *R. v. Kingston upon Thames R.B.C., ex p. T.* [1994] 1 F.L.R. 798 at 817.

[75] *R. on app. A. v. Lambeth LBC* [2002] 1 F.L.R. 353, CA *per* Laws L.J. at para. 44.

[76] *R. v. Birmingham C. C., ex p. A.* [1997] 2 F.L.R. 841, QBD; *R. v. East Sussex C. C., ex p. W.* [1998] 2 F.L.R. 1082, QBD.

[77] *R. v. Somerset C. C., ex p. Prospects Care Services* [2000] 1 F.L.R. 636, QBD at 641 *per* Dyson J.; *R. v. Hampshire C. C., ex p. H.* [1999] 2 F.L.R. 359, CA at 372 *per* Butler-Sloss L.J.

[78] H.R.A. 1998, s.4(2).

[79] This can include a failure to act: *Re S.(F.C.)* [2002] 1 F.L.R. 815, HL, 10 at para. 49 *per* Lord Nicholls.

[80] H.R.A. 1998, s.7(1). Proceedings may be brought in either the country court which made the original care order or the High Court: *Re W. and B.; Re W.* [2001] 2 F.L.R. 582, CA *per* Hale L.J. at para. 75. Alternatively, under s.7(1) (b) a party could raise the matter in any Children Act proceedings

explored.[81] The court can grant such relief or order as it considers appropriate including any remedy available in judicial review, injunctions and damages.[82] The High Court may also exercise its powers under the inherent jurisdiction to ensure compliance with Convention rights but remains bound by the restrictions in the Children Act 1989, s.100. In *Re M*[83] the court quashed a decision to abandon plans for a baby subject to a care order to live with either of his parents in favour of a placement with the maternal grandmother or adoption because the parents' Article 8 rights had been breached by failure to involve them in the decision-making. It also arranged for a further hearing to reconsider the new care plan. And in *R. ota L. v. Manchester City Council*[84] (a judicial review application) the court struck down the local authority policy of paying short-term relative carers less than local authority foster carers on the basis that this was unreasonable, failed to take account of the duty to safeguard the child's welfare and breached Article 8 together with Article 14. The authority was order to pay damages under the 1998 Act. These cases highlight the importance of the Human Rights Act in raising awareness about the possibility of challenging local authority decisions, extending the grounds on which claims can be made, establishing a new mechnism for claims, and improving the remedies available.

(e) The European Court of Human Rights[85]

22–076 The incorporation of the European Convention on Human Rights into U.K. law reduces the need for the Court in Strasbourg but it remains the last resort for those who have been unable to get redress for a breach of a Convention rights. In the past, the European Court provided the only means of challenging decisions which, though lawful under domestic law, breached the Convention. It has been highly influential in the development of child care law but cost and delay of taking cases to Europe meant that it could rarely remedy breaches to the right to family life.[86]

---

[81] *Re S.(F.C.)* [2002] 1 F.L.R. 815, HL, at para. 62 *per* Lord Nicholls.

[82] H.R.A. 1998, s.8.

[83] *Re M. (Care: Challenging Decisions by Local Authority)* [2001] 2 F.L.R. 1300, FD.

[84] [2002] 2 F.L.R. 43.

[85] H. Swindells *et al., Family Law and the Human Rights Act 1998* (1999); J. Fortin, *Children's Rights and the Developing Law* (1998); U. Kilkelly, *The Child and the European Convention on Human Rights* (1999) and above para. 17–013.

[86] Cases took at least five years and cost £30,000, see J. Fortin, "The Human Rights Act 1998: human rights for children too" in *The new handbook of children's rights* (B. Franklin ed., 2001), p. 120.

CHAPTER 23

ADOPTION

I. INTRODUCTION

23–001 Adoption is the legal process[1] whereby a court irrevocably extinguishes the legal ties between a child[2] and the natural parents or guardians and creates analogous ties between the child and the adopters.[3] "Simple adoptions", revocable or incomplete transfers of parental responsibility which exist in some countries cannot be made; "special guardianship" is the nearest equivalent.[4] Some foreign "simple adoptions" are treated as full adoptions.[5] A court order is always required; so called *de facto* adoptions, arrangements where the child lives permanently with people who have put themselves *in loco parentis* to the child, are ineffective to give the carers parental responsibility, to remove that of the parents,[6] or to change the child's status although they are not without legal effect.[7]

Adoption in England and Wales[8] is entirely the creature of statute. It was introduced by the Adoption of Children Act 1926 and is now governed by the Adoption Act 1976 which is expected to be replaced by the Adoption and Children Act 2002 from a date to be appointed (currently planned to be 2004). This concept of adoption differs sharply from that in some civil law systems

---

[1] This is more restrictive than the dictionary definition see: Shorter O.E.D. "to take voluntarily into any relationship . . . especially that of a son."

[2] The courts will be able to grant orders on applications made before the child reached age 18 so long as he or she is under 19 years: Adoption and Children Act 2002, s.47(9), 49(4).

[3] Adoption and Children Act 2002, s.46, 67 (Adoption Act 1976, ss.12, 39); see generally *per* Lord Simon of Glaisdale. *O'Connor v. A & B* [1971] 1 W.L.R. 1227, 1235–6 and *Re B (adoption: jurisdiction to set aside)* [1995] 2 F.L.R. 1, CA, *per* Swinton Thomas L.J at p. 8.

[4] Children Act 1989, s.14A-14G added by Adoption and Children Act 2002, s.115.

[5] Simple adoptions are recognised under the Hague Convention on Intercountry Adoption, Art. 26 but Central Authorities seek to ensure that the parents consent to a full adoption where the receiving State is England and Wales. The High Court has a power to treat a "simple adoption" as other than a full adoption where this would be more favourable to the child: Adoption and Children Act 2002, s.88.

[6] Children Act 1989, ss.2(9),(11), 3(5). Such an agreement is not enforceable but would justify reasonable action by the carers "for the purposes of safeguarding or promoting the child's welfare."

[7] See, *e.g. Brock v. Wollams* [1949] 2 K.B. 388 (informally adopted child a "member of family of adopter" for purposes of the Rent Acts), *cf. Joram Developments Ltd v. Sharratt* [1979] 1 W.L.R. 928, H.L.; *Re Callaghan (dec'd)* [1985] 1 F.L.R. 116 (adult child treated as a "child of the family" could apply under the Inheritance (Provision for Family and Dependants) Act 1975, s.1(1)(d)); *R. v. Immigration Appeal Tribunal, ex p. Ali* [1987] 2 F.L.R. 220, *de facto* adoption in a country where legal adoption did not exist could satisfy test in Immigration Rules but see now Statement of Changes in Immigration Rules (1993–4) H.C. 395, paras 310–316.

[8] This is also the case in Scotland and Northern Ireland where similar provisions apply see: Adoption (Scotland) Act 1978; Adoption (Northern Ireland) Order 1987.

which inherited the Roman Law concepts of *adoptio* and *adrogatio*. In the United Kingdom, adoption is associated with the desire to nurture a child as the natural child of the adopters. Hence, although adoption has important effects on citizenship, succession and other legal rights, these rights must be incidental to the factual relationship of dependence between the parent and child.[9] In contrast, in some foreign systems[10] adoption may be used to confer succession rights on the adopted person as in the striking case of *Bedinger v. Graybill's trustee*[11] where the man adopted his wife so that she could succeed to settled property as his child and heir at law. This is particularly so in civil law systems under which certain relatives are entitled to a *legitima portio* or share of a deceased person's property.[12] Islamic systems do not recognise adoption in the sense of a complete transfer of a child to a new family but have developed the concept of *Kafalah* to provide substitute family care for children.[13]

23–002 Adoption may be seen as providing for children, for those who wish to be parents and even for parents who are unable or unwilling to care for their children. Varying emphasis has been given to these three elements in the past and to the three sets of participants in the adoption triangle.[14] But now the fundamental purpose of adoption is as a service for children, to provide a new permanent family by severance of the legal links with the birth family and the creation of new legal ties.[15] Adoption has become the placement of choice for some abused or neglected children, many of whom have disabilities[16] or behavioural problems, compulsorily removed from their families and for whom return home is considered contrary to their welfare. Indeed through the introduction of new legislation, procedures and standards, the government is seeking to promote the wider use of adoption for looked after children who cannot return to their birth families.[17]

---

[9] See: *Re B (Adoption Order: Nationality)* [1999] 1 F.L.R. 907 HL where adoption was granted to enable grandparents to continue to care for their 16-year-old Jamaican grandchild whose mother lived in poverty and father had died; *Re W (Adoption: Non-patrial)* [1986] Fam. 54 where adoption was refused when it was sought in order to give a 17 year old boy from Hong Kong British citizenship.

[10] For a full comparative analysis, see H. D. Krause, "Creation of Relations of Kinship" in *International Encyclopedia of Comparative Law*, Vol. IV, Chap. 6.

[11] 302 S.W. (2nd) 594 (1957) (Court of Appeals, Kentucky).

[12] *e.g.* the attempt of Somerset Maugham (then aged 88) to adopt his male secretary in order to defeat the claim of his only daughter Lady John Hope.

[13] D. Pearl and W. Menski, *Muslim Family Law* (3rd ed.; 1998) p. 410 *et seq.*; Van Bueren (1995), pp. 94 *et seq.*; see also: K. Beevers and S Ebrahimi, "Iranian child protection law—towards a concept of adoption" [2002] *I.F.L.* 166.

[14] *e.g.*, in 1975, concern for the rights and welfare of adopted adults justified breaching the confidentiality birth mothers had been given and providing a system of access to birth records, see below.

[15] D.H. and W.O., *Interdepartmental Review of Adoption Law* (1992), para. 3.1.

[16] H. Argent, *Find me a family* (1984); Adoption agencies are arranging adoptive placements for babies born with AIDS, see D. Batty, *The implications of AIDS for children in care* (BAAF, 1987).

[17] *Adoption: a new approach* (2000 Cm. 5017) para. 1.13; P.I.U. *Prime Minister's Review Adoption* (2000) p. 5.

Increasingly, children who are placed for adoption have families with whom they have emotional links, so that adoption has to be seen in terms of losses as well as gains.[18] A new form of adoption termed "open adoption"[19] is developing, where some links with the former family continue after adoption, and this brings into question the distinction between adoption, special guardianship and residence orders.

Adoption is still regarded by some as a service for childless families; but there are few babies placed with agencies for adoption. Placement, except with relatives, by those not registered as adoption agencies is illegal.[20] However, babies are available overseas; the practice of intercountry adoption has developed to meet the needs of adults and to provide for destitute children. Intercountry adoption has only recently become significant in England but is the most common form of adoption in some Western countries. A Convention to regulate intercountry adoption was drawn up by the Hague Conference on Private International Law in 1993. This has been signed by the United Kingdom and will be implemented by the Adoption (Intercountry Aspects) Act 1999 and the Adoption and Children Act 2002.[21]

23–003 Alternative methods of relieving childlessness: artificial insemination by donor (AID), treatments for female infertility and surrogacy raise some similar issues to adoption such as whether children should have a right to know their origins, the obligation of the parents to tell the child and whether the birth parents (or donors) should have the right to secrecy.[22] Adoption law and practice have had some influence on these matters, and this is another area where the European Convention on Human Rights can be expected to shape legal developments.[23]

Reform of adoption law has been under discussion since 1989[24]; a White

---

[18] J. Triseliotis, "Some moral and practical issues in adoption work" (1993) Vol. 13, No. 2 *Adoption and Fostering* 21, 23; and in relation to in family adoption: *Re B (Adoption by One Natural Parent to Exclusion of Other)* [2001] 1 F.L.R. 589 at para. 14 *per* Hale L.J.

[19] See A. Mullender, *Open Adoption* (1991); M. Ryburn, *Open adoption: research theory and practice* (1994); SSI, *Moving goal posts: a study of post adoption contact in the North of England* (1995); R. Parker, *Adoption: messages from research* (1999) Chap. 5 and below, para. 23.056.

[20] Adoption and Children Act 2002, s.92, 93 (Adoption Act 1976, s.11). *Re Adoption Application (Non-patrial: Breach of Procedures)* [1993] 1 F.L.R. 947; *Gatehouse v. Robinson and Robinson* [1986] 1 F.L.R. 504; *Re MW (Adoption: Surrogacy)* [1995] 2 F.L.R. 759.

[21] see below, para. 23.047.

[22] K. O'Donovan, "A right to know one's parentage?" (1988) 2 *Int. J. of Law & Fam.* 27; E. Haimes, "What can artificial reproduction learn from adoption" (1988) 2 *Int. J. of Law & Fam.* 46; Human Fertilization & Embryology: A framework for legislation Cm. 259 (1987), paras 82, 83 and below, para. 23.071.

[23] *Rose v. Secretary of State for Health and the Human Fertility and Embryology Authority* [2002] 2 F.L.R. 962, FD.

[24] See Inter-departmental Review of Adoption Law Discussion papers, 1: *The nature and effect of adoption* (1990); 2: *Agreement and Freeing* (1991); 3: *The adoption process* (1991); 4; *Intercountry adoption* (1992); *Report to ministers of an inter-departmental working group* (1992); *Placement for adoption* (1994); *The future of adoption panels* (1994). Inter-departmental Review of Adoption Law Background papers 1: *International perspectives* (1990), 2. *Review of Research relating to adoption* (1990); 3: *Intercountry adoption* (1992). Scottish law was also reviewed see Scottish Office, *The Future of Adoption Law in Scotland* (1993), some amendments to Scottish law were included in the Children (Scotland) Act 1995.

Paper was published in 1993[25] and a draft bill in 1996[26] but Parliamentary time was not made available. In 2000, the Prime Minister announced the Government's commitment to modernising adoption,[27] a new White Paper[28] was produced and a second bill introduced to Parliament.[29] A third bill, which draws heavily on the earlier two but takes more account of the complex human rights issues, was introduced at the beginning of the 2001–2002 session. Following heated debate and considerable amendment, the Adoption of Children Act 2002 was enacted at the very end of the session; it is expected to be implemented in 2004. Much of the detail has been left to regulations but some indication of the content of these was given by ministers during the debates. Alongside the new legislation, the Department of Health has introduced Adoption Standards,[30] practice guidance[31] and established a register of children needing adoptive families and prospective adopters to facilitate placement,[32] and the President of the Family Division has issued guidance designed to reduce delays and improve the service from the higher courts in adoption.[33] This chapter explains the law as reformed by the Adoption and Children Act 2002. An account of the earlier law is found in the sixth edition of this work.

The history and development of adoption

23–004 Adoption was reluctantly[34] introduced into English law following the recommendation of the Tomlin Report[35] in order to provide legal security for those involved in *de facto* arrangements which had become increasingly common.[36] The Adoption of Children Act 1926 permitted adoption without parental consent and required independent scrutiny of all cases. It did not ensure the child's full integration into the adoptive family; inheritance rights in the birth family were

---

25 *Adoption: the future* Cm. 2288 (1993).

26 D.H. and W.O., *Adoption—a service for children* (1996).

27 Performance and Innovation Unit, *Prime Minister's Review Adoption* (2000).

28 *Adoption: a new approach* Cm. 5017 (2000).

29 Bill 66 (2000-2001). This was largely to ensure wide consultation see: Select Committee on the Adoption and Children Bill (2001 H.C. 431); for a critique see S. Harris-Short [2001] C.F.L.Q. 405.

30 D.H., *National Adoption Standards for England* (2001); these will have the status of statutory guidance to local authorities from April 1, 2003: LAC (2001) 33, para. 10.

31 Details of guidance can be found on the Department of health web site: www.doh.gov.uk/adoption.

32 s.125; The Adoption and Children Act Register is run by Norwood Family Adoption Agency.

33 *Adoption Proceedings—a new approach* (2001). This does not apply to family proceedings courts. Certain county courts have been designated adoption centres and the importance of active case management confirmed.

34 The Report of the Committee on Child Adoption Cmd. 1254 (1921) (The Hopkinson Report) was followed by six unsuccessful bills; see N. Lowe, "English adoption law: past, present and future" in S. Katz *et al., Cross currents* (2000) 307; S. Cretney, "Adoption from contract to status" in S. Cretney, *Law, law reform and the family* (1998) 184 and *Family Law in the Twentieth Century—a history* (2003), Chap. 17.

35 The Report of the Child Adoption Committee Cmd. 2401 (1925), Cmd. 2469 (1926).

36 I. Pinchbeck & M. Hewitt, *Children in English Society*, Vol. 2, pp. 605-7 (1973). The lack of a legal framework which meant that children might be reclaimed when they reached working age, or that birth parents might be forced to take them away was thought to discourage adoption. The application of the welfare principle should theoretically have provided security but this was far from certain, see: *Re Thain* [1926] Ch. 676.

not replaced.[37] Over the next half century adoption law was repeatedly under scrutiny and a number of themes can be identified in three major reports on law and practice.[38] Adoption was developed from a private or amateur activity to form part of the child care service offered by local authorities and professional adoption agencies.[39] Increased emphasis was placed on protecting children—advertising was controlled,[40] children were fully integrated into adoptive families by the provision of inheritance rights,[41] and placements were supervised by local authorities.[42] The importance of identity was recognised and adopted adults were permitted access to their birth records and with it the possibility of tracing birth relatives.[43] Step-parent adoption which could distort family relationships was discouraged.[44] Adoption came to be seen as a method of providing homes for children (not merely legalising existing arrangements) and changes were made to facilitate this. The grounds for dispensing with agreement were expanded by legislation, the "freeing for adoption" process was devised so that the giving of agreement could be separated from placement[45] and provision was made for financial allowances for adopters.[46]

The character of adoption also changed markedly, particularly during the last quarter of the Twentieth Century.[47] Abortion, welfare benefits and the end of the stigma of single parenthood provided alternatives for birth parents so that very few babies were relinquished for adoption. Local authorities began to view adoption as an option for older children who could not return to their families

---

[37] Adoption of Children Act 1926, ss.2(3), 5(2); although there was a general power to dispense with consent it was interpreted narrowly, Cretney *op cit.* 194; attitudes to inheritance had delayed the introduction of adoption in England, see J. Triseliotis (1995) 2 *Adoption & Fostering* 37, 39.

[38] (a) Report of the Departmental Committee on Adoption Societies & Agencies Cmd. 5499 (1937) (Horsburgh Report) resulted in the Adoption of Children (Regulation) Act 1939; (b) Report of the Departmental Committee on the Adoption of Children Cmd. 9240 (1954) (Hurst Report) resulted in the Adoption Act 1958; (c) Report of the Departmental Committee on the Adoption of Children Cmnd. 5107 (1972) (Houghton Report) resulted in the Children Act 1975 and the law was then consolidated in the Adoption Act 1976 although parts of this were not implemented until the 1980s. For a general account, see C. Walby & B. Symons, *Who am I?* (1990), Chap. 1.

[39] Voluntary adoption societies pressed for the introduction of legal adoption but substantial numbers of placements were made directly by parents or by third parties, often doctors and vicars, see: Houghton Report, para. 81 *et seq.* Local authorities were permitted to arrange adoptions for children by the Adoption Act 1949, s.7(2) and required to provide an adoption service from 1988 by the Adoption Act 1976, s.1. The Children Act 1975 outlawed third party placements and required higher standards and some smaller agencies closed, see Adoption Agencies Regulations 1983, S.I. 1983 No. 1964.

[40] Adoption Act 1976, s.58; *cf.* advertisements by agencies have become an important method of finding families for hard to place children: P. Sawbridge, *Parents for Children* (BAAF, 1983), paper 2.

[41] Adoption of Children Act 1949, ss.9, 10; Children Act 1975, Sched. 1, para. 5.

[42] Adoption of Children Act 1949, s.5; Hurst Report, para 67. Step-parent adoptions were exempted from welfare supervision in the 1958 Act, s.3 until the recommendations of the Houghton Committee were implemented. Local authorities should supervise all non-agency cases; adoption agencies should supervise their own placements: para. 240.

[43] Houghton Committee, paras 303-6 and J. Triseliotis, *In search of origins* (1973); Adoption Act 1976, s.26.

[44] Houghton Committee, para.107; Children Act 1975, s.10(3); Adoption Act 1976, s.14(3) (repealed by Children Act 1989); J. Masson *et al.*, *Mine yours or ours?* (1983).

[45] Houghton Report, paras 173 *et seq.*; Children Act 1975, s.14; Adoption Act 1976, s.18.

[46] Houghton Report, para. 93; Adoption Act 1976, ss.57(4), 57A; Adoption Allowance Regulations 1991 (S.I. 1991 No. 2030).

[47] See N. Lowe in S. Katz *et al.* (eds) *Cross currents, op cit.*

after abuse, and increasingly these arrangements were made without the agreement of parents.[48] By the late 1980s, research and practice were showing the value of more open arrangements in adoption,[49] there was growing recognition of the need to involve birth parents in the adoption process[50] and the Contact Register was established to facilitate contact between adopted adults and their birth relatives.[51] The emphasis in the Children Act 1989 on local authorities working with families of looked after children conflicted with the idea of non-consensual adoption, the proportion of children adopted from care declined. But concern about the poor life chances of children brought up in care compared with those in secure families and the belief that it was possible to find more adoptive families for looked after children encouraged the promotion of adoption and created the impetus for reform.[52] In order to ensure the opportunity of family life for as many children as possible, less restrictive attitudes were needed to the selection of adopters, and adoption orders could not be restricted to married couples and single people.[53] It was also recognised that caring for children adopted from care placed extra demands on parents and that post adoption services could enhance the well-being of adopters, adopted people and birth parents, and help maintain placements.[54]

II. EFFECTS OF ADOPTION ORDERS

A. Adoption orders

23–005 The Adoption and Children Act 2002 defines an adoption order as an order giving parental responsibility for a child to the adopters.[55] Adoptive parents may make any decision which other parents may make, including emigrating and appointing a testamentary guardian[56]; they are not subject to supervision by the courts or any other agency. With one exception where a 'step-parent' adopts

---

[48] Parker (1999) *op cit*. Chap. 1.

[49] Review of Adoption Law (1992), Foreword.

[50] Review of Adoption Law (1992), para. 1.4.

[51] Children Act 1989, Sched. 10, para. 21; Adoption Act 1976, s.51A.

[52] Prime Minister's Review (2000) pp. 5–7 and annex 4; *Adoption: a new approach* (2000), Chap. 2; J. Selwyn and W. Sturgess, *International overview of adoption* (2000) and the polemics published by the Institute of Economic Affairs: P. Morgan, *Adoption and the care of children* (1998) and P. Morgan (ed.) *Adoption: the continuing debate* (1999).

[53] LAC (98)20, paras 43 *et seq*.; Select Committee on Adoption and Children Bill (2000–1 H.C. 431-ii) evidence of B.A.A.F. para. 9.1. and Hansard, *Commons*, May 16, 2002, Vol. 385, col. 976 *et seq*. Report; *Lords*, Vol. 639, col. 865, October, 18, 2002, Report; *Commons* Vol. 392, col. 24 *et seq*. November, 4, 2002 (Commons Consideration of Lords Amendments); *Lords* Vol. 641, col. 569 *et seq*. November 5, 2002 (Lords Consideration of of Commons Amendments) and below para. 23.019.

[54] LAC (98)20, para. 54; N. Lowe *et al*., *Supporting adoption* (1999); *Adoption: a new approach* (2000), Chap. 6 and Adoption and Children Act 2002, ss.3(3) and 4.

[55] s.46(1) re-enacting Adoption Act 1976, s.12(1) as amended by the Children Act 1989, Sched. 10, para. 3.

[56] Adoption and Children Act 2002, s.67; Children Act 1989, ss.3, 5.

their partner's child,[57] the making of an adoption order extinguishes the parental responsibility of any other person,[58] any order under the Children Act 1989 and any duty to pay maintenance except in so far as it relates to a period prior to the adoption.[59] The legislation states that an adopted child is to be treated as "the legitimate child of the adopter or adopters" and, where he or she is adopted by a couple,[60] "as the child of the relationship of the couple" and is not the child of any other person.[61] Unlike other orders relating to children, adoption does not cease to have effect when the child reaches age 18.

The consequences of adoption cannot be seen in purely legal terms. It is well recognised that adoption confers "an extra and psychologically and emotionally important sense of 'belonging'." It is said that there is a real benefit to the parent/child relationship in knowing that each is legally bound to the other and that the relationship is free from interference from outsiders.[62] This has justified allowing adoption without the agreement of the natural parents. However, adoption is not the only way of showing a child that a relationship is secure, nor will adoption necessarily ensure that a relationship is maintained with the adoptive parents.[63] Also, whereas it is possible to be objective about legal consequences the same cannot be said about emotional ones.

In three cases: succession rights, citizenship and the prohibited degrees of marriage, the general principles are modified by statutory rules.

1. Succession

23–006 Since 1950 an adopted child has lost any right to inherit on the intestacy of the birth parents but gained a corresponding right from the adoptive parents.[64] Adoption did not removed rights already vested in possession[65] but wills and deeds were interpreted to exclude adopted children from general gifts made before the adoption. The Children Act 1975 removed the restrictions on the succession rights of adopted children where deeds were made or deaths occurred on or after January 1, 1976.[66] Special rules are, however, required for cases where a gift

---

[57] Adoption and Children Act 2002, ss.51(2), 67(3)(b). Partner is defined in s.144(4)–(7) and includes a spouse or another person (of either sex) living with the parent in an enduring family relationship.

[58] s.46(3)(b).

[59] Adoption and Children Act 2002, s.46(2)(d) re-enacting Adoption Act 1976, s.12(2). A trust which expressly provides for continuance is unaffected: s.46(4) re-enacting s.12(4)

[60] Or by one of a couple who is the partner of the child's parent, ss.51(2), 67(2)(b).

[61] Adoption and Children Act 2002, s.67(1)–(3) re-enacting Adoption Act 1976, s.39 (with amendments to take account of adoption by partners).

[62] *Re H (Adoption Non-patrial)* [1996] 1 F.L.R. 717 at 726, *per* Holman J.

[63] Comprehensive statistics on adoption disruptions are not available but a study of 1500 placements found that 9% broke down before the order was made and another 8% subsequently see Parker (1999), *op cit.* p. 10.

[64] Adoption of Children Act 1949; Adoption and Children Act 2002, s.67(1)–(3) effectively re-enacting Adoption Act 1976, s.39(1).

[65] *Staffordshire County Council v. B* [1998] 1 F.L.R. 261 ChD (this includes an interest expectant on one vested in possession). Adoption and Children Act 2002, s.69(4) enacts this rule.

[66] Adoption Act 1976, ss.39, 42 introduced by the Children Act 1975, Sched. 1. The Adoption and Children Act 2002, s.69 and Sched. 4, para. 17 maintains this regime. It does not apply to peerages: s.71 re-enacting s.44(1). Twenty-three peers and 6 Baronets have adopted children: *Hansard*

depends upon the date of birth of an adopted person or seniority as against other children in the adoptive family. It is provided that where a disposition "depends on the date of birth" of a child, it has to be constructed as if (a) the adopted child had been born on the date of adoption, and (b) two or more children adopted on the same date had been born on that date in the order of their actual births.[67] Thus, if the will of a testator contains a gift "to the eldest son of X," and X had a natural child A born in 1980 and an adopted child B born in 1978 but adopted in 1981, A would take as the eldest child. However, these rules do not "affect any reference to the age of a child."[68] Thus, if the same testator gave his residuary estate "to the children of X at 25" B, the adopted child, would take in 2003 and not 25 years after the adoption. It also seems that B would benefit from a gift to "the first child of X to attain 25".[69]

2. Citizenship

23–007 The British Nationality Act 1981[70] provides that where an adoption order is made by a court in the United Kingdom in respect of a child who is not a British citizen, he or she acquires British citizenship from the date of the adoption if the adopter is a British citizen. British Nationality is also conferred on Convention adoptions that take place overseas provided that the adopters are habitually resident in the United Kingdom and at least one of them is a British citizen.[71] A child who has British Nationality does not cease to be entitled to it because of adoption by a foreigner.[72] The government and the courts have been concerned that adoption should not be used to evade immigration rules.

Children adopted overseas may enter for settlement if the adoption was due to the parents' inability to care for them, there has been a genuine transfer of parental responsibility and the adoption was not arranged to facilitate the child's entry to the United Kingdom.[73] Children are admitted *for* adoption at the discretion of the Home Secretary.[74] The Home Office must be notified of adoption

Commons Special Standing Committee on Adoption and Children Bill, 11th session, December 6, 2001,

[67] Adoption and Children Act 2002, s.69(2) re-enacting Adoption Act 1976, s.42(2).

[68] *ibid.*

[69] There are special rules applying to children who are adopted by one of their own parents as a sole adoptive parent: Adoption and Children Act 2002, s.67(4) re-enacting Adoption Act 1976, s.43.

[70] s.1(5).

[71] Adoption (Intercountry Aspects) Act 1999, s.7 amending British Nationality Act 1981, s.1(5). Under the Hague Convention on Intercountry Adoption, Art. 5 Convention adoptions may only take place if the Central Authorities of the receiving state have determined that the child will be free to enter and reside permanently in that state. In the case of other overseas adoptions by a British adopter application may be made for citizenship by registration under the Home Secretary's discretionary powers, British Nationality Act 1981, s.3(1).

[72] Adoption and Children Act 2002, s.74(2) the general principle in s.67 (Adoption Act 1976, s.39) does not apply for the purposes of the British Nationality Act 1981.

[73] Statement of changes in Immigration Rules (1994 H.C. 395), para. 314.

[74] Adoption applicants and those who have obtained a recognised adoption order overseas must apply for entry clearance before bringing the child to the U.K.: D.H. *Intercountry adoption guide* (2001), paras 5.10 *et seq.* Entry clearance is granted if the adoption application is likely to be granted. The local authority must notify the Home Office about any application to adopt a child from overseas where entry clearance was not obtained, para. 9D.

applications where citizenship may be in issue.[75] Despite Home Office concerns, general considerations about maintaining effective immigration controls are unlikely to justify refusing any adoption order that will confer real benefits on a child during childhood.[76]

3. Prohibited degrees

23–008 For the purposes of the prohibited degree of marriage, adoption does not destroy the prohibitions arising from birth to the child's natural parents.[77] If an adopted person (however innocently) marries a child of the natural parents, the marriage is void.[78] An adopted person and the adoptive parents are prohibited from marrying (even if the child is subsequently adopted by someone else)[79] but there are no further bars on marrying within the adoptive family. Hence an adopted child may legally marry a natural or adopted child of the adoptive family. This seems a curious exception to the principle that adoption integrates the child fully into the adoptive family. However, the approach to marriage between affines is now more liberal and it would be difficult to justify the imposition of the stricter rules which apply to consanguinity.[80]

Revocation

23–009 Adoption orders are irrevocable; where adoptive relationships breakdown[81] the parents retain parental responsibility unless and until a further adoption order is made.[82] It has been said that the edifice of adoption would be gravely shaken if adoption orders could be set aside.[83] This is clearly so if revocation could occur during childhood but the continued imposition of a legal identity on an adult may appear unjust:—

---

[75] D.H., *Intercountry adoption guide—practice and procedures* (2001), para. 5.17; *Re H (a minor) (adoption: non-patrial)* [1982] Fam. 121; *Re W (A Minor) (Adoption: Non-patrial)* [1986] Fam. 54.

[76] *Re B (Adoption Order: Nationality)* [1999] 1 F.L.R. 907 at p. 910 *per* Lord Hoffman; benefits occurring after the age of 18 can be considered: *Re D (Adoption Order: Validity)* [1991] Fam. 137 but will not be sufficient, at p. 911.

[77] Adoption and Children Act 2002, s.74(1) re-enacting Adoption Act 1976, s.47(1); a similar approach is taken to incest.

[78] The Registrar-General can verify relationships for an adopted person intending to marry: Adoption and Children Act 2002, s.79(7) re-enacting Adoption Act 1976, s.51(2).

[79] Marriage Act 1949, Sched. 1, Pt I as amended by the Children Act 1975, Sched. 3, para. 8.

[80] Houghton Report, paras 329–333; see also Marriage (Prohibited Degrees of Relationships) Act 1986. A new offence of familial sexual abuse has been proposed which would apply equally to adoptive and birth parents, and also between adoptive siblings under 18: H.O., *Setting the boundaries* (2000) para. 5.6.1–4. These recommendations have been included in the Sexual Offences Bill 2003, c1.30.

[81] The term 'disruptions' is given to such breakdowns whether they occur before or after the order has been made. There are no accurate statistics but see above n. 63 and N. Lowe *et al., Supporting adoption* (1999), Chap. 12.

[82] Adoption and Children Act 2002, s.46(5). Charges may be levied on the adoptive parents if the child becomes looked after by a local authority: Children Act 1989, Sched. 3, Pt III. Wardship may be used in an exceptional case: *Re O (Wardship: Adopted Child)* [1978] Fam. 196, CA, but this case should not be cited as a precedent *per* Ormerod L.J. at p. 205.

[83] *Re B (Adoption: Setting Aside)* [1995] 1 F.L.R. 1 at 7 *per* Sir Stephen Brown P.

> In *Re B (Adoption: Setting Aside)*[84] a baby whose mother was English Roman Catholic and whose father was a Kuwaiti Muslim was placed by the matron of a mother and baby home with a Jewish couple who were told that the baby's father was Jewish. When they discovered that the boy was not Jewish they arranged to have him admitted to the Jewish faith. The boy was brought up as Jewish and later emigrated to Israel. There he was assumed because of his appearance to be an Arab; and he was forced to leave. He made inquiries about his origin and wanted to have the adoption order revoked so that he could take on a Arab identity and be accepted in Kuwait. His application and his appeal were refused.

Exceptionally, an adoption order may be annulled on appeal; where a father agreed to a step-parent adoption in ignorance of his wife's fatal illness the court was prepared to allow an appeal outside the time limit and return the children to his care.[85] Also where there was a "plethora of irregularities going to the heart of the adoption process" an intercountry adoption was set aside but the child remained with the family under wardship.[86] A child may also be able to re-establish a legal link with a natural parent or other member of the birth family by applying for a residence order in their favour.[87]

B. Registration of adoption

23–010 The Registrar General maintains an Adopted Children Register; the index to this like the index to the Register of Births is open to public search.[88] On adoption the child's birth certificate is replaced with a certified copy of the entry in the Register[89]; this gives the child's names (normally with the adoptive parents' surname) and is sufficient evidence of date and place of birth.[90] A short form of birth certificate giving the child's name and date of birth may be issued. Where this is used, no one, including the child, can see that the child is adopted.[91] The small number of adoptions each year means that it might be possible for a parent to discover the child's new name by identifying the entry in the Adopted Children Register and thus to trace the child. The court may not prevent an adoption being included on the register but under its inherent jurisdiction, could restrict

---

[84] [1995] 1 F.L.R. 1, FD; [1995] 2 F.L.R. 1, CA.

[85] *Re M (Minors) (Adoption)* [1991] 1 F.L.R. 458. It was accepted that the father gave his agreement by mistake.

[86] *Re K (Adoption and Wardship)* [1997] 2 F.L.R. 221 CA.

[87] *Re T (A Minor) (Wardship: Representation)* [1994] Fam. 49 and above, para. 17.017. In theory this option is also available to a parent and could be appropriate if the adoption failed.

[88] The register itself is not open to search, Adoption and Children Act 2002, s.77(2), 79(2) re-enacting Adoption Act 1976, s.50(1), (3).

[89] Adoption and Children Act 2002, Sched. 1, para. 1 re-enacting Adoption Act 1976, Sched. 1, para. 1. Provision is also made for entries in relation to registrable foreign adoptions, para. 3.

[90] Adoption and Children Act 2002, s.77(4)(5) re-enacting Adoption Act 1976, s.50(2).

[91] Births and Deaths Registration Act 1953, s.33; Registration of Births and Deaths Regulations 1987, S.I 1987 No. 2088, reg. 64 and Form 21.

the Registrar General from providing a copy of the adoption certificate whilst the child is under 18.[92]

C. Access to birth and adoption records[93]

23–011 The Registrar General is required to keep records so that it is possible to trace the original birth registration of an adopted person,[94] but until November 26, 1976 a person adopted in England or Wales[95] had no right to this information. Following a recommendation of the Houghton Committee[96] which recognised that some adopted people wished to know more about their background, provision was made for adopted adults to obtain access to the original birth certificate. Because of concerns for natural mothers who had been promised confidentiality when they relinquished their babies,[97] those adopted before the Children Act 1975 were required to undergo counselling before obtaining this.[98] The numbers of adoptees who have received their records has greatly exceeded expectations; it is estimated that a third of all adopters will do so at some time in their lives.[99]The Act provided no absolute right to birth records information; the Registrar General could refuse it if there are public policy reasons[1]:—

> In *R. v. Registrar General, ex p. Smith*,[2] Smith, the adopted person, was detained in Broadmoor following his convictions for murder of a stranger and manslaughter of a cell-mate. He was thought to suffer from psychiatric illness and had extreme hatred for his adoptive parents. He applied for a copy of his original birth certificate, but after receiving medical advice that his mother might be in danger if he were released, the Registrar-General

---

[92] *Re X (A Minor) (Adoption)* [1994] 2 F.L.R. 450 CA; *President's Direction* [1999] 1 F.L.R. 315. For adoptions made after the implementation of the 2002 Act access to birth records is via the adoption agency or local authority, ss.60, 79; any order preventing disclosure would in the future have to be against the agency.

[93] Leaflets about access to birth records under the 1976 Act scheme have been prepared by the Department of Health for adopted people and counsellors: Leaflets ACR 100, ACR 101 (for people living outside the U.K.), ACR 113. They are reproduced in *Guidance* Vol. 9, annex B. This scheme is preserved for adoptions before the "appointed day" in the 2002 Act by Adoption and Children Act 2002, Sched. 2.

[94] Adoption and Children Act 2002, s.79 re-enacting Adoption Act 1976, s.50(4).

[95] Children Act 1975, s.26; Scottish law permitted access to birth records at age 17. See now Adoption (Scotland) Act 1978, s.45(5). Research into the operation of the Scottish system convinced the Houghton Committee that access could be permitted: see J. Triseliotis, *In Search of Origins* (1973).

[96] Houghton Report, para. 303 and recommendation 77.

[97] See E. Haimes & N. Timms, *Adoption, identity & social policy* (1985), pp. 17–18.

[98] Adoption Act 1976, s.51(7); but a person who knew their original name could obtain their birth certificate in the normal way. From 1991 provision was made for counselling overseas: s.51(8). D.H. leaflet ACR 114 lists organisations in Australia, Canada, New Zealand and South Africa which provide counselling. Counselling was voluntary for other adopted people. The need for counselling was graphically portrayed in the film *Secrets and Lies* (1995).

[99] R. Rushbrooke, *Population Trends* 104 (2001), p. 31. This does not include those adoptees who obtained records without using s.51.

[1] *R. v. Registrar-General, ex p. Smith* [1991] 2 Q.B. 393, CA. The High Court has the power to order non-disclosure on the application of the adoption agency, s.60(2)(a),(3).

[2] [1991] 2 Q.B. 393, CA.

refused to provide it. Smith sought judicial review of the decision but the refusal was upheld and his appeal refused.

The birth certificate provides little information but the full names of the mother, and sometimes the father, often make it possible to trace them. Detailed information about the adoption is held by the agency, the local authority which supervised the placement and the court[3] and might be released. Adopted adults could apply to the court for the name of the agency that arranged their placement and the local authority which supervised it.[4] Adoption agencies had discretion to disclose information from adoption records but practice varied widely.[5] These provisions were not only used by adopted people, some birth relatives, particularly mothers sought assistance in to find out how their (adult) children were faring. Intermediary services were established by some voluntary organisations, via these it was possible for some birth relatives to obtain information and even initiate contact. Provision was also made for other people to apply to the court for an order permitting the disclosure of information from the register.[6] Orders were only granted if the applicant could establish truly exceptional circumstances,[7] for example, to allow medical information to be passed to someone who might have inherited a genetic disorder or to allow a reunion between elderly siblings adopted separately.

23–012 The White paper acknowledged the right of all adopted people to information about their family history and proposed that access to specific material in adoption records should be covered in the legislation.[8] However, when the Adoption and Children Bill was introduced it provided a restrictive scheme for access to information based on "data protection philosophy and human rights" which precluded the disclosure of identifying information, including the birth certificate, without consent.[9] These proposals caused consternation amongst adoption agencies who considered that adopted people had a right to know their birth

---

[3] Adoption Rules 1984, r. 53(4). This power was provided to enable adopted people to make inheritance claims where adoption did not end these rights in the natural family: Haimes and Timms, p. 13.

[4] Adoption Act 1976, s.50(5); Adoption Rules 1984 (S.I. 1984 No. 265), r. 53(3)(b)(ii).

[5] Adoption Agencies Regulations 1983, reg. 15(2); LAC (84) 3; the discretion must be exercised reasonably: *Gunn-Russo v. Nugent Care Society* [2002] 1 F.L.R. 1 Q.B.D. (a general refusal to disclose over 50 years after the adoption without considering documents individually was unreasonable). D.H., *Draft Adoption Standards—adopted adults and their birth siblings* (2001) states "Agencies will advise and help adopted adults and their birth siblings separated by adoption who wish to initiate communication. . ." G3; Agencies should have policies on information sharing, para. 13; see also *D v. Registrar General* [1996] 1 F.L.R. 707, where Westminster City Council's policy of refusing information led the applicant to seek an order.

[6] Adoption Act 1976, s.50(5); applications are rare—only 1 or 2 a year: D. Howe and J. Feast, *Adoption, search and reunion* (2000) p. 9.

[7] *D v. Registrar General* [1997] 1 F.L.R. 715 CA birth mother's application refused because there was no benefit to the adopted person overruling *Re H (Adoption: Disclosure of Information)* [1995] 1 F.L.R. 236 (information disclosed where sibling had genetic disorder). Some Adoption Agencies were less restrictive in their attitude to providing information: Clarke Hall and Morrison 2, 3 para. 302.

[8] Cm. 5017, paras 6.44 *et seq.*; *Prime Minister's Review* (2000) paras 3.136 *et seq.* and p. 50.

[9] Adoption and Children Bill, cl. 53–60 and Chap. 5, Special Standing Committee 2nd sitting, Memorandum of the Department of Health and oral evidence of James Paton, Department of Health.

identity and were not convinced that the existing scheme for access posed risks for birth parents, even in the context of adoption of abused children.[10] The government put forward major amendments to meet their objections. From the implementation of the new Act, adopted adults will be able to obtain details from the adoption agency in order to access their original birth certificate, and they will have the right to copies of specific documents from the court which made the order.[11] In exceptional circumstances, where the agency wishes to withhold identifying information it can seek an order from the High Court.[12] In other circumstances, where disclosure of "protected information" is sought, the agency will have discretion to withhold it and must take reasonable steps to obtain the views of the person concerned, and in the case of information about a child, their parents.[13] Agencies will also be required to keep specific information about adoptions, to disclose it to adopters and adopted adults, and may disclose any non-identifying information in the course of their work, for example, during post-adoption counselling.[14] Regulations will set out when agencies must offer or provide counselling and there will be further direction of disclosure through the Adoption Standards and practice guidance.[15]

The adoption contact register

23–013 Until 1991 there was no official way for birth relatives to signal their interest in contact from those who had been adopted although assistance was provided by NORCAP (the National Organisation for Counselling Adoptees and Parents). NORCAP established a register for this purpose, an intermediary service to facilitate exchange of information or contact, and support groups. It also campaigned for better services for birth relatives.[16] The Children Act 1989 required the Registrar General to maintain an Adoption Contact Register.[17] This provides a safe and confidential way for birth parents and other relations to assure an adopted person that contact would be welcome and give a current address. A person adopted in England or Wales who has sufficient details about their birth,

[10] Memorandum and oral evidence of BAAF, 2nd sitting; Memorandum from NORCAP, 4th sitting; 18th sitting, col. 689 *et seq.*

[11] Adoption and Children Act 2002, s.60(4). The documents will be prescribed by regulations and may be limited to a copy of the order.

[12] s.60(3). The adopted person will also be entitled to specific information which the agency was required to provide for the adopters, s.60(2)(b).

[13] ss.61, 62. Protected information is information which is or includes identifying information, s.57(1)–(3). The child's welfare is the paramount consideration in deciding whether to proceed with an application for disclosure, s.62(6). Where disclosure is agreed at adoption, for example where a mother leaves a letter for an adopted child to receive at age 18 or in the event of her death, the agency will not need to carry out these checks, s.57(5).

[14] Adoption and Children Act 2002, ss.56, 58. Regulations will prescribe circumstances when and to whom information must be disclosed.

[15] ss.63, 64; D.H., *Draft Standards: adopted adults and their birth siblings* (2001); D.H., *Intermediary services for birth relatives: practice guidance* (2000).

[16] The powerlessness of birth mothers and the sense of loss they experience is graphically described in D. Howe *et al.*, *Half a million women* (1992).

[17] Adoption Act 1976, s.51A added by the Children Act 1989, s.88 and Sched. 10, para. 21; *Guidance* Vol. 9, annex B. and D.H. Leaflet ACR 110, para. 2; Adoption and Children Act 2002, s.80. See also, A. Mullender and S. Kearn, *I'm here waiting* (1997) the researchers were critical of the impersonal service and the lack of publicity for the Adoption Contact Register.

may register their wish to contact relatives.[18] Relatives who know the details of an adopted person's birth may also register.[19] A fee is charged for this service.[20] Where there is a match the Registrar General gives the adopted person the relative's name and address but no information can be provided to any relative.[21] In the first 10 years of this service 20,000 adoptees and 8,500 relatives registered but only just over 500 matches were made.[22] Far more people establish contact in other ways, most who do so, or who are contacted are positive about the experience although not all relationships are maintained.[23] The Review of Adoption Law recommended that the Register be extended to allow birth parents and relatives to indicate their wish not to be contacted[24]; this was not included in the Adoption and Children Bill 2002. By restricting access to birth records, the original Bill would have allowed birth parents to prevent an adopted person using the Contact Register.

These provisions operate within a context where there is now considerable openness with exchange of information (usually via the adoption agency) and even contact between the birth family and the adopters before and after the adoption order has been made. The statutory regime thus represents the minimum access to information for those affected by domestic adoptions in England and Wales. Far less information may be available for those involved in adoption at earlier times but special provision has been made in the 2002 Act following a sustained campaign from NORCAP.[25] It criticised the limited assistance available to those who wished to make contact with adult relatives who had been adopted as children and campaigned to place (licensed) intermediary services on a statutory footing with rights to access information to assist such people. The government was unwilling to impose a duty on adoption agencies to provide intermediary services because this might draw resources from their main work of making placements. However, it finally accepted a scheme which will allow registered adoption support agencies to act as intermediaries and obtain information from the Registrar General, adoption agencies and the courts.[26] Where a person was adopted through an adoption agency the intermediary will be able to establish the name of the agency from the Registrar General and then

---

[18] Adoption and Children Act 2002, s.80(2) re-enacting Adoption Act 1976, s.51A(4).

[19] Adoption and Children Act 2002, s.80(5) re-enacting Adoption Act 1976, s.51A(6): relatives need to know enough to obtain a birth certificate of the person who has been adopted.

[20] s.80(6) and Adopter Persons (Contact Register) (Fees) Rules 1991 (S.I. 1991 No. 952).

[21] Adoption and Children Act 2002, ss.80(6)(a), 81(3) re-enacting Adoption Act 1976, s.51A(9), (11).

[22] J. Haskey, *Population Trends* 106, 15, 16 see also J. Haskey and R. Errington, *Population Trends* 104, 18. By contrast, the NORCAP register contains 50,000 entries and has made 750 links in 19 years.

[23] Howe and Feast (2000) *op cit*.

[24] Review of Adoption Law (1992), para. 31.5; this was accepted in Cm. 2288, para. 4.22—see draft Adoption Bill 1996, cl. 65(2).

[25] NORCAP, Memorandum submitted to Select Committee on Adoption and Children Bill, para. 2.14 *et seq*., Commons Committee, 4th Sitting, November 21, 2001; Lords Report, Vol. 639, cols 935–938 October, 18, 2002; Commons Consideration of Lords Amendments, Vol. 392, cols 102–3.

[26] Adoption and Children Act 2002, s.98. The Minister stated that the government intended to consult adoption stakeholders on the detail of the regulations, Hansard, *Commons*, November 4, 2002, Vol. 392, col. 102.

approach the agency for further information; in non-agency cases information may be available from the local authority or the court.[27] Regulations will preclude the intermediary disclosing information without the informed consent of the adopted adult.[28] However, direct discussion between the intermediary and the adopted person may facilitate the passing of information, even where he or she does not want contact.

Information is also limited in many international adoptions. Where children have been abandoned, their date of birth and parents' identities may be unknown; some countries protect mothers from identification because of the stigma of giving birth outside marriage. Even where identifying details are collected, records may be sealed preventing any disclosure of, for example, the original birth certificate. The Hague Convention requires the competent authorities in each State to preserve any information they hold about the child's or parent's identity. Access to this is generally determined by the law of the State holding the information but there can be no disclosure of the identity of the birth parents unless this is permitted in the State of origin.[29]

III. PROVISION OF ADOPTION SERVICES

23–014 Adoption is strictly regulated in England and Wales; only local authorities and registered adoption societies can run adoption agencies and arrangements for adoption can only made by adoption agencies or by a person acting under a High Court order.[30] The provision of adoption support services is also regulated.[31] The formalisation of adoption always requires a court order.[32] There are restrictions on who may adopt but the main responsibility for determining the suitability of prospective adopters falls on adoption agencies.

A. Organisation of Adoption Services

Local authority responsibilities

23–015 The Adoption and Children Act 2002, s. 3 requires each local authority to maintain an Adoption Service, to make arrangements for adoption and to provide adoption support services in conjunction with their other services and local adoption societies. Local authorities must prepare and publish a plan for the provision

---

27 Adoption and Children Act 2002, ss.64(4), 65(1), 98(2), (3).

28 Hansard, *Commons*, November 4, 2002, Vol. 391, col. 102, Jacqui Smith, Minister of State, Department of Health.

29 Hague Adoption Convention, Arts 16(2), 30. Preserving information allows for access should the law be relaxed in future.

30 Adoption and Children Act 2002, s.92(1). It is a criminal offence for other persons to undertake certain steps in connection with adoption, s.93(1).

31 Adoption and Children Act 2002, s.8; Care Standards Act 2000, s.4(7A).

32 But adoptions made in specific overseas jurisdictions are valid without further proceedings in England and Wales, see below, paras 23.048 and 23.049.

of adoption services.[33] Although these services are under local control they are subject to considerable direction by the Secretary of State, through regulations and guidance, including the National Adoption Standards. The Department of Health monitors local authority adoption activity to ensure that targets are met, and has established the Adoption and Permanence Taskforce to assist local authorities to develop services. The National Care Standards Commission has responsibility for inspecting local authority adoption services.[34] In Wales, adoption policy is a matter for the Welsh Assembly.

In relation to individual children it looks after, a local authority must consider whether to make an adoption plan, and if it does, obtain parental consent or apply for a placement order.[35] It must consider whether to approve prospective adopters and to make placements with them. It must also assess needs for adoption support services and decide whether to provide them.[36]

Adoption societies

23–016 Voluntary organisations can operate as adoption agencies if they are registered with the National Care Standards Commission.[37] They must comply with detailed regulations about their management, financial position, practice (including record keeping), and with National Standards.[38] Adoption societies work alongside local authorities and may facilitate the adoption of looked after children by undertaking assessments and identifying suitable adopters. The National Adoption Register is run by an adoption society.

Adoption agencies are required to operate adoption panels which include members independent of the agency to consider adoption plans, the approval of prospective adopters and the matching of children with them.[39] Agencies can make decisions only after taking into account the recommendations of the panel.[40]

B. The role of the court

23–017 The courts play a vital role in dealing with adoption.[41] They ensure that all the parties to an adoption are listened to and treated fairly before orders are made, they consider whether plans for adoption are in the best interests of children, approve such plans in care or placement order proceedings, and make adoption

---

[33] s.5.

[34] Care Standards Act 2000, Pt 2. This body will apply the National Minimum Standards for Adoption when inspecting services.

[35] s.22 and see para. 23.041, below.

[36] s.4, and para. 23.022, below.

[37] s.2. For profit organisations may not be registered as adoption societies but can be registered as Adoption Support Agencies: Adoption and Children Act 2002, s.8(1).

[38] Regulations made under Adoption and Children Act 2002, ss.9 and 10. Adoption Agencies are currently subject to the Adoption Agencies Regulations 1983; S.I. 1983 No. 1964.

[39] Adoption Agencies Regulations 1983, S.I. 1983 No. 1964 regs 5, 5A. New regulations will be issued. For details of the panel system and proposals for change see: D.H., *Adopter preparation and assessment and the operation of adoption panels: a fundamental review* (2002).

[40] reg. 11.

[41] Cm. 5017, para. 8.1.

orders. Officers from CAFCASS have responsibility to ensure that those consenting to adoption understand the effects of their actions, they represent children where they are parties to the proceedings and provide welfare reports.[42] Although the Prime Minister's Review questioned whether court proceedings were necessary for straightforward adoptions, the White Paper accepted that it was extremely difficult to identify such adoptions, and that the significance of adoption justified the involvement of the courts.[43] Adoption involves both judicial functions such as determining disputes about welfare, consent and contact, and the conferring of the new status on the adopters and child.[44]

All three levels of court have jurisdiction in adoption. Court rules require applications which discharge care orders to be made to the court which made that order[45] but allow transfer to the level of court appropriate to the case. The majority of adoption orders are made in county courts. Concerns about delay and inefficiency led the President of the Family Division to issue guidance to increase specialism in the higher courts and to ensure active management of adoption cases.[46] Specific county courts have been designated as Adoption Centres[47]; only designated adoption judges can make county court adoption orders. However, the family proceedings court retains jurisdiction in adoption and charges lower fees.

C. Eligibility and suitability of adopters

23–018 No one has the right to adopt[48]; adoption law sets out eligibility rules for adopters and, where an adoption agency is involved,[49] the applicants must also satisfy it of their suitability. As part of the compromise reached to allow adoption by unmarried and same-sex couples, provision was made for regulations to limit agency discretion in determining the suitability of prospective adopters.[50]

Eligibility

23–019 The Adoption and Children Act 2002 lays down the following rules (and conditions about domicile or habitual residence which are beyond the scope of this book[51]:—

---

42 This will be provided by the rules, s.100(3); for the position before the implementation of the 2002 Act see: Adoption Rules 1984, rr. 5, 6, 17 and 18.

43 PIU Report (2000), paras 4.14 and 7.21; Cm. 5017, para. 8.32.

44 The final hearing may end with "an adoption ceremony".

45 Children (Allocation of Proceedings) Order 1991, S.I. 1991 No. 1677, art. 14.

46 *President's Direction, Adoption proceedings—a new approach* (2001). Despite some confusion it remains possible for the judge hearing care proceedings to make an order freeing the child for adoption.

47 County court adoption proceedings should be made in or transferred to such courts, *President's Direction* (2001), p. 2.

48 Jacqui Smith, Minister of State, Department of Health, Hansard *Commons* Vol. 392, col. 96 (Commons Consideration of Lords Amendments, November 4, 2002).

49 This includes all agency placements and intercountry adoptions where the official procedures are followed, but not "in family" adoptions, see below para. 23.047.

50 Adoption and Children Act 2002, s.45.

51 Adoption and Children Act, s.49(2)(3). For an explanation, see Cheshire and North's *Private International Law* (13th ed., 1999), p. 134 *et seq*.

(i) An adoptive parent must be at least 21 years of age (a parent adopting his or her own child with their partner need only be 18 years of age).[52]

(ii) If a couple wish to adopt jointly they must either be married or "living as partners in an enduring family relationship."[53]

(iii) Single people may adopt[54]; if a sole applicant is married an order can only be made if the court is satisfied that his or her spouse cannot be found, or is incapable by reason of ill-health of applying, or that the spouses have separated and the separation is likely to be permanent.[55]

(iv) In addition, regulations preclude an adoption agency placing any child for adoption or fostering in a household where any person over the age of 18 has been convicted or cautioned for a specified offence.[56]

Adoption has always been open to both married couples and single people, but only one member of an unmarried couple could become an adoptive parent, their partner could obtain a more limited legal relationship with the adopted child by a residence order.[57] When originally introduced to Parliament the Adoption and Children Bill retained the requirement of marriage for adoption by couples although it allowed for special guardianship orders in favour of unmarried couples.[58] Child welfare organisations expressed concerns that allowing adoption by one member of a couple was confusing for children, off-putting for prospective adopters and would make it more difficult to recruit the additional adopters needed.[59] Nevertheless, the Government took the view that unmarried couples should not be permitted to adopt until a status had been devised which would provide a formal legal relationship.[60] However, an amendment was accepted by the Commons to permit adoption by unmarried couples.[61] This proved very contentious not least because it allowed adoption by same-sex couples. The supporters accepted that this was a natural development from adoption by single people living in relationships; that an adoptive family was better for a child than growing up in state care; and that children should have a parental

---

52 Adoption and Children Act 2002, s.50.

53 Adoption and Children Act 2002, s.144(4). A joint adoption order may be made in favour of a separated married couple: *Re WM (Adoption: Non-patrial)* [1997] 1 F.L.R. 132, FD and where the unmarried partner of a parent applies to adopt alone their relationship with the parent need not be "enduring".

54 For a review of such adoptions see, M. Owen, *Novices, old hands and professionals: adoption by single people* (1999).

55 Adoption and Children Act 2002, s.51(3).

56 Adoption Agencies Regulations 1983, (S.I. 1983 No 1964) reg. 8A and Sched. 2. added by the Children (Protection from Offenders)(Miscellaneous Amendments) Regulations 1997 (S.I. 1997 No. 2308), see D.H. Circular LAC(97)17 and C. Smith [2000] *J.S.W.F.L.* 367. These provisions were introduced following the conviction of Roger Saint for serious offences against children.

57 Children Act 1989, s.8; *Re W (Adoption: Homosexual Adopter)* [1997] 2 F.L.R. 406 FD; *Re T, Petitioner* [1997] SLT 724, Ct of Sess. (IH).

58 Children Act 1989, ss.14A–14G added by Adoption and Children Act 2002.

59 See for example, memorandum from BAAF, Special Standing Committee on Adoption and Children Bill, November 20, 2001. Only 1 of the 30 organisations submitting evidence supported retention of the marriage requirement.

60 There were two Private Member's Bills before Parliament to establish such a relationship but it was clear that neither would be enacted during the 2001–2 session.

61 At Report Stage, Hansard, *Commons* Vol. 385, cols 976–1007, (May 16, 2002) amendment tabled by David Hinchliffe, M.P.

relationship with both parties. The objectors stressed the vulnerability of adopted children and the instability of relationships outside marriage; children's need for two parents of opposite sexes; and the possibility of increasing the pool of prospective adopters in other ways. The Lords rejected the amendment, a further amendment which would have allowed adoption by unmarried, heterosexual couples was not moved.[62] The Joint Committee on Human Rights concluded that the Bill as amended by the Lords was not compatible with human rights.[63] The amendment was re-introduced in the Commons with government support and passed again.[64] A further attempt in the Lords to restrict adoption was unsuccessful.[65] Under the Adoption and Children Act 2002 both members of an unmarried or same-sex couple may become joint adoptive parents.[66]

Suitability

23–020 Adopter assessment is designed to safeguard the children involved[67] but prospective adopters have some rights, they must be given clear information about adoption and treated fairly, openly and with respect.[68] Adoption agencies recruit prospective adopters, develop their understanding of adoption through individual and group activities and assess their suitability to adopt.[69] A detailed report must be prepared for the agency's adoption panel[70] which makes recommendations about approval. The agency decides whether to approve but must take the panel's recommendation into account.[71] Approximately 95 per cent of applicants

---

[62] By Lord Jenkins of Roding see Hansard, *Lords* Vol. 639, col. 910 (Report Stage, October 18, 2002).

[63] Joint Committee on Human Rights, *24th Report*, 2002. In its 9th Report (HC 475) the Committee had found that the original Bill was compatible but the decisions of the European Court of Human Rights in *Frette v. France* App. No. 36515/97 and of the South African Constitutional Court in *Du Toit and de Vos v. Minister for Population Development and others*, judgment September 10, 2002 led the Committee to reconsider. Given the practice of permitting adoption by one member of a homosexual couple, restricting adoption by unmarried couples was likely to breach the Art. 8 rights of both children and prospective adopters when taken with Art. 14.

[64] Despite a three-line whip imposed on Conservative Members, Hansard, *Commons*, Vol. 392, cols 24–99, Commons Consideration of Lords Amendments, November 4, 2002.

[65] Hansard, *Lords*, Vol. 641, cols 569–624, Lords Consideration of Commons Amendments, November 5, 2002.

[66] It seems likely that some adoptions will be delayed pending the implementation of this provision and that some families will seek re-adoption so that the child can have a relationship with both adults. There is no simplified system for such adoptions. The U.K. must abrogate the European Convention on Adoption which limits joint adoption to married couples.

[67] D.H., *Adopter preparation and assessment and the operation of adoption panels: a fundamental review* (October 2002), Foreword.

[68] D.H., *National Adoption Standards for England* (2001) Standards B 1–7.

[69] This assessment is frequently referred to as "the home study" and covers details of the applicants' relationship, their health, life-style etc., and personal references. The Department of Health is considering issuing guidance about the issues to be explored in adopter assessment: D.H., *Adopter preparation and assessment and the operation of adoption panels: a fundamental review* (2002). Adoption and Children Act 2002, s.45 provides for the regulation of agency decisions about the suitability of prospective adopters.

[70] The applicants should be given the report at least 28 days before the meeting and allowed to comment on it, and to attend the panel meeting, *National Adoption Standards for England* (2001), Standard B6. The Adoption Agencies Regulations 1983, reg. 11 only requires such notification and representations where the agency proposes not to approve the applicants.

[71] Adoption Agencies Regulations 1983, regs 8, 10(1)(b) and 11A.

put to panel are approved but some others withdraw or are counselled out before a formal report is made.

Following a commitment in the White Paper intended to increase prospective adopters' confidence in agency decisions,[72] the 2002 Act established a new system of review. "Qualifying determinations", for example decisions about the suitability of applicants, will be subject to independent review under a mechanism to be established by regulations.[73] Complaints may be made to local authorities in respect of other decisions[74]; judicial review remains an option only where these systems fail to correct untenable decisions or faulty procedure.[75]

Matching

23–021 Once applicants have been approved the agency considers whether there are children waiting for adoption locally who might be a suitable match. The applicants are given brief details of such children. If the applicants wish to proceed the adoption panel considers the match and makes a recommendation. After the agency decision-maker has approved the match the placement can be made.[76] Prospective applicants should be provided with more information about the child at each stage of the process so that they can decide whether to proceed.[77] Before the child is placed the applicants should be provided with a full report of the child's history, needs, health and other matters relevant to his or her care. A local authority which fails to disclose information may be liable to the adopters for losses suffered because of this:—

> In *A and B v. Essex County Council*[78] the local authority placed a boy with the adopters without informing them that his experienced foster carers considered him to have an "enormous behaviour problem . . . an uncontrollable, vicious child" and that a child psychiatrist had recommended child guidance and 24 hour supervision. The court accepted that the adopters would not have proceeded with the placement had they known this. They boy damaged the adopters' home, caused them much distress and led to them suffering psychiatric illness. The court held that the local authority was liable for the damage experienced before the order was finalised but not subsequently.[79] The damage suffered subsequently was not due to the local authority's failure to provide information—even if the adopters had

---

[72] 2000 Cm. 5107, para. 6.23.

[73] Adoption and Children Act 2002, s.12. This will replace the second hearing by the panel provided in the Adoption Agencies Regulations 1983.

[74] Children Act 1989, s.26(3B) (added by Adoption and Children Act 2002, s.117, and above, para. 22.071.

[75] see above, paras 22.074–075.

[76] Adoption Agencies Regulation 1983, regs 10–11A, similar provision can be expected in the new regulations.

[77] Jacqui Smith, Minister of State, Department of Health, Special Standing Committee 14th Session, December 18, 2002, col. 720 *et seq.* Details of the required information will be set out in regulations made under s.9 The Adoption Agencies Regulations 1983, regs 12 and 13A require information to be provided before placement and after the order has been made.

[78] [2002] EWHC 2709 (QB).

[79] The court relied on the decision in *Phelps v. Hillingdon L.B.C.* [2001] 2 A.C. 619.

been given further information after the placement, their commitment to the child was such that they would probably have proceeded with the placement. The boy was accommodated by the local authority.

D. Adoption Support

23–022 Originally adoption was viewed as creating relationships which could replace and mirror birth relationships. While placements largely concerned healthy babies, it was natural to expect adopters to take full responsibility and manage without further support. However, changes in understanding about adoption and in adoption practice, particularly the wish to secure permanent homes for children with special needs and sibling groups, led to a questioning of this approach and recognition of the importance of supporting adoption.[80] The task of adoptive parenting has become more complex with the placement of children with special needs and the maintenance of links with birth relations, support may be required by adopters and children after the adoption order had been made. Without support carers may be unwilling to adopt; unsupported adopters may be unable to cope putting placements at risk of breakdown. Support for adoption may be financial or practical, enabling the adopters to purchase additional services they think their family needs or providing assistance that they agency considers appropriate.

The Houghton Committee recommended the introduction of adoption allowances and the availability of social work support for those who sought access to their birth records.[81] The Adoption Act 1976 placed a duty on local authorities to establish an adoption service designed to meet the needs of (amongst others) "children who have been adopted" and "persons who have adopted"[82]; it thus provided the legal framework for post-adoption services.[83] However there was little guidance about what post-adoption services should be provided; provision of services was patchy.[84] There was considerable opposition to providing adopters with allowances that were not available to birth parents, but pilot schemes were introduced under the Adoption Act 1976 and, following an amendment in the Children Act 1989, a general scheme was introduced.[85] Agencies were permitted to pay an allowance in circumstances set out in regulations where adoption was not otherwise practicable.[86] The system was inflexible; allowances could not be paid where difficulties arose only after the adoption. There were wide variations in the information provided to prospective adopters about finan-

---

[80] For a comprehensive discussion of this development see: N. Lowe *et al.*, *Supporting adoption reframing the approach* (1999) and N. Lowe, "The changing face of adoption—the gift/donation model versus the contract/services model" [1997] *C.F.L.Q.* 371.

[81] 1972 Cmnd. 5107, paras 93–95 and recommendation 17, para. 304.

[82] Adoption Act 1976, s.1.

[83] See Lowe *et al.* (1999), p. 32.

[84] Lowe *et al.* (1999), p. 34 quoting *Inter-departmental Review of Adoption, Discussion Paper 3* (1990).

[85] Adoption Act 1976, s.57; Children Act 1989, s.88 and Sched 10, para. 25 adding Adoption Act 1976, s.57A and Adoption Allowances Regulations 1991, S.I. 1991 No. 2030.

[86] For example, where it was desirable to place a child with siblings or the child needed special care which required greater expenditure, reg. 2.

cial support, the willingness of agencies to pay, the assessment of means, and the amounts paid.[87]

Research on adoption in the 1990s highlighted the challenges faced by adopters, identified substantial unmet support needs during and after the adoption process, and revealed wide variation between authorities in the practical and financial support provided.[88] Despite government encouragement, many local authorities confined their post adoption services to provision of allowances and counselling.[89] Lowe and colleagues argued that agency mindset in providing services had failed to keep pace with the changes in adoption and stressed that adoption should not be regarded as ending the state's obligations to looked after children. There should be explicit duties to provide post adoption support and agencies should make agreements with adopters and children about support.[90] The Prime Minister's Review considered that the lack of consistent support acted as a disincentive to local authorities placing children for adoption outside their area and contributed to delay and drift. In order to improve the success of adoptive placements, the government promised "to support a better deal for adopters" by giving all adoptive families a right to an assessment for post adoption support services and imposing a clear duty on local authority social services departments to provide post adoption support.[91] The term "adoption support" is now used to include services concerned with adoption both before and after the adoption is finalised.[92]

23–023 The new scheme for adoption allowances is being implemented from April 2003.[93] The National Adoption Standards for England require local authorities to provide or commission a comprehensive range of adoption services. Details of the required services will be set out in regulations[94] and supported by practice guidance.[95] The Adoption and Children Act imposes a duty on local authorities to make and participate in arrangements for the provision of adoption support services.[96] It gives specific persons[97] the right to request an assessment of their needs for adoption support,[98] but does not require the local authority to ensure that needs are met.[99] Where there are needs for health or education services, the

---

[87] N. Lowe *et al., Supporting adoption* (1999), Chap. 14; PIU Report (2000) para. 3.121.

[88] Lowe *et al.* (1999); see also R. Parker (ed.), *Adoption: messages from research* (1999).

[89] PIU Report (2000) para. 3.124 citing Cm. 2288 paras 4.23, 4.25.

[90] Lowe *et al.* (1999), pp. 429, 434; PIU Report (2000) paras 3.118–3.122.

[91] Cm. 5017, paras 6.26–7.

[92] D.H., *Providing effective adoption support-consultation paper* (2002) p. 3.

[93] D.H., *Adoption The draft Adoption Support Services (Local Authorities)(Transitory and Transitional Provisions)(England) Regulations 2003 and draft accompanying guidance* (2002). This early implementation will not include the full range of support services for ste-parent adoptions, or services for adopted adults and birth relatives, p. 5.

[94] Adoption and Children Act 2002, s.4(7).

[95] National Standards (2001), E1, E6; D.H., *Providing effective adoption support—consultation* (2002), para. 3.

[96] s.3(2). "The main financial implications of the Adoption and Children Bill lie in adoption support." Jacqui Smith, Minister of State, Hansard, *Commons*, Vol. 376, col. 133w.

[97] "a) children who may be adopted, their parents and guardians, b) persons wishing to adopt a child, and c) adopted persons, their parents, natural parents and former guardians", s.3(1).This right may be extended to others by regulations, s.4(7)(a) and there is a discretion to assess others, s.4(3).

[98] *cf.* Children Act 1989, s.17.

[99] s.4(1), (4). Where it decides to provide services it must prepare a plan and keep this under review.

local authority must notify the relevant body; and where another local authority could help they may be requested to help and must comply if this is consistent with the exercise of their functions.[1]

The position of special guardians[2] and their children is even weaker. Although local authorities must make arrangements for support services, unless specific provision is made in regulations, they have no duty to assess an individual's needs.[3]

There are many parallels between this scheme and Part III of the Children Act 1989 which has failed to secure family support services for many children in need and been subject to considerable recent litigation.[4] Although committed to supporting adoption, the government was concerned not to provide greater rights than to family support services.[5] The Act only imposes a "target duty" to provide adoption services which is unenforceable through the courts unless it crystallises.[6] In deciding whether or not to meet a person's needs, the local authority must not act unreasonably and must comply with its human rights responsibilities. Where refusal of services undermines the art. 8 right to respect for family life, for example because the adoption is at risk of breakdown or contact will cease, the local authority's decision can be challenged. Post adoption services fall into two categories, services which relate to general needs, for example because of the child's behavioural problems, and services which relate specifically to adoption, for example birth records counselling. In relation to general services, local authorities must take care not to discriminate by providing easier, or more difficult access to services for adoptive families than for other families of children in need. Those dissatisfied with services or the lack of them may use the complaints process.[7]

IV. PRINCIPLES IN ADOPTION LAW

Welfare

23–024 The Adoption and Children Act 2002, section 1 provides that, "[W]henever a court or adoption agency is coming to a decision relating to the adoption of a child the paramount consideration . . . must be the child's welfare, throughout

---

[1] s.4(9)–(11) but the House of Lords has refused to order co-operation from a housing authority under Children Act 1989, s.27 see: *R v. Northavon D.C. ex p. Smith* [1994] 2 F.L.R. 671 and above, para. 22.013.

[2] see above para. 18.043 and below, para. 23.058.

[3] Children Act 1989, s.14F(1),(2). There is a strong non-discrimination argument that similar provision should be made where looked-after children become subject to special guardianship rather than adoption, also where relatives become special guardians where children would otherwise have to be looked after by a local authority.

[4] see above, paras 22.007–009 and 22.013.

[5] Lord Hunt, Parliamentary Under-Secretary, Department of Health, Hansard, *Lords* Vol. 636, cols CWH76-80, Grand Committee, June 27, 2002.

[6] *R. (on the application of) A v. Lambeth L.B.C.* [2002] 1 F.L.R. 353 at para. 26 *per* Laws L.J. Assessment appears insufficient for this because the local authority is specifically permitted to determine whether to provide services, s.4(4).

[7] see above para. 22.071; s.26(3B) extends this to representations about adoption services.

his life." This provision replaces a more limited test which only gave "first consideration to the need to safeguard and promote" welfare throughout childhood[8] and did not apply a simple welfare test to determine whether a child could be adopted without parental consent. Parents were expected to give great weight to the welfare of their children but their consent to adoption could only be dispensed with on specific grounds, including that they were withholding it unreasonably.[9] The 1993 White Paper recommended that the child's welfare in adulthood should also be considered, and the 1996 Bill also made welfare the basis for dispensing with parental consent.[10] The 2000 proposals followed this approach to ensure coherence with planning for the child's needs under the Children Act 1989 and to promote permanence within the context of the belief, set out in the Prime Minister's Review, that adoption delivers benefits to most children and to society.[11] This welfare test applies to agency decisions about placement, removal from placement, contact and post adoption support, and to court decisions about placement and adoption orders, or alternative orders which might be made in these proceedings, such as special guardianship or residence orders. It does not apply to the court's decision to dispense with a parent's consent to adoption[12]; consent may be dispensed with "where the child's welfare requires" this.[13] Benefits largely experienced in adulthood such as citizenship may now tip the balance in favour of adoption, nor should the fact that the child will soon be 18 weaken the case for adoption.[14]

Further guidance is provided in the form of a checklist similar to that in the Children Act 1989. This includes matters particularly relevant to adoption decisions such as the likely effect on the child of becoming an adopted person, the likelihood of relationships with relatives continuing, the willingness and ability of relatives to meet the child's needs and their wishes and feelings regarding the child.[15] In this context, "relatives" includes parents, who are thus recognised for their potential contribution to the child's welfare, not because parenthood gives them rights. Parents cannot prevent an adoption where this best meets their child's needs. The importance for welfare of protecting the child's

---

[8] Adoption Act 1976, s.6.

[9] Adoption Act 1976, s.16(2). "[T]he fact that a reasonable parent does pay regard to the welfare of his child must enter into the question of reasonableness as a relevant factor." *Re W (an infant)* [1971] A.C. 682, 699 *per* Lord Hailsham. For this reason Dr Cretney took the view that the non application of the welfare test made no difference to the decision to dispense with consent, see 4th edition of this work, p. 455.

[10] Cm. 2288 para. 4.2; *Adoption—a service for children* (1996) para. 4.1.

[11] PIU Review, paras 9, 2.81, 4.8 and 8.2–3. Concern was expressed that the courts gave "the benefit of doubt to birth parents" para. 3.62; Cm. 5017 paras 1.20–1, 2.11, 4.14.

[12] Adoption and Children Act 2002, s.1(7) does not include dispensing with consent within its definition of "a decision relating to the adoption of a child", cl. 1(8)(c) which had this effect was removed at Report Stage: Hansard, *Commons* May 16, 2002, Vol. 385, col. 959.

[13] s.52(1)(b).

[14] cf. *Re B (adoption order: nationality)* [1999] 1 F.L.R. 907 at p. 911 *per* Lord Hoffman, "Benefits which will accrue only after the end of childhood are not welfare benefits to which first consideration must be given."

[15] s.1(4)(c), (f). Relationships in this context are not limited to legal relationships, s.1(8)(a). Therefore where continuing contact is crucial to welfare, if arrangements have been agreed between the adopters and the agency to allow contact with birth relatives, or between siblings placed separately, adoption may nevertheless be in the child's interests.

identity is underlined by a duty on adoption agencies when placing a child to give due consideration to the child's religious persuasion, racial origin and cultural and linguistic background.[16] Adoption practice gives considerable emphasis to professional assessments of the child's needs but the law recognises that the child's own views about arrangements are important to welfare decisions, and this is stressed in the Adoption Standards.[17]

Consent

23–025 Parental consent has been a mainstay of adoption law and is required under international law.[18] Adoption was conceived as a "court-sanctioned contract" which necessarily required the consent of the parties, but the 1926 Act allowed parental consent to be dispensed with.[19] Although widely drawn, these powers were narrowly interpreted until a decision in 1947[20] which was followed by legislation redefining the grounds for dispensing with consent. Apart from specific grounds which had their origin in the Poor Law, the 1949 Act allowed consent to be dispensed with where it was unreasonably withheld. This "piece of machinery" invented to determine whether the advantages of adoption were sufficient to override parental objections[21] became the main ground and was used in more than half of all cases where orders were made without consent.[22]

The Adoption and Children Act 2002 provides a general power to dispense with consents[23] but parental consent still has crucial importance in the adoption process. Where each parent has consented to the child's placement for adoption and not withdrawn their consent, an adoption agency can place the child without obtaining a placement order from a court.[24] And in such cases, withdrawal of consent necessitates a local authority application for a placement order or the child's return to the parents (if he or she is not placed for adoption or the agency considers return to be in the child's interests).[25]

---

16 s.1(5). A similar provision applies to all decisions by local authorities in relation to looked after children, Children Act 1989, s.22(5)(c). The formulation "due consideration" allows the agency to prefer same-race placements but in line with previous guidance (LAC 98(20) paras 11–18) not to the exclusion of any adoption for a child who would benefit from family placement.

17 s.1(4)(a); D.H., *National Adoption Standards for England* (2001) A4.

18 Review of Adoption Law (1992), Discussion paper No. 2, *Agreement and Freeing* (1991), para. 80 (see also Background paper No. 1, *International perspectives* (1990)). The relevant treaties include The European Convention on Human Rights, the European Convention on Adoption and the Hague Convention on Intercountry adoption.

19 Cretney, *op cit.* p. 193.

20 *ibid.* citing *H v. H* [1947] K.B 463, 466, DC.

21 *Re C (a minor)(adoption: parental agreement: contact)* [1993] 2 F.L.R. 260, 272 *per* Steyn and Hoffman L. JJ.

22 Parker (1999), *op cit.* p. 69 citing Malos and Milsom; Review of Adoption Law, Discussion paper No. 2, *Agreement and Freeing* (1991) para. 37.

23 s.52(1) and see below.

24 s.19(1). But not if care proceedings are pending, s.19(3).

25 s.22(1), 31, 32. But it is an offence for anyone other than the agency to remove the child, s.30(1), (3), (8). All agency decisions are subject to the welfare test in s.1 but an adoption society has no power to seek a placement order and continue with inchoate adoption plans if consent is withdrawn. In contrast, local authorities are under a duty to seek placement orders where they are satisfied children ought to be placed for adoption but they do not have the authority of parental consent to do so, s.22(1).

Whose consent?

23–026 Adoption requires the consent of all parents or guardians, but "parent" is defined only to include parents with parental responsibility so the consent of some fathers is not required. The extension of parental responsibility to fathers jointly registering the birth will reduce the numbers whose consent is not required.[26] Where the father only obtains parental responsibility after the child has been placed for adoption with the mother's consent, he is treated as having given consent on the same terms as the mother.[27] Only guardians appointed under the Children Act 1989 are able to give consent, so where a child from overseas is adopted in England, the agreement of a person or institution who had rights under a foreign order is not required.[28] The child's consent is not required. Following the recommendation of the Review of Adoption Law,[29] the 1996 draft Bill included provisions requiring the agreement of children aged 12 years or over[30] but this was criticised by adoption agencies who considered that having to "sign away" their birth families placed too great a burden on children.[31] Nevertheless, courts and agencies must have regard to the child's wishes and feelings as part of the welfare checklist; court rules will give children party status in placement order proceedings and will allow them to apply to be parties in adoption[32] but it is not clear that this ensures sufficient attention is given to children's views about whom they live with and the legal arrangements for this.[33] Particularly, issues of contact with siblings may not receive adequate attention[34] if children are not represented.

---

[26] Children Act 1989, s.4(1)(a), (1A) added by Adoption and Children Act 2002, s.112. In 2000, only a third of adoptions were of children of married parents, ONS, FM2, table 6.1a.

[27] s.52(9)(10). The father may withdraw this consent but this may not be effective if an application for adoption has already been made, s.52(4).

[28] cl. 131(1) this is a different definition from that in the 1976 Act which allowed the court to hold that the consent of the Director of the Romanian orphanage was required in *Re AGN (adoption: foreign adoption)* [2000] 2 F.L.R. 431. FD not following *Re D (adoption: foreign adoption)* [1999] 2 F.L.R. 865 FD; *Re J (Adoption: Consent of Foreign Public Authority)* [2002] 2 F.L.R. 618, FD (consent of Jordanian care authority not required).

[29] Review of Adoption Law (1992), paras 9.5–6, 12.9. Also that children should be represented, paras 37.2 *et seq.*

[30] Draft Adoption Bill 1996, cll. 41(7), 46(3). There is a similar provision in Scots Law: Adoption (Scotland) Act 1978, s.12(8).

[31] Select Committee on the Adoption and Children Bill 2001 (H.C.P 431 ii) evidence of BAAF, para. 10.2.

[32] 2002 Bill EN, para. 279; Special Standing Committee 2001–2, 24th session, January 17, 2002, col. 905. "[The government] will need to ensure that children are not unnecessarily made party to proceedings, because involvement can be stressful for them." Jacqui Smith, Minister of State, Department of Health. If children are parties they are likely to be represented by a children's guardian.

[33] For example, Cm. 5017, para. 5.11 gives a case example where a 13-year-old girl does not want adoption but to remain with foster carers and her 9-year-old sister and see her birth family. It suggests special guardianship for both children without any reference to the views of the younger girl.

[34] The court must consider arrangements for contact before making placement or adoption orders, ss.27(4) and 46(6).

Consent to what?

23–027 Until 1984 the consent required was to a specific adoption but adoption agencies and adopters preferred not to let birth parents know who would be caring for the child, and from 1949 the identity of the adopters could be concealed.[35] The Houghton Committee recommended a new procedure "freeing for adoption" so that birth parents could finalise their consent before adopters had been found, and this was included in the 1976 Act.[36] In practice, freeing did not work as intended and seemed to contribute to delay.[37] By the time the freeing provisions were implemented there were few consensual baby placements for which it was largely intended. When freeing applications were made, children were often already placed with prospective adopters so that, in contested cases, the process neither allowed parents to challenge the adoption plan nor protected the adopters from conflict. For these reasons the 1992 Review proposed its abolition and a new system whereby the court made "placement orders" to authorise the child's placement for adoption.[38]

(a) consent and placement

23–028 A child can only be placed for adoption if each parent consents to the child's placement, either with identified prospective adopters or anyone chosen by the agency, or a placement order is obtained.[39] Placement orders also require parental consent but where this is refused, or is withdrawn, the court may dispense with it and make the order.[40] Foster carers may still apply to adopt without either the consent of the parents or the local authority obtaining a placement order if they have looked after the child for at least 12 months.[41] Further consent is required to the adoption order unless a placement order has been obtained.[42]

(b) consent and adoption

23–029 Consent to the adoption order may also be specific or general, and may be given at the same time as consent to placement, or subsequently. Where advance con-

---

35 Cretney, *op. cit.* 190–2 and Cretney (2003) Chap. 17, n.101 and accompanying text. For this reason *de facto* adoptions were not always formalised although some birth parents were asked to sign consent forms in blank without the adopters' names being included.

36 Houghton Committee, paras 173–183, 221–224. The process also protected adopters from disputes with parents but this was given less emphasis see: J. Rowe, "Freeing and adoption from a historical perspective" (1984) 2 *Adoption and Fostering* 10.

37 N. Lowe *et al.*, *Report of the research into the law and practice of freeing for adoption* (1993).

38 Review of Adoption Law (1992) paras 14.6–14.9; Cm. 2288, para. 4.8–9. The original proposals for placement orders were considered too cumbersome and were modified following further consultation: D.H., *Placement for adoption—a consultation document* (1994) and again for the 2002 Act.

39 s.19(1), 21.

40 s.21(3), 52.

41 s.42(4) but if the child were only accommodated a person with parental responsibility could remove the child under Children Act 1989, ss.20(8)–(5)(a) and any person could remove the child with leave of the court, s.38(5)(b). Foster carers who have cared for the child for five years have greater security, s.38(2), (3).

42 s.47. An order from Scotland or Northern Ireland freeing the child for adoption is also sufficient, s.47(6).

sent is given the parent need take no further part in the proceedings but can notify the agency that he or she wishes to be informed of any adoption application.[43] Consent given in advance may be withdrawn but this is ineffective if an application for an adoption order has already been made.[44] Unless there is a placement order, an adoption order can only be made if the requisite consents are given, there is no opposition to adoption from someone who has given consent in advance, or the court is satisfied that the consent should be dispensed with.[45] A person who has given consent to adoption cannot oppose the adoption without leave of the court, nor may a parent or guardian do so where a placement order has been obtained, and leave can only be given where there has been a change of circumstances.[46] Through these provisions it is intended to ensure that most decisions about consent are taken earlier in the process and to reduce delay by excluding objections from those who initially consented to adoption or had their objections to placement overridden by a court.

Consents must be given "unconditionally and with full understanding of what it involved".[47] It follows that parents cannot bargain consent for contact, nor may adopters give inducements for consent.[48] Information about the effect of adoption is provided on the consent form, and consents must be witnessed by a CAFCASS officer but this may not be adequate to protect a parent under stress.[49] The former provision and the consent form which required consent to be "freely" given was criticised on the basis that it discouraged parents from consenting by suggesting that they willingly gave up responsibility for their child rather than were resigned to doing so in the child's interests. The government has suggested that the form should be changed to encourage consent, reduce contested adoptions and speed up the process.[50] However, it seems unlikely that merely rewording the consent form will have such a substantial effect.

In cases of intercountry adoption, the child's State of Origin may allow both simple and full adoption; the Hague Convention allows conversion of simple adoptions in the Receiving State but only if the necessary consent has been

---

[43] s.20(4); EN para. 68. Under the freeing procedures a parent could make a declaration of no further involvement and this also precluded an application for revocation of the order, Adoption Act 1976, ss.19, 20.

[44] ss.20(3), 52(4).

[45] ss.20(1)(2), 47(2).

[46] s.47(2)(b), (3), (4)(b), (5). For example, the mother in *Scott v. U.K.* [2000] 1 F.L.R. 958 might have successfully contested the adoption as she had overcome her addiction to alcohol between the freeing order (placement order) and the adoption but it would be open to the court to dispense with her consent.

[47] s.52(5).

[48] ss.52(5), 92(1),(4). Making, offering or receiving such a payment is an offence, s.95(3). It does not necessarily preclude an adoption order *cf.* Adoption Act 1976, s.24(2) but the High Court can retrospectively authorise an excepted payment: *Re MW (Adoption: Surrogacy)* [1995] 2 F.L.R. 759, FD.

[49] ss.52(7), 102(1). In *Re A (Adoption: Agreement: Procedure)* [2001] 2 F.L.R. 455, CA where the use of the same form for consent to adoption and freeing and the rapid pace of the process had confused the mother, a 15-year-old Kosovan rape victim. But in *Re D (Adoption: Freeing Order)* [2001] 1 F.L.R. 403, FD (not a freeing case) the court accepted the mother's agreement even though it had not been witnessed because she refused to see the CAFCASS officer.

[50] Parker (1999) *op cit.* p. 68; PIU Review, paras 3.64-3.65; Cm. 5017, paras 8.27–8; Special Select Committee Report 2001 (H.C.P 431 ii) evidence of BAAF, para. 10.1; No new form has been issued but the word "freely" was removed at Report Stage.

given.[51] Where this is not the case, a Convention adoption is still treated as a full adoption but the High Court has power to give it different effect where this would benefit the child.[52] In the case of simple adoptions from non-Convention countries a further consent will be required for an adoption order in the U.K.[53]

When must consent be given?

23–030 The mother's consent to adoption is only valid if the child is at least 6 weeks old when it is given.[54] This ensures that she has had time to recover from the birth before making such an important decision. Where the law of the child's State of Origin allows consent to be given earlier this will not be valid for any adoption order made in England or Wales.[55] No such protection is given to fathers, nor in respect of a decision to consent to placement. Thus a mother could consent to her child's placement at birth and change her mind within a relatively short time but be unable to reclaim the child. She would be free to oppose the adoption, but the passage of time, the baby's relationship with the adopters and lack of relationship with the mother would be likely to encourage the court to dispense with her consent.[56]

Dispensing with consent

23–031 The changes relating to dispensing with consent sweep away most of the earlier case law, replacing all but one of the previous grounds with a welfare test. The Review of Adoption Law expressed concern at the limited weight given to the parental views and recommended that adoption should be permitted against the parents' wishes where the adoption plan had been approved by the court and the advantages to the child of becoming a member of a new family by adoption were "so significantly better" than any other option as to justify this, or the parent could not be found or was incapable of giving consent.[57] However, all the subsequent bills used a different formula.

Under the Adoption of Children Act 2002 the court can make placement or adoption orders without parental consent on two separate grounds:—

23–032 Section 52(1)(a) "the parent or guardian cannot be found or is incapable of giving consent".

---

[51] Art. 27. The Central Authority seeks to ensure that the parents consent to a full adoption where the Receiving State is England and Wales. The High Court has a power to treat a simple adoption as other than a full adoption where this would be more favourable to the child: Adoption and Children Act 2002, s.88; EN para. 195.

[52] s.88(2).

[53] *Re G (Foreign Adoption: Consent)* [1995] 2 F.L.R. 528, FD.

[54] s.52(3). This protection was introduced by the Adoption Act 1949, s.3(4) and is reflected in the European Convention on Adoption 1967.

[55] In *Re A (Adoption of Russian Child)* [2000] 1 F.L.R. 539 the court dispensed consent where the mother had signed the form shortly after the birth. A Convention adoption made in the state of origin would be valid providing the consent was given after birth and acceptable in that state, Hague Convention, Art. 4(c)(iv).

[56] ss.30(1), 47(5); EN para. 122.

[57] Review of Adoption Law (1992), paras 12.1, 12.6 and Chap. 15; Cm. 2288, paras 4.9 *et seq.* and 5.4–5. D.H., *Placement for Adoption* (1994), para. 3.3.

This provision repeats one in earlier law[58] which was used in only a small percentage of cases.[59] It may be used where the whereabouts of a person whose consent is required are unknown and cannot be discovered, or where he or she lacks the mental capacity to give agreement.[60] Notice of the proceedings must normally be served on each person whose consent is required[61]; and if this is not done the decision may be challenged.[62] Where there is no known address[63] for a person, very thorough inquiries should be made and assistance sought from appropriate government departments; it may be necessary to advertise in newspapers. However, if there are no practical means of communicating with a person whose consent is required they "cannot be found" even if their whereabouts are actually known:—

> In *Re A (Adoption of Russian Child)*,[64] a child was brought to the U.K. after a Russian adoption order, made with the mother's consent given only two days after the birth. The adopters applied for adoption in England and needed a valid consent. The judge obtained advice that any contact with the mother would violate her rights and that disclosure of the fact of adoption was a criminal offence. Considering the problems this might cause for the adopters who had business interests in Russia, he accepted that it was neither reasonable nor practical to contact the mother and dispensed with her consent.

23–032/1 Section 52(1)(b) "the welfare of the child requires the consent to be dispensed with."

The Department of Health noted in 1996 that because the welfare test has to be considered in all court adoption decisions, making welfare the principal ground for dispensing with consent added little.[65] However, it took the view requiring the court to find that the advantages of adoption were "so significantly greater"[66] could create confusion but added nothing because the court had to apply the European Convention of Human Rights.[67] This approach was heavily

---

[58] Adoption Act 1926, s.2(3); Adoption Act 1976, s.16(2)(a).

[59] For 11% of non-agreeing mothers and 5% of non-agreeing fathers in Murch's study, see: Review of Adoption Law, Discussion paper No. 2, *Agreement & Freeing* (1991), p. 26.

[60] In *Re L (A Minor) (Adoption: Parental Agreement)* [1987] 1 F.L.R. 400 the court was unwilling to accept the mother's psychiatrist's certificate that she was so incapable; the fact that the parent is irrational is insufficient. Minority does not *per se* prevent a person having the capacity to consent.

[61] The requirements as to service are set out in the Adoption Rules 1984; non-compliance is an irregularity: C.P.R. 1998, r. 3.10 and the court has a power to dispense with service.

[62] Under the H.R.A. 1998 or by granting leave out of time: *Re F (R) (An Infant)* [1970] 1 Q.B. 385 the applicants made numerous attempts to contact the mother but did not ask her father whose address they knew. Concern about a possible challenge to the adoption led the court to direct that a father whose consent was not required should be notified: *Re R (Adoption: Father's Involvement)* [2001] 1 F.L.R. 302, CA.

[63] If there is a known address the parent can be found: *Re B* [1988] 1 Q.B. 12; but see below.

[64] [2000] 1 F.L.R. 539 FD. For an earlier example see *Re R (adoption)* [1967] 1 W.L.R. 34.

[65] D.H. and W.O., *Adoption a service for children* (1996), para. 4.1.

[66] Suggested in the Adoption Review (1992), para. 12.6.

[67] Special Standing Committee, November 20, 2001, James Paton, Department of Health, "the test . . . would not be trivial or low."

criticised by adoption and social work professionals on the basis that fear of losing their children could deter families from seeking social services support and thus undermine the Children Act 1989. A simple welfare test gave insufficient weight to the families' views; and there should be a clear limit to the State's right to intervene.[68] This formulation appears to remove any possibility of taking account of parents' rights or interests. Whereas parents could take a different view of their child's welfare and not be unreasonable[69] the court now imposes an objective view of what the child's welfare requires. However, adoption without parental consent must be a proportionate response to the child's welfare needs,[70] and so it will be necessary to compare adoption plans within any proposals from the family.[71] At the placement order stage, the crucial issues will be the prospects for rehabilitation and the availability of suitable carers within the family. The application will only be sought because the local authority thinks the child ought to be placed for adoption, contesting parents will thus be challenging a professional assessment about their child's welfare and will need expert evidence.[72] The local authority will need a care order or to prove the significant harm test; the parents' failure as carers will already have been established for the court. Considerable emphasis is placed on acting without delay[73] but where there is some prospect of care within the family, the time taken to complete adoption plans needs to be considered alongside the time for the family to show its abilities. Where the issue is the legal arrangements for care, the court must be satisfied that adoption is a better arrangement than residence or special guardianship which both allow the parents to retain their status and legal relationship with the child.[74] However, if the adopters have made their commitment to the child on the basis that adoption is intended and are unwilling to care for the child without an adoption order, the court is likely to dispense with parental consent. But it may take a different view where a child objects to adoption.[75]

---

[68] Special Select Committee (H.C.P. 431) Memoranda of evidence from BAAF, para.11, BASW, paras 1–5, ADSS, cl. 44, FRG, para.1. Particular concern was expressed because until it was amended in Committee, the bill allowed placement orders to be made without satisfaction of the "significant harm test" in Children Act 1989, s.31(2).

[69] Adoption Act 1989, s.16(2)(b). For a detailed discussion of the working of this provision see 6th edition of this work, p. 923 *et seq*.

[70] Art. 8(2); *Re C and B (Care Order: Future Harm)* [2001] 1 F.L.R. 611 CA; *Re O (Supervision Order)* [2001] 1 F.L.R. 923, CA at para. 28 *per* Hale L.J.

[71] One difficulty with this, noted by the Family Rights Group is that members of the extended family may be unwilling to put themselves forward until it is clear that a care order will be made. By this time plans for adoptive placements may be well advanced.

[72] see J. Brophy *et al., Expert evidence in child protection litigation* (1999).

[73] Adoption and Children Act 2002, s.1(3). Reduction of delay was a major reason for reducing opportunities to object to adoption, PIU Review paras 3.47 *et seq*.; Cm. 5017 para. 8.28.

[74] Adoption has been seen as offering few advantages and carrying the disadvantage of ending links with the family: *Re H; Re W (Adoption: Parental Agreement)* (1983) 4 F.L.R. 614; *Re P (adoption: freeing order)* [1994] 2 F.L.R. 1000, CA *cf. Re C (Adoption Order: conditions)* [1989] A.C. 1; *Re A (A Minor) (Adoption: Parental Consent)* [1987] 2 All E.R. 81; and see J. Triseliotis "Open adoption—the evidence examined" in M. Adcock *et al., Exploring openness in adoption* (1993).

[75] See *Re M (Adoption or Residence Order)* [1998] 1 F.L.R. 570 CA where the child's objections led to the local authority withdrawing support for adoption and the court refused the order on the basis that the mother, who could not care for her daughter was not unreasonable in refusing consent. If there is a placement order, the prospective adopters may have a legitimate expectation of adoption.

23–032/2 The Act restricts the circumstances when a parent can oppose an adoption if he or she has previously agreed to a placement or a placement order has been made.[76] The question of dispensing with parental consent to adoption rather than placement will generally be confined to cases where there is no placement order, for example in agency cases where consent was given to placement; applications by foster carers or family members; and intercountry adoptions where the official procedures have not been complied with.[77] Where consent was originally given, the court may be easily satisfied that adoption is in the child's interests. There may be a case for arguing that the child's welfare does not require adoption given the security that can be obtained through other arrangements, but this may be less persuasive where the parent initially agreed. In "in family" cases it may be particularly difficult to establish that adoption is required for the child's welfare given that it involves losses rather than gains.[78]

Human Rights

23–033 Closed adoption effected in the face of parental opposition requires overriding justification if the European Convention on Human Rights, Art. 8 is not to be breached.[79] But the recognition of the crucial importance of a *de facto* family ties with carers by adoption, even without the consent of the parents, may be justified in the interests of the child and the carers.[80] And adoption with the consent of a parent cannot breach his or her rights.[81] The requirement that adoption orders are only granted where they are in the child's interests is sufficient to ensure that adoption is proportionate to the child's needs.[82] Concerns to ensure compliance with the Convention were instrumental in shaping the Adoption and Children Act 2002, particularly in removing the discrimination between married and unmarried and same-sex couples.[83] Adoption also raises Art. 8 issues for those who are adopted. An adopted person who has been denied access to information about the identity of birth parents and who cannot therefore establish her family history has challenged the French system for allowing mothers to give up their children anonymously.[84] Parents must be sufficiently involved

---

76 s.47(2)(c), (3), (4)(c), (5); leave of the court is required which can only be given if there has been a change in circumstances, s.47(7).

77 Where official procedures have been followed a valid consent will have been given, this is required not only for adoption under the Hague Convention but for entry clearance where a child is to be adopted in the U.K.: D.H., *Intercountry adoption guide—practice and procedures* (2001), paras 5.12–5.15.

78 *Re B (Adoption by One Natural Parent to the Exclusion of Other)* [2001] 1 F.L.R. 5898 CA *per* Hale L.J. at para. 12 (reversed for other reasons [2002] 1 F.L.R.196 H.L.).

79 H. Swindells *et al., Family Law and the Human Rights Act 1998* (1999), para. 9.63; *P, C and S v. U.K.* [2002] 2 F.L.R. 631 E.Ct.H.R. at para. 118.

80 *Soderback v. Sweden* [1999] 1 F.L.R. 250 E.Ct.H.R. a step-parent adoption.

81 *Re B (Adoption by One Natural Parent to the Exclusion of Other)* [2002] 1 F.L.R.196 H.L. *per* Lord Nicholls at para 29.

82 *ibid., per* Ld. Nicholls at paras 30–32; for a critique of the House of Lord's approach to the Convention, see: S. Harris-Short [2002] *C.F.L.Q.* 325, 336.

83 Joint Committee on Human Rights, *24th Report*, 2002, see para 23.019, above.

84 *Odievre v. France* App. No. 42326/98. The introduction of anonymous birth is being discussed in Germany but has been delayed pending the case in Strasbourg. Anonymous birth is not permitted in England and Wales but those born as a result of egg or sperm donation has no rights of access to information about their genetic parents, see para. 23.071, below.

in decisions which lead to an adoption plan,[85] and their rights to a fair hearing demand competent representation by a lawyer instructed to protect the applicants rights, for example by ensuring that issues of contact are fully considered.[86]

> In *P, C and S v. U.K*[87] the local authority became concerned about the welfare of the couple's unborn baby because the mother had been prosecuted in the U.S.A. for harming her older child. This boy had suffered repeated hospital admissions because of illness induced by being given laxatives. The local authority arranged a psychiatric assessment of the couple but before it was received the mother gave birth following an emergency caesarean. The local authority obtained a without notice emergency protection order and removed the baby shortly after birth. The baby was never returned to the couple although they were allowed contact. The parents' lawyers withdrew at the beginning of the four week contested care hearing, the judge allowed only a short adjournment and case proceeded without the parents being represented. A week after the care order was made the judge heard the freeing proceedings, again without parental representation. The European Court of Human Rights found that the Art. 8 rights of the parents and the child had been breached and that the trials had been unfair. The need for speed in making arrangements for babies did not justify proceeding in this way. It was crucial for the parents to be able to put forward their case as favourably as possible.[88]

Although their consent may not be required, fathers must generally be involved in the adoption process. Adoption agencies are required to to consult fathers about their views.[89] Where a father has "family life" in respect of the child he must be sufficiently involved in decision making and his article 6 rights must be protected. Only in exceptional cases is it appropriate not to notify the father, the mother's desire for confidentiality is insufficient to justify non-disclosure.[90]

> In *Re M (adoption: rights of natural father)*[91] the local authority applied for and was granted a direction that the father need not be contacted about the adoption of a child he had been told was still born. The father had convictions for serious offences including rape and had assaulted the mother in front of their older child on his last visit and the mother feared for her safety and he child's should the father learn of her deception.

---

[85] *Scott v. U.K.* [2000] 1 F.L.R. 958 E.Ct.H.R. (application found inadmissible)

[86] *P, C and S v. U.K.* [2002] 2 F.L.R. 631 E.Ct.H.R. at paras 96–100. The court also found that the lack of representation in the care and freeing proceedings breached Art. 8, at paras 137–8. The parents were awarded compemsation but the court considered it inappropriate to award damages to the child who was unaware of the proceedings and had no legal ties to the parents following the adoption.

[87] [2002] 2 F.L.R. 631 E.Ct.H.R.

[88] at para.136.

[89] Adoption Agencies Regulations 1983, regs 7(1),(2) and Sched 1, Part III.

[90] *Re H; Re G (Adoption: Consultation of Unmarried Fathers)* [2001] 1 F.L.R. 646 FD; *Re R (Adoption: Father's Involvement)* [2001] 1 F.L.R. 302 CA,

[91] [2001] 1 F.L.R. 745, FD.

Confidentiality

23–034 Adoptions have been cloaked in secrecy in order to protect the parties from any stigma and to prevent interference in the child's upbringing. Information collected by adoption agencies[92] and for the courts is confidential[93] and can be disclosed only as permitted by the legislation.[94] Court proceedings take place in private and may be arranged so that the parties do not see each other.[95] The applicants may apply for a serial number so that their identity cannot be discovered by the child's parents.[96] But a birth parent cannot keep their identity secret from the adopters or the child.[97] Assessments of the applicants and the birth family are confidential. The court may exceptionally order that their contents are not disclosed where this is justified by the risk of significant harm to the child[98] but in most cases the needs of a fair trial demand that there are no restrictions on disclosure to the parties.[99] A children's guardian cannot be refused copies of local authority adoption assessments in Children Act 1989 proceedings.[1]

V. MODERN ADOPTION PRACTICE

The use of adoption

23–035 Although adoption has a single meaning and its effects apply equally to all adoptions, there are distinct policies, laws and practices which apply to the different circumstances in which adoption is used:— relinquishment or baby placement, public law adoptions, intercountry adoptions and "in family" adoptions. These will now be considered in turn.

---

[92] Adoption Agencies Regulations 1983, r. 14(1).

[93] Adoption Rules 1984, rr. 17(8), 18(11) and 22(5).

[94] Adoption and Children Act 2002, ss.54–65, see para. 23.012, above. Regulations will require agencies to give prospective adopters information about the child's background, Lords Grand Committee Vol. 637, col. CWH 274, Lord McIntosh. See also D.H., *National Adoption Standards for England* (2001) C2 and F13. Where a local authority fails to disclose information and the prospective adopters suffer damage it may be liable in negligence: *A and B v. Essex C.C.* [2002] EWHC 2707 Q.B.

[95] Adoption Rules 1984 (S.I. 1984 No. 265), rr. 10(3), 23(3).

[96] r. 14; *Re X (Adoption: Confidential Procedure)* [2002] 2 F.L.R. 476, CA. In such cases The Review of Adoption Law, Discussion Paper No. 1, *The nature and effects of adoption* (1990), para. 102 suggested that the procedure might be being used too readily and that leave should be required.

[97] The Houghton Committee recommended this although they considered that natural parents needed less protection: para. 298, recommendation 74.

[98] *Re D (Adoption Reports: Confidentiality)* [1995] 2 F.L.R. 687, H.L. at 700, *per* Lord Mustill; *Re K (Adoption: Disclosure of Information)* [1997] 2 F.L.R. 74, FD but note placement with an applicant convicted of such offences is no longer permissible.

[99] *Re R (Care: Disclosure: Nature of Proceedings)* [2002] 1 F.L.R. 755, 776 H *per* Charles J.; and see *Re X (Adoption: Confidential Procedure)* [2002] 2 F.L.R. 476 CA.

[1] *Manchester C.C. v. T* [1994] Fam. 181, CA.

1. Relinquishment or baby placement

23–036 Early adoption practice focussed on the placement of babies, mostly born outside marriage, who had been handed over by their mothers. Adoption societies accepted healthy white babies[2] and placed them with married couples, many of whom sought adoption because of infertility. Local authorities also arranged the adoption of children with the agreement of parents who could not care for them.[3] In 1968, the peak year for adoptions, baby adoptions accounted for three-quarters of all adoptions by non-parents and approximately one in five illegitimate children were adopted.[4] Although placement was a voluntary act, harsh family and social pressures on women who became pregnant outside marriage and the lack of financial support for lone motherhood effectively forced women to hand over their babies for adoption.[5] The availability of effective contraception, the Abortion Act 1967 and changes in social attitudes to unmarried mothers led to a dramatic decline in this use of adoption. It is now unusual; each year about 50 mothers place their children with adoption agencies because of their own circumstances or the child's severe disabilities.[6]

Freeing for adoption

23–037 Until the child was adopted parental responsibility continued and consent could be withdrawn. The Houghton Committee thought this prevented mothers planning for their future, encouraged indecisiveness and caused anxiety for prospective adopters. They therefore recommended that parents should be able to choose to relinquish parental responsibility in favour of an adoption agency at an early stage in the adoption.[7] The court would decide whether or not to accept the mother's decision. The Children Act 1975 made provision for "freeing orders" but the system was not implemented until 1984.[8] By this time these voluntary placements had all but disappeared; freeing was largely used to protect prospective adopters from contests with birth parents.[9]

The 1992 Review recommended that a "placement order" should be required before an adoption agency could place a child with prospective adopters.[10] However, the proposals for uncontested adoptions were revised and the need for a

---

[2] For a brief account of the development of practice see: Houghton Report, *op. cit.* paras 22–26.

[3] N. Lowe, "English adoption law: past present and future" in Katz *et al.*, *Cross currents* (2000) 306, 318.

[4] Lowe (2000), *op. cit.*, p. 316 and R. Leete, "Adoption trends and illegitimate births 1951–1977" (1978) 14 *Populations Trends* 9–16.

[5] D. Howe *et al.*, *Half a million women* (1992). Lowe (2000), *op. cit.*, n. 46 found that single mothers were subject to family pressure even in the late 1980s.

[6] Parker (1999), *op cit.* p. 4.

[7] Houghton Report, *op. cit.* paras 168–186; J. Rowe, "Freeing for adoption a historical perspective" (1984) 8 *Adoption and Fostering*, 2, 10.

[8] Children Act 1975, s.14; Adoption Act 1976, s.18. For a detailed account of freeing see 6th edition of this work 907–911.

[9] See generally: N. Lowe *et al.*, *Report of the research into the use and practice of the freeing for adoption provisions* (1993).

[10] para. 14.8. In uncontested cases it was proposed that the order could be made without a full hearing, para 15.1(d).

placement order removed because of concerns about delaying adoptions. Subsequent Reviews did not consider these adoptions; the new provisions largely are based on those in the 1996 Bill[11] but make special provision for the placement of children under the age of six weeks.[12]

Relinquishment under the Adoption and Children Act 2002

23–038 The Act abolishes freeing and allows agencies to place children for adoption with parental consent.[13] It seeks to protect both birth parents and prospective adopters and to avoid delays by enabling final agreement to adoption to be given at an early stage and removing the need for court proceedings to ratify this before the adoption order is made. Parents will be able to agree to adoption when they agree to placement; they may withdraw their consent and reclaim the child but only where there is no application for a placement order.[14] Adoption Societies will not be able to press on with an adoption if parents withdraw their agreement at an earlier stage.[15] Consent to placement gives the agency parental responsibility for the child, it does not remove the parent's parental responsibility but allows the agency to restrict their exercise of it.[16] Authority to place[17] ends contact orders; the government's preferred approach is for agreements to be made about contact at this stage but there is a wide power to make contact orders.[18] Parents consenting to adoption may specify they do not wish to be informed about any application for adoption[19] and can thus choose to take no further part in the process.

Under this scheme, the protection of the parent's rights, and the child's right to be brought up by the parent rest on the skills of the agency to ensure that the parent fully understands and wants adoption for her child.[20] This is supplemented by the requirement that consent to placement and adoption are witnessed by a

---

[11] D.H., *Placement for adoption* (1994) paras 4.2 *et seq*.; Adoption Bill 1996, cl. 19; Adoption and Children Act 2002, s.19.

[12] Adoption and Children Act 2002, s.18(1). The mother's consent is ineffective if given less than six weeks from the birth, s.52(3).

[13] Sched. 5 and s.19. New Adoption Agencies Regulations will set out the consent requirements where a baby is placed for adoption before the age of six weeks. If the mother then disappears the adoption can proceed but it will be necessary to dispense with the mother's consent, Baroness Andrews, Hansard *Lords* Vol. 640, col. 211, Third Reading, October 30, 2002.

[14] ss.20(1), (3), 32(1), 52(4); withdrawal of consent to placement or adoption is ineffective if given after an application for an adoption order has been made. Parents who originally consented can only oppose the adoption with leave of the court on the basis of a change of circumstances after consent was given, s.47(2)–(7).

[15] A local authority could seek a placement order, ss.22, 32(1).

[16] s.25(1), (4). The effect of consenting to placement is analogous to that of a care order. Once the child is placed the prospective adopters also acquire parental responsibility to the extent determined by the agency.

[17] *i.e.* consent to placement or a placement order.

[18] s.26(3) sets out who may apply for contact, relatives will not need the leave of the court; the court may make orders without application, s.26(4).

[19] s.20(4).

[20] The Agency also has duties to counsel the child's father: Adoption Agencies Regulations 1983, S.I. 1983 No. 1964, reg. 7(1)(3); *Re R (Adoption: Father's Involvement)* [2001] 1 F.L.R. 302, CA.

CAFCASS officer.[21] Where adoption seems the obvious solution to immense difficulties such safeguards may not prove adequate.[22]

2. Public law adoptions

23–039 The adoption of children from state care, with or without their parents' agreement, has been the focus of the recent debates on adoption. Changes in law and practice have aimed to increase these adoptions and reduce the time taken to achieve them in order to provide new, permanent families quickly for children who cannot return home. This form of adoption is common in North America[23] but unusual in most of Europe where public care is generally regarded as temporary and intended to restore children to their families.[24] The promotion of adoption for children in care reflects the view, backed by considerable research, that state care rarely provides the necessary security, and that the well-being even of older children can be improved through adoption[25] It rests on the belief that children's needs can justify a complete and involuntary severance of parental ties.

The practice of arranging adoption for looked after children developed in the 1970s. The Houghton Committee noted that there was a sizeable number of children accommodated by local authorities whose parents' unwillingness to agree to adoption deprived them of the security of a settled home life. It proposed that local authorities and adoption societies should be able to apply to the court for an order dispensing with parental consent with a view to a child's future adoption.[26] Rowe and Lambert's study *Children who wait*[27] emphasised the importance of planning for children in long-term care and "permanency planning" became part of social work practice in some local authorities. The Children Act 1975 increased local authority powers over children they looked after, but the introduction of "freeing for adoption" was delayed until 1984, and only in 1988 were all local authorities required to run a comprehensive adoption service.[28] From this time there was a substantial increase in the number of adoptions from care.[29]

---

[21] s.104.

[22] *Re A (Adoption: Agreement: Procedure)* [2001] 2 F.L.R. 455 (freeing order revoked on appeal, the mother, a 15-year-old Kosovan rape victim, had not understood what she was signing).

[23] Under the Adoption and Safe Families Act 1997, States are required to make reasonable efforts to secure a permanent placement and strict time limits are set for permanency hearings, see: J. Selwyn and W. Sturgess, *International overview of adoption* (2001) and M. Guggenheim, "Child welfare policy and practice in the United States 1950–2000" in S. Katz *et al.*, *op cit.* 547, 559.

[24] See for example, *Johansen v. Norway* (1996) 23 E.H.R.R. 33 but "there are circumstances . . . where a young baby might be adopted in conformity with Art. 8 of the Convention" *P, C and S v. U.K.* [2002] 2 F.L.R. 631 at para. 122.

[25] Parker (1999), *op cit.* pp 10–18; B. Tizard, *Adoption—a second chance* (1977); J. Thoburn, *Success and failure in permanent family placement* (1990); J. Gibbons, *Development after physical abuse in early childhood* (1995); J. Triseliotis, "Long-term foster care or adoption? The evidence examined" [2002] *Child and Family Soc. Wk.* 22.

[26] Houghton Report, paras 221–225 and recommendation 53.

[27] J. Rowe and L. Lambert, *Children who wait* (ABAFA, 1973).

[28] Parker (1999), *op. cit.* pp. 2–4; Lowe, *op. cit.* p. 322.

[29] Parker (1999), *op. cit.* p. 4; PIU Report (2000) Fig. 2.1.

Following the implementation of the Children Act 1989 these adoptions declined, the emphasis on working in partnership with families and on rehabilitation diverted attention from adoption. More prosaically, resources committed to implementing the Act or ensuring the compliance with child protection procedures were not available to develop adoption services.[30] There were wide variations between local authorities in the proportion of children leaving care for adoption, and in the time taken to match children to adopters.[31]

The Department of Health began to focus local authority attention on the importance of adoption for children in public care, first by issuing a Circular on adoption[32] and then including "maximizing the contribution [of] adoption" as an objective in the *Quality Protects* programme.[33] In 2000, the Prime Minister's Review concluded that more use could be made of adoption to meet the needs of looked after children. The White Paper set new targets, supported by central government funding, to increase by 40 per cent the number of looked after children adopted by 2004–5.[34] In the year ending March 2002, approximately 6 per cent of the looked after population, 3,400 children, were adopted, an increase of 47 per cent over the number in March 1999.[35]

Despite these increases, the legal framework for adoptions from care remained unsatisfactory. The freeing for adoption procedure failed to secure speedy adoptions or to ensure that parental consent was given or dispensed with before the child's placement.[36] Freeing orders also left children in legal limbo without any individual who had parental responsibility for them.[37] The 1992 Adoption Review had recommended the abolition of freeing and that the court's approval should be obtained by a placement order whenever adoption was planned.[38] The 1996 draft Bill on which the first 2001 Bill was based, required adoption agencies to apply for a placement order if they were satisfied that the child should be adopted but did not have parental consent, or where the plan for a child in care proposed adoption.[39] However, no conditions were set for placement orders; unlike care orders they would be granted solely on the basis of the child's welfare. These provisions proved highly controversial; it was unfair to parents that they risked losing a child via adoption merely because they had sought help from a local authority. In order to meet objections, the second Bill restricted applications for placement orders to local authorities and made proof of the

---

[30] The PIU Report identified barriers to adoption at all stages of the process, Chap. 3 but did not find evidence of a conscious anti-adoption culture, para 6.6; Cm. 5017 para. 2.21 noted variation between councils in the quality of management of adoption.

[31] SSI, *For children's sake: an SSI inspection of Local authority adoption services—Part I* (1996) *Part II* (1997).

[32] LAC (98) *20 Adoption—achieving the right balance* (1998).

[33] Published in September 1998 see: D.H., *The Government's objectives for children's social services* (1999).

[34] Cm. 5017 p. 5.

[35] D.H., *Statistical Bulletin children adopted from care in England 2001/2002* (2002).

[36] N. Lowe *et al., Freeing for adoption* (1993).

[37] This was a particular problem if no adoption placement was found. A substantial, but unknown, number of children remained subject to freeing orders, the provisions for revocation of freeing were unsatisfactory: *Re C (Adoption: Freeing Order)* [1999] 1 F.L.R. 348, FD.

[38] Review of Adoption Law (1992) para. 14.8; Cm. 2288, para. 4.8.

[39] cl. 23.

threshold conditions for a care order a precondition unless the child was an orphan.[40]

Planning adoption

23–040 A plan for adoption must be based on an assessment that the birth family is unable to meet the child's needs within a reasonable time, and that adoption is likely to provide the best means for doing so.[41] Parents must be sufficiently involved in the planning process but need not be included in all meetings where adoption is considered.[42] There are wide variations in the use made of adoption by different local authorities which are not explained by the differences in their care populations.[43] However, children under the age of four years, and those without direct contact with their parents or other family members are more likely to have a plan for adoption than for long term fostering.[44] Plans must be realistic. Although it is said that no child is unadoptable it may be impossible to identify a family willing to adopt a particular child. A central register of children awaiting adoptive placement and approved adopters has been set up in order to maximize the chances of finding homes for children, but there remains a shortage of families and individuals willing and able to parent older children with disabilities or behavioural problems.

Focusing too long on rehabilitation can delay or deny a settled home but giving it too little attention undermines the child's and parents' rights to family life. Time scales for planning are not included in legislation but the National Adoption Standards expect local authorities to agree a plan for permanence at the child's four month statutory review and to match children who have an adoption plan with prospective adopters within six months of the court order.[45] Developments in practice are being made to improve permanency planning. Twin-tracking, simultaneous work with the family on rehabilitation whilst preparing for permanent placement elsewhere, aims to reduce the time taken to secure a home for the child.[46] Concurrent planning aims to to minimise the number of placements prior to adoption by placing the child with foster carers, approved as adopters, who have agreed to work with the agency and the parents for the child's rehabilitation. Only if this is unsuccessful will the placement become an adoptive placement. Such arrangements depend on the commitment and integrity of the carers and the supervision of the agency.[47]

---

[40] Adoption and Children Act 2002, s.21(2).

[41] Adoption and Children Act 2002, s.1(1), (2), (4).

[42] *Scott v. U.K.* [2000] 1 F.L.R. 958 E.Ct.H.R. (mother's application under Art. 8 declared inadmissible).

[43] N. Lowe and M. Murch, *The plan for the child* (2002) p. 141 *et seq.*

[44] N. Lowe and M. Murch (2002), *op. cit.* Chap. 3 (based on a study of 113 children aged under 12 who had been continuously looked after for the previous 12 months).

[45] D.H., *National Adoption Standards for England* (2001) Standards A2, A3; Review of Children's Cases Regulations 1991, S.I. 1991 No. 895.

[46] This approach has the approval of the courts: *Re D and K (Care Plan: Twin Track Planning)* [1999] 2 F.L.R. 872 FD; *Re R (Child of Teenage Mother)* [2000] 2 F.L.R. 660, FD.

[47] Currently there are only pilot schemes see E. Monck, 25 (2001) *Adoption and Fostering* 1, 67 and E. Monck *et al.*, *The role of concurrent planning* (2003). Their ability to achieve rehabilitation to the birth family remains unclear.

Adoption from care under the Adoption and Children Act 2002—placement orders

23–041 The placement order process seeks to protect the parents' rights by requiring court scrutiny of the local authority's adoption plan before the placement is made. A local authority must seek a placement order whenever it is satisfied that a looked after child ought to be adopted but parental agreement has not been given.[48] Unless the child is already subject to a care order, the court can only make a placement order if the significant harm test[49] is proved and parental agreement is given or dispensed with.[50] These proceedings provide an opportunity for parents and other family members to challenge the plan for adoption; the court must be satisfied that it is better for the child's welfare to make the placement order than not to do.[51] The seriousness of the matter at stake demands that parents are given a fair hearing, including representation for these proceedings.[52]

23–041/1 The placement order facilitates the adoption plan by giving the local authority parental responsibility[53] and ending existing orders for contact.[54] Before making a placement order, the court must consider the agency's proposals for contact and may make orders for contact subject to any conditions.[55] It can therefore continue family contact pending the adoption.[56] The placement order also prohibits anyone other than the local authority removing the child from the adopters, and restricts further opportunities to prevent the adoption.[57] A parent or guardian can only apply to revoke the order or oppose the adoption with the leave of the court and this can only be given where there has been a change of circumstances after the placement order was made.[58] Section 8, supervision and special guardianship orders may not generally be made in respect of a child subject to a placement order.[59] The existence of a placement order should reassure prospective adopters that the plan for adoption has been approved by the court, and that parental opposition will only exceptionally be able to undermine this.

---

48 s.22(1)(2). Placement order applications are not required for looked after children who are orphans s.21(2)(c) nor where the adoption is started by foster carers giving notice of intention to adopt, s.22(5).

49 Children Act 1989, s.31(2), see above para. 22.027 *et seq*.

50 s.21(2)(3). For the grounds for dispensing with agreement see above, para. 23.031.

51 s.1(6).

52 *P, C and S v. U.K.* [2002] 2 F.L.R. 631 (a case where a freeing order was made in respect of a child of unrepresented parents).

53 s.25(1). The agency has power to restrict the parental responsibility of the parents and the prospective adopters, s.25(4).

54 s.26(1), *i.e.* orders under Children Act 1989, ss.8 or 34, s.26(6).

55 s.27(4)(5). The provisions in ss.26 and 27 are modelled on Children Act 1989, s.34 but a wider group of relatives may apply for contact without obtaining the leave of the court.

56 The arrangements for contact after adoption will largely depend on the attitude of the adopters, see below, para. 23.057.

57 ss.34(1) and 47(4), (5).

58 ss.24(2), (3), 47(4), (5), (7).

59 ss.26(2)(a), 29(3)–(5). There is no restriction on granting a residence or special guardianship order in favour of a person who has leave, or making orders after the placement order has been revoked, s.24(1)–(4), see below, para. 23.058.

Revocation of placement orders

23–042 Where it is in the child's interest, for example because there is no longer a plan for adoption, the placement order may be revoked. Any person, including the adoption agency may apply for revocation but parents require the leave of the court.[60] Where the court refuses adoption it has discretion whether or not to revoke the placement order.[61] Where the child was in care, revocation of the placement order allows the care order to take effect so the local authority retains control over the future plan for the child.[62]

Adoption from care under the Adoption and Children Act 2002—by foster carers

23–043 Foster carers may seek to adopt the child they are looking after whether or not a placement order has been made. Adoption by foster carers may proceed with the support of the agency.[63] Alternatively, foster carers can give notice to the local authority of their intention to adopt and apply for an adoption order, but only after the child has had his or her home with them for at least 12 months.[64] If the child is removed from the carers, the adoption plan would be undermined. Where the child is only accommodated, parents retain their right to remove the child from the foster carers, but once the foster carers have looked after the child for a year they can apply for a residence order and seek directions that the child should remain with them pending the full hearing.[65] In addition, where the child has lived with the applicants for five years and intention to adopt has been given, the child can only be removed with leave of the court or by the local authority exercising its statutory powers.[66] Any decision by the local authority to remove the child must be made in accordance with its responsibility to safeguard and promote the child's welfare.[67]

3. Intercountry adoptions[68]

23–044 Intercountry adoption began as an altruistic response towards orphans and the

---

[60] s.24(1), (2). Parents could only seek revocation of freeing after one year; there was no provision for a revocation application by the agency but the inherent jurisdiction could be invoked: *Re C (Adoption: Freeing Order)* [1999] 1 F.L.R. 348, FD.

[61] s.24(4).

[62] s.29(1); *cf.* the position regarding revocation of freeing orders: *Re G (Adoption: Freeing Order)* [1997] 2 F.L.R. 202, HL.

[63] Some agencies did not encourage adoption by foster carers, Parker (1999) p. 131, citing Lowe *et al.* (1999).

[64] ss.42(4), 44.

[65] Children Act 1989, s.10(5A) added by Adoption and Children Act 2002, Sched. 3 para. 56.

[66] s.38(2)(3), re-enacting Adoption Act 1976, s.28. For example, the local authority could remove the child where the placement was not suitable, Fostering Services Regulations 2002, S.I. 2002 No. 57, reg. 36.

[67] Children Act 1989, s.22(3)–(5); *R. v. Devon County Council, ex p. O* [1997] 2 F.L.R. 388 Q.B.D., above para. 22.074.

[68] See P. Selman (ed.) *Intercountry adoption* (2000); J. Rosenblatt, *International Adoption* (1995); Inter-departmental Review of Adoption Law, Background Paper 3, *Intercountry adoption* (1992) and Discussion Paper No. 4, *Intercountry Adoption* (1992); UNICEF, *Intercountry adoption, Innocenti Digest* 4 (1998).

abandoned children of servicemen in World War II, the Korean War and the Vietnam War. It developed because of the decline in babies available for adoption in receiving countries, the abandonment and institutionalisation of children due to extreme poverty in countries of origin, increased awareness that children overseas could be adopted, and the growth of intermediaries and agencies willing to arrange such adoptions.[69] Now over 30,000 children from 50 countries are adopted outside their countries of origin each year. The U.S.A. is the main receiving country, the main countries of origin are Russia, China Vietnam, Columbia and Guatemala.[70]

Compared with the rest of Western Europe, the number of these adoptions in the U.K. is low; only approximately 300 orders are made each year.[71] Intercountry adoption is also a recent development in the U.K.; there were few such adoptions before the revolution in Romania in December 1989 exposed the plight (and availability) of neglected children in orphanages.[72] In contrast to much of Western Europe, official attitudes to intercountry adoption have been largely negative or neutral in the U.K. There is no official programme bringing children here for adoption, and until 1998 some local authorities refused to assess would-be adopters.[73] Unlike other adoptions of unrelated children in the U.K., intercountry adoptions are not arranged through adoption agencies regulated or registered here. U.K. adoption agencies have focussed on developing adoption for older British children and are concerned about the welfare of children adopted transracially and transculturally.[74] The complexities of procedures for intercountry adoption and the lack of sources of information about them meant that in about one quarter of all cases formal procedures were not followed.[75] This has led to increasing concern about the suitability of the arrangements made and the welfare of the children involved.[76]

The adoption of children internationally has long raised legal concerns about

---

[69] J. Masson, "Intercountry adoption: a global problem or a global solution" (2001) *J. International Affairs* 141, 143.

[70] P. Selman, "The demographic history of intercountry adoption" in P. Selman (ed.) *Intercountry adoption* (2000). Compared with their small populations, there is substantial resort to intercountry adoption in Scandanavian countries.

[71] *Second Report to the U.N. Committee on the Rights of the Child by the U.K.* (1999), para. 7.23.8. In 2001 the Department of Health received assessment reports for 326 intending overseas adopters—see www.doh.gov.uk/adoption.

[72] P. Thurman, "Intercountry adoption—a view from the House of Commons" in M. Humphrey and H. Humphrey (eds.) *Intercountry adoption practical experiences* (1993) p. 138; D.C.C. and I.S.S., *The adoption of Romanian children by foreigners* (1991) in Inter-departmental Review of Adoption, Discussion paper 4 (1992).

[73] see LAC (98)20 para. 52. The obligations of local authorities in relation to intercountry adoptions were clarified by the Adoption (Intercountry Aspects) Act 1999, s.9, see now Adoption and Children Act 2002, s.2(8).

[74] J. Masson, "The 1999 Reform of Intercountry adoption in the United Kingdom: new solutions and old problems" [2000] F.L.Q. 221, 225–6; B.A.A.F., *Policy statement on intercountry adoption* (1998).

[75] Adoption (Intercountry Aspects) Act 1999 E.N. paras 4–5.

[76] There have been a series of international statements seeking to promote good practice in adoption including the U.N. Declaration on Social and Legal Principles relating to the Protection and Welfare of Children (1986) A/41/898; U.N. CRC (1989) Art. 21; Hague Convention on the Protection of Children and Co-operation in Respect of Intercountry Adoption (1993); European Parliament Resolution (1996) A4-0392 and Council of Europe Parliamentary Assembly Recommendation 1443 (2000).

the power of the courts to make orders in respect of adopters or children from other jurisdictions, the recognition of orders, and the child's status for the purpose of immigration and inheritance rights.[77] Also, the Home Office has been concerned that adoption should not be used as a mechanism for avoiding immigration control; it has restricted entry for settlement to children whose (foreign) adoption is recognised and children who are to be adopted in the U.K. Also, the adoption must be due to the inability of the birth parents to care for the child and there must be a genuine transfer of responsibility to the adoptive parents.[78]

The growth of intercountry adoption has also raised ethical concerns.[79] Practices have tended to focus on the requirements of adults, rather than the needs of children. Although adoption can provide individual children with a materially better life, it removes them from their culture and may expose them to racism. It also removes some impetus (and possibly financial assistance) for the provision of better child care services in the home country, and may encourage abandonment, child sale and kidnapping.[80] For these reasons the U.N. Convention on the Rights of the Child states that intercountry adoption may be considered as an "alternative means of care" if the child cannot be cared for "in any suitable manner" in the country of origin.[81] In the U.K. the lack of agency control has meant that adopters have not been subject to as rigorous assessment as those adopting domestically. Adopters have also been exploited by unscrupulous intermediaries who charge high fees to facilitate adoptions overseas.[82] The government has sought to ensure that the same principles and safeguards apply as in domestic adoptions[83] but in practice, there has been a two-tier system with lower standards and ineffective controls against abuses in intercountry adoption.[84]

The Hague Convention[85]

23–045 In 1988, the Hague Conference on Private International Law decided to establish a Special Commission to attempt to develop a new[86] international conven-

---

77 J. Van Loon, *Report on Intercountry Adoption*, Hague Conference on International Law (1990).

78 Immigration Rules H.C. 395 para. 310 for entry following adoption, para. 316A for entry for the purpose of adoption in the U.K., see Macdonald (5th ed. 2001) para. 11.84 *et seq. De facto* adoptions are considered outside the rules, para. 11.97.

79 J. Triseliotis, "Intercountry adoption—global trade or global gift" (2000) *Adoption and Fostering* 24, 2, 45.

80 Abuses have led a number of countries to declare a moratorium on intercountry adoptions. DNA tests are used in some cases to ensure that the person giving consent to the adoption is the child's mother.

81 Art. 21(b). See also Hague Convention, *Preamble* paras 2 and 3. For a discussion of the subsidiarity principle in intercountry adoption see J. Masson (2001) *op cit.* p. 157–160 and *Report of the Special Commission on the practical operation of the Hague Convention*, December 2000, para. 24 *et seq.*

82 UNICEF, *op cit.* p. 8.

83 1993 Cm. 2288, para. 6.10; D.H. *Intercountry adoption practice* (1997) para. 2.4.

84 *Re C (Adoption: Legality)* [1999] 1 F.L.R. 370, 362 *per* Johnson J.; and see J. Masson (2000), *op cit.* p. 232–3.

85 Copies of the Convention, Reports of the Special Commissions and details of ratifications can be found on the Hague Convention website: www.hcch.net.

86 The Hague Convention on Jurisdiction, Applicable Law and Recognition of Decrees Relating to Adoption 1965 had been largely ineffective because it was ratified only by Austria, Switzerland and the U.K. Almost no Convention adoptions were ever made.

tion on intercountry adoption. The Permanent Bureau was concerned about the dramatic increase in the number of international adoptions, the complex human and legal problems involved, the insufficiency of domestic laws and the need for a multilateral approach, particularly one which included the states from which children came for adoption. There was a need to establish legally binding standards and a system of supervision to ensure that these were observed. Good communication between the authorities in countries of origin and destination was essential to secure co-operation between them and confidence in the decisions made.[87] The meetings of the Special Commission involved 33 States which were Members of the Hague Conference and 24 non-member States as well as a large number of NGOs concerned with adoption and child welfare. The Convention was completed in 1993 and came into force in 1995. It has been ratified or acceded to by over 50 countries, including both sending and receiving countries. The three countries with the most intercountry adoptions, the U.S.A., China and Russia have indicated their interest in implementing the Convention.

The Convention has three objectives:— to establish safeguards to ensure that intercountry adoptions take place in the best interests of the child; to establish a system of co-operation between countries in order to prevent abduction, sale and trafficking in children; and to secure the recognition of adoptions made under the Convention.[88] By establishing a system of international co-operation it is intended to raise standards and eliminate abuses. Adoptions following the Convention's procedures will be more child-centred, simpler for prospective adopters and of certain effect.[89] These advantages should make Convention adoptions more attractive and discourage intending adopters from seeking children in jurisdictions where procedures remain unregulated.

The Convention applies where a child who is habitually resident in one Contracting State is moved for or after adoption by a person who is habitually resident in another Contracting State.[90] Adoptions can only take place after the competent authorities in the child's state have established that the child is "adoptable" and those in the prospective adopter's state have established that they are eligible and suitable to adopt.[91] A child is only "adoptable" if adoption overseas is in his or her best interests, the required informed consents have been given freely and without inducements, and consideration has been given to the child's wishes and opinions.[92] The Receiving State must also have determined that the child will be able to enter and reside there.[93] Contracting States must designate a Central Authority to discharge the duties under the Convention. These include promoting co-operation over intercountry adoption internally, providing information to other Central Authorities and the Permanent Bureau about

---

[87] G. Parra-Aranguren, *Explanatory Report on the Convention on protection of children and co-operation in respect of intercountry adoption* (1993), paras 6–7.

[88] Art. 1.

[89] W. Duncan, "The Hague Convention on Protection of Children and Co-operation in Respect of Intercountry adoption its birth and prospects" in P. Selman, *op cit.* p. 40, 46.

[90] Art. 2.

[91] Arts 4 and 5.

[92] Art. 4.

[93] Art. 5(c).

the law in their country, and eliminating obstacles to the operation of the Convention.[94] Central Authorities may delegate to other public authorities or accredited bodies, duties in respect of individual adoptions such as the collection and exchange of information about the child and the applicants, and measures to prevent abuses of adoption practice.[95]

Despite the fact that "private" adoptions arranged without the involvement of an accredited agency have been regarded as more at risk of abuse,[96] the Hague Convention allows individual intermediaries to undertake some of the functions of Central Authorities where the domestic law of the country allows this.[97] However, an individual State can declare that it will not allow children habitually resident there to be adopted through such arrangements, and the formal reports on eligibility and adoptability remain the responsibility of Central Authorities or other official bodies.[98] These provisions represent a compromise between the American free-market approach and the more regulated approach operating in Europe and in some Asian sending countries.[99] It was thought that the U.S.A. would be unlikely to ratify the Convention if individuals, often lawyers, could not continue to arrange adoptions, and that a Convention which excluded the major receiving State would be ineffective.[1]

23–046 Prospective adopters must apply for intercountry adoption via the Central Authority in their State of habitual residence. A "homestudy" report must be prepared on the applicants, their background, reasons for adopting and the children for whom they are qualified to care. This is transmitted to the child's State where a comparable report is prepared on the child. This is forwarded to the Central Authority in the applicants' State together with proof of the required consents. The Convention forbids any contact between the applicants and the child's parents or carer until after their consent has been given, the child's adoptability has been established and the applicants have been found eligible and suitable to adopt. This is intended to prevent abuses such as direct approaches to parents or orphanages by people wanting to adopt, and the opportunity for money to be offered or requested to facilitate an adoption.[2] The adoption can only progress if the prospective adopters accept the selected child and both Central Authorities agree.[3] The adoption order can either be made in the child's or the applicant's State. However, if the child enters the applicants' State before the adoption order is made and the placement breaks down, the Central Authority there must protect the child, consult with the Central Authority child's State

---

[94] Arts 6 and 7.
[95] Arts 8, 9.
[96] UNICEF (1998) p. 8.
[97] Art. 22 functions under Arts 15 to 21 can be delegated.
[98] Art. 22(1)(5). If there is no declaration the State accepts private arrangements.
[99] Parra-Aranguren Report paras 242, 373 *et seq*. Euradopt, an organisation of European adoption agencies has agreed a set of ethical rules which should apply to all adoptions: www.euradopt.org.
[1] W. Duncan, "Regulating intercountry adoption—an international perspective" in A. Bainham and D. Pearl (eds) *Frontiers of Family Law* (1993); W. Duncan, "The Hague Convention on the protection and co-operation in respect of intercountry adoption" (1993) 3 *Adoption and Fostering* 7.
[2] Art. 29; and see Parra-Aranguren Report, paras 495 *et seq*.
[3] Arts 14–17.

of origin about alternative placements and, as a last resort, return the child to it.[4] An adoption made under the Convention is recognised in all other Convention countries. Recognition may only be refused if the adoption is "manifestly contrary to public policy, taking into account the welfare of the child."[5]

The Convention forbids "improper financial or other gain" from intercountry adoption activities but reasonable costs and expenses are permitted.[6] However, the Special Commission in December 2000 noted excessive legal fees, particularly in some South American countries and where the lawyer also identified a child for adoption. The Commission recommended that information about costs should provided in advance and that agency accreditation should ensure financial controls.[7] Some orphanages also sought donations and there were suggestions that the highest donors obtained children. The Special Commission was divided between those who thought that donations should not be condoned and those who accepted that support for child care services could be an acceptable part of the cost of providing adoption services. The Permanent Bureau suggested a compromise which accepted contributions providing the amount was notified in advance, the purpose was clear and proper accounts were kept.[8]

It is too soon to judge whether the Convention will successfully regulate intercountry adoption and improve practice. There are currently wide variations in practice; some States have large numbers of accredited agencies and operate few controls on them, in others arrangements are closely supervised by the Central Authority or a well-established agency. A large number of children are adopted from non-Convention countries. The fact that applicants remain willing to adopt from countries with poor standards creates "a market for children" in those states[9] and undermines the work of the Convention. Concerns about abuses in Guatemala led UNICEF to propose that Convention countries should suspend all intercountry adoptions from there but there is no power in the Convention to do this. The Special Commission agreed that states should seek to apply the same safeguards in arrangements with non-Convention countries and encourage such states to join the Convention.[10]

Intercountry Adoption in England and Wales

23–047 The Adoption (Intercountry Aspects) Act 1999 was passed to give effect to

[4] Art. 21. If the placement breaks down after adoption the domestic law of the receiving State determines what should occur. In England and Wales the child would become looked after by a local authority and the adopters would be responsible for making a contribution to the cost, see para 22.063 above and Children Act 1989, Sched. 2, pt 3.

[5] Art. 24. This should be interpreted very restrictively, Parra-Aranguren Report, para. 426. The adoption of a refugee child where no attempts have been made to trace the family who are subsequently located could be contrary to public policy, see *Report of the Special Commission on the Implementation of the Intercountry Adoption Convention* October 1994 and *Re K (Adoption and Wardship)* [1997] 2 F.L.R. 221, FD and CA.

[6] Art. 32. Central Authorities have responsibilities for preventing this, Art. 8.

[7] *Report of the Special Commission on the practical operation of the Hague Convention*, December 2000, paras 37–41.

[8] *ibid.* para. 42–47.

[9] *Report of the Special Commission on the practical operation of the Hague Convention*, December 2000, para. 52.

[10] *ibid.* para 48–57.

the Hague Convention in England, Wales and Scotland[11]; most of its provisions were incorporated into the Adoption and Children Act 2002.[12] Depending on the country of origin of the child, one of three separate regimes[13] applies to intercountry adoptions in the U.K. But in all cases the same process, based on that operated by the Department of Health for many years,[14] is used for determining the eligibility and suitability of the applicants and regulating entry to the country for or after adoption. These controls are backed by criminal sanctions. Only adoption agencies may make arrangements for adoption; a person who undertakes an assessment, or arranges a placement commits an offence.[15] A person who brings a child to the U.K. without previously obtaining notification of approval from the Department of Health also commits and offence.[16]

Intending adopters must be assessed and approved by a local authority or voluntary adoption agency[17]; "home studies" provided by independent social workers cannot be used.[18] Applicants are approved to adopt from a specific country, if they wish to adopt from elsewhere they must demonstrate that they fully understand the cultural and other needs of a child from that country and obtain a new approval from the agency.[19] The process of approval involves counselling and assessment, referral to the agency's adoption panel for a recommendation and notification of the applicants. Where the applicants are approved the agency notifies the Secretary of State[20] who decides whether to endorse the application. Adoption specialists in the Department of Health review the reports provided by the agency, if they are satisfied a Certificate of Eligibility is issued and forwarded to the relevant body in the applicant's chosen country.[21] Judicial review is not available where the applicants are rejected by the Department acting on professional advice.[22]

There is no single process for finding a suitable child. Applicants may use the services of an overseas agency or an intermediary and in some countries it

---

[11] ss.1, 4, 5. The Convention, whose implementation has been promised by British Governments since 1993 is now scheduled for implementation "in mid 2003". In Northern Ireland the Convention is implemented by the Adoption (Intercountry Aspects) Act Northern Ireland 2001.

[12] ss.1, 2, 7 and Sched. 1 (the text of the Convention) remain in force. This was originally a Private Member's Bill promoted by Mark Oaten M.P. following failure by successive governments to provide Parliamentary time to implement the Convention having announced its intention to do so in 1993, Cm. 2288, para. 6.29.

[13] Convention adoptions, Designated country adoptions and Non-Convention adoptions, discussed below.

[14] see: D.H., *Intercountry adoption guide—practice and procedures* (2001).

[15] Adoption and Children Act 2002, ss.92–94.

[16] Adoption and Children Act 2002, ss.83(7), (8) re-enacting Adoption Act 1976, s.56A, added by Adoption (Intercountry Aspects Act 1999, s.14; Adoption of Children from Overseas Regulations 1991, 1991 S.I. No 1251.

[17] Adoption of Children from Overseas Regulations 2001, 2001 S.I. No 1251, reg. 3 (comparable regulations apply in Wales); currently only two agencies provide this service in England: Parents and Children Together and the Doncaster Adoption and Family Welfare Society.

[18] Adoption and Children Act 2002, s.94(1). This restriction was introduced by the Adoption (Intercountry Aspects) Act 1999, s.13.

[19] D.H., *Intercountry adoption guide—practice and procedures* (2001) para. 6.6.

[20] Adoption is a devolved responsibility, the Secretary of State's functions are exercised in Wales by the National Assembly for Wales.

[21] D.H., *Intercountry adoption guide* (2001) *op cit.* paras 5.3–5.6.

[22] *R v. Secretary of State for Health, ex p. Luff* [1992] 1 F.L.R. 59, FD.

remains possible to identify a child directly through an orphanage.[23] When a child has been matched with the applicants they are informed and must decide whether or not to accept. If they do they must arrange to travel to the child's country and continue the process there. They must obtain entry clearance to bring the child to the U.K. Before granting this, the immigration officer checks with the Department of Health that the required procedures have been followed and either a recognised adoption order has been obtained or that it is likely that a court in England will grant the order.[24] Where the child has not been adopted, the applicants must complete the process by adopting here. Even where an order has been obtained some countries require further reports on the child's welfare.[25]

Adoptions under the Hague Convention

23–048 The Central Authority for England is the Secretary of State for Health; communications can be sent to the Department of Health in relation to any part of Great Britain.[26] Adoption societies whose approval covers intercountry adoption are accredited bodies but local authorities, as public authorities with responsibility to provide adoption services, deal with the majority of cases.[27] Detailed provisions defining "Convention adoption orders" and setting out the conditions which must be satisfied before such an order can be made are provided by regulations.[28] Where at least one of the adopters is a British citizen, a "Convention adoption"[29] gives the child British citizenship; there are no restrictions on the adopters bringing the child to the U.K.[30] Similarly, prospective adopters may bring a child from a Convention country to the U.K. for adoption, providing that they have followed the required procedures in the U.K. and completed the necessary stages in the child's home state.[31] The High Court has power to annul adoptions made under the Convention which are contrary to public policy.[32]

Designated country adoptions

23–049 Where a child is adopted overseas in a country listed in the Adoption (Designation of Overseas Adoptions) Order 1973[33] the order is recognised as

---

[23] There are restrictions on advertising adoption but these cannot prevent intending adopters from locating children via internet advertisements if these are not held by an internet service provider in the U.K., s.123. The Kilshaws identified the twins through an advert placed by an overseas agency see *Flintshire C.C. v. K* [2001] 2 F.L.R. 476, FD.

[24] D.H., *Intercountry adoption guide* (2001), *op cit.* paras 5.7–5.15.

[25] D.H., *Intercountry adoption guide* (2001), para. 5.56.

[26] Adoption (Intercountry Aspects) Act 1999, s.2(1), (2). In Wales, the National Assembly for Wales performs these functions and in Scotland, the Secretary of State within the Scottish Executive.

[27] Adoption (Intercountry Aspects) Act 1999, s.2(3), (4); Adoption and Children Act 2002, s.2(8), 3.

[28] To be made under Adoption (Intercountry Aspects) Act 1999, s.1.

[29] *i.e.* an adoption made in a Convention country outside the British Islands.

[30] Adoption (Intercountry Aspects) Act 1999, s.7 amending British Nationality Act 1981, s.1.

[31] To be set out in regulations made under Adoption (Intercountry Aspects) Act 1999, s.1.

[32] Adoption and Children Act 2002, s.89(1) implementing Art. 24, above. Similarly, a Convention adoption can be annulled by the state which made it, s.91.

[33] 1973 S.I. No. 19. Designated countries include many but not all Commonwealth Countries, members of the European Union and some other European Countries, the U.S.A. and China. Inclusion in the list does not indicate that the country applies similar standards to those in the U.K. or that

an adoption order in the U.K.[34] so long as it is valid in the country where it was made.[35] The applicants do not need to re-adopt the child[36] but must have complied with the formal procedures set out in regulations, unless the adoption was completed more than six months before the entry to the U.K.[37]

Other intercountry adoptions

23–050 Where the child has not been adopted in either a Convention or Designated country an adoption order must be obtained from a court in the U.K. The applicants must notify their local authority of their intention to adopt within 14 days of entering the U.K.,[38] until the notification is made the child is a private foster child.[39] The local authority must investigate and prepare a report for the court.[40] No application can be made until the child has had his home with the applicants for the required period,[41] and the order can only be made if the court is satisfied that the local authority has had sufficient opportunities to see the child with the applicants.[42] These provisions are intended to ensure local authorities are aware of children brought in for adoption. Prior to their introduction the courts could be faced with applications from unsuitable people with established relationships with the child so that there was no alternative to granting an adoption order.[43]

---

there is a bilateral agreement with the U.K. relating to intercountry adoption. The list will be revised following the implementation of the Hague Convention, Adoption and Children Bill 2002, E.N. para. 10. Countries will only appear on the new list if their adoption practices meet specific requirements, Jacqui Smith, Hansard, *Commons*, May 20, 2002, Vol. 386, col. 25, Adoption and Children Bill, Report Stage.

[34] The adoption is an "overseas adoption" Adoption and Children Act 2002, s.87(1), (2)(b).

[35] In *Flintshire C.C. v. K* [2001] 2 F.L.R. 476, FD the order was defective because the parties did not satisfy the residence requirements to allow jurisdiction in Arkansas, a state chosen for the proceedings because of its lax adoption rules. The High Court may annul an overseas adoption on public policy grounds, s.89(1).

[36] There are some advantages of doing so see: R. Cordery, "Re-adoption in the U.K.—a guide for families who have adopted children in China" [2000] *I.F.L* 74. The child obtains British citizenship by registration, see above para. 23. 007.

[37] Adoption and Children Act 2002, s.83(1)(b), (3).

[38] Adoption of Children from Overseas Regulations 2001, 2001 S.I. No 1251, reg. 3(3). It is an offence to fail to do so, s.83(7).

[39] Children Act 1989, Pt IX.

[40] Adoption and Children Act 2002, s.44(5).

[41] s.42(5). In non agency, non-step-parent cases where the applicants are not local authority foster parents the probationary period is three years. But s.81(6) provides that requirements in Chap. 3 of the Act may be modified for overseas adoptions. The government proposes that the probationary period should be six months where applicants have complied with the proper procedures and 12 months in other cases, Jacqui Smith, Hansard, *Commons*, May 20, 2002 Vol. 386, col. 23, Adoption and Children Bill, Report Stage.

[42] s.42(7).

[43] "Except in the very unusual case where there is a claim for the return of the child by the natural family, in all reported cases welfare considerations have led the court to [grant the order]." *per* Johnson J. *Re C (Adoption: Legality)* [1999] 1 F.L.R. 370, 382; see also *Re R (No. 1) (Intercountry Adoption)* [1999] 1 F.L.R. 1014, FD; *Re AW (Adoption Application)* [1993] 1 F.L.R. 62.

Adoption overseas of UK resident children[44]

23–051 As a consequence of concerns about the effects of the child migration programme[45] adoption overseas is rarely considered appropriate for children in the U.K. and is subject to considerable safeguards. Such adoptions may be arranged with relatives overseas or where carers, temporarily resident in the U.K., return overseas. Children may not be removed from the U.K. for adoption overseas except by parents, step-parents or relatives unless an order has been obtained granting the applicant parental responsibility.[46] Removing a child contrary to these provisions is an offence.

4. "In family" adoptions

23–052 Although never intended to re-order legal relationships within families, adoption orders have been used for this purpose since 1927. Some parents, step-parents, grand-parents and other relatives have felt that the status adoption gives provides advantages for them and their child relatives. At different times these adoptions have been favoured with less regulation or discouraged with increased controls. Alternative orders[47] have been made available but have not proved attractive; the majority of relative carers look after children without formal arrangements but adoption orders were sought by approximately 1500 step-parents in 2001.[48]

Adoption by a parent

23–053 In the 1950s when the stigma of illegitimacy was great; unmarried mothers were advised to adopt their own children in order to conceal the illegitimacy, improve the child's status and prevent the father interfering.[49] Adoption orders to unmarried mothers were anomalous since they did not end the father's obligation to support the child.[50] Although these parental adoptions were rare, the Houghton Committee recommended that they should be made only in exceptional circumstances and should end the father's obligation to maintain.[51] Provisions to this effect were

---

44 The provisions also apply to Commonwealth citizens present in the U.K. Such children may be in the U.K because of the historic links between the countries and may need the same protection as those habitually resident here.

45 See above, para. 22.068.

46 Adoption and Children Act 2002, s.84, 85. The order must be made by the High Court under s.84; s.85 does not apply where the court has given permission for the emigration of a looked after child under Children Act 1989, Sched. 2, para. 19.

47 Joint custody and custodianship introduced by the Children Act 1975, replaced by residence orders by the Children Act 1989 and supplemented special guardianship orders in Adoption and Children Act 2002, s.115.

48 *Judicial Statistics 2001*, table 5.4. Statistics are not kept for the numbers of adoptions by parents and relatives.

49 M. Kornitzer, *Child Adoption in the Modern World* (1952), pp. 56, 319; M. Kornitzer, *Child Adoption* (1958), p. 111.

50 Adoption Act 1958, s.15.

51 1972 Cmnd. 5107, para. 102; in 1970 there were 84 orders in favour of mothers and 11 in favour of fathers, (App B). Only 13 orders were made in 1978: *First Report to Parliament on the Children Act 1975* (H.C. 268, 1979–80), para. 27.

introduced in the Children Act 1975 and have been repeated in subsequent legislation.[52] This use of adoption remains controversial:—

> In *Re B (Adoption: Natural Parent)*[53] the mother requested that social services place her child for adoption, saying that the father was overseas. By chance the father's whereabouts were known by the social worker, he was contacted and he offered to care for the child. The mother agreed to this arrangement and only expressed a slight reservation when he applied to adopt the child. The application was transferred to the High Court and the Official Solicitor was appointed. He opposed the application on the basis that it only served to end the mother's relationship with the child and did not therefore safeguard the child's welfare. The order was made; the mother's rejection of the child at birth justified making the order.[54] The Court of Appeal allowed the appeal by the Official Solicitor. Hale L.J. stated that only some reason such as death, disappearance or anonymous sperm donation could justify adoption by one parent. Ending in law the mother child relationship was a disproportionate response to the child's needs and contrary the child's article 8 rights.[55] A residence order was granted, the father was given unfettered powers to take the child abroad and the mother was barred from making any applications without leave. The father appealed. The House of Lords restored the adoption order on the basis that the Court of Appeal had exceeded its power to review the judge's discretion. It rejected the narrow interpretation of the circumstances in which adoption could be granted to a parent and, with less than convincing reasoning, held that an order which was in the child's best interests could not breach the child's rights.[56]

Such an adoption order in favour of a parent has no effect on the child's entitlement to property which depends on a relationship with that parent.[57]

Adoption by parent and step-parent

23–054 Step-parent adoptions are far more common[58] but only a tiny minority of step-families use adoption (or any other order) to regularise their position. Adop-

---

[52] Adoption and Children Act 2002, s.51(4). The court must record the reason for granting the order.

[53] [2002] 1 F.L.R. 196, HL reversing [2001] 1 F.L.R. 589, CA and upholding the order made in *B v. P (Adoption by Unmarried Father)* [2000] 2 F.L.R. 717, FD.; see also Harris-Short [2002] *C.F.L.Q.* 325.

[54] [2000] 2 F.L.R. 721H *per* Bracewell J.

[55] [2001] 1 F.L.R. 589 at paras 34–40. This assumes that "family life" exists between a both who has rejected the child at birth and her child a point accepted by the House of Lords [2002] 1 F.L.R. 196 at para. 30, and see above, para 23.033.

[56] [2002] 1 F.L.R. 196 at paras 17–19, 23 and 31. The child's welfare was not paramount under the Adoption Act 1976, even if it were a marginal improvement in welfare would not necessarily justify a lifelong change of status, the effects of which could not possibly be determined when the order was made.

[57] Adoption and Children Act 2002, s.67(4).

[58] 1500 orders, just over a third of adoptions were in favour of a parent and step-parent in 2001 but there were over 14,000 orders in 1975: see Masson *et al.*, (1983), p. 12.

tion orders in favour of a parent and step-parent are subject to most of the requirements which apply to other adoptions[59] and have the same effect as other adoption orders. The child is legally integrated into the new family, cutting the links with the natural family. The birth parent and step-parent become the child's legal adoptive parents; the original birth certificate is replaced with an adoption certificate and, if the applicants are mother and step-father as is most common,[60] the child's surname is usually changed. The Houghton Committee considered that such adoptions were inappropriate and could be damaging because they destroyed beneficial links with the non-adopting parent and could be used to conceal the child's past.[61] There was only very limited anecdotal evidence for this view[62] which ignored the fact that many of the children had no contact with their other parent. Following recommendations by the Committee, the Children Act 1975 provided alternative orders, joint custody or custodianship and required the court to make these where they were better than adoption.[63] This led to an immediate fall in step-parent adoption applications even where no alternative was available, and a sharp increase in unsuccessful applications.[64] There were wide variations in the success rates in different courts; judges and social workers were uncertain when adoption was appropriate.[65] The Children Act 1989 repealed the restriction introduced in the 1975 Act; residence orders replaced joint custody and custodianship and were available to all step-parents. The 2002 Act once again requires the court to be satisfied that the order it makes is better than any alternative order, or making no order at all.[66]

Despite changes in law and practice emphasising the enduring nature of parenthood,[67] the Review of Adoption Law considered that it was inappropriate to prevent step-parent adoption. This could be a suitable arrangement where a child had no relationship with one side of his or her family. However, it was anomalous to require a birth parent to adopt their own children in order for their spouse to adopt, so a new form of adoption order should be provided.[68] The Adoption and Children Act 2002, enables the partner of the parent to adopt the child alone.[69] Where such an order is made the step-parent becomes a legal parent but

---

[59] The age limit for the child's parent (but not step-parent) is 18: Adoption and Children Act 2002, s.50(2)(a); the probationary period is six months, s.42(3).

[60] 96 per cent of applications were made by mothers and step-fathers in the largest study of these adoption: see Masson *et al.* (1983), p. 46.

[61] 1972 Cmnd. 5107, para. 105. For a discussion of different approaches to step-parent adoption see J. Masson, "Step-parent adoption" in P. Bean (ed.) *Adoption* (1984).

[62] The report of the Association of Child Care Officers, *Adoption: the Way Ahead* (1969) and I. Goodacre, *Adoption policy and practice* (1966) were relied on by the Committee.

[63] 1972 Cmnd. 5107, paras 106–110; ss.10(3) and 37(1); these sections were implemented on November 26, 1976 and December 1, 1985 respectively.

[64] Masson *et al.* (1983), tables 7.5 & 7.6.

[65] See *Re S (Infants) (Adoption by Parent)* [1977] Fam. 173; *Re D (Adoption by Step Parent)* [1980] 2 F.L.R. 102. For a discussion of the judicial approaches in the case law, see J. Priest, "Step-parent adoptions: What is the law?" [1982] *J.S.W.L.* 285 and R. W. Rawlings, "Law reform with tears" (1982) 45 *M.L.R.* 637.

[66] Adoption and Children Act 2002, s.1(6).

[67] Children Act 1989, s.2, 3 and 33; Child Support Act 1991.

[68] Review of Adoption Law (1992), paras 19.2–3.

[69] s.52(2). Adoption is only available to one of the parents and in practice this must be the parent with care, s.42(7).

their spouse retains their status and relationship with the child.[70] The Act thus allows co-parenting arrangements between a parent and their gay, lesbian or heterosexual partner to be formalised through adoption and without changing the status of the birth parent.[71] This form of order exists alongside the traditional form of step-parent adoption, and although the court can grant alternative orders under the Children Act, it is not clear that it can grant an adoption order in favour of only one of joint applicants. Couples seeking to create a legal relationship between a child and the parent's partner should be advised that only the partner need apply for adoption.[72]

The Review of Adoption Law also acknowledged that adoption might be inappropriate where the step-parent had little interest in the child or because adoption could undermine relationships with the extended family. It proposed a simpler alternative to discourage adoption applications.[73] Married step-parents should be able to share parental responsibility by an agreement with both natural parents, registered with the court, or under a court order. The Adoption and Children Act 2002 makes provision for this.[74] In contrast with adoption, this provision does not enable an unmarried or same-sex partner to obtain parental responsibility for a step-child by agreement. The government took the view that the acquisition of parental responsibility by such people should always be subject to court scrutiny.[75]

The court is now provided with a confusing array of orders with quite similar effect in law but which may be viewed very differently by the applicants.[76] When hearing an adoption application the court must consider the whole range of its powers and may make a residence order or special guardianship order (but not parental responsibility under s.4A) even though no application has been made.[77] The child's welfare is paramount but the court will need to consider the impact of the order on the other parent and the effect of granting an irrevocable adoption order to a step-parent whose relationship with the parent may break down, because these necessarily impact on the child's welfare. Both granting and refusing an order in favour of a step-parent may interfere with rights to family life. The step-parent may have a relationship with the child which ought to be recognised even though doing so will end a parent's legal relationship.[78] It is comparatively unusual for orders to be made, particularly where a parent

---

[70] s.67(2)(b).

[71] No corresponding change has been signalled in relation to parenting orders, Human Fertilisation and Embryology Act 1990, s.30, see para. 23.069, below.

[72] No explanation was given why both forms of step-parent adoption were thought desirable. The comparable provisions in the Adoption (Scotland) Act 1978 which are limited to married couples provides that even where both parties adopt the parent retains their pre-existing parental rights and responsibilities, s.15(1)(aa).

[73] Review of Adoption Law (1992), paras.19.2–3; Cm. 2288, para. 5.20.

[74] s.112, adding Children Act 1989, s.4A.

[75] The government's original proposal, set out in a letter to Peers in June 2002, would have allowed s.4A agreements in favour of heterosexual partners but required a court order for a same-sex partner.

[76] Applicants may not be satisfied if they are given a different order from that they sought; adoption has emotional connotations derived from its established position in society, substitute orders have not so far been able to match this.

[77] Adoption and Children Act 2002, s.1(6); Children Act 1989, ss.4A(1)(b), 8(3), 10(1), 14A(6)(b).

[78] *Soderback v. Sweden* [1999] 1 F.L.R. 230.

with parental responsibility objects. But there are cases where the child's need for security, the child's wish to be adopted, the strength of the relationship with the step-parent and the lack of positive involvement from the other natural parent justify adoption.[79] However, these adoptions are given thorough consideration.[80] Applicants may be counselled against seeking adoption,[81] and applications which undermine valuable relationships or do not include all the children are likely to be refused.[82]

Adoption by grand-parents or other relatives

23–055 Grandparents, aunts, uncles and other relatives[83] may also seek to adopt a child. In most cases this will be the result of informal arrangements made in the family; local authorities do place children with relatives, but these arrangements rarely lead to adoption.[84] The Houghton Committee also opposed adoption by relatives because of the possibility of distortion of family relationships, for example adoption by grandparents would turn the child's mother into a sister.[85] Custodianship was made available but the Children Act 1989 replaced this with the residence order. The Review of Adoption Law did not want to rule out adoption by relatives but considered that there were few situations where it provided clear advantages or a residence order was inadequate.[86] The Adoption and Children Act 2002 requires adoption to be the better option[87] and applies the same restrictions to these applications as apply to non-agency applications by strangers. Relatives must have cared for the child for at least three of the previous five years, or have the leave of the court, before making an application.[88] They are required to notify the local authority and are subject to investigation.[89] The alternative of a residence order is available without satisfying these conditions but applicants may need the leave of the court.[90]

The Prime Minister's Review also identified special guardianship as better

---

[79] *Re B (Adoption: Father's Objection)* [1999] 2 F.L.R. 215, CA *per* Butler-Sloss L.J. (order granted and appealed refused; father had twice kidnapped his son and been involved in over 140 court applications in respect of him). And see *Re PJ (Adoption: Practice on Appeal)* [1998] 2 F.L.R. 252, CA where the violent father's appeal against dispensing with his consent was allowed but the Court of Appeal exercising its own (pragmatic) discretion allowed the orders to stand.

[80] This was not the case in the past and is not always expected by applicants, see *Masson et al.* (1983).

[81] DHSS Circular LAC 84(10), para. 60.

[82] *Re P (Minors) (Adoption)* [1989] 1 F.L.R. 1, CA.

[83] Adoption and Children Act 2002, s.144; great uncles and great aunts are not relatives. *Re C (minors) (wardship: adoption)* [1989] 1 F.L.R. 222.

[84] M. Murch *et al.*, *Pathways to adoption* (1993), p. 11; only 7% of the sample of applications were by relatives, 80% of these resulted in orders: p. 20. Fostering under a care order, a residence order or special guardianship provide more suitable arrangements for most cases.

[85] 1973 Cmnd. 5107, para. 111.

[86] Review of Adoption Law (1992), paras 6.3, 20.1–204.

[87] s.1(6).

[88] Adoption and Children Act 2002, s.42(5), (6).

[89] s.44(2)–(5).

[90] Children Act 1989, ss.9(3),10(5). The court is to be given power to direct that the order lasts until the child is aged 18, Adoption and Children Act, s.114, adding Children Act 1989, s.12(5)(6). There is no provision for *intervivos* guardianship as proposed by Cm. 2288, paras 5.4, 5.23–24.

than adoption for some children being cared for by their wider birth family.[91] Relatives will be able to strengthen their legal position by obtaining a special guardianship order if they already have a residence order, have cared for the child for three years or have the consent of everyone with parental responsibility.[92] The court may grant a residence order or a special guardianship order when considering an adoption application and must give paramount consideration to the child's welfare throughout his life when choosing between these.[93] The determining factor could be the legal effects adoption has in adulthood.

> In *Re W (A Minor) (Adoption: Custodianship: Access)*[94] the Court of Appeal upheld a decision to dispense with the agreement of a mentally handicapped mother to the adoption of her child by her parents although contact between the other and child was continuing. The grandparents had cared for the child since birth. The mother's limited ability and lack of relationship with the child justified an order to secure the child's care. Adoption was more appropriate because it enabled the grandparents to appoint a testamentary guardian. However, this could now be achieved by special guardianship.[95]

Open Adoption

23–056 Adoption has traditionally been a closed and secretive process[96] in which birth parents and adoptive parents are unaware of each other's identities, and the child's adoptive status is concealed from all but the child and the adoptive family.[97] Adoption law originally gave birth parents access to the identity of the adopters but professional practices and legislation reinforced the closed nature of adoption.[98] In the 1970s there was increased recognition of the adopted person's need for information about their background in order to form a positive self-identity.[99] Later studies revealed the desire and need of those who had relinquished children for adoption to know that their child was placed successfully.[1] Adoption agencies began to develop more open adoption practices, and it is now accepted that adoption plans should include arrangements for maintaining links with their birth families.[2]

---

[91] PIU, *Adoption* (2000), para 5.8. For an explanation of special guardianship see, para. 18.043, above.

[92] Children Act 1989, s.14A(5)(b), (c).

[93] Children Act 1989, ss.10(1), 14A(6); Adoption and Children Act 2002, s.1(2)(6).

[94] [1988] 1 F.L.R. 175, CA.

[95] Children Act 1989, s.14G(4)(b) amending Children Act 1989, s.5(4)

[96] Review of Adoption Law (1992), para. 4.1.

[97] The arrangements for court proceedings and for registration of adoption facilitate this.

[98] M. Ryburn "Secrecy and openness in adoption—an historical perspective" (1995) 29 *Social Policy and Administration* 150; S. Cretney, *Family law in the Twentieth Century* (2003) Chap. 17.

[99] Following the publication of J. Triseliotis, *In search of origins* (1973) and the introduction of access to birth records, see above para. 23.011.

[1] Howe *et al.* (1992); D. Howe and J. Feast, *Adoption, search and reunion* (2000). These ideas have been accepted in the 2002 Act with provision for intermediaries to assist parents to make contact with their adult birth children, s.98.

[2] Adoption Standards (2001) Standard A11, C4, D7.

Openness can take many different forms including greater involvement of the birth parents in the plan of adoption and selection of adoptive parents; indirect contact involving the passing of information after adoption between adults with the adoption agency acting as a "letter box"; or direct contact between the child and natural parents or other relatives.[3] Arrangements in an individual case may become more or less open as time passes.[4] It has been suggested that where contact has survived the original care order it is likely to survive into adoption.[5] At least 70 per cent of adopted children have some form of contact with their birth families.[6]

Openness is said to have the following advantages: it may facilitate better arrangements for the child's care, reduce the sense of rejection the adopted child feels, ensure the adopters and the child have more information about the child's background and encourage the birth family to support the adoption plan.[7] There is research evidence that some adopters feel their relationships with their adoptive children benefit from contact with birth relatives but others feel their position is undermined.[8] Adopted children have indicated that they would like more contact with their families.[9] But there is concern that contact is imposed to placate the birth parents, irrespective of the child's welfare,[10] that placements will be destabilised,[11] and that prospective adopters will withdraw if they are expected to maintain contact.

23–056/1 Contact cannot be bargained for parental consent.[12] Although it is possible for the courts to make a section 8 contact order when making an adoption order,[13] they are extremely reluctant to do so. Where the adopters agree to contact an order is regarded as unnecessary.[14] Where they do not, the imposition of

---

[3] Review of Adoption Law (1992), para. 4.2; for details of the range of policies and practices see: SSI, *Moving goalposts* (1995). Contact with maternal relatives is far more common than with paternal relatives, E. Neil, "The reasons why young children are placed for adoption" (2000) *Child and Fam. Soc. Wk.* 303, 314.

[4] Review of Adoption Law (1992), para. 5.3 suggests that contact may diminish but others have suggested that it is likely to develop as trust develops between the adopters and the birth parents, see M. Beek [1994] 2 *Adoption and Fostering* 36; R. McRoy [1991] 4 *Adoption and Fostering* 99.

[5] M. Richards [1994] 4 *Adoption and Fostering* 5 at 6; In Ryburn's study of contested adoptions nearly half had some ongoing contact, M. Ryburn (ed.) *Contested Adoption* (1994) p. 141; M. Ryburn [1994] 4 *Adoption and Fostering* 30. In Neil's study contact was less common where children had been relinquished as babies, see (2000) *Child and Fam. Soc. Wk.* 303, 311.

[6] Unpublished research cited in D.H., *Providing effective adoption consultation paper* (2002), p. 15; see also Parker (1999) p. 47.

[7] Review of Adoption Law (1992), para. 4.4. Lowe *et al.* (1999) p. 324 also note that contact can help children to settle and allay their anxieties about the well-being of birth relatives.

[8] Thoburn (1990), pp. 85, 89; M. Ryburn, *Open adoption* (1994); Lowe *et al.* (1999) p. 281. Lowe *et al.* suggest various conditions before adopters feel comfortable with contact and see the benefits for their children:— birth relatives must approve of the adoption; adopters must accept that the child may need to see birth relatives; all parties must feel secure about the adoption and the adopters need to communicate pro contact attitudes to their children, p. 324.

[9] C. Thomas *et al.*, *Adopted children speaking* (1999) Chap. 8.

[10] Lowe *et al.* (1999) p. 313.

[11] SSI, *Moving goalposts* (1995), p. 28; for a case example of action to support the adoptive parents see: *Re O (contempt: committal)* [1995] 2 F.L.R. 767.

[12] Consent must be unconditional, s.52(5) and above para. 23.029, but parents may feel more able to support adoption knowing that some contact will continue.

[13] For the position when a placement order is made see above para. 23.041.

[14] *Re T (Adoption: Contact)* [1995] 2 F.L.R. 251, CA.

contact is viewed as incompatible with adopters' complete parental responsibility.[15] Agencies are encouraged to negotiate written agreements about contact between parents or relatives and prospective adopters, and to clarify their role in providing support for these.[16] These arrangements are not enforceable. Also, it is unclear that children's interests in maintaining contact with relatives, particularly siblings placed separately, are protected in such arrangements. Unless children are represented in the adoption proceedings the court may remain unaware of the importance of contact to them.[17] Where the effect of adoption is to terminate relationships with siblings, the court will need to be satisfied that formal arrangements for contact are not required to protect each child's Article 8 rights.

Applications for contact after adoption require leave and the court will only grant this where the adopters' decision is sufficiently contrary to the child's welfare or unreasonable to justify overriding their discretion.[18] An appeal against refusal of leave was allowed where the adopters reneged on their agreement to provide an annual report to the adopted children's adult half sister.[19] But leave was refused for an application on behalf of a nine year adopted girl who wanted contact with her half brother, adopted into a different family.[20]

VI. ORDERS IN ADOPTION PROCEEDINGS

23–057 A court hearing an adoption application must always consider the whole range of powers available to it under the Adoption and Children Act 2002 and the Children Act 1989. It must not make an order unless this would be better for the child than not doing so[21] but may make section 8 orders or special guardianship orders without an application.[22] Three major decisions are involved:— 1) whether to order adoption, special guardianship or residence or make no order at all; 2) whether or not to make orders for contact; and 3) whether to impose any other conditions on the adoption. These decisions must all be made giving paramount consideration to the child's welfare,[23] and in the case of decision

---

15 *Re C (Adoption: Conditions)* [1989] A.C. 1; adopters should be in the "driving seat" *Re T (Adoption: Contact)* [1995] 2 F.L.R. 251, CA at p. 253 *per* Butler-Sloss L.J. The approach is quite different where birth parents separate see: CASC, *Making contact work* (2002), above para. 19.052.

16 Baroness Andrews, Hansard, *Lords*, Vol. 639, col. 669, Adoption and Children Bill, Report Stage, October 15, 2002.

17 Children are not automatically parties to their adoption proceedings.

18 *Re S (Contact: Application by Sibling)* [1998] 2 F.L.R. 897, FD.

19 *Re T (Adopted Children: Contact)* [1995] 2 F.L.R. 792, CA. Applications for leave after adoption should be designed to ensure that the adopters are not disturbed *per* Balcombe L.J. at p. 798–9; *Re E (Adopted Child: Contact Leave)* [1995] 1 F.L.R. 57 leave refused where a social worker had promised the birth parents a photograph of their child.

20 *Re S (Contact: Application by Sibling)* [1998] 2 F.L.R. 897, FD.

21 Adoption and Children Act 2002, s. (6); Children Act 1989, s.1(5) and above para. 19.003.

22 Children Act 1989, ss.10(1)(b), 14A(6)(b). A step parent can get parental responsibility in this manner without an application but an order under s.4A requires an application.

23 Children Act 1989, s.1(1); Adoption and Children Act 2002, s.1(2),(7) and above, Chap. 20.

relating to the adoption of a child, this means welfare "throughout his life"[24] and includes (inter alia) the likely effect of ceasing to be a member of the original family and being an adopted person.[25]

The judge or magistrates considering the application will have reports from the agency or local authority[26] and possibly the assistance of a CAFCASS officer.[27] They may also have evidence from the applicants, the birth parents, relatives and, if they have been made parties, the children.[28] The government expects that most issues surrounding adoption will have been resolved before the adoption hearing[29] but the courts' approach to making alternative orders will be crucial.

1. Adoption, special guardianship or residence?

23–058 It is important to recognise that there is more than one way of securing legal permanence,[30] and that special guardianship or residence, supported by other orders as required, may be more appropriate than adoption.[31] However, there are major differences between the effects of these orders. Adoption ends the child's legal relationship with the birth family and the status of the parents, and enables his or her full legal integration into the new family, with lifelong effect, giving a new and irrevocable status which effects citizenship and inheritance rights. Special guardians may appear very like parents during childhood, they can make almost all decisions about the child's upbringing and may be permitted to change the child's name, but their power is limited in some respects.[32] Special guardianship does not change the child's status nor give inheritance rights but provision for this may be made by will. There is considerable legal security for the arrangement; parents, children and some others can only apply for revocation of the order with the leave of the court,[33] and parents also require leave to seek a residence order during special guardianship.[34] The position of non-parents with

---

[24] s.1(2) and above, para. 23.024.

[25] s.1(4)(c).

[26] These are currently termed "Sched. 2 reports" Adoption Rules 1984, r. 22 and Sched. 2.

[27] Adoption and Children Act 2002, s.102.

[28] Rules will require parents to be notified of the proceedings, s.141(3)(4), but unless the court requires, the person need not attend. In practice parents are unlikely to attend where they have not been given leave to contest the application and any concerns about contact have been dealt with informally. It is not intended to designate adoption proceedings as "specified proceedings", Baroness Scotland, Parliamentary Secretary, Lord Chancellor's Department, Hansard, *Lords* Vol. 639 col. 1345, Adoption and Children Bill, *Report Stage*, October 23, 2002.

[29] Baroness Scotland, Hansard, *Lords* Vol. 639 col. 1345, Adoption and Children Bill, *Report Stage*, October 23, 2002.

[30] *Re B (Adoption Order)* [2001] 2 F.L.R. 26, 31 *per* Hale L.J. But in *Re O (Transracial Adoption)* [1995] 2 F.L.R. 597, at 607–8 Thorpe J. considered that the advice of the guardian that security could be achieved by residence was "inherently fallacious".

[31] A discussion of these issues in an earlier context remains relevant, see: M. Adcock and R. White, "Adoption, custodianship; or fostering" (1985) 4 *Adoption and Fostering* 14, 15.

[32] For example they require consent of those with parental responsibility for a name change or to remove the child from the U.K. for more than three months, s.14C(3) added by Adoption and Children Act 2002, s.115.

[33] Children Act 1989, s.14D added by Adoption and Children Act 2002, s.115.

[34] Children Act 1989, s.10(7A) added by Adoption and Children Act 2002, Sched. 3, para. 56(d).

residence orders is more limited[35] but the court can direct that the order lasts until the child reaches age 18 and if it does so, the order cannot be varied or discharged without leave.[36] In either case, parents may continue to apply for contact, prohibited steps and specific issue orders without leave unless the court has imposed restrictions under section 91(14).[37] Overall those who obtain only special guardianship or residence orders have a more limited legal relationship with the child and less protection against further court proceedings by the parents. And where there is only a residence order, the carers have no rights to be assessed for support services and can only seek family support under Children Act 1989, Part III.[38] Special guardianship has been introduced with the intention of providing more security and support that has been available through residence orders.[39] It is likely that it will replace residence orders for long term foster carers and many relative carers.

Despite the more limited relationship created by special guardianship there will be circumstances where one of these orders is more in the child's interests than adoption.[40] Particularly where there a good reasons for the child retaining full membership of the original family; for example, where adoption would distort family relationships by excluding a parent,[41] or by placing a parent in the position of a sibling, or where the child has a strong wish to retain the formal parent child link:—

> In *Re M (Adoption or Residence order)*[42] the local authority placed a girl aged nine years with a couple. Contact was arranged with the girls' family four times a year. The couple applied to adopt; although the girl was happy to remain with the applicants she did not wish to be adopted. The local authority withdrew its support for adoption and suggested rehabilitating the girl to her mother. The couple then suggested that they should seek residence instead of adoption, but changed their minds after the mother applied for residence. The mother's application for residence was dismissed, her consent was dispensed with an adoption order made. On appeal, the court dismissed the adoption application on the basis that the mother was not refusing her consent unreasonably. Despite the couple's threat to reject the

---

[35] see above, paras 18.041 and 19.014. The main difference is the length of time the child can be taken outside the U.K. without consent of those with parental responsibility or the court.

[36] Children Act 1989, s.12(5)(6). There is no restriction on applications for residence orders comparable to that applying where there is a special guardianship order.

[37] see above, para. 19.026.

[38] see above, paras 22.07–009 and 23.022.

[39] D.H., *Friends and family care (kinship care) current policy framework, issues and options, discussion paper* (2002), para. 50.

[40] *Re B (Adoption Order)* [2001] 2 F.L.R. 26, CA (where the foster carer had a good relationship with the parents and was content to have a residence order).

[41] *Re B (Adoption: Natural Parent)* [2002] 1 F.L.R. 196, HL. The Court of Appeal's judgment in this case (reversed for other reasons) indicates concern about the use of adoption by one parent to exclude the other, see above para. 23.053. Special guardianship is not available to parents but they may obtain residence orders which will normally end at age 16, Children Act 1989, ss.12(5) and 14A(2)(b), added by Adoption and Children Act 2002, ss.114 and 115.

[42] [1998] 1 F.L.R. 370, CA.

girl unless an adoption order was made; a residence order was granted with restrictions on further applications by the mother.

Where a child can obtain the same level of care and security through special guardianship and wants to retain the legal relationship with their birth family, it will be difficult for the court to be satisfied that adoption is in the child's best interests, and even more difficult to be satisfied that the child's welfare requires that parental consent be dispensed with.[43] However, the child's age and ability to understand the change of status that adoption brings mean that in most cases greater weight is likely to be given to the applicant's views than those of the child. Security and status are matters where perception and feelings may be more important than the formal effect of orders. Carers may want adoption so as to be prepared for unlikely occurrences, such as emigration or their own premature deaths, not merely to have an arrangement which will work in the ordinary course of events. If there is no prospect of return to the family of origin and the child is young, adoption may reflect the fact that the carers are the child's only effective parents.[44] But this will not always be the case where there is substantial contact between the birth family and the carers and each is able to recognise the others' value to the child. Where the natural parents harbour unrealistic hopes of rehabilitation or are in conflict with the carers, residence may not provide adequate security for the child.[45] But an adoption application may increase the conflict, at least in the short term. Adoption will alter the child's identity which may be inappropriate, particularly where this damages links to culture or community. In some cases adoption may be essential because of the additional power it gives the adoptive parents.[46] Adoption remains attractive because the concept is well established and understood in the community.[47] Developments of more open models of adoption may fit within the legal framework of special guardianship or residence but whilst adoption is understood as a superior status with general community support, applicants are likely to seek it, not the alternatives.

2. Contact orders

23–059 Before making an adoption order the court must consider whether there should be arrangements for allowing any person contact with the child,[48] this reflects

---

[43] Adoption and Children Act 2002, s.52(1).

[44] *Re B (Adoption Order)* [2001] 2 F.L.R. 26, CA; *Re A (A minor) (Adoption: Parental Consent)* [1987] 2 All E.R. 81, CA; *Re S (A Minor) (Adoption or Custodianship)* [1987] 2 F.L.R. 331, CA.

[45] *Re M (A minor) (Custodianship: Jurisdiction)* [1987] 1 W.L.R. 162, CA.

[46] *Re W (Adoption: Custodianship: Access)* [1988] 1 F.L.R. 175, CA (the need to appoint a guardian).

[47] Custodianship was not seen as attractive by foster carers and there were few applications: see E. Bullard, E. Malos *et al. Custodianship: caring for other people's children* (1991). Special guardianship may be more in keeping with Islamic Law which supports the retention of legal links with the birth family.

[48] Adoption and Children Act 2002, s.46(6).

as major change in policy,[49] recognising open adoption and the importance of maintaining relationships with members of the child's birth family.[50] The court may make section 8 contact orders but rarely does so, preferring that contact arrangements should be agreed by the adopters and under their control.[51] Contact orders may, of course be made alongside special guardianship or residence orders, but there is no specific injunction on the court to consider doing so. Where contact arrangements are well established an order may still be advantageous because it will make clear to all concerned that arrangements should continues despite the acquisition of parental responsibility by the carers. If the local authority played a major role in facilitating contact for a child in care before the special guardianship order was granted this should be continued as part of the support package.[52]

3. Other conditions

23–060 Following the recommendation of the Adoption Law Review, the power to make adoption orders subject to "such terms and conditions as the court thinks fit"[53] has not been retained. Conditions were rarely used[54] and only exceptionally imposed on adopters without their consent because, by undermining them, the security of the child could be threatened.[55] Where conditions are appropriate the court may impose them on the adopters or the birth parents by making prohibited steps or specific issue orders. The court may not include an injunction as a term of an adoption order.[56] Where it is necessary to protect the adopters and child against harassment by members of the birth family, the High Court may grant an injunction under its inherent jurisdiction,[57] any court could exercise powers under the Family Law Act 1996, Pt IV[58] or action could be taken under the Protection from Harassment Act 1997.[59]

---

[49] In *Re C (A Minor)(Adoption Conditions)* [1989] A.C. 1 the House of Lords accepted that a contact condition (in favour of contact with siblings) could be included in an adoption order.

[50] See above, para. 23.056.

[51] See above, para. 23.056. It thereby avoids any problems of enforcement see above para. 19.052.

[52] Children Act 1989, s.14F, and above, para. 23.023. The court could alternatively make a family assistance order: *Re E (Family Assistance Order)* [1999] 1 F.L.R. 512, FD, above para. 19.025.

[53] Review of Adoption Law (1992), para. 5.8; Cm. 2288, para. 4.6; Adoption Act 1976, s.12(6).

[54] *Re J (A Minor) (Adoption Conditions)* [1973] Fam. 106; *Re C (A Minor) (Adoption Order: Conditions)* [1989] A.C.1 are the leading examples, both concern conditions about contact.

[55] *Re S (A Minor) (Blood Transfusion)* [1994] 2 F.L.R. 416 at 421 *per* Waite L.J. (The appeal of adopters who were Jehovah's Witnesses against the imposition of a condition (given as an undertaking) to permit blood transfusions was allowed.)

[56] *Re D (A Minor) (Adoption Order: Validity)* [1991] Fam. 137.

[57] *Re O (Minors) (Adoption: Injunction)* [1993] 2 F.L.R. 737 an injunction made in wardship proceedings prior to the adoption does not automatically survive the adoption order. (The parents were later imprisoned for breach of the injunction: *Re O (Contempt: Committal)* [1995] 2 F.L.R. 767, CA.) Where the adopters do not wish to apply the local authority has been allowed to do so on the basis that the Children Act 1989, s.100(4) was satisfied; *Re O* (above) and *Re X (A Minor) (Adoption Details: Disclosure)* [1994] 2 F.L.R. 450 at 453, CA.

[58] See above, para. 10.019 *et seq.*

[59] See above, para. 10.002 *et seq.*

Interim orders

23–061 The power to grant interim adoption orders[60] has not been re-enacted. The Review of Adoption Law doubted whether an order with the emotional significance of adoption should ever be granted as a temporary measure and considered interim orders to be unnecessary because the court can make residence orders.[61] In agency cases the prospective adopters will already have parental responsibility under the placement order or agreement.[62]

Restrictions on making orders

23–062 Procedural requirements in non-agency cases for the notification of the local are enforced by precluding the making of adoption orders where notice has not been given.[63] However, there is no longer any statutory restriction on making an adoption order where an illegal payment has been made.[64] Although the court regarded permitting such adoptions as tantamount to ratifying the sale of a child for adoption,[65] it could authorise illegal payments and did so where it considered adoption in the child's interests.[66] The issue of payment remains relevant to determining whether adoption is in the child's interests,[67] and in Convention cases, the court could annul the adoption on the basis that it was contrary to public policy.[68]

Refusal of adoption no longer requires automatic return of the child. If the agency wishes to terminate the placement it must serve notice in the normal way.[69] Where an adoption order has been refused the court may not hear any further application for adoption by the same applicants unless it appears proper to do so because of a change in circumstances.[70] The ending of objections from the parents or the child, or even the passage of time could justify a further application by long-term carers.

---

[60] Adoption Act 1976, s.25.

[61] Review of Adoption Law, Discussion Paper No. 3, *The adoption process* (1991), para. 199.

[62] Adoption and Children Act 2002, s.25(3).

[63] Adoption and Children Act 2002, s.44.

[64] Adoption Act 1976, s.24(2); Adoption and Children Act 2002, s.95.

[65] *per* Booth J. in *Re C (A Minor) (Adoption Application)* [1993] 1 F.L.R. 87 at 94, 101. (The application for adoption was withdrawn in this case and the child made a ward of court with a view to rehabilitation with her mother.)

[66] *Re Adoption Application* [1987] Fam. 81; *Re A (Adoption Placement)* [1988] 2 F.L.R. 133; *Re MW (Adoption: Surrogacy)* [1995] 2 F.L.R. 759; *Re AW (Adoption Applications)* [1993] 1 F.L.R. 64.

[67] Being the subject of a commercial transaction is likely to be harmful to the child, past unscrupulous action on the part of prospective adopters may indicate likely future harm to the child, s.1(4)(e).

[68] Adoption and Children Act 2002, s.89.

[69] Adoption Act 1976, s.30—this was considered unsatisfactory by the Review of Adoption Law, Discussion Paper No. 3, *The adoption process* (1991) para. 174; Adoption and Children Act 2002, s.35.

[70] Adoption and Children Act 2002, s.48. This applies where the first application was made in any part of the U.K. or in the Isle of Man or Channel Islands.

VII. SURROGACY

A. Introduction

23–063 Surrogacy is the practice whereby one woman carries a child for another with the intention that the child should be handed over after birth.[71] "Full" surrogacy arrangements involve semen and egg donation, by the commissioning parents and use of in vitro fertilization techniques so that the child is genetically related to both of them[72]; "partial" surrogacy, where the surrogate is inseminated artificially by the commissioning father, is more common.[73] Where surrogacy occurs the commissioning parents want to be the child's social parents; although they may be the child's genetic parents they can only acquire the legal status of parents[74] by taking some further step which in the case of the mother necessitates court proceedings.

The extent to which surrogacy has been practised in the past is unknown but it is likely that intra-family arrangements were made; the provision of a baby for a childless relative is not uncommon in some Asian communities. In the early 1980s, commercial surrogacy agencies started to operate in the USA[75] and by the mid 1980s it looked as if they would develop in Europe.[76] In Britain, a committee, chaired by Dame Mary Warnock was established in 1982 to examine the social, ethical and legal implications of developments in the field of assisted reproduction. Surrogacy was among the topics it considered. The majority of the committee was convinced that the danger of exploitation in surrogacy outweighed its potential benefits.[77] In order to minimise surrogacy they proposed that all agencies involved in it and any professional who assisted (but not the parties) should be criminally liable.[78] They acknowledged that this would not eradicate private agreements, which they thought should be unenforceable, and recommended that the law should be clarified in this respect.[79] They made proposals about the parentage of children born through assisted reproduction, but

---

[71] Report of the Committee of Inquiry into Human Fertilization and Embryology (Warnock Report) Cmnd. 9314 (1984), para. 8.1, 216; G. Douglas, *Law, fertility and reproduction* (1991); D. Morgan "Surrogacy: an introductory essay" in R. Lee & D. Morgan (eds), *Birth Rights: Law and ethics at the beginning of life* (1989).

[72] *ibid.* M. Wright, "Surrogacy and adoption: problems and possibilities" (1986) 16 *Fam. Law* 109, 110 gives some case examples. F. Price and R. Cook, "The donor, the recipient and the child—human egg donation in UK licensed centres" [1995] *C.F.L.Q.* 145. For an explanation of some of the modern reproductive methods, see Government White Paper, *Human Fertilization and Embryology: A framework for legislation*: Cm. 259 (1987), Annex A and the website of the Human Fertilization and Embryology Authority: www.hfea.gov.uk.

[73] The child's legal status and the commissioning father's relationship with the child differ if artificial insemination or licensed treatment services are used: Human Fertilization and Embryology Act 1990, s.28(2)(3); *Re D (Parental Responsibility: IVF Baby)* [2001] 1 F.L.R. 972, CA; *U v. W (A-G. Intervening)* [1997] 2 F.L.R. 282, FD and above p. 525.

[74] Human Fertilization and Embryology Act 1990, ss.27, 28 and above, paras 18. 002–3.

[75] D. Morgan, "Surrogacy—giving it an understood name" [1985] *J.S.W.L.* 216 at 227.

[76] J. Zipper, "What else is new? Reproductive technologies and custody politics" in C. Smart and S. Sevenhuijsen (eds), *Child Custody and the Politics of Gender* (1989), p. 264.

[77] Cmnd. 3194, para. 8.17.

[78] Cmnd. 3194, para. 8.18.

[79] Cmnd. 3194, para. 8.19.

not about the protection of children born following surrogacy arrangements. Two members of the committee dissented[80] taking the view that surrogacy would be beneficial on some occasions and thus gynaecologists should be able to refer couples to non-commercial, licensed agencies which would provide counselling and match prospective parties.[81] This would discourage unsatisfactory "do-it-yourself arrangements." The minority also recommended that adoption should be available to secure the status of the parents even where the surrogate was paid for her services.[82] The Warnock Report was heavily criticised for failing to understand the complexity of the issues surrounding assisted reproduction and considering that the problems of surrogacy could be solved by making it illegal.[83] The incomplete implementation of either of the report's approaches to surrogacy created a policy vacuum and led to haphazard development.[84]

23–064 In January 1985 the birth of baby Cotton[85] following a commercial surrogacy arrangement produced a "moral panic". The Government introduced legislation which became the Surrogacy Arrangements Act 1985.[86] This made it illegal for third parties to negotiate or facilitate any surrogacy for payment[87] and banned advertisement for, or of, surrogacy services.[88] It appears to have prevented the growth of commercial surrogacy agencies in Britain. However, the Act does not affect non-commercial agencies, nor does it regulate negotiations directly between the carrying mother and the commissioning parents.

In 1986 a Government Green Paper canvassed views on human infertility services and embryo research.[89] The responses showed widespread agreement about the problems of surrogacy and the importance of the child's welfare but no consensus about the most constructive role legislation might play in dealing with this.[90] The Government concluded that legislation should give no encouragement to non-commercial or private surrogacy but that it was not appropriate, nor in the child's best interests, to extend the criminal sanctions in the 1985 Act. However, it considered that views were still developing on these issues and that they should be kept under review. The Human Fertilization and Embryology Act 1990[91] established a statutory licensing authority, the Human Fertilization

---

[80] Dr David Davies and Dr Wendy Greengross.

[81] Warnock Report, *Expression of Dissent: A Surrogacy.*

[82] *ibid.* para. 7.

[83] J. Priest (1985) 48 *M.L.R.* 73; M. Wright (1986) 16 Fam. Law 109.

[84] Brazier Report: *Surrogacy—Review for Health Ministers of current arrangements for payment and regulation* Cm. 4088 (1998) i, para. 3.

[85] *Re C (A Minor) (Ward Surrogacy)* [1985] F.L.R. 846. The local authority obtained a place of safety order (Children and Young Persons Act 1969, s.28) but the commissioning parents made the child a ward of court. They were permitted to take the child permanently to the USA. The DHSS issued Circular (85)12 to advise local authorities of their responsibilities; see also K. Cotton and D. Winn, *Baby Cotton: For Love and Money* (1985).

[86] M.D.A. Freeman, *Current Law Annotation to Surrogacy Arrangements Act 1985* (1985).

[87] s.2. Payment could still be made to the mother for producing a diary about her pregnancy. A private Members' Bill, the Surrogacy Arrangements (Amendment) Bill which would have outlawed this was unsuccessful.

[88] s.3.

[89] *Legislation on human infertility services and embryo research* Cm. 46 (1986).

[90] *Human Fertilization and Embryology: A framework for legislation* Cm. 259 (1987), para. 72.

[91] A comprehensive account of this Act is beyond the scope of this text: see D. Morgan, *Current Law Annotated Statutes* and G. Douglas, *Law, Fertility and Reproduction* (1991).

and Embryology Authority, to regulate research and treatment in human infertility and embryology.[92] The Act regulates surrogacy by bringing medicalized surrogacy services within the control of HFEA,[93] by determining who legally are the child's parents[94] and by enabling commissioning parents to become legal parents through obtaining a court order, the parental order.[95]

In 1998, the Brazier Committee reviewed the law relating to surrogacy. It justified further controls backed by new legislation on the basis of the potential risks to all parties, including the child. It considered that payments created a danger that women would be enticed to act as surrogates, commodified children and contravened society's norms; it proposed that only genuine, documented expenses should be permitted.[96] Surrogacy agencies should be registered, operate only on a non-profit basis and be required to comply with a Code of Practice.[97] The committee did not seek to outlaw arrangements made without an agency, even between strangers[98] but proposed that the commissioning adults should only be able to obtain a parental order where they had complied with the legislation and code.[99] If implemented, these proposals may lead to the closure of agencies but rather than ending surrogacy for strangers they could encourage riskier (illegal) commercial arrangements.[1]

The extent to which surrogacy is practice in the U.K. is unclear. A quarter of licensed fertility clinics have been involved in surrogacy arrangements and each year about 40 parental orders are granted conferring status on the commissioning parents. The majority of these relate to arrangements made without a licensed clinic.[2] The numbers of British women who act as surrogates for couples elsewhere and of British couples who use surrogates overseas are not known; it is estimated that in approximately 5 per cent of arrangements the birth mother refuses to hand over the child.[3]

B. Surrogacy and adoption

23–065 There are four main parallels which may be drawn between surrogacy and adoption.[4] First, surrogacy is seen as an alternative to adoption which has become

[92] Human Fertilization and Embryology Act 1990, ss.5, 8.

[93] s.8 and Sched. 2. The HFEA keeps surrogacy under review but only has control over the activities of licensed clinics.

[94] ss.27–29.

[95] s.30.

[96] Brazier Report: *Surrogacy—Review for Health Ministers of current arrangements for payment and regulation* (1998) Cm. 4068, i paras 4–9.

[97] *ibid.*

[98] This contrasts with the law of adoption; only placements with relatives can be made without an agency, Adoption and Children Act 2002, s.92(1), (4).

[99] Cm. 4068, p. 72 para. 9(vii). Adoption would remain available subject to approval by the High Court.

[1] M. Freeman "Does surrogacy have a future after Brazier?" (1999) *Med. L. Rev* 7, pp. 1, 8, 10.

[2] Cm. 4068, paras 1.23, 1.27, 1.31.

[3] Cm. 4068, para. 3.5.

[4] See G. Douglas & N. Lowe "Becoming a parent in English Law" (1992) 108 *L.Q.R.* 414; B. Hale, *From the test tube to the coffin* (1996) 15, 28 *et seq.*; E. Blyth *et al.*, "The implications of adoption for donor offspring following donor-assisted conception" [2001] *Child and Family Soc. Wk.* 295.

necessary because of the shortage of babies for adoption.[5] For some it is a preferred way of alleviating infertility because it enables them to have a child who is genetically related to one or both of them. Secondly, the practice of surrogacy, like adoption, is subject to control by professionals and regulatory bodies in order to safeguard the welfare of children.[6] Commercial arrangements for both surrogacy and adoption are illegal; payment of money other than expenses may preclude an order which gives the child's carers the status of parent.[7] Surrogacy arrangements may currently be made without the involvement of any agency[8] but the Brazier Committee proposed in 1998 that surrogacy agencies should, like adoption agencies, be regulated.[9] Thirdly, the commissioning parents are not the child's legal parents[10] but can only acquire that status by a court process based on adoption, or adoption itself.[11] Fourthly, issues of secrecy and of access to information about birth arise in surrogacy arrangements and other forms of assisted Reproduction[12] as they do in adoption, but those who were born following gamete donation have more limited rights to knowledge of their origins.[13]

C. Enforceability of surrogacy contracts

23–066 The Surrogacy Arrangements Act 1985, s.1A[14] provides that "No surrogacy arrangement is enforceable by or against any of the persons making it". Thus no action may be brought to enforce payment or its return if the child is not

---

5 See L. Harding, "The debate on surrogate motherhood" [1985] *J.S.W.L.* 37, 42.

6 Human Fertilization and Embryology Authority, *Code of Practice* (5th. ed. 2001); G. Douglas, "Assisted reproduction and the welfare of the child" [1993] *C.L.P.* 53, 67; E. Jackson "Conception and the irrelevance of the welfare of the child" [2002] *M.L.R.* 176: scrutiny of those applying for assisted reproduction treatment is markedly less searching than for prospective adopters.

7 *Re MW (Adoption: Surrogacy)* [1995] 2 F.L.R. 759, above para. 23.062 and below.

8 Although the use of *in vitro* fertilization techniques is impractical outside a clinic and offences will be committed by an unlicensed clinic using such techniques, partial surrogacy with artificial insemination or intercourse occurs legally but the legal effects may be different. Human Fertilization and Embryology Act 1990, s.28(6) and *Re Q (Parental Order)* [1996] 1 F.L.R. 369.

9 Cm. 4068, p. 72, para 9.

10 See above but the commissioning father could be the legal father: Human Fertilization and Embryology Act 1990, s.28; *Re B (parentage)* [1996] 2 F.L.R. 15 *cf. Re Q (parental order)* [1996] 1 F.L.R. 369 where the commissioning father was not the sperm donor and the court found that he had not been treated "together with" the surrogate mother when she received A.I.D.

11 Human Fertilization and Embryology Act 1990, s.30(9); Parental Orders (Human Fertilization and Embryology) Regulations 1994, S.I. 1994 No. 2767.

12 *Human Fertilization and Embryology: A framework for legislation* Cm. 259 (1987), paras 81–86. It has been suggested that there should be a contact register for donor offspring and donors but this raises huge practical difficulties, see: HFEA, *Response to Department of Health's consultation on donor information* (2002).

13 This is currently under review, see para. 23.071, below.

14 Added by Human Fertilization and Embryology Act 1990, s.36. The common law offence of child sale may also be committed. The Warnock Committee took this view but wanted the matter clarified (Cmnd. 9314, para. 8.19).

handed over.[15] Agreements cannot be made to transfer parental responsibility[16]; any dispute about the residence of a child referred to the courts would be decided applying the welfare principle in section 1 of the Children Act 1989. The emphasis given to maintaining the status quo means that commissioning parents are unlikely to succeed in obtaining a court order transferring residence to them:—

> In *Re P (Minors) (Wardship Surrogacy)*[17] an Asian father commissioned a white single parent to bear a child for him and his wife. Twins were born following artificial insemination but the mother refused to hand them over. The children, aged five months at the hearing, were made wards of court and the father applied for care and control. Arnold J. acknowledged that the father's home was materially and intellectually superior and recognised the value of links with the children's Asian culture. However, he refused to order that the children should live with their father because these advantages did not outweigh the disadvantage of leaving their mother with whom they were bonded.

The likely outcome is less clear if the surrogate mother changes her mind after handing over the baby:—

> In *Re W (A Minor) (Residence Order)*[18] the mother who had had a brief relationship with the father handed the baby to the father shortly after birth and signed a parental responsibility agreement. A few days later she regretted her actions and applied *ex parte* for a residence order. Her application was refused but her appeal was allowed so that she had care of the child pending a full hearing. Lord Donaldson M.R. stated that there was a "rebuttable presumption that a baby should be with its mother."[19]

Disputes arising out of surrogacy arrangements do not require wardship proceedings although these may be desirable.[20] Applications may be made under

---

[15] In *W and B v. H (Child Abduction: Surrogacy)* [2002] 1. F.L.R. 1008; *(No. 2)* [2002] 2 F.L.R. 252 Hedley J. dismissed a Hague Convention application for the return of twins born in England as a result of a surrogacy agreement in California even though, under Californian law, the commissioning parents were the legal parents and had obtained there a pre-birth determination of custody. The children were not habitually resident in California and therefore were not unlawfully retained in England. In the second case, he ordered the children's summary return to California on the basis that they had no real connection with England (the only country they had ever lived in and of which they were citizens) so that the issue of their parentage and care could be determined by the Californian Court. The issues that this raised under the H.R.A. 1998 were apparently not argued.

[16] Children Act 1989, s.2(9).

[17] [1987] 2 F.L.R. 421; a similar approach was taken in the notorious American case *In Re Baby M*, 217 N.J. Super 313, 525 A. 2d 1128; (on appeal), 537 A. 2d 1127 but the commissioning parents obtained custody of the child.

[18] [1992] 2 F.L.R. 332, CA. This was not a surrogacy case although the facts were not that different from partial surrogacy.

[19] At p. 336.

[20] The court's power to control publicity may be desirable but the inherent jurisdiction cannot be used for that reason alone, see above, para 19.049.

the Children Act 1989, but a commissioning parent who is not the child's legal parent, will require leave.[21]

D. Regulation of surrogacy practice

23–067 The creation in the U.K. of embryos outside the body and the storage of gametes is prohibited except under a licence granted by the Human Fertilization and Embryology Authority.[22] Consequently, full surrogacy and partial surrogacy using stored gametes[23] can only legally be undertaken in a licensed clinic. It is a condition of a licence that:

> "a woman shall not be provided with treatment services unless account has been taken of the welfare of any child who may be born as a result of the treatment (including the need of that child for a father), and of any other child who may be affected by the birth".[24]

This provision which was introduced, to neutralise opposition in Parliament from M.P.s concerned about the treatment of single or lesbian women has been severely criticised.[25] Jackson has argues that the provision is incompatible with the European Convention on Human Rights because it fails to respect Article 8 rights. By assuming that infertile couples require external assessment to qualify as parents, it fails to accord them proper moral respect. It is nonsensical to use a welfare test to allocate publicly funded fertility services because it involves determining whether a child's welfare will be served by his or own conception.[26] It can also be discriminatory by attributing adverse life chances of a group to individuals who may not share those characteristics.[27] Even if there is a moral basis for requiring such assessments, clinics have insufficient powers to undertake them because they are forbidden from communicating with third parties about provision of treatment.[28]

The Code of Practice states that centres should take all responsible steps to ascertain who the legal parents would be, bear in mind their commitment to

---

[21] Children Act 1989, s.10(5).

[22] Human Fertilization and Embryology Act 1990, ss.3(1), 4(1). For an outline of regulation in Europe see: D. Langdridge and E. Blyth, "Regulation of assisted conception services in Europe: implications of the new reproductive technologies for 'the family' " [2001] *J.S.W.F.L.* 45.

[23] The term gamete covers both sperm and eggs. Storage of gametes is required so that they can be tested for HIV, etc.

[24] Human Fertilization and Embryology Act 1990, s.13(5); and see B. Hale *op cit.* p. 35; E. Blyth, "Children's welfare, surrogacy and social work" (1993) 23 *Brit. J. Soc. Wk.* 259 and E. Jackson, "Conception and the irrelevance of welfare" [2002] *M.L.R.* 176.

[25] Jackson (2002), *op. cit.* p. 195.

[26] *ibid.* pp. 187, 193, 199. She also suggests that Art. 12 may be breached but acknowledges that the Court of Appeal has suggested otherwise: *R. (on the application of Mellor) v. Secretary of State for the Home Department* [2001] 2 F.L.R. 1158, CA.

[27] Jackson (2002), *op. cit.* p. 193; G. Douglas, "Assisted reproduction and the welfare of the child" [1993] C.L.P. 53, 69.

[28] Human Fertilization and Embryology Act 1990, s.33; Douglas (1993), *op cit.* p. 65. Centres must make inquiries of each prospective parents and, *with their consent*, may seek information about them from other sources. There is no requirement for police or other checks before treatment is provided.

bringing up children and take account of possible attitudes of other members of the family towards the child.[29] Assisted conception techniques should only be considered where it is physically impossible or highly undesirable for medical reasons for the commissioning mother to carry the child.[30] Only a minority of clinics provide treatment in surrogacy cases.[31] In cases of surrogacy, centres should bear in mind that either the carrying mother or the commissioning parents may become the child's legal parents.[32] In practice, it appears that there is little assessment of individual's fitness to be parents; the legal requirement to consider the child's welfare does not appear to have made clinics change their approach in deciding whom they will treat.[33]

If surrogacy occurs outside a licensed clinic, the sperm donor will be the child's legal father.[34] This provision was intended to discourage informal sperm donation but does not discourage partial surrogacy because this is what the commissioning parents want. However, if the commissioning father is infertile, treatment of the surrogate in a licensed clinic has advantages because it can ensure that he is the child's legal father.[35] In either case the commissioning father must obtain parental responsibility in the usual way.[36]

Local authorities are required to investigate cases of surrogacy which come to their attention to ensure that the child is not at risk.[37] However there is some confusion about what is the appropriate approach where the commissioning parents are not ideal but the birth mother is content and the circumstances do not justify court proceedings:—

> In *Re H (A Minor) (s.37 Direction)*[38] the mother reached an agreement with a lesbian couple during her pregnancy that they should bring up her child. Prior to the birth, they inquired at the social services department about adopting the child and were informed that private placements were illegal. The child was born at their home and cared for by them. They asked for registration as private foster parents but this was refused because one of the women had a recent conviction for violence. In addition to making inquiries in connection with the fostering application, the social worker also counselled the mother and advised her to stop visiting the child. The couple applied, with the mother's consent, for a residence order.[39] The court

---

29 Human Fertilization and Embryology Authority, *Code of Practice* (2001), paras 3.13 and 3.15.

30 *ibid.* para. 3.16.

31 G. Douglas (1993), *op cit.* p. 63. More clinics were willing to treat surrogates after the 1990 Act but this is probably due to the more relaxed attitude of the BMA: BMA, *Surrogacy, ethical considerations* (1989).

32 Code of Practice, para. 3.15b.

33 G. Douglas (1993), *op cit.* pp. 65–67.

34 Human Fertilization and Embryology Act 1990, s.28(2)(3); *U v. W (A-G. Intervening)* [1997] 2 F.L.R. 282, FD.

35 s.28(3).

36 Children Act 1989, s.4 (as amended, see paras 18.034–18.036) if he is the legal father under Human Fertilization and Embryology Act 1990, s.28 but not married to the mother.

37 DHSS Circular (85)12 published in the wake of the *Kim Cotton* case.

38 [1993] 2 F.L.R. 541. This is not a surrogacy case but the facts were similar.

39 If one of the carers had a residence order the arrangement would not be private fostering: Children Act 1989, s.66.

was concerned about the welfare of the child, particularly because one of the applicants had mental health problems and both had a history of broken relationships. It made a residence order but directed that the local authority should undertake a section 37 investigation and suggested that the grounds of a care order were probably met.[40] By the time the matter was reconsidered by the court the child would have lived with the applicants for a year and had no contact with the mother for six months.

Alternative, possibly more suitable, arrangements for the child may be impeded if the child has become settled in the commissioning parents' home.

E. Acquisition of the status of parent

23–068 During the passage of the Human Fertilization and Embryology Bill attention was drawn to the fact that both commissioning parents could only obtain parental responsibility by adopting the child. This process was considered, by some, to be unnecessarily complex because the applicants who had determined that the child would be created were often the genetic parents.[41] Also, adoption was problematic unless the commissioning father was the child's legal father because it is illegal to place or receive an unrelated child for adoption except via an adoption agency.[42] A provision was hurriedly drafted to create parental orders[43] but its implementation was delayed while a suitable process was devised. Section 30 was implemented on November 1, 1994; regulations based on adoption legislation, explain the effects of a parental order.[44] The proceedings are based on adoption proceedings.[45]

Parental orders

23–069 The Human Fertilization and Embryology Act, s.30 enables married commissioning parents to obtain a parental order if at least one of them is the child's genetic parent.[46] A parental order gives the applicants the status of parents and extinguishes the parental responsibility of everyone else.[47] The parental order must be sought within six months of the birth of the child, the child must be living with the applicants and the legal parents (including a father who does not

---

[40] *Re H (A minor) (s.37 Direction)* [1993] 2 F.L.R. 541 at 548 *per* Scott Baker J.

[41] *Re W (Minors) (Surrogacy)* [1991] 1 F.L.R. 385. The case was settled by the commissioning parents undertaking to apply for a parental order (see below) as soon as possible.

[42] Adoption and Children Act 2002, s.92(4). If the original placement were a private foster placement, adoption could occur after three years: s.42(5), but this too can be problematic: see *Re H (A Minor) (s.37 Direction)* [1993] 2 F.L.R. 541.

[43] Human Fertilization and Embryology Act, s.30.

[44] Parental Orders (Human Fertilization and Embryology) Regulations 1994, S.I. 1994 No. 2767.

[45] See Family Proceedings (Amendment No. 2) Rules 1994, S.I. 1994 No. 2165; Family Proceedings Courts (Children Act 1989) (Amendment) Rules 1994 , S.I. 1994 No. 2166. Amendments are required for the provisions remain in line with adoption. If changes are not made unmarried and same-sex couples will have to seek adoption.

[46] s.30(1). Parental orders are available in either full or partial surrogacy.

[47] Parental Order (Human Fertilization and Embryology) Regulations 1994, Sched. 1; a useful account is provided in Department of Health Guidance notes to the provisions (1994).

have parental responsibility) must agree unconditionally to the making of the order.[48] There are no provisions, comparable to those in adoption, for the dispensing of agreement but if a person cannot be found, or is incapable of giving it, their agreement is not required.[49] This means the use of anonymously donated gametes does not prevent the applicants from seeking a parental order.[50]

Applications are made to the family proceedings court but may be transferred to a higher court. Under the original regulations the child's welfare was the "first consideration"[51] but Department of Health guidance suggests that it may be helpful to consider the welfare checklist in the Children Act 1989, s.1.[52] The Brazier Committee recommended that the child's welfare should be paramount,[53] this is the welfare test applied by the Adoption and Children Act 2002, and new regulations are needed to avoid inconsistency for example to allow unmarried couples to obtain parental orders.

A "parental order reporter", a CAFCASS officer is appointed to investigate the case[54] including advising the court about alternatives; the role of the reporter is restricted by limited access to information from a clinic carrying out the treatment.[55] But it has been said that reporters may presume that the child's welfare has been given adequate consideration where treatment occurred in a licensed clinic.[56] Guidance indicates that a recommendation against the making of an order is exceptional.[57] A parental order may not be made in any case where payments have been made other than to cover expenses, unless these payments have been authorised by the court.[58] However, the courts have been willing to authorise payments in order to safeguard the welfare of the child.[59] Parental order proceedings are family proceeding so the court may make any section 8 order with or without an application.[60] If an order is refused an appeal may be made to the High Court.[61]

---

[48] Human Fertilization and Embryology Act 1990, s.30(2)(3)(5).

[49] s.30(6).

[50] If the treatment occurred in a licensed clinic the anonymous semen donor would not be the child's father: s.28.

[51] The regulations originally applied Adoption Act 1976, s.6.

[52] LAC (94)25. This will apply to any s.8 orders made instead of or additionally to the parental order.

[53] Cm. 4068, ii para. 7 but the Report was not entirely consistent see Freeman (1999) *op cit.* p. 13.

[54] These are specified proceedings: Children Act 1989, s.42(6)(i). Only exceptionally difficult, unusual or sensitive cases should be referred to CAFCASS Legal: *CAFCASS Practice Note* [2001] 2 F.L.R. 151, para. 8.

[55] J. Timms, *Children's representation* (1995), p. 301; the 1990 Act was amended by the Human Fertilization and Embryology (Disclosure of Information) Act 1992, s.1 to increase the information available for parental order proceedings.

[56] *ibid.* p. 298, but this does not seem to accord with what is known about clinic practice see Douglas (1993), *op. cit.* pp. 65–67 and Jackson (2002), *op cit.* p. 194.

[57] LAC(94) 25.

[58] s.30(7). See above, para 23.062, for the approach of the courts to comparable provisions in adoption. A survey for the Brazier Report found payments up to £12,000 and averaging nearly £4,000. In *Re MW (Adoption: Surrogacy)* [1995] 2 F.L.R. 759 the court authorised a payment of £7,500 to a surrogate mother and made an adoption order after dispensing with her consent.

[59] *Re C (Application by Mr and Mrs X Under s.30 of the Human Fertilization and Embryology Act 1990)* [2002] 1 F.L.R. 909, FD. If the child's welfare is paramount there will be few if any circumstances where discretion would not be exercised to authorise the payment.

[60] Children Act 1989, s.10(1); Human Fertilization and Embryology Act 1990, s.30(8)(a).

[61] Parental Orders (Human Fertilization and Embryology) Regulations (1994), Sched. 1, para. 5(b) applying Adoption Act 1976, s.63(2).

When a parental order is made the child's birth is re-registered with the commissioning parents as the child's legal parents.[62] The child's status is comparable with that obtained by adoption.[63] The making of a parental order does not affect the inheritance of honours and other dispositions are construed as if the child was born on the date the parental order was obtained.[64]

All applicants who meet the basic qualifications for a parental order are likely to be successful. A number of factors account for this:—sympathy for the applicants (they have usually only turned to surrogacy because of a misfortune of biology which means the woman is unable to carry a pregnancy); a belief that they are entitled to the child (at least one of them is the child's genetic parent); recognition that it is only a legal device which defines others as the child's parents; and the general acceptance of the notion that biological reproduction is a qualification for parenthood all combine to make substantial scrutiny of consensual and non-commercial arrangements unacceptable.[65]

Adoption

23–070 Where the conditions for a parental order are not satisfied, for example the birth mother refuses her agreement, the time limit has passed or neither of the commissioning adults is genetically related to the child, the status of parent can be acquired by adoption. But a placement with unrelated adopters, even with the genetic father and his wife breaches the law relating to private placements.[66] Applications for adoption are subject to more substantial scrutiny; the local authority must be notified of intention to adopt, must investigate the suitability of the prospective adopters and the welfare of the child, and report to the court hearing the application.[67] However, the court may be faced with a *fait accompli* so that it is necessary for the child's welfare to make the order.

Where neither a parental order nor adoption is available the commissioning adults may secure their position through a residence order.[68]

---

[62] Parental Orders (Human Fertilization and Embryology) Regulations 1994, Sched. 1, para. 4(a) applying Adoption Act 1976, s.50.

[63] Parental Orders (Human Fertilization and Embryology) Regulations 1994, Sched. 1, para. 2 applying Adoption Act 1976, s.39.

[64] Parental Orders (Human Fertilization and Embryology) Regulations 1994, Sched. 1, para. 3 applying Adoption Act 1976, ss.42–46.

[65] See D. Morgan, "A surogacy issue: who is the other mother?" (1994) 8 *Int. J. of Law and Fam.* 386 and Jackson (2002) *op. cit.*

[66] see above, para. 23.014.

[67] Adoption and Children Act 2002, s.44(1)(5)(6). Arguable any regulations made under s.45 will not apply because the local authority makes its report as local authority, not as an adoption agency.

[68] *Re H (A minor) (s.37 Direction)* [1993] 2 F.L.R. 541.

F. Knowledge of origins[69]

23–071 The Warnock Committee considered that non-identifying information about the donor should be made available to a child born as a result of AID at age 18.[70] The Government sought further views on the issues of confidentiality and access to information about origins.[71] Most respondents supported a right for children to have some information about their genetic parents and some argued, by analogy with adoption, for a right to know the identity of genetic parents.[72] Although it recognised that views may change, the Government considered that adults should only be able to know that they were born following gamete or embryo donation and have certain non-identifying information about the donor.[73] Legislation enables those over 18 to discover from the Human Fertilization and Embryology Authority whether they were or may have been born in consequence of treatment services.[74] However, unless a person has been told of the circumstances of their conception he or she will not know that the HFEA holds information.[75] The applicant may be told whether someone other than the legal parents is a genetic parent or whether an intended spouse is or may be a genetic relation but may not obtain any information which identifies a gamete donor.[76] A child who is the subject of a parental order may on reaching the age of 18 obtain a copy of their original birth certificate but this will not show the genetic parents where gamete donation was used.[77] These provisions are kept under review; the Department of Health issued a consultation paper at the beginning of 2002.[78]

The current approach reflects the ambivalence felt by legislators and professionals to assisted reproduction.[79] Although secrecy protects the child from information about his or her origins which may be upsetting, it is permitted for

---

[69] See generally K. O'Donovan "A right to know one's parentage?" (1988) 2 *Int. J. Law & Fam.* 27; E. Haimes, " 'Secrecy': What can artificial reproduction learn from adoption?" (1988) 2 *Int. J. Law & Fam.* 46; M. Freeman, "The new birth right? Identity and the child of the reproduction revolution" (1996) 4 *Int J. of children's rights* 273; S. Wilson, "Identity, genealogy and the social family: the case of donor insemination" (1997) 11 *Int. J. Law Pol. and Fam.* 270; E. Blyth *et al.*, "The implications of adoption for donor offspring following donor-assisted conception" [2001] *Child and Family Soc. Wk.* 295.

[70] Warnock Report, para. 4.21.

[71] Cm. 46 (1986), paras 31, 32.

[72] Cm. 259 (1987), paras 81 *et seq.*

[73] *ibid.* See also *per* Lord Chancellor, Hansard, *Lords*, Vol. 516, col. 1477 (Human Fertilization and Embryology Bill, Report Stage).

[74] Human Fertilization and Embryology Act 1990, s.31 requires the authority to keep a register of treatment provided. Some clinics hold information for the period before this.

[75] A large study of donor insemination families found that less than 10% of mothers had had told the child by the age of 12 years and 75% had decided not to do so: S. Golombok *et al.* cited in D.H., *Donor information consultation* (2002), para. 1.25.

[76] Human Fertilization and Embryology Act 1990, s.31(4)(5). There is a power to make regulations to allow disclosure of other information but disclosure which identifies the donor is forbidden except in defined circumstances: s.33 as amended by the Human Fertilization and Embryology (Disclosure of Information) Act 1992, s.1 and no regulations have been made.

[77] Parental Orders (Human Fertilization and Embryology) Regulations 1994, Sched. 1, para. 4(b).

[78] Human Fertilization and Embryology Act 1990, s.8; D.H., *Donor information consultation* (2002).

[79] Haimes, *op cit.* p. 60.

the convenience of the donor[80] and the recipient parents; the child, unlike the adults, may lose information which is culturally, psychologically and medically useful.[81] The HFEA's response to the Department of Health consultation indicated that it supported moves towards ending donor anonymity, but that this should not be applied retrospectively,[82] or on an optional basis for future donors.[83] The Human Rights Act 1998 may require legislation to allow those born as a result of gamete donation to establish their genetic identity. It has been held that article 8 is engaged by the issue of access to such information, but detailed consideration of the claims is awaiting government decisions at the conclusion of the consultation exercise.[84] These are very sensitive issues requiring a careful balancing of the rights of donors, legal parents and children. But as with adoption in 1975, openness is likely to be imposed at some point in the future.[85]

---

[80] Concern has been expressed that donors would not come forward if they were not given confidentiality. In Sweden there was a decline in donors after confidentiality was abolished for AID but this was only temporary. Sperm used by the NHS is frequently imported from Denmark.

[81] O'Donovan, *op cit.* p. 29. O'Donovan argues that the state should be required to disclose to the child.

[82] There is no intention to make future disclosure rules retrospective: D.H. (2002) *op cit.* para 1.3. If any regulations were made under s.31 allowing disclosure of identifiable information they would only apply to future donations.

[83] HFEA, *Response to the Department of Health's consultation on donor information* (2002).

[84] *Rose v. Secretary of State for Health and the HFEA* [2002] 2 F.L.R. 962, FD. The applications concerned persons conceived both before and after the introduction of the 1990 Act.

[85] A small number of jurisdictions (Austria, Sweden, Switzerland and Victoria in Australia) give donor offspring a right to discover the identity of their genetic parent, Blyth *et al.* (2001) *op cit.* p. 296.

INDEX